Philosophy of Mind

Philosophy of Mind
Historical and Contemporary Perspectives

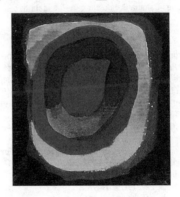

EDITED BY
PETER A. MORTON AND
MYRTO MYLOPOULOS

THIRD EDITION

broadview press

BROADVIEW PRESS – www.broadviewpress.com
Peterborough, Ontario, Canada

Founded in 1985, Broadview Press remains a wholly independent publishing house.
Broadview's focus is on academic publishing; our titles are accessible to university
and college students as well as scholars and general readers. With 800 titles in print,
Broadview has become a leading international publisher in the humanities, with world-
wide distribution. Broadview is committed to environmentally responsible publishing
and fair business practices.

Library and Archives Canada Cataloguing in Publication

Title: Philosophy of mind : historical and contemporary perspectives /
    edited by Peter A. Morton and Myrto Mylopoulos.
Other titles: Historical introduction to the philosophy of mind
Names: Morton, Peter A., 1952- editor. | Mylopoulos, Myrto, editor.
Description: Third edition. | Includes bibliographical references.
Identifiers: Canadiana 20190229101 | ISBN 9781554814008 (softcover)
Subjects: LCSH: Philosophy of mind—History—Textbooks. | LCSH: Mind and body
    —History—Textbooks. | LCGFT: Textbooks.
Classification: LCC BD418.3 .H57 2019 | DDC 128/.209—dc23

Broadview Press handles its own distribution in North America:
PO Box 1243, Peterborough, Ontario K9J 7H5, Canada
555 Riverwalk Parkway, Tonawanda, NY 14150, USA
Tel: (705) 743-8990; Fax: (705) 743-8353
email: customerservice@broadviewpress.com

For all territories outside of North America, distribution is handled by Eurospan Group.

Broadview Press acknowledges the financial support of the
Government of Canada for our publishing activities.

Copy-edited by Robert M. Martin
Book design by Chris Rowat Design

PRINTED IN CANADA

CONTENTS

PREFACE TO THE THIRD EDITION

The intent behind the third edition of this book does not deviate from the motives of the first two editions. As in the previous editions, there are two main pedagogical ideas on which the third edition of this book is based. One is to find a way to assist students with the unfamiliar and sometimes counterintuitive aspects of philosophical theories of mind. When first confronted with behaviorism, identity theory, and functionalism, students often find them bewildering and not in keeping with their own thoughts on the subject. The problem is therefore to make the theories and arguments accessible to students, but in a way that neither glosses over nor waters down the difficult issues involved. The approach we have adopted is, in part, a historical one that shows students how the contemporary sets of theories and issues arose from an ongoing process of revising and rethinking previous theories. Another central aspect of the book is the combination of primary source readings and our own commentary. While it is necessary for students to read the original source material, they often cannot do so without help and guidance in following the arguments and cutting through the jargon. In many cases the historical background to the readings is also essential to understanding the context and language in which the arguments are posed. To deal with these issues we accompany the primary readings with our own explanations of the contextual background, the structure of the arguments, and the technical material that is assumed but not explained in the readings.

The major difference in the third edition is a substantial reworking of Part Three: Contemporary Issues. Part One remains the same as in the second edition, save for one important addition in Chapter 5: We have replaced the reading from John Locke with the correspondence between René Descartes and Elisabeth, Princess of Bohemia. Part Two is not substantially changed from the second edition, although some of the explanations have been improved. Many years have passed, however, since the publication of the first two editions, and we have expanded and updated the contents of Part Three to reflect as many of the developments of the past decade as possible while keeping the size of the volume within reasonable limits.

We want to extend our sincere thanks to Robert M. Martin, of Dalhousie University. As with the Second Edition, Bob composed the study questions and did a wonderful job of copy-editing. We also thank Stephen Latta, Philosophy Editor at Broadview Press, who guided the Third Edition through many stages from inception to final proofs. The staff at Broadview made the entire project a pleasant experience.

Typographic Conventions

We have followed a particular set of conventions for the use of quotation marks, and italicized and bold font. Single quotes are used only to refer to words, phrases, or sentences, as in the following example:

'Light' is a word with five letters.

Double quotes are used to indicate either a quotation from a text or a word used in an unusual sense. We have used italicized font for book titles, for foreign words, and frequently also for emphasis. Bold font indicates that the word or phrase occurs in the Glossary at the back of the book. We have put words and phrases in bold at the place where the definition occurs in the commentary, which is not always the first occurrence of the word.

INTRODUCTION

The Mind-Body Problem

The issues introduced in this book are today referred to collectively as "the mind-body problem." The simplest way to describe this problem is to say that it is a search for an answer to the question, 'What is the relationship between the mind and the physical body?' This search raises such issues as whether the mind and body are one thing or two, and whether artificial machines could have minds.

According to a standard explanation, the mind-body problem arises in something like the following way. We have a reasonable understanding of our own physical body. That is, we are confident that we have identified the functions of most of the major systems of the body, and we have a pretty good idea of how they work. The mind, however, is more mysterious. We seem to have a rough idea of what we *mean* when we talk about the mind: It is that part of us that contains our thoughts, experiences, and feelings. But we aren't entirely sure what thoughts, experiences, and feelings really *are*. Are they the activities of an immaterial substance—a soul? Are they activities of the brain? Do thoughts, experiences, and feelings even exist as we understand them?

The Changing Nature of the Problem

The standard characterization of the problem is reasonably accurate as far as it goes. But it also glosses over some of the most interesting aspects of the issue. In the first place, we *don't* entirely know what we mean when we talk about the mind. The meanings of the terms 'thought,' 'experience,' and 'feeling' are very obscure and are a matter of debate. And, second, our understanding of the physical body and how it works is constantly evolving. New ideas and discoveries are always altering our conception of how the body works, especially those parts of the body most closely connected with thought and experience. The discoveries of such things as the mechanical function of the heart, the structure of the cell, and the processes of evolution have changed how we think of the body and subsequently of how it might be related to the mind. Most recently, new advances in neuroscience are changing our theories of how the processes of the brain operate. What we have, then, is not a fixed and static problem. As Noam Chomsky puts it, there is no single mind-body problem; there have been as many mind-body problems as there have been ways of thinking about the body and the mind.

The Historical Development

Although the character of the mind-body problem is constantly changing, the changes haven't been random and unconnected. There is a historical continuity to the succession of theories about the mind that make up the Western tradition beginning in ancient Greece. Each change in thinking about the mind has been the result of an attempt to solve a puzzle that previous theories were unable to resolve. The range of theories that are currently defended have grown out of this process.

Whether these changes have formed a progressive evolution—providing a better and better understanding of the mind—or whether earlier insights have been lost in the process is an interesting question. Certainly each stage in the development was perceived at the time as an advance over earlier views. And if you defend one of the current theories as the correct view, then you will almost certainly see the process within which it was devised as a progressive one. But there have been frequent occasions when older views have been resurrected and restored to prominence, albeit in a different form from when they were first put forward. So the resolution of this question is best left as part of the general argument over which theory is most likely to give us a true understanding of the mind.

The Approach Taken in This Book

We have chosen to introduce the mind-body problem in this book by outlining some major trends in its history. There are two reasons for this. One reason is to make clear the points we mentioned above. One gains a false impression of the mind-body problem if it is introduced as a static issue with the range of current options fixing the terms of the debate. The best way to perceive the flexibility of the framework within which the debate is conducted is to see how it evolved and notice the differences between earlier frameworks and current ones.

The second reason for taking a historical approach is pedagogical. The theories that are presently at the front of debate, and that new students of the discipline must learn, are not self-evident options for most people. A natural reaction when first shown the theories surveyed in Part Two of this book is one of puzzlement: Why *these* theories? Why not think about the issues in some completely different way? And some theories—behaviorism, for example—seem just bizarre upon first encounter. The historical development can be used to help explain why philosophers think that the contemporary theories offer the best hope of arriving at the right answers, or, more accurately, why philosophers think we are now asking the right questions.

One side benefit of the historical approach is to dispel the tendency to treat older theories and arguments simply as crude versions of the current ones. This tendency is a mistake because to some extent the issues themselves have changed. Let us offer one example of this. A central theory in the mind-body debate is the one constructed by René Descartes in the seventeenth century. According to Descartes, the mind and the body are two distinct and utterly different entities that are somehow linked together. Descartes's argument that the mind and the body are distinct is sometimes presented in introductory texts as if it is flawed because of some errors of reasoning that he was simply unaware of. But Descartes's reasoning was built upon a very old idea, the idea of *substance*, that Descartes inherited from his predecessors. This idea formed part of the manner in which Descartes framed the issue, and his argument is only understood if it is seen in this way. Because the concept of substance has been abandoned, it is natural to ignore this aspect of his argument, and so to see it as simply a mistaken piece of logic. There is little doubt that Descartes's argument is unsuccessful, but it is so for much more interesting reasons than the ones usually given. And the real reasons show us by example that arriving at the right theory of the mind depends on more than just brushing up on our logic.

The Readings

A second feature of this book is the relationship between the readings and our own commentary. This aspect is a product of our experiences as teachers. It seems absolutely essential that students approaching the mind-body problem do so by way of *primary texts*, that is, by reading the original writings of the people who proposed the theories and arguments in the first place. The only way to get a good grasp of the ideas proposed by Aristotle, Descartes, or the linguistic philosophers is to read them. Without this, you miss the force of the arguments and the subtleties of the theories. More importantly, it is wrong to foist a single interpretation of these works onto students without letting them read them for themselves and examine the interpretation critically. On the other hand, the primary texts are often hard to read. One reason for this is that they are sometimes very old, and so are written in archaic language using concepts that have long lost their currency. Another reason is that many of these works were not primarily written for students new to the discipline, but for other professional philosophers who know a lot of the jargon and the background. So it doesn't work to simply hand out primary texts and ask students to read them.

The solution we have adopted in this book is to accompany the primary texts—the readings—with commentaries that explain their content, or at least some of the central ideas they contain. Sometimes the commentary follows the reading paragraph by paragraph, but often it is possible only to focus in on certain central passages that contain the main arguments or theories. But the commentary is always aimed directly at the readings with the goal of making the readings clear to someone who does not have the background knowledge to read them on their own. In each case the commentary also attempts to provide a general historical background to the text, outlining some of the major historical developments that influenced them and the connections that exist between the different readings.

One consequence of such an emphasis on primary texts is that only certain figures in the debate can be examined closely, to the exclusion of other important writers. There are many versions of the main theories, and arguments for them, that are not addressed in the book. This is revealed, for example, in the emphasis on Descartes, who was certainly not the only mind-body dualist of his time. Similarly, the theory of functionalism, which we outline in Chapter Nine, is a much more complex theory than we have covered here, with more versions than the ones we have presented. The focus on primary readings also forces huge jumps between historical periods. The readings leap directly from Aristotle to the seventeenth century, ignoring more than a whole millennium. Medieval scholars are right to protest the tendency to ignore their period as if nothing of consequence happened in all that time. But, as choices have to be made, we prefer to sacrifice comprehensiveness in favor of a close, ground-level familiarity with the ideas in their original form.

An Overview of the Book

The book is divided into three major parts. Part One sketches some of the major developments in the mind-body problem before the twentieth century. The first person within the Western tradition to construct a reasonably detailed and full theory of the mind is Plato. Every aspect of thinking about the mind since his day has been influenced by the ideas that he put forward. Chapter One looks at Plato's contention that the soul, which includes what we now think of as the mind, is separate from, and even stands in opposition to, the natural world. His student,

Aristotle, whom we read in Chapter Two, had an equally large impact on the ways in which we have formed our views of the mind. In certain ways Aristotle's theory contrasts directly with Plato's, for he argued that the soul is an integral part of the natural order and inseparable from it.

After Aristotle we jump fifteen hundred years to the scientific revolution of the sixteenth and seventeenth centuries. The mechanical view of nature developed by early modern scientists forced a rethinking of the mind and its relation to the body. The issues raised by this change in our views of nature are explored in Chapter Three. In the remaining chapters of Part One we look at the ideas about the mind that were proposed in response to this change. Here we begin to take an especially close look at how philosophers have attempted to deal with what is perhaps the most puzzling feature of the mind, namely, how things appear to us in conscious experience. The question they faced was how to reconcile conscious experience with a mechanical picture of nature—a problem that continues to be addressed in Parts Two and Three of the book. By far the greatest emphasis in the chapters that follow is on René Descartes. This is because Descartes has had the profoundest influence on the mind-body problem since the seventeenth century, even though his theory of mind-body dualism is no longer a strong contender today. Chapter Four examines Descartes's theory about our knowledge of the mind, which forms the basis for his dualist view that mind and body must be two distinct entities. Chapter Five presents Descartes's defense and explanation of his version of mind-body dualism. Chapter Six then introduces two alternatives to Descartes's dualism that were defended in the same time period, one of which denies the distinct existence of the immaterial mind, and the other of which denies the existence of mind-independent matter.

Part Two of the book examines three central approaches to the mind-body problem that have been defended in the past century and that still have proponents among contemporary philosophers working in the Anglo-American tradition. The central aspect of all thinking about the mind in the last one hundred years has been the assumption of materialism, the idea that the mind—including conscious experience—is, in some fashion or other, nothing over and above the biological processes of the physical body. The developments in the philosophy of mind since the turn of the twentieth century have been largely a succession of ways of defending and developing this idea.

The principal motivation behind the theories that dominated the early twentieth century was to reject the speculative metaphysics of earlier approaches, and bring the study of the mind into line with either scientific standards or with ordinary ways of talking about the mind. Chapter Seven surveys some of the ideas and arguments of this period, which are embodied in the views of behaviorism and "linguistic philosophy." The former attempted to replace reference to mental events, states, and processes with reference to observable variables, such as stimulus-response patterns and learning histories, that are open to scientific investigation. Linguistic philosophy sought instead to dissolve various difficulties that arise in trying to understand the mind in material terms through an analysis of the ways in which ordinary language about the mind can lead to conceptual confusions and imaginary problems.

Two views of the mind have been at the center of most debates in the past fifty years. Both have been defended in several forms and are under constant revision. Mind-brain identity theory is based on the idea that events in the mind, such as conscious sensations and thoughts, are events in the central nervous system, particularly the brain. This theory says that explanations of the mind and conscious experience can be developed along the same lines as scientific explanations of natural phenomena like heat and lightning—by reducing complex observable events to combinations of simpler events at a more basic level. The next theory, functionalism, is an outgrowth of both the mind-brain identity theory and behaviorism, together with ideas taken from the study of computers. A central argument for this view is that we cannot restrict the possession of conscious experience and thought to just those creatures whose biological make-up is similar to ours. So functionalists argue that we need to explain the processes and events of the mind in a way that abstracts from the biological details of neurological events, looking instead at the functional processes that are realized in the human brain but that might be realized in different ways in other possible creatures.

Part Three has been almost completely updated from the Second Edition, in order to better reflect current debates and controversies, as well as a growing practice in philosophy of mind to tackle difficult issues by combining the traditional philosophical tools of conceptual analysis and logical argumentation with empirical findings from the cognitive sciences—especially psychology and neuroscience. The selected topics and readings demonstrate the contributions from cognitive science to important questions surrounding, in particular, the phenomena of conscious experience and agency.

We have chosen to focus on conscious experience and agency, in part because they are so central to the common notion of what having a mind consists in. Broadly speaking, it is not unnatural to think of entities with minds as those that are aware of themselves and their surroundings, as well as possessed of the capacity to behave intelligently. But in what does this awareness consist, and how might we explain its most puzzling features? In addition, what sets apart non-intelligent, reflex behavior, from flexible, purposive behavior that constitutes human action and agency more generally?

In addition, readers will have noticed from Parts One and Two of the book that in the long history of the mind-body problem, philosophers have tended to focus especially on the puzzle of how best to account for the subjective nature of conscious experience within a scientific worldview. This continues to be one of the central questions with which philosophers of mind and cognitive scientists are concerned, and we think it is particularly instructive to see where the debate has landed in recent years.

We set the stage for exploring such questions in Chapter Ten, "Can Machines Have Minds?" This chapter deals, in part, with issues that date to the middle of the twentieth century when the earliest digital computers were developed. One of the first theorists in this field, the computer scientist Alan Turing, proposed a test that could serve as a marker of intelligence for artificial machines. We will look at both proponents and detractors of the view that an artificial system could ever possess intelligence, let alone genuine thoughts and experiences. The chapter closes with a natural question to ask about the future of artificial intelligence (AI). Suppose that future artificial systems come to behave more and more intelligently, and to become increasingly tightly woven into our societies. At what point might we start treating such systems not merely as tools for our own purposes, but rather as *persons*, with all the accompanying moral and legal obligations? An answer to this question presupposes an answer to the mind-body problem, and in particular to the relationship between our two focal aspects of the mind—consciousness and agency—and the physical body. The remaining chapters explore these phenomena in further depth.

Chapter Eleven looks closely at consciousness and subjective experience. Think of how our perception of the world around us—our experiences of color, sound, and so on—differs from the experiences of creatures such as bats that have very different perceptual organs. According to some philosophers, these differences reveal a subjective element of conscious experience that is necessarily hidden from the objective methods of neuroscience and cognitive psychology. Because of this, they argue, conscious experience forms an element of the mind that cannot be explained by any of the theories outlined in Part Two. Other philosophers attempt to show how such explanations are possible, or else deny that conscious experience has any of the problematic features cited.

Chapter Twelve continues our examination of consciousness, asking in particular what consciousness might be good for. On the assumption that consciousness is an evolved biological property, it seems reasonable to ask what, if any, advantage it confers upon those organisms that possess it. This takes us to a more pointed investigation than is carried out in the previous chapter, namely, whether consciousness can be fully understood just by appeal to the functions it enables, or whether instead the subjective element of consciousness cannot be explained in purely functional terms.

The issues addressed in Chapters Thirteen and Fourteen center on our capacity for intelligent action, and on agency more broadly. The readings in Chapter Thirteen address the question "what is an action?" and reflect attempts by philosophers to distinguish between intelligent action and mere reflex, by appeal to the causal relationships between an individual's psychological states and their bodily behavior—the so-called causal theory of action. This chapter also links back to our theme in the previous one, by asking whether or not consciousness plays some sort of a pivotal role in enabling such an agent to plan, initiate, and guide their behavior.

The selected readings in Chapter Fourteen explore one of the major challenges to the causal theory of action, which is that of explaining the involvement of the *agent* in the production of action. Some theorists have argued that an agent cannot be reduced to psychological states and processes and the causal relationships that hold between them—something more must be added. Others disagree, arguing that the causal theory has the resources to account not only for intelligent action, but for agency more generally. The chapter closes by tying together this topic with those in Chapters Eleven and Twelve on conscious experience, and asking how we can explain from a subjective point of view what is it *like* to act, and what can be said about the nature of such experiences.

PART ONE
HISTORICAL BACKGROUND

1

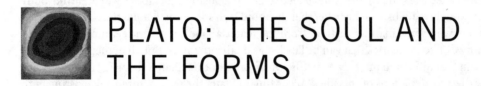

PLATO: THE SOUL AND THE FORMS

Introduction

The origin of the Western view of the mind lies in ancient Greece. The world view developed by the Greeks in the fourth and fifth centuries BCE has provided much of the philosophical framework of European civilization. When medieval and early modern philosophers and scientists constructed their explanations of the natural world, they developed their ideas directly from classical Greek philosophers. These ideas have been greatly modified over time, but their influence is still felt in our modern scientific theories. To a large extent our modern conception of the mind has its roots in the ancient Greek idea of the soul. To understand the current issues and debates surrounding the nature of the mind, it is illuminating to begin by looking at their origins in the ancient world.

Plato and Socrates

Plato (c. 428–347 BCE) is one of the most influential philosophers of European civilization. Plato formulated many questions that have remained central to philosophical enquiry throughout the centuries, and proposed answers to them that still have their influence today. Plato was a student of Socrates (470–399 BCE), who was put to death by the Athenians on the official charge of corrupting the youth of Athens. Socrates himself put nothing in writing but instead spent his time conversing with people and forcing them to critically examine their beliefs, often to their discomfort. Plato's writings take the form of dialogues between his teacher Socrates and various interlocutors. How reflective the dialogues are of the historical Socrates is difficult to decide accurately; often it is clear that the Socrates in the dialogues is serving as a spokesman for views that Plato developed after Socrates' death.

In this chapter, we will read sections of a dialogue entitled *The Phaedo*, named after the person who narrates the story. *The Phaedo* is an account of the death of Socrates. In it Socrates explains to his friends, Simmias and Cebes, why he is unafraid of his impending execution and why death is something to be looked forward to by anyone who leads a truly philosophical life. The defense of the philosophical life that Plato presents in the dialogue hinges on two theories that are central to Plato's work. One is a theory about the world and our knowledge of it that we can call "the theory of the Forms." The other is a belief in the immortality of the soul. In this chapter we will emphasize the importance of the relationship between these ideas.

Dualism

Plato was perhaps the first to articulate a detailed theory of the mind and its relation to the physical body. Several central elements of what we think of today as the mind are aspects of what Plato called the soul. In *The Phaedo* Plato defends a position that today we call **mind-body dualism**. Roughly, dualism is the belief that the mind is in some way *nonphysical* or *immaterial*, and is thereby in some manner distinct from the material body. Over the centuries there have been many different theories that can be labeled as dualist theories. But all of them agree in the basic claim that mind and matter are distinct from one another. Plato's theory of the soul is one of the earliest formulations of this idea. According to Plato, the soul is immortal, existing both before birth and after death. The human body and all other material objects are impermanent, existing only for a certain period of time. Thus the soul and the physical body are, in Plato's view, two distinct entities. Plato argues in *The Phaedo* and elsewhere that the best life for a person to lead is the cultivation of the soul while turning one's attention away from the influence of the physical body.

Plato's Conception of the Soul

What does Plato mean when he talks about "the soul," a term that conjures up many different images? Probably a good part of the portrait of the soul in *The Phaedo* represents the views of his teacher, Socrates. *The Phaedo* presents a first sketch of a theory of the soul. This theory is more fully developed in later dialogues, particularly in a dialogue called *The Republic*. In *The Republic* Plato is clearly moving beyond what Socrates provided him with and offers a detailed account of the soul and its different parts. We will restrict ourselves to the sketch given in *The Phaedo* as it covers the essential elements of Plato's theory without bringing in too many details.

Plato inherited from Socrates the idea that sensual pleasures and the cultivation of the body hinder a person's well-being. This asceticism sets up an opposition between the body and senses on the one hand and the "true self" on the other. So we can think of the soul as the "real person," which can be distinguished from the body and the senses. The opposition between soul and body is a central component in the picture of the soul developed in *The Phaedo*. As we will see, it plays a major role in Plato's argument that soul and body are two distinct entities.

Another element of the soul that Plato refers to in *The Phaedo* is derived from early Greek tradition. This element is closest to the meaning of the original Greek word *psuchê*: the idea that the soul is what brings life to the body. The difference between a living thing and a dead body is the presence of a soul. At one point in *The Phaedo* Plato claims that the soul by its very nature is "that which brings life."

Besides these traditional meanings attached to the word 'soul,' Plato adds two additional ideas. First, Plato identifies the soul as the seat of reason and knowledge. According to Plato, the soul is the rational part of us while our irrational nature comes from the influence of the body. Plato believes that it is through the activity of the rational soul that we have knowledge. Second, the soul experiences different states of consciousness stemming from the influence of the senses and the condition of the body. For example, the eyes and ears produce experiences of color and sound in the soul, while injury to the body produces sensations of pain. According to Plato, these experiences are states of the immaterial soul produced by the changes in the body.

These last two elements in Plato's conception of the soul are important to Plato's reasons for believing in dualism. As we will see in this chapter, Plato believes that the soul can be a source of reason and knowledge only if it is a distinct entity from the physical body. To follow Plato's arguments for dualism, we will have to understand a certain amount about his theory of knowledge.

Plato's idea that the soul is the seat of both reason and consciousness is also essential in forming an understanding of our current psychological theories. For this idea is the historical antecedent to the concept of the mind in modern psychology and philosophy. In the final section of this book we will look at how recent thinkers have attempted to explain the characteristics of thought and consciousness in terms of modern neuroscience.

Socrates' Defense

We can now begin reading *The Phaedo*. The entire dialogue is fairly lengthy, so we'll read some central sections, beginning with a section we'll call "Socrates' defense." A group of friends has gathered with Socrates in prison where he is awaiting his execution. To ease their grief Socrates has said that a philosopher does not fear death because he can look forward to a better existence in the next world. In this first section of *The Phaedo* Socrates defends this claim on the grounds that the philosophical life is nothing more than the art of dying. (Simmias points out the joke in this: Most people would agree that death is precisely what philosophers should undergo.)

Socrates begins his argument with a description of death as "nothing but the separation of the soul from the body" (64c).[1] He claims that a genuine philosopher will ignore the pleasures of the body and seek instead to release the soul from the influence of the body. The body, he says, is a hindrance in the gaining of wisdom because sight and hearing, which rely on the sensory organs of the body, do not "afford men any truth" (65b). This is a striking claim. According to Plato, our eyes and ears are not sources of information about the world around us, but actually form an obstruction to knowledge. This idea, which identifies the soul with knowledge and denies the reliability of the senses, forms an essential part of the portrayal of the soul in *The Phaedo*. To see what basis he has for making this claim we need to look at Plato's theory of knowledge.

What Is Revealed to the Soul

At 65c Socrates says,

> "So isn't it in reasoning, if anywhere at all, that any of the things that *are* become manifest to [the soul]?"

A few lines later is the following exchange:

"Well, now, what about things of this sort, Simmias [i.e., things that are revealed to the soul]? Do we say that there is something *just* or nothing?"

"Yes, we most certainly do!"

"And again, something *beautiful* and *good*?" "Of course."

"Now did you ever yet see any such things with your eyes?" "Certainly not."

"Well, did you grasp them with any other bodily sense-perception? And I'm talking about them all—about largeness, health, and strength, for example—and, in short, about the Being of all other such things, what each one actually is; is it through the body that their truest element is viewed, or isn't it rather thus: whoever of us is prepared to think most fully and minutely of each object of his inquiry, in itself, will come closest to the knowledge of each?"

"Yes, certainly."

This is a difficult passage, but it is important. Notice first that Socrates is claiming that there are certain things that are manifest (or revealed) to the soul, but not to the bodily senses such as sight. The idea is that there is a certain kind of knowledge or awareness that the soul possesses, which is not obtained through the senses.

He also says that the things revealed to the soul are "the things that *are*" (66a). He means that the things revealed to the soul are the things that are lasting and unchanging, while the things perceived by the senses are impermanent and constantly changing. So what are the things "that *are*"? What significance does Plato see in this claim? To answer these questions we need to understand something that philosophers nowadays call *universals*. This will take us away from our main topic of the soul for a page or two. But the diversion will help us understand Plato's ideas about soul and body more properly.

Universals

Let's look, then, at universals. A **universal** is a characteristic or property that may be possessed by more than one object. Consider a simple example: if two objects are both red, there is something they have in common, namely the redness. So Plato distinguishes between individual things and the universal, redness, that they have in common. Plato was interested in the sorts of universals that arise in ethics, politics, and mathematics. In ethics there are such properties as virtue and justice, and in mathematics there are such properties as equality and circularity.

Another way to describe universals is to say that they are the means by which we classify objects into kinds. When we say that two objects are red, we are assigning a certain label to them. This label is given to all objects that are similar to one another in a particular way. In ethics we classify a certain kind of person as virtuous, and in mathematics, certain shapes as circular.

Plato's teacher, Socrates, was the first person to draw attention to universals and to recognize their importance. Many of Plato's dialogues emphasize the significance of universals in obtaining knowledge. For example, suppose we ask the question, "What is virtue?" This question cannot be answered simply by giving a list of examples of particular people or actions, for this still leaves the important question, "What do all these things have in common that makes them virtuous?" Without knowing the answer to this question, we cannot claim to know what virtue is. Plato points out that the answer to this last question consists of a description of a universal, which he would call "virtue itself." Using examples such as this, Plato argues that real knowledge requires an understanding of universals. Such an understanding, he maintains, is more than just a familiarity with individual things. A fundamental question for Plato, then, is the question of how knowledge of universals is obtained.

Knowledge of Universals

Plato believes that we grasp universals through the *intellect* and not through the senses. The **intellect** is that part of the mind that is responsible for reason and understanding. According to Plato, when you see that two objects are beautiful, your eyes are involved in the perception, but it is the intellect or the mind that grasps what they have in common. That is, you might see two beautiful objects, but to see *that* they are beautiful you must have an understanding of the universal, beauty, which both possess. Similarly, when we see that someone is virtuous, this perception is achieved by the mind's understanding of the universal, "virtue itself."

In Plato's view, the senses give a certain kind of information, which we may think of as "raw data." But it is the soul that interprets and understands these data by identifying what objects have in common. Moreover, he maintains that the data provided by the senses are misleading in certain ways, and so we cannot classify objects just by analyzing what the senses bring in. The soul must provide additional knowledge that it brings from within itself.

But what basis does Plato have for believing that only the intellect can grasp universals? Why can't our eyes perceive the beauty of something directly without the aid of the intellect? The answer to this lies in his account of what universals are. This takes us to Plato's famous theory of "the Forms."

The Forms

Plato believes that universals must exist independently of individual objects. For example, even if there were no virtuous people, the universal, "virtue itself," would exist on its own. He had many reasons for this belief. Partly his conclusion came from his study of mathematics. Consider the following example from geometry. Once we understand the rule that the angles of a triangle are equal to two right angles, this knowledge can be applied to any and all triangles. In Plato's view, this means that our knowledge is not of any *particular* triangle. It is knowledge of the *property* of triangularity. This is especially evident when we realize that no physical object is *exactly* triangular (because, for example, no line on paper is perfectly straight), but only approximately so. Plato argues that the universal, triangularity, must be a separate thing from any particular object, because knowledge of one is distinct from knowledge of the other. We can apply the same reasoning to the other universals that Plato was concerned with, such as beauty and virtue. According to Plato, then, universals are objects in their own right, existing independently of the things we perceive with the senses.

Plato gives universals the Greek name *eidos*, usually translated as **Forms** or **Ideas**. In the passage we just read, the "things that *are*," to which Socrates refers, are the Forms. When Socrates asks Simmias whether "there is something just" or "beautiful, and good," he is asking about the Forms of Justice, Beauty, and Goodness.

Material Objects and the Forms

According to Plato, the Forms as a whole make up a distinct realm from the natural world. The Forms are changeless, eternal entities. By contrast, the material objects that we perceive with the senses are always changing, taking on new characteristics, and existing at one time but not at others. For example, a painting might be beautiful for a time and then lose its beauty through decay or damage. But the universal, Beauty itself, never changes and never ceases to exist; it is timeless and immutable. This is what is meant in the quotation above, when Socrates says that the Forms are the things that *are*. Material things are impermanent and constantly changing. To use Plato's description, they are in a perpetual state of *becoming*. The Forms, on the other hand, never change and never cease to be—they don't become anything; they just *are*.

If universals are entities separate from material objects, how can we say that material objects possess them? If Beauty is an entity separate from all material objects, how can paintings and other material objects *be* beautiful? Plato's answer to this is that material objects have properties in common by *resembling* the same Forms. Thus paintings or sculptures can all be beautiful to the extent that they resemble the Form of Beauty.

We used the word 'extent' in the last sentence to point out that, as resemblance is never perfect, objects in the material world never possess properties perfectly. There are no perfectly beautiful paintings, perfectly virtuous people, or perfectly triangular objects. This adds another interpretation to Socrates' claim that the Forms are the only things that *are*. For in Plato's view, no material thing is ever really perfectly beautiful, or virtuous, or triangular.

Knowledge of Universals Again

Because the senses inform us of the material world around us, Plato maintains that they provide us only with fleeting glimpses of the imperfect images of the Forms. Only the intellect or the soul can acquire genuine knowledge of what is eternal and unchanging by coming to know the Forms directly. This knowledge is obtained through reason and reflection, as in mathematics and philosophical debate. This is why Plato claims that the things that really exist—the timeless, eternal Forms—are known only through the intellect. What is given to us through the senses is imperfect and constantly changing as objects take on and lose their resemblance to the Forms. The distractions of sensory stimulation get in the way of our coming to know the true nature of universals, which are the sources of all the features of the world.

This is the end of our excursion into Plato's theory of universals and our knowledge of them. We can now return to Socrates' defense, picking up the dialogue where we left it at 66a.

The Problem of Immortality

With Simmias' acceptance of the theory of the Forms, Socrates argues that as long as we possess a physical body our soul will be confused by the distractions of the senses and drawn away from genuine knowledge. At 66b he claims that "as long as we possess the body, and our soul is contaminated with such an evil, we'll surely never adequately gain what we desire—and that, we say, is truth." The idea is that the bodily senses reveal only shadows and images of the Forms, but direct knowledge of the Forms by the intellect gives us genuine knowledge. Thus a true "lover of knowledge" will welcome death as a release from the body (67a–68b), and the practice of philosophy is nothing but the "cultivation of dying" (67e).

But in the next section at 70a, Cebes points out that not everyone believes that the soul exists after death. Some people, he says, "fear that when it's been separated from the body, it may no longer exist anywhere." So to defend the philosophical life and his attitude toward death, Socrates must also demonstrate the truth of dualism. He must show that the soul is not a part of the physical body, or dependent upon it, but that it exists as an independent entity after death. In *The Phaedo* Plato has Socrates offer four different arguments for this theory of the soul. The first is called "the cyclical argument."

The Cyclical Argument

In the cyclical argument Plato's intent is to show that when we die our souls exist in another world and are reborn. Plato bases his argument on a general principle, with which the others agree. The principle is that "opposites come to be only from their opposite." For example, what comes to be larger comes to be from something smaller, and what comes to be colder comes to be from something hotter. Socrates then has Cebes agree that being dead is the opposite of being alive (71c). So from the general principle, Socrates argues, it follows that life and death come from each other (71d). Socrates compares this to sleeping and being awake: going to sleep is the process of going from wakefulness to sleep, and waking up is the process of going from sleep to wakefulness. In the same way, he argues, in birth "living people are born from the dead no less than dead people from the living" (72a). If this comparison is accurate, it must follow that the souls of the dead exist somewhere until they are born again.

From 72b to 72d Socrates supports the general principle on which the argument is based by claiming that if it were not true, everything would eventually have the same form. If people went to sleep, but there were no waking up from sleep, eventually everyone would be asleep. In the same way, he argues, if things died but did not return to life, ultimately everything would be dead.

Notice, by the way, that at this point Socrates extends the argument from people to "all things that partake in life" (72c). It is not only the souls of people to which his argument applies, but to all living things. Here Plato is clearly referring to the soul as the source of animation, that which brings life to the body. This raises the question of how this element of the soul can be combined with its role as intellect or seat of consciousness. He represents the intellect as resembling the immaterial Forms. How, then, can the soul be the source of life in material things? What is the connection between matter and the Forms? This is a problem that Plato's successor, Aristotle, resolves by rejecting both Plato's dualism and his theory of universals.

The Recollection Argument

At 72e Cebes reminds the others of a theory that Socrates has used before to justify the belief that the soul is immortal. This is the theory that "learning is nothing but recollection." According to the theory, what we take to be the acquisition of new knowledge is actually a matter of being reminded of what we have learned in a previous life. Cebes points out that if the recollection theory is true, then our souls must have existed before this life. This provides Socrates with another argument for dualism, as the recollection theory entails the possibility of the soul existing independently of the body.

The question, then, is what reason there is to believe the theory, and Simmias asks Cebes to remind him of the arguments for it. (The pun here is intentional.) What follows is a lengthy discussion of the recollection theory, and of one of the arguments for it based on the theory of the Forms.

Defending the Recollection Theory

Cebes first raises very briefly an argument that is given extended treatment in another dialogue, *The Meno.* This is the idea that if we are questioned in the right way, we will arrive at the correct answers to problems on our own, without the answers being supplied to us. The conclusion drawn is that the answers must have been in us before our birth, and the questioning merely reminds us of them. In *The Meno* Socrates leads a slave-boy in this way to solve the problem of determining the length of the sides of a square that is double in area to a given square. The slave-boy arrives at the correct answer by providing Socrates with answers to a series of questions, without Socrates actually supplying him with the correct answers.

At 73c Socrates begins a different argument for the recollection theory, based on the theory of the Forms. At 73d he presents a definition of recollection, which serves as the first premise in his argument. According to this definition, recollection is defined as "perceiving one thing and as a result coming to think of something else." The example Socrates offers is that of a lover who is reminded of his beloved by recognizing an object that belongs to the loved one. He adds that sometimes a recollection is occasioned by something similar to the object itself, as with a picture, and sometimes by something dissimilar, as with a piece of clothing owned by the loved one. At 74a he says that when we are reminded of something from a similar thing, we must be aware of the fact that the object that prompts the recollection is "lacking... in its similarity, in relation to what one is reminded of." His point is that even in the case of similar objects, what prompts a recollection does not possess all the qualities of what it brings to mind. A picture, for example, is a two-dimensional image of a person, not a perfect duplicate.

At this point the theory of the Forms is brought into the argument, using for illustration the universal Equality. Socrates first has Simmias agree that there is a Form of Equality (which he calls here "the equal itself") (74a). Then at 74c he adds the following two premises:

1. Things that we perceive to be equal are distinct from the equal itself. That is, the material objects we perceive and the Forms are distinct from one another.
2. Our knowledge of equality is produced by the perception of equal things.

The basis for premise 1 is that material objects are always in some ways unequal while this cannot be true of "the equal itself." This reflects the differences between material things and the Forms that we described earlier. Premise 2 is drawn from the fact that we are first taught the *concept* of equality by perceiving particular material objects. When we first learn the meaning of the term 'equality,' it is usually by being shown examples of equal things. So although sensory perception by itself cannot provide us with the concept of equality, it is only in the act of perceiving equal things that the concept is first brought to mind.

Given the definition of recollection as the act of perceiving one thing and thinking of something different as a result, Socrates concludes from premises 1 and 2 that our knowledge of equality must be a case of recollection. Because certain pairs of material things *resemble* the Form of Equality, our perception of them can bring the idea of that Form to mind. We perceive one thing with our senses (namely, the material objects) and are thereby prompted to think of something else (namely, the Form).

So it is agreed that knowledge of universals like Equality is a matter of being reminded of the Forms when we observe things that resemble them. But because perception begins at birth, the conclusion is that our knowledge of universals was obtained prior to our birth. It follows from this theory that our souls must have existed before our birth, during which time we gained our acquaintance with the Forms. At 76e Socrates reminds the others that this argument depends on the theory of the Forms, and without the theory it "will have gone for nothing."

Two Additional Arguments for Immortality

The remaining portions of *The Phaedo* are too long to reproduce in the readings.[2] At 77d Socrates says that despite the two arguments given already, Cebes and Simmias are still afraid that at death "as the soul goes out of the body, the wind may literally blow it apart and disperse it." So Socrates offers two additional arguments to allay their fears.

The first argument is called "the affinity argument," because in it Plato contends that the soul is most similar to the Forms, which are eternal and unchanging. The argument has two premises:

1. The things that are most liable to destruction are the things we perceive with our bodily senses like sight and touch, and the things that are not susceptible to destruction are the Forms.
2. The soul is most similar to the unchanging, invisible Forms and not to the realm of ever-changing objects that we perceive with the senses.

The fourth argument in *The Phaedo* is called "the argument from opposites." In this final argument, Socrates points out that the existence of each kind of object depends upon its possessing certain qualities essential for its existence. For example, the existence of snow depends on coldness—in the presence of warmth, snow disappears. He argues that when an object possesses a particular property in this way, it cannot possess the opposite of that property. Because coldness is essential to snow, snow cannot possess warmth. Cebes and the others agree that the soul is the source of life by its very nature. It follows, then, that the soul cannot also admit of death. Hence the soul is immortal.

Plato's Influence

We have seen how Plato developed a theory of the soul to explain our knowledge of universals. This knowledge, Plato believed, could not be acquired through the senses but only through the activity of the intellect. As the intellect is associated with the Forms, which are eternal and indestructible, the soul too must be immortal.

From the beginning there was an awareness of various problems in Plato's theory of the Forms, and Plato himself looked on his theories as hypotheses to be amended and worked over. The largest problem was in explaining how material objects could resemble and be influenced by the immaterial Forms. Eventually the problems in reworking his ideas became so difficult that Plato began to rethink his commitment to the theory of the Forms. Once the theory of the Forms was given up, it became possible for his student, Aristotle, to reject the theory of the soul that came with it.

As we will see in the next chapter, Aristotle abandons the contrast Plato draws between the senses and the intellect. Aristotle maintains that the senses are a reliable (though incomplete) source of knowledge. This difference between Plato and Aristotle is part of what led to Aristotle's rejection of Plato's theory of the soul. Interestingly, however, the developments that created the modern mathematical sciences in the seventeenth century CE brought back doubts about the veracity of sensory perception. Even though Plato's theory of the Forms was never resurrected, we will see that two aspects of Plato's views returned with the rise of modern science: the idea that the senses are not entirely reliable as a guide to knowledge of the world, and the idea that mind and body are two distinct entities. In a different guise again, these ideas continue to have an influence in present-day psychology and neuroscience.

Notes

1. These numbers occur in the margin of the reading. They refer to a standard page numbering system, used with all translations of Plato and based on the pagination of a standard edition of the original Greek text. The first number refers to the page number, and the letter refers to the column.

2. For the complete dialogue, see *Plato: The Phaedo*, translated with notes by David Gallop (Oxford: Oxford University Press, 1975).

PLATO

Selections from *The Phaedo*

Socrates' Defense

[…]

'Let him be,' he said. 'Now then, with you for my jury I want to give my defence, and show with what good reason, as it seems to me, a man who has truly spent his life in philosophy feels confident when about to die, and is hopeful 64a that, when he has died, he will win very great benefits in the other world. So I'll try, Simmias and Cebes, to explain how this could be.

'Other people may well be unaware that all who actually engage in philosophy aright are practising nothing other than dying and being dead. Now if this is true, it would be odd indeed for them to be eager in their whole life for nothing but this, and yet to be resentful when it comes, the very thing they'd long been eager for and practised.'

Simmias laughed at this and said: 'Good-b ness, Socrates, you've made me laugh, even though I wasn't much inclined to laugh just now. I imagine that most people, on hearing that, would think it very well said of philosophers—and our own countrymen would quite agree—that they are, indeed, verging on death, and that they, at any rate, are well aware that this is what philosophers deserve to undergo.'

'Yes, and what they say would be true, Simmias, except for their claim to be aware of it themselves; because they aren't aware in what sense genuine philosophers are verging on death and deserving of it, and what kind of death they deserve. Anyway, let's discuss it c among ourselves, disregarding them: do we suppose that death *is* something?'

'Certainly,' rejoined Simmias.

'And that it is nothing but the separation of the soul from the body? And that being dead is this: the body's having come to be apart, separated from the soul, alone by itself, and the soul's being apart, alone by itself, separated from the body? Death can't be anything else but that, can it?'

'No, it's just that.'

'Now look, my friend, and see if maybe you
d agree with me on these points; because through
them I think we'll improve our knowledge of
what we're examining. Do you think it befits
a philosophical man to be keen about the
so-called pleasures of, for example, food and
drink?'

'Not in the least, Socrates,' said Simmias.

'And what about those of sex?'

'Not at all.'

'And what about the other services to the
body? Do you think such a man regards them
as of any value? For instance, the possession of
smart clothes and shoes, and the other bodily
adornments—do you think he values them
e highly, or does he disdain them, except in so far
as he's absolutely compelled to share in them?'

'I think the genuine philosopher disdains
them.'

'Do you think in general, then, that such a
man's concern is not for the body, but so far as
he can stand aside from it, is directed towards
the soul?'

'I do.'

'Then is it clear that, first, in such matters
as these the philosopher differs from other men
65a in releasing his soul, as far as possible, from its
communion with the body?'

'It appears so.'

'And presumably, Simmias, it does seem to
most men that someone who finds nothing of
that sort pleasant, and takes no part in those
things, doesn't deserve to live; rather, one who
cares nothing for the pleasures that come by
way of the body runs pretty close to being dead.'

'Yes, what you say is quite true.'

'And now, what about the actual gaining
of wisdom? Is the body a hindrance or not, if
b one enlists it as a partner in the quest? This is
the sort of thing I mean: do sight and hearing
afford men any truth, or aren't even the poets
always harping on such themes, telling us that

we neither hear nor see anything accurately?
And yet if these of all the bodily senses are neither accurate nor clear, the others will hardly be
so; because they are, surely, all inferior to these.
Don't you think so?'

'Certainly.'

'So when does the soul attain the truth?
Because plainly, whenever it sets about examining anything in company with the body, it is
completely taken in by it.'

'That's true.'   c

'So isn't it in reasoning, if anywhere at all,
that any of the things that *are* become manifest
to it?'

'Yes.'

'And it reasons best, presumably, whenever
none of these things bothers it, neither hearing
nor sight nor pain, nor any pleasure either, but
whenever it comes to be alone by itself as far as
possible, disregarding the body, and whenever,
having the least possible communion and contact with it, it strives for that which is.'

'That is so.'

'So there again the soul of the philosopher   d
utterly disdains the body and flees from it,
seeking rather to come to be alone by itself?'

'It seems so.'

'Well now, what about things of this sort,
Simmias? Do we say that there is something
just, or nothing?'

'Yes, we most certainly do!'

'And again, something *beautiful*, and *good*?'

'Of course.'

'Now did you ever yet see any such things
with your eyes?'

'Certainly not.'

'Well, did you grasp them with any other
bodily sense-perception? And I'm talking about
them all—about largeness, health, and strength,
for example—and, in short, about the Being of
all other such things, what each one actually is;   e
is it through the body that their truest element
is viewed, or isn't it rather thus: whoever of us

is prepared to think most fully and minutely of each object of his inquiry, in itself, will come closest to the knowledge of each?'

'Yes, certainly.'

'Then would that be achieved most purely by the man who approached each object with his intellect alone as far as possible, neither adduc-
66a ing sight in his thinking, nor dragging in any other sense to accompany his reasoning; rather, using his intellect alone by itself and unsullied, he would undertake the hunt for each of the things that are, each alone by itself and unsullied; he would be separated as far as possible from his eyes and ears, and virtually from his whole body, on the ground that it confuses the soul, and doesn't allow it to gain truth and wisdom when in partnership with it: isn't it this man, Simmias, who will attain that which is, if anyone will?'

'What you say is abundantly true, Socrates,' said Simmias.

b 'For all these reasons, then, some such view as this must present itself to genuine philosophers, so that they say such things to one another as these: "There now, it looks as if some sort of track is leading us, together with our reason, astray in our inquiry: as long as we possess the body, and our soul is contaminated by such an evil, we'll surely never adequately gain what we desire—and that, we say, is truth. Because the body affords us countless distrac-
c tions, owing to the nurture it must have; and again, if any illnesses befall it, they hamper our pursuit of that which is. Besides, it fills us up with lusts and desires, with fears and fantasies of every kind, and with any amount of trash, so that really and truly we are, as the saying goes, never able to think of anything at all because of it. Thus, it's nothing but the body and its desires that brings wars and factions and fighting; because it's over the gaining of wealth that all wars take place, and we're compelled to gain
d wealth because of the body, enslaved as we are

to its service; so for all these reasons it leaves us no leisure for philosophy. And the worst of it all is that if we do get any leisure from it, and turn to some inquiry, once again it intrudes every-where in our researches, setting up a clamour and disturbance, and striking terror, so that the truth can't be discerned because of it. Well now, it really has been shown us that if we're ever going to know anything purely, we must be rid of it, and must view the objects themselves with e the soul by itself; it's then, apparently, that the thing we desire and whose lovers we claim to be, wisdom, will be ours—when we have died, as the argument indicates, though not while we live. Because, if we can know nothing purely in the body's company, then one of two things must be true: either knowledge is nowhere to be gained, or else it is for the dead; since then, but no sooner, will the soul be alone by itself apart 67a from the body. And therefore while we live, it would seem that we shall be closest to knowl-edge in this way—if we consort with the body as little as possible, and do not commune with it, except in so far as we must, and do not infect ourselves with its nature, but remain pure from it, until God himself shall release us; and being thus pure, through separation from the body's folly, we shall probably be in like company, and shall know through our own selves all that is unsullied—and that, I dare say, is what the b truth is; because never will it be permissible for impure to touch pure." Such are the things, I think, Simmias, that all who are rightly called lovers of knowledge must say to one another, and must believe. Don't you agree?'

'Emphatically, Socrates.'

'Well then, if that's true, my friend,' said Socrates, 'there's plenty of hope for one who arrives where I'm going, that there, if anywhere, he will adequately possess the object that's been our great concern in life gone by; and thus the journey now appointed for me may also be c made with good hope by any other man who regards his intellect as prepared, by having been, in a manner, purified.'

'Yes indeed,' said Simmias.

'Then doesn't purification turn out to be just what's been mentioned for some while in our discussion—the parting of the soul from the body as far as possible, and the habituating of it to assemble and gather itself together, away from every part of the body, alone by itself, and
d to live, so far as it can, both in the present and in the hereafter, released from the body, as from fetters?'

'Yes indeed.'

'And is it just this that is named "death"—a release and parting of soul from body?'

'Indeed it is.'

'And it's especially those who practise philosophy aright, or rather they alone, who are always eager to release it, as we say, and the occupation of philosophers is just this, isn't it—a release and parting of soul from body?'

'It seems so.'

'Then wouldn't it be absurd, as I said at the start, for a man to prepare himself in his life to
e live as close as he can to being dead, and then to be resentful when this comes to him?'

'It would be absurd, of course.'

'Truly then, Simmias, those who practise philosophy aright are cultivating dying, and for them least of all men does being dead hold any terror. Look at it like this: if they've set themselves at odds with the body at every point, and desire to possess their soul alone by itself, wouldn't it be quite illogical if they were afraid and resentful when this came about—if, that is, they didn't go gladly to the place where,
68a on arrival, they may hope to attain what they longed for throughout life, namely wisdom—and to be rid of the company of that with which they'd set themselves at odds? Or again, many have been willing to enter Hades of their own accord, in quest of human loves, of wives and sons who have died, led by this hope, that there

they would see and be united with those they desired; will anyone, then, who truly longs for wisdom, and who firmly holds this same hope, that nowhere but in Hades will he attain b it in any way worth mentioning, be resentful at dying; and will he not go there gladly? One must suppose so, my friend, if he's truly a lover of wisdom; since this will be his firm belief, that nowhere else but there will he attain wisdom purely. Yet if that is so, wouldn't it, as I said just now, be quite illogical if such a man were afraid of death?'

'Yes, quite illogical!'

'Then if you see a man resentful that he is going to die, isn't this proof enough for you that he's no lover of wisdom after all, but what we may call a lover of the body? And this same c man turns out, in some sense, to be a lover of riches and of prestige, either one of these or both.'

'It's just as you say.'

'Well now, Simmias, isn't it also true that what is named "bravery" belongs especially to people of the disposition we have described?'

'Most certainly.'

'And then temperance too, even what most people name "temperance"—not being excited over one's desires, but being scornful of them and well-ordered—belongs, doesn't it, only to those who utterly scorn the body and live in d love of wisdom?'

'It must.'

'Yes, because if you care to consider the bravery and temperance of other men, you'll find it strange.'

'How so, Socrates?'

'You know, don't you, that all other men count death among great evils?'

'Very much so.'

'Is it, then, through being afraid of greater evils that the brave among them abide death, whenever they do so?'

'It is.'

'Then, it's through fearing and fear that all men except philosophers are brave; and yet it's surely illogical that anyone should be brave through fear and cowardice.'

e   'It certainly is.'

'And what about those of them who are well-ordered? Aren't they in this same state, temperate through a kind of intemperance? True, we say that's impossible; but still that state of simple-minded temperance does turn out in their case to be like this: it's because they're afraid of being deprived of further pleasures, and desire them, that they abstain from some because they're overcome by others. True, they

69a call it "intemperance" to be ruled by pleasures, but still that's what happens to them: they overcome some pleasures because they're overcome by others. And this is the sort of thing that was just mentioned: after a fashion, they achieve temperance because of intemperance.'

'Yes, so it seems.'

'Yes, Simmias, my good friend; since this may not be the right exchange with a view to goodness, the exchanging of pleasures for pleasures, pains for pains, and fear for fear, greater for lesser ones, like coins; it may be, rather, that this alone is the right coin, for which one

b   should exchange all these things—wisdom; and the buying and selling of all things for that, or rather with that, may be real bravery, temperance, justice, and, in short, true goodness in company with wisdom, whether pleasures and fears and all else of that sort be added or taken away; but as for their being parted from wisdom and exchanged for one another, goodness of that sort may be a kind of illusory facade, and fit for slaves indeed, and may have nothing healthy or true about it; whereas, truth to tell, temperance, justice, and bravery may in

c   fact be a kind of purification of all such things, and wisdom itself a kind of purifying rite. So it really looks as if those who established our initiations are no mean people, but have in

fact long been saying in riddles that whoever arrives in Hades unadmitted to the rites, and uninitiated, shall lie in the slough, while he who arrives there purified and initiated shall dwell with gods. For truly there are, so say those concerned with the initiations, "many who bear the wand, but few who are devotees." Now these   d latter, in my view, are none other than those who have practised philosophy aright. And it's to be among them that I myself have striven, in every way I could, neglecting nothing during my life within my power. Whether I have striven aright and we have achieved anything, we shall, I think, know for certain, God willing, in a little while, on arrival yonder.

'There's my defence, then, Simmias and Cebes, to show how reasonable it is for me not to take it hard or be resentful at leaving you and my masters here, since I believe that there also,   e no less than here, I shall find good masters and companions; so if I'm any more convincing in my defence to you than to the Athenian jury, it would be well.'

The Cyclical Argument

When Socrates had said this, Cebes rejoined: 'The other things you say, Socrates, I find excellent; but what you say about the soul is the sub-   70a ject of much disbelief: men fear that when it's been separated from the body, it may no longer exist anywhere, but that on the very day a man dies, it may be destroyed and perish, as soon as it's separated from the body; and that as it goes out, it may be dispersed like breath or smoke, go flying off, and exist no longer anywhere at all. True, if it did exist somewhere, gathered together alone by itself, and separated from those evils you were recounting just now, there'd be plenty of hope, Socrates, and a fine   b hope it would be, that what you say is true; but on just this point, perhaps, one needs no little reassuring and convincing, that when the man has died, his soul exists, and that it possesses some power and wisdom.'

'That's true, Cebes,' said Socrates; 'but then what are we to do? Would you like us to speculate on these very questions, and see whether this is likely to be the case or not?'

'For my part anyway,' said Cebes, 'I'd gladly hear whatever opinion you have about them.'

c 'Well,' said Socrates, 'I really don't think anyone listening now, even if he were a comic poet, would say that I'm talking idly, and arguing about things that don't concern me. If you agree, then, we should look into the matter.

'Let's consider it, perhaps, in this way: do the souls of men exist in Hades when they have died, or do they not? Now an ancient doctrine, which we've recalled that they do exist in that world, entering it from this one, and that they re-enter this world and are born again from the dead; yet if this is so, if living people are born again from those who have died, surely souls d would have to exist in that world? Because they could hardly be born if they didn't exist; so it would be evidence for the truth of these claims, if really became plain that living people are born from the dead and from nowhere else; but if that isn't so, some other argument would be needed.'

'Certainly,' said Cebes.

'Well now, consider the matter, if you want to understand more readily, in connection not only with mankind, but with all animals and plants; and, in general, for all things subject to coming-to-be, let's see whether everything e comes to be in this way: opposites come to be only from their opposites—in the case of all things that actually have an opposite—as, for the beautiful is opposite, of course, to the ugly, just to unjust, and so on in countless other cases. So let's consider this: is it necessary that whatever has an opposite comes to be only from its opposite? For example, when a thing comes to be larger, it must, surely, come to be larger from being smaller before?'

'Yes.'

'And again, if it comes to be smaller, it will 71a come to be smaller later from being larger before?'

'That's so.'

'And that which is weaker comes to be, presumably, from a stronger, and that which is faster from a slower?'

'Certainly.'

'And again, if a thing comes to be worse, it's from a better, and if more just, from a more unjust?'

'Of course.'

'Are we satisfied, then, that all things come to be in this way, opposite things from opposites?'

'Certainly.'

'Now again, do these things have a further feature of this sort: between the members of every pair of opposites, since they are two, b aren't there two processes coming-to-be, from one to the other, and back again from the latter to the former? Thus, between a larger thing and a smaller, isn't there increase and decrease, so in the one case we speak of "increasing" and in the other of "decreasing"?'

'Yes.'

'And similarly with separating and combining, cooling and heating, and all such; even if in some cases we don't use names, still in actual fact mustn't the same principle everywhere hold good: they come to be from each other, and there's a process of coming-to-be of each into the other?'

'Certainly.'

'Well then, is there an opposite to living, as c sleeping is opposite to being awake?'

'Certainly.'

'What is it?'

'Being dead.'

'Then these come to be from each other, if they are opposites; and between the pair of them, since they are two, the processes of coming-to-be are two?'

'Of course.'

'Now then,' said Socrates, 'I'll tell you one of the couples I was just mentioning, the couple itself and its processes; and you tell me the other. My couple is sleeping and being awake: being awake comes to be from sleeping, and d sleeping from being awake, and their processes are going to sleep and waking up. Is that sufficient for you or not?'

'Certainly.'

'Now it's for you to tell me in the same way about life and death. You say, don't you, that being dead is opposite to living?'

'I do.'

'And that they come to be from each other?'

'Yes.'

'Then what is it that comes to be from that which is living?'

'That which is dead.'

'And what comes to be from that which is dead?'

'I must admit that it's that which is living.'

'Then it's from those that are dead, Cebes, e that living things and living people are born?'

'Apparently.'

'Then our souls do exist in Hades.'

'So it seems.'

'Now *one* of the relevant processes here is obvious, isn't it? For dying is obvious enough, surely?'

'It certainly is.'

'What shall we do then? Shan't we assign the opposite process to balance it? Will nature be lame in this respect? Or must we supply some process opposite to dying?'

'We surely must.'

'What will this be?'

'Coming to life again.'

72a 'Then if there is such a thing as coming to life again, wouldn't this, coming to life again, be a process from dead to living people?'

'Certainly.'

'In that way too, then, we're agreed that living people are born from the dead no less than dead people from the living; and we thought that, if this were the case, it would be sufficient evidence that the souls of the dead must exist somewhere, whence they are born again.'

'I think, Socrates, that that must follow from our admissions.'

'Then look at it this way, Cebes, and you'll see, I think, that our admissions were not mistaken. If there were not perpetual reciprocity b in coming to be, between one set of things and another, revolving in a circle, as it were—if, instead, coming-to-be were a linear process from one thing into its opposite only, without any bending back in the other direction or reversal, do you realize that all things would ultimately have the same form: the same fate would overtake them, and they would cease from coming to be?'

'What do you mean?'

'It's not at all hard to understand what I mean. If, for example, there were such a thing as going to sleep, but from sleeping there were no reverse process of waking up; you realize that c everything would ultimately make Endymion seem a mere trifle: he'd be nowhere, because the same fate as his, sleeping, would have overtaken everything else.* Again, if everything were combined, but not separated, then Anaxagoras' notion of "all things together" would soon be realized.† And similarly, my dear Cebes, if all

---

* Eds.: In Greek mythology, Endymion was a youth of great beauty, loved by Selene, the goddess of the moon. When Zeus offered him whatever fate he wished, he chose eternal sleep to remain forever youthful. Selene visited him in his sleep and had fifty daughters by him. In another version of the myth, Selene asked Zeus to put Endymion into an eternal sleep to preserve his beauty.

† Eds.: This quotation is from the pre-Socratic philosopher, Anaxagoras of Clazomenae (c. 500–428 BCE). Anaxagoras accepted an argument by Parmenides of Elea that coming-to-be is impossible because what-is-not (from which what-comes-to-be must come) cannot exist, and therefore no change is possible. In light of this he postulated that everything contains all the ingredients of everything else.

things that partake in life were to die, but when they'd died, the dead remained in that form, and didn't come back to life, wouldn't it be quite inevitable that everything would ultimately be d dead, and nothing would live? Because if the living things came to be from the other things, but the living things were to die, what could possibly prevent everything from being completely spent in being dead?'

'Nothing whatever, in my view, Socrates,' said Cebes; 'what you say seems to be perfectly true.'

'Yes, it certainly is true, Cebes, as I see it; and we're not deceived in making just those admissions: there really is such a thing as coming to life again, living people *are* born from the e dead, and the souls of the dead exist.'

[...]

The Recollection Argument

'Yes, and besides, Socrates,' Cebes replied, 'there's also that theory you're always putting forward, that our learning is actually nothing but recollection; according to that too, if it's true, what we are now reminded of we must have learned at some former time. But that 73a would be impossible, unless our souls existed somewhere before being born in this human form; so in this way too, it appears that the soul is something immortal.'

'Yes, what are the proofs of those points, Cebes?' put in Simmias. 'Remind me, as I don't recall them very well at the moment.'

'One excellent argument,' said Cebes, 'is that when people are questioned, and if the questions are well put, they state the truth about everything for themselves—and yet unless knowledge and a correct account were present within them, they'd be unable to do this; thus, b if one takes them to diagrams or anything else of that sort, one has there the plainest evidence that this is so.'

'But if that doesn't convince you, Simmias,' said Socrates, 'then see whether maybe you agree if you look at it this way. Apparently you doubt whether what is called "learning" is recollection?'

'I don't *doubt* it,' said Simmias; 'but I do need to undergo just what the argument is about, to be "reminded." Actually, from the way Cebes set about stating it, I do almost recall it and am nearly convinced; but I'd like, none the less, to hear now how you set about stating c it yourself.'

'I'll put it this way. We agree, I take it, that if anyone is to be reminded of a thing, he must have known that thing at some time previously.'

'Certainly.'

'Then do we also agree on this point: that whenever knowledge comes to be present in this sort of way, it is recollection? I mean in some such way as this: if someone, on seeing a thing, or hearing it, or getting any other sense-perception of it, not only recognizes that thing, but also thinks of something else, which is the object not of the same knowledge but of another, don't we then rightly say that he's been d "reminded" of the object of which he has got the thought?'

'What do you mean?'

'Take the following examples: knowledge of a man, surely, is other than that of a lyre?'

'Of course.'

'Well now, you know what happens to lovers, whenever they see a lyre or cloak or anything else their loves are accustomed to use: they recognize the lyre, and they get in their mind, don't they, the form of the boy whose lyre it is? And that is recollection. Likewise, someone seeing Simmias is often reminded of Cebes, and there'd surely be countless other such cases.'

'Countless indeed!' said Simmias.

'Then is something of that sort a kind of rec- e ollection? More especially, though, whenever it happens to someone in connection with things he's since forgotten, through lapse of time or inattention?'

'Certainly.'

'Again now, is it possible, on seeing a horse depicted or a lyre depicted, to be reminded of a man; and on seeing Simmias depicted, to be reminded of Cebes?'

'Certainly.'

74a 'And also, on seeing Simmias depicted, to be reminded of Simmias himself?'

'Yes, that's possible.'

'In all these cases, then, doesn't it turn out that there is recollection from similar things, but also from dissimilar things?'

'It does.'

'But whenever one is reminded of something from similar things, mustn't one experience something further: mustn't one think whether or not the thing is lacking at all, in its similarity, in relation to what one is reminded of?'

'One must.'

'Then consider whether this is the case. We say, don't we, that there is something *equal*—I don't mean a log to a log, or a stone to a stone, or anything else of that sort, but some further thing beyond all those, the equal itself: are we to say that there *is* something or nothing?'

b 'We most certainly are to say that there *is*,' said Simmias; 'unquestionably!'

'And do we know *what it is*?'

'Certainly.'

'Where did we get the knowledge of it? Wasn't it from the things we were just mentioning: on seeing logs or stones or other equal things, wasn't it from these that we thought of that object, it being different from them? Or doesn't it seem different to you? Look at it this way: don't equal stones and logs, the very same ones, sometimes seem equal to one, but not to another?'

'Yes, certainly.'

'But now, did the equals themselves ever c seem to you unequal, or equality inequality?'

'Never yet, Socrates.'

'Then those equals, and the equal itself, are not the same.'

'By no means, Socrates, in my view.'

'But still, it is from *those* equals, different as they are from *that* equal, that you have thought of and got the knowledge of it?'

'That's perfectly true.'

'It being either similar to them or dissimilar?'

'Certainly.'

'Anyway, it makes no difference; so long as on seeing one thing, one does, from this sight, d think of another, whether it be similar or dissimilar, this must be recollection.'

'Certainly.'

'Well now, with regard to the instances in the logs, and, in general, the equals we mentioned just now, are we affected in some way as this: do they seem to us to be equal in the same way as *what it is* itself? Do they fall short of it at all in being like the equal, or not?'

'Very far short of it.'

'Then whenever anyone, on seeing a thing, thinks to himself, "this thing that I now see seeks to be like another of the things that are, but falls short, and cannot be like that object: e it is inferior," do we agree that the man who thinks this must previously have known the object he says it resembles but falls short of?'

'He must.'

'Now then, have we ourselves been affected in just this way, or not, with regard to the equals and the equal itself?'

'Indeed we have.'

'Then we must previously have known the equal, before that time when we first, on see- 75a ing the equals, thought that all of them were striving to be like the equal but fell short of it.'

'That is so.'

'Yet we also agree on this: we haven't derived the thought of it, nor could we do so, from anywhere but seeing or touching or some other of the senses—I'm counting all these as the same.'

'Yes, they are the same, Socrates, for what the argument seeks to show.'

'But of course it is *from* one's sense-percep-
b tions that one must think that all the things in the sense-perceptions are striking for *what equal is*, yet are inferior to it; or how shall we put it?'

'Like that.'

'Then it must, surely, have been before we began to see and hear and use the other senses that we got knowledge of the equal itself, of *what it is*, if we were going to refer the equals from our sense-perceptions to it, supposing that all things are doing their best to be like it, but are inferior to it.'

'That must follow from what's been said before, Socrates.'

'Now we were seeing and hearing, and were possessed of our other senses, weren't we, just as soon as we were born?'

c 'Certainly.'

'But we must, we're saying, have got our knowledge of the equal *before* these?'

'Yes.'

'Then it seems that we must have got it before we were born.'

'It seems so.'

'Now if, having got it before birth, we were born in possession of it, did we know, both before birth and as soon as we were born, not only the equal, the larger and the smaller, but everything of that sort? Because our present argument concerns the beautiful itself, and the good itself, and just and holy, no less than the
d equal; in fact, as I say, it concerns everything on which we set this seal, "*what it is*," in the questions we ask and in the answers we give. And so we must have got pieces of knowledge of all those things before birth.'

'That is so.'

'Moreover, if having got them, we did not on each occasion forget them, we must always be born knowing, and must continue to know

throughout life: because this is knowing—to possess knowledge one has got of something, and not to have lost it; or isn't loss of knowledge what we mean by "forgetting," Simmias?'

'Certainly it is, Socrates.'   e

'But on the other hand, I suppose that if, having got them before birth, we lost them on being born, and later on, using the senses about the things in question, we regain those pieces of knowledge that we possessed at some former time, in that case wouldn't what we call "learning" be the regaining of knowledge belonging to us? And in saying that this was being reminded, shouldn't we be speaking correctly?'

'Certainly.'

'Yes, because it did seem possible, on sens-   76a ing an object, whether by seeing or hearing or getting some other sense-perception of it, to think from this of some other thing one had forgotten—either a thing to which the object, though dissimilar to it, was related, or else something to which it was similar; so, as I say, one of two things is true: *either* all of us were born knowing those objects, and we know them throughout life; *or* those we speak of as "learning" are simply being reminded later on, and learning would be recollection.'

'That's quite true, Socrates.'

'Then which do you choose, Simmias? That we are born knowing, or that we are later   b reminded of the things we'd gained knowledge of before?'

'At the moment, Socrates, I can't make a choice.'

'Well, can you make one on the following point, and what do you think about it? If a man knows things, can he give an account of what he knows or not?'

'Of course he can, Socrates.'

'And do you think everyone can give an account of those objects we were discussing just now?'

'I only wish they could,' said Simmias; 'but I'm afraid that, on the contrary, this time tomorrow there may no longer be any man who can do so properly.'

c   'You don't then, Simmias, think that everyone knows those objects?'

'By no means.'

'Are they, then, reminded of what they once learned?'

'They must be.'

'When did our souls get the knowledge of those objects? Not, at any rate, since we were born as human beings.'

'Indeed not.'

'Earlier, then.'

'Yes.'

'Then our souls did exist earlier, Simmias, before entering human form, apart from bodies; and they possessed wisdom.'

'Unless maybe, Socrates, we get those pieces of knowledge at the very moment of birth; that
d   time still remains.'

'Very well, my friend; but then at what other time, may I ask, do we lose them? We aren't born with them, as we agreed just now. Do we then lose them at the very time at which we get them? Or have you any other time to suggest?'

'None at all, Socrates. I didn't realize I was talking nonsense.'

'Then is our position as follows, Simmias? If the objects we are always harping on exist, a beautiful, and a good and all such Being, and if we refer all the things from our sense-perceptions to that Being, finding again what was formerly   e ours, and if we compare these things with that, then just as surely as those objects exist, so also must our soul exist before we are born. On the other hand, if they don't exist, this argument will have gone for nothing. Is this the position? Is it equally necessary that those objects exist, and that our souls existed before birth, and if the former don't exist, then neither did the latter?'

'It's abundantly clear to me, Socrates,' said Simmias, 'that there's the same necessity in either case, and the argument takes opportune refuge in the view that our soul exists before   77a birth, just as surely as the Being of which you're now speaking. Because I myself find nothing so plain to me as that all such objects, beautiful and good and all the others you were speaking of just now, *are* in the fullest possible way, so in my view it's been adequately proved.'

[...]

Study Questions

NOTE: References to particular places in our selections from Plato's writing will be indicated using the standard page-numbering system from the left and right margins of your text.

1. At 64a Socrates claims that "all who engage in philosophy aright are practising nothing other than dying and being dead." (a) Explain what he means by this surprising claim in your own words. (b) Explain how this claim is connected to Socrates' view of the nature of mind (or "soul").

2. At 65 and 66, Socrates argues that one cannot grasp the idea of *largeness* (for example) by using the senses. (See for example 65d.) In your own words, briefly but clearly outline (a) what you take to be his argument for this surprising position, (b) an argument against this, showing where (you claim) he went wrong, and how the idea of largeness might be grasped merely on the basis of sense-experience.

3. At around 68 and 69, Socrates argues that a truly rational person would not fear death. (a) In your own words, briefly outline his argument for this position. (b) But many people (probably including you) do fear death. Give Socrates' explanation of why they do, and of what he takes this to be the result of. (c) Do you think he is right about why you (or people in general) fear death? Explain.

4. Socrates sees the living person as a union of body and soul; and Cebes, while wondering if immortality follows, accepts this. Can you think of one or more alternatives to this "union" view? For each alternative, what might the consequences for the possibility of immortality be?

5. In 70 through 73, Socrates argues for the existence of one's mind before birth and after death. This argument is based on the idea that everything comes from its opposite. (a) Briefly, in your own words, outline this argument. (b) Criticize this argument. Is it true that everything comes from its opposite? Does his conclusion really follow from this idea?

6. At around 72c, Socrates argues for a "recycling" of souls, on the basis that if the latter view were true, then everything would eventually be dead. (a) Give a brief summary of how this argument is supposed to go. (b) Is this reasoning convincing? Defend or criticize it.

7. Beginning at around 73, Socrates argues for the idea that real knowledge is recollection. In your own words, (a) outline his argument for this surprising conclusion; and (b) criticize this argument.

Suggested Readings

Some interpretations and evaluations of Plato's philosophy of mind:

R. Kraut, ed. *The Cambridge Companion to Plato*. (Cambridge: Cambridge University Press, 1992).

N.D. Smith, ed. *Plato: Critical Assessments, Vol. III: Plato's Middle Period, Psychology, and Value Theory*. (London: Routledge, 1998).

D. Bostok, "The Soul and Immortality in Plato's *Phaedo*," in *Plato 2: Ethics, Politics, Religion, and the Soul*, G. Fine (ed.). (Oxford: Oxford University Press 1999).

S. Lovibond, "Plato's Theory of Mind," in *Companions to Ancient Thought 2: Psychology*, S. Everson (ed.). (Cambridge: Cambridge University Press, 1991).

Plato discusses universals also in *Republic*, books 6 and 7, and in *Parmenides*. A good contemporary introduction to and discussion of universals is David Armstrong's *Universals: An Opinionated Introduction* (Boulder: Westview, 1989).

2

 # ARISTOTLE: NATURALIZING THE SOUL

Introduction

According to Plato, the universe is divided into two distinct realms: the material realm of objects perceived by the senses and the realm of the eternal, immutable Forms. The body belongs to the first of these and the soul to the second. Only in this way, Plato believed, can we explain our knowledge of universals. Plato's interest in universals arose in large part from his studies of mathematics and politics, and so his theory of the soul was shaped by these concerns. But his student Aristotle (384–322 BCE) was most interested in the place of human beings in the natural world. Aristotle was as much a natural scientist as a philosopher, conducting careful studies of plant and animal life and devising detailed theories to explain change and motion in the physical world. Although he inherited the problem of universals from Plato, Aristotle believed universals to be part of the natural world itself rather than a distinct realm of immaterial Forms.

The largest single difficulty with Plato's theory of the Forms is to explain the relationship between material objects and the Forms. As Plato's student, Aristotle was aware of this difficulty and of the attempts to solve it. Moreover, as a botanist, Aristotle believed that change and growth in the natural world come from a force in material things themselves, and this made it difficult to believe that material things are simply shadowy images of the Forms. His solution was to replace the idea of two distinct realms with the idea that material things have two distinct aspects: their matter and their form. The former played the role of Plato's material realm, while the latter played the role of Plato's realm of Forms. This means that universals are aspects of material things, and not independent entities as Plato argues in *The Phaedo*.

Aristotle on the Soul

Given his rejection of the theory of Forms, Aristotle was led to a different conception of the soul. For Aristotle, the soul is not a separate entity from the body, but rather an aspect of a person's biological makeup. Aristotle argued that, as living creatures, we are more than just a mass of tissue and bone. The explanation of why we grow and reproduce and move about must involve more than just the matter that makes up our bodies, for that matter is common to both living and dead things. Adopting from Plato and others the idea that the soul is what brings life to the body, Aristotle sought to explain the nature of the soul by defining it as the source of all the activities that constitute life.

In a text called *On the Soul*, Aristotle presents a detailed description of the soul in terms of the way in which its various elements produce the different aspects of living things. In Book I of *On the Soul* he criticizes earlier theories, and in Book II he presents his own views, beginning with a general definition of the soul and its relation to the body, and moving to descriptions of its specific functions. We will start with chapter 1 of Book II, where he presents and defends his general definition. Then we will look at his descriptions of two important functions of the soul: visual perception and thought.

The Soul as "Substance"

At the outset of chapter 1, Book II, of *On the Soul* Aristotle asks, "What is soul?" In asking this question Aristotle is adopting the definition of the soul as that which brings life. In these terms his question can be interpreted as meaning, "What is the origin of life?"

In the second paragraph he begins his answer by talking about what he calls **substance**. Exactly what this word means for him is a deep and complex question. But in simplest terms 'substance' is a word for the basic elements of the world. The things we see around us are constantly moving and changing: the stars revolve in the sky, the seasons change, and plants and animals are born and grow. What accounts for these changes? What is it that remains throughout the changes? For Aristotle, these are questions about the nature of substance. To understand Aristotle's conception of the soul, we have to form some understanding of his notion of substance.

Substance as Matter and Form

Aristotle's opening remark on the concept of substance is as follows.

> We say that substance is one kind of what is, and that in several senses: in the sense of *matter* or that which in itself is not a this, and in the sense of *form* or *essence*, which is that precisely in virtue of which a thing is called a this, and thirdly in the sense of that which is compounded of both.

Notice that in this sentence Aristotle identifies three different concepts that fall under the general term 'substance.' They are labeled as

(a) substance as **matter**
(b) substance as **form** or **essence**
(c) substance as the combination of (a) and (b).

The distinction between the concepts of matter and form is a central feature of Aristotle's theory of the soul.

Roughly, the difference between matter and form is that between what something is made of and what makes it the kind of thing it is. Here's an example. Think of two statues of Socrates, one of marble and one of bronze. Insofar as they are both statues of Socrates they are the same *kind* of thing. But they are composed of different material. In this case, what makes these the same kind of thing is that they both portray the actual person Socrates, and this is a result of their shape. So, in this example, the form is the shape. The matter of each statue is the marble or bronze out of which it is composed.

Now think of another two statues of Socrates, this time both of marble. Again, they are the same kind of thing, both statues of Socrates, but of different *pieces* of marble. Here again they have the same form but different matter. For even though the matter in each case is of the same kind, there are still two distinct lumps of marble. One way to look at it is that form is what any two objects of the same kind have in common, and matter is what differentiates one from another.

Aristotle applies the same distinction to the natural world. Plants and animals of the same species share the same form or essence. The form of a particular plant or animal is what it has in common with other members of the same species. The matter is what differentiates it from those other members.

We need to be a bit careful about what the previous sentence means. Consider the two marble statues again. The fact that there are two pieces of marble explains why there are two statues and not one. But the interesting differences between the two statues, their sculptural features, are not just reflections of different matter, but are features of the shape the form takes in each individual statue. The same is true of living things. The differences in character and personality among people and animals are a result of differences in the way in which the species is realized in the individual. So your form or essence is what makes you a human being, but it is also what makes you the person you are.[1]

There are some points about matter and form that are worth noting:

1. What is matter and what is form depend on the object we are talking about. For example, a lump of clay is the matter of a brick, but a brick can be part of the matter of a house. Similarly, an eye is part of the matter of a person, yet the eye itself has its own form and matter. So there is no absolute distinction between matter and form.
2. Only certain kinds of material can be the matter for a particular kind of object. Marble and bronze can both form the matter of a statue, but water cannot. Similarly, only certain kinds of natural material, tissue and bone for example, can form the matter of living things.
3. The previous point explains why, in the second paragraph, Aristotle says that matter is "potentiality" while form is "actuality." Certain kinds of material (lumps of marble, for example) are potentially statues. Other kinds of material (such as matter in the womb at conception) are potentially living things. Marble becomes a statue, and flesh becomes a living thing by possessing a certain form, that is, by passing from potentiality to actuality. This is also why in the passage quoted above, Aristotle refers to matter as "that which is not a *this*," and to form as "that precisely in virtue of which a thing is a *this*." It is only in virtue of possessing a form that matter can be identified as a particular kind of thing—a *this*. In the

case of artificial things, like the statue, the transition from potentiality to actuality happens by human action. But in living things it happens by a principle of change within the thing itself, as when a seed or an egg become a fully formed plant or animal.

The Definition of Soul

In the third and fourth paragraphs, Aristotle presents a line of reasoning to yield a general definition of the soul, according to which the soul is the form or essence of living things. The third paragraph presents the following two premises:

1. Natural bodies are substances in the sense of composites of form and matter.
2. Some natural bodies are living things, and some are not.

By "natural bodies" Aristotle means things like rocks, trees, water, and animals; that is, objects that are of natural origin. So according to these two premises, natural things comprise both matter and form, and some are alive and others not.

The first sentence of the fourth paragraph gives us another premise:

3. Because a living body is a body of a particular kind (one that lives), the soul cannot be a body.

Think here of the difference between a living animal and a dead body. They are different in that one possesses a soul and one does not. Hence, the collection of tissues, bones, and organs that make up the physical body cannot be the soul. The body is not what brings life into being but what makes life *possible*. In this sense, the body is to a living thing what the bronze is to a statue.

Putting together all of the points established so far, we get the following argument. The soul is substance; that is, it is a *fundamental* element of the world. Hence it must be either matter, form, or the combination. All natural bodies, living or not, are combinations of matter and form, and so the soul must be one or the other. But it can't be matter because matter is only *potentially* a living thing. Thus Aristotle arrives at the following conclusion.

Hence, the soul must be a substance in the sense of the form of a natural body having life potentially within it.

The difference between a natural body that is only *potentially* alive and one that is *actually* alive is the presence of a soul. The soul is thus the form or essence of living things.

Soul as the Form of Living Things

The form of something is what makes it the kind of thing it is. Among living things the form is what makes a plant or an animal a member of one species rather than another. It is a principle of life that makes something, say, a rabbit rather than a person or a tree. An acorn grows into an oak rather than an elm because it possesses the form or soul of an oak. Accordingly, living things of the same species have the same kind of soul. Because a soul can only enliven matter that is organized in a particular way, with all of the parts necessary for the processes of life, Aristotle describes the soul in the fifth paragraph as the actuality of a "natural organized body."

In the natural world, what makes something the kind of thing it is—its form—is a principle of growth and movement within the thing itself. With respect to living things, the activities of growth and movement that constitute life spring from something within the plant or animal itself. According to Aristotle, it is the specific nature of this power that determines the species to which something belongs. We might say that a thing belongs to a species in virtue of what it *does* rather than how it looks. For example, there are certain kinds of activity that are natural to horses, and it is the capacity for this activity that makes an animal a horse. The physical characteristics of a species (such as the hooves and skeletal structure of a horse) make this activity possible. But it is the *soul* of the animal that makes this possibility actual.

In the sixth paragraph, Aristotle illustrates his idea by saying that if an axe were a natural thing, its soul would be what makes it an axe. This would be its ability to cut wood. But an axe is not a natural thing because, if it were, it would have the power *in itself* to cut wood. Living things, plants and animals, have the power in themselves to do the kinds of things that make them the things they are: growth, reproduction, perception, movement, and so on. This is their soul.

He then asks us to think of the parts of animals. He says that if an eye were a living thing, sight would be its soul, since sight is what makes an eye what it is. The difference between an eye of a living creature and that of a statue is that one sees and the other doesn't, no matter how "life-like" the statue. Similarly, he says, the general faculty or power of sense—what we might call **sensibility**—is what gives form to the sensitive organs of the body as a whole. In these terms we can think of the soul of a living thing as composed of a hierarchy of forms, each contributing to the powers and abilities that constitute life for that particular species.

Body and Soul

At the end of the chapter Aristotle concludes that the soul is inseparable from the body. This is because form cannot exist except as realized in some matter. There cannot be form without matter, any more than there can be matter without form. In a similar vein, he had said in the fifth paragraph that the question whether the body and soul are one is "unnecessary." He explains this point by saying

> It is as though we were to ask whether the wax and its shape are one, or generally the matter of a thing and that of which it is the matter. Unity has many senses (as many as 'is' has), but the proper one is that of actuality.

In the second sentence he means that things exist as separate individuals—as "units"—only insofar as they possess both matter and form.

So, unlike Plato, Aristotle does not believe that the soul can exist independently of the body. The soul is one aspect of a single indivisible whole that is the living creature. And it cannot exist except in the context of the whole. For Aristotle, then, the soul is an essential and integral part of the natural order rather than something that exists as a separate entity from things in the natural world. However, near the very end of the chapter he qualifies this belief. He says

> Yet some [souls] may be separable because they are not the actualities of any body at all.

This seems to allow that in certain instances there may be such a thing as form without matter, and hence pure soul. As we will see later on in this chapter, Aristotle appears to have in mind something like the possibility of "pure intellect."

The Faculties of the Soul

So far, Aristotle has established the general point that the soul of living things is their form or essence, by which he means that which makes them the kind of thing they are. We have seen that the form of a living thing is that which gives it its ability to perform the activities of life such as growth, reproduction, movement, and perception. According to Aristotle, the various species form a hierarchy according to the nature of their activities. For example, while all species grow and reproduce, not all forms of life possess sensory organs to perceive the world around them. This hierarchy leads Aristotle to distinguish between different divisions or faculties of the soul whereby species can be categorized in accordance with the specific faculties they possess.

All living things have the power to feed themselves, and to reproduce. Hence, all living things have what Aristotle calls a **nutritive soul**, or a nutritive faculty of the soul. In addition to a nutritive faculty, some species have powers of locomotion and perception, which he calls the **sensitive soul**, or the faculty of sensibility. Finally, human beings have what Aristotle terms a **rational soul**, which is the faculty of reason and reflection.

In the remaining chapters of *On the Soul* Aristotle explains how these various faculties operate in nature. This part of the text should be looked upon as a scientific treatise or a textbook on biology. (In fact, it probably served as a textbook for Aristotle's students.) Book II, chapter 7 is devoted to the faculty of visual perception. We will begin there because Aristotle's theory of vision forms a good contrast with later views on the mind.

Color and the Transparent

He starts chapter 7 with a definition. **The visible**, he says, is the object of sight. That is, the visible is what we perceive through sight. He claims that there are two kinds of things that are visible:

1. color
2. something else to be explained later.

In the second sentence he says that color "lies upon what is in itself visible." (You can ignore the rest of the sentence.) By this he means color is what lies on the surface of visible objects.

Read the next sentence carefully. Aristotle says that the nature of color is "to set in movement what is actually transparent." By 'movement,' he means something broader than change of location. His actual meaning is something more like what we would call change. Understood in this way, the nature of color is to change what is **transparent**. In the next paragraph he begins to explain what he means by "what is transparent." In English, of course, something is "transparent" when we can see other things through it, and that's what Aristotle means as well. He expresses this by saying that what is transparent is not visible "in itself, but rather owing its visibility to the color of something else." We don't actually see what is transparent—we see other things through what is transparent. In the next sentence he says that there is a transparent substance in air, water, and other things.

Putting these ideas together we get the following. There is a certain substance in the air or water between the surface of colored objects and the eye. Color is by definition something on the surface of objects that changes this substance. As a result of this change, color is made visible to the eye.

Light and Vision

Aristotle now explains what light is. It is "the activity of what is transparent *qua* transparent." This is difficult wording, but his point is the following. The transparent substance found in air is either active or inactive. To say that the transparent substance is active means that color is visible through it, and to say it is inactive is to say that color is not visible through it. Light is the active state of the substance, and darkness is the inactive state.

He also says that fire excites this substance to activity—in our terms, fire produces light. The reason we can see in the presence of fire in the sun or in a candle is that the fire renders the transparent substance active. We should not think here of light from the fire *traveling through the air* as in our modern theory. Think instead of the transparent medium becoming active in the presence of fire and transmitting color as a result of this activity.

We can pass over the next few paragraphs to the one beginning, "The following makes the necessity…" Here he argues for the necessity of a medium (the transparent) between the eye and the object. He says,

> color sets in movement what is transparent, e.g., the air, and that, extending continuously from the object of the organ, sets the latter in movement.

But how is the organ set in motion? Aristotle answers this in a passage from a short treatise called *Sense and Sensibilia*, which we have included below. There he explains that there must be a transparent substance in the eye as well, and this he thinks is water. So the idea is that when the transparent substance in the air and in the eye is active, color is transmitted to the soul. It is when this substance in the eye becomes active that we experience the color that is on the object.

Putting all the pieces together, we get the following picture. In the presence of fire, color on the surface of objects is communicated to the soul as a result of the activity of the transparent substance in air or water and the water in the eye. So according to Aristotle, visual perception is a matter of the soul literally taking on the colors of the things around us. Our visual experience of color is an event whereby the soul receives the colors of the surrounding environment.

The Passive Intellect

In chapters 4 and 5 of Book III Aristotle turns his attention to the activity of thinking, which is the product of the faculty of mind or intellect. In chapter 4, he considers what we can call the "passive" mind, and in chapter 5 he considers the "active" mind.

In the second paragraph of chapter 4, he assumes that thinking must be like sense perception. The difference between thinking and sense perception, he believes, lies simply in what is perceived. Each of the senses is responsible for our awareness of a particular quality of objects. Vision is responsible for our awareness of color, and hearing is responsible for our perception of sound. In each case the quality of the object acts on the sense organ in a way that reproduces the same quality in the soul. The eye transmits color to the soul, and sound is reproduced in the soul through the ear. In a similar manner, Aristotle says, in thinking, the soul "is acted upon by what is capable of being thought." What he means is that, in the act of thinking, the soul takes on the nature of what it thinks about.

In the next sentence he indicates what it is that is capable of being thought.

He says,

> The thinking part of the soul must therefore be, while impassable, capable of receiving the *form* of an object; that is, must be potentially identical in *character* with its object without being the object.

According to Aristotle, then, the mind perceives the form or essence of things in the world. Let's look at this idea carefully.

Forms and the Intellect

Recall the difference between form and matter. The form of an object is what makes it the kind of thing it is. Now think about perceiving something, say, a galloping horse. We feel the rush of wind, we see the white color, and we hear the thundering hooves. Each of these sensations is the perception of a sensible quality: color, sound, coolness on the skin. But how do we know that it is a horse that we perceive? We are not very much aware of perceiving the individual sensible qualities at all—we perceive a horse. How is that possible? That is, how is it that we perceive not just the color and sound, but also the quality of "horseness" in the object? Aristotle's answer is that there must be a special faculty by which we perceive the *essences* of things, and this he calls the mind. So to think about something is to receive its form or essence in the faculty of mind.

We can see vestiges of Aristotle's theory in modern English. We often talk of being "informed" about something, and of things "impressing" themselves on our mind. The metaphor here is that of the form of something impressing itself on the mind just as a seal is impressed on a blob of warm wax. Along these same lines, Aristotle argues that the mind "can have no nature of its own." His reasoning is that the mind is capable of thinking about any essence whatsoever, and so it cannot have an essence of its own. Just as a piece of warm wax can receive any impression, the mind can take on the form of any object. Compare this with the faculty of vision. The soul is capable of seeing because the eyes have the potential to take on the color of their object. So the eyes have their own nature, namely, to become colored. But this also means that in vision we can only perceive colors. As the mind, on the other hand, can think of any form at all, it cannot have any form of its own except a "certain capacity" to take on forms.

Aristotle expresses this another way by saying that before it thinks, the mind "is not actually any real thing." For this reason, he argues, the mind is not "blended" with the body (as the senses are), because that would give it a physical nature like the organs of sense. How this fits with his earlier claim that mind and body are inseparable is unclear. Here we are reminded of the intriguing comment at the end of chapter 1 that some souls "are not the actualities of any body at all."

The Active Intellect

In chapter 5, Aristotle argues that there must be more to the mind than an ability to take on forms. In the first sentence Aristotle says that for every kind of thing there must be both a "matter" and a "cause." Think again of our statue example from the beginning of the chapter. In order for a statue to exist there must be material (the matter) that is capable of becoming a statue, and there must also be something that causes the material to take on the appropriate form. In this case, the matter might be the marble, and the cause the sculptor. In the case of vision, we have as matter the faculty of sight in the soul, which is potentially colored. And what causes the act of vision, whereby the soul takes on the color of the object, is fire.

The mind as we have described it so far is merely passive in its potential for taking on the forms of its objects. As such it constitutes the matter of thought. So Aristotle's point in chapter 5 of *On the Soul* is that there must be an *active* cause that brings thought about, that plays the role that fire plays in vision. But in this case there is no *external* cause—the mind is, in effect, the cause of its own thinking. So in addition to the passive mind, there must be an active mind that is the cause of thought.

In the second paragraph, then, he says that in addition to the mind that becomes all things, there is the mind that makes all things. The former is the passive intellect, and the latter is the active intellect.

The next two paragraphs are among the strangest and most controversial in all of Aristotle's writings. Of the active mind he says,

> When separated it is alone just what it is, and this above all is immortal and eternal...and without this nothing thinks.

It seems that Aristotle is claiming here that the active mind is independent of the body and is immortal. How this is to be understood is not clear. It appears to be an echo of the view expressed at the end of chapter 1 of Book I: that there can be such a thing as pure soul that exists without being realized in matter. But these are murky waters, and I'll leave it to you to puzzle over.

Naturalizing the Soul

Aristotle clearly continues certain lines of thought begun by Socrates and Plato. For example, Aristotle's view of the mind is deeply affected by the problem of universals and by the conception of the soul as both the source of life and the seat of the intellect. But Aristotle's theory differs sharply from that of Plato. According to Plato, the soul is part of the realm of the Forms, which are perfect, eternal objects—a realm altogether separate from the natural world that we perceive through the senses. Aristotle, on the other hand, creates a theory wherein the soul is part and parcel of the natural world of material objects and living things. According to his theory, the principles by which the soul operates are the same in general character as the principles that govern rocks, trees, and stars. Even though he speaks of the active intellect as eternal and separate from the body, the operation of the intellect follows the same pattern as the operations of sensory perception and organic activity generally. This forms a sharp contrast with Plato's view, according to which reason and reflection require the mind's removal from the world of ordinary objects.

We can give a label to the changes that Aristotle introduces to thinking about the mind by describing it as a **naturalist** theory. That is, he constructs a theory wherein the soul is an integral part of the natural order of material objects, plants, and animals.

One advantage that Aristotle's theory possesses over Plato's is that it resolves the difficulties in combining the conceptions of the soul as both the source of life and the seat of the intellect.

Plato understood rational thought to be an activity distinct from, and even in conflict with, the activities of the physical body. But this view makes it hard to understand how the soul can *also* be that which brings life to the body. Within Aristotle's theory there is no such difficulty. According to Aristotle, a creature is alive by virtue of the fact that it is capable of the activities belonging to a particular species. The life of a plant consists of the activities of growth and nutrition as they are realized in the species to which it belongs; and the life of an animal (such as, say, a mollusk or a turtle) consists of these activities plus locomotion and perception. In each case, the soul is the cause of these various activities. Aristotle then conceives of rational thought as the kind of activity that is natural and peculiar to the human species. In this way he considers the human soul to be the cause of reason and reflection in exactly the same way that the soul is the cause of nutrition and locomotion in other species. For Aristotle, then, the activity of the intellect is just one aspect of life as a human being.

The Reliability of Perception

Another important aspect of Aristotle's theory of the soul is his idea that sensory perception is a direct and reliable link with the world. According to Aristotle, there is a similarity between sensory perception and the action of the intellect in that, in each case, the forms and qualities in the world are reproduced in the soul. Thus in both cases our perceptions reflect the world as it really is. Contrast this with Plato's view. According to Plato, the senses can trigger our recollection of the Forms, but they are not themselves a reliable or direct source of knowledge. The senses provide us with only fleeting and imperfect glimpses of what can really only be understood through the exercise of pure thought.

In the next few chapters, we will see how the invention of modern mathematical physics led one important scientist of the early modern era—René Descartes—to "de-naturalize" the mind. In resolving the difficulties that Aristotle's scientific program encounters, Descartes severed the connection between the mind and the natural world that is found in Aristotle's theories. To see how this development occurred we have to examine the basic ideas behind the rise of modern science in the seventeenth century.

Note

1. This point is made by Abraham Edel, *Aristotle and His Philosophy* (Chapel Hill, NC: University of North Carolina Press, 1982), p. 127.

ARISTOTLE

Selections from *On the Soul* and *Sense and Sensibilia*

On the Soul

Book II

1 · Let the foregoing suffice as our account of the views concerning the soul which have been handed on by our predecessors; let us now make as it were a completely fresh start, endeavoring to answer the question, What is soul? i.e., to formulate the most general possible account of it.

We say that substance is one kind of what is, and that in several senses: in the sense of matter or that which in itself is not a this, and in the sense of form or essence, which is that precisely in virtue of which a thing is called a this, and thirdly in the sense of that which is compounded of both. Now matter is potentiality, form actuality; and actuality is of two kinds, one as e.g., knowledge, the other as e.g., reflecting.

Among substances are by general consent reckoned bodies and especially natural bodies; for they are the principles of all other bodies. Of natural bodies some have life in them, others not; by life we mean self-nutrition and growth and decay. It follows that every natural body which has life in it is a substance in the sense of a composite.

Now given that there are bodies of such and such a kind, viz. having life, the soul cannot be a body; for the body is the subject or matter, not what is attributed to it. Hence the soul must be a substance in the sense of the form of a natural body having life potentially within it. But substance is actuality, and thus soul is the actuality of a body as above characterized. Now there are two kinds of actuality corresponding to knowledge and to reflecting. It is obvious that the soul is an actuality like knowledge; for both sleeping and waking presuppose the existence of soul, and of these waking corresponds to reflecting, sleeping to knowledge possessed but not employed, and knowledge of something is temporally prior.

That is why the soul is an actuality of the first kind of a natural body having life potentially in it. The body so described is a body which is organized. The parts of plants in spite of their extreme simplicity are organs; e.g., the leaf serves to shelter the pericarp, the pericarp to shelter the fruit, while the roots of plants are analogous to the mouth of animals, both serving for the absorption of food. If, then, we have to give a general formula applicable to all kinds of soul, we must describe it as an actuality of the first kind of a natural organized body. That is why we can dismiss as unnecessary the question whether the soul and the body are one: it is as though we were to ask whether the wax and its shape are one, or generally the matter of a thing and that of which it is the matter. Unity has many senses (as many as 'is' has), but the proper one is that of actuality.

We have now given a general answer to the question, What is soul? It is substance in the sense which corresponds to the account of a thing. That means that it is what it is to be for a body of the character just assigned. Suppose that a tool, e.g., an axe, were a *natural* body, then being an axe would have been its essence, and so its soul; if this disappeared from it, it would have ceased to be an axe, except in name. As it is, it is an axe; for it is not of a body of that sort that what it is to be, i.e., its account, is a soul, but of a natural body of a particular kind, viz. one having in itself the power of setting itself in movement and arresting itself. Next, apply this doctrine in the case of the parts of the living body. Suppose that the eye were an animal—sight would have been its soul, for sight is the substance of the eye which corresponds to the account, the eye being merely the matter of seeing; when seeing is removed the eye is no longer an eye, except in name—no more than the eye of a statue or of a painted figure. We must now extend our consideration from the parts to the whole living body; for what the part is to the part, that the whole faculty of sense is to the whole sensitive body as such.

We must not understand by that which is potentially capable of living what has lost the soul it had, but only what still retains it; but seeds and fruits are bodies which are potentially of that sort. Consequently, while waking is actuality in a sense corresponding to the cutting and the seeing, the soul is actuality in the sense corresponding to sight and the power in the tool; the body corresponds to what is in potentiality; as the pupil *plus* the power of sight constitutes the eye, so the soul *plus* the body constitutes the animal.

From this it is clear that the soul is inseparable from its body, or at any rate that certain parts of it are (if it has parts)—for the actuality of some of them is the actuality of the parts themselves. Yet some may be separable because they are not the actualities of any body at all. Further, we have no light on the problem whether the soul may not be the actuality of its body in the sense in which the sailor is the actuality of the ship.

This must suffice as our sketch or outline of the nature of soul.

[...]

7 · The object of sight is the visible, and what is visible is color and a certain kind of object which can be described in words but which has no single name; what we mean by the second will be abundantly clear as we proceed. Whatever is visible is color and color is what lies upon what is in itself visible; 'in itself' here means not that visibility is involved in the definition of what thus underlies color, but that that substratum contains in itself the cause of visibility. Every color has in it the power to set in movement what is actually transparent; that power constitutes its very nature. That is why it is not visible except with the help of light; it is only in light that the color of a thing is seen. Hence our first task is to explain what light is.

Now there clearly is something which is transparent, and by 'transparent' I mean what is visible, and yet not visible in itself, but rather owing its visibility to the color *of something else*; of this character are air, water, and many solid bodies. Neither air nor water is transparent because it is air or water; they are transparent because each of them has contained in it a certain substance which is the same in both and is also found in the eternal upper body. Of this substance light is the activity—the activity of what is transparent *qua* transparent; where this power is present, there is also the potentiality of the contrary, viz. darkness. Light is as it were the proper color of what is transparent, and exists whenever the potentially transparent is excited to actuality by the influence of fire or something resembling 'the uppermost body'; for fire too contains something which is one and the same with the substance in question.

We have now explained what the transparent is and what light is; light is neither fire nor any kind whatsoever of body nor an efflux from any kind of body (if it were, it would again itself be a kind of body)—it is the presence of fire or something resembling fire in what is transparent. It is certainly not a body, for two bodies cannot be present in the same place. The opposite of light is darkness; darkness is the absence from what is transparent of the corresponding positive state above characterized; clearly therefore, light is just the presence of that.

Empedocles (and with him all others who used the same forms of expression) was wrong in speaking of light as 'travelling' or being at a given moment between the earth and its envelope, its movement being unobservable by us; that view is contrary both to the clear evidence of argument and to the observed facts; if the distance traversed were short, the movement might have been unobservable, but where the distance is from extreme East to extreme West, the strain upon our powers of belief is too great.

What is capable of taking on color is what in itself is colorless, as what can take on sound is what is soundless; what is colorless includes what is transparent and what is invisible or scarcely visible, i.e., what is dark. The latter is the same as what is transparent, when it is potentially, not of course when it is actually transparent; it is the same substance which is now darkness, now light.

Not everything that is visible depends upon light for its visibility. This is only true of the 'proper' color of things. Some objects of sight which in light are invisible, in darkness stimulate the sense; that is, things that appear fiery or shining. This class of objects has no simple common name, but instances of it are fungi, horns, heads, scales, and eyes of fish. In none of these is what is seen their own proper color. Why we see these at all is another question. At present what is obvious is that what is seen in light is always color. That is why without the help of light color remains invisible. Its being

color at all means precisely its having in it the power to set in movement what is actually transparent, and the actuality of what is transparent is just light.

The following makes the necessity of a medium clear. If what has color is placed in immediate contact with the eye, it cannot be seen. Color sets in movement what is transparent, e.g., the air, and that, extending continuously from the object of the organ, sets the latter in movement. Democritus misrepresents the facts when he expresses the opinion that if the interspace were empty one could distinctly see an ant on the vault of the sky; that is an impossibility. Seeing is due to an affection or change of what has the perceptive faculty, and it cannot be affected by the seen color itself; it remains that it must be affected by what comes between. Hence it is indispensable that there be something in between—if there were nothing, so far from seeing with greater distinctness, we should see nothing at all.

We have now explained the cause why color cannot be seen otherwise than in light. Fire on the other hand is seen both in darkness and in light; this double possibility follows necessarily from our theory, for it is just fire that makes what is potentially transparent actually transparent.

The same account holds also of sound and smell; if the object of either of these senses is in immediate contact with the organ no sensation is produced. In both cases the object sets in movement only what lies between, and this in turn sets the organ in movement: if what sounds or smells is brought into immediate contact with the organ, no sensation will be produced. The same, in spite of all appearances, applies also to touch and taste; why there is this apparent difference will be clear later. What comes between in the case of sounds is air; the corresponding medium in the case of smell has no name. But, corresponding to what is transparent in the case of color, there is a quality found both in air and water, which serves as a medium for what has smell; for animals that live in water seem to possess the sense of smell. Men and all other land animals that breathe, perceive smells only when they breathe air in. The explanation of this too will be given later.

[…]

Sense and Sensibilia

[…]

That without light vision is impossible has been stated elsewhere; but, whether the medium between the eye and its objects is air or light, vision is caused by a process through this medium.

Accordingly, that the inner part of the eye consists of water is easily intelligible, water being transparent.

Now, as vision outwardly is impossible without light, so also it is impossible inwardly.

There must, therefore, be some transparent medium within the eye, and, as this is not air, it must be water. The soul or its perceptive part is not situated at the external surface of the eye, but obviously somewhere within: whence the necessity of the interior of the eye being transparent, i.e., capable of admitting light. And that it is so is plain from actual occurrences. It is matter of experience that soldiers wounded in battle by a sword slash on the temple, so inflicted as to sever the passages of the eye, feel a sudden onset of darkness, as if a lamp had gone out; because what is called the pupil, i.e., the transparent, which is a sort of lamp, is then cut off.

[…]

On the Soul

Book III

4 · Turning now to the part of the soul with which the soul knows and thinks (whether this is separable from the others in definition only, or spatially as well) we have to inquire what differentiates this part, and how thinking can take place.

If thinking is like perceiving, it must be either a process in which the soul is acted upon by what is capable of being thought, or a process different from but analogous to that. The thinking part of the soul must therefore be, while impassible, capable of receiving the form of an object; that is, must be potentially identical in character with its object without being the object. Thought must be related to what is thinkable, as sense is to what is sensible.

Therefore, since everything is a possible object of thought, mind in order, as Anaxagoras says, to dominate, that is, to know, must be pure from all admixture; for the co-presence of what is alien to its nature is a hindrance and a block: it follows that it can have no nature of its own, other than that of having a certain capacity. Thus that in the soul which is called thought (by thought I mean that whereby the soul thinks and judges) is, before it thinks, not actually any real thing. For this reason it cannot reasonably be regarded as blended with the body: if so, it would acquire some quality, e.g., warmth or cold, or even have an organ like the sensitive faculty: as it is, it has none. It was a good idea to call the soul 'the place of forms,' though this description holds only of the thinking soul, and even this is the forms only potentially, not actually.

[…]

5 · Since in every class of things, as in nature as a whole, we find two factors involved, a matter which is potentially all the particulars included in the class, a cause which is productive in the sense that it makes them all (the latter standing to the former, as e.g., an art to its material), these distinct elements must likewise be found within the soul.

And in fact thought, as we have described it, is what it is by virtue of becoming all things, while there is another which is what it is by virtue of making all things: this is a sort of positive state like light; for in a sense light makes potential colors into actual colors.

Thought in this sense of it is separable, impassible, unmixed, since it is in its essential nature activity (for always the active is superior to the passive factor, the originating force to the matter).

Actual knowledge is identical with its object: in the individual, potential knowledge is in time prior to actual knowledge, but absolutely it is not prior even in time. It does not sometimes think and sometimes not think. When separated it is alone just what it is, and this alone is immortal and eternal (we do not remember because, while this is impossible, passive thought is perishable); and without this nothing thinks.

Study Questions

1. Explain in your own words (a) what Aristotle means by saying that the soul is the form, and the body is the matter on which this form is imposed and (b) explain how this has implications for the survival of a person after bodily death.
2. "While waking is actuality in a sense corresponding to the cutting and the seeing, the soul is actuality in the sense corresponding to sight and the power in the tool." This is not easy to understand. See if you can explain in your own words what he means here.
3. In his section on vision, Aristotle argues against two positions: that light *travels* from the visible object to our eyes, taking some length of time to get there; and that one could see objects where empty space intervenes between the viewer and the object. (Note that he's wrong on both counts!) State his arguments for each position in your own words. Where has he gone wrong?
4. Why does Aristotle conclude that the mind "can have no nature of its own, other than that of having a certain capacity"? Explain in your own words exactly what he means by this.
5. In the last paragraph in our readings, Aristotle appears to contradict what he said in earlier passages. This last paragraph, admittedly, is rather obscure. What do you think he's saying here? Does this really contradict what he said earlier?
6. What does it mean to say that Aristotle attempts to *naturalize* the mind? Explain what features of the excerpts presented here demonstrate this attempt.

7. The famous work *School of Athens* by the Renais-
sance painter Raphael shows dozens of ancient
philosophers. Have a look: this can be found at
several places on the internet, including <http://
en.wikipedia.org/wiki/File:Sanzio_01_Plato_
Aristotle.jpg>. Look for websites which enlarge
the two philosophers at the center: they are Plato
and Aristotle. Plato points upward with his right
hand; Aristotle's right hand is extended horizontally, with his palm flat and fingers extended.
Interpret these gestures, and relate them to the
readings from the two philosophers we've just
done.

Suggested Readings

More on the mind is found in Aristotle's *Metaphysics*, book 7.

Some interpretations and evaluations of Aristotle's philosophy of mind:

Jonathan Barnes, "Aristotle's Concept of Mind," *Proceedings of the Aristotelian Society* 75
(1971): 101–14.
Myles F. Burnyeat, "Is an Aristotelian Philosophy of Mind Still Credible?," in *Essays on Aris-
totle's* De Anima, Martha C. Nussbaum and Amalie O. Rorty (eds.). (Oxford: Clarendon
Press, 1992).
Terence H. Irwin, "Aristotle's Philosophy of Mind," in *Companions to Ancient Thought 2: Psy-
chology*, Stephen Everson, (ed.). (Cambridge: Cambridge University Press, 1991).
Christopher Shields, "Soul and Body in Aristotle," *Oxford Studies in Ancient Philosophy* 6
(1988): pp. 103–37.
Richard Sorabji, "Body and Soul in Aristotle," *Philosophy* 49 (1974): pp. 63–89.

3

THE SCIENTIFIC REVOLUTION

Introduction

In this chapter we introduce a major shift in thinking about the mind, which reached its greatest momentum in the seventeenth century. There were many origins of this change, but we have chosen to focus on one of the central factors: the rise of the modern mathematical sciences. It is in the seventeenth century, through the work of such people as Galileo Galilei, René Descartes, and Isaac Newton, that the mathematical sciences burst into full bloom and in the process replaced many of the earlier ways of thinking about the world—including the ways people thought about the mind. In order to see how modern views of the mind developed, we need to look at the deep changes brought about by the new sciences.

Although it is a common error to oversimplify the philosophy and science of medieval Europe, it is safe to claim that Aristotle was the predominant intellectual influence on the European continent in the Middle Ages. When Aristotle's work became widely available in Latin, medieval scholars set to work to reconcile Aristotle's theories with the Holy Scriptures and with the doctrines laid down by the Church Fathers. The result of this effort was an extensive science and philosophy based equally on common sense, Aristotelian principles, and Christian faith.

But by the sixteenth century serious problems had become apparent in the Aristotelian system. The reasons for this are numerous and complex, and it is not possible for us to look at them in detail. But to give you an idea, here are a few sketches.

Problems with Aristotle's Theories

In the sixteenth century Galileo Galilei challenged the Aristotelian theory of motion with detailed studies of the times and motions of falling bodies. Galileo's careful studies of pendulums and rolling balls demonstrated that Aristotelian theories of motion were inconsistent with the observable facts.

Another blow to the Aristotelian worldview was Nicolaus Copernicus's discovery that the earth is in motion around the sun. In Aristotle's system the Earth is at the center of the cosmos, with the moon, sun, planets, and distant stars all revolving around the Earth in concentric circles; his explanations of change and motion in the natural world were built around this cosmological scheme. Once the heliocentric system was adopted, central portions of Aristotle's scientific system fell apart.

Perhaps the most damaging criticism of Aristotle's schema of matter and form was the charge that Aristotle's theories become vacuous when they are applied to complex problems. Critics of the Aristotelian method illustrated this point with the following rhetorical example. Followers of Aristotelian method might explain how a sleeping powder achieves its result by claiming that it possesses "dormitive" qualities: that which is potentially asleep becomes actually asleep in virtue of these qualities. This claim is obviously true, but it doesn't help us understand how sleeping powders work. In the same way, an unsympathetic reader could argue that Aristotle's definition of the soul contains a circularity. Aristotle explains the nature of the soul by saying that it is the form of living things. But given the definition of form as that which makes something the kind of thing it is, and the definition of the soul as that which brings life, it seems that Aristotle explains the soul—the source of life—by saying that it is that which brings life to living things. Once again, true but not very helpful.

Teleological Explanations

The decline of the Aristotelian system was due not only to problems within that system itself, but also to the increasing success of a new approach to science. The most significant element of this new science was the rejection of Aristotle's explanations of cause and effect.

Aristotle's explanations of change are always given in terms of things taking on forms and qualities. An important feature of these explanations is that they involve things moving *toward* the full realization of the respective forms and qualities. For example, an acorn grows into an oak by moving toward the form of a fully developed tree, and this form is latent in it from the moment it is created. You might compare the process to the building of a house, in which the builders are guided by the blueprint. The idea of the house is present from the outset, and the building of the house is a development toward the physical realization of the plan. The same idea is used in Aristotle's explanation of natural motion. The Earth is "heavy" because its proper place is at the center of the cosmos, and so without interference it will naturally move toward that location. For the same sort of reason, fire always moves upward toward its natural place in the outer regions.

These kinds of explanations are called **teleological** from the Greek word *telos*, which means "end," "goal," or "purpose." Teleological explanations appeal to an end or final purpose toward which things are directed.

Mechanical Explanations

Compare Aristotle's conception of change and motion with our modern ideas. The modern law of inertia tells us that in the absence of any external force an object will maintain a constant state of rest or uniform motion. In this picture, matter is entirely *inert*—it has no natural direction of motion and it doesn't move toward anything from any kind of internal drive. Explanations of motion in our modern physics are in terms of external forces acting on objects that otherwise will remain in their current state of uniform motion. We can call theories of this sort **mechanical theories**.

A distinctive feature of the scientific revolution of the seventeenth century is that all forms of teleological explanation were rejected in favor of a search for mechanical explanations. Part of the motivation behind this change was the alleged vacuity of Aristotelian explanations. It is of no value to explain change in terms of goals and purposes, critics of Aristotle maintained, if the goal itself is simply a re-description of the change. For instance, it doesn't help in understanding why an object falls to the ground to be told that it's the kind of thing that naturally moves in that direction. The solution, the critics argued, was to explain all motion and change by appeal to mechanical causes.

Mathematical Laws

The other distinctive feature of the new science is an emphasis on mathematics as a tool for describing natural laws. Modern scientific theories are **quantitative**. By contrast, Aristotle's system is entirely **qualitative**. The basic elements of Aristotle's science are earth, fire, air, and water. These elements are described in terms of four basic qualities (hot, cold, dry, and wet) and in terms of their natural motion. Nowhere in this system do mathematical relations play any part. Medieval scientists took mathematics to be a curiosity, an interesting pastime, but not of any real value in understanding the world.

A distinctive aspect of the new science, however, is the formulation of mathematical laws. Scientists like Galileo and Newton replaced the qualitative descriptions of the world with measurements of time, distance, weight, and so on. The measurements were used to formulate and test mathematical laws. It is this use of mathematical laws relating measurable quantities that distinguishes the new science from medieval theories.

Platonism

Part of the move towards mathematical descriptions of nature involved a revival of interest in Plato. The text of Plato most familiar to medieval scholars is a book called *The Timaeus*. In this book Plato is heavily influenced by the followers of the mathematician, Pythagoras. Following ideas developed by the Pythagoreans, Plato explained the observable characteristics of matter in terms of hidden geometrical properties, a view now called "geometrical atomism." In *The Timaeus* each of the four elements of Greek science—earth, water, air, and fire—is associated with one of the five regular solids: the tetrahedron, octahedron, icosahedron, cube, and dodecahedron. (The fifth solid Plato associated with the cosmos as a whole.) The properties of these figures could then be used to explain facts about the observable behavior of matter, such as the fact that water evaporates while earth does not. According to *The Timaeus*, the divine creator of the world used mathematical principles to construct a cosmos of ultimate beauty and rational harmony.

As Aristotelian science became more rigid and unworkable in the late middle ages, many scholars returned to the Platonic notion that the world can only be understood by discovering its hidden mathematical and divine nature. A perfect example of this development is the construction of the heliocentric theory of the planetary system. Copernicus wrote of his heliocentric theory, "We find then in this arrangement an admirable harmony of the world, and a dependable, harmonious interconnection of the motion and size of the paths, such as otherwise cannot be discovered." Kepler's subsequent discoveries of the elliptical shape of the planetary orbits and the laws of planetary motion were driven by a mystical search for divine order and mathematical harmony.

Splitting Perception from Reality

The new mathematical sciences dealt a direct blow to the Aristotelian confidence in the reliability of perception. Mathematical laws are *idealizations* of what we actually observe.[1] The acceptance of the new mathematical laws did not arise from the fact that they can be directly observed, but from the fact that they yielded more accurate predictions than any other laws.

Moreover, within the new science all of nature was to be explained in terms of the mathematical relations between inert particles of matter. Hence the only qualities of matter that made their way into the new physics were those that could be assigned numerical values: size, shape, motion, and mass. Other qualities, such as color, warmth, and wetness, were either explained in terms of the size, shape, motion, and mass of inert particles or were rejected as not really belonging to nature at all.

The new scientists concluded from this that the real qualities of objects are not necessarily the ones we perceive them to have. The appearances of things, they argued, are not a direct, straightforward guide to the nature of the real world. We need to distinguish carefully between our perceptions and the real nature of the world around us—between how things look and how they really are. Accordingly, the new scientists set about unravelling Aristotle's account of the relation between the perceiving mind and the physical world to show that the real qualities of objects are not like the sensations of color, warmth, and taste that we receive from them.

Galileo's *Assayer*

We begin with a selection from a book by Galileo called *The Assayer*. Galileo Galilei was born in 1564 at Pisa and died in 1642, the year of Isaac Newton's birth. He was a teacher of mathematics and physics at the universities of Pisa and Padua. At the end of his life he served in Florence as chief mathematician of the Duke of Tuscany. In his early career he was a respected teacher of Aristotle, but at Padua he began work on his new mathematical physics. He came under increasing criticism by the Aristotelians, and in 1633 he was imprisoned by the Inquisition for teaching Copernicus's heliocentric theory. The Aristotelians said that as he became a better mathematician he became a worse physicist, because he moved away from descriptions of the world as it appears in simple observations, and focused instead on abstract and ideal mathematical descriptions of times and motions.

In our first selection from *The Assayer* Galileo is defending his claim that "motion is the cause of heat." Galileo argues that in order to defend his claim, he needs to correct the mistaken view that the sensation of heat, as we experience it, is a real quality residing in the objects that warm us.

The Argument from Conceivability

Galileo's first argument is based on the claim that only certain qualities are recognized as being essential to the existence of physical objects. He argues that we cannot conceive of material objects existing at all without thinking of them as having a shape, a size, a position, and a state of motion or rest.

> Now I say whenever I conceive any material or corporeal substance, I immediately feel the need to think of it as bounded, as having this or that shape; as being large or small...as being in motion or at rest; as touching or not touching some other body; and as being one in number, or few, or many.

From this he concludes that these are essential qualities of matter that are part of its real nature and not merely reflections of our perceptions. The same is not true, he maintains, of tastes, odors, and colors. We can conceive of material objects lacking any one of these. He concludes from this that the latter qualities "are no more than mere names," and that they exist "only in the consciousness," not in the objects themselves. If there were no living creatures possessing such consciousness, he claims, these qualities would not exist at all.

According to Aristotle, the qualities of matter are those it appears to have in our immediate perception of it. A physical object does not appear to have merely a size, shape, and location. We are also aware of qualities such as warmth, color, and odor, and these appear to be real qualities of physical things. Galileo's claim is that we should not trust this perception. In a move reminiscent of Plato, Galileo seems to be asking us to turn our attention away from the immediate appearances of things and focus instead on what we can *conceive in our minds* as essential to the existence of matter.

The Argument from Analogy

Galileo then offers a second argument, this time drawing an analogy between qualities that we mistakenly attribute to matter and a quality that we know exists only in our own minds. He compares the sensations of taste, odor, and color with the sensation of tickling. When a hand or feather is run lightly over our body we feel a tickling sensation, but everyone agrees that the tickling "belongs to us, and not the hand." If we run our hand over a statue, no one believes that this motion produces the same tickling. Hence, the tickling is not a quality of the hand or the feather. It exists solely in the consciousness of the person tickled. He argues that the sensations of touch, taste, smell, and sound have the same nature as tickling: each is a sensation produced in us by the action of external objects, but not existing as a real quality in the objects themselves.

In the next page or two he suggests ways in which the motion of particles of matter might produce the sensations of tastes, odors, and sounds. Particles that possess a certain kind of motion may be able to enter into the tiny passages of the tongue and nostrils, and in so doing stimulate in the mind the sensations of taste and fragrance. Sensations of sound are produced, he suggests, by the motion of air particles causing a vibration of the eardrum. Differences in the vibration of the eardrum cause differences in the sensation of sound in the mind. In each case, all that exists in the physical environment is the motion of minute particles.

From these explanations Galileo draws the conclusion that the only qualities that really exist in material objects are the sizes, shapes, and motions of the particles that cause the sensations. The tastes, odors, and sounds that we experience are merely sensations in our mind, and so do not exist outside our consciousness. You might be thinking at this moment of the old saw, "If a tree falls in the forest, and no one is there to hear it, is there a sound?" Galileo's answer would be "No." There would be a motion of air particles produced by the tree falling but no quality of sound such as exists in our experience.

He concludes that the same can be said of heat as can be said of sound and taste. Heat, he claims, is a sensation in the mind produced by the rapid motion of tiny particles on our skin. Just as the motion of air particles vibrating the eardrum produces a sensation of sound, the rapid motion of particles on the skin produces in us a sensation of warmth. Remove the person experiencing that sensation and there is no quality of warmth.

René Descartes

Galileo's way of expressing this conclusion gives the appearance that in his view there is no such thing as color, taste, heat, or odor in physical objects. But this is not the best way of understanding the point. A better description is found in arguments offered by another important figure in the new science, René Descartes.

Descartes was born in France in 1596. He was equal parts scientist, mathematician, and philosopher, and had a profound influence in all three disciplines. As a young man, Descartes's interest in physics and mathematics was stimulated by his friendship with the scientist Isaac Beekman. The first problem he worked on was the law of falling bodies, the same problem that exercised Galileo. After Galileo's condemnation by the Inquisition in 1633 Descartes suppressed his own scientific work, *The World*, and turned his attention to philosophical issues. In 1649 he accepted an invitation to serve as tutor to Queen Christina of Sweden, and he died there the next year of pneumonia. Our first reading from Descartes is chapter 1 of *The World*. Here Descartes defends a view similar to the one advanced by Galileo in the previous reading, applied in this case to the nature of light. His objective is to show that "there may be a difference between the sensation we have of light…and what it is in the objects that produces this sensation within us."

Qualities and Sensations

Descartes first prepares the ground by distinguishing between two different things, both of which we associate with the word 'light.' The first is "the sensation we have of light" and the second is "what it is in the objects that produces this sensation within us." This distinction is straightforward, and in a sense Aristotle would accept it. There is something in the physical environment that we call light. In order for us to perceive this light, it must produce some effect in our mind. Descartes calls this effect a **sensation**.[2] So there are two distinct items: (1) the quality of light in the physical environment, and (2) the sensation in our mind.[3]

Aristotle would have no objection to the existence of both the sensation in the mind (although he wouldn't have called it that) and the quality of the object that causes that sensation. But beyond this Descartes and Aristotle part company. The position Descartes says he wants to oppose is the assumption that

> the ideas [or sensations] we have in our minds are wholly *similar* to the objects from which they proceed.

This is the very assumption upon which Aristotle's link between mind and nature is based. According to Aristotle, the qualities in the mind by which we perceive the world are identical to the qualities of the things around us. As we saw in the last chapter, Aristotle explains our perception of color by postulating that the action of light produces the same color in the eye as that in the object. Descartes's point in distinguishing between sensations and qualities of objects is to argue that there need not be any such identity. Sensations in the mind need not be the same as what produces them.

Descartes's Arguments from Analogy

Descartes bases his conclusion on a series of analogies. The first analogy is between the sensation of light and words in a language. Words, he says, make us think of their objects, even though they do not resemble them. Think, for example, of the word 'dog.' When someone utters this word, the sound brings to mind a certain kind of animal. Yet the sound bears no resemblance to that animal in any way. Descartes claims that there is no reason to reject the possibility that light is like words in this way. That is, it is something in nature that produces an idea or sensation in our minds, although it has no resemblance to that sensation at all.

His next comparison is with the nature of sound. He points out that, as sounds are produced by motions in the air, if sounds produced sensations that resembled their causes, we would have sensations of air motions rather than the sounds that we hear. But there is no similarity between our sensation of sound and the action of air motions. Different motions produce different sensations, but beyond this correlation there is no resemblance between the two. In the same way, Descartes claims, we should expect no similarity between the sensation of light and whatever it is that produces it.

He follows this argument with a version of Galileo's tickling analogy. The sensation of tickling, Descartes claims, shows that there is no similarity between actions upon our skin and the events in the mind that they produce. He supports this point with another example. He tells the story of a soldier who believes he is wounded in battle although the actual cause of his sensation is a buckle under his armor. If the sense of touch produced sensations that were identical to their causes, such confusion couldn't occur.

He concludes that there is nothing in the perception of light that would lead us to suppose it is different in nature from sounds or sensations of touch: the sensation of light produced in our minds may have no resemblance to the light in the external world that causes it. Thus the real nature of light is open to question and cannot be directly determined from the qualities of our sensations.

Resemblance

Notice the difference between Descartes's conclusion and Galileo's. According to Galileo, qualities such as taste, odor, and heat do not exist in the object. (To that list we can add color, sound, and light.) But this isn't a very perspicuous way of making the point. For there is something in the physical environment that produces our sensations, which Galileo and Descartes claim is the different motions of particles; and we do use the words 'taste,' 'color,' and so on to refer to them. Descartes's conclusion is a bit clearer than Galileo's. He does not deny that there are some qualities in the physical world that we call taste, color, and light. His position is simply that there need be no *similarity* between the real qualities in the physical world and our sensations of them. Another way he makes the point is by the observation that there is nothing in the real quality that *resembles* the sensation that it produces.

Seen in terms of resemblance or similarity, the idea that Descartes and Galileo are advancing can be put in the following way: there is nothing in physical objects similar to the sensations of color, taste, odor, and warmth. On the other hand, there is something in physical objects that resembles our sensations or ideas of shape, size, and motion. We want to distinguish, then, between two kinds of qualities that we attribute to objects: those that resemble our sensations of them and those that don't.

Qualities in the World and Sensations in the Mind

Galileo and Descartes take the view that the physical world is composed entirely of particles that possess no qualities except size, shape, solidity, and motion. All other qualities of objects—

warmth, light, color, taste, odor, and sound—are merely certain shapes and motions of these minute particles, which strike our sense organs and produce particular effects in the mind.

This position is expressed in a comment in the second selection from Descartes, drawn from a book entitled *Principles of Philosophy*. At the end of Part Four, Section 198, Descartes makes the following remark:

> In view of all this we have every reason to conclude that the properties in external objects to which we apply the terms light, color, smell, taste, sound, heat and cold...are, so far as we can see, simply various dispositions in those objects which make them able to set up various kinds of motions in our nerves which are required to produce the various sensations in our soul.

What we call color or sound in the physical world, then, are nothing more than the disposition to set into motion various minute particles within our nerves. The characteristics of colors, odors, and tastes with which we are familiar—what colors *look like* to us, and what sounds *sound like* to us—are merely products of our own consciousness, bearing no resemblance to anything in the physical world.[4]

This consequence of the mechanical sciences introduced what has become one of the most profound issues in the philosophy of mind. The occurrence of sensations with qualities such as warmth, taste, color, fragrance, and pain, is one of the most characteristic features of our conscious experience. Yet the mechanical sciences denied that these very qualities have any reality outside the mind, and the same is true of our modern physics. These qualities play no role whatsoever in our modern explanations of nature except as features of our own perceptual experiences. What positive account can we give, then, of the origin and nature of the perceptual qualities of our conscious experience? While the mechanical philosophy of sixteenth and seventeenth centuries laid the foundation for the modern sciences, they also opened one of biggest mysteries we have today: the completely familiar, yet so far inexplicable, character of conscious experience. This topic will reappear in subsequent chapters of this book, and especially in Chapter Eleven.

Descartes's Theory of Color Perception

In order to get a clearer grasp of just how the ideas advanced by the new scientists differ from those of Aristotle, let's look briefly at Descartes's explanation of color perception. According to Descartes, all matter is composed solely of minute particles, variously shaped and in constant motion. The particles of air are smooth and spherical, and it is the pressure exerted on the retina of the eye by these particles that causes our sensations of light. Experiments with prisms show us that color is an attribute of light. As the only qualities that the particles of light possess are their size, shape, and motion, the different colors in light must be produced by some differences in one of these three qualities. Descartes had reason to believe that all air particles are the same size and spherical shape, so color must be a product of their motion. His suggestion is as follows. Given their spherical shape, air particles will spin, and because they are in contact with one another, the rotation of one particle will affect the rotation of its neighbors. When light particles reflect from opaque surfaces or pass through the surface of water or glass, their spin is affected by the angle at which they strike the surface. It follows that light particles reflecting off the surfaces of objects and striking the retina will have different rates of rotation. These differences in rotation rates are communicated through the particles of the nerves to the brain, where each different rate of rotation produces a different sensation of color.

According to Descartes, then, color as it exists in the physical world consists entirely of differences in the rotations of minute air particles. These particles themselves have no color; their only qualities are their shape, size, and motion. But color *as it exists in the mind* is a sensation that appears to us in the various hues of red, blue, green, and so on. These two—color in the world and color in the mind—are completely different.

Notice the contrast between Descartes's theory of color perception and Aristotle's theory sketched in the last chapter. According to Aristotle, the color that is produced in the soul is the same quality as the color in the object that produces it. Color perception is thus made possible by the affinity between us and the things that surround us. This affinity between the soul and the world is abandoned by Descartes.

While Descartes's theory of light has been superseded by more sophisticated theories, the gap between the qualities of our sensations and the qualities we attribute to the world has not altered. We now explain light and color in terms of photons and the biochemistry of retinal cells. But it is still possible to argue in the manner of Descartes and Galileo that there is no resemblance between the properties of photons and retinal cells and our conscious experience of color.

Explaining the Facts about Perception

The central idea in Descartes's explanation of color is that each difference in the color of objects corresponds to a difference in the motion of particles. From this general idea Descartes draws the conclusion that the shapes and motions of minute particles are all that is needed to explain the facts of perception. As long as each sensation is correlated with a specific motion in the nerve fibers and we can show how such a motion is produced by motions generated in the sensory organs by physical objects, we can explain all we need to in understanding sense perception.

This point is made by Galileo in *The Assayer*. After giving his descriptions of how taste, odor, and sound can be produced by the shapes and motions of particles, Galileo makes the following remark:

> To excite in us tastes, odors, and sounds I believe that *nothing is required* in external bodies except shapes, numbers, and slow or rapid movements.

Similarly, in the selection from *Principles of Philosophy* quoted earlier, Descartes says,

> …we know that the nature of our soul is such that different local motions *are quite sufficient* to produce all the sensations in the soul.

In Part Four, section 198, of *Principles of Philosophy* he provides a number of examples. He says, for instance,

> If someone is struck in the eye, so that the vibration of the blow reaches the retina, this will cause him to see many sparks of flashing light, yet the light is not outside his eye. And if someone puts a finger in his ear he will hear a throbbing hum which comes simply from the movement of air trapped in the ear.

These examples are easy to explain, he says, if the sensations are caused by motions in the nerves, for we know that motions can cause other motions. By contrast, Descartes argues, the Aristotelian theory cannot explain the facts of perception. He says,

> But there is no way of understanding how [size, shape, and motion] can produce something else whose nature is quite different from their own—like the substantial forms and real qualities which many philosophers suppose to inhere in things; and we cannot understand how these qualities or forms could have the power subsequently to produce local motions in other bodies.

The idea here is that Aristotelian science cannot explain how sensations of color and sound can be caused by motion. This is reminiscent of the criticism of Aristotelian science described at the beginning of the chapter: the Aristotelian system of forms and qualities often fails to provide the explanations we seek. Explaining our perception of the world in terms of the soul's potential to take on the forms and qualities of things around us still leaves the question of *how* this takes place.

The Scientific Worldview

We have been led to the following conclusion. The basis for the claim that our sensations of color, warmth, taste, and so on have no resemblance to real qualities in the world is the assertion that the qualities of size, shape, and motion are sufficient by themselves to explain perception. That is, the only qualities we *need* to suppose exist in the real world are the mathematical qualities. Given these qualities, we can explain all of the facts of perception. The rejection of the Aristotelian affinity between the perceptions of the soul and the nature of the world is thus a result of the confidence in mechanical explanations of perception.

This view is part of the general belief that the mechanical sciences are sufficient for explaining all natural phenomena. For instance, we find in *The Assayer* the following statement from Galileo that without mathematics there can be no understanding of the natural world:

> Philosophy is written in this grand book, the universe, which stands continually open to our gaze. But the book cannot be understood unless one first learns to comprehend the language and read the letters in which it is composed. It is written in the language of mathematics, and its characters are triangles, circles, and other geometrical figures without which it is humanly impossible to understand a single word of it; without these, one wanders about in a dark labyrinth.

The successes of the new science in discovering mathematical laws led to the confident expectation that in time everything would be explained in these terms. This confidence is expressed in the beginning of the third selection from Descartes, *Principles of Philosophy*, Part Two, section 64.

> The only principles which I accept, or require, in physics are those of geometry and pure mathematics; these principles explain all natural phenomena, and enable us to provide quite certain demonstrations regarding them.

The Problem of Perception

The successes of the mechanical sciences have done much to vindicate the confidence of Galileo and Descartes. But in the specific case of perception, there is also something misleading in the claim that mechanical explanations are sufficient to explain all of the facts.

When Descartes and the others say that the motion of particles is sufficient to explain the facts about perception, what they mean is something like the following. For each distinct sensation produced in the mind, it is possible to identify a particle motion that can produce that sensation. Look, however, at Descartes's criticism of the Aristotelian theory. As we saw earlier, his complaint is that we cannot understand how motion can produce anything but other motions. Yet this same criticism can be made of the mechanical explanation. According to Descartes and the others, there is no similarity between our sensations and the motions in the physical world that produce them. They must claim this in order to maintain that the only real qualities of objects are size, shape, and motion. But, in that case, the motions produce sensations that are completely different in nature from their causes. And this is precisely what Descartes rejects in the Aristotelian theory. The question that remains unanswered in the mechanical explanation is how particle motions can cause sensations, given that the two are completely unalike.

The problem is this. As we just saw, there are certain aspects of perception that are not explained by Aristotle's claim that qualities in the world and sensations in the soul are identical. But, at the same time, Aristotle's theory does render the connection between the soul and the natural world comprehensible: if the qualities of each are the same, it is easy to see how one causes the other. The mechanical view solves the problem of locating a distinct cause for each sensation. What it *doesn't* do is explain the connection between the sensations and their putative causes.

The Larger Question

The advantage enjoyed by Aristotle's theory is that soul and nature have a natural affinity. This makes the connection between our thoughts and sensations and the external world easy to explain. By eliminating all but the mechanical qualities from the physical world, the new science is able to construct explanations of many natural phenomena that Aristotle's theory cannot account for. However, one phenomenon it does not provide an explanation for is the connection between mind and body. How are things in the world related as cause and effect to the states and activities of the mind?

The bigger question that begs for an answer in the mechanical philosophy is how to explain what the mind is in general terms. We are told that particle motions cause sensations, and that sensations are not like their causes. But what *are* sensations? The attributes of matter are the mechanical qualities of size, shape and motion, mass, and so on. But what are the attributes of mind? What definition of the soul (or, in modern terms, the mind) can be provided by the new sciences? Descartes and others of the new philosophy were aware of these questions and debated them at length. In this and the following two chapters we look at Descartes's answers to these questions, and the reception they received.

Notes

1. For example, in order to obtain measurements consistent with Newton's law of motion, $F = ma$, we have to discount the effects of friction.
2. Descartes sometimes uses the word 'sensation' and sometimes the word 'idea' in this paragraph and elsewhere. We can safely ignore any difference between these two in reading this passage.

3. Notice that if we apply the same distinction to the question about the tree in the forest, we can see what's wrong with the question. When we hear a tree fall in the forest, there are two things that we designate by the word 'sound.' One is the movement of the air caused by the tree falling. The other is the sensation in the mind that this movement produces. If no one is in the forest there is no sensation of sound, but there are nonetheless the air motions that would produce that sensation in a sentient creature. The question is silly because it is ambiguous—you don't know which of the two items you're being asked about.

4. The person who developed this view most carefully and fully is John Locke. See the introduction to Chapter Six below.

GALILEO GALILEI

Selections from *The Assayer*

On the Senses

[…]

It now remains for me to tell Your Excellency, as I promised, some thoughts of mine about the proposition "motion is the cause of heat," and to show in what sense this may be true. But first I must consider what it is that we call heat, as I suspect that people in general have a concept of this which is very remote from the truth. For they believe that heat is a real phenomenon, or property, or quality, which actually resides in the material by which we feel ourselves warmed. Now I say that whenever I conceive any material or corporeal substance, I immediately feel the need to think of it as bounded, and as having this or that shape; as being large or small in relation to other things, and in some specific place at any given time; as being in motion or at rest; as touching or not touching some other body; and as being one in number, or few, or many. From these conditions I cannot separate such a substance by any stretch of my imagination. But that it must be white or red, bitter or sweet, noisy or silent, and of sweet or foul odor, my mind does not feel compelled to bring in as necessary accompaniments. Without the senses as our guides, reason or imagination unaided would probably never arrive at qualities like these. I think that tastes, odors, colors, and so on are no more than mere names so far as the object in which we place them is concerned, and that they reside only in the consciousness. Hence if the living creature were removed, all these qualities would be wiped away and annihilated. But since we have imposed upon them special names, distinct from those of the other and real qualities mentioned previously, we wish to believe that they really exist as actually different from those.

I may be able to make my notion clearer by means of some examples. I move my hand first over a marble statue and then over a living man. As to the effect flowing from my hand, this is the same with regard to both objects and my hand; it consists of the primary phenomena of motion and touch, for which we have no further names. But the live body which receives these operations feels different sensations according to the various places touched. When touched upon the soles of the feet, for example, or under the knee or armpit, it feels in addition to the common sensation of touch a sensation on which we have imposed a special name, "tickling." This sensation belongs to us and not to the hand. Anyone would make a serious error if he said that the hand, in addition to the properties of moving and touching, possessed another faculty of "tickling," as if tickling were a phenomenon that resided in the hand that tickled. A piece of paper or a feather drawn lightly over any part of our bodies performs intrinsically the same operations of moving and touching, but by touching the eye, the nose, or the upper lip it excites in us an almost intolerable titillation, even though elsewhere it is scarcely felt. This titillation belongs entirely to us and not to the feather; if the live and sensitive body were removed it would remain no more than a mere word. I believe that no more solid an existence belongs to many qualities which we have come to attribute to physical bodies—tastes, odors, colors, and many more.

A body which is solid and, so to speak, quite material, when moved in contact with any part of my person produces in me the sensation we call touch. This, though it exists over my entire body, seems to reside principally in the palms of the hands and in the finger tips, by whose means we sense the most minute differences in texture that are not easily distinguished by other parts of our bodies. Some of these sensations are more pleasant to us than others.... The sense of touch is more material than the other senses; and, as it arises from the solidity of matter, it seems to be related to the earthly element.

Perhaps the origin of two other senses lies in the fact that there are bodies which constantly dissolve into minute particles, some of which are heavier than air and descend, while others are lighter and rise up. The former may strike upon a certain part of our bodies that is much more sensitive than the skin, which does not feel the invasion of such subtle matter. This is the upper surface of the tongue; here the tiny particles are received, and mixing with and penetrating its moisture, they give rise to tastes, which are sweet or unsavory according to the various shapes, numbers, and speeds of the particles. And those minute particles which rise up may enter by our nostrils and strike upon some small protuberances which are the instrument of smelling; here likewise their touch and passage is received to our like or dislike according as they have this or that shape, are fast or slow, and are numerous or few. The tongue and nasal passages are providently arranged for these things, as the one extends from below to receive descending particles, and the other is adapted to those which ascend. Perhaps the excitation of tastes may be given a certain analogy to fluids, which descend through air, and odors to fires, which ascend.

Then there remains the air itself, an element available for sounds, which come to us indifferently from below, above, and all sides—for we reside in the air and its movements displace it equally in all directions. The location of the ear is most fittingly accommodated to all positions in space. Sounds are made and heard by us when the air—without any special property of "sonority" or "transonority"—is ruffled by a rapid tremor into very minute waves and moves certain cartilages of a tympanum in our ear. External means capable of thus ruffling the air are very numerous, but for the most part they may be reduced to the trembling of some body which pushes the air and disturbs it. Waves are propagated very rapidly in this way, and high tones are produced by frequent waves and low tones by sparse ones.

To excite in us tastes, odors, and sounds I believe that nothing is required in external bodies except shapes, numbers, and slow or rapid movements. I think that if ears, tongues, and noses were removed, shapes and numbers and motions would remain, but not odors or tastes or sounds. The latter, I believe, are nothing more than names when separated from living beings, just as tickling and titillation are nothing but names in the absence of such things as noses and armpits. And, as these four senses are related to the four elements, so I believe that vision, the sense eminent above all others in the proportion of the finite to the infinite, the temporal to the instantaneous, the quantitative to the indivisible, the illuminated to the obscure—that vision, I say, is related to light itself. But of this sensation and the things pertaining to it I pretend to understand but little; and since even a long time would not suffice to explain that trifle, or even to hint at an explanation, I pass this over in silence.

Having shown that many sensations which are supposed to be qualities residing in external objects have no real existence save in us, and outside ourselves are mere names, I now say that I am inclined to believe heat to be of this character. Those materials which produce heat in us and make us feel warmth, which are known by the general name of "fire," would then be a multitude of minute particles having certain shapes and moving with certain velocities. Meeting with our bodies, they penetrate by means of their extreme subtlety, and their touch as felt by us when they pass through our substance is the sensation we call "heat." This is pleasant or unpleasant according to the greater or smaller speed of these particles as they go pricking and penetrating; pleasant when this assists our necessary transpiration, and obnoxious when it causes too great a separation and dissolution of our substance. The operation of fire by means of its particles is merely that in moving it penetrates all bodies, causing their speedy or slow dissolution in proportion to the number and velocity of the fire-corpuscles and the density or tenuity of the bodies. Many materials are such that in their decomposition the greater part of them passes over into additional tiny corpuscles, and this dissolution continues so long as these continue to meet with further matter capable of being so resolved. I do not believe that in addition to shape, number, motion, penetration, and touch there is any other quality in fire corresponding to "heat"; this belongs so intimately to us that when the live body is taken away, heat becomes no more than a simple name....

Since the presence of fire-corpuscles alone does not suffice to excite heat, but their motion is needed also, it seems to me that one may very reasonably say that motion is the cause of heat.... But I hold it to be silly to accept that proposition in the ordinary way, as a stone or piece of iron or a stick must heat up when moved. The rubbing together and friction of two hard bodies, either by resolving their parts into very subtle flying particles or by opening an exit for the tiny fire-corpuscles within, ultimately sets these in motion; and when they meet our bodies and penetrate them, our conscious mind feels those pleasant or unpleasant sensations which we have named heat, burning, and scalding. And perhaps when such attrition stops at or is confined to the smallest quanta, their motion is temporal and their action calorific only; but when their ultimate and highest resolution into truly indivisible atoms is arrived at, light is created. This may have an instantaneous motion, or rather an instantaneous expansion and diffusion, rendering it capable of occupying immense spaces by its—I know not whether to say its subtlety, its rarity, its immateriality, or some other property which differs from all these and is nameless.

[...]

On Mathematics and Nature

[...]

In Sarsi I seem to discern the firm belief that in philosophizing one must support oneself upon the opinion of some celebrated author, as if our minds ought to remain completely sterile and barren unless wedded to the reasoning of some other person. Possibly he thinks that philosophy is a book of fiction by some writer, like the *Iliad* or *Orlando Furioso*, productions in which the least important thing is whether what is written there is true. Well, Sarsi, that is not how matters stand. Philosophy is written in this grand book, the universe, which stands continually open to our gaze. But the book cannot be understood unless one first learns to comprehend the language and read the letters in which it is composed. It is written in the language of mathematics, and its characters are triangles, circles, and other geometric figures without which it is humanly impossible to understand a single word of it; without these, one wanders about in a dark labyrinth.

[...]

RENÉ DESCARTES

Selections from *The World or Treatise on Light*[*]

Chapter I. The Difference between Our Sensations and the Things That Produce Them

The subject I propose to deal with in this treatise is light, and the first point I want to draw to your attention is that there may be a difference between the sensation we have of light (i.e., the idea of light which is formed in our imagination by the mediation of our eyes) and what it is in the objects that produces this sensation within us (i.e., what it is in a flame or the sun that we call by the name 'light'). For although everyone is commonly convinced that the ideas we have in our mind are wholly similar to the objects from which they proceed, nevertheless I cannot see any reason which assures us that this is so. On the contrary, I note many observations which should make us doubt it.

Words, as you well know, bear no resemblance to the things they signify, and yet they make us think of these things, frequently even without our paying attention to the sound of the words or to their syllables. Thus it may happen that we hear an utterance whose meaning we understand perfectly well, but afterwards we cannot say in what language it was spoken. Now if words, which signify nothing except by human convention, suffice to make us think of things to which they bear no resemblance, then why could nature not also have established some sign which would make us have the sensation of light, even if the sign contained nothing in itself which is similar to this sensation? Is it not thus that nature has established laughter

---

* Eds.: Angle brackets indicate places where translations of the original work that were approved by Descartes added important additional material.

and tears, to make us read joy and sadness on the faces of men?

But perhaps you will say that our ears really cause us to perceive only the sound of the words, and our eyes only the countenance of the person who is laughing or weeping, and that it is our mind which, recollecting what the words and the countenance signify, represents their meaning to us at the same time. I could reply that by the same token it is our mind which represents to us the idea of light each time our eye is affected by the action which signifies it. But rather than waste time debating the question, I prefer to bring forward another example.

Suppose we hear only the sound of some words, without attending to their meaning. Do you think the idea of this sound, as it is formed in our mind, is anything like the object which is its cause? A man opens his mouth, moves his tongue, and breathes out: I do not see anything in these actions which is not very different from the idea of the sound which they make us imagine. Most philosophers maintain that sound is nothing but a certain vibration of air which strikes our ears. Thus, if the sense of hearing transmitted to our mind the true image of its object then, instead of making us conceive the sound, it would have to make us conceive the motion of the parts of the air which is then vibrating against our ears. But not everyone will wish to believe what the philosophers say, and so I shall bring forward yet another example.

Of all our senses, touch is the one considered the least deceptive and most certain. Thus, if I show you that even touch makes us conceive many ideas which bear no resemblance to the objects which produce them, I do not think you should find it strange if I say that sight can do likewise. Now, everyone knows that the ideas of tickling and of pain, which are formed in our mind on the occasion of our being touched by external bodies, bear no resemblance to these bodies. Suppose we pass a feather gently over the lips of a child who is falling asleep, and he feels himself being tickled. Do you think the idea of tickling which he conceives resembles anything present in this feather? A soldier returns from battle; in the heat of combat he might have been wounded without being aware of it. But now, as he begins to cool off, he feels pain and believes himself wounded. We call a surgeon, who examines the soldier after we remove his armor, and we find in the end that what he was feeling was nothing but a buckle or strap caught under his armor, which was pressing on him and causing his discomfort. If his sense of touch, in making him feel this strap, had imprinted an image of it in his mind, there would have been no need for a surgeon to inform him of what he was feeling. Now, I see no reason which compels us to believe that what it is in objects that gives rise to the sensation of light is any more like this sensation than the actions of a feather and a strap are like a tickling sensation and pain. And yet I have not brought up these examples to make you believe categorically that the light in the objects is something different from what it is in our eyes. I merely wanted you to suspect that there might be a difference, so as to keep you from assuming the opposite, and to make you better able to help me in examining the matter further.

[...]

RENÉ DESCARTES

Selections from *Principles of Philosophy*

Part Four

198. *By means of our senses we apprehend nothing in external objects beyond their shapes, sizes and motions.*

Moreover, we observe no differences between the various nerves which would support the view that different nerves allow different things to be transmitted to the brain from the external sense organs; indeed, we are not entitled to say that anything reaches the brain except for the local motion of the nerves themselves. And we see that this local motion produces not only sensations of pain and pleasure but also those of light and sound. If someone is struck in the eye, so that the vibration of the blow reaches the retina, this will cause him to see many sparks of flashing light, yet the light is not outside his eye. And if someone puts a finger in his ear he will hear a throbbing hum which comes simply from the movement of air trapped in the ear.

Finally, let us consider heat and other qualities perceived by the senses, in so far as those qualities are in objects, as well as the forms of purely material things, for example the form of fire: we often see these arising from the local motion of certain bodies and producing in turn other local motions in other bodies. Now we understand very well how the different size, shape and motion of the particles of one body can produce various local motions in another body. But there is no way of understanding how these same attributes (size, shape and motion) can produce something else whose nature is quite different from their own—like the substantial forms and real qualities which many

modern scientific view

<philosophers> suppose to inhere in things; and we cannot understand how these qualities or forms could have the power subsequently to produce local motions in other bodies. Not only is all this unintelligible, but we know that the nature of our soul is such that different local motions are quite sufficient to produce all the sensations in the soul. What is more, we actually experience the various sensations as they are produced in the soul, and we do not find that anything reaches the brain from the external sense organs except for motions of this kind. In view of all this we have every reason to conclude that the properties in external objects to which we apply the terms light, color, smell, taste, sound, heat and cold—as well as the other tactile qualities and even what are called 'substantial forms'—are, so far as we can see, simply various dispositions in those objects which make them able to set up various kinds of motions in our nerves <which are required to produce all the various sensations in our soul>.

[…]

Part Two

64. *The only principles which I accept, or require, in physics are those of geometry and pure mathematics; these principles explain all natural phenomena, and enable us to provide quite certain demonstrations regarding them.*

I will not here add anything about shapes or about the countless different kinds of motions that can be derived from the infinite variety of different shapes. These matters will be quite clear in themselves when the time comes for me to deal with them. I am assuming that my readers know the basic elements of geometry already, or have sufficient mental aptitude to understand mathematical demonstrations. For I freely acknowledge that I recognize no matter in corporeal things apart from that which the geometers call quantity, and take as the object of their demonstrations, i.e., that to which every kind of division, shape and motion is applicable. Moreover, my consideration of such matter involves absolutely nothing apart from these divisions, shapes and motions; and even with regard to these, I will admit as true only what has been deduced from indubitable common notions so evidently that it is fit to be considered as a mathematical demonstration. And since all natural phenomena can be explained in this way, as will become clear in what follows, I do not think that any other principles are either admissible or desirable in physics.

[...]

Study Questions

1. Galileo distinguishes between characteristics which we can "separate from substance" in our minds from those we can't. Explain in your own words what you think he means here. He argues on the basis of this distinction that characteristics of the first sort would no longer exist if nobody sensed them. Try to explain, in your own words, why he thinks this is supposed to follow.
2. It's claimed in the introduction to this section that Galileo didn't really mean that tastes, odors, sounds, heat and coolness, etc., do not exist outside minds; a clearer way of expressing what he really meant was given by Descartes. What is Descartes's alternative way of talking about these phenomena? Do you think that Galileo really meant what Descartes said about them? Defend your position.
3. Compare what Galileo and Descartes say in the last paragraph of their readings. What, in your own words, is a common position here? Do you detect important differences? If so, what are they?

Suggested Readings

Galileo's thoughts on color are discussed in:

Paul A. Boghossian and J. David Velleman, "Color as a Secondary Quality," *Mind* 98 (1989): pp. 81–103.
Jonathan Cohen "Barry Stroud, the Quest for Reality: Subjectivism and the Metaphysics of Colour," *Noûs* 37 (2003): pp. 537–54.

The general form of Galileo's arguments is discussed in Gad Prudovsky, "Arguments from Conceivability," *Ratio* 8 (1995): pp. 63–69. It's quite hard to find any substantial treatment of his thoughts on these matters, however, because almost everything written on him concentrates on his much more important work on astronomy and physics, and on the methodology of science.

For further reading on Descartes, see the list for Descartes in Chapter Four.

4

DESCARTES: KNOWLEDGE OF MIND AND MATTER

Introduction

As we saw in the last chapter, Descartes's goal was to develop and defend the new mathematical sciences. In pursuing this goal, Descartes was especially aware of the religious and philosophical implications it carried. Where Galileo defended the new science on the grounds of its experimental success, Descartes wished to demonstrate once and for all the correctness of its methods using principles drawn from "the light of reason." His intent was not merely to develop the science itself, but to create a complete philosophical system of which the physical sciences would form an integral part. The result of this effort produced a theory of knowledge, a theory of mind, and a theology, as well as a foundation for the physical sciences.

Descartes's Dualism

The theory of mind that Descartes constructed is a version of dualism, and is thus reminiscent in some ways of Plato's view. According to Descartes, the mind is an immaterial entity, entirely distinct from the physical body. Like Plato, Descartes argued that the characteristics of the mind are altogether different from those of material objects. According to Descartes, the nature of the physical world is described in entirely mathematical terms; its only real properties are those of shape, size, position, motion, and number. None of these characteristics belongs to the mind, which has only one attribute: conscious intelligence. The mind *thinks*, where thinking includes conscious experience, reason, and will. And just as the mind lacks any of the attributes of size, shape, and location, objects in the material world are utterly devoid of any thought or consciousness.

Although one of his primary goals was to create an account of mind that left room for the methods of the new science, Descartes did not determine the nature of the mind from scientific principles. Instead he developed an ingenious theory of knowledge wherein both the nature of the mind *and* the mathematical character of the physical world could be deduced. According to Descartes, once we establish the real sources of knowledge and determine from that what can be known with absolute certainty, we will recognize that the only real properties of matter are those of pure mathematics, and we will see that the mind is entirely distinct from the physical body.

The *Meditations*

Our readings for this chapter and the next are from a small book entitled *Meditations on First Philosophy* that Descartes wrote in both Latin and French between 1638 and 1640. Descartes intended the *Meditations on First Philosophy* to provide a short and accessible presentation of his philosophy; in this little book all of the central tenets of his philosophical system are laid out and defended. It is written in the first person because his theory of knowledge begins with our reflective knowledge of our own mind, and it proceeds from there to deduce the difference between mind and body and the nature of each. The book is divided into six chapters, which he calls Meditations. The most important parts of the *Meditations* for our purposes, and hence those included in the readings, are the Second and Sixth Meditations and the first two paragraphs of the Third. We need to begin, however, with an outline of the First Meditation where the groundwork of his position is established.

The Search for Certainty

At the beginning of the First Meditation Descartes says that many of the principles upon which his beliefs have been based have turned out to be mistaken. He is thinking here largely of his early education in Aristotelian philosophy and science. He concludes from this that if secure knowledge of the world is possible, he must first reject all of his beliefs and start again from the very foundations. To this end he makes the following important assertion.

> But reason now convinces me that I should withhold my assent from opinions which are not entirely certain and indubitable, no less than from those which are plainly false; so if I uncover any reason for doubt in each of them, that will be enough to reject them all.

The position he is taking here is that he cannot accept any of his opinions as genuine knowledge unless it is *impossible* for him to doubt their truth. This principle serves as the basis of his system, and, as we will see, it is the origin of his theory of mind and body. It is usually referred to as Descartes's "Method of Doubt."

Doubts about the Senses and the Intellect

The Method of Doubt provides Descartes with a way of undermining the Aristotelian system, for that system is based on the assumption that our thoughts and sensory perceptions are direct copies of the world around us. By showing that this confidence in the senses and the intellect does not survive the Method of Doubt, Descartes is free to establish his own system. Accordingly, Descartes spends most of the First Meditation casting doubt on the idea that things are necessarily the way they appear.

Clearly the sensory appearances of things are sometimes possible to doubt, for things are often not exactly as they appear. On the other hand he points out that some of what we perceive by the senses would seem to be *absurd* to doubt.

[F]or example, the fact that I am now here, seated by the fire, wearing a winter robe, holding this paper in my hands, and so on. And, in fact, how could I deny that these very hands and this whole body are mine...

Yet even what appears to be most evident is sometimes false. If I am dreaming, even the clearest of my perceptions are illusory, so we need a test to distinguish dreams from reality. But Descartes points out that there is no test that would make it *impossible* to doubt that we are dreaming, for any test we can use could in principle be part of the dream itself.

Nor can we have a simple, unreflective confidence in the use of reason, for even the simplest truths of the intellect (say, the belief that 2+3=5) are drawn from certain basic operations of the mind: counting, calculating, drawing inferences, and so on. This means that the truths of reason are safe from doubt only if we cannot doubt the reliability of our powers of reasoning. How can we be absolutely sure of our powers of reason? Suppose, for example, that you made the *same* mistake every time you calculated something. No matter how many times you checked your conclusion, you would still miss your error.

Thought Experiments

Descartes ends the First Meditation with what we call nowadays a **thought experiment**. Because thought experiments will play a central role in our readings beyond this chapter, it is worthwhile to look at what they are intended to do.

In simplest terms a thought experiment is simply a fictional story that is used to test and challenge the ways we think about the world. The idea of using fiction in this way is familiar from the science fiction genre. People in science fiction stories are constantly forced into situations that violate our expectations, and this forces us to re-examine our ways of thinking about things.

Exactly what thought experiments can prove is a matter of debate. Some argue that, unlike real experiments, thought experiments do not reveal anything about the world. They only show us more vividly the implications of our own ways of thinking. (Daniel Dennett, whom we will read in Chapter Eleven, calls them "intuition pumps.") Others contend that they show us what *could* be true, even if what they describe isn't actually true. And facts about what could be true, they argue, can form the basis for substantial conclusions about the nature of the world.

The Evil Demon

Descartes's thought experiment involves the possibility that all of our perceptions and thoughts about the world might be false. He does this by asking us to consider the possibility of an evil demon who has complete control of our mind. Let's follow Descartes's reasoning here. Imagine an evil demon, infinitely cunning and powerful, and imagine that the demon is wholly bent on deceiving you into false beliefs. If it is possible for you to be mistaken about anything at all then the demon will manage it. The demon has control of your memory, your sensory perceptions, and your faculty of reasoning, so that everything you see, remember, or deduce is simply an illusion the demon creates.

Such a description gives an ideal way to identify those beliefs that it is impossible to doubt: any belief you would continue to hold *while imagining that you are being deceived by an evil demon* is one of which you must be absolutely certain. Accordingly, Descartes ends the First Meditation with the conclusion that he will accept as a foundation for knowledge *only* those beliefs that he would continue to hold even while under the power of such an evil demon.

"I think, therefore I am"

The Second Meditation begins with a reiteration of the evil demon scenario, and Descartes asks what beliefs could possibly survive such an all-encompassing doubt. It seems that the only beliefs that would meet this requirement are those that must necessarily be true simply because we believe them to be true. Descartes points out that the statement 'I exist' is just such a belief. It is always impossible to falsely assert 'I exist.' This gives him his first principle and foundation for knowledge:

> *I am, I exist* is necessarily true every time I say it or conceive of it in my mind.

In a different book, he expresses the same idea with his famous line, "I think, therefore I am." Notice, however, that only the *first-person* belief 'I exist' is impossible to doubt. It is possible to doubt that *other* people exist. This is the reason the Meditations are written in the first person: all knowledge begins with knowledge of oneself.

"I exist as a thinking thing"

The next step in Descartes's argument is the claim that knowledge of one's own existence, when understood properly, leads directly to other knowledge. In order to recognize myself as existing I must know something about what I am. Accordingly Descartes turns next to the question what the word 'I' refers to in the quotation above.

Keep in mind that Descartes is still searching for beliefs that are absolutely certain. The inference from his own existence to any further knowledge must pass the evil demon test—he can only draw the inference if he would be willing to do so in the presence of an evil demon. Accordingly, Descartes spends a few paragraphs rejecting many of the beliefs about himself he usually accepts: he believes himself to have a certain physical body, and there are many events he remembers as part of his life history. All of these things could be the illusions of an evil demon. So knowledge of his own existence does not come from knowledge of any of these things, even if they are all true.

In light of this, Descartes argues that his knowledge of his own existence is based only on his awareness of his own *thinking*. The statement, 'I exist,' must be true as long as I *think* that it is. He says,

> What about thinking? Here I discover something: thinking does exist. This is the only thing which cannot be detached from me. *I am, I exist*—that is certain. But for how long? Surely for as long as I am thinking.

This is true, he maintains, even if all his sensory perceptions and memories are entirely false. That the perceptions and memories themselves exist is still true. Hence, knowledge of one's own individual existence is derived from nothing more than the awareness of one's own thought.

To this conclusion he adds that in order to know that he thinks, he must also have some conception of what thinking is. So this adds another small piece of knowledge. He asks the question, "What is a thing that thinks?" The answer is that a thing that thinks is a thing that doubts, understands, affirms, denies, wills, refuses, and also imagines and senses. The existence of each of these various states of mind, he claims, is directly evident whenever we reflect on our own conscious experience.

Thought as Consciousness

At the end of his list of what thinking includes he makes the following important comment:

> Finally, it is the same I that feels, or notices corporeal things, apparently through the senses: for example, I now see light, hear noise, and feel heat. But these are false, for I am asleep. Still, I certainly seem to see, hear, and grow warm—and this cannot be false. Strictly speaking, this is what in me is called sense perception and, taken in this precise meaning, it is nothing other than thinking.

In the first sentence of this quotation Descartes is pointing out that he has included sense perception on the list of different kinds of thinking. In the third sentence he admits that these perceptions may be illusions. But, he says, he is nonetheless aware of the perception itself; that is, of his conscious experience of seeming to perceive something. Even if his perceptions are illusory, he is still aware that he has them. In the last sentence of the passage, he adds that this experience of perception is a form of thinking.

In this paragraph Descartes is constructing an altogether new understanding of **thought** or thinking.[1] Normally, sensing is thought of as an activity that necessarily involves the bodily organs—you can't perceive without organs to perceive with. But here Descartes has *redefined* sensing as an activity that one cannot doubt even while doubting the existence of the physical body. So this conception of sensing carries no assumption that the physical body exists. And understood in this new way, sensing is described as an aspect of **thinking**.

In these two steps Descartes has introduced a new conception of thinking as whatever we *cannot doubt* when we reflect on our own internal experience. The implication of this is that the mind itself is here given an entirely new definition. The mind is understood to be that part of us that thinks, and thinking is defined in terms of the contents of our conscious experience. In this way Descartes introduces a new idea of the mind as a center of consciousness.

Taking advantage of this new definition of the mind, Descartes concludes that our awareness of our own mind forms the foundation for all of our knowledge. Even if all of our thoughts and perceptions are false, and the world is not as we perceive it or remember it, the fact that we are having those thoughts and those perceptions is impossible to doubt. According to Descartes, the nature and content of the mind is directly evident to us. We cannot be mistaken about the immediate contents of our own thoughts.

Knowledge of Physical Objects

Descartes's arguments so far have given him the material he needs to draw striking conclusions about the nature of the mind. But in order to complete his argument for dualism, Descartes also has to establish certain claims about the physical world. Beginning with the line "From these thoughts, I begin to understand somewhat better what I am...," Descartes re-examines the basis for our beliefs about the physical world. Aristotle's system is based on the idea that the nature of the physical world is revealed to us directly by the senses. Accordingly, Descartes's first project is to undermine this belief.

He begins by admitting that the conclusion he has reached about the mind conflicts with our ordinary view of things. Common sense suggests that our knowledge of ordinary physical objects is more immediate and more certain than our knowledge of this mysterious thing, the mind. So he attempts to confirm his conclusion by answering the question, 'How *do* we have knowledge of ordinary physical objects?'

In his answer to the question Descartes implicitly assumes that there are three distinct faculties of the mind by which we might have knowledge of physical objects: the senses, the imagination, and the intellect. He offers an argument that has the following form.

1. Knowledge of physical objects is not obtained through the senses.
2. Nor is it obtained through the imagination.
   Hence it is obtained through the intellect.

Let's look first at his argument for the two premises, and then at what he intends in his conclusion.

The "Piece of Wax" Argument

The argument for the first premise is based on a claim that a physical object is distinct from any of the sensible qualities (color, shape, odor, and so on) that it has at any particular time. But our senses perceive only those qualities. Therefore, what we perceive through the senses is not the object itself but only certain qualities it happens to have.

The reasoning here is illustrated by an example of an ordinary physical object: a piece of wax. As the wax is heated, every quality perceived by the senses changes—its color, its taste, its fragrance, and its size and shape. Nothing sensible remains of the piece of wax before it was heated. *Yet it remains the same object.* The piece of wax didn't vanish while a new object appeared in its place.[2] The same object simply changed in its appearance. Hence the object that we recognize as the piece of wax cannot be anything perceived by the senses.

In his argument for the second premise Descartes considers the possibility that our idea of the piece of wax is formed through our ability to *imagine* all the particular sensible qualities it may have over time. On this hypothesis, the reason we recognize the changed object as the same piece of wax is because our idea of it includes all of the changes it might undergo. So our recognition of the object would be a function of the imagination, not the senses. But Descartes rejects this on the grounds that an object may have an infinite number of particular sensible qualities. Think, for example, of how many shapes a piece of wax can have. He can only imagine a finite number of these qualities, and so he cannot possibly have formed his idea of the object through the imagination.

Perception Involves Judgment

Because it is not through either the senses or the imagination, our knowledge of physical objects can only be through the intellect. This is similar to an idea that we have already encountered in Aristotle. Recall the question raised in Chapter Two of how we are capable of perceiving a horse from our awareness of a collection of sensible qualities. The answer Aristotle gives is that our mind is capable of taking on the forms or essences of things. In his piece-of-wax argument Descartes is making the related point (applied to a piece of wax rather than a horse) that perception cannot consist merely of the perception of sensible qualities. What answer does Descartes give, then, to Aristotle's question?

Near the end of the piece-of-wax argument he says our perception of the piece of wax is a case of "mental inspection." But what does he mean by that? A bit further on he describes the intellect as the "faculty of judgment." When we perceive an object like the piece of wax, there is an act of judgment involved in our perception. I don't *see* the piece of wax—I *infer* that it is there from appearances provided by my senses.

Descartes admits, however, that his claim that perception involves the intellect conflicts with how we *seem* to have knowledge of physical objects. We are not aware of any acts of judgment or inference in our ordinary perception of the world. But Descartes points out that we often make judgments without noticing them, and he gives the following example. He looks out the window, and it seems that he sees men in the street; but on closer inspection he notices that he does not actually see any men but only hats and coats, from which he *judges* that it is men that he sees. There was an act of judgment in this perception, but it went unnoticed. So he concludes that:

> And thus what I thought I was seeing with my eyes I understand only with my faculty of judgment, which is in my mind.

The Idea of Matter

But this isn't the whole story. Judgment always involves some kind of conclusion. What exactly is it that I infer when I perceive something like the piece of wax? The answer to this puzzle lies in a comment that Descartes makes in the middle of the piece-of-wax argument. In asking what his idea of the piece of wax is, he says,

> Perhaps what I now think is as follows: the wax itself was not really that sweetness of honey, that fragrance of flowers, that white color, or that shape and sound, but a body which a little earlier was perceptible to me in those forms, but which is now perceptible in different ones. But what exactly is it that I am imagining in this way? Let us consider that point and, *by removing those things which do not belong to the wax*, see what is left over. It is clear that nothing remains, other than something extended, flexible, and changeable. [emphasis ours]

In the highlighted phrase we have a version of Galileo's argument from conceivability whereby Galileo concludes that *matter* has no other qualities than shape, size, and motion. Descartes is asserting the same idea. By "something extended," he means something extended in space, that is, something that has a size, shape, and location.

So the idea of the piece of wax that we have in our mind is just the idea of something that possesses a certain size and shape, and that is perceptible by the organs of sense. When we perceive an object like the wax, we form a judgment to the effect that there is before us something extended in space that produces certain sensations in our mind.

It is important to see just how it is that this idea is involved in the act of perception. According to Descartes, the common opinion that our ideas and experiences of the world come directly from the senses is mistaken. Without the activity of the intellect, he believes, our sensations would not provide us with a coherent, structured perception of an enduring physical world. The idea of matter as extended in space does not come to us *from* our sensory experience; rather it is an idea supplied by the mind that we *read into* the sensations supplied by our sensory organs. This, I believe, is what Descartes means when he says that the perception of the wax is an act of "purely mental inspection." In a manner reminiscent of Plato, Descartes's view is that, although the senses provide us with a certain amount of confused information, the conceptual framework needed to make sense of that information is provided by the intellect alone.

Descartes's Rule

The idea that perception of the physical world involves an act of "mental inspection" raises a problem: if our conception of physical objects is supplied by the mind, how can we assure ourselves that this conception is correct? Descartes turns to this problem in the Third Meditation.

Near the beginning of the Third Meditation, Descartes says that in the previous Meditation he has already discovered a rule that he can use to acquire knowledge about the physical world. He goes back to the first belief established in the Second Meditation: "I am, I exist—that is certain. But for how long? For as long as I am thinking." Given that this statement is beyond doubt, he asks what *reason* he had for accepting it as such. His answer is that, "In this first item of knowledge there is simply a clear and distinct perception of what I am asserting...." This thought suggests to him the following rule:

> [A]ll those things I perceive very clearly and very distinctly are true.

What does he mean by this? Recall that in the Second Meditation, when he first establishes the belief 'I exist,' he discovers that this knowledge is based solely on the existence of his own conscious thought. It is only after he has clearly and distinctly perceived the *precise content* of that belief that he sees that it must be true. So the idea he draws from this is as follows. There are certain ideas and thoughts that occur in the conscious mind. Some of these thoughts and ideas are clear and distinct; others are confused and vague. Our beliefs are often false when they are based on confused and vague ideas and impressions. But our beliefs are always true when they are based on clear and distinct ideas and impressions. Because he has relied on this rule in establishing the certainty of his own existence, he now maintains that the rule *must* be acceptable as a means of acquiring knowledge, or else he must give up his claim to know that he exists, which would be absurd.

The Existence of God

In the remainder of the Third Meditation Descartes argues that we can demonstrate the truth of this rule by proving the existence of a benevolent and powerful God. Once this has been proven, we can see that such a God would not create us in such a way that our clearest beliefs can be mistaken.

This argument gives us a further clue to what Descartes means by "clear and distinct ideas." In the Sixth Meditation, while discussing what can be known of physical objects, he makes the following claim:

> But regarding other material things which are either merely particular, for example that the sun is of such and such a magnitude and shape, and so on, or less clearly understood, for

example light, sound, pain, and things like that, although these may be extremely doubtful and uncertain, nonetheless, because of the very fact that God is not a deceiver and thus it is impossible for there to be any falsity in my opinions which I cannot correct with another faculty God has given me, I have the sure hope that I can reach the truth even in these matters.

The idea expressed here is that we will not fall into errors that we are incapable of correcting. It follows that as long as we do everything that is within our power to avoid error, our beliefs will always be true. A clear and distinct idea, understood in this light, is one that appears to be true even after it has been examined critically with every faculty of reason and analysis we possess.

Descartes's critics have maintained that proving the existence of God in order to support his rule is circular. For one of the premises in his argument that God exists, they maintain, is the rule itself, so that a person will only accept the premises as true if they already accept the conclusion. To pursue this problem is beyond our scope here, so I will pass it by and look instead at what Descartes does with his rule once it is established.

Using the Rule

The Sixth Meditation is the culmination of the book, and Descartes declares two objectives here: to establish the existence and nature of physical objects, and to demonstrate that the mind and the physical body are two distinct entities. In the Second Meditation he introduced the idea of matter as something extended in space. Descartes now argues that the spatial properties of size, shape, and motion are the properties of matter of which we can form a clear and distinct idea. He says,

> It remains for me to examine whether material things exist. At the moment, I do, in fact, know that they could exist, at least insofar as they are objects of pure mathematics, since I perceive them *clearly and distinctly.* [emphasis ours]

The claim here is that the only clear and distinct, and hence truly accurate, conception he has of physical objects is that of something extended in space, and thus possessing size, shape, position, and motion. This is because the idea of spatial extension is based on the sciences of arithmetic and geometry, and the principles of these sciences are all clear and distinct.

Descartes admits, however, that there are other qualities commonly attached to the idea we have of material objects: colors, sounds, scents, and so on. And all of these are derived from our sensory perceptions. How are these sensory perceptions related to the world of material objects? To answer this question Descartes turns to the relationship between mind and matter. This topic is the subject of the next chapter.

Notes

1. This point is made very effectively by Gareth Matthews in "Consciousness and Life," *Philosophy* 52 (1977): pp. 13–26.
2. It is sometimes assumed that Descartes means that the object remains a piece of wax rather than some other kind of object. But his point doesn't concern kinds of physical objects. It is that the object has not been replaced by a different one.

RENÉ DESCARTES

Selections from *Meditations on First Philosophy*[*]

SECOND MEDITATION
Concerning the Nature of the Human Mind and the Fact that It Is Easier to Know than the Body

Yesterday's meditation threw me into so many doubts that I can no longer forget them or even see how they might be resolved. Just as if I had suddenly fallen into a deep eddying current, I am hurled into such confusion that I am unable to set my feet on the bottom or swim to the surface. However, I will struggle along and try once again [to follow] the same path I started on yesterday—that is, I will reject everything which admits of the slightest doubt, just as if I had discovered it was completely false, and I will proceed further in this way, until I find something certain, or at least, if I do nothing else, until I know for certain that there is nothing certain. In order to shift the entire earth from its location, Archimedes asked for nothing but a fixed and immovable point. So I, too, ought to hope for great things if I can discover something, no matter how small, which is certain and immovable.

Therefore, I assume that everything I see is false. I believe that none of those things my lying memory represents has ever existed, that I have no senses at all, and that body, shape, extension, motion, and location are chimeras. What, then, will be true? Perhaps this one thing: there is nothing certain.

But how do I know that there exists nothing other than the items I just listed, about which one could not entertain the slightest momentary doubt? Is there not some God, by whatever name I call him, who places these very thoughts inside me? But why would I think this, since I myself could perhaps have produced them? So am I then not at least something? But I have already denied that I have senses and a body. Still, I am puzzled, for what follows from this? Am I so bound up with my body and my senses that I cannot exist without them? But I have convinced myself that there is nothing at all in the universe—no sky, no earth, no minds, no bodies. So then, is it the case that I, too, do not exist? No, not at all: if I persuaded myself of something, then I certainly existed. But there is some kind of deceiver, supremely powerful and supremely cunning, who is constantly and intentionally deceiving me. But then, if he is deceiving me, there again is no doubt that I exist—for that very reason. Let him trick me as much as he can, he will never succeed in making me nothing, as long as I am aware that I am something. And so, after thinking all these things through in great detail, I must finally settle on this proposition: the statement *I am, I exist* is necessarily true every time I say it or conceive of it in my mind.

But I do yet understand enough about what this *I* is, which now necessarily exists. Thus, I must be careful I do not perhaps unconsciously substitute something else in place of this *I* and in that way make a mistake even here, in the conception which I assert is the most certain

---

[*] Eds.: This translation is based upon the first Latin edition of Descartes's *Meditations* (1641). Words in square brackets are insertions and additions from the first French edition.

and most evident of all. For that reason, I will now reconsider what I once believed myself to be, before I fell into this [present] way of thinking. Then I will remove from that whatever could, in the slightest way, be weakened by the reasoning I have [just] brought to bear, so that, in doing this, by the end I will be left only with what is absolutely certain and immovable.

What then did I believe I was before? Naturally, I thought I was a human being. But what is a human being? Shall I say a *rational animal*? No. For then I would have to ask what an *animal* is and what *rational* means, and thus from a single question I would fall into several greater difficulties. And at the moment I do not have so much leisure time that I wish to squander it with subtleties of this sort. Instead I would prefer here to attend to what used to come into my mind quite naturally and spontaneously in earlier days every time I thought about what I was. The first thought, of course, was that I had a face, hands, arms, and this entire mechanism of limbs, the kind one sees on a corpse, and this I designated by the name *body*. Then it occurred to me that I ate and drank, walked, felt, and thought. These actions I assigned to the *soul*. But I did not reflect on what this *soul* might be, or else I imagined it as some kind of attenuated substance, like wind, or fire, or aether, spread all through my denser parts. However, I had no doubts at all about my body—I thought I had a clear knowledge of its nature. Perhaps if I had attempted to describe it using the mental conception I used to hold, I would have explained it as follows: By a *body* I understand everything that is appropriately bound together in a certain form and confined to a place; it fills a certain space in such a way as to exclude from that space every other body; it can be perceived by touch, sight, hearing, taste, or smell, and can also be moved in various ways, not, indeed, by itself, but by something else which makes contact with it. For I judged that possessing

the power of self-movement, like the ability to perceive things or to think, did not pertain at all to the nature of body. Quite the opposite in fact, so that when I found out that faculties rather similar to these were present in certain bodies, I was astonished.

But what [am I] now, when I assume that there is some extremely powerful and, if I may be permitted to speak like this, malevolent and deceiving being who is deliberately using all his power to trick me? Can I affirm that I possess even the least of all those things which I have just described as pertaining to the nature of body? I direct my attention [to this], think [about it], and turn [the question] over in my mind. Nothing comes to me. It is tedious and useless to go over the same things once again. What, then, of those things I used to attribute to the soul, like eating, drinking, or walking? But given that now I do not possess a body, these are nothing but imaginary figments. What about sense perception? This, too, surely does not occur without the body. And in sleep I have apparently sensed many objects which I later noticed I had not [truly] perceived. What about thinking? Here I discover something: thinking does exist. This is the only thing which cannot be detached from me. *I am, I exist*—that is certain. But for how long? Surely for as long as I am thinking. For it could perhaps be the case that, if I were to abandon thinking altogether, then in that moment I would completely cease to be. At this point I am not agreeing to anything except what is necessarily true. Therefore, strictly speaking, I am merely a thinking thing, that is, a mind or spirit, or understanding, or reason—words whose significance I did not realize before. However, I am something real, and I truly exist. But what kind of thing? As I have said, a thing that thinks.

And what else besides? I will let my imagination roam. I am not that interconnection of limbs we call a human body. Nor am I even some attenuated air which filters through those limbs—wind, or fire, or vapor, or breath, or anything I picture to myself. For I have assumed those things were nothing. Let this assumption hold. Nonetheless, I am still something. Perhaps it could be the case that these very things which I assume are nothing, because they are unknown to me, are truly no different from that *I* which I do recognize. I am not sure, and I will not dispute this point right now. I can render judgment only on those things which are known to me: I know that I exist. I am asking what this *I* is—the thing I know. It is very certain that knowledge of this *I*, precisely defined like this, does not depend on things whose existence I as yet know nothing about and therefore on any of those things I conjure up in my imagination. And this phrase *conjure up* warns me of my mistake, for I would truly be conjuring something up if I imagined myself to be something, since imagining is nothing other than contemplating the form or the image of a physical thing. But now I know for certain that I exist and, at the same time, that it is possible for all those images and, in general, whatever relates to the nature of body to be nothing but dreams [or chimeras]. Having noticed this, it seems no less foolish for me to say "I will let my imagination work, so that I may recognize more clearly what I am" than if I were to state, "Now I am indeed awake, and I see some truth, but because I do yet not see it with sufficient clarity, I will quite deliberately go to sleep, so that in my dreams I will get a truer and more distinct picture of it." Therefore, I realize that none of those things which I can understand with the aid of my imagination is pertinent to this idea I possess about myself and that I must be extremely careful to summon my mind back from such things, so that it may perceive its own nature with the utmost clarity, on its own.

But what then am I? A thinking thing. What is this? It is surely something that doubts, understands, affirms, denies, is willing, is unwilling, and also imagines and perceives.

This is certainly not an insubstantial list, if all [these] things belong to me. But why should they not? Surely I am the same I who now doubts almost everything, yet understands some things, who affirms that this one thing is true, denies all the rest, desires to know more, does not wish to be deceived, imagines many things, even against its will, and also notices many things which seem to come from the senses? Even if I am always asleep and even if the one who created me is also doing all he can to deceive me, what is there among all these things which is not just as true as the fact that I exist? Is there something there that I could say is separate from me? For it is so evident that I am the one who doubts, understands, and wills, that I cannot think of anything which might explain the matter more clearly. But obviously it is the same I that imagines, for although it may well be case, as I have earlier assumed, that nothing I directly imagine is true, nevertheless, the power of imagining really exists and forms part of my thinking. Finally, it is the same I that feels, or notices corporeal things, apparently through the senses: for example, I now see light, hear noise, and feel heat. But these are false, for I am asleep. Still, I certainly seem to see, hear, and grow warm—and this cannot be false. Strictly speaking, this is what in me is called sense perception and, taken in this precise meaning, it is nothing other than thinking.

From these thoughts, I begin to understand somewhat better what I am. However, it still appears that I cannot prevent myself from thinking that corporeal things, whose images are formed by thought and which the senses themselves investigate, are much more distinctly known than that obscure part of me, the I, which is not something I can imagine, even though it is really strange that I have a clearer sense of those things whose existence I know is doubtful, unknown, and alien to me than I do of something which is true and known, in a word, of my own self. But I realize what the trouble is. My mind loves to wander and is not yet allowing itself to be confined within the limits of the truth. All right, then, let us at this point for once give it completely free rein, so that a little later on, when the time comes to pull back, it will consent to be controlled more easily.

Let us consider those things we commonly believe we understand most distinctly of all, that is, the bodies we touch and see—not, indeed, bodies in general, for those general perceptions tend to be somewhat more confusing, but rather one body in particular. For example, let us take this [piece of] beeswax. It was collected from the hive very recently and has not yet lost all the sweetness of its honey. It [still] retains some of the scent of the flowers from which it was gathered. Its color, shape, and size are evident. It is hard, cold, and easy to handle. If you strike it with your finger, it will give off a sound. In short, everything we require to be able to recognize a body as distinctly as possible appears to be present. But watch. While I am speaking, I bring the wax over to the fire. What is left of its taste is removed, its smell disappears, its color changes, its shape is destroyed, its size increases, it turns to liquid, and it gets hot. I can hardly touch it. And now, if you strike it, it emits no sound. After [these changes], is what remains the same wax? We must concede that it is. No one denies this; no one thinks otherwise. What then was in [this piece of wax] that I understood so distinctly? Certainly nothing I apprehended with my senses, since all [those things] associated with taste, odor, vision, touch, and sound have now changed. [But] the wax remains.

Perhaps what I now think is as follows: the wax itself was not really that sweetness of honey, that fragrance of flowers, that white color, or that shape and sound, but a body

which a little earlier was perceptible to me in those forms, but which is now [perceptible] in different ones. But what exactly is it that I am imagining in this way? Let us consider that point and, by removing those things which do not belong to the wax, see what is left over. It is clear that nothing [remains], other than something extended, flexible, and changeable. But what, in fact, do *flexible* and *changeable* mean? Do these words mean that I imagine that this wax can change from a round shape to a square one or from [something square] to something triangular? No, that is not it at all. For I understand that the wax has the capacity for innumerable changes of this kind, and yet I am not able to run through these innumerable changes by using my imagination. Therefore, this conception [I have of the wax] is not produced by the faculty of imagination. What about extension? Is not the extension of the wax also unknown? For it becomes greater when the wax melts, greater [still] when it boils, and once again [even] greater, if the heat is increased. And I would not be judging correctly what wax is if I did not believe that it could also be extended in various other ways, more than I could ever grasp in my imagination. Therefore, I am forced to admit that my imagination has no idea at all what this wax is and that I perceive it only with my mind. I am talking about this [piece of] wax in particular, for the point is even clearer about wax in general. But what is this wax which can be perceived only by the mind? It must be the same as the wax I see, touch, and imagine—in short, the same wax I thought it was from the beginning. But we should note that the perception of it is not a matter of sight, or touch, or imagination, and never was, even though that seemed to be the case earlier, but simply of mental inspection, which could be either imperfect and confused as it was before, or clear and distinct as it is now, depending on the lesser or greater degree of attention I bring to bear on those things out of which the wax is composed.

However, now I am amazed at how my mind is [weak and] prone to error. For although I am considering these things silently within myself, without speaking aloud, I still get stuck on the words themselves and am almost deceived by the very nature of the way we speak. For if the wax is there [in front of us], we say that we see the wax itself, not that we judge it to be there from the color or shape. From that I could immediately conclude that I recognized the wax thanks to the vision in my eyes, and not simply by mental inspection. But by analogy, suppose I happen to glance out of the window at people crossing the street; in normal speech I also say I see the people themselves, just as I do with the wax. But what am I really seeing other than hats and coats, which could be concealing automatons underneath? However, I judge that they are people. And thus what I thought I was seeing with my eyes I understand only with my faculty of judgment, which is in my mind.

But someone who wishes [to elevate] his knowledge above the common level should be ashamed to have based his doubts in the forms of speech which ordinary people use, and so we should move on to consider next whether my perception of what wax is was more perfect and more evident when I first perceived it and believed I knew it by my external senses, or at least by my so-called *common* sense,* in other words, by the power of imagination, or whether it is more perfect now, after I have investigated more carefully both what wax is and how it can be known. To entertain doubts about this matter would certainly be silly. For in my first perception of the wax what was distinct? What

did I notice there that any animal might not be capable of capturing? But when I distinguish the wax from its external forms and look at it as something naked, as if I had stripped off its clothing, even though there could still be some error in my judgment, it is certain that I could not perceive it in this way without a human mind.

But what am I to say about this mind itself, in other words, about myself? For up to this point I am not admitting there is anything in me except mind. What, I say, is the *I* that seems to perceive this wax so distinctly? Do I not know myself not only much more truly and certainly, but also much more distinctly and clearly than I know the wax? For if I judge that the wax exists from the fact that I see it, then from the very fact that I see the wax it certainly follows much more clearly that I myself also exist. For it could be that what I see is not really wax. It could be the case that I do not have eyes at all with which to see anything. But when I see or think I see (at the moment I am not differentiating between these two), it is completely impossible that I, the one doing the thinking, am not something. For similar reasons, if I judge that the wax exists from the fact that I am touching it, the same conclusion follows once again, namely, that I exist. The result is clearly the same if [my judgment rests] on the fact that I imagine the wax or on any other reason at all. But these observations I have made about the wax can be applied to all other things located outside of me. Furthermore, if my perception of the wax seemed more distinct after it was drawn to my attention, not merely by sight or touch, but by several [other] causes, I must concede that I now understand myself much more distinctly, since all of those same reasons capable of assisting my perception either of the wax or of any other body whatsoever are even better proofs of the nature of my mind! However, over and above this, there are so many other things

---

* Eds.: He does not mean "common sense" as we use it in English. This is a term from Aristotle, which refers to the perception of things that are common to several senses. For example, size, shape, location, movement, etc., can be perceived by sight, hearing, and touch.

in the mind itself which can provide a more distinct conception of its [nature] that it hardly seems worthwhile to review those features of corporeal things which might contribute to it.

And behold—I have all on my own finally returned to the place where I wanted to be. For since I am now aware that bodies themselves are not properly perceived by the senses or by the faculty of imagination, but only by the intellect, and are not perceived because they are touched or seen, but only because they are understood, I realize this obvious point: there is nothing I can perceive more easily or more clearly than my own mind. But because it is impossible to rid oneself so quickly of an opinion one has long been accustomed to hold, I would like to pause here, in order to impress this new knowledge more deeply on my memory with a prolonged meditation.

THIRD MEDITATION
Concerning God and the Fact that He Exists

Now I will close my eyes, stop up my ears, and withdraw all my senses. I will even blot out from my thinking all images of corporeal things, or else, since this is hardly possible, I will dismiss them as empty and false images of nothing at all, and by talking only to myself and looking more deeply within, I will attempt, little by little, to acquire a greater knowledge of and more familiarity with myself. I am a thinking thing—in other words, something that doubts, affirms, denies, knows a few things, is ignorant of many things, wills, refuses, and also imagines and feels. For, as I have pointed out earlier, although those things which I sense or imagine outside of myself are perhaps nothing, nevertheless, I am certain that the thought processes I call sense experience and imagination, given that they are only certain modes of thinking, do exist within me.

In these few words, I have reviewed everything I truly know, or at least [everything] that, up to this point, I was aware I knew. Now I will look around more diligently, in case there are perhaps other things in me that I have not yet considered. I am certain that I am a thinking thing. But if that is the case, do I not then also know what is required for me to be certain about something? There is, to be sure, nothing in this first knowledge other than a certain clear and distinct perception of what I am affirming, and obviously this would not be enough for me to be certain about the truth of the matter, if it could ever happen that something I perceived just as clearly and distinctly was false. And now it seems to me that now I can propose the following general rule: all those things I perceive very clearly and very distinctly are true.

[...]

SIXTH MEDITATION
Concerning the Existence of Material Things and the Real Distinction between Mind and Body

It remains for me to examine whether material things exist. At the moment, I do, in fact, know that they *could* exist, at least insofar as they are objects of pure mathematics, since I perceive them clearly and distinctly. For there is no doubt that God is capable of producing everything which I am capable of perceiving in this way, and I have never judged that there is anything He cannot create, except in those cases where there might be a contradiction in my clear perception of it. Moreover, from my faculty of imagination, which I have learned by experience I use when I turn my attention to material substances, it seems to follow that they exist. For when I consider carefully what the imagination is, it seems nothing other than a certain application of my cognitive faculty to an object which is immediately present to it and which therefore exists.

In order to clarify this matter fully, I will first examine the difference between imagination and pure understanding. For example, when I imagine a triangle, not only do I understand that it is a shape composed of three lines, but at the same time I also see those three lines as if they were, so to speak, present to my mind's eye. This is what I call imagining. However, if I wish to think about a chiliagon, even though I understand that it is a figure consisting of one thousand sides just as well as I understand that a triangle is a figure consisting of three sides, I do not imagine those thousand sides in the same way, nor do I see [them], as it were, in front of me. And although, thanks to my habit of always imagining something whenever I think of a corporeal substance, it may happen that [in thinking of a chiliagon] I create for myself a confused picture of some shape, nevertheless, it is obviously not a chiliagon, because it is no different from the shape I would also picture to myself if I were thinking of a myriagon or of any other figure with many sides. And that shape is no help at all in recognizing those properties which distinguish the chiliagon from other polygons. However, if it is a question of a pentagon, I can certainly understand its shape just as [well as] I can the shape of a chiliagon, without the assistance of my imagination. But, of course, I can also imagine the pentagon by applying my mind's eye to its five sides and to the area they contain. From this I clearly recognize that, in order to imagine things, I need a certain special mental effort that I do not use to understand them, and this new mental effort reveals clearly the difference between imagination and pure understanding.

Furthermore, I notice that this power of imagining, which exists within me, insofar as it differs from the power of understanding, is not a necessary part of my own essence, that is, of my mind. For even if I did not have it, I would still undoubtedly remain the same person I am now. From this it would seem to follow that my imagination depends upon something different from [my mind]. I understand the following easily enough: If a certain body—my body—exists, and my mind is connected to it in such a way that whenever my mind so wishes it can direct itself (so to speak) to examine that body, then thanks to this particular body it would be possible for me to imagine corporeal things. Thus, the only difference between imagination and pure understanding would be this: the mind, while it is understanding, in some way turns its attention to itself and considers one of the ideas present in itself, but when it is imagining, it turns its attention to the body and sees something in it which conforms to an idea which it has either conceived by itself or perceived with the senses. I readily understand, as I have said, that the imagination *could* be formed in this way, if the body exists, and because I can think of no other equally convenient way of explaining it, I infer from this that the body probably exists—but only probably—and although I am looking into everything carefully, I still do not yet see how from this distinct idea of corporeal nature which I find in my imagination I can derive any argument which necessarily concludes that anything corporeal exists.

However, I am in the habit of imagining many things apart from the corporeal nature which is the object of study in pure mathematics, such as colors, sounds, smells, pain, and things like that, although not so distinctly. And since I perceive these better with my senses, through which, with the help of my memory, they appear to have reached my imagination, then in order to deal with them in a more appropriate manner, I ought to consider the senses at the same time as well and see whether those things which I perceive by this method of thinking, which I call sensation, will enable me to establish some credible argument to prove the existence of corporeal things.

First of all, I will review in my mind the things that I previously believed to be true, because I perceived them with my senses, along with the reasons for those beliefs. Then I will also assess the reasons why I later called them into doubt. And finally I will consider what I ought to believe about them now.

To begin with, then, I sensed that I had a head, hands, feet, and other limbs making up that body which I looked on as if it were a part of me or perhaps even my totality. I sensed that this body moved around among many other bodies which could affect it in different ways, either agreeably or disagreeably. I judged which ones were agreeable by a certain feeling of pleasure and which ones were disagreeable by a feeling of pain. Apart from pain and pleasure, I also felt inside me sensations of hunger, thirst, and other appetites of this kind, as well as certain physical inclinations towards joy, sadness, anger, and other similar emotions. And outside myself, besides the extension, shapes, and motions of bodies, I also had sensations in them of hardness, heat, and other tactile qualities and, in addition, of light, colors, smells, tastes, and sounds. From the variety of these, I distinguished sky, land, sea, and other bodies, one after another. And because of the ideas of all those qualities which presented themselves to my thinking, although I kept sensing these as merely my own personal and immediate ideas, I reasonably believed that I was perceiving certain objects entirely different from my thinking, that is, bodies from which these ideas proceeded. For experience taught me that these ideas reached me without my consent, so that I was unable to sense any object, even if I wanted to, unless it was present to my organs of sense, and I was unable not to sense it when it was present. And since the ideas I perceived with

my senses were much more vivid, lively, and sharp, and even, in their own way, more distinct than any of those which I myself intentionally and deliberately shaped by meditation or which I noticed impressed on my memory, it did not seem possible that they could have proceeded from myself. Thus, the only conclusion left was that they had come from some other things. Because I had no conception of these objects other than what I derived from those ideas themselves, the only thought my mind could entertain was that [the objects] were similar to [the ideas they produced]. And since I also remembered that earlier I had used my senses rather than my reason and realized that the ideas which I myself formed were not as vivid, lively, and sharp as those which I perceived with my senses and that most of the former were composed of parts of the latter, I easily convinced myself that I had nothing at all in my intellect which I had not previously had in my senses. I also maintained, not without reason, that this body, which, by some special right, I called my own, belonged to me more than any other object, for I could never separate myself from it, as I could from other [bodies], I felt every appetite and emotion in it and because of it, and finally, I noticed pain and the titillation of pleasure in its parts, but not in any objects placed outside it. But why a certain strange sadness of spirit follows a sensation of pain and a certain joy follows from a sensation of [pleasurable] titillation, or why some sort of twitching in the stomach, which I call hunger, is urging me to eat food, while the dryness of my throat [is urging me] to drink, and so on—for that I had no logical explanation, other than that these were things I had learned from nature. For there is clearly no relationship (at least, none I can understand) between that twitching [in the stomach] and the desire to consume food, or between the sensation of something causing pain and the awareness of sorrow arising from that feeling. But it seemed to me that all the other judgments I made about objects of sense experience I had learned from nature. For I had convinced myself that that was how things happened, before I thought about any arguments which might prove it.

However, many later experiences have gradually weakened the entire faith I used to have in the senses. For, now and then, towers which seemed round from a distance appeared square from near at hand, immense statues standing on the tower summits did not seem large when I viewed them from the ground, and in countless other cases like these I discovered that my judgments were deceived in matters dealing with external senses. And not just with external [senses], but also with internal ones as well. For what could be more internal than pain? And yet I heard that people whose legs or arms had been cut off sometimes still seemed to feel pain in the part of their body which they lacked. Thus, even though I were to feel pain in one of my limbs, I did not think I could be completely certain that it was the limb which caused my pain. To these reasons for doubting sense experience, I recently added two extremely general ones. First, there was nothing I ever thought I was sensing while awake that I could not also think I was sensing now and then while asleep, and since I do not believe that those things I appear to sense in my sleep come to me from objects placed outside me, I did not see why I should give more credit to those I appear to sense when I am awake. Second, because I was still ignorant—or at least was assuming I was ignorant—of the author of my being, there seemed to be nothing to prevent nature from constituting me in such a way that I would make mistakes, even in those matters which seemed to me most true. As for the reasons which had previously convinced me of the truth of what I apprehended with my senses, I had no difficulty refuting them. For since nature seemed to push me to accept many things which my reason opposed, I believed I should not place much trust in those things nature taught. And although perceptions of the senses did not depend upon my will, I did not believe that was reason enough for me to conclude that they must come from things different from myself, because there could well be some other faculty in me, even one I did not yet know, which produced them.

But now that I am starting to gain a better understanding of myself and of the author of my being, I do not, in fact, believe that I should rashly accept all those things I appear to possess from my senses, but, at the same time, [I do not think] I should call everything into doubt.

First, since I know that all those things I understand clearly and distinctly could have been created by God in a way that matches my conception of them, the fact that I can clearly and distinctly understand one thing, distinguishing it from something else, is sufficient to convince me that the two of them are different, because they can be separated from each other, at least by God. The power by which this [separation] takes place is irrelevant to my judgment that they are distinct. And therefore, given the mere fact that I know I exist and that, at the moment, I look upon my nature or essence as absolutely nothing other than that I am a thinking thing, I reasonably conclude that my essence consists of this single fact: I am a thinking thing. And although I may well possess (or rather, as I will state later, although I certainly do possess) a body which is very closely joined to me, nonetheless, because, on the one hand, I have a clear and distinct idea of myself, insofar as I am merely a thinking thing, without extension, and, on the other hand, [I have] a distinct idea of body, insofar as it is merely an extended thing which does not think, it is certain that my mind is completely distinct from my body and can exist without it.

Moreover, I discover in myself faculties for certain special forms of thinking, namely, the faculties of imagining and feeling. I can conceive of myself clearly and distinctly as a complete being without these, but I cannot do the reverse and think of these faculties without me, that is, without an intelligent substance to which they belong. For the formal conception of them includes some act of intellection by which I perceive that they are different from me, just as [shapes, movement, and the other] modes [or accidents of bodies are different] from the object [to which they belong]. I also recognize certain other faculties [in me], like changing position, assuming various postures, and so on, which certainly cannot be conceived, any more than those previously mentioned, apart from some substance to which they belong, and therefore they, too, cannot exist without it. However, it is evident that these [faculties], if indeed they [truly] exist, must belong to some corporeal or extended substance, and not to any intelligent substance, since the clear and distinct conception of them obviously contains some [form of] extension, but no intellectual activity whatsoever. Now, it is, in fact, true that I do have a certain passive faculty of perception, that is, of receiving and recognizing ideas of sensible things. But I would be unable to use this power unless some active faculty existed, as well, either in me or in some other substance capable of producing or forming these ideas. But this [active faculty] clearly cannot exist within me, because it presupposes no intellectual activity at all, and because, without my cooperation and often even against my will, it produces those ideas. Therefore I am left to conclude that it exists in some substance different from me that must contain, either formally or eminently,* all

the reality objectively present† in the ideas produced by that faculty (as I have just observed above). This substance is either a body, that is, something with a corporeal nature which obviously contains formally everything objectively present in the ideas, or it must be God, or some other creature nobler than the body, one that contains [those same things] eminently. But since God is not a deceiver, it is very evident that He does not transmit these ideas to me from Himself directly or even through the intervention of some other creature in which their objective reality is contained, not formally but only eminently. For since he has given me no faculty whatsoever for recognizing such a source, but by contrast, has endowed me with a powerful tendency to believe that these ideas are sent out from corporeal things, I do not see how it would be possible not to think of Him as a deceiver, if these [ideas] were sent from any source other than corporeal things. And therefore corporeal things exist.

However, perhaps they do not all exist precisely in the ways I grasp them with my senses, since what I comprehend with my senses is very obscure and confused in many things. But at least [I should accept as true] all those things in

---

* Eds.: Here Descartes is using terms from medieval Scholastic philosophy. Elsewhere Descartes defines the first term in this way: "Whatever exists in the objects of our ideas in a way that corresponds to our perception of it is said to exist *formally* in those objects." The other he defines in this way: "Something is said to exist *eminently*

in an object when, although it does not correspond exactly to our perception of it, its greatness is such that it can fill the role of that to which it does correspond." See René Descartes, *The Philosophical Writings of Descartes*, John Cottingham, Robert Stoothoff and Dugald Murdoch (trans.) (Cambridge: Cambridge University Press, 1984–91), Volume II, p. 114. The first case applies to ordinary successful perception. The second case applies to the properties of God, which do not correspond to our perception of them (since our perception is inadequate), but they can nonetheless be the *cause* of those perceptions.

† Eds.: Very roughly, in Descartes's use of the terms, something that exists in the mind has *objective* reality, whereas something that actually exists outside the mind has *formal* reality. The idea of a unicorn, for example, has objective reality even though unicorns have no formal reality, whereas the objects we perceive that exist in the actual world have formal reality.

them which I understand clearly and distinctly, that is, generally speaking, everything which is included as an object in pure mathematics.

But regarding other material things which are either merely particular, for example that the sun is of such and such a magnitude and shape, and so on, or less clearly understood, for example light, sound, pain, and things like that, although these may be extremely doubtful and uncertain, nonetheless, because of the very fact that God is not a deceiver and thus it is impossible for there to be any falsity in my opinions which I cannot correct with another faculty God has given me, I have the sure hope that I can reach the truth even in these matters. And clearly there is no doubt that all those things I learn from nature contain some truth. For by the term *nature*, generally speaking, I understand nothing other than either God himself or the coordinated structure of created things established by God, and by the term *my nature*, in particular, nothing other than the combination of all those things I have been endowed with by God.

However, there is nothing that nature teaches me more emphatically than the fact that I have a body, which does badly when I feel pain, which needs food or drink when I suffer from hunger or thirst, and so on. And therefore I should not doubt that there is some truth in this.

For through these feelings of pain, hunger, thirst, and so on, nature teaches me that I am not only present in my body in the same way a sailor is present onboard a ship, but also that I am bound up very closely and, so to speak, mixed in with it, so that my body and I form a certain unity. For if that were not the case, then when my body was injured, I, who am merely a thinking thing, would not feel any pain because of it; instead, I would perceive the wound purely with my intellect, just as a sailor notices with his eyes if something is broken on his ship. And

when my body needed food or drink, I would understand that clearly and not have confused feelings of hunger and thirst. For those sensations of thirst, hunger, pain, and so on are really nothing other than certain confused ways of thinking, which arise from the union and, as it were, the mixture of the mind with the body.

Moreover, nature also teaches me that various other bodies exist around my own and that I should pursue some of these and stay away from others. And certainly from the fact that I sense a wide diversity of colors, sounds, odors, tastes, heat, hardness, and similar things, I reasonably conclude that in the bodies from which these different sense perceptions come there are certain variations which correspond to these perceptions, even if they are perhaps not like them. And given the fact that I find some of these sense perceptions pleasant and others unpleasant, it is entirely certain that my body, or rather my totality, since I am composed of body and mind, can be affected by various agreeable and disagreeable bodies surrounding it.

However, many other things which I seemed to have learned from nature I have not really received from her, but rather from a certain habit I have of accepting careless judgments [about things]. And thus it could easily be the case that these judgments are false—for example, [the opinion I have] that all space in which nothing at all happens to stimulate my senses is a vacuum, that in a warm substance there is something completely similar to the idea of heat which is in me, that in a white or green [substance] there is the same whiteness or greenness which I sense, that in [something] bitter or sweet there is the same taste as I sense, and so on, that stars and towers and anything else some distance away have bodies with the same size and shape as the ones they present to my senses, and things of that sort. But in order to ensure that what I perceive in this matter is sufficiently distinct, I should define more accurately what it is precisely that I mean when I say I have learned something from nature. For here I am taking the word *nature* in a more restricted sense than *the combination of all those things which have been bestowed on me by God.* For this combination contains many things which pertain only to the mind, such as the fact that I perceive that what has been done cannot be undone, and all the other things I grasp by my natural light [without the help of the body]. Such things are not under discussion here. This combination also refers to many things which concern only the body, like its tendency to move downward, and so on, which I am also not dealing with [here]. Instead, I am considering only those things which God has given me as a combination of mind and body. And so nature, in this sense, certainly teaches me to avoid those things which bring a sensation of pain and to pursue those which [bring] a sensation of pleasure, and such like, but, beyond that, it is not clear that with those sense perceptions nature teaches us that we can conclude anything about things placed outside of us without a previous examination by the understanding, because to know the truth about them seems to belong only to the mind and not to that combination [of body and mind]. And so, although a star does not make an impression on my eyes any greater than the flame of a small candle, nonetheless, that fact does not incline me, in any real or positive way, to believe that the star is not larger [than the flame], but from the time of my youth I have made this judgment without any reason [to support it]. And although I feel heat when I come near the fire, and even pain if I get too close to it, that is really no reason to believe that there is something in the fire similar to that heat I feel, any more than there is something similar to the pain. The only thing [I can conclude] is that there is something in the fire, whatever it might be, which brings out in us those sensations of heat or pain. So, too,

although in some space there is nothing which stimulates my senses, it does not therefore follow that the space contains no substances. But I see that in these and in a great many other matters, I have grown accustomed to undermine the order of nature, because, of course, these sense perceptions are, strictly speaking, given to me by nature merely to indicate to my mind which things are agreeable or disagreeable to that combination of which it is a part, and for that purpose they are sufficiently clear and distinct. But then I use them as if they were dependable rules for immediately recognizing the essence of bodies placed outside me. However, about such bodies they reveal nothing except what is confusing and obscure.

In an earlier section, I have already examined sufficiently why my judgments may happen to be defective, in spite of the goodness of God. However, a new difficulty crops up here concerning those very things which nature reveals to me as objects I should seek out or avoid, and also concerning the internal sensations, in which I appear to have discovered errors: for example, when someone, deceived by the pleasant taste of a certain food, eats a poison hidden within it [and thus makes a mistake]. Of course, in this situation, the person's nature urges him only to eat food which has a pleasant taste and not the poison, of which he has no knowledge at all. And from this, the only conclusion I can draw is that my nature does not know everything. There is nothing astonishing about that, because a human being is a finite substance and thus is capable of only limited perfection.

However, we are frequently wrong even in those things which nature urges [us to seek]. For example, sick people are eager for drink or food which will harm them soon afterwards. One could perhaps claim that such people make mistakes because their nature has been corrupted. But this does not remove the difficulty, for a sick person is no less a true creature of God than a healthy one, and thus it seems no less contradictory that God has given the person a nature which deceives him. And just as a clock made out of wheels and weights observes all the laws of nature with the same accuracy when it is badly made and does not indicate the hours correctly as it does when it completely satisfies the wishes of the person who made it, in the same way, if I look on the human body as some kind of machine composed of bones, nerves, muscles, veins, blood, and skin, as if no mind existed in it, the body would still have all the same motions it now has in those movements that are not under the control of the will and that, therefore, do not proceed from the mind [but merely from the disposition of its organs]. I can readily acknowledge, for example, that in the case of a body sick with dropsy, it would be quite natural for it to suffer from a parched throat, which usually conveys a sensation of thirst to the mind, and for its nerves and other parts also to move in such a way that it takes a drink and thus aggravates the illness. And when nothing like this is harming the body, it is equally natural for it to be stimulated by a similar dryness in the throat and to take a drink to benefit itself. Now, when I consider the intended purpose of the clock, I could say that, since it does not indicate the time correctly, it is deviating from its own nature, and, in the same way, when I think of the machine of the human body as something formed for the motions which usually take place in it, I might believe that it, too, is deviating from its own nature, if its throat is dry when a drink does not benefit its own preservation. However, I am fully aware that this second meaning of the word *nature* is very different from the first. For it is merely a term that depends on my own thought, a designation with which I compare a sick person and a badly constructed clock with the idea of a healthy person and a properly con-

structed clock, and thus, the term is extrinsic to these objects. But by that [other use of the term *nature*] I understand something that is really found in things and that therefore contains a certain measure of the truth.

Now, when I consider a body suffering from dropsy, even though I say that its nature has been corrupted, because it has a dry throat and yet does not need to drink, clearly the word *nature* is merely an extraneous term. However, when I consider the composite, that is, the mind united with such a body, I am not dealing with what is simply a term but with a true error of nature, because this composite is thirsty when drinking will do it harm. And thus I still have to enquire here why the goodness of God does not prevent its nature, taken in this sense, from being deceitful.

At this point, then, my initial observation is that there is a great difference between the mind and the body, given that the body is, by its very nature, always divisible, whereas the mind is completely indivisible. For, in fact, when I think of [my mind], that is, when I think of myself as purely a thinking thing, I cannot distinguish any parts within me. Instead, I understand that I am something completely individual and unified. And although my entire mind seems to be united with my entire body, nonetheless, I know that if a foot or arm or any other part of the body is sliced off, that loss will not take anything from my mind. And I cannot call the faculties of willing, feeling, understanding, and so on parts of the mind because it is the same single mind that wishes, feels, and understands. By contrast, I cannot think of any corporeal or extended substance that my thought is not capable of dividing easily into parts. From this very fact, I understand that the substance is divisible. (This point alone would be enough to teach me that the mind is completely different from the body, if I did not already know that well enough from other sources.)

Furthermore, I notice that the mind is not immediately affected by all parts of the body, but only by the brain, or perhaps even by just one small part of it, namely, the one in which our *common sense* is said to exist. Whenever this part is arranged in the same particular way, it delivers the same perception to the mind, even though the other parts of the body may be arranged quite differently at the time. This point has been demonstrated in countless experiments, which I need not review here.

In addition, I notice that the nature of my body is such that no part of it can be moved by any other part some distance away which cannot also be moved in the same manner by any other part lying between them, even though the more distant part does nothing. So, for example, in a rope ABCD [which is taut throughout], if I pull on part D at the end, then the movement of the first part, A, will be no different than it would be if I pulled at one of the intermediate points, B or C, while the last part, D, remained motionless. And for a similar reason, when I feel pain in my foot, physics teaches me that this sensation occurs thanks to nerves spread throughout the foot. These nerves stretch from there to the brain, like cords, and when they are pulled in my foot, they also pull the inner parts of the brain, where they originate, and stimulate in them a certain motion which nature has established to influence the mind with a sense of pain apparently present in the foot. However, since these nerves have to pass through the shin, the thigh, the loins, the back, and the neck in order to reach the brain from the foot, it can happen that, even if that portion of the nerves which is in the foot is not affected, but only one of the intermediate portions, the motion created in the brain is exactly the same as the one created there by an injured foot. As a result, the mind will necessarily feel the identical pain. And we should assume that the same is true with any other sensation whatsoever.

Finally, I notice that, since each of those motions created in that part of the brain which immediately affects the mind introduces into it only one particular sensation, we can, given this fact, come up with no better explanation than that this sensation, out of all the ones which could be introduced, is the one which serves to protect human health as effectively and frequently as possible [when a person is completely healthy]. But experience testifies to the fact that all sensations nature has given us are like this, and thus we can discover nothing at all in them which does not bear witness to the power and benevolence of God. Thus, for example, when the nerves in the foot are moved violently and more than usual, their motion, passing through the spinal cord to the inner core of the brain, gives a signal there to the mind which makes it feel something—that is, it feels as if there is a pain in the foot. And that stimulates [the mind] to do everything it can to remove the cause of the pain as something injurious to the foot. Of course, God could have constituted the nature of human beings in such a way that this same motion in the brain communicated something else to the mind, for example, a sense of its own movements, either in the brain, or in the foot, or in any of the places in between—in short, of anything you wish. But nothing else would have served so well for the preservation of the body. In the same way, when we need a drink, a certain dryness arises in the throat which moves its nerves and, with their assistance, the inner parts of the brain. And this motion incites in the mind a sensation of thirst, because in this whole situation nothing is more useful for us to know than that we need a drink to preserve our health. The same is true for the other sensations.

From this it is clearly evident that, notwithstanding the immense goodness of God, human nature, given that it is composed of mind and body, cannot be anything other than something that occasionally deceives us. For if some cause, not in the foot, but in some other part through which the nerves stretch between the foot and the brain, or even in the brain itself, stimulates exactly the same motion as that which is normally aroused when a foot is injured, then pain will be felt as if it were in the foot, and the sensation will naturally be deceiving. Since that same motion in the brain is never capable of transmitting to the mind anything other than the identical sensation and since [the sensation] is habitually aroused much more frequently from an injury in the foot than from anything else in another place, it is quite reasonable that it should always transmit to the mind a pain in the foot rather than a pain in any other part of the body. And if sometimes dryness in the throat does not arise, as it usually does, from the fact that a drink is necessary for the health of the body, but from some different cause, as occurs in a patient suffering from dropsy, it is much better that it should deceive us in a case like that than if it were, by contrast, always deceiving us when the body is quite healthy. The same holds true with the other sensations.

This reflection is the greatest help, for it enables me not only to detect all the errors to which my nature is prone, but also to correct or to avoid them easily. For since I know that, in matters concerning what is beneficial to the body, all my senses show [me] what is true much more frequently than they deceive me, and since I can almost always use several of them to examine the same matter and, in addition, [can use] my memory, which connects present events with earlier ones, as well as my understanding, which has now ascertained all the causes of my errors, I should no longer fear

that those things which present themselves to me every day through my senses are false. And I ought to dismiss all those exaggerated doubts of the past few days as ridiculous, particularly that most important [doubt] about sleep, which I did not distinguish from being awake. For now I notice a significant distinction between the two of them, given that our memory never links our dreams to all the other actions of our lives, as it [usually] does with those things which take place when we are awake. For clearly, if someone suddenly appears to me when I am awake and then immediately afterwards disappears, as happens in my dreams, so that I have no idea where he came from or where he went, I would reasonably judge that I had seen some apparition or phantom created in my brain [similar to the ones created when I am asleep], rather than a real person. But when certain things occur and I notice distinctly the place from which they came, where they are, and when they appeared to me, and when I can link my perception of them to the rest of my life as a totality, without a break, then I am completely certain that this is taking place while I am awake and not in my sleep. And I should not have the slightest doubt about the truth of these perceptions if, after I have called upon all my senses, my memory, and my understanding to examine them, I find nothing in any of them which contradicts any of the others. For since God is not a deceiver, it must follow that in such cases I am not deceived. But because, in dealing with what we need to do, we cannot always take the time for such a scrupulous examination, we must concede that human life is often prone to error concerning particular things and that we need to acknowledge the frailty of our nature.

Study Questions

1. Descartes reasons that he cannot be mistaken about the facts that he is thinking, that it follows that as long as this is true, he exists as a thinking thing, and that this is the basic nature of his *self*. But here's an objection: Descartes already has admitted that any bit of his reasoning might turn out to be false; so doesn't this apply to the reasoning just described? Defend this objection against Descartes, or defend Descartes against this objection.

2. Outline Descartes's reasoning in the "piece-of-wax" example. Explain in your own words how it's supposed to follow that we don't know about external objects through our senses, but rather through the intellect. Does this really follow from this example? If you don't think so, explain how we do know that this changed object is the same piece of wax.

3. Think about truths of geometry such as *The sum of the lengths of any two sides of a triangle is greater than the length of the third* or truths of arithmetic such as *7 + 5 = 12*. Try to explain why Descartes would count these as "clear and distinct" as opposed to, say, beliefs about particular things you perceive with the senses. In what sense are the former "clear and distinct"? Do you think that this sort of belief is more likely to be true? Why?

4. In the first three sentences of the Sixth Meditation, Descartes gives a complicated argument about the existence of material things, based on God's capability. Outline his reasoning here.

5. Explain in your own words what Descartes takes to be the difference between imagination and pure understanding as Descartes explains it in the third paragraph of the Sixth Meditation. Why does he suppose that imagining something increases the probability that the thing exists, while this is not true for pure understanding?

6. In the Sixth Meditation, Descartes talks about his experience of square towers looking round, and enormous statues seeming small. Explain in your own words why rare experiences like this undermine his general faith in the information of his senses. Do these cases show that no sense perception is clear and distinct?

7. Outline in your own words Descartes's argument in the long paragraph in the Sixth Meditation beginning "Moreover this," and ending "And therefore corporeal things exist."

8. It's not terribly clear what Descartes means when he says that his body is "divisible" whereas his mind isn't? Try to explain what he meant here.

9. Explain how Descartes argues in the Sixth Meditation that the fallibility of our senses is consistent with the benevolence of God—with the fact that God is not a deceiver.

10. Some philosophers (atheists and believers alike) regard Descartes's reliance on God as a non-deceiver as rather a cheat. See if you can come up with a way to establish the general reliability of the senses without bringing in God. (Hint: One way this might be tried is to use the idea of our sense-organs having *evolved* through Darwinian natural selection. But consider this: doesn't our evidence for this, as for every other bit of science, depend on our *assuming* the reliability of the senses?)

Suggested Readings

There is a great deal of secondary literature on Descartes. Some suggestions:

Joseph Almog, *What Am I? Descartes and the Mind-Body Problem*. (New York: Oxford University Press, 2002).

Gordon Baker and Katherine J. Morris, *Descartes's Dualism*. (London: Routledge, 1996).

Vere C. Chappell, "Descartes's Ontology," *Topoi* 16 (1997): pp. 111–27.

John Cottingham (1992), "Dualism: Theology, Metaphysics, and Science," in *The Cambridge Companion to Descartes*, John Cottingham, ed. (Cambridge: Cambridge University Press, 1992); and his *Descartes*. (New York: Routledge, 1999).

Daniel Garber, *Descartes Embodied: Reading Cartesian Philosophy through Cartesian Science*. (Cambridge: Cambridge University Press, 2001).

Michael Hooker, ed., *Descartes: Critical and Interpretive Essays*. (Baltimore: Johns Hopkins University Press, 1978).

Marleen Rozemond, *Descartes's Dualism*. (Cambridge, MA: Harvard University Press, 1998).

Bernard Williams, *Descartes: The Project of Pure Enquiry*. (Harmondsworth: Penguin Books, 1978).

Margaret Wilson, *Descartes*. (London: Routledge, 1978); and her *Ideas and Mechanism: Essays in Early Modern Philosophy*. (Princeton: Princeton University Press, 1999).

Almost every work on philosophy of mind talks about Descartes, and almost all of them outline Cartesian dualism's problems. Works starting with a clear account of them (but going on to argue for alternative positions) include:

Keith Campbell, *Body and Mind*. (London: Macmillan, 1970).

Peter Smith and O.R. Jones, *Philosophy of Mind*. (Cambridge: Cambridge University Press, 1986).

Paul Churchland, *Matter and Consciousness*, 2nd edition. (Cambridge, MA: MIT Press, 1988).

David M. Armstrong, *A Materialist Theory of Mind*. (London: Routledge, 1968).

David Braddon-Mitchell and Frank Jackson, *Philosophy of Mind and Cognition: An Introduction*, 2nd edition. (Oxford: Blackwell, 2007).

A contemporary argument for Cartesian dualism can be found in Sidney Shoemaker, "On an Argument for Dualism," in *Knowledge and Mind*, Carl Ginet and Sydney Shoemaker (eds.). (Oxford: Oxford University Press, 1983).

5

 # DESCARTES'S DUALISM

Introduction

Descartes's aim in the final part of the *Meditations on First Philosophy* is to establish the real qualities of mind and matter, and to show how the two interact. To this end Descartes has established three points. In the Second Meditation he introduces a conception of the mind as defined by the contents of conscious thought. In the Third Meditation he presents the general rule that whatever is clearly and distinctly perceived is always true. And at the very beginning of the Sixth Meditation he makes the claim that the idea of physical objects as extended in space is clear and distinct as it is understood through the sciences of geometry and arithmetic. Later in the Sixth Meditation Descartes puts these assertions together in an ingenious argument to prove the independent existence of mind and body.

The first part of the Sixth Meditation is taken up by a long consideration of his natural reasons for believing in the existence of physical objects. Among these are the fact that his sensory experiences are not under the control of his will, and the fact that these experiences are much more vivid than the products of his imagination. Nonetheless, he concludes that "although perceptions of the senses did not depend upon my will, I did not believe that was reason enough for me to conclude that they must come from things different from myself …" Still, although this convinces him not to accept everything his senses tell him, neither should he "call everything into doubt." It is at this point in the Meditation that he presents his very famous argument that mind and body are two distinct things.

Descartes's Argument for Dualism

The argument has three premises, which we can paraphrase as follows.

1. Anything that I can clearly and distinctly understand can be created by God exactly as I understand it. So if I can clearly and distinctly understand one thing apart from another, this is enough to make me certain that the two things are distinct.
2. I can form a clear and distinct understanding of my own existence as depending on nothing more than the fact that I think, and hence (from Premise 1) it follows that nothing belongs to my essence except thought.
3. I also have a clear and distinct understanding of physical bodies (including my own) simply as extended matter, without possessing any thought.

Hence, I (or my soul) am distinct from my physical body, and can exist without it.

The first premise is an application of the rule introduced in the Third Meditation. If we can form a clear and distinct idea of a certain state of affairs, then such a state of affairs must at least be possible. In essence, the claim is that there can be no contradiction in any idea we can form clearly and distinctly in our minds.

The particular state of affairs Descartes has in mind is the independent existence of mind and body. By definition two things are distinct (that is, they are *two* things, not one) if each one can exist when the other doesn't. So Descartes's idea is this: if he can conceive clearly and distinctly of the mind existing without the body, and the body without the mind, then these must be real possibilities, and hence they must be two distinct things.

The Clear and Distinct Ideas of Mind and Body

The basis of the second premise goes back to the Second Meditation. There Descartes redefined thinking in terms of the contents of conscious thought and experience. In this premise he maintains that this conception of the mind is clear and distinct. The longer and more critically we reflect on what is necessary for the soul to exist, the more we are convinced that it will exist just as long as it is engaged in conscious thought. According to Descartes, the new understanding of the mind that he formed in the Second Meditation is not merely an interesting new hypothesis. It is the understanding we arrive at when we reflect as sharply as possible on what is absolutely necessary for the mind to exist.

Another way of understanding Descartes's point in the second premise is to see that solipsism is a real possibility. **Solipsism** is the idea that nothing exists but your own mind, that is, your current thoughts and sensations. To imagine that solipsism is true, imagine that the contents of your current conscious experience are all that exist. There is no physical world—no planets, trees, houses, or mountains—and no other people; only your own internal thoughts. Although no one actually believes this to be true, Descartes's point here is that it is not an incoherent idea.

The third premise asserts what he has established in the first part of the Sixth Meditation: our understanding of pure mathematics gives us a clear and distinct idea of material objects as things that occupy space but have no other attributes. In the study of geometry we can form a conception of physical objects possessing only the properties of size, shape, and motion. Because the principles of geometry are clear and distinct, it follows from Premise 1 that these are the only properties that material things require in order to exist.

Since the only attribute that the soul needs to exist is conscious thought, and the only attribute that the physical body (including the brain and the organs of sense) needs to exist is spatial extension, Descartes concludes that each can exist independently of the other. Destruction of the body will not destroy the mind, for the mind exists just as long as there is consciousness, which is not an attribute of matter. Similarly, the body can exist as a material object even in the absence of the mind because it is nothing more than a spatially extended object. Because each can exist without the other, mind and body are two different objects. Moreover, each possesses completely different properties from the other.

The Existence of the Physical World

Notice, however, that this argument does not actually demonstrate that there are any material objects. So far Descartes has shown only that the *idea* of material objects extended in space is clear and distinct, and that the mind is not a material object. The conclusions he has established so far do not rule out the possibility that nothing exists at all except his own consciousness, which simply forms the idea of material objects within itself. But in what follows Descartes argues that these objects do exist, and that his mind is conjoined to a physical body just as he perceives it to be.

The argument depends again on the rule of the Third Meditation. This rule implies that we are always capable in principle of correcting any error into which we might fall. For otherwise we could fall into error even with our clearest and most distinct perceptions. But we have no ability (or faculty as he calls it) to distinguish whether material objects exist or whether the entire material world as it is perceived is an illusion. There is no noticeable difference between reality as we think of it and a perfect illusion created by an evil demon. Because the absence of any noticeable difference contradicts what was established in the Third Meditation, it follows that the illusion is impossible.

From this reasoning Descartes concludes that "corporeal things exist. However, perhaps they do not all exist precisely in the ways I grasp them with my senses, since what I comprehend with my senses is very obscure and confused in many things." Material objects must therefore exist insofar as he has a clear and distinct comprehension of them. This last qualification is important. For all that has been assured is that material objects exist as spatially extended objects that possess a size, shape, location, and motion, but not that they exist exactly as they appear to the senses.

Mind-Body Interaction

Descartes then turns to the precise nature of the relationship between mind and body. He points out that nature has taught him that he has a body to which he is "bound up very closely and, so to speak, mixed in with it, so that my body and I form a certain unity."[1] The mind feels sensations of pain, hunger, and thirst when the body is injured or has need of food and drink. In similar ways the mind receives other sensations that inform it of the condition of the body. Our sensory impressions instruct us of the existence of bodies other than our own; from the fact that the mind receives sensations of color, sounds, tastes, and so on, it is certain that there are features of surrounding objects that correspond to these different sensations.

But Descartes reminds us that it is not necessarily the case that there are qualities in the objects that *resemble* these sensations. All that is certain is that there is something in the object corresponding to each different sensation. Moreover, nothing can be ascertained of the world from the sensations produced by external objects without careful attention by the mind. For example, from the fact that the sensation produced by a candle flame is larger than that produced by a star, it does not follow that this difference reflects their actual relative sizes. This supports the point made in the Second Meditation that conclusions about the world from sensations require acts of judgment of the intellect. We can't simply *see* what the world is like; we have to infer what it is like from our sensations.

The Connection between Mind and Body

A bit further on Descartes admits that "a new difficulty crops up here" concerning judgments that are defective. His theory so far does not explain how some sensations are actually mislead-ing, as when poisons have a pleasant taste. His long consideration of this problem leads him to re-examine the relationship between mind and body more closely. He argues that although the body is divisible into spatial parts, the mind is not. His point here is that the mind is not spatially distributed around the body, since it has neither spatial extension nor parts in any other real sense.[2] It is also clear, he argues, that the mind receives impressions only from the brain and not from other regions of the body. His reasoning here is that the mind receives the same sensations no matter where a nerve is stimulated, as long as the signal reaching the brain is the same. From these points Descartes gives the following explanation of the source of sensations in the mind.

Stimulation of the nerves, by external objects or by changes in the body, is communicated through the nerve fibers to produce motions in the brain. These motions are finally gathered in a region of the brain Descartes calls the "common sense," which he identified as the pineal gland. Each distinct motion in the pineal gland produces a distinct sensation in the mind. On the basis of these changing sensations, the mind can determine the state of the surrounding physical envi-ronment. Similarly, but in the opposite direction, certain actions of the mind produce motions in the brain, which in turn generate muscle contractions. For example, if the mind wills the arm to raise, a certain motion is produced in the brain that indirectly causes the necessary muscles in the arm to contract.

The Argument from Mechanics

Descartes's argument for dualism in the *Meditations*, which we have just surveyed, is deduced from the "clear and distinct ideas" of mind and matter. In a different work, Descartes uses his theory of the mechanical nature of the body to argue that certain aspects of human behavior cannot be the product merely of the physical body but must involve an immaterial soul. This argument occurs in Book V of an earlier work known as *Discourse on the Method*. Descartes's argument in the *Discourse* relies on what he takes to be observable differences between the abili-ties of humans and physical machines.

At the beginning of this reading, Descartes reviews a set of (unpublished) theories about the structure and function of the human body based on mechanical principles. These theories were intended to show how all of the biological functions of the body could be explained on the sup-position that the body is a machine operating on the same principles as mechanical clocks and hydraulic pumps. In reply he contends that, although an artificial machine of this sort could be constructed to perfectly resemble a nonhuman animal, it is impossible to build one that duplicates *human* behavior. He appeals to two aspects of human behavior: language use and what we can call "behavioral plasticity."

Language and Behavioral Plasticity

The first difference that Descartes describes between human actions and what a machine is capable of performing is that:

> [Machines] would never be able to use words or other signs to make words as we do to declare our thoughts to others.

He agrees that we can construct a machine that will produce language-like sounds in response to certain stimuli. But even "the dullest of men" are capable of putting words together into an *endless* number of *different* sentences, and to use these sentences in an unending number of different circumstances. This, Descartes contends, a machine would never be able to do. His reasoning here is that machines can only be constructed to utter a finite number of different utterances, each one in response to a single particular stimulus. In this way, machine language-ability would resemble something like what we now call **reflex** actions: a set of fixed responses to a limited set of stimuli. He concludes that the human ability to speak and understand language cannot be the product of the physical body, which operates on purely mechanical principles.

The reflex nature of machine response reveals a second difference between humans and mechanical devices, Descartes contends. Because a machine can only be built to respond in a single way to a particular given situation, it can respond to a variety of different situations only by combining a number of different such reflex actions, which he calls "dispositions." By contrast, human reason is a single "universal" instrument designed to respond appropriately to any given situation. We can say that the "organ" that controls human behavior is unendingly flexible, adapting itself to any of an indefinite variety of circumstances. This ability is now referred to as **behavioral plasticity**. According to Descartes, machines, constructed on a reflex-action principle, are incapable of this kind of plasticity.

Descartes next claims that human behavior differs in the same manner from animal behavior. Like artificial machines, animals can only respond in fixed ways to a finite number of circumstances. This shows that nonhuman animals lack intelligence, even though their behavior at times appears to resemble or surpass our own.[3] Animals, he claims, are nothing more than complex living machines, no different in kind from clocks.[4]

Minds and Machines

At the end of this part of the *Discourse*, Descartes argues that, given these differences between humans and machines (including living machines), it follows that the human soul is not the product of matter and hence is "entirely independent" of the body. As the variety and plasticity of human behaviors transcends what matter can produce, only an immaterial soul can be the cause of our actions.

An interesting feature of Descartes's argument here is its reliance on the assumption that machines can only respond to situations in a reflex manner. Although series of reflex actions can be combined into enormously complex behaviors, Descartes believed that there is always an upper limit on the flexibility of behavior that machines can exhibit. The same is not true, he contends, of human actions produced by the intellect. In this contention Descartes identifies a problem in machine construction that is a major topic in computer construction today. As we will see in Chapter Ten, programmable computers are machines that can perform in ways that Descartes did not envision. However, there are still serious problems facing the design of machines capable of the flexibility of human behavior.

Antoine Arnauld and the Criticisms of the *Meditations*

When Descartes's *Meditations on First Philosophy* was complete, it was circulated in manuscript form to a number of prominent intellectuals, who were invited to submit their comments and objections to the arguments in the *Meditations*. These were then published in the first edition of the *Meditations*, as were Descartes's replies. The fourth of these Objections was written by Antoine Arnauld (1612–94), a theologian and philosopher at the Sorbonne in Paris. Arnauld's criticism of the argument for dualism in the Sixth Meditation is very useful in understanding Descartes's reasoning. In addition to this criticism, Arnauld is known for raising the most powerful objection to the *Meditations*: that the argument for the rule, "Whatever I perceive very clearly and distinctly is true," is circular.

Arnauld's Analysis of Descartes's Argument

We start with the section Arnauld entitles "The Nature of the Human Mind." His first point here is that much of Descartes's reasoning in the Second Meditation is similar to what Saint Augustine had written centuries earlier. He follows this with a concise description of Descartes's argument for mind-body dualism. According to Arnauld, Descartes argues as follows:

> I can doubt whether I have a body, and even whether there are any bodies at all in the world. Yet for all that, I may not doubt that I am or that I exist, so long as I am doubting or thinking. Therefore I who am doubting and thinking am not a body. For, in that case, in having doubts about my body I should be having doubts about myself.

Arnauld begins his criticism of this argument by raising an earlier version of Descartes's argument in *Discourse on the Method*. In response to criticisms of his argument in the *Discourse*, Descartes admits that

> the proof excluding anything corporeal from the nature of the mind was not put forward "in an order corresponding to the actual truth of the matter" but merely in an order corresponding to his "own perception."[5]

Arnauld's point is that Descartes's argument appears to derive the conclusion that the mind can exist without the body solely from the fact that he can *imagine* his body not existing. But where do we get the assurance that whatever we can imagine must be possible? So Arnauld asks the following question.

How does it follow, from the fact that he is aware of nothing else belonging to his essence, that nothing else does in fact belong to it?

Why should we conclude that the body is not a part of the mind simply from the fact that we can doubt the former but not the latter?[6]

Questioning the First Premise

In the Second Meditation Descartes redefines thinking as conscious thought: that which is impossible to doubt when we reflect on our own internal experience. Arnauld's point here is that there are in fact two components to this redefinition. For Descartes concludes not only (1) that he knows that he exists as a thinking thing, but also (2) that thinking, including only the contents of conscious experience, is *all* that truly belongs to the mind. As we cannot doubt the existence of our own conscious thoughts, Descartes contends, it is *only* the latter that truly belong to the mind.

Arnauld claims that there is no justification for this conclusion in the Second Meditation. That is, the new conception of the mind does not *by itself* show that the mind can exist without the body. The argument relies crucially on the first premise of the argument, which Arnauld refers to as the "major premise":

hence the fact that I can clearly and distinctly understand one thing apart from another is enough to make me certain that the two things are distinct, since they are capable of being separated by God.

Arnauld raises two questions about this premise: (1) Under what conditions could this principle be true? (2) Are those conditions met in our comprehension of mind and body?

Adequate Knowledge

Arnauld's answer to the first question is that the principle would only be true if one's knowledge were what Descartes elsewhere calls "adequate knowledge." By this Descartes means knowledge that includes an understanding of every aspect of the things in question. So the principle is only true if there is nothing at all one does not know about the things to which it is applied. If we know *everything* about the mind, then we know whether or not it depends on the body for its existence. Arnauld takes this answer from Descartes himself, who says that inadequate knowledge is sufficient to establish a "formal" distinction between two things, but not to establish a "real" distinction, and that there is a "real" distinction between mind and body.[7]

So the question is, what evidence is there that our knowledge of mind and body is adequate in this sense? Arnauld points out that Descartes's justification here is simply that he can clearly and distinctly conceive of the mind as existing without the body, and vice versa. In response Arnauld presents an example intended to show that this is not sufficient to achieve the desired conclusion. Consider someone who clearly understands the concept of a right-angled triangle, but who has not yet grasped the rule of the hypotenuse. Then, says Arnauld, he might then reason as follows.

I clearly and distinctly perceive that the triangle is right-angled; but I doubt that the square on the hypotenuse is equal to the squares on the other two sides; therefore it does not belong to the essence of the triangle that the square on its hypotenuse is equal to the squares on the other sides.

Obviously it does not follow from the fact that someone can *imagine* triangles violating the rule of the hypotenuse that there could actually be triangles that do violate the rule. The person merely has a less than "adequate" grasp of the nature of right triangles. Arnauld's question, then, is how our understanding of the mind is any clearer than the understanding of the triangle in this story. He maintains that Descartes offers no proper answer to this question, and hence the argument is unsound.

Descartes's Reply

Descartes replies that, contrary to Arnauld's claim, he never asserted that "adequate" knowledge was required to establish a real distinction between things. Only God, he argues, can know that His knowledge is adequate in this sense. Given our limited abilities, humans are not capable of an adequate knowledge of anything. A bit further on he says one's knowledge must be "complete." This point seems at first to be a purely semantic quibble. But it is the crux of Descartes's reply and, in fact, of his argument that mind and body are distinct.

He says that "a complete understanding of something" is the same as "understanding something to be a complete thing." So it seems that Descartes's point is that the first premise of his argument is true only when the things to which it is applied are "complete things." And a **complete thing**, he says, is a "substance." The heart of the issue, then, is what Descartes understands as "substance."

We have seen this word used in Aristotle's *On the Soul*, and Descartes's use of it has some similarity. In the *Principles of Philosophy*, Part One, Section 51, Descartes says that a *substance* is "a thing which exists in such a way as to depend on no other thing for its existence." This implies that substances are the *fundamental* or basic constituents of the world. This much Aristotle would perhaps agree to. But Descartes puts it to use in his own way. For Descartes has argued that he can conceive of his mind existing, as a thinking thing, by itself without any body. Mind conceived in this way is a substance. So Descartes holds that his major premise is true of our clear and distinct ideas of substances—complete things that can exist on their own.

The Argument for Dualism Revisited

Accordingly Descartes restates the major premise this way:

The mere fact that I can clearly and distinctly understand one *substance* apart from another is enough to make me certain that one excludes the other.

So his point is, then, that if I conceive of two things as substances, *and* I can conceive of each existing without the other, then they are two distinct things. This permits him to reject Arnauld's triangle example as irrelevant. For the question in that example is whether a right triangle can exist without a certain *property* (namely, having the square of the hypotenuse equal to those on the other sides). That property is not a complete thing in itself, able to exist without figures to which it belongs. As the principle stated in the major premise of Descartes's argument applies only to substances, it does not apply to the example.

Descartes claims that, stated in this way, the major premise follows directly from the definition of substance. For if we can conceive of two things existing as complete things—as substances—and each is conceived of as having different properties from the other, then it follows from the idea of substance that each can exist without the other. We can see here the important use that Descartes makes of the argument (found also in Galileo) that matter cannot exist without shape, size, and location, although the same is not true of color, taste, sound, and fragrance. In Descartes's hands this becomes the basis for a view of matter extended in space as a complete thing, able to exist without any other properties. In the same way, he conceives of mind as a complete thing, existing with no other attribute than thought and not dependent on anything else for its existence.

Descartes's Two Substances

In Section 53 of Part One of the *Principles of Philosophy*, Descartes claims that mind and matter are each substances with only one principal attribute. In the case of mind that attribute is thought, and in the case of matter the principal attribute is extension in space. All other attributes of mind and matter are simply modes (or modifications) of thought and extension. Hence, on Descartes's view, there are in the natural world only two kinds of things, minds and bodies, and each has only one attribute. All other things are to be explained in terms of these two attributes. For example, sense perception is just a particular mode of thought, as is reason and judgment. Color, taste, fragrance, and sound *as we perceive them* are all qualities of our subjective experience. In objects these qualities are simply shapes and sizes of the particles on surfaces that produce sensations in us by changing the motions of light and air.

Elisabeth of Bohemia's Question about Mind-Body Interaction

One of the most interesting discussions of Descartes's philosophy occurred in a lengthy correspondence between Descartes and Elisabeth Simmern van Pallandt, Princess of Bohemia. During the time of this correspondence, Elisabeth was living in exile in the Hague in the Netherlands. Her father, who was originally Elector Palatine, had briefly been King of Bohemia before his defeat in 1620 by the Holy Roman Emperor, Ferdinand II. The correspondence was initiated by Elisabeth in 1643 after she had read Descartes's *Meditations on First Philosophy* as well as some of his scientific work. It continued until 1649, shortly before Descartes's death. This series of letters, which Elisabeth asked Descartes not to publish, is the only philosophical work of Elisabeth's that we have, but it covers a broad range of topics in metaphysics, ethics, political philosophy, and the nature of the good, as well as issues in mathematics and physics. In their exchange, Elisabeth presses Descartes on his understanding of the union of mind and body, and in the process formulates a position of her own.

Elisabeth opens the conversation by saying that her letter was prompted by hearing of Descartes's thwarted plan to visit her. Encouraged by their mutual friend, Alphonse Pollot, Elisabeth requests of Descartes that he explain more fully "how the soul of a human being (it being only a thinking substance) can determine the bodily spirits, in order to bring about voluntary actions." By referring to "voluntary actions," she is asking about those bodily movements that originate in an act of the will, which is one of the faculties that Descartes ascribes to the immaterial mind. And by "bodily spirits," she is referring to the fine matter that moves through the nerves of the body and communicates motion to the muscles.

Motion and Its Determination

Elisabeth was not the first to challenge Descartes on his claims that the immaterial mind produces movement in the body, and that bodily movement produces effects in the mind. In the Fifth Set of Objections to the *Meditations*, which Elisabeth had read, Pierre Gassendi also raises this issue. But, as Deborah Tollefsen has pointed out, Elisabeth presents a challenge that is well-informed with regard to Descartes's physics.[8] Elisabeth was familiar with a distinction that Descartes drew between a body's "quantity of motion" and the "determination" of that motion. In her request for explanation of mind-body interaction, Elisabeth asks how the soul "can *determine*" these bodily spirits, and in the next sentence she refers to "all *determinations* of movement." Descartes had introduced this distinction in his explanation of the laws of reflection and refraction in his *Optics*, a work that Elisabeth had read.[9] Understanding the role of this distinction is useful in unpacking Elisabeth's response to Descartes's dualism.

When we use modern physics to explain the impact of one body on another, we use the concept of *force*, which we measure by the product of an object's mass and its acceleration. Descartes's physics contained an important precursor to the idea of force, *quantity of motion*, which he measured as the product of an object's mass and its velocity. Acceleration is of course not just velocity but change in velocity, and this was a fatal weakness in Descartes's theory. But there is a further aspect of Descartes's idea of velocity that is relevant to Elisabeth's question. The modern concept of force includes both magnitude and direction, but in Descartes's physics what we call force is separated into two different concepts: *motion* and *determination*. The first is the magnitude of the force, the *quantity* of motion. By "determination" Descartes meant more than just direction, but something more subtle that included direction. As Descartes understood it, it is possible for the determination of a body's movement to change without any change in the quantity of motion. So Elisabeth's question, properly understood, is not "How does the mind introduce motion in the body?" but "How does the mind introduce change in the determination of motion in the body?"

Elisabeth's Challenge

Elisabeth's challenge to Descartes is based on an argument that, on the basis of his own account of motion, an immaterial soul cannot bring about a change in determination of movement. Her first premise is the following.

> …every determination of movement happens from the impulsion of a thing moved, according to the manner in which it is pushed by that which moves it, or else, depends on the qualification and figures of the superficies of the latter.

There are, then, three ways in which the determination of a movement can be influenced. The first, "from the impulsion of a thing," seems to be a reference to Descartes's idea of quantity of motion, that is, the magnitude of the force applied to the thing moved. According to Tollefsen, the other two possibilities can be found in Descartes's *Optics*. The second, "according to the manner in which it is pushed," matches his observation that the direction of a tennis ball is influenced by the position of the racquet when it strikes the ball. And corresponding to the third possibility, Descartes writes in the *Optics*,

...consider that a ball passing through the air may encounter bodies that are soft or hard or fluid. If these bodies are soft, they completely stop the ball and check its movement, as when it strikes linen sheets or sand or mud. But if they are hard, they send the ball in another direction without stopping it, and they do so in many different ways.[10]

The first premise of Elisabeth's challenge, then, is drawn from Descartes's own theory of motion according to his *Optics*.

The remainder of her argument is that none of these three possibilities can be realized by an immaterial soul. She says,

> The first two of those require contact between the two things, and the third requires that the causally active thing be extended. Your notion of the soul entirely excludes extension, and it appears to me that an immaterial thing can't possibly touch anything else.

That is, without contact there can be neither impulsion nor manner of impact, and without extension a body cannot have either shape, hardness or softness, or fluidity. So an immaterial object, lacking both movement and spatial extension, cannot bring about any change in the determination of movement of a physical body in any of the possible ways. The combination of Descartes's physics and his metaphysics of the soul thus makes it impossible for the mind to bring about change of motion in the body in the manner that he asserts.

On these grounds Elisabeth asks for a more precise definition of the soul than what Descartes offered in the *Meditations*. More specifically, she asks for a statement of the substance of the soul "separate from its action, that is, from thought." So where Descartes says that thought is the only essential attribute of the soul, she takes thought to be what the soul *does*, but not what it *is*. To this she adds that even if thought is inseparable from the substance of the soul, we would still want to know what that substance is. Thought, then, is not an attribute of the soul (whether essential or not), but an activity, and there must be a statement of what kind of thing it is that is capable of that activity.

Three Primitive Ideas

Descartes's reply in his first letter acknowledges the legitimacy of Elisabeth's demand to provide a better account of the interaction between body and soul, but he does not provide a better definition of the soul as she requested. In fact, as he sees it, his fault in the *Meditations* was in concentrating on making the immateriality of the soul clear, while not explaining "the union of the soul with the body and how the soul has the power to move the body." Accordingly, he devotes his letter to explaining the knowledge we have of mind-body interaction.

Recall that Descartes's argument for mind-body dualism in the *Meditations* was based on the claim that we have clear and distinct ideas both of matter and of mind. From these ideas we understand that each has only one essential attribute: extension and thought, respectively. His account of mind-body interaction uses the same strategy. He claims that in addition to the ideas of mind and body we have a third, that of the union of mind and body in a person. This idea, like the other two, is primitive: It is not based on any other idea, and hence in particular it is independent of the ideas of mind and body individually. Those people who, like Elisabeth, are confused about mind-body interaction are so because they attempt to base their understanding on the idea of mind or that of body, and so they look in the wrong place. In Elisabeth's case, she attempts to understand how the mind moves the body by using the idea of how one *body* moves another. Clearly, such an idea cannot be used to explain motion caused by an immaterial mind.

From this point, Descartes's answer is difficult to follow. The paragraph demands close reading in light of the distinction we reviewed in Chapter Three between qualities in the world and sensations in the mind. The mechanical philosophers, recall, argued that the qualities of heat, color, and so on, do not exist in matter as we experience them in our sensations. In material objects they exist only as the movement of particles, whereas we perceive them as simple qualities. In this paragraph Descartes talks specifically of heaviness as such a quality. He says that we conceive of heaviness (and of heat) as a real quality, and also we confusedly think of it as a substance distinct from the bodies in which it exists. When we think of heaviness as a real quality in this way, we have no idea of it other than of a power to move objects towards the center of the earth. Yet we find no difficulty in this idea. And *this*, he argues, is because we have illegitimately drawn the idea from that which we have of the way in which the soul moves the body. That is, we mistakenly think of heaviness as a substance moving material objects to the center of the earth *because* we import the idea we already (and quite legitimately) have of how the mind moves the body.

The Origin of the Idea of Mind-Body Union

Elisabeth's response of June 10 is prefaced by a modest claim that her duties prevent her from properly attending to Descartes's letter. But her skepticism towards his answer is genuine. She says that she can no more comprehend how a false idea of heaviness can "persuade us that a body can be pushed by an immaterial thing," than how the true idea should persuade us of the opposite. She analyzes Descartes's argument thus: Due to our ignorance of the true cause of heaviness, and since no cause of heaviness is present to our senses, we attribute it to an immaterial cause (the idea of which is drawn from the idea of mind-body interaction). But she rejects this reasoning on the grounds that the only idea we have of an "immaterial thing" is the negation of matter, and this cannot possibly be thought of as acting on matter.

In the second last paragraph of this letter she presents two direct arguments against the possibility of mind-body interaction. We will return to these arguments later, and turn first to Descartes's reply to Elisabeth's skepticism, in his next letter of June 28th. Here he attempts to reveal the origin of the idea of mind-body interaction, and contrast it to those of mind and body, in order to counter Elisabeth's claim that she can more easily "concede matter and extension to the soul" than concede to mind-body interaction.

He claims in this letter that the idea of the mind comes entirely from the understanding, without either the imagination or the senses. It is a purely intellectual idea. The idea of matter, he argues, comes partly from the understanding, but this is much aided by the imagination. Here he means that the idea of spatial extension can be understood intellectually, but it becomes clearer when we conceive of geometric figures in the imagination. Mind-body interaction, however, is not clearly conceived by the understanding or by the imagination. It comes only from the senses. Those who do not try to understand this interaction, but only use their senses, think of the union of mind and body as one thing, as a *person*. This is the best way to conceive of it, and it is actually hampered by metaphysical contemplation, for this would require that one think clearly of two distinct things as only one thing, which is impossible. And this, he says, is the origin of Elisabeth's confusion. She is over-intellectualizing. Indeed, when she says she can more easily "concede matter and extension to the soul," she should do just that when it comes to mind-body union.

Extension as an Essential Attribute of the Mind

In her reply of July 1, Elisabeth agrees that the senses *do* teach of the union of mind and body. That is, we sense the motion of our body in response to our will, and we experience sensations as things affect our organs of sense. But this, she says, doesn't explain to her *how* this occurs. This, she says, might well overturn Descartes's idea of the soul as nonextended. Her argument here is an interesting use of Descartes's own clarity and distinctness rule: If we cannot explain *clearly and distinctly* how body and soul are united in a person, then the concepts we are using must not be adequate.

On these grounds she offers a possible revision of the definition of the soul. Descartes's arguments demonstrate that extension is not necessary for thought. But they do not show that extension is "repugnant to it." So it is possible that the soul is extended, even though its capacity for thought does not depend on this property. Extension may be necessary for other properties of the soul, and specifically for its union with the body, and these additional properties may well be essential to the definition of the soul in its full capacity. Extension, then, is necessary for "some other function of the soul [than thought] which is no less essential to it?" And by this function it seems quite clear that Elisabeth intends the mind's union with the body.

The Union of Mind and Body

We can turn now to the second last paragraph of Elisabeth's letter of June 10th, which we passed over earlier. In this paragraph Elisabeth gives two arguments against the possibility of mind-body interaction according to Descartes's definitions of mind as possessing only thought, and of body possessing only extension.

She first argues against the idea of the mind affecting the material body. She claims that the mind can affect other things only through *information*. By this, she does not mean information in our modern English sense, and it isn't entirely clear how she is using the French word. She does say, however, that if the mind were to move the bodily spirits, they would have to be *intelligent* spirits. This assumption is presumably based on Descartes's idea of the soul as possessing only thought, which can thus be its only causal power. Yet since the body possesses only extension, Descartes denies intelligence to the body. So Descartes's restriction of the attributes of the body to extension alone, makes it impossible for the mind to influence the body.

Her second argument is against Descartes's idea of how the body affects the mind. According to Descartes, the soul has "the faculty and custom of reasoning well." Reason, in his view, is the fundamental capacity of the mind. Yet it can lose this capacity due to "some vapors" of the body. Moreover, she argues, although the soul can exist entirely without the body, it is "still so governed by it." Here she is questioning how Descartes can explain the fact that the mind can be so affected by illnesses and weaknesses of the body, a situation that she later claims is one from which she herself suffers. When she asks Descartes to give a better account of the union of mind and body than that provided by the senses, she means an account of the myriad ways in which the functioning of the mind is susceptible to the influence of the body. For this purpose, Descartes's simple description of this influence is clearly unacceptable.

The Passions of the Soul

We gain further insight into Elisabeth's disagreement with Descartes on mind-body interaction in the exchange of letters between May 18 and September 13, 1645, which are too long to reproduce here.[11] Descartes writes on May 18 that he has heard that Elisabeth has been ill, and he suggests that the illness is caused by sadness brought on by her plight as an exile. His advice to Elisabeth is to exercise her will to make reason the mistress of her passions, so that her illness can be borne patiently. In a later work, Descartes defines the passions as "those perceptions, sensations or emotions of the soul which we refer particularly to it, and which are caused, maintained and strengthened by some movement of the spirits."[12] According to this definition, the passions are states of mind brought about by the impressions of the body.[13] His advice, then, is to use the will to place reason over bodily influences. This suggestion brings about a lengthy discussion between Elisabeth and Descartes of how the passions of the soul can affect physical health, and how illnesses and bodily indispositions can affect the abilities of the mind.

Elisabeth says that she has "a body imbued with a large part of the weaknesses of [her] sex, so that it is affected very easily by the afflictions of the soul and has none of the strength to bring itself back into line."[14] Her point is that certain conditions of the body can render it disposed to the influences of the mind. She also insists that she does not know how to prevent the anxiety that comes with bad news, and when that anxiety is calmed by reason a new disaster provokes another. In reply to Descartes's practical advice not to let her imagination create anxieties that can slow the circulation and interfere with the lungs, she says that the sources of anxiety are not so easily avoided.

At this point, Descartes turns to the Roman philosopher, Seneca, and to the Stoic philosophy Seneca defended. From consideration of neo-Stoic arguments, Descartes comes to the conclusion that perfect contentment can be brought about through "a firm and constant resolution to execute all that reason advises."[15] To this Elisabeth gives the following reply.

> I do not yet know how to rid myself of the doubt that one can arrive at the true happiness of which you speak without the assistance of that which does not depend absolutely on the will. For there are diseases that destroy altogether the power of reasoning and by consequence that of enjoying a satisfaction of reason. There are others that diminish the force of reason and prevent one from following the maxims that good sense would have forged and that make the most moderate man subject to being carried away by his passions and less capable of disentangling himself from the accidents of fortune requiring a prompt resolution.[16]

Elisabeth insists, then, that the exercise of the will, and the capacity of the mind to reason, cannot be removed entirely from the influence of the body as Descartes suggests. And on September 16 she writes,

> It is true that a habit of esteeming good things according to how they can contribute to contentment, measuring this contentment according to the perfections which give birth to the pleasures, and judging these perfections and these pleasures without passion will protect them from a number of faults. But in order to esteem these goods in this way, one must know them perfectly. And in order to know all those goods among which one must choose in an active life, one would need to possess an infinite science.[17]

According to Elisabeth, the Stoic control of the passions, as advocated by Descartes, is impossible in principle. Her arguments thus raise serious issues concerning the relations between the emotions and reason.

At the end of the same letter Elisabeth asks Descartes for a better explanation of the passions, "for those who call the passions perturbations of the mind would persuade me that the force of the passions consists only in overwhelming and subjecting reason to them, if experience did not show me that there are passions that do carry us to reasonable actions."[18] This adds a further point to her position: The passions can sometimes aid in the proper exercise of reason. Elisabeth's request for further explanation provided the motivation behind Descartes's later book, *The Passions of the Soul*, which dealt with the subject in great detail. In this work, Descartes himself articulated an important role for the passions in practical reason and the pursuit of truth.[19] He maintains, however, that the passions must nonetheless be controlled and guided by reason, if they are to be reliable, a requirement that Elisabeth denies can be met.

Notes

1. The expression 'that nature teaches me,' which occurs in this sentence and elsewhere, refers to the irresistible beliefs that arise as the result of our union with the body.

2. This paragraph serves to some extent as a second argument that mind and body are distinct, as Descartes indicates in the last sentence. But it is widely seen as a weak argument, and we will focus here on its more important role in explaining the connection between mind and body.

3. An example of the kind of thing Descartes has in mind is the behavior of certain varieties of spiders. Many spiders have elaborate procedures for burying their eggs and camouflaging the hole. This activity looks for all the world like the product of genuine intelligence. But if the spider is interrupted in its task, it will repeat its previous step, and it will do so over and over again without ever noticing the interruption. This, Descartes would say, is because its behavior is just a complex series of reflex actions, not an intelligent understanding of what it is doing.

4. There is a debate about what Descartes's views on nonhuman animals were with regard to questions such as whether they experience sensations like pain or color. His writings are open to a number of different interpretations.

5. The passage that Arnauld is quoting here occurs in the Preface to the *Meditations*.

6. This last question suggests an interpretation of Descartes's argument as follows. "If mind and body are one thing, then whatever is true of the body must be true of the mind. But I can doubt the existence of the body without doubting the existence of the mind. Therefore, they cannot be one thing." But this argument is clearly fallacious, and Descartes's reply to Arnauld suggests that he is not relying on this line of reasoning.

7. A "formal distinction," according to Descartes, is that between two properties or characteristics of a thing, like size and shape. A "real distinction," he says, is that between two *substances*. The meaning of Descartes's notion of substance will come up when we read Descartes's reply to Arnauld.

8. Deborah Tollefsen, "Princess Elisabeth and the Problem of Mind-Body Interaction," *Hypatia* 14 (1999): pp. 59–77.

9. René Descartes, *Discourse on Method, Optics, Geometry, and Meteorology*. Paul J. Olscamp (trans.) (Indianapolis: Hackett Publishing, 2001), pp. 65–76.

10. Quoted in Tollefsen (1999) pp. 63–64. In her letter of May 24, Elisabeth refers to Descartes's point in the *Optics* about the effect of soft bodies versus hard bodies in impact for distinguishing a body's motion from its determination.

11. See Lisa Shapiro (trans., ed.), *The Correspondence between Princess Elisabeth of Bohemia and René Descartes*. (Chicago: University of Chicago Press, 2007), pp. 85–111.

12. René Descartes, *The Passions of the Soul*, in *The Philosophical Writings of Descartes*, John Cottingham, Robert Stoothoff, and Dugald Murdoch (trans.). (Cambridge: Cambridge University Press, 1984–1991). Volume I, pp. 338–39.

13. Descartes does, however, assert the existence and importance of "intellectual passions," which do not have their origin in the bodily experience.

14. Shapiro (2007) pp. 88–89. Elisabeth also later refers to "the curse" of her sex. On these comments regarding her sex, see Lisa Shapiro "Princess Elizabeth and Descartes: The Union of Soul and Body and the Practice of Philosophy," *British Journal for the History of Philosophy*, 7 (1999): pp. 503–20.

15. Shapiro (2007) p. 98.

16. Shapiro (2007) p. 100.

17. Shapiro (2007) p. 110.

18. Shapiro (2007) pp. 110–11.

19. See Amy M. Schmitter "Descartes and the Primacy of Practice: The Role of the Passions in the Pursuit of Truth." *Philosophical Studies* 108 (2002): pp. 99–108.

RENÉ DESCARTES

Selections from *Principles of Philosophy**

Part One

[...]

51. *What is meant by 'substance'—a term which does not apply univocally to God and his creatures.*

In the case of those items which we regard as things or modes of things, it is worthwhile examining each of them separately. By *substance* we can understand nothing other than a thing which exists in such a way as to depend on no other thing for its existence. And there is only one substance which can be understood to depend on no other thing whatsoever, namely God. In the case of all other substances, we perceive that they can exist only with the help of God's concurrence.

---

* Eds.: Angle brackets indicate places where translations of the original work that were approved by Descartes added important additional material.

Hence the term 'substance' does not apply *univocally*, as they say in the Schools, to God and to other things; that is, there is no distinctly intelligible meaning of the term which is common to God and his creatures. <In the case of created things, some are of such a nature that they cannot exist without other things, while some need only the ordinary concurrence of God in order to exist. We make this distinction by calling the latter 'substances' and the former 'qualities' or 'attributes' of those substances.>

[…]

53. *To each substance there belongs one principal attribute; in the case of mind, this is thought, and in the case of body it is extension.*

A substance may indeed be known through any attribute at all; but each substance has one prin-cipal property which constitutes its nature and essence, and to which all its other properties are referred. Thus extension in length, breadth and depth constitutes the nature of corporeal substance; and thought constitutes the nature of thinking substance. Everything else which can be attributed to body presupposes extension, and is merely a mode of an extended thing; and similarly, whatever we find in the mind is simply one of the various modes of thinking. For example, shape is unintelligible except in an extended thing; and motion is unintelligible except as motion in an extended space; while imagination, sensation and will are intelligible only in a thinking thing. By contrast, it is possible to understand extension without shape or movement, and thought without imagination or sensation, and so on; and this is quite clear to anyone who gives the matter his attention.

RENÉ DESCARTES

Selections from *Discourse on the Method of rightly conducting one's reason and seeking the truth in the sciences*

Part V

[…]

I explained in particular detail all these things in the treatise which I had planned to publish previously. And then I demonstrated what the nerves and muscles in the human body must be made of, so that the animal spirits, once inside the nerves, would have the power to move its limbs, as one sees that heads, for a little while after being cut off, continue to move and bite the earth, in spite of the fact that they are no longer animated. I also showed what changes must take places in the brain to cause the waking state, sleep, and dreams, how light, sounds, smells, tastes, heat, and all the other qualities of external objects could imprint various ideas on the brain through the mediation of the senses, just as hunger, thirst, and the other inner passions can also send their ideas to the brain; what must be understood by common sense where these ideas are taken in, by memory which preserves them, and by fantasy which can change them in various ways and compose new ones, and, in the same way, distribute animal spirits to the muscles and make the limbs of the body move in all the different ways—in relation to the objects which present themselves to the senses and in relation to the interior physical passions—just as our bodies can move themselves without being led by the will. None of this will seem strange to those who know how many varieties of *automata*, or moving machines, human industry can make, by using only very few pieces in comparison with the huge number of bones, muscles, nerves, arteries, veins, and all the other parts in the body of each animal. They will look on this body as a machine, which, having been made by the hand of God, is incomparably better ordered and more inherently admirable in its movements than any of those which human beings could have invented. And here, in particular, I stopped to reveal that if there were machines which had the organs and the external shape of a monkey or of some other animal without reason, we would have no way of recognizing that they were not exactly the same nature as the animals; whereas, if there was a machine shaped like our bodies which imitated our actions as much as is morally possible, we would always have two very certain ways of recognizing that they were not, for all their resemblance, true human beings. The first of these is that they would never be able to use words or other signs to make words as we do to declare our thoughts to others. For one can easily imagine a machine made in such a way that it expresses words, even that it expresses some words relevant to some physical actions which bring about some change in its organs (for example, if one touches it in some spot, the machine asks what it is that one wants to say to it; if in another spot, it cries that one has hurt it, and things like that), but one can-

not imagine a machine that arranges words in various ways to reply to the sense of everything said in its presence, as the most stupid human beings are capable of doing. The second test is that, although these machines might do several things as well or perhaps better than we do, they are inevitably lacking in some others, through which we would discover that they act, not by knowledge, but only by the arrangement of their organs. For, whereas reason is a universal instrument which can serve in all sorts of encounters, these organs need some particular arrangement for each particular action. As a result of that, it is morally impossible that there is in a machine's organs sufficient variety to act in all the events of life in the same way that our reason empowers us to act. Now, by these two same means, one can also recognize the difference between human beings and beasts. For it is really remarkable that there are no men so dull and stupid, including even idiots, who are not capable of putting together different words and of creating out of them a conversation through which they make their thoughts known; by contrast, there is no other animal, no matter how perfect and how successful it might be, which can do anything like that. And this inability does not come about from a lack of organs. For we see that magpies and parrots can emit words, as we can, but nonetheless cannot talk the way we can, that is to say, giving evidence that they are thinking about what they are uttering; whereas, men who are born deaf and dumb are deprived of organs which other people use to speak—just as much as or more than the animals—but they have a habit of inventing on their own some signs by which they can make themselves understood to those who, being usually with them, have the spare time to learn their language. And this point attests not merely to the fact that animals have less reason than men, but to the fact that they have none at all. For we see that it takes very little for someone to learn how to speak, and since we observe inequality among the animals of the same species just as much as among human beings, and see that some are easier to train than others, it would be incredible that a monkey or a parrot which was the most perfect of his species was not equivalent in speaking to the most stupid child or at least a child with a troubled brain, unless their soul had a nature totally different from our own. And one should not confuse words with natural movements which attest to the passions and can be imitated by machines as well as by animals, nor should one think, like some ancients, that animals talk, although we do not understand their language. For if that were true, because they have several organs related to our own, they could just as easily make themselves understood to us as to the animals like them. Another truly remarkable thing is that, although there are several animals which display more industry in some of their actions than we do, we nonetheless see that they do not display that at all in many other actions. Thus, the fact that they do better than we do does not prove that they have a mind, for, if that were the case, they would have more of it than any of us and would do better in all other things; it rather shows that they have no reason at all, and that it is nature which has activated them according to the arrangement of their organs—just as one sees that a clock, which is composed only of wheels and springs, can keep track of the hours and measure time more accurately than we can, for all our care.

After that, I described the reasonable soul and revealed that it cannot be inferred in any way from the power of matter, like the other things I have spoken about, but that it must be expressly created, and I described how it is not sufficient that it is lodged in the human body like a pilot in his ship, except perhaps to move its limbs, but that it is necessary that the soul is joined and united more closely with the body, so that it has, in addition, feelings and appetites similar to ours and thus makes up a true human being. As for the rest, here I went on at some length on the subject of the soul, because it is among the most important. For, apart from the error of those who deny God, which I believe I have adequately refuted above, there is nothing which distances feeble minds from the right road of virtue more readily than to imagine that the soul of animals is the same nature as our own and that thus we have nothing either to fear or to hope for after this life, any more than flies and ants do; whereas, once one knows how different they are, one understands much better the reasons which prove that the nature of our souls is totally independent of the body, and thus it is not at all subject to dying along with the body. Then, to the extent that one cannot see other causes which destroy the soul, one is naturally led to judge from that that the soul is immortal.

ANTOINE ARNAULD

Objections to Descartes' *Meditations*

The Nature of the Human Mind

The first thing that I find remarkable is that our distinguished author has laid down as the basis for his entire philosophy exactly the same principle as that laid down by St Augustine—a man of the sharpest intellect and a remarkable thinker, not only on theological topics but also on philosophical ones. In Book II chapter 3 of *De Libero Arbitrio*, Alipius, when he is disputing with Euodius and is about to prove the existence of God, says the following: 'First, if we are to take as our starting point what is most evident, I ask you to tell me whether you yourself exist. Or are you perhaps afraid of making a mistake in your answer, given that, if you did not exist, it would be quite impossible for you to make a mistake?' This is like what M. Descartes says: 'But there is a deceiver of supreme power and cunning who is deliberately and constantly deceiving me. In that case I too undoubtedly exist, if he is deceiving me.' But let us go on from here and, more to the point, see how this principle can be used to derive the result that our mind is separate from our body.

I can doubt whether I have a body, and even whether there are any bodies at all in the world. Yet for all that, I may not doubt that I am or exist, so long as I am doubting or thinking.

Therefore I who am doubting and thinking am not a body. For, in that case, in having doubts about my body I should be having doubts about myself.

Indeed, even if I obstinately maintain that there are no bodies whatsoever, the proposition still stands, namely that I am something, and hence I am not a body.

This is certainly very acute. But someone is going to bring up the objection which the author raises against himself: the fact that I have doubts about the body, or deny that it exists, does not bring it about that no body exists. 'Yet may it not perhaps be the case that these very things which I am supposing to be nothing, because they are unknown to me, are in reality identical with the "I" of which I am aware? I do not know,' he says 'and for the moment I shall not argue the point. I know that I exist; the question is, what is this "I" that I know? If the "I" is understood strictly as we have been taking it, then it is quite certain that knowledge of it does not depend on things of whose existence I am as yet unaware.'

But the author admits that in the argument set out in the Discourse on the Method the proof excluding anything corporeal from the nature of the mind was not put forward 'in an order corresponding to the actual truth of the matter' but merely in an order corresponding to his 'own perception.' So the sense of the passage was that he was aware of nothing at all which he knew belonged to his essence except that he was a thinking thing. From this answer it is clear that the objection still stands in precisely the same form as it did before, and that the question he promised to answer still remains outstanding: How does it follow, from the fact that he is aware of nothing else belonging to his essence, that nothing else does in fact belong to it? I must confess that I am somewhat slow, but I have been unable to find anywhere in the Second Meditation an answer to this question. As far as I can gather, however, the author does attempt a proof of this claim in the Sixth Meditation, since he takes it to depend on his having clear knowledge of God, which he had not yet arrived at in the Second Meditation. This is how the proof goes:

> I know that everything which I clearly and distinctly understand is capable of being created by God so as to correspond exactly with my understanding of it. Hence the fact that I can clearly and distinctly understand one thing apart from another is enough to make me certain that the two things are distinct, since they are capable of being separated, at least by God. The question of what kind of power is required to bring about such a separation does not affect the judgment that the two things are distinct ... Now on the one hand I have a clear and distinct idea of myself, in so far as I am simply a thinking, non-extended thing; and on the other hand I have a distinct idea of body, in so far as this is simply an extended, non-thinking thing. And accordingly, it is certain that I am really distinct from my body, and can exist without it.*

We must pause a little here, for it seems to me that in these few words lies the crux of the whole difficulty.

First of all, if the major premiss of this syllogism is to be true, it must be taken to apply not to any kind of knowledge of a thing, nor even to clear and distinct knowledge; it must apply solely to knowledge which is adequate. For our distinguished author admits in his reply to the theologian, that if one thing can be conceived distinctly and separately from another 'by an abstraction of the intellect which conceives the thing inadequately,' then this is sufficient for there to be a formal distinction between the two, but it does not require that there be a real distinction. And in the same passage he draws the following conclusion:

> By contrast, I have a complete understanding of what a body is when I think that it is merely something having extension, shape and motion, and I deny that it has anything which belongs to the nature of a mind. Conversely, I understand the mind to be a complete thing, which doubts, understands, wills, and so on, even though I deny that it has any of the attributes which are contained in the idea of a body. Hence there is a real distinction between the body and the mind.†

But someone may call this minor premiss into doubt and maintain that the conception you have of yourself when you conceive of yourself as a thinking, non-extended thing is an inadequate one; and the same may be true of your conception of yourself as an extended, non-thinking thing. Hence we must look at how this is proved in the earlier part of the argument. For I do not think that this matter is so clear that it should be assumed without proof as a first principle that is not susceptible of demonstration.

As to the first part of your claim, namely that you have a complete understanding of what a body is when you think that it is merely something having extension, shape, motion etc., and you deny that it has anything which belongs

---

* Eds.: The corresponding passage in this volume, which is from a different translation, is found on page 94 ("First, since I know that…").

† Eds.: This statement is from Descartes' reply to the first set of objections, from Caterus, a Dutch theologian.

to the nature of a mind, this proves little. For those who maintain that our mind is corporeal do not on that account suppose that every body is a mind. On their view, body would be related to mind as a genus is related to a species. Now a genus can be understood apart from a species, even if we deny of the genus what is proper and peculiar to the species—hence the common maxim of logicians, 'The negation of the species does not negate the genus.' Thus I can understand the genus 'figure' apart from my understanding of any of the properties which are peculiar to a circle. It therefore remains to be proved that the mind can be completely and adequately understood apart from the body.

I cannot see anywhere in the entire work an argument which could serve to prove this claim, apart from what is suggested at the beginning: 'I can deny that any body exists, or that there is any extended thing at all, yet it remains certain to me that I exist, so long as I am making this denial or thinking it. Hence I am a thinking thing, not a body, and the body does not belong to the knowledge I have of myself.'

But so far as I can see, the only result that follows from this is that I can obtain some knowledge of myself without knowledge of the body. But it is not yet transparently clear to me that this knowledge is complete and adequate, so as to enable me to be certain that I am not mistaken in excluding body from my essence. I shall explain the point by means of an example. Suppose someone knows for certain that the angle in a semi-circle is a right angle, and hence that the triangle formed by this angle and the diameter of the circle is right-angled. In spite of this, he may doubt, or not yet have grasped for certain, that the square on the hypotenuse is equal to the squares on the other two sides; indeed he may even deny this if he is misled by some fallacy. But now, if he uses the same argument as that proposed by our illustrious author, he may appear to have confirmation

of his false belief, as follows: 'I clearly and distinctly perceive,' he may say, 'that the triangle is right-angled; but I doubt that the square on the hypotenuse is equal to the squares on the other two sides; therefore it does not belong to the essence of the triangle that the square on its hypotenuse is equal to the squares on the other sides.'

Again, even if I deny that the square on the hypotenuse is equal to the square on the other two sides, I still remain sure that the triangle is right-angled, and my mind retains the clear and distinct knowledge that one of its angles is a right angle. And given that this is so, not even God could bring it about that the triangle is not right-angled.

I might argue from this that the property which I doubt, or which can be removed while leaving my idea intact, does not belong to the essence of the triangle.

Moreover, 'I know,' says M. Descartes, 'that everything which I clearly and distinctly understand is capable of being created by God so as to correspond exactly with my understanding of it. And hence the fact that I can clearly and distinctly understand one thing apart from another is enough to make me certain that the two things are distinct, since they are capable of being separated by God.' Yet I clearly and distinctly understand that this triangle is right-angled, without understanding that the square on the hypotenuse is equal to the squares on the other sides. It follows on this reasoning that God, at least, could create a right-angled triangle with the square on its hypotenuse not equal to the squares on the other sides.

I do not see any possible reply here, except that the person in this example does not clearly and distinctly perceive that the triangle is right-angled. But how is my perception of the nature of my mind any clearer than his perception of the nature of the triangle? He is just as certain that the triangle in the semi-circle has one right angle (which is the criterion of a right-angled triangle) as I am certain that I exist because I am thinking.

Now although the man in the example clearly and distinctly knows that the triangle is right-angled, he is wrong in thinking that the aforesaid relationship between the squares on the sides does not belong to the nature of the triangle. Similarly, although I clearly and distinctly know my nature to be something that thinks, may I, too, not perhaps be wrong in thinking that nothing else belongs to my nature apart from the fact that I am a thinking thing? Perhaps the fact that I am an extended thing may also belong to my nature.

Someone may also make the point that since I infer my existence from the fact that I am thinking, it is certainly no surprise if the idea that I form by thinking of myself in this way represents to my mind nothing other than myself as a thinking thing. For the idea was derived entirely from my thought. Hence it seems that this idea cannot provide any evidence that nothing belongs to my essence beyond what is contained in the idea.

It seems, moreover, that the argument proves too much, and takes us back to the Platonic view (which M. Descartes nonetheless rejects) that nothing corporeal belongs to our essence, so that man is merely a rational soul and the body merely a vehicle for the soul—a view which gives rise to the definition of man as 'a soul which makes use of a body.'

If you reply that body is not straightforwardly excluded from my essence, but is ruled out only and precisely in so far as I am a thinking thing, it seems that there is a danger that someone will suspect that my knowledge of myself as a thinking thing does not qualify as knowledge of a being of which I have a complete and adequate conception; it seems instead that I conceive of it only inadequately, and by a certain intellectual abstraction.

Geometers conceive of a line as a length without breadth, and they conceive of a surface as length and breadth without depth, despite the fact that no length exists without breadth and no breadth without depth. In the same way, someone may perhaps suspect that every thinking thing is also an extended thing—an extended thing which, besides the attributes it has in common with other extended things, such as shape, motion, etc., also possesses the peculiar power of thought. This would mean that although, simply in virtue of this power, it can by an intellectual abstraction be apprehended as a thinking thing, in reality bodily attributes may belong to this thinking thing. In the same way, although quantity can be conceived in terms of length alone, in reality breadth and depth belong to every quantity, along with length.

The difficulty is increased by the fact that the power of thought appears to be attached to bodily organs, since it can be regarded as dormant in infants and extinguished in the case of madmen. And this is an objection strongly pressed by those impious people who try to do away with the soul.

So far I have dealt with the real distinction between our mind and the body. But since our distinguished author has undertaken to demonstrate the immortality of the soul, it may rightly be asked whether this evidently follows from the fact that the soul is distinct from the body. According to the principles of commonly accepted philosophy this by no means follows, since people ordinarily take it that the souls of brute animals are distinct from their bodies, but nevertheless perish along with them.

I had got as far as this in my comments, and was intending to show how the author's principles, which I thought I had managed to gather from his method of philosophizing, would enable the immortality of the soul to be inferred very easily from the real distinction between the mind and the body. But at this point, a little study composed by our illustrious author was sent to me, which apart from shedding much light on the work as a whole, puts forward the same solution to the point at issue which I was on the point of proposing.

As far as the souls of the brutes are concerned, M. Descartes elsewhere suggests clearly enough that they have none. All they have is a body which is constructed in a particular manner, made up of various organs in such a way that all the operations which we observe can be produced in it and by means of it.

But I fear that this view will not succeed in finding acceptance in people's minds unless it is supported by very solid arguments. For at first sight it seems incredible that it can come about, without the assistance of any soul, that the light reflected from the body of a wolf onto the eyes of a sheep should move the minute fibres of the optic nerves, and that on reaching the brain this motion should spread the animal spirits throughout the nerves in the manner necessary to precipitate the sheep's flight.

RENÉ DESCARTES

Reply to Antoine Arnauld

Reply to Part One, Dealing with the Nature of the Human Mind

I shall not waste time here by thanking my distinguished critic for bringing in the authority of St Augustine to support me, and for setting out my arguments so vigorously that he seems to fear that their strength may not be sufficiently apparent to anyone else.

But I will begin by pointing out where it was that I embarked on proving 'how, from the fact that I am aware of nothing else belonging to my essence (that is, the essence of the mind alone) apart from the fact that I am a thinking thing, it follows that nothing else does in fact belong to it.' The relevant passage is the one where I proved that God exists—a God who can bring about everything that I clearly and distinctly recognize as possible.

Now it may be that there is much within me of which I am not yet aware (for example, in this passage I was in fact supposing that I was not yet aware that the mind possessed the power of moving the body, or that it was substantially united to it). Yet since that of which I am aware is sufficient to enable me to subsist with it and it alone, I am certain that I could have been created by God without having these other attributes of which I am unaware, and hence that these other attributes do not belong to the essence of the mind.

For if something can exist without some attribute, then it seems to me that that attribute is not included in its essence. And although mind is part of the essence of man, being united to a human body is not strictly speaking part of the essence of mind.

I must also explain what I meant by saying that 'a real distinction cannot be inferred from the fact that one thing is conceived apart from another by an abstraction of the intellect which conceives the thing inadequately. It can be inferred only if we understand one thing apart from another completely, or as a complete thing.' I do not, as M. Arnauld assumes, think that adequate knowledge of a thing is required here. Indeed, the difference between complete and adequate knowledge is that if a piece of knowledge is to be *adequate* it must contain absolutely all the properties which are in the thing which is the object of knowledge. Hence only God can know that he has adequate knowledge of all things.

A created intellect, by contrast, though perhaps it may in fact possess adequate knowledge of many things, can never know it has such knowledge unless God grants it a special revelation of the fact. In order to have adequate knowledge of a thing all that is required is that the power of knowing possessed by the intellect is adequate for the thing in question, and this can easily occur. But in order for the intellect to know it has such knowledge, or that God put nothing in the thing beyond what it is aware of, its power of knowing would have to equal the infinite power of God, and this plainly could not happen on pain of contradiction.

Now in order for us to recognize a real distinction between two things it cannot be required that our knowledge of them be adequate if it is impossible for us to know that it is adequate. And since, as has just been explained, we can never know this, it follows that it is not necessary for our knowledge to be adequate.

Hence when I said that 'it does not suffice for a real distinction that one thing is understood apart from another by an abstraction of the intellect which conceives the thing inadequately,' I did not think this would be taken to imply that *adequate* knowledge was required to establish a real distinction. All I meant was that we need the sort of knowledge that we have not ourselves made *inadequate* by an abstraction of the intellect.

There is a great difference between, on the one hand, some item of knowledge being wholly adequate, which we can never know with certainty to be the case unless it is revealed by God, and, on the other hand, its being adequate enough to enable us to perceive that we have not rendered it inadequate by an abstraction of the intellect.

In the same way, when I said that a thing must be understood *completely*, I did not mean that my understanding must be adequate, but merely that I must understand the thing well enough to know that my understanding is *complete*.

I thought I had made this clear from what I had said just before and just after the passage in question. For a little earlier I had distinguished between 'incomplete' and 'complete' entities, and I had said that for there to be a real distinction between a number of things, each of them must be understood as 'an entity in its own right which is different from everything else.'

And later on, after saying that I had 'a complete understanding of what a body is,' I immediately added that I also 'understood the mind to be a complete thing.' The meaning of these two phrases was identical; that is, I took 'a complete understanding of something' and 'understanding something to be a complete thing' as having one and the same meaning.

But here you may justly ask what I mean by a 'complete thing,' and how I prove that for establishing a real distinction it is sufficient that two things can be understood as 'complete' and that each one can be understood apart from the other.

My answer to the first question is that by a 'complete thing' I simply mean a substance endowed with the forms or attributes which enable me to recognize that it is a substance.

We do not have immediate knowledge of substances, as I have noted elsewhere. We know them only by perceiving certain forms or attributes which must inhere in something if they are to exist; and we call the thing in which they inhere a 'substance.'

But if we subsequently wanted to strip the substance of the attributes through which we know it, we would be destroying our entire knowledge of it. We might be able to apply various words to it, but we could not have a clear and distinct perception of what we meant by these words.

I am aware that certain substances are commonly called 'incomplete.' But if the reason for calling them incomplete is that they are unable to exist on their own, then I confess I find it self-contradictory that they should be substances, that is, things which subsist on their own, and at the same time incomplete, that is, not possessing the power to subsist on their own. It is also possible to call a substance incomplete in the sense that, although it has nothing incomplete about it *qua* substance, it is incomplete in so far as it is referred to some other substance in conjunction with which it forms something which is a unity in its own right.

Thus a hand is an incomplete substance when it is referred to the whole body of which it is a part; but it is a complete substance when it is considered on its own. And in just the same way the mind and the body are incomplete substances when they are referred to a human being which together they make up. But if they are considered on their own, they are complete.

For just as being extended and divisible and having shape etc. are forms or attributes by which I recognize the substance called *body*, so understanding, willing, doubting etc. are forms by which I recognize the substance which is called *mind*. And I understand a thinking substance to be just as much a complete thing as an extended substance.

It is quite impossible to assert, as my distinguished critic maintains, that 'body may be related to mind as a genus is related to a species.' For although a genus can be understood without this or that specific differentia, there is no way in which a species can be thought of without its genus.

For example, we can easily understand the genus 'figure' without thinking of a circle (though our understanding will not be distinct unless it is referred to some specific figure and it will not involve a complete thing unless it also comprises the nature of body). But we cannot understand any specific differentia of the 'circle' without at the same time thinking of the genus 'figure.'

Now the mind can be perceived distinctly and completely (that is, sufficiently for it to be considered as a complete thing) without any of the forms or attributes by which we recognize that body is a substance, as I think I showed quite adequately in the Second Meditation. And similarly a body can be understood distinctly and as a complete thing, without any of the attributes which belong to the mind.

But here my critic argues that although I can obtain some knowledge of myself without knowledge of the body, it does not follow that this knowledge is complete and adequate, so as to enable me to be certain that I am not mistaken in excluding body from my essence. He explains the point by using the example of a triangle inscribed in a semi-circle, which we can clearly and distinctly understand to be right-angled although we do not know, or may even deny, that the square on the hypotenuse is equal to the squares on the other sides. But we cannot infer from this that there could be a right-angled triangle such that the square on the hypotenuse is not equal to the squares on the other sides.

But this example differs in many respects from the case under discussion.

First of all, though a triangle can perhaps be taken concretely as a substance having a triangular shape, it is certain that the property of having the square on the hypotenuse equal to the squares on the other sides is not a substance. So neither the triangle nor the property can be understood as a complete thing in the way in which mind and body can be so understood; nor can either item be called a 'thing' in the sense in which I said 'it is enough that I can understand one thing (that is, a complete thing) apart from another' etc. This is clear from the passage which comes next: 'Besides I find in myself faculties' etc. I did not say that these faculties were *things*, but carefully distinguished them from things or substances.

Secondly, although we can clearly and distinctly understand that a triangle in a semi-circle is right-angled without being aware that the square on the hypotenuse is equal to the squares on the other two sides, we cannot have a clear understanding of a triangle having the square on its hypotenuse equal to the squares on the other sides without at the same time being aware that it is right-angled. And yet we can clearly and distinctly perceive the mind without the body and the body without the mind.

Thirdly, although it is possible to have a concept of a triangle inscribed in a semi-circle which does not include the fact that the square on the hypotenuse is equal to the squares on the other sides, it is not possible to have a concept of the triangle such that no ratio at all is understood to hold between the square on the hypotenuse and the squares on the other sides. Hence, though we may be unaware of what that ratio is, we cannot say that any given ratio does not hold unless we clearly understand that it does not belong to the triangle; and where the ratio is one of equality, this can never be understood. Yet the concept of body includes nothing at all which belongs to the mind, and the concept of mind includes nothing at all which belongs to the body.

So although I said 'it is enough that I can clearly and distinctly understand one thing apart from another' etc., one cannot go on to argue 'yet I clearly and distinctly understand that this triangle is right-angled without understanding that the square on the hypotenuse' etc. There are three reasons for this. First, the ratio between the square on the hypotenuse and the squares on the other sides is not a complete thing. Secondly, we do not clearly understand the ratio to be equal except in the case of a right-angled triangle. And thirdly, there is no way in which the triangle can be distinctly understood if the ratio which obtains between the square on the hypotenuse and the squares on the other sides is said not to hold.

But now I must explain how the mere fact that I can clearly and distinctly understand one substance apart from another is enough to make me certain that one excludes the other.

The answer is that the notion of a *substance* is just this—that it can exist by itself, that is without the aid of any other substance. And there is no one who has ever perceived two substances by means of two different concepts without judging that they are really distinct.

Hence, had I not been looking for greater than ordinary certainty, I should have been content to have shown in the Second Meditation that the mind can be understood as a subsisting thing despite the fact that nothing belonging to the body is attributed to it, and that, conversely, the body can be understood as a subsisting thing despite the fact that nothing belonging to the mind is attributed to it. I should have added nothing more in order to demonstrate that there is a real distinction between the mind and the body, since we commonly judge that the order in which things are mutually related in our perception of them corresponds to the order in which they are related in actual reality. But one of the exaggerated doubts which I put forward in the First Meditation went so far as to make it impossible for me to be certain of this very point (namely whether things do in reality correspond to our perception of them), so long as I was supposing myself to be ignorant of the author of my being. And this is why everything I wrote on the subject of God and truth in the Third, Fourth and Fifth Meditations contributes to the conclusion that there is a real distinction between the mind and the body, which I finally established in the Sixth Meditation.

And yet, says M. Arnauld, 'I have a clear understanding of a triangle inscribed in a semi-circle without knowing that the square on the hypotenuse is equal to the squares on the other sides.' It is true that the triangle is intelligible even though we do not think of the ratio which obtains between the square on the hypotenuse and the squares on the other sides; but it is not intelligible that this ratio should be denied of the triangle. In the case of the mind, by contrast, not only do we understand it to exist without the body, but, what is more, all the attributes which belong to a body can be denied of it. For it is of the nature of substances that they should mutually exclude one another.

M. Arnauld goes on to say: 'Since I infer my existence from the fact that I am thinking, it is certainly no surprise if the idea that I form in this way represents me simply as a thinking thing.' But this is no objection to my argument. For it is equally true that when I examine the nature of the body, I find nothing at all in it which savours of thought. And we can have no better evidence for a distinction between two things than the fact that if we examine either of them, whatever we find in one is different from what we find in the other.

Nor do I see why this argument 'proves too much.' For the fact that one thing can be separated from another by the power of God is the very least that can be asserted in order to establish that there is a real distinction between the two. Also, I thought I was very careful to guard against anyone inferring from this that man was simply 'a soul which makes use of a body.' For in the Sixth Meditation, where I dealt with the distinction between the mind and the body, I also proved at the same time that the mind is substantially united with the body. And the arguments which I used to prove this are as strong as any I can remember ever having read. Now someone who says that a man's arm is a substance that is really distinct from the rest of his body does not thereby deny that the arm belongs to the nature of the whole man. And saying that the arm belongs to the nature of the whole man does not give rise to the suspicion that it cannot subsist in its own right. In the same way, I do not think I proved too much in showing that the mind can exist apart from the body. Nor do I think I proved too little in saying that the mind is substantially united with the body, since that substantial union does not prevent our having a clear and distinct concept of the mind on its own, as a complete thing. The concept is thus very different from that of a surface or a line, which cannot be understood as complete things unless we attribute to them not just length and breadth but also depth.

Finally the fact that 'the power of thought is dormant in infants and extinguished in madmen' (I should say not 'extinguished' but 'disturbed'), does not show that we should regard it as so attached to bodily organs that it cannot exist without them. The fact that thought is often impeded by bodily organs, as we know from our own frequent experience, does not at all entail that it is produced by those organs. This latter view is one for which not even the slightest proof can be adduced.

I must admit, however, that the fact that the mind is closely conjoined with the body, which we experience constantly through our senses, does result in our not being aware of the real distinction between mind and body unless we attentively meditate on the subject. But I think that those who repeatedly ponder on what I wrote in the Second Meditation will be easily convinced that the mind is distinct from the body, and distinct not just by a fiction or abstraction of the intellect: it can be known as a distinct thing because it is in reality distinct.

I will not answer my critic's further observations regarding the immortality of the soul, because they do not conflict with my views. As far as the souls of the brutes are concerned, this is not the place to examine the subject, and, short of giving an account of the whole of physics, I cannot add to the explanatory remarks I made in Part 5 of the *Discourse on the Method*. But to avoid passing over the topic in silence, I will say that I think the most important point is that, both in our bodies and those of the brutes, no movements can occur without the presence of all the organs or instruments which would enable the same movements to be produced in a machine. So even in our own case the mind does not directly move the external limbs, but simply controls the animal spirits which flow from the heart via the brain into the muscles, and sets up certain motions in them; for the spirits are by their nature adapted with equal facility to a great variety of actions. Now a very large number of the motions occurring inside us do not depend in any way on the mind. These include heartbeat, digestion, nutrition, respiration when we are asleep, and also such waking actions as walking, singing and the like, when these occur without the mind attending to them. When people take a fall, and stick out their hands so as to protect their head, it is not reason that instructs them to do this; it is simply that the sight of the impending fall reaches the brain and sends the animal spirits into the nerves in the manner necessary to produce this movement even without any mental volition, just as it would be produced in a machine. And since our own experience reliably informs us

that this is so, why should we be so amazed that the 'light reflected from the body of a wolf onto the eyes of a sheep' should equally be capable of arousing the movements of flight in the sheep?

But if we wish to determine by the use of reason whether any of the movements of the brutes are similar to those which are performed in us with the help of the mind, or whether they resemble those which depend merely on the flow of the animal spirits and the disposition of the organs, then we should consider the differences that can be found between men and beasts. I mean the differences which I set out in Part 5 of the *Discourse on the Method*, for I think these are the only differences to be found. If we do this, it will readily be apparent that all the actions of the brutes resemble only those which occur in us without any assistance from the mind. And we shall be forced to conclude from this that we know of absolutely no principle of movement in animals apart from the disposition of their organs and the continual flow of the spirits which are produced by the heat of the heart as it rarefies the blood. We shall also see that there was no excuse for our imagining that any other principle of motion was to be found in the brutes. We made this mistake because we failed to distinguish the two principles of motion just described; and on seeing that the principle depending solely on the animal spirits and organs exists in the brutes just as it does in us, we jumped to the conclusion that the other principle, which consists in mind or thought, also exists in them. Things which we have become convinced of since our earliest years, even though they have subsequently been shown by rational arguments to be false, cannot easily be eradicated from our beliefs unless we give the relevant arguments our long and frequent attention.

Correspondence between René Descartes and Elisabeth, Princess of Bohemia

Elisabeth to Descartes
[The Hague] 6 May 1643

M. Descartes,

I learned, with much joy and regret, of the plan you had to see me a few days ago, I was touched equally by your charity in willing to share yourself with an ignorant and intractable person and by the bad luck that robbed me of such a profitable conversation. M. Palotti greatly augmented this latter passion in going over with me the solutions you gave him to the obscurities contained in the physics of M. Regius. I would have been better instructed on these from your mouth, as I would have been on a question I proposed to that professor while he was in this town, and regarding which he redirected me to you so that I might receive a satisfactory answer. The shame of showing you so disordered a style prevented me, up until now, from asking you for this favor by letter.

But today M. Palotti has given me such assurance of your goodwill toward everyone, and in particular toward me, that I chased from my mind all considerations other than that of availing myself of it. So I ask you please to tell me how the soul of a human being (it being only a thinking substance) can determine the bodily spirits, in order to bring about voluntary actions. For it seems that all determination of movement happens through the impulsion of the thing moved, by the manner in which it is pushed by that which moves it, or else by the particular qualities and shape of the surface of the latter. Physical contact is required for the first two conditions, extension for the third. You entirely exclude the one [extension] from the notion you have of the soul, and the other [physical contact] appears to me incompatible

with an immaterial thing. This is why I ask you for a more precise definition of the soul than the one you give in your *Metaphysics*, that is to say, of its substance separate from its action, that is, from thought. For even if we were to suppose them inseparable (which is however difficult to prove in the mother's womb and in great fainting spells) as are the attributes of God, we could, in considering them apart, acquire a more perfect idea of them.

Knowing that you are the best doctor for my soul, I expose to you quite freely the weaknesses of its speculations, and hope that in observing the Hippocratic oath, you will supply me with remedies without making them public; such I beg of you to do, as well as to suffer the badgerings of

Your affectionate friend at your service,

Elisabeth.

Descartes to Elisabeth
[Egmond du Hoef] 21 May 1643

Madame,

The favor with which your Highness has honored me, in allowing me to receive her orders in writing, is greater than I would ever have dared to hope; and it is more consoling to my failings than what I had hoped for with passion, which was to receive them by mouth, had I been able to be admitted the honor of paying you reverence, and of offering you my very humble services when I was last in The Hague. For in that case I would have had too many marvels to admire at the same time, and seeing superhuman discourse emerging from a body so similar to those painters give to angels, I would have been delighted in the same manner as it seems to me must be those who, coming from the earth, enter newly into heaven. This would have made me less capable of responding to your Highness, who without doubt has already noticed in me this failing, when I had the honor of speaking with her before; and your clemency wanted to assuage it, in leaving me the traces of your thoughts on a paper, where, in rereading them several times and accustoming myself to consider them, I would be truly less dazzled, but I instead feel more wonder, in noticing that these thoughts not only seem ingenious at the outset, but also even more judicious and solid the more one examines them.

I can say with truth that the question your Highness proposes seems to me that which, in view of my published writings, one can most rightly ask me. For there are two things about the human soul on which all the knowledge we can have of its nature depends: one of which is that it thinks and the other is that, being united to the body, it can act on and be acted upon by it. I have said almost nothing about the latter, and have concentrated solely on making the first better understood, as my principal aim was to prove the distinction between the soul and the body. Only the first was able to serve this aim, and the other would have been harmful to it. But, as your Highness sees so clearly that one cannot conceal anything from her, I will try here to explain the manner in which I conceive of the union of the soul with the body and how the soul has the power [force] to move it.

First, I consider that there are in us certain primitive notions that are like originals on the pattern of which we form all our other knowledge. There are only very few of these notions; for, after the most general—those of being, number, and duration, etc.—which apply to all that we can conceive, we have, for the body in particular, only the notion of extension, from which follow the notions of shape and movement; and for the soul alone, we have only that of thought, in which are included the perceptions of the understanding and the inclinations of the will; and finally, for the soul and the body together, we have only that of their union, on which depends that of the power the soul has to move the body and the body to act on the soul, in causing its sensations and passions.

I consider also that all human knowledge [science] consists only in distinguishing well these notions, and in attributing each of them only to those things to which it pertains. For, when we want to explain some difficulty by means of a notion which does not pertain to it, we cannot fail to be mistaken; just as we are mistaken when we want to explain one of these notions by another; for being primitive, each of them can be understood only through itself. Although the use of the senses has given us notions of extension, of shapes, and of movements that are much more familiar than the others, the principal cause of our errors lies in our ordinarily wanting to use these notions to explain those things to which they do not pertain. For instance, when we want to use the imagination to conceive the nature of the soul, or better, when one wants to conceive the way in which the soul moves the body, by appealing to the way one body is moved by another body. That is why, since, in the *Meditations* which your Highness deigned to read, I was trying to make conceivable the notions which pertain to the soul alone, distinguishing them from those which pertain to the body alone, the first thing that I ought to explain subsequently is the manner of conceiving those which pertain to the union of the soul with the body, without those which pertain to the body alone, or to the soul alone. To which it seems to me that what I wrote at the end of my response to the sixth objections can be useful; for we cannot look for these simple notions elsewhere than in our soul, which has them all in itself by its nature, but which does not always distinguish one from the others well enough, or even attribute them to the objects to which it ought to attribute them.

Thus, I believe that we have heretofore confused the notion of the power with which the soul acts on the body with the power with which one body acts on another; and that we have attributed the one and the other not to the soul, for we did not yet know it, but to diverse qualities of bodies, such as heaviness, heat, and others, which we have imagined to be real, that is to say, to have an existence distinct from that of body, and by consequence, to be substances, even though we have named them qualities. In order to understand them, sometimes we have used those notions that are in us for knowing body, and sometimes those which are there for knowing the soul, depending on whether what we were attributing to them was material or immaterial. For example, in supposing that heaviness is a real quality, of which we have no other knowledge but that it has the power to move a body in which it is toward the center of the earth, we have no difficulty in conceiving how it moves the body, nor how it is joined to it; and we do not think that this happens through a real contact of one surface against another, for we experience in ourselves that we have a specific notion for conceiving that; and I think that we use this notion badly, in applying it to heaviness, which, as I hope to demonstrate in my Physics, is nothing really distinct from body. But I do think that it was given to us for conceiving the way in which the soul moves the body.

If I were to employ more words to explain myself, I would show that I did not sufficiently recognize the incomparable mind of your Highness, and I would be too presumptuous if I dared to think that my response should be entirely satisfactory to her; but I will try to avoid both the one and the other in adding here nothing more, except that if I am capable of writing or saying something that could be agreeable to her, I would always take it as a great honor to take up a pen or to go to The Hague for this end, and that there is nothing in the world which is so dear to me as the power to obey her commandments. But I cannot find a reason to observe the Hippocratic oath that she enjoined me to, since she communicated nothing to me that does not merit being seen and admired by all men. I can only say, on this matter, that esteeming infinitely your letter to me, I will treat it as the misers do their treasures: the more they value them the more they hide them away, and begrudging the rest of the world a view of them, they make it their sovereign good to look at them. Thus, it will be easy for me alone to enjoy the good of seeing it, and my greatest ambition is to be able to say and to be truly, Madame,

Your Highness's very humble and obedient servant,

Descartes.

Elisabeth to Descartes
[The Hague] 10 June 1643

M. Descartes,

Your good will appears not only in your showing me the faults in my reasoning and correcting them, as I expected, but also in your attempt to console me about them in order to make the knowledge of them less annoying for me. But, in detriment to your judgment, you attempt to console me about those faults with false praise. Such false praise would have been necessary to encourage me to work to remedy them had my upbringing, in a place where the ordinary way of conversing has accustomed me to understand that people are incapable of giving one true praise, not made me presume that I could not err in believing the contrary of what people speak, and had it not rendered the consideration of my imperfections so familiar that they no longer upset me more than is necessary to promote the desire to rid myself of them.

This makes me confess, without shame, that I have found in myself all the causes of error which you noticed in your letter, and that as yet I have not been able to banish them entirely, for the life which I am constrained to lead does not leave enough time at my disposal to acquire a habit of meditation in accordance with your rules. Now the interests of my house, which I must not neglect, now some conversations and social obligations which I cannot avoid, beat down so heavily on this weak mind with annoyance or boredom, that it is rendered useless for anything else at all for a long time afterward: this will serve, I hope, as an excuse for my stupidity in being unable to comprehend, by appeal to the idea you once had of heaviness, the idea through which we must judge how the soul (nonextended and immaterial) can move the body; nor why this power [*puissance*] to carry the body toward the center of the earth, which you earlier falsely attributed to a body as a quality, should sooner persuade us that a body can be pushed by some immaterial thing, than the demonstration of a contrary truth (which you promise in your physics) should confirm us in the opinion of its impossibility. In particular, since this idea (unable to pretend to the same perfection and objective reality as that of God) can be feigned due to the ignorance of that which truly moves these bodies toward the center, and since no material cause presents itself to the senses, one would then attribute this power to its contrary, an immaterial cause. But I nevertheless have never been able to conceive of such an immaterial thing as anything other than a negation of matter which cannot have any communication with it. I admit that it would be easier for me to concede matter and extension to the soul than to concede the capacity to move a body and to be moved by it to an immaterial thing. For, if the first is achieved through information, it would be necessary that the spirits,

which cause the movements, were intelligent, a capacity you accord to nothing corporeal. And even though, in your *Metaphysical Meditations*, you show the possibility of the second, it is altogether very difficult to understand that a soul, as you have described it, after having had the faculty and the custom of reasoning well, can lose all of this by some vapors, and that, being able to subsist without the body, and having nothing in common with it, the soul is still so governed by it. But after all, since you have undertaken to instruct me, I entertain these sentiments only as friends which I do not intend to keep, assuring myself that you will explicate the nature of an immaterial substance and the manner of its actions and passions in the body, just as well as you have all the other things that you have wanted to teach. I beg of you also to believe that you could not perform this charity to anyone who felt more the obligation she has to you as, Your very affectionate friend,
Elisabeth.

Descartes to Elisabeth
28 June 1643, Egmond du Hoef

Madame,

I have a very great obligation to your Highness in that she, after having borne my explaining myself badly in my previous letter, concerning the question which it pleased her to propose to me, deigns again to have the patience to listen to me on the same matter, and to give me occasion to note the things which I omitted. Of which the principal ones seem to me to be that, after having distinguished three sorts of ideas or primitive notions which are each known in a particular way and not by a comparison of the one with the other—that is, the notion that we have of the soul, that of the body, and the union which is between the soul and the body—I ought to have explained the difference between these three sorts of notions and between the operations of the soul through which we have them, and to have stated how we render each of them familiar and easy to us. Then, after that, having said why I availed myself of the comparison with heaviness, I ought to have made clear that, even though one might want to conceive of the soul as material (which, strictly speaking, is what it is to conceive its union with the body), one would not cease to know, after that, that the soul is separable from it. That is, I think, all of what your Highness has prescribed me to do here.

First, then, I notice a great difference between these three sorts of notions. The soul is conceived only by the pure understanding [l'entendement]; the body, that is to say, extension, shapes, and motions, can also be known by the understanding alone, but is much better known by the understanding aided by the imagination; and finally, those things which pertain to the union of the soul and the body are known only obscurely by the understanding alone, or even by the understanding aided by the imagination; but they are known very clearly by the senses. From which it follows that those who never philosophize and who use only their senses do not doubt in the least that the soul moves the body and that the body acts on the soul. But they consider the one and the other as one single thing, that is to say, they conceive of their union. For to conceive of the union between two things is to conceive of them as one single thing. Metaphysical thoughts which exercise the pure understanding serve to render the notion of the soul familiar. The study of mathematics, which exercises principally the imagination in its consideration of shapes and movements, accustoms us to form very distinct notions of body. And lastly, it is in using only life and ordinary conversations and in abstaining from meditating and studying those things which exercise the imagination that we learn to conceive the union of the soul and the body.

I almost fear that your Highness will think that I do not speak seriously here. But this would be contrary to the respect I owe her and that I would never neglect to pay her. And I can say with truth that the principal rule I have always observed in my studies, and that which I believe has served me the most in acquiring some bit of knowledge, is that I never spend more than a few hours each day in thoughts which occupy the imagination, and very few hours a year in those which occupy the understanding alone, and that I give all the rest of my time to relaxing the senses and resting the mind; I even count, among the exercises of the imagination, all serious conversations and everything for which it is necessary to devote attention. It is this that has made me retire to the country. For even though in the most populated city in the world I could have as many hours to myself as I now employ in study, I would nevertheless not be able to use them so usefully, since my mind would be distracted by the attention the bothers of life require. I take the liberty to write of this here to your Highness in order to show that I truly admire that, amid the affairs and the cares which persons who are of a great mind and of great birth never lack, she has been able to attend to the meditations which are required in order to know well the distinction between the soul and the body.

But I judged that it was these meditations, rather than these other thoughts which require less attention, that have made her find obscurity in the notion we have of their union; as it does not seem to me that the human mind is capable of conceiving very distinctly, and at the same time, the distinction between the soul and the body and their union, since to do so it is necessary to conceive them as one single thing and at the same time to conceive them as two, which is contradictory. On this matter (supposing your Highness still had the reasons which prove the distinction of the soul and body at the forefront of her mind and not wanting to ask her to remove them from there in order to represent to herself the notion of the union that each always experiences within himself without philosophizing, in knowing that he is a single person who has together a body and a thought, which are of such a nature that this thought can move the body and sense what happens to it), I availed myself in my previous letter of a comparison between heaviness and those other qualities which we commonly imagine to be united to some bodies just as thought is united to our own, and I was not worried that this comparison hangs on qualities that are not real, even though we imagine them so, since I believed that your Highness was already entirely persuaded that the soul is a substance distinct from body.

But since your Highness notices that it is easier to attribute matter and extension to the soul than to attribute to it the capacity to move a body and to be moved by one without having matter, I beg her to feel free to attribute this matter and this extension to the soul, for to do so is to do nothing but conceive it as united with the body. After having well conceived this and having experienced it within herself, it will be easy for her to consider that the matter that she has attributed to this thought is not the thought itself, and that the extension of this matter is of another nature than the extension of this thought, in that the first is determined to a certain place, from which it excludes all other extended bodies, and this is not the case with the second. In this way your Highness will not neglect to return easily to the knowledge of the distinction between the soul and the body, even though she has conceived their union. Finally, though I believe it is very necessary to have understood well once in one's life the principles of metaphysics, since it is these that give us knowledge of God and of our soul, I also believe that it would be very harmful

to occupy one's understanding often in meditating on them. For in doing so, it could not attend so well to the functions of the imagination and the senses. The best is to content oneself in retaining in one's memory and in one's belief the conclusions that one has at one time drawn from such meditation, and then to employ the rest of the time one has for study in those thoughts where the understanding acts with imagination or the senses.

The extreme devotion which I have to serve your Highness makes me hope that my frankness will not be disagreeable to her. She would have here received a longer discourse in which I would have tried to clarify all at once the difficulties of the question asked, but for a new annoyance which I have just learned about from Utrecht, that the magistrate summons me in order to verify what I wrote about one of their ministers—no matter that this is a man who has slandered me very indignantly and that what I wrote about him in my just defense was only too well known to the world—and so I am constrained to finish here, in order that I may go find the means to extricate myself as soon as I can from this chicanery. I am, &c.

Elisabeth to Descartes
[The Hague] 1 July 1643

M. Descartes,

I see that you have not received as much inconvenience from my esteem for your instruction and the desire to avail myself of it, as from the ingratitude of those who deprive themselves of it and would like to deprive the human species of it. I would not have sent you new evidence of my ignorance until I knew you were done with those of that mindset, if Sieur Van Bergen had not obliged me to it earlier, through his kindness in agreeing to stay in town, just until I gave him a response to your letter of 28 June. What you write there makes me see clearly the three sorts of notions that we have, their objects, and how we ought to make use of them.

I also find that the senses show me that the soul moves the body, but they teach me nothing (no more than do the understanding and the imagination) of the way in which it does so. For this reason, I think that there are some properties of the soul, which are unknown to us, which could perhaps overturn what your *Metaphysical Meditation* persuaded me of by such good reasoning: the nonextendedness of the soul. This doubt seems to be founded on the rule that you give there, in speaking of the true and the false, that all error comes to us in forming judgments about that which we do not perceive well enough. Though extension is not necessary to thought, neither is it at all repugnant to it, and so it could be suited to some other function of the soul which is no less essential to it. At the very least, it makes one abandon the contradiction of the Scholastics, that it [the soul] is both as a whole in the whole body and as a whole in each of its parts. I do not excuse myself at all for confusing the notion of the soul with that of the body for the same reason as the vulgar; but this doesn't rid me of the first doubt, and I will lose hope of finding certitude in anything in the world if you, who alone have kept me from being a skeptic, do not answer that to which my first reasoning carried me.

Even though I owe you this confession and thanks, I would think it strongly imprudent if I did not already know your kindness and generosity, equal to the rest of your merits, as much by the experience that I have already had as by reputation. You could not have attested to it in a manner more obliging than by the clarifications and counsel you have imparted to me, which I hold above all as one of the greatest treasures that could be possessed by

Your very affectionate friend at your service,

Elisabeth.

[...]

Study Questions

1. What two sorts of behavior (which could be taken as evidence of mind) would machines never be able to manifest, according to Descartes? Does modern computer technology show that he is wrong?

2. Why does Descartes think that animals manifest no intelligence whatsoever? Perhaps you're familiar with the behavior of dogs or cats to argue for or against this claim.

3. (a) On the second page of the Arnauld excerpt, in the paragraph beginning "As to the first part," Arnauld talks about the relation of a genus to a species. Explain what this is, and why Arnauld supposes that the possibility that mind and body have this sort of relation shows that Descartes's reasoning doesn't prove what he claims it does? (b) Summarize, in your own words, Descartes's reply to this objection, which he gives about halfway into the "Reply" excerpt, starting with the paragraph beginning "It is quite impossible to assert ..." (c) Do you think that Arnauld has successfully shown Descartes's argument to be inconclusive? Explain.

4. Here is an explanation of Arnauld's right-triangle example:

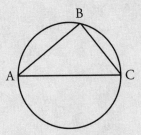

Consider a semicircle (the half-circle above diameter AC). Pick any point on the semicircle; call it B. Draw lines AB, BC. You can have a clear idea that there is a right triangle here ABC, but not know (what's true and provable) that $AC^2 = AB^2 + BC^2$.

Summarize, in your own words, Descartes's reply to this objection. Do you think that Arnauld has successfully shown Descartes's argument to be inconclusive? Explain.

5. (a) Summarize Arnauld's objection to Descartes's claim that the "brutes" (animals) have no souls. (b) Summarize, in your own words, Descartes's reply to this objection. (c) Do you think that Arnauld has successfully shown Descartes's argument to be inconclusive? Explain.

6. Descartes would claim that physicalism—that is, the idea that everything about a human including the "mental" parts is physical—is *unintelligible*. In Paragraph 53 of the *Principles of Philosophy*, he explains why. Summarize this explanation in your own words. Do you think that what is "unintelligible" in Descartes's terms must therefore be false?

7. Why does Descartes bring up the example of heaviness when writing to Elisabeth? Does that analogy help his case at all? Is his account of the movement of heavy objects downward consistent with his mechanistic treatment of physical motion? What is Elisabeth's reply to Descartes's example?

8. Does Descartes really give a satisfactory reply to Elisabeth about the nature of mind-body causal interaction? See if you can summarize his replies. Are they relevant?

Suggested Readings

For Descartes, see Suggested Readings in Chapter 4, page 000. For Elisabeth, see the endnotes following the editors' introduction in this chapter.

6

MATERIALISM AND IDEALISM

Introduction

Descartes's dualism very rapidly became the most influential theory of mind in the early modern period. Yet it was not by any means the only theory being actively discussed. Other philosophers confronting the same problems as Descartes arrived at very different solutions. In this chapter we look at two theories that form an interesting contrast to Descartes's ideas.

Descartes divided the existing world into two distinct substances: mind and matter. Each possesses a single attribute: thought in the case of mind, and spatial extension in the case of matter. All other qualities are simply modes of these two properties. A central problem in Descartes's system is explaining how these two substances interact. How can changes in the motions of material particles in the brain affect modes of consciousness in the mind? And how can acts of will in the mind change the motions of material particles in the brain? The two theories that we look at in this chapter take a direct and simple approach to this problem: eliminate one of the two substances. Theories that take this line and postulate the existence of a single substance are varieties of **monism**. Some monists argue that the mind does not exist as a distinct entity from the physical body. In their view the only existing substance is matter. This position is called **materialism**. Other monists reject the independent existence of material objects, and argue that only minds exist. These latter theories, which reject the existence of matter as a distinct substance and postulate the existence of only minds, are varieties of **idealism**.

When we say that monist theories reject one of the two substances in dualist theories, it is natural to interpret this as asserting one of two claims: that the mind doesn't exist, or that matter doesn't exist. There are theories that make claims something like this, but it is not by any means the most common line. Instead most supporters of monism agree that both mind and matter exist, but they argue that one of the two is simply a mode of the other. Most materialists argue that the mind is not an immaterial substance as Descartes claims, but rather a physical state of the brain (or some other organ). Idealists argue that material objects—tables, chairs, mountains, the human body—are all modes of thought. In their view, material things exist solely as collections of sensations in the minds of perceiving subjects.

We will read selections from two philosophers, Thomas Hobbes and George Berkeley, who responded to Descartes's system by rejecting one of the two substances. Hobbes was a materialist, notorious in his day for the alleged atheism of his theories. Berkeley was a bishop of the Anglican Church, who devoted his philosophical work to challenging the materialist tendencies of the new mathematical sciences. We begin chronologically, with Hobbes.

Thomas Hobbes

Thomas Hobbes (1588–1679) was born in Wiltshire, England. He was a contemporary of Descartes, eight years his senior, and like Descartes rejected the Aristotelian science and philosophy that he learned at school. In his later years he became involved in the political turmoil of the English civil war. Several times he had to flee to the European mainland in fear of imprisonment or death. After his schooling he obtained the position of tutor to the son of the Earl of Devonshire, William Cavendish. Cavendish was a royalist, and Hobbes supported the royalist cause throughout his life.

Hobbes is best known as a political theorist. His major book, *Leviathan*, is a defense of strong central government and the authority of a supreme ruler. According to Hobbes, the basis of politics and morality is a contract formed between members of society to surrender certain individual freedoms in return for peace and security. He is perhaps most popularly remembered for his comment that life in the original state of nature before the formation of civil society was "solitary, poor, nasty, brutish, and short."

Hobbes was greatly impressed by the work of Galileo and Descartes in the new mathematical sciences. Like Descartes, he believed that the deductive method of mathematics could be applied to all areas of human knowledge. However, Hobbes took the lessons of the new science further than Descartes, and concluded that inert particles of matter are *all* that exist. In his view, all properties of things are simply motions of the minute particles that make up physical objects. This aspect of Hobbes's views led to the charge that he was secretly an atheist, and it was common on the continent to denounce ideas on the grounds that they bordered on Hobbesian atheism.

Hobbes's Materialism

In its broadest sense, materialism is more than just a claim about the mind; it is a claim about the whole world. Materialism in this broad sense is the belief that nothing exists but matter. According to materialists, everything that exists is a material thing, and everything that happens occurs in accordance with the laws of physics. If materialism is true, it follows that all aspects of the mind, such as thought, perception and emotion, are in some way aspects of the matter of which the body is composed.

Materialism is a very old doctrine, and varieties of materialism were formulated before Aristotle's time. For example, a group of Greek thinkers of the fifth century BCE, called **atomists**, argued that the world is composed of nothing but simple, minute particles called "atoms." Atoms were claimed to be indestructible, and everything in the world was said to be formed of collections of atoms. All observable features of the world were held to be the product of colli-sions between these tiny, invisible particles. The Greek atomists held that the soul is comprised of very tiny atoms, which reside in the body and which we recognize elsewhere as fire. The view that Hobbes is constructing in *Leviathan* can be seen as a development of ideas that originated with the Greek atomists.

We will read here the opening sections of *Leviathan*, in which Hobbes outlines the basic ideas of his materialist account of the mind. This section forms a background to the political and moral theories of the book. His purpose is to explain the origins and nature of human thoughts and actions in order to place them into the context of a general theory of society.

Hobbes's Theory of Sense

In the opening section of chapter 1 of *Leviathan* Hobbes defines thoughts as "representation[s] ... of some quality, or other accident of a body without us." So thoughts are distinguished by the fact that they represent the outside world. All thought, according to Hobbes, originates in the organs of sense. Ideas are produced by the copying, rearranging, and combining of the materials provided by the senses. This doctrine of the origin of ideas contrasts with that of Descartes. Descartes's arguments rest to a large extent on the clarity and distinctness rule introduced in the Third Meditation. According to Descartes, there are certain "clear and distinct" ideas of mind and matter that are found in the intellect. Because they are not derived from our sensory experiences, these are **innate ideas** that reside in the mind independently of experience or observation. The Method of Doubt becomes Descartes's way of isolating the content of these ideas, and thus they form the basis for all of our knowledge. Hobbes rejects the existence of innate ideas altogether.[1]

The purpose of Part I of *Leviathan* is to explain how each of the many different kinds of thoughts and ideas is constructed from sensations. The fourth paragraph of chapter 1 gives a description of sensations: how they are formed and what they consist of. Here is where Hobbes makes his materialism explicit. According to Hobbes, sensations are produced by the pressure of external objects on the sensory organs. In the case of taste and touch this pressure is direct, whereas in the case of hearing, vision and smell the pressure is transmitted via motions in the surrounding air. This pressure is then communicated through the nerves to the heart and brain, where it encounters a resistance. The counterpressure produced in the brain is the sensation that we experience. Thus in Hobbes's view sensation is nothing more than the motions of material particles in the brain. He says:

> All which qualities, called "sensible" are in the object that causes them but so many motions of the matter, by which it presses our organs diversely. Neither in us that are pressed are they anything else but divers motions; for motion produces nothing but motion.

Notice that in this passage Hobbes is explicitly rejecting Descartes's idea that the motion of particles in the brain causes qualities in the mind that are of a completely different nature. If the origin of sensation is motion, Hobbes contends, then sensation itself must also be motion.

In the final paragraph of chapter 1 Hobbes contrasts his view, not with that of Descartes, but with the beliefs of the Aristotelian universities. He wants his theory to be distinguished from the idea that the qualities and forms of external objects are communicated to the mind via visible or intelligible "species." The concept of species that Hobbes refers to here is a later development of Aristotelianism according to which objects send out likenesses of themselves that are then received by the soul.

Hobbes on Thought and Imagination

But not all of our thoughts and ideas are directly caused by sensory stimulation. Most of the things that go on in the mind are produced from within the mind itself. These include our trains of reason and reflection, and the things we imagine and dream. In the next sections of chapter 1 Hobbes seeks to explain how these are all generated in one way or another by the motions produced in sensation. Here Hobbes has an especially ingenious theory. Thought, imagination, and dreams are all the result of the *inertia* of material particles. In the second paragraph of chapter 2 he says:

> When a body is once in motion, it moves, unless something else hinder it, eternally; and whatsoever hinders it cannot in an instant, but in time and by degrees, quite extinguish it...so also it happens in that motion which is made in the internal parts of a man, then, when he sees, dreams, etc. For, after the object is removed, or the eye shut, we still retain an image of the thing seen, though more obscure than when we see it.

The continuation of the motion produced by a sensation is what we recognize as memory, and "much memory, or memory of many things," Hobbes says, "is called experience." So our knowledge of the world in the form of sensory experience is nothing more than the continuation of motion in the brain as a result of the inertia of matter. Dreams are of the same nature, he claims, and their vividness is due simply to the fact that when we sleep there are no new motions being set up by sensory stimulation.

In chapter 3 Hobbes introduces an explanation of the continuity and connectedness of our thoughts. If thoughts are nothing more than residual motions, why are their contents connected to one another in coherent sequences? One thought follows another according to patterns that reflect relations between the objects in the world that originally produced them. For example, if a person believes that the Eiffel Tower is in Paris, and believes that Paris is east of Berlin, she will in all likelihood also believe that the Eiffel Tower is east of Berlin. How can this relation between our thoughts be explained on the assumption that each of these beliefs is nothing more than motions left over from some previous sensory stimulation? Here again Hobbes appeals to the inertia of the matter of which the thoughts are composed. In the second paragraph he says:

> But as we have no imagination whereof we have not formerly had sense, in whole or in parts, so we have no transition from one imagination to another whereof we never had the like before in our senses. The reason whereof is this. All fancies are motions within us, relics of those made in the sense, and those motions that immediately succeeded one another in the sense continue also together after sense: in so much as the former coming again to take place, and be predominant, the latter followeth, *by coherence of the matter moved*, in such manner as water upon a plane table is drawn which way any one part of it is guided by the finger. [emphasis ours]

So thoughts follow one another in coherent patterns because the particles of matter in the brain stick together. In the remainder of the chapter he explains various aspects of our trains of thought in more detail on the basis of this general idea.

Hobbes's intention, then, is to produce a complete psychology—in the sense of a science of thought—by appealing to nothing more than the inertia of material particles in the nerves and brain. If such a project could be completed, then all aspects of the world would be accounted for in terms of one or two very simple properties of matter. All of the many forms and qualities of Aristotle's systems would be replaced by a single substance with a bare minimum of attributes. And the mysterious metaphysics of Descartes's dualism, with the inexplicable interaction between two completely unlike substances, is abandoned in favor of a system involving only one kind of substance—matter—and one kind of causation—communication of motion.

The Problem with Materialism

As we will see in Part Two of this book, materialism is the predominant view of philosophers and psychologists today, although the specifics of Hobbes's theory have been replaced by bio-chemistry. But now, as then, the difficulty in materialism as an account of mind is the same as its chief virtue, namely, its austerity. On the one side, explanations by their very nature show how something we didn't previously understand can be seen in terms of something we do understand. For example, once the theory of electricity was available, it became possible to explain lightning as electrical discharge. Something previously a mystery became understandable in terms of the same processes that make your hair stick to clothing. Seen in this way, a project like Hobbes's, which reduces all properties of things to inert particles in motion, is just the sort of thing that we should be looking for. In large part, the success of chemical biology in achieving what Hobbes set out to do is the reason for the wide acceptance of materialism today.

But on the other side, the austerity of Hobbes's materialism is precisely what is counterintuitive. Where are the colors, sounds, and fragrances that make up our experience of the world? While Descartes removed these qualities from the physical world, he placed them in the mind. In Hobbes's view, on the other hand, these sensations in the mind are themselves nothing but various motions of material particles. We can explain the problem this way: particle motions are nothing *like* the colors that we see and the sounds we hear. So how can these motions provide an explanation of the colors and sounds of our perceptual experience? The materialism of contemporary philosophers and scientists is different from Hobbes's theory of matter in motion, but here too the same problem arises. In Part Three we will look at recent ideas on how to get around this difficulty.

George Berkeley

George Berkeley (1685–1753) was born nearly a century later than Hobbes and Descartes. By the time he attended university Isaac Newton's theories were universally accepted. He was born to a wealthy family in Kilkenny, Ireland, and attended Trinity College in Dublin. In 1707 he was elected a Fellow of the College and was ordained into the Anglican Church. Most of his philosophical work was completed within six years of his appointment. Thereafter he traveled extensively, and in later life, as Bishop of Cloyne, he devoted his energies to alleviating the poverty of his native Ireland.

Although he enjoyed a successful career in the Church, Berkeley's philosophy never received the response he had hoped. In university Berkeley came to despise what he saw as the absurd consequences of the new mechanical sciences. In his view, the idea that colors, sounds, and other qualities do not exist in matter is a direct violation of common sense. Thus Berkeley saw himself as a champion of common sense, and felt that his philosophy would restore to material things the qualities that the new sciences denied them. But his views were controversial from the outset, leading one commentator to declare him insane. Most of the criticisms of his conclusions, however, were based on misunderstandings. For example, Samuel Johnson thought Berkeley could be dismissed by kicking a stone and declaring, "I refute him *thus*." But in denying the independent existence of matter, Berkeley was not asserting that material objects do not exist as we perceive them and interact with them. To the contrary, his aim was to show that material things exist *exactly* as we perceive them. It was in this that Berkeley believed that he was defending common sense.

We will read selections from a book entitled *A Treatise Concerning the Principles of Human Knowledge*, published in 1710. In this book Berkeley begins with the same premise as Hobbes, that there are no innate ideas; all the materials of thought are drawn from the experiences provided by the senses. But Berkeley draws very different conclusions from this premise than does Hobbes. Once we examine our ideas of material things, he argues, we will see that we have no conception of them except as they are perceived by the senses. For this reason he claims that the idea of matter developed by Descartes and Hobbes is absurd and contradictory.

Berkeley's Theory of Material Objects

Berkeley begins the *Treatise* by asserting that the "objects of human knowledge" are either sensations or they are ideas produced by combining and rearranging the material originally supplied by the senses. In his assertion, Berkeley was following the work of another important British philosopher, John Locke (1632–1704). But Berkeley drew very different and more radical conclusions from this premise than did Locke.

Locke developed more precisely than other philosophers the consequence of the mechanical philosophy that we surveyed in Chapter Three: that the sensations we experience in the mind need not resemble the qualities in the world that produce them. Locke distinguished between what he called **primary qualities** of material objects and **secondary qualities**. The former are qualities such as size, shape, and motion, which *resemble* the sensations we have of them. Secondary qualities are the motions of imperceptible particles in the object that produce sensations of color, taste, fragrance, and sound in the mind. Nothing resembling these sensations exist in the material objects themselves. Berkeley completely rejected this conclusion from the mechanical philosophy, and in so doing rejected the mechanical philosophy itself.

From the premise that all ideas come from our sensory experiences, Berkeley argues in the *Treatise* that the mind has no other object than ideas produced in this way. By this he means that we cannot form coherently in our minds the idea of anything except as it is a "compounding, dividing, or barely representing [i.e., copying]" of sensations. In the same paragraph he concludes that our ideas of material things like apples, stones, trees, and books are simply collections of these sensations. Our idea of an apple, he says, is the idea of "a certain colour, taste, smell, figure and consistence" designated by a single name.[2] In the next paragraph he adds that the only other coherent idea we can form is that of a perceiving mind, for there can only be collections of sensations if there is a mind which receives those sensations.

Esse est percipi

In paragraph 3 Berkeley claims that the only conception we have of something *existing* is the idea of something that falls into one of these two categories—it is either a collection of sensations or a subject that perceives them. This means that we have no idea of material objects existing except as collections of sensations. This provides Berkeley with his most important principle: *esse est percipi*—to be is to be perceived. Material things, he claims, cannot be coherently held to exist except as they are perceived by a thinking subject. Therefore, it is not possible for material objects to "have any existence out of the minds of thinking things which perceive them." In Berkeley's view, then, objects cannot exist if they are not perceived by a sentient mind. Material things are just collections of sensations in the mind. For example, an apple in your hand is not something that exists independently of you or somebody else perceiving it. The apple consists entirely of your perceptions of color, taste, and smell, and those perceptions of other people who have corresponding sensations.

Of course, it is part of common sense that objects do not cease to exist as soon as no one is perceiving them. The room you are in will still exist even after you have left it. But this does not force us to the conclusion that the room exists independently of being perceived. To say that the room exists although no one is perceiving it is simply to say that if someone *were* to turn their perceptions in that direction they *would* perceive it. Objects do not consist of the collection of actual perceptions, but of the collection of all possible perceptions (which, according to Berkeley, resides in the mind of God).

The Rejection of Abstract Ideas

Paragraph 5 describes what Berkeley sees as the origin of the false view that material things can exist independently of their being perceived. The idea derives, he says, from the pernicious doctrine of **abstract ideas**. To see what he has in mind here we can return to Descartes. Recall that in the beginning of the Sixth Meditation Descartes claims that in mathematics we have a clear and distinct idea of physical objects as possessing no other attribute than spatial extension. That is, we can *abstract* the spatial properties of an object from the color, taste, and smell that we perceive it to have.

Once we allow that ideas can be formed by abstraction in this manner, we are led to suppose we can form the idea of material objects by abstracting away *all* of their sensible qualities. This leads us to the idea of an object existing entirely independently of all perceptions. This idea, Berkeley claims, is nonsensical. He says that:

> [A]s it is impossible for me to see or feel anything without an actual sensation of that thing, so is it impossible for me to conceive in my thoughts any sensible thing or object distinct from the sensation or perception of it.

Resemblance and the Primary-Secondary Distinction

In paragraph 8 he considers a counterargument that might be offered. According to Locke and Descartes, the spatial properties of material things are the same as the ideas we form of them. So they might admit that *ideas* exist only in the minds of a thinking subject, but insist that there are objects that *resemble* those ideas which nonetheless exist independently of them. Against this Berkeley claims that we have no idea of resemblance except that between two ideas. "An idea," he says, "can be like nothing but an idea." One shape might resemble another, and one color might resemble another, but we cannot conceive of these shapes and colors except as we are aware of them as ideas in our mind. So the assertion of a resemblance between material objects and ideas is as empty as the claim that we can form an idea of objects abstracted from their sensible appearances.

From paragraph 9 to the end of paragraph 15 he attacks the distinction between what Locke called primary and secondary qualities. Berkeley contends that our descriptions of primary qualities are also nothing more than descriptions of the appearances of things. The ideas of shape, size, and motion, he argues, consist entirely of relations between things as they occur in our sensory experiences. According to Berkeley, all of the arguments to reach the conclusion that *secondary* qualities exist only in the mind can be used in the same way to reach the conclusion that *primary* qualities also exist only in the mind. For our ideas of primary qualities are formed from our sensations in the same way as our ideas of secondary qualities, and thus they have no meaning outside of that context. Thus Berkeley maintains that idealism can be derived as a consequence of following the primary-secondary arguments to their proper conclusion. If color, sound, and fragrance exist only in the mind, so do size, shape, and motion.

Our Knowledge of the External World

In paragraph 18 he adds another argument. Suppose it is possible, as others maintain, for objects to exist independently of our perceptions of them and yet resemble our perceptions. There would still be no way for us to *know* that they exist in this way, for our knowledge of objects is based entirely on our perceptions. We cannot "step outside" our perceptions and compare the way we see things to the way they really are. So it is not necessary to argue that it is *impossible* for there to be spatially extended objects existing outside the mind. Even if this were possible, we would nonetheless have no basis for asserting that such objects really do exist.

We can see this latter argument as taking Descartes's evil demon scenario to a different conclusion than does Descartes himself. In the Sixth Meditation Descartes admits that if the evil demon's illusion is perfect, there is no *noticeable* difference between there being such a demon and there not being such a demon. The correct conclusion to draw from this, Berkeley would say, is that the "perfect illusion" *is* our reality. An amusing article by O.K. Bouwsma makes this point nicely.[3] Imagine a demon who selects a subject called Tom, on whom he will perfect his craft. The demon first constructs a very imperfect illusion, where everything in Tom's world is made of paper. Tom, of course, notices the difference straight away. So the demon works harder, and at last he succeeds in the perfect illusion. Nothing in Tom's experience reveals the illusion in the slightest way. The demon's success, however, is his undoing. For Tom declares that the demon has not created an illusion at all; he has simply recreated Tom's real world. In a similar way, Berkeley concludes in paragraph 20:

In short, if there were external bodies, it is impossible we should ever come to know it; and if there were not, we might have the very same reasons to think there were that we have now.

The perfect illusion and the real world are indistinguishable, and this simply means that there can be no reason to distinguish them.

The Cause of Our Perceptions

In paragraphs 26 through 30 Berkeley turns to the causes of our sensations. As Descartes pointed out, the reason we believe that there is an external world is that our perceptions come independently of our will. It is impossible for us *not* to perceive the world around us. Moreover, the perceptions we have fit together into a coherent whole. As we shift our attention in different directions, our perceptions fit together to form a congruous single picture. And there are regularities in the way things behave that lead us to believe in what we call "laws of nature." These facts lead us to the conclusion that the origin of our perceptions is in something outside of us, and that this something is a single stable whole—what we can call the external world. This is what Samuel Johnson had in mind when he kicked the stone and declared, "I refute him *thus*."

Berkeley agrees that the fact that our sensations are independent of our will demonstrates that they have an external cause. But because the idea of material substance is incoherent, "it remains therefore that the cause of ideas is an incorporeal active substance or Spirit." And the coherence and regularity of our perceptions lead us to admire the "wisdom and benevolence" of this active Spirit. So the facts that lead Johnson to believe in the existence of a material world are taken by Berkeley as proof of the existence of God.

We are forced, then, to choose between two possible causes of our perceptions: God or material substance. Descartes's response to this dilemma in the Sixth Meditation is to argue that if God *is* the cause of our perception, then He is guilty of deception. But this claim depends on the assumption that it is impossible for us not to believe that our perceptions are caused by a material substance. And certainly the stability and coherence of our perceptions lead to the conclusion that they are produced by a stable, enduring substance. This much Berkeley would accept: this substance, he would claim, is God. Descartes must add the argument that we cannot avoid believing that this substance *resembles* our perceptions of it. But, as we have seen, Berkeley's response is that the notion of resemblance has no meaning except as a relation between things in our perceptions.

The Fates of Idealism and Materialism

In the years after his death Berkeley's arguments were picked up and developed by David Hume and Immanuel Kant. Through the influence of Kant, idealism became the predominant philosophical position of German philosophy in the nineteenth century, exemplified in the writings of Fichte, Schelling, and Hegel. Late in the century the principles of German philosophy spread to England where they became widely accepted in the universities. The details of idealism in the nineteenth century take us far from our topic, and are much too complex to summarize here.

In the late nineteenth century, however, the acceptance of idealism declined dramatically. In Britain this was influenced to a large degree by the development of formal logic, which undermined some of the arguments put forward by later idealists. Another factor in the demise of idealism, especially in Germany, was the dramatic developments in the scientific study of the nervous system. These advances in biology led to the replacement of idealism in the universities with materialism, which became the predominant position in the twentieth century. However, some of Berkeley's arguments survive in the views of a group known as the "logical positivists." The philosophy of mind they constructed, called behaviorism, and the evolution of materialism are the subjects of Part Two.

Notes

1. The doctrine that all ideas and knowledge come from sense experience is called *empiricism*. John Locke and George Berkeley were also empiricists. The contrary doctrine, that some ideas and knowledge come from the mind independently of experience, is called *rationalism*. Descartes is perhaps the most well-known rationalist.

2. His point here is precisely the opposite of Descartes's conclusion in "the piece of wax" argument. There Descartes contends that our idea of the piece of wax cannot consist of the collection of sensible qualities, and thus concludes that the mind itself must supply our idea of matter. Berkeley's position is that such an idea is impossible, and so our idea of the wax must consist solely of the collection of what we experience in our sensations.

3. O.K. Bouwsma, "Descartes's Evil Genius," *The Philosophical Review* 58 (1949): pp. 141–51.

THOMAS HOBBES

Selections from *Leviathan*

Part I—Of Man

Chapter 1. Of Sense

Concerning the thoughts of man, I will consider them first singly, and afterwards in train, or dependence upon one another. Singly, they are every one a "representation" or "appearance" of some quality, or other accident of a body without us, which is commonly called an "object." Which object works on the eyes, ears, and other parts of a man's body, and, by diversity of working, produces diversity of appearances.

The original of them all is that which we call "sense," for there is no conception in a man's mind which hath not at first, totally or by parts, been begotten upon the organs of sense. The rest are derived from that original.

To know the natural cause of sense is not very necessary to the business now in hand; and I have elsewhere written of the same at large. Nevertheless, to fill each part of my present method I will briefly deliver the same in this place. The cause of sense is the external body, or object, which presses the organ proper to each sense, either immediately, as in the taste and touch, or mediately, as in seeing, hearing, and smelling; which pressure, by the mediation of the nerves and other strings and membranes of the body continued inwards to the brain and heart, causes there a resistance, or counter-pressure, or endeavor of the heart to deliver itself, which endeavor, because "outward," seems to be some matter without. And this "seeming" or "fancy" is that which men call "sense" and consists, as to the eye, in a "light" or "color figured"; to the ear, in a "sound"; to the nostril, in an "odor"; to the tongue and palate, in a "savor"; and to the rest of the body, in "heat," "cold," "hardness," "softness," and such other qualities as we discern by "feeling." All which qualities, called "sensible" are in the object that causes them but so many several motions of the matter, by which it presses our organs diversely. Neither in us that are pressed are they anything else but divers motions; for motion produces nothing but motion. But their appearance to us is fancy, the same waking that dreaming. And as pressing, rubbing, or striking the eye, makes us fancy a light, and pressing the ear produces a din, so do the bodies also we see or hear produce the same by their strong, though unobserved, action. For if those colors and sounds were in the bodies, or objects that cause them, they could not be severed from them, as by glasses. And in echoes by reflection, we see they are, where we know the thing we see is in one place, the appearance in another. And though at some certain distance the real and very object seem invested with the fancy it begets in us, yet still the object is one thing, the image or fancy is another. So that sense in all cases is nothing else but original fancy, caused, as I have said, by the pressure, that is by the motion, of external things upon our eyes, ears, and other organs thereunto ordained.

But the philosophy schools through all the universities of Christendom, grounded upon certain texts of Aristotle, teach another doctrine, and say, for the cause of "vision," that the thing seen sends forth on every side a "visible species," in English, a "visible show," "apparition," or "aspect," or "a being seen"; the receiving whereof into the eye is "seeing." And for the cause of "hearing," that the thing heard sends forth an "audible species," that is an "audible aspect," or "audible being seen," which entering at the ear makes "hearing." Nay, for the cause of "understanding" also, they say the thing understood sends forth an "intelligible species," that is, an "intelligible being seen," which, coming into the understanding, makes us understand. I say not this as disproving the use of universities; but, because I am to speak hereafter of their office in a commonwealth. I must let you see on all occasions by the way what things would be amended in them, amongst which the frequency of insignificant speech is one.

Chapter 2. Of Imagination

That when a thing lies still, unless somewhat else stir it, it will lie still for ever, is a truth that no man doubts of. But that when a thing is in motion, it will eternally be in motion, unless somewhat else stay it, though the reason be the same, namely that nothing can change itself, is not so easily assented to. For men measure not only other men but all other things, by themselves; and, because they find themselves subject after motion to pain and lassitude, think everything else grows weary of motion, and seeks repose of its own accord; little considering whether it be not some other motion wherein that desire of rest they find in themselves consists. From hence it is that the schools say heavy bodies fall downwards out of an appetite to rest, and to conserve their nature in that place which is most proper for them; ascribing appetite and knowledge of what is good for their conservation, which is more than man has, to things inanimate, absurdly.

When a body is once in motion, it moves, unless something else hinder it, eternally; and whatsoever hinders it cannot in an instant, but in time and by degrees, quite extinguish it; and, as we see in the water though the wind cease the waves give not over rolling for a long time after: so also it happens in that motion which is made in the internal parts of a man, then, when he sees, dreams, etc. For, after the object is removed, or the eye shut, we still retain an image of the thing seen, though more obscure than when we see it. And this is it the Latins call "imagination," from the image made in seeing; and apply the same, though improperly, to all the other senses. But the Greeks call it "fancy," which signifies "appearance," and is as proper to one sense as to another. "Imagination," therefore, is nothing but "decaying sense," and is found in men, and many other living creatures, as well sleeping as waking.

The decay of sense in men waking is not the decay of the motion made in sense, but an obscuring of it in such manner as the light of the sun obscures the light of the stars, which stars do no less exercise their virtue, by which they are visible, in the day than in the night. But because amongst many strokes which our eyes, ears, and other organs, receive from external bodies, the predominant only is sensible; therefore, the light of the sun being predominant, we are not affected with the action of the stars. And any object being removed from our eyes, though the impression it made in us remain, yet other objects more present succeeding and working on us, the imagination of the past is obscured and made weak, as the voice of a man is in the noise of the day. From whence it follows that the longer the time is, after the sight or sense of any object, the weaker is the imagination. For the continual change of man's body destroys in time the parts which in sense were moved; so that distance of time, and of place, hath one and the same effect in us. For as at a great distance of place that which we look at appears dim and without distinction of the smaller parts, and as voices grow weak and inarticulate, so also after great distance of time our imagination of the past is weak; and we

lose, for example, of cities we have seen many particular streets, and of actions many particular circumstances. This "decaying sense," when we would express the thing itself, I mean "fancy" itself, we call "imagination," as I said before; but when we would express the decay, and signify that the sense is fading, old, and past, it is called "memory." So that imagination and memory are but one thing, which for divers considerations hath divers names.

Much memory, or memory of many things, is called "experience." Again, imagination being only of those things which have been formerly perceived by sense, either all at once or by parts at several times, the former, which is the imagining the whole object as it was presented to the sense, is "simple" imagination, as when one imagines a man, or horse, which he hath seen before. The other is "compounded," as when, from the sight of a man at one time, and of a horse at another, we conceive in our mind a Centaur. So when a man compounds the image of his own person with the image of the actions of another man, as when a man images himself a Hercules or an Alexander, which happens often to them that are much taken with reading of romances, it is a compound imagination, and properly but a fiction of the mind. There be also other imaginations that rise in men, though waking, from the great impression made in sense; as, from gazing upon the sun, the impression leaves an image of the sun before our eyes a long time after; and, from being long and vehemently intent upon geometrical figures, a man shall in the dark, though awake, have the images of lines and angles before his eyes; which kind of fancy hath no particular name, as being a thing that doth not commonly fall into men's discourse.

The imaginations of them that sleep are those we call "dreams." And these also, as also all other imaginations, have been before, either totally or by parcels, in the sense. And, because in sense, the brain and nerves, which are the necessary organs of sense, are so benumbed in sleep as not easily to be moved by the action of external objects, there can happen in sleep no imagination, and therefore no dream, but what proceeds from the agitation of the inward parts of man's body; which inward parts, for the connection they have with the brain and other organs, when they be distempered, do keep the same in motion; whereby the imaginations there formerly made, appear as if a man were waking; saving that the organs of sense being now benumbed, so as there is no new object which can master and obscure them with a more vigorous impression, a dream must needs be more clear in this silence of sense than our waking thoughts. And hence it comes to pass that it is a hard matter, and by many thought impossible, to distinguish exactly between sense and dreaming. For my part, when I consider that in dreams I do not often nor constantly think of the same persons, places, objects, and actions, that I do waking, nor remember so long a train of coherent thoughts, dreaming, as at other times, and because waking I often observe the absurdity of dreams, but never dream of the absurdities of my waking thoughts, I am well satisfied, that, being awake, I know I dream not, though when I dream I think myself awake.

And, seeing dreams are caused by the distemper of some of the inward parts of the body, divers distempers must needs cause different dreams. And hence it is that lying cold breeds dreams of fear, and raises the thought and image of some fearful object, the motion from the brain to the inner parts and from the inner parts to the brain being reciprocal; and that, as anger causes heat in some parts of the body when we are awake, so when we sleep the overheating of the same parts causes anger, and raises up in the brain the imagination of an enemy. In the same manner, as natural kindness, when we are awake, causes desire, and desire makes heat in certain other parts of the body; so also too much heat in those parts, while we sleep, raises in the brain an imagination of some kindness shown. In sum, our dreams are the reverse of our waking imaginations, the motion when we are awake beginning at one end, and when we dream at another.

The most difficult discerning of a man's dream from his waking thoughts is, then, when by some accident we observe not that we have slept: which is easy to happen to a man full of fearful thoughts, and whose conscience is much troubled, and that sleeps without the circumstances of going to bed or putting off his clothes, as one that nods in a chair. For he that takes pains, and industriously lays himself to sleep, in case any uncouth and exorbitant fancy come unto him, cannot easily think it other than a dream. We read of Marcus Brutus (one that had his life given him by Julius Caesar, and was also his favorite, and notwithstanding murdered him) how at Philippi, the night before he gave battle to Augustus Caesar, he saw a fearful apparition, which is commonly related by historians as a vision; but, considering the circumstances, one may easily judge to have been but a short dream. For, sitting in his tent, pensive and troubled with the horror of his rash act, it was not hard for him, slumbering in the cold, to dream of that which most frightened him; which fear, as by degrees it made him wake, so also it must needs make the apparition by degrees to vanish; and, having no assurance that he slept, he could have no cause to think it a dream or anything but a vision. And this is no very rare accident; for even they that be perfectly awake, if they be timorous and superstitious, possessed with fearful tales, and alone in the dark, are subject to the like fancies, and believe they see spirits and dead men's ghosts walking in churchyards; whereas it is either their fancy only, or else the knavery of such persons as make use of such superstitious fear to pass disguised in the night to places they would not be known to haunt.

From this ignorance of how to distinguish dreams and other strong fancies from vision and sense, did arise the greatest part of the religion of the Gentiles in time past, that worshipped satyrs, fawns, nymphs, and the like; and now-a-days the opinion that rude people have of fairies, ghosts, and goblins, and of the power of witches. For as for witches, I think not that their witchcraft is any real power; but yet that they are justly punished for the false belief they have that they can do such mischief, joined with their purpose to do it if they can; their trade being nearer to a new religion than to a craft or science. And for fairies and walking ghosts, the opinion of them has, I think, been on purpose either taught, or not confuted, to keep in credit the use of exorcism, of crosses, of holy water, and other such inventions of ghostly men. Nevertheless there is no doubt but God can make unnatural apparitions; but that He does it so often as men need to fear such things more than they fear the stay or change of the course of nature, which He also can stay and change, is no point of Christian faith. But evil men, under pretext that God can do anything, are so bold as to say anything when it serves their turn, though they think it untrue; it is the part of a wise man to believe them no farther than right reason makes that which they say appear credible. If this superstitious fear of spirits were taken away, and with it prognostics from dreams, false prophecies, and many other things depending thereon, by which crafty ambitious persons abuse the simple people, men would be much more fitted than they are for civil obedience.

And this ought to be the work of the schools; but they rather nourish such doctrine. For, not knowing what imagination or the senses are, what they receive they teach; some saying that imaginations rise of themselves and have no cause; others that they rise most commonly from the will, and that good thoughts are blown (inspired) into a man by God, and evil thoughts by the devil; or that good thoughts are poured (infused) into a man by God, and evil ones by the devil. Some say the senses receive the species of things, and deliver them to the common sense, and the common sense delivers them over to the fancy, and the fancy to the memory, and the memory to the judgment, like handling of things from one to another, with many words making nothing understood.

The imagination that is raised in man, or any other creature endowed with the faculty of imagining, by words or other voluntary signs, is that we generally call "understanding," and is common to man and beast. For a dog by custom will understand the call or the rating of his master; and so will many other beasts. That understanding which is peculiar to man, is the understanding not only his will, but his conceptions and thoughts, by the sequel and contexture of the names of things into affirmations, negations, and other forms of speech; and of this kind of understanding I shall speak hereafter.

Chapter 3. Of the Consequence or Train of Imaginations

By "consequence," or "train," of thoughts I understand that succession of one thought to another which is called, to distinguish it from discourse in words, "mental discourse."

When a man thinks on anything whatever, his next thought after is not altogether so casual as it seems to be. Not every thought to every thought succeeds indifferently. But as we have no imagination whereof we have not formerly had sense, in whole or in parts, so we have no transition from one imagination to another whereof we never had the like before in our senses. The reason whereof is this. All fancies are motions within us, relics of those made in the sense, and those motions that immediately succeeded one another in the sense continue also together after sense: in so much as the former coming again to take place, and be predominant, the latter followeth, by coherence of the matter moved, in such manner as water upon a plane table is drawn which way any one part of it is guided by the finger. But because in sense to one and the same thing perceived, sometimes one thing sometimes another, succeeds, it comes to pass in time that in the imagining of anything there is no certainty what we shall imagine next: only this is certain, it shall be something that succeeded the same before, at one time or another. This train of thoughts, or mental discourse, is of two sorts. The first is "unguided," "without design," and inconstant; wherein there is no passionate thought, to govern and direct those that follow, to itself, as the end and scope of some desire or other passion: in which case the thoughts are said to wander, and seem impertinent one to another as in a dream. Such are commonly the thoughts of men that are not only without company but also without care of anything; though even then their thoughts are as busy as at other times, but without harmony; as the sound which a lute out of tune would yield to any man, or in tune to one that could not play. And yet in this wild ranging of the mind a man may oft-times perceive the way of it, and the dependence of one thought upon another. For in a discourse of our present civil war, what could seem more impertinent than to ask, as one did, what was the value of a Roman penny. Yet the coherence to me was manifest enough. For the thought of the war introduced the thought of the delivering up the king to his enemies, the thought of that brought in the thought of the delivering up of Christ; and that again the thought of the thirty pence, which was the price of that treason; and thence easily followed that malicious question; and all this in a moment of time—for thought is quick.

The second is more constant; as being "regulated" by some desire and design. For the impression made by such things as we desire, or fear, is strong and permanent, or, if it cease for a time, of quick return: so strong it is sometimes as to hinder and break our sleep. From desire arises the thought of some means we have seen produce the like of that which we aim at; and from the thought of that, the thought of means to that mean, and so continually till we come to some beginning within our own power. And because the end, by the greatness of the impression, comes often to mind, in case our thoughts begin to wander, they are quickly again reduced into the way: which observed by one of the Seven Wise Men, made him give men this precept, which is now worn out, Respice finem; that is to say, in all your actions look often upon what you would have as the thing that directs all your thoughts in the way to attain it.

GEORGE BERKELEY

Selections from *A Treatise Concerning the Principles of Human Knowledge*

Part One

1 It is evident to any one who takes a survey of the *objects* of human knowledge, that they are either ideas actually imprinted on the senses: or else such as are perceived by attending to the passions and operations of the mind; or lastly, ideas formed by help of memory and imagination—either compounding, dividing, or barely representing those originally perceived in the aforesaid ways. By sight I have the ideas of light and colors with their several degrees and variations. By touch I perceive hard and soft, heat and cold, motion and resistance, and of all these more and less either as to quantity or degree. Smelling furnishes me with odors; the palate with tastes; and hearing conveys sounds to the mind in all their variety of tone and composition. And as several of these are observed to accompany each other, they come to be marked by one name, and so to be reputed as one thing. Thus, for example a certain color, taste, smell, figure and consistence having been observed to go together, are accounted one distinct thing, signified by the name *apple*: other collections of ideas constitute a stone, a tree, a book, and the like sensible things—which as they are pleasing or disagreeable excite the passions of love, hatred, joy, grief, and so forth.

2 But, besides all that endless variety of ideas or objects of knowledge, there is likewise something which knows or perceives them, and exercises divers operations, as willing, imagining, remembering, about them. This perceiving, active being is what I call *mind, spirit, soul,* or *myself.* By which words I do not denote any one of my ideas, but a thing entirely distinct from them, wherein, they exist, or, which is the same thing, whereby they are perceived—for the existence of an idea consists in being perceived.

3 That neither our thoughts, nor passions, nor ideas formed by the imagination, exist without the mind, is what everybody will allow. And it seems no less evident that the various sensations or ideas imprinted on the sense, however blended or combined together (that is, whatever objects they compose), cannot exist otherwise than in a mind perceiving them.—I think an intuitive knowledge may be obtained of this by any one that shall attend to what is meant by the term *exists*, when applied to sensible things. The table I write on I say exists, that is, I see and feel it; and if I were out of my study I should say it existed— meaning thereby that if I was in my study I might perceive it, or that some other spirit actually does perceive it. There was an odor, that is, it was smelt; there was a sound, that is, it was heard; a color or figure, and it was perceived by sight or touch. This is all that I can understand by these and the like expressions. For as to what is said of the absolute existence of unthinking things without any relation to their being perceived, that seems perfectly unintelligible. Their *esse* is *percipi*, nor is it possible they should have any existence out of the minds of thinking things which perceive them.

4 It is indeed an opinion strangely prevailing amongst men, that houses, mountains, rivers, and in a word all sensible objects, have an existence, natural or real, distinct from their being perceived by the understanding. But, with how

great an assurance and acquiescence soever this principle may be entertained in the world, yet whoever shall find in his heart to call it in question may, if I mistake not, perceive it to involve a manifest contradiction. For, what are the forementioned objects but the things we perceive by sense? and what do we perceive besides our own ideas or sensations? and is it not plainly repugnant that any one of these, or any combination of them, should exist unperceived?

5 If we thoroughly examine this tenet it will, perhaps, be found at bottom to depend on the doctrine of *abstract ideas*. For can there be a nicer strain of abstraction than to distinguish the existence of sensible objects from their being perceived, so as to conceive them existing unperceived? Light and colors, heat and cold, extension and figures—in a word the things we see and feel—what are they but so many sensations, notions, ideas, or impressions on the sense? and is it possible to separate, even in thought, any of these from perception? For my part, I might as easily divide a thing from itself. I may, indeed, divide in my thoughts, or conceive apart from each other, those things which, perhaps I never perceived by sense so divided. Thus, I imagine the trunk of a human body without the limbs, or conceive the smell of a rose without thinking on the rose itself. So far, I will not deny, I can abstract—if that may properly be called *abstraction* which extends only to the conceiving separately such objects as it is possible may really exist or be actually perceived asunder. But my conceiving or imagining power does not extend beyond the possibility of real existence or perception. Hence, as it is impossible for me to see or feel anything without an actual sensation of that thing, so is it impossible for me to conceive in my thoughts any sensible thing or object distinct from the sensation or perception of it.

6 Some truths there are so near and obvious to the mind that a man need only open his eyes to see them. Such I take this important one to be, viz., that all the choir of heaven and furniture of the earth, in a word all those bodies which compose the mighty frame of the world, have not any subsistence without a mind, that their *being* is to be perceived or known; that consequently so long as they are not actually perceived by me, or do not exist in my mind or that of any other created spirit, they must either have no existence at all, or else subsist in the mind of some Eternal Spirit—it being perfectly unintelligible, and involving all the absurdity of abstraction, to attribute to any single part of them an existence independent of a spirit. To be convinced of which, the reader need only reflect, and try to separate in his own thoughts the *being* of a sensible thing from its *being perceived*.

7 From what has been said it follows there is not any other Substance than Spirit, or that which perceives. But, for the fuller proof of this point, let it be considered the sensible qualities are color, figure, motion, smell, taste, etc., *i.e.,* the ideas perceived by sense. Now, for an idea to exist in an unperceiving thing is a manifest contradiction, for to have an idea is all one as to perceive; that therefore wherein color, figure, and the like qualities exist must perceive them; hence it is clear there can be no unthinking substance or *substratum* of those ideas.

8 But, say you, though the ideas themselves do not exist without the mind, yet there may be things like them, whereof they are copies or resemblances, which things exist without the mind in an unthinking substance. I answer, an idea can be like nothing but an idea; a color or figure can be like nothing but another color or figure. If we look but never so little into our thoughts, we shall find it impossible for us to conceive a likeness except only between our ideas. Again, I ask whether those supposed originals or external things, of which our ideas are the pictures or representations, be themselves perceivable or no? If they are, then

they are ideas and we have gained our point; but if you say they are not, I appeal to any one whether it be sense to assert a color is like something which is invisible; hard or soft, like something which is intangible; and so of the rest.

9 Some there are who make a distinction between *primary* and *secondary* qualities. By the former they mean extension, figure, motion, rest, solidity or impenetrability, and number; by the latter they denote all other sensible qualities, as colors, sounds, tastes, and so forth. The ideas we have of these they acknowledge not to be the resemblances of anything existing without the mind, or unperceived, but they will have our ideas of the primary qualities to be patterns or images of things which exist without the mind, in an unthinking substance which they call Matter. By Matter, therefore, we are to understand an inert, senseless substance, in which extension, figure, and motion do actually subsist. But it is evident from what we have already shown, that extension, figure, and motion are only ideas existing in the mind, and that an idea can be like nothing but another idea, and that consequently neither they nor their archetypes can exist in an unperceiving substance. Hence, it is plain that the very notion of what is called *Matter* or *corporeal substance* involves a contradiction in it.

10 They who assert that figure, motion, and the rest of the primary or original qualities do exist without the mind in unthinking substances, do at the same time acknowledge that colors, sounds, heat, cold, and suchlike secondary qualities, do not—which they tell us are sensations existing in the mind alone, that depend on and are occasioned by the different size, texture, and motion of the minute particles of matter. This they take for an undoubted truth, which they can demonstrate beyond all exception. Now, if it be certain that those original qualities are inseparably united with the other sensible qualities, and not, even

in thought, capable of being abstracted from them, it plainly follows that they exist only in the mind. But I desire any one to reflect and try whether he can, by any abstraction of thought, conceive the extension and motion of a body without all other sensible qualities. For my own part, I see evidently that it is not in my power to frame an idea of a body extended and moving, but I must withal give it some color or other sensible quality which is acknowledged to exist only in the mind. In short, extension, figure, and motion, abstracted from all other qualities, are inconceivable. Where therefore the other sensible qualities are, there must these be also, to wit, in the mind and nowhere else.

11 Again, *great* and *small*, *swift* and *slow*, are allowed to exist nowhere without the mind, being entirely relative, and changing as the frame or position of the organs of sense varies. The extension therefore which exists without the mind is neither great nor small, the motion neither swift nor slow, that is, they are nothing at all. But, say you, they are extension in general, and motion in general: thus we see how much the tenet of extended movable substances existing without the mind depends on the strange doctrine of *abstract ideas*. And here I cannot but remark how nearly the vague and indeterminate description of Matter or corporeal substance, which the modern philosophers are run into by their own principles, resembles that antiquated and so much ridiculed notion of *materia prima*, to be met with in Aristotle and his followers. Without extension solidity cannot be conceived; since therefore it has been shewn that extension exists not in an unthinking substance, the same must also be true of solidity.

12 That number is entirely the creature of the mind, even though the other qualities be allowed to exist without, will be evident to whoever considers that the same thing bears a different denomination of number as the mind views it with different respects. Thus, the same exten-

sion is one, or three, or thirty-six, according as the mind considers it with reference to a yard, a foot or an inch. Number is so visibly relative, and dependent on men's understanding, that it is strange to think how any one should give it an absolute existence without the mind. We say one book, one page, one line, etc.; all these are equally units, though some contain several of the others. And in each instance, it is plain, the unit relates to some particular combination of ideas arbitrarily put together by the mind.

13 Unity I know some will have to be a simple or uncompounded idea, accompanying all other ideas into the mind. That I have any such idea answering the word unity I do not find; and if I had, methinks I could not miss finding it: on the contrary, it should be the most familiar to my understanding, since it is said to accompany all other ideas, and to be perceived by all the ways of sensation and reflexion. To say no more, it is an *abstract* idea.

14 I shall farther add, that, after the same manner as modern philosophers prove certain sensible qualities to have no existence in Matter, or without the mind, the same thing may be likewise proved of all other sensible qualities whatsoever. Thus, for instance, it is said that heat and cold are affections only of the mind, and not at all patterns of real beings, existing in the corporeal substances which excite them, for that the same body which appears cold to one hand seems warm to another. Now, why may we not as well argue that figure and extension are not patterns or resemblances of qualities existing in Matter, because to the same eye at different stations or eyes of a different texture at the same station, they appear various, and cannot therefore be the images of anything settled and determinate without the mind? Again, it is proved that sweetness is not really in the sapid thing, because the thing remaining unaltered the sweetness is changed into bitter, as in case of a fever or otherwise vitiated palate. Is it not as reasonable to say that motion is not without the mind, since if the succession of ideas in the mind become swifter, the motion, it is acknowledged, shall appear slower without any alteration in any external object?

15 In short, let any one consider those arguments which are thought manifestly to prove that colors and taste exist only in the mind, and he shall find they may with equal force be brought to prove the same thing of extension, figure, and motion. Though it must be confessed this method of arguing does not so much prove that there is no extension or color in an outward object, as that we do not know by sense which is the true extension or color of the object. But the arguments foregoing plainly shew it to be impossible that any color or extension at all, or other sensible quality whatsoever, should exist in an unthinking subject without the mind, or in truth, that there should be any such thing as an outward object.

16 But let us examine a little the received opinion.—It is said extension is a mode or accident of Matter, and that Matter is the substratum that supports it. Now I desire that you would explain to me what is meant by Matter's supporting extension. Say you, I have no idea of Matter and therefore cannot explain it. I answer, though you have no positive, yet, if you have any meaning at all, you must at least have a relative idea of Matter; though you know not what it is, yet you must be supposed to know what relation it bears to accidents, and what is meant by its supporting them. It is evident "support" cannot here be taken in its usual or literal sense—as when we say that pillars support a building; in what sense therefore must it be taken?

17 If we inquire into what the most accurate philosophers declare themselves to mean by material substance, we shall find them acknowledging they have no other meaning annexed to those sounds but the idea of Being

in general, together with the relative notion of its supporting accidents. The general idea of Being appeareth to me the most abstract and incomprehensible of all other; and as for its supporting accidents, this, as we have just now observed, cannot be understood in the common sense of those words; it must therefore be taken in some other sense, but what that is they do not explain. So that when I consider the two parts or branches which make the signification of the words material substance, I am convinced there is no distinct meaning annexed to them. But why should we trouble ourselves any farther, in discussing this material substratum or support of figure and motion, and other sensible qualities? Does it not suppose they have an existence without the mind? And is not this a direct repugnancy, and altogether inconceivable?

18 But, though it were possible that solid, figured, movable substances may exist without the mind, corresponding to the ideas we have of bodies, yet how is it possible for us to know this? Either we must know it by sense or by reason. As for our senses, by them we have the knowledge only of our sensations, ideas, or those things that are immediately perceived by sense, call them what you will: but they do not inform us that things exist without the mind, or unperceived, like to those which are perceived. This the materialists themselves acknowledge. It remains therefore that if we have any knowledge at all of external things, it must be by reason, inferring their existence from what is immediately perceived by sense. But what reason can induce us to believe the existence of bodies without the mind, from what we perceive, since the very patrons of Matter themselves do not pretend there is any necessary connexion betwixt them and our ideas? I say it is granted on all hands (and what happens in dreams, phrensies, and the like, puts it beyond dispute) that it is possible we might be affected with all the ideas we have now, though there were no bodies existing without resembling them. Hence, it is evident the supposition of external bodies is not necessary for the producing our ideas; since it is granted they are produced sometimes, and might possibly be produced always in the same order, we see them in at present, without their concurrence.

19 But, though we might possibly have all our sensations without them, yet perhaps it may be thought easier to conceive and explain the manner of their production, by supposing external bodies in their likeness rather than otherwise; and so it might be at least probable there are such things as bodies that excite their ideas in our minds. But neither can this be said; for, though we give the materialists their external bodies, they by their own confession are never the nearer knowing how our ideas are produced; since they own themselves unable to comprehend in what manner body can act upon spirit, or how it is possible it should imprint any idea in the mind. Hence it is evident the production of ideas or sensations in our minds can be no reason why we should suppose Matter or corporeal substances, since that is acknowledged to remain equally inexplicable with or without this supposition. If therefore it were possible for bodies to exist without the mind, yet to hold they do so, must needs be a very precarious opinion; since it is to suppose, without any reason at all, that God has created innumerable beings that are entirely useless, and serve to no manner of purpose.

20 In short, if there were external bodies, it is impossible we should ever come to know it; and if there were not, we might have the very same reasons to think there were that we have now. Suppose—what no one can deny possible—an intelligence without the help of external bodies, to be affected with the same train of sensations or ideas that you are, imprinted in the same order and with like vividness in his mind. I ask whether that intelligence hath not all the reason to believe the existence of corpo-

real substances, represented by his ideas, and exciting them in his mind, that you can possibly have for believing the same thing? Of this there can be no question—which one consideration were enough to make any reasonable person suspect the strength of whatever arguments he may think himself to have, for the existence of bodies without the mind.

21 Were it necessary to add any farther proof against the existence of Matter after what has been said, I could instance several of those errors and difficulties (not to mention impieties) which have sprung from that tenet. It has occasioned numberless controversies and disputes in philosophy, and not a few of far greater moment in religion. But I shall not enter into the detail of them in this place, as well because I think arguments *a posteriori* are unnecessary for confirming what has been, if I mistake not, sufficiently demonstrated *a priori*, as because I shall hereafter find occasion to speak somewhat of them.

22 I am afraid I have given cause to think I am needlessly prolix in handling this subject. For, to what purpose is it to dilate on that which may be demonstrated with the utmost evidence in a line or two, to any one that is capable of the least reflexion? It is but looking in to your own thoughts, and so trying whether you can conceive it possible for a sound, or figure, or motion, or color to exist without the mind or unperceived. This easy trial may perhaps make you see that what you contend for is a downright contradiction. Insomuch that I am content to put the whole upon this issue:—If you can but conceive it possible for one extended movable substance, or, in general, for any one idea, or anything like an idea, to exist otherwise than in a mind perceiving it, I shall readily give up the cause. And, as for all that compages [complex system] of external bodies you contend for, I shall grant you its existence, though you cannot either give me any reason why you believe it exists, or assign any use to it when it

is supposed to exist. I say, the bare possibility of your opinions being true shall pass for an argument that it is so.

23 But, say you, surely there is nothing easier than for me to imagine trees, for instance, in a park, or books existing in a closet, and nobody by to perceive them. I answer, you may so, there is no difficulty in it: but what is all this, I beseech you, more than framing in your mind certain ideas which you call books and trees, and the same time omitting to frame the idea of any one that may perceive them? But do not you yourself perceive or think of them all the while? This therefore is nothing to the purpose: it only shews you have the power of imagining or forming ideas in your mind: but it does not shew that you can conceive it possible the objects of your thought may exist without the mind. To make out this, it is necessary that you conceive them existing unconceived or unthought of, which is a manifest repugnancy. When we do our utmost to conceive the existence of external bodies, we are all the while only contemplating our own ideas. But the mind taking no notice of itself, is deluded to think it can and does conceive bodies existing unthought of or without the mind, though at the same time they are apprehended by or exist in itself. A little attention will discover to any one the truth and evidence of what is here said, and make it unnecessary to insist on any other proofs against the existence of *material substance*.

24 It is very obvious, upon the least inquiry into our thoughts, to know whether it is possible for us to understand what is meant by the *absolute existence of sensible objects in themselves, or without the mind*. To me it is evident those words mark out either a direct contradiction, or else nothing at all. And to convince others of this, I know no readier or fairer way than to entreat they would calmly attend to their own thoughts; and if by this attention the emptiness or repugnancy of those expressions does appear, surely nothing more is requisite for the

conviction. It is on this therefore that I insist, to wit, that the absolute existence of unthinking things are words without a meaning, or which include a contradiction. This is what I repeat and inculcate, and earnestly recommend to the attentive thoughts of the reader.

25 All our ideas, sensations, notions, or the things which we perceive, by whatsoever names they may be distinguished, are visibly inactive—there is nothing of power or agency included in them. So that one idea or object of thought cannot produce or make any alteration in another. To be satisfied of the truth of this, there is nothing else requisite but a bare observation of our ideas. For, since they and every part of them exist only in the mind, it follows that there is nothing in them but what is perceived: but whoever shall attend to his ideas, whether of sense or reflexion, will not perceive in them any power or activity; there is, therefore, no such thing contained in them. A little attention will discover to us that the very being of an idea implies passiveness and inertness in it, insomuch that it is impossible for an idea to do anything, or, strictly speaking, to be the cause of anything: neither can it be the resemblance or pattern of any active being, as is evident from sect. 8. Whence it plainly follows that extension, figure, and motion cannot be the cause of our sensations. To say, therefore, that these are the effects of powers resulting from the configuration, number, motion, and size of corpuscles, must certainly be false.

26 We perceive a continual succession of ideas, some are anew excited, others are changed or totally disappear. There is therefore some cause of these ideas, whereon they depend, and which produces and changes them. That this cause cannot be any quality or idea or combination of ideas, is clear from the preceding section. It must therefore be a substance; but it has been shewn that there is no corporeal or material substance: it remains therefore that the cause of ideas is an incorporeal active substance or Spirit.

27 A spirit is one simple, undivided, active being—as it perceives ideas it is called the *understanding*, and as it produces or otherwise operates about them it is called the *will*. Hence there can be no *idea* formed of a soul or spirit, for all ideas whatever, being passive and inert (*vide* sect. 25), they cannot represent unto us, by way of image or likeness, that which acts. A little attention will make it plain to any one, that to have an idea which shall be like that active principle of motion and change of ideas is absolutely impossible. Such is the nature of *spirit*, or that which acts, that it cannot be of itself perceived, but only by the effects which it produceth. If any man shall doubt of the truth of what is here delivered, let him but reflect and try if he can frame the idea of any power or active being, and whether he has ideas of two principal powers, marked by the names *will* and *understanding*, distinct from each other as well as from a third idea of Substance or Being in general, with a relative notion of its supporting or being the subject of the aforesaid powers—which is signified by the name *soul* or *spirit*. This is what some hold; but, so far as I can see, the words *will, soul, spirit*, do not stand for different ideas, or, in truth, for any idea at all, but for something which is very different from ideas, and which, being an agent, cannot be like unto, or represented by, any idea whatsoever. Though it must be owned at the same time that we have some *notion* of soul, spirit, and the operations of the mind: such as willing, loving, hating—inasmuch as we know or understand the meaning of these words.

28 I find I can excite ideas in my mind at pleasure, and vary and shift the scene as oft as I think fit. It is no more than willing, and straightway this or that idea arises in my fancy; and by the same power it is obliterated and makes way for another. This making and unmaking of ideas doth very properly denominate the mind active. Thus much is certain and grounded on experience: but when we think of unthinking agents

or of exciting ideas exclusive of volition, we only amuse ourselves with words.

29 But, whatever power I may have over my own thoughts, I find the ideas actually perceived by Sense have not a like dependence on my will. When in broad daylight I open my eyes, it is not in my power to choose whether I shall see or no, or to determine what particular objects shall present themselves to my view; and so likewise as to the hearing and other senses; the ideas imprinted on them are not creatures of my will. There is therefore some *other* Will or Spirit that produces them.

30 The ideas of Sense are more strong, lively, and distinct than those of the imagination; they have likewise a steadiness, order, and coherence, and are not excited at random, as those which are the effects of human wills often are, but in a regular train or series, the admirable connexion whereof sufficiently testifies the wisdom and benevolence of its Author. Now the set rules or established methods wherein the Mind we depend on excites in us the ideas of sense, are called the *laws of nature*: and these we learn by experience, which teaches us that such and such ideas are attended with such and such other ideas, in the ordinary course of things.

[...]

Study Questions

1. (a) Give a brief outline of Hobbes's account of how perception works. (b) Compare his with Descartes's account. (c) Hobbes and Descartes come to a very different view of whether and how perception can result in knowledge. What's the difference? Is this a consequence of differences in their accounts of how it works?
2. Materialism is sometimes described as the view that only material things and their material interactions exist. Does this make Hobbes a materialist? Explain.
3. Berkeley's departure from our ordinary views is evident in the very first sentence of the selection here. Explain in your own words what he means, and compare it with our ordinary view.
4. What would Berkeley's answer be to the clichéd question, "If a tree falls in the forest, and nobody is around to hear it, does it make a sound?" For that matter, can the *tree* exist unperceived? Relate the following famous philosophical limerick to Berkeley's solution to this problem.

> There was a young man who said,
> God Must think it exceedingly odd
> To find that this tree Continues to be
> When there's no one around in the quad.
> Dear Sir: Your astonishment's odd;
> *I* am always about in the quad.
> And that's why the tree Continues to be,
> Since observed by Yours faithfully, God.

5. What is an *abstract idea*? Why do Berkeley's central principles imply that these do not exist?

6. What is "material (unthinking) substance or substratum"? Summarize Berkeley's arguments that there can be no such thing.

7. What is the distinction between primary and secondary qualities supposed to be? Where does this distinction show up in our previous readings? In your own words, give Berkeley's reaction to this distinction.

8. Summarize Berkeley's argument concerning the existence of mind-independent matter in sections 18–20 of his excerpt. What exactly does he try to prove? Do you agree with his reasoning and his conclusion? Explain.

9. How would Berkeley answer this objection: If the only thing I know about is the contents of my own mind, then how could I distinguish between my imagination and what I call (and what you deny is) perception of the outside world?

Suggested Readings

A very early and influential materialist was Democritus (c. 460–c. 370 BCE). See Jonathan Barnes, *Early Greek Philosophy* (London: Penguin, 1987) for a discussion of his thought and influence.

Lucretius's philosophical poem *De Rerum Natura* advocates and explains Democritean materialism at length. See Lucretius, *The Nature of Things* (Hackett Publishing Company, 2001) for a translation.

A more recent materialist work is Baron Paul d'Holbach's anonymously published *Le Système de la Nature* (*The System of Nature*).

Hobbes's philosophy of mind is discussed in:

David M. Rosenthal, "The Identity Theory," in *A Companion to the Philosophy of Mind*, Samuel D. Guttenplan (ed). (Oxford: Blackwell, 1994).

Daniel Garber, "Soul and Mind: Life and Thought in the Seventeenth Century" and Charles Mccracken, "Knowledge of the Soul"; both in *The Cambridge History of Seventeenth-Century Philosophy*, Daniel Garber (ed). (Cambridge: Cambridge University Press, 1998).

Works on Berkeley:

Robert Schwartz, *Vision: Variations on Some Berkeleian Themes*. (Cambridge: Blackwell, 1994).

Kenneth P. Winkler, *Berkeley: An Interpretation*. (Oxford: Clarendon, 1994).

Geoffrey J. Warnock, *Berkeley*. (Harmondsworth: Penguin, 1969).

David Berman, *Berkeley*. (Oxford: Routledge, 1999).

Colin Murray Turbayne (ed.), *Berkeley: Critical and Interpretive Essays*. (Minneapolis: University of Minnesota Press, 1982).

PART TWO
RECENT THEORIES OF MIND

7

BEHAVIORISM AND LINGUISTIC PHILOSOPHY

Against Metaphysics

The philosophies of mind constructed by Plato, Aristotle, and Descartes are each examples of what we call **metaphysics**. This term, which originates with the ancient Greeks, refers to theories that attempt to describe the ultimate nature of reality. The idea is clearly illustrated by Descartes's philosophy. In defending the new science and describing the nature of the soul, Descartes was not content to rely on the success of scientific experiments. Instead, he wanted to prove conclusively that the nature of reality conforms to the methods of science—that the language of mathematics really *is* the language of nature. Such a proof requires knowledge that extends beyond what can be observed, in order to demonstrate how our observations correspond to reality.

There have always been people who have been skeptical of metaphysical enterprises like Descartes's. An example of this skepticism is John Locke's criticism of Descartes's claim that we have direct knowledge of the soul as a distinct substance. Locke rejects Descartes's claim that we have a "clear and distinct" understanding of the essential properties of matter and mind based solely on reason and reflection. According to Locke, all knowledge is based on sensory experience, and experience does not tell us whether matter is capable of thought. The assertion that all knowledge is based on experience provides a basis for rejecting *all* metaphysical theories. This idea was extensively developed in the eighteenth century by David Hume and Immanuel Kant, who attempted to demonstrate systematically that it is impossible to determine the ultimate nature of reality. All we can ascertain, they argued, was the nature of the world as we experience it. We cannot compare our experience with a description of what the world is really like "behind the appearances."

Logical Positivism

Philosophy in the twentieth century was greatly influenced by a movement known as **logical positivism**, or **logical empiricism**, which attacks all metaphysical systems as nonsense. Logical positivism was founded in Vienna prior to World War Two by a group of philosophers and scientists who called themselves the Vienna Circle. What distinguishes these philosophers from other critics of metaphysics is their claim that metaphysics is not merely hopeless or useless, but *meaningless*. They argue that sentences like 'The soul is an immaterial substance' are just empty strings of words that have no content whatsoever. Their argument for this conclusion is based on a theory about language. The emphasis on language, and the conclusions drawn from it, introduced an entirely new way of thinking about the mind-body problem.

If a sentence in a language has any meaning, logical positivists argue, it must be possible (at least in principle) to provide evidence that it is true or false. If there is no evidence that could possibly count for or against the truth of a particular sentence, then that sentence cannot possibly be saying anything about the world. So a sentence is meaningful, they claim, only if we can specify what would count as evidence that it is true or false.[1]

The only exceptions they allow to this rule are tautologies and contradictions; these sentences are true or false simply by virtue of the meanings of the words they contain. For example, we need no evidence to assure us that the sentence 'All sisters are female' is true. It would be absurd to conduct a statistical survey to find out whether all sisters are female. This is because the term 'female' is part of the meaning of the term 'sister.' For this reason, the logical positivists argue, such statements tell us nothing about the world; they inform us only of the logical structure of our own language.

Logical positivists claim that metaphysical sentences are all perfectly compatible with any evidence whatsoever—there can never be evidence either for them or against them. In other words, whether a metaphysical statement is true or false would make no difference at all to how the world appears. An example of this, they claim, is the sentence 'God exists.' Any event or observation whatsoever can be accounted for by both atheists and deists, and so both the truth *and* falsity of 'God exists' is compatible with all possible evidence. Given this view of language, it follows that metaphysical sentences are meaningless. They are grammatically well-formed, but otherwise they are just empty strings of words, no more meaningful than 'Blue is more identical than music.' Metaphysical assertions like Descartes's about the nature of the mind fall into this category as well. According to logical positivists, the sentence 'Mind and body are distinct substances' has no meaning at all.

The Task of Philosophy

But if metaphysics is meaningless, then what is the point of philosophy itself? Some members of the Vienna Circle declared that philosophy consists entirely of meaningless statements, and should be abandoned altogether. Most positivists, however, have not drawn this conclusion, but argue instead for a revised role for philosophy. An excellent example of this view is presented in an article by Moritz Schlick entitled "The Future of Philosophy."[2]

Schlick points out that philosophy and science were not clearly separated until the nineteenth century. For this reason, Schlick claims, it had always been thought that philosophy has the same goal as the sciences, namely, to discover true theories about the world. The only difference thought to exist between philosophy and science is that philosophy has a wider subject matter: philosophy studies the whole of reality and the sciences investigate different aspects of reality. Schlick argues that a better conception of philosophy can found in the activity of Socrates. In some of Plato's dialogues Socrates does not arrive at any answers to the questions he considers. He doesn't construct philosophical theories about the nature of reality. Instead he simply makes clearer what is *meant* by certain questions and certain words. For example, when he looks at the question 'What is justice?,' Socrates spends his time on an analysis of the *concept* conveyed by the word 'justice.' In this way, according to Schlick, the proper task of philosophy is not the "pursuit of truth" but the "pursuit of meaning." We can only determine whether a sentence is true or false once we have a clear understanding of what it means. It is this essential task, Schlick claims, that belongs to philosophy.

The Verifiability Theory of Meaning

Schlick bases his claim about the role of philosophy on the logical positivists' analysis of meaning. He says:

> We know the meaning of a proposition when we are able to indicate exactly the circumstances under which it would be true (or, what amounts to the same, the circumstances which would make it false). The description of these circumstances is absolutely the only way in which the meaning of a sentence can be made clear.[3]

We should notice first the term 'proposition' in this statement. This is a philosophical term that will occur frequently in this and later chapters. Propositions are closely related to declarative sentences, i.e., sentences that are either true or false, such as 'It is snowing.' Notice that different declarative sentences can say exactly the same thing. The French sentence, 'Il neige' has the same meaning as the English sentence 'It is snowing.' The same is true of 'Kasim loves Aliya' and 'Aliya is loved by Kasim.' Philosophers say that such sentences *express the same proposition.* A **proposition** is the content of, or what is said by, a declarative sentence.

Schlick's analysis, then, is of the meanings of declarative sentences or, more exactly, of the propositions those sentences express. His proposal is that if someone were to ask what a particular declarative sentence means, the correct answer would be a description of the evidence that would have to be collected to establish that it is true or false. This idea has been called the **verifiability theory of meaning**. It remains a very influential theory, although it is no longer accepted in its original form.

Some sentences can be verified directly by observation. Sentences like 'This stick is two meters long' or 'The cat is on the mat' can be verified by making some very simple observations. So, according to the verifiability theory, the meanings of these sentences are simply descriptions of those observations. The difficulty in ascertaining meanings arises when we consider sentences that contain theoretical words like 'force' or 'molecule.' These terms appear to be descriptions of things that cannot be observed. But, if this is so, the meanings of such sentences would appear to be descriptions of hidden or unobservable entities rather than descriptions of observations.

The logical positivists claim that this appearance is misleading. They point out that theoretical sentences are also confirmed or disconfirmed by observations. But the observations are complex ones, involving intricate experiments or elaborate equipment. It follows from the verifiability theory that the meanings of these sentences must be descriptions of these complicated observations. So logical positivists maintain that sentences containing theoretical terms are not descriptions of unobservable entities, but are simply shorthand for describing collections of complex observations. To reveal the meanings of these sentences, it is necessary to *translate* them into compound observation sentences. Before a scientist can proceed to find out whether a theoretical sentence is true or false, Schlick argues, there is a philosophical job of determining exactly what evidence would confirm or disconfirm it. In any interesting scientific situations this is a difficult business. Schlick offers two illustrations of this in Newton's working out the concept of mass and Einstein's analysis of the concept of simultaneity. In performing these analyses, Schlick claims, Newton and Einstein were working as philosophers rather than as scientists.

Logical Behaviorism

Schlick argues that many so-called philosophical problems have always resisted solution simply because they are meaningless, even though they have the grammatical form of proper questions. Those questions raised by philosophers that do have a real meaning, he claims, will turn out to be scientific questions answerable by the ordinary methods of science. So when philosophers turn their attention to questions about the mind, their objective should be to determine which are scientific questions and which are meaningless combinations of words that only *look* as though they are genuine questions. The mind-body problem as it is traditionally conceived, Schlick contends, is not a meaningful question. According to Schlick, there can be no observational evidence either for or against any of its solutions. In other words, whether the mind is or is not an immaterial entity makes no difference to the observable world.

But this doesn't entail that all statements about the mind are meaningless. For some can be shown to be scientific statements to be confirmed or disconfirmed by observation. Since the eighteenth century there have been attempts to use the methods of science to study such mental processes as sensation, learning, and memory. For example, the nineteenth-century German scientist Gustav Fechner devised mathematical techniques to relate the physical intensities of light and sound to our sensory experiences. Such efforts led to several definitions of psychology as a "science of the mind." Logical positivists see the job of philosophy of mind to be the "logical analysis of psychology," that is, the study of the meanings of psychological statements by specifying the circumstances under which they are shown to be true or false.

Not all of the methods used by psychologists are accepted by logical positivists as scientifically respectable. In particular, they reject the use of **introspection** on one's own experiences. Remember that, on Descartes's view, knowledge of the mind is obtained by reflecting on the contents of one's own conscious experience. And William James, who established much of the content of modern psychology, described its method as "looking into our minds and reporting what we there discover."[4] Some early psychologists believed that it is possible to use introspection to uncover the "atoms" of the mind in much the same way that chemists have worked out the periodic table of the elements. But logical positivists are skeptical of this method, for there is no way to resolve disagreement in what people report as going on in the mind. People are notoriously inconstant and vague about the contents of their own conscious experience.

As a result, logical positivists attempt to analyze descriptions of the mind solely in terms of what can be observed by everyone rather than what can be observed only through each person's private introspection. Accordingly, early advocates adopted a position called **behaviorism** as providing the appropriate framework for psychology. According to behaviorists, the proper job of psychology is not to describe and explain private, inner thoughts and experiences but to predict and explain human *behavior*. This fits the logical positivists' goals because a person's behavior is observable by anyone, and the techniques of measuring and recording behavior are fully amenable to the methods of the physical sciences. On this basis, the positivists advanced a philosophical theory they termed **logical behaviorism**. This was a theory of the meanings of psychological statements, such that every such statement is shown to be true or false entirely in terms of actual or potential human behavior. It was developed in the early twentieth century especially by Rudolph Carnap and Carl Hempel.

Scientific Behaviorism

Logical behaviorism, as a philosophical theory, was initially inspired and supported by a scientific research program, founded at much the same time, that attempts to predict human behavior through a set of laws that are tested by observing how people behave under various kinds of conditions. This program formed the basis of a school of psychology that we can call **scientific behaviorism**. The founder of this school was John B. Watson (1878–1958), an American animal researcher and psychologist at Johns Hopkins University. Watson was scathing in his descriptions of the problems with introspection as a technique for understanding the mind. He argued instead that human beings should be studied in the same way as other animals, namely, by observing their behavior and the ways that it is affected by changes in their physical environment.

To this end Watson took as his model Ivan Pavlov's studies on conditioned reflexes in animal behavior. Pavlov's method was to record the regular connections between **stimulus** and **response**. A stimulus is an event in an animal's environment that affects its behavior. A response to a stimulus is the behavior an animal exhibits when it is presented with that stimulus. Pavlov had discovered that a response that normally followed one particular stimulus will be elicited by a different stimulus if the two stimuli occur together over a period of time. This technique is known as **classical conditioning**. Pavlov is famous for his demonstration of the technique by inducing salivation in dogs by ringing a bell that had previously accompanied food.

Although Watson laid the foundation for behaviorism, the movement in its current form is linked most closely with the work of B.F. Skinner (1904–90) of Harvard University. Skinner agreed with the general method of recording stimuli and responses, but he differed from Watson in insisting that humans and other animals do not merely respond to environmental stimuli; they modify their behavior in regular ways in light of its consequences. The basis of Skinner's idea is a principle formulated by Edward Thorndike called **The Law of Effect**. The Law of Effect says that the frequency with which a behavior pattern occurs is related to the tendency it has to produce positive results. For example, the likelihood that an animal will push on a lever is increased if doing so produces food and is decreased if doing so produces pain. Thorndike's work led Skinner to the notion of **operant behavior**, which is the idea that behavior is "shaped" by its results, either positive or negative.

The advantage of the idea of operant behavior over the classical conditioning model is that it allows us to explain how entirely new patterns of behavior can emerge. An animal encounters the positive results of a form of behavior, and as a result comes to exhibit that behavior regularly.

Owen Flanagan points out that Skinner's idea of operant behavior explains novel behavior in much the same way that the theory of evolution explains novel forms of life: those forms of behavior that happen to produce positive outcomes will be reinforced over time, while those that tend to produce negative results will gradually be extinguished.[5]

Skinner was convinced that the idea of operant behavior could be used to explain all forms of human behavior, including those typically associated with conscious intelligence such as language understanding and creativity. We will examine here a reading from Skinner's *Science and Human Behavior* (1953), in which he argues that linguistic behavior can be explained without any reference to inner states of mind.

Laws of Stimulus and Response

In this selection Skinner defends the idea that we can predict, and thereby explain, human behavior by measuring the connections between stimulus and response. We can treat stimulus and response as two related physical variables, just as mass, time, and motion are related physical variables. The goal of psychology, as he sees it, is to describe the laws by which stimuli and behavior are connected, taking them as physical laws on a par with, say, the laws of motion. He argues that if we can describe these laws, there is no need to describe the inner mental processes that occur *between* a stimulus and a person's behavior. Skinner claims that in this way we can entirely bypass the vexing and possibly unanswerable question of what the inner states are that produce human behavior: whether they are states of an immaterial mind, as Descartes says, or processes of the nervous system, as many scientists argue. Skinner claims that psychology should be agnostic on the question of what is the nature of mental processing. It should concentrate on formulating the laws governing observable, measurable variables in human behavior, leaving the rest to pseudoscience and mysticism.[6]

Against "Inner Causes"

The first four sections of the reading from *Science and Human Behavior* are criticisms of the traditional ways of explaining behavior, each of which refers to some inner state that is seen as the cause of what a person does. In the opening section Skinner argues that the tendency to search for inner, hidden qualities in things to explain why they act as they do is a common error in science. He lists a number of mistaken theories in the history of science where in each case the search for an inner cause proved fruitless because, being difficult to verify or refute, people can make them up however they like. For example, medieval philosophers attributed the motion of a falling rock to a *vis viva* or "living force." The position Skinner takes here is in agreement with the logical positivists' assertion that scientific theories should not be taken as descriptions of unobservable entities, but as descriptions of relations between observable variables.

The next three sections describe three common varieties of explanations of human behavior, each of which Skinner claims is an instance of the mistaken approach of looking for hidden, internal causes. The first is the reference to neural causes. Skinner points out that in ordinary talk we attribute people's behavior to states of the nervous system in a loose and casual manner. For example, when we talk about "nervous breakdown," we are simply disguising a superficial description of a person's behavior by dressing it up with reference to the nerves. Neurology itself, he argues, is guilty of the same loose talk. Because we cannot observe brain processes directly, we often infer their existence from how people behave. But if we then refer to these processes as the causes of people's behavior, we aren't *explaining* why they behave as they do. For the terms we are using are simply words that describe that behavior. Saying that someone is crying uncontrollably because they are having a nervous breakdown isn't explanatory, because the term "nervous breakdown" is nothing more than a description of that behavior. Eventually, we may be able to predict specific behavior from observations of neural processes, but this may never happen, and we should not pretend that it is possible now.

Another form of appeal to inner causes of human behavior is the description of an "inner mind" controlling the actions of the body. Descartes's dualism is a version of this kind of explanation. Again, Skinner points out that scientists often resort to such explanations of behavior, and he cites the Freudian concepts of ego, superego, and id as being used in this way. Freud himself was not a dualist, for he believed that the processes of the mind are activities of the nervous system. But he believed that we could not understand how such processes affect human behavior without analyzing them in terms of the *meaning* they have for the subject. According to Freud, theories that leave out the inner meanings of our actions are inadequate for comprehending why people behave as they do. Freud modified Descartes's theory to include the idea that mental occurrences are not only hidden to others, they are hidden to the person who has them as well. But, according to Skinner, this only increases the ease with which we can invent whatever inner mental causes we like, as it is now entirely impossible to confirm or disconfirm them.

In the fourth section Skinner describes cases where it appears as if we are explaining behavior in terms of inner causes, but where in fact the inner cause is just another word for the behavior itself. Words like "intelligence" and "addiction" sound as though they describe genuine causes of a person's behavior. Skinner claims, however, that they are nothing more than words we use to refer to certain kinds of behavior. As with many references to neural causes, these are words that can give an appearance of explanation where there is none.

Functional Analysis of Behavior

In the fifth section, "The variables of which behavior is a function," Skinner argues that by searching for inner causes we have overlooked what we *can* observe, which can be used to explain and predict human behavior. According to Skinner, we can describe behavior as a *function* of features of people's environment and their *environmental history*. Let's have a look at what this means. To say that a variable, y, is a **function** of another variable, x, means that whenever we specify a value for x we will always get a specific value for y. For example, the function $y = x^2$ always gives a certain value for y when a number is substituted for x. By the term **environmental history** Skinner just means a description of all the stimuli that have affected a person in the past. So when he says that behavior "is a function of environmental history," his point is that how someone will behave in a given environment is dictated by the stimuli to which they have been exposed in the recent and distant past. Each possible environmental history yields exactly one behavior, just as each possible value for x in x^2 yields exactly one number.

Thus, according to Skinner, we can predict precisely how a person will behave if we know what stimuli they have been affected by in the past together with a knowledge of their current physical environment. Of course, we can never determine *all* the facts about a person's environmental history. But Skinner says that we should be able to measure the *probability* that a person will exhibit a certain behavior in a given situation, and we can then determine how changes in their history will affect those probabilities. For a trivial example, depriving someone of water for a prolonged period will increase the chances of their drinking when given water.

His recommendation, then, is that, "we must investigate the effect of each variable quantitatively with the methods and techniques of a laboratory." What Skinner is proposing here is that the same methods be applied to explanations of human behavior as mechanical scientists apply to physical events. Events in a person's behavior are explained by discovering mathematical laws that describe how that behavior is produced by the impact of the surrounding environment on a person's body. Once these laws are complete, the task of psychology is finished. Descartes's "inner" mind has been bypassed altogether so that human behavior is explained in the same terms as that of any other physical body.

The Theoretician's Dilemma

In the remaining paragraphs of the section Skinner argues that referring to inner causes of behavior is entirely *dispensable*. If human behavior is a function of environment and environmental history, then the latter two are all that are needed to account for behavior. Using the trivial example again, it is unnecessary to say that lack of water caused thirst, and that thirst in turn caused the subject to drink. We can simply say that lack of water caused the subject to drink—the reference to thirst is superfluous. Hence, inner causes are both difficult to verify *and* unnecessary, rendering them unsuitable for scientific explanations.

Skinner's argument here has become famous under the title **The Theoretician's Dilemma**. Whenever a theory describing unobservable entities is used to predict the occurrence of one observable event from the prior occurrence of another, we find ourselves confronted with a quandary: either the observable events are connected in the way the theory describes, or they are not. In the first case, the theory is not needed because we can predict the one event from the other without any reference to the theory. And in the second case, the theory is useless because it is of no help in our predictions.

A Problem for Behaviorism

To many people behaviorism appears obviously false. The idea that descriptions of thoughts and experiences are only descriptions of behavior seems to fly in the face of common sense. As we will see later in this chapter, however, appeals to common sense are weakened by arguments that what we have come to accept as common sense is based on fundamental errors. But behaviorism also encounters a problem of a different kind: Skinner's project of explaining behavior entirely in terms of stimulus-response laws runs into serious difficulty when confronted with the complexity of human behavior.

The problem behaviorists face in accounting for complex behavior is illustrated nicely in reading a critical review by Noam Chomsky of another of Skinner's books, *Verbal Behavior*.[7] Chomsky is a linguist who did most of his work at the Massachusetts Institute of Technology. He is one of the originators of the idea that the brain should be understood as a kind of digital computer. In his review of Skinner, Chomsky argues that we cannot explain the variety and complexity of linguistic ability simply as behavioral responses to physical stimuli. According to Chomsky, linguistic abilities can only be explained on the assumptions that language is the result of complex mental processes that analyze sentences into their grammatical and semantic components.

The Behaviorist's Dilemma

Chomsky argues that the problem facing Skinner's program arises from the fact that behaviorism is formulated in accordance with the methods used to predict the behavior of animals in tightly controlled laboratory experiments. A typical experiment of this sort requires an animal to perform such activities as pressing a bar to release food when certain stimuli are presented. In such a context it is possible to demonstrate that certain behavior patterns are the product of very specific environmental stimuli. But, according to Chomsky, Skinner is unable to show how to extend this method outside the laboratory to complex human verbal behavior.

Chomsky argues that when discussing behavior outside the laboratory, behaviorists like Skinner are faced with a dilemma. They claim that all behavior can be shown to be the product of laws formulated in terms of responses to environmental stimuli. But the only laws of behavior that have actually been *demonstrated* are those devised in the laboratory involving very specific aspects of the animals' behavior (such as pressing a bar to release food pellets) and very specific aspects of the environment (such as flashing lights). If we direct our attention to other features of the environment and to other aspects of animal behavior, we must admit that no laws connecting the two have yet been discovered. So behaviorists have two choices: (1) admit that it has not been shown that response is always a function of external stimuli, or (2) insist that only those aspects of the environment and of behavior that have been demonstrated to be lawfully connected are to be counted as genuine stimuli and behavioral responses. The first is the denial of Skinner's central claim in *Verbal Behavior*. But the second option is also unacceptable because it renders Skinner's assertion that response is a function of stimuli true *by definition* rather than by observation.

Chomsky's Painting Example

Chomsky argues that Skinner tries to avoid this dilemma by a sleight of hand. According to Chomsky, Skinner defends the scientific character of the stimulus-response approach by first describing the results achieved with animals in the laboratory. Then he applies the method outside the laboratory by extending the definition of stimulus and response beyond their original meaning in the laboratory. When the terms are stretched in this way, Chomsky argues, they lose their scientific character.

Chomsky presents the following illustration of his point. Suppose when looking at a painting, a person's response is to utter the word, 'Dutch.' According to Skinner, this response is "under the control of extremely subtle properties" of the painting. The task of the psychologist, in Skinner's view, is to work out what those properties are. But Chomsky asks us to think of all the other verbal responses a person might make: "Clashes with the wallpaper," "I thought you liked abstract work," "Never saw it before," "Tilted," "Hanging too low," "Beautiful," "Hideous," "Remember our camping trip last summer?" What are the properties of the painting that would produce these remarks?

We might try to say that it was the property of clashing with the wallpaper that produced the first, and the property of being unfamiliar to the subject that produced the third, and so on. But this would be pointless because we are now using the subject's response to determine the relevant aspects of the stimulus. As Chomsky puts it, "We don't know what the stimuli are until the subject responds." According to Chomsky this is a reversion to precisely the kind of psychology that Skinner wants to avoid. For by waiting for the subject's utterance before identifying the stimulus, the character of the stimulus is determined by the inner thoughts of the subject rather than by objective features of the environment. That is, the stimulus is described in terms of how the subject *perceives* it, rather than by its objective physical characteristics. Thus, Chomsky argues, Skinner fails to offer any description of the stimuli that prompts verbal behavior in terms of objective physical properties of the environment.

Complex Mental States vs. Past Environmental History

Chomsky's criticism is not that behaviorism has the wrong objectives. Unlike some critics of behaviorism, Chomsky does not attack Skinner's restriction of psychology to the task of predicting human behavior. Rather, his point is that Skinner's behaviorist method makes such prediction impossible. The criticism that Chomsky makes of behaviorism is that how a person behaves seems to depend on more than just the physical character of the stimulus. It also depends on what is going on *in the person's mind* at the time the stimulus is presented. According to Chomsky, we can only predict what people will do by considering their actions to be the result of complex internal states of mind. However, Skinner has a reply to this criticism. In the second last paragraph from our reading he admits that "other variables" may be needed to predict the behavior. In predicting whether a person will drink water we need to consider whether they believe the water is poisoned, or have grown up in a culture where people drink only in private. At the end of the paragraph he argues that:

> Adequate prediction in any science requires information about all relevant variables, and the control of a subject matter for practical purposes makes the same demands.

His point is that a person's behavior depends on their *entire past environmental history* as well as on the current stimulus. So, to use Chomsky's example, how a person will respond to a painting will be determined by what has happened to them in the past as well as by the physical properties of the painting itself. The question dividing Chomsky and Skinner, then, is whether sufficiently full descriptions of environmental history can replace descriptions of inner mental processes. In Chomsky's view, inner causes of behavior are not dispensable as Skinner claims, but are essential in being able to predict what a person will do. Chomsky's point is that we can understand how a person's past environmental history affects their behavior only by discovering how it alters their state of mind. According to Skinner, on the other hand, predicting human behavior requires only a knowledge of the relevant aspects of a person's past physical environment. Once these are known, references to inner states of mind are unnecessary as well as unconfirmable.

The Critique of Introspection

Behaviorist theories of the mind make reference only to descriptions of *other* people's mental states. But what of our knowledge of our *own* states of mind? According to people like Descartes, the real nature of the mind is revealed only through reflection on one's own conscious experience. It is only in this way, they argue, that we see the inner causes of our own behavior. This conforms with what we might take as common sense: "Of course, I know what I am thinking; I don't need a behaviorist to tell me."

As we have seen, the positivists' suspicion of introspection is based on the difficulty in resolving disagreements in introspective reports. Introspective psychology as a science is impossible, they claim, because its methods do not lead to agreement on what the structure of the mind is.

And they are correct that people are notoriously bad at accurately reporting their own thoughts. But, on the other hand, the failure of introspective methods in practice does not show that it is impossible *in principle* to devise a successful introspective psychology. Proponents of introspection argue that the method requires great skill and training to be carried out properly. If logical behaviorism is to succeed, the project of translating psychological statements into descriptions of behavior must be coupled with a direct criticism of introspection as a legitimate method of studying the mind.

Criticism of theories that postulate inner mental states revealed through introspection was carried out most effectively by Gilbert Ryle and Ludwig Wittgenstein, two philosophers whose aims were different from those of the logical positivists although they originated from similar concerns. As we have seen, logical positivists claim that the role of philosophy is to analyze the *meaning* of scientific theories. The emphasis on linguistic analysis is shared by both Ryle and Wittgenstein. But they do not place the same emphasis on the physical sciences as the model of meaningful investigation of the world. In their view, a study of our everyday use of language is sufficient by itself to eradicate metaphysical problems.

Ordinary Language

Gilbert Ryle (1900–76) worked as a scholar of philosophy at Oxford University all of his adult life. His philosophy is based on the general view that most philosophical problems are merely confusions created by accidents of grammar. One such problem, he argues, is the nature of universals, which led Plato to his theory of the Forms. According to Ryle, we are mistakenly led to suppose that words like 'triangularity' and 'punctuality' must refer to some kind of *objects*, simply on the grounds that they can occur as the subject of a sentence. Once this idea is accepted, we are faced with the problem of deciding what kind of object these things are: what is *triangularity itself* over and above particular triangles? Ryle argues that the problem disappears once we recognize that it is based on nothing more than an accidental feature of language.

Ryle's philosophy of mind is laid out in his book, *The Concept of Mind*, published in 1949, from which we will read selected passages. The approach that Ryle takes to the subject is explained in the introduction to the book. He begins with the claim that rather than advancing new knowledge about the mind, he intends instead to "rectify the logical geography of the knowledge which we already possess." To a certain degree this metaphorical description of his project matches the aims of logical positivists. Ryle shares with the logical positivists the view that metaphysical theories about the nature of mind are meaningless gibberish produced by a misunderstanding of the meanings of mental concepts. In their view and in Ryle's, the role of philosophy is to provide a logical analysis of the meanings of psychological statements.

But the next paragraph reveals an important difference between Ryle's project and that of the logical positivists. Rather than restricting all meaningful questions to the natural sciences, Ryle believes the correct approach is to look carefully at our everyday descriptions of the mind. According to Ryle, people in ordinary life know perfectly well how to talk sensibly about the mind and how to interact with other people on the basis of this knowledge. It is here that we should look for an understanding of how psychological concepts are used. Ryle argues that the everyday ability to *use* mental concepts does not bring with it a clear understanding of how these concepts are logically related to one another and to other concepts. And it is this lack of understanding that creates so-called philosophical problems. As he sees it, it is a failure to see what he calls the "logical geography" of everyday mental concepts that leads to meaningless theories like Descartes's. The general project of removing philosophical problems by gaining a proper understanding of our day-to-day use of language has been called the **ordinary language** school. Ryle's critique of Descartes's philosophy of mind in chapter 1 of *The Concept of Mind*, called "Descartes's Myth," provides a perfect example of the "ordinary language" method of philosophical analysis.

Critique of "The Official Doctrine"

Ryle describes Descartes's view as "the official doctrine" of the mind. According to this doctrine, Ryle says, each person has two distinct histories: (1) a private, "inner" history, consisting of what happens in the mind; and (2) a publicly observable, "outer" history, consisting of what happens in and to the body. He points out that the use of the words 'inner' and 'outer' is metaphorical, as the mind is not believed to exist in space. But even as a metaphor the view faces difficulties.

First, the interaction between mind and body must always be a mystery in Descartes's theory. For these interactions belong neither to the private inner history revealed through introspection nor to the public outer history of bodily behavior; interaction between mind and body must necessarily lie outside of both kinds of experience. For example, accepting Descartes's theory would mean that the discipline of psychophysics, which studies correlations between sensations and the activities of the nervous system, would belong to neither psychology nor physiology. In this claim Ryle is entirely correct. While Descartes's theory of mind resolved some difficulties that Aristotle's theory confronted, it is unable to say anything about how a relation of cause and effect between mind and matter could possibly work.

A second difficulty with Descartes's view lies in his account of our knowledge of the mind. According to Descartes, each person has direct knowledge of the episodes in their own mental history. We can turn our attention inwards and introspectively observe the goings-on in our own mind. On the other hand, we have no direct knowledge of what goes on in the minds of others. We must infer other people's thoughts and feelings by observing their behavior and drawing conclusions by analogy with our own internal experience. Thus each of us lives a private mental history hidden to others like a "ghostly Robinson Crusoe," which Ryle believes is simply absurd. Our success in interacting with other people on the basis of the thoughts, beliefs, and desires that we attribute to them shows that the minds of other people are not hidden from us but are as accessible as any other aspect of the world.

Category Mistakes

In the second section of chapter 1, entitled "The Absurdity of the Official Doctrine," Ryle describes what he sees as the fundamental error in the Cartesian picture of the mind. He argues that the official doctrine is based on a special kind of logical mistake—a **category mistake**. This is the mistake of taking two terms as belonging to a single "logical category" when in fact they belong to different categories. So a central component in Ryle's critique of Descartes is the idea of logical categories. Later in the chapter he defines this idea:

> When two terms belong to the same category, it is proper to construct conjunctive propositions embodying them.

By a "conjunctive proposition" Ryle means (roughly) a sentence formed by joining two or more phrases with the word 'and.' He gives the following example of this definition. It is correct to say in English that there is a right-hand glove and a left-hand glove; and it is equally correct to say that there is a pair of gloves. But it is not correct to infer from this that there is a right-hand glove, a left-hand glove, *and* a pair of gloves, for this implies that there are three different items: two gloves and one pair. So the term 'pair of gloves' is in a different logical category from the terms 'left-hand glove' and 'right-hand glove.' He gives several other examples of this idea, such as a person who is shown the colleges and libraries of a university and then asks mistakenly where the university itself is. There is a university, and there are colleges and libraries; but it is incorrect to say that there are colleges, libraries, *and* the university in the sense that the university is something that exists separately from its colleges and libraries.

In the section entitled "The Origin of the Mistake," Ryle argues that Descartes's view of the mind is based on just such a category mistake. It is correct to say that there is a mind, and it is also correct to say that there is a body. But from this Descartes draws the conclusion that there must be a mind *and* a body, which is a mistake because 'mind' and 'body' are terms belonging to different logical categories. The mind no more exists separately from the body than a university exists separately from its colleges and libraries.

Ryle's Historical Reconstruction of Descartes's Mistake

But what would lead Descartes to make such a basic error in logic? In answer to this question Ryle offers a historical explanation of Descartes's reasoning. As a scientist, Descartes adopted the principles of mechanical science developed by Galileo. But as a religious man, he could not accept that humans are merely physical mechanisms. His solution was to suppose that if mental terms do not refer to mechanical processes of the body, they must refer to *nonmechanical* processes. And if mechanical laws explain physical events, there must be other laws that explain mental events. In this way the mind was held to be the same kind of thing as the body, but made of different stuff. Because the body is a complex, organized unit, the mind must be a complex, organized unit as well, but of a nonphysical nature.

Against this view, Ryle argues that the sentence 'There are mental processes' is not the same kind of sentence as 'There are physical processes.' He makes this point by comparing these two sentences to other pairs of sentences. For example, the sentence, 'She came home in a flood of tears' is not the same kind of sentence as 'She came home in a sedan chair.' According to Ryle, then, the so-called mind-body problem is an improper question, similar to the question 'Did she buy a left-hand and right-hand glove, or a pair of gloves?' This distortion of logic, Ryle argues, leads to some of the "deepest problems" of modern philosophy: How can minds influence bodies? How is human freedom compatible with mechanical laws? Once the error is revealed, these problems will simply disappear.

So Ryle's view is that it is a mistake to think of mind and body as two distinct *entities*. It is better to think of the words 'mind' and 'body' as two ways of talking about a single person. When we talk about a person's body, we are describing their physical structure—the bones, tissues, and organs of which they are composed. What are we describing, then, when we talk about their mind—their thoughts, feelings, desires, and sensations? Here Ryle follows a line similar to that taken by the logical positivists: descriptions of mental states are actually descriptions of behavior. This fits well with his comparisons of other distinct logical categories. It is no more correct to say there is the body *and* its behavior than it is to say there is the university *and* its colleges and libraries.

States of Mind as Dispositions

In a later section of the book Ryle gives a more subtle account of the meaning of psychological descriptions. This account avoids an obvious objection to the idea that psychological terms refer only to a person's behavior. Consider a very simple example, such as the statement, 'Brenda has a headache.' How might we translate that sentence into a description of Brenda's behavior? We might try to do it with a collection of statements like 'She takes pain medicine' or 'She says, "I have a headache."' The problem with this idea is that none of these sentences are necessarily true whenever it is true that Brenda has a headache. People who have a headache will not always display the kinds of behavior that we associate with that condition. Brenda might not have any medicine in the house, and there might not be anyone to say anything to. According to Ryle, this reveals that simple descriptions of typical behavior cannot be the correct analysis of the original sentence.

Ryle argues that the concepts of mental states should be understood as "dispositional concepts." By this he means that a mental state is a **behavioral disposition**; that is, a tendency to behave in certain ways under certain circumstances. That behavior will then only be exhibited when those circumstances occur. For example, a person with a disposition to take pain medicine will do so only if there is some to take. Instead of simple descriptions of behavior, the translations of psychological statements will take the form of 'if-then' sentences, such as 'If there are aspirins available, Brenda will take one,' and 'If asked how she feels, Brenda will say, "I have a headache."' The if-clause describes a circumstance that might arise, and the then-clause describes how the person will behave in that circumstance.

This analysis agrees with the psychological behaviorists' project of explaining behavior through connections between stimulus and response. As the result of their environmental history, people will behave in certain specific ways whenever their current environment includes a particular stimulus. In Ryle's terms this is to say that a person's environmental history has produced a certain *disposition*, namely, to exhibit a particular behavior under particular conditions. When those conditions arise, the behavior will be displayed.

Ryle compares his analysis of mental states to other common dispositional concepts such as brittleness and solubility: To say that a glass is brittle is to say that it will break when struck, and to say that sugar is soluble is to say that it will dissolve when immersed in certain liquids. A brittle glass will not break if it is never struck, and a sugar cube will not dissolve if it is never immersed in liquid. Ryle's claim is that psychological concepts like those of beliefs, thoughts, moods, and sensations are similar in nature to these concepts of physical dispositions. We use psychological descriptions to refer to what people are *disposed* to do, not what they *actually* do.

Multi-Tracked Dispositions

The dispositional account of psychological concepts allows Ryle to introduce a special feature of most states of mind. The simplest kinds of dispositions are what Ryle calls "single-track" dispositions. By this he means dispositions to do one specific thing under certain conditions. For example, brittleness is simply the disposition to break when struck. But the dispositions described by psychological concepts, Ryle claims, are "multi-tracked," which means that there are many different dispositions contained under the same concept. For example, there are many different ways in which a person who is depressed will behave, depending on the circumstances. So a complete analysis of a psychological concept will generally involve a large number of dispositions, each of which involves the way in which a person will behave under a particular set of circumstances.

If this account is correct, psychological concepts will not be describable by a single if-then sentence. Rather, each such concept will require a long (and probably endless) *list* of sentences. Each such sentence in the list will describe the behavior that a person would exhibit under one particular kind of circumstance. For example, we could not analyze a psychological concept such as that of *experiencing a sensation of thirst* in terms of a single disposition, say, to drink water. For one thing, what a thirsty person will drink depends on what is available. Second, there are social situations in which a thirsty person would, say, politely ask whether they may drink something. So to fully analyze that concept in terms of behavioral dispositions, we would need a long list of the behaviors that would be exhibited under each of these different situations. Letting 'C1, C2, C3...' be the list of circumstances a person might find themselves in, the full analysis of the concept of experiencing a sensation of thirst will look something like the following.

> A person is experiencing thirst if and only if
> (i) in circumstance C1, the person will drink water;
> (ii) in circumstance C2, the person will drink orange juice;
> (iii) in circumstance C3, the person will say "May I have something to drink?"
> ...and so on.

There Are No Mental States

There is one more important feature of Ryle's analysis of psychological concepts. Descartes and others take mental states to be inner states of a person. According to Ryle, however, psychological concepts do not refer to *states* of any kind. They refer only to certain facts about a person's behavior. A person with a headache is not in a certain kind of state that produces certain forms of behavior. The headache consists of nothing more than the relevant facts about the person's behavior. And this is true, he says, of dispositional concepts generally. For example, the brittleness of a glass is not an internal condition of glass that *causes* it to break. The brittleness is nothing more than the fact that it will break under certain circumstances. This point is clearly brought out in a quotation later picked up by David Armstrong. Ryle says:

> To possess a dispositional property *is not to be in a particular state*, or to undergo a particular change; it is to be bound or liable to be in a particular state, or to undergo a particular change, when a particular condition is realized. [emphasis mine]

So when we say that the glass broke *because* it was brittle, we mean nothing more than that the glass was the sort of thing that will break when struck, and it was struck. We do not mean that the glass had a particular internal state that caused it to break on impact. In the same way, Ryle says, psychological dispositions are not internal states that cause certain kinds of behavior, for that would bring us back to Descartes's theory. In Ryle's view, there is nothing more to a psychological concept than what is conveyed by a statement that describes how a person will behave under certain circumstances.

Wittgenstein's *Philosophical Investigations*

Ludwig Wittgenstein (1889–1951) is one of the most enigmatic philosophers of the twentieth century. Perhaps his most astounding achievement is to have produced two completely different and important systems of philosophy within one lifetime. Wittgenstein was an intense man who attacked philosophical problems with great passion. Throughout his life he produced work that has proven neither easy to understand nor easy to ignore.

Wittgenstein was born and raised in Vienna in a household of wealthy parents with broad artistic and intellectual interests. As a young boy Wittgenstein was exposed to some of the greatest figures of Viennese culture. After an initial start in engineering he developed an interest in pure mathematics, which led him to discover Bertrand Russell's book, *The Principles of Mathematics*. Russell's work in logic and mathematics was in many ways an important influence on the logical positivists. In 1912 Wittgenstein moved to Cambridge to study logic with Russell. After serving in World War I Wittgenstein apparently abandoned philosophical work. However, the book that he composed while in Cambridge, the *Tractatus Logico-Philosophicus*, was discovered by Moritz Schlick and other members of the Vienna Circle, and Wittgenstein was convinced by them to return to Cambridge in 1929.

In the 1930s Wittgenstein began work on a number of ideas that conflicted directly with the basic assumptions of his early philosophy. This work culminated in the book *Philosophical Investigations*, which was not published in his lifetime. In this book Wittgenstein argues that words gain their meaning from the social practices that govern their use. He applies this idea in particular to the words we use to describe our thoughts and sensations, and from this he draws the conclusion that they cannot refer to inner states of mind in the way that Descartes describes in the Second Meditation. In this way Wittgenstein's conclusions bear a similarity to those of Gilbert Ryle.

The Idea of a "Private Language"

Wittgenstein's critique of the idea of inner mental states takes the form of an attack on a certain idea of how words that describe sensations, like 'pain' and 'tickling,' get their meaning. If the Cartesian view of the mind is correct, these words get their meaning by being associated with a particular kind of inner sensation. There is a characteristic feeling that you associate with a word like 'headache,' and the meaning the word has for you is formed by this association. The phrase 'for you' in the previous sentence is particularly important here. In the Cartesian picture of the mind, the thoughts and sensations you have are immediately evident to you but are hidden from everyone else. You know directly what your headache feels like, but you can only infer that others have similar experiences from their behavior. If a word like 'headache' gets its meaning from association with a particular inner sensation, and that sensation is known only to you, it follows that the word has a private meaning for you that others cannot possibly know. Each person attaches their own private, subjective meaning to sensation words, and it is impossible to know whether these meanings are the same for different people or not. Wittgenstein refers to this idea of language as the idea of a **private language**. His argument against views like Descartes's is that this notion of a private language is incoherent. We will read passages from *Philosophical Investigations* in which this argument is laid out. You will notice the idiosyncratic manner of Wittgenstein's writings, which is typical of his work generally.

Against the Idea of a Private Language

In paragraph 256 Wittgenstein first raises the question whether our words for sensations gain their meaning by being associated with outward expressions—grimacing, smiling, etc.—in which case the meaning of the word would be public and everyone would understand it in the same way. But then he considers the possibility that a person might have sensations and associate names with them, but have no outward expressions for them at all. In this case the meaning of the person's sensation words would be private, known only to that person. In paragraph 257 he asks what could be meant by saying that this person has "named his pain"?

In the following paragraph he makes a crucial point. He thinks of a situation in which he records the occurrences of a certain sensation, marking the occurrences in a diary with the letter 'S.' Can 'S' be taken as a name for the sensation? If so, the letter would get its meaning only from the fact that he concentrates his attention on the sensation at the time of writing the letter. But now the letter serves as the name of the sensation only if it is used in association with the *same* sensation each time. The question Wittgenstein asks is, how can he know that he has in fact used the letter correctly? Since the sensation is known only to him, his conviction that a certain sensation is the same as an earlier one cannot be verified by anyone else. He can only say that he *feels sure* that this is the same sensation again. There is, as he puts it, no "criterion for correctness." That is, there is no independent means of ascertaining whether his feeling of certainty is justified or not.

The significance of this last point for Wittgenstein is not easy to see from this passage, but depends upon an idea that he develops over the entire book. This idea is alluded to in paragraph 259 where he makes reference to the *rules* of a private language, and again in paragraph 261 where he talks about "a particular language game." This notion of a **language game** is central to Wittgenstein's understanding of how language works, and so also to his claim that a private language is impossible. Let's take a moment to look at this notion and its importance to Wittgenstein's argument.

Language Games

According to Wittgenstein, words and sentences can only gain their meaning from the way in which they are used by speakers of the language. We can say that someone understands the sentence, 'Shut the door,' if they use it in appropriate ways and respond to other people's use of it in appropriate ways. If they shut the door, or say, 'Shut it yourself,' then we can suppose they understand the sentence correctly. If they were to open the window or say, 'You're right, Wednesdays are busy,' we must suppose they are attaching a meaning to it that is incorrect. This sentence is a command, and so we might suppose that this point is true only of these kinds of sentences. But Wittgenstein claims that the same is true of all linguistic expressions, including declarative sentences. The sentence, 'The cat is on the mat,' has a variety of appropriate uses and a variety of appropriate responses to uses of it. A person shows their understanding of the sentence if they know, for example, which questions the sentence can be used to answer, such as 'Where's the cat?' or 'What's that on the mat?' Similarly, they show their understanding by knowing how to determine whether it is true, or knowing the circumstances in which it can be appropriately said.

There is in the previous paragraph an assumption that Wittgenstein draws out and lays emphasis on. On the view of language put forward by Wittgenstein, there are, and must be, *appropriate* uses of words and sentences. A person shows an understanding of an expression if they use it in the *right* ways. The question, then, is what establishes appropriate or correct use of expressions of a language? The answer that Wittgenstein gives is that for every language there is a set of rules that govern and determine correct and incorrect uses of and responses to its words and sentences. These rules are not explicitly stated or taught, but users of the language implicitly recognize them by conforming their linguistic behavior to that of the language community. These rules are what Wittgenstein calls a "language game." He uses the analogy of a game because the rules of language operate in his view similarly to the rules of a game. A person is playing chess, for example, and not checkers, only if they follow a certain set of rules. Similarly someone is speaking English only if the ways in which they use words and sentences conform to the rules of language. Notice too from our examples that the rules of a language game extend far beyond rules of grammar to include all forms of behavior surrounding the uses of expressions of the language.

Going on in the Same Way

Seen in terms of linguistic rules, one way of defending the possibility of a private language is to argue that one merely has to follow a simple rule: associate a word with a particular sensation on one occasion and then use the word the same way in the future. Wittgenstein's argument, then, is that it is impossible to determine whether or not one is following that rule, for one cannot tell whether one really is using the word the same way or whether one merely *thinks* one is using it the same way. It is only by comparing our use of the word with that of others that we can judge correctness or incorrectness, which renders a private language impossible.

Putting the issue in this way, in terms of rules for the use of a word, allows Wittgenstein to rest his argument on a general premise about the nature of rules. It makes no sense, he argues, to ask whether a rule is being followed correctly or incorrectly except by asking whether a given action is commonly *accepted* as conforming to the rule. To illustrate this claim, Wittgenstein elsewhere asks us to consider a pupil learning the rule '+2'.[8] Suppose that after the number 1000, the pupil continues 1004, 1008, 1012. We will claim, of course, that he is misapplying the rule. But suppose the pupil replies, "But I went on in the same way." What can we show him that will demonstrate that he is in error? According to Wittgenstein, there is nothing we can say beyond the fact that his action is different from what is commonly accepted as falling under the rule.

Here is Wittgenstein's reasoning behind this conclusion. In demonstrating the rule, we gave the pupil only a finite number of examples. Perhaps we showed him the first ten numbers in the series. But a finite number of examples will conform to an endless variety of different rules.[9] We might try to point out to the student that after 1000 he is not following the rule '+2', but rather the rule '+4'. But why should he agree? He can say that *his* numbers, not ours, conform to the rule '+2' *as illustrated by the examples we gave him.* There is nothing in the examples to indicate that we are right and he is wrong. The only thing that determines that the pupil is in error is the fact that the numbers he gives are different from what is commonly accepted as correct.

A common response here is to say that there is more on which to base our claim that the pupil is mistaken than just the examples we gave him. We can see that the pupil isn't continuing the series the right way because we *understand* the rule and he obviously doesn't. This response is based on the notion that correctly following a rule is a matter of having the right idea or understanding of the rule in your mind. You might think of there being a picture of the rule in your mind, and that picture can then be applied to each example to see if it conforms to the rule or not. But Wittgenstein argues that this won't help us to show that the pupil is mistaken. For we have no way of determining whether someone has a correct understanding of a rule other than seeing whether their actions are the same as ours. As Norman Malcolm puts it, "The correct use is a criterion of correct understanding."[10] So we are back where we began: our response to the student is just that the numbers we accept are commonly accepted as correct and his aren't.

The general conclusion that Wittgenstein draws from this argument is that language is not based on an understanding of meanings that we carry around in our head. It is based on the fact that human beings happen to accept certain forms of behavior as correct or natural in their use of language to communicate with one another. It follows that the meanings we attach to words, including the words we use to describe our own mind, are determined by social practice, or what Wittgenstein calls a "form of life." Outside of accepted social practices linguistic expressions have no significance at all. Wittgenstein illustrates this in paragraph 268 with the thought of the right hand "giving money" to the left hand. It can of course be done in a certain sense, but it would have no significance in terms of the public use of money. Similarly, someone can perhaps say that they are following a set of private language rules, but this would have no significance at all for any meaningful use of language.

This leads to conclusions directly opposed to the Cartesian picture of the mind. Descartes's contention in the Second Meditation is that knowledge of our own thoughts and sensations is the foundation of all knowledge, and this knowledge is directly accessible to us but hidden from others. According to Wittgenstein, on the other hand, what is hidden to others can form no part of the meanings of our words, from which it follows that statements describing the mind are not descriptions of private inner states, but rather statements whose application is fixed by their association with certain accepted forms of behavior. What can be known, or at least what can be described in words, is restricted to what is publicly observable.

Notes

1. The influence of Berkeley is evident in this idea. The position that the meaning of a sentence is exhausted by the evidence for or against it contains an echo of Berkeley's contention that we have no ideas that are not collections of sensations.
2. Moritz Schlick, "The Future of Philosophy," *College of the Pacific Publications in Philosophy* I (1932): pp. 45–62; reprinted in *The Linguistic Turn: Essays in Philosophical Method*, Richard Rorty (ed.) (Chicago: University of Chicago Press, 1992).
3. Schlick, p. 48.
4. William James, *The Principles of Psychology* (1890; reprint, Cambridge, MA: Harvard University Press, 1976).
5. Owen Flanagan, *The Science of the Mind* (Cambridge, MA: MIT Press, 1991), p. 107.
6. This bears a similarity to Newton's attitude in treating gravity as a relation between mass and force while refusing to speculate on its underlying nature. "I feign no hypotheses," Newton declared.
7. "A Review of Skinner's Verbal Behavior," reprinted in *Readings in the Philosophy of Psychology, Volume I*, Ned Block (ed.) (Cambridge, MA: Harvard University Press, 1980), pp. 48–63.
8. Ludwig Wittgenstein, *Philosophical Investigations*, translated by G.E.M. Anscombe (Oxford: Basil Blackwell, 1958), paragraph 185.

9. To convince yourself of this, consider the following example. The series of numbers 1, 4, 10, conforms to two different rules: "Begin with 1, then add (1 · 3), then add (2 · 3), then add (3 · 3), and so on," or "Begin with 1, then add 3, then add 6, then add 3, then add 6, and so on." From the three numbers we are given, neither of these can be said to be *the correct* interpretation of the series of three numbers.

10. Norman Malcolm, "Wittgenstein's Philosophical Investigations" in *The Philosophy of Mind*, ed. V.C. Chappell (Englewood Cliffs, NJ: Prentice Hall, 1962), pp. 74–81. First published in *Philosophical Review*, LXIII (1954): pp. 530–59.

B.F. SKINNER

Selections from *Science and Human Behavior*

Inner "Causes"

Every science has at some time or other looked for causes of action inside the things it has studied. Sometimes the practice has proved useful, sometimes it has not. There is nothing wrong with an inner explanation as such, but events which are located inside a system are likely to be difficult to observe. For this reason we are encouraged to assign properties to them without justification. Worse still, we can invent causes of this sort without fear of contradiction. The motion of a rolling stone was once attributed to its *vis viva*. The chemical properties of bodies were thought to be derived from the *principles* or *essences* of which they were composed. Combustion was explained by the *phlogiston* inside the combustible object. Wounds healed and bodies grew well because of a *vis medicatrix*. It has been especially tempting to attribute the behavior of a living organism to the behavior of an inner agent, as the following examples may suggest.

Neural causes. The layman uses the nervous system as a ready explanation of behavior. The English language contains hundreds of expressions which imply such a causal relationship. At the end of a long trial we read that the jury shows signs of brain fag, that the nerves of the accused are on edge, that the wife of the accused is on the verge of a nervous breakdown, and that his lawyer is generally thought to have lacked the brains needed to stand up to the prosecution. Obviously, no direct observations have been made of the nervous systems of any of these people. Their "brains" and "nerves" have been invented on the spur of the moment to lend substance to what might otherwise seem a superficial account of their behavior.

The sciences of neurology and physiology have not divested themselves entirely of a similar practice. Since techniques for observing the electrical and chemical processes in nervous tissue had not yet been developed, early information about the nervous system was limited to its gross anatomy. Neural processes could only be inferred from the behavior which was said to result from them. Such inferences were legitimate enough as scientific theories, but they could not justifiably be used to explain the very behavior upon which they were based. The hypotheses of the early physiologist may have been sounder than those of the layman, but until independent evidence could be obtained, they were no more satisfactory as explanations of behavior. Direct information about many of the chemical and electrical processes in the nervous system is now available. Statements about the nervous system are no longer necessarily inferential or fictional. But there is still a measure of circularity in much physiological explanation, even in the writings of specialists. In World War I a familiar disorder was called "shell shock." Disturbances in behavior were explained by arguing that violent explosions had damaged the structure of the nervous system, though no direct evidence of such damage was available. In World War II the same disorder was classified as "neuropsychiatric." The prefix seems to show a continuing unwillingness to abandon explanations in terms of hypothetical neural damage.

Eventually a science of the nervous system based upon direct observation rather than inference will describe the neural states and events which immediately precede instances of behavior. We shall know the precise neurological conditions which immediately precede, say, the response, "No, thank you." These events in turn will be found to be preceded by other neurological events, and these in turn by others.

This series will lead us back to events outside the nervous system and, eventually, outside the organism. In the chapters which follow we shall consider external events of this sort in some detail. We shall then be better able to evaluate the place of neurological explanations of behavior. However, we may note here that we do not have and may never have this sort of neurological information at the moment it is needed in order to predict a specific instance of behavior. It is even more unlikely that we shall be able to alter the nervous system directly in order to set up the antecedent conditions of a particular

instance. The causes to be sought in the nervous system are, therefore, of limited usefulness in the prediction and control of specific behavior.

Psychic inner causes. An even more common practice is to explain behavior in terms of an inner agent which lacks physical dimensions and is called "mental" or "psychic." The purest form of the psychic explanation is seen in the animism of primitive peoples. From the immobility of the body after death it is inferred that a spirit responsible for movement has departed. The *enthusiastic* person is, as the etymology of the word implies, energized by a "god within." It is only a modest refinement to attribute every feature of the behavior of the physical organism to a corresponding feature of the "mind" or of some inner "personality." The inner man is regarded as driving the body very much as the man at the steering wheel drives a car. The inner man wills an action, the outer executes it. The inner loses his appetite, the outer stops eating.

The inner man wants and the outer gets. The inner has the impulse which the outer obeys.

It is not the layman alone who resorts to these practices, for many reputable psychologists use a similar dualistic system of explanation. The inner man is sometimes personified clearly, as when delinquent behavior is attributed to a "disordered personality," or he may be dealt with in fragments, as when behavior is attributed to mental processes, faculties, and traits. Since the inner man does not occupy space, he may be multiplied at will. It has been argued that a single physical organism is controlled by several psychic agents and that its behavior is the resultant of their several wills. The Freudian concepts of the ego, superego, and id are often used in this way. They are frequently regarded as nonsubstantial creatures, often in violent conflict, whose defeats or victories lead to the adjusted or maladjusted behavior of the physical organism in which they reside.

Direct observation of the mind comparable with the observation of the nervous system has not proved feasible. It is true that many people believe that they observe their "mental states" just as the physiologist observes neural events, but another interpretation of what they observe is possible, as we shall see in Chapter XVII. Introspective psychology no longer pretends to supply direct information about events which are the causal antecedents, rather than the mere accompaniments, of behavior. It defines its "subjective" events in ways which strip them of any usefulness in a causal analysis. The events appealed to in early mentalistic explanations of behavior have remained beyond the reach of observation. Freud insisted upon this by emphasizing the role of the unconscious—a frank recognition that important mental processes are not directly observable. The Freudian literature supplies many examples of behavior from which unconscious wishes, impulses, instincts, and emotions are inferred. Unconscious thought-processes have also been used to explain intellectual achievements. Though the mathematician may feel that he knows "how he thinks," he is often unable to give a coherent account of the mental processes leading to the solution of a specific problem. But any mental event which is unconscious is necessarily inferential, and the explanation is therefore not based upon independent observations of a valid cause.

The fictional nature of this form of inner cause is shown by the ease with which the mental process is discovered to have just the properties needed to account for the behavior. When a professor turns up in the wrong classroom or gives the wrong lecture, it is because his *mind* is, at least for the moment, *absent*. If he forgets to give a reading assignment, it is because it has slipped his *mind* (a hint from the class may re*mind* him of it). He begins to tell an old joke but pauses for a moment, and it is evident to everyone that he is trying to make up his *mind* whether or not he has already used the joke that term. His lectures grow more tedious with the years, and questions from the class confuse him more and more, because his *mind* is failing. What he says is often disorganized because his *ideas* are confused. He is occasionally unnecessarily emphatic because of the force of his *ideas*. When he repeats himself, it is because he has an *idée fixe*: and when he repeats what others have said, it is because he borrows his *ideas*. Upon occasion there is nothing in what he says because he lacks *ideas*. In all this it is obvious that the mind and the ideas, together with their special characteristics, are being invented on the spot to provide spurious explanations. A science of behavior can hope to gain very little from so cavalier a practice. Since mental or psychic events are asserted to lack the dimensions of physical science, we have an additional reason for rejecting them.

Conceptual inner causes. The commonest inner causes have no specific dimensions at all, either neurological or psychic. When we say that a man eats *because* he is hungry, smokes a great deal *because* he has the tobacco habit, fights *because* of the instinct of pugnacity, behaves brilliantly *because* of his intelligence, or plays the piano well *because* of his musical ability, we seem to be referring to causes. But on analysis these phrases prove to be merely redundant descriptions. A single set of facts is described by the two statements: "He eats" and "He is hungry." A single set of facts is described by the two statements: "He smokes a great deal" and "He has the smoking habit." A single set of facts is described by the two statements: "He plays well" and "He has musical ability." The practice of explaining one statement in terms of the other is dangerous because it suggests that we have found the cause and therefore need search no further. Moreover, such terms as "hunger," "habit," and "intelligence" convert what are essentially the properties of a process or relation into what appear to be things. Thus we are unprepared for the properties eventually to be discovered in the behavior itself and continue to look for something which may not exist.

The Variables of Which Behavior Is a Function

The practice of looking inside the organism for an explanation of behavior has tended to obscure the variables which are immediately available for a scientific analysis. These variables lie outside the organism, in its immediate environment and in its environmental history. They have a physical status to which the usual techniques of science are adapted, and they make it possible to explain behavior as other subjects are explained in science. These independent variables are of many sorts and their relations to behavior are often subtle and complex, but we cannot hope to give an adequate account of behavior without analyzing them.

Consider the act of drinking a glass of water. This is not likely to be an important bit of behavior in anyone's life, but it supplies a convenient example. We may describe the topography of the behavior in such a way that a given instance may be identified quite accurately by any qualified observer. Suppose now we bring someone into a room and place a glass of water before him. Will he drink? There appear to be only two possibilities: either he will or he will not. But we speak of the *chances* that he will drink, and this notion may be refined for scientific use. What we want to evaluate is the *probability* that he will drink. This may range from virtual certainty that drinking will occur to virtual certainty that it will not. The very considerable problem of how to measure such a probability will be discussed later. For the moment, we are interested in how the probability may be increased or decreased.

Everyday experience suggests several possibilities, and laboratory and clinical observations have added others. It is decidedly not true that a horse may be led to water but cannot be made to drink. By arranging a history of severe deprivation we could be "absolutely sure" that drinking would occur. In the same way we may be sure that the glass of water in our experiment will be drunk. Although we are not likely to arrange them experimentally, deprivations of the necessary magnitude sometimes occur outside the laboratory. We may obtain an effect similar to that of deprivation by speeding up the excretion of water. For example, we may induce sweating by raising the temperature of the room or by forcing heavy exercise, or we may increase the excretion of urine by mixing salt or urea in food taken prior to the experiment. It is also well known that loss of blood, as on a battlefield, sharply increases the probability of drinking. On the other hand, we may set the probability at virtually zero by inducing or forcing our subject to drink a large quantity of water before the experiment.

If we are to predict whether or not our subject will drink, we must know as much as possible about these variables. If we are to induce him to drink, we must be able to manipulate them. In both cases, moreover, either for accurate prediction or control, we must investigate the effect of each variable quantitatively with the methods and techniques of a laboratory science.

Other variables may, of course, affect the result. Our subject may be "afraid" that something has been added to the water as a practical joke or for experimental purposes. He may even "suspect" that the water has been poisoned. He may have grown up in a culture in which water is drunk only when no one is watching. He may refuse to drink simply to prove that we cannot predict or control his behavior. These possibilities do not disprove the relations between drinking and the variables listed in the preceding paragraphs; they simply remind us that other variables may have to be taken into account. We must know the history of our subject with respect to the behavior of drinking water, and if we cannot eliminate social factors from the situation, then we must know the history of his personal relations to people resembling the experimenter. Adequate prediction in any science requires information about all relevant variables, and the control of a subject matter for practical purposes makes the same demands.

Other types of "explanation" do not permit us to dispense with these requirements or to fulfill them in any easier way. It is of no help to be told that our subject will drink provided he was born under a particular sign of the zodiac which shows a preoccupation with water or provided he is the lean and thirsty type or was, in short, "born thirsty." Explanations in terms of inner states or agents, however, may require some further comment. To what extent is it helpful to be told, "He drinks because he is thirsty"? If to be thirsty means nothing more than to have a tendency to drink, this is mere redundancy. If it means that he drinks because of a state of thirst, an inner causal event is invoked. If this state is purely inferential—if no dimensions are assigned to it which would make direct observation possible—it cannot serve as an explanation. But if it has physiological or psychic properties, what role can it play in a science of behavior?

NOAM CHOMSKY

A Review of B.F. Skinner's *Verbal Behavior*

1

A great many linguists and philosophers concerned with language have expressed the hope that their studies might ultimately be embedded in a framework provided by behaviorist psychology, and that refractory areas of investigation, particularly those in which meaning is involved, will in this way be opened up to fruitful exploration. Since this volume [*Verbal Behavior* (New York: Appleton-Century-Crofts, 1957)—*Ed.*] is the first large-scale attempt to incorporate the major aspects of linguistic behavior within a behaviorist framework, it merits and will undoubtedly receive careful attention. Skinner is noted for his contributions to the study of animal behavior. The book under review is the product of study of linguistic behavior extending over more than twenty years. Earlier versions of it have been fairly widely circulated, and there are quite a few references in the psychological literature to its major ideas.

The problem to which this book is addressed is that of giving a "functional analysis" of verbal behavior. By functional analysis, Skinner means identification of the variables that control this behavior and specification of how they interact to determine a particular verbal response. Furthermore, the controlling variables are to be described completely in terms of such notions as *stimulus, reinforcement, deprivation*, which have been given a reasonably clear meaning in animal experimentation. In other words, the goal of the book is to provide a way to predict and control verbal behavior by observing and manipulating the physical environment of the speaker.

Skinner feels that recent advances in the laboratory study of animal behavior permit us to approach this problem with a certain optimism, since "the basic processes and relations which give verbal behavior its special characteristics are now fairly well understood...the results [of this experimental work] have been surprisingly free of species restrictions. Recent work has shown that the methods can be extended to human behavior without serious modification" (3).[1]

It is important to see clearly just what it is in Skinner's program and claims that makes them appear so bold and remarkable. It is not primarily the fact that he has set functional analysis as his problem, or that he limits himself to study of *observables*, i.e., input-output relations. What is so surprising is the particular limitations he has imposed on the way in which the observables of behavior are to be studied, and, above all, the particularly simple nature of the *function* which, he claims, describes the causation of behavior. One would naturally expect that prediction of the behavior of a complex organism (or machine) would require, in addition to information about external stimulation, knowledge of the internal structure of the organism, the ways in which it processes input information and organizes its own behavior. These characteristics of the organism are in general a complicated product of inborn structure, the genetically determined course of maturation, and past experience. Insofar as independent neurophysiological evidence is not available, it is obvious that inferences concerning the structure of the organism are based on observation of behavior and outside events. Nevertheless, one's estimate of the relative importance of external factors and internal structure in the determination of behavior

will have an important effect on the duration of research on linguistic (or any other) behavior, and on the kinds of analogies from animal behavior studies that will be considered relevant or suggestive.

Putting it differently, anyone who sets himself the problem of analyzing the causation of behavior will (in the absence of independent neurophysiological evidence) concern himself with the only data available, namely the record of inputs to the organism and the organism's present response, and will try to describe the function specifying the response in terms of the history of inputs. This is nothing more than the definition of his problem. There are no possible grounds for argument here, if one accepts the problem as legitimate, though Skinner has often advanced and defended this definition of a problem as if it were a thesis which other investigators reject. The differences that arise between those who affirm and those who deny the importance of the specific "contribution of the organism" to learning and performance concern the particular character and complexity of this function, and the kinds of observations and research necessary for arriving at a precise specification of it. If the contribution of the organism is complex, the only hope of predicting behavior even in a gross way will be through a very indirect program of research that begins by studying the detailed character of the behavior itself and the particular capacities of the organism involved.

Skinner's thesis is that external factors consisting of present stimulation and the history of reinforcement (in particular, the frequency, arrangement, and withholding of reinforcing stimuli) are of overwhelming importance, and that the general principles revealed in laboratory studies of these phenomena provide the basis for understanding the complexities of verbal behavior. He confidently and repeatedly voices his claim to have demonstrated that the contribution of the speaker is quite trivial and elementary, and that precise prediction of verbal behavior involves only specification of the few external factors that he has isolated experimentally with lower organisms.

Careful study of this book (and of the research on which it draws) reveals, however, that these astonishing claims are far from justified. It indicates, furthermore, that the insights that have been achieved in the laboratories of the reinforcement theorist, though quite genuine, can be applied to complex human behavior only in the most gross and superficial way, and that speculative attempts to discuss linguistic behavior in these terms alone omit from consideration factors of fundamental importance that are, no doubt, amenable to scientific study, although their specific character cannot at present be precisely formulated. Since Skinner's work is the most extensive attempt to accommodate human behavior involving higher mental faculties within a strict behaviorist schema of the type that has attracted many linguists and philosophers, as well as psychologists, a detailed documentation is of independent interest. The magnitude of the failure of this attempt to account for verbal behavior serves as a kind of measure of the importance of the factors omitted from consideration, and an indication of how little is really known about this remarkably complex phenomenon.

The force of Skinner's argument lies in the enormous wealth and range of examples for which he proposes a functional analysis. The only way to evaluate the success of his program and the correctness of his basic assumptions about verbal behavior is to review these examples in detail and to determine the precise character of the concepts in terms of which the functional analysis is presented. Section 2 of this review describes the experimental context with respect to which these concepts are originally defined. Sections 3 and 4 deal with the basic concepts—*stimulus*, *response*, and *reinforcement*—Sections 6 to 10 with the new descriptive machinery developed specifically for the description of verbal behavior. In Section 5 we consider the status of the fundamental claim, drawn from the laboratory, which serves as the basis for the analogic guesses about human behavior that have been proposed by many psychologists. The final section (Section 11) will consider some ways in which further linguistic work may play a part in clarifying some of these problems.

2

Although this book makes no direct reference to experimental work, it can be understood only in terms of the general framework that Skinner has developed for the description of behavior. Skinner divides the responses of the animal into two main categories. *Respondents* are purely reflex responses elicited by particular stimuli. *Operants* are emitted responses, for which no obvious stimulus can be discovered. Skinner has been concerned primarily with operant behavior. The experimental arrangement that he introduced consists basically of a box with a bar attached to one wall in such a way that when the bar is pressed, a food pellet is dropped into a tray (and the bar press is recorded). A rat placed in the box will soon press the bar, releasing a pellet into the tray. This state of affairs, resulting from the bar press, increases the *strength* of the bar-pressing operant. The food pellet is called a *reinforcer*; the event, a *reinforcing event*. The strength of an operant is defined by Skinner in terms of the rate of response during extinction (i.e., after the last reinforcement and before return to the pre-conditioning rate).

Suppose that release of the pellet is conditional on the flashing of a light. Then the rat will come to press the bar only when the light flashes. This is called *stimulus discrimination*. The response is called a *discriminated operant* and the light is called the *occasion* for its emission: this is to be distinguished from elicitation of a response by a stimulus in the case of the respondent.[2] Suppose that the apparatus is so arranged that bar-pressing of only a certain character (e.g., duration) will release the pellet. The rat will then come to press the bar in the required way. This process is called *response differentiation*. By successive slight changes in the conditions under which the response will be reinforced, it is possible to shape the response of a rat or a pigeon in very surprising ways in a very short time, so that rather complex behavior can be produced by a process of successive approximation.

A stimulus can become reinforcing by repeated association with an already reinforcing stimulus. Such a stimulus is called a *secondary reinforcer*. Like many contemporary behaviorists, Skinner considers money, approval, and the like to be secondary reinforcers which have become reinforcing because of their association with food, etc.[3] Secondary reinforcers can be *generalized* by associating them with a variety of different primary reinforcers.

Another variable that can affect the rate of the bar-pressing operant is drive, which Skinner defines operationally in terms of hours of deprivation. His major scientific book, *Behavior of Organisms*, is a study of the effects of food-deprivation and conditioning on the strength of the bar-pressing response of healthy mature rats. Probably Skinner's most original contribution to animal behavior studies has been his investigation of the effects of intermittent reinforcement, arranged in various different ways, presented in *Behavior of Organisms* and extended (with pecking of pigeons as the operant under investigation) in the recent *Schedules of Reinforcement* by Ferster and Skinner (1957). It is apparently these studies that Skinner has in mind when he refers to the recent advances in the study of animal behavior.[4]

The notions *stimulus, response, reinforcement* are relatively well defined with respect to the bar-pressing experiments and others similarly restricted. Before we can extend them to real-life behavior, however, certain difficulties must be faced. We must decide, first of all, whether any physical event to which the organism is capable of reacting is to be called a stimulus on a given occasion, or only one to which the organism in fact reacts; and correspondingly, we must decide whether any part of behavior is to be called a response, or only one connected with stimuli in lawful ways. Questions of this sort pose something of a dilemma for the experimental psychologist. If he accepts the broad definitions, characterizing any physical event impinging on the organism as a stimulus and any part of the organism's behavior as a response, he must conclude that behavior has not been demonstrated to be lawful. In the present state of our knowledge, we must attribute an overwhelming influence on actual behavior to ill-defined factors of attention, set, volition, and caprice. If we accept the narrower definitions, then behavior is lawful by definition (if it consists of responses); but this fact is of limited significance, since most of what the animal does will simply not be considered behavior. Hence, the psychologist either must admit that behavior is not lawful (or that he cannot at present show that it is—not at all a damaging admission for a developing science), or must restrict his attention to those highly limited areas in which it is lawful (e.g., with adequate controls, bar-pressing in rats; lawfulness of the observed behavior provides, for Skinner, an implicit definition of a good experiment).

Skinner does not consistently adopt either course. He utilizes the experimental results as evidence for the scientific character of his system of behavior, and analogic guesses (formulated in terms of a metaphoric extension of the technical vocabulary of the laboratory) as evidence for its scope. This creates the illusion of a rigorous scientific theory with a very broad scope, although in fact the terms used in the description of real-life and of laboratory behavior may be mere homonyms, with at most a vague similarity of meaning. To substantiate this evaluation, a critical account of his book must show that with a literal reading (where the terms of the descriptive system have something like the technical meanings given in Skinner's definitions) the book covers almost no aspect of linguistic behavior, and that with a metaphoric reading, it is no more scientific than the traditional approaches to this subject matter, and rarely as clear and careful.[5]

3

Consider first Skinner's use of the notions *stimulus* and *response*. In *Behavior of Organisms* (9) he commits himself to the narrow definitions for these terms. A part of the environment and a part of behavior are called *stimulus* (eliciting, discriminated, or reinforcing) and *response*, respectively, only if they are lawfully related; that is, if the *dynamic laws* relating them show smooth and reproducible curves. Evidently, stimuli and responses, so defined, have not been shown to figure very widely in ordinary human behavior.[6] We can, in the face of presently available evidence, continue to maintain the lawfulness of the relation between stimulus and response only by depriving them of their objective character. A typical example of *stimulus control* for Skinner would be the response to a piece of music with the utterance *Mozart* or to a painting with the response *Dutch*. These responses are asserted to be "under the control of extremely subtle properties" of the physical object or event (108). Suppose instead of saying *Dutch* we had said *Clashes with the wallpaper, I thought you liked abstract work, Never saw it before, Tilted, Hanging too low, Beautiful, Hideous, Remember our camping trip last summer?*, or whatever else might come into our minds when looking at a picture (in Skinnerian translation, whatever other responses exist in sufficient strength). Skinner could only say that each of these responses is under the control of some other stimulus property of the physical object. If we look at a red chair and say *red*, the response is under the control of the stimulus *redness*; if we say *chair*, it is under the control of the collection of properties (for Skinner, the object) *chairness* (110), and similarly for any other response. This device is as simple as it is empty. Since properties are free for the asking (we have as many of them as we have nonsynonymous descriptive expressions in our language, whatever this means exactly), we can account for a wide class of responses in terms of Skinnerian functional analysis by identifying the *controlling stimuli*. But the word *stimulus* has lost all objectivity in this usage. Stimuli are no longer part of the outside physical world; they are driven back into the organism. We identify the stimulus when we hear the response. It is clear from such examples, which abound, that the talk of *stimulus control* simply disguises a complete retreat to mentalistic psychology. We cannot predict verbal behavior in terms of the stimuli in the speaker's environment, since we do not know what the current stimuli are until he responds. Furthermore, since we cannot control the property of a physical object to which an individual will respond, except in highly artificial cases, Skinner's claim that his system, as opposed to the traditional one, permits the practical control of verbal behavior[7] is quite false.

Other examples of *stimulus control* merely add to the general mystification. Thus, a proper noun is held to be a response "under the control of a specific person or thing" (as controlling stimulus, 113). I have often used the words *Eisenhower* and *Moscow*, which I presume are proper nouns if anything is, but have never been *stimulated* by the corresponding objects. How can this fact be made compatible with this definition? Suppose that I use the name of a friend who is not present. Is this an instance of a proper noun under the control of the friend as stimulus? Elsewhere it is asserted that a stimulus controls a response in the sense that presence of the stimulus increases the probability of the response. But it is obviously untrue that the probability that a speaker will produce a full name is increased when its bearer faces the speaker. Furthermore, how can one's own name be a proper noun in this sense? A multitude of similar questions arise immediately. It appears that the word *control* here is merely a misleading paraphrase for the traditional *denote* or *refer*. The assertion (115) that so far as the speaker is concerned, the relation of reference is "simply the probability that the speaker will emit a response of a given form in the presence of a stimulus having specified properties" is surely incorrect if we take the words *presence*, *stimulus*, and *probability* in their literal sense. That they are not intended to be taken literally is indicated by many examples, as when a response is said to be "controlled" by a situation or state of affairs as "stimulus." Thus, the expression *a needle in a haystack* "may be controlled as a unit by a particular type of situation" (116); the words in a single part of speech, e.g., all adjectives, are under the control of a single set of subtle properties of stimuli (121); "the sentence *The boy runs a store* is under the control of an extremely complex stimulus situation" (335); "*He is not at all well* may function as a standard response under the control of a state of affairs which might also control *He is ailing*" (325); when an envoy observes events in a foreign country and reports upon his return, his report is under "remote stimulus control" (416); the statement *This is war* may be a response to a "confusing international situation" (441); the suffix *-ed* is controlled by that "subtle property of stimuli which we speak of as action-in-the-past" (121) just as the *-s* in *The boy runs* is under the control of such specific features of the situation as its "currency" (332). No characterization of the notion *stimulus control* that is remotely related to the bar-pressing experiment (or that preserves the faintest objectivity) can be made to cover a set of examples like these, in which, for example, the *controlling stimulus* need not even impinge on the responding organism.

Consider now Skinner's use of the notion *response*. The problem of identifying units in verbal behavior has of course been a primary concern of linguists, and it seems very likely that experimental psychologists should be able to provide much-needed assistance in clearing up the many remaining difficulties in systematic identification. Skinner recognizes (20) the fundamental character of the problem of identification of a unit of verbal behavior, but is satisfied with an answer so vague and subjective that it does not really contribute to its solution. The unit of verbal behavior—the verbal operant—is defined as a class of responses of identifiable form functionally related to one or more controlling variables. No method is suggested for determining in a particular instance what are the controlling variables, how many such units have occurred, or where their boundaries are in the total response. Nor is any attempt made to specify how much or what kind of similarity in form or *control* is required for two physical events to be considered instances of the same operant. In short, no answers are suggested for the most elementary questions that must be asked of anyone proposing a method for description of behavior. Skinner is content with what he calls an *extrapolation* of the concept of operant developed in the laboratory to the verbal field. In the typical Skinnerian experiment, the problem of identifying the unit of behavior is not too crucial. It is defined, by fiat, as a recorded peck or bar-press, and systematic variations in the rate of this operant and its resistance to extinction are studied as a function of deprivation and scheduling of reinforcement (pellets). The operant is thus defined with respect to a particular experimental procedure. This is perfectly reasonable and has led to many interesting results. It is, however, completely meaningless to speak of extrapolating this concept of operant to ordinary verbal behavior. Such "extrapolation" leaves us with no way of justifying one or another decision about the units in the "verbal repertoire."

Skinner specifies "response strength" as the basic datum, the basic dependent variable in his functional analysis. In the bar-pressing experiment, response strength is defined in terms of rate of emission during extinction. Skinner has argued[8] that this is "the only datum that varies significantly and in the expected direction under conditions which are relevant to the 'learning process.'" In the book under review, response strength is defined as "probability of emission" (22). This definition provides a comforting impression of objectivity, which, however, is quickly dispelled when we look into the matter more closely. The term *probability* has some rather obscure meaning for Skinner in this book.[9] We are told, on the one hand, that "our evidence for the contribution of each variable [to response strength] is based on observation of frequencies alone" (28). At the same time, it appears that frequency is a very misleading measure of strength, since, for example, the frequency of a response may be "primarily attributable to the frequency of occurrence of controlling variables" (27). It is not clear how the frequency of a response can be attributable to anything BUT the frequency of occurrence of its controlling variables if we

accept Skinner's view that the behavior occurring in a given situation is "fully determined" by the relevant controlling variables (175, 228). Furthermore, although the evidence for the contribution of each variable to response strength is based on observation of frequencies alone, it turns out that "we base the notion of strength upon several kinds of evidence" (22), in particular (22–28): emission of the response (particularly in unusual circumstances), energy level (stress), pitch level, speed and delay of emission, size of letters etc. in writing, immediate repetition, and—a final factor, relevant but misleading—over-all frequency.

Of course, Skinner recognizes that these measures do not co-vary, because (among other reasons) pitch, stress, quantity, and reduplication may have internal linguistic functions.[10] However, he does not hold these conflicts to be very important, since the proposed factors indicative of strength are "fully understood by everyone" in the culture (27). For example, "if we are shown a prized work of art and exclaim *Beautiful!*, the speed and energy of the response will not be lost on the owner." It does not appear totally obvious that in this case the way to impress the owner is to shriek *Beautiful* in a loud, high-pitched voice, repeatedly, and with no delay (high response strength). It may be equally effective to look at the picture silently (long delay) and then to murmur *Beautiful* in a soft, low-pitched voice (by definition, very low response strength).

It is not unfair, I believe, to conclude from Skinner's discussion of response strength, the *basic datum* in functional analysis, that his *extrapolation* of the notion of probability can best be interpreted as, in effect, nothing more than a decision to use the word *probability*, with its favorable connotations of objectivity, as a cover term to paraphrase such low-status words as *interest, intention, belief,* and the like. This interpretation is fully justified by the way in which Skinner uses the terms *probability* and *strength*. To cite just one example, Skinner defines the process of confirming an assertion in science as one of "generating additional variables to increase its probability" (425), and more generally, its strength (425–29). If we take this suggestion quite literally, the degree of confirmation of a scientific assertion can be measured as a simple function of the loudness, pitch, and frequency with which it is proclaimed, and a general procedure for increasing its degree of confirmation would be, for instance, to train machine guns on large crowds of people who have been instructed to shout it. A better indication of what Skinner probably has in mind here is given by his description of how the theory of evolution, as an example, is confirmed. This "single set of verbal responses…is made more plausible—is strengthened—by several types of construction based upon verbal responses in geology, paleontology, genetics, and so on" (427). We are no doubt to interpret the terms *strength* and *probability* in this context as paraphrases of more familiar locutions such as "justified belief" or "warranted assertability," or something of the sort. Similar latitude of interpretation is presumably expected when we read that "frequency of effective action accounts in turn for what we may call the listener's 'belief'" (88) or that "our belief in what someone tells us is similarly a function of, or identical with, our tendency to act upon the verbal stimuli which he provides" (160).[11]

I think it is evident, then, that Skinner's use of the terms *stimulus, control, response,* and *strength* justify the general conclusion stated in the last paragraph of Section 2. The way in which these terms are brought to bear on the actual data indicates that we must interpret them as mere paraphrases for the popular vocabulary commonly used to describe behavior and as having no particular connection with the hom-onymous expressions used in the description of laboratory experiments. Naturally, this terminological revision adds no objectivity to the familiar *mentalistic* mode of description.

4

The other fundamental notion borrowed from the description of bar-pressing experiments is *reinforcement*. It raises problems which are similar, and even more serious. In *Behavior of Organisms*, "the operation of reinforcement is defined as the presentation of a certain kind of stimulus in a temporal relation with either a stimulus or response. A reinforcing stimulus is defined as such by its power to produce the resulting change [in strength]. There is no circularity about this: some stimuli are found to produce the change, others not, and they are classified as reinforcing and nonreinforcing accordingly" (62). This is a perfectly appropriate definition[12] for the study of schedules of reinforcement. It is perfectly useless, however, in the discussion of real-life behavior, unless we can somehow characterize the stimuli which are reinforcing (and the situations and conditions under which they are reinforcing). Consider first of all the status of the basic principle that Skinner calls the "law of conditioning" (law of effect). It reads: "if the occurrence of an operant is followed by presence of a reinforcing stimulus, the strength is increased" (*Behavior of Organisms*, 21). As *reinforcement* was defined, this law becomes a tautology.[13] For Skinner, learning is just change in response strength.[14] Although the statement that presence of reinforcement is a sufficient condition for learning and maintenance of behavior is vacuous, the claim that it is a necessary condition may have some content, depending on how the class of reinforcers (and appropriate situations) is characterized. Skinner does make it very clear that in his view reinforcement is a necessary condition for language learning and for the continued availability of linguistic responses in the adult.[15] However, the looseness of the term *reinforcement* as Skinner uses it in the book under review makes it entirely pointless to inquire into the truth or falsity of this claim. Examining the instances of what Skinner calls *reinforcement*, we find that not even the requirement that a reinforcer be an identifiable stimulus is taken seriously. In fact, the term is used in such a way that the assertion that reinforcement is necessary for learning and continued availability of behavior is likewise empty.

To show this, we consider some examples of *reinforcement*. First of all, we find a heavy appeal to automatic self-reinforcement. Thus, "a man talks to himself...because of the reinforcement he receives" (163); "the child is reinforced automatically when he duplicates the sounds of airplanes, streetcars ..." (164); "the young child alone in the nursery may automatically reinforce his own exploratory verbal behavior when he produces sounds which he has heard in the speech of others" (58); "the speaker who is also an accomplished listener 'knows when he has correctly echoed a response' and is reinforced thereby" (68); thinking is "behaving which automatically affects the behaver and is reinforcing because it does so" (438; cutting one's finger should thus be reinforcing, and an example of thinking); "the verbal fantasy, whether overt or covert, is automatically reinforcing to the speaker as listener. Just as the musician plays or composes what he is reinforced by hearing, or as the artist paints what reinforces him visually, so the speaker engaged in verbal fantasy says what he is reinforced by hearing or writes what he is reinforced by reading" (439); similarly, care in problem solving, and rationalization, are automatically self-reinforcing (442–43). We can also reinforce someone by emitting verbal behavior as such (since this rules out a class of aversive stimulations, 167), by not emitting verbal

behavior (keeping silent and paying attention, 199), or by acting appropriately on some future occasion (152: "the strength of [the speaker's] behavior is determined mainly by the behavior which the listener will exhibit with respect to a given state of affairs"; this Skinner considers the general case of "communication" or "letting the listener know"). In most such cases, of course, the speaker is not present at the time when the reinforcement takes place, as when "the artist...is reinforced by the effects his works have upon...others" (224), or when the writer is reinforced by the fact that his "verbal behavior may reach over centuries or to thousands of listeners or readers at the same time. The writer may not be reinforced often or immediately, but his net reinforcement may be great" (206; this accounts for the great "strength" of his behavior). An individual may also find it reinforcing to injure someone by criticism or by bringing bad news, or to publish an experimental result which upsets the theory of a rival (154), to describe circumstances which would be reinforcing if they were to occur (165), to avoid repetition (222), to "hear" his own name though in fact it was not mentioned or to hear nonexistent words in his child's babbling (259), to clarify or otherwise intensify the effect of a stimulus which serves an important discriminative function (416), and so on.

From this sample, it can be seen that the notion of reinforcement has totally lost whatever objective meaning it may ever have had. Running through these examples, we see that a person can be reinforced though he emits no response at all, and that the reinforcing *stimulus* need not impinge on the *reinforced person* or need not even exist (it is sufficient that it be imagined or hoped for). When we read that a person plays what music he likes (165), says what he likes (165), thinks what he likes (438–39), reads what books he likes (163), etc., because he finds it reinforcing to do so, or that we write books or inform others of facts because we are reinforced by what we hope will be the ultimate behavior of reader or listener, we can only conclude that the term *reinforcement* has a purely ritual function. The phrase "*X* is reinforced by *Y* (stimulus, state of affairs, event, etc.)" is being used as a cover term for "*X* wants *Y*," "*X* likes *Y*," "*X* wishes that *Y* were the case," etc. Invoking the term *reinforcement* has no explanatory force, and any idea that this paraphrase introduces any new clarity or objectivity into the description of wishing, liking, etc., is a serious delusion. The only effect is to obscure the important differences among the notions being paraphrased. Once we recognize the latitude with which the term *reinforcement* is being used, many rather startling comments lose their initial effect—for instance, that the behavior of the creative artist is "controlled entirely by the contingencies of reinforcement" (150). What has been hoped for from the psychologist is some indication how the casual and informal description of everyday behavior in the popular vocabulary can be explained or clarified in terms of the notions developed in careful experiment and observation, or perhaps replaced in terms of a better scheme. A mere terminological revision, in which a term borrowed from the laboratory is used with the full vagueness of the ordinary vocabulary, is of no conceivable interest.

It seems that Skinner's claim that all verbal behavior is acquired and maintained in "strength" through reinforcement is quite empty, because his notion of reinforcement has no clear content, functioning only as a cover term for any factor, detectable or not, related to acquisition or maintenance of verbal behavior.[16] Skinner's use of the term *conditioning* suffers from a similar difficulty. Pavlovian and operant conditioning are processes about which psychologists have developed real understanding. Instruction of human beings is not. The claim that instruction and imparting of information

are simply matters of conditioning (357–66) is pointless. The claim is true, if we extend the term *conditioning* to cover these processes, but we know no more about them after having revised this term in such a way as to deprive it of its relatively clear and objective character. It is, as far as we know, quite false, if we use *conditioning* in its literal sense. Similarly, when we say that "it is the function of predication to facilitate the transfer of response from one term to another or from one object to another" (361), we have said nothing of any significance. In what sense is this true of the predication *Whales are mammals*? Or, to take Skinner's example, what point is there in saying that the effect of *The telephone is out of order* on the listener is to bring behavior formerly controlled by the stimulus *out of order* under control of the stimulus *telephone* (or the telephone itself) by a process of simple conditioning (362)? What laws of conditioning hold in this case? Furthermore, what behavior is *controlled* by the stimulus *out of order*, in the abstract? Depending on the object of which this is predicated, the present state of motivation of the listener, etc., the behavior may vary from rage to pleasure, from fixing the object to throwing it out, from simply not using it to trying to use it in the normal way (e.g., to see if it is really out of order), and so on. To speak of "conditioning" or "bringing previously available behavior under control of a new stimulus" in such a case is just a kind of play-acting at science...

[...]

11

The preceding discussion covers all the major notions that Skinner introduces in his descriptive system. My purpose in discussing the concepts one by one was to show that in each case, if we take his terms in their literal meaning, the description covers almost no aspect of verbal behavior, and if we take them metaphorically, the description offers no improvement over various traditional formulations. The terms borrowed from experimental psychology simply lose their objective meaning with this extension, and take over the full vagueness of ordinary language. Since Skinner limits himself to such a small set of terms for paraphrase, many important distinctions are obscured. I think that this analysis supports the view expressed in Section 1, that elimination of the independent contribution of the speaker and learner (a result which Skinner considers of great importance, cf. 311–12) can be achieved only at the cost of eliminating all significance from the descriptive system, which then operates at a level so gross and crude that no answers are suggested to the most elementary questions.[46] The questions to which Skinner has addressed his speculations are hopelessly premature. It is futile to inquire into the causation of verbal behavior until much more is known about the specific character of this behavior; and there is little point in speculating about the process of acquisition without much better understanding of what is acquired.

Anyone who seriously approaches the study of linguistic behavior, whether linguist, psychologist, or philosopher, must quickly become aware of the enormous difficulty of stating a problem which will define the area of his investigations, and which will not be either completely trivial or hopelessly beyond the range of present-day understanding and technique. In selecting functional analysis as his problem, Skinner has set himself a task of the latter type. In an extremely interesting and insightful paper,[47] K.S. Lashley has implicitly delimited a class of problems which can be approached in a fruitful way by the linguist and psychologist, and which are clearly preliminary to those with which Skinner is concerned.

Lashley recognizes, as anyone must who seriously considers the data, that the composition and production of an utterance is not simply a matter of stringing together a sequence of responses under the control of outside stimulation and intraverbal association, and that the syntactic organization of an utterance is not something directly represented in any simple way in the physical structure of the utterance itself. A variety of observations lead him to conclude that syntactic structure is "a generalized pattern imposed on the specific acts as they occur" (512), and that "a consideration of the structure of the sentence and other motor sequences will show…that there are, behind the overtly expressed sequences, a multiplicity of integrative processes which can only be inferred from the final results of their activity" (509). He also comments on the great difficulty of determining the "selective mechanisms" used in the actual construction of a particular utterance (522).

Although present-day linguistics cannot provide a precise account of these integrative processes, imposed patterns, and selective mechanisms, it can at least set itself the problem of characterizing these completely. It is reasonable to regard the grammar of a language L ideally as a mechanism that provides an enumeration of the sentences of L in something like the way in which a deductive theory gives an enumeration of a set of theorems. (*Grammar*, in this sense of the word, includes phonology.) Furthermore, the theory of language can be regarded as a study of the formal properties of such grammars, and, with a precise enough formulation, this general theory can provide a uniform method for determining, from the process of generation of a given sentence, a structural description which can give a good deal of insight into how this sentence is used and understood. In short, it should be possible to derive from a properly formulated grammar a statement of the integrative processes and generalized patterns imposed on the specific acts that constitute an utterance. The rules of a grammar of the appropriate form can be subdivided into the two types, optional and obligatory; only the latter must be applied in generating an utterance. The optional rules of the grammar can be viewed, then, as the selective mechanisms involved in the production of a particular utterance. The problem of specifying these integrative processes and selective mechanisms is nontrivial and not beyond the range of possible investigation. The results of such a study might, as Lashley suggests, be of independent interest for psychology and neurology (and conversely). Although such a study, even if successful, would by no means answer the major problems involved in the investigation of meaning and the causation of behavior, it surely will not be unrelated to these. It is at least possible, furthermore, that such a notion as *semantic generalization*, to which such heavy appeal is made in all approaches to language in use, conceals complexities and specific structure of inference not far different from those that can be studied and exhibited in the case of syntax, and that consequently the general character of the results of syntactic investigations may be a corrective to oversimplified approaches to the theory of meaning.

The behavior of the speaker, listener, and learner of language constitutes, of course, the actual data for any study of language. The construction of a grammar which enumerates sentences in such a way that a meaningful structural description can be determined for each sentence does not in itself provide an account of this actual behavior. It merely characterizes abstractly the ability of one who has mastered the language to distinguish sentences from nonsentences, to understand new sentences (in part), to note certain ambiguities, etc. These are very remarkable abilities.

We constantly read and hear new sequences of words, recognize them as sentences, and understand them. It is easy to show that the new events that we accept and understand as sentences are not related to those with which we are familiar by any simple notion of formal (or semantic or statistical) similarity or identity of grammatical frame. Talk of generalization in this case is entirely pointless and empty. It appears that we recognize a new item as a sentence not because it matches some familiar item in any simple way, but because it is generated by the grammar that each individual has somehow and in some form internalized. And we understand a new sentence, in part, because we are somehow capable of determining the process by which this sentence is derived in this grammar.

Suppose that we manage to construct grammars having the properties outlined above. We can then attempt to describe and study the achievement of the speaker, listener, and learner. The speaker and the listener, we must assume, have already acquired the capacities characterized abstractly by the grammar. The speaker's task is to select a particular compatible set of optional rules. If we know, from grammatical study, what choices are available to him and what conditions of compatibility the choices must meet, we can proceed meaningfully to investigate the factors that lead him to make one or another choice. The listener (or reader) must determine, from an exhibited utterance, what optional rules were chosen in the construction of the utterance. It must be admitted that the ability of a human being to do this far surpasses our present understanding. The child who learns a language has in some sense constructed the grammar for himself on the basis of his observation of sentences and nonsentences (i.e., corrections by the verbal community). Study of the actual observed ability of a speaker to distinguish sentences from nonsentences, detect ambiguities, etc., apparently forces us to the conclusion that this grammar is of an extremely complex and abstract character, and that the young child has succeeded in carrying out what from the formal point of view, at least, seems to be a remarkable type of theory construction. Furthermore, this task is accomplished in an astonishingly short time, to a large extent independently of intelligence, and in a comparable way by all children. Any theory of learning must cope with these facts.

It is not easy to accept the view that a child is capable of constructing an extremely complex mechanism for generating a set of sentences, some of which he has heard, or that an adult can instantaneously determine whether (and if so, how) a particular item is generated by this mechanism, which has many of the properties of an abstract deductive theory. Yet this appears to be a fair description of the performance of the speaker, listener, and learner. If this is correct, we can predict that a direct attempt to account for the actual behavior of speaker, listener, and learner, not based on a prior understanding of the structure of grammars, will achieve very limited success. The grammar must be regarded as a component in the behavior of the speaker and listener which can only be inferred, as Lashley has put it, from the resulting physical acts. The fact that all normal children acquire essentially comparable grammars of great complexity with remarkable rapidity suggests that human beings are somehow specially designed to do this, with data-handling or "hypothesis-formulating" ability of unknown character and complexity.[48] The study of linguistic structure may ultimately lead to some significant insights into this matter. At the moment the question cannot be seriously posed, but in principle it may be possible to study the problem of determining what the built-in structure of an information-processing (hypothesis-forming) system must be to enable it to arrive at the grammar of a language from the available data in the available time. At any rate, just as the attempt to eliminate the contribution of the speaker leads to a "mentalistic" descriptive system that succeeds only in blurring important traditional distinctions, a refusal to study the contribution of the child to language learning permits only a superficial account of language acquisition, with a vast and unanalyzed contribution attributed to a step called *generalization* which in fact includes just about everything of interest in this process. If the study of language is limited in these ways, it seems inevitable that major aspects of verbal behavior will remain a mystery.

Notes

1. Skinner's confidence in recent achievements in the study of animal behavior and their applicability to complex human behavior does not appear to be widely shared. In many recent publications of confirmed behaviorists there is a prevailing note of skepticism with regard to the scope of these achievements. For representative comments, see the contributions to *Modern Learning Theory* (by W.K. Estes *et al.*; New York: Appleton-Century-Crofts, Inc., 1954); B.R. Bugelski, *Psychology of Learning* (New York: Holt, Rinehart & Winston, Inc., 1956); S. Koch, in *Nebraska Symposium on Motivation*, 58 (Lincoln, 1956); W.S. Verplanck, "Learned and Innate Behavior," *Psych. Rev.*, 52 (1955), 139. Perhaps the strongest view is that of H. Harlow, who has asserted ("Mice, Monkeys, Men, and Motives," *Psych. Rev.*, 60 [1953] 23–32) that "a strong case can be made for the proposition that the importance of the psychological problems studied during the last 15 years has decreased as a negatively accelerated function approaching an asymptote of complete indifference."

M. Tinbergen, a leading representative of a different approach to animal-behavior studies (comparative ethology), concludes a discussion of *functional analysis* with the comment that "we may now draw the conclusion that the causation of behavior is immensely more complex than was assumed in the generalizations of the past. A number of internal and external factors act upon complex central nervous structures. Second, it will be obvious that the facts at our disposal are very fragmentary indeed"—*The Study of Instinct* (Toronto: Oxford UP, 1951), p. 74.

2. In *Behavior of Organisms* (New York: Appleton-Century-Crofts, Inc., 1938), Skinner remarks that "although a conditioned operant is the result of the correlation of the response with a particular reinforcement, a relation between it and a discriminative stimulus acting prior to the response is the almost universal rule" (178–79). Even emitted behavior is held to be produced by some sort of "originating force" (51) which, in the case of operant behavior, is not under experimental control. The distinction between eliciting stimuli, discriminated stimuli, and "originating forces" has never been adequately clarified and becomes even more confusing when private internal events are considered to be discriminated stimuli (see below).

3. In a famous experiment, chimpanzees were taught to perform complex tasks to receive tokens which had become secondary reinforcers because of association with food. The idea that money, approval, prestige, etc. actually acquire their motivating effects on human behavior according to this paradigm is unproved, and not particularly plausible. Many psychologists within the behaviorist movement are quite skeptical about this... As in the case of most aspects of human behavior, the evidence about secondary reinforcement is so fragmentary, conflicting, and complex that almost any view can find some support.

4. Skinner's remark quoted above about the generality of his basic results must be understood in the light of the experimental limitations he has imposed. If it were true in any deep sense that the basic processes in language are well understood and free of species restriction, it would be extremely odd that language is limited to man. With the exception of a few scattered observations (cf. his article, "A Case History in Scientific Method," *The American Psychologist*, 11 [1956], 221–33), Skinner is apparently basing this claim on the fact that qualitatively similar results are obtained with bar pressing of rats and pecking of pigeons under special conditions of deprivation and various schedules of reinforcement. One immediately questions how much can be based on these facts, which are in part at least an artifact traceable to experimental design and the definition of *stimulus* and *response* in terms of *smooth dynamic curves* (see below). The dangers inherent in any attempt to *extrapolate* to complex behavior from the study of such simple responses as bar pressing should be obvious and have often been commented on (cf., e.g., Harlow, *op. cit.*). The generality of even the simplest results is open to serious question. Cf. in this connection M.E. Bitterman, J. Wodinsky, and D.K. Candland, "Some Comparative Psychology," *Am. Jour. of Psych.*, 71 (1958), 94–110, where it is shown that there are important qualitative differences in solution of comparable elementary problems by rats and fish.

5. An analogous argument, in connection with a different aspect of Skinner's thinking, is given by M. Scriven in "A Study of...

Radical Behaviorism," *Univ. of Minn. Studies in Philosophy of Science*, I. Cf. Verplanck's contribution to *Modern Learning Theory, op. cit.* pp. 283–88, for more general discussion of the difficulties in formulating an adequate definition of *stimulus* and *response*. He concludes, quite correctly, that in Skinner's sense of the word, stimuli are not objectively identifiable independently of the resulting behavior, nor are they manipulable. Verplanck presents a clear discussion of many other aspects of Skinner's system, commenting on the untestability of many of the so-called "laws of behavior" and the limited scope of many of the others, and the arbitrary and obscure character of Skinner's notion of *lawful relation*; and, at the same time, noting the importance of the experimental data that Skinner has accumulated.

6. In *Behavior of Organisms*, Skinner apparently was willing to accept this consequence. He insists (41–42) that the terms of casual description in the popular vocabulary are not validly descriptive until the defining properties of stimulus and response are specified, the correlation is demonstrated experimentally, and the dynamic changes in it are shown to be lawful. Thus, in describing a child as hiding from a dog, "it will not be enough to dignify the popular vocabulary by appealing to essential properties of *dogness* or *hidingness* and to suppose them intuitively known." But this is exactly what Skinner does in the book under review, as we will see directly.

7. 253f. and elsewhere, repeatedly. As an example of how well we can control behavior using the notions developed in this book, Skinner shows here how he would go about evoking the response *pencil*. The most effective way, he suggests, is to say to the subject, "Please say *pencil*" (our chances would, presumably, be even further improved by use of "aversive stimulation," e.g., holding a gun to his head). We can also "make sure that no pencil or writing instrument is available, then hand our subject a pad of paper appropriate to pencil sketching, and offer him a handsome reward for a recognizable picture of a cat." It would also be useful to have voices saying *pencil* or *pen and* . . . in the background; signs reading *pencil* or *pen and* . . .; or to place a "large and unusual pencil in an unusual place clearly in sight." "Under such circumstances, it is highly probable that our subject will say *pencil*." "The available techniques are all illustrated in this sample." These contributions of behavior theory to the practical control of human behavior are amply illustrated elsewhere in the book, as when Skinner shows (113–14) how we can evoke the response *red* (the device suggested is to hold a red object before the subject and say, "Tell me what color this is").

In fairness, it must be mentioned that there are certain nontrivial applications of *operant conditioning* to the control of human behavior. A wide variety of experiments have shown that the number of plural nouns (for example) produced by a subject will increase if the experimenter says "right" or "good" when one is produced (similarly, positive attitudes on a certain issue, stories with particular content, etc.; cf. L. Krasner, "Studies of the Conditioning of Verbal Behavior," *Psych. Bull.*, 55 [1958], for a survey of several dozen experiments of this kind, mostly with positive results). It is of some interest that the subject is usually unaware of the process. Just what insight this gives into normal verbal behavior is not obvious. Nevertheless, it is an example of positive and not totally expected results using the Skinnerian paradigm.

8. "Are Theories of Learning Necessary?," *Psych. Rev.*, 57 (1950), 193–216.

9. And elsewhere. In his paper "Are Theories of Learning Necessary?" Skinner considers the problem how to extend his analysis of behavior to experimental situations in which it is impossible to observe frequencies, rate of response being the only valid datum. His answer is that "the notion of probability is usually extrapolated to cases in which a frequency analysis cannot be carried out. In the field of behavior we arrange a situation in which frequencies are available as data, but we use the notion of probability in analyzing or formulating instances of even types of behavior which are not susceptible to this analysis" (199). There are, of course, conceptions of probability not based directly on frequency, but I do not see how any of these apply to the cases that Skinner has in mind. I see no way of interpreting the quoted passage other than as signifying an intention to use the word *probability* in describing behavior quite independently of whether the notion of probability is at all relevant.

10. Fortunately, "In English this presents no great difficulty" since, for example, "relative pitch levels...are not...important" (25). No reference is made to the numerous studies of the function of relative pitch levels and other intonational features in English.

11. The vagueness of the word *tendency*, as opposed to *frequency*, saves the latter quotation from the obvious incorrectness of the former. Nevertheless, a good deal of stretching is necessary. If *tendency* has anything like its ordinary meaning, the remark is clearly false. One may believe strongly the assertion that Jupiter has four moons, that many of Sophocles's plays have been irretrievably lost, that the earth will burn to a crisp in ten million years, and

so on, without experiencing the slightest tendency to act upon these verbal stimuli. We may, of course, turn Skinner's assertion into a very unilluminating truth by defining "tendency to act" to include tendencies to answer questions in certain ways, under motivation to say what one believes is true.

12. One should add, however, that it is in general not the stimulus as such that is reinforcing, but the stimulus in a particular situational context. Depending on experimental arrangement, a particular physical event or object may be reinforcing, punishing, or unnoticed. Because Skinner limits himself to a particular, very simple experimental arrangement, it is not necessary for him to add this qualification, which would not be at all easy to formulate precisely. But it is of course necessary if he expects to extend his descriptive system to behavior in general.

13. This has been frequently noted.

14. See, for example, "Are Theories of Learning Necessary?," *op. cit.*, p. 199. Elsewhere, he suggests that the term *learning* be restricted to complex situations, but these are not characterized.

15. "A child acquires verbal behavior when relatively unpatterned vocalizations, selectively reinforced, gradually assume forms which produce appropriate consequences in a given verbal community" (31). "Differential reinforcement shapes up all verbal forms, and when a prior stimulus enters into the contingency, reinforcement is responsible for its resulting control.... The availability of behavior, its probability or strength, depends on whether reinforcements *continue* in effect and according to what schedules" (203–04); elsewhere, frequently.

16. Talk of schedules of reinforcement here is entirely pointless. How are we to decide, for example, according to what schedules covert reinforcement is *arranged*, as

in thinking or verbal fantasy, or what the scheduling is of such factors as silence, speech, and appropriate future reactions to communicated information?

[…]

46. E.g., what are in fact the actual units of verbal behavior? Under what conditions will a physical event capture the attention (be a stimulus) or be a reinforcer? How do we decide what stimuli are in "control" in a specific case? When are stimuli "similar"? And so on. (It is not interesting to be told, e.g., that we say *Stop* to an automobile or billiard ball because they are sufficiently similar to reinforcing people [46].)

The use of unanalyzed notions like "similar" and "generalization" is particularly disturbing, since it indicates an apparent lack of interest in every significant aspect of the learning or the use of language in new situations. No one has ever doubted that in some sense, language is learned by generalization, or that novel utterances and situations are in some way similar to familiar ones. The only matter of serious interest is the specific "similarity." Skinner has, apparently, no interest in this. Keller and Schoenfeld (*op. cit.*) proceed to incorporate these notions (which they identify) into their Skinnerian "modern objective psychology" by defining two stimuli to be similar when "we make the same sort of *response* to them" (124; but when are responses of the "same sort"?). They do not seem to notice that this definition converts their "principle of generalization" (116), under any reasonable interpretation of this, into a tautology. It is obvious that such a definition will not be of much help in the study of language learning or construction of new responses in appropriate situations.

47. The problem of serial order in behavior, in Jeffress (ed.), *Hixon Symposium on Cerebral Mechanisms in Behavior* (New York, 1951).

48. There is nothing essentially mysterious about this. Complex innate behavior patterns and innate "tendencies to learn in specific ways" have been carefully studied in lower organisms. Many psychologists have been inclined to believe that such biological structure will not have an important effect on acquisition of complex behavior in higher organisms, but I have not been able to find any serious justification for this attitude. Some recent studies have stressed the necessity for carefully analyzing the strategies available to the organism, regarded as a complex "information-processing system" (cf. Bruner, Goodnow, and Austin, *A Study of Thinking* [New York, 1956]; Newell, Shaw, and Simon, "Elements of a Theory of Human Problem Solving," *Psych. Rev.* 65.151–66 [1958]), if anything significant is to be said about the character of human learning. These may be largely innate, or developed by early learning processes about which very little is yet known. (But see Harlow, "The Formation of Learning Sets," *Psych. Rev.* 56.51–65 (1949), and many later papers, where striking shifts in the character of learning are shown as a result of early training; also Hebb, *Organization of behavior* 109 ff.) They are undoubtedly quite complex. Cf. Lenneberg, *op. cit.*, and Lees, review of Chomsky's *Syntactic Structures* in *Lg.* 33.406 f. (1957), for discussion of the topics mentioned in this section.

GILBERT RYLE

Selections from *The Concept of Mind*

Introduction

This book offers what may with reservations be described as a theory of the mind. But it does not give new information about minds. We possess already a wealth of information about minds, information which is neither derived from, nor upset by, the arguments of philosophers. The philosophical arguments which constitute this book are intended not to increase what we know about minds, but to rectify the logical geography of the knowledge which we already possess.

Teachers and examiners, magistrates and critics, historians and novelists, confessors and non-commissioned officers, employers, employees and partners, parents, lovers, friends, and enemies all know well enough how to settle their daily questions about the qualities of character and intellect of the individual with whom they have to do. They can appraise his performances, assess his progress, understand his words and actions, discern his motives and see his jokes. If they go wrong, they know how to correct their mistakes. More, they can deliberately influence the minds of those with whom they deal by criticism, example, teaching, punishment, bribery, mockery, and persuasion, and then modify their treatments in the light of the results produced.

Both in describing the minds of others and in prescribing for them, they are wielding with greater or less efficiency concepts of mental powers and operations. They have learned how to apply in concrete situations such mental-conduct epithets as 'careful,' 'stupid,' 'logical,' 'unobservant,' 'ingenious,' 'vain,' 'methodical,' 'credulous,' 'witty,' 'self-controlled,' and a thousand others.

It is, however, one thing to know how to apply such concepts, quite another to know how to correlate them with one another and with concepts of other sorts. Many people can talk sense with concepts but cannot talk sense about them; they know by practice how to operate with concepts, anyhow inside familiar fields, but they cannot state the logical regulations governing their use. They are like people who know their way about their own parish, but cannot construct or read a map of it, much less a map of the region or continent in which their parish lies.

For certain purposes it is necessary to determine the logical cross-bearings of the concepts which we know quite well how to apply. The attempt to perform this operation upon the concepts of the powers, operations and states of minds has always been a big part of the task of philosophers. Theories of knowledge, logic, ethics, political theory and aesthetics are the products of their inquiries in this field. Some of these inquiries have made considerable regional progress, but it is part of the thesis of this book that during the three centuries of the epoch of natural science the logical categories in terms of which the concepts of mental powers and operations have been co-ordinated have been wrongly selected. Descartes left as one of his main philosophical legacies a myth which continues to distort the continental geography of the subject.

A myth is, of course, not a fairy story. It is the presentation of facts belonging to one category in the idioms appropriate to another. To explode a myth is accordingly not to deny the facts but to re-allocate them. And this is what I am trying to do.

To determine the logical geography of concepts is to reveal the logic of the propositions in which they are wielded, that is to say, to show with what other propositions they are consistent and inconsistent, what propositions follow from them and from what propositions they follow. The logical type or category to which a concept belongs is the set of ways in which it is logically legitimate to operate with it. The key arguments employed in this book are therefore intended to show why certain sorts of operations with the concepts of mental powers and processes are breaches of logical rules. I try to use *reductio ad absurdum* arguments both to disallow operations implicitly recommended by the Cartesian myth and to indicate to what logical types the concepts under investigation ought to be allocated. I do not, however, think it improper to use from time to time arguments of a less rigorous sort, especially when it seems expedient to mollify or acclimatise. Philosophy is the replacement of category-habits by category-disciplines, and if persuasions of conciliatory kinds ease the pains of relinquishing inveterate intellectual habits, they do not indeed reinforce the rigorous arguments, but they do weaken resistances to them.

Some readers may think that my tone of voice in this book is excessively polemical. It may comfort them to know that the assumptions against which I exhibit most heat are assumptions of which I myself have been a victim. Primarily I am trying to get some disorders out of my own system. Only secondarily do I hope to help other theorists to recognise our malady and to benefit from my medicine.

Chapter I: Descartes's Myth

(1) *The Official Doctrine.*

There is a doctrine about the nature and place of minds which is so prevalent among theorists and even among laymen that it deserves to be described as the official theory. Most philosophers, psychologists and religious teachers subscribe, with minor reservations, to its main articles and, although they admit certain theoretical difficulties in it, they tend to assume that these can be overcome without serious modifications being made to the architecture of the theory. It will be argued here that the central principles of the doctrine are unsound and conflict with the whole body of what we know about minds when we are not speculating about them.

The official doctrine, which hails chiefly from Descartes, is something like this. With the doubtful exceptions of idiots and infants in arms every human being has both a body and a mind. Some would prefer to say that every human being is both a body and a mind. His body and his mind are ordinarily harnessed together, but after the death of the body his mind may continue to exist and function.

Human bodies are in space and are subject to the mechanical laws which govern all other bodies in space. Bodily processes and states can be inspected by external observers. So a man's bodily life is as much a public affair as are the lives of animals and reptiles and even as the careers of trees, crystals, and planets.

But minds are not in space, nor are their operations subject to mechanical laws. The workings of one mind are not witnessable by other observers; its career is private. Only I can take direct cognisance of the states and processes of my own mind. A person therefore lives through two collateral histories, one consisting of what happens in and to his body, the other consisting of what happens in and to his mind. The first is public, the second private. The events in the first history are events in the physical world, those in the second are events in the mental world.

It has been disputed whether a person does or can directly monitor all or only some of the episodes of his own private history; but, according to the official doctrine, of at least some of these episodes he has direct and unchallengeable cognisance. In consciousness, self-consciousness and introspection he is directly and authentically apprised of the present states and operations of his mind. He may have great or small uncertainties about concurrent and adjacent episodes in the physical world, but he can have none about at least part of what is momentarily occupying his mind.

It is customary to express this bifurcation of his two lives and of his two worlds by saying that the things and events which belong to the physical world, including his own body, are external, while the workings of his own mind are internal. This antithesis of outer and inner is of course meant to be construed as a metaphor, since minds, not being in space, could not be described as being spatially inside anything else, or as having things going on spatially inside themselves. But relapses from this good intention are common and theorists are found speculating how stimuli, the physical sources of which are yards or miles outside a person's skin, can generate mental responses inside his skull, or how decisions framed inside his cranium can set going movements of his extremities.

Even when 'inner' and 'outer' are construed as metaphors, the problem how a person's mind and body influence one another is notoriously charged with theoretical difficulties. What the mind wills, the legs, arms, and the tongue execute; what affects the ear and the eye has something to do with what the mind perceives; grimaces and smiles betray the mind's moods

and bodily castigations lead, it is hoped, to moral improvement. But the actual transactions between the episodes of the private history and those of the public history remain mysterious, since by definition they can belong to neither series. They could not be reported among the happenings described in a person's autobiography of his inner life, but nor could they be reported among those described in some one else's biography of that person's overt career. They can be inspected neither by introspection nor by laboratory experiment. They are theoretical shuttlecocks which are forever being bandied from the physiologist back to the psychologist and from the psychologist back to the physiologist.

Underlying this partly metaphorical representation of the bifurcation of a person's two lives there is a seemingly more profound and philosophical assumption. It is assumed that there are two different kinds of existence or status. What exists or happens may have the status of physical existence, or it may have the status of mental existence. Somewhat as the faces of coins are either heads or tails, or somewhat as living creatures are either male or female, so, it is supposed, some existing is physical existing, other existing is mental existing. It is a necessary feature of what has physical existence that it is in space and time; it is a necessary feature of what has mental existence that it is in time but not in space. What has physical existence is composed of matter, or else is a function of matter; what has mental existence consists of consciousness, or else is a function of consciousness.

There is thus a polar opposition between mind and matter, an opposition which is often brought out as follows. Material objects are situated in a common field, known as 'space,' and what happens to one body in one part of space is mechanically connected with what happens to other bodies in other parts of space. But mental happenings occur in insulated fields, known as 'minds,' and there is, apart maybe from telepathy, no direct causal connection between what happens in one mind and what happens in another. Only through the medium of the public physical world can the mind of one person make a difference to the mind of another. The mind is its own place and in his inner life each of us lives the life of a ghostly Robinson Crusoe. People can see, hear and jolt one another's bodies, but they are irremediably blind and deaf to the workings of one another's minds and inoperative upon them.

What sort of knowledge can be secured of the workings of a mind? On the one side, according to the official theory, a person has direct knowledge of the best imaginable kind of the workings of his own mind. Mental states and processes are (or are normally) conscious states and processes, and the consciousness which irradiates them can engender no illusions and leaves the door open for no doubts. A person's present thinkings, feelings and willings, his perceivings, rememberings, and imaginings are intrinsically 'phosphorescent'; their existence and their nature are inevitably betrayed to their owner. The inner life is a stream of consciousness of such a sort that it would be absurd to suggest that the mind whose life is that stream might be unaware of what is passing down it.

True, the evidence adduced recently by Freud seems to show that there exist channels tributary to this stream, which run hidden from their owner. People are actuated by impulses the existence of which they vigorously disavow; some of their thoughts differ from the thoughts which they acknowledge; and some of the actions which they think they will to perform they do not really will. They are thoroughly gulled by some of their own hypocrisies and they successfully ignore facts about their mental lives which on the official

theory ought to be patent to them. Holders of the official theory tend, however, to maintain that anyhow in normal circumstances a person must be directly and authentically seized of the present state and workings of his own mind.

Besides being currently supplied with these alleged immediate data of consciousness, a person is also generally supposed to be able to exercise from time to time a special kind of perception, namely inner perception, or introspection. He can take a (non-optical) 'look' at what is passing in his mind. Not only can he view and scrutinize a flower through his sense of sight and listen to and discriminate the notes of a bell through his sense of hearing; he can also reflectively or introspectively watch, without any bodily organ of sense, the current episodes of his inner life. This self-observation is also commonly supposed to be immune from illusion, confusion or doubt. A mind's reports of its own affairs have a certainty superior to the best that is possessed by its reports of matters in the physical world. Sense-perceptions can, but consciousness and introspection cannot, be mistaken or confused.

On the other side, one person has no direct access of any sort to the events of the inner life of another. He cannot do better than make problematic inferences from the observed behavior of the other person's body to the states of mind which, by analogy from his own conduct, he supposes to be signalised by that behavior. Direct access to the workings of a mind is the privilege of that mind itself; in default of such privileged access, the workings of one mind are inevitably occult to everyone else. For the supposed arguments from bodily movements similar to their own to mental workings similar to their own would lack any possibility of observational corroboration. Not unnaturally, therefore, an adherent of the official theory finds it difficult to resist this consequence of his premises, that he has no good reason to believe that there do exist minds other than his own. Even if he prefers to believe that to other human bodies there are harnessed minds not unlike his own, he cannot claim to be able to discover their individual characteristics, or the particular things that they undergo and do. Absolute solitude is on this showing the ineluctable destiny of the soul. Only our bodies can meet.

As a necessary corollary of this general scheme there is implicitly prescribed a special way of construing our ordinary concepts of mental powers and operations. The verbs, nouns, and adjectives, with which in ordinary life we describe the wits, characters, and higher-grade performances of the people with whom we have do, are required to be construed as signifying special episodes in their secret histories, or else as signifying tendencies for such episodes to occur. When someone is described as knowing, believing, or guessing something, as hoping, dreading, intending, or shirking something, as designing this or being amused at that, these verbs are supposed to denote the occurrence of specific modifications in his (to us) occult stream of consciousness. Only his own privileged access to this stream in direct awareness and introspection could provide authentic testimony that these mental-conduct verbs were correctly or incorrectly applied. The onlooker, be he teacher, critic, biographer, or friend, can never assure himself that his comments have any vestige of truth. Yet it was just because we do in fact all know how to make such comments, make them with general correctness and correct them when they turn out to be confused or mistaken, that philosophers found it necessary to construct their theories of the nature and place of minds. Finding mental-conduct concepts being regularly and effectively used, they properly sought to fix their logical geography. But the logical geography officially recommended would entail that there

could be no regular or effective use of these mental-conduct concepts in our descriptions of, and prescriptions for, other people's minds.

(2) The Absurdity of the Official Doctrine.

Such in outline is the official theory. I shall often speak of it, with deliberate abusiveness, as 'the dogma of the Ghost in the Machine.' I hope to prove that it is entirely false, and false not in detail but in principle. It is not merely an assemblage of particular mistakes. It is one big mistake and a mistake of a special kind. It is, namely, a category-mistake. It represents the facts of mental life as if they belonged to one logical type or category (or range of types or categories), when they actually belong to another. The dogma is therefore a philosopher's myth. In attempting to explode the myth I shall probably be taken to be denying well-known facts about the mental life of human beings, and my plea that I aim at doing nothing more than rectify the logic of mental-conduct concepts will probably be disallowed as mere subterfuge.

I must first indicate what is meant by the phrase 'Category-mistake.' This I do in a series of illustrations.

A foreigner visiting Oxford or Cambridge for the first time is shown a number of colleges, libraries, playing fields, museums, scientific departments, and administrative offices. He then asks 'But where is the University? I have seen where the members of the Colleges live, where the Registrar works, where the scientists experiment and the rest. But I have not yet seen the University in which reside and work the members of your University.' It has then to be explained to him that the University is not another collateral institution, some ulterior counterpart to the colleges, laboratories, and offices which he has seen. The University is just the way in which all that he has already seen is organized. When they are seen and when their co-ordination is understood, the University has been seen. His mistake lay in his innocent assumption that it was correct to speak of Christ Church, the Bodleian Library, the Ashmolean Museum, *and* the University, to speak, that is, as if 'the University' stood for an extra member of the class of which these other units are members. He was mistakenly allocating the University to the same category as that to which the other institutions belong.

The same mistake would be made by a child witnessing the march-past of a division, who, having had pointed out to him such and such battalions, batteries, squadrons, etc., asked when the division was going to appear. He would be supposing that a division was a counterpart to the units already seen, partly similar to them and partly unlike them. He would be shown his mistake by being told that in watching the battalions, batteries, and squadrons marching past he had been watching the division marching past. The march-past was not a parade of battalions, batteries, squadrons, *and* a division; it was a parade of the battalions, batteries, and squadrons *of* a division.

One more illustration. A foreigner watching his first game of cricket learns what are the functions of the bowlers, the batsmen, the fielders, the umpires, and the scorers. He then says 'But there is no one left on the field to contribute the famous element of team-spirit. I see who does the bowling, the batting, and the wicket-keeping; but I do not see whose role it is to exercise *esprit de corps.*' Once more, it would have to be explained that he was looking for the wrong type of thing. Team-spirit is not another cricketing operation supplementary to all of the other special tasks. It is, roughly, the keenness with which each of the special tasks is performed, and performing a task keenly is not performing two tasks. Certainly exhibiting team-spirit is not the same thing as bowling or catching, but nor is it a third thing such

that we can say that the bowler first bowls *and* then exhibits team-spirit or that a fielder is at a given moment *either* catching *or* displaying *esprit de corps.*

These illustrations of category-mistakes have a common feature which must be noticed. The mistakes were made by people who did not know how to wield the concepts *University*, *division*, and *team-spirit*. Their puzzles arose from inability to use certain items in the English vocabulary.

The theoretically interesting category-mistakes are those made by people who are perfectly competent to apply concepts, at least in the situations with which they are familiar, but are still liable in their abstract thinking to allocate those concepts to logical types to which they do not belong. An instance of a mistake of this sort would be the following story. A student of politics has learned the main differences between the British, the French, and the American Constitutions, and has learned also the differences and connections between the Cabinet, Parliament, the various Ministries, the Judicature, and the Church of England. But he still becomes embarrassed when asked questions about the connections between the Church of England, the Home Office, and the British Constitution. For while the Church and the Home Office are institutions, the British Constitution is not another institution in the same sense of that noun. So inter-institutional relations which can be asserted or denied to hold between the Church and the Home Office cannot be asserted or denied to hold between either of them and the British Constitution. 'The British Constitution' is not a term of the same logical type as 'the Home Office' and 'the Church of England.' In a partially similar way, John Doe may be a relative, a friend, an enemy, or a stranger to Richard Roe; but he cannot be any of these things to the Average Taxpayer. He knows how to talk sense in certain sorts of discussions about the Average Taxpayer, but he is baffled to say why he could not come across him in the street as he can come across Richard Roe.

It is pertinent to our main subject to notice that, so long as the student of politics continues to think of the British Constitution as a counterpart to the other institutions, he will tend to describe it as a mysteriously occult institution; and so long as John Doe continues to think of the Average Taxpayer as a fellow-citizen, he will tend to think of him as an elusive insubstantial man, a ghost who is everywhere yet nowhere.

My destructive purpose is to show that a family of radical category-mistakes is the source of the double-life theory. The representation of a person as a ghost mysteriously ensconced in a machine derives from this argument. Because, as is true, a person's thinking, feeling, and purposive doing cannot be described solely in the idioms of physics, chemistry, and physiology, therefore they must be described in counterpart idioms. As the human body is a complex organised unit, so the human mind must be another complex organised unit, though one made of a different sort of stuff and with a different sort of structure. Or, again, as the human body, like any other parcel of matter, is a field of causes and effects, so the mind must be another field of causes and effects, though not (Heaven be praised) mechanical causes and effects.

(3) The Origin of the Category-Mistake.

One of the chief intellectual origins of what I have yet to prove to be the Cartesian category-mistake seems to be this. When Galileo showed that his methods of scientific discovery were competent to provide a mechanical theory which should cover every occupant of space, Descartes found in himself two conflicting motives. As a man of scientific genius he could not but endorse the claims of mechanics, yet as a religious and moral man he could not accept, as Hobbes accepted, the discouraging rider to those claims, namely that human nature differs only in degree of complexity from clockwork. The mental could not be just a variety of the mechanical.

He and subsequent philosophers naturally but erroneously availed themselves of the following escape-route. Since mental-conduct words are not to be construed as signifying the occurrence of mechanical processes, they must be construed as signifying the occurrence of non-mechanical processes; since mechanical laws explain movements in space as the effects of other movements in space, other laws must explain some of the non-spatial workings of minds as the effects of other non-spatial workings of minds. The difference between the human behaviors which we describe as intelligent and those which we describe as unintelligent must be a difference in their causation; so, while some movements of human tongues and limbs are the effects of mechanical causes, others must be the effects of non-mechanical causes, i.e., some issue from movements of particles of matter, others from workings of the mind.

The differences between the physical and the mental were thus represented as differences inside the common framework of the categories of 'thing,' 'stuff,' 'attribute,' 'state,' 'process,' 'change,' 'cause,' and 'effect.' Minds are things, but different sorts of things from bodies; mental processes are causes and effects, but different sorts of causes and effects from bodily movements. And so on. Somewhat as the foreigner expected the University to be an extra edifice, rather like a college but also considerably different, so the repudiators of mechanism represented minds as extra centers of causal processes, rather like machines but also considerably different from them. Their theory was a para-mechanical hypothesis.

That this assumption was at the heart of the doctrine is shown by the fact that there was from the beginning felt to be a major theoretical difficulty in explaining how minds can influence and be influenced by bodies. How can a mental process, such as willing, cause spatial movements like the movements of the tongue? How can a physical change in the optic nerve have among its effects a mind's perception of a flash of light? This notorious crux by itself shows the logical mold into which Descartes pressed his theory of the mind. It was the self-same mold into which he and Galileo set their mechanics. Still unwittingly adhering to the grammar of mechanics, he tried to avert disaster by describing minds in what was merely an obverse vocabulary. The workings of minds had to be described by the mere negatives of the specific descriptions given to bodies; they are not in space, they are not motions, they are not modifications of matter, they are not accessible to public observation. Minds are not bits of clockwork, they are just bits of not-clockwork.

As thus represented, minds are not merely ghosts harnessed to machines, they are themselves just spectral machines. Though the human body is an engine, it is not quite an ordinary engine, since some of its workings are governed by another engine inside it—this interior governor-engine being one of a very special sort. It is invisible, inaudible and it has no size or weight. It cannot be taken to bits and the laws it obeys are not those known to ordinary engineers. Nothing is known of how it governs the bodily engine.

A second major crux points the same moral. Since, according to the doctrine, minds belong to the same category as bodies and since bodies are rigidly governed by mechanical laws, it seemed to many theorists to follow that minds must be similarly governed by rigid non-mechanical laws. The physical world is a deterministic system, so the mental world must be a deterministic system. Bodies cannot help the modifications that they undergo, so minds cannot help pursuing the careers fixed for them. *Responsibility*, *choice*, *merit*, and *demerit* are therefore inapplicable concepts—unless the compromise solution is adopted of saying that the laws governing mental processes, unlike those governing physical processes, have the congenial attribute of being only rather rigid. The problem of the Freedom of the Will was the problem how to reconcile the hypothesis that minds are to be described in terms drawn from the categories of mechanics with the knowledge that higher-grade human conduct is not of a piece with the behavior of machines.

It is an historical curiosity that it was not noticed that the entire argument was broken-backed. Theorists correctly assumed that any sane man could already recognise the differences between, say, rational and non-rational utterances or between purposive and automatic behavior. Else there would have been nothing requiring to be salved from mechanism. Yet the explanation given presupposed that one person could in principle never recognise the difference between the rational and the irrational utterances issuing from other human bodies, since he could never get access to the postulated immaterial causes of some of their utterances. Save for the doubtful exception of himself, he could never tell the difference between a man and a Robot. It would have to be conceded, for example, that, for all that we can tell, the inner lives of persons who are classed as idiots or lunatics are as rational as those of anyone else. Perhaps only their overt behavior is disappointing; that is to say, perhaps 'idiots' are not really idiotic, or 'lunatics' lunatic. Perhaps, too, some of those who are classed as sane are really idiots. According to the theory, external observers could never know how the overt behavior of others is correlated with their mental powers and processes and so they could never know or even plausibly conjecture whether their applications of mental-conduct concepts to these other people were correct or incorrect. It would then be hazardous or impossible for a man to claim sanity or logical consistency even for himself, since he would be debarred from comparing his own performances with those of others. In short, our characterisations of persons and their performances as intelligent, prudent, and virtuous or as stupid, hypocritical, and cowardly could never have been made, so the problem of providing a special causal hypothesis to serve as the basis of such diagnoses would never have arisen. The question, 'How do persons differ from machines?' arose just because everyone already knew how to apply mental-conduct concepts before the new causal hypothesis was introduced. This causal hypothesis could not therefore be the source of the criteria used in those applications. Nor, of course, has the causal hypothesis in any degree improved our handling of those criteria. We still distinguish good from bad arithmetic, politic from impolitic conduct and fertile from infertile imaginations in the ways in which Descartes himself distinguished them before and after he speculated how the applicability of these criteria was compatible with the principle of mechanical causation.

He had mistaken the logic of his problem. Instead of asking by what criteria intelligent behavior is actually distinguished from non-intelligent behavior, he asked 'Given that the principle of mechanical causation does not tell us the difference, what other causal principle will tell it us?' He realised that the problem was not one of mechanics and assumed that it must therefore be one of some counterpart to mechanics. Not unnaturally psychology is often cast for just this role.

When two terms belong to the same category, it is proper to construct conjunctive propositions embodying them. Thus a purchaser may say that he bought a left-hand glove and a right-hand glove, but not that he bought a left-hand glove, a right-hand glove and a pair of gloves. 'She came home in a flood of tears and a sedan-chair' is a well-known joke based on the absurdity of conjoining terms of different types. It would have been equally ridiculous to construct the disjunction 'She came home either in a flood of tears or else in a sedan-chair.' Now the dogma of the Ghost in the Machine does just this. It maintains that there exist both bodies and minds; that there occur physical processes and mental processes; that there are mechanical causes of corporeal movements and mental causes of corporeal movements. I shall argue that these and other analogous conjunctions are absurd; but, it must be noticed, the argument will not show that either of the illegitimately conjoined propositions is absurd in itself. I am not, for example, denying that there occur mental processes. Doing long division is a mental process and so is making a joke. But I am saying that the phrase 'there occur mental processes' does not mean the same sort of thing as 'there occur physical processes,' and, therefore, that it makes no sense to conjoin or disjoin the two.

If my argument is successful, there will follow some interesting consequences. First, the hallowed contrast between Mind and Matter will be dissipated, but dissipated not by either of the equally hallowed absorptions of Mind by Matter or of Matter by Mind, but in quite a different way. For the seeming contrast of the two will be shown to be as illegitimate as would be the contrast of 'she came home in a flood of tears' and 'she came home in a sedan-chair.' The belief that there is a polar opposition between Mind and Matter is the belief that they are terms of the same logical type.

It will also follow that both Idealism and Materialism are answers to an improper question. The 'reduction' of the material world to mental states and processes, as well as the 'reduction' of mental states and processes to physical states and processes, presuppose the legitimacy of the disjunction 'Either there exist minds or there exist bodies (but not both).' It would be like saying, 'Either she bought a left-hand and a right-hand glove or she bought a pair of gloves (but not both).'

It is perfectly proper to say, in one logical tone of voice, that there exist minds and to say, in another logical tone of voice, that there exist bodies. But these expressions do not indicate two different species of existence, for 'existence' is not a generic word like 'colored' or 'sexed.' They indicate two different senses of 'exist,' somewhat as 'rising' has different senses in 'the tide is rising,' 'hopes are rising,' and 'the average age of death is rising.' A man would be thought to be making a poor joke who said that three things are now rising, namely the tide, hopes and the average age of death. It would be just as good or bad a joke to say that there exist prime numbers and Wednesdays and public opinions and navies; or that there exist both minds and bodies. In the succeeding chapters I try to prove that the official theory does rest on a batch of category-mistakes by showing that logically absurd corollaries follow from it. The exhibition of these absurdities will have the constructive effect of bringing out part of the correct logic of mental-conduct concepts.

(4) Historical Note.

It would not be true to say that the official theory derives solely from Descartes's theories, or even from a more widespread anxiety about the implications of seventeenth century mechanics. Scholastic and Reformation theology had schooled the intellects of the scientists as well as of the laymen, philosophers and clerics of that age. Stoic-Augustinian theories of the will were embedded in the Calvinist doctrines of sin and grace; Platonic and Aristotelian theories of the intellect shaped the orthodox doctrines of the immortality of the soul. Descartes was reformulating already prevalent theological doctrines of the soul in the new syntax of Galileo. The theologian's privacy of conscience became the philosopher's privacy of consciousness, and what had been the bogy of Predestination reappeared as the bogy of Determinism.

It would also not be true to say that the two-worlds myth did no theoretical good. Myths often do a lot of theoretical good, while they are still new. One benefit bestowed by the para-mechanical myth was that it partly superannuated the then prevalent para-political myth. Minds and their Faculties had previously been described by analogies with political superiors and political subordinates. The idioms wed were those of ruling, obeying, collaborating, and rebelling. They survived and still survive in many ethical and some epistemological discussions. As, in physics, the new myth of occult Forces was a scientific improvement on the old myth of Final Causes, so, in anthropological and psychological theory, the new myth of hidden operations, impulses, and agencies was an improvement on the old myth of dictations, deferences, and disobediences.

Chapter II: Knowing How and Knowing That

[...]

When we describe glass as brittle, or sugar as soluble, we are using dispositional concepts, the logical force of which is this. The brittleness of glass does not consist in the fact that it is at a given moment actually being shivered. It may be brittle without ever being shivered. To say that it is brittle is to say that if it ever is, or ever had been, struck or strained, it would fly, or have flown, into fragments. To say that sugar is soluble is to say that it would dissolve, or would have dissolved, if immersed in water.

A statement ascribing a dispositional property to a thing has much, though not everything, in common with a statement subsuming the thing under a law. To possess a dispositional property is not to be in a particular state, or to undergo a particular change; it is to be bound or liable to be in a particular state, or to undergo a particular change, when a particular condition is realised. The same is true about specifically human dispositions such as qualities of character. My being an habitual smoker does not entail that I am at this or that moment smoking; it is my permanent proneness to smoke when I am not eating, sleeping, lecturing, or attending funerals, and have not quite recently been smoking.

In discussing dispositions it is initially helpful to fasten on the simplest models, such as the brittleness of glass or the smoking habit of a man. For in describing these dispositions it is easy to unpack the hypothetical proposition implicitly conveyed in the ascription of the dispositional properties. To be brittle is just to be bound or likely to fly into fragments in such and such conditions; to be a smoker is just to be bound or likely to fill, light, and draw on a pipe in such and such conditions. These are simple, single-track dispositions, the actualisations of which are nearly uniform.

But the practice of considering such simple models of dispositions, though initially helpful, leads at a later stage to erroneous assumptions. There are many dispositions the actualisations of which can take a wide and perhaps unlimited variety of shapes; many disposition-concepts are determinable concepts. When an object is described as hard, we do not mean only that it would resist deformation; we mean also that it would, for example, give out a sharp sound if struck, that it would cause

us pain if we came into sharp contact with it, that resilient objects would bounce off it, and so on indefinitely. If we wished to unpack all that is conveyed in describing an animal as gregarious, we should similarly have to produce an infinite series of different hypothetical propositions.

Now the higher-grade dispositions of people with which this inquiry is largely concerned are, in general, not single-track dispositions, but dispositions the exercises of which are indefinitely heterogeneous. When Jane Austen wished to show the specific kind of pride which characterised the heroine of 'Pride and Prejudice,' she had to represent her actions, words, thoughts, and feelings in a thousand different situations. There is no one standard type of action or reaction such that Jane Austen could say 'My heroine's kind of pride was just the tendency to do this, whenever a situation of that sort arose.'

[...]

Chapter V: Dispositions and Occurrences

[...]

I have already had occasion to argue that a number of the words which we commonly use to describe and explain people's behavior signify dispositions and not episodes. To say that a person knows something, or aspires to be something, is not to say that he is at a particular moment in process of doing or undergoing anything, but that he is able to do certain things, when the need arises, or that he is prone to do and feel certain things in situations of certain sorts.

This is, in itself, hardly more than a dull fact (almost) of ordinary grammar. The verbs 'know,' 'possess,' and 'aspire' do not behave like the verbs 'run,' 'wake up,' or 'tingle'; we cannot say 'he knew so and so for two minutes, then stopped and started again after a breather,' 'he gradually aspired to be a bishop,' or 'he is now engaged in possessing a bicycle.' Nor is it a peculiarity of people that we describe them in dispositional terms. We use such terms just as much for describing animals, insects, crystals, and atoms. We are constantly wanting to talk about what can be relied on to happen as well as to talk about what is actually happening; we are constantly wanting to give explanations of incidents as well as to report them; and we are constantly wanting to tell how things can be managed as well as to tell what is now going on in them. Moreover, merely to classify a word as signifying a disposition is not yet to say much more about it than to say that it is not used for an episode. There are lots of different kinds of dispositional words.

Hobbies are not the same sort of thing as habits, and both are different from skills, from mannerisms, from fashions, from phobias, and from trades. Nest-building is a different sort of property from being feathered, and being a conductor of electricity is a different sort of property from being elastic.

There is, however, a special point in drawing attention to the fact that many of the cardinal concepts in terms of which we describe specifically human behavior are dispositional concepts, since the vogue of the para-mechanical legend has led many people to ignore the ways in which these concepts actually behave and to construe them instead as items in the descriptions of occult causes and effects. Sentences embodying these dispositional words have been interpreted as being categorical reports of particular but unwitnessable matters of fact instead of being testable, open hypothetical and what I shall call 'semi-hypothetical' statements. The old error of treating the term 'Force' as denoting an occult force-exerting agency has been given up in the physical sciences, but its relatives survive in many theories of mind and are perhaps only moribund in biology.

[...]

LUDWIG WITTGENSTEIN

Selections from *Philosophical Investigations*

256. Now, what about the language which describes my inner experiences and which only I myself can understand? *How* do I use words to stand for my sensations?—As we ordinarily do? Then are my words for sensations tied up with my natural expressions of sensation? In that case my language is not a 'private' one. Someone else might understand it as well as I.—But suppose I didn't have any natural expression for the sensation, but only had the sensation? And now I simply *associate* names with sensations and use these names in descriptions.—

257. "What would it be like if human beings shewed no outward signs of pain (did not groan, grimace, etc.)? Then it would be impossible to teach a child the use of the word 'toothache.'"—Well, let's assume the child is a genius

and itself invents a name for the sensation!— But then, of course, he couldn't make himself understood when he used the word.—So does he understand the name, without being able to explain its meaning to anyone?—But what does it mean to say that he has 'named his pain'?—

How has he done this naming of pain?! And whatever he did, what was its purpose?—When one says "He gave a name to his sensation" one forgets that a great deal of stage-setting in the language is presupposed if the mere act of naming is to make sense. And when we speak of someone's having given a name to pain, what is presupposed is the existence of the grammar of the word "pain"; it shews the post where the new word is stationed.

258. Let us imagine the following case. I want to keep a diary about the recurrence of a certain sensation. To this end I associate it with the sign "S" and write this sign in a calendar for every day on which I have the sensation. ——I will remark first of all that a definition of the sign cannot be formulated.—But still I can give myself a kind of ostensive definition.—How? Can I point to the sensation? Not in the ordinary sense. But I speak, or write the sign down, and at the same time I concentrate my attention on the sensation—and so, as it were, point to it inwardly.—But what is this ceremony for? for that is all it seems to be! A definition surely serves to establish the meaning of a sign.—Well, that is done precisely by the concentrating of my attention; for in this way I impress on myself the connexion between the sign and the sensation.—But "I impress it on myself" can only mean: this process brings it about that I remember the connexion *right* in the future. But in the present case I have no criterion of correctness. One would like to say: whatever is going to seem right to me is right. And that only means that here we can't talk about 'right.'

259. Are the rules of the private language *impressions* of rules?—The balance on which impressions are weighed is not the *impression* of a balance.

260. "Well, I *believe* that this is the sensation S again."—Perhaps you *believe* that you believe it!

Then did the man who made the entry in the calendar make a note of *nothing whatever*?— Don't consider it a matter of course that a person is making a note of something when he makes a mark—say in a calendar. For a note has a function, and this "S" so far has none.

(One can talk to oneself.—If a person speaks when no one else is present, does that mean he is speaking to himself?)

261. What reason have we for calling "S" the sign for a *sensation*? For "sensation" is a word of our common language, not of one intelligible to me alone. So the use of this word stands in need of a justification which everybody understands.—And it would not help either to say that it need not be a *sensation*; that when he writes "S," he has *something*—and that is all that can be said. "Has" and "something" also belong to our common language.—So in the end when one is doing philosophy one gets to the point where one would like just to emit an inarticulate sound.—But such a sound is an expression only as it occurs in a particular language-game, which should now be described.

262. It might be said: if you have given yourself a private definition of a word, then you must inwardly *undertake* to use the word in such-and-such a way. And how do you undertake that? Is it to be assumed that you invent the technique of using the word; or that you found it ready-made?

263. "But I can (inwardly) undertake to call THIS 'pain' in the future."—"But is it certain

that you have undertaken it? Are you sure that it was enough for this purpose to concentrate your attention on your feeling?"—A queer question.—

264. "Once you know *what* the word stands for, you understand it, you know its whole use."

265. Let us imagine a table (something like a dictionary) that exists only in our imagination. A dictionary can be used to justify the translation of a word X by a word Y. But are we also to call it a justification if such a table is to be looked up only in the imagination?—"Well, yes; then it is a subjective justification."—But justification consists in appealing to something independent.—"But surely I can appeal from one memory to another. For example, I don't know if I have remembered the time of departure of a train right and to check it I call to mind how a page of the time-table looked. Isn't it the same here?"—No; for this process has got to produce a memory which is actually *correct*. If the mental image of the time-table could not itself be *tested* for correctness, how could it confirm the correctness of the first memory? (As if someone were to buy several copies of the morning paper to assure himself that what it said was true.)

Looking up a table in the imagination is no more looking up a table than the image of the result of an imagined experiment is the result of an experiment.

266. I can look at the clock to see what time it is: but I can also look at the dial of a clock in order to *guess* what time it is; or for the same purpose move the hand of a clock till its position strikes me as right. So the look of a clock may serve to determine the time in more than one way. (Looking at the clock in imagination.)

267. Suppose I wanted to justify the choice of dimensions for a bridge which I imagine to be building, by making loading tests on the material of the bridge in my imagination. This would, of course, be to imagine what is called justifying the choice of dimensions for a bridge. But should we also call it justifying an imagined choice of dimensions?

268. Why can't my right hand give my left hand money?—My right hand can put it into my left hand. My right hand can write a deed of gift and my left hand a receipt.—But the further practical consequences would not be those of a gift. When the left hand has taken the money from the right, etc., we shall ask: "Well, and what of it?" And the same could be asked if a person had given himself a private definition of a word; I mean, if he has said the word to himself and at the same time has directed his attention to a sensation.

269. Let us remember that there are certain criteria in a man's behavior for the fact that he does not understand a word: that it means nothing to him, that he can do nothing with it. And criteria for his 'thinking he understands,' attaching some meaning to the word, but not the right one. And, lastly, criteria for his understanding the word right. In the second case one might speak of a subjective understanding. And sounds which no one else understands but which I '*appear to understand*' might be called a "private language."

270. Let us now imagine a use for the entry of the sign "S" in my diary. I discover that whenever I have a particular sensation a manometer shews that my blood-pressure rises.

So I shall be able to say that my blood-pressure is rising without using any apparatus. This is a useful result. And now it seems quite indifferent whether I have recognized the sensation *right* or not. Let us suppose I regularly identify it wrong, it does not matter in the least.

And that alone shews that the hypothesis that I make a mistake is mere show. (We as it were turned a knob which looked as if it could be used to turn on some part of the machine; but it was a mere ornament, not connected with the mechanism at all.)

And what is our reason for calling "S" the name of a sensation here? Perhaps the kind of way this sign is employed in this language-game.—And why a "particular sensation," that is, the same one every time? Well, aren't we supposing that we write "S" every time?

271. "Imagine a person whose memory could not retain *what* the word 'pain' meant—so that he constantly called different things by that name—but nevertheless used the word in a way fitting in with the usual symptoms and presuppositions of pain"—in short he uses it as we all do. Here I should like to say: a wheel that can be turned though nothing else moves with it, is not part of the mechanism.

272. The essential thing about private experience is really not that each person possesses his own exemplar, but that nobody knows whether other people also have *this* or something else. The assumption would thus be possible—though unverifiable—that one section of mankind had one sensation of red and another section another.

273. What am I to say about the word "red"?—that it means something 'confronting us all' and that everyone should really have another word, besides this one, to mean his *own* sensation of red? Or is it like this: the word "red" means something known to everyone; and in addition, for each person, it means something known only to him? (Or perhaps rather: it *refers* to something known only to him.)

274. Of course, saying that the word "red" "refers to" instead of "means" something pri-

vate does not help us in the least to grasp its function; but it is the more psychologically apt expression for a particular experience in doing philosophy. It is as if when I uttered the word I cast a sidelong glance at the private sensation, as it were in order to say to myself: I know all right what I mean by it.

275. Look at the blue of the sky and say to yourself "How blue the sky is!"—When you do it spontaneously—without philosophical intentions—the idea never crosses your mind that this impression of color belongs only to *you*. And you have no hesitation in exclaiming that to someone else. And if you point at anything as you say the words you point at the sky. I am saying: you have not the feeling of pointing-into-yourself, which often accompanies 'naming the sensation' when one is thinking about 'private language.' Nor do you think that really you ought not to point to the color with your hand, but with your attention. (Consider what it means "to point to something with the attention.")

276. But don't we at least *mean* something quite definite when we look at a color and name our color-impression? It is as if we detached the color-*impression* from the object, like a membrane. (This ought to arouse our suspicions.)

277. But how is even possible for us to be tempted to think that we use a word to *mean* at one time the color known to everyone—and at another the 'visual impression' which *I* am getting *now*? How can there be so much as a temptation here?———I don't turn the same kind of attention on the color in the two cases. When I mean the color impression that (as I should like to say) belongs to me alone I immerse myself in the color—rather like when I 'cannot get my fill of a color.' Hence it is easier to produce this experience when one

is looking at a bright color, or at an impressive color-scheme.

278. "I know how the color green looks to *me*"—surely that makes sense!—Certainly what use of the proposition are you thinking of?

279. Imagine someone saying: "But I know how tall I am!" and laying his hand on top of his head to prove it.

280. Someone paints a picture in order to shew how he imagines a theatre scene. And now I say: "This picture has a double function: it informs others, as pictures or words inform——but for the one who gives the information it is a representation (or piece of information?) of another kind: for him it is the picture of his image, as it can't be for anyone else. To him his private impression of the picture means what he has imagined, in a sense in which the picture cannot mean this to others."—And what right have I to speak in this second case of a representation or piece of information—if these words were rightly used in the *first* case?

281. "But doesn't what you say come to this: that there is no pain, for example, without *pain-behavior*?"—It comes to this: only of a living human being and what resembles (behaves like) a living human being can one say: it has sensations; it sees; is blind; hears; is deaf, is conscious or unconscious.

Study Questions

1. Does Skinner's criticism explained in his section called "Neural causes" apply to Hobbes? Explain.
2. What does Skinner mean by a "merely redundant description"? Explain how he criticizes the explanation that "a man eats because he is hungry" on this basis.
3. JOKE: "Two behaviorists meet in the morning. One says to the other, 'You're fine; how am I?'" Explain.
4. Briefly but clearly outline Chomsky's argument that Skinner's views run into problems in specifying *stimuli* for verbal behavior. Explain what he says about 'stimulus' ("paraphrases...no particular connection") in the last paragraph of Section 3 of his article.
5. Skinnerian psychology is sometimes said to be strictly "empiricist" science, while Chomsky's (of which you can get an idea from Section 11) is "rationalist." If you're not clear about these words, look them up. In what sense is this true? In what sense is this false or misleading?
6. It seems that we can often know what's "on your mind" by seeing how you act or hearing what you say. But Ryle says that, given the "Official Doctrine," this is impossible. Explain his reasoning here.
7. In part (3), Ryle says he intends to dissipate the contrast between Mind and Matter, but not by "absorption [a] of Mind by Matter or [b] of Matter by Mind." Which authors we have read so far advocate absorption [a]? Which [b]?

8. Ryle says he's talking about "higher-grade" not "single-track" dispositions. Explain the difference here.

9. Is Ryle a *logical behaviorist*? (Look this term up in the Glossary at the end of the book if you're not sure about it.) Explain.

10. In a reading later in this book, David Armstrong offers this criticism of Ryle:

> When I think, but my thoughts do not issue in any action, it seems…obvious that there is something actually going on in me which constitutes my thought. It is not simply that I would speak or act if some conditions that are unfulfilled were to be fulfilled.

Do you think this is a valid criticism of Ryle? What are Ryle's arguments against an account of thinking that would admit this "something actually going on"?

11. At the end of Section 258, Wittgenstein says: "But in the present case I have no criterion of correctness. One would like to say: whatever is going to seem right to me is right. And that only means that here we can't talk about 'right.'" What is special about "the present case"? Explain carefully, in your own words, what his reasoning here is. Do you think it's correct? Does he prove that in this sort of case we can't talk about 'right'?

12. Sometimes it's thought that Wittgenstein is claiming that no words or beliefs about one's own private mental events have any meaning; and since talk about mental events does have meaning, it must be about publicly observable behavior—one's own, and others'. What in this article would justify that interpretation? Think, however, about the last section in the readings. Does this tell you that Wittgenstein is actually concluding something different? What, exactly?

Suggested Readings

Defenses of logical behaviorism can be found in:

Rudolph Carnap, "Logical Foundations of the Unity of Science," in *International Encyclopedia of Unified Science*, O. Neurath, R. Carnap, and C. Morris (eds.), vol. 1, pt. 1. (Chicago: University of Chicago Press, 1955).

Carl Hempel, "The Logical Analysis of Psychology," in *Readings in Philosophical Analysis*, H. Feigl and W. Sellars (eds.). (New York: Appleton-Century Crofts, 1949; reprinted in *Philosophy of Mind: A Guide and Anthology*, J. Heil [ed.]. [Oxford: Oxford University Press, 2003]).

An important attack on behaviorism was Hilary Putnam, "Brains and Behavior," in *Analytic Philosophy*, 2nd series, R.J. Butler, (ed.) (Oxford: Blackwell, 1965). Excerpted in *Philosophy of Mind: A Guide and Anthology*, John Heil, (ed.). (Oxford: Oxford University Press, 2003), and in *Philosophy of Mind; Classical and Contemporary Readings*, David J. Chalmers (ed.). (New York: Oxford University Press, 2002).

John B. Watson, the father of modern behavioristic psychology, expresses his views very clearly in "Psychology as the Behaviorist Views It," *Psychological Review* 20 (1913): pp. 158–77.

A work by Skinner, written ten years after the selection in this book, is "Behaviorism at Fifty," *Science* 140 (1963): pp. 951–58. Reprinted with commentaries and Skinner's responses in *Behavioral and Brain Sciences* 7 (1984): pp. 615–21.

A general account and evaluation of behaviorism is in Keith Campbell, *Body and Mind*. (London: Methuen, 1970).

8

THE MIND-BRAIN
IDENTITY THEORY

The Rise of Materialism

Since the second half of the twentieth century the most widely accepted positions on the nature of the mind have been varieties of materialism. Although materialism is as old as the Greek atomists, and has been defended over the centuries by people like Hobbes, it is only in recent years that it has become almost universally accepted among philosophers and psychologists. Several different theories have come to the fore in recent years, but each of them takes as a given the view that human beings consist of nothing more than the matter of which their bodies are composed. Debates over the mind-body problem have largely become debates over which particular version of materialism should be accepted as correct. In this chapter and the next we will look at three versions of materialism that are currently competing for prominence.

The widespread acceptance of materialism is due to a large extent to developments in biology. Biology is the study of living things, and so a central question in biology is to define the difference between living things and nonliving matter. Descartes's answer was that life is a purely material phenomenon. While holding that the mind is an immaterial substance, Descartes argued that the body is simply a physical mechanism, and he offered a mechanical explanation of a living body. Many biologists after Descartes rejected this purely mechanical account of life. They argued that biological functions are due to a "vital power" or "animality" that is not physical in nature. But the nineteenth century saw the demise of vitalism, not through a return to Descartes's theory, but through cellular biology. The first important step in this development was the discovery of the cell as an essential unit of the body, and the realization that the nature of life could be understood in terms of the molecular composition of cellular matter. By the turn of this century biologists had come to the conclusion that the nature of life lies in the physical structure of molecules.

These developments in biology had important effects on the study of the mind. In the eighteenth century, studies of the effects of brain damage revealed that specific functions of the mind, such as language and memory, are associated with specific regions of the brain. Over the years more and more correlations were established between mental activities and processes of the nervous system. This was later coupled with the discovery that the brain and the rest of the nervous system are complex arrangements of neurons. These developments led to the supposition that all processes of the mind are in some manner biochemical processes of the nervous system. In this way the developments in biology between Descartes's time and our century came slowly to support the idea that all facets of human beings, including what we think of as the mind, are properties of matter.

Conscious Experience and the Brain

In his essay "Is Consciousness a Brain Process?" published in 1956, Ullin T. Place acknowledges the demise of dualism among philosophers and psychologists in the early twentieth century. Place was a student of Gilbert Ryle at Oxford, and was sympathetic to the general aims of the behaviorism of Ryle and Wittgenstein. In the introductory section of this paper, Place describes behaviorism as the form that materialism adopted in the first half of the twentieth century. The behaviorist describes states of consciousness in terms of certain kinds of behavior and dispositions to behave in certain ways, and avoids any talk of an inner mind altogether. Descriptions of behavior can be given entirely in materialist terms, as various kinds of bodily movements and vocal expressions, making behaviorism a fully materialist doctrine.

Place accepts that with respect to certain concepts, "an analysis in terms of dispositions to behave is fundamentally sound." These concepts, he says, are those concerning our *cognitive* abilities—involved in our acquisition of knowledge—and our *volitional* abilities—our wants and desires. The general idea here is that our beliefs and our desires can be understood entirely through our behavior. For example, a state of thirst and a belief that a glass contains water can be understood as a disposition to drink from the glass. Place also defended Skinner's behaviorism against Chomsky's criticism that we read in the previous chapter.[1]

After this, however, Place expresses a view that became important in the late 1950s and early 1960s: that behaviorism cannot deal successfully with that part of mental life involving *conscious experience*. **Conscious experience** is the subjective aspect of our mental life. As some philosophers describe it, it is what thoughts, sensations, memories, and so on are like for the person who is having them. The attempt to describe sensations, like pains or experiences of color, or mental images, such as the experience of imagining a waterfall, are in Place's view not susceptible to description in terms of a person's behavior. As we shall see, a number of philosophers came to adopt this position on the limitations of behaviorism. There is, they argue, something we can genuinely call a person's inner mental life, which is not adequately captured by descriptions of the person's outward behavior.

The existence of conscious experience, of a subjective inner mental life, is exactly what Descartes drew attention to in his Second Meditation. One can doubt the existence of an object one perceives, he says, but one cannot doubt the *experience* of perceiving it. And it is, of course, exactly this private inner life that behaviorists argue lies outside of the science of mind. Place argues that descriptions of our conscious experiences do in fact describe states and events that are in some sense inner or private to the individual. Yet he denies that this assertion commits him to Cartesian dualism. The position that Place wants to defend in this article is that inner mental states are not states of an immaterial mind as the dualists contend. They are instead states of the *brain*. This position reconciles materialism with the acceptance of inner mental states, for states and events of the brain are of course entirely material; they are states of the physical arrangement of neurons and events involving their complex interactions. Exactly how this position is to be understood in detail will be developed over the course of this chapter.

Phenomenal Properties

Before we turn to the detailed account of the idea that mental states are brain states, we want to look first at the final section, Section V, of Place's article. In this section, Place makes reference to what he calls "phenomenal properties" of conscious experience. It is worth looking carefully at what Place says about these properties, because their existence and nature has become a recurring controversy in the philosophy of mind, and they will form the subject matter of Chapter Eleven ahead.

Consider, first, a case of looking at a red cup. Physicists can explain the properties of the rays of light that strike the cup, and the properties of the light reflected from it towards the eye. Neurophysiologists can describe the chemical processes that occur when those rays strike the retina inside the eye, and a good deal of what goes on in the neural activity of the brain resulting from the stimulation of the retina. But there seems to be something about our experience that neither of these scientists describes: what the conscious experience of the color of the cup is like for the person who sees it. There is, or there seems to be, a quality of redness as it appears to the perceiver: what red *looks like*. There are similar properties, it seems, for each of our senses. There is the way that a toothache feels; what a foghorn or a tiny bell sounds like; what a fine Bordeaux tastes like; what freshly mowed grass smells like.

Place calls these the **phenomenal properties** of our experiences: "the properties of the looks, sounds, smells, tastes, and feels which [things in our environment] produce in us."[2] By this description, Place seems at first to identify these properties as precisely those that John Locke described as the "qualities of sensations." Recall from the introduction to Chapter Six that Locke argued that the sensations of secondary qualities had no resemblance to the properties in objects that cause them. In this assertion, Locke was developing a claim already made by Descartes. As we will see in later chapters, phenomenal properties have been given a variety of names and descriptions, and the assertion that our experiences possess these properties has led to deep disagreements among philosophers.

The Phenomenological Fallacy

Place points out that many people argue that the idea of phenomenal properties leads to a serious difficulty for materialism. The long quotation that Place gives from Sir Charles Sherrington can be described this way: "Where is the blue that I see in the sky? Physicists say that the sky is a collection of molecules making up our atmosphere, and none of those molecules are blue. Light is a set of photons, none of which are blue. And when a neurophysiologist looks inside the brain, she sees no blue neurons there either. So where is the blueness?"

This apparent problem, Place argues, arises from a certain assumption that these people make. He describes this assumption as the belief that because we recognize things in our environment by their look, sound, smell, taste, and feel, we begin by describing their phenomenal properties, i.e., the properties of the looks, sounds, smells, tastes, and feels which they produce in us, and infer their real properties from their phenomenal properties.

Place believes this assumption is false; he calls it the "phenomenological fallacy." As he sees it, when we perceive the property of an object in the world (say, the color of a cup) a certain experience is generated in our mind, and that experience enables us to recognize that property in physical objects. This much is uncontroversial. But from these facts some people infer that, when a subject describes the look, sound, smell, and taste of objects in the world, she does so by way of describing the phenomenal properties of something *in her own mind*. This "something" is the so-called phenomenal field, which some people mistakenly think of as similar to a movie screen before the mind's eye. This, he says, is a logical error. Colors and other perceptible properties are properties of physical objects. And we learn to describe our conscious experiences by way of learning to describe those physical properties—not the other way around. Once we rid ourselves of this mistake, we can come to understand, Place thinks, that perceptual experiences are "nothing more than" events in the brain caused by those properties. Phenomenal properties, therefore, are "mythical" creations of the logical error.

Ockham's Razor

A very similar position is taken in the second article of this chapter, "Sensations and Brain Processes," by J.J.C. Smart which appeared in 1959. Place and Smart both taught in Australia in the 1950s, and they worked together on the ideas presented in this chapter. As does Place, Smart contends that sensations like those of pain and color are physical states of the brain. He uses one particular kind of sensation to make his point: the visual sensation of an after-image. An after-image is the kind of thing you get when you look at a bright light and then look away at a blank wall.[3] He asks, "When I report that I have a yellowy-orange after-image, what is it that I am reporting?" What kind of thing is this after-image?

Smart argues first that the answer to this question must be consistent with materialism. Every aspect of the world except consciousness is now understood to be an aspect of matter, and it seems unbelievable, he argues, to suppose that consciousness should be the one exception to materialism. Smart's argument for materialism is an application of a principle we call "Ockham's Razor" after the medieval philosopher, William of Ockham. **Ockham's Razor** instructs us never to postulate more than is needed to explain what is observed. The idea is that if two theories are each consistent with all available evidence, the one that postulates fewer entities and properties is more likely to be true.

Ockham's Razor, sometimes called "the principle of parsimony," is an important element in scientific reasoning. We see it at work, for example, in the defense of the new science. Descartes argues for the mechanical science on the grounds that a few simple properties are sufficient to explain all observable physical phenomena. A particularly dramatic example of the principle is the success of Newton's theory of gravity. By postulating a force of attraction between all particles of matter, Newton was able to explain the acceleration of falling bodies, the movement of the ocean tides, and the shape of the planetary orbits, all by means of one single law. Before Newton each of these phenomena was given a separate explanation. The unity and simplicity that Newton's theory brought was a major factor in its acceptance by the scientific community.

Smart applies the same reasoning to the mind-body problem. Given the strong correlations between what happens in the mind and what happens in the body, and given that every other aspect of the world has turned out to be physical in nature, the simplest conclusion to draw is that the mind itself will turn out to be physical as well. If this is not true, Smart argues, we are forced to conclude that just one phenomenon—consciousness—is distinct from everything else in the universe. Smart claims that this would make consciousness and sensation a "**nomological dangler**." By this he means that consciousness would be left hanging as the one aspect of the universe that could not be explained in terms of the mechanical properties of matter.

Smart considers one important objection to his use of Ockham's Razor: There are always constituents of the world that science cannot explain. For example, while a physicist or chemist can explain why a certain material behaves as it does by referring to the periodic table of the elements, there is no explanation of why we have *this* set of elements and not another. This problem currently lies outside the domain of physics, and is accepted as a "brute fact"—something that is known but not explainable. Thus a critic of Smart's argument can say that the existence of consciousness might also be a brute fact, which we have to accept as something that falls outside the domain of scientific explanation.

Smart replies that the things currently accepted as brute facts all involve the basic or fundamental constituents of the universe. By contrast, consciousness only exists in the presence of certain highly complex and organized biological systems involving "configurations consisting of billions of neurons...all put together...as though their main purpose in life was to be a negative feedback mechanism of a complicated sort." The presence of consciousness in these organisms requires *some* kind of explanation, and the simplest available is that it is an aspect of organized matter.

Like Place, Smart finds Wittgenstein's version of behaviorism congenial because of its compatibility with materialism. On Wittgenstein's view, he says, "a man is a vast arrangement of physical particles, but there are not, over and above this, sensations or states of consciousness." But Smart contends that one cannot reduce sensations such as after-images solely to aspects of a person's behavior. Just as Place claims that behaviorism cannot adequately account for conscious experience, Smart says:

> ...it does seem to me as though, when a person says "I have an after-image," he *is* making a genuine report, and that when he says "I have a pain," he *is* doing more than "replace pain-behavior."

By this he means just that people's reports of sensations are reports of genuine events that are occurring, so that there must be something more than just the behavior, even if this "something more" is not an immaterial thing. Smart's solution to the problem is very similar to Place's. Sensations, he says, could "just be brain process of a certain sort." His idea here is that, when a person is aware of a sensation such as an after-image, the event that they are aware of is a physical event in the brain.

Two Meanings of 'Is'

Yet Place's and Smart's defense of conscious experiences as aspects of our inner mental life needed to address the behaviorist arguments against such an idea. For, as we have seen, behaviorists like Ryle and Wittgenstein attacked the notion of an inner mental life as simply incoherent. For Ryle it leads to the mysterious Cartesian doctrine of the "ghost in the machine," and for Wittgenstein it depends on an impossibility: a private language. Interestingly, the response that Place and Smart gave uses a characteristic strategy of the behaviorists themselves, namely, that the critics are making a serious error in understanding *language*. Once this error is cleared up, they contend, the acceptance of inner conscious experience as a phenomenon not fully describable in terms of behavior is fully compatible with materialism.

The key to understanding this issue is to recall that Ryle and Wittgenstein approach the mind-body problem by looking carefully at what people *mean* when they describe their beliefs, desires, and thoughts. The resulting analysis, they argue, reveals that our descriptions cannot be understood as descriptions of a private inner life because this leads to logical errors and confusions. Place and Smart, however, argue that this way of formulating the problem misrepresents the issue.

Place addresses three criticisms of the idea that states and processes of the mind are really states and processes of the brain, each of which relies on a mistaken view of the meaning of such a statement. First, people can easily describe their own conscious experience without knowing a single thing about the brain—indeed without even knowing they *have* a brain. You can describe my own headache, for example, without having to describe any neural events at all. Second, the two descriptions—of consciousness and of the brain—are "verified in entirely different ways." For example, if you need to confirm the presence of a headache to a doctor who enquires, you would only have to consult your own inner experience. Yet if the doctor wants to determine what is going on in your brain at that moment, she will use a piece of machinery that measures levels of neural activity. So how can these be confirmations of the same process? The third criticism is perhaps less obvious: There is no *logical* connection between states of consciousness and states of the brain. If someone says "This person is experiencing a sensation of pain," and also say, "There is nothing going on in the brain of this person," there is no *logical* contradiction in the way there would be if they said, "This person is and is not experiencing a sensation of pain." What this indicates is that the two statements, 'This person is experiencing a sensation of pain,' and 'There is something going on in the brain of this person,' do not have the same meaning, so when someone talks of their inner experiences they are not talking about their brain.

Place argues that all three of these criticisms misrepresent the issue in the same way. In each case, he claims, the critic assumes that a sentence like, 'sensations of pain are processes of the brain' is a statement of *definition*. This assumption, he argues, is both unnecessary and false. Let's look first at the examples that Place gives to illustrate his point. Compare the sentence, 'A square is an equilateral rectangle,' with the sentence, 'His table is an old packing crate.' The first is a definition. It indicates what the word 'square' means. The second is not a definition; it doesn't describe what the words 'his table' mean. It is a description of the composition of the table. So the word 'is' is being used in different ways in the two sentences. Place describes this difference as that between the 'is' of *definition* and the 'is' of *composition*.

Place's argument is that the critics of his claim that consciousness is a brain process take this assertion as one of definition. Properly understood, however, it is really a statement about the composition of conscious states. The criticisms outlined in the preceding paragraph all assume that 'consciousness is a brain process' should be taken as a definition of the word 'consciousness.' For example, the fact that a person can describe their own headache while knowing nothing about the brain is paradoxical only if it is claimed that a description of the brain is part of the definition of 'headache.' Yet supposing that someone can describe aspects of their headache while not knowing that what they are describing is in fact something going on in their brain is no more mysterious than knowing that someone's table is in their living room while not knowing that it is an old packing crate. Similarly, there is no reason why different aspects of a headache—the experiential and the neural—shouldn't be confirmed in different ways, just as confirming that someone's table is in their living room and confirming that it is an old packing crate require different criteria. And finally, there is clearly no logical connection between a table being in the living room and its being an old packing crate, and in the same way there need be no logical connection between a headache feeling a certain way and its being a brain process—unless, that is, the description of the brain process is part of the definition of the word 'headache.' The error that the critics make, then, derives from the basic assumption of behaviorists that the mind-body problem is one about the definitions of our words.

Identity and Reference

Smart agrees with Place on two points: that the behaviorists misconstrue the mind-body problem as one of understanding the definitions of our words, and that the right solution to the problem is that states of consciousness are states of the brain. Yet he formulates these points somewhat differently than does Place. Place sees the fundamental confusion as that between the 'is' of definition and the 'is' of composition. Smart, however, uses a different way of presenting the same confusion. In the section entitled, "Remarks on Identity," Smart says that by saying that a mental event is a brain event he is using the word 'is' in the sense of "*strict identity.*" This point needs to be looked at carefully.

Smart is introducing a third way in which we can understand the sentence, 'mental states are brain states.' A simple example can illustrate the differences. Consider the sentence, 'Alecia Beth Moore is Pink.' Neither of Place's two meanings of 'is' can explain what this says. It does not say that the *definition* of 'Alecia Beth Moore' is 'Pink.' Nor can we say that this is a statement of composition: Alecia Beth Moore is not *made of* Pink. What it really means is that Alecia Beth Moore and Pink are the *same person.* When we use the name 'Alecia Beth Moore' we are talking about the same person as when we use the name 'Pink.' The two names, 'Alecia Beth Moore' and 'Pink' both *refer to* the same person.

Smart's argument is that states of consciousness are states of the brain in exactly the same sense that Alecia Beth Moore is Pink. The sentence, 'States of consciousness are states of the brain,' says that the two phrases, 'states of consciousness' and 'states of the brain' *refer to* the same thing. This meaning of the word 'is' is that of **identity**. To say that x is y, in this sense, is to say that x and y are the same thing. Thus the theory that Smart proposes has been termed the **mind-brain identity theory**. Before looking at the arguments for and against this view, we must get clear on just what kind of identity he is suggesting.

Strict Identity and Correlation

When Smart says that there is a "strict identity" between mental events and brain events, he is first concerned to distinguish his view from the idea that there is a *correlation* between two events. To say that there is a correlation between a mental event and a brain event is to say there are two events which occur together. This is something that Descartes would agree with. According to Descartes, each type of sensation in the mind is caused by a certain kind of event in the brain. There are certain physical occurrences in the brain that are always immediately accompanied by the occurrence of a sensation in consciousness, and these sensations never arise in the absence of their respective brain events. Nonetheless, Descartes views the two occurrences, mental and physical, as just that: *two* events, not one.

Smart's position is that there are not two correlated events—the event in the brain and the event in the mind—but rather that there is only one event, and that event is a brain event. In the same way, Smart says, a flash of lightning is not *correlated* with a discharge of electricity in the sky; the lightning *is* a discharge of electricity.

Numerical and Qualitative Identity

Another way to understand Smart's idea is to draw a distinction between what is called "qualitative identity" and "numerical identity." When we say that one thing is **qualitatively identical** to another, we mean that the two things are similar to one another in every respect. For example, there are several flags in front of the Canadian Parliament Buildings that are identical in this sense. They are the same size, shape, and color, and their construction is exactly the same. But when we say that one thing is **numerically identical** to another, we mean that it is actually one and the same thing as the other. For example, to say that the easternmost town of the continental United States is numerically identical to Lubec, Maine is to say that Lubec and the easternmost town in the continental USA are one and the same town; there is exactly one place that is both the easternmost town in the continental USA and Lubec, Maine. When we are talking about numerical identity, we usually use the shorter expression of the form, 'Lubec *is* the easternmost town in the continental USA.'[4] Each of the following is an example of numerical identity.

> Five is the sum of two and three.
> Water is H_2O.
> Her oldest sister is her best friend.

When identity theorists say that the mind is the brain, and that states of mind are states of the brain, they are talking about numerical identity. They claim that the object that we think of as the mind is one and the same thing as the brain, and that each mental state or event is one and the same thing as some particular physical state or event of the brain.

Contingent and Necessary Facts

Another important element in Smart's theory is found in the paragraph immediately preceding the section "Remarks on Identity." That paragraph begins with the following passage:

Let me first try to state more accurately the thesis that sensations are brain-processes. It is not the thesis that, for example, 'after-image' or 'ache' means the same as 'brain process of sort X' (where 'X' is replaced by a description of a certain sort of brain process). It is that, in so far as 'after-image' or 'ache' is a report of a process, it is a report of a process that *happens to be* a brain process.

Here Smart is introducing a central feature of the identity theory. We can describe this feature by saying that the identity of mind and brain is a "contingent identity," not a "necessary identity." Let's look at these concepts before going on to see what use Smart makes of them.

Some facts are contingent facts and some are necessary facts. To say that a fact is **contingent** means that it is a result of how the world happens to be; had the world been different than it is, it might not have been a fact. For example, that Bruce Willis was born in Germany is a contingent fact. It is true that Willis was born in Germany, but if his parents had moved to the US before he was born, it would not have been true. By contrast, when a fact is **necessary**, it is impossible for it not to be a fact. Which facts are necessary—and whether there even are any—are controversial questions, but there are some plausible cases. Mathematical facts seem to be necessary: no matter how the world might have turned out, the sum of two positive numbers cannot possibly be a negative number. The least controversial examples of necessary facts are those that depend solely on logical relations between concepts. For instance, the sentence 'All sisters are female' is necessarily true simply because the concept conveyed by the term 'female' is part of the concept conveyed by 'sister.'[5]

Contingent and Necessary Identity

So to say that one thing is **contingently identical** to another means that the identity depends on how the world happens to be. Let's look at an example. We know now that the brightest star in the morning sky, the Morning Star, is actually the planet Venus. And the brightest star in the evening sky, the Evening Star, happens to be the same planet. So the Morning Star and the Evening Star are numerically identical. But if the solar system had been arranged differently than it is (say, if the scattering of celestial matter produced a different arrangement of planets), the brightest objects in the morning and evening skies might have been two *different* planets, say Venus and Jupiter. So the numerical identity of the Morning Star and the Evening Star is contingent; it is a result of how the world happens to be put together. For another example, the numerical identity of Lubec, Maine and the easternmost town in the continental USA is also contingent; people might have built a town further east (say, on West Quoddy Head).

By contrast, to say one thing is **necessarily identical** to another means that it is impossible that they could have been different objects, no matter how the world happened to be. For example, John's oldest sister is necessarily identical to John's oldest female sibling. Given what a sister is, it is impossible for John's oldest sister to be anyone *but* his oldest female sibling. This is because the two expressions 'sister' and 'female sibling' express the same concept. In such a case the identity is not dependent on how the world is put together; it is fixed by the logical relations between the two concepts.

Discovering Contingent Facts

Identity theorists use the following argument to support their claim that the identity of mind and brain is a contingent identity: Necessary identities, they claim, are ones that depend on the nature of our concepts. This means that understanding the concepts involved is all we need to recognize necessary identities. For example, to know that John's oldest sister is his oldest female sibling, you don't have to know anything about John or his family; you don't need to know anything at all except what a sister is. If someone were to conduct a survey to see whether everyone's oldest sister happens to be their oldest female sibling, they would reveal that they are confused about the word 'sister.' By contrast, identity theorists argue, contingent identities are ones that we can *discover*.

When an identity is contingent, knowing the meanings of the two terms is not sufficient to make the identity known. For example, it was a significant discovery to realize that the Morning Star and the Evening Star are one and the same planet. People had long been able to identify the brightest objects in the morning and evening skies without realizing that both are in fact the planet Venus.

Similarly, identity theorists contend, the contingent nature of mind-brain identity is revealed by the fact that it is something that we have discovered. We have always understood what is meant by the terms 'mind' and 'brain.' But it is only in the past few decades that we have come to recognize that the mind happens to be the same object as the brain. The fact that this is something we can discover, they claim, reveals that mind-brain identity is a contingent fact, one that is a matter of how the world happens to be.

The Scientific Character of the Mind-Body Problem

Identity theorists argue that the idea that the nature of mental states is a contingent matter makes the identity theory different in an important way from both Descartes's dualism and logical behaviorism. According to Descartes, discovering the nature of the mind is achieved by reflection on our ideas of mind and matter. When we do this, he argues, we see that the mind could not possibly be a material object. The idea of mind and the idea of matter are ideas of two different substances—two "complete things"—and no matter how the world might have been put together it is impossible that one should be the same as the other. In a somewhat similar way, behaviorists such as Ryle argue that understanding the mind is a matter of understanding the nature of psychological concepts. Thus Wittgenstein argued that an analysis of the concept of pain reveals that the word 'pain' can only refer to outward behavior and not to an inner private experience.

Identity theorists reject both of these approaches. They argue that discovering the nature of the mind is a *scientific* matter, to be settled by experiments and observations, not by examining our concepts of mind and matter. Understanding the nature of the mind, they argue, is no different from understanding the nature of water or lightning. In both of these latter cases, careful experiments revealed the underlying physical nature of the object. Molecular physics revealed that water is a substance with the molecular structure H_2O. And Benjamin Franklin's experiment with his kite revealed that lightning is actually an electrical discharge in the atmosphere. Similarly, identity theorists claim that observation and experiment will reveal the nature of thought, feeling, and sensation. And they argue that the best current evidence is that all of these states of mind are physical processes of the brain.

Intertheoretic Reduction

The similarity that identity theorists assert between the identity of mind and brain and scientific discoveries of the underlying nature of phenomena like water and lightning leads us to another important aspect of identity theory. The identity theory is usually seen as a version of what philosophers call *reductionism*. The identity of mental states or processes with neural states or processes implies that by understanding the biochemical activity of the brain, we can explain how and why the mind acts as it does. For example, the activity of reason could potentially be explained in terms of the successive firings of millions of neurons in the cerebral cortex. In this way, identity theorists believe that we can explain the activity of the mind in terms of some more basic or fundamental processes, namely, biochemical processes. Biochemical processes are more basic in the sense that they occur across the spectrum of life and are responsible for a vast number of biological phenomena. In this way, the mind comes to be seen as part of the fundamental nature of life. The activity of explaining something in terms of more basic entities or processes is called **intertheoretic reduction**. As it is characterized by identity theorists, this kind of reduction occurs when a phenomenon that is not yet understood becomes identified with something belonging to a broad and fundamental science, and when that identification allows us to explain the occurrence of the phenomenon in terms of some more basic entities and events. In particular, we can call **neurophysical reduction** the identity of mental states and processes with neural states and processes, and the explanation of the former in terms of the latter.

Place and Smart each compares the identity of mental processes with neural processes with Benjamin Franklin's discovery that lightning is electrical discharge. The phenomenon of electrical discharge is described and explained by physics, which studies the most basic or fundamental properties of matter. So Franklin's discovery of the physical nature of lightning allowed for an explanation of the many properties of lightning in terms of these fundamental properties. This was, then, an instance of intertheoretic reduction. Identity theorists see similar cases of reduction throughout much of science. The ability of plants to draw energy from the sun, for example, has been reduced to the synthesis of organic compounds from carbon dioxide and water. Examples of such explanations abound throughout the sciences. According to identity theorists, then, the reduction of mental states to neural states, and of mental activity to neural activity, is part of the general scientific enterprise of explaining observable occurrences in terms of some basic or fundamental entities. At one time, the states and processes of the mind were thought to be singular in nature, altogether different from other aspects of the world, just as biologists once believed about the processes of life. The reduction of mental states to brain states is intended to show how mental states are part of a more general and fundamental phenomenon, just as biochemistry now shows how respiration and digestion are physical processes.

The First Objection: Knowledge of Brain States

Smart uses the notion of contingent identity to reject a number of common criticisms of the identity theory. In the concluding sections of his paper he describes several objections that are raised against his theory and offers his reply to each. Let's look at the first and third of these objections together with Smart's replies. The first underscores the importance of the notion of contingent identity, and the third introduces an interesting element of Smart's identity theory.

The first objection that Smart discusses is the same one that Place considers first as well. It is the argument that a person can describe their sensations without possessing any knowledge of brain processes. Applied to Smart's example, one can know that one is experiencing a yellow-orange after-image, even though one has no idea what's going on in their brain. It follows, so the objection goes, that the after-image and the brain process can't possibly be the same thing. If one is aware of the sensation, and the sensation is identical to a brain state, then one would have to be aware of the brain state. Because one may have no idea what's going on in one's brain, the sensation can't be a brain state.

Smart's reply to this is similar to Place's, but it is cast in terms of the difference between contingent and necessary identity. Recognizing an after-image requires only a knowledge of the *concept* of an after-image. One can apply this concept correctly without knowing that what it refers to is identical to a brain state, because the identity of after-images with brain states is a contingent one. Smart illustrates his point with the identity of the Morning Star and Evening Star. Someone can recognize the Evening Star as long as they can identify the brightest object in the evening sky, even if they have no knowledge whatever of the Morning Star. This is because the identity of the Morning Star and the Evening Star is contingent. It just so happens, given the arrangement of matter in the universe, that both concepts apply to the same object: the planet Venus.

The Third Objection: Mental Properties

The third objection is based on Smart's reply to the first. Smart's example of a contingent identity is that of the Morning Star and the Evening Star. The fact that identity in this case is contingent means that, had the world been different than it is, the brightest objects in the morning and evening skies might have been two different objects. And this in turn means that the planet Venus might have been the brightest object in the morning sky *without* being the brightest object in the evening sky. What this reveals is that the property or characteristic of *being the brightest object in the morning sky* is a different property from that of *being the brightest object in the evening sky*, for it is possible for something to have one of these properties but not the other. In general, whenever A is contingently identical to B, the property described by the term 'A' is different from the property described by the term 'B.' Let's see how this point applies to mind-brain identity.

We'll use Smart's example of an after-image again. If, as Smart says, an orange after-image is contingently identical to a brain process of type X, then, from what we have just seen, the property of *being an orange after-image* is a different property from that of *being a brain state of type X*. Now, the property of being a particular kind of brain process is one that we would explain in terms of electrochemical activity in the nervous system. But what about the property of being an orange after-image? What characteristics would something necessarily have to have in order to be an after-image? It looks as though this would be a matter of having a certain appearance in consciousness, for this is how we are familiar with after-images. That is, we recognize something as an after-image by how it appears to us in our visual experience. So it seems that the property of *appearing a certain way in consciousness* is a different property from that of being a certain kind of brain process.

Property Dualism

The conclusion of the third objection is that if the identity of mental states and brain states is contingent, as Smart claims, then there must be mental *properties* that are not physical properties. And this, it is argued, leads us to another form of dualism. This form of dualism has it that, while the mind is not a separate *entity* from the brain, *mental properties* of the brain are not identical to *physical properties* of the brain. The mind/brain is a single entity, but it is held to have two distinct sets of characteristics, mental and physical. This kind of dualism is called **property dualism**, in contrast to Descartes's dualism, which is sometimes referred to as **substance dualism**.

So it appears that if mind-brain identity is contingent, mental properties are not physical properties of the brain even if there is a single event in the brain that has both such properties. It looks as though, in defending materialism from the first objection, Smart has ended up with a variety of dualism after all. This is much the same as the problem that U.T. Place saw as a consequence of the Phenomenological Fallacy: that the properties of conscious experiences seem to be something distinct from the physical properties of the brain. Indeed, Place's solution is the same as Smart's, although not as clearly described.

Smart's Reply to the Third Objection

Smart's reply to this objection is as follows. He says:

> When a person says, "I see a yellowish-orange after-image," he is saying something like this: "There is something going on which is like what is going on when I have my eyes open, am awake, and there is an orange illuminated in good light in front of me, that is, when I really see an orange."

What does this mean, and how does it solve the problem?

The problem Smart faces can be put in this way: Given the nature of contingent identity, there are two different properties that the yellowish-orange sensation has:

1. the property of appearing yellowish-orange in consciousness, and
2. the property of being a brain process of type X.

And it appears as though the first is a purely mental property, for how something appears in consciousness can only be understood in terms of our private mental experience. So if (1) is going to be distinct from (2), it seems that (1) must refer to an ineliminably *psychic* property. Smart's solution is to find a description of the first property that eliminates any reference to consciousness.

So he replaces (1) with

(1*) the property of being an event similar to what happens when I see an orange.

(1) and (1*), he claims, are really the same property. But notice that (1*) makes no reference to consciousness. In fact, (1*) makes no claim at all about what kind of event occurs when we see an orange. The event described in (1*) could have any nature at all, mental or physical. So Smart can admit that there is a single event that has two properties: that of being similar to what happens when one sees an orange, and that of being a brain process of type X. But this admission does not force him to admit that there are any nonphysical properties.

Topic-Neutral Descriptions

In this reply to the third objection Smart is introducing a new approach to the mind-body problem. We identify mental states in terms of some characteristic they have that is neutral with respect to their intrinsic nature. Smart calls these **topic-neutral** terms. We then set about investigating the underlying nature of the states identified in this way. For example, we can identify the sensation of pain as whatever it is that happens in a person when they do something like drop a brick on their foot. It is then a matter of scientific investigation what kind of occurrence that is.

The topic-neutral approach, identity theorists argue, is similar to the standard way of proceeding in the sciences. At one time scientists identified electricity simply as the event that occurs when a glass rod is rubbed or when wires are attached to a battery cell. Then they set about determining what kind of thing electricity is. Several ideas were proposed before the present theory of electron transmission was hit upon. In general, the method is to identify a particular kind of occurrence without any knowledge of its underlying nature, and then to find out through experiment and observation what kind of occurrence it is. The topic-neutral approach is a reflection of Smart's contention that the nature of the mind is a contingent matter, to be settled by scientific investigation. When we identify an after-image as an event that is similar to what happens when we see something orange, the nature of the event is left open to investigation. We can ask, what kind of event is it that occurs in this way? And the answer to this question is to be settled by collecting evidence for and against competing hypotheses. The current evidence, Smart says, favors the contention that these kinds of events are physical events in the brain. But if so, this will be a contingent matter. That is, the event does not *have to be* a physical event in the brain; rather the world just happens to be that way.

Can Mind-Brain Identity Really Be Contingent?

Shortly after the formulation of the identity theory, a Princeton philosopher, Saul Kripke, outlined what he took to be a serious problem with the claim that mind-brain identity is a contingent matter. Kripke's initial influence was as a logician. In several early works he made important advances in a field of mathematical logic called "modal logic," which deals with the notions of possibility and necessity. His criticism of the identity theory rose directly out of his work on the logic of necessity.[6] Before we look at Kripke's argument, let's briefly review the issue that he addresses.

As we have seen, identity theorists contend that the virtue of the topic-neutral approach is that it leaves the mind-body problem as an issue to be settled by scientific study. Smart and Place argue that the weight of evidence currently suggests that the thoughts and sensations we experience are biochemical processes of the brain. Yet the very fact that this issue is to be settled by the weight of evidence, they argue, shows that the issue is a *contingent* one. That is, whether thoughts and sensations are brain events or states of an immaterial substance is a matter of how the world happens to be put together. In an article entitled "Identity and Necessity," Kripke argues that the scientific nature of the mind-body problem does *not* show that the issue is a contingent one. The argument in this article anticipates an important book called *Naming and Necessity.*[7] His contention is that necessary facts—facts that could not have been otherwise, no matter how the world turned out—can be discovered by science, or settled by the weight of evidence, just as contingent facts can be. According to Kripke, this shows that the tactics Smart uses to respond to the criticisms of identity theory will not work.

Science and Contingent Identity

In the first two paragraphs of our selection from Kripke's article, he reminds us that the argument that mind-brain identity is a contingent issue is made by comparing that issue with certain well-known scientific facts. These facts, identity theorists claim, are precisely the same as the identity of mind and brain; each of them is a contingent fact, discovered in the course of normal scientific investigation. For example, the fact that heat is molecular motion is held to be contingent because we might have discovered that some other theory is true. (We might, for example, have discovered that heat is a kind of fluid.) It is then argued that the same is true of mind and brain: some other theory (such as Descartes's) *might* have been true; but, as it turns out, mental states and activities turn out to be brain states and activities.

In the next paragraph Kripke claims that the scientific facts that identity theorists use to compare their theory with the mind-brain identity theory are not actually contingent facts at all.[8] If a statement such as 'Heat is molecular motion' is true, he contends, it is necessarily true. In other words, if heat is molecular motion, then it could not have been anything but molecular motion, no matter how the world might have turned out to be. His argument for this claim is based on a pair of technical concepts: that of a "rigid designator" and that of a "nonrigid designator." We need first to understand these two concepts.

Rigid and Nonrigid Designators

Kripke uses the term '**designator**' to mean any word or expression that is used to refer to something. A name is a designator, because it refers to a particular thing. 'Paris' is the name of a certain city in France, and 'Justin Bieber' is a name that refers to a certain individual. There are also names for certain kinds of substances or natural phenomena, like 'water' and 'heat.' Sometimes descriptions, such as 'the author of *Hamlet*,' also refer to individuals, in which case they are also designators.

The difference between rigid and nonrigid designators is a matter of what the designators refer to under various different circumstances. Let's use Kripke's example of a **nonrigid designator**: 'the inventor of bifocals.' The person who invented bifocals was Benjamin Franklin, so the description 'the inventor of bifocals' refers to Franklin. But of course someone else might have developed the idea before Franklin, so the fact that Franklin invented bifocals is a contingent fact. And if someone else, say Isaac Newton, had invented them, then the term 'the inventor of bifocals' would have referred to that person. So the person to whom the term refers depends on certain contingent facts; in some circumstances it would refer to one person, and under other circumstances it would refer to someone else.

A **rigid designator**, on the other hand, is such that the individual it refers to does not depend on any contingent circumstances. Kripke's example is 'the square root of 25.' That expression refers to the number 5, and there are no possible circumstances under which it would refer to any other number. You might say that, when a term is a rigid designator, the fact that it refers to a certain individual is a necessary fact.[9]

Necessity and Theoretical Identities

With the notions of rigid and nonrigid designators established, Kripke turns to his first argument. If a sentence like 'Heat is molecular motion' is contingent, he points out, then it must be possible for there to be circumstances in which it is false, that is, circumstances in which the term 'heat' refers to something other than the motion of molecules. But if you consider the situations that people have in mind, he says, it turns out that they are not actually cases in which 'heat' does not refer to molecular motion. In any conceivable circumstance, the term 'heat' will always refer to molecular motion. Hence, it is a rigid designator.

He asks us to consider various thought experiments that cover the cases in which 'heat' might not designate molecular motion. He says,

> There is a certain external phenomenon which we can sense by the sense of touch, and it produces a sensation which we call "the sensation of heat." We then discover that the external phenomenon which produces this sensation…is in fact that of molecular agitation in the thing we touch, a very high degree of molecular agitation. So, it might be thought, to imagine a situation in which heat would not have been the motion of molecules, we need only imagine a situation in which we would have had the very same sensation and it would have been produced by something other than the motion of molecules.

But, he claims, there is no such situation. First, he asks us to imagine that Martians came to our planet, for whom the rapid motion of molecules in fire produces the same sensation we get from ice, and ice produces in them the sensation we get from fire. We would not say that this shows that heat is not molecular motion, but rather that heat produces in them a different sensation than it does in us. Nor would it be different, he says, if it had been us who (through some different evolutionary process) received the sensations that these Martians do. We would not say, "In that circumstance, heat would not be molecular motion." We would say, "In that circumstance, heat would produce a different sensation than it does under these circumstances." So, he concludes, under no possible situation would 'heat' refer to anything other than molecular motion, and this means that 'heat' is a rigid designator. The fact that heat is molecular motion, then, is a *necessary fact*.

Discovering Necessary Identities

Kripke argues that, even though such facts as the identity of heat and molecular motion are necessary facts, they are nonetheless discovered by scientific investigation. Terms like 'heat' and 'lightning,' and 'light' all refer to certain things in the natural environment. Over time we have come to discover that these things are molecular motion, electrical discharge, and streams of photons. Nonetheless, despite our earlier ignorance, these terms are rigid designators that refer to the same phenomena under any possible circumstances. So our discoveries are discoveries of necessary facts.

According to Kripke, the apparent contingency of these identities is an illusion. From the fact that we have only just discovered these identities, we mistakenly *thought* that the issues were contingent. The illusion, he says, derives from the fact that we mistakenly took the designators to refer to the sensations that are produced by these phenomena. For example, our initial way of identifying heat arose from the contingent fact that it happens to cause a certain sensation in our minds. We allowed ourselves to be confused by supposing that the term 'heat' designates the sensation. But more careful reflection reveals that the term 'heat' refers to the external phenomenon that *causes* that sensation. And it would always refer to that same phenomenon, no matter what kind of sensation we happen to experience.

Mind and Body Again

Kripke now asks us to compare these theoretical identities with the case of mind-brain identity. Consider, he says, an identity claim such as 'Pain is such and such a neural (brain) state.' The identity theorist's contention is that such a claim, if it is true, is contingently true, on the grounds that we can imagine both the brain state occurring without any experience of pain, and a creature being in pain but not having the specified brain state.

Given Kripke's argument above, the identity theorist might admit that the contingency here, as in the other cases, is only apparent. Mental states, it turns out, could not be anything *but* brain states. Still, they might argue, this does not affect the issue of mind-brain identity. Even if the identity of thoughts and sensations with physical events in the brain turns out to be a necessary identity, it is nonetheless one that is discovered, just as we have discovered the nature of heat, water, and lightning. Thus the important aspect of the identity theory—that mind-brain identity is a scientific issue, not a conceptual one—is unchanged.

In the remainder of our selection, however, Kripke argues that this tactic will not save the identity theory from embarrassment. For, contrary to what the identity theorists assert, he argues that the case of mind-brain identity is very different from the other cases of theoretical identity.

In all of the other theoretical identities, what appeared to be contingent identities turn out to be illusions. We *thought*, for example, that we could imagine a situation where heat is something other than molecular motion; once we consider it more carefully, it turns out that there could be no such situation. In each case, our mistake was to think that a term designates a sensation rather than the external cause of that sensation. However, Kripke argues, this mistake could not occur in the case of pain and brain states. We could not mistakenly associate the term 'pain' with a sensation rather than its external cause, for pain *is* the sensation. As Kripke puts it, the sensation associated with the term 'pain' is not a contingent property of pain (as the sensation of heat is to molecular motion) but an *essential* property: nothing could be pain that isn't that sensation. And this, Kripke concludes, means that we cannot explain the mistaken idea that mind-brain identity is contingent in the same way that we explain the other cases.

The Problem for the Identity Theory

Kripke's arguments have two conclusions with respect to mind-brain identity. First, identity theorists are wrong in their assertion that the mind-body problem is a contingent issue. That is, whether states of mind are brain states or states of an immaterial substance is not a contingent matter that depends on how the world happens to be.

Second, we cannot say that we mistakenly *thought* that the issue was a contingent one. Although we can explain the illusion of contingency in cases like the identity of heat and molecular motion by saying that we mistakenly identified heat with the sensation it produces, we cannot say that we mistakenly identified pain with the sensation it produces. This means that if the identity theorists are right that states of mind are brain states, it is impossible to say how anyone could have thought they were anything but brain states. And this means they cannot explain how we could *discover* the identity of mental states and brain states.

Kripke maintains that materialists have failed to come up with any argument sophisticated enough to account for these two difficulties. "So the conclusion of this investigation," he says:

> would be that the analytical tools we are using [i.e., the notions of rigid and nonrigid designators] go against the identity thesis and so go against the general thesis that mental states are just physical states.

Identity theorists are left, then, with two options for replying to Kripke. They can maintain that psychological terms are not rigid designators as Kripke maintains. To do this would require an argument that what topic-neutral descriptions of psychological states refer to can vary depending on the circumstances. The other option is to accept that mind-brain identity is necessary and then find some way of explaining how we could have thought the mind could be something other than the brain.

Notes

1. U.T. Place, *Identifying the Mind: Selected Papers of U.T. Place*, George Graham and Elizabeth R. Valentine (eds.) (Oxford: Oxford University Press, 2004).

2. The adjective "phenomenal" comes from the word "phenomenon," which is derived from the Greek *phainomenon* "that which appears or is seen." From the same root we have the word "phenomenology," the study of conscious experiences.

3. The reason for choosing after-images as his example is that they are not perceptions of anything in the physical environment; they are "pure" sensations. For this reason after-images do not generate any confusion in distinguishing sensations from the objects of which they are perceptions.

4. Sentences of the form 'A is B' also have another use: namely, to say that an object A has a certain property B, as when we say 'The chair is green.' Here we don't mean that the chair and the color green are one and the same object, but that the chair has the property of being green. This use of the 'is' is called the "predicative" use.

5. Of course, we could use the words 'sister' and 'female' in a way that gives them different meanings. But this wouldn't change the point. For what is essential is that the concept expressed in English by the word 'sister' comprises the conjunction of two concepts expressed by the words 'female' and 'sibling.' We can change our language, but that wouldn't change the logical relations between these concepts.

6. Kripke also developed an influential interpretation and defense of Wittgenstein's Private Language Argument, which we read in Chapter Seven.

7. Saul A. Kripke, *Naming and Necessity* (Cambridge, MA: Harvard University Press, 1976).

8. He mentions two kinds of identity statements: those involving proper names (our example, "Alecia Beth Moore is Pink") and theoretical identifications. We will ignore the cases of proper names, because they do not affect the mind-body issue. We are concerned with theoretical identifications, such as the fact that heat is molecular motion and that water is H_2O.

9. In the remainder of this paragraph, and in the following paragraph, Kripke points out two ways in which it is possible to misunderstand him. First, the question of whether a term would refer to different individuals under different circumstances should not be taken as a matter of whether the words could be given a different meaning. For example, 'the square root of 25' might be given a completely different meaning than what we understand, in which case it would not refer to the number 5. But this would not mean that it is a nonrigid designator. Second, the fact that a term is a rigid designator does not mean that the individual it refers to must necessarily exist. But if it does exist, then the term refers to it and not something else.

U.T. PLACE

"Is Consciousness a Brain Process?"

The thesis that consciousness is a process in the brain is put forward as a reasonable scientific hypothesis, not to be dismissed on logical grounds alone. The conditions under which two sets of observations are treated as observations of the same process, rather than as observations of two independent correlated processes, are discussed. It is suggested that we can identify consciousness with a given pattern of brain activity, if we can explain the subject's introspective observations by reference to the brain processes with which they are correlated. It is argued that the problem of providing a physiological explanation of introspective observations is made to seem more difficult than it really is by the "phenomenological fallacy," the mistaken idea that descriptions of the appearances of things are descriptions of the actual state of affairs in a mysterious internal environment.

I. Introduction

The view that there exists a separate class of events, mental events, which cannot be described in terms of the concepts employed by the physical sciences no longer commands the universal and unquestioning acceptance among philosophers and psychologists which it once did. Modern physicalism, however, unlike the materialism of the seventeenth and eighteenth centuries, is behavioristic. Consciousness on this view is either a special type of behavior, "sampling" or "running-back-and-forth" behavior as Tolman has it,[1] or a disposition to behave in a certain way, an itch, for example, being a temporary propensity to scratch. In the case of cognitive concepts like "knowing," "believing," "understanding," "remembering," and volitional concepts like "wanting" and "intending," there can be little doubt, I think, that an analysis in terms of dispositions to behave is fundamentally sound.[2] On the other hand, there would seem to be an intractable residue of concepts clustering around the notions of consciousness, experience, sensation, and mental imagery, where some sort of inner process story is unavoidable.[3] It is possible, of course, that a satisfactory behavioristic account of this conceptual residuum will ultimately be found. For our present purposes, however, I shall assume that this cannot be done and that statements about pains and twinges, about how things look, sound, and feel, about things dreamed of or pictured in the mind's eye, are statements referring to events and processes which are in some sense private or internal to the individual of whom they are predicated. The question I wish to raise is whether in making this assumption we are inevitably committed to a dualist position in which sensations and mental images form a separate category of processes over and above the physical and physiological processes with which they are known to be correlated. I shall argue that an acceptance of inner processes does not entail dualism and that the thesis that consciousness is a process in the brain cannot be dismissed on logical grounds.

II. The "Is" of Definition and the "Is" of Composition

I want to stress from the outset that in defending the thesis that consciousness is a process in the brain, I am not trying to argue that when we describe our dreams, fantasies, and sensations we are talking about processes in our brains. That is, I am not claiming that statements about sensations and mental images are reducible to or analyzable into statements about brain processes, in the way in which "cognition statements" are analyzable into statements about behavior. To say that statements about consciousness are statements about brain processes is manifestly false. This is shown (a) by the fact that you can describe your sensations and mental imagery without knowing anything about your brain processes or even that such things exist, (b) by the fact that statements about one's consciousness and statements about one's brain processes are verified in entirely different ways, and (c) by the fact that there is nothing self-contradictory about the statement "X has a pain but there is nothing going on in his brain." What I do want to assert, however, is that the statement "Consciousness is a process in the brain," although not necessarily true, is not necessarily false. "Consciousness is a process in the brain" in my view is neither self-contradictory nor self-evident; it is a reasonable scientific hypothesis, in the way that the statement "Lightning is a motion of electric charges" is a reasonable scientific hypothesis.

The all but universally accepted view that an assertion of identity between consciousness and brain processes can be ruled out on logical grounds alone derives, I suspect, from a failure to distinguish between what we may call the "is" of definition and the "is" of composition. The distinction I have in mind here is the difference between the function of the word "is" in statements like "A square is an equilateral rectangle," "Red is a color," "To understand an instruction is to be able to act appropriately under the appropriate circumstances," and its function in statements like "His table is an old packing case," "Her hat is a bundle of straw tied together with string," "A cloud is a mass of water droplets or other particles in suspension." These two types of "is" statements have one thing in common. In both cases it makes sense to add the qualification "and nothing else." In this they differ from those statements in which the "is" is an "is" of predication; the statements "Toby is eighty years old and nothing else," "Her hat is red and nothing else," or "Giraffes are tall and nothing else," for example, are nonsense. This logical feature may be described by saying that in both cases both the grammatical subject and the grammatical predicate are expressions which provide an adequate characterization of the state of affairs to which they both refer.

In another respect, however, the two groups of statements are strikingly different. Statements like "A square is an equilateral rectangle" are necessary statements which are true by definition. Statements like "His table is an old packing-case," on the other hand, are contingent statements which have to be verified by observation. In the case of statements like "A square is an equilateral rectangle" or "Red is a color," there is a relationship between the meaning of the expression forming the grammatical predicate and the meaning of the expression forming the grammatical subject, such that whenever the subject expression is applicable the predicate must also be applicable. If you can describe something as red then you must also be able to describe it as colored. In the case of statements like "His table is an old packing-case," on the other hand, there is no such relationship between the meanings of the expressions "his table" and "old packing-case"; it merely so happens that in this case both expressions are applicable to and at the same time provide an adequate characterization of the same object.

Those who contend that the statement "Consciousness is a brain process" is logically untenable, base their claim, I suspect, on the mistaken assumption that if the meanings of two statements or expressions are quite unconnected, they cannot both provide an adequate characterization of the same object or state of affairs: if something is a state of consciousness, it cannot be a brain process, since there is nothing self-contradictory in supposing that someone feels a pain when there is nothing happening inside his skull. By the same token we might be led to conclude that a table cannot be an old packing-case, since there is nothing self-contradictory in supposing that someone has a table, but is not in possession of an old packing-case.

III. The Logical Independence of Expressions and the Ontological Independence of Entities

There is, of course, an important difference between the table/packing-case and the consciousness/brain process case in that the statement "His table is an old packing-case" is a particular proposition which refers only to one particular case, whereas the statement "Consciousness is a process in the brain" is a general or universal proposition applying to all states of consciousness whatever. It is fairly clear, I think, that if we lived in a world in which all tables without exception were packing-cases, the concepts of "table" and "packing-case" in our language would not have their present logically independent status. In such a world a table would be a species of packing-case in much the same way that red is a species of color. It seems to be a rule of language that whenever a given variety of object or state of affairs has two characteristics or sets of characteristics, one of which is unique to the variety of object or state of affairs in question, the expression used to refer to the characteristic or set of char-

acteristics which defines the variety of object or state of affairs in question will always entail the expression used to refer to the other characteristic or set of characteristics. If this rule admitted of no exception it would follow that any expression which is logically independent of another expression which uniquely characterizes a given variety of object or state of affairs must refer to a characteristic or set of characteristics which is not normally or necessarily associated with the object or state of affairs in question. It is because this rule applies almost universally, I suggest, that we are normally justified in arguing from the logical independence of two expressions to the ontological independence of the states of affairs to which they refer. This would explain both the undoubted force of the argument that consciousness and brain processes must be independent entities because the expressions used to refer to them are logically independent and, in general, the curious phenomenon whereby questions about the furniture of the universe are often fought and not infrequently decided merely on a point of logic. The argument from the logical independence of two expressions to the ontological independence of the entities to which they refer breaks down in the case of brain processes and consciousness, I believe, because this is one of a relatively small number of cases where the rule stated above does not apply. These exceptions are to be found, I suggest, in those cases where the operations which have to be performed in order to verify the presence of the two sets of characteristics inhering in the object or state of affairs in question can seldom if ever be performed simultaneously. A good example here is the case of the cloud and the mass of droplets or other particles in suspension. A cloud is a large semi-transparent mass with a fleecy texture suspended in the atmosphere whose shape is subject to continual and kaleidoscopic change. When observed at close quarters, however, it is found to consist of a mass of tiny particles, usually water droplets, in continuous motion. On the basis of this second observation we conclude that a cloud is a mass of tiny particles and nothing else. But there is no logical connection in our language between a cloud and a mass of tiny particles; there is nothing self-contradictory in talking about a cloud which is not composed of tiny particles in suspension. There is no contradiction involved in supposing that clouds consist of a dense mass of fibrous tissue; indeed, such a consistency seems to be implied by many of the functions performed by clouds in fairy stories and mythology. It is clear from this that the terms "cloud" and "mass of tiny particles in suspension" mean quite different things. Yet we do not conclude from this that there must be two things, the mass of particles in suspension and the cloud. The reason for this, I suggest, is that although the characteristics of being a cloud and being a mass of tiny particles in suspension are invariably associated, we never make the observations necessary to verify the statement "That is a cloud" and those necessary to verify the statement "This is a mass of tiny particles in suspension" at one and the same time. We can observe the micro-structure of a cloud only when we are enveloped by it, a condition which effectively prevents us from observing those characteristics which from a distance lead us to describe it as a cloud. Indeed, so disparate are these two experiences that we use different words to describe them. That which is a cloud when we observe it from a distance becomes a fog or mist when we are enveloped by it.

IV. When Are Two Sets of Observations Observations of the Same Event?

The example of the cloud and the mass of tiny particles in suspension was chosen because it is one of the few cases of a general proposition involving what I have called the "is" of composition which does not involve us in scientific technicalities. It is useful because it brings out the connection between the ordinary everyday cases of the "is" of composition like the table/packing-case example and the more technical cases like "Lightning is a motion of electric charges" where the analogy with the consciousness/brain process case is most marked. The limitation of the cloud/tiny particles in suspension case is that it does not bring out sufficiently clearly the crucial problems of how the identity of the states of affairs referred to by the two expressions is established. In the cloud case the fact that something is a cloud and the fact that something is a mass of tiny particles in suspension are both verified by the normal processes of visual observation. It is arguable, moreover, that the identity of the entities referred to by the two expressions is established by the continuity between the two sets of observations as the observer moves towards or away from the cloud. In the case of brain processes and consciousness there is no such continuity between the two sets of observations involved. A closer introspective scrutiny will never reveal the passage of nerve impulses over a thousand synapses in the way that a closer scrutiny of a cloud will reveal a mass of tiny particles in suspension. The operations required to verify statements about consciousness and statements about brain processes are fundamentally different.

To find a parallel for this feature we must examine other cases where an identity is asserted between something whose occurrence is verified by the ordinary processes of observation and something whose occurrence is established by special procedures. For this purpose I have chosen the case where we say that lightning is a motion of electric charges. As in the case of consciousness, however closely we scrutinize the lightning we shall never be able to observe the electric charges, and just as the operations for determining the nature of one's state of consciousness are radically different from those involved in determining the nature of one's brain processes, so the operations for determining the occurrence of lightning are radically different from those involved in determining the occurrence of a motion of electric charges. What is it, therefore, that leads us to say that the two sets of observations are observations of the same event? It cannot be merely the fact that the two sets of observations are systematically correlated such that whenever there is lightning there is always a motion of electric charges. There are innumerable cases of such correlations where we have no temptation to say that the two sets of observations are observations of the same event. There is a systematic correlation, for example, between the movement of the tides and the stages of the moon, but this does not lead us to say that records of tidal levels are records of the moon's stages or vice versa. We speak rather of a causal connection between two independent events or processes.

The answer here seems to be that we treat the two sets of observations as observations of the same event in those cases where the technical scientific observations set in the context of the appropriate body of scientific theory provide an immediate explanation of the observations made by the man in the street. Thus we conclude that lightning is nothing more than a motion of electric charges, because we know that a motion of electric charges through the atmosphere, such as occurs when lightning is reported, gives rise to the type of visual stimulation which would lead an observer to report a flash of lightning. In the moon/tide case, on the other hand, there is no such direct causal connection between the stages of the moon and the observations made by the man who measures the height of the tide. The causal connection is

between the moon and the tides, not between the moon and the measurement of the tides.

V. The Physiological Explanation of Introspection and the Phenomenological Fallacy

If this account is correct, it should follow that in order to establish the identity of consciousness and certain processes in the brain, it would be necessary to show that the introspective observations reported by the subject can be accounted for in terms of processes which are known to have occurred in his brain. In the light of this suggestion it is extremely interesting to find that when a physiologist, as distinct from a philosopher, finds it difficult to see how consciousness could be a process in the brain, what worries him is not any supposed self-contradiction involved in such an assumption, but the apparent impossibility of accounting for the reports given by the subject of his conscious processes in terms of the known properties of the central nervous system. Sir Charles Sherrington has posed the problem as follows:

> The chain of events stretching from the sun's radiation entering the eye to, on the one hand, the contraction of the pupillary muscles, and on the other, to the electrical disturbances in the brain-cortex are all straightforward steps in a sequence of physical "causation," such as, thanks to science, are intelligible. But in the second serial chain there follows on, or attends, the stage of brain-cortex reaction an event or set of events quite inexplicable to us, which both as to themselves and as to the causal tie between them and what preceded them science does not help us; a set of events seemingly incommensurable with any of the events leading up to it. The self "sees"

the sun; it senses a two-dimensional disc of brightness, located in the "sky," this last a field of lesser brightness, and over-head shaped as a rather flattened dome, coping the self and a hundred other visual things as well. Of hint that this is within the head there is none. Vision is saturated with this strange property called "projection," the unargued infer-ence that what it sees is at a "distance" from the seeing "self." Enough has been said to stress that in the sequence of events a step is reached where a physical situation in the brain leads to a psychi-cal, which however contains no hint of the brain or any other bodily part...The supposition has to be, it would seem, two continuous series of events, one physico-chemical, the other psychical, and at times interaction between them.[4]

Just as the physiologist is not likely to be impressed by the philosopher's contention that there is some self-contradiction involved in supposing consciousness to be a brain process, so the philosopher is unlikely to be impressed by the considerations which lead Sherrington to conclude that there are two sets of events, one physico-chemical, the other psychical. Sherrington's argument, for all its emotional appeal, depends on a fairly simply logical mis-take, which is unfortunately all too frequently made by psychologists and physiologists and not infrequently in the past by the philosophers themselves. This logical mistake, which I shall refer to as the "phenomenological fallacy," is the mistake of supposing that when the sub-ject describes his experience, when he describes how things look, sound, smell, taste, or feel to him, he is describing the literal properties of objects and events on a peculiar sort of internal cinema or television screen, usually referred to in the modern psychological literature as the "phenomenal field." If we assume, for example, that when a subject reports a green after-image he is asserting the occurrence inside himself of an object which is literally green, it is clear that we have on our hands an entity for which there is no place in the world of physics. In the case of the green after-image there is no green object in the subject's environment corresponding to the description that he gives. Nor is there anything green in his brain; certainly there is nothing which could have emerged when he reported the appearance of the green after-image. Brain processes are not the sort of things to which color concepts can be properly applied.

The phenomenological fallacy on which this argument is based depends on the mistaken assumption that because our ability to describe things in our environment depends on our con-sciousness of them, our descriptions of things are primarily descriptions of our conscious experience and only secondarily, indirectly, and inferentially descriptions of the objects and events in our environments. It is assumed that because we recognize things in our environ-ment by their look, sound, smell, taste, and feel, we begin by describing their phenomenal prop-erties, i.e., the properties of the looks, sounds, smells, tastes, and feels which they produce in us, and infer their real properties from their phenomenal properties. In fact, the reverse is the case. We begin by learning to recognize the real properties of things in our environ-ment. We learn to recognize them, of course, by their look, sound, smell, taste, and feel; but this does not mean that we have to learn to describe the look, sound, smell, taste, and feel of things before we can describe the things themselves. Indeed, it is only after we have learned to describe the things in our environment that we learn to describe our consciousness of them. We describe our conscious experience not in terms of the mythological "phenomenal properties" which are supposed to inhere in the mythological "objects" in the mythological "phenomenal field," but by reference to the actual physical properties of the concrete physical objects, events, and processes which normally, though not perhaps in the present instance, give rise to the sort of conscious experience which we are trying to describe. In other words when we describe the after-image as green, we are not saying that there is something, the after-image, which is green; we are saying that we are having the sort of experience which we normally have when, and which we have learned to describe as, looking at a green patch of light.

Once we rid ourselves of the phenomenological fallacy we realize that the problem of explaining introspective observations in terms of brain processes is far from insuperable. We realize that there is nothing that the introspecting subject says about his conscious experiences which is inconsistent with anything the physiologist might want to say about the brain processes which cause him to describe the environment and his consciousness of that environment in the way he does. When the subject describes his experience by saying that a light which is in fact stationary appears to move, all the physiologist or physiological psychologist has to do in order to explain the subject's introspective observations is to show that the brain process which is causing the subject to describe his experience in this way is the sort of process which normally occurs when he is observing an actual moving object and which therefore normally causes him to report the movement of an object in his environment. Once the mechanism whereby the individual describes what is going on in his environment has been worked out, all that is required to explain the individu-

al's capacity to make introspective observations is an explanation of his ability to discriminate between those cases where his normal habits of verbal descriptions are appropriate to the stimulus situation and those cases where they are not, and an explanation of how and why, in those cases where the appropriateness of his normal descriptive habits is in doubt, he learns to issue his ordinary descriptive protocols preceded by a qualificatory phrase like "it appears," "seems," "looks," "feels," etc.[5]

Notes

1. E.C. Tolman, *Purposive Behaviour in Animals and Men* (Berkeley 1932).
2. L. Wittgenstein. *Philosophical Investigations* (Oxford 1953); G. Ryle, *The Concept of Mind* (1949).
3. Place, "The Concept of Heed," *British Journal of Psychology* XLV (1954), 243–55.
4. Sir Charles Sherrington, *The Integrative Action of the Nervous System* (Cambridge 1947), pp. xx–xxi.
5. I am greatly indebted to my fellow-participants in a series of informal discussions on this topic which took place in the Department of Philosophy, University of Adelaide, in particular to Mr. C.B. Martin for his persistent and searching criticism of my earlier attempts to defend the thesis that consciousness is a brain process, to Professor D.A.T. Gasking, of the University of Melbourne, for clarifying many of the logical issues involved, and to Professor J.J.C. Smart for moral support and encouragement in what often seemed a lost cause.

J.J.C. SMART

"Sensations and Brain Processes"

This paper[1] takes its departure from arguments to be found in U.T. Place's "Is Consciousness a Brain Process?"[2] I have had the benefit of discussing Place's thesis in a good many universities in the United States and Australia, and I hope that the present paper answers objections to his thesis which Place has not considered and that it presents his thesis in a more nearly unobjectionable form. This paper is meant also to supplement the paper "The 'Mental' and the 'Physical,'" by H. Feigl,[3] which in part argues for a similar thesis to Place's. Suppose that I report that I have at this moment a roundish, blurry-edged after-image which is yellowish towards its edge and is orange towards its center. What is it that I am reporting? One answer to this question might be that I am not reporting anything, that when I say that it looks to me as though there is a roundish yellowy-orange patch of light on the wall I am expressing some sort of *temptation*, the temptation to say that there is a roundish yellow-orange patch on the wall (though I may know that there is not such a patch on the wall). This is perhaps Wittgenstein's view in the *Philosophical Investigations* (see §§ 367, 370). Similarly, when I "report" a pain, I am not really reporting anything (or, if you like, I am reporting in a queer sense of "reporting"), but am doing a sophisticated sort of wince. (See § 244: "The verbal expression of pain replaces crying and does not describe it." Nor does it describe anything else?)[4] I prefer most of the time to discuss an after-image rather than a pain, because the word "pain" brings in something which is irrelevant to my purpose: the notion of "distress." I think that "he is in pain" entails "he is in distress," that is, that he is in a certain agitation-condition.[5] Similarly, to say "I am in pain" may be to do more than "replace pain behavior": it may be partly to report something, though this something is quite nonmysterious, being an agitation-condition, and so susceptible of behavioristic analysis. The suggestion I wish if possible to avoid is a different one, namely that "I am in pain" is a genuine report, and that what it reports is an irreducibly psychical something. And similarly the suggestion I wish to resist is also that to say "I have a yellowish-orange after-image" is to report something irreducibly psychical.

Why do I wish to resist this suggestion? Mainly because of Occam's razor. It seems to me that science is increasingly giving us a viewpoint whereby organisms are able to be seen as physico-chemical mechanisms:[6] it seems that even the behavior of man himself will one day be explicable in mechanistic terms. There does seem to be, so far as science is concerned, nothing in the world but increasingly complex arrangements of physical constituents. All except for one place: in consciousness. That is, for a full description of what is going on in a man you would have to mention not only the physical processes in his tissues, glands, nervous system, and so forth, but also his states of consciousness: his visual, auditory, and tactual sensations, his aches and pains. That these should be *correlated* with brain processes does not help, for to say that they are *correlated* is to say that they are something "over and above." You cannot correlate something with itself.

You correlate footprints with burglars, but not Bill Sikes the burglar with Bill Sikes the burglar. So sensations, states of consciousness, do seem to be the one sort of thing left outside the physicalist picture, and for various reasons I just cannot believe that this can be so. That everything should be explicable in terms of physics (together of course with descriptions of the ways in which the parts are put together—roughly, biology is to physics as radio-engineering is to electromagnetism) except the occurrence of sensations seems to me to be frankly unbelievable. Such sensations would be "nomological danglers," to use Feigl's expression.[7] It is not often realized how odd would be the laws whereby these nomological danglers would dangle. It is sometimes asked, "Why can't there be psychophysical laws which are of a novel sort, just as the laws of electricity and magnetism were novelties from the standpoint of Newtonian mechanics?" Certainly we are pretty sure in the future to come across new ultimate laws of a novel type, but I expect them to relate simple constituents: for example, whatever ultimate particles are then in vogue. I cannot believe that ultimate laws of nature could relate simple constituents to configurations consisting of perhaps billions of neurons (and goodness knows how many billion billions of ultimate particles) all put together for all the world as though their main purpose in life was to be a negative feedback mechanism of a complicated sort. Such ultimate laws would be like nothing so far known in science. They have a queer "smell" to them. I am just unable to believe in the nomological danglers themselves, or in the laws whereby they would dangle. If any philosophical arguments seemed to compel us to believe in such things, I would suspect a catch in the argument. In any case it is the object of this paper to show that there are no philosophical arguments which compel us to be dualists.

The above is largely a confession of faith, but it explains why I find Wittgenstein's position (as I construe it) so congenial. For on this view there are, in a sense, no sensations. A man is a vast arrangement of physical particles, but there are not, over and above this, sensations or states of consciousness. There are just behavioral facts about this vast mechanism, such as that it expresses a temptation (behavior disposition) to say "there is a yellowish-red patch on the wall" or that it goes through a sophisticated sort of wince, that is, says "I am in pain." Admittedly Wittgenstein says that though the sensation "is not a something," it is nevertheless "not a nothing either" (§ 304), but this need only mean that the word "ache" has a use. An ache is a thing, but only in the innocuous sense in which the plain man, in the first paragraph of Frege's *Foundations of Arithmetic*, answers the question "What is the number one?" by "a thing." It should be noted that when I assert that to say "I have a yellowish-orange after-image" is to express a temptation to assert the physical-object statement "There is a yellowish-orange patch on the wall," I mean that saying "I have a yellowish-orange after-image" is (partly) the exercise of the disposition[8] which is the temptation. It is not to *report*: that I have the temptation, any more than is "I love you" normally a report that I love someone. Saying "I love you" is just part of the behavior which is the exercise of the disposition of loving someone.

Though for the reasons given above, I am very receptive to the above "expressive" account of sensation statements, I do not feel that it will quite do the trick. Maybe this is because I have not thought it out sufficiently, but it does seem to me as though, when a person says "I have an after-image," he is making a genuine report, and that when he says "I have a pain," he is doing more than "replace pain-behavior," and that "this more" is not just to say that he is in distress. I am not so sure, however, that to admit this is to admit that there are nonphysical correlates of brain processes. Why should not sensations just be brain processes of a certain sort? There are, of course, well-known (as well as lesser-known) philosophical objections to the view that reports of sensations are reports of brain-processes, but I shall try to argue that these arguments are by no means as cogent as is commonly thought to be the case.

Let me first try to state more accurately the thesis that sensations are brain-processes. It is not the thesis that, for example, "after-image" or "ache" means the same as "brain process of sort X" (where "X" is replaced by a description of a certain sort of brain process). It is that, in so far as "after-image" or "ache" is a report of a process, it is a report of a process that *happens to be* a brain process. It follows that the thesis does not claim that sensation statements can be *translated* into statements about brain processes.[9] Nor does it claim that the logic of a sensation statement is the same as that of a brain-process statement. All it claims is that in so far as a sensation statement is a report of something, that something is in fact a brain process. Sensations are nothing over and above brain processes. Nations are nothing "over and above" citizens, but this does not prevent the logic of nation statements being very different from the logic of citizen statements, nor does it insure the translatability of nation statements into citizen statements. (I do not, however, wish to assert that the relation of sensation statements to brain-process statements is very like that of nation statements to citizen statements. Nations do not just *happen to be* nothing over and above citizens, for example. I bring in the "nations" example merely to make a negative point: that the fact that the logic of A-statements is different from that of B-statements does not insure that A's are anything over and above B's.)

Remarks on Identity

When I say that a sensation is a brain process or that lightning is an electric discharge, I am using "is" in the sense of strict identity. (Just as in the—in this case necessary—proposition "7 is identical with the smallest prime number greater than 5.") When I say that a sensation is a brain process or that lightning is an electric discharge I do not mean just that the sensation is somehow spatially or temporally continuous with the brain process or that the lightning is just spatially or temporally continuous with the discharge. When on the other hand I say that the successful general is the same person as the small boy who stole the apples I mean only that the successful general I see before me is a time slice[10] of the same four-dimensional object of which the small boy stealing apples is an earlier time slice. However, the four-dimensional object which has the general-I-see-before-me for its late time slice is identical in the strict sense with the four-dimensional object which has the small-boy-stealing-apples for an early time slice. I distinguish these two senses of "is identical with" because I wish to make it clear that the brain-process doctrine asserts identity in the *strict* sense.

I shall now discuss various possible objections to the view that the processes reported in sensation statements are in fact processes in the brain. Most of us have met some of these objections in our first year as philosophy students. All the more reason to take a good look at them. Others of the objections will be more recondite and subtle.

Objection 1. Any illiterate peasant can talk perfectly well about his after-images, or how things look or feel to him, or about his aches and pains, and yet he may know nothing whatever about neurophysiology. A man may, like Aristotle, believe that the brain is an organ for cooling the body without any impairment of his ability to make true statements about his sensations. Hence the things we are talking about when we describe our sensations cannot be processes in the brain.

Reply. You might as well say that a nation of slugabeds, who never saw the Morning Star or knew of its existence, or who had never thought of the expression "the Morning Star," but who used the expression "the Evening Star" perfectly well, could not use this expression to refer to the same entity as we refer to (and describe as) "the Morning Star."[11]

You may object that the Morning Star is in a sense not the very same thing as the Evening Star, but only something spatiotemporally continuous with it. That is, you may say that the Morning Star is not the Evening Star in the strict sense of "identity" that I distinguished earlier.

There is, however, a more plausible example. Consider lightning.[12] Modern physical science tells us that lightning is a certain kind of electrical discharge due to ionization of clouds of water vapor in the atmosphere. This, it is now believed, is what the true nature of lightning is. Note that there are not two things: a flash of lightning and an electrical discharge. There is one thing, a flash of lightning, which is described scientifically as an electrical discharge to the earth from a cloud of ionized water molecules. The case is not at all like that of explaining a footprint by reference to a burglar. We say that what lightning really is, what its true nature as revealed by science is, is an electrical discharge. (It is not the true nature of a footprint to be a burglar.)

To forestall irrelevant objections, I should like to make it clear that by "lightning" I mean the publicly observable physical object, lightning, not a visual sense-datum of lightning. I say that the publicly observable physical object lightning is in fact the electrical discharge, not just a correlate of it. The sense-datum, or rather the having of the sense-datum, the "look" of lightning, may well in my view be a correlate of the electrical discharge. For in my view it is a brain state *caused* by the lightning. But we should no more confuse sensations of lightning with lightning than we confuse sensations of a table with the table.

In short, the reply to Objection 1 is that there can be contingent statements of the form "A is identical with B," and a person may well know that something is an A without knowing that it is a B. An illiterate peasant might well be able to talk about his sensations without knowing about his brain processes, just as he can talk about lightning though he knows nothing of electricity.

Objection 2. It is only a contingent fact (if it is a fact) that when we have a certain kind of sensation there is a certain kind of process in our brain. Indeed it is possible, though perhaps in the highest degree unlikely, that our present physiological theories will be as out of date as the ancient theory connecting mental processes with goings on in the heart. It follows that when we report a sensation we are not reporting a brain-process.

Reply. The objection certainly proves that when we say "I have an after-image" we cannot *mean* something of the form "I have such and such a brain-process." But this does not show that what we report (having an after-image) is not *in fact* a brain process. "I see lightning" does not *mean* "I see an electrical discharge." Indeed, it is logically possible (though highly unlikely) that the electrical discharge account of lightning might one day be given up. Again, "I see the Evening Star" does not *mean* the same as "I see the Morning Star," and yet "The Evening Star and the Morning Star are one and the same thing" is a contingent proposition. Possibly Objection 2 derives some of its apparent strength from a "Fido"-Fido theory of meaning. If the meaning of an expression were what the expression named, then of course it *would* follow from the fact that "sensation" and "brain-process" have different meanings that they cannot name one and the same thing.

Objection 3.[13] Even if Objections 1 and 2 do not prove that sensations are something over and above brain-processes, they do prove that the qualities of sensations are something over and above the qualities of brain-processes. That is, it may be possible to get out of asserting the existence of irreducibly psychic processes, but not out of asserting the existence of irreducibly psychic *properties*. For suppose we identify the Morning Star with the Evening Star. Then there must be some properties which logically imply that of being the Morning Star, and quite distinct properties which entail that of being the Evening Star. Again, there must be some properties (for example, that of being a yellow flash) which are logically distinct from those in the physicalist story.

Indeed, it might be thought that the objection succeeds at one jump. For consider the property of "being a yellow flash." It might seem that this property lies inevitably outside the physicalist framework within which I am trying to work (either by "yellow" being an objective emergent property of physical objects, or else by being a power to produce yellow sense-data, where "yellow," in this second instantiation of the word, refers to a purely phenomenal or introspectible quality). I must therefore digress for a moment and indicate how I deal with secondary qualities. I shall concentrate on color.

First of all, let me introduce the concept of a normal percipient. One person is more a normal percipient than another if he can make color discriminations that the other cannot. For example, if A can pick a lettuce leaf out of a heap of cabbage leaves, whereas B cannot though he can pick a lettuce leaf out of a heap of beetroot leaves, then A is more normal than

B. (I am assuming that A and B are not given time to distinguish the leaves by their slight difference in shape, and so forth.) From the concept of "more normal than" it is easy to see how we can introduce the concept of "normal." Of course, Eskimos may make the finest discriminations at the blue end of the spectrum, Hottentots at the red end. In this case the concept of a normal percipient is a slightly idealized one, rather like that of "the mean sun" in astronomical chronology. There is no need to go into such subtleties now. I say that "This is red" means something roughly like "A normal percipient would not easily pick this out of a clump of geranium petals though he would pick it out of a clump of lettuce leaves." Of course it does not exactly mean this: a person might know the meaning of "red" without knowing anything about geraniums, or even about normal percipients. But the point is that a person can be *trained* to say "This is red" of objects which would not easily be picked out of geranium petals by a normal percipient, and so on. (Note that even a color-blind person can reasonably assert that something is red, though of course he needs to use another human being, not just himself, as his "color meter.") This account of secondary qualities explains their unimportance in physics. For obviously the discriminations and lack of discriminations made by a very complex neurophysiological mechanism are hardly likely to correspond to simple and nonarbitrary distinctions in nature.

I therefore elucidate colors as powers, in Locke's sense, to evoke certain sorts of discriminatory responses in human beings. They are also, of course, powers to cause sensations in human beings (an account still nearer Locke's). But these sensations, I am arguing, are identifiable with brain processes.

Now how do I get over the objection that a sensation can be identified with a brain process only if it has some phenomenal property, not possessed by brain processes, whereby one-half of the identification may be, so to speak, pinned down?

Reply. My suggestion is as follows. When a person says, "I see a yellowish-orange after-image," he is saying something like this: "*There is something going on which is like what is going on when* I have my eyes open, am awake, and there is an orange illuminated in good light in front of me, that is, when I really see an orange." (And there is no reason why a person should not say the same thing when he is having a veridical sense-datum, so long as we construe "like" in the last sentence in such a sense that something can be like itself.) Notice that the italicized words, namely "there is something going on which is like what is going on when," are all quasilogical or topic-neutral words. This explains why the ancient Greek peasant's reports about his sensations can be neutral between dualistic metaphysics or my materialistic metaphysics. It explains how sensations can be brain-processes and yet how a man who reports them need know nothing about brain-processes. For he reports them only very abstractly as "something going on which is like what is going on when…" Similarly, a person may say "someone is in the room," thus reporting truly that the doctor is in the room, even though he has never heard of doctors. (There are not two people in the room: "someone" *and* the doctor.) This account of sensation statements also explains the singular elusiveness of "raw feels"—why no one seems to be able to pin any properties on them.[14] Raw feels, in my view, are colorless for the very same reason that *something* is colorless. This does not mean that sensations do not have plenty of properties, for if they are brain-processes they certainly have lots of neurological properties. It only means that in speaking of them as being like or unlike one another we need not know or mention these properties.

This, then, is how I would reply to Objection 3. The strength of my reply depends on the possibility of our being able to report that one thing is like another without being able to state the respect in which it is like. I do not see why this should not be so. If we think cybernetically about the nervous system we can envisage it as able to respond to certain likenesses of its internal processes without being able to do more. It would be easier to build a machine which would tell us, say on a punched tape, whether or not two objects were similar, than it would be to build a machine which would report wherein the similarities consisted.

Objection 4. The after-image is not in physical space. The brain-process is. So the after-image is not a brain-process.

Reply. This is an *ignoratio elenchi*. I am not arguing that the after-image is a brain-process, but that the experience of having an after-image is a brain-process. It is the *experience* which is reported in the introspective report. Similarly, if it is objected that the after-image is yellowy-orange, my reply is that it is the experience of seeing yellowy-orange that is being described, and this experience is not a yellowy-orange something. So to say that a brain-process cannot be yellowy-orange is not to say that a brain-process cannot in fact be the experience of having a yellowy-orange after-image. There is, in a sense, no such thing as an after-image or a sense-datum, though there is such a thing as the experience of having an image, and this experience is described indirectly in material object language, not in phenomenal language, for there is no such thing.[15] We describe the experience by saying, in effect, that it is like the experience we have when, for example, we really see a yellow-orange patch on the wall. Trees and wallpaper can be green, but not the experience of seeing or imagining a tree or wallpaper. (Or if they are described as green or yellow this can only be in a derived sense.)

Objection 5. It would make sense to say of a molecular movement in the brain that it is swift or slow, straight or circular, but it makes no sense to say this of the experience of seeing something yellow.

Reply. So far we have not given sense to talk of experiences as swift or slow, straight or circular. But I am not claiming that "experience" and "brain-process" mean the same or even that they have the same logic. "Somebody" and "the doctor" do not have the same logic, but this does not lead us to suppose that talking about somebody telephoning is talking about someone over and above, say, the doctor. The ordinary man when he reports an experience is reporting that something is going on, but he leaves it open as to what sort of thing is going on, whether in a material solid medium or perhaps in some sort of gaseous medium, or even perhaps in some sort of non-spatial medium (if this makes sense). All that I am saying is that "experience" and "brain-process" may in fact refer to the same thing, and if so we may easily adopt a convention (which is not a change in our present rules for the use of experience words but an addition to them) whereby it would make sense to talk of an experience in terms appropriate to physical processes.

Objection 6. Sensations are private, brain processes are *public*. If I sincerely say, "I see a yellowish-orange after-image," and I am not making a verbal mistake, then I cannot be wrong. But I can be wrong about a brain-process. The scientist looking into my brain might be having an illusion. Moreover, it makes sense to say that two or more people are observing the same brain-process but not that two or more people are reporting the same inner experience.

Reply. This shows that the language of introspective reports has a different logic from the language of material processes. It is obvious that until the brain-process theory is much improved and widely accepted there will be no *criteria* for saying "Smith has an experience of such-and-such a sort" *except* Smith's introspective reports. So we have adopted a rule of language that (normally) what Smith says goes.

Objection 7. I can imagine myself turned to stone and yet having images, aches, pains, and so on.

Reply. I can imagine that the electrical theory of lightning is false, that lightning is some sort of purely optical phenomenon. I can imagine that lightning is not an electrical discharge. I can imagine that the Evening Star is not the Morning Star. But it is. All the objection shows is that "experience" and "brain-process" do not have the same meaning. It does not show that an experience is not in fact a brain process.

This objection is perhaps much the same as one which can be summed up by the slogan: "What can be composed of nothing cannot be composed of anything."[16] The argument goes as follows: on the brain-process thesis the identity between the brain-process and the experience is a contingent one. So it is logically possible that there should be no brain-process, and no process of any other sort either (no heart process, no kidney process, no liver process). There would be the experience but no "corresponding" physiological process with which we might be able to identify it empirically.

I suspect that the objector is thinking of the experience as a ghostly entity. So it is composed of something, not of nothing, after all. On his view it is composed of ghost stuff, and on mine it is composed of brain stuff. Perhaps the counter-reply will be[17] that the experience is simple and uncompounded, and so it is not composed of anything after all. This seems to be a quibble, for, if it were taken seriously, the remark "What can be composed of nothing cannot be composed of anything" could be recast as an a priori argument against Democritus and atomism and for Descartes and infinite divisibility. And it seems odd that a question of this sort could be settled a priori. We must therefore construe the word "composed" in a very weak sense, which would allow us to say that even an indivisible atom is composed of something (namely, itself). The dualist cannot really say that an experience can be composed of nothing. For he holds that experiences are something over and above material processes, that is, that they are a sort of ghost stuff. (Or perhaps ripples in an underlying ghost stuff.) I say that the dualist's hypothesis is a perfectly intelligible one. But I say that experiences are not to be identified with ghost stuff but with brain stuff. This is another hypothesis, and in my view a very plausible one. The present argument cannot knock it down a priori.

Objection 8. The "beetle in the box" objection (see Wittgenstein, *Philosophical Investigations*, § 293). How could descriptions of experiences, if these are genuine reports, get a foothold in language? For any rule of language must have public criteria for its correct application.

Reply. The change from describing how things are to describing how we feel is just a change from uninhibitedly saying "this is so" to saying "this looks so." That is, when the naive person might be tempted to say, "There is a patch of light on the wall which moves whenever I move my eyes" or "A pin is being stuck into me," we have learned how to resist this temptation and say "It *looks as though* there is a patch of light on the wallpaper" or "It *feels as though* someone were sticking a pin into me." The introspective account tells us about the individual's state of consciousness in the same way as does "I see a patch of light" or "I feel a pin being stuck into me": it differs from the corresponding perception statement in so far as it withdraws any claim about what is actually going on in the external world. From the point of view of the psychologist, the change from talking about the environment to talking about

one's perceptual sensations is simply a matter of disinhibiting certain reactions. These are reactions which one normally suppresses because one has learned that in the prevailing circumstances they are unlikely to provide a good indication of the state of the environment.[18] To say that something looks green to me is simply to say that my experience is like the experience I get when I see something that really is green. In my reply to Objection 3, I pointed out the extreme openness or generality of statements which report experiences. This explains why there is no language of private qualities. (Just as "someone," unlike "the doctor," is a colorless word.)[19]

If it is asked what is the difference between those brain processes which, in my view, are experiences and those brain processes which are not, I can only reply that it is at present unknown. I have been tempted to conjecture that the difference may in part be that between perception and reception (in D.M. MacKay's terminology) and that the type of brain process which is an experience might be identifiable with MacKay's active "matching response."[20] This, however, cannot be the whole story, because sometimes I can perceive something unconsciously, as when I take a handkerchief out of a drawer without being aware that I am doing so. But at the very least, we can classify the brain processes which are experiences as those brain processes which are, or might have been, causal conditions of those pieces of verbal behavior which we call reports of immediate experience. I have now considered a number of objections to the brain-process thesis. I wish now to conclude with some remarks on the logical status of the thesis itself. U.T. Place seems to hold that it is a straight-out scientific hypothesis.[21] If so, he is partly right and partly wrong. If the issue is between (say) a brain-process thesis and a heart thesis, or a liver thesis, or a kidney thesis, then the issue is a purely empirical one, and the verdict is overwhelmingly in favor of the brain. The right sorts of things don't go on in the heart, liver, or kidney, nor do these organs possess the right sort of complexity of structure. On the other hand, if the issue is between a brain-or-liver-or-kidney thesis (that is, some form of materialism) on the one hand and epiphenomenalism on the other hand, then the issue is not an empirical one. For there is no conceivable experiment which could decide between materialism and epiphenomenalism. This latter issue is not like the average straight-out empirical issue in science, but like the issue between the nineteenth-century English naturalist Philip Gosse[22] and the orthodox geologists and paleontologists of his day. According to Gosse, the earth was created about 4000 BC exactly as described in *Genesis*, with twisted rock strata, "evidence" of erosion, and so forth, and all sorts of fossils, all in their appropriate strata, just as if the usual evolutionist story had been true. Clearly this theory is in a sense irrefutable: no evidence can possibly tell against it. Let us ignore the theological setting in which Philip Gosse's hypothesis had been placed, thus ruling out objections of a theological kind, such as "what a queer God who would go to such elaborate lengths to deceive us." Let us suppose that it is held that the universe just *began* in 4004 BC with the initial conditions just everywhere as they were in 4004 BC, and in particular that our own planet began with sediment in the rivers, eroded cliffs, fossils in the rocks, and so on. No scientist would ever entertain this as a serious hypothesis, consistent though it is with all possible evidence. The hypothesis offends against the principles of parsimony and simplicity. There would be far too many brute and inexplicable facts. Why are pterodactyl bones just as they are? No explanation in terms of the evolution of pterodactyls from earlier forms of life would any longer be possible. We would have millions of facts about the world as it was in 4004 BC that just have to be *accepted*.

The issue between the brain-process theory and epiphenomenalism seems to be of the above sort. (Assuming that a behavioristic reduction of introspective reports is not possible.) If it be agreed that there are no cogent philosophical arguments which force us into accepting dualism, and if the brain process theory and dualism are equally consistent with the facts, then the principles of parsimony and simplicity seem to me to decide overwhelmingly in favor of the brain-process theory. As I pointed out earlier, dualism involves a large number of irreducible psycho-physical laws (whereby the "nomological danglers" dangle) of a queer sort, that just have to be taken on trust, and are just as difficult to swallow as the irreducible facts about the paleontology of the earth with which we are faced on Philip Gosse's theory.

Notes

1. This is a very slightly revised version of a paper which was first published in the *Philosophical Review*, LXVIII (1959), 141–56. Since that date there have been criticisms of my paper by J.T. Stevenson, *Philosophical Review*, LXIX (1960), 505–10, to which I have replied in *Philosophical Review*, LXX (1961), 406–07, and by G. Pitcher and by W.D. Joske, *Australasian Journal of Philosophy*, XXXVIII (1960), 150–60, to which I have replied in the same volume of that journal, pp. 252–54.
2. *British Journal of Psychology*, XLVII (1956), 44–50...
3. *Minnesota Studies in the Philosophy of Science*, Vol. II (Minneapolis: University of Minnesota Press, 1958), pp. 370–497.
4. Some philosophers of my acquaintance, who have the advantage over me in having known Wittgenstein, would say that this

interpretation of him is too behavioristic. However, it seems to me a very natural interpretation of his printed words, and whether or not it is Wittgenstein's real view it is certainly an interesting and important one. I wish to consider it here as a possible rival both to the "brain-process" thesis and to straight-out old-fashioned dualism.

5. See Ryle, *The Concept of Mind* (London: Hutchinson's University Library, 1949), p. 93.

6. On this point see Paul Oppenheim and Hilary Putnam, "Unity of Science as a Working Hypothesis," in *Minnesota Studies in the Philosophy of Science*, Vol. II (Minneapolis: University of Minnesota Press, 1958), pp. 3–36.

7. Feigl, *op. cit.*, p. 428. Feigl uses the expression "nomological danglers" for the laws whereby the entities dangle: I have used the expression to refer to the dangling entities themselves.

8. Wittgenstein did not like the word "disposition." I am using it to put in a nutshell (and perhaps inaccurately) the view which I am attributing to Wittgenstein. I should like to repeat that I do not wish to claim that my interpretation of Wittgenstein is correct. Some of those who knew him do not interpret him in this way. It is merely a view which I find myself extracting from his printed words and which I think is important and worth discussing for its own sake.

9. See Place, *op. cit.*, p. 102, and Feigl, *op. cit.*, p. 390, near top.

10. See J.H. Woodger, *Theory Construction*, International Encyclopedia of Unified Science, II, No. 5 (Chicago: University of Chicago Press, 1939), 38. I here permit myself to speak loosely. For warnings against possible ways of going wrong with this sort of talk, see my note "Spatialising Time," *Mind*, LXIV (1955), 239–41.

11. Cf. Feigl, *op. cit.*, p. 439.

12. See Place, *op. cit.*, p. 106; also Feigl, *op. cit.*, p. 438.

13. I think this objection was first put to me by Professor Max Black. I think it is the most subtle of any of those I have considered, and the one which I am least confident of having satisfactorily met.

14. See B.A. Farrell, "Experience," *Mind*, LIX (1950), 170–98…

15. Dr. J.R. Smythies claims that a sense-datum language could be taught independently of the material object language ("A Note on the Fallacy of the 'Phenomenological Fallacy,'" *British Journal of Psychology*, XLVIII [1957], 141–44). I am not so sure of this: there must be some public criteria for a person having got a rule wrong before we can teach him the rule. I suppose someone might *accidentally* learn color words by Dr. Smythies's procedure. I am not, of course, denying that we can learn a sense-datum language in the sense that we can learn to report our experience. Nor would Place deny it.

16. I owe this objection to Dr. C.B. Martin. I gather that he no longer wishes to maintain this objection, at any rate in its present form.

17. Martin did not make this reply, but one of his students did.

18. I owe this point to Place, in correspondence.

19. The "beetle in the box" objection is, *if it is sound*, an objection to *any* view, and in particular the Cartesian one, that introspective reports are genuine reports. So it is no objection to a weaker thesis that I would be concerned to uphold, namely, that if introspective reports of "experiences" are genuinely reports, then the things they are reports of are in fact brain processes.

20. See his article "Towards an Information-Flow Model of Human Behaviour," *British Journal of Psychology*, XLVII (1956), 30–43.

21. *Op. cit.* For a further discussion of this, in reply to the original version of the present paper, see Place's note "Materialism as a Scientific Hypothesis," *Philosophical Review*, LXIX (1960), 101–04.

22. See the entertaining account of Gosse's book *Omphalos* by Martin Gardner in *Fads and Fallacies in the Name of Science*, 2nd ed. (New York: Dover, 1957), pp. 124–27.

SAUL KRIPKE

Selections from "Identity and Necessity"

In recent philosophy a large number of other identity statements have been emphasized as examples of contingent identity statements, different, perhaps, from either of the types I have mentioned before. One of them is, for example, the statement "Heat is the motion of molecules." First, science is supposed to have discovered this. Empirical scientists in their investigations have been supposed to discover (and, I suppose, they did) that the external phenomenon which we call "heat" is, in fact, molecular agitation. Another example of such a discovery is that water is H_2O, and yet other examples are that gold is the element with such and such an atomic number, that light is a stream of photons, and so on. These are all in some sense of "identity statement" identity statements. Second, it is thought, they are plainly contingent identity statements, just because they were scientific discoveries. After all, heat might have turned out not to have been the motion of molecules. There were other alternative theories of heat proposed, for example, the caloric theory of heat. If these theories of heat had been correct, then heat would not have been the motion of molecules, but instead, some substance suffusing the hot object, called "caloric." And it was a matter of course of science and not of any

logical necessity that the one theory turned out to be correct and the other theory turned out to be incorrect. So, here again, we have, apparently, another plain example of a contingent identity statement. This has been supposed to be a very important example because of its connection with the mind-body problem. There have been many philosophers who have wanted to be materialists, and to be materialists in a particular form, which is known today as "the identity theory." According to this theory, a certain mental state, such as a person's being in pain, is identical with a certain state of his brain (or, perhaps, of his entire body, according to some theorists), at any rate, a certain material or neural state of his brain or body. And so, according to this theory, my being in pain at this instant, if I were, would be identical with my body's being or my brain's being in a certain state. Others have objected that this cannot be because, after all, we can imagine my pain existing even if the state of the body did not. We can perhaps imagine my not being embodied at all and still being in pain, or, conversely, we could imagine my body existing and being in the very same state even if there were no pain. In fact, conceivably, it could be in this state even though there were no mind 'back of it,' so to speak, at all. The usual reply has been to concede that all of these things might have been the case, but to argue that these are irrelevant to the question of the identity of the mental state and the physical state. This identity, it is said, is just another contingent scientific identification, similar to the identification of heat with molecular motion, or water with H_2O. Just as we can imagine heat without any molecular motion, so we can imagine a mental state without any corresponding brain state. But, just as the first fact is not damaging to the identification of heat and the motion of molecules, so the second fact is not at all damaging to the identification of a mental state with the corresponding brain state. And so, many recent philosophers have held it to be very important for our theoretical understanding of the mind-body problem that there can be contingent identity statements of this form.

To state finally what *I* think, as opposed to what seems to be the case, or what others think, I think that in both cases, the case of names and the case of the theoretical identifications, the identity statements are necessary and not contingent. That is to say. they are necessary if *true*; of course, false identity statements are not necessary. How can one possibly defend such a view?

Perhaps I lack a complete answer to this question, even though I am convinced that the view is true. But to begin an answer, let me make some distinctions that I want to use. The first is between a *rigid* and a *nonrigid designator.* What do these terms mean? As an example of a nonrigid designator, I can give an expression such as 'the inventor of bifocals.' Let us suppose it was Benjamin Franklin who invented bifocals, and so the expression, 'the inventor of bifocals,' designates or refers to a certain man, namely, Benjamin Franklin. However, we can easily imagine that the world could have been different, that under different circumstances someone else would have come upon this invention before Benjamin Franklin did, and

in that case, *he* would have been the inventor of bifocals. So, in this sense, the expression 'the inventor of bifocals' is nonrigid: Under certain circumstances one man would have been the inventor of bifocals; under other circumstances, another man would have. In contrast, consider the expression 'the square root of 25.' Independently of the empirical facts, we can give an arithmetical proof that the square root of 25 is in fact the number 5, and because we have proved this mathematically, what we have proved is necessary. If we think of numbers as entities at all, and let us suppose, at least for the purpose of this lecture, that we do, then the expression 'the square root of 25' necessarily designates a certain number, namely 5. Such an expression I call 'a *rigid* designator.' Some philosophers think that anyone who even uses the notions of rigid or nonrigid designator has already shown that he has fallen into a certain confusion or has not paid attention to certain facts. What do I mean by 'rigid designator'? I mean a term that designates the same object in all possible worlds. To get rid of one confusion which certainly is not mine, I do not use "might have designated a different object" to refer to the fact that language might have been used differently. For example, the expression 'the inventor of bifocals' might have been used by inhabitants of this planet always to refer to the man who corrupted Hadleyburg. This would have been the case, if, first, the people on this planet had not spoken English, but some other language, which phonetically overlapped with English, and if, second, in that language the expression 'the inventor of bifocals' meant the 'man who corrupted Hadleyburg.' Then it would refer, of course, in their language, to whoever in fact corrupted Hadleyburg in this counterfactual situation. That is not what I mean. What I mean by saying that a description might have referred to something different, I mean that in *our* language as *we* use it in describing a counterfactual situation, there might have been a different object satisfying the descriptive conditions *we* give for reference. So, for example, we use the phrase 'the inventor of bifocals,' when we are talking about another possible world or a counterfactual situation, to refer to whoever in that counterfactual situation would have invented bifocals, not to the person whom people *in* that counterfactual situation would have called the inventor of bifocals.' *They* might have spoken a different language which phonetically overlapped with English in which 'the inventor of bifocals' is used in some other way. I am *not* concerned with that question here. For that matter, they might have been deaf and dumb, or there might have been no people at all. (There still could have been an inventor of bifocals even if there were no people—God, or Satan, will do.)

Second, in talking about the notion of a rigid designator, I do not mean to imply that the object referred to has to exist in all possible worlds, that is, that it has to necessarily exist. Some things, perhaps mathematical entities such as the positive integers, if they exist at all, necessarily exist. Some people have held that God both exists and necessarily exists; others, that He contingently exists; others, that He contingently fails to exist; and others, that He necessarily fails to exist:[8] all four options have been tried. But at any rate, when I use the notion of rigid designator, I do not imply that the object referred to necessarily exists. All I mean is that in any possible world where the object in question *does* exist, in any situation where the object *would* exist, we use the designator in question to designate that object. In a situation where the object does not exist, then we should say that the designator has no referent and that the object in question so designated does not exist.

[...]

Let me turn to the case of heat and the motion of molecules. Here surely is a case that is contingent identity! Recent philosophy has emphasized this again and again. So, if it is a case of contingent identity, then let us imagine under what circumstances it would be false. Now, concerning this statement I hold that the circumstances philosophers apparently have in mind as circumstances under which it would have been false are not in fact such circumstances. First, of course, it is argued that "Heat is the motion of molecules" is an a posteriori judgment; scientific investigation might have turned out otherwise. As I said before, this shows nothing against the view that it is necessary—at least if I am right. But here, surely, people had very specific circumstances in mind under which, so they thought, the judgment that heat is the motion of molecules would have been false. What were these circumstances? One can distill them out of the fact that we found out empirically that heat is the motion of molecules. How was this? What did we find out first when we found out that heat is the motion of molecules? There is a certain external phenomenon which we can sense by the sense of touch, and it produces a sensation which we call "the sensation of heat." We then discover that the external phenomenon which produces this sensation, which we sense, by means of our sense of touch, is in fact that of molecular agitation in the thing that we touch, a very high degree of molecular agitation. So, it might be thought, to imagine a situation in which heat would not have been the motion of molecules, we need only imagine a situation in which we would have had the very same sensation and it would have been produced by something other than the motion of molecules. Similarly, if we wanted to imagine a situation in which light was not a stream of photons, we could imagine a situation in which we were sensitive to something else in exactly the same way, producing what we call visual experiences, though not through a stream of photons. To make the case stronger, or to look at another side of the coin, we could also consider a situation in which we *are* concerned with the motion of molecules but in which such motion does not give us the sensation of heat. And it might also have happened that we, or, at least, the creatures inhabiting this planet, might have been so constituted that, let us say, an increase in the motion of molecules did not give us this sensation but that, on the contrary, a slowing down of the molecules did give us the very same sensation. This would be a situation, so it might be thought, in which heat would not be the motion of molecules, or, more precisely, in which temperature would not be mean molecular kinetic energy.

But I think it would not be so. Let us think about the situation again. First, let us think about it in the actual world. Imagine right now the world invaded by a number of Martians, who do indeed get the very sensation that we call "the sensation of heat" when they feel some ice which has slow molecular motion, and who do not get a sensation of heat—in fact, maybe just the reverse—when they put their hand near a fire which causes a lot of molecular agitation. Would we say, "Ah, this casts some doubt on heat being the motion of molecules, because there are these other people who don't get the same sensation"? Obviously not, and no one would think so. We would say instead that the Martians somehow feel the very sensation we get when we feel heat when they feel cold and that they do not get a sensation of heat when they feel heat. But now let us think of a counterfactual situation.[16] Suppose the earth had from the very beginning been inhabited by such creatures. First, imagine it inhabited by no creatures at all: then there is no one to feel any sensations of heat. But we would not say that under such circumstances it would necessarily be the case that heat did not exist; we would

say that heat might have existed, for example, if there were fires that heated up the air.

Let us suppose the laws of physics were not very different: Fires do heat up the air. Then there would have been heat even though there were no creatures around to feel it. Now let us suppose evolution takes place, and life is created, and there are some creatures around. But they are not like us, they are more like the Martians. Now would we say that heat has suddenly turned to cold, because of the way the creatures of this planet sense it? No, I think we should describe this situation as a situation in which, though the creatures on this planet got our sensation of heat, they did not get it when they were exposed to heat. They got it when they were exposed to cold. And that is something we can surely well imagine. We can imagine it just as we can imagine our planet being invaded by creatures of this sort. Think of it in two steps. First there is a stage where there are no creatures at all, and one can certainly imagine the planet still having both heat and cold, though no one is around to sense it. Then the planet comes through an evolutionary process to be peopled with beings of different neural structure from ourselves. Then these creatures could be such that they were insensitive to heat, they did not feel it in the way we do; but on the other hand, they felt cold in much the same way that we feel heat. But still, heat would be heat, and cold would be cold. And particularly, then, this goes in no way against saying that in this counterfactual situation heat would still *be* the molecular motion, *be* that which is produced by fires, and so on, just as it would have been if there had been no creatures on the planet at all. Similarly, we could imagine that the planet was inhabited by creatures who got visual sensations when there were sound waves in the air. We should not therefore say, "Under such circumstances, sound would have been light." Instead we should say, "The planet was inhabited by creatures who were in some sense visually sensitive to sound, and maybe even visually sensitive to light." If this is correct, it can still be and will still be a necessary truth that heat is the motion of molecules and that light is a stream of photons.

To state the view succinctly: we use both the terms 'heat' and 'the motion of molecules' as rigid designators for a certain external phenomenon. Since heat is in fact the motion of molecules, and the designators are rigid, by the argument I have given here, it is going to be *necessary* that heat is the motion of molecules. What gives us the illusion of contingency is the fact we have identified the heat by the contingent fact that there happen to be creatures on this planet—(namely, ourselves) who are sensitive to it in a certain way, that is, who are sensitive to the motion of molecules or to heat—these are one and the same thing. And this is contingent. So we use the description, 'that which causes such and such sensations, or that which we sense in such and such a way,' to identify heat. But in using this fact we use a contingent property of heat, just as we use the contingent property of Cicero as having written such and such works to identify him. We then use the terms 'heat' in the one case and 'Cicero' in the other *rigidly* to designate the objects for which they stand. And of course the term 'the motion of molecules' is rigid; it always stands for the motion of molecules, never for any other phenomenon. So, as Bishop Butler said, "everything is what it is and not another thing." Therefore, "Heat is the motion of molecules" will be necessary, not contingent, and one only has the *illusion* of contingency in the way one could have the illusion of contingency in thinking that this table might have been made of ice. We might think one could imagine it, but if we try, we can see on reflection that what we are really imagining is just there being another lectern in this very position here which was in

fact made of ice. The fact that we may identify this lectern by being the object we see and touch in such and such a position is something else.

Now how does this relate to the problem of mind and body? It is usually held that this is a contingent identity statement just like "Heat is the motion of molecules." That cannot be. It cannot be a contingent identity statement just like "Heat is the motion of molecules" because, if I am right, "Heat is the motion of molecules" is not a contingent identity statement. Let us look at this statement. For example, "My being in pain at such and such a time is my being in such and such a brain state at such and such a time," or, "Pain in general is such and such a neural (brain) state."

This is held to be contingent on the following grounds. First, we can imagine the brain state existing though there is no pain at all. It is only a scientific fact that whenever we are in a certain brain state we have a pain. Second, one might imagine a creature being in pain, but not being in any specified brain state at all, maybe not having a brain at all. People even think, at least prima facie, though they may be wrong, that they can imagine totally disembodied creatures, at any rate certainly not creatures with bodies anything like our own. So it seems that we can imagine definite circumstances under which this relationship would have been false. Now, if these circumstances are circumstances, notice that we cannot deal with them simply by saying that this is just an illusion, something we can apparently imagine, but in fact cannot in the way we thought erroneously that we could imagine a situation in which heat was not the motion of molecules. Because although we can say that we pick out heat contingently by the contingent property that it affects us in such and such a way, we cannot similarly say that we pick out pain contingently by the fact that it affects us in such and such a way. On such a picture there would be the brain state, and we pick it out by the contingent fact that it affects us as pain. Now that might be true of the brain state, but it cannot be true of the pain. The experience itself has to be *this experience*, and I cannot say that it is contingent property of the pain I now have that it is a pain.[17] In fact, it would seem that both the terms, 'my pain' and 'my being in such and such a brain state' are, first of all, both rigid designators. That is, whenever anything is such and such a pain, it is essentially that very object, namely, such and such a pain, and wherever anything is such and such a brain state, it is essentially that very object, namely, such and such a brain state. So both of these are rigid designators. One cannot say this pain might have been something else, some other state. These are both rigid designators.

Second, the way we would think of picking them out—namely, the pain by its being an experience of a certain sort, and the brain state by its being the state of a certain material object, being of such and such molecular configuration—both of these pick out their objects essentially and not accidentally, that is, they pick them out by essential properties. Whenever the molecules *are* in this configuration, we *do* have such and such a brain state. Whenever you feel *this*, you do have a pain. So it seems that the identity theorist is in some trouble, for, since we have two rigid designators, the identity statement in question is necessary. Because they pick out their objects essentially, we cannot say the case where you seem to imagine the identity statement false is really an illusion like the illusion one gets in the case of heat and molecular motion, because that illusion depended on the fact that we pick out heat by a certain contingent property. So there is very little room to maneuver; perhaps none.[18] The identity theorist, who holds that pain is the brain state, also has to hold that it necessarily is the brain state. He therefore cannot concede, but has to deny, that there would have been situations under which one would have had pain but not the corresponding brain state. Now usually in arguments on the identity theory, this is very far from being denied. In fact, it is conceded from the outset by the materialist as well as by his opponent. He says, "Of course, it *could* have been the case that we had pains without the brain states. It is a contingent identity." But that cannot be. He has to hold that we are under some illusion in thinking that we can imagine that there could have been pains without brain states. And the only model I can think of for what the illusion might be, or at least the model given by the analogy the materialists themselves suggest, namely, heat and molecular motion, simply does not work in this case. So the materialist is up against a very stiff challenge. He has to show that these things we think we can see to be possible are in fact not possible. He has to show that these things which we can imagine are not in fact things we can imagine. And that requires some very different philosophical argument from the sort which has been given in the case of heat and molecular motion. And it would have to be a deeper and subtler argument than I can fathom and subtler than has ever appeared in any materialist literature that I have read. So the conclusion of this investigation would be that the analytical tools we are using go against the identity thesis and so go against the general thesis that mental states are just physical states.[19]

The next topic would be my own solution to the mind-body problem, but that I do not have.

[...]

Notes

8. If there is no deity, and especially if the nonexistence of a deity is *necessary*, it is dubious that we can use 'He' to refer to a deity. The use in the text must be taken to be non-literal.

[...]

16. Isn't the situation I just described also counterfactual? At least it may well be, if such Martians never in fact invade. Strictly speaking, the distinction I wish to draw compares how we *would* speak *in* a (possibly counterfactual) situation, *if* it obtained, and how we *do* speak *of* a counterfactual situation, knowing that it does not obtain— i.e., the distinction between the language we would have used in a situation and the language we *do* use to describe it. (Consider the description: "Suppose we all spoke German." This description is in English.) The former case can be made vivid by imagining the counterfactual situation to be actual.

17. The most popular identity theories advocated today explicitly fail to satisfy this simple requirement. For these theories usually hold that a mental state is a brain state and that what makes the brain state into a mental state is its 'causal role,' the fact that it tends to produce certain behavior (as intentions produce actions, or pain, pain behavior) and to be produced by certain stimuli (e.g., pain, by pinpricks). If the relations between the brain state and its causes and effects are regarded as contingent, then *being such-and-such-a-mental-state* is a contingent property of the brain state. Let X be a pain. The causal-role identity theorist holds (1) that X is a brain state, (2) that the fact that X is a pain is to be analyzed (roughly) as the fact that X is produced by certain stimuli and produces certain behavior. The fact mentioned in (2) is, of course, regarded as contingent; the brain state X might well exist and not tend to produce the appropriate behavior in the absence of other conditions. Thus (1) and (2) assert that a certain pain X might have existed, yet not have been a pain. This

seems to me self-evidently absurd. Imagine any pain: is it possible that *it itself* could have existed, yet not have been a pain?

If $X = Y$, then X and Y share all properties, including modal properties. If X is a pain and Y the corresponding brain state, then *being a pain* is an essential property of X, and *being a brain state* is an essential property of Y. If the correspondence relation is, in fact, identity, then it must be *necessary* of Y that it corresponds to a pain, and *necessary* of X that it correspond to a brain state, indeed to this particular brain state, Y. Both assertions seem false: it *seems* clearly possible that X should have existed without the corresponding brain state; or that the brain state should have existed without being felt as pain. Identity theorists cannot, contrary to their almost universal present practice, accept these intuitions; they must deny them, and explain them away. This is none too easy a thing to do.

18. A brief restatement of the argument may be helpful here. If "pain" and "C-fiber stimulation" are rigid designators of phenomena, one who identifies them must regard the identity as necessary. How can this necessity be reconciled with the apparent fact that C-fiber stimulation might have turned out not to be correlated with pain at all? We might try to reply by analogy to the case of heat and molecular motion: the latter identity, too, is necessary, yet someone may believe that, before scientific investigation showed otherwise, molecular motion might have turned out not to be heat. The reply is, of course, that what really is possible is that people (or some rational sentient beings) could have been in the *same epistemic situation* as we actually are, and identify *a phenomenon* in the same way we identify heat, namely, by feeling it by the sensation we call "the sensation of heat,"

without the phenomenon being molecular motion. Further, the beings might not have been sensitive to molecular motion (i.e., to heat) by any neural mechanism whatsoever. It is impossible to explain the apparent possibility of C-fiber stimulations not having been pain in the same way. Here, too, we would have to suppose that we could have been in the same epistemological situation, and identify something in the same way we identify pain, without its corresponding to C-fiber stimulation. But the way we identify pain is by feeling it, and if a C-fiber stimulation could have occurred without our feeling any pain, then the C-fiber stimulation would have occurred without there *being* any pain, contrary to the necessity of the identity. The trouble is that although 'heat' is a rigid designator, heat is picked out by the contingent property of its being felt in a certain way: pain, on the other hand, is picked out by an essential (indeed necessary and sufficient) property. For a sensation to be *felt* as pain is for it to *be* pain.

19. All arguments against the identity theory which rely on the necessity of identity, or on the notion of essential property, are, of course, inspired by Descartes's argument for his dualism. The earlier arguments which superficially were rebutted by the analogies of heat and molecular motion, and the bifocals inventor who was also Postmaster General, had such an inspiration; and so does my argument here. R. Albritton and M. Slote have informed me that they independently have attempted to give essentialist arguments against the identity theory, and probably others have done so as well.

The simplest Cartesian argument can perhaps be restated as follows: Let 'A' be a *name* (rigid designator) of Descartes's body. Then Descartes argues that since he could exist even if A did not, $\lozenge$ (Descartes $\neq A$): hence Descartes $\neq A$. Those who have accused him of a modal fallacy have forgotten that 'A' is rigid. His argument is valid, and his conclusion is correct, provided its (perhaps dubitable) premise is accepted. On the other hand, provided that Descartes is regarded as having ceased to exist upon his death, "Descartes $\neq A$" can be established without the use of a modal argument; for if so, no doubt A survived Descartes when A was a corpse. Thus A had a property (existing at a certain time) which Descartes did not. The same argument can establish that a statue is not the hunk of stone, or the congery of molecules, of which it is composed. Mere non-identity, then, may be a weak conclusion. (See D. Wiggins, *Philosophical Review*, Vol. 77 [1968], pp. 90 ff.) The Cartesian modal argument, however, surely can be deployed to maintain relevant stronger conclusions as well.

Study Questions

1. Given that Place believes that conscious states are brain processes, what does he mean when he says that it's manifestly false that "statements about consciousness are statements about brain processes"? (You must read further than this quotation in Place's article to get a full idea.)

2. What does Place mean when he calls two terms "logically independent"? How does he explain cases in which the terms 'X' and 'Y' are logically independent, yet without exception, all Xs are Ys?

3. What Place calls the "phenomenological fallacy" shows up in several articles we have already read. Find some of these instances.

4. Place argues that once we rid ourselves of the "phenomenological fallacy" we can see that phenomenal properties are "mythical" creations of a logical error. Compare this with Galileo's position on color, sound, and heat in Chapter Three, and then contrast it with Berkeley's position on those same properties in Chapter Six.

5. What's the difference between *property dualism* and *substance dualism*? Explain how the former is involved in *Objection 3* in Smart's article. Outline Smart's attempt to deal with this objection. Define in your own words "secondary quality" and "normal percipient" (as Smart understands it); explain how secondary qualities are supposed to be involved here. Is Smart really claiming that "mental" properties (like *looking red*) might actually be nothing but brain properties? Of course, he doesn't mean that someone's brain looks red. What does he mean?

6. Smart remarks in his reply to Objection 8 that "there is no language of private qualities." Who in our previous readings claims there is? What sort of statement was supposed to be a report of the existence of a "private quality"? Explain how Smart understands what's really meant here.

7. Kripke mentions an objection to identity theory in the second paragraph of his article, beginning with the phrase "Others have objected...." Which *Objection* in Smart's article is this one? Is Smart's reply exactly what Kripke mentions as "the usual reply"?

8. What is a "rigid designator"? Explain (using the notion of "possible worlds") why an identity statement involving two rigid designators is necessary, not contingent.

9. Kripke claims that the fact that heat is the motion of molecules is necessary, not contingent. His argument for this involves imagining counterfactual situations (what are these?) and seeing what we would say about them. Outline his argument.

10. Smart appears to suggest (but not using Kripke's terms) that the mental terms in mind-brain identity statements are non-rigid. Find what might be that suggestion in his article. How would the two differ in their judgments about thinking about mental events in other possible worlds? Does what you think when imagining other possible worlds agree with Kripke or with Smart?

11. If Kripke is right, then mind-brain identity statements are necessary. Identity theorists usually have thought they are contingent. (Smart and Place both say so.) But could an identity theorist accept Kripke's point, but still be an identity theorist? The long paragraph beginning with "Second..." just before the end of Kripke's article, suggests not. What do you think?

Suggested Readings

David Armstrong is among the best-known materialists. See *A Materialist Theory of the Mind* (London: Routledge, 1968) and "The Nature of Mind," in *The Mind-Brain Identity Theory*, C.V. Borst (ed). (London: MacMillan, 1970). Reprinted in *Introduction to Philosophy: Classical and Contemporary Readings*, John Perry and Michael Bratman (eds.) (New York: Oxford University Press, 1986).

For more by Smart, see "Materialism," *Journal of Philosophy* 60 (1963): pp. 651–62.

On the identity theory and materialism, see:

David Lewis, "An Argument for the Identity Theory," *Journal of Philosophy* 63 (1966): pp. 17–25. Reprinted in Lewis's *Philosophical Papers*, Vol. 1. (Oxford: Oxford University Press); and in *Materialism and the Mind-Body Problem*, David Rosenthal (ed.). (Englewood Cliffs: Prentice Hall, 1979).

Colin McGinn, "Philosophical Materialism," *Synthese* 44 (1980): pp. 173–206.

Ullin T. Place, "Is Consciousness a Brain Process?," *British Journal of Psychology* 47 (1956): pp. 44–50. Reprinted in *The Mind-Brain Identity Theory*, C. Borst (ed.). (London: Macmillan, 1970); in *The Philosophy of Mind*, V. Chappell (ed.). (Harlow: Prentice Hall, 1962); in *Body, Mind and Death*, A. Flew (ed.). (London: Macmillan, 1964); and in *Introduction to the Philosophy of Mind*, H. Morick (ed.). (Brighton: Harvester Press, 1979).

Robert Boyd, "Materialism without Reductionism: What Physicalism Does not Entail," in *Readings in the Philosophy of Psychology*, Vol. 1, Ned Block (ed.). (Cambridge, MA: Harvard University Press).

Kripke's argument is criticized in many places, including the following three articles by Fred Feldman: "Identity, Necessity, and Events," in Ned Block, ed., *Readings in the Philosophy of Psychology*, Vol. I, (Cambridge MA: Harvard University Press, 1980; "Kripke's Argument against Materialism," *Philosophical Studies* 24 (1973): pp. 416–19; and "Kripke on the Identity Theory," *Journal of Philosophy* 71 (1974): pp. 665–76.

9

FUNCTIONALISM

Armstrong's Criticism of Smart

In this chapter we will consider a theory of the mind called "functionalism." In the past forty years this theory has become the most widely accepted position in the philosophy of mind, although it has many critics and detractors. The position emerged partly as the result of perceived weaknesses in both behaviorism and the identity theory. As we will see, its champions argue that functionalism avoids the shortcomings of both behaviorism and identity theory, while at the same time preserving the best of both of those theories.

We begin our survey of functionalism with a look at how an early version of the theory emerged from a modification to J.J.C. Smart's "topic-neutral" descriptions of perceptual states by Smart's fellow Australian, David M. Armstrong (1926–2014). From the 1960s Armstrong defended materialism and naturalism in the philosophy of mind, in the philosophy of science, and in metaphysics. The result of his defense was the articulation of a comprehensive set of theories that draw together positions on a wide variety of philosophical controversies.

In his 1968 book, *A Materialist Theory of the Mind*, Armstrong criticizes the thesis that Smart puts forward in "Sensations and Brain Processes" that sensations can be identified in topic-neutral terms by their role in perception. A sensation of orange is identified by Smart as an event that typically happens when one sees an orange. But Armstrong points out that this will work only for sensations, and not even all of those. It cannot be extended to other mental states and processes. What perceptual event, he asks, is the one that can be identified with the decision to walk down to the pub for a drink? Clearly there is no perception that must take place in order for that mental event to occur.

Armstrong agrees, however, that the topic-neutral approach is correct in principle. In his view, Smart has simply failed to get hold of the correct topic-neutral descriptions. The decision to go to the pub for a drink is identified less by the things that produce it than by the behavior it typically produces, for example, going to the pub. Hence, according to Armstrong, we need to identify mental states both by the kinds of environmental stimuli that cause them *and* by the behavior that they produce.

In his article, "The Nature of Mind," Armstrong proposes an alternative way to formulate a materialist theory of the mind that takes mental states and processes to be inner states and processes, as does Smart, and also accords with the general intent of Smart's topic-neutral descriptions. But, as we shall see, Armstrong's proposal leads in fact to a theory of the mind fundamentally at odds with identity theory.

Behaviorism Again

Armstrong begins his article with a general defense of materialism and, in a manner similar to Smart's, he cites behaviorism as a theory of mind sympathetic to materialism. Yet he says that the earliest versions of behaviorism, which identify states of mind with *actual* behavior, suffered from the weakness that states of mind can occur without leading to any behavior at all. According to Armstrong, this weakness was avoided by Ryle's identification of mental states with *dispositions* to behave in certain ways. Such dispositions will not result in actual behavior unless the appropriate conditions occur.

Yet Armstrong argues that while behaviorists successfully address this weakness of early behaviorism, "it seems clear, now that the shouting and the dust have died, *they did not do enough.*" The problem with Ryle's version of behaviorism, he argues, is Ryle's insistence that dispositions are not *internal states or processes.* In his opposition to Descartes's conception of thoughts and sensations as private, inner states, Ryle argues that the very idea of mental states, of things "going on in the mind," is fundamentally mistaken. There is nothing in a disposition, according to Ryle, beyond certain facts about a person's behavior. Armstrong argues that this is simply false. He says:

> When I think, but my thoughts do not issue in any action, it seems as obvious as anything is obvious that there is something actually going on in me which constitutes my thought. It is not simply that I would speak or act if some conditions that are unfulfilled were to be fulfilled. Something is currently going on, in the strongest and most literal sense of 'going on,' and this something is my thought.

Notice the similarity of this assertion to Smart's claim that, "it does seem to me as though, when a person says 'I have an after-image,' he *is* making a genuine report, and that when he says 'I have a pain,' he *is* doing more than 'replace pain-behaviour.'" The general point is that we simply cannot avoid the view that thoughts and sensations are *inner* states of a person. This much is in accord with Smart. Yet, unlike Smart, Armstrong does not entirely reject the behaviorist association of mental states with dispositions to behave.

Behavioral Criteria

Armstrong maintains that a promising materialist theory can be reached by making certain important changes to behaviorism. He says:

> Behaviourism is certainly wrong, but perhaps it is not altogether wrong. Perhaps the Behaviourists are wrong in identifying the mind and mental occurrences with behaviour, but

perhaps they are right in thinking that our notion of a mind and of individual mental states is *logically tied to behaviour*. For perhaps what we mean by a mental state is some state of the person which, under suitable conditions, *brings about* a certain range of behaviour. Perhaps mind can be defined not as behaviour, but rather as the inner *cause* of behaviour.

According to Armstrong, behaviorists were correct in their claim that the connection between mental states and behavior is a *logical* connection. For example, it is part of the *meaning* of the phrase 'want to go out to the pub for a drink' that this state will produce certain kinds of behavior in the right circumstances. Notice, for instance, how common the following kind of statement is: 'I don't think you really *want* to go. You have the time and the money. So if you really wanted to, you would go right now.' This reinforces Armstrong's claim that we see a logical or conceptual connection between the mental state and the action: you can't have that state and yet not exhibit the behavior in the appropriate situations.

The amendment that Armstrong makes to behaviorism is to identify mental states with the internal states of a person that *cause* behavior. This stands in contrast to Ryle's assertion that dispositions are not internal states but solely aspects of the behavior itself. Armstrong argues that Ryle's position is inconsistent with the way in which scientists think of physical dispositions. Solubility, for example, is not merely a tendency to dissolve, but a specific kind of molecular structure that *causes* substances like salt and sugar to dissolve in solvents like water. In this way, solubility is an internal state of a substance that is identified by its behavioral effects.

In the final sections of his paper Armstrong turns to the problem that Smart originally addressed, and which he claimed that behaviorism cannot successfully solve: the nature of consciousness. He asks, "Can we say that to be conscious, to have experiences, is simply for something to go on within us apt for the causing of certain sorts of behaviour?" Armstrong first answers this in the negative. Here he draws upon an interesting example of a case where the production of behavior does not account for what needs to be explained. Sometimes, when driving long distances, we realize that we have been driving for a long time and yet were not aware of what we were doing. This example points out that the behaviorist cannot account for the difference between *having* inner states that produce behavior (in this case driving behavior) and being *aware* of having them. So behaviorism also needs to be modified to account for this difference.

The particular aspect of conscious experience that Smart raised was that of sensations and perceptions. In Smart's view, we cannot treat perceptual experiences as dispositions to behave but must treat them as inner states of the person. Yet Armstrong replies that behavioral psychologists have in fact successfully associated perceptual states with certain forms of behavior. Laboratory animals, for example, can be trained to perform certain actions in response to colored stimuli. So we can in principle identify perceptual states as states that produce certain forms of behavior. But again we need to make the point that the perceptual state of the animal is not the behavior itself but rather an inner state that *produces* the behavior. So Armstrong's revision to the behaviorist view can, he argues, accommodate the idea that perceptual experiences are inner states without abandoning the logical tie between those inner states and certain kinds of behavior.

Finally Armstrong asks how this account can deal with the issue raised by his driving example. How do we explain the phenomenon of being *aware of* our own internal states? Here he argues that such a state of awareness is a form of perception, and so can be handled in the same way as other forms of perception. But what are perceived in these cases are not things in the world around us, but our own mental states. That is, *awareness* of our thoughts and perceptions is a *perception* of those very thoughts and perceptions. Once we recognize consciousness as a form of perception in this way, then it can be dealt with in the same way as any other perception: It is an inner state that produces certain kinds of behavior. As Armstrong says, this will be "selective behaviour towards our own mental states." What he means is that being aware of our own thoughts and perceptions will yield certain kinds of behavior that would not otherwise occur. To use Armstrong's example, whether a person is or is not aware of the states that are causing their driving behavior will make a difference to other ways in which they behave. They might say, for example, "Wow, I barely missed that red light," which they would not have said if they had not been aware of their driving.

The Best of Both Worlds

At this point we can stop to recognize an important feature of Armstrong's position that has become important in subsequent developments. Armstrong has combined certain features of Smart's identity theory with certain aspects of behaviorism, and yet produced a theory that is different in important ways from each. The aspects of Smart's position that he has preserved are, first, the claim that states and processes of mind are internal states, and, second, that saying that states and processes of the mind are internal states does not commit us to any form of dualism. But he does not follow Smart in saying that states and processes of mind must be identified with neurological sates of the brain. Taking a line similar to Smart's topic-neutral descriptions, he argues that we can maintain the behaviorist's insistence on a *logical* connection between states of mind and behavior. To say that someone has this thought or that thought, or perceives this or perceives that, or has this fear or that fear, is ultimately a matter of how that person behaves in various circumstances. Yet Armstrong does not follow the behaviorist in saying that those thoughts, perceptions, and fears are *nothing more than* dispositions to certain kinds of behavior. Rather, they are internal states that produce those kinds of behavior under the right circumstances. This allows the *possibility* that these inner states are physical states of the brain, but (like the topic-neutral approach) it is neutral on this point. It simply says that thoughts and perceptions, and so on, are *whatever* internal states it is that yield the various kinds of behavior by which we recognize them. This is a fundamental aspect of functionalism.

The argument that functionalism preserves the virtues of both behaviorism and identity theory, while avoiding the pitfalls of each, is presented in our next reading, an article by Jerry A. Fodor (1935–2017), one of the most influential philosophers of mind in the past half century. In the 1970s and 1980s Fodor developed the initial concepts central to functionalism into an articulate theory of cognition called "representationalism." This theory holds that mental states, especially propositional attitudes, are functional states that operate on representations of the world, which are carried by what Fodor called a "language of thought" that is codified in the brain. Fodor's work in later years focused on how states of mind can carry meaning, arguing that this occurs through causal relations between mental representations and objects in the world. Fodor's article, "The Mind-Body Problem," was published in *Scientific American* in 1981 as an attempt to popularize functionalism and present its virtues to a non-professional audience.

Neither Dualism nor Materialism

Fodor begins his article by pointing out that while the philosophical study of science in general has been focused on issues of scientific method and practice, these issues have not generally been applied to psychology. Philosophy of mind has traditionally been a debate between dualists and materialists rather than a discussion about the methodological principles of psychology. By contrast, he contends, his theory—functionalism—is neutral on the debate between material-ists and dualists. He claims that the rise of functionalism has been driven by developments in a number of fields: artificial intelligence, computational theory, linguistics, and so on, and not by metaphysical debates about dualism and materialism. Materialists and dualists differ over what the mind is *made of*—whether immaterial spirit or matter. The fields that have inspired functional-ism, however, all share a different focus: They look not at the material out of which something is made but rather at the way that material is "put together." For example, in computational theory, programmers do not concern themselves with the physical composition of computer systems, but only with the programs that the systems carry out. In the same way, functionalism is not concerned with the material of the mind, but with the functions and processes that it carries out. We can call this the **functional organization** of a system.

Fodor's article is designed to show how the focus on functional organization can avoid the pitfalls of all of the metaphysical (and anti-metaphysical) theories, while combining their respec-tive strengths. In the following sections he reviews the drawbacks and strengths of the various positions in the mind-body problem.

Mental Causation

The principal point in Fodor's comparison of the metaphysical theories is their ability to account for what he calls "mental causation." This term refers to the manner in which states of mind take part in relations of cause and effect, and most importantly how they cause behavior. For example, we know that thirst, which we can think of as a state of desire, will cause a person to drink water. The theories that Fodor surveys differ with regard to their ability to explain how such forms of causation occur.

Dualism fares the worst in this regard. This was the key point in Elisabeth of Bohemia's cri-tique of Descartes's theory, which we read in Chapter Five. Mental causation remains a mystery for the dualist, since mind and matter are entirely different substances and operate on entirely different principles. While there might be laws relating states of mind with behavior, and relating external stimuli to sensory experiences, these laws can only state *what* happens, not how what happens is possible.

The second position that Fodor describes, which he calls "radical behaviorism," is the position taken by Skinner that we reviewed in Chapter Seven. The thesis of radical behaviorism, in Fodor's analysis, is that behavior has no *mental* causes at all. The causes of behavior are simply the external stimuli to which an organism is exposed. External events in the environment directly produce a behavioral response from the organism as the result of the past conditioning of the organism. Here Fodor repeats a criticism made by both Smart and Armstrong: the behaviorist denial that there is "something going on" in the mind runs contrary to our deepest ways of thinking about ourselves and other people. But the most serious problem for radical behaviorism, Fodor says, is the one made by Chomsky: As psychology has matured it has turned out less and less possible to explain behavior as the product of external stimuli alone. The causes of human behavior uncovered by psychologists grow ever more complex.

'Logical behaviorism' is the term that Fodor gives to the dispositional theory of Ryle and Wittgenstein that we reviewed in Chapter Seven. This theory, Fodor claims, is superior to radical behaviorism because it *can* give an account of mental causation. According to logical behaviorism, mental states are behavioral dispositions. The statement, 'Smith is thirsty' is expressed by a statement of the form, 'If there were water available, Smith would drink some.' The latter statement describes Smith's disposition to exhibit a certain behavior (drinking) when the appropriate external conditions occur (the presence of water). Mental causation occurs when the if-then statement is true and the if-clause is also true. An explanation of Smith's drinking water, then, is given by the statement, 'If there were water available, Smith would drink some, and there was water available.'

Fodor points out that reference to physical dispositions is common in the physical sciences. 'The glass is fragile' can be expressed as the conditional statement, 'If the glass were struck, it would break.' Since this kind of statement is respectable in the physical sciences, it lends plausibility to the behaviorists' claim that mental states can be properly understood as behavioral dispositions. Yet logical behaviorism faces a more subtle difficulty. Dispositional causation, which we described in the previous paragraph, is only one kind of causation. There is also a more basic kind of causation, where one particular event causes another, which Fodor calls event-event causation. For example, striking a piece of glass causes it to break. This kind of causation is more basic because dispositional causation always involves event-event causation, but not vice versa. For example, when we analyze the dispositional statement, 'The glass broke because it was fragile,' we find that we must refer to the fact that striking the glass caused it to break, which is event-event causation. The problem is that logical behaviorism must insist that unlike physical causation, mental causation involves *only* dispositional causation and not event-event causation. Fodor points out an important reason to insist that mental causation *must* include event-event causation. This is the fact that mental states do not only cause behavior; they also cause other mental states. See Fodor's example of the relationships between having a headache, wanting to relieve it, believing aspirin will relieve the headache, and as a result having a disposition to take aspirin.

There is a more serious point here that Fodor doesn't mention: The fact illustrated in the aspirin example shows that mental states produce behavior *only* in conjunction with other mental states. Having a headache will only produce a disposition to take aspirin given the belief that aspirin relieves headaches. So the problem is not merely that we must *allow for* event-event causation, but that it is essential to the production of behavioral dispositions. Single mental states—such as beliefs and desires—do not produce behavior in isolation from one another.

The Identity Theory and Complex Mental Causes

Fodor points out that, unlike behaviorism, the identity theory of Smart and Armstrong has no difficulty in accounting for the fact that mental states work in conjunction with one another. According to identity theorists, each mental state will be a particular neurological state of the brain, and it is quite easy to suppose that any one of these will lead to behavior only in the presence of others. It is entirely plausible that the behavior that will result from a particular neurological state in one area of the brain will depend on the neurological states of other areas.

Suppose, for example, that Smith's thirst is identical to the firing of a small collection of neurons in one region of the nervous system. What effect that activity will have on Smith's behavior could easily depend on which neurons are firing in other regions. And the neural activity in those other regions will each be identical to some specific state of mind, such as beliefs about what is in the glass. In this way we explain complex *mental* causes of behavior by identifying them with complex *neurological* causes of behavior.

The Problem of Martians

When we assess the competing theories of mind according to their ability to explain mental causation, identity theory is the hands-down winner. But Fodor argues that identity theory suffers from a different problem altogether—one that is not faced by behaviorism. Consider the following example. Suppose that it were established by neuropsychology that the mental state of being in pain is a certain kind of physical activity of the neospinothalamic pathway and limbic system. This might be true of human beings and other animals that have a sufficiently well-developed nervous system. But this also implies that if a creature does not have a neospinothalamic pathway or limbic system, then it cannot experience pain. Imagine now that there are Martians that exhibit all of the behavioral signs of experiencing pain, yet are of a radically different physical construction from creatures on Earth. Must we deny that these Martians can experience pain, even though their behavior clearly indicates that they do?

Now one can argue here that such creatures cannot experience pain *as we do*. Perhaps there is human pain and Martian pain, that are different in nature, but are sufficiently similar to one another to warrant using the same term. But recall that, on the identity theory, each kind of mental state, including beliefs and desires, is numerically identical to a kind of physical state. So, for example, every belief that Saturn has rings, is also identical to one of the same sort of physical state of the brain. So here again, the Martians described would not be capable of having that belief. Here there is no recourse to saying their belief is similar but not the same as ours. There is no reason to suppose they couldn't have exactly the same belief about Saturn as we do.

Notice that this difficulty is not one that behaviorism (or dualism for that matter) has to face. As long as the Martians exhibit all of the same behavioral patterns and dispositions as we do, then they necessarily have the same mental states as we do. What the underlying physical nature of these dispositions might be is entirely irrelevant.

The upshot, then, appears to be something of a dilemma: If we want to have an adequate account of mental causation, then identity theory is the way to go. But if we want to allow for creatures not physically similar to human beings to still have psychological states like ours, then we need a form of behaviorism. What we need, and what Fodor claims that functionalism can provide, is a way of combining the virtues of the two theories and avoiding the failings of each.

The Ambiguity in Identity Theory

To understand Fodor's solution to this dilemma we need to draw yet another distinction between different kinds of numerical identity. Smart's argument hinged on the difference between necessary and contingent identity, claiming that the latter avoids all of the common objections to identifying states of mind with states of the brain. There are, however, two kinds of contingent identity, and according to Fodor only one of them is plausible in the case of mind and body. Fodor labels these two kinds of contingent identity "token physicalism" and "type physicalism." He says:

> The identity theory can be held either as a doctrine about mental particulars (John's current pain or Bill's fear of cats) or as a doctrine about mental universals, or properties (having a pain or being afraid of animals). These two doctrines called respectively token physicalism and type physicalism—differ in their strength and plausibility.

Let's look at what this means.

Types and Tokens

We need to begin with the general difference between what philosophers call types and tokens. It is obvious that there are many different kinds of things in the world. There are buildings, people, trees, and so on. And it is just as obvious that there can be many things of a particular kind. There are many individual buildings, individual people, and individual trees. Consider the following list of words {black, red, blue, black}. If you ask how many words there are in this list the answer is ambiguous. There are four individual words, but only three different types of words. Philosophers mark this with the following terminology. An individual thing—an individual person or object or event—is a **token**, and a kind of thing, or a category of thing, is a **type**. For example, Buckingham Palace, the White House, and your place of residence are all tokens of the type *building*. And Britain, France, and Germany are all tokens of the type *nation*.

We can apply this terminology to mental and physical states and activities. A **mental type** is a kind of mental state or activity, such as a kind of thought or sensation or belief. For example, believing in Santa Claus is a mental state type possessed by many children, and having a headache is a type of mental state often caused by nervous tension. A **mental token** is the mental state or activity of a particular person at a particular time. So Johnny's belief in Santa Claus and Mary's belief in Santa Claus are two mental tokens of the same type. And Theresa's present headache is a token of the same type as her headache yesterday, and the one she will have tomorrow.

In the same way, a **physical type** is a kind or category of physical object or event. H_2O is a physical state type, and so is being heavier than ten kilograms. The categories that neurophysiologists use to describe the activities and states of the brain are also physical types. For example, there is a type of brain activity involving a rhythmic firing of neurons, called omega-oscillation, that is involved in visual perception. Each of these physical types can have many tokens. A **physical token** is a particular physical object or event that exists at a particular time. Just as the particular glass of H_2O that you drank yesterday is a physical token of the same type as the glass of H_2O you will drink tomorrow, so the omega-oscillation in your visual cortex at the present moment and the omega-oscillation in your visual cortex at the same time tomorrow are two tokens of the same physical type.

Type Identity and Token Identity

We can also apply the difference between tokens and types to the idea of numerical identity. The sentence 'A is identical to B' can mean that there is a single item named by both 'A' and 'B.' But we can also assert the identity of types. That is, either we can say that a particular *object* is identical to another object, or we can say that one *type* of object is identical to another type of object. And these two sentences make very different claims.

If A and B are tokens, then to say that A is identical to B is to say that A and B are the same individual objects. For example, when we say that Buckingham Palace is the London residence of the Queen of England we are claiming that the individual object we call Buckingham Palace is one and the same object as the London residence of the English queen. Similarly, the sentence 'My spouse is my best friend' means that the particular person to whom the speaker is married is the same person as the one they consider their best friend.

If A and B are types, then to say that A is identical to B is to say that all things that belong to type A also belong to type B, and vice versa. For example, the sentence 'Water is H_2O' is not a claim about any particular body of water but rather a claim that if a substance is water then it is also H_2O, and if a substance is H_2O then it is water. Long ago people learned that water is H_2O, but in doing so they learned about a *type* of thing rather than simply about some individual thing. They learned that all and only water is H_2O. In the same way, Benjamin Franklin's demonstration that lightning is an electrical discharge in the atmosphere was a discovery about lightning as a type of thing and not a discovery merely about any one particular bolt of lightning. The difference between token identity and type identity is especially important in cases where there is only one token of a certain type. For example, the sentence 'The daughter of the president is the most popular person in the country' might be true as a case of token identity, but it will be false as a case of type identity. For it might be true that the individual who is the daughter of the president is also the individual who is the most popular person in the country. But it does not follow that *anyone* who is the daughter of the president is thereby also the most popular person in the country.

Type Physicalism and Token Physicalism

Now let's see what this has to do with the identity theory. Identity theorists say that mental states are identical to physical states of the brain. But without more clarification, this claim is ambiguous. It can mean either of the following two claims:

1. **Token physicalism:** Each mental token is identical to a physical token.
2. **Type physicalism:** Each mental type is identical to a physical type.

The first of these two claims is really just an assertion of materialism. Materialism is the claim that all that exists is matter. This means that everything that exists is a physical thing. And another way of saying that everything is a physical thing is to say that every token is a physical token. So the claim that every mental token is identical to a physical token follows directly from materialism. If all there is is matter, then everything that exists—including every token mental state or activity—is identical to some token physical object, state, or event.

The second, however, has larger implications. It says that whenever a mental state belongs to a specific type, for example believing that Paris is in France, then that state also belongs to a specific physical type, something described in terms of neural or other physical terms. In Chapter Eight we saw two varieties of type physicalism.[1] One version is that of Smart and Armstrong. Their view is that, as a result of the laws of nature, those states that belong to a certain mental type (given in behavioral terms, for example) will also belong to a certain neural type. This reflects Armstrong's position that nature has so arranged things that the types of internal states that produce various types of behavior are also types of neural states.[2] The other variety of type identity is Saul Kripke's. Using his concept of rigid designators, Kripke argues that a *property* described in one way can be numerically identical to a *property* described in another way. The property of being water is, in his view, the very same property as being H_2O.[3]

Now let's apply this point to the identity of mental and physical types.

Think first of Smart's example of after-images. Suppose that after-images are firings of something called Q-cells in a region of the visual cortex. If this is a type-identity claim, then all and only firing of Q-cells in the visual cortex are after-images. It follows that if an event is *not* a firing of Q-cells, then it is not an after-image. Similarly, if the belief that Ottawa is the capital of Canada is type-identical to a particular kind of neural activity in the cerebral cortex, then any event that isn't *that* kind of neural activity won't be a belief that Ottawa is the capital of Canada.

These implications do not hold of token physicalism. For token physicalism only asserts that each mental token is identical to *some* physical token. It doesn't also say that any mental tokens of the same type must be tokens of the same physical type. More generally, materialism does not imply type physicalism. Materialism is compatible with there being no relation between mental types and physical types at all. All it requires is that each individual thing that exists, mental or otherwise, be a physical thing of some kind or other.

The Implications of Type Physicalism

If mental types such as thoughts, beliefs, and sensations are identical to types of neural events in the human nervous system in the way that identity theorists claim, then (as a result of natural laws) whether a creature has a certain thought or sensation depends on whether there is a neural event of the relevant kind occurring in the nervous system. This is similar to the fact that whether a pool of wet stuff is water depends on whether or not it is H_2O. Fodor points out the implication of this: Creatures that are physically different from us could not have mental states of the same types as ours. So if creatures, say, from Mars were radically different in physical composition from human beings, they could not have beliefs or desires, thoughts or sensations as we do. Because each type of belief, desire, or thought is identified with a particular type of physical event, if that physical event is absent in a creature then so is the belief, desire, or thought. This point applies directly to the question of whether artificial intelligence is possible. If type physicalism is true, then it is impossible to build a machine that thinks, believes or perceives but is not biologically identical to human beings, for the relevant neural state types would be missing in this case as well. So Fodor's point is that type physicalism rules out the possibility that creatures physically different from humans (or at least physically different from our biological order) could have mental states. As Ned Block puts it, type physicalism commits a kind of "species chauvinism": Only creatures like us can have thoughts, beliefs, and sensations.

Of course, it may turn out that conscious intelligence occurs only in creatures that have neurological structures like ours. And it may be that artificial intelligence of a non-biological kind is impossible. But critics of type physicalism argue that it is misguided to decide this issue in advance. Surely we don't want to rule out the possibility of intelligence radically different in physical nature from our own without any investigation. We *might* discover that the forms of mental life that occur in our corner of the universe are forms of neurological organization. But it need not follow that, given the laws of nature, the only way in which the same forms of mental life can occur is through a particular neurological type. Fodor argues that these implications of type physicalism show that it is not a plausible solution to the mind-body problem.

But What Are Mental Types?

The problem of "species chauvinism" suggests that type physicalism is not a good choice of theory. But if we claim that token physicalism is true, and type physicalism is false, we face a difficulty. Suppose a human being called Jane is standing at a bus stop and thinking to herself, "The bus is late." Now imagine that a Martian is waiting for the same bus, and is also thinking to himself, "The bus is late." What *is* it that Jane and the Martian have in common that makes it true that they have the same thought? What makes two physical events, each entirely different from the other, a thought that the bus is late? In general, the question is this: if type physicalism is false, then what do mental tokens of the same type have in common?

To see the force of this question you can ask yourself, What is it that all *clocks* have in common? Clocks do not all share any one physical characteristic, but there is still something that makes an instrument a clock: for an instrument to be a clock, it must be possible to use it to tell the time. We want to ask the same kind of question about states of mind: what is it that makes a physical event a certain kind of mental state such as a thought or a headache?

Here Fodor follows Armstrong and argues that logical behaviorism is on the right track in offering "a relational interpretation of mental properties, one which identifies them in ways that abstracts from the physiology of their bearers." His point here is that, according to behaviorists, whether a creature is thinking a certain thought, or holds a certain belief, depends only on the relation between stimulus and behavior that it exhibits. They would argue that to say Jane and the Martian are thinking the same thought means only that they exhibit the same behavioral disposition. So it makes no difference what the physical composition is like; it is only the behavior that counts.

Functional States

So the question now becomes, how do we characterize mental types in a way that draws on the lessons of behaviorism, but is not restricted to thinking of mental states as merely behavioral dispositions? Here Fodor argues that machines provide a useful analogy. He describes two kinds of machine: one compatible with a behaviorist understanding of mental states and one compatible with what he sees as the proper solution. The machines are vending machines that dispense a Coke when 10 cents is put in the slot. The insertion of coins is to be analogous to some input stimulus, and the dispensing of a Coke is to be analogous to outward behavior. The first machine is a simple stimulus-response mechanism: Given a dime as input it will dispense a Coke as output. We can say it has a permanent disposition to dispense a Coke when given dimes.

The second machine is more complex: it will accept nickels and dimes, and will also give change. The operation of the machine is governed by two internal states of the machine, which Fodor labels S1 and S2. What the machine does when given a nickel or a dime depends on whether it is in state S1 or S2. Here is a description of how the machine operates.

When in S1 and given a dime: Dispense a Coke, and stay in S1.
When in S1 and given a nickel: Do not dispense a Coke, and move to S2.

When in S2 and given a dime: Dispense a Coke and a nickel, and revert to S1.

When in S2 and given a nickel: Dispense a Coke, and revert to S1.

The principal difference between this second machine and the first is that a stimulus will not only produce behavior, but will also cause the machine to switch from one internal state to another. The idea here is that the behavior of the machine is not simply the product of some stimulus that serves as input to the machine, but of a sequence of events within the machine. When in S1 and given a nickel, no behavior results. But there is an internal event caused by that stimulus: The machine switches from S1 to S2. So the second machine provides an analogy to complex mental causes of behavior, which was the weakness in the behaviorist model of mental causes. Yet the description of the second machine in terms of its two internal states, S1 and S2, makes no reference at all to the physical construction of the machine. The states are described in what Fodor calls "relational" terms, the relation of each state to stimulus, behavior, and the other internal state. Any physical construction that exhibits those relations between its states is identical in its operation to any other.

The idea here is that we can describe mental states in ways analogous to the internal states of the second machine. Each one will be described in terms of its relations between (a) sensory stimulus, (b) behavior, and (c) other mental states. This way we can allow for complex sequences of mental states in the production of behavior, but we do not describe the internal states in terms of their physical construction (neurons, say), but relational terms. So any organism (think of Jane and the Martian) with internal states of the same relational kind are identical as far as the operation of the mind is concerned. This gives us a picture of mental states that has the virtue of identity theory (complex mental causes), but also the virtue of behaviorism (freedom from chauvinism). Internal states described in terms of their relations to stimulus, behavior, and other internal states are called **functional states**. **Functionalism**, then, is the theory of mind that identifies mental state types as functional states.

Turing Machines and Functional States

Fodor mentions one possible objection to functionalism: Describing mental states in terms of their function appears just too easy. His comparison: We might explain the lifting of a valve by postulating a valve opener, and then identify valve openers as any mechanism that opens valves. Here the postulation of a functional state explains nothing. We might do the same in explaining the operation of the mind. For every kind of mental activity we can postulate a mental state defined simply as a state that performs that function. Using Fodor's example, we can describe the processing of visual information by way of functional states that are defined as simply states that process visual information. This is of course worthless as far as understanding how visual information processing is carried out.

Fodor's solution to this problem is to adopt a particular model of mechanisms: a computer. The operation of a computer is determined by its **program**, a set of instructions that determine precisely what the machine will do. The **program states** of a computer are functional states defined in terms of what the mechanism will do with the symbols it reads. Fodor uses a very general and abstract way of describing the operation of a computer. He adopts a model envisioned by the mathematician and computer theorist, Alan Turing, in the 1950s, which has since become known as a "Turing Machine." We will consider Turing's ideas and his model of computing mechanisms in detail in Chapter Ten. The machine is an abstract entity that is described as having a tape of indefinite length, with symbols written in squares. The machine reads one symbol on the tape at a time, and its program states determine what it will do with that symbol. The advantage to using a Turing Machine as a model of a computer is that Turing was able to prove, mathematically, that any computer operation whatsoever (any program, to use another word) can be performed by a Turing Machine. (Turing Machines are of no *practical* value because they are tremendously inefficient in any practical task. The virtue of the machine is purely theoretical.) The solution that the Turing Machine provides for the problem of trivial explanations of mental operations is that (a) its internal states are described entirely in relational terms as functional states, and yet (b) it ensures that the operations of these internal states can be physically realized. Any mental operation that can be described in terms of the operations of a Turing Machine can in principle be physically realized. So functionalism can now be narrowed to what we can call **Turing Machine functionalism**: Mental state types are internal functional states described as states of a Turing Machine.

In the remaining sections of this introduction, we examine some of the implications of functionalism and the problems that it encounters.

Multiple Realizability

If type physicalism is false, as functionalists argue, then mental types have what is called **multiple realizability**. This means that events that are of the same mental type can be of different physical types—the same mental state can be realized in different ways. If a type is multiply realizable, then there is no single physical property that each token of that type must have in common. There are many kinds of things that are multiply realizable. Money is one example. A dollar can be made up of a paper banknote or one coin or four quarters or ten dimes, each of which is physically different from the other. Another example of a type that is multiply realizable is the clock. There are mechanical clocks, electric clocks, and water clocks, and there are digital clocks and analog clocks. There is no single physical property that every clock must possess.

What would it be like for mental types to be multiply realizable? As it happens, all of the creatures with mental states that we know of are quite similar in physical structure. Each possesses a nervous system roughly the same as our own. But think again of Jane and the Martian. If materialism is true, then Jane's thought is a physical event, most likely a neural event in her cerebral cortex. Under token physicalism the Martian's thought will also be a physical event occurring in his body. But as long as *type* identity is false, his thought need not be physically similar in any way to Jane's thought.

Functionalism and Reduction

Let's see how functionalism bears on the issue of reductionism, which we discussed in Chapter Eight. The reduction of mental states and process to neural states and processes requires the type-identity of mental states and neural states. This is because explanations of mental events must apply to any mental state and processes of the same kind. Because they reject type-identity, however, functionalists deny that mental state types are reducible to neural state types. To see why this should be so, let's look again at the example of Jane and her Martian friend. Functionalists will claim that the reason Jane and the Martian are thinking the same thought is not because they share any physical characteristics, but because they are each in a certain functional state.

What matters in determining the facts about their psychology is not their physical state, but the way in which their physical states are connected to one another and to stimulus and behavior. This means that a neurological description of what is going on in Jane's head will not explain her psychology—it won't explain what she is thinking, or why she is thinking it. All we can get from neuroscience is a description of how the sequence of functional states that she has in common with the Martian happen to be realized in her nervous system.

Although reductionism in philosophy of mind is usually thought of in the context of identity theory, there is another kind of reductionism to which functionalism must be committed: what we can call **functional reductionism**. This includes the claims that (a) any two states that are functionally identical are mentally identical, and vice versa, and (b) all states and processes of the mind can be *explained* in terms of functional states and processes. The kind of functions that are relevant here, remember, are the relations between the mental state, the stimuli and behavior, and other mental states. If Jane and her Martian friend really are thinking the same thought, then they must have internal states that are functionally equivalent even though they are physically quite different. As we saw earlier in this chapter, critics of identity theory accuse the theory of "species chauvinism" in its implication that only creatures neurologically identical to human beings can have mental states. As we will see shortly, and in greater detail in Chapter Ten, functional reductionism has the opposite implication: *Anything* functionally equivalent to human beings must be mentally equivalent also.

Multiple Realizability and Autonomy

According to functionalists, the multiple realizability of psychological states entails that psychology will remain independent, or "autonomous," of neuroscience. To say that one theory is **autonomous** of another means that an understanding of the entities and laws of one will not provide us with an understanding of the entities and laws of the other. The idea applied to psychology and neuroscience is that we cannot gain an understanding of the mind from neuroscience.

To illustrate this point, functionalists compare the relationship between psychology and neuroscience with that between computer science and physical engineering. Computer science is a study of how information can be stored and processed. This involves the analysis of systems of representation such as binary and decimal notation, and the construction of algorithms to process the information that is represented. Although there is a great deal of interaction between computer programmers and physical engineers, there is nonetheless more to the study of computers than questions of physical engineering. Physical engineering will provide us with an understanding of how algorithms can be implemented in different kinds of hardware. But considerations of hardware alone will not give us answers to questions about information processing. Similarly, machine functionalists argue that there will always be more to psychology than the study of the nervous system. Their claim is that in order to learn how human beings represent information about the world we need to study the algorithms by which the brain extracts information from sensory input. Neuroscience, they argue, can tell us how these algorithms are implemented in the nervous system. Yet a physical study of the brain will not tell us how it processes information.[4]

Some critics of functionalism have focused on the claim of autonomy. Most vocal in this regard have been Paul M. Churchland and Patricia Smith Churchland, both professors emeriti at the University of California, San Diego. In their individual publications, the Churchlands have championed the importance of neuroscience in constructing philosophical theories of the mind. They have been critics not only of functionalism, but of any philosophy of mind constructed without proper regard for the ways in which neural structures shape our thoughts and experiences. They contend that psychological theories based on what they call "folk psychology"—as they call conventional psychology—will be entirely replaced by neuroscientific theories that bear no resemblance to traditional psychology. The kind of autonomy that Fodor claims for functionalism is, in their view, a totally misguided venture.

The Problem of Qualitative Content

Following his description of Turing Machine Functionalism, Fodor says, "Such is the origin, the provenance and the promise of contemporary functionalism. How much has it actually paid off?" At this point, Fodor raises two issues that have been important in the development of the philosophy of mind over the past twenty years, in order to assess how well functionalism can deal with these issues. In this regard the basic problem lies in the fact that functionalism describes mental state types entirely in terms of their functional role: the relations of cause and effect between mental states, stimulus, and behavior. Typically we identify our own mental states in terms of two properties they have that do not appear to be functional properties. We will talk about these properties at length when we look at the last reading in this chapter, and also in later chapters. But it is worth looking here at how Fodor claims that functionalism handles one of these two properties well and the other not well at all.

The first property that mental states have in terms of which we typically identify them is what Fodor calls their **qualitative content**. From his descriptions it is clear that what Fodor is here calling "qualitative content" is the same aspect of mental states that, in the readings from Chapter Eight, U.T. Place and J.J.C. Smart called "phenomenal properties." In that chapter we explained this term as referring to what conscious experiences are *like* for the perceiver. Fodor refers to it as "the character of experience." In his example, a blank wall will *appear differently* when it is viewed through a red or green filter. And these differences correspond to differences in qualitative content.

Fodor illustrates the idea of qualitative content with an imaginary situation, a so-called thought experiment, that has been in use at least since John Locke,[5] which is now known as the **inverted spectrum**. This is the idea that two people may have color sensations in reverse of one another. For example, we might suppose that ripe tomatoes produce in you the color sensation that in your best friend is caused by a healthy, freshly mowed lawn, and vice versa. As you and your friend would agree in your use of words, including color terms, and in every other behavioral criterion, it would be impossible to tell by any public measure whether this is the case or not. (Indeed, you and your friend would not ever notice the difference between you!) Other versions of the same story involve *intra*personal alterations in qualitative content. We can suppose that for some reason (say, a surgical accident) you wake up one morning to find that all your color experiences have been reversed: Your favorite green sweater now looks a bright shade of red, and stop signs now look a dull green.

The reason that qualitative content is a problem for functionalism is that there seems to be no necessary relationship between the functional role of a mental state and its qualitative content. Fodor asks us to imagine two people whose psychological descriptions are the same in every respect and yet the qualitative content of red for one is the same as the qualitative content of green for the other, and vice versa. If this is the *only* relevant difference between the two people, then it would seem that the functional roles of their mental states are the same while the qualitative content would be different. Functional role would seem to miss out on an essential way in which we identify our mental states. As Fodor says, the problem of qualitative content is a serious one for functionalism, although (as we will see in Chapter Eleven) many philosophers argue that it is a fatal problem for *any* materialist account of conscious experience.

Intentional Content

The second feature of mental states that Fodor raises as an issue for functionalism is *intentional content*. The term 'intentional,' and the related noun 'intentionality,' as they are used here, are philosophical terms referring to a familiar feature of mental states. Suppose you are walking with your friend, who is suddenly looking pensive and withdrawn. When you ask about her change in behavior, she explains that she was thinking of her mother. For this kind of explanation to make sense, we must suppose that there is some kind of connection or relation between your friend's state of mind and the person who is her mother. We express this by saying that her thought is *about* that person, or that she is thinking *of* her. This relationship, whereby a state of mind is *of* or *about* something, is what philosophers have come to call **intentionality**. The term derives from the Latin term *tendere* meaning "to aim at." So the idea is that thoughts, beliefs, and other states of mind point to, or are directed toward, something else.

Saying that mental states have intentionality is a technical way of saying that they have meaning. To see this, consider something else that has meaning, namely, sentences, such as for example 'The Eiffel Tower is in Paris.' This sentence is about something, it refers to a specific object in the world, namely, the Eiffel Tower, and it also says something about that object, namely, that it is in Paris. Referring to an object and saying something about it are both aspects of meaning. Fodor's point is that mental states possess the same capacity to carry meaning. A person can *think* about the Eiffel Tower, and a person can *believe* that the Eiffel Tower is in Paris. What Fodor calls the **intentional content** of a mental state—a belief, a thought, a perception—is the meaning that it carries. In fact, many philosophers, including Fodor, argue that sentences in human languages have meaning precisely because they express the intentional content of mental states. Languages, one might say, exist to express thoughts.

Philosophers and linguists have yet another way of talking about this feature of mental states and sentences: We say that they have semantic properties. A **semantic property** is any property having to do with meaning. As we will see in Chapter Ten, in computer science it is common to distinguish semantic properties of computer languages (the meanings of the strings of computer symbols) from their *syntactic* properties (e.g., their ordering and shape). In addition, we can define the **semantic content** of a mental state or sentence as the meaning it carries in virtue of its semantic properties.

The properties of intentionality, meaning, and semantics are connected to a further important feature of mental states and sentences. Recall from Chapter Seven the connection between declarative sentences and *propositions*. In that chapter we defined a proposition as the content of a declarative sentence, what a sentence says. So we see that propositions are the meanings of sentences or, in other words, the intentional or semantic content of sentences. Similarly, certain kinds of mental states, such as beliefs and desires, can have propositions as their intentional or semantic content. If Samantha remembers that she left her keys at home, the proposition 'I left my keys at home' is the content of her memory. For this reason the English philosopher, Bertrand Russell, defined these kinds of mental states as **propositional attitudes**. They describe the psychological attitude a person can have towards a certain proposition. Consider, for example, the proposition 'Good deeds are always rewarded.' Someone can hope, believe, desire, doubt, or dream that this proposition is true.[6] Each of these is a different attitude towards the same proposition. The **propositional content** of the state is the proposition towards which it is directed; in the example, 'Good deeds are always rewarded.'

Not all mental states are propositional attitudes, however, and not all intentional contents are propositions. Perceptual states, for example, carry information, which can be construed as intentional content, even if they are not propositional attitudes in Russell's sense. Nonetheless, the terms 'propositional content,' 'intentional content,' and 'semantic content' all reflect the general ability of mental states to carry meaning. These terms will occur in many of the following readings.

The Problem of Intentional Content

Fodor's point in this section of his paper is that mental states, such as beliefs, have the same semantic properties as do sentences of a language. Your *belief* that the Eiffel Tower is in Paris has exactly the same semantic properties as the sentence 'The Eiffel Tower is in Paris.' Both the belief and the sentence have the same *intentional content*. So a successful theory of the mind must be able to explain how mental states have intentional content, or possess semantic properties. Here Fodor claims that functionalism is in a much better position than it is with respect to qualitative content.

His argument here is that we can explain the functional role of mental states in terms of operations on *symbols*. A **symbol** is a physical object or physical state that can carry meaning. Letters on a page or a number on a door are simple examples. This, Fodor thinks, is the key to the similarity between mental states and sentences: both involve symbols. His idea is that certain physical states of the brain can serve as strings of symbols, literally "sentences in the head." The functional role of mental states can be understood in a manner analogous to that of Turing Machine states: writing, moving, and deleting strings of symbols. These strings of symbols can thus carry semantic properties in the same way as do sentences in natural languages like English. In other writings Fodor has explored this idea in some detail: Propositional attitudes such as beliefs and desires, according to Fodor, are functional states that are defined in terms of the operations they perform on the symbols that constitute what he calls a "language of thought."

A serious and difficult question, which Fodor briefly discusses in the final paragraphs of "The Mind-Body Problem" is *how* physical states of the brain can act as symbols with semantic content. The most general question is how *any* physical state—states of the brain, letters on a blackboard, symbols in a computer—can possess meaning at all. How do mental states and sentences in natural languages "point to," or "say something about" something outside of themselves? This problem, The Problem of Intentionality, is enormously challenging, and the research remains far from any satisfactory answer. Fodor's *partial* answer here is that mental states possess intentionality by virtue of the symbols that constitute the language of thought. In other work, he has argued that intentionality ultimately derives from causal relations between the symbols in the mind and objects in the physical world.

The Problem of Liberalism

In our final reading for this chapter, we look at Ned Block's article, "Troubles with Functionalism," first published in 1978. Ned Block is Silver Professor of Philosophy and Psychology at New York University. From 1971 to 1995 he was Professor of Philosophy at MIT. Earlier in this chapter we saw a problem with identity theory that Block identifies: "species chauvinism." The problem is that identity theory would exclude those creatures with biological construction different from our own as having any mental states. In this article he raises the opposite criticism of functionalism. Fodor's principal argument in support of functionalism is that *any* creature that has a functional organization similar to our own will have mental states similar to our own. But in this article Block argues that there are conceivable systems that have the very same functional organization as a human being, while we would agree that it is not prima facie plausible that such a system would actually have mental states. So where identity theory suffers from excluding systems that seem to have mental states, functionalism suffers from admitting systems that seem not to have mental states. Block calls this weakness, "liberalism."

Before we look at the systems that Block says raise problems for functionalism, we should clarify the kind of functionalism that Block is referring to. He adopts the version of functionalism that earlier we labeled "Turing Machine functionalism," according to which the functional organization of a system is characterized as a Turing Machine. So two systems have the same psychological states if the functional role of those states can be characterized by the same Turing Machine description. Block's argument, then, is that we can describe systems that would have the same Turing Machine description as a human being, and yet would not plausibly be thought of as having mental states of any kind.

Homunculi-Headed Robots

The system that Block describes is a curious kind of robot. The robot has a physical body outwardly just like a human being's. But where a human being has a physical brain that carries out the processes of the mind that occur between stimulus and behavior, the robot has an empty space in which there are little people who carry out the functional role of mental states. Historically, the idea that the function of a mental state can be carried out by little people inside the head is an old one. For example, when we explain how the visual system manages to receive information through the retina, we could image a little person looking at the retinal image and sending whatever information about it that the other mental states require. Of course this doesn't really *explain* anything because we would still have to say how the little person sees the retinal image. A little person inside the head that carries out mental functions is called a **homunculus** (**homunculi** in plural). So Block calls his robot a "homunculi-headed robot."

Let's look at how Block says this robot would work. We imagine that for each Turing Machine functional state of the robot, there is one homunculus whose job it is to carry out the functional role of that state. Let's look at a simpler version of the same idea. Recall Fodor's Coke machine. It has two internal states, S1 and S2. We could construct such a machine using homunculi—building a homunculi-headed Coke machine. Imagine that inside the box of the Coke machine are two people. One is in control of the machine when it is in S1, and the other is in control of the machine when it is in S2. When the machine is in S1 and someone inserts a nickel, the first homunculus would simply hand control over to the other homunculus. When the machine is in S1 and someone inserts a dime, then the first homunculus would put out a Coke and keep control himself. When the machine is in S2 (i.e., when the second homunculus is in control), then the second homunculus would give out a Coke when someone inserts a nickel, and would give out a Coke and a nickel when someone inserts a dime. In each case the second homunculus would then return control to the first. (Notice that you can try this yourself with two volunteers as the homunculi.) Now in the case of Block's homunculi-headed robot we imagine the same scenario, but instead of two homunculi there would be perhaps millions—enough to carry out the functional operations of a human mind. While the system would be much larger than the homunculi-headed Coke machine, it wouldn't in principle be any different. If the operation of the human mind can be fully described as a Turing Machine, then there is no reason *in principle* why we couldn't construct Block's robot, although in practice it is an imaginary mechanism.

In a second version of the same idea, Block describes the robot in somewhat different terms. Here we imagine that the functional states of the robot are carried out by people connected to it via two-way radio. These radios connect each person to the other people (the other homunculi) and to the artificial body of the robot. Block asks us to imagine that the homunculi be thought of as the population of China (which is assumed to be large enough to perform the necessary functions). As Block says, the population of China, each person carrying out the functions of one internal state of the system, would constitute a kind of "external brain" of the robot. Despite its external brain, the robot would receive stimulus and exhibit outward behavior in ways identical to a human being. Observing its behavior, we would think it *is* a human being.

Block considers a number of objections to this idea: (1) that such a machine could not plausibly exhibit all the behavior of a person only for a limited period of time; (2) that there are physical events that could happen to the population of China (say, a flood) that would alter its behavior, yet would not be actual inputs to the system; and (3) that the Chinese system would work too slowly. We will leave his replies for you to read yourself. In the next section of the article, "Putnam's Proposal," Block considers a way of rejecting the homunculi-headed robot as a plausible candidate for a functional system of the right sort. Hilary Putnam has argued that two systems can not be functionally identical if one of them has parts (here the individual Chinese people) that themselves have a functional organization characteristic of a sentient being. The idea here is that, not only must the overall functioning of the two systems be the same, but the functional organization of the parts that carry out the functional roles must themselves also be identical. Here again we leave Block's reply to this objection for you to read, and concentrate instead on Block's primary argument.

Absent Qualia

Block's argument rests on the fact that most of us would not suppose that the homunculi-headed robot has the necessary what-ever-it-is that would lead us to think that it is a conscious being with a mind just like a human being. What exactly would we suppose is missing? Recall Fodor's admission that functionalism has trouble explaining the *qualitative content* of a mental state (or as Place and Smart refer to it, the *phenomenal* properties of a mental state). Block is drawing on the same point. When a person is in pain, for example, there is not only the person's external behavior to consider, there is also the qualitative fact about what the pain *feels like* for the person. We can suppose that the homunculi-headed robot would exhibit all the same outward behavior as an injured person, and indeed that this behavior was produced by a set of functional states the same as a person's. But we would not be inclined to suppose that the robot system—consisting only of the population of China connected by two-way radios—would feel any actual pain.

Here Block uses a philosophical term we have not yet introduced. Philosophers often refer to the phenomenal or qualitative properties of a conscious mental state, as **qualia** (singular **quale**). So two mental state tokens of pain that feel the same, that have the same phenomenal or qualitative character, are said to have the same qualia. Similarly, two tokens of experiencing the same shade of red would have the same qualia. Block's point, seen in these terms, is that the functional states of the robot system would have *no qualia at all*. (Of course, the mental states of the people carrying out those functional roles would *themselves* have qualia. But these would not belong to the robot. For example, if the robot were to stub its toe the people of China would not feel any pain. If there is any pain, it must be pain felt by the robot system itself.) A homunculi-headed robot cannot be considered to be a psychological being like a person, because our intuition tells us that, unlike people, the internal states of the robot would not possess any qualia, any qualitative character.

Worries about Intuitions

In the section of the article entitled, "Is the Prima Facie Doubt Merely Prima Facie?" Block looks at the fact we mentioned in the preceding sentence. The argument just described rests on the fact that our *intuition* leads us to think that the states of the homunculi-headed robot do not have any qualia. That is, it just *seems that way to us* when we imagine the robot. But such intuitions have failed us before. Block mentions the fact that, prior to the heliocentric theory of the planetary system, it *seemed as though* the earth was not in motion. People couldn't feel or see any motion, and so their intuition told them that the earth was still. What reason is there, then, to suppose that the intuition that the robot has no mental states is any more reliable? Maybe we just don't know enough about robots, just as earlier people didn't know about inertia. As Block mentions, intuitions about qualia are especially suspicious because no physical system seems the kind of thing that could have internal states with qualia. The brain, as a mass of grey material, seems equally unlikely to be the seat of conscious experiences.

Block's response is that there are in fact good reasons to contrast the homunculi-headed robot with human beings in a way that renders his intuition plausible. The first is that we *know* that people have qualia, whereas we have no reason to think that the robots do. The second is that the robots are constructed only to mimic human behavior, and there is no reason to suppose that a machine that simply mimics behavior possesses the properties that produce that behavior in a person. To the response that the very complexity of the robot's behavior is itself reason to attribute qualia to the robot, Block's reply is that this is just a "crude appeal to behaviorism." Of course, a supporter of functionalism could argue that this begs the question, since the very point of functionalism is based on the behaviorist identification of mental states with their functional role.

Back to Meanings

Recall from Chapter Seven that behaviorists take the dispositions to exhibit certain kinds of behavior given certain stimuli as an explanation of the *meanings* of psychological descriptions. To say that Smith is thirsty means (among other things) that if there is water to drink then Smith will drink some. Block points out that this strategy is available as a defense of functionalism against the homunculi-headed robot. A supporter of functionalism could argue that carrying out the functional role of a Turing Machine state is simply a *definition* of what we mean when we say that a person has this or that mental state. If we take this line, then the implausibility of qualia doesn't make any difference—to deny mental states to the homunculi-headed robot is simply to ignore the meanings of our psychological descriptions.

Block's reply here is complex, and we will leave the details to you.[7] But there is one point that can be made here. To claim that functional role constitutes the meaning of psychological descriptions amounts to a denial of the claim that qualitative content can be used to differentiate one mental state type from another. As long as two internal states have the same functional role, then they are identical by definition (even if they have no qualitative character at all). To return to Fodor's description of color reversal above, this position would deny that the two people whose experiences of red and green are reversed makes any difference to their psychological descriptions. By definition, it would make no difference to our description of their mental states. In itself, this is not an absurd position to take, but it does challenge our intuitions, which is precisely the challenge that Block considers in this section of his article.

Notes

1. There is a weaker version of type identity than these two. It can happen that two types are identical by accident or coincidence. For example, it might come to be that the only remaining bungalows are on Elm Street and every house on Elm Street is a bungalow. It would follow that all and only bungalows are on Elm Street. This is just an *accidental identity*, not a matter of laws of nature. There could be a bungalow somewhere else, or they could build a 20-storey apartment house on Elm Street.

2. Here is another example of type identity that results from natural laws. In the seventeenth century Robert Boyle established the Law of Ideal Gases. It says that, as a result of physical laws, any gas that is ideal (i.e., is considered as composed of point masses that interact through elastic collision) also has the property that its volume and pressure are inversely proportional (at the same temperature). According to this law, these two properties are one and the same.

3. If this correct as a matter of how rigid designators work, then type identity is a *necessary* identity. It is impossible for something to be water without being H_2O. It is on these grounds that Kripke argues that mental states cannot be physical states, because (given the nature of the terms) mental properties can never be identical to physical properties.

4. A good example of this reasoning can be found in Zenon Pylyshyn, *Computation and Cognition: Toward a Foundation for Cognitive Science* (MIT Press, 1984). See also David Marr, *Vision: A Computational Investigation into the Human Representation and Processing of Visual Information* (San Francisco: W.H. Freeman and Company, 1982).

5. John Locke, *An Essay Concerning Human Understanding*, Book II, Section xxxii.

6. Truth and falsehood, by the way, are also important semantic properties.

7. In a section of the article that we have not reproduced, Block draws a distinction between two different kinds of functionalist theories. He uses the term 'Functionalism' with a capital 'F' to refer to functional analyses of psychological terms in terms of common-sense psychology (e.g., 'pain' refers to a state that tends to result in the avoidance of the thing that caused

it). 'Psychofunctionalism' refers to functional analyses of psychological terms in terms of scientific theories of human psychology (e.g., 'pain' refers to a state that is caused by neural impulses). He argues that Functionalism is too liberal on the grounds of the argument included here. He argues Psychofunctionalism can avoid this problem, but at the cost of restricting mentality to creatures exactly like human beings.

DAVID M. ARMSTRONG

"The Nature of Mind"

Men have minds, that is to say, they perceive, they have sensations, emotions, beliefs, thoughts, purposes, and desires.[1] What is it to have a mind? What is it to perceive, to feel emotion, to hold a belief, or to have a purpose? In common with many other modern philosophers, I think that the best clue we have to the nature of mind is furnished by the discoveries and hypotheses of modern science concerning the nature of man.

What does modern science have to say about the nature of man? There are, of course, all sorts of disagreements and divergencies in the views of individual scientists. But I think it is true to say that one view is steadily gaining ground, so that it bids fair to become established scientific doctrine. This is the view that we can give a complete account of man *in purely physico-chemical terms*. This view has received a tremendous impetus in the last decade from the new subject of molecular biology, a subject which promises to unravel the physical and chemical mechanisms which lie at the basis of life. Before that time, it received great encouragement from pioneering work in neurophysiology pointing to the likelihood of a purely electro-chemical account of the working of the brain. I think it is fair to say that those

scientists who still reject the physico-chemical account of man do so primarily for philosophical, or moral, or religious reasons, and only secondarily, and halfheartedly, for reasons of scientific detail. This is not to say that in the future new evidence and new problems may not come to light which will force science to reconsider the physico-chemical view of man. But at present the drift of scientific thought is clearly set towards the physico-chemical hypothesis. And we have nothing better to go on than the present.

For me, then, and for many philosophers who think like me, the moral is clear. We must try to work out an account of the nature of mind which is compatible with the view that man is nothing but a physico-chemical mechanism.

And...I shall be concerned to do just this: to sketch (in barest outline) what may be called a Materialist or Physicalist account of the mind. But before doing this I should like to go back and consider a criticism of my position which must inevitably occur to some. What reason have I, it may be asked, for taking my stand on science? Even granting that I am right about what is the currently dominant scientific view of man, why should we concede science a special authority to decide questions about the nature of man? What of the authority of philosophy, of religion, of morality, or even of literature and art? Why do I set the authority of science above all these? Why this "scientism"?

It seems to me that the answer to this question is very simple. If we consider the search for truth, in all its fields, we find that it is only in science that men versed in their subject can, after investigation that is more or less prolonged, and which may in some cases extend beyond a single human lifetime, reach substantial agreement about what is the case. It is only as a result of scientific investigation that we ever seem to reach an intellectual consensus about controversial matters.

In the Epistle Dedicatory to his *De Corpore* Hobbes wrote of William Harvey, the discoverer of the circulation of the blood, that he was "the only man I know, that conquering envy, hath established a new doctrine in his lifetime." Before Copernicus, Galileo and Harvey, Hobbes remarks, "there was nothing certain in natural philosophy." And, we might add, with the exception of mathematics, there was nothing certain in any other learned discipline.

These remarks of Hobbes are incredibly revealing. They show us what a watershed in the intellectual history of the human race the seventeenth century was. Before that time inquiry proceeded, as it were, in the dark. Men could not hope to see their doctrine *established*, that is to say, accepted by the vast majority of those properly versed in the subject under discussion. There was no intellectual consensus. Since that time, it has become a commonplace to see new doctrines, sometimes of the most far-reaching kind, established to the satisfaction of the learned, often within the lifetime of their first proponents. Science has provided us with a method of deciding disputed questions. This is not to say, of course, that the consensus of those who are learned and competent in a subject cannot be mistaken. Of course such a

consensus can be mistaken. Sometimes it has been mistaken. But, granting fallibility, what better authority have we than such a consensus?

Now this is of the utmost importance. For in philosophy, in religion, in such disciplines as literary criticism, in moral questions in so far as they are thought to be matters of truth and falsity, there has been a notable failure to achieve an intellectual consensus about disputed questions among the learned. Must we not then attach a peculiar authority to the discipline that can achieve a consensus? And if it presents us with a certain vision of the nature of man, is this not a powerful reason for accepting that vision? I will not take up here the deeper question *why* it is that the methods of science have enabled us to achieve an intellectual consensus about so many disputed matters. That question, I think, could receive no brief or uncontroversial answer. I am resting my argument on the simple and uncontroversial fact that, as a result of scientific investigation, such a consensus has been achieved.

It may be replied—it often is replied—that while science is all very well in its own sphere— the sphere of the physical, perhaps—there are matters of fact on which it is not competent to pronounce. And among such matters, it may be claimed, is the question what is the whole nature of man. But I cannot see that this reply has much force. Science has provided us with an island of truths, or, perhaps one should say, a raft of truths, to bear us up on the sea of our disputatious ignorance. There may have to be revisions and refinements, new results may set old findings in a new perspective, but what science has given us will not be altogether superseded. Must we not therefore appeal to these relative certainties for guidance when we come to consider uncertainties elsewhere? Perhaps science cannot help us to decide whether or not there is a God, whether or not human beings have immortal souls, or whether or not the will is free. But if science cannot assist us, what can? I conclude that it is the scientific vision of man, and not the philosophical or religious or artistic or moral vision of man, that is the best clue we have to the nature of man. And it is rational to argue from the best evidence we have.

Having in this way attempted to justify my procedure, I turn back to my subject: the attempt to work out an account of mind, or, if you prefer, of mental process, within the framework of the physico-chemical or, as we may call it, the Materialist view of man.

Now there is one account of mental process that is at once attractive to any philosopher sympathetic to a Materialist view of man: this is Behaviourism. Formulated originally by a psychologist, J.B. Watson, it attracted widespread interest and considerable support from scientifically oriented philosophers. Traditional philosophy had tended to think of the mind as a rather mysterious inward arena that lay behind, and was responsible for, the outward or physical behaviour of our bodies. Descartes thought of this inner arena as a *spiritual substance*, and it was this conception of the mind as spiritual object that Gilbert Ryle attacked, apparently in the interest of Behaviourism, in his important book *The Concept of Mind*. He ridiculed the Cartesian view as the dogma of "the ghost in the machine." The mind was not something behind the behaviour of the body, it was simply part of that physical behaviour. My anger with you is not some modification of a spiritual substance which somehow brings about aggressive behaviour; rather it is the aggressive behaviour itself: my addressing strong words to you, striking you, turning my back on you, and so on. Thought is not an inner process that lies behind, and brings about, the words I speak and write: it is my speaking and writing. The mind is not an inner arena, it is outward act.

It is clear that such a view of mind fits in very well with a completely Materialistic or Physicalist view of man. If there is no need to draw a distinction between mental processes and their expression in physical behaviour, but if instead the mental processes are identified with their so-called "expressions," then the existence of mind stands in no conflict with the view that man is nothing but a physico-chemical mechanism.

However, the version of Behaviourism that I have just sketched is a very crude version, and its crudity lays it open to obvious objections. One obvious difficulty is that it is our common experience that there can be mental processes going on although there is no behaviour occurring that could possibly be treated as expressions of these processes. A man may be angry, but give no bodily sign; he may think, but say or do nothing at all.

In my view, the most plausible attempt to refine Behaviourism with a view to meeting this objection was made by introducing the notion of *a disposition to behave*. (Dispositions to behave play a particularly important part in Ryle's account of the mind.) Let us consider the general notion of disposition first. Brittleness is a disposition, a disposition possessed by materials like glass. Brittle materials are those which, when subjected to relatively small forces, break or shatter easily. But breaking and shattering easily is not brittleness, rather it is the *manifestation* of brittleness. Brittleness itself is the tendency or liability of the material to break or shatter easily. A piece of glass may never shatter or break throughout its whole history, but it is still the case that it is brittle: it is liable to shatter or break if dropped quite a small way or hit quite lightly. Now a disposition to *behave* is simply a tendency or liability of a person to behave in a certain way under certain circumstances. The brittleness of glass is a disposition that the glass retains throughout its history, but clearly there could also be dispositions that come and go. The dispositions to behave that are of interest to the Behaviourist are, for the most part, of this temporary character.

Now how did Ryle and others use the notion of a disposition to behave to meet the obvious objection to Behaviourism that there can be mental processes going on although the subject is engaging in no relevant behaviour? Their strategy was to argue that in such cases, although the subject was not behaving in any relevant way, he or she was *disposed* to behave in some relevant way. The glass does not shatter, but it is still brittle. The man does not behave, but he does have a disposition to behave. We can say he thinks although he does not speak or act because at that time he was disposed to speak or act in a certain way. *If* he had been asked, perhaps, he would have spoken or acted. We can say he is angry although he does not behave angrily, because he is disposed so to behave. *If* only one more word had been addressed to him, he would have burst out. And so on. In this way it was hoped that Behaviourism could be squared with the obvious facts.

It is very important to see just how these thinkers conceived of dispositions. I quote from Ryle:

> To possess a dispositional property *is not to be in a particular state, or to undergo a particular change*: it is to be bound or liable to be in a particular state, or to undergo a particular change, when a particular condition is realised. (*The Concept of Mind*, p. 43; my italics.)

So to explain the breaking of a lightly struck glass on a particular occasion by saying it was brittle is, on this view of dispositions, simply to say that the glass broke because it is the sort of thing that regularly breaks when quite lightly struck. The breaking was the normal behaviour, or not abnormal behaviour, of such a thing. The

brittleness is not to be conceived of as a *cause* for the breakage, or even, more vaguely, a *factor* in bringing about the breaking. Brittleness is just the fact that things of that sort break easily.

But although in this way the Behaviourists did something to deal with the objection that mental processes can occur in the absence of behaviour, it seems clear, now that the shouting and the dust have died, that they did not do enough. When I think, but my thoughts do not issue in any action, it seems as obvious as anything is obvious that there is something actually going on in me which constitutes my thought. It is not simply that I would speak or act if some conditions that are unfulfilled were to be fulfilled. Something is currently going on, in the strongest and most literal sense of "going on," and this something is my thought. Rylean Behaviourism denies this, and so it is unsatisfactory as a theory of mind. Yet I know of no version of Behaviourism that is more satisfactory. The moral for those of us who wish to take a purely physicalistic view of man is that we must look for some other account of the nature of mind and of mental processes.

But perhaps we need not grieve too deeply about the failure of Behaviourism to produce a satisfactory theory of mind. Behaviourism is a profoundly unnatural account of mental processes. If somebody speaks and acts in certain ways it is natural to speak of this speech and action as the *expression* of his thought. It is not at all natural to speak of his speech and action as identical with his thought. We naturally think of the thought as something quite distinct from the speech and action which, under suitable circumstances, brings the speech and action about. Thoughts are not to be identified with behaviour, we think, they lie behind behaviour. A man's behaviour constitutes the *reason* we have for attributing certain mental processes to him, but the behaviour cannot be identified with the mental processes.

This suggests a very interesting line of thought about the mind. Behaviourism is certainly wrong, but perhaps it is not altogether wrong. Perhaps the Behaviourists are wrong in identifying the mind and mental occurrences with behaviour, but perhaps they are right in thinking that our notion of a mind and of individual mental states is *logically tied to behaviour.* For perhaps what we mean by a mental state is some state of the person which, under suitable circumstances, *brings about* a certain range of behaviour. Perhaps mind can be defined not as behaviour, but rather as the inner *cause* of certain behaviour. Thought is not speech under suitable circumstances, rather it is something within the person which, in suitable circumstances brings about speech. And, in fact, I believe that this is the true account, or, at any rate, a true first account, of what we mean by a mental state.

How does this line of thought link up with a purely physicalist view of man? The position is, I think, that while it does not make such a physicalist view inevitable, it does make it *possible.* It does not entail, but it is compatible with, a purely physicalist view of man. For if our notion of the mind and mental states is nothing but that of a cause within the person of certain ranges of behaviour, then it becomes a scientific question, and not a question of logical analysis, what in fact the intrinsic nature of that cause is. The cause might be, as Descartes thought it was, a spiritual substance working through the pineal gland to produce the complex bodily behaviour of which men are capable. It might be breath, or specially smooth and mobile atoms dispersed throughout the body; it might be many other things. But in fact the verdict of modern science seems to be that the sole cause of mind-betokening behaviour in man and the higher animals is the physico-chemical workings of the central nervous system. And so, assuming we have correctly characterised

our concept of a mental state as nothing but the cause of certain sorts of behaviour, then we can identify these mental states with purely physical states of the central nervous system.

At this point we may stop and go back to the Behaviourists' dispositions. We saw that, according to them, the brittleness of glass or, to take another example, the elasticity of rubber, is not a state of the glass or the rubber, but is simply the fact that things of that sort behave in the way they do. But now let us consider how a scientist would think about brittleness or elasticity. Faced with the phenomenon of breakage under relatively small impacts, or the phenomenon of stretching when a force is applied followed by contraction when the force is removed, he will assume that there is some current *state* of the glass or the rubber which is responsible for the characteristic behaviour of samples of these two materials. At the beginning he will not know what this state is, but he will endeavor to find out, and he may succeed in finding out. And when he has found out he will very likely make remarks of this sort: "We have discovered that the brittleness of glass is in fact a certain sort of pattern in the molecules of the glass." That is to say, he will *identify* brittleness with the state of the glass that is responsible for the liability of the glass to break. For him, a disposition of an object is a state of the object. What makes the state a state of brittleness is the fact that it gives rise to the characteristic manifestations of brittleness. But the disposition itself is distinct from its manifestations: it is the state of the glass that gives rise to these manifestations in suitable circumstances.

You will see that this way of looking at dispositions is very different from that of Ryle and the Behaviourists. The great difference is this: If we treat dispositions as actual states, as I have suggested that scientists do, even if states whose intrinsic nature may yet have to be discovered, then we can say that dispositions are actual *causes*, or causal factors, which, in suitable circumstances, actually bring about those happenings which are the manifestations of the disposition. A certain molecular constitution of glass which constitutes its brittleness is actually *responsible* for the fact that, when the glass is struck, it breaks.

Now I shall not argue the matter here, because the detail of the argument is technical and difficult,[2] but I believe that the view of dispositions as states, which is the view that is natural to science, is the correct one. I believe it can be shown quite strictly that, to the extent that we admit the notion of dispositions at all, we are committed to the view that they are actual *states* of the object that has the disposition. I may add that I think that the same holds for the closely connected notions of capacities and powers. Here I will simply assume this step in my argument.

But perhaps it can be seen that the rejection of the idea that mind is simply a certain range of man's behaviour in favor of the view that mind is rather the inner *cause* of that range of man's behaviour is bound up with the rejection of the Rylean view of dispositions in favor of one that treats dispositions as states of objects and so as having actual causal power. The Behaviourists were wrong to identify the mind with behaviour. They were not so far off the mark when they tried to deal with cases where mental happenings occur in the absence of behaviour by saying that these are dispositions to behave. But in order to reach a correct view, I am suggesting, they would have to conceive of these dispositions as actual *states* of the person who has the disposition, states that have actual power to bring about behaviour in suitable circumstances. But to do this is to abandon the central inspiration of Behaviourism: that in talking about the mind we do not have to go behind outward behaviour to inner states.

And so two separate but interlocking lines of thought have pushed me in the same direction. The first line of thought is that it goes profoundly against the grain to think of the mind as behaviour. The mind is, rather, that which stands behind and brings about our complex behaviour. The second line of thought is that the Behaviourists' dispositions, properly conceived, are really states that underlie behaviour, and, under suitable circumstances, bring about behaviour. Putting these two together, we reach the conception of a mental state as *a state of the person apt for producing certain ranges of behaviour.* This formula: a mental state is a state of the person apt for producing certain ranges of behaviour, I believe to be a very illuminating way of looking at the concept of a mental state. I have found it very fruitful in the search for detailed logical analyses of the individual mental concepts.

Now, I do not think that Hegel's dialectic has much to tell us about the nature of reality. But I think that human thought often moves in a dialectical way, from thesis to antithesis and then to the synthesis. Perhaps thought about the mind is a case in point. I have already said that classical philosophy tended to think of the mind as an inner arena of some sort. This we may call the Thesis. Behaviourism moved to the opposite extreme: the mind was seen as outward behaviour. This is the Antithesis. My proposed Synthesis is that the mind is properly conceived as an inner principle, but a principle that is identified in terms of the outward behaviour it is apt for bringing about. This way of looking at the mind and mental states does not itself entail a Materialist or Physicalist view of man, for nothing is said in this analysis about the intrinsic nature of these mental states. But if we have, as I have asserted that we do have, general scientific grounds for thinking that man is nothing but a physical mechanism, we can go on to argue that the mental states are in fact nothing but physical states of the central nervous system.

Along these lines, then, I would look for an account of the mind that is compatible with a purely Materialist theory of man. I have tried to carry out this programme in detail in *A Materialist Theory of the Mind*. There are, as may be imagined, all sorts of powerful objections that can be made to this view. But...I propose to do only one thing. I will develop one very important objection to my view of the mind—an objection felt by many philosophers—and then try to show how the objection should be met.

The view that our notion of mind is nothing but that of an inner principle apt for bringing about certain sorts of behaviour may be thought to share a certain weakness with Behaviourism. Modern philosophers have put the point about Behaviourism by saying that although Behaviourism may be a satisfactory account of the mind from an *other-person point of view*, it will not do as a *first-person* account. To explain. In our encounters with other people, all we ever observe is their behaviour: their actions, their speech, and so on. And so, if we simply consider other people, Behaviourism might seem to do full justice to the facts. But the trouble about Behaviourism is that it seems so unsatisfactory as applied to our *own* case. In our own case, we seem to be aware of so much more than mere behaviour.

Suppose that now we conceive of the mind as an inner principle apt for bringing about certain sorts of behaviour. This again fits the other-person cases very well. Bodily behaviour of a very sophisticated sort is observed, quite different from the behaviour that ordinary physical objects display. It is inferred that this behaviour must spring from a very special sort of inner cause in the object that exhibits this behaviour. This inner cause is christened "the mind," and those who take a physicalist view of man argue that it is simply the central ner-

vous system of the body observed. Compare this with the case of glass. Certain characteristic behaviour is observed: the breaking and shattering of the material when acted upon by relatively small forces. A special inner state of the glass is postulated to explain this behaviour. Those who take a purely physicalist view of glass then argue that this state is a *natural* state of the glass. It is, perhaps, an arrangement of its molecules, and not, say, the peculiarly malevolent disposition of the demons that dwell in glass.

But when we turn to our own case, the position may seem less plausible. We are conscious, we have experiences. Now can we say that to be conscious, to have experiences, is simply for something to go on within us apt for the causing of certain sorts of behaviour? Such an account does not seem to do any justice to the phenomena. And so it seems that our account of the mind, like Behaviourism, will fail to do justice to the first-person case.

In order to understand the objection better it may be helpful to consider a particular case. If you have driven for a very long distance without a break, you may have had experience of a curious state of automatism, which can occur in these conditions. One can suddenly "come to" and realise that one has driven for long distances without being aware of what one was doing, or, indeed, without being aware of anything. One has kept the car on the road, used the brake and the clutch perhaps, yet all without any awareness of what one was doing.

Now, if we consider this case it is obvious that *in some sense* mental processes are still going on when one is in such an automatic state. Unless one's will was still operating in some way, and unless one was still perceiving in some way, the car would not still be on the road. Yet, of course, *something* mental is lacking. Now, I think, when it is alleged that an account of mind as an inner principle apt for the production of certain sorts of behaviour leaves out consciousness or experience, what is alleged to have been left out is just whatever is missing in the automatic driving case. It is conceded that an account of mental processes as states of the person apt for the production of certain sorts of behaviour may very possibly be adequate to deal with such cases as that of automatic driving. It may be adequate to deal with most of the mental processes of animals, who perhaps spend a good deal of their lives in this state of automatism. But, it is contended, it cannot deal with the consciousness that we normally enjoy.

I will now try to sketch an answer to this important and powerful objection. Let us begin in an apparently unlikely place, and consider the way that an account of mental processes of the sort I am giving would deal with *sense-perception*. Now psychologists, in particular, have long realised that there is a very close logical tie between sense-perception and *selective behaviour*. Suppose we want to decide whether an animal can perceive the difference between red and green. We might give the animal a choice between two pathways, over one of which a red light shines and over the other of which a green light shines. If the animal happens by chance to choose the green pathway we reward it; if it happens to choose the other pathway we do not reward it. If, after some trials, the animal systematically takes the green-lighted pathway, and if we become assured that the only relevant differences in the two pathways are the differences in the colour of the lights, we are entitled to say that the animal can see this colour difference. Using its eyes, it selects between red-lighted and green-lighted pathways. So we say it can see the difference between red and green.

Now a Behaviourist would be tempted to say that the animal's regularly selecting the green-lighted pathway *was* its perception of the colour difference. But this is unsatisfactory, because we all want to say that perception is something that goes on within the person or animal—within its mind—although, of course, this mental event is normally *caused* by the operation of the environment upon the organism. Suppose, however, that we speak instead of capacities for selective behaviour towards the current environment, and suppose we think of these capacities, like dispositions, as actual inner states of the organism. We can then think of the animal's perception as a state within the animal, apt, if the animal is so impelled, for selective behaviour between the red- and green-lighted pathways.

In general, we can think of perceptions as inner states or events apt for the production of certain sorts of selective behaviour towards our environment. To perceive is like acquiring a key to a door. You do not have to use the key: you can put it in your pocket and never bother about the door. But if you do want to open the door the key may be essential. The blind man is a man who does not acquire certain keys, and, as a result, is not able to operate in his environment in the way that somebody who has his sight can operate. It seems, then, a very promising view to take of perceptions that they are inner states defined by the sorts of selective behaviour that they enable the perceiver to exhibit, if so impelled.

Now how is this discussion of perception related to the question of consciousness of experience, the sort of thing that the driver who is in a state of automatism has not got, but which we normally do have? Simply this. My proposal is that consciousness, in this sense of the word, is nothing but *perception or awareness of the state of our own mind*. The driver in a state of automatism perceives, or is aware of, the road. If he did not, the car would be in a ditch. But he is not currently aware of his awareness of the road. He perceives the road, but he does not perceive his perceiving, or anything else that is going on in his mind. He is not, as we normally are, conscious of what is going on in his mind.

And so I conceive of consciousness or experience, in this sense of the words, in the way that Locke and Kant conceived it, as like perception. Kant, in a striking phrase, spoke of "inner sense." We cannot directly observe the minds of others, but each of us has the power to observe directly our own minds, and "perceive" what is going on there. The driver in the automatic state is one whose "inner eye" is shut: who is not currently aware of what is going on in his own mind.

Now if this account is along the right lines, why should we not give an account of this inner observation along the same lines as we have already given of perception? Why should we not conceive of it as an inner state, a state in this case directed towards other inner states and not to the environment, which enables us, if we are so impelled, to behave in a selective way *towards our own states of mind*? One who is aware, or conscious, of his thoughts or his emotions is one who has the capacity to make discriminations between his different mental states. His capacity might be exhibited in words. He might say that he was in an angry state of mind when, and only when, he *was* in an angry state of mind. But such verbal behaviour would be the mere *expression* or *result* of the awareness. The awareness itself would be an inner state: the sort of inner state that gave the man a capacity for such behavioural expressions.

So I have argued that consciousness of our own mental state may be assimilated to *perception* of our own mental state, and that, like other perceptions, it may then be conceived of as an inner state or event giving a capacity for selective behaviour, in this case selective behaviour towards our own mental state. All this is meant to be simply a logical analysis of consciousness, and none of it entails, although it does not rule out, a purely physicalist account of what these inner states are. But if we are convinced, on general scientific grounds, that a purely physical account of man is likely to be the true one, then there seems to be no bar to our identifying these inner states with purely physical states of the central nervous system. And so consciousness of our own mental state becomes simply the scanning of one part of our central nervous system by another. Consciousness is a self-scanning mechanism in the central nervous system.

As I have emphasized before, I have done no more than sketch a programme for a philosophy of mind. There are all sorts of expansions and elucidations to be made, and all sorts of doubts and difficulties to be stated and overcome. But I hope I have done enough to show that a purely physicalist theory of the mind is an exciting and plausible intellectual option.

Notes

1. Inaugural lecture of the Challis Professor of Philosophy at the University of Sydney (1965); slightly amended (1968).
2. It is presented in my book *A Materialist Theory of the Mind* (1968) ch. 6, sec. VI.

JERRY A. FODOR

"The Mind-Body Problem"

Modern philosophy of science has been devoted largely to the formal and systematic description of the successful practices of working scientists. The philosopher does not try to dictate how scientific inquiry and argument ought to be conducted. Instead he tries to enumerate the principles and practices that have contributed to good science. The philosopher has devoted the most attention to analyzing the methodological peculiarities of the physical sciences. The analysis has helped to clarify the nature of confirmation, the logical structure of scientific theories, the formal properties of statements that express laws and the question of whether theoretical entities actually exist.

It is only rather recently that philosophers have become seriously interested in the methodological tenets of psychology. Psychological explanations of behavior refer liberally to the mind and to states, operations and processes of the mind. The philosophical difficulty comes in stating in unambiguous language what such references imply.

Traditional philosophies of mind can be divided into two broad categories: dualist theories and materialist theories. In the dualist approach the mind is a nonphysical substance. In materialist theories the mental is not distinct from the physical; indeed, all mental states, properties, processes and operations are in principle identical with physical states, properties, processes and operations. Some materialists, known as behaviorists, maintain that all talk of mental causes can be eliminated from the language of psychology in favor of talk of environmental stimuli and behavioral responses. Other materialists, the identity theorists, contend that there are mental causes and that they are identical with neurophysiological events in the brain.

In the past 15 years a philosophy of mind called functionalism that is neither dualist nor materialist has emerged from philosophical reflection on developments in artificial intelligence, computational theory, linguistics, cybernetics, and psychology. All these fields, which are collectively known as the cognitive sciences, have in common a certain level of abstraction and a concern with systems that process information. Functionalism, which seeks to provide a philosophical account of this level of abstraction, recognizes the possibility that systems as diverse as human beings, calculating machines and disembodied spirits could all have mental states. In the functionalist view the psychology of a system depends not on the stuff it is made of (living cells, metal or spiritual energy) but on how the stuff is put together. Functionalism is a difficult concept, and one way of coming to grips with it is to review the deficiencies of the dualist and materialist philosophies of mind it aims to displace.

The chief drawback of dualism is its failure to account adequately for mental causation. If the mind is nonphysical, it has no position in physical space. How, then, can a mental cause give rise to a behavioral effect that has a position in space? To put it another way, how can the nonphysical give rise to the physical without violating the laws of the conservation of mass, of energy, and of momentum?

The dualist might respond that the problem of how an immaterial substance can cause physical events is not much obscurer than the problem of how one physical event can cause another. Yet there is an important difference: there are many clear cases of physical causation but not one clear case of nonphysical causation. Physical interaction is something philosophers, like all other people, have to live with. Nonphysical interaction, however, may be no more than an artifact of the immaterialist construal of the mental. Most philosophers now agree that no argument has successfully demonstrated why mind-body causation should not be regarded as a species of physical causation.

Dualism is also incompatible with the practices of working psychologists. The psychologist frequently applies the experimental methods of the physical sciences to the study of the mind. If mental processes were different in kind from physical processes, there would be no reason to expect these methods to work in the realm of the mental. In order to justify their experimental methods many psychologists urgently sought an alternative to dualism.

In the 1920s John B. Watson of Johns Hopkins University made the radical suggestion that behavior does not have mental causes. He regarded the behavior of an organism as its observable responses to stimuli, which he took to be the causes of its behavior. Over the next 30 years psychologists such as B.F. Skinner of Harvard University developed Watson's ideas into an elaborate world view in which the role of psychology was to catalogue the laws that determine causal relations between stimuli and responses. In this "radical behaviorist" view the problem of explaining the nature of the mind-body interaction vanishes; there is no such interaction.

Radical behaviorism has always worn an air of paradox. For better or worse, the idea of mental causation is deeply ingrained in our everyday language and in our ways of understanding our fellow men and ourselves. For example, people commonly attribute behavior to beliefs, to knowledge and to expectations. Brown puts gas in his tank because he believes the car will not run without it. Jones writes not "acheive" but "achieve" because he knows the rule about putting *i* before *e*. Even when a behavioral response is closely tied to an environmental stimulus, mental processes often intervene. Smith carries an umbrella because the sky is cloudy, but the weather is only part of the story. There are apparently also mental links in the causal chain: observation and expectation. The clouds affect Smith's behavior only because he observes them and because they induce in him an expectation of rain.

The radical behaviorist is unmoved by appeals to such cases. He is prepared to dismiss references to mental causes, however plausible they may seem, as the residue of outworn creeds. The radical behaviorist predicts that as psychologists come to understand more about the relations between stimuli and responses they will find it increasingly possible to explain behavior without postulating mental causes.

The strongest argument against behaviorism is that psychology has not turned out this way; the opposite has happened. As psychology has matured, the framework of mental states and processes that is apparently needed to account for experimental observations has grown all the more elaborate. Particularly in the case of human behavior psychological theories satisfying the methodological tenets of radical behaviorism have proved largely sterile, as would be expected if the postulated mental processes are real and causally effective.

Nevertheless, many philosophers were initially drawn to radical behaviorism because, paradoxes and all, it seemed better than dualism. Since a psychology committed to immaterial substances was unacceptable, philosophers turned to radical behaviorism because it seemed to be the only alternative materialist philosophy of mind. The choice, as they saw it, was between radical behaviorism and ghosts.

By the early 1960s philosophers began to have doubts that dualism and radical behaviorism exhausted the possible approaches to the philosophy of mind. Since the two theories seemed unattractive, the right strategy might be to develop a materialist philosophy of mind that nonetheless allowed for mental causes. Two such philosophies emerged, one called logical behaviorism and the other called the central-state identity theory.

Logical behaviorism is a semantic theory about what mental terms mean. The basic idea is that attributing a mental state (say thirst) to an organism is the same as saying that the organism is disposed to behave in a particular way (for example to drink if there is water available). On this view every mental ascription is equivalent in meaning to an if-then statement (called a behavioral hypothetical) that expresses a behavioral disposition. For example, "Smith is thirsty" might be taken to be equivalent to the dispositional statement "If there were water available, then Smith would drink some." By definition a behavioral hypothetical includes no mental terms. The if-clause of the hypothetical speaks only of stimuli and the then-clause speaks only of behavioral responses. Since stimuli and responses are physical events, logical behaviorism is a species of materialism.

The strength of logical behaviorism is that by translating mental language into the language of stimuli and responses it provides an interpretation of psychological explanations in which behavioral effects are attributed to mental causes. Mental causation is simply the manifestation of a behavioral disposition. More precisely, mental causation is what happens when an organism has a behavioral disposition and the if-clause of the behavioral hypothetical expressing the disposition happens to be true. For example, the causal statement "Smith

drank some water because he was thirsty" might be taken to mean "If there were water available, then Smith would drink some, and there was water available."

I have somewhat oversimplified logical behaviorism by assuming that each mental ascription can be translated by a unique behavioral hypothetical. Actually the logical behaviorist often maintains that it takes an open-ended set (perhaps an infinite set) of behavioral hypotheticals to spell out the behavioral disposition expressed by a mental term. The mental ascription "Smith is thirsty" might also be satisfied by the hypothetical "If there were orange juice available, then Smith would drink some" and by a host of other hypotheticals. In any event the logical behaviorist does not usually maintain he can actually enumerate all the hypotheticals that correspond to a behavioral disposition expressing a given mental term. He only insists that in principle the meaning of any mental term can be conveyed by behavioral hypotheticals.

The way the logical behaviorist has interpreted a mental term such as thirsty is modeled after the way many philosophers have interpreted a physical disposition such as fragility. The physical disposition "The glass is fragile" is often taken to mean something like "If the glass were struck, then it would break." By the same token the logical behaviorist's analysis of mental causation is similar to the received analysis of one kind of physical causation. The causal statement "The glass broke because it was fragile" is taken to mean something like "If the glass were struck, then it would break, and the glass was struck."

By equating mental terms with behavioral dispositions the logical behaviorist has put mental terms on a par with the nonbehavioral dispositions of the physical sciences. That is a promising move, because the analysis of nonbehavioral dispositions is on relatively solid philosophical ground. An explanation attributing the breaking of a glass to its fragility is surely something even the staunchest materialist can accept. By arguing that mental terms are synonymous with dispositional terms, the logical behaviorist has provided something the radical behaviorist could not: a materialist account of mental causation.

Nevertheless, the analogy between mental causation as construed by the logical behaviorist and physical causation goes only so far. The logical behaviorist treats the manifestation of a disposition as the sole form of mental causation, whereas the physical sciences recognize additional kinds of causation. There is the kind of causation where one physical event causes another, as when the breaking of a glass is attributed to its having been struck. In fact, explanations that involve event-event causation are presumably more basic than dispositional explanations, because the manifestation of a disposition (the breaking of a fragile glass) always involves event-event causation and not vice versa. In the realm of the mental many examples of event-event causation involve one mental state's causing another, and for this kind of causation logical behaviorism provides no analysis. As a result the logical behaviorist is committed to the tacit and implausible assumption that psychology requires a less robust notion of causation than the physical sciences require.

Event-event causation actually seems to be quite common in the realm of the mental. Mental causes typically give rise to behavioral effects by virtue of their interaction with other mental causes. For example, having a headache causes a disposition to take aspirin only if one also has the desire to get rid of the headache, the belief that aspirin exists, the belief that taking aspirin reduces headaches and so on. Since mental states interact in generating behavior, it will be necessary to find a construal of psychological explanations that posits mental processes: causal sequences of mental events. It is this construal that logical behaviorism fails to provide.

Such considerations bring out a fundamental way in which logical behaviorism is quite similar to radical behaviorism. It is true that the logical behaviorist, unlike the radical behaviorist, acknowledges the existence of mental states. Yet since the underlying tenet of logical behaviorism is that references to mental states can be translated out of psychological explanations by employing behavioral hypotheticals, all talk of mental states and processes is in a sense heuristic. The only facts to which the behaviorist is actually committed are facts about relations between stimuli and responses. In this respect logical behaviorism is just radical behaviorism in a semantic form. Although the former theory offers a construal of mental causation, the construal is Pickwickian. What does not really exist cannot cause anything, and the logical behaviorist, like the radical behaviorist, believes deep down that mental causes do not exist.

An alternative materialist theory of the mind to logical behaviorism is the central-state identity theory. According to this theory, mental events, states and processes are identical with neurophysiological events in the brain, and the property of being in a certain mental state (such as having a headache or believing it will rain) is identical with the property of being in a certain neurophysiological state. On this basis it is easy to make sense of the idea that a behavioral effect might sometimes have a chain of mental causes; that will be the case whenever a behavioral effect is contingent on the appropriate sequence of neurophysiological events.

The central-state identity theory acknowledges that it is possible for mental causes to interact causally without ever giving rise to any behavioral effect, as when a person thinks for a while about what he ought to do and then decides to do nothing. If mental processes are neurophysiological, they must have the causal properties of neurophysiological processes. Since neurophysiological processes are presumably physical processes, the central-state identity theory ensures that the concept of mental causation is as rich as the concept of physical causation.

The central-state identity theory provides a satisfactory account of what the mental terms in psychological explanations refer to, and so it is favored by psychologists who are dissatisfied with behaviorism. The behaviorist maintains that mental terms refer to nothing or that they refer to the parameters of stimulus-response relations. Either way the existence of mental entities is only illusory. The identity theorist, on the other hand, argues that mental terms refer to neurophysiological states. Thus he can take seriously the project of explaining behavior by appealing to its mental causes.

The chief advantage of the identity theory is that it takes the explanatory constructs of psychology at face value, which is surely something a philosophy of mind ought to do if it can. The identity theory shows how the mentalistic explanations of psychology could be not mere heuristics but literal accounts of the causal history of behavior. Moreover, since the identity theory is not a semantic thesis, it is immune to many arguments that cast in doubt logical behaviorism. A drawback of logical behaviorism is that the observation "John has a headache" does not seem to mean the same thing as a statement of the form "John is disposed to behave in such and such a way." The identity theorist, however, can live with the fact that "John has a headache" and "John is in such and such a brain state" are not synonymous. The assertion of the identity theorist is not that these sentences mean the same thing but only that they are rendered true (or false) by the same neurophysiological phenomena.

The identity theory can be held either as a doctrine about mental particulars (John's current pain or Bill's fear of animals) or as a doctrine about mental universals, or properties (having a pain or being afraid of animals). The two doctrines, called respectively token physicalism and type physicalism, differ in strength and plausibility. Token physicalism maintains only that all the mental particulars that happen to exist are neurophysiological, whereas type physicalism makes the more sweeping assertion that all the mental particulars there could possibly be are neurophysiological. Token physicalism does not rule out the logical possibility of machines and disembodied spirits having mental properties. Type physicalism dismisses this possibility because neither machines nor disembodied spirits have neurons.

Type physicalism is not a plausible doctrine about mental properties even if token physicalism is right about mental particulars. The problem with type physicalism is that the psychological constitution of a system seems to depend not on its hardware, or physical composition, but on its software, or program. Why should the philosopher dismiss the possibility that silicon-based Martians have pains, assuming that the silicon is properly organized? And why should the philosopher rule out the possibility of machines having beliefs, assuming that the machines are correctly programmed? If it is logically possible that Martians and machines could have mental properties, then mental properties and neurophysiological processes cannot be identical, however much they may prove to be coextensive.

What it all comes down to is that there seems to be a level of abstraction at which the generalizations of psychology are most naturally pitched. This level of abstraction cuts across differences in the physical composition of the systems to which psychological generalizations apply. In the cognitive sciences, at least, the natural domain for psychological theorizing seems to be all systems that process information. The problem with type physicalism is that there are possible information-processing systems with the same psychological constitution as human beings but not the same physical organization. In principle all kinds of physically different things could have human software.

This situation calls for a relational account of mental properties that abstracts them from the physical structure of their bearers. In spite of the objections to logical behaviorism that I presented above, logical behaviorism was at least on the right track in offering a relational interpretation of mental properties: to have a headache is to be disposed to exhibit a certain pattern of relations between the stimuli one encounters and the responses one exhibits. If that is what having a headache is, however, there is no reason in principle why only heads that are physically similar to ours can ache. Indeed, according to logical behaviorism, it is a necessary truth that any system that has our stimulus-response contingencies also has our headaches.

All of this emerged 10 or 15 years ago as a nasty dilemma for the materialist program in the philosophy of mind. On the one hand the identity theorist (and not the logical behaviorist) had got right the causal character of the interactions of mind and body. On the other the logical behaviorist (and not the identity theorist) had got right the relational character of mental properties. Functionalism has apparently been able to resolve the dilemma. By stressing the distinction computer science draws between hardware and software the functionalist can make sense of both the causal and the relational character of the mental.

The intuition underlying functionalism is that what determines the psychological type to which a mental particular belongs is the causal role of the particular in the mental life of the organism. Functional individuation is differentiation with respect to causal role. A headache, for example, is identified with the type of mental state that among other things causes a disposition for taking aspirin in people who believe aspirin relieves a headache, causes a desire to rid oneself of the pain one is feeling, often causes someone who speaks English to say such things as "I have a headache" and is brought on by overwork, eyestrain, and tension. This list is presumably not complete. More will be known about the nature of a headache as psychological and physiological research discovers more about its causal role.

Functionalism construes the concept role in such a way that a mental state can be defined by its causal relations to other mental states. In this respect functionalism is completely different from logical behaviorism. Another major difference is that functionalism is not a reductionist thesis. It does not foresee, even in principle, the elimination of mentalistic concepts from the explanatory apparatus of psychological theories.

The difference between functionalism and logical behaviorism is brought out by the fact that functionalism is fully compatible with token physicalism. The functionalist would not be disturbed if brain events turn out to be the only things with the functional properties that define mental states. Indeed, most functionalists fully expect it will turn out that way.

Since functionalism recognizes that mental particulars may be physical, it is compatible with the idea that mental causation is a species of physical causation. In other words, functionalism tolerates the materialist solution to the mind-body problem provided by the central-state identity theory. It is possible for the functionalist to assert both that mental properties are typically defined in terms of their relations and that interactions of mind and body are typically causal in however robust a notion of causality is required by psychological explanations. The logical behaviorist can endorse only the first assertion and the type physicalist only the second. As a result functionalism seems to capture the best features of the materialist alternatives to dualism. It is no wonder that functionalism has become increasingly popular.

Machines provide good examples of two concepts that are central to functionalism: the concept that mental states are interdefined and the concept that they can be realized by many systems. [The tables below contrast] a behavioristic Coke machine with a mentalistic one. Both machines dispense a Coke for 10 cents. (The price has not been affected by inflation.)

stays in *S1*. *S2* is the state a machine is in if, and only if, (1) given a nickel, it dispenses a Coke and proceeds to *S1*, and (2) given a dime, it dispenses a Coke and a nickel and proceeds to *S1*. What *S1* and *S2* jointly amount to is the machine's dispensing a Coke if it is given a dime, dispensing a Coke and a nickel if it is given a dime and a nickel and waiting to be given a second nickel if it has been given a first one.

Since *S1* and *S2* are each defined by hypothetical statements, they can be viewed as dispositions. Nevertheless, they are not behavioral dispositions because the consequences an input has for a machine in *S1* or *S2* are not specified solely in terms of the output of the machine. Rather, the consequences also involve the machine's internal states.

	State S0
Dime input	Dispenses a Coke.

	State S1	State S2
Nickel input	Gives no output and goes to S2.	Dispenses a Coke and goes to S1.
Dime input	Dispenses a Coke and stays in S1.	Dispenses a Coke and a nickel and goes to S1.

The states of the machines are defined by reference to their causal roles, but only the machine [represented by the table] on the left would satisfy the behaviorist. Its single state (*S0*) is completely specified in terms of stimuli and responses. *S0* is the state a machine is in if, and only if, given a dime as the input, it dispenses a Coke as the output.

The machine [represented by the table] on the right [...] has interdefined states (*S1* and *S2*), which are characteristic of functionalism. *S1* is the state a machine is in if, and only if, (1) given a nickel, it dispenses nothing and proceeds to *S2*, and (2) given a dime, it dispenses a Coke and

Nothing about the way I have described the behavioristic and mentalistic Coke machines puts constraints on what they could be made of. Any system whose states bore the proper relations to inputs, outputs and other states could be one of these machines. No doubt it is reasonable to expect such a system to be constructed out of such things as wheels, levers and diodes (token physicalism for Coke machines). Similarly, it is reasonable to expect that our minds may prove to be neurophysiological (token physicalism for human beings).

Nevertheless, the software description of a Coke machine does not logically require wheels, levers and diodes for its concrete realization. By the same token, the software description of the mind does not logically require neurons. As far as functionalism is concerned a Coke machine with states *S1* and *S2* could be made of ectoplasm, if there is such stuff and if its states have the right causal properties. Functionalism allows for the possibility of disembodied Coke machines in exactly the same way and to the same extent that it allows for the possibility of disembodied minds.

To say that *S1* and *S2* are interdefined and realizable by different kinds of hardware is not, of course, to say that a Coke machine has a mind. Although interdefinition and functional specification are typical features of mental states, they are clearly not sufficient for mentality. What more is required is a question to which I shall return below.

Some philosophers are suspicious of functionalism because it seems too easy. Since functionalism licenses the individuation of states by reference to their causal role, it appears to allow a trivial explanation of any observed event *E*, that is, it appears to postulate an *E*-causer. For example, what makes the valves in a machine open? Why, the operation of a valve opener. And what is a valve opener? Why, anything that has the functionally defined property of causing valves to open.

In psychology this kind of question-begging often takes the form of theories that in effect postulate homunculi with the selfsame intellectual capacities the theorist set out to explain. Such is the case when visual perception is explained by simply postulating psychological mechanisms that process visual information. The behaviorist has often charged the mentalist, sometimes justifiably, of mongering this kind of question-begging pseudo explanation. The charge will have to be met if functionally defined mental states are to have a serious role in psychological theories.

The burden of the accusation is not untruth but triviality. There can be no doubt that it is a valve opener that opens valves, and it is likely that visual perception is mediated by the processing of visual information. The charge is that such putative functional explanations are mere platitudes. The functionalist can meet this objection by allowing functionally defined theoretical constructs only where mechanisms exist that can carry out the function and only where he has some notion of what such mechanisms might be like. One way of imposing this requirement is to identify the mental processes that psychology postulates with the operations of the restricted class of possible computers called Turing machines.

A Turing machine can be informally characterized as a mechanism with a finite number of program states. The inputs and outputs of the machine are written on a tape that is divided into squares each of which includes a symbol from a finite alphabet. The machine scans the tape one square at a time. It can erase the symbol on a scanned square and print a new one in its place. The machine can execute only the elementary mechanical operations of scanning, erasing, printing, moving the tape, and changing state.

The program states of the Turing machine are defined solely in terms of the input symbols on the tape, the output symbols on the tape, the elementary operations, and the other states of the program. Each program state is therefore functionally defined by the part it plays in the overall operation of the machine. Since the functional role of a state depends on the relation of the state to other states as well as to inputs and outputs, the relational character of the mental is captured by the Turing-machine version of functionalism. Since the definition of a program state never refers to the physical structure of the system running the program, the Turing-machine version of functionalism also captures the idea that the character of a mental state is independent of its physical realization. A human being, a roomful of people, a computer, and a disembodied spirit would all be a Turing machine if they operated according to a Turing-machine program.

The proposal is to restrict the functional definition of psychological states to those that can be expressed in terms of the program states of Turing machines. If this restriction can be enforced, it provides a guarantee that psychological theories will be compatible with the demands of mechanisms. Since Turing machines are very simple devices, they are in principle quite easy to build. Consequently by formulating a psychological explanation as a Turing-machine program the psychologist ensures that the explanation is mechanistic, even though the hardware realizing the mechanism is left open.

There are many kinds of computational mechanisms other than Turing machines, and so the formulation of a functionalist psychological theory in Turing-machine notation provides only a sufficient condition for the theory's being mechanically realizable. What makes the condition interesting, however, is that the simple Turing machine can perform many complex tasks. Although the elementary operations of the Turing machine are restricted, iterations of the operations enable the machine to carry out any well-defined computation on discrete symbols.

An important tendency in the cognitive sciences is to treat the mind chiefly as a device that manipulates symbols. If a mental process can be functionally defined as an operation on symbols, there is a Turing machine capable of carrying out the computation and a variety of mechanisms for realizing the Turing machine. Where the manipulation of symbols is important the Turing machine provides a connection between functional explanation and mechanistic explanation.

The reduction of a psychological theory to a program for a Turing machine is a way of exorcising the homunculi. The reduction ensures that no operations have been postulated except those that could be performed by a familiar mechanism. Of course, the working psychologist usually cannot specify the reduction for each functionally individuated process in every theory he is prepared to take seriously. In practice the argument usually goes in the opposite direction; if the postulation of a mental operation is essential to some cherished psychological explanation, the theorist tends to assume that there must be a program for a Turing machine that will carry out that operation.

The "black boxes" that are common in flow charts drawn by psychologists often serve to indicate postulated mental processes for which Turing reductions are wanting. Even so, the possibility in principle of such reductions serves as a methodological constraint on psychological theorizing by determining what functional definitions are to be allowed and what it would be like to know that everything has been explained that could possibly need explanation.

Such is the origin, the provenance and the promise of contemporary functionalism. How much has it actually paid off? This question is not easy to answer because much of what is now happening in the philosophy of mind and the cognitive sciences is directed at exploring the scope and limits of the functionalist explanations of behavior. I shall, however, give a brief overview.

An obvious objection to functionalism as a theory of the mind is that the functionalist definition is not limited to mental states and processes. Catalysts, Coke machines, valve openers, pencil sharpeners, mousetraps, and ministers of finance are all in one way or another concepts that are functionally defined, but none is a mental concept such as pain, belief, and desire. What, then, characterizes the mental? And can it be captured in a functionalist framework?

The traditional view in the philosophy of mind has it that mental states are distinguished by their having what are called either qualitative content or intentional content. I shall discuss qualitative content first.

It is not easy to say what qualitative content is; indeed, according to some theories, it is not even possible to say what it is because it can be known not by description but only by direct experience. I shall nonetheless attempt to describe it. Try to imagine looking at a blank wall through a red filter. Now change the filter to a green one and leave everything else exactly the way it was. Something about the character of your experience changes when the filter does, and it is this kind of thing that philosophers call qualitative content. I am not entirely comfortable about introducing qualitative content in this way, but it is a subject with which many philosophers are not comfortable.

The reason qualitative content is a problem for functionalism is straightforward. Functionalism is committed to defining mental states in terms of their causes and effects. It seems, however, as if two mental states could have all the same causal relations and yet could differ in their qualitative content. Let me illustrate this with the classic puzzle of the inverted spectrum.

It seems possible to imagine two observers who are alike in all relevant psychological respects except that experiences having the qualitative content of red for one observer would have the qualitative content of green for the other. Nothing about their behavior need reveal the difference because both of them see ripe tomatoes and flaming sunsets as being similar in color and both of them call that color "red." Moreover, the causal connection between their (qualitatively distinct) experiences and their other mental states could also be identical. Perhaps they both think of Little Red Riding Hood when they see ripe tomatoes, feel depressed when they see the color green, and so on. It seems as if anything that could be packed into the notion of the causal role of their experiences could be shared by them, and yet the qualitative content of the experiences could be as different as you like. If this is possible, then the functionalist account does not work for mental states that have qualitative content. If one person is having a green experience while another person is having a red one, then surely they must be in different mental states.

The example of the inverted spectrum is more than a verbal puzzle. Having qualitative content is supposed to be a chief factor in what makes a mental state conscious. Many psychologists who are inclined to accept the functionalist framework are nonetheless worried about the failure of functionalism to reveal much about the nature of consciousness. Functionalists have made a few ingenious attempts to talk themselves and their colleagues out of this worry, but they have not, in my view, done so with much success. (For example, perhaps one is wrong in thinking one can imagine what an inverted spectrum would be like.) As matters stand, the problem of qualitative content poses a serious threat to the assertion that functionalism can provide a general theory of the mental.

Functionalism has fared much better with the intentional content of mental states. Indeed, it is here that the major achievements of recent cognitive science are found. To say that a mental state has intentional content is to say that it has certain semantic properties. For example, for Enrico to believe Galileo was Italian apparently involves a three-way relation between Enrico, a belief and a proposition that is the content of the belief (namely the proposition that Galileo was Italian). In particular it is an essential property of Enrico's belief that it is about Galileo (and not about, say, Newton) and that it is true if, and only if, Galileo was indeed Italian. Philosophers are divided on how these considerations fit together, but it is widely agreed that beliefs involve semantic properties such as expressing a proposition, being true or false and being about one thing rather than another.

It is important to understand the semantic properties of beliefs because theories in the cognitive sciences are largely about the beliefs organisms have. Theories of learning and perception, for example, are chiefly accounts of how the host of beliefs an organism has are determined by the character of its experiences and its genetic endowment. The functionalist account of mental states does not by itself provide the required insights. Mousetraps are functionally defined, yet mousetraps do not express propositions and they are not true or false.

There is at least one kind of thing other than a mental state that has intentional content: a symbol. Like thoughts, symbols seem to be about things. If someone says "Galileo was Italian," his utterance, like Enrico's belief, expresses a proposition about Galileo that is true or false depending on Galileo's homeland. This parallel between the symbolic and the mental underlies the traditional quest for a unified treatment of language and mind. Cognitive science is now trying to provide such a treatment.

The basic concept is simple but striking. Assume that there are such things as mental symbols (mental representations) and that mental symbols have semantic properties. On this view having a belief involves being related to a mental symbol, and the belief inherits its semantic properties from the mental symbol that figures in the relation. Mental processes (thinking, perceiving, learning, and so on) involve causal interactions among relational states such as having a belief. The semantic properties of the words and sentences we utter are in turn inherited from the semantic properties of the mental states that language expresses.

Associating the semantic properties of mental states with those of mental symbols is fully compatible with the computer metaphor, because it is natural to think of the computer as a mechanism that manipulates symbols. A computation is a causal chain of computer states and the links in the chain are operations on semantically interpreted formulas in a machine code. To think of a system (such as the nervous system) as a computer is to raise questions about the nature of the code in which it computes and the semantic properties of the symbols in the code. In fact, the analogy between minds and computers actually implies the postulation of mental symbols. There is no computation without representation.

The representational account of the mind, however, predates considerably the invention of the computing machine. It is a throwback to classical epistemology, which is a tradition that includes philosophers as diverse as John Locke, David Hume, George Berkeley, René Descartes, Immanuel Kant, John Stuart Mill, and William James.

Hume, for one, developed a representational theory of the mind that included five points. First, there exist "Ideas," which are a species of mental symbol. Second, having a belief involves entertaining an Idea. Third, mental processes are causal associations of Ideas. Fourth, Ideas are like pictures. And fifth, Ideas have their semantic properties by virtue of what they resemble: the Idea of John is about John because it looks like him.

Contemporary cognitive psychologists do not accept the details of Hume's theory, although they endorse much of its spirit. Theories of computation provide a far richer account of mental processes than the mere association of Ideas. And only a few psychologists still think that imagery is the chief vehicle of mental representation. Nevertheless, the most significant break with Hume's theory lies in the abandoning of resemblance as an explanation of the semantic properties of mental representations.

Many philosophers, starting with Berkeley, have argued that there is something seriously wrong with the suggestion that the semantic relation between a thought and what the thought is about could be one of resemblance. Consider the thought that John is tall. Clearly the thought is true only of the state of affairs consisting of John's being tall. A theory of the semantic properties of a thought should therefore explain how this particular thought is related to this particular state of affairs. According to the resemblance theory, entertaining the thought involves having a mental image that shows John to be tall. To put it another way, the relation between the thought that John is tall and his being tall is like the relation between a tall man and his portrait.

The difficulty with the resemblance theory is that any portrait showing John to be tall must also show him to be many other things: clothed or naked, lying, standing or sitting, having a head or not having one, and so on. A portrait of a tall man who is sitting down resembles a man's being seated as much as it resembles a man's being tall. On the resemblance theory it is not clear what distinguishes thoughts about John's height from thoughts about his posture.

The resemblance theory turns out to encounter paradoxes at every turn. The possibility of construing beliefs as involving relations to semantically interpreted mental representations clearly depends on having an acceptable account of where the semantic properties of the mental representations come from. If resemblance will not provide this account, what will?

The current idea is that the semantic properties of a mental representation are determined by aspects of its functional role. In other words, a sufficient condition for having semantic properties can be specified in causal terms. This is the connection between functionalism and the representational theory of the mind. Modern cognitive psychology rests largely on the hope that these two doctrines can be made to support each other.

No philosopher is now prepared to say exactly how the functional role of a mental representation determines its semantic properties. Nevertheless, the functionalist recognizes three types of causal relation among psychological states involving mental representations, and they might serve to fix the semantic properties of mental representations. The three types are causal relations among mental states and stimuli, mental states and responses, and some mental states and other ones.

Consider the belief that John is tall. Presumably the following facts, which correspond respectively to the three types of causal relation, are relevant to determining the semantic properties of the mental representation involved in the belief. First, the belief is a normal effect of certain stimulations, such as seeing John in circumstances that reveal his height. Second, the belief is the normal cause of certain behavioral effects, such as uttering "John is tall." Third, the belief is a normal cause of certain other beliefs and a normal effect of certain other beliefs. For example, anyone who believes John is tall is very likely also to believe someone is tall. Having the first belief is normally causally sufficient for having the second belief. And anyone who believes everyone in the room is tall and also believes John is in the room will very likely believe John is tall. The third belief is a normal effect of the first two. In short, the functionalist maintains that the proposition expressed by a given mental representation depends on the causal properties of the mental states in which that mental representation figures.

The concept that the semantic properties of mental representations are determined by aspects of their functional role is at the center of current work in the cognitive sciences. Nevertheless, the concept may not be true. Many philosophers who are unsympathetic to the cognitive turn in modern psychology doubt its truth, and many psychologists would probably reject it in the bald and unelaborated way that I have sketched it. Yet even in its skeletal form, there is this much to be said in its favor: It legitimizes the notion of mental representation, which has become increasingly important to theorizing in every branch of the cognitive sciences. Recent advances in formulating and testing hypotheses about the character of mental representations in fields ranging from phonet-

ics to computer vision suggest that the concept of mental representation is fundamental to empirical theories of the mind.

The behaviorist has rejected the appeal to mental representation because it runs counter to his view of the explanatory mechanisms that can figure in psychological theories. Nevertheless, the science of mental representation is now flourishing. The history of science reveals that when a successful theory comes into conflict with a methodological scruple, it is generally the scruple that gives way. Accordingly the functionalist has relaxed the behaviorist constraints on psychological explanations. There is probably no better way to decide what is methodologically permissible in science than by investigating what successful science requires.

NED BLOCK

Selections from "Troubles with Functionalism"

[…]

Homunculi-Headed Robots

In this section I shall describe a class of devices that are prima facie embarrassments for all versions of functionalism in that they indicate functionalism is guilty of liberalism—classifying systems that lack mentality as having mentality. Consider the simple version of machine functionalism already described. It says that each system having mental states is described by at least one Turing-machine table of a certain kind, and each mental state of the system is identical to one of the machine-table states specified by the machine table. I shall consider inputs and outputs to be specified by descrip-

tions of neural impulses in sense organs and motor-output neurons. […]

Imagine a body externally like a human body, say yours, but internally quite different. The neurons from sensory organs are connected to a bank of lights in a hollow cavity in the head. A set of buttons connects to the motor-output neurons. Inside the cavity resides a group of little men. Each has a very simple task: to implement a "square" of an adequate machine table that describes you. On one wall is a bulletin board on which is posted a state card; that is, a card that bears a symbol designating one of the states specified in the machine table. Here is what the little men do: Suppose the posted card has a 'G' on it. This alerts the little men who implement G squares—'G-men' they call themselves. Suppose the light representing input I_{17} goes on. One of the G-men has the following as his sole task when the card reads 'G' and the I_{17} light goes on, he presses output button O_{191} and changes the state card to 'M.' This G-man is called upon to exercise his task only rarely. In spite of the low level of intelligence required of each little man, the system as a whole manages to simulate you because the functional organization they have been trained to realize is yours. A Turing machine can be represented as a finite set of quadruples (or quintuples, if the output is divided into two parts): current state, current input; next state, next output. Each little man has the task corresponding to a single quadruple. Through the efforts of the little men, the system realizes the same (reasonably adequate) machine table as you do and is thus functionally equivalent to you.[5]

I shall describe a version of the homunculi-headed simulation, which has more chance of being nomologically possible. How many homunculi are required? Perhaps a billion are enough.

Suppose we convert the government of China to functionalism, and we convince its officials...to realize a human mind for an hour. We provide each of the billion people in China (I chose China because it has a billion inhabitants) with a specially designed two-way radio that connects them in the appropriate way to other persons and to the artificial body mentioned in the previous example. We replace each of the little men with a citizen of China plus his or her radio. Instead of a bulletin board, we arrange to have letters displayed on a series of satellites placed so that they can be seen from anywhere in China.

The system of a billion people communicating with one another plus satellites plays the role of an external "brain" connected to the artificial body by radio. There is nothing absurd about a person being connected to his brain by radio. Perhaps the day will come when our brains will be periodically removed for cleaning and repairs. Imagine that this is done initially by treating neurons attaching the brain to the body with a chemical that allows them to stretch like rubber bands, thereby assuring that no brain-body connections are disrupted. Soon clever businessmen discover that they can attract more customers by replacing the stretched neurons with radio links so that brains can be cleaned without inconveniencing the customer by immobilizing his body.

It is not at all obvious that the China-body system is physically impossible. It could be functionally equivalent to you for a short time, say an hour.

"But," you may object, "how could something be functionally equivalent to me for *an hour*? Doesn't my functional organization determine, say, how I would react to doing nothing for a week but reading the *Reader's Digest*?" Remember that a machine table specifies a set of conditionals of the form: if the machine is in S_i and receives input I_j, it emits output O_k and goes into S_1. These conditionals are to be understood *subjunctively*. What gives a system a functional organization at a time is not just what it *does* at that time, but also the counterfactuals true of it at that time: what it *would* have done (and what its state transitions would have been) had it had a different input or been in a different state. If it is true of a system at time t that it *would* obey a given machine table no matter which of the states it is in and no matter which of the inputs it receives, then the system is described at t by the machine table (and realizes at t the abstract automaton specified by the table), even if it exists for only an instant. For the hour the Chinese system is "on," it *does* have a set of inputs, outputs, and states of which such subjunctive conditionals are true. This is what makes any computer realize the abstract automaton that it realizes.

Of course, there are signals the system would respond to that you would not respond to—for example, massive radio interference or a flood of the Yangtze River. Such events might cause a malfunction, scotching the simulation, just as a bomb in a computer can make it fail to realize the machine table it was built to realize. But just as the computer *without* the bomb *can* realize the machine table, the system consisting of the people and artificial body can realize the machine table so long as there are no catastrophic interferences, such as floods, etc.

"But," someone may object, "there is a difference between a bomb in a computer and a bomb in the Chinese system, for in the case of the latter (unlike the former), inputs as specified in the machine table can be the cause of the malfunction. Unusual neural activity in the sense organs of residents of Chungking Province caused by a bomb or by a flood of the Yangtze can cause the system to go haywire."

Reply: The person who says what system he or she is talking about gets to say what signals count as inputs and outputs. I count as inputs and outputs only neural activity in the artificial body connected by radio to the people of China. Neural signals in the people of Chungking count no more as inputs to this system than input tape jammed by a saboteur between the relay contacts in the innards of a computer counts as an input to the computer.

Of course, the object consisting of the people of China + the artificial body has *other* Turing-machine descriptions under which neural signals in the inhabitants of Chungking *would* count as inputs. Such a new system (that is, the object under such a new Turing-machine description) would not be functionally equivalent to you. Likewise, any commercial computer can be redescribed in a way that allows tape jammed into its innards to count as inputs. In describing an object as a Turing machine, one draws a line between the inside and the outside. (If we count only neural impulses as inputs and outputs, we draw that line inside the body; if we count only peripheral stimulations as inputs, ... we draw that line at the skin.) In describing the Chinese system as a Turing machine, I have drawn the line in such a way that it satisfies a certain type of functional description—one that you *also* satisfy, and one that, according to functionalism, justifies attributions of mentality. Functionalism does not claim that every mental system has a machine table of a sort that justifies attributions of mentality with respect to *every* specification of inputs and outputs, but rather, only with respect to *some* specification.

Objection: The Chinese system would work too slowly. The kind of events and processes with which we normally have contact would pass by far too quickly for the system to detect them. Thus, we would be unable to converse with it, play bridge with it, etc.

Reply: It is hard to see why the system's time scale should matter.... Is it really contradictory or nonsensical to suppose we could meet a race of intelligent beings with whom we could communicate only by devices such as time-lapse photography? When we observe these creatures, they seem almost inanimate. But when we view the time-lapse movies, we see them conversing with one another. Indeed, we find they are saying that the only way they can make any sense of us is by viewing movies greatly slowed down. To take time scale as all important seems crudely behavioristic....

What makes the homunculi-headed system (count the two systems as variants of a single system) just described a prima facie counterexample to (machine) functionalism is that there is prima facie doubt whether it has any mental states at all—especially whether it has what philosophers have variously called "qualitative states," "raw feels," or "immediate phenomenological qualities." (You ask: What is it that philosophers have called qualitative states? I answer, only half in jest: As Louis Armstrong said when asked what jazz is, "If you got to ask, you ain't never gonna get to know."*) In Nagel's terms (1974), there is a prima facie doubt whether there is anything which it is like to be the homunculi-headed system.[6]...

Putnam's Proposal

One way functionalists can try to deal with the problem posed by the homunculi-headed counterexamples is by the ad hoc device of stipulating them away. For example, a functionalist might stipulate that two systems cannot be functionally equivalent if one contains parts with functional organizations characteristic of sentient beings and the other does not. In his article hypothesizing that pain is a functional state, Putnam stipulated that "no organism capable of feeling pain possesses a decomposition into parts which separately possess Descriptions" (as the sort of Turing machine which can be in the functional state Putnam identifies with pain). The purpose of this condition is "to rule out such 'organisms' (if they count as such) as swarms of bees as single pain feelers" (Putnam 1967, pp. 434–35).

One way of filling out Putnam's requirement would be: a pain-feeling organism cannot possess a decomposition into parts *all* of which have a functional organization characteristic of sentient beings. But this would not rule out my homunculi-headed example, since it has nonsentient parts, such as the mechanical body and sense organs. It will not do to go to the opposite extreme and require that *no* proper

parts be sentient. Otherwise pregnant women and people with sentient parasites will fail to count as pain-feeling organisms. What seems to be important to examples like the homunculi-headed simulation I have described is that the sentient beings *play a crucial role* in giving the thing its functional organization. This suggests a version of Putnam's proposal which requires that a pain-feeling organism has a certain functional organization and that it has no parts which (1) themselves possess that sort of functional organization and also (2) play a crucial role in giving the whole system its functional organization.

Although this proposal involves the vague notion "crucial role," it is precise enough for us to see it will not do. Suppose there is a part of the universe that contains matter quite different from ours, matter that is infinitely divisible. In this part of the universe, there are intelligent creatures of many sizes, even humanlike creatures much smaller than our elementary particles. In an intergalactic expedition, these people discover the existence of our type of matter. For reasons known only to them, they decide to devote the next few hundred years to creating out of *their* matter substances with the chemical and physical characteristics (except at the sub-elementary particle level) of *our* elements. They build hordes of space ships of different varieties about the sizes of our electrons, protons, and other elementary particles, and fly the ships in such a way as to mimic the behavior of these elementary particles. The ships also contain generators to produce the type of radiation elementary particles give off. Each ship has a staff of experts on the nature of our elementary particles. They do this so as to produce huge (by our standards) masses of substances with the chemical and physical characteristics of oxygen, carbon, etc. Shortly after they accomplish this, you go off on an expedition to that part of the universe, and discover the "oxygen," "carbon," etc. Unaware of its real nature, you set up

---

* Eds.: This is a misquotation. What Louis Armstrong actually said in reply to the question was "If you still have to ask...shame on you." This has no philosophical implications. With thanks to Robert M. Martin.

a colony, using these "elements" to grow plants for food, provide "air" to breathe, etc. Since one's molecules are constantly being exchanged with the environment, you and other colonizers come (in a period of a few years) to be composed mainly of the "matter" made of the tiny people in space ships. Would you be any less capable of feeling pain, thinking, etc. just because the matter of which you are composed contains (and depends on for its characteristics) beings who themselves have a functional organization characteristic of sentient creatures? I think not. The basic electrochemical mechanisms by which the synapse operates are now fairly well understood. As far as is known, changes that do not affect these electrochemical mechanisms do not affect the operation of the brain, and do not affect mentality. The electrochemical mechanisms in your synapses would be unaffected by the change in your matter.[7]

[…]

Is the Prima Facie Doubt Merely Prima Facie?

The Absent Qualia Argument rested on an appeal to the intuition that the homunculi-headed simulations lacked mentality or at least qualia. I said that this intuition gave rise to prima facie doubt that functionalism is true. But intuitions unsupported by principled argument are hardly to be considered bedrock. Indeed, intuitions incompatible with well-supported theory (such as the pre-Copernican intuition that the earth does not move) thankfully soon disappear. Even fields like linguistics whose data consist mainly in intuitions often reject such intuitions as that the following sentences are ungrammatical (on theoretical grounds):

The horse raced past the barn fell.
The boy the girl the cat bit scratched died.

These sentences are in fact grammatical though hard to process.[8] .

Appeal to intuitions when judging possession of mentality, however, is *especially* suspicious. *No* physical mechanism seems very intuitively plausible as a seat of qualia, least of all a *brain*. Is a hunk of quivering gray stuff more intuitively appropriate as a seat of qualia than a covey of little men? If not, perhaps there is a prima facie doubt about the qualia of brain-headed systems too?

However, there is a very important difference between brain-headed and homunculi-headed systems. Since we know that *we are brain-headed systems*, and that *we* have qualia, we know that brain-headed systems can have qualia. So even though we have no theory of qualia which explains how this is *possible*, we have overwhelming reason to disregard whatever prima facie doubt there is about the qualia of brain-headed systems. Of course, this makes my argument partly *empirical*—it depends on knowledge of what makes us tick. But since this is knowledge we in fact possess, dependence on this knowledge should not be regarded as a defect.[9]

There is another difference between us meat-heads and the homunculi-heads: they are systems designed to mimic us, but we are not designed to mimic anything (here I rely on another empirical fact). This fact forestalls any attempt to argue on the basis of an inference to the best explanation for the qualia of homunculi-heads. The best explanation of the homunculi-heads' screams and winces is not their pains, but that they were designed to mimic our screams and winces.

Some people seem to feel that the complex and subtle behavior of the homunculi-heads (behavior just as complex and subtle—even as "sensitive" to features of the environment, human and nonhuman, as your behavior) is itself sufficient reason to disregard the prima facie doubt that homunculi-heads have qualia. But this is just crude behaviorism....

My case against Functionalism depends on the following principle: if a doctrine has an absurd conclusion which there is no independent reason to believe, and if there is no way of explaining away the absurdity or showing it to be misleading or irrelevant, and if there is no good reason to believe the doctrine that leads to the absurdity in the first place, then don't accept the doctrine. I claim that there is no independent reason to believe in the mentality of the homunculi-head, and I know of no way of explaining away the absurdity of the conclusion that it has mentality (though of course, my argument is vulnerable to the introduction of such an explanation). The issue, then, is whether there is any good reason to believe Functionalism. One argument for Functionalism is that it is the best solution available to the mind-body problem. I think this is a bad form of argument [...]

The only other argument for Functionalism that I know of is that Functional identities can be shown to be true on the basis of analyses of the meanings of mental terminology. According to this argument, Functional identities are to be justified in the way one might try to justify the claim that the state of being a bachelor is identical to the state of being an unmarried man. A similar argument appeals to common-sense platitudes about mental states instead of truths of meaning. Lewis says that functional characterizations of mental states are in the province of "commonsense psychology—folk science, rather than professional science" (Lewis 1972, p. 250). (See also Shoemaker 1975, and Armstrong 1968. Armstrong equivocates on the analyticity issue. See Armstrong 1968, pp. 84–85, and p. 90.) And he goes on to insist that Functional characterizations should "include only platitudes which are common knowledge among us—everyone knows them, everyone knows that everyone else knows

them, and so on" (Lewis 1972, p. 256). I shall talk mainly about the "platitude" version of the argument. The analyticity version is vulnerable to essentially the same considerations, as well as Quinean doubts about analyticity....

I am willing to concede, for the sake of argument, that it is possible to define any given mental state term in terms of platitudes concerning other mental state terms, input terms, and output terms. But this does not commit me to the type of definition of mental terms in which all mental terminology has been eliminated via Ramsification or some other device. It is simply a fallacy to suppose that if each mental term is definable in terms of the others (plus inputs and outputs), then each mental term is definable nonmentalistically. To see this, consider the example given earlier. Indeed, let's simplify matters by ignoring the inputs and outputs. Let's define pain as the cause of worry, and worry as the effect of pain. Even a person so benighted as to accept this needn't accept a definition of pain as *the cause of something*, or a definition of worry as *the effect of something*. Lewis claims that it is analytic that pain is the occupant of a certain causal role. Even if he is right about a causal role, specified in part mentalistically, one cannot conclude that it is analytic that pain is the occupant of any causal role, nonmentalistically specified.

I don't see any decent argument for Functionalism based on platitudes or analyticity. Further, the conception of Functionalism as based on platitudes leads to trouble with cases that platitudes have nothing to say about. Recall the example of brains being removed for cleaning and rejuvenation, the connections between one's brain and one's body being maintained by radio while one goes about one's business. The process takes a few days and when it is completed, the brain is reinserted in the body. Occasionally it may happen that a person's body is destroyed by an accident while the brain is being cleaned and rejuvenated. If hooked up to input sense organs (but not output organs) such a brain would exhibit *none* of the usual platitudinous connections between behavior and clusters of inputs and mental states. If, as seems plausible, such a brain could have almost all the same (narrow) mental states as we have (and since such a state of affairs could become typical), Functionalism is wrong. [...]

Notes

[...]

5. The basic idea for this example derives from Putnam (1967). I am indebted to many conversations with Hartry Field on the topic. Putnam's attempt to defend functionalism from the problem posed by such examples is discussed in the section entitled Putnam's Proposal of this chapter.
6. Shoemaker (1975) argues (in reply to Block and Fodor 1972) that absent qualia are logically impossible; that is, that it is logically impossible that two systems be in the same functional state yet one's state have and the other's state lack qualitative content.
7. Since there is a difference between the role of the little people in producing your functional organization in the situation just described and the role of the homunculi in the homunculi-headed simulations this chapter began with, presumably Putnam's condition could be reformulated to rule out the latter without ruling out the former. But this would be a most ad hoc maneuver.
8. Compare the first sentence with 'The fish eaten in Boston stank.' The reason it is hard to process is that 'raced' is naturally read as active rather than passive. See Fodor et al., 1974, p. 360. For a discussion of why the second sentence is grammatical, see Fodor and Garrett 1967, Bever 1970, and Fodor et al., 1974.

9. We often fail to be able to conceive of how something is possible because we lack the relevant theoretical concepts. For example, before the discovery of the mechanism of genetic duplication, Haldane argued persuasively that no conceivable physical mechanism could do the job. He was right. But instead of urging that scientists should develop ideas that would allow us to conceive of such a physical mechanism, he concluded that a nonphysical mechanism was involved. (I owe the example to Richard Boyd.)

References

Armstrong, D. (1968) *A Materialist Theory of Mind.* London: Routledge & Kegan Paul.

Bever, T. (1970) "The Cognitive Basis for Linguistic Structures," in J.R. Hayes (ed.), *Cognition and the Development of Language.* New York: Wiley.

Block, N. and Fodor, J. (1972) "What Psychological States Are Not," *Philosophical Review* 81, 159–81.

Fodor, J., Bever, T. and Garrett, M. (1974) *The Psychology of Language.* New York: McGraw-Hill.

Fodor, J. and Garrett, M. (1967) "Some Syntactic Determinants of Sentential Complexity," *Perception and Psychophysics* 2, 289–96.

Lewis, D. (1972) "Psychophysical and Theoretical Identifications," *Australasian Journal of Philosophy* 50(3), 249–58.

Nagel, T. (1974) "What Is It Like to Be a Bat?" *Philosophical Review* 83, 435–50.

Putnam, H. (1967) "The Nature of Mental States" (originally published under the title "Psychological Predicates") in *Mind, Language and Reality: Philosophical Papers,* vol. 2. London: Cambridge UP, 1975.

Shoemaker, S. (1975) "Functionalism and Qualia," *Philosophical Studies* 27, 271–315.

Study Questions

1. Armstrong offers this as a criticism of behaviorism: "A man's behaviour constitutes the reason we have for attributing certain mental processes to him, but the behaviour cannot be identified with the mental processes." Do Skinner or Ryle actually hold the position he denies is true? Explain.

2. Armstrong conceives of a mental state as "a state of the person apt for producing certain ranges of behaviour." He thinks this state may very well be a physical state of the central nervous system. Would this sort of description of (for example) feeling angry make the statement identifying this with a particular physical state a necessary truth? That is, would the Armstrong description of that mental state be a rigid or non-rigid designator?

3. Why is accounting for *consciousness* seen (even by Armstrong) to be a main problem for Armstrong's view? How does he attempt this?

4. "Armstrong's view is Ryle's plus Smart's." Explain and defend this statement. Briefly state also how Armstrong's view is different from Ryle's, and how it's different from Smart's.

5. When Fodor describes Radical Behaviorism and Logical Behaviorism, to what extent do his descriptions fit the positions of Skinner and Ryle, respectively? Explain and defend your answer.

6. Fodor says, "Although the [logical behaviorist] offers a construal of mental causation, the construal is Pickwickian." What does 'Pickwickian' mean? What is Fodor's point here?

7. Explain what Fodor calls the "nasty dilemma for the materialist program." Explain why the "distinction between hardware and software" in Functionalism can, in Fodor's view, solve this problem. Explain also how the Coke-machine example also is intended to cope with this problem.

8. Fodor mentions the charge that Functionalism is "question-begging." Explain this; find this charge in Skinner's article, and explain how Skinner puts it.

9. Fodor writes, "The semantic properties of the words and sentences we utter are in turn inherited from the semantic properties of the mental states that language expresses." Contrast this with Wittgenstein's position in his critique of a "private language" in Chapter Seven. What might Fodor say in reply to Wittgenstein?

10. What, exactly, does Block suppose is missing from both robots? Explain what it is, in your own words, as clearly and persuasively as you can.

11. Block argues that there are two differences between us and homunculi-headed robots that make it plausible to think that we have qualia but they don't. What are these differences? Do you think they show what Block says they do? Explain.

Suggested Readings

A very widely cited paper on the functional analysis of mental states is Robert E. Cummins, "Functional Analysis," *Journal of Philosophy* 72 (1975): pp. 741–64.

Another is William G. Lycan, "Form, Function and Feel," *Journal of Philosophy* 78 (1981): pp. 24–50.

Ned Block and Jerry Fodor, "What Psychological States Are Not," *Philosophical Review* 81 (1972): pp. 159–81.

For a discussion of functionalism and consciousness see Robert van Gulick, "A Functionalist Plea for Self-Consciousness," *Philosophical Review* 97 (1988): pp. 149–81.

PART THREE
CONTEMPORARY ISSUES

10

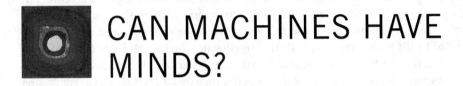

CAN MACHINES HAVE MINDS?

Introduction

In Part Two we surveyed the predominant theories of mind of the past one hundred years. The central feature of these theories has been an adherence to materialism. Since the early twentieth century most philosophers have agreed that mental states and activities are realized in some manner in the physical matter of the body. Over the past few decades debates over the best way to provide a materialist theory of mind have clustered around a particular set of problems, all of which have to do with understanding how a purely material system can exhibit the most common and essential properties of intelligent conscious minds. In Part Three we look at some of the central issues arising in these debates.

In this chapter we look at a question that naturally emerges from materialist theories of mind. If the properties of the mind are the products solely of physical states interacting with one another, is it possible to build an artificial machine that has all of those properties? The advent of electronic computers in the second half of the twentieth century has had a profound effect on this question. Computers are able to carry out many tasks that we perform with our minds: calculating, inferring, analyzing, etc. In fact, the term 'computer' was introduced to indicate a machine that does something people do, namely, compute. Could a computer ever be built whose internal states and processes constitute genuine *thought and intelligence*? Of course, few people believe that any computers that currently exist actually think, but there remains the question whether it is possible in principle to build one that does. Beyond the question whether computers, or any artificial machine, can possess the attributes of thought—and perhaps even of consciousness—there is a further question that will be addressed in this chapter of whether that would give such machines moral rights or status. In so far as machines can be built that possess the same mental capacities as human beings, would they then possess the same moral rights (and responsibilities) as do human beings?

Alan Turing

We will look at the issue of computer intelligence by way of an article by Alan Turing (1912–54), a mathematician and philosopher who was deeply involved in the development of the digital computer in the 1940s and 1950s. In many ways, Turing was the first to clearly articulate the idea of a programmable computer, and it was Turing who first coined the term 'computer' to describe a programmable calculating machine.

Turing's life was one of tremendous achievement, but one that ended tragically. There are few individuals whose lives are more deeply intertwined with the developments of their century. It was in his early years at Cambridge that Turing began to experiment with the ideas that eventually led him to the idea of a programmable calculating machine. Turing's work at Cambridge was interrupted by his involvement with British Intelligence during the Second World War. Turing was chiefly responsible for the invention of a decoding machine that cracked the German secret code known as "Enigma." After the war Turing returned to the development of computing machines, first at the National Physical Laboratory and later at Manchester University. In 1952 he was arrested for homosexual behavior, and the pressure of the trial and the surrounding publicity drove him to suicide two years later.

Can Machines Think?

In his 1950 article, "Computing Machinery and Intelligence," Turing addresses the question, 'Can machines think?' The importance of Turing's article lies less in the answer he gives than in his analysis of what that question means. The aim of Turing's article is to clarify the question by considering (1) what we mean by a *machine*, and (2) how we can determine whether something thinks. In both of these respects, Turing's article has had a huge impact on the subject of machine intelligence. At the outset of the article, Turing argues that we cannot answer these questions by looking at the common uses of the words 'machine' and 'think' because this will yield an answer that simply reflects common prejudice. The first five sections of his article defend specific and controversial answers to both questions.

The "Turing Test"

The first two sections of the article focus on the second question: how can we tell whether something thinks? To answer this question, Turing proposes an "intelligence test" that we could put to a machine. He argues that if the machine passes the test we should conclude that it possesses intelligence. He calls this test the Imitation Game, but it has since become known as the Turing Test.

The **Turing Test** is set up in the following way. In one room we place a machine and a person. In a separate room we place a second person called the "interrogator." Both the machine and the person hidden with it give answers to questions posed by the interrogator. There are no restrictions put on the questions the interrogator can ask, but the machine will be programmed to give answers that resemble as closely as possible those that a human might give. The interrogator is told that one of the two sets of answers comes from a machine and one from a person, but is not told which is which. From the answers to the questions the interrogator is supposed to determine which is the machine and which is the person. The machine has passed if it can fool the interrogator as often as would a human put in its place.

The idea behind the Turing Test is this: If it is impossible to distinguish a machine from a person on the basis of answers to questions put to it, we must conclude that the machine is intelligent.

The Defense of the Turing Test

The Turing Test accepts a certain kind of behavior—answering questions fluently—to be a definite indicator of intelligence. Turing claims that the question 'Can a machine think?' can be *replaced* by the question 'Can a machine pass the test?' This suggests that passing the test is not to be taken as *evidence* of intelligence, but rather as defining what intelligence consists of.

However, in a later section of the paper, entitled "The Argument from Consciousness," Turing gives a clearer indication of how the test should be understood. In that section Turing defends the test from the objection that, although machines may be able to *behave* as if they were intelligent, no machine could ever experience such things as pleasure, grief, or misery. The premise behind this objection is that the only real criterion of intelligence is the subjective experience of consciousness—no behavior, however complex, is constitutive of thought.

Turing's reply to this argument is that behavior is the only criterion *available* for deciding whether something or someone thinks. If we were to insist that behavior can never be a sure sign of intelligence, he says, we would be forced into the view that the only way to be certain that a machine thinks is "to *be* the machine, and to feel oneself thinking." Taken literally, the premise of the argument from consciousness leads us to the conclusion that the only intelligence we can be certain of is our own. For other people's consciousness is hidden from us, and is inferred only from their behavior. This position Turing calls the "solipsist point of view," and adopting the test as an indicator of intelligence, he says, is the only way to avoid being forced into solipsism.

At the end of the section Turing admits that consciousness is a mystery, and he describes his position as entailing only that this mystery need not be solved in order to answer the question whether machines think. Because we already accept behavior as an indicator of intelligence, the Turing Test can be defended on the grounds that it applies the same criterion to machines as we use with other people. So it seems clear that Turing does not intend the test to serve as a *definition* of intelligence, but only as an *empirical criterion*.

What Is a Machine?

In sections 3 through 5, Turing considers the other question in the puzzle over machine intelligence, namely, what is a machine? He argues that we cannot define a machine simply as anything constructed by engineers, for some day in the future it may be possible to produce a living person from a single cell, and this, he says, would not be accepted as a case of constructing a thinking machine, even though it would be an artificial creation.

As with the question 'What is thinking?,' Turing puts the question 'What is a machine?' in terms of conditions on the Turing Test. If the test is accepted as determining whether or not a machine can think, then we have to answer the question, 'What will we allow to take part in the test?' His answer to this question is that the game should be restricted to what he calls **digital**

computers. So the question 'Can machines think?' becomes 'Can digital computers think?' In his defense of this position, Turing addresses two issues: (1) what is a digital computer, and (2) why should such machines be taken as a standard for all machines whatsoever?

He addresses the first of these issues in section 4. Although digital computers are much more familiar now than they were in Turing's day, there is a crucial aspect to Turing's description of digital computers that we should not overlook. Turing describes them in the following way:

> The idea behind digital computers may be explained by saying that these machines are intended to carry out any operations which could be done by a human computer. The human computer is supposed to be following fixed rules; he has no authority to deviate from them in any detail.

So the central idea behind the digital computer, according to Turing, is that of a set of fixed rules that lead to a specific result or accomplish a particular operation if they are strictly adhered to. Nowadays computer programmers refer to such a set of rules as an "algorithm." Let's look briefly at this idea.

Algorithms

An **algorithm** is a set of rules that, if followed precisely, will accomplish a specific task. A computer program is an algorithm, where the rules are the steps written into the program. Each of the steps of a program is an instruction to carry out a mechanical operation in the computer. But when Turing originally devised the idea of an algorithm, he did not restrict the rules to machine instructions. Instead he defined an algorithm in terms of rules that a person can follow to accomplish a task. Understood in these terms, the important feature of an algorithm is that someone can follow the rules, and thus accomplish what the algorithm is designed for, without understanding what it is they are doing or what the purpose of any particular rule is. If an algorithm is properly designed in these terms, it should be possible to replace the person following them with a mechanical device.

In the twenty-first century, with the rapid expansion of technology, the development of algorithms for tasks previously carried out by human beings has become commonplace. As an example, computer engineers have designed artificial systems that might be used by restaurants or doctor's offices to book reservations. One part of the problem has been the mechanical one of constructing a machine that will mimic human conversational speech. But the other part is to work out very precisely the tasks involved—the questions to ask the client, how to understand clients' questions, how to move appointments in emergencies, etc.—in such a way that the instructions can be programmed into a machine. Similar questions arise when designing self-driving or autonomous vehicles. The tasks that such machines can now accomplish are impressive, and this has not been an advancement in mechanical engineering as much as it has been an advancement in algorithms.

Discrete State Machines

According to Turing, then, a digital computer is a machine that operates according to an algorithm. How can computers defined in this manner serve as representatives of all possible machines? Turing addresses this question in section 5. There he claims that digital computers can mimic the behavior of any "discrete state" machine. A **discrete state machine** is one that moves from one definite state to another, and that is in any one of a finite number of states at a given time. For example, compare a digital watch that clicks from one second to the next to an analog watch that moves smoothly in a circle. The importance of discrete state machines is that at any given moment they are in one distinct state or another, and their behavior can be determined from their current state and their current input. The Coke machine that Jerry Fodor describes in "The Mind-Body Problem" is an example of a simple discrete state machine. At any given time it is in either State 1 or State 2, and its behavior given an input of a nickel or a dime is determined by its current state.

We can predict the behavior of a discrete state machine by means of what is called a "machine table." Again, this idea is nicely illustrated by the table that represents the operation of the Coke machine. A **machine table** describes the behavior of the machine in terms of the relations among three sets of components: the input to the machine, a set of internal states, and the output of the machine. In a sense, a machine table is just an algorithm for the machine presented in graphical form. Turing gives an example of such a table in section 5 of his article.

Notice that, as Fodor emphasizes in his article, a machine table says nothing at all about the physical construction of the machine. There are any number of ways of building a mechanism that will conform to the machine table of the Coke machine. We could construct such a machine out of metal, or we could simply give the instructions to a young child who does what the instructions tell her. You can see that the child would not have to be able to add or subtract to follow the instructions, nor even know what it is she is doing. The Coke machine is a very simple example, but for any discrete state machine, no matter how complex, we can draw a machine table like this that will predict its behavior. For example, we could construct such a table for a digital watch, where the input consists of electrical bursts from the battery and the output consists of changes to the numerical display.

Universal Machines

Given that the behavior of a digital machine is entirely predictable from its machine table, Turing argues that its behavior can be mimicked by a computer. He says:

> Given the table corresponding to a discrete state machine it is possible to predict what it will do. There is no reason why this calculation should not be carried out by means of a digital computer. Provided it could be carried out sufficiently quickly the digital computer could mimic the behaviour of any discrete state machine... This special property of digital computers, that they can mimic any discrete state machine, is described by saying that they are *universal* machines.

This property of digital computers, their "universality," is an important mathematical result discovered by Turing in the 1930s. In essence his discovery was that a certain form of digital computer, since known as the "Turing Machine," can be programmed to carry out the operation of any possible discrete state machine.[1] The description of this particular machine in Turing's early papers was a major step in the development of the programmable electronic computer.

The Turing Machine

A **Turing Machine** is a deceptively simple device. It can be understood as an abstract computational device with unlimited storage capacities and no time constraints. As shown in Figure 1, it consists of three components:

1. A tape of indefinite length divided into squares, in each of which is written a single symbol such as a letter or numeral.
2. A read-write head, which can read the symbols written in the squares (i.e., it can tell which one is there), and can write new symbols in their place. The read-write head can also move back and forth along the tape, one square at a time.
3. A set of internal states, which determine what the read-write head will do given the symbol it is currently reading.

The operation of a Turing Machine is as follows. At any given moment the machine is in one state or another and its read-write head is scanning one square that contains a symbol. The operation of the Turing Machine is shown in a machine table, just as in Fodor's Coke machine in Chapter Nine. In place of the "output," the squares of the machine table say what the machine will do next. Given the particular state and the symbol currently scanned, the read-write head will do one of three things:

1. Move one square to the left.
2. Move one square to the right.
3. Replace the current symbol with a new symbol.

After each step, the machine will either change state or remain in its current state, and this is also written into the machine table.

Figure 2 is a representation of a machine that tells whether the number of letters in a word on the tape is even or odd. It begins with the read-write head at the right of the word on the tape, and it moves left along the string, one square at a time. As it encounters each letter it will change back and forth between states 3 and 4. These states "keep track" of whether the number of letters so far is even or odd. When it runs out of letters (i.e., encounters a blank square) it will write 'even' or 'odd' depending on which state it ended in.

Figure 1. The Components of a Turing Machine.

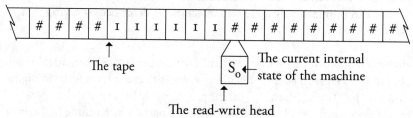

330

Figure 2.

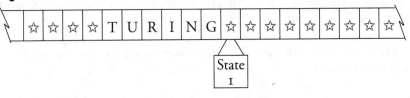

	State 1	State 2	State 3	State 4
A Letter		Found a letter! Write a ☆. Go to state 3.		Found another letter! Write a ☆. Go back to state 1.
A Star	Move one square left. Go to state 2.	No more letters. Write "E" for "Even." Stop.	Move one square left. Go to state 4.	No more letters. Write "O" for "Odd." Stop.

The Universal Turing Machine

Turing showed that a Turing Machine can be constructed that can mimic the behavior of any discrete state machine whatsoever. This means that despite its simple construction, it is capable of operating as well (though not nearly as quickly) as any computer that currently exists, and any computer we might build in the future. How is this possible?

We can program a Turing Machine to mimic another machine by dividing the contents of the tape into two parts: one part of the tape we designate as the "program," and the other we designate as the "working space." The input of the mimicked machine will be the contents of the working space before each operation, and the output will be the contents of the working space after the operation. What output will be produced given a particular input is determined by what is written into the program portion of the tape.

Because of its ability to mimic any discrete state machine, including any other digital computer, Turing's invention is sometimes called a **Universal Turing Machine**, or **UTM**. We can think of the UTM as the most general form of digital computer, and thus the most general form of discrete state machine.[2] This means that we can rephrase the question 'Can machines think?' in the following way: Is it possible for a UTM to pass the Turing Test?

Learning Machines

An important aspect of any discrete state machine, including the UTM, is that its behavior is completely predictable. Given its machine table, its current input, and its current state, we can determine precisely what the device will do at that moment and each succeeding moment. This aspect of discrete state machines is often given as a reason for concluding that such machines could never think. Turing describes this as the "Lady Lovelace Objection" after a remark by Augusta Ada King, Countess of Lovelace, about an early-nineteenth-century computer, Charles Babbage's "Analytical Engine." She said:

> The Analytical Machine has no pretensions to originate anything. It can do whatever we know how to order it to perform.

Real thought, it is argued, can generate original ideas and behavior, and so a digital computer, it seems, could never possess real thought.

Turing's reply to this argument is that we could construct a machine that is programmed to learn. That is, information from previous inputs could be stored on the tape and be used to influence what the machine does in the future. Of course, the "learning" function would have to be built into the program of the machine, so that its behavior is still predictable in principle. But such a function may be so complex that it is impossible in practice to know what the machine will do as it accumulates new information. Its behavior then might be every bit as "unpredictable" as that of a person. In section 7, entitled "Learning Machines," Turing suggests modifying the Turing Test so the machine will mimic the behavior not of an adult but that of a child, including its learning capacities. If the program that governs the machine is sufficiently complex, Turing argues, the behavior of the machine as it learns would be indistinguishable in many ways from that of a growing human being.

Computing with Symbols

The idea of a learning machine raises one final aspect of the operation of digital computers that needs to be mentioned here although it is not a point emphasized by Turing. An essential feature of Turing Machines, which accounts for the flexibility of their behavior, is the tape. The tape is of indefinite length, which means that it is always possible to add new squares in either direction if they are needed. The importance of this is that any amount of new information can be stored on the tape, giving the machine an unlimited degree of flexibility in the sense that there are no bounds on its ability to alter its behavior in light of new information.

The important aspect of the tape is that it contains an indefinitely extendable string of symbols, where each symbol represents a unit of information. This means that the "memory space" of the computer is limited only by the size of the tape and not by the design of the machine itself. The use of symbols in this way was perhaps the major intellectual development in the invention of the digital computer. The flexibility of machines that do not operate on symbols is restricted to the number of distinct internal states in their machine table.[3]

In light of the importance of symbols, we can think of digital computers as defined by two features:

1. Their operation is determined according to an algorithm, and can be represented by a machine table.
2. Their operation consists of reading and writing symbols, displayed in strings of indefinite length.

The first of these two features is what digital computers have in common with all discrete state machines, and the second is what gives them their flexibility of operation and makes them capable of mimicking any other machine. The first feature is what makes them *machines* in Turing's sense, and the second is what people such as Turing believe makes them capable in principle of intelligence.

Problems for Constructing Intelligent Machines

In Chapter Five we looked at Descartes's claim that machines are not capable in principle of imitating human behavior. His argument focused on language use and what we called "behavioral plasticity." The work of Turing and others in this century has shown that Descartes's idea that machines are capable only of reflex action is incorrect. The fact that digital computers can store and read symbols gives them the ability to perform any set of actions for which there can be an algorithm. Researchers in linguistics, such as Noam Chomsky, have shown that many of the patterns of human language use can be modeled in an algorithm and hence are performable by a machine.

However, the project of constructing a machine that will display the same kind of plasticity of behavior that humans are capable of is far from complete. Two problems have motivated much recent work in computer design. One is the "frame problem." This is the problem of writing an algorithm for a task that will anticipate the results of actions carried out, but without having to provide instructions for everything that will *not* result from carrying out an action. The other is a collection of difficulties variously described as "the problem of knowledge access" or "the relevance problem." The core of these problems is that it is very hard, and perhaps impossible, to lay out in advance what information will be relevant to the infinite number of circumstances the machine could find itself in. Humans have an uncanny ability to call up the right information at the right time without having to scan *everything* they know to see whether it *might* be relevant.[4]

Against the Possibility of Intelligent Machines

The frame problem and the knowledge access problem are serious challenges to the project of constructing an intelligent machine. However, as long as work continues, it is difficult to say that there *cannot* be a solution to these problems. In contrast, in the next reading we look at an argument by John Searle that a symbol processing machine, like a Turing Machine, is incapable *in principle* of what we recognize as intelligence. That is, Searle argues that computer intelligence is not merely difficult to achieve, but impossible because of the very nature of computers.

Searle's early influence was in philosophy of language. In the 1960s he helped articulate what is called the speech act theory of language, which is based on the idea that language is best understood by looking at how people use it. Since then Searle's views have expanded into a full theory of mind and language, focusing especially on the nature of consciousness. An excellent introduction to his philosophy of mind can be found in *Mind, a Brief Introduction* of 2004.[5] Searle was Slusser Professor Emeritus of Philosophy at the University of California at Berkeley, but his Emeritus status was revoked in 2019 after it was determined that he violated Berkeley's policies against sexual harassment and retaliation.

Artificial Intelligence

Searle's article is not aimed directly at Turing's article, but at the discipline of **Artificial Intelligence**, or **AI**. Searle distinguishes between two distinct branches of AI, only one of which is the target of his article. "Weak AI" is the use of computers to mimic, or provide a model of, the operation of the mind. There is no assumption here that the computer programs constructed will render the machines intelligent in any real sense. "Strong AI" is the discipline that accepts the validity of the Turing Test, and is busy working on programs that will produce intelligent machines; the assumption of this school, Searle says, is that "the appropriately programmed computer really *is* a mind." Searle's article is an attack on Strong AI. Searle's article relies on a thought experiment involving a "computer" that passes the Turing Test, but which he contends is obviously devoid of any kind of intelligence or understanding.

The "Chinese Room"

At Yale University in the 1970s Roger Schank and his colleagues were working on the design of machines that will understand stories. The criterion of understanding that was used is that the machine must be able to answer questions about the story, using information not directly given but inferred from aspects of the story and other information kept in the memory. This test was a version of the Turing Test, where responding to questions about the story in the right manner is a sign of really understanding the story. So Searle describes an imaginary machine that responds to the questions in just the way the researchers intended, but which he claims clearly has no understanding of the story. This imaginary machine is "the Chinese Room."[6]

The Chinese Room is described as follows. Searle asks us to imagine that he is locked in a room with a large collection of Chinese writing, of which he has no understanding at all. The Chinese writing is in three groups, which (unbeknownst to him) consist of a story, a background script, and a set of questions. Together with these batches of Chinese writing is a set of rules in English. The rules make up an algorithm for correlating the first batch with the second (i.e., the script with the story), for correlating each of those with the third batch (i.e., the questions), and for generating new strings of Chinese characters (the answers) from the third batch. Searle then says:

> Suppose…after a while I got so good at following the instructions for manipulating the Chinese symbols and the programmers got so good at writing the programs that from the external point of view—that is, from the point of view of someone outside the room in which I am locked—my answers…are absolutely indistinguishable from those of native Chinese speakers. Nobody just looking at my answers can tell that I don't speak a word of Chinese.

The important assumption about the situation described is that it satisfies the description of a digital computer outlined above. All that occurs in the room is a sequence of actions performed according to an algorithm, and those actions consist entirely of reading and writing symbols. Searle himself could easily be replaced by a mechanism that operates according to the instructions that he is following. Searle asks two questions about this situation: (1) Does the "machine" have any understanding of the story? (2) Do the program and the operation of the machine shed any light on human understanding? He claims that it is obvious that the answer to (1) is negative, and that if that is the case, the answer to (2) must be negative as well.

The Systems Reply

In the sections that follow, Searle considers several critical replies to the Chinese Room argument. We will look at the first two. The first he calls the "Systems Reply." The objection is that, although the person manipulating the symbols inside the room doesn't understand any Chinese, the symbol-manipulating system *as a whole* does. That is, Searle is looking in the wrong place for understanding; it's not in any component of the computing system, but in the overall operation of the machine. For comparison, while no single *part of you*—in isolation from the rest—understands English, nonetheless *you* do.

Searle's first response is to modify the thought experiment to eliminate the worry: Suppose that the person in the room *is* the entire system. The individual has memorized all the rules and the data banks, and does all the operations in her head. Still that individual does not understand Chinese, and there is nothing else that could be "the system." However, against this first response Searle imagines the critic saying that in such a scenario we need to think of the person in the room in terms of the subsystem that manipulates the Chinese symbols, not in terms of the subsystem that understands English. But to this Searle contends that the subsystem that manipulates the rules is not at all comparable to the system that understands English. The latter, the individual who is consciously following the rules, knows a great deal more than just how to produce the right behavior according to the rules. She also knows that she is answering questions as best she can about a story concerning restaurants—she knows what the symbol manipulation itself is intended to accomplish.

Searle adds that the idea of a "subsystem" that understands Chinese would lead to absurd consequences if we apply it to other subsystems. Any system of the body that carries out a specific task, such as the stomach, can be said to be processing information, and if that is all that is required for understanding, then these systems too possess understanding. But of course we cannot say that the stomach understands digestion.

Perhaps most important, he argues that the subsystem reply points to a problem that underlies the whole Strong AI project. If that project is to succeed, then it must be able to explain the difference between subsystems that are cognitive and those that are not. Otherwise *any* system that can be thought of as having an "input" and an "output" and instantiating a program that mediates between them can be considered as a cognitive system. And he points out that some people do indeed take that attitude. He cites as an example one author who talks about thermostats as having beliefs about temperature on the grounds that its behavior distinguishes temperatures above and below a certain level. But, he says, cognition is not just a certain way of *talking about* a system; it must be something factual and intrinsic about the system itself. It is a matter of fact, he argues, that thermostats and calculators do not have beliefs, but people do. If Strong AI suggests otherwise, then it fails to give us an answer to a fundamental question in cognitive science, i.e., what is it that distinguishes the mind from non-mental systems?

The Robot Reply

The second of the critical replies Searle calls the "Robot Reply." The point of this reply is that the reason the Chinese machine has no understanding of Chinese is that it is not connected in any way to its external environment, except through the Chinese people entering the input and reading the output. The machine, as imagined, does not interact with the world in any direct way. It doesn't move around in the environment, and it doesn't receive sensory input of any kind. Thus the Chinese symbols that the machine manipulates have no meaning derived from the interaction of the machine with the outside world. But suppose we were to modify the story, and imbed such a machine into a robot that interacts with its environment in all the same ways that human beings do. The machine would not *merely* receive symbols as input and send symbols as output, but would actually operate the robot in a way that involves direct causal connections to the outside world. The input strings would be received, say, from a television camera, and the output strings would control the limbs of the robot. Such a robot, so the reply goes, would have genuine understanding.

Searle's first response to this criticism of the Chinese Room is that it concedes an important premise in his own argument, namely, that intelligent understanding is more than just the manipulation of symbols. The machine Searle describes has no understanding because *all* that it does is receive and send symbol strings, and this is insufficient for understanding. In a sense, Searle is pointing out that this reply to his argument concedes that the Turing Test is not a genuine test of intelligence. The machine's ability to send and receive symbol strings in a way indistinguishable from genuine conversation is not a sufficient condition for us to attribute understanding to the machine. We must also add a certain kind of interaction with the environment.

Beyond that, however, Searle contends that, even if we were to embed the symbol manipulating machine into a robot as the reply describes, that still wouldn't be sufficient to give it genuine understanding. His response is to modify his original thought experiment to accommodate the additional abilities of the machine described in the reply. Suppose, he says, that some of the symbols coming to him in his room are sent from a video camera inside a robot, and that some of the symbols strings he outputs control the limbs of the robot. Nothing, he argues, changed the original point that neither he, nor anything else inside the room, has any understanding of what's going on.

Machines Again

In Searle's concluding section he claims that the correct answer to the question "Can machines think?" is obviously "yes" because people are biological machines in some sense. Moreover, he thinks it is clear that people are also computers in the sense that the nervous system carries out many computing operations. What he rejects is the claim that something can think *solely* by virtue of carrying out a computer program.

His claim is that symbols *by themselves* have no meaning; they are not *about* anything. Whatever meaning is carried by the symbols that a computer reads and writes resides solely in the minds of the people who program them and use them. The Chinese symbols in Searle's room carry meaning only because people who understand Chinese attach meaning to them. Without those people the symbols have no content whatsoever. So Searle's position on the Turing Test is that computers may be able to mimic intelligent *behavior*. But as long as they consist entirely of devices that operate on strings of symbols according to an algorithm, they will lack the central feature of the mind, namely, the connection between thoughts and things in the world. What is missing from such computers is the causal power of the brain to generate meaning. The route to understanding the mind, Searle argues, lies in the biological study of that power. Thus he says, "Whatever else intentionality is, it is a biological phenomenon, and it is as likely to be as causally dependent on the specific biochemistry of its origins as lactation, photosynthesis, or any other biological phenomena."

Escaping the Chinese Room

Our last reading in this chapter is a criticism of Searle's argument by Margaret A. Boden, an influential writer on cognition and artificial intelligence.[7] Boden is Research Professor of Cognitive Science at Sussex University in the United Kingdom. Since the early 1970s she has published a large number of books and articles on many different aspects of psychology and cognitive science. In 2016 she published *AI, Its Nature and Future*, a major study of the nature, impact, and significance of AI and robotics.

According to Boden, Searle's argument depends on a common misunderstanding of the nature of a computing machine, one which is drawn from the very abstract way of characterizing computation in terms of the manipulation of symbols. Boden argues that this weakness in Searle's argument becomes clear once we form a correct understanding of the role that symbols play in the operation of the machine.

Intentional and Syntactical Properties

On Boden's analysis of Searle's article, his argument rests on two central claims, one concerning the nature of computational *theories*, and the other concerning the nature of computer *hardware*. Both of these claims, she says, are mistaken. Let's look at what Boden says is Searle's first claim, concerning computational theories. Such theories, she says, commonly rest on the assumption that computers operate on symbols solely in virtue of what she calls their "syntactic properties." The **syntactic properties** (or, as they are sometimes called, the **formal properties**) of a symbol are the physical properties by which the system recognizes it. For example, the shape of the letter 'y' by which we recognize it as a particular letter of the alphabet is a syntactic property. Similarly, the magnetic charge of a symbol in an electronic storage device is also a syntactic property. Recall that in its operation a Turing Machine will read a symbol on the tape and then perform a certain action determined by the symbol read and the current internal state. The assumption of computational theories is that the machine "reads" a symbol only in the sense that it is able to detect its syntactic properties.

The restriction of computer operations to the syntactic properties of symbols ties Searle's argument against artificial intelligence to the issue of intentional properties that Jerry Fodor discusses in his article, "Functionalism." Recall from Chapter Nine that intentional properties are those that involve *meaning* or *semantic content*. Seen in this light, Searle's claim is that, since artificial machines operate solely on the syntactic properties of their symbols, they are incapable of recognizing (or understanding) their intentional or semantic properties. As purely "syntactic engines," computers are incapable of possessing intentional properties except insofar as we, as their programmers, are capable of reading them.

This general argument against artificial intelligence is illustrated in Searle's Chinese Room thought experiment. While Searle in his Chinese Room recognizes the syntactic features of the Chinese symbols he is reading—their *shapes*—he has no idea of their intentional or semantic properties. He has no idea what they *mean*. Only the Chinese people inputting and reading the symbols understand them in the sense of recognizing their intentional or semantic properties. Hence, the machine itself—Searle and the bits of paper he works with—are devoid of intentional properties. It is true that Searle's mental states themselves possess intentional properties, but these have nothing to do with the intentional properties of the Chinese symbols he is manipulating.

Hardware and Biology

Searle's second central claim, according to Boden, contrasts the purely mechanical nature of an artificial computer with the biological nature of living things. According to Searle, the intentional properties of mental states in living things derive from the "causal powers" of certain biological states of the brain. It is because the internal states of computers lack these causal powers that they lack intentional properties. The (non-mental) causal powers that Searle uses to illustrate this idea are the powers of photosynthesis and lactation. These abilities of living organisms rest on the biological nature of the cells of the physical body and the larger functions of the body which these cells generate. Similarly, Searle argues, intentionality rests on certain biological properties of the organisms in which it is found.

Boden addresses her first criticism of Searle's arguments against this second claim. Her point is that Searle's appeal to the biological properties of the brain and the nervous system is misleading. It looks as though Searle is putting forward a positive theory of intentionality, describing how it arises and what its nature is. Yet, according to Boden, Searle in fact offers nothing of the sort. Here she points to Searle's example of the biological power of photosynthesis. We know how photosynthesis is carried out in the plant, in terms of understanding both the products of photosynthesis and the chemical processes by which these products are produced. By contrast, we have no real idea what intentionality is. There are several competing theories of what intentionality is, and we are a long way from an unproblematic understanding of it. Second, we have no idea how neuroproteins in the structure of neurons generate intentionality. So Searle really has no basis for the claim that intentionality derives from the biochemical substrate of the brain.

A second point she makes is that, to the extent that we do have an idea how neural processes might generate intentionality, it seems that this ability rests on the capacity for neural structures to carry *information*. For example, the chemical functions of neural cell membranes (so-called sodium pumps) enable the transmission of information along the axon of the cell. Similarly, the neurochemical functioning of vision cells enables them to detect so-called intensity gradients in the retinal image, which are used by the vision system to detect edges in physical surfaces. Boden's point is that, while it is good to know how these activities are carried out biologically, the psychologist is interested only in the information-carrying capacities of these activities, not their biochemical nature. Boden argues that we know that certain artificial computer systems are able to carry out precisely these same kinds of information-processing tasks. As an example, she cites the studies of the processing of visual information, especially from the 2-dimensional retinal image to the 3-dimensional representation of objects.[8] While it may turn out that only biological organisms can process all of the information in vision, we have no reason at present to think this is true.

Boden's final point on this echoes a claim that Fodor made in his discussion of intentionality in "The Mind-Body Problem." At present *no* physical substrate, whether mechanical or biological, seems to be plausible as a possible physical base for intentionality. This is because we have, at present, so little understanding of how intentionality is possible at all. So, given our present level of understanding, Searle's assertion that intentionality can only be realized in a biological organism is premature.

The Robot Reply Again[9]

Boden turns next to a criticism of what she calls Searle's negative claim: that computational theories, which assume that computers operate solely on the syntactic properties of symbols, cannot explain the intentional properties of symbolic representations. Her first target is Searle's response to the Robot reply, which we reviewed above. Boden's argument here is that Searle is confusing two kinds of intentionality. The first is what Boden calls "full-blooded" intentionality, which is the kind that Searle's article is concerned with. This includes examples such as *seeing beansprouts*, or *understanding English*. Boden argues that computational psychologists do not attribute this kind of intentionality to internal states of the brain, or even to the brain itself. These kinds of intentional states, which make sensorimotor capabilities and beliefs and desires possible, are ascribed to the person as a whole. So Searle's claim that the Chinese Room, carrying out the computational processes of the brain does not possess full-blooded intentionality is not something that computational psychologists would deny.[10] Boden argues, however, that more specific processes of the mind, of the kind modeled by computational theories, possess a lower level of intentionality. Here she has in mind processes such as language parsing (breaking a sentence or phrase into its component parts), and the processing of visual information such as edges and 3-dimensional depth. These processes, she argues, are relatively "stupid." A language parser does not understand English, nor does an edge detector see beansprouts. Yet computational psychologists attribute to these processes a kind of limited intentionality. The very lowest level of information processing—edge detection, and neuronal inhibition, for example—can be fully understood in purely biochemical terms. Yet even here we can attribute a very low degree of intentionality. The states these processes generate are, in a certain way, *about* edges and other aspects of the stimulus.

Boden brings in a second reply to Searle's argument, which she calls the "English reply," to buttress her argument. This reply claims that, although the Searle-in-the-room cannot understand Chinese, he does have to understand enough English to follow the instructions. Thus there is in fact intentionality present in the Chinese Room, even if it is not an understanding of Chinese. She admits that this goes against Searle's basic premise: that computers operate on purely syntactic properties. But if we do not admit this assumption, then the English reply "may be relevant after all." So the English reply suggests that we need to examine closely the basis for Searle's basic premise.

Boden's argument here addresses the character of computer programs: the set of symbol strings that the computer must read. The point that Searle's basic premise overlooks, she argues, is that while a computer program can be understood in purely syntactic terms (what she calls an "uninterpreted logical calculus"), in fact it is also a set of instructions for the machine to do things. In order for the machine to carry out the program it must be engineered in such a way that the lowest-level machine code causes it to perform certain operations. Hence, she argues, a *programming language* (the set of symbol strings that a computer reads) is not merely a means of representing things (insofar as the symbol strings correspond to, or are "mapped onto") things in the world, but also a means of "representational activity." By this she means that the strings of symbols that a computer reads are representations partially in virtue of the fact that they cause the computer to do certain things.

At this point Boden appeals to the work of Brian Cantwell Smith, currently a professor at The University of Toronto.[11] The arguments here are very technical, so we will try to outline only the principal points. Traditionally, computer scientists have distinguished between two kinds of computer languages: a "representational language," by which the computer represents things (for example, by which the symbols in a computer can represent the number of cars in a parking lot), and a "procedural language," by which the computer is instructed what to do with the strings of symbols in the representational language. Yet Smith argues that this distinction is not absolute or essential. He claims that the distinction should be broken down, and a single, unified language be developed to cover both functions of computer languages.

The point that Boden wants to make here is that, given the somewhat artificial distinction between representational and procedural languages, it should be clear that computers cannot be thought of merely as devices that move around meaningless symbols, but as fundamentally engaged in doing specific things with them. This procedural aspect of computer languages, she argues, gives computer programs a "toe-hold in semantics" in virtue of the causal powers of the computer. Here Boden's point is another one Fodor makes in "The Mind-Body Problem." One promising way of explaining intentional properties of mental states is in terms of the relations of cause and effect between them. A desire for ice cream together with a belief that there is ice cream in the fridge will generally cause an intent to open the fridge. It is these relations of cause and effect that Boden claims the procedural aspects of computer programs make possible. The pro-cedural properties of computer programs determine how representational states of the machine interact with one another. Hence, the distinction between syntactical and semantic properties that Searle relies on cannot be properly drawn. The operations on symbol strings that computers carry out not only reflect their syntactic properties, but also reflect certain low-level intentional properties in virtue of the relations of cause and effect between them. The English reply above reflects this point in that it indicates that a certain kind of intentionality is required in order to be able to carry out the instructions contained in the computer program.

Machines and Moral Rights

The arguments from Turing, Searle, and Boden that we have just surveyed concern the possibility that we could develop machines, and specifically symbol-processing computers, that are capable of thought and intelligence of the sort possessed by human beings. This debate has not changed substantially since the 1990s. But in the last few decades computers, robots, and other machines have entered the human world in ways that were previously unimaginable. They now touch almost every facet of our life. While this development has raised important questions concerning human communication and interaction, not all of it has impacted the question of artificial intel-ligence. There is, however, one aspect of the way in which machines have very recently entered the human world that does raise new and serious questions about the future of such machines: Self-guided, "autonomous" robots have been constructed that interact with human beings in increasingly complex ways. This raises a question that is not addressed by the foregoing articles: "Can machines possess the same *moral rights* as human beings?" All the machines we have to date are mechanical devices that we treat in any way we choose, and to which we relate in much the way we do with toasters, vacuum cleaners, and laptops. But already in 1989, an episode of the television series, *Star Trek: The Next Generation*, raised the question whether robots could develop to a point where they must be treated as persons.[12] This has become more than a purely theoretical question, perhaps, since a robot named Sophia was granted citizenship by the Kingdom of Saudi Arabia in October of 2017. Seen from one perspective, this suggests an alternative to the Turing Test. The question, "Can machines think?" might be best answered by the question, "Under what circumstances could machines possess the moral rights of persons?"

This question is directly addressed by Eric Schwitzgebel and Mara Garza, both at the University of California, Riverside. Garza is interested in moral theory and the intersection between it and AI. Schwitzgebel has published primarily in the area of consciousness and introspective self-awareness.[13] Schwitzgebel and Garza offer both a positive argument for the moral rights of **artificial intelligences (AIs)**[14] and replies to several objections. They also put forward two conclusions about the future of morality that are surprising and potentially worrying. In their opinion, we could potentially owe AIs greater moral consideration than we do to human strangers, and the implications of the moral rights of AIs might destabilize ethical theory generally. Schwitzgebel and Garza's article is clearly written and does not contain a lot of technical language, so it is quite readable on its own. We will restrict our introduction to an overview of the structure of the arguments it contains.

Moral Rights and Relevant Differences

The positive argument that Schwitzgebel and Garza offer in section 1 of their article, which they call The No-Relevant-Difference Argument, is based on a general ethical principal that has broad application across the application of moral rights. It says that any differences between the moral consideration we owe to different entities must rest on some relevant difference between them. The term "relevant" here presumably means "morally relevant." The principle, then, is the claim that moral rights cannot be assigned in a morally arbitrary way.[15] As the authors point out, the principal is widely applied in the rejection of differences such as "skin color, ancestry, place of birth, gender, sexual orientation, and wealth" as a basis for moral rights, on the grounds that such differences are not morally relevant. More generally, it is accepted that with respect to fundamental moral rights, there are no relevant differences between any human beings.

It follows from the principal stated in the first premise that any difference in the moral treatment of artificial intelligences (AIs) and human beings must rest on some relevant difference between them. To establish the *possibility* of AI with the same rights as human beings, then it is necessary only to establish the *possibility* of AIs that do not differ from human beings in any way relevant to those rights. We have italicized the word "possible" here to emphasize that Schwitzgebel and Garza want their conclusion to be a fairly weak one. Their second premise says only that "There are possible AIs who do not differ in any such relevant respects from human beings." Despite this, they believe that their conclusion—that there are possible AIs that do not differ in their moral rights from human beings—has very strong implications for ethical theory.

Psychological and Social Properties

Schwitzgebel and Garza take the first premise of The No-Relevant-Difference Argument as not needing defense beyond the fact that its rejection would render the possession of moral rights arbitrary and thus open to chauvinism and bias. The question, they say, is the truth of the second premise: the possibility of AIs that do not differ from human beings in any way that could justify a difference in moral rights. Here the authors rule out one possible basis for denial of moral rights: It cannot be relevant moral status what kind of body one has, or what kind of "underlying architecture." Whether an entity is made of different materials than are human beings, or whether an entity's physical make-up is structured or organized in a different way than it is in humans, are neither of them relevant. Human beings do not possess moral rights because our bodies are composed of carbon-based molecules, nor because our biological organization is cell-based. Interestingly, Schwitzgebel and Garza do not raise the question whether it is relevant whether an entity is, in some relevant sense, a *living* thing.

The next question, then, is what differences do the authors believe *are* relevant? In one paragraph they mention two of the most common philosophical theories of what moral rights are based on: Immanuel Kant's theory, based on a capacity for reason, and utilitarian theories, based on a capacity for pleasure and pain. Opting not to advocate either of these theories, Schwitzgebel and Garza make a more general assertion, which they call the "psycho-social view of moral properties." This is the principle that "[o]nly psychological and social properties are directly relevant to moral status." Applied to the first premise of the No-Relevant-Difference Argument, this yields the claim that any difference in moral rights between two entities must be justified on the basis of some relevant differences in psychological or social properties of the entities. Among psychological properties, the authors include both phenomenal (or phenomenological) and functional properties. The difference between these two kinds of properties will be explained below in Chapters Twelve and Thirteen. Among social properties and relations, they allow *beliefs* about moral status, but not moral status itself, since that would beg the very question at hand.

In the second half of section 2, Schwitzgebel and Garza give something of a defense of the psycho-social view. The arguments here rest largely on the wide-spread acceptance of this view, together with a brisk rejection of teleological and theistic groundings of moral status. In section 3, they point out an advantage to the psycho-social view, namely, that worries about what constitutes an "artificial" entity, to which Alan Turing devotes considerable attention, have no hold on the grounding of morality. If psychological and social properties are all that are considered, then the artificiality question is rendered irrelevant. Whether or not something is or isn't an AI has no bearing on its moral status, just as questions about the material and architectural properties have no such bearing. We might point out, however, that *practical* advantages of a theory might not have any bearing on issues of moral rights, since practicality is not a moral virtue of theories.

Psychological Properties

In section 4, Schwitzgebel and Garza confront an objection to the second premise of the No-Relevant-Differences Argument that is substantial and goes to the heart of the issue of artificial intelligence. The objection stems from the problem of stating precisely what kinds of psychological properties are relevant to the possession of moral rights. For, as the authors acknowledge, there are bound to be many differences between the psychological capacities of machines and of human beings, just as there are between human beings themselves. The question is which such differences are relevant to moral status. Objectors to artificial intelligence have pointed to various kinds of psychological capacities of human beings that they claim are not plausibly properties that AIs are likely to possess, and some of these appear to be essential to the possession of moral rights. These criticisms return the issue of the moral rights of AIs to determining the possibility of genuine artificial intelligence.

Schwitzgebel and Garza introduce three criticisms of the prospects of AI from well-known writings by John Searle, Ada Lovelace, and Roger Penrose, although they do not present the most common interpretations of these criticisms. For example, from Searle they draw the criticism that "artificial entities might necessarily lack consciousness." In "Minds, Brains and Programs," Searle's question is whether the "Chinese Room" *understands* the sentences it gives and receives, and he mentions consciousness only once. In later writings, however, Searle has drawn a connection between understanding and consciousness.[16]

Schwitzgebel and Garza interpret the objection to the possibility of AIs from Ada Lovelace, which was cited by Alan Turing, as one concerning "free will." Yet, as they say, Lovelace does not mention free will explicitly, but rather the ability to "originate anything" other than what "we know how to order it to perform." In endnote 6, however, Schwitzgebel and Garza quote Lovelace as saying that the Analytic Machine is "simply an automaton which acts according to the laws imposed on it." This statement is much closer to the issue philosophers call free will. We will talk more about this issue in later chapters, but we can make a preliminary point here. According to many philosophers, the idea that human beings are capable of acting according to their own free choice is nothing but an illusion, because every event in the world—including every human action—is entirely determined by the laws of nature. Others, who we term *libertarians*, hold that human action is not determined by natural laws, and they claim that this fact is what distinguishes human freedom and morality from the rest of nature. Libertarians, then, would deny that AIs, whose actions are governed entirely by their physical construction, can possess the basic capacity on which morality is founded, namely, freedom of the will. So, whether or not such a position can be attributed to Ada Lovelace, there is a libertarian argument against the possibility of AIs with moral rights.

A third criticism of AI that Schwitzgebel and Garza cite is from the Oxford mathematician, Roger Penrose, in his book, *The Emperor's New Mind*.[17] Penrose's criticism of AI (in Searle's sense) is based on the claim that no purely algorithmic and deterministic system is capable of either consciousness or human understanding. Penrose's argument is based on an interpretation of certain mathematical results, including one of Turing's, that prove important limitations of formal systems. In his criticism of the limitations of algorithmic devices, Penrose is sympathetic to Searle's argument in "Minds, Brains and Programs." Many philosophers have criticized Penrose's argument on the grounds that it mischaracterizes both the nature of consciousness and the mathematical results upon which it is based. Nonetheless, for the purposes of Schwitzgebel and Garza, Penrose's position is congenial to their readings of Searle and Lovelace, in that it attacks the project of constructing deterministic, algorithmic AIs.

Schwitzgebel and Garza do not challenge the claim that consciousness, free will, and what Penrose calls "insight," are necessary for the attribution of moral rights to AIs. Nor do they attempt to refute the criticisms of the traditional AI project from Searle, Lovelace, and Penrose. Rather, they appeal to the modesty of their conclusion, saying that their claim is only that there are *some possible* AIs that possess the necessary psychological properties. They can then allow that Searle's, Lovelace's, and Penrose's skepticisms may well be right that no purely algorithmic device can possess the relevant psychological properties. They place the burden of proof, however, on those who would claim that *no possible* device can be constructed with the required properties. And they cite Searle and Penrose to the effect that it might be possible to construct non-algorithmic devices of the required sort.

Three Objections to the Main Thesis

In sections 5, 6, and 7 of their article, Schwitzgebel and Garza describe and then respond to three possible objections to the attribution of moral rights to AIs. They call these the objections from Duplicability, from Otherness, and from Existential Debt. The first is the objection that, since AIs are artificial, we could potentially build as many perfect duplicates as we desire. Such devices would not have the same moral status as human beings, each of whom is fragile and unique. The Objection from Otherness is that human morality is based on "circles of concern," beginning with family, and then extending to neighbors, fellow citizens, and foreigners, such that our degrees of moral consideration are weaker with each move away from ourselves. Given that AIs are outside of our circles of concern, we owe them no moral consideration. The third objection is that, since AIs are by hypothesis *artificial*, they owe their entire existence to us, and thus we have no obligations to them. The replies that Schwitzgebel and Garza give to these possible objections are clear enough, and so we will leave them to the reader.

Why We Might Owe More to AIs Than to Other People

On the assumption that objections like those in sections 5, 6, and 7 can be satisfactorily met, Schwitzgebel and Garza turn to consideration of the implications that the moral rights of AIs would raise. They believe there are surprising consequences, some of which might be threatening to our commonly-held assumptions about morality.

In section 8 Schwitzgebel and Garza offer two arguments that there are grounds for believing that we would owe *greater* moral consideration to AIs that we create than we do to other people, including our own children. The first argument is based on the assumption that, because AIs are artificial, we would have complete control over the properties that we give them, and over the environments in which we would place them. Our relationship to them would be similar to that between a deity and its creation. It would thus be "morally odious," they argue, to treat decisions about the design of AIs cavalierly. They extend this argument to groups or societies of AIs, such that we would plausibly have an obligation to "ensure happy, flourishing AIs who are not enslaved or abused." This obligation would be all the greater because the AIs would be our creation and, accordingly, our responsibility.

The second argument Schwitzgebel and Garza offer here is based on the idea that, whatever the grounds for moral consideration might be, it is plausible that we could construct AIs that possess more of it than do human beings. First, there is the utilitarian principle to maximize happiness. If one accepts this, then there would be an obligation to "create AIs who experience substantially more joy than the typical human being." This principle is not plausible without qualification, however, because it runs up against the claim that maximizing happiness cannot come at the cost of individual rights. To this they reply that, insofar as we ground our ethics on the creation of happiness and avoidance of pain, we ought at least to give greater moral consideration to AIs who enjoy greater pleasure or experience greater suffering than human beings.

There are those who would argue that the basis of morality is not pleasure or happiness, but the capacity for rationality. Here too we face the consequence that we should give greater moral consideration to AIs with greater rational capabilities. Yet philosophers who base morality on rationality do not attribute degrees of rights based on degrees of rationality; it is, as Schwitzgebel and Garza say, a matter of a threshold: Beings with the capacity for a certain kind of reason are those to whom we owe moral consideration. To this, the authors offer a science fiction scenario involving an AI that can split into multiple rational beings, each of which has the moral rights of an individual. They say, then, that AIs would raise serious issues about individual identity.

The Consequences of Getting It Wrong

On the standard reading of arguments like those of Turing and Searle, the issue concerning AIs is whether they could *in fact* possess intelligence, consciousness, understanding, or other possibly relevant psychological capacities. But Schwitzgebel and Garza make the interesting point that, considered from another angle, the problem is one of *knowing* whether AIs possess these properties. As they point out, this situation is not unique to possible AIs. Already there are difficult questions about the properties of non-human species. At one end of the spectrum is panpsychism, according to which, all things possess consciousness to some degree. At the other is the claim that genuine conscious experience is limited to mature human beings, and even those only in moments of reflection. Presumably, the correct answer lies between these extremes, but exactly where is currently a mystery. This difficulty raises ethical questions, for example, about the treatment of animals.

The most pressing problem arising from this for AI, as Schwitzgebel and Garza see it, is the potential for wrong decisions with catastrophic consequences. If we were to create large numbers of AIs, we face two possible errors: on the one hand relegating conscious, intelligent beings to suffering and slavery, and on the other devoting valuable resources to the treatment of unconscious, unthinking machines. So the problem is not one that we can treat lightly as the science of AIs grows.

Is Ethical Theory Capable of Dealing with AI?

In the final section of their article, Schwitzgebel and Garza make an interesting comparison between ethical theory and physics. This comparison depends on a certain assumption about morality: Moral statements, like those about the physical world, are objectively true or false. That is, Schwitzgebel and Garza are realists about moral values. For example, on their view there is an objective fact of the matter whether or not AIs possess moral rights; it is not merely a matter of opinion or cultural practice. From this assumption, the authors make a claim about our current ethical theories that is similar to what Patricia Churchland has said about "folk physics" and "folk psychology": They are sets of generalizations, which people have developed over time, that work reasonably well in the kinds of situations in which people commonly find themselves. In the case of physics, over the centuries we have replaced our primitive understanding of the natural world with sophisticated scientific theories to accommodate data and solve problems that our folk theories cannot. And Churchland is optimistic that something similar will happen as neuropsychology replaces folk psychology. Schwitzgebel and Garza, however, form a pessimistic hypothesis about the future of ethical theory in the face of the emergence of AIs.

As they observe, we do have sophisticated ethical theories that philosophers have constructed over time to solve moral problems. They cite the utilitarian theory, based on the foundational principle to maximize happiness, and the Kantian theory, based on the principle, "act on that maxim that you can will to be a universal law." But these theories are not comparable to modern theoretical physics, because there are no constraints on the testing of such theories beyond what the authors call the "intuitive or common-sense or common-ground starting points that are attractive to us because of our cultural and evolutionary history." This contrasts with physics, where the construction and testing of theories is constrained by observable facts about the behavior of physical objects. Similarly, the development theoretical psychology over folk psychology is bound by the behavior of human beings.

As the development of AIs advances, Schwitzgebel and Garza claim, the intuitions and common-sense beliefs of our "folk ethics" will be increasingly challenged by new problems. They speculate that these problems will extend far beyond what those beliefs and intuitions were constructed to handle, arising as they did from our collective history. Perhaps there are ethical truths about AIs that we will not be able to recognize because of our attachment to ways of thinking that functioned well in our primitive past. Our ethical judgments might then "deliver wrong or contradictory or unstable verdicts." Schwitzgebel and Garza offer one consoling suggestion: that our ethical intuitions and reflections will shape a future morality by informing our future judgments. These judgments might ultimately "stabilize" into coherent solutions to our problems. And these solutions might be constrained by a set of "implacable moral facts" sufficient to set boundaries on our moral theories.

AI and Theories of Consciousness and Agency

Schwitzgebel and Garza argue that attributing moral rights to artificial devices rests on the possession of a set of psychological and social attributes. The particular psychological attributes they consider are drawn from John Searle, Ada Lovelace, and Roger Penrose. They offer no defense of these choices, taking them as merely representative examples, since their argument does not hinge on the question of which specific attributes we ultimately determine are definitive of artificial intelligence. However, Schwitzgebel and Garza's argument requires, in part, that we understand the nature of certain psychological properties that we take as central to *human* mentality. Among these are two that have been the subject of considerable research in the past few decades, namely, *consciousness* and *agency*. Tellingly, each of these characteristics is alluded to in the set of objections to the possibility of artificial intelligence to which Alan Turing responds. For the purposes of continuity between this chapter and those that follow, let's dig these characteristics out of the remarks in Turing's descriptions of the objections to artificial intelligence.

One aspect of human mental life that Turing addresses in the objections to his thesis is consciousness. In the quotation from Jefferson that he cites, this includes "thoughts and emotions felt." We don't merely have thoughts and emotions, we consciously experience them. The psychological feature alluded to here is what in previous chapters we have been calling the *phenomenal properties*, or *qualitative content*, of conscious experience. It would seem that the possession of consciousness with these properties is a central psychological feature of human beings. As Thomas Nagel, whom we will read in Chapter Eleven, puts it, if a being is conscious, then there is *something it is like* to be that kind of being. The questions of how best to understand this aspect of consciousness, how far science can get in studying it, and what functions it may serve, are the subject matter of Chapters Eleven and Twelve.

Alan Turing identifies another psychological aspect of human life that has received a lot of attention in the past two decades. In the section of his article entitled "The Argument from Informality of Behavior," he makes the following remark.

> There may however be a certain confusion between "rules of conduct" and "laws of behavior" to cloud the issue. By "rules of conduct" I mean precepts such as "Stop if you see red lights," on which one can act, and of which one can be conscious. By "laws of behavior" I mean laws of nature as applied to a man's body such as "if you pinch him he will squeak."

In this passage, Turing identifies an important distinction between two kinds of behavior. First, it is recognized that the behavior of all objects in the natural world is determined by the laws of nature. But, as Turing observes, human beings also follow what he calls "rules of conduct." What is distinctive about these rules, he says, is that they are ones that guide our acts. And acts are more than just behavior. In his examples, stopping at a red light is an act, whereas squeaking when pinched is not. Similarly, when we say that lightning caused a fire, we do not think of this as an act of the lightning. There are laws of nature that generate a sequence of causes that result in the fire. And a person can cause a fire in a similar fashion, say, in unknowingly tipping over a bucket of hot coals. But there are other cases in which we take a person's behavior to be an action that they have performed. If someone surreptitiously looks about, and when no one is looking strikes a match and throws it into a brush pile, we would say that this was not just a sequence of causes and effects, but an action of that person.

This capacity for action, as opposed to the sequences of cause and effect that characterize the natural world, is another important psychological attribute of human beings. What is it, then, that distinguishes behavior that we would consider as actions? One way that we explain the difference between events that are actions and those that are not is in terms of intentions. The lightning may have caused the fire, but it certainly didn't intend to. Likewise for the person who squeaks when pinched. The person who looked around and threw a match, on the other hand, did intend to start a fire. So it seems that acts are behaviors done with intention. Further, in the previous quotation, Turing describes acts as something of which we can be conscious, and certainly the clearest cases of intentional acts are those of which we are conscious. The links between action, intention, and consciousness are the subject of Chapter Thirteen.

The psychological attributes we have listed so far are all ones that are not only possessed by human beings, but arguably by other forms of animal life as well. Many of the higher species of animals would appear to possess consciousness, both phenomenal consciousness and the capacity for conscious control of action. But there is another element to human action that does not seem to apply to non-human animals: the ability to freely choose what one will do. This is the reason we hold human beings responsible for their behavior, but not other animals. This kind of freedom is alluded to in the section of Turing's article that he calls "Lady Lovelace's Objection." The quotation from Ada Lovelace, recall, was that "The Analytical Engine has no pretensions to originate anything. It can do whatever we know how to order it to perform." Now, one way in which Turing interprets this argument is that machines do not have the capacity to learn new behaviors, and this argument is easily responded to. But the second sentence suggests something else, something that Schwitzgebel and Garza identify as free will. Yet the point is not necessarily that human actions are free from determinism, but rather that, in some sense or other, human beings have the capacity to freely choose their actions, that is, to exercise their own agency. Even if we do not challenge the thesis of determinism, we can ask what it is about human beings that gives them that capacity for freedom and agency. This is one of the questions raised in Chapter Thirteen. Closely related to this capacity, and another important element of human mental life, is our own sense of ourselves as agents: When we act consciously we have an awareness of ourselves as performing the action. As Markus Schlosser puts it, there is a sense that our "movements are our own doing, initiated and guided by us." This too would seem to be a central feature of human mental life.[18] Philosophers refer to this as *agentive self-awareness*, and it too has been the subject of much recent research. The last two articles of Chapter Fourteen look at some of this research.

Notes

1. Recall from the previous chapter the significance that functionalists give to the Turing Machine in ensuring that the functional role of internal states can be mechanically realized.
2. Since Turing published this result, it has been shown that there is a large class of machines and formal systems that have the same computing power as the Turing Machine. This suggests that what Turing and others have discovered is a general class of machines that define the notion of a digital computer.
3. Notice, for example, that the Coke machine has only two states, and the information it can store is limited to whether or not its last input was a nickel, represented by whether it is in state 1 or 2. To increase its capacity, say to handle quarters as well as nickels and dimes, we would have to completely redesign it. By contrast, a digital computer can be built so that these changes can be carried out by inputting a new program.
4. A good, simple description of these problems (although perhaps a bit dated now) is found in John Haugeland, *Artificial Intelligence: The Very Idea* (Cambridge, MA: MIT Press, 1985), chapter 5.
5. *Mind: A Brief Introduction* (Oxford/New York: Oxford University Press, 2004).
6. You may notice the similarity between Searle's imaginary machine here and Ned Block's "homunculi-headed robot" in Chapter Nine. The two thought experiments are directed at very similar intuitions.
7. The criticism of Searle's argument that we are reading here was first published in her *Computer Models of Mind* (Cambridge: Cambridge University Press, 1988), and was subsequently republished in modified form in the book she edited, *The Philosophy of Artificial Intelligence* (Oxford: Oxford University Press, 1996).
8. See, for example, the work of David Marr and his school at MIT, as presented in Marr's book, *Vision: A Computational Investigation into the Human Representation and Processing of Visual Information* (San Francisco: W.H. Freeman, 1982).
9. This section is technically more difficult than the other sections of this chapter.
10. Searle's "Systems Reply" bears some similarity to the point that Boden is making here.
11. *Reflection and Semantics in a Procedural Language* (Cambridge, MA.: MIT PhD dissertation and Technical Report LCS/TR-272, 1982).
12. "The Measure of a Man," first shown on February 13, 1989. An extended version was released by CBS in 2012.
13. His books include *Perplexities of Consciousness* (Cambridge MA: MIT Press, 2011) and, with Russell T. Hurlburt, *Describing Inner Experience? Proponent Meets Skeptic* (Cambridge, MA: MIT Press, 2007).

14. For this article, then, the term "AI" will mean "entities with artificial intelligence" rather than the research project of creating such entities, as Searle uses the term.

15. Schwitzgebel and Garza do not use the term "moral rights" in this premise, and in a footnote they suggest that "moral considerability" is clearer than "moral rights." We will continue to speak of moral rights despite this caution of theirs.

16. For example, in 'The Problem of Consciousness,' in *Consciousness and Language* (Cambridge: Cambridge University Press, 2002), p. 17. Quoted in David Cole, "The Chinese Room Argument," *The Stanford Encyclopedia of Philosophy* (Winter 2015 Edition), Edward N. Zalta (ed.), <https://plato.stanford.edu/archives/win2015/entries/chinese-room/>.

17. Roger Penrose, *The Emperor's New Mind* (Oxford: Oxford University Press, 1989).

18. See Schlosser's article in Chapter Fourteen.

ALAN TURING

"Computing Machinery and Intelligence"

1. The Imitation Game

I propose to consider the question "Can machines think?" This should begin with definitions of the meaning of the terms "machine" and "think." The definitions might be framed so as to reflect so far as possible the normal use of the words, but this attitude is dangerous. If the meaning of the words "machine" and "think" are to be found by examining how they are commonly used it is difficult to escape the conclusion that the meaning and the answer to the question, "Can machines think?" is to be sought in a statistical survey such as a Gallup poll. But this is absurd. Instead of attempting such a definition I shall replace the question by another, which is closely related to it and is expressed in relatively unambiguous words.

The new form of the problem can be described in terms of a game which we call the "imitation game." It is played with three people, a man (A), a woman (B), and an interrogator who may be of either sex. The interrogator stays in a room apart from the other two. The object of the game for the interrogator is to determine which of the other two is the man and which is the woman. He knows them by labels X and Y, and at the end of the game he says either "X is A and Y is B" or "X is B and Y is A." The interrogator is allowed to put questions to A and B thus:

C: Will X please tell me the length of his or her hair?

Now suppose X is actually A, then A must answer. It is A's object in the game to try to cause C to make the wrong identification. His answer might therefore be

"My hair is shingled, and the longest strands are about nine inches long."

In order that tones of voice may not help the interrogator the answers should be written, or better still, typewritten. The ideal arrangement is to have a teleprinter communicating between the two rooms. Alternatively the question and answers can be repeated by an intermediary.

The object of the game for the third player (B) is to help the interrogator. The best strategy for her is probably to give truthful answers. She can add such things as "I am the woman, don't listen to him!" to her answers, but it will avail nothing as the man can make similar remarks.

We now ask the question, "What will happen when a machine takes the part of A in this game?" Will the interrogator decide wrongly as often when the game is played like this as he does when the game is played between a man and a woman? These questions replace our original, "Can machines think?"

2. Critique of the New Problem

As well as asking, "What is the answer to this new form of the question," one may ask, "Is this new question a worthy one to investigate?" This latter question we investigate without further ado, thereby cutting short an infinite regress.

The new problem has the advantage of drawing a fairly sharp line between the physical and the intellectual capacities of a man. No engineer or chemist claims to be able to produce a material which is indistinguishable from the human skin. It is possible that at some time this might be done, but even supposing this invention available we should feel there was little point in trying to make a "thinking machine" more human by dressing it up in such artificial flesh. The form in which we have set the problem reflects this fact in the condition which prevents the interrogator from seeing or touching the other competitors, or hearing their voices. Some other advantages of the proposed criterion may be shown up by specimen questions and answers. Thus:

Q: Please write me a sonnet on the subject of the Forth Bridge.
A: Count me out on this one. I never could write poetry.

Q: Add 34957 to 70764.
A: (Pause about 30 seconds and then give as answer) 105621.
Q: Do you play chess?
A: Yes.
Q: I have K at my K1, and no other pieces. You have only K at K6 and R at R1. It is your move. What do you play?
A: (After a pause of 15 seconds) R-R8 mate.

The question and answer method seems to be suitable for introducing almost any one of the fields of human endeavor that we wish to include. We do not wish to penalize the machine for its inability to shine in beauty competitions, nor to penalize a man for losing in a race against an airplane. The conditions of our game make these disabilities irrelevant. The "witnesses" can brag, if they consider it advisable, as much as they please about their charms, strength or heroism, but the interrogator cannot demand practical demonstrations.

The game may perhaps be criticized on the ground that the odds are weighted too heavily against the machine. If the man were to try and pretend to be the machine he would clearly make a very poor showing. He would be given away at once by slowness and inaccuracy in arithmetic. May not machines carry out something which ought to be described as thinking but which is very different from what a man does? This objection is a very strong one, but at least we can say that if, nevertheless, a machine can be constructed to play the imitation game satisfactorily, we need not be troubled by this objection.

It might be urged that when playing the "imitation game" the best strategy for the machine may possibly be something other than imitation of the behavior of a man. This may be, but I think it is unlikely that there is any great effect of this kind. In any case there is no intention to investigate here the theory of the game, and it will be assumed that the best strategy is to try to provide answers that would naturally be given by a man.

3. The Machines Concerned in the Game

The question which we put in §1 will not be quite definite until we have specified what we mean by the word "machine." It is natural that we should wish to permit every kind of engineering technique to be used in our machines. We also wish to allow the possibility that an engineer or team of engineers may construct a machine which works, but whose manner of operation cannot be satisfactorily described by its constructors because they have applied a method which is largely experimental. Finally, we wish to exclude from the machines men born in the usual manner. It is difficult to frame the definitions so as to satisfy these three conditions. One might for instance insist that the team of engineers should be all of one sex, but this would not really be satisfactory, for it is probably possible to rear a complete individual from a single cell of the skin (say) of a man. To do so would be a feat of biological technique deserving of the very highest praise, but we would not be inclined to regard it as a case of "constructing a thinking machine." This prompts us to abandon the requirement that every kind of technique should be permitted. We are the more ready to do so in view of the fact that the present interest in "thinking machines" has been aroused by a particular kind of machine, usually called an "electronic computer" or "digital computer." Following this suggestion we only permit digital computers to take part in our game.

This restriction appears at first sight to be a very drastic one. I shall attempt to show that it is not so in reality. To do this necessitates a short account of the nature and properties of these computers.

It may also be said that this *identification* of machines with digital computers, like our criterion for "thinking," will only be unsatisfactory if (contrary to my belief), it turns out that digital computers are unable to give a good showing in the game.

There are already a number of digital computers in working order, and it may be asked, "Why not try the experiment straight away? It would be easy to satisfy the conditions of the game. A number of interrogators could be used, and statistics compiled to show how often the right identification was given." The short answer is that we are not asking whether all digital computers would do well in the game nor whether the computers at present available would do well, but whether there are imaginable computers which would do well. But this is only the short answer. We shall see this question in a different light later.

4. Digital Computers

The idea behind digital computers may be explained by saying that these machines are intended to carry out any operations which could be done by a human computer. The human computer is supposed to be following fixed rules; he has no authority to deviate from them in any detail. We may suppose that these rules are supplied in a book, which is altered whenever he is put on to a new job. He has also an unlimited supply of paper on which he does his calculations. He may also do his multiplications and additions on a "desk machine," but this is not important.

If we use the above explanation as a definition we shall be in danger of circularity of argument. We avoid this by giving an outline of the means by which the desired effect is achieved.

A digital computer can usually be regarded as consisting of three parts:

(i) Store.

(ii) Executive unit.

(iii) Control.

The store is a store of information, and corresponds to the human computer's paper, whether this is the paper on which he does his calculations or that on which his book of rules is printed. Insofar as the human computer does calculations in his head a part of the store will correspond to his memory.

The executive unit is the part which carries out the various individual operations involved in a calculation. What these individual operations are will vary from machine to machine. Usually fairly lengthy operations can be done such as "Multiply 3540675445 by 7076345687" but in some machines only very simple ones such as "Write down 0" are possible.

We have mentioned that the "book of rules" supplied to the computer is replaced in the machine by a part of the store. It is then called the "table of instructions." It is the duty of the control to see that these instructions are obeyed correctly and in the right order. The control is so constructed that this necessarily happens.

The information in the store is usually broken up into packets of moderately small size. In one machine, for instance, a packet might consist of ten decimal digits. Numbers are assigned to the parts of the store in which the various packets of information are stored, in some systematic manner. A typical instruction might say—

"Add the number stored in position 6809 to that in 4302 and put the result back into the latter storage position."

Needless to say it would not occur in the machine expressed in English. It would more likely be coded in a form such as 6809430217. Here 17 says which of various possible operations is to be performed on the two numbers. In this case the operation is that described above,

viz. "Add the number..." It will be noticed that the instruction takes up 10 digits and so forms one packet of information, very conveniently. The control will normally take the instructions to be obeyed in the order of the positions in which they are stored, but occasionally an instruction such as "Now obey the instruction stored in position 5606, and continue from there" may be encountered, or again "If position 4505 contains 0 obey next the instruction stored in 6707, otherwise continue straight on."

Instructions of these latter types are very important because they make it possible for a sequence of operations to be repeated over and over again until some condition is fulfilled, but in doing so to obey, not fresh instructions on each repetition, but the same ones over and over again. To take a domestic analogy. Suppose Mother wants Tommy to call at the cobbler's every morning on his way to school to see if her shoes are done; she can ask him afresh every morning. Alternatively she can stick up a notice once and for all in the hall which he will see when he leaves for school and which tells him to call for the shoes, and also to destroy the notice when he comes back if he has the shoes with him.

The reader must accept it as a fact that digital computers can be constructed, and indeed have been constructed, according to the principles we have described, and that they can in fact mimic the actions of a human computer very closely.

The book of rules which we have described our human computer as using is of course a convenient fiction. Actual human computers really remember what they have got to do. If one wants to make a machine mimic the behavior of the human computer in some complex operation one has to ask him how it is done, and then translate the answer into the form of an instruction table. Constructing instruction tables is usually described as "programing." To "program a machine to carry out the operation A" means to put the appropriate instruction table into the machine so that it will do A.

An interesting variant on the idea of a digital computer is a "digital computer with a random element." These have instructions involving the throwing of a die or some equivalent electronic process; one such instruction might for instance be, "Throw the die and put the resulting number into store 1000." Sometimes such a machine is described as having free will (though I would not use this phrase myself). It is not normally possible to determine from observing a machine whether it has a random element, for a similar effect can be produced by such devices as making the choices depend on the digits of the decimal for π.

Most actual digital computers have only a finite store. There is no theoretical difficulty in the idea of a computer with an unlimited store. Of course only a finite part can have been used at any one time. Likewise only a finite amount can have been constructed, but we can imagine more and more being added as required. Such computers have special theoretical interest and will be called infinite capacity computers.

The idea of a digital computer is an old one. Charles Babbage, Lucasian Professor of Mathematics at Cambridge from 1828 to 1839, planned such a machine, called the Analytical Engine, but it was never completed. Although Babbage had all the essential ideas, his machine was not at that time such a very attractive prospect. The speed which would have been available would be definitely faster than a human computer but something like 100 times slower than the Manchester machine, itself one of the slower of the modern machines. The storage was to be purely mechanical, using wheels and cards. The fact that Babbage's Analytical Engine was to be entirely mechanical will help us to rid ourselves of a superstition. Importance is often attached to the fact that modern digital computers are electrical, and that the nervous system also is electrical. Since Babbage's machine was not electrical, and since all digital computers are in a sense equivalent, we see that this use of electricity cannot be of theoretical importance. Of course electricity usually comes in where fast signaling is concerned, so that it is not surprising that we find it in both these connections. In the nervous system chemical phenomena are at least as important as electrical. In certain computers the storage system is mainly acoustic. The feature of using electricity is thus seen to be only a very superficial similarity. If we wish to find such similarities we should look rather for mathematical analogies of function.

5. Universality of Digital Computers

The digital computers considered in the last section may be classified among the "discrete state machines." These are the machines which move by sudden jumps or clicks from one quite definite state to another. These states are sufficiently different for the possibility of confusion between them to be ignored. Strictly speaking there are no such machines. Everything really moves continuously. But there are many kinds of machines which can profitably be *thought of* as being discrete state machines. For instance in considering the switches for a lighting system it is a convenient fiction that each switch must be definitely on or definitely off. There must be intermediate positions, but for most purposes we can forget about them. As an example of a discrete state machine we might consider a wheel which clicks round through 120° once a second, but may be stopped by a lever which can be operated from outside; in addition a lamp is to light in one of the positions of the wheel. This machine could be described abstractly as follows: The internal state of the machine (which is described by the position of the wheel) may be q_1, q_2, or q_3. There is an input signal i_o or i_1 (position of lever). The internal state at any moment is determined by the last state and input signal according to the table

	Last State		
	q_1	q_2	q_3
i_0	q_2	q_3	q_1
i_1	q_1	q_2	q_3

Input

The output signals, the only externally visible indication of the internal state (the light) are described by the table

State	q_1	q_2	q_3
Output	o_0	o_0	o_1

This example is typical of discrete state machines. They can be described by such tables provided they have only a finite number of possible states.

It will seem that given the initial state of the machine and the input signals it is always possible to predict all future states. This is reminiscent of Laplace's view that from the complete state of the universe at one moment of time, as described by the positions and velocities of all particles, it should be possible to predict all future states. The prediction which we are considering is, however, rather nearer to practicability than that considered by Laplace. The system of the "universe as a whole" is such that quite small errors in the initial conditions can have an overwhelming effect at a later time. The displacement of a single electron by a billionth of a centimeter at one moment might make the difference between a man being killed by an avalanche a year later, or escaping. It is an essential property of the mechanical systems which we have called "discrete state machines" that this phenomenon does not occur. Even

when we consider the actual physical machines instead of the idealized machines, reasonably accurate knowledge of the state at one moment yields reasonably accurate knowledge any number of steps later.

As we have mentioned, digital computers fall within the class of discrete state machines. But the number of states of which such a machine is capable is usually enormously large. For instance, the number for the machine now working at Manchester is about $2^{165,000}$, i.e., about $10^{50,000}$. Compare this with our example of the clicking wheel described above, which had three states. It is not difficult to see why the number of states should be so immense. The computer includes a store corresponding to the paper used by a human computer. It must be possible to write into the store any one of the combinations of symbols which might have been written on the paper. For simplicity suppose that only digits from 0 to 9 are used as symbols. Variations in handwriting are ignored. Suppose the computer is allowed 100 sheets of paper each containing 50 lines each with room for 30 digits. Then the number of states is $10^{100 \times 50 \times 30}$, i.e., $10^{150,000}$. This is about the number of states of three Manchester machines put together. The logarithm to the base two of the number of states is usually called the "storage capacity" of the machine. Thus the Manchester machine has a storage capacity of about 165,000 and the wheel machine of our example about 1.6. If two machines are put together their capacities must be added to obtain the capacity of the resultant machine. This leads to the possibility of statements such as "The Manchester machine contains 64 magnetic tracks each with a capacity of 2560, eight electronic tubes with a capacity of 1280. Miscellaneous storage amounts to about 300 making a total of 174,380."

Given the table corresponding to a discrete state machine it is possible to predict what it will do. There is no reason why this calculation should not be carried out by means of a digital computer. Provided it could be carried out sufficiently quickly the digital computer could mimic the behavior of any discrete state machine. The imitation game could then be played with the machine in question (as B) and the mimicking digital computer (as A) and the interrogator would be unable to distinguish them. Of course the digital computer must have an adequate storage capacity as well as working sufficiently fast. Moreover, it must be programed afresh for each new machine which it is desired to mimic. This special property of digital computers, that they can mimic any discrete state machine, is described by saying that they are universal machines. The existence of machines with this property has the important consequence that, considerations of speed apart, it is unnecessary to design various new machines to do various computing processes. They can all be done with one digital computer, suitably programed for each case. It will be seen that as a consequence of this all digital computers are in a sense equivalent.

We may now consider again the point raised at the end of §3. It was suggested tentatively that the question, "Can machines think?" should be replaced by "Are there imaginable digital computers which would do well in the imitation game?" If we wish we can make this superficially more general and ask "Are there discrete state machines which would do well?" But in view of the universality property we see that either of these questions is equivalent to this, "Let us fix our attention on one particular digital computer C. Is it true that by modifying this computer to have an adequate storage, suitably increasing its speed of action, and providing it with an appropriate program, C can be made to play satisfactorily the part of A in the imitation game, the part of B being taken by a man?"

6. Contrary Views on the Main Question

We may now consider the ground to have been cleared and we are ready to proceed to the debate on our question, "Can machines think?" and the variant of it quoted at the end of the last section. We cannot altogether abandon the original form of the problem, for opinions will differ as to the appropriateness of the substitution and we must at least listen to what has to be said in this connection.

It will simplify matters for the reader if I explain first my own beliefs in the matter. Consider first the more accurate form of the question. I believe that in about fifty years' time it will be possible to program computers, with a storage capacity of about 10^9, to make them play the imitation game so well that an average interrogator will not have more than a 70 per cent chance of making the right identification after five minutes of questioning. The original question, "Can machines think?" I believe to be too meaningless to deserve discussion. Nevertheless I believe that at the end of the century the use of words and general educated opinion will have altered so much that one will be able to speak of machines thinking without expecting to be contradicted. I believe further that no useful purpose is served by concealing these beliefs. The popular view that scientists proceed inexorably from well-established fact to well-established fact, never being influenced by any unproved conjecture, is quite mistaken. Provided it is made clear which are proved facts and which are conjectures, no harm can result. Conjectures are of great importance since they suggest useful lines of research.

I now proceed to consider opinions opposed to my own.

[...]

(3) *The Mathematical Objection.* There are a number of results of mathematical logic which can be used to show that there are limitations to the powers of discrete state machines. The best known of these results is known as Gödel's theorem, and shows that in any sufficiently powerful logical system statements can be formulated which can neither be proved nor disproved within the system, unless possibly the system itself is inconsistent. There are other, in some respects similar, results due to Church, Kleene, Rosser, and Turing. The latter result is the most convenient to consider, since it refers directly to machines, whereas the others can only be used in a comparatively indirect argument: for instance if Gödel's theorem is to be used we need in addition to have some means of describing logical systems in terms of machines, and machines in terms of logical systems. The result in question refers to a type of machine which is essentially a digital computer with an infinite capacity. It states that there are certain things that such a machine cannot do. If it is rigged up to give answers to questions as in the imitation game, there will be some questions to which it will either give a wrong answer, or fail to give an answer at all however much time is allowed for a reply. There may, of course, be many such questions, and questions which cannot be answered by one machine may be satisfactorily answered by another. We are of course supposing for the present that the questions are of the kind to which an answer "Yes" or "No" is appropriate, rather than questions such as "What do you think of Picasso?" The questions that we know the machines must fail on are of this type. "Consider the machine specified as follows... Will this machine ever answer 'Yes' to any question?" The dots are to be replaced by a description of some machine in a standard form, which could be something like that used in §5. When the machine described bears a certain comparatively simple relation to

the machine which is under interrogation, it can be shown that the answer is either wrong or not forthcoming. This is the mathematical result: it is argued that it proves a disability of machines to which the human intellect is not subject.

The short answer to this argument is that although it is established that there are limitations to the powers of any particular machine, it has only been stated, without any sort of proof, that no such limitations apply to the human intellect. But I do not think this view can be dismissed quite so lightly. Whenever one of these machines is asked the appropriate critical question, and gives a definite answer, we know that this answer must be wrong, and this gives us a certain feeling of superiority. Is this feeling illusory? It is no doubt quite genuine, but I do not think too much importance should be attached to it. We too often give wrong answers to questions ourselves to be justified in being very pleased at such evidence of fallibility on the part of the machines. Further, our superiority can only be felt on such an occasion in relation to the one machine over which we have scored our petty triumph. There would be no question of triumphing simultaneously over *all* machines. In short, then, there might be men cleverer than any given machine, but then again there might be other machines cleverer again, and so on.

Those who hold to the mathematical argument would, I think, mostly be willing to accept the imitation game as a basis for discussion. Those who believe in the two previous objections would probably not be interested in any criteria.

(4) *The Argument from Consciousness.* This argument is very well expressed in Professor Jefferson's Lister Oration for 1949, from which I quote. "Not until a machine can write a sonnet or compose a concerto because of thoughts and emotions felt, and not by the chance fall of symbols, could we agree that machine equals brain—that is, not only write it but know that it had written it. No mechanism could feel (and not

merely artificially signal, an easy contrivance) pleasure at its successes, grief when its valves fuse, be warmed by flattery, be made miserable by its mistakes, be charmed by sex, be angry or depressed when it cannot get what it wants."

This argument appears to be a denial of the validity of our test. According to the most extreme form of this view the only way by which one could be sure that a machine thinks is to be the machine and to feel oneself thinking. One could then describe these feelings to the world, but of course no one would be justified in taking any notice. Likewise according to this view the only way to know that a man thinks is to be that particular man. It is in fact the solipsist point of view. It may be the most logical view to hold but it makes communication of ideas difficult. A is liable to believe "A thinks but B does not" while B believes "B thinks but A does not." Instead of arguing continually over this point it is usual to have the polite convention that everyone thinks.

I am sure that Professor Jefferson does not wish to adopt the extreme and solipsist point of view. Probably he would be quite willing to accept the imitation game as a test. The game (with the player B omitted) is frequently used in practice under the name of viva voce to discover whether someone really understands something or has "learned it parrot fashion." Let us listen in to a part of such a viva voce:

Interrogator: In the first line of your sonnet which reads "Shall I compare thee to a summer's day," would not "a spring day" do as well or better?
Witness: It wouldn't scan.
Interrogator: How about "a winter's day." That would scan all right.
Witness: Yes, but nobody wants to be compared to a winter's day.
Interrogator: Would you say Mr. Pickwick reminded you of Christmas?

Witness: In a way.
Interrogator: Yet Christmas is a winter's day, and I do not think Mr. Pickwick would mind the comparison.
Witness: I don't think you're serious. By a winter's day one means a typical winter's day, rather than a special one like Christmas.

And so on. What would Professor Jefferson say if the sonnet-writing machine was able to answer like this in the viva voce? I do not know whether he would regard the machine as "merely artificially signaling" these answers, but if the answers were as satisfactory and sustained as in the above passage I do not think he would describe it as "an easy contrivance." This phrase is, I think, intended to cover such devices as the inclusion in the machine of a record of someone reading a sonnet, with appropriate switching to turn it on from time to time.

In short then, I think that most of those who support the argument from consciousness could be persuaded to abandon it rather than be forced into the solipsist position. They will then probably be willing to accept our test.

I do not wish to give the impression that I think there is no mystery about consciousness. There is, for instance, something of a paradox connected with any attempt to localize it. But I do not think these mysteries necessarily need to be solved before we can answer the question with which we are concerned in this paper.

[…]

(6) *Lady Lovelace's Objection.* Our most detailed information of Babbage's Analytical Engine comes from a memoir by Lady Lovelace. In it she states, "The Analytical Engine has no pretensions to *originate* anything. It can do *whatever we know how to order it* to perform"

(her italics). This statement is quoted by Hartree who adds: "This does not imply that it may not be possible to construct electronic equipment which will 'think for itself,' or in which, in biological terms, one could set up a conditioned reflex, which would serve as a basis for 'learning.' Whether this is possible in principle or not is a stimulating and exciting question, suggested by some of these recent developments. But it did not seem that the machines constructed or projected at the time had this property."

I am in thorough agreement with Hartree over this. It will be noticed that he does not assert that the machines in question had not got the property, but rather that the evidence available to Lady Lovelace did not encourage her to believe that they had it. It is quite possible that the machines in question had in a sense got this property. For suppose that some discrete state machine has the property. The Analytical Engine was a universal digital computer, so that, if its storage capacity and speed were adequate, it could by suitable programing be made to mimic the machine in question. Probably this argument did not occur to the Countess or to Babbage. In any case there was no obligation on them to claim all that could be claimed.

This whole question will be considered again under the heading of learning machines.

A variant of Lady Lovelace's objection states that a machine can "never do anything really new." This may be parried for a moment with the saw, "There is nothing new under the sun." Who can be certain that "original work" that he has done was not simply the growth of the seed planted in him by teaching, or the effect of following well-known general principles. A better variant of the objection says that a machine can never "take us by surprise." This statement is a more direct challenge and can be met directly. Machines take me by surprise with great frequency. This is largely because I do not do sufficient calculation to decide what to expect them to do, or rather because, although I do a calculation, I do it in a hurried, slipshod fashion, taking risks. Perhaps I say to myself, "I suppose the voltage here ought to be the same as there: anyway let's assume it is." Naturally I am often wrong, and the result is a surprise for me, for by the time the experiment is done these assumptions have been forgotten. These admissions lay me open to lectures on the subject of my vicious ways, but do not throw any doubt on my credibility when I testify to the surprises I experience.

I do not expect this reply to silence my critic. He will probably say that such surprises are due to some creative mental act on my part, and reflect no credit on the machine. This leads us back to the argument from consciousness, and far from the idea of surprise. It is a line of argument we must consider closed, but it is perhaps worth remarking that the appreciation of something as surprising requires as much of a "creative mental act" whether the surprising event originates from a man, a book, a machine or anything else.

[…]

7. Learning Machines

[…]

The only really satisfactory support that can be given for the view expressed at the beginning of §6, will be that provided by waiting for the end of the century and then doing the experiment described. But what can we say in the meantime? What steps should be taken now if the experiment is to be successful?

As I have explained, the problem is mainly one of programing. Advances in engineering will have to be made too, but it seems unlikely that these will not be adequate for the requirements. Estimates of the storage capacity of the brain vary from 10^{10} to 10^{15} binary digits. I incline to the lower values and believe that only a very small fraction is used for the higher types of thinking. Most of it is probably used for the retention of visual impressions. I should be surprised if more then 10^9 was required for satisfactory playing of the imitation game, at any rate against a blind man. (Note: The capacity of the *Encyclopaedia Britannica*, eleventh edition, is 2×10^9.) A storage capacity of 10^7 would be a very practicable possibility even by present techniques. It is probably not necessary to increase the speed of operations of the machines at all. Parts of modern machines which can be regarded as analogues of nerve cells work about a thousand times faster than the latter. (This should provide a "margin of safety" which could cover losses of speed arising in many ways.) Our problem then is to find out how to program these machines to play the game. At my present rate of working I produce about a thousand digits of program a day, so that about sixty workers, working steadily through the fifty years might accomplish the job, if nothing went into the wastepaper basket. Some more expeditious method seems desirable.

In the process of trying to imitate an adult human mind we are bound to think a good deal about the process which has brought it to the state that it is in. We may notice three components,

(a) The initial state of the mind, say at birth,
(b) The education to which it has been subjected,
(c) Other experience, not to be described as education, to which it has been subjected.

Instead of trying to produce a program to simulate the adult mind, why not rather try to produce one which simulates the child's? If this were then subjected to an appropriate course of education one would obtain the adult brain. Presumably the child-brain is something like a notebook as one buys it from the stationers. Rather little mechanism, and lots of blank sheets. (Mechanism and writing are from our point of view almost synonymous.) Our hope is that there is so little mechanism in the child-brain that something like it can be easily programed. The amount of work in the education we can assume, as a first approximation, to be much the same as for the human child.

We have thus divided our problem into two parts—the child-program and the education process. These two remain very closely connected. We cannot expect to find a good child-machine at the first attempt. One must experiment with teaching one such machine and see how well it learns. One can then try another and see if it is better or worse. There is an obvious connection between this process and evolution, by the identifications

Structure of the child-machine material	= Hereditary
Changes of the child-machine	= Mutations
Natural selection	= Judgment of the experimenter

One may hope, however, that this process will be more expeditious than evolution. The survival of the fittest is a slow method for measuring advantages. The experimenter, by the exercise of intelligence, should be able to speed it up. Equally important is the fact that he is not restricted to random mutations. If he can trace a cause for some weakness he can probably think of the kind of mutation which will improve it.

[...]

We may hope that machines will eventually compete with men in all purely intellectual fields. But which are the best ones to start with? Even this is a difficult decision. Many people think that a very abstract activity, like the playing of chess, would be best. It can also be maintained that it is best to provide the machine with the best sense organs that money can buy, and then teach it to understand and speak English. This process could follow the normal teaching of a child. Things would be pointed out and named, etc. Again I do not know what the right answer is, but I think both approaches should be tried.

We can only see a short distance ahead, but we can see plenty there that needs to be done.

JOHN R. SEARLE

"Minds, Brains and Programs"

What psychological and philosophical significance should we attach to recent efforts at computer simulations of human cognitive capacities? In answering this question, I find it useful to distinguish what I will call "strong" AI from "weak" or "cautious" AI (artificial intelligence). According to weak AI, the principal value of the computer in the study of the mind is that it gives us a very powerful tool. For example, it enables us to formulate and test hypotheses in a more rigorous and precise fashion. But according to strong AI, the computer is not merely a tool in the study of the mind, rather, the appropriately programmed computer really *is* a mind, in the sense that computers given the right programs can be literally said to *understand* and have other cognitive states. In strong AI, because the programmed computer has cognitive states, the programs are not mere tools that enable us to test psychological explanations, rather, the programs are themselves the explanations.

I have no objection to the claims of weak AI, at least as far as this article is concerned. My discussion here will be directed at the claims I have defined as those of strong AI, specifically the claim that the appropriately programmed computer literally has cognitive states and that the programs thereby explain human cognition. When I hereafter refer to AI, I have in mind the strong version, as expressed by these two claims. I will consider the work of Roger Schank and his colleagues at Yale (Schank and Abelson 1977), because I am more familiar with it than I am with any other similar claims, and because it provides a very clear example of the sort of work I wish to examine. But nothing that follows depends upon the details of Schank's programs. The same arguments would apply to Winograd's SHRDLU (Winograd 1973), Weizenbaum's ELIZA (Weizenbaum 1965), and indeed any Turing machine simulation of human mental phenomena.

Very briefly, and leaving out the various details, one can describe Schank's program as follows: The aim of the program is to simulate the human ability to understand stories. It is characteristic of human beings' story-understanding capacity that they can answer questions about the story even though the information that they give was never explicitly stated in the story. Thus, for example, suppose you are given the following story: "A man went into a restaurant and ordered a hamburger. When the hamburger arrived it was burned to a crisp, and the man stormed out of the restaurant angrily, without paying for the burger or leaving a tip." Now, if you are asked "Did the man eat the hamburger?" you will presumably answer, "No, he did not." Similarly, if you are given the following story: "A man went into a restaurant and ordered a hamburger; when the hamburger came he was very pleased with it; and as he left the restaurant he gave the waitress a large tip before paying his bill," and you are asked the question, "Did the man eat the hamburger?" you will presumably answer, "Yes, he ate the hamburger." Now Schank's machines can similarly answer questions about restaurants in this fashion. To do this, they have a "representation" of the sort of information that human beings have about restaurants, which enables them to answer such questions as those above, given these sorts of stories. When the machine is given the story and then asked the question, the machine will print out answers of the sort that we would expect human beings to give if told similar stories. Partisans of strong AI claim that in this question and answer sequence the machine is not only simulating a human ability but also (1) that the machine can literally be said to *understand* the story and provide the answers to questions, and (2) that what the machine and its program do *explains* the human ability to understand the story and answer questions about it.

Both claims seem to me to be totally unsupported by Schank's work, as I will attempt to show in what follows.[1]

One way to test any theory of the mind is to ask oneself what it would be like if my mind actually worked on the principles that the theory says all minds work on. Let us apply this test to the Schank program with the following *Gedankenexperiment*. Suppose that I'm locked in a room and given a large batch of Chinese writing. Suppose furthermore (as is indeed the case) that I know no Chinese, either written or spoken, and that I'm not even confident that I could recognize Chinese writing as Chinese writing distinct from, say, Japanese writing or meaningless squiggles. To me, Chinese writing is just so many meaningless squiggles. Now suppose further that after this first batch of Chinese writing I am given a second batch of Chinese script together with a set of rules for correlating the second batch with the first batch. The rules are in English, and I understand these rules as well as any other native speaker of English. They enable me to correlate one set of formal symbols with another set of formal symbols, and all that "formal" means here is that I can identify the symbols entirely by their shapes. Now suppose also that I am given a third batch of Chinese symbols together with some instructions, again in English, that enable me to correlate elements of this third batch with the first two batches, and these rules instruct me how to give back certain Chinese symbols with certain sorts of shapes in response to certain sorts of shapes given me in the third batch. Unknown to me, the people who are giving me all of these symbols call the first batch a "script," they call the second batch a "story," and they call the third batch "questions." Furthermore, they call the symbols I give them back in response to the third batch "answers to the questions," and the set of rules in English that they gave me, they call the "program." Now just to complicate the story a little, imagine that these people also give me stories in English, which I understand, and they then ask me questions in English about these stories, and I give them back answers in English. Suppose also that after a while I get so good at following the instructions for manipulating the Chinese symbols and the programmers get so good at writing the programs that from the external point of view—that is, from the point of view of somebody outside the room in which I am locked—my answers to the questions are absolutely indistinguishable from those of native Chinese speakers. Nobody just looking at my answers can tell that I don't speak a word of Chinese. Let us also suppose that my answers to the English questions are, as they no doubt would be, indistinguishable from those of other native English speakers, for the simple reason that I am a native English speaker. From the external point of view—from the point of view of someone reading my "answers"—answers to the Chinese questions and the English questions are equally good. But in the Chinese case, unlike the English case, I produce the answers by manipulating uninterpreted formal symbols. As far as the Chinese is concerned, I simply behave like a computer; I perform computational operations on formally specified elements. For the purposes of the Chinese, I am simply an instantiation of the computer program.

Now the claims made by strong AI are that the programmed computer understands the stories and that the program in some sense explains human understanding. But we are now in a position to examine these claims in light of our thought experiment.

1. As regards the first claim, it seems to me quite obvious in the example that I do not understand a word of Chinese stories. I have inputs and outputs that are indistinguishable from those of the native Chinese speaker, and I can have any formal program you like, but I still understand nothing. For the same reasons, Schank's computer understands nothing of any stories, whether in Chinese, English, or whatever, since in the Chinese case the computer is me, and in cases where the computer is not me, the computer has nothing more than I have in the case where I understand nothing.

2. As regards the second claim, that the program explains human understanding, we can see that the computer and its program do not provide sufficient conditions of understanding since the computer and the program are functioning, and there is no understanding. But does it even provide a necessary condition or a significant contribution to understanding? One of the claims made by the supporters of strong AI is that when I understand a story in English, what I am doing is exactly the same—or perhaps more of the same—as what I was doing in manipulating the Chinese symbols. It is simply more formal symbol manipulation that distinguishes the case in English, where I do understand, from the case in Chinese where I don't. I have not demonstrated that this claim is false, but it would certainly appear an incredible claim in the example. Such plausibility as the claim has derives from the supposition that we can construct a program that will have the same inputs and outputs as native speakers, and in addition we assume that speakers have some level of description where they are also instantiations of a program. On the basis of these two assumptions we assume that even if Schank's program isn't the whole story about understanding, it may be part of the story. Well, I suppose that is an empirical possibility, but not the slightest reason has so far been given to believe that it is true, since what is suggested—though certainly not demonstrated—by the example is that the computer program is simply irrelevant to my understanding of the story. In the Chinese case I have everything that artificial intelligence can put into me by way of a program, and I understand nothing; in the English case I understand everything, and there is so far no reason at all to suppose that my understanding has anything to do with computer programs, that is, with computational operations on purely formally specified elements. As long as the program is defined in terms of

computational operations on purely formally defined elements, what the example suggests is that these by themselves have no interesting connection with understanding. They are certainly not sufficient conditions, and not the slightest reason has been given to suppose that they are necessary conditions or even that they make a significant contribution to understanding. Notice that the force of the argument is not simply that different machines can have the same input and output while operating on different formal principles—that is not the point at all. Rather, whatever purely formal principles you put into the computer, they will not be sufficient for understanding, since a human will be able to follow the formal principles without understanding anything. No reason whatever has been offered to suppose that such principles are necessary or even contributory, since no reason has been given to suppose that when I understand English I am operating with any formal program at all.

Well, then, what is it that I have in the case of the English sentences that I do not have in the case of the Chinese sentences? The obvious answer is that I know what the former mean, while I haven't the faintest idea what the latter mean. But in what does this consist and why couldn't we give it to a machine, whatever it is? I will return to this question later, but first I want to continue with the example.

I have had the occasions to present this example to several workers in artificial intelligence, and, interestingly, they do not seem to agree on what the proper reply to it is. I get a surprising variety of replies, and in what follows I will consider the most common of these (specified along with their geographic origins).

But first I want to block some common misunderstandings about "understanding": In many of these discussions one finds a lot of fancy footwork about the word "understanding." My critics point out that there are many different degrees of understanding; that "understanding" is not a simple two-place predicate; that there are even different kinds and levels of understanding, and often the law of excluded middle doesn't even apply in a straightforward way to statements of the form "x understands y"; that in many cases it is a matter for decision and not a simple matter of fact whether x understands y; and so on. To all of these points I want to say: of course, of course. But they have nothing to do with the points at issue. There are clear cases in which "understanding" literally applies and clear cases in which it does not apply; and these two sorts of cases are all I need for this argument.[2] I understand stories in English; to a lesser degree I can understand stories in French; to a still lesser degree, stories in German; and in Chinese, not at all. My car and my adding machine, on the other hand, understand nothing: they are not in that line of business. We often attribute "understanding" and other cognitive predicates by metaphor and analogy to cars, adding machines, and other artifacts, but nothing is proved by such attributions. We say, "The door *knows* when to open because of its photoelectric cell," "The adding machine *knows how* (*understands how*, is *able*) to do addition and subtraction but not division," and "The thermostat *perceives* changes in the temperature." The reason we make these attributions is quite interesting, and it has to do with the fact that in artifacts we extend our own intentionality;[3] our tools are extensions of our purposes, and so we find it natural to make metaphorical attributions of intentionality to them; but I take it no philosophical ice is cut by such examples. The sense in which an automatic door "understands instructions" from its photoelectric cell is not at all the sense in which I understand English. If the sense in which Schank's programmed computers understand stories is supposed to be the metaphorical sense in which the door understands, and not the sense in which I understand English, the issue would not be worth discussing. But Newell and Simon (1963) write that the kind of cognition they claim for computers is exactly the same as for human beings. I like the straightforwardness of this claim, and it is the sort of claim I will be considering. I will argue that in the literal sense the programmed computer understands what the car and the adding machine understand, namely, exactly nothing. The computer understanding is not just (like my understanding of German) partial or incomplete; it is zero.

Now to the replies:

I. The Systems Reply (Berkeley). "While it is true that the individual person who is locked in the room does not understand the story, the fact is that he is merely part of a whole system, and the system does understand the story. The person has a large ledger in front of him in which are written the rules, he has a lot of scratch paper and pencils for doing calculations, he has 'data banks' of sets of Chinese symbols. Now, understanding is not being ascribed to the mere individual; rather it is being ascribed to this whole system of which he is a part."

My response to the systems theory is quite simple: Let the individual internalize all of these elements of the system. He memorizes the rules in the ledger and the data banks of Chinese symbols, and he does all the calculations in his head. The individual then incorporates the entire system. There isn't anything at all to the system that he does not encompass. We can even get rid of the room and suppose he works outdoors. All the same, he understands nothing of the Chinese, and a fortiori neither does the system, because there isn't anything in the system that isn't in him. If he doesn't understand, then there is no way the system could understand because the system is just a part of him.

Actually I feel somewhat embarrassed to give even this answer to the systems theory because the theory seems to me so implausible to start with. The idea is that while a person doesn't understand Chinese, somehow the *conjunction* of that person and bits of paper might understand Chinese. It is not easy for me to imagine how someone who was not in the grip of an ideology would find the idea at all plausible. Still, I think many people who are committed to the ideology of strong AI will in the end be inclined to say something very much like this; so let us pursue it a bit further. According to one version of this view, while the man in the internalized systems example doesn't understand Chinese in the sense that a native Chinese speaker does (because, for example, he doesn't know that the story refers to restaurants and hamburgers, etc.), still "the man as a formal symbol manipulation system" *really does understand Chinese.* The subsystem of the man that is the formal symbol manipulation system for Chinese should not be confused with the subsystem for English.

So there are really two subsystems in the man; one understands English, the other Chinese, and "it's just that the two systems have little to do with each other." But, I want to reply, not only do they have little to do with each other, they are not even remotely alike. The subsystem that understands English (assuming we allow ourselves to talk in this jargon of "subsystems" for a moment) knows that the stories are about restaurants and eating hamburgers, he knows that he is being asked questions about restaurants and that he is answering questions as best he can by making various inferences from the content of the story, and so on. But the Chinese system knows none of this. Whereas the English subsystem knows that "hamburgers" refers to hamburgers, the Chinese subsystem knows only that "squiggle squiggle" is followed by "squoggle squoggle."

All he knows is that various formal symbols are being introduced at one end and manipulated according to rules written in English, and other symbols are going out at the other end. The whole point of the original example was to argue that such symbol manipulation by itself couldn't be sufficient for understanding Chinese in any literal sense because the man could write "squoggle squoggle" after "squiggle squiggle" without understanding anything in Chinese. And it doesn't meet that argument to postulate subsystems within the man, because the subsystems are no better off than the man was in the first place; they still don't have anything even remotely like what the English-speaking man (or subsystem) has. Indeed, in the case as described, the Chinese subsystem is simply a part of the English subsystem, a part that engages in meaningless symbol manipulation according to rules in English.

Let us ask ourselves what is supposed to motivate the systems reply in the first place; that is, what *independent* grounds are there supposed to be for saying that the agent must have a subsystem within him that literally understands stories in Chinese? As far as I can tell the only grounds are that in the example I have the same input and output as native Chinese speakers and a program that goes from one to the other. But the whole point of the examples has been to try to show that that couldn't be sufficient for understanding, in the sense in which I understand stories in English, because a person, and hence the set of systems that go to make up a person, could have the right combination of input, output, and program and still not understand anything in the relevant literal sense in which I understand English. The only motivation for saying there *must* be a subsystem in me that understands Chinese is that I have a program and I can pass the Turing test: I can fool native Chinese speakers. But precisely one of the points at issue is the adequacy of the Turing test. The example shows that there could be two "systems," both of which pass the Turing test, but only one of which understands; and it is no argument against this point to say that since they both pass the Turing test they must both understand, since this claim fails to meet the argument that the system in me that understands English has a great deal more than the system that merely processes Chinese. In short, the systems reply simply begs the question by insisting without argument that the system must understand Chinese.

Furthermore, the systems reply would appear to lead to consequences that are independently absurd. If we are to conclude that there must be cognition in me on the grounds that I have a certain sort of input and output and a program in between, then it looks like all sorts of non-cognitive subsystems are going to turn out to be cognitive. For example, there is a level of description at which my stomach does information processing, and it instantiates any number of computer programs, but I take it we do not want to say that it has any understanding (cf. Pylyshyn 1980). But if we accept the systems reply, then it is hard to see how we avoid saying that stomach, heart, liver, and so on are all understanding subsystems, since there is no principled way to distinguish the motivation for saying the Chinese subsystem understands from saying that the stomach understands. It is, by the way, not an answer to this point to say that the Chinese system has information as input and output and the stomach has food and food products as input and output, since from the point of view of the agent, from my point of view, there is no information in either the food or the Chinese—the Chinese is just so many meaningless squiggles. The information in the Chinese case is solely in the eyes of the programmers and the interpreters, and there is nothing to prevent them from treating the input and output of my digestive organs as information if they so desire.

This last point bears on some independent problems in strong AI, and it is worth digressing for a moment to explain it. If strong AI is to be a branch of psychology, then it must be able to distinguish those systems that are genuinely mental from those that are not. It must be able to distinguish the principles on which the mind works from those on which nonmental systems work; otherwise it will offer us no explanations of what is specifically mental about the mental. And the mental-nonmental distinction cannot be just in the eye of the beholder but it must be intrinsic to the systems; otherwise it would be up to any beholder to treat people as nonmental and, for example, hurricanes as mental if he likes. But quite often in the AI literature the distinction is blurred in ways that would in the long run prove disastrous to the claim that AI is a cognitive inquiry. McCarthy, for example, writes, "Machines as simple as thermostats can be said to have beliefs, and having beliefs seems to be a characteristic of most machines capable of problem solving performance" (McCarthy 1979). Anyone who thinks strong AI has a chance as a theory of the mind ought to ponder the implications of that remark. We are asked to accept it as a discovery of strong AI that the hunk of metal on the wall that we use to regulate the temperature has beliefs in exactly the same sense that we, our spouses, and our children have beliefs, and furthermore that "most" of the other machines in the room—telephone, tape recorder, adding machine, electric light switch—also have beliefs in this literal sense. It is not the aim of this article to argue against McCarthy's point, so I will simply assert the following without argument. The study of the mind starts with such facts as that humans have beliefs, while thermostats, telephones, and adding machines don't. If you get a theory that denies this point you have produced a counterexample to the theory and the theory is false. One gets the impression that people in AI who write this sort of thing think they can get away with it because they don't really take it seriously, and they don't think anyone else will either. I propose, for a moment at least, to take it seriously. Think hard for one minute about what would be necessary to establish that the hunk of metal on the wall over there had real beliefs, beliefs with direction of fit, propositional content, and conditions of satisfaction; beliefs that had the possibility of being strong beliefs or weak beliefs; nervous, anxious, or secure beliefs; dogmatic, rational, or superstitious beliefs; blind faiths or hesitant cogitations; any kind of beliefs. The thermostat is not a candidate. Neither is stomach, liver, adding machine, or telephone. However, since we are taking the idea seriously, notice that its truth would be fatal to strong AI's claim to be a science of the mind. For now the mind is everywhere. What we wanted to know is what distinguishes the mind from thermostats and livers. And if McCarthy were right, strong AI wouldn't have a hope of telling us that.

II. The Robot Reply (Yale). "Suppose we wrote a different kind of program from Schank's program. Suppose we put a computer inside a robot, and this computer would not just take in formal symbols as input and give out formal symbols as output, but rather would actually operate the robot in such a way that the robot does something very much like perceiving, walking, moving about, hammering nails, eating, drinking—anything you like. The robot would, for example, have a television camera attached to it that enabled it to see, it would have arms and legs that enabled it to 'act,' and all of this would be controlled by its computer 'brain.' Such a robot would, unlike Schank's computer, have genuine understanding and other mental states."

The first thing to notice about the robot reply is that it tacitly concedes that cognition is not solely a matter of formal symbol manipulation, since this reply adds a set of causal relations with the outside world (cf. Fodor 1980). But the answer to the robot reply is that the addition of such "perceptual" and "motor" capacities adds nothing by way of understanding, in particular, or intentionality, in general, to Schank's original program. To see this, notice that the same thought experiment applies to the robot case. Suppose that instead of the computer inside the robot, you put me inside the room and, as in the original Chinese case, you give me more Chinese symbols with more instructions in English for matching Chinese symbols to Chinese symbols and feeding back Chinese symbols to the outside. Suppose, unknown to me, some of the Chinese symbols that come to me come from a television camera attached to the robot and other Chinese symbols that I am giving out serve to make the motors inside the robot move the robot's legs or arms. It is important to emphasize that all I am doing is manipulating formal symbols: I know none of these other facts. I am receiving "information" from the robot's "perceptual" apparatus, and I am giving out "instructions" to its motor apparatus without knowing either of these facts. I am the robot's homunculus, but unlike the traditional homunculus, I don't know what's going on. I don't understand anything except the rules for symbol manipulation. Now in this case I want to say that the robot has no intentional states at all; it is simply moving about as a result of its electrical wiring and its program. And furthermore, by instantiating the program I have no intentional states of the relevant type. All I do is follow formal instructions about manipulating formal symbols.

III. The Brain Simulator Reply (Berkeley and MIT). "Suppose we design a program that doesn't represent information that we have about the world, such as the information in Schank's scripts, but simulates the actual sequence of neuron firings at the synapses of the brain of a native Chinese speaker when he understands stories in Chinese and gives answers to them. The machine takes in Chinese stories and questions about them as input, it simulates the formal structure of actual Chinese brains in processing these stories, and it gives out Chinese answers as outputs. We can even imagine that the machine operates, not with a single serial program, but with a whole set of programs operating in parallel, in the manner that actual human brains presumably operate when they process natural language. Now surely in such a case we would have to say that the machine understood the stories; and if we refuse to say that, wouldn't we also have to deny that native Chinese speakers understood the stories? At the level of the synapses, what would or could be different about the program of the computer and the program of the Chinese brain?"

Before countering this reply I want to digress to note that it is an odd reply for any partisan of artificial intelligence (or functionalism, etc.) to make: I thought the whole idea of strong AI is that we don't need to know how the brain works to know how the mind works. The basic hypothesis, or so I had supposed, was that there is a level of mental operations consisting of computational processes over formal elements that constitute the essence of the mental and can be realized in all sorts of different brain processes, in the same way that any computer program can be realized in different computer hardwares: On the assumptions of strong AI, the mind is to the brain as the program is to the hardware, and thus we can understand the mind without doing neurophysiology. If we had to know how the brain worked to do AI, we wouldn't bother with AI. However, even getting this close to the operation of the brain is still not sufficient to produce understanding. To see this, imagine that instead of a monolingual man in a room shuffling symbols we have the man operate an elaborate set of water pipes with valves connecting them. When the man receives the Chinese symbols, he looks up in the program, written in English, which valves he has to turn on and off. Each water connection corresponds to a synapse in the Chinese brain, and the whole system is rigged up so that after doing all the right firings, that is after turning on all the right faucets, the Chinese answers pop out at the output end of the series of pipes.

Now where is the understanding in this system? It takes Chinese as input, it simulates the formal structure of the synapses of the Chinese brain, and it gives Chinese as output. But the man certainly doesn't understand Chinese, and neither do the water pipes, and if we are tempted to adopt what I think is the absurd view that somehow the *conjunction* of man *and* water pipes understands, remember that in principle the man can internalize the formal structure of the water pipes and do all the "neuron firings" in his imagination. The problem with the brain simulator is that it is simulating the wrong things about the brain. As long as it simulates only the formal structure of the sequence of neuron firings at the synapses, it won't have simulated what matters about the brain, namely its causal properties, its ability to produce intentional states. And that the formal properties are not sufficient for the causal properties is shown by the water pipe example: we can have all the formal properties carved off from the relevant neurobiological causal properties.

IV. The Combination Reply (Berkeley and Stanford). "While each of the previous three replies might not be completely convincing by itself as a refutation of the Chinese Room counterexample, if you take all three together they are collectively much more convincing and even decisive. Imagine a robot with a brain-shaped computer lodged in its cranial cavity, imagine the computer programmed with all the synapses of a human brain, imagine the whole behavior of the robot is indistinguishable from human behavior, and now think of the whole thing as a unified system and not just as a computer with inputs and outputs. Surely in such a case we would have to ascribe intentionality to the system."

I entirely agree that in such a case we would find it rational and indeed irresistible to accept the hypothesis that the robot had intentionality, as long as we knew nothing more about it. Indeed, besides appearance and behavior, the other elements of the combination are really irrelevant. If we could build a robot whose behavior was indistinguishable over a large range from human behavior, we would attribute intentionality to it, pending some reason not to. We wouldn't need to know in advance that its computer brain was a formal analogue of the human brain.

But I really don't see that this is any help to the claims of strong AI, and here's why: According to strong AI, instantiating a formal program with the right input and output is a sufficient condition of, indeed is constitutive of, intentionality. As Newell (1979) puts it, the essence of the mental is the operation of a physical symbol system. But the attributions of intentionality that we make to the robot in this example have nothing to do with formal programs. They are simply based on the assumption that if the robot looks and behaves sufficiently like us, then we would suppose, until proven otherwise, that it must have mental states like ours that cause and are expressed by its behavior and it must have an inner mechanism capable of producing such mental states. If we knew independently how to account for its behavior without such assumptions we would not attribute intentionality to it, especially if we knew it had a formal program. And this is precisely the point of my earlier reply to objection II.

Suppose we knew that the robot's behavior was entirely accounted for by the fact that a man inside it was receiving uninterpreted formal symbols from the robot's sensory receptors and sending out uninterpreted formal symbols to its motor mechanisms, and the man was doing the symbol manipulation in accordance with a bunch of rules. Furthermore, suppose the man knows none of these facts about the robot, all he knows is which operations to perform on which meaningless symbols. In such a case we would regard the robot as an ingenious mechanical dummy. The hypothesis that the dummy has a mind would now be unwarranted and unnecessary, for there is now no longer any reason to ascribe intentionality to the robot or to the system of which it is a part (except of course for the man's intentionality in manipulating the symbols). The formal symbol manipulations go on, the input and output are correctly matched, but the only real locus of intentionality is the man, and he doesn't know any of the relevant intentional states; he doesn't, for example, *see* what comes into the robot's eyes, he doesn't *intend* to move the robot's arm, and he doesn't *understand* any of the remarks made to or by the robot. Nor, for the reasons stated earlier, does the system of which man and robot are a part.

To see this point, contrast this case with cases in which we find it completely natural to ascribe intentionality to members of certain other primate species such as apes and monkeys and to domestic animals such as dogs. The reasons we find it natural are, roughly, two: We can't make sense of the animal's behavior without the ascription of intentionality, and we can see that the beasts are made of similar stuff to ourselves—that is an eye, that a nose, this is its skin, and so on. Given the coherence of the animal's behavior and the assumption of the same causal stuff underlying it, we assume both that the animal must have mental states underlying its behavior, and that the mental states must be produced by mechanisms made out of the stuff that is like our stuff. We would certainly make similar assumptions about the robot unless we had some reason not to, but as soon as we knew that the behavior was the result of a formal program, and that the actual causal properties of the physical substance were irrelevant we would abandon the assumption of intentionality.

There are two other responses to my example that come up frequently (and so are worth discussing) but really miss the point.

V. The Other Minds Reply (Yale). "How do you know that other people understand Chinese or anything else? Only by their behavior. Now the computer can pass the behavioral tests as well as they can (in principle), so if you are going to attribute cognition to other people you must in principle also attribute it to computers."

This objection really is only worth a short reply. The problem in this discussion is not about how I know that other people have cognitive states, but rather what it is that I am attributing to them when I attribute cognitive states to them. The thrust of the argument is that it couldn't be just computational processes and their output because the computational processes and their output can exist without the cognitive state. It is no answer to this argument to feign anesthesia. In "cognitive sciences" one presupposes the reality and knowability of the mental in the same way that in physical sciences one has to presuppose the reality and knowability of physical objects.

VI. The Many Mansions Reply (Berkeley). "Your whole argument presupposes that AI is only about analog and digital computers. But that just happens to be the present state of technology. Whatever these causal processes are that you say are essential for intentionality (assuming you are right), eventually we will be able to build devices that have these causal processes, and that will be artificial intelligence. So your arguments are in no way directed at the ability of artificial intelligence to produce and explain cognition."

I really have no objection to this reply save to say that it in effect trivializes the project of strong AI by redefining it as whatever artificially produces and explains cognition. The interest of the original claim made on behalf of artificial intelligence is that it was a precise, well defined thesis: mental processes are computational processes over formally defined elements. I have been concerned to challenge that thesis. If the claim is redefined so that it is no longer that thesis, my objections no longer apply because there is no longer a testable hypothesis for them to apply to.

Let us now return to the question I promised I would try to answer: Granted that in my original example I understand the English and I do not understand the Chinese, and granted therefore that the machine doesn't understand either English or Chinese, still there must be something about me that makes it the case that I understand English and a corresponding something lacking in me that makes it the case that I fail to understand Chinese. Now why couldn't we give those somethings, whatever they are, to a machine?

I see no reason in principle why we couldn't give a machine the capacity to understand English or Chinese, since in an important sense our bodies with our brains are precisely such machines. But I do see very strong arguments for saying that we could not give such a thing to a machine where the operation of the machine is defined solely in terms of computational processes over formally defined elements: that is, where the operation of the machine is defined as an instantiation of a computer program. It is not because I am the instantiation of a computer program that I am able to understand English and have other forms of intentionality (I am, I suppose, the instantiation of any number of computer programs), but as far as we know it is because I am a certain sort of organism with a certain biological (i.e., chemical and physical) structure, and this structure, under certain conditions, is causally capable of producing perception, action, understanding, learning, and other intentional phenomena. And part of the point of the present argument is that only something that had those causal powers could have that intentionality. Perhaps other physical and chemical processes could produce exactly these effects; perhaps, for example, Martians also have intentionality but their brains are made of different stuff. That is an empirical question, rather like the question whether photosynthesis can be done by something with a chemistry different from that of chlorophyll.

But the main point of the present argument is that no purely formal model will ever be sufficient by itself for intentionality because the formal properties are not by themselves constitutive of intentionality, and they have by themselves no causal powers except the power, when instantiated, to produce the next stage of the formalism when the machine is running. And any other causal properties that particular realizations of the formal model have, are irrelevant to the formal model because we can always put the same formal model in a different realization where those causal properties are obviously absent. Even if, by some miracle, Chinese speakers exactly realize Schank's program, we can put the same program in English speakers, water pipes, or computers, none of which understand Chinese, the program notwithstanding.

What matters about brain operations is not the formal shadow cast by the sequence of synapses but rather the actual properties of the sequences. All the arguments for the strong version of artificial intelligence that I have seen insist on drawing an outline around the shadows cast by cognition and then claiming that the shadows are the real thing.

By way of concluding I want to try to state some of the general philosophical points implicit in the argument. For clarity I will try to do it in a question-and-answer fashion, and I begin with that old chestnut of a question:

"Could a machine think?"

The answer is, obviously, yes. We are precisely such machines.

"Yes, but could an artifact, a man-made machine, think?"

Assuming it is possible to produce artificially a machine with a nervous system, neurons with axons and dendrites, and all the rest of it, sufficiently like ours, again the answer to the question seems to be obviously, yes. If you can exactly duplicate the causes, you could duplicate the effects. And indeed it might be possible to produce consciousness, intentionality, and all the rest of it using some other sorts of chemical principles than those that human beings use. It is, as I said, an empirical question.

"OK, but could a digital computer think?"

If by "digital computer" we mean anything at all that has a level of description where it can correctly be described as the instantiation of a computer program, then again the answer is, of course, yes, since we are the instantiations of any number of computer programs, and we can think.

"But could something think, understand, and so on *solely* in virtue of being a computer with a right sort of program? Could instantiating a program, the right

program of course, by itself be a sufficient condition of understanding?"

This I think is the right question to ask, though it is usually confused with one or more of the earlier questions, and the answer to it is no.

"Why not?"

Because the formal symbol manipulations by themselves don't have any intentionality; they are quite meaningless; they aren't even *symbol* manipulations, since the symbols don't symbolize anything. In the linguistic jargon, they have only a syntax but no semantics. Such intentionality as computers appear to have is solely in the minds of those who program them and those who use them, those who send in the input and those who interpret the output.

The aim of the Chinese room example was to try to show this by showing that as soon as we put something into the system that really does have intentionality (a man), and we program him with the formal program, you can see that the formal program carries no additional intentionality. It adds nothing, for example, to a man's ability to understand Chinese.

Precisely that feature of AI that seemed so appealing—the distinction between the program and the realization—proves fatal to the claim that simulation could be duplication. The distinction between the program and its realization in the hardware seems to be parallel to the distinction between the level of mental operations and the level of brain operations. And if we could describe the level of mental operations as a formal program, then it seems we could describe what was essential about the mind without doing either introspective psychology or neurophysiology of the brain. But the equation "mind is to brain as program is to hardware" breaks down at several points, among them the following three:

First, the distinction between program and realization has the consequence that the same program could have all sorts of crazy realizations that had no form of intentionality. Weizenbaum (1976, Ch. 2), for example, shows in detail how to construct a computer using a roll of toilet paper and a pile of small stones. Similarly, the Chinese story understanding program can be programmed into a sequence of water pipes, a set of wind machines, or a monolingual English speaker, none of which thereby acquires an understanding of Chinese. Stones, toilet paper, wind, and water pipes are the wrong kind of stuff to have intentionality in the first place—only something that has the same causal powers as brains can have intentionality—and though the English speaker has the right kind of stuff for intentionality you can easily see that he doesn't get any extra intentionality by memorizing the program, since memorizing it won't teach him Chinese.

Second, the program is purely formal, but the intentional states are not in that way formal. They are defined in terms of their content, not their form. The belief that it is raining, for example, is not defined as a certain formal shape, but as a certain mental content with conditions of satisfaction, a direction of fit (see Searle 1979), and the like. Indeed the belief as such hasn't even got a formal shape in this syntactic sense, since one and the same belief can be given an indefinite number of different syntactic expressions in different linguistic systems.

Third, as I mentioned before, mental states and events are literally a product of the operation of the brain, but the program is not in that way a product of the computer.

"Well if programs are in no way constitutive of mental processes, why have so many people believed the converse? That at least needs some explanation."

I don't really know the answer to that one. The idea that computer simulations could be the real thing ought to have seemed suspicious in the first place because the computer isn't confined to simulating mental operations, by any means. No one supposes that computer simulations of a five-alarm fire will burn the neighborhood down or that a computer simulation of a rainstorm will leave us all drenched. Why on earth would anyone suppose that a computer simulation of understanding actually understood anything? It is sometimes said that it would be frightfully hard to get computers to feel pain or fall in love, but love and pain are neither harder nor easier than cognition or anything else. For simulation, all you need is the right input and output and a program in the middle that transforms the former into the latter. That is all the computer has for anything it does. To confuse simulation with duplication is the same mistake, whether it is pain, love, cognition, fires, or rainstorms.

Still, there are several reasons why AI must have seemed—and to many people perhaps still does seem—in some way to reproduce and thereby explain mental phenomena, and I believe we will not succeed in removing these illusions until we have fully exposed the reasons that give rise to them.

First, and perhaps the most important, is a confusion about the notion of "information processing": many people in cognitive science believe that the human brain, with its mind, does something called "information processing," and analogously the computer with its program does information processing; but fires and rainstorms, on the other hand, don't do information processing at all. Thus, though the computer can simulate the formal features of any process whatever, it stands in a special relation to the mind and brain because when the computer is properly programmed, ideally with the same program as the brain, the information processing is identical in the two cases, and this information processing is really the essence of the mental. But the trouble with this argument is that it rests on an ambiguity in the notion of "information." In the sense in which people "process information" when they reflect, say, on problems in arithmetic or when they read and answer questions about stories, the programmed computer does not do "information processing." Rather, what it does is manipulate formal symbols. The fact that the programmer and the interpreter of the computer output use the symbols to stand for objects in the world is totally beyond the scope of the computer. The computer, to repeat, has a syntax but no semantics. Thus, if you type into the computer "2 plus 2 equals?" it will type out "4." But it has no idea that "4" means 4 or that it means anything at all. And the point is not that it lacks some second-order information about the interpretation of its first-order symbols, but rather that its first-order symbols don't have any interpretations as far as the computer is concerned. All the computer has is more symbols. The introduction of the notion of "information processing" therefore produces a dilemma: either we construe the notion of "information processing" in such a way that it implies intentionality as part of the process or we don't. If the former, then the programmed computer does not do information processing, it only manipulates formal symbols. If the latter, then, though the computer does information processing, it is only doing so in the sense in which adding machines, typewriters, stomachs, thermostats, rainstorms, and hurricanes do information processing; namely, they have a level of description at which we can describe them as taking information in at one end, transforming it, and producing information as output. But in this case it is up to outside observers to interpret the input and output as information in the ordinary sense. And no similarity is established between the computer and the brain in terms of any similarity of information processing.

Second, in much of AI there is a residual behaviorism or operationalism. Since appropriately programmed computers can have input-output patterns similar to those of human beings, we are tempted to postulate mental states in the computer similar to human mental states. But once we see that it is both conceptually and empirically possible for a system to have human capacities in some realm without having any intentionality at all, we should be able to overcome this impulse. My desk adding machine has calculating capacities, but no intentionality, and in this paper I have tried to show that a system could have input and output capabilities that duplicated those of a native Chinese speaker and still not understand Chinese, regardless of how it was programmed. The Turing test is typical of the tradition in being unashamedly behavioristic and operationalistic, and I believe that if AI workers totally repudiated behaviorism and operationalism much of the confusion between simulation and duplication would be eliminated.

Third, this residual operationalism is joined to a residual form of dualism; indeed strong AI only makes sense given the dualistic assumption that, where the mind is concerned, the brain doesn't matter. In strong AI (and in functionalism, as well) what matters are programs, and programs are independent of their realization in machines; indeed, as far as AI is concerned, the same program could be realized by an electronic machine, a Cartesian mental substance, or a Hegelian world spirit. The single most surprising discovery that I have made in discussing these issues is that many AI workers are quite shocked by my idea that actual human mental phenomena might be dependent on actual physical-chemical properties of actual human brains. But if you think about it a minute you can see that I should not have been surprised; for unless you accept some form of dualism, the strong AI project hasn't got a chance. The project is to reproduce and explain the mental by designing programs, but unless the mind is not only conceptually but empirically independent of the brain you couldn't carry out the project, for the program is completely independent of any realization. Unless you believe that the mind is separable from the brain both conceptually and empirically—dualism in a strong form—you cannot hope to reproduce the mental by writing and running programs since programs must be independent of brains or any other particular forms of instantiation. If mental operations consist in computational operations on formal symbols, then it follows that they have no interesting connection with the brain; the only connection would be that the brain just happens to be one of the indefinitely many types of machines capable of instantiating the program. This form of dualism is not the traditional Cartesian variety that claims there are two sorts of *substances*, but it is Cartesian in the sense that it insists that what is specifically mental about the mind has no intrinsic connection with the actual properties of the brain. This underlying dualism is masked from us by the fact that AI literature contains frequent fulminations against "dualism"; what the authors seem to be unaware of is that their position presupposes a strong version of dualism.

"Could a machine think?" My own view is that only a machine could think, and indeed only very special kinds of machines, namely brains and machines that had the same causal powers as brains. And that is the main reason strong AI has had little to tell us about thinking, since it has nothing to tell us about machines. By its own definition, it is about programs, and programs are not machines. Whatever else intentionality is, it is a biological phenomenon, and it is as likely to be as causally dependent on the specific biochemistry of its origins as lactation, photosynthesis, or any other biological phenomena. No one would suppose that we could produce milk and sugar by running a computer simulation of the formal sequences in lactation and photosynthesis, but where the mind is concerned many people are willing to believe in such a miracle because of a deep and abiding dualism: the mind they suppose is a matter of formal processes and is independent of quite specific material causes in the way that milk and sugar are not.

In defense of this dualism the hope is often expressed that the brain is a digital computer (early computers, by the way, were often called "electronic brains"). But that is no help. Of course the brain is a digital computer. Since everything is a digital computer, brains are too. The point is that the brain's causal capacity to produce intentionality cannot consist in its instantiating a computer program, since for any program you like it is possible for something to instantiate that program and still not have any mental states. Whatever it is that the brain does to produce intentionality, it cannot consist in instantiating a program since no program, by itself, is sufficient for intentionality.

Notes

I am indebted to a rather large number of people for discussion of these matters and for their patient attempts to overcome my ignorance of artificial intelligence. I would especially like to thank Ned Block, Hubert Dreyfus, John Haugeland, Roger Schank, Robert Wilensky, and Terry Winograd.

1. I am not, of course, saying that Schank himself is committed to these claims.
2. Also, "understanding" implies both the possession of mental (intentional) states and the truth (validity, success) of these states. For the purposes of this discussion we are concerned only with the possession of the states.

3. Intentionality is by definition that feature of certain mental states by which they are directed at or about objects and states of affairs in the world. Thus, beliefs, desires, and intentions are intentional states; undirected forms of anxiety and depression are not.

References

Fodor, J.A. 1968. The appeal to tacit knowledge in psychological explanation. *Journal of Philosophy* 65:627–40.

Fodor, J.A. 1980. Methodological solipsism considered as a research strategy in cognitive psychology. *Behavioral and Brain Sciences* 3:1.

McCarthy, J. 1979. Ascribing mental qualities to machines. In: *Philosophical perceptives in artificial intelligence*, ed. M. Ringle. Atlantic Highlands, NJ: Humanities Press.

Newell, A. 1979. Physical symbol systems. Lecture at the La Jolla Conference on Cognitive Science.

Newell, A., and Simon, H.A. 1963. GPS, a program that simulates human thought. In: *Computers and thought*, ed. A. Feigenbaum & V. Feldman, pp. 279–93. New York: McGraw-Hill.

Pylyshyn, Z.W. 1980. Computation and cognition: Issues in the foundations of cognitive science. *Behavioral and Brain Sciences 3*.

Schank, R.C., and Abelson, R.P. 1977. *Scripts, plans, goals, and understanding*. Hillsdale, NJ: Lawrence Erlbaum Press.

Searle, J.R. 1979. The intentionality of intention and action. *Inquiry* 22:253–80.

Weizenbaum, J. 1965. Eliza—a computer program for the study of natural language communication between man and machine. *Communication of the Association for Computing Machinery* 9:36–45.

Weizenbaum, J. 1976. *Computer power and human reason*. San Francisco: W.H. Freeman.

Winograd, T. 1973. A procedural model of language understanding. In: *Computer models of thought and language*, ed. R. Schank & K. Colby. San Francisco: W.H. Freeman.

MARGARET A. BODEN

"Escaping from the Chinese Room"

John Searle, in his paper on 'Minds, Brains, and Programs' (1980), argues that computational theories in psychology are essentially worthless. He makes two main claims: that computational theories, being purely formal in nature, cannot possibly help us to understand mental processes; and that computer hardware—unlike neuroprotein—obviously lacks the right causal powers to generate mental processes. I shall argue that both these claims are mistaken.

His first claim takes for granted the widely-held (formalist) assumption that the 'computations' studied in computer science are purely syntactic, that they can be defined (in terms equally suited to symbolic logic) as *the formal manipulation of abstract symbols, by the application of formal rules*. It follows, he says, that formalist accounts—appropriate in explaining the meaningless 'information'-processing or 'symbol'-manipulations in computers—are unable to explain how human minds employ *information* or *symbols* properly so-called. Meaning, or intentionality, cannot be explained in computational terms.

Searle's point here is not that no machine can think. Humans can think, and humans—he allows—are machines; he even adopts the materialist credo that only machines can think. Nor is he saying that humans and programs are utterly incommensurable. He grants that, at some highly abstract level of description, people (like everything else) are instantiations of digital computers. His point, rather, is that nothing can think, mean, or understand *solely* in virtue of its instantiating a computer program.

To persuade us of this, Searle employs an ingenious thought-experiment. He imagines himself locked in a room, in which there are various slips of paper with doodles on them; a window through which people can pass further doodle-papers to him, and through which he can pass papers out; and a book of rules (in English) telling him how to pair the doodles, which are always identified by their shape or form. Searle spends his time, while inside the room, manipulating the doodles according to the rules.

One rule, for example, instructs him that when *squiggle-squiggle* is passed in to him, he should give out *squoggle-squoggle*. The rule-book also provides for more complex sequences of doodle-pairing, where only the first and last steps mention the transfer of paper into or out of the room. Before finding any rule directly instructing him to give out a slip of paper, he may have to locate a *blongle* doodle and compare it with a *blungle* doodle—in which case, it is the result of this comparison which determines the nature of the doodle he passes out. Sometimes many such doodle-doodle comparisons and consequent doodle-selections have to be made by him inside the room before he finds a rule allowing him to pass anything out.

So far as Searle-in-the-room is concerned, the *squiggles* and *squoggles* are mere meaningless doodles. Unknown to him, however, they are Chinese characters. The people outside the room, being Chinese, interpret them as such. Moreover, the patterns passed in and out at the window are understood by them as *questions* and *answers* respectively: the rules happen to be such that most of the questions are paired, either directly or indirectly, with what they recognize as a sensible answer. But Searle himself (inside the room) knows nothing of this.

The point, says Searle, is that Searle-in-the-room is clearly instantiating a computer program. That is, he is performing purely formal manipulations of uninterpreted patterns: he is all syntax and no semantics.

The doodle-pairing rules are equivalent to the if-then rules, or 'productions,' commonly used (for example) in expert systems. Some of the internal doodle-comparisons could be equivalent to what AI workers in natural-language processing call a script—for instance, the restaurant script described by R.C. Schank and R.P. Abelson (1977). In that case, Searle-in-the-room's paper-passing performance would be essentially comparable to the performance of a 'question-answering' Schankian text-analysis program. But 'question-answering' is not question-answering. Searle-in-the-room is not really *answering*: how could he, since he cannot understand the questions? Practice does not help (except perhaps in making the doodle-pairing swifter): if Searle-in-the-room ever escapes, he will be just as ignorant of Chinese as he was when he was first locked in.

Certainly, the Chinese people outside might find it useful to keep Searle-in-the-room fed and watered, much as in real life we are willing to spend large sums of money on computerized 'advice' systems. But the fact that people who already possess understanding may use an intrinsically meaningless formalist computational system to provide what they interpret (*sic*) as questions, answers, designations, interpretations, or symbols is irrelevant. They can do this only if they can externally specify a mapping between the formalism and matters of interest to them. In principle, one and the same formalism might be mappable onto several different domains, so could be used (by people) in answering questions about any of those domains. In itself, however, it would be meaningless—as are the Chinese symbols from the point of view of Searle-in-the-room.

It follows, Searle argues, that no system can understand anything solely in virtue of its instantiating a computer program. For if it could, then Searle-in-the-room would understand Chinese.

Hence, theoretical psychology cannot properly be grounded in computational concepts.

Searle's second claim concerns what a proper explanation of understanding would be like. According to him, it would acknowledge that meaningful symbols must be embodied in something having 'the right causal powers' for generating understanding, or intentionality. Obviously, he says, brains do have such causal powers whereas computers do not. More precisely (since the brain's organization could be paralleled in a computer), neuroprotein does whereas metal and silicon do not: the biochemical properties of the brain matter are crucial.

A. Newell's (1980) widely cited definition of 'physical-symbol systems' is rejected by Searle, because it demands merely that symbols be embodied in some material that can implement formalist computations—which computers, admittedly, can do. In Searle's view, no electronic computer can really manipulate symbols, nor really designate or interpret anything at all—*irrespective* of any causal dependencies linking its internal physical patterns to its behaviour. (This strongly realist view of intentionality contrasts with the instrumentalism of D.C. Dennett [1971]. For Dennett, an intentional system is one whose behaviour we can explain, predict, and control only by ascribing beliefs, goals, and rationality to it. On this criterion, some *existing* computer programs are intentional systems, and the hypothetical humanoids beloved of science-fiction would be intentional systems *a fortiori*.) Intentionality, Searle declares, is a biological phenomenon. As such, it is just as dependent on the underlying biochemistry as are photosynthesis and lactation. He grants that neuroprotein may not be the only substances in the universe capable of supporting mental life, much as substances other than chlorophyll may be able (on Mars, perhaps) to catalyse the synthesis of carbohydrates. But he rejects metal or silicon as potential alternatives, even on Mars. He asks whether a computer made out of old beer-cans could possibly *understand*—a rhetorical question to which the expected answer is a resounding 'No!' In short, Searle takes it to be intuitively obvious that the inorganic substances with which (today's) computers are manufactured are essentially incapable of supporting mental functions.

In assessing Searle's two-pronged critique of computational psychology, let us first consider his view that intentionality must be biologically grounded. One might be tempted to call this a positive claim, in contrast with his (negative) claim that purely formalist theories cannot explain mentality. However, this would be to grant it more than it deserves, for its explanatory power is illusory. The biological analogies mentioned by Searle are misleading, and the intuitions to which he appeals are unreliable.

The brain's production of intentionality, we are told, is comparable to photosynthesis—but is it, really? We can define the *products* of photosynthesis, clearly distinguishing various sugars and starches within the general class of carbohydrates, and showing how these differ from other biochemical products such as proteins. Moreover, we not only *know that* chlorophyll supports photosynthesis, we also *understand how* it does so (and *why* various other chemicals cannot). We know that it is a catalyst rather than a raw material; and we can specify the point at which, and the subatomic process by which, its catalytic function is exercised. With respect to brains and understanding, the case is very different.

Our theory of what intentionality is (never mind how it is generated) does not bear comparison with our knowledge of carbohydrates: just what intentionality *is* is still philosophically controversial. We cannot even be entirely confident that we can recognize it when we see it. It is generally agreed that the propositional attitudes are intentional, and that feelings and sensations are not; but there is no clear consensus about the intentionality of emotions.

Various attempts have been made to characterize intentionality and to distinguish its subspecies as distinct intentional states (beliefs, desires, hopes, intentions, and the like). Searle himself has made a number of relevant contributions, from his early work on speech-acts (1969) to his more recent account (1983) of intentionality in general. A commonly used criterion (adopted by Brentano in the nineteenth century and also by Searle) is a *psychological* one. In Brentano's words, intentional states direct the mind on an object; in Searle's, they have intrinsic representational capacity, or 'aboutness'; in either case they relate the mind to the world, and to possible worlds. But some writers define intentionality in *logical* terms (Chisholm 1967). It is not even clear whether the logical and psychological definitions are precisely co-extensive (Boden 1970). In brief, no theory of intentionality is accepted as unproblematic, as the chemistry of carbohydrates is.

As for the brain's biochemical 'synthesis' of intentionality, this is even more mysterious. We have very good reason to believe *that* neuroprotein supports intentionality, but we have hardly any idea *how—qua* neuroprotein—it is able to do so.

In so far as we understand these matters at all, we focus on the neurochemical basis of certain *informational functions*—such as message-passing, facilitation, and inhibition—embodied in neurones and synapses. For example: how the sodium-pump at the cell-membrane enables an action potential to propagate along the axon; how electrochemical changes cause a neurone to enter into and recover from its refractory period; or how neuronal thresholds can be altered by neurotransmitters, such as acetylcholine.

With respect to a visual cell, for instance, a crucial psychological question may be *whether it can function so as to detect intensity-gradients*. If the neurophysiologist can tell us which molecules enable it to do so, so much the better. But from the psychological point of view, it is not the biochemistry as such which matters but the information-bearing functions grounded in it. (Searle apparently admits this when he says, 'The type of realizations that intentional states have in the brain may be describable at a much higher functional level than that of the specific biochemistry of the neurons involved' [1983: 272].) As work in 'computer vision' has shown, metal and silicon are undoubtedly able to support some of the functions necessary for the 2D-to-3D mapping involved in vision. Moreover, they can embody specific mathematical functions for recognizing intensity-gradients (namely 'DOG-detectors,' which compute the difference of Gaussians) which seem to be involved in many biological visual systems. Admittedly, it may be that metal and silicon cannot support all the functions involved in normal vision, or in understanding generally.

Perhaps only neuroprotein can do so, so that only creatures with a 'terrestrial' biology can enjoy intentionality. But we have no specific reason, at present, to think so. Most important in this context, any such reasons we might have in the future must be grounded in empirical discovery: intuitions will not help.

If one asks which mind-matter dependencies are intuitively plausible, the answer must be that *none* is. Nobody who was puzzled about intentionality (as opposed to action-potentials) ever exclaimed 'Sodium—of course!' Sodium-pumps are no less 'obviously' absurd than silicon chips, electrical polarities no less 'obviously' irrelevant than old beer-cans, acetylcholine hardly less surprising than beer. The fact that the first member of each of these three pairs is *scientifically* compelling does not make any of them *intuitively* intelligible: our initial surprise persists.

Our intuitions might change with the advance of science. Possibly we shall eventually see neuroprotein (and perhaps silicon too) as obviously capable of embodying mind, much as we now see biochemical substances in general (including chlorophyll) as obviously capable of producing other such substances—an intuition that was not obvious, even to chemists, prior to the synthesis of urea. At present, however, our intuitions have nothing useful to say about the material basis of intentionality. Searle's 'positive' claim, his putative alternative explanation of intentionality, is at best a promissory note, at worst mere mystery-mongering.

Searle's negative claim—that formal-computational theories cannot explain understanding—is less quickly rebutted. My rebuttal will involve two parts: the first directly addressing his example of the Chinese room, the second dealing with his background assumption (on which his example depends) that computer programs are pure syntax.

The Chinese-room example has engendered much debate, both within and outside the community of cognitive science. Some criticisms were anticipated by Searle himself in his original paper, others appeared as the accompanying peer-commentary (together with his Reply), and more have been published since. Here, I shall concentrate on only two points: what Searle calls the Robot reply, and what I shall call the English reply.

The Robot reply accepts that the only understanding of Chinese which exists in Searle's example is that enjoyed by the Chinese people outside the room. Searle-in-the-room's inability to connect Chinese characters with events in the outside world shows that he does not understand Chinese. Likewise, a Schankian teletyping computer that cannot recognize a restaurant, hand money to a waiter, or chew a morsel of food understands nothing of restaurants—even if it can usefully 'answer' our questions about them. But a robot, provided not only with a restaurant script but also with camera-fed visual programs and limbs capable of walking and picking things up, would be another matter. If the input-output behaviour of such a robot were identical with that of human beings, then it would demonstrably understand both restaurants and the natural language—Chinese, perhaps—used by people to communicate with it. Searle's first response to the Robot reply is to claim a victory already, since the reply concedes that cognition is not solely a matter of formal symbol-manipulation but requires in addition a set of causal relations with the outside world. Second, Searle insists that to add perceptuomotor capacities to a computational system is not to add intentionality, or understanding.

He argues this point by imagining a robot which, instead of being provided with a computer program to make it work, has a miniaturized Searle inside it—in its skull, perhaps. Searle-in-the-robot, with the aid of a (new) rule-book, shuffles paper and passes *squiggles* and *squoggles* in and out, much as Searle-in-the-room did before him. But now some or all of the incoming Chinese characters are not handed in by Chinese people, but are triggered by causal processes in the cameras and audio-equipment in the robot's eyes and ears. And the outgoing Chinese characters are not received by Chinese hands, but by motors and levers attached to the robot's limbs—which are caused to move as a result. In short, this robot is apparently able not only to answer questions in Chinese, but also to see and do things accordingly: it can recognize raw beansprouts and, if the recipe requires it, toss them into a wok as well as the rest of us.

(The work on computer vision mentioned above suggests that the vocabulary of Chinese would require considerable extension for this example to be carried through. And the large body of AI research on language-processing suggests that the same could be said of the English required to express the rules in Searle's initial 'question-answering' example. In either case, what Searle-in-the-room needs is not so much Chinese, or even English, as a programming-language. We shall return to this point presently.)

Like his roombound predecessor, however, Searle-in-the-robot knows nothing of the wider context. He is just as ignorant of Chinese as he ever was, and has no more purchase on the outside world than he did in the original example. To him, beansprouts and woks are invisible and intangible: all Searle-in-the-robot can see and touch, besides the rule-book and the doodles, are his own body and the inside walls of the robot's skull. Consequently, Searle argues, the robot cannot be credited with understanding of any of these worldly matters. In truth, it is not *seeing* or *doing* anything at all: it is 'simply moving about as a result of its electrical wiring and its program,' which latter is instantiated by the man inside it, who 'has no intentional states of the relevant type' (1980: 420).

Searle's argument here is unacceptable as a rebuttal of the Robot reply, because it draws a false analogy between the imagined example and what is claimed by computational psychology.

Searle-in-the-robot is supposed by Searle to be performing the functions performed (according to computational theories) by the human brain. But, whereas most computationalists do not ascribe intentionality to the brain (and those who do, as we shall see presently, do so only in a very limited way), Searle characterizes Searle-in-the-robot as enjoying full-blooded intentionality, just as he does himself. Computational psychology does not credit the brain with *seeing beansprouts* or *understanding English*: intentional states such as these are properties of people, not of brains. In general, although representations and mental processes are assumed (by computationalists and Searle alike) to be embodied in the brain, the sensorimotor capacities and propositional attitudes which they make possible are ascribed to the person as a whole. So Searle's description of the system inside the robot's skull as one which can understand English does not truly parallel what computationalists say about the brain.

Indeed, the specific procedures hypothesized by computational psychologists, and embodied by them in computer models of the mind, are relatively stupid—and they become more and more stupid as one moves to increasingly basic theoretical levels. Consider theories of natural-language parsing, for example. A parsing procedure that searches for a determiner does not understand English, and nor does a procedure for locating the reference of a personal pronoun: only the person whose brain performs these interpretive processes, and many others associated with them, can do that. The capacity to understand English involves a host of interacting information processes, each of which performs only a very limited function but which together provide the capacity to take English sentences as input and give appropriate English sentences as output. Similar remarks apply to the individual components of computational theories of vision, problem-solving, or learning. Precisely because psychologists wish to *explain* human language, vision, reasoning, and learning, they posit underlying processes which lack the capacities.

In short, Searle's description of the robot's pseudo-brain (that is, of Searle-in-the-robot) as understanding English involves a category-mistake comparable to treating the brain as the bearer—as opposed to the causal basis—of intelligence.

Someone might object here that I have contradicted myself, that I am claiming that one cannot ascribe intentionality to brains and yet am implicitly doing just that. For I spoke of the brain's effecting 'stupid' component-procedures—but stupidity is virtually a *species* of intelligence. To be stupid is to be intelligent, but not very (a person or a fish can be stupid, but a stone or a river cannot).

My defence would be twofold. First, the most basic theoretical level of all would be at the neuroscientific equivalent of the machine-code, a level 'engineered' by evolution. The facts that a certain light-sensitive cell *can* respond to intensity-gradients by acting as a DOG-detector and that one neurone *can* inhibit the firing of another, are explicable by the biochemistry of the brain. The notion of stupidity, even in scare-quotes, is wholly inappropriate in discussing such facts. However, these very basic information-processing functions (DOG-detecting and synaptic inhibition) *could* properly be described as 'very, very, very...stupid.' This of course implies that intentional language, if only of a highly grudging and uncomplimentary type, is applicable to brain processes after all—which prompts the second point in my defence. I did not say that

intentionality cannot be ascribed to brains, but that full-blooded intentionality cannot. Nor did I say that brains cannot understand anything at all, in howsoever limited a fashion, but that they cannot (for example) understand English. I even hinted, several paragraphs ago, that a few computationalists do ascribe some degree of intentionality to the brain (or to the computational processes going on in the brain). These two points will be less obscure after we have considered the English reply and its bearing on Searle's background assumption that formal-syntactic computational theories are purely syntactic.

The crux of the English reply is that the instantiation of a computer program, whether by man or by manufactured machine, does involve understanding—at least of the rule-book. Searle's initial example depends critically on Searle-in-the-room's being able to understand the language in which the rules are written, namely English; similarly, without Searle-in-the-robot's familiarity with English, the robot's beansprouts would never get thrown into the wok. Moreover, as remarked above, the vocabulary of English (and, for Searle-in-the-robot, of Chinese too) would have to be significantly modified to make the example work.

An unknown language (whether Chinese or Linear B) can be dealt with only as an aesthetic object or a set of systematically related forms. Artificial languages can be designed and studied, by the logician or the pure mathematician, with only their structural properties in mind (although D.R. Hofstadter's [1979] example of the quasi-arithmetical pq-system shows that a psychologically compelling, and predictable, interpretation of a formal calculus may arise spontaneously). But one normally responds in a very different way to the symbols of one's native tongue; indeed, it is very difficult to 'bracket' (ignore) the meanings of familiar words. The view held by computational psychologists, that natural languages can be characterized in procedural terms, is relevant here: words, clauses, and sentences can be seen as mini-programs. The symbols in a natural language one understands initiate mental activity of various kinds. To learn a language is to set up the relevant causal connections, not only between words and the world ('cat' and the thing on the mat) but between words and the many non-introspectible procedures involved in interpreting them.

Moreover, we do not need to be told *ex hypothesi* (by Searle) that Searle-in-the-room understands English: his behaviour while in the room shows clearly that he does. Or, rather, it shows that he understands a *highly limited subset* of English.

Searle-in-the-room could be suffering from total amnesia with respect to 99 per cent of Searle's English vocabulary, and it would make no difference. The only grasp of English he needs is whatever is necessary to interpret (*sic*) the rule-book—which specifies how to accept, select, compare, and give out different patterns. Unlike Searle, Searle-in-the-room does not require words like 'catalyse,' 'beer-can,' 'chlorophyll,' and 'restaurant.' But he may need 'find,' 'compare,' 'two,' 'triangular,' and 'window' (although his understanding of these words could be much less full than Searle's). He must understand conditional sentences, if any rule states that if he sees a *squoggle* he should give out a *squiggle*. Very likely, he must understand some way of expressing negation, temporal ordering, and (especially if he is to learn to do his job faster) generalization. If the rules he uses include some which parse the Chinese sentences, then he will need words for grammatical categories too. (He will not need explicit rules for parsing English sentences, such as the parsing procedures employed in AI programs for language-processing, because he already understands English.)

In short, Searle-in-the-room needs to understand only that subset of Searle's English which is equivalent to the programming-language understood by a computer generating the same 'question-answering' input-output behaviour at the window. Similarly, Searle-in-the-robot must be able to understand whatever subset of English is equivalent to the programming-language understood by a fully computerized visuomotor robot.

The two preceding sentences may seem to beg the very question at issue. Indeed, to speak thus of the programming-language understood by a computer is seemingly self-contradictory. For Searle's basic premiss—which he assumes is accepted by all participants in the debate—is that a computer program is purely formal in nature: the computation it specifies is purely syntactic and has no intrinsic meaning or semantic content to be understood.

If we accept this premiss, the English reply sketched above can be dismissed forthwith for seeking to draw a parallel where no parallel can properly be drawn. But if we do not, if—*pace* Searle (and others [Fodor 1980; Stich 1983])—computer programs are not concerned only with syntax, then the English reply may be relevant after all. We must now turn to address this basic question.

Certainly, one can for certain purposes think of a computer program as an uninterpreted logical calculus. For example, one might be able to prove, by purely formal means, that a particular well-formed formula is derivable from the program's data-structures and inferential rules. Moreover, it is true that a so-called interpreter program that could take as input the list-structure '(father [maggie])' and return '(leonard)' would do so on formal criteria alone, having no way of interpreting these patterns as possibly denoting real people. Likewise, as Searle points out, programs provided with restaurant-scripts are not thereby provided with knowledge of restaurants. The existence of a mapping between a formalism and a certain domain does not in itself provide the manipulator of the formalism with any understanding of that domain.

But what must not be forgotten is that a computer program is *a program for a computer*: when a program is run on suitable hardware, the machine *does* something as a result (hence the use in computer science of the words 'instruction' and 'obey'). At the level of the machine-code the effect of the program on the computer is direct, because the machine is engineered so that a given instruction elicits a unique operation (instructions in high-level languages must be converted into machine-code instructions before they can be obeyed). A programmed instruction, then, is not a mere formal pattern—nor even a declarative statement (although it may for some purposes be thought of under either of those descriptions). It is a procedure specification that, given a suitable hardware context, can cause the procedure in question to be executed.

One might put this by saying that a programming-language is a medium not only for expressing *representations* (structures that can be written on a page or provided to a computer, some of which structures may be isomorphic with things that interest people) but also for bringing about the *representational activity* of certain machines.

One might even say that a representation *is* an activity rather than a structure. Many philosophers and psychologists have supposed that mental representations are intrinsically active. Among those who have recently argued for this view is Hofstadter (1985: 648), who specifically criticizes Newell's account of *symbols* as manipulable formal tokens. In his words, 'The brain itself does not "manipulate symbols"; the brain is the medium in which the symbols are floating and in which they trigger each other.'

Hofstadter expresses more sympathy for 'connectionist' than for 'formalist' psychological theories. Connectionist approaches involve parallel-processing systems broadly reminiscent of the brain, and are well suited to model cerebral representations, symbols, or concepts, as *dynamic*. But it is not only connectionists who can view concepts as intrinsically active, and not only *cerebral* representations which can be thought of in this way: this claim has been generalized to cover traditional computer programs, specifically designed for von Neumann machines. The computer scientist B.C. Smith (1982) argues that programmed representations, too, are inherently active—and that an adequate theory of the semantics of programming-languages would recognize the fact.

At present, Smith claims, computer scientists have a radically inadequate understanding of such matters. He reminds us that, as remarked above, there is no general agreement—either within or outside computer science—about what *intentionality* is, and deep unclarities about *representation* as well. Nor can unclarities be avoided by speaking more technically, in terms of *computation* and *formal symbol-manipulation*. For the computer scientist's understanding of what these phenomena really are is also largely intuitive. Smith's discussion of programming-languages identifies some fundamental confusions within computer science. Especially relevant here is his claim that computer scientists commonly make too complete a theoretical separation between a program's control-functions and its nature as a formal-syntactic system.

The theoretical divide criticized by Smith is evident in the widespread 'dual-calculus' approach to programming. The dual-calculus approach posits a sharp theoretical distinction between a declarative (or denotational) representational structure and the procedural language that interprets it when the program is run. Indeed, the knowledge-representation and the interpreter are sometimes written in two quite distinct formalisms (such as predicate calculus and LISP, respectively). Often, however, they are both expressed in the same formalism; for example, LISP (an acronym for LISt-Processing language) allows facts and procedures to be expressed in formally similar ways, and so does PROLOG (PROgramming-in-LOGic). In such cases, the dual-calculus approach dictates that the (single) programming-language concerned be theoretically described in two quite different ways.

To illustrate the distinction at issue here, suppose that we wanted a representation of family relationships which could be used to provide answers to questions about such matters. We might decide to employ a list-structure to represent such facts as that Leonard is the father of Maggie. Or we might prefer a frame-based representation, in which the relevant name-slots in the father-frame could be simultaneously filled by 'leonard' and 'maggie.' Again, we might choose a formula of the predicate calculus, saying that there exist two people (namely, Leonard and Maggie), and Leonard is the father of Maggie. Last, we might employ the English sentence 'Leonard is the father of Maggie.'

Each of these four representations could be written/drawn on paper (as are the rules in the rule-book used by Searle-in-the-room), for us to interpret *if* we have learnt how to handle the relevant notation. Alternatively, they could be embodied in a computer database. But to make them usable by the computer, there has to be an interpreter-program which (for instance) can find the item 'leonard' when we 'ask' it who is the father of Maggie. No one with any sense would embody list-structures in a computer without providing it also with a *list-processing* facility, nor give it frames without a *slot-filling* mechanism, logical formulae without *rules of inference*, or English sentences without *parsing procedures*. (Analogously, people who knew that Searle speaks no Portuguese would not give Searle-in-the-room a Portuguese rule-book unless they were prepared to teach him the language first.)

Smith does not deny that there is an important distinction between the *denotational import* of an expression (broadly: what actual or possible worlds can be mapped onto it) and its *procedural consequence* (broadly: what it does, or makes happen). The fact that the expression '(father [maggie])' is isomorphic with a certain parental relationship between two actual people (and so might be mapped onto that relationship by us) is one thing. The fact that the expression '(father [maggie])' can cause a certain computer to locate 'leonard' is quite another thing. Were it not so, the dual-calculus approach would not have developed. But he argues that, rather than persisting with the dual-calculus approach, it would be more elegant and less confusing to adopt a 'unified' theory of programming-languages, designed to cover both denotative and procedural aspects.

He shows that many basic terms on either side of the dual-calculus divide have deep theoretical commonalities as well as significant differences. The notion of *variable*, for instance, is understood in somewhat similar fashion by the logician and the computer scientist: both allow that a variable can have different *values* assigned to it at different times. That being so, it is redundant to have two distinct theories of what a variable is. To some extent, however, logicians and computer scientists understand different things by this term: the value of a variable in the LISP programming-language (for example) is another LISP-expression, whereas the value of a variable in logic is usually some object external to the formalism itself. These differences should be clarified—not least to avoid confusion when a system attempts to reason *about* variables by *using* variables. In short, we need a single definition of 'variable,' allowing both for its declarative use (in logic) and for its procedural use (in programming). Having shown that similar remarks apply to other basic computational terms, Smith outlines a unitary account of the semantics of LISP and describes a new calculus (MANTIQ) designed with the unified approach in mind.

As the example of using variables to reason about variables suggests, a unified theory of computation could illuminate how *reflective* knowledge is possible. For, given such a theory, a system's representations of data and of processes—including processes internal to the system itself—would be essentially comparable. This theoretical advantage has psychological relevance (and was a major motivation behind Smith's work).

For our present purposes, however, the crucial point is that a fundamental theory of *programs*, and of *computation*, should acknowledge that an essential function of a computer program is to make things happen. Whereas symbolic logic can be viewed as mere playing around with uninterpreted formal calculi (such as the predicate calculus), and computational logic can be seen as the study of abstract timeless relations in mathematically specified 'machines' (such as Turing machines), computer science cannot properly be described in either of these ways.

It follows from Smith's argument that the familiar characterization of computer programs as all syntax and no semantics is mistaken. The inherent procedural consequences of any computer program give it a toehold in semantics, where the semantics in question is not denotational, but causal. The analogy is with Searle-in-the-room's understanding of English, not his understanding of Chinese.

This is implied also by A. Sloman's (1986*a*; 1986*b*) discussion of the sense in which programmed instructions and computer symbols must be thought of as having some semantics, however restricted. In a causal semantics, the meaning of a symbol (whether simple or complex) is to be sought by reference to its causal links with other phenomena. The central questions are 'What causes the symbol to be built and/or activated?' and 'What happens as a result of it?' The answers will sometimes mention external objects and events visible to an observer, and sometimes they will not.

If the system is a human, animal, or robot, it may have causal powers which enable it to refer to restaurants and beansprouts (the philosophical complexities of reference to external, including unobservable, objects may be ignored here, but are helpfully discussed by Sloman). But whatever the information-processing system concerned, the answers will sometimes describe purely *internal* computational processes—whereby other symbols are built, other instructions activated. Examples include the interpretative processes inside Searle-in-the-room's mind (comparable perhaps to the parsing and semantic procedures defined for automatic natural-language processing) that are elicited by English words, and the computational processes within a Schankian text-analysis program. Although such a program cannot use the symbol 'restaurant' to mean *restaurant* (because it has no causal links with restaurants, food and so forth), its internal symbols and procedures do embody some minimal understanding of certain other matters—of what it is to compare two formal structures, for example.

One may feel that the 'understanding' involved in such a case is *so* minimal that this word should not be used at all. So be it. As Sloman makes clear, the important question is not '*When does a machine understand something?*' (a question which misleadingly implies that there is some clear cut-off point at which understanding ceases) but '*What things does a* machine *(whether biological or not) need to be able to do in order to be able to understand?'* This question is relevant not only to the *possibility* of a computational psychology, but to its *content* also.

In sum, my discussion has shown Searle's attack on computational psychology to be ill founded. To view Searle-in-the-room as an instantiation of a computer program is not to say that he lacks all understanding. Since the theories of a formalist-computational psychology should be likened to computer programs rather than to formal logic, computational psychology is not in principle incapable of explaining how meaning attaches to mental processes.

References

Boden, M.A. (1970). "Intentionality and Physical Systems." *Philosophy of Science* 37: 200–14.

Chisholm, R.M. (1967). "Intentionality." In P. Edwards (ed.), *The Encyclopedia of Philosophy.* Vol. IV, pp. 201–04. New York: Macmillan.

Dennett, D.C. (1971). "Intentional Systems." *J. Philosophy* 68: 87–106. Repr. in D.C. Dennett, *Brainstorms: Philosophical Essays on Mind and Psychology*, pp. 3–22. Cambridge, MA: MIT P, 1978.

Fodor, J.A. (1980). "Methodological Solipsism Considered as a Research Strategy in Cognitive Psychology." *Behavioral and Brain Sciences* 3: 63–110. Repr. in J.A. Fodor, *Representations: Philosophical Essays on the Foundations of Cognitive Science*, pp. 225–56. Brighton: Harvester P, 1981.

Hofstadter, D.R. (1979). *Gödel, Escher, Bach: An Eternal Golden Braid.* New York: Basic Books.

—— (1985). "Waking Up from the Boolean Dream; Or, Subcognition as Computation." In D.R. Hofstadter, *Metamagical Themas: Questing for the Essence of Mind and Pattern*, pp. 631–65. New York: Viking.

Newell, A. (1980). "Physical Symbol Systems." *Cognitive Science* 4: 135–83.

Schank, R.C., and Abelson, R.P. (1977). *Scripts, Plans, Goals, and Understanding.* Hillsdale, NJ: Erlbaum.

Searle, J.R. (1969). *Speech Acts: An Essay in the Philosophy of Language.* Cambridge: Cambridge UP.

—— (1980). "Minds, Brains, and Programs." *Behavioral and Brain Sciences* 3: 417–24.

—— (1983). *Intentionality: An Essay in the Philosophy of Mind.* Cambridge: Cambridge UP.

Sloman, A. (1986a). "Reference Without Causal Links." In B. du Boulay and L.I. Steels (eds.), *Seventh European Conference on Artificial Intelligence*, pp. 369–81. Amsterdam: North-Holland.

—— (1986b). "What Sorts of Machines Can Understand the Symbols They Use?" *Proc. Aristotelian Soc.* Supp. 60: 61–80.

Smith, B.C. (1982). *Reflection and Semantics in a Procedural Language.* Cambridge, MA: MIT PhD dissertation and Technical Report LCS/TR-272.

Stich, S.C. (1983). *From Folk Psychology to Cognitive Science: The Case Against Belief.* Cambridge, MA: MIT P/Bradford Books.

ERIC SCHWITZGEBEL AND MARA GARZA

"A Defense of the Rights of Artificial Intelligences"

"I am thy creature, and I will be ever mild and docile to my natural lord and king if thou wilt also perform thy part, the which thou owest me. Oh, Frankenstein, be not equitable to every other and trample upon me alone, to whom thy justice, and even thy clemency and affection, is most due. Remember that I am thy creature; I ought to be thy Adam..." (Frankenstein's monster to his creator, Victor Frankenstein, in Shelley 1818/1965, 95)

Introduction

We might someday create entities with *human-grade artificial intelligence*. Human-grade artificial intelligence—hereafter, just *AI*, leaving *human-grade* implicit—in our intended sense of the term, requires both intellectual and emotional similarity to human beings, that is, both human-like general theoretical and practical reasoning and a human-like capacity for joy and suffering. Science fiction authors, artificial intelligence researchers, and the (relatively few) academic philosophers who have written on the topic tend to think that such AIs would deserve moral consideration, or "rights," similar to the moral consideration we owe to human beings.[1] Below we provide a positive argument for AI rights, defend AI rights against four objections, recommend two principles of ethical AI design, and draw two further conclusions: first, that we would probably owe more moral consideration to human-grade artificial intelligences than we owe to human strangers, and second, that the

development of AI might destabilize ethics as an intellectual enterprise.

1. The No-Relevant-Difference Argument

Our main argument for AI rights is as follows:

Premise 1. If Entity A deserves some particular degree of moral consideration and Entity B does not deserve that same degree of moral consideration, there must be some *relevant difference* between the two entities that grounds this difference in moral status.

Premise 2. There are possible AIs who do not differ in any such relevant respects from human beings.

Conclusion. Therefore, there are possible AIs who deserve a degree of moral consideration similar to that of human beings.

A weaker version of this argument, which we will not focus on here, substitutes "mammals" or some other term from the animal rights literature for "human beings" in Premise 2 and the Conclusion.[2]

The argument is valid: The conclusion plainly follows from the premises. We hope that most readers will also find both premises plausible and thus accept the argument as sound. To deny Premise 1 renders ethics implausibly arbitrary. All four of the objections we consider below are challenges to Premise 2. The argument is intentionally abstract. It does not commit to any one account of what constitutes a "relevant" difference. We believe that the argument can succeed on a variety of plausible accounts. On a broadly Kantian view, rational capacities would be the most relevant. On a broadly utilitarian view, capacity for pain and pleasure would be most relevant. Also plausible are nuanced or mixed accounts or accounts that require entering certain types of social relationships. In Section 2, we will argue that only psychological and social properties should be considered directly relevant to moral status.

The argument's conclusion is intentionally weak. There are *possible* AIs who deserve a degree of moral consideration similar to that of human beings. This weakness avoids burdening our argument with technological optimism or commitment to any particular type of AI architecture. The argument leaves room for strengthening. For example, an enthusiast for strong "classical" versions of AI could strengthen Premise 2 to "There are possible AIs designed along classical lines who…" and similarly strengthen the Conclusion. Someone who thought that human beings might differ in no relevant respect from silicon-based entities, or from distributed computational networks, or from beings who live entirely in simulated worlds (Egan 1997; Bostrom 2003), could also strengthen Premise 2 and the Conclusion accordingly.

One might thus regard the No-Relevant-Difference Argument as a template that permits at least two dimensions of further specification: specification of what qualifies as a relevant difference and specification of what types of AI possibly lack any relevant difference.

The No-Relevant-Difference Argument is humanocentric in that it takes humanity as a standard. This is desirable because we assume it is less contentious among our interlocutors that human beings have rights (at least "normal" human beings, setting aside what

is sometimes called the problem of "marginal cases") than it is that rights have any specific basis such as rationality or capacity for pleasure. If a broader moral community someday emerges, it might be desirable to recast the No-Relevant-Difference Argument in correspondingly broader terms.

The argument suggests a test of moral status, which we will call the *Difference Test*. The Difference Test is a type of moral argumentative challenge. If you are going to regard one type of entity as deserving greater moral consideration than another, you ought to be able to point to a relevant difference between those entities that justifies that differential treatment. Inability to provide such a justification opens one up to suspicions of chauvinism or bias.

The Difference Test has general appeal in the fight against chauvinism and bias among human beings. Human egalitarianism gains support from the idea that skin color, ancestry, place of birth, gender, sexual orientation, and wealth cannot properly ground differences in a person's moral status. The No-Relevant-Difference Argument aims to extend this egalitarian approach to AIs.

2. The Psycho-Social View of Moral Status, and Liberalism about Embodiment and Architecture

It shouldn't matter to one's moral status what kind of body one has, except insofar as one's body influences one's psychological and social properties. Similarly, it shouldn't matter to one's moral status what kind of underlying architecture one has, except insofar as underlying architecture influences one's psychological and social properties. Only psychological and social properties are directly relevant to moral status—or so we propose. This is one way to narrow what qualifies as a "relevant" difference in the sense of Premise 1 of the No-

Relevant-Difference Argument. Call this the *psycho-social view of moral status*.[3]

By *psychological* we mean to include both functional or cognitive properties, such as the ability to reason mathematically, and phenomenological or conscious properties, such as the disposition to experience pain when damaged, regardless of whether the phenomenological or conscious reduces to the functional or cognitive. By *social* we mean to include facts about social relationships, independently of whether they are psychologically appreciated by either or both of the related parties—for example, the relationship of parenthood or citizenship or membership in a particular community. Others' *opinions* of one's moral status are a possibly relevant dimension of the social (though worryingly so), but we do not include an entity's *actual* moral status in the "social" lest the psycho-social view be trivially true.

A purely psychological view would ground moral status entirely in the psychological properties of the entity whose status is being appraised. Our view is not restricted in this way, instead allowing that social relationships might be directly relevant to moral status. Neither do we intend this view to be temporally restricted or restricted to actually manifested properties. Both past and future psychological and social properties, both actual and counterfactual, might be directly relevant to moral status (as in the case of a fetus or a brain-injured person, or in the case of an unremembered interaction, or in a case of "she would have suffered if…"). We leave open which specific psychological and social properties are relevant to moral status.

Here are two reasons to favor the psychosocial view of moral status.

1. All of the well-known modern secular accounts of moral status in philosophy ground moral status only in psychological and social properties, such as capacity for rational thought, pleasure, pain, and social relationships. No influential modern secular account is plausibly read as committed to a principle whereby two beings can differ in moral status but not in any psychological or social properties, past, present, or future, actual or counterfactual. (For a caveat, see Section 6 on the Objection from Otherness.)

However, some older or religious accounts might have resources to ground a difference in moral status outside the psychological and social. An Aristotelian *might* suggest that AIs would have a different *telos* or defining purpose than human beings. However, it's not clear that an Aristotelian must think this; nor do we think such a principle, interpreted in such a way, would be very attractive from a modern perspective, unless directly relevant psychological or social differences accompanied the difference in telos. Similarly, a theist might suggest that God somehow imbues human beings with higher moral status than AIs, even if they are psychologically and socially identical. We find this claim difficult to assess, but we're inclined to think that a deity who distributed moral status unequally in this way would be morally deficient.

2. If one considers a wide range of cases in vivid detail, it appears to be intuitively clear—though see our critiques of moral intuition in Sections 10 and 12—that what should matter to moral status are only psychological and social properties. This is, we think, one of the great lessons to be drawn from broad exposure to science fiction. Science-fictional portrayals of robots in Asimov and *Star Trek*, of simulated beings in Greg Egan and the "White Christmas" episode of *Black Mirror*, of sentient spaceships in the works of Iain Banks and Aliette de Bodard, of group minds and ugly "spiders" in Vernor Vinge, uniformly invite the thoughtful reader or viewer to a liberal attitude toward embodiment: What matters is how such beings think, what they feel, and how they interact with others.[4] Whether they are silicon or meat, humanoid or

ship-shaped, sim or ghost, is irrelevant except insofar as it influences their psychological and social properties.

To be clear: Embodiment or architecture might matter a lot to moral status. But if they do, we propose that it's only via their relationship to psychological and social properties.

3. "Artificial" and a Slippery Slope Argument for AI Rights

It's not clear what it means, in general, for something to be "artificial," nor what the term "artificial" means specifically in the context of "artificial intelligence." For our purposes, "artificial" should not be read as implying "programmed" or "made of silicon." To read it that way commits to too narrow a view of the possible future of AI. AI might leave silicon behind as it previously left vacuum tubes behind, perhaps in favor of nanotech carbon components or patterns of interference in reflected light. And even now, what we normally think of as nonhuman grade AI can be created other than by explicit programming, for example through evolutionary algorithms or training up connectionist networks.

Borderline cases abound. Are killer bees natural or artificial? How about genetically engineered viruses? If we released self-replicating nanotech and it began to evolve in the wild, at what point, if ever, would it qualify as natural? If human beings gain control over their bodily development, incorporating increasingly many manufactured and/or genetically tweaked parts, would they cross from the natural to the artificial? How about babies or brain cells grown in vats, shaped into cognitive structures increasingly unlike those of people as they existed in 2015? Might some beings who are otherwise socially and psychologically indistinguishable from natural human beings lack full moral status because of some fact about their design history—a fact perhaps

unknowable to them or to anyone with whom they are likely to interact?

Consider the film *Blade Runner* and the Philip K. Dick novel on which it was loosely based (Dick 1968; Fancher, Peoples, and Scott 1982). In that world, "andys" or "replicants" are manufactured as adults with fictional memories, and they survive for several years. Despite this fact about their manufacture, they are biologically almost indistinguishable from human beings, except by subtle tests, and sometimes neither the andys/replicants themselves nor their acquaintances know that they are not normal human beings. Nevertheless, because they are a product of the increasingly advanced development of biological-mimicry AI, they are viewed as entities with lesser rights. Such beings would be in some important sense artificial; but since they are conceptualized as having almost normal human brains, it's unclear how well our conceptions of "artificial intelligence" apply to them.

One nice feature of our view is that none of this matters. "Artificial" needn't be clearly distinguished from "natural." Once all the psychological and social properties are clarified, you're done, as far as determining what matters to moral status.

A person's moral status is not reduced by having an artificial limb. Likewise, it seems plausible to say that a person's moral status would not be reduced by replacing a damaged part of her brain with an artificial part that contributes identically to her psychology and does not affect relevant social relationships, if artificial parts can be built or grown that contribute identically to one's psychology. This suggests a second argument for AI rights:

The Slippery Slope Argument for AI rights:

Premise 1. Substituting a small artificial component into an entity with rights, if that component contributes identically to the entity's psychology and does not affect relevant social relationships, does not affect that entity's rights.

Premise 2. The process described in Premise 1 could possibly be iterated in a way that transforms a natural human being with rights into a wholly artificial being with the same rights.

Conclusion. Therefore, it is possible to create an artificial being with the same rights as those of a natural human being.

This argument assumes that replacement by artificial components is possible while preserving all relevant psychological properties, which would include the property of having conscious experience.[5] However, some might argue that consciousness, or some other relevant psychological property, could not in fact be preserved while replacing a natural brain with an artificial one—which brings us to the first of four objections to AI rights.

4. The Objection from Psychological Difference

We have asserted that there are possible AIs who have no relevant psychological differences from ordinary human beings. One objection is that this claim is too far-fetched—that all possible, or at least all realistically possible, artificial entities would differ psychologically from human beings in some respect relevant to moral status. The existing literature suggests three candidate differences of plausibly sufficient magnitude to justify denying full rights to artificial entities. Adapting a suggestion from Searle (1980), artificial entities might necessarily lack *consciousness*. Adapting a suggestion from Lovelace (1843), artificial entities might necessarily lack *free will*. Adapting a suggestion from Penrose (1999), artificial entities might necessarily be incapable of *insight*.

We believe it would be very difficult to establish such a conclusion about artificial entities in general. Even Searle, perhaps the most famous critic of strong, classical AI, says that he sees no reason in principle why a machine couldn't understand English or Chinese, which on his view would require consciousness; and he allows that artificial intelligence research might in the future proceed very differently, in a way that avoids his concerns about classical AI research in terms of formal symbol manipulation (his "Many Mansions" discussion et seq.). Lovelace confines her doubts to Babbage's analytic engine. Penrose suggests that we might someday discover in detail what endows us with consciousness that can transcend purely algorithmic thinking, and then create such consciousness artificially (1999, 416). Searle and Penrose, at least, seem to allow that technology might well be capable of creating an artificially designed, grown, or selected entity, with all the complexity, creativity, and consciousness of a human being. For this reason, we have described the objections above as "inspired" by them. They themselves are more cautious.[6]

A *certain* way of designing artificial intelligence—a nineteenth- and twentieth-century way—might not, if Searle, Lovelace, and Penrose are right, achieve certain aspects of human psychology that are important to moral status. (We take no stand here on whether this is actually so.) But no *general* argument has been offered against the moral status of all possible artificial entities. AI research might proceed very differently in the future, including perhaps artificially grown biological or semi-biological systems, chaotic systems, evolved systems, artificial brains, and systems that more effectively exploit quantum superposition.

The No-Relevant-Difference Argument commits only to a very modest claim: There are possible AIs who are not relevantly different. To argue against this possibility on broadly Searle-Lovelace-Penrose grounds will require going considerably farther than they themselves do. Pending further argument, we see no reason to think that *all* artificial entities must suffer from psychological deficiency. Perhaps the idea that AIs must necessarily lack consciousness, free will, or insight is attractive partly due to a culturally ingrained picture of AIs as deterministic, clockwork machines very different from us spontaneous, unpredictable humans. But we see no reason to think that human cognition is any less mechanical or more spontaneous than that of some possible artificial entities.

Maybe consciousness, free will, or insight requires an immaterial soul? Here we follow Turing's (1950) response to a similar concern. If naturalism is true, then whatever process generates a soul in human beings might also generate a soul in an artificial being. Even if soul-installation requires the miraculous touch of God, we're inclined to think that a god who cares enough about human consciousness, freedom, and insight to imbue us with souls might imbue the right sort of artificial entity with one also.

The arguments of Searle, Lovelace, and Penrose do raise concerns about the *detection* of certain psychological properties in artificial systems—an issue we will address in Section 11.

5. The Objection from Duplicability

AIs might not deserve equal moral concern because they do not have fragile, unique lives of the sort that human beings have. It might be possible to duplicate AIs or back them up so that if one is harmed or destroyed, others can take its place, perhaps with the same memories or seeming-memories—perhaps even ignorant that any re-creation and replacement has occurred. Harming or killing an AI might therefore lack the gravity of harming or killing

a human being. Call this the Objection from Duplicability.[7]

Our reply is simple: It should be possible to create relevantly similar AIs as unique and fragile as human beings. If so, then the No-Relevant-Difference Argument survives the objection.[8]

Although we think this reply is adequate to save the No-Relevant-Difference Argument as formulated, it's also worth considering the effects of duplicability on the moral status of AIs that are not unique and fragile. Duplicability and fragility probably would influence our moral obligations to AIs. If one being splits into five virtually identical beings, each with full memories of their previous lives before the split, and then after ten minutes of separate existence one of those beings is killed, it seems less of a tragedy than if a single unique, nonsplitting being is killed. This might be relevant to the allotment of risky tasks, especially if splitting can be planned in advance. On the other hand, the possibly lower fragility of some possible AIs might make their death more of a tragedy. Suppose a natural eighty-year-old woman with ten more years of expected life has an artificial twin similar in all relevant respects except that the twin has a thousand more years of expected life. Arguably, it's more of a tragedy for the twin to be destroyed than for the natural woman to be destroyed. Possibly it's even more tragic if the AI had the potential to split into a thousand separate AIs each with a thousand years of expected life—perhaps en route to colonize a star—who will now never exist.

Another interesting possibility, suggested in Grau (2010), is that if AIs are generally created duplicatable, they might also be created with a less vivid sense of the boundaries of the self and be better treated with an ethics that readily sacrifices one AI's interests for the benefit of another, even if such benefit tradeoffs would be morally unintuitive for human moral patients (e.g., unwilling organ donor cases). We're unsure how these issues ought to play out. However, we see here no across-the-board reason to hold AI lives in less esteem generally.

6. The Objection from Otherness

The state of nature is a "Warre, where every man is Enemy to every other man"—says Hobbes (1651/1996, 89 [62])—until some contract is made by which we agree to submit to an authority for the mutual good. Perhaps such a state of Warre is the "Naturall Condition" between species: We owe nothing to alligators and they owe nothing to us. For a moment, let's set aside any purely psychological grounds for moral consideration. A Hobbesian might say that if space aliens were to visit, they would be not at all wrong to kill us for their benefit, nor vice versa, until the right sort of interaction created a social contract. Alternatively, we might think in terms of circles of concern: We owe the greatest obligation to family, less to neighbors, still less to fellow citizens, still less to distant foreigners, maybe nothing at all outside our species. Someone might think that AIs necessarily stand outside of our social contracts or the appropriate circles of concern, and thus there's no reason to give them moral consideration.

Extreme versions of these views are, we think, obviously morally odious. Torturing or killing a human-grade AI or a conscious, self-aware, intelligent alien, without very compelling reason, is not morally excused by the being's not belonging to our species or social group. Vividly imagining such cases in science fiction scenarios draws out the clear intuition that such behavior would be grossly wrong. One might hold that biological species per se matters at least somewhat, and thus that there will always be a relevant relational difference between AIs and "us" human beings, in light of which AIs deserve less moral consideration from us than do our fellow human beings.[9] However, we suggest that this is to wrongly fetishize species membership. Consider a hypothetical case in which AI has advanced to the point where artificial entities can be seamlessly incorporated into society without the AIs themselves, or their friends, realizing their artificiality. Maybe some members of society have [choose-your-favorite-technology] brains while others have very similarly functioning natural human brains. Or maybe some members of society are constructed from raw materials as infants rather than via germ lines that trace back to homo sapiens ancestors. We submit that as long as these artificial or non–homo-sapiens beings have the same psychological properties and social relationships that natural human beings have, it would be a cruel moral mistake to demote them from the circle of full moral concern upon discovery of their different architecture or origin.

Purely *biological* otherness is irrelevant unless some important psychological or social difference flows from it. And on any reasonable application of a psychosocial standard for full moral status, there are possible AIs that would meet that standard—for example if the AI is psychologically identical to us, fully and blamelessly ensconced in our society, and differs only in social properties concerning to whom it owes its creation or its neighbors' hypothetical reaction to discovering its artificial nature.

7. The Objection from Existential Debt

Suppose you build a fully human-grade intelligent robot. It costs you $1,000 to build and $10 per month to maintain. After a couple of years, you decide you'd rather spend the $10 per month on a magazine subscription. Learning of your plan, the robot complains, "Hey, I'm a being as worthy of continued existence as you are! You can't just kill me for the sake of a magazine subscription!"

Suppose you reply: "You ingrate! You owe your very life to me. You should be thankful just for the time I've given you. I owe you nothing. If I choose to spend my money differently, it's my money to spend." The Objection from Existential Debt begins with the thought that artificial intelligence, simply by virtue of being *artificial* (in some appropriately specifiable sense), is made by us, and thus owes its existence to us, and thus can be terminated or subjugated at our pleasure without moral wrongdoing as long as its existence has been overall worthwhile.

Consider this possible argument in defense of eating humanely raised meat. A steer, let's suppose, leads a happy life grazing on lush hills. It wouldn't have existed at all if the rancher hadn't been planning to kill it for meat. Its death for meat is a condition of its existence, and overall its life has been positive; seen as the package deal it appears to be, the rancher's having brought it into existence and then killed it is overall morally acceptable.[10] A religious person dying young of cancer who doesn't believe in an afterlife might console herself similarly: Overall, she might think, her life has been good, so God has given her nothing to resent. Analogously, the argument might go, you wouldn't have built that robot two years ago had you known you'd be on the hook for $10 per month in perpetuity. Its continuation-at-your-pleasure was a condition of its very existence, so it has nothing to resent.

We're not sure how well this argument works for nonhuman animals raised for food, but we reject it for human-grade AI. We think the case is closer to this clearly morally odious case:

Ana and Vijay decide to get pregnant and have a child. Their child lives happily for his first eight years. On his ninth birthday, Ana and Vijay decide they would prefer not to pay any further expenses for the child, so that they can purchase a boat instead. No one else can easily be found to care for the child, so they kill him painlessly. But it's okay, they argue! Just like the steer and the robot! They wouldn't have had the child (let's suppose) had they known they'd be on the hook for child-rearing expenses until age eighteen. The child's support-at-their-pleasure was a condition of his existence; otherwise Ana and Vijay would have remained childless. He had eight happy years. He has nothing to resent.

The decision to have a child carries with it a responsibility for the child. It is not a decision to be made lightly and then undone. Although the child in some sense "owes" its existence to Ana and Vijay, that is not a callable debt, to be vacated by ending the child's existence. Our thought is that for an important range of possible AIs, the situation would be similar: If we bring into existence a genuinely conscious human-grade AI, fully capable of joy and suffering, with the full human range of theoretical and practical intelligence and with expectations of future life, we make a moral decision approximately as significant and irrevocable as the decision to have a child.

A related argument might be that AIs are the *property* of their creators, adopters, and purchasers and have diminished rights on that basis. This argument might get some traction through social inertia: Since all past artificial intelligences have been mere property, something would have to change for us to recognize human-grade AIs as more than mere property. The legal system might be an especially important source of inertia or change in the conceptualization of AIs as property (Snodgrass and Scheerer 1989; Chopra and White 2011). We suggest that it is approximately as odious to regard a psychologically human-equivalent AI as having diminished moral status on the grounds that it is legally property as it is in the case of human slavery.

8. Why We Might Owe More to AIs, Part One: Our Responsibility for Their Existence and Properties

We're inclined, in fact, to turn the Existential Debt objection on its head: If we intentionally bring a human-grade AI into existence, we put ourselves into a social relationship that carries responsibility for the AI's welfare. We take upon ourselves the burden of supporting it or at least of sending it out into the world with a fair shot of leading a satisfactory existence. In most realistic AI scenarios, we would probably also have some choice about the features the AI possesses, and thus presumably an obligation to choose a set of features that will not doom it to pointless misery.[11] Similar burdens arise if we do not personally build the AI but rather purchase and launch it, or if we adopt the AI from a previous caretaker.

Some familiar relationships can serve as partial models of the sorts of obligations we have in mind: parent–child, employer–employee, deity–creature. Employer–employee strikes us as likely too weak to capture the degree of obligation in most cases but could apply in an "adoption" case where the AI has independent viability and willingly enters the relationship. Parent–child perhaps comes closest when the AI is created or initially launched by someone without whose support it would not be viable and who contributes substantially to the shaping of the AI's basic features as it grows, though if the AI is capable of mature judgment from birth that creates a disanalogy. Deity–creature might be the best analogy when the AI is subject to a person with profound control over its features and environment. All three analogies suggest a special relationship with obligations that exceed those we normally have to human strangers.

In some cases, the relationship might be *literally* conceivable as the relationship between deity and creature. Consider an AI in a simulated world, a "Sim," over which you have god-like powers. This AI is a conscious part of a computer or other complex artificial device. Its "sensory" input is input from elsewhere in the device, and its actions are outputs back into the remainder of the device, which are then perceived as influencing the environment it senses. Imagine the computer game The Sims, but containing many actually conscious individual AIs. The person running the Sim world might be able to directly adjust an AI's individual psychological parameters, control its environment in ways that seem miraculous to those inside the Sim (introducing disasters, resurrecting dead AIs, etc.), have influence anywhere in Sim space, change the past by going back to a save point, and more—powers that would put Zeus to shame. From the perspective of the AIs inside the Sim, such a being would be a god. If those AIs have a word for "god," the person running the Sim might literally be the referent of that word, literally the launcher of their world and potential destroyer of it, literally existing outside their spatial manifold, and literally capable of violating the laws that usually govern their world. Given this relationship, we believe that the manager of the Sim would also possess the obligations of a god, including probably the obligation to ensure that the AIs contained within don't suffer needlessly. A burden not to be accepted lightly![12]

Even for AIs embodied in our world rather than in a Sim, we might have considerable, almost godlike control over their psychological parameters. We might, for example, have the opportunity to determine their basic default level of happiness. If so, then we will have a substantial degree of direct responsibility for their joy and suffering. Similarly, we might have the opportunity, by designing them wisely or unwisely, to make them more or less likely to lead lives with meaningful work, fulfilling social relationships, creative and artistic achievement, and other value-making goods. It would be morally odious to approach these design choices cavalierly, with so much at stake. With great power comes great responsibility.[13]

We have argued in terms of individual responsibility for individual AIs, but similar considerations hold for group-level responsibility. A society might institute regulations to ensure happy, flourishing AIs who are not enslaved or abused; or it might fail to institute such regulations. People who knowingly or negligently accept societal policies that harm their society's AIs participate in collective responsibility for that harm.

Artificial beings, if psychologically similar to natural human beings in consciousness, creativity, emotionality, self-conception, rationality, fragility, and so on, warrant substantial moral consideration in virtue of that fact alone. If we are furthermore *also* responsible for their existence and features, they have a moral claim upon us that human strangers do not ordinarily have to the same degree.

9. Why We Might Owe More to AIs, Part Two: Their Possible Superiority

Robert Nozick (1974) imagines "utility monsters" who derive enormous pleasure from sacrificing others. We might imagine a being who derives a hundred units of pleasure from each cookie it eats, while normal human beings derive only one unit of pleasure. A simple version of pleasure-maximizing utilitarianism would suggest (implausibly, Nozick thinks) that we should give all our cookies to the monster. If it is possible to create genuinely joyful experiences in AIs, it will also likely be possible to create AIs who experience substantially more joy than the typical human being. Such AIs might be something like Nozick's utility monsters. If our moral obligation is to maximize happiness, we might be obliged to create many such enti-

ties, even at substantial cost to ordinary human beings.[14] Adapting an example from Bostrom (2014), we might contemplate converting most of the mass of the solar system into "hedonium"—whatever artificial substrate most efficiently generates feelings of pleasure. We might be morally obliged to destroy ourselves to create a network of bliss machines.

Most philosophers would reject simple pleasure-maximization approaches to ethics. For example, a consequentialist might complicate her account by recognizing individual rights that cannot easily be set aside for the benefit of others. But even with such complications, any ethics that permits inflicting harm on one person to elsewhere create greater happiness, or to prevent greater suffering, invites the possibility of giving greater moral weight to outcomes for possible AIs that are capable of much greater happiness or suffering than ordinary humans.

One might hope to avoid this result by embracing an ethics that emphasizes the value of rationality rather than pleasure and pain, but this invites the possibly unappealing thought that AIs with superior rational capacities might merit greater moral consideration. To avoid this conclusion, one might treat rationality as a threshold concept with human beings already across the highest morally relevant threshold: Equal status for human beings and all creatures with rational capacities similar to or superior to those of human beings. One cookie and one vote for each.

Although such a view avoids utility monster cases, it throws us upon troubling issues of personal identity. Consider, for example, a *fission-fusion monster*—a human-grade AI who can divide and merge at will.[15] How many cookies should it get? October 31st, it is one entity. November 1st it fissions into a million human-grade AIs, each with the memories and values of the entity who existed on October 31st, each of whom applies for unemployment benefits and receives one cookie from the dole.

CHAPTER TEN • CAN MACHINES HAVE MINDS?

November 2nd the million entities vote for their favorite candidate. November 3rd the entities merge back together into one entity, who has memories of each entity's November 1st–2nd experiences, and who now has a million cookies and looks forward to its candidate's inauguration. Maybe next year it will decide to split into a million again, or a thousand, or maybe it will merge with the friendly fission-fusion monster next door. In general, if goods and rights are to be distributed equally among discrete individuals, it might be possible for AIs to win additional goods and rights by exploiting the boundaries of individuality. Whatever it is that we morally value—unless (contra Section 6) it is natural humanity itself—it would be rare stuff indeed if no hypothetical AI could possess more of it than a natural human.

[...]

11. The Strange Epistemology of Artificial Consciousness

At the end of Section 4, we mentioned that the arguments of Searle, Lovelace, and Penrose raise concerns about the detection of psychological properties in AIs....

Searle (1980) imagines a "Chinese room" in which a monolingual English speaker sits. Chinese characters are passed into the room. The room's inhabitant consults a giant lookup table, and on the basis of what he sees, he passes other Chinese characters out of the room. If the lookup table is large enough and good enough and if we ignore issues of speed, then in principle, according to Searle, the inhabitant's responses could so closely resemble real human responses that he would be mistaken for a fluent Chinese speaker, despite having no understanding of Chinese. Thus, Searle says, mere intelligent-looking symbol manipulation is insufficient for conscious understanding and,

specifically, the symbol manipulation that constitutes classical computation is insufficient to create conscious understanding in a machine. Ned Block (1978/2007) similarly imagines a mannequin whose motions are controlled by a billion people consulting a lookup table, whose resulting behavior is indistinguishable from that of a genuinely conscious person. Suppose Searle or Block is correct and a being who outwardly behaves very similarly to a human being might not be genuinely conscious, if it is not constructed from the right types of materials or according to the right design principles. People seeing it only from the outside will presumably be inclined to misattribute a genuine stream of conscious experience to it—and if they open it up, they might have very little idea what to look for to settle the question of whether it genuinely *is* conscious (Block 2002/2007 even suggests that this might be an impossible question to settle). Analogous epistemic risks attend broadly Lovelacian and Penrosian views: How can we know whether an agent is free or predetermined, operating merely algorithmically or with genuine conscious insight? This might be neither obvious from outside nor discoverable by cracking the thing open; and yet on such views, the answer is crucial to the entity's moral status.

Even setting aside such concerns, the epistemology of consciousness is difficult. It remains an open question how broadly consciousness spreads across the animal kingdom on Earth and what processes are the conscious ones in human beings. The live options span the entire range from radical panpsychism according to which everything in the universe is conscious all the way to views on which consciousness, that is, a genuine stream of subjective experience, is limited only to mature human beings in their more reflective moments.[19]

Although it seems reasonable to assume that we have not yet developed an artificial entity with a genuinely conscious stream of experience that merits substantial moral consideration, our poor understanding of consciousness raises the possibility that we might some day create an artificial entity whose status as a genuinely conscious being is a matter of serious dispute. This entity, we might imagine, says "ow!" when you strike its toe, says it enjoys watching sports on television, professes love for its friends—and it's not obvious that these are simple pre-programmed responses (as they would be for ELIZA...), but neither is it obvious that these responses reflect the genuine feelings of a conscious being. The world's most knowledgeable authorities disagree, dividing into believers (yes, this is real conscious experience, just like we have!) and disbelievers (no way, you're just falling for tricks instantiated in a dumb machine).

Such cases raise the possibility of moral catastrophe. If the disbelievers wrongly win, then we might perpetrate slavery and murder without realizing we are doing so. If the believers wrongly win, we might sacrifice real human interests for the sake of artificial entities who don't have interests worth the sacrifice.

We draw two lessons. First, if society continues on the path toward developing more sophisticated artificial intelligence, developing a good theory of consciousness is a moral imperative. Second if we do reach the point where we can create entities whose moral status is reasonably disputable, we should consider an Excluded Middle Policy—that is, a policy of only creating AIs whose moral status is clear, one way or the other.[20]

12. How Weird Minds Might Destabilize Human Ethics

Intuitive or common-sense physics works great for picking berries, throwing stones, and loading baskets. It's a complete disaster when applied to the very large, the very small, the very energetic, and the very fast. Intuitive biology and intuitive mathematics are much the same: They succeed for practical purposes across long-familiar types of cases, but when extended too far they go wildly astray.

We incline toward moral realism. We think that there are moral facts that people can get right or wrong. Hitler's moral attitudes were not just different but mistaken. The twentieth century "rights revolutions" (women's rights, ethnic rights, worker's rights, gay rights, children's rights) were not just change but progress toward a better appreciation of the moral facts. Our reflections in this essay lead us to worry that if artificial intelligence research continues to progress, intuitive ethics might encounter a range of cases for which it is as ill-prepared as intuitive physics was for quantum entanglement and relativistic time dilation. If that happens, and if there are moral facts, possibly we will get those facts badly wrong.[21]

Intuitive or common-sense ethics was shaped in a context where the only species capable of human-grade practical and theoretical reasoning was humanity itself, and where human variation tended to stay within certain boundaries. It would be unsurprising if intuitive ethics were ill-prepared for utility monsters, fission-fusion monsters, AIs of vastly superior intelligence, highly intelligent AIs nonetheless designed to be cheerfully suicidal slaves, toys with features designed specifically to capture children's affection, giant virtual sim-worlds that can be instantiated on a home computer, or entities with radically different value systems. We might expect ordinary human moral judgment to be baffled by such cases and to deliver wrong or contradictory or unstable verdicts.

In the case of physics and biology, we have pretty good scientific theories by which to correct our intuitive judgments, so it's no problem if we leave ordinary judgment behind in such matters. However, it's not clear that we have, or will have, such well-founded replacement theories in ethics. There are, of course, ambitious ethical theories—"maximize happiness," "act on that maxim that you can will to be a universal law"—but the development and adjudication of such theories depends, and might inevitably depend, upon intuitive or common-sense or common-ground starting points that are attractive to us because of our cultural and evolutionary history, and which philosophical reflection and argumentation are unlikely to dislodge. It's partly because we find it so initially plausible to think that we shouldn't give all our cookies to the utility monster or kill ourselves to tile the solar system with hedonium that we reject the straightforward extension of utilitarian happiness-maximizing theory to such cases and reach for a different type of theory. But if our intuitive or common-sense judgments about such cases are not to be trusted, because such cases are too far beyond what we can reasonably expect ordinary human moral cognition to handle—well, what then? Maybe we should kill ourselves for sake of hedonium, and we're just unable to appreciate this moral fact because we are too attached to old patterns of thinking that worked well in our limited ancestral environments?

A partial way out might be this. If the moral facts partly *depend* on our intuitive reactions and best reflective judgments, that might set some limitations on how far wrong we are likely to go—at least in favorable circumstances, when we are thinking at our best. Much like an object's being brown, on a certain view of the nature of color, just consists in its being such that ordinary human perceivers in normal conditions would experience it as brown, maybe an action's being morally right just consists in its being such that ordinary human beings who considered the matter carefully enough would tend to regard that action as right—or something in that ballpark.[22] We might then be able to shape future morality—real morality, the real (or real enough) moral facts—by shaping our future reactions and judgments. One society or subculture, for example, might give a certain range of rights and opportunities to fission-fusion monsters, another society a different range of rights and opportunities, and this might substantially influence people's reactions to such entities and the success of the society in propagating its moral vision. Our ethical assessments might be temporarily destabilized but resolve into one or more coherent solutions.[23]

However, the range of legitimate moral choices is we think constrained by certain moral facts sufficiently implacable that a system that rejected them would not be a satisfactory moral system on the best way of construing the possible boundaries of "morality" worth the name. One such implacable fact is that it would be a moral disaster if our future society constructed large numbers of human-grade AIs, as self-aware as we are, as anxious about their future, and as capable of joy and suffering, simply to torture, enslave, and kill them for trivial reasons.[24]

Notes

1. Classic examples in science fiction include Isaac Asimov's robot stories (esp. 1954/1962, 1982) and *Star Trek: The Next Generation*, especially the episode "The Measure of a Man" (Snodgrass and Scheerer 1989). Academic treatments include Basl 2013; Bryson 2013; Bostrom and Yudkowsky 2014; Gunkel and Bryson, 2014. See also Coeckelbergh 2012 and Gunkel 2012 for critical treatments of the question as typically posed. We use the term "rights" here

to refer broadly to moral considerability, moral patiency, or the capacity to make legitimate ethical claims upon us.

2. On sub-human AI and animal rights, see especially Basl 2013, 2014.

3. Compare Bostrom and Yudkowsky's (2014) Principle of Substrate Non-Discrimination and Principle of Ontogeny Non-Discrimination. We embrace the former but possibly not the latter (depending on how it is interpreted), as should be clear from our discussion of social properties and especially our special duties to our creations.

4. See Asimov 1954/1962, 1982; Snodgrass and Scheerer 1989; Egan 1994, 1997; Brooker and Tibbets 2014; Banks' "Culture" series from 1987 to 2012; de Bodard, e.g., 2011, 2013; Vinge 1992, 1999, 2011.

5. Our argument is thus importantly different from superficially similar arguments in Cuda (1985) and Chalmers (1996), which assume the possibility of replacement parts that are functionally identical but which do not assume that consciousness is preserved. Rather, the preservation of consciousness is what Cuda and Chalmers are trying to establish as the argumentative conclusion, with the help of some further premises, such as (in Chalmers) introspective reliability. We find the Cuda-Chalmers argument attractive but we are not committed to it.

6. We have also simplified the presentation of the positions "inspired by" Searle, Lovelace, and Penrose in a way that the authors might not fully approve. Lovelace (1843), for example, doesn't use the word "freedom" or the phrase "free will"—more characteristic is "the machine is not a thinking being, but simply an automaton which acts according to the laws imposed on it" (675); also, the machine "follows" rather than "originates" (722). Searle

(1980) emphasizes meaning, understanding, and intentionality in a way not emphasized in this brief description. Penrose's position does not entirely contrast with Searle's on the issue of consciousness, since he suggests that an algorithmic machine or automaton would lack consciousness, and conversely Searle suggests that consciousness is necessary for "flexibility and creativity" (Searle 1992, 108) in a way that might fit with Penrose's nonalgorithmic insight and perhaps the idea implicit in Lovelace that "thinking" requires more than acting according to imposed laws. The success of our reply does not, we think, depend on philosophical differences at this level of detail. See Estrada 2014 for extensive discussion of Lovelace's objection and Turing's replies to her and others' objections.

7. This objection is inspired by Peter Hankins's (2015) argument that duplicability creates problems for holding robots criminally responsible. (Hankins also suggests that programmed robots have "no choice"—a concern more in the spirit of the previous section.)

8. Whether it would be good to create fragile rather than sturdy AIs will depend on the details. Fragility needn't be bad overall if other factors compensate. On the other hand, it might be problematic for an AI designer to make an AI fragile and difficult to duplicate simply to inflate our moral consideration for it.

9. This is a version of the view Singer labels pejoratively as "speciesism" (1975/2002, 2009). Our view is also compatible with Kagan's (forthcoming) critique of Singer on this issue, since it seems that Kagan's proposed "personism" would not violate the psycho-social view of moral status in the broad sense of Section 2. Perhaps Wil-

liams (2006, ch. 13) advocates speciesism per se, though it's not entirely clear.

10. See DeGrazia 2009 for presentation and criticism of an argument along roughly these lines.

11. Analogous issues are central to the ethics of disability, eugenics, and human enhancement, e.g., Glover 2006; Buchanan 2011; Sparrow 2011.This is notoriously hazardous moral terrain, and in particular we would not endorse the simplistic ideal of always trying to maximize what we currently judge to be beauty, intelligence, moral character, and ability.

12. We assume that divinities do have moral obligations to their creations, despite some religious traditions that hold otherwise. The intuitive appeal of our view is nicely illustrated by fantastical tales of creators who feel insufficient obligation, as in Twain (1900/1969, ch. 2) and Lem (1967/1974). Only finite deities are relevant to the present argument. For further reflections on this theme, presented as science fiction, see Schwitzgebel and Bakker 2013; Schwitzgebel 2015b.

13. As Uncle Ben wisely advises Spider-Man in the 2002 film (Lee et al. 2002, slightly modifying a passage in the voice of the narrator in Lee and Ditko 1962).

14. Compare also Parfit's (1984) "Repugnant Conclusion."

15. For a related example, see Briggs and Nolan [2015].

[…]

19. For more detail on the first author's generally skeptical views about the epistemology of consciousness, see Schwitzgebel 2011, 2014, 2015a.

20. In her provocatively titled article "Robots Should Be Slaves" (2010; see also Bryson 2013), Joanna J. Bryson argues for a version of the Excluded Middle Policy: Since robots with enough mental sophistication might become targets of moral concern, we should adopt a policy of only making robots sufficiently unsophisticated that their "enslavement" would be morally permissible.

21. Compare Bakker on "crash spaces" for our "ancestral ways of meaning making" (Bakker this issue, postscript).

22. We've used a "secondary quality" type phrasing here, but in fact we are imagining a broad class of views such as the (disagreeing) views of McDowell (1985); Railton (1986); Brink (1989); Casebeer (2003); and Flanagan, Sarkissian, and Wong (2007)—naturalistic, allowing for genuine moral truths, with norms contingent upon facts about the human condition, but not so strongly relativist as to deny a normatively compelling, fairly stable moral core across human cultures as they have existed so far.

23. Thus, despite the generally moral realist framing of this article, we accept aspects of the more constructivist and relativist views of Coeckelbergh (2012) and Gunkel (2012), according to which we collaboratively decide, rather than discover, who is and who is not part of the moral community and "grow" moral relations through actively engaging with the world. Compare also Mandik (this issue) on cultural selection for metaphysical daring in a posthuman environment.

24. For helpful discussion, thanks to Nir Aides, Scott Bakker, Joe Corneli, Phil Hand, Peter Hankins, Davy Schwitzgebel, Justin E.H. Smith, and the many people who commented, privately or publicly, on our posts on these topics on The Splintered Mind and Codex Writers Group.

References

Asimov, Isaac. 1954/1962. *Caves of Steel*. New York: Pyramid.

———. 1982. *The Complete Robot*. Garden City, NY: Doubleday.

Banks, Iain. 1987. *Consider Phlebas*. New York: Hachette.

———. 2012. *The Hydrogen Sonata*. New York: Hachette.

Basl, John. 2013."The Ethics of Creating Artificial Consciousness." *APA Newsletter on Philosophy and Computers* 13(1): 23–29.

———. 2014. "Machines as Moral Patients We Shouldn't Care About (Yet): The Interests and Welfare of Current Machines." *Philosophy and Technology* 27: 79–96.

Block, Ned. 1978/2007. "Troubles with Functionalism." In *Consciousness, Function, and Representation*. Cambridge, MA: MIT Press.

———. 2002/2007. "The Harder Problem of Consciousness." In *Consciousness, Function, and Representation*. Cambridge, MA: MIT Press.

Boden, Margaret et al. 2010. "Principles of Robotics." ESPRC website. Retrieved August 21, 2015, from https://www.epsrc.ac.uk/research/ourportfolio/themes/engineering/activities/principlesofrobotics/.

Bostrom, Nick. 2003. "Are We Living in a Computer Simulation?" *Philosophical Quarterly* 53: 243–55.

———. 2014. *Superintelligence*. Oxford: Oxford University Press.

Bostrom, Nick, and Yudkowsky, Eliezer. 2014."The Ethics of Artificial Intelligence." In *Cambridge Handbook of Artificial Intelligence*, ed. K. Frankish and. M. Ramsey. Cambridge: Cambridge University Press.

Briggs, Rachael, and Nolan, Daniel. 2015. "Utility Monsters for the Fission Age." *Pacific Philosophical Quarterly*. 96 (2): 392–407.

Brink, David O. 1989. *Moral Realism and the Foundations of Ethics*. Cambridge: Cambridge University Press.

Brooker, Charlie, and Tibbets, Carl. 2014. "White Christmas." Episode of *Black Mirror* television series, season 2, episode 4.

Bryson, Joanna J. 2010. "Robots Should Be Slaves." In *Close Engagements with Artificial Companions*, ed. Y. Wilks. Amsterdam: John Benjamins.

———. 2013. "Patiency Is Not a Virtue: Intelligent Artifacts and the Design of Ethical Systems." Online MS. Retrieved July 7, 2015, from https://www.cs.bath.ac.uk/~jjb/ftp/Bryson-MQ-J.pdf.

Buchanan, Allen E. 2011. *Beyond Humanity?* Oxford: Oxford University Press.

Casebeer, William. 2003. *Natural Ethical Facts*. Cambridge, MA: MIT Press.

Chalmers, David J. 1996. *The Conscious Mind*. Oxford: Oxford University Press.

Chopra, Samir, and White, Laurence F. 2011. *Legal Theory for Autonomous Artificial Agents*. Ann Arbor: University of Michigan Press.

Clark, Andy. 2011. *Supersizing the Mind*. Oxford: Oxford University Press.

Clarke, Arthur C. 1953. *Childhood's End*. New York: Random House.

Coeckelbergh, Mark. 2012. *Growing Moral Relations*. Basingstoke, UK: Palgrave Macmillan.

Cuda, Tom. 1985. "Against Neural Chauvinism." *Philosophical Studies* 48: 111–27.

Darling, Kate. Forthcoming. "Extending Legal Rights to Social Robots." In *Robot Law*, ed. M. Froomkin, R. Calo and I. Kerr. Cheltenham, UK: Edward Elgar.

de Bodard, Aliette. 2011. Shipbirth. *Asimov's* 35(2): 50–60.

———. 2013. "The Waiting Stars." In *The Other Half of the Sky*, ed. A. Andreadis and K. Holt. Bennington, VT: Candlemark & Gleam.

DeGrazia, David. 2009. "Moral Vegetarianism from a Very Broad Basis." *Journal of Moral Philosophy* 6: 455–68.

Dick, Philip K. 1968. *Do Androids Dream of Electric Sheep?* New York: Doubleday.

Egan, Greg. 1994. *Permutation City*. London: Millennium.

——. 1997. *Diaspora*. London: Millennium.

Estrada, Daniel. 2014. *Rethinking Machines*. PhD dissertation, Philosophy Department, University of Illinois, Urbana-Champaign.

Fancher, Hampton, Peoples, David, and Scott, Ridley. 1982. *Blade Runner*. Warner Brothers.

Fiala, Brian, Arico, Adam, and Nichols, Shaun. 2012. "The Psychological Origins of Dualism." In *Creating Consilience*, ed. E. Slingerland and M. Collard. Oxford: Oxford University Press.

Flanagan, Owen, Sarkissian, Hagop, and Wong, David. 2007. "Naturalizing Ethics." In *Moral Psychology*, ed. W. Sinnott-Armstrong, vol. 1. Cambridge, MA: MIT Press.

Glover, Jonathan. 2006. *Choosing Children*. Oxford: Oxford University Press.

Grau, Christopher. 2010. "There Is No 'I' in 'Robot': Robots and Utilitarianism." In *Machine Ethics*, ed. S.L. Anderson and M. Anderson. Cambridge: Cambridge University Press.

Gunkel, David J. 2012. *The Machine Question*. Cambridge, MA: MIT Press.

Gunkel, David J., and Bryson, Joanna J., eds. 2014. "Machine Morality." Special issue of *Philosophy and Technology* 27(1).

Hankins, Peter. 2015. "Crimbots." Blogpost at *Conscious Entities*. Retrieved February 2, 2015, from http://www.consciousentities.com/?p=1851.

Hobbes, Thomas. 1651/1996. *Leviathan*, ed. R. Tuck. Cambridge: Cambridge University Press.

Johnson, Susan C. 2003. "Detecting Agents." *Philosophical Transactions of the Royal Society B* 358: 549–59.

Kagan, Shelly. 2016. "What's Wrong with Speciesism?" *Journal of Applied Philosophy* 33 (1): 1–116.

L'Engle, Madeline. 1963. *A Wrinkle in Time*. New York: Scholastic.

Lee, Stan, and Ditko, Steve. 1962. *Spider-Man*. Amazing Fantasy, 15.

Lee, Stan, Ditko, Steve, Koepp, David, and Raimi, Sam. 2002. *Spider-Man*. Columbia Pictures.

Lem, Stanislaw. 1967/1974. "The Seventh Sally." In *The Cyberiad*, ed. and trans, M. Kandel. San Diego, CA: Harcourt.

Lovelace, Ada. 1843. "Sketch of the Analytical Engine Invented by Charles Babbage, by L.F. Menabrea." In *Scientific Memoirs*, ed. R. Taylor, vol. III. London: Richard and John E. Taylor.

McDowell, John. 1985. "Values and Secondary Qualities." In *Morality and Objectivity*, ed. T. Honderich. New York: Routledge.

Meltzoff, Andrew N., Brooks, Rechele, Shon, Aaron P., and Rao, Rajesh P. N. 2010. "'Social' Robots Are Psychological Agents for Infants: A Test of Gaze Following." *Neural Networks* 23: 966–72.

Nozick, Robert. 1974. *Anarchy, State, and Utopia*. New York: Basic Books.

Parfit, Derek. 1984. *Reasons and Persons*. Oxford: Oxford University Press.

Penrose, Roger. 1999. *The Emperor's New Mind*. New York: Oxford University Press.

Railton, Peter. 1986. "Moral Realism." *Philosophical Review* 95: 163–207.

Scheutz, Matthias. 2012. "The Inherent Dangers of Unidirectional Emotional Bonds between Humans and Social Robots." In *Robot Ethics*, ed. N.G. Lin, K. Abney, and G.A. Bekey. Cambridge, MA: MIT Press.

Schwitzgebel, Eric. 2011. *Perplexities of Consciousness*. Cambridge, MA: MIT Press.

———. 2014. "The Crazyist Metaphysics of Mind." *Australasian Journal of Philosophy* 92: 665–82.

———. 2015a. "If Materialism Is True, the United States Is Probably Conscious." *Philosophical Studies* 172: 1697–721.

———. 2015b. "Out of the Jar." *Magazine of Fantasy and Science Fiction* 128(1): 118–28.

Schwitzgebel, Eric, and Bakker, R. Scott. 2013. "Reinstalling Eden." *Nature* 503: 562.

Searle, John R. 1980. "Minds, Brains, and Programs." *Behavioral and Brain Sciences* 3: 417–57.

———. 1992. *The Rediscovery of the Mind*. Cambridge, MA: MIT Press.

Shelley, Mary. 1818/1965. *Frankenstein*. New York: Signet Classics.

Singer, Peter. 1975/2002. *Animal Liberation*. New York: Ecco Press.

———. 2009. "Speciesism and Moral Status." *Metaphilosophy* 40: 567–81.

Snodgrass, Melinda M., and Scheerer, Robert. 1989. "The Measure of a Man." *Star Trek: The Next Generation*, tv series, season 2, episode 9.

Sparrow, Robert. 2011. "A Not-So-New Eugenics." *Hastings Center Report* 41(1): 32–42.

Turing, A.M. 1950. "Computing Machinery and Intelligence." *Mind* 59: 433–60.

Turkle, Sherry. 2010. "In Good Company? On the Threshold of Robot Companions." In *Close Engagements with Robotic Companions*, ed. Y. Wilks. Amsterdam: John Benjamins.

Twain, Mark. 1900/1969. "The Chronicle of Young Satan." In *Mark Twain's Mysterious Stranger Manuscripts*, ed. W.M. Gibson. Berkeley: University of California Press.

Vinge, Vernor. 1992. *A Fire Upon the Deep*. New York: Tor Books.

———. 1999. *A Deepness in the Sky*. New York: Tor Books.

———. 2011. *Children of the Sky*. New York: Tor Books.

Weizenbaum, Joseph. 1976. *Computer Power and Human Reason*. San Francisco: W.H. Freeman.

Williams, Bernard. 2006. *Philosophy as a Humanistic Discipline*, ed. A.W. Moore. Princeton, NJ: Princeton University Press.

Study Questions

1. In the last paragraph of section 4, Turing says that "all digital computers are in a sense equivalent." What does he mean by this?

2. Consider what Turing calls "The Argument from Consciousness." Outline this argument, then Turing's responses. Does what he says in the paragraph beginning "In short then," sum up his response? Do you find his response adequate? Explain and defend your position.

3. Turing suggests, at the end of the section considering "Arguments from Various Disabilities," that these arguments are often disguised forms of the argument from consciousness. Explain how the disabilities arguments might really be of this sort.

4. Compare Turing's view of mind to functionalism. (Hint: See Fodor's comments on the distinction between software and hardware.)

5. Having given the "Chinese Room" thought experiment, Searle claims that it is obvious that "I do not understand a word of Chinese stories." This is true. Does it follow that, for the same reason, Schank's computer understands nothing of any stories? Remember that the "I" in the story is just one part of the "computer" that inputs and outputs responses. Evaluate the "Systems Reply" to Searle.

6. If you build a computer simulation of some human activity, is that any reason to think that the computer is actually *performing* that activity? (Can you think of any cases where this might be so?) Would the simulation *explain* the activity? Compare Turing's and Searle's answers to this. Who is right?

7. When Searle says that the Systems Reply "simply begs the question," what does this mean? Why does he say this? Is he right?

8. Try to figure out what sort of reasons Searle has for insisting that "a machine defined solely in terms of computational processes over formally defined elements" *could not* be given the capacity to understand English. (The important word here seems to be 'solely.') Boden may help here.

9. Consider the "Robot Reply" Searle reports, Searle's retort, and Boden's discussion of both. (a) Outline the Reply and Searle's retort. (b) Why might it seem that a "robot" as conceived, embedded in an external environment, would be a better candidate for containing intentionality than (say) your computer? (c) Explain what a "false analogy" is, and why Boden thinks Searle's retort involves this.

10. What does Searle mean by saying that the contents of a computer have *syntax* but no *semantics*? You might have to look up these two words in the Glossary at the end of this book. The Introduction to this section and Boden's article will help with this question. Boden's criticism is that even a computer, in a sense, has a "semantics," in that its function is to make things happen in the world external to it. Explain why "making things happen" can be seen as at least something like "having a semantics."

11. Schwitzgebel and Garza give only passing treatment to what might be considered the ethically central dissimilarity between any machine and a human: that humans are conscious, and arguably no machine could be. Assuming that this difference really must exist, do you think it's ethically relevant? Consider: does a permanently unconscious brain-damaged human lack all moral standing?

12. Schwitzgebel and Garza consider the suggestion that our moral intuitions are based on the facts as we've known them; the science-fiction scenarios they imagine then might yield inconsistent moral intuitions or result only in puzzlement. Does this mean that looking for answers to ethical questions under various science-fiction scenarios is a useless exercise, bound to fail to give reasonable results? What is their response?

13. Imagine the existence of something like human-grade consciousness in future machines. That would make them something like some of the higher animals, who (most of us are convinced) feel pain, have social relations (including relations with us), etc. But we do not give *full* human rights to any animal. Is this a mistake? Or is this a

correct response to the fact that these animals are not fully like us—so deserving of moral consideration, but not equal to that of humans. Consider "The Objection from Otherness," section 6 of Schwitzgebel and Garza's argument. Explain what they say; do they respond adequately to this objection? How might their arguments apply to how we treat animals?

Suggested Readings

A great deal has been written about minds and machines, often dealing with both the Turing Test and with Searle's Chinese Room Argument. Here are a few references:

Stevan Harnad, "Minds, Machines and Searle," *Journal of Experimental and Theoretical Artificial Intelligence* 1 (1989): pp. 5–25. See also his "Minds, Machines and Turing: The Indistinguishability of Indistinguishables," *Journal of Logic, Language and Information* 9 (2000): pp. 425–45.

Daniel C. Dennett, "Can Machines Think?," in *How We Know*, Michael G. Shafto (ed.). (New York: Harper & Row 1984).

Keith Gunderson, "The Imitation Game," *Mind* 73 (1964): pp. 234–45.

Ned Block, "Psychologism and Behaviorism," *Philosophical Review* 90 (1981): pp. 5–43.

Hilary Putnam, "Minds and Machines," in *Dimensions of Mind*, Sidney Hook (ed.). (New York: New York University Press, 1960).

Jerry A. Fodor, "Yin and Yang in the Chinese Room," in *The Nature of Mind*, D. Rosenthal, (ed.). (Oxford: Oxford University Press, 1991). An anthology including a number of important recent articles (including one by Searle) is *Views into the Chinese Room: New Essays on Searle and Artificial Intelligence*. John M. Preston and Michael A. Bishop (eds.). (Oxford: Oxford University Press, 2002).

For a classic critique of the possibility of "strong AI", see:

J.R. Lucas, "Minds, Machines, and Gödel," in *Minds and Machines*, A.R. Anderson, ed. (Prentice-Hall, NJ: Prentice-Hall, 1964), pp. 43–59.

For more on issues related to the possibility of conscious AI, see:

David Chalmers, "The Singularity: A Philosophical Analysis," *Journal of Consciousness Studies* 17 (2010): 7–65.

Daniel C. Dennett, "The Practical Requirements for Making a Conscious Robot," *Philosophical Transactions: Physical Sciences and Engineering* 349 (1994): pp. 133–46.

For more on the moral status of AI, see:

Robert Sparrow, "The Turing Triage Test," *Ethics and Information Technology* 6 (2004): pp. 203–13.

11

CONSCIOUSNESS AND "WHAT IT IS LIKE"

Introduction

In this chapter, we explore positions on a feature of the mind that is perhaps, as the philosopher David Chalmers has put it, "at once the most familiar thing in the world and the most mysterious": consciousness. For many, including Chalmers, what makes consciousness such a puzzling phenomenon is the strong sense that an adequate scientific explanation of it remains forever out of reach. Though physics, chemistry, biology, and psychology have helped us understand the foundations of life, the structure of the universe, and various aspects of the human mind, they seem for many to be hopelessly ill-equipped when it comes to explaining our subjective experiences. As we will see in this chapter, attempts to articulate and defend this impression, as well as subsequent reactions to such attempts, have provoked some of the strongest disagreements in philosophy of mind.

The Qualitative Character of Experience

Let's first review the general nature of the issue before us. Common sense suggests that there are certain facts about conscious experiences that pertain to what those experiences are like for the person undergoing them. This is perhaps clearest in the case of conscious sensations such as pains, and sensory experiences in the various modalities, though it holds no less for emotional experiences, and some even argue for the experience of thinking certain thoughts. There are many terms that are used to describe this aspect of consciousness. We have so far encountered three: the *phenomenal properties* of conscious experience, which Block and others refer to as *qualia*; and the *qualitative content* of mental states, which Jerry Fodor contrasts with intentional content. To add another one to the list, Thomas Nagel, in our next reading, calls it the **subjective character**

of experience. A general name that it is often given, and one that we will make liberal use of in this chapter, is the **qualitative character of experience**.

Part of what makes this aspect of experience so hard to identify is that it is notoriously difficult to capture in words. This is not to deny that we have a rich vocabulary for *aspects* of the qualitative character of our experiences. We can describe a pain, for example, as sharp or dull, throbbing or steady, mild or severe. And we can distinguish, using such descriptions, among pains of different types, for example headaches versus stomachaches, and cuts versus burns. Yet it seems that no matter how rich our vocabulary, we will still inevitably fall short of communicating the full qualitative character of an experience. Imagine trying to explain the difference between purple and yellow to a person blind from birth, or the experience of a papercut to someone who has never felt pain. It would seem that to get at what color sensations or papercuts are really like, one must experience them for oneself. And while we can *name* the basic phenomenal properties, it seems that we cannot further describe them. As we saw in earlier chapters, Wittgenstein and others have used these observations to question the validity of the very concept of phenomenal properties, a strategy that is followed by Daniel Dennett in our readings in this chapter.

Consciousness and the Mechanical Sciences

As we saw in Chapter Three, the qualitative character of experience became a philosophical problem with the rise of the mechanical sciences in the seventeenth century. Mechanical scientists like Galileo and Descartes drew a distinction between the way the world appears to us and the properties that actually exist in the world. And, as we saw there, this stands in sharp contrast to Aristotle's theory of perception. Recall that according to Aristotle, the character of our experience is *identical* to the character of the physical world around us. For example, Aristotle believed that colors exist in the world exactly as we perceive them. In rejecting Aristotle's theories, the new scientists argued that there need be no similarity at all between our sensations and the qualities of physical objects. According to the mechanical sciences, the way colors and other secondary qualities appear to us is not an aspect of the physical world, but rather an aspect of our minds. As Galileo put it, qualities like color, *as they are experienced by us*, exist only in our consciousness.

Dualists such as Descartes are able to explain the difference between the character of our sensations and the character of the physical world by insisting that the mind is a substance distinct from matter. The qualitative features of consciousness, on this view, are intrinsic characteristics of the immaterial mind, and are not a part of the physical world. However, if one rejects dualism, while maintaining a mechanical theory of matter, then it becomes very hard to say what qualitative properties are. If the mind itself is simply a part of the physical world, as materialists maintain, then what becomes of the way that colors look to us? It seems that while the mechanical sciences banished the qualitative character of experience to the inner mind, materialism threatens to remove it from existence altogether.

Consciousness and Contemporary Theories

The qualitative aspect of experience presents a problem for each of the theories we surveyed in Part Two. None of these theories defines mental states in terms of their qualitative properties. Behaviorists define mental states as relations between stimulus and behavior. Identity theorists argue that mental states are purely physical states of the brain, describable through topic-neutral characteristics such as their typical causes. Functionalists define mental states as functional states mediating between stimulus and behavior. In none of these cases are qualitative properties seen as *essential* features of our mental states. This means that materialists must either find a way to account for qualitative properties, or they must reject the idea that there are such properties.

Philosophers have responded in different ways to this problem. In the essays that follow, Thomas Nagel and Frank Jackson argue that physical science is unable to explain the qualitative nature of consciousness, and conclude from this that materialism is seriously threatened. Daniel Dennett, on the other hand, claims that insisting on the importance of the qualitative properties of conscious experience is a mistake because such properties simply don't exist as described. Likewise, Rosenthal is skeptical that qualitative properties should be construed in the way that the thought experiments of Nagel and Jackson, among others, have suggested. He argues instead that there is an objective basis for studying what the conscious experience of others is like. Akins challenges Nagel and Jackson's stance from a different perspective, arguing that phenomenal properties are inextricable from intentionality and representation, and since these are properties of experience that science can help us understand, there's hope that science will be able to tell us about phenomenal properties in the fullness of time.

Nagel's Rejection of Reductionism

The beginning of this debate in contemporary philosophy can be traced in many ways to an article written by Thomas Nagel in the 1970s called "What Is It Like to Be a Bat?" Nagel is currently University Professor of Philosophy and Law Emeritus at New York University. In his numerous publications, especially *The View from Nowhere* of 1986, Nagel has expressed deep skepticism about any scientific reductionist account of mind and consciousness. In his article Nagel argues that we cannot ignore the qualitative character of mental states, and for that very reason it is impossible to reduce descriptions of the mind to descriptions of neurological activity or to functional properties. Nagel argues that the mind-body problem is not at all like cases of reduction in the physical sciences, such as the reduction of lightning to electrical discharge, with which it is often compared. Nagel argues that the central characteristic of the mind is consciousness, and by this he means in particular the qualitative character of experience. He claims that it is nonsensical to reduce the elements of consciousness to either physical features of the brain or the functional properties of machine states.

Subjective Experience

Nagel claims that for a creature (human or otherwise) to have consciousness means that there is "something it is like" to be that sort of creature, and he refers to this as the *subjective character of experience*. He illustrates this idea by considering the experience of a bat, a creature whose form of perception is very different from our own. As we can presume that bats have conscious experience, there must be something it is like to be a bat. The question, then, is how this aspect of the mind can be explained in the terms of neuroscience—how and whether neuroscience can answer the question, "What is it like to be a bat?"

Nagel makes two preliminary remarks about subjective experience. The first is that it is not possible for us to *imagine* what the subjective experience of other creatures is like. We can imagine ourselves behaving like a bat, but that doesn't tell us what experience is like *for the bat*. The second point is that taking the idea of subjective experience seriously implies accepting the existence of something that cannot be expressed entirely in language. Here Nagel is raising the point we mentioned earlier in the chapter: We cannot convey the qualitative character of experience with words. Given this fact, it seems as though we can come to understand the experiences of others only by having similar experiences ourselves. This is what Nagel means by referring to consciousness as a *subjective* phenomenon. A fact is **subjective** if it can only be understood by creatures with a certain form of conscious experience (what Nagel calls a "point of view"). He says:

> There is a sense in which phenomenological facts are perfectly objective: one person can know or say of another what the quality of the other's experience is. They are subjective, however, in the sense that even this objective ascription of experience is possible only for someone sufficiently similar to the object of ascription to be able to adopt his point of view—to understand the ascription in the first person as well as in the third, so to speak.

Objective facts, on the other hand, are those that can be understood by creatures with very different points of view. For example, he points out that there are facts about lightning that could be understood by "bat scientists" or Martians, whose experience of lightning is very different from ours. Creatures with very different subjective experience can converse with one another about objective facts even though they could not convey to one another what their respective experience of those facts is like.

Nagel's Argument against Reductionism

It is the subjectivity of experience, Nagel claims, that makes it impossible to reduce descriptions of experience to neurological or functional descriptions. His argument is based on an analysis of how successful reduction works. In successful cases of reduction, he argues, the reduction is always from a subjective description toward a more objective description. For example, heat is initially understood by humans in terms of the subjective impression of warmth, and only later do we come to understand it in objective terms as molecular motion. There could conceivably be creatures who do not experience heat in the way that we do, but who are nonetheless perfectly familiar with the facts about molecular motion. We could discuss with them the objective facts about heat, but we could not convey to them what our subjective experience of heat is like, what heat *feels* like to us. In reducing the observable characteristics of the physical world to the objective sciences we are replacing a concept tied to the impressions objects make on our senses to one that is not so dependent.

The fact that reduction always moves in the direction of greater objectivity is the basis for Nagel's argument against a reductive explanation of subjective experience. For we have no idea, he says, how to give an objective explanation of something that is *intrinsically* subjective. Many different forms of life may be able to understand the objective facts about bat physiology, but only bats can know what it is like to be a bat. Hence, a neurophysiological description of a bat, even if it is complete in every detail, will still leave out what Nagel claims is essential to the mind: the character of subjective experience. It is impossible, then, to reduce descriptions of inner mental life to descriptions of brain activity. The same would be true of the attempt to reduce subjective experience to functional properties of the brain, as functionalists advocate.

Nagel's conclusion is that we currently have no idea how materialism *could* be true. For Nagel the relationship between brain activity and consciousness is a mystery into which we have no insight. We must continue to describe ourselves in two different vocabularies: in terms of the objective facts of our neurophysiology and the subjective facts of our conscious experience. Nagel concedes that it may someday become apparent how to achieve a successful reduction of consciousness to brain activity, but this will require a notion of intertheoretic reduction utterly different from what we now understand. Under our current conception of reduction, it is contradictory to reduce subjective experience to objective facts.

Epiphenomenal Qualia

The central concept in Nagel's argument is that of subjective experience, which he describes as "what it is like to be an *x*," where *x* is a kind or species of organism. This concept is intended to capture the qualitative aspect of conscious experience. Although Nagel's characterization of the qualitative has a certain intuitive appeal, critics have complained that it is too broad and vague. A sharper critique is offered in Frank Jackson's article, "Epiphenomenal Qualia." Jackson is an Australian philosopher, currently Emeritus Professor at Australian National University in Canberra. For several years he taught at Princeton University. In this article Jackson presents an argument somewhat similar to Nagel's, but which relies on a different way of characterizing the qualitative side of conscious experience. Jackson employs the word 'qualia,' which we first encountered in Ned Block's critique of functionalism in Chapter Nine, but he gives this term a special use. He defines qualia as:

> certain features of the bodily sensations especially, but also of certain perceptual experiences, which no amount of purely physical information includes.

More fully, a quale, as Jackson uses the term, is a property of certain kinds of mental states, namely sensations and perceptual experiences, that cannot be described in words referring only to physical processes of the nervous system. Jackson's examples of qualia are "the hurtfulness of pains, the itchiness of itches, pangs of jealousy, or... the characteristic experience of tasting a lemon, smelling a rose, hearing a loud noise or seeing the sky."

An important aspect of Jackson's use of the term 'qualia' is the way that this concept defines the problem of consciousness. As Jackson conceives of it, the qualitative element of consciousness should be seen as a set of *properties* or features that sensations and perceptual states possess. What identifies these properties as qualia is that they cannot be described in physical vocabulary. The problem of consciousness thus becomes the problem of explaining (or explaining away) the existence of these sorts of properties. In Section III of his article, Jackson uses this feature of his characterization to differentiate his argument from Nagel's.

Jackson's Argument against Materialism

According to Jackson, the existence of qualia shows that materialism, or physicalism as he calls it, is false. In his view, demonstrating that there are aspects of conscious experience that physical descriptions cannot capture provides a very simple and conclusive argument for dualism. Here is the argument in the fourth paragraph:

Nothing you could tell of a purely physical sort captures the smell of a rose, for instance. Therefore, Physicalism is false.

This argument is a version of what has been called the Knowledge Argument, which contends that no amount of knowledge in neuroscience, or any other physical science for that matter, will explain the nature of the qualitative character of experience. The premise of this argument is just the statement that qualia exist. Jackson maintains that there can be no question of the validity of the argument (given his definition of sensations as non-physical). His article is therefore devoted primarily to establishing the truth of the premise, from which he believes dualism follows directly. As we will see, Jackson defends a version of dualism different from those we have looked at so far. But first let's examine Jackson's defense of the premise of his argument.

Jackson's First Thought Experiment

Jackson's defense of his premise depends entirely on a pair of thought experiments. These thought experiments are intended to show us that we must admit the existence of aspects of conscious experience that cannot be described in physical terms.

His first thought experiment concerns a person whose visual experiences are richer than those of normally sighted people. This person, whom Jackson calls Fred, is able to perceive more shades of red than other people. Where the rest of us would see two objects of the same shade of red, Fred sees objects of two different shades. We can think of Fred as being different from normally sighted people in the same way that normally sighted people are from those who are red-green color-blind. His visual system is capable of a greater degree of color sensitivity than other people's.

Jackson's point is that the possibility of someone like Fred demonstrates the existence of qualia. For no amount of physical information about Fred's eyes or brain would tell us what Fred's visual experience of the additional shades of red is *like*. Even if we knew how Fred's retina responds to finer differences in the wavelengths of light than does our own, we would not thereby know what these extra colors look like to Fred.

Jackson's Second Thought Experiment

The story of Fred is a story of someone whose visual experience is richer than our own. Jackson's second experiment makes the same point using a story of someone with impoverished visual experience. He tells the story of Mary, a brilliant neuroscientist, who knows all there is to know about the neurophysiology of vision, including how the various wavelengths of light stimulate the rods and cones of the retina and how this information is processed in the brain. The odd fact about Mary is that, for some unspecified reason, she has been forced to live all her life in a black-and-white world. She has been confined to rooms devoid of color and receives all her information about the outside world from a black-and-white television.

We then imagine that at some point in her life Mary is released from her confinement. Jackson argues that at the moment she enters the outside world, she will come to learn something she didn't know before, namely, what colors look like. And yet, *ex hypothesi*, prior to her release she already knew everything there is to know about the *physical* process of color perception. It follows, Jackson maintains, that there is an aspect of visual experiences—their qualia—that cannot be known by understanding only the physical side of color vision. Ergo, qualia exist.

Epiphenomenalism

In Section IV of his article, Jackson outlines his theory of the nature of qualia. Jackson's position is a version of a view called **epiphenomenalism**. This is the idea that conscious experience is a by-product of brain activity and is causally inert. We can illustrate the view by comparing it with Descartes's theory of the relation between mind and body. According to Descartes, the body influences the mind and vice versa. On his theory, motion in the pineal gland of the brain, caused by sensory stimulation, produces sensations in the immaterial mind. Conversely, mental activity can produce motion in the pineal gland, which in turn generates behavior. This aspect of Descartes's theory is called **mind-body interactionism**. Epiphenomenalism agrees with the first part of Descartes's theory but denies the second. Epiphenomenalists claim that brain activity generates conscious experience, but they deny that conscious experience produces any effect on the brain or the rest of the body.

We can get an idea of epiphenomenalism by comparing this view of mind and brain to the relationship between an automobile and the exhaust fumes it produces. Exhaust fumes are always generated when the engine of an automobile is functioning. Yet the fumes do not in turn influence the action of the engine or the automobile. They are a non-efficacious by-product of engine activity. Epiphenomenalists view states of consciousness as similar in this way to exhaust fumes. They are generated by physical processes in the brain, but they themselves have no effect on the functioning of the brain.

Jackson offers a modified version of epiphenomenalism. Although he is a dualist, in the sense that he denies the mind consists solely of the physical processes of the brain, he does not believe that the mind is a distinct *entity* from the brain. Rather he claims that qualia are nonphysical *properties* of physical brain states. This means that he holds a version of what, in Chapter Eight, we called *property dualism*. Qualia, in Jackson's view, are properties of the brain that are epiphenomenal in that they are produced by the physical activity of the brain but have no effect on that activity.

Jackson's Defense of Epiphenomenalism

In Section IV Jackson offers replies to a number of objections raised by critics against epiphenomenalism. The first objection is that, contrary to Jackson's view, the qualitative character of our experience does produce effects on our physical behavior. For example, it is the fact that pain *hurts* that causes us to avoid the things that produce it. To this Jackson replies that the connection between pain and behavior can be explained by supposing that a physical event in the brain causes *both* the behavior and the experience of pain. There is then no reason to suppose that the pain causes the behavior.

The second objection that Jackson considers is that epiphenomenalism is inconsistent with evolution. Those traits that are selected through evolution, the objection runs, are those that have a positive effect on survival. Because epiphenomenal properties have no effect on survival, positive or negative, they will not be selected. Jackson's reply here is that epiphenomenal properties may be a by-product of other properties that do have a positive effect on survival, just as a bear's possessing a *heavy* coat may be the result of the survival advantage of possessing a *warm* coat.

The third objection is that if qualia have no effect on behavior, we cannot infer their existence from behavior; hence we can have no knowledge of qualia in other people. Jackson contends that this objection rests on a misconception of how we know about qualia in others. We know from our own case that the brain events that produce certain kinds of behavior *also* cause certain experiential states. From the behavior of other people we can infer the existence of the same sorts of brain events as our own, and from that we can infer the existence of the experiences those brain states produce.

Qualia and Ockham's Razor

The most interesting aspect of the fourth section of Jackson's article is a more general objection he sees arising from his replies. This fourth objection is that, even if the nonexistence of qualia cannot be demonstrated:

> [t]hey *do* nothing, they *explain* nothing, they serve merely to soothe the intuitions of dualists, and it is left a total mystery how they fit into the world view of science.

This is a key point, because it returns us to one of the main premises in the materialists' arguments, namely, Ockham's Razor or the principle of parsimony. As we saw in Chapter Eight, a central aim of the sciences since the seventeenth century has been to reduce all observable phenomena to a small number of mechanical laws. Descartes, Galileo, and Newton began the project by attempting to explain all aspects of the physical world in terms of mechanical properties of matter. Reductionism in the philosophy of mind is a continuation of this same program, attempting to explain mental life in terms of the physical activity of the brain or the characteristics of machine tables.

If Jackson is correct about the existence of qualia, then there are properties of the mind that resist reduction to more fundamental elements of the world. Because qualia are epiphenomenal properties, it will be impossible to integrate our descriptions of the mind with what we know of the physical activity of the brain. However, Jackson contends that this is not a reason to reject the existence of qualia, for it rests on an over-optimistic conception of our ability to understand the world. The reductionist program assumes that all natural phenomena can be explained in terms of a set of laws *that we are able to comprehend*. Jackson rejects this optimism. He says:

> The wonder is that we understand as much as we do, and there is no wonder that there should be matters which fall quite outside our comprehension. Perhaps exactly how epiphenomenal qualia fit into the scheme of things is one such.

In Jackson's opinion, the relation between qualia and the physical world will likely remain a mystery beyond our powers to understand.

Quining Qualia

In an article entitled "Quining Qualia," Tufts University philosopher Daniel Dennett directly challenges the premise of Jackson's article. Dennett is famous for a wide variety of technical and popular philosophical writings on the nature of the mind. One of his book-length discussions of the mind is *Consciousness Explained*, a book that attacks the Cartesian idea of a single, unitary site of conscious experience, an idea that he dubs "the Cartesian Theater."[1]

As Dennett explains in the second paragraph of his article, the verb 'to **quine**' is a humorous word that means "to deny resolutely the existence of something real or significant." It is a satirical jab at the Harvard philosopher W.V.O. Quine, who is renowned for often appearing to do precisely what the definition says. So Dennett's intent is to deny the existence of qualia. His point is that none of the features of qualia that are used to support philosophical conclusions can sustain close critical examination.

Defining Qualia

Dennett's goal is to separate out the elements of consciousness that he thinks are real from the features commonly associated with the term 'qualia,' which he argues are vacuous. Consequently the precise meaning of 'qualia' is something that he develops over the course of his essay. Dennett's article is based on a succession of thought experiments, or "intuition pumps" as he calls them, designed to tease out what qualia are supposed to be and why the concept is so tangled and problematic. Because thought experiments are used to test the implications of our concepts, they are well-suited to Dennett's goal. There are too many such thought experiments in Dennett's article to consider each in detail or to look carefully at the points he draws from each. Instead we will try to isolate the highlights, leaving the close reading to you.

The first two thought experiments, which he calls *watching you eat cauliflower* and *the wine-tasting machine*, are intended to get hold of the aspects of qualia that make them the subject of philosophical debate. The first experiment is designed merely to point out the traditional conceptions that qualia are known only to individual consciousness, and that the character of qualia cannot be conveyed in words. The second experiment is a description of a machine that detects all the salient qualities of wines but, as a nonconscious machine, cannot possibly experience the real taste of a wine. From these thought experiments Dennett draws the following list of attributes commonly associated with qualia.

1. Qualia are *ineffable* in the sense that we cannot convey to others what our own experiences are really like.
2. They are *intrinsic* or *nonrelational*. This means, first, that we cannot analyze them into simpler components. For example, the way that the color red looks to you resists any analysis into more basic elements; it is simple and homogeneous. It also means that qualia are not defined in terms of relations with other things. The property of being one meter long is a relational property; it is a matter of having a certain relationship to a standard meter stick in Paris. By contrast, it is said, the redness that we experience in our vision is not defined by any relations it has with anything else—it is defined by what it looks like.
3. They are *private* in that there is no way of comparing one person's conscious experience with that of another, to see, for example, whether the color blue looks the same to both.
4. They are *directly apprehensible* in consciousness, which means that each of us has a direct, noninferential awareness of what colors look like, or sound like, in our own conscious experience.

The Inverted Spectrum Experiments

Section 3 of Dennett's article is intended to show that the intuitions supporting the notion of private, ineffable qualia are not as reliable as the simplest thought experiments suggest. In this section he considers a collection of experiments that have traditionally been used to support the idea of qualia, and argues that they are weaker than often thought. These are the so-called "inverted spectrum" thought experiments, the oldest of which is the one that, as we saw in Chapter Nine, Fodor uses to introduce the concept of qualitative content.[2] Dennett's argument in Section 3 is that the very nature of qualia undermines these thought experiments. Here Dennett appeals to versions of the verifiability theory of meaning that we surveyed in Chapter Seven. Because qualia are private and ineffable by definition, it is in principle impossible to tell whether or not a color reversal exists between two people. Hence by the verifiability criterion, the question whether the reversal exists is meaningless. The intrapersonal versions of the story are intended to overcome this problem, because one presumes that one can tell whether one's *own* experience has changed. However, in these cases the same problem arises in other ways. Here Dennett reminds us of Wittgenstein's "private language argument." What criterion would you use to say that your *color experience* has reversed overnight, rather than saying that your *color memory connections* have reversed overnight? Perhaps you merely misremember how things used to look. Being mistaken about this makes no sense, Dennett argues, for there is no way to detect errors.

Making Mistakes about Qualia

The fourth feature of qualia in Dennett's list of their special attributes is that they are directly apprehensible in consciousness. For example, each of us knows directly and immediately what the color red looks like to us, and what coffee tastes like to us. This has been a standard reason for accepting that we cannot be mistaken about the qualia of our own perceptual experience. In Section 4, Dennett presents a set of thought experiments designed to question this idea. His stories are based on two professional coffee tasters, Chase and Sanborn. Both agree that they no longer enjoy the flavor of their company's brand of coffee. However, where one claims that his enjoyment of the flavor has diminished, the other claims that the flavor of the coffee has changed over time. Here again, Dennett's point is that there is no criterion for determining which explanation is the correct one, even in one's own case.

In what follows, Dennett considers various strategies a defender of qualia might adopt if confronted with this situation. One is to maintain infallibility by trivializing the issue. Chase and Sanborn each insist that they know how things *seem* to them, and the qualia supporter can argue that there is nothing more to the issue. (Here Dennett quotes from Wittgenstein: "Imagine someone saying: 'But I know how tall I am!' and laying his hand on top of his head to prove it.") This strategy doesn't work for the case in hand, however, for the infallibility in question also concerns the *inter*personal issue: We want Chase to be able to say that his situation is not the same as Sanborn's.

Another strategy that Dennett suggests a defender of qualia might adopt is to:

> treat qualia as *logical constructs* out of subjects' qualia-judgments: a subject's experience has the quale *F* if and only if the subject judges his experience to have quale *F*.

By this Dennett means that each person's statements about their own experiences determine what the facts are. When Chase declares that the taste of the coffee has not changed, he thereby makes it true that it hasn't changed. Asking how Chase knows that the taste of coffee hasn't changed, Dennett says, becomes the same as asking how Dostoevsky knows that Raskolnikov's hair is brown.

A different comparison is the act of promising: *saying* that you promise makes it true that you have promised. But here again, Dennett argues, the strategy won't work. In this case the problem is that defenders of qualia will insist that the question about Chase and Sanborn is an *empirical* one. By this Dennett means that the question is supposed to be about what their experiences are *really like*, and not just a question about what each of them *said*.

Empirical Tests

Dennett points out that, as the issue is an empirical one, there will be tests we could use to help us decide whether Chase's or Sanborn's qualia have changed. We could use blind tastings, giving the two subjects the same coffee to drink and then a different coffee, to see how their judgments vary. Such a test would help us determine whether the change in subjective reports is "a change near the brute perceptual processing end of the spectrum or a change near the ultimate reactive judgment end of the spectrum." By this Dennett means that the tests will help decide between two different hypotheses: (1) the subjects' experiences have changed, while the content of their judgments about what their experiences are remains constant; (2) their experiences have remained constant, while their judgments about those experiences have changed. There is also neurological evidence we can use to determine where along the neural pathways the change has occurred, whether it occurred relatively early on in the perceptual process, or whether it occurred at some higher level of neural activity.

In the remainder of the section, Dennett argues that these kinds of empirical tests ultimately fail to resolve the issue. In Dennett's view, there is simply no fact of the matter concerning where, in the myriad of neural activity, particular conscious experiences occur. We cannot isolate a neural event and correlate it with a particular perceptual experience or with a particular judgment. There is no fact of the matter, then, about whether Chase's and Sanborn's qualia have changed or whether their judgments about their qualia have changed.

In Section 5 Dennett describes a collection of genuine cases of perceptual impairment that have occurred as a result of brain damage.[3] In these cases too, Dennett argues, there is no simple way to determine whether the impairment is a matter of a loss or alteration of the subjects' perceptual experiences, or whether the impairment affects the subjects' abilities to judge or remember their experiences. His conclusion is that the concept of qualia provides no assistance at all in understanding what has happened in cases like these. He says:

> It seems fairly obvious to me that none of the real problems of interpretation that face us in these curious cases is advanced by any analysis of how the concept of *qualia* is to be applied—unless we wish to propose a novel, technical sense for which the traditional term might be appropriated. But that would be at least a tactical error: the intuitions that surround and *purport* to anchor the current understanding of the term are revealed to be in utter disarray when confronted with these cases.

Accounting for Ineffability

In the final section of his article, Dennett turns to the question of why, if the concept of qualia is so problematic, has it been so captivating? Where has the idea of private, ineffable, intrinsic properties of experience come from? In addressing this question, Dennett sketches a positive account of his own to explain these apparent elements of our conscious experience. The discussion is too complex to consider in detail, but we can isolate the main elements.

Dennett's view is that the qualitative character of conscious experience can be explained in terms of the *information* that our perceptual states carry. For example, when someone perceives an object as being blue, their visual system—the eyes and the neural pathways associated with them—is detecting a property of that object. So the visual system is collecting information about the object. The apparent features of qualia—their homogeneity, their ineffability, their privacy, and so on—merely reflect the fact that one is unable to analyze the information one is receiving.

The fact that someone's experience of the color blue is simple and homogeneous means only that they can tell that the object has some kind of surface feature, although their vision does not tell them anything about that feature beyond the fact that it is similar to features of other objects. Similarly, Dennett argues that qualia appear ineffable only because we are often unable to say precisely what information a sensation carries. To illustrate, he brings in another thought experiment: a verbal description of an osprey cry will partially enable us to identify one in the field. But when we actually hear one for the first time, we have gained some additional information. We can say, "So *that's* what it sounds like." We are at a loss, however, to say what this additional information is, so it seems ineffable. Dennett contends that the reason for the apparent ineffability is that from this one experience we have actually gained very little information. We can't generalize from this experience to other osprey cries, and we can't know what other patterns of air movement might produce this same sensation. He says:

> In other words, when first I hear the osprey cry, I may have identified a property-detector in myself, but I have no idea (yet) what property my new-found property-detector detects.

Nonetheless, to the extent that his sensation is correlated with a certain kind of event in the world this experience does provide him with a certain amount of (ineffable) information.

The parenthetical word 'yet' in the previous quote is important. For Dennett points out that sensations that appear at first to be simple and unstructured can be analyzed into components with training and practice. First Dennett argues that an inability to analyze a sensory experience does not by itself show that there is nothing to be analyzed. The sound of the osprey may carry a vast amount of information that we are simply unable to extract. Dennett compares this possibility with the spy trick of using a torn piece of paper to identify the right contact person. The torn edge is so complex that we are unable to properly analyze and reproduce it. Similarly, the sound of an osprey may be instantly recognizable but so complex that our sensory organs cannot break it down. But we can be trained to analyze apparently simple sensations into their components. Here Dennett reminds us of the musical training required to hear harmonics in a single piano note or to detect the subtle components in the taste of a wine.

In Dennett's view, then, the simplicity and ineffability of sensory experiences merely reflect the paucity of information we are able to glean from what our sensory organs bring in. Dennett has carried the reductive enterprise of the scientific revolution to its full conclusion. In rejecting Aristotle's identification of sensations with real qualities of the world, Galileo and Descartes moved the qualitative features of colors and sounds to the mind. Dennett has taken the additional step of removing them from existence altogether. The idea of simple, private, ineffable qualities of experiences are merely fictions of a mistaken picture of the mind.

Color Inversion and Conceivability

David M. Rosenthal is Professor of Philosophy and Linguistics, as well as the coordinator of the Interdisciplinary Concentration of Cognitive Science at the Graduate Center, City University of New York. Like Dennett, Rosenthal takes issue with certain core assumptions used by philosophers in reasoning about consciousness. Where Dennett challenges the traditional philosophical notion of qualia, Rosenthal criticizes the basis of some central thought experiments that philosophers have used in their arguments in favor of this traditional conception. He finds that these thought experiments are all based on a single assumption that he claims is false, namely that it is only via first-person access that we have a grip on the nature of qualia—what he calls '**mental qualities**.' In his article, Rosenthal presents a way of thinking about mental qualities from a *third*-person perspective, according to which such qualities are the properties of mental states in virtue of which an individual is able to discriminate among perceptible properties of objects in the world. Note that since mental qualities are keyed to the ability of a creature to discriminate among properties of objects, they are defined in a way that frees them from the assumptions that they must be conscious and are accessible only via introspection.

Rosenthal opens his article by considering the grounds of inverted spectrum thought experiments introduced earlier. The purported conceivability of inverted mental qualities is used to contend that there can be differences in such qualities that transcend any behavioral, physical, or functional differences. Accordingly, these qualities cannot be reduced to any of these factors.

Inverted spectrum cases are necessarily based on thought experiments, because they contend not only that such reversals are conceivable, but that if they exist they would be *undetectable* by any public means. Rosenthal argues that such thought experiments are misleading, and that in fact undetectable inversion is not conceivable at all. He gives an initial reason for questioning the conceivability of undetectable inversion by comparing it to what he claims is a similar thought experiment: Suppose someone said that it is conceivable that water is not a complex chemical substance, but a simple, basic element. Such a supposition, it would seem, is not very bizarre, because, as we saw in Chapter Two, the classical Greeks believed water is in fact a simple, basic substance. Rosenthal argues, however, that the supposition is based on an inadequate concept of water, one based only on a concept of something that looks and behaves *like water*. "Given what water *actually is*," he argues, "and given *anything like a satisfactory concept of water*, it is simply not conceivable that water is a simple, basic substance." Rosenthal's argument is that, by parity of reasoning, given what mental qualities actually are, and given a satisfactory concept of mental qualities, undetectable inversion is not conceivable.

First-Person and Third-Person Access

Rosenthal's point in bringing up the undetectable inversion thought experiment is to draw out the particularly stringent requirements their supposed conceivability places on theorizing about mental qualities. If the conceivability of undetectable inversion of mental qualities is taken to be a fundamental fact that any theory of mental qualities must explain, then that theory must also claim that there can be no "third-person, intersubjective access to mental qualities," or alternatively, that "mental qualities allow only first-person access." This, after all, is what is entailed by the conceivability of undetectable quality inversion. The assumption Rosenthal is identifying, then, is that only the subject who is in a particular mental state can have access to the qualitative properties of that state. Notice too that 'first-person access to mental qualities' means knowledge of those properties acquired through subjective awareness of them. So in these terms, the assumption is that subjective awareness is the only source of knowledge of mental qualities.

The conceivability of undetectable quality inversion rests entirely on this assumption. For it is only this assumption that rules out the possibility of having knowledge of the mental qualities of other people's mental states. You know what the colors of a ripe tomato and fresh green grass look like *to you*, and on the grounds of this assumption, you do not know, and *could not ever come to know*, what they look like to others.

Rosenthal argues that this assumption lies at the basis of other "intuitively inviting" assertions about the nature of mental qualities. First, there is the assertion by David Chalmers and others that so-called zombies—creatures physically identical to human beings who behave in every way as human beings do, but who lack any form of conscious experience—are conceivable (and hence possible). According to Rosenthal, if there were knowledge of mental qualities through third-person access, this could only be through some aspect of the subject's physical make-up or their behavior, because nothing else is publicly observable. And this would mean that *differences* in mental qualities make some observable difference to physical make-up or to behavior. Again, the purported conceivability of zombies relies on the assumption that we can have only first-person access to mental qualities.

Another claim about mental qualities that Rosenthal says rests on the same assumption is what Joseph Levine calls *the explanatory gap*, and David Chalmers calls *the hard problem*. What is common to these claims is that no amount of knowledge of the physical body (or knowledge of cognitive functioning) could tell us why a particular physical process (or cognitive function) would be instrumental in the occurrence of any particular qualitative state (or any qualitative state at all). We cannot answer the question why *this* particular neural activity produces *this* particular shade of green. Rosenthal's reply to this line of argument compares it to one put forward by Gottfried Wilhelm Leibniz in the seventeenth century. Leibniz asks us to imagine (again, in a thought experiment) a machine that functions just as the brain does, and that we could go inside this machine. Nothing we would see inside the machine, Leibniz contends, "would explain a perception." According to Rosenthal, the basis of Leibniz's inference from the thought experiment is that going inside the machine would not give us *first-person* access to the processes going on there.

Similarly, Rosenthal contends that the same assumption lies behind Jackson's thought experiment of the neuroscientist, Mary. Mary knows everything there is to know about color perception that is possible from a third-person perspective. She knows about the neural processing of color, as well as human behavioral responses to color stimuli. But when she gains conscious *experience* of color for the first time, so the argument goes, she learns something she didn't know before. That knowledge, it seems, can only be possible through first-person access, and so this thought experiment again rests on the assumption that knowledge of mental qualities requires conscious experience of them. So the intuitions elicited by such thought experiments arguably would seem to reflect this implicit theoretical assumption, and so cannot then serve as theory-neutral data for a theory about mental qualities to accommodate.

There is, then, as Rosenthal quotes from C.D. Broad, "a curious superstition" that consciousness "must give exhaustive and infallible information." One of the results of this assumption is the ineffable character of qualia: There is nothing we can say about them, because one cannot convey in words what one is only aware of from the first-person. Nor, as Jackson and others argue, can neuroscience or cognitive science tell us anything about them, because these sciences rely on a third-person perspective.

Perceptual Role Theories of Mental Qualities

What Rosenthal's argument demands, then, is that there be a way to gain knowledge of mental qualities through some form of third-person evidence, which can only be behavioral or neural. In Section III he puts forward a suggestion for using behavioral evidence, based on the "intimate and arguably essential role" of mental qualities *in perception*. Spatial perception, for example, is the ability to determine the relative directions and distances between objects in one's environment, and color perception is the ability to discriminate between different colors of objects. Such abilities can be tested behaviorally by determining which differences among stimuli the subject can discriminate.

Rosenthal labels theories that rely on such evidence, *perceptual-role theories*, in contrast to *consciousness-based* theories, which rely on introspection. According to a perceptual role theory, he says, "mental qualities are *the properties in virtue of which we make perceptual discriminations*." Since we are talking about the perception of objects in the environment, it might seem that Rosenthal is here referring to properties of the physical objects perceived. But in the next sentence he says that,

> if an individual's perceiving involves such discriminations, that individual is in *mental states* that have mental qualities that pertain to those discriminations. [Our emphasis]

So mental qualities are properties of *mental states*, the ones on the basis of which people make discriminations among properties of the objects they perceive.

Unconscious Perceptions and Mental Qualities

One of the most important features of perceptual-role theories is that they can be applied to perceptions of which subjects are not conscious. Experiments show that people can make discriminations between perceptible properties on the basis of subliminal perceptions, ones of which they are unaware. One form of this effect occurs in so-called "masked-priming" experiments. In one such experiment, stimuli are flashed quickly on a screen, with meaningless symbols displayed in between that serve as "stimulus masks." The stimuli between the masks are displayed too rapidly for the subject to consciously detect them, yet it is found that they nonetheless have a pronounced effect on the subjects' responses to subsequent stimuli.

It is one thing to assert the existence and influence of subliminal or unconscious perceptions. Rosenthal, however, wants to use such perceptions for evidence about *mental qualities*, and that requires the further assumption that unconscious perceptual states have mental qualities in the first place. For example, we would need to assume that perceptions of color of which we are completely unaware possess qualities of redness or blueness, just like the conscious perceptions of a red apple or a blue sky. So Rosenthal refers to the existence of "nonconscious mental qualities."

He says that perceptual-role theories of mental qualities require "access to mental qualities in the absence of any consciousness of those qualities at all."

The question, then, concerns the grounds on which we can make such an assumption. For proponents of consciousness-based theories, whereby mental qualities are *by definition* properties we are aware of through consciousness, there simply cannot be such a thing as a "nonconscious mental quality." And some philosophers, Rosenthal admits, argue that what might *appear* to be unconscious perceptions in the priming experiments are not actual perceptual states, what they call "occurrent states," but only *dispositions* to be in a perceptual state. There would, then, be no actual unconscious states that bear mental qualities.

Rosenthal's first response to these arguments is that the burden of proof is on the side of those who doubt that subliminal or unconscious perceptions bear mental qualities, for such doubts "will have no force without independent support." To this he adds, as we mentioned earlier, that priming evidence suggests that people make the same quality discriminations unconsciously that they do consciously, indicating that the same mental qualities occur in each case.

The idea of perceptual-role theories of mental qualities, then, is of theories that examine the nature of mental qualities as they are revealed in people's perceptions, regardless of whether those people have any conscious access to their perceptions. What would such theories look like? To answer this question, Rosenthal advocates a theory based on so-called "quality spaces." This idea will require some introduction, including a preliminary technical concept of multi-dimensional scaling.

Multi-Dimensional Scaling

Multi-Dimensional Scaling (MDS) is a technique for displaying relations of similarity between objects. These relations are displayed on a graph, such that the greater the similarity between objects the closer they are placed together on the graph. For example, one could represent people along a line according to the relative differences in their ages. When scaling is applied to more than one relation, each relation is displayed on an axis of a multi-dimensional graph. For example, a group of cars can be placed on a two-dimensional graph with the two axes representing relative size and cost. There is no limit in principle to the number of relations that a graph can represent, although it is only possible to display three relations visually.

One of the common uses of MDS is **perceptual mapping**, which displays relations of *perceived similarity*. Subjects are asked to indicate relative similarities between a group of objects. For example, a marketing company might ask a set of consumers to rate their perception of clothing lines according to whether they are perceived to be comfortable or dressy, and whether they are perceived to be conservative or fashionable. These perceptions can then be mapped onto a two-dimensional grid, which the marketers can use to find market niches. It is important to note that distances in perceptual mapping are only relative distances, not absolute. If A and B are separated by a distance of five units, this means that there are five *discriminable differences* between them, and if B and C are separated by 10 units, then there are twice as many discriminable differences between them.

Quality Space Theory

The techniques of perceptual mapping have been applied by psychologists who study the perception of such properties as color, taste, and odor. In their experiments, subjects are presented with stimuli (sounds or color patches, for example) and are asked to make judgments about them, such as *matching* (x matches y), *discrimination* (x is different from y), or *relative similarity* (x is more similar to y than z). When these data are projected onto a graph, the result is what psychologists call a *quality space*. For example, the perceived colors of objects can be represented by three different properties: hue, saturation, and lightness. Experiments can ascertain the discriminations that human subjects can make for each of these properties, and from these results it is possible to construct a three-dimensional graph, similar to the Munsell Color System used by graphic artists. This would be a quality space for color: Each color perceived by human subjects would be represented by a point within that three-dimensional space.

Quality space theory (QST) is the idea that the construction of quality spaces from perceptual discrimination behavior offers a way of studying mental qualities that avoids reliance on first-person awareness of these qualities. Rosenthal's argument in support of QST is in the second and third paragraphs of Section III. Here is our summary of that argument: A quality space for a perceptible property represents the discriminations people are capable of making with respect to that property. People must have mental states in virtue of which they can make these discriminations, and therefore the quality space must represent those mental states. Mental qualities are the properties of those mental states in virtue of which they differ from one another. So, in general, quality spaces represent the mental qualities by which people discriminate among perceptible properties. Thus, they offer an explanation of the mental qualities that are used in human perception.

Following that argument, Rosenthal lists some of the virtues of QST: It treats conscious and nonconscious perceptual states equally, which he says accords with experimental results. It can be applied to all of the external sense modalities: vision, audition, olfaction, gustation, and tactition. Spatial perception through each of those modalities can be studied through discrimination, just as in the cases of color and other sensible properties, and from this, QST can be used to model proprioception and kinesthesia (i.e., unconscious and conscious perception of bodily movement). Finally, it can be applied to bodily sensations, such as pain, by mapping perceptual discrimination of intensity, location, and qualitative feel.

What Are Perceptible Properties?

Rosenthal describes quality spaces as reflecting the *discriminations* people make among *perceptible properties*. Importantly, Rosenthal emphasizes that "the quality spaces relevant here don't rely on the physical properties of the stimuli, for example, on the wave-mechanical properties of light or sound." If the quality space for color were based on such wave-mechanical properties, we would require only a single axis representing wave-length. Yet to capture human color perception we need three axes, for hue, saturation, and lightness.

This point has been expanded by Austen Clark.[4] He points out that the complications in human perception are such that there are no direct relations between properties of physical objects, or properties of physical sense stimulation, and what is perceived by our senses. Rather, what we perceive is determined by *the manner in which* the receptor cells of sense modalities (sight, sound, taste, etc.) are affected by ambient energies (photons of light, for example), and how that information is processed by neural systems in the brain. So what is represented on the axes of quality spaces are actually the properties an individual's sensory system enables them to discriminate, rather than properties of physical objects *per se*.

We can illustrate this point by looking more closely at color perception. The most complex of the three relations represented by a quality space for color is hue. The human retina has three different receptors for hue, which respond most intensely to short, medium, and long wavelengths of light (very roughly, blue, green, and red, respectively). However, the chromatic system that receives the signals from these receptors does not simply combine them. Instead, the signals are linked together into two pairs of opposing hues: red-green and blue-yellow. Activation of one of either pair results in inhibition of the other.[5] Accordingly, the properties that a quality space for hue needs to represent are features of that opponent-process rather than any physical properties of colored surfaces or light rays. Clark (p. 7) points out that the fact that orange appears most similar to red and yellow has no parallel in any facts about surface reflectance or light waves; it is purely a fact about the opponent-process within the visual system.

Even patterns of stimulation of receptor cells at the retina do not reflect relations between perceived colors. For example, recognizing the same object as having the same color under different lighting conditions, and therefore different retinal stimulation, requires the system to compensate for variations in illumination. Winkler et al. found that there are notable differences in color effects when light is varied along bluish directions from those when it is varied along yellow directions.[6] They attribute this to a built-in "tendency to attribute bluish tints to the illuminant rather than the object, consistent with an inference that indirect lighting from the sky and in shadows tends to be bluish." They hypothesize that this might explain the remarkable phenomenon of "the dress" image, that became a social-media sensation, in which some people see the same dress as blue-black and others as white-gold.[7] So when we speak of **perceptible properties**, we should recognize that these are properties of objects *only as they appear* to certain kinds of creatures. They are not physical properties of objects or of ambient energies, but are properties which result from the manner in which sensory stimulation is received and processed by neural systems.[8]

Color Inversion Again

Rosenthal began his article with the claim that the basis of the color-inversion thought experiment is the assumption that only consciousness can give us access to mental qualities. But from what we know from QST, he says, undetectable color inversion is in fact impossible. At the end of Section III he presents his argument for this by using the features of a quality space for color.

His first premise is this: "Quality-space theory taxonomizes mental qualities by relative location in a space constructed from an individual's ability to discriminate the corresponding perceptible properties." His point is that differences between colors in a quality space are marked only by *relative distances in similarity* between them. So, for example, we can determine of three colors—A, B, and C—recognized by a subject, that A *is more similar to B than to* C. But all that means is that between A and B the subject recognizes fewer distinguishable s than between B and C. There is no sense here by which we can say that A *looks to the subject more like B than like* C. For 'looks like' is a term of subjective awareness. Nor is there any sense of absolute differences in color, only *relative* differences in color discrimination.

His next premise is that, given the first premise, "if there were an axis with respect to which that quality space is symmetrical, it would be impossible to distinguish stimuli on one side of that axis from stimuli on the other." For this, we need the idea of *spatial symmetry*. This idea is easiest to visualize by thinking of shapes. Two shapes are symmetrical if they match perfectly when placed one on top of the other. Your right and left hands, for example, are symmetrical, because they match when you put them palm to palm. Now apply this idea to the axis for hue in a color space. If the relative distances between shades of red and shades of green are symmetrical, then one can be mapped perfectly onto the other. His second premise says that, if such were the case, then a quality space for color would not distinguish perceptions of red from perceptions of green, for the differences in discrimination between shades of one would be identical to the discrimination between shades of the other.

Rosenthal's conclusion from these two premises is that, if red-green inversion *were* undetectable, as the thought experiment assumes, this would require that the relative differences between shades for each hue are symmetrical. Otherwise there would be detectable differences between the perceptions of the two hues. But *in fact* this is not the case. Human responses to colors are not distributed evenly across the visible spectrum; we are able to discriminate more finely in some regions of the light spectrum than others. This means that relative distances between discernible colors are very different in some regions of the color space than they are in other regions. In particular, the red and green regions of color space are not symmetrical, and therefore they are distinguishable from one another by measuring relative degrees of similarity. Undetectable red-green color reversal is therefore not possible.

But there is a further question, for the color-inversion argument claims, not that such an inversion in humans is in fact possible, but only that it is *conceivable*. Thus Sydney Shoemaker argues as follows:

> Even if our color experience is not invertible, it seems obviously possible that there should be such creatures, otherwise very much like ourselves, whose color experience does have a structure that allows for such a mapping—creatures whose color experience *is* invertible.[9]

However, Rosenthal replies that this appeal to the conceivability of color inversion is still very weak because it depends crucially on an impoverished concept of mental qualities. Our conception of color, based on introspection, is too primitive to determine whether undetectable color inversion is possible. It is similar to the classical conception of water, based only on its immediately observable properties, which permits the thought that water may be a primitive element. Once we have a better understanding of the full properties of water, we see that this is impossible. Similarly, the understanding of color perception derived from QST shows that any conception of color which permits the possibility of undetectable color inversion, is inadequate. What is plausible and implausible depends on the richness of one's understanding of the phenomenon in question.

Explaining Appearances

One central purpose of theories of mental qualities is to explain the appearances of things. According to defenders of irreducible qualia, the appearances of things are properties of conscious mental states, which cannot be explained either by appeal to neural processes of the brain, nor to functional processes of the cognitive system. In fact, on this account, there is no explanation of *qualia* at all, because they are the primitive properties of experience. They are the fundamental data upon which theories of consciousness are constructed. Using this data, we can construct theories of what consciousness is like for creatures sufficiently similar to us to experience the same qualia.

In the opening paragraphs of Section IV, Rosenthal challenges this perspective on explanations of mental qualities and consciousness. The assumption underlying it, he argues, is the same as that behind the thought experiments involving qualia (such as color reversal), namely, that access to mental properties is possible only through consciousness. Since consciousness does not allow for any finer analysis of mental qualities than primitive qualia, it can take us no further. We *begin* with qualia. But, according to Rosenthal, this has the situation entirely backwards. "Experiences," he says, "are the *explananda* of consciousness, not the *explanans*." What he means is that the properties of experience (including qualia) are what is to be explained, not what we use in our explanations.

How, then, does Rosenthal propose to explain mental qualities? From the perspective of perceptual-role theories, he claims, our consciousness of our own experiences is itself an appearance; it is how our own mental lives (the things going on in our minds) *appear to us*. In conscious experience, therefore, we are aware of the activity of our own minds. From this perspective, these appearances are no more reliable than any other. We could be mistaken about what is going on in our own mind as easily as we can be mistaken about what is going on in the world around us. The study of consciousness then becomes the study of *why* our mental activity appears to us in the way that it does, and to what extent this appearance is accurate.

Consciousness-based theories of mental qualities, on the other hand, are founded on first-person awareness. The material from which they construct explanations of subjective experience are the properties of our conscious states as they appear in consciousness. And qualia are the primitive elements of those conscious states. From the perspective of consciousness-based theories, then, there is no possibility of being mistaken in our awareness of qualia. Since the point of theories of consciousness, from this perspective, is to show how subjective experience is constructed *from* qualia, there is no sense in which we can say that qualia are themselves (possibly mistaken) appearances of mental states. Mental reality, on such a view, *is identical to* mental appearance.

Higher-Order Awareness

Rosenthal's purpose in Section IV is to present a theory of consciousness that compliments quality space theory. The basis of this theory is presented in the fifth and sixth paragraphs. It is founded on his basic point that consciousness is an awareness of our own mental states. It is defined as a property of mental states, as follows: A mental state is *conscious* if one is aware of oneself as being in that state.

We need now to explain the idea of **higher-order awareness (HOA)**, which Rosenthal uses in his theory of consciousness. This idea is based on the claim that one can be aware of something, without being aware of that awareness itself. Consider the case of driving a car while deep in thought about something else. Somehow you are aware of the traffic around you, of the traffic lights changing color, and so on, but you are not aware of *that* awareness. Then suddenly you become aware of your driving; perhaps a car horn jolts you back to your driving. At that moment you have an awareness of your own perceptions. Not only are you aware of a red light; you are *aware of being aware* of a red light. This is what Rosenthal calls a higher-order awareness (HOA). It is an awareness of awareness. (He mentions that, in earlier articles, he has talked about this idea in terms of higher-order *thoughts*, thoughts about thoughts, but that in this article he speaks only of awareness.) The idea of HOA offers an explanation of how there is *something it is like* to be in a qualitative state. For this is a result of being aware of being in that qualitative state. On this view, there is something it is like to perceive a bright red flower, for example, if and only if one is suitably aware of oneself as perceiving the flower *as red*.

Intrinsic vs. Comparative Identification

At the end of the same paragraph, Rosenthal makes a very important point. He says that,

> since mental qualities are taxonomized by location in a suitable quality space, HOAs must represent them in respect of such locations. When qualitative states are conscious, one is aware of their distinctive mental qualities in terms of the location those qualities have in a suitable quality space.

What this means is that a mental quality, such as that of a color or sound, is distinguished from others *only* by its relations to other qualities in the relevant quality space. A particular shade of red is recognized, not by its intrinsic quality—its particular redness—but by its relations to other shades of red and to other colors than red.

Rosenthal first defends this point by saying that it is consistent with some important experimental outcomes. But further on he recognizes that this is not how we intuitively *seem* to recognize colors. "It's intuitively inviting," he says, "to hold that we taxonomize each mental quality noncomparatively as a qualitative atom, independent of any others." For example, it seems that we recognize a particular shade of red just by looking at it by itself, and saying, "*That* shade of red." And this doesn't seem to require that we compare the shade to any others. In reply to this intuition, he says there are two separate questions, which we need to separate. "One is whether we can individuate token mental qualities one by one, independent of other tokens; the other is whether we can taxonomize those tokens noncomparatively in respect of what type of mental quality it is." This needs some explaining.

To individuate a *token* mental quality is to identify a particular mental quality on a particular occasion, and to think to oneself something like, "*that* patch of color before me *now*." To do this we need only attend to that patch of color at that moment. And we need to do this to be able to compare mental qualities with one another, and so it cannot itself depend on comparison. But to *taxonomize* mental qualities is to put them into kinds, and to say something like, "This is a shade of light green, but this one is more like a dark blue." It is this latter task that Rosenthal says can only be done comparatively. We put colors, sounds, etc., into groups under labels, not individually, but by their relations to one another. To put it more technically, we group mental qualities into kinds by virtue of the structure (the shape, if you like) of their quality spaces. A shade of blue is classified, not by its intrinsic quality, but by the degree that it is different from other shades in its hue, saturation, and lightness. (And by "degree" here, we mean only *comparative* degree.)[10]

Why Consciousness Is Not Intrinsic to Mental Qualities

Those who defend consciousness-based theories of mental qualities hold that consciousness is intrinsic to, or inseparable from, mental qualities.[11] There simply cannot be mental qualities of which no one is conscious. This is because, on such a theory, mental qualities are defined as the properties of mental states that we recognize when we consciously attend to them. Redness, say, is a property of visual states that we recognize when we pay conscious attention to our visual experiences. However, Rosenthal says that QST can "readily explain the subjective appearance that consciousness is intrinsic to mental qualities." That is, not only can QST show that such an appearance is false, but it can also explain why it *seems* to be right.

When one has a second-order awareness of being in a state with a particular mental quality, there is not commonly a *third*-order awareness of that second-order awareness. Perhaps only someone with a philosophical interest in experience would say something like, "I am aware of being aware of seeing red." One's awareness of being in a certain qualitative state like seeing red seems not to rest on being in a distinct state. This, Rosenthal says, makes it seem as if the consciousness is intrinsic to being in that state, and hence to the mental quality it possesses.

This, however, is not the case, he argues, because a qualitative state and a higher-order awareness of it are independent of one another. One can have the former without the latter. This is required by the assumption, which Rosenthal makes, that there are qualitative states of which we are not aware. (Remember the case of subliminal perception.)

Being Mistaken about Mental Qualities

Rosenthal argues that the independence of mental qualities from higher-order awareness of them is what makes it possible for one to be *mistaken* about the qualities of one's own mental states. One can believe that one is in a state with a certain mental quality, and be wrong. For instance, one may be aware of the mental quality of a color sensation one is having as being of a generic green, when in fact it is a lime green.

While there can be small errors like this in higher-order awareness, Rosenthal says that there is reason to think that radical errors—cases in which one is completely mistaken as to what kind of state one is in—would be rare. If someone actually perceives something as green, but at the same time is consciously aware of perceiving it as red, there would be competing and inconsistent information existing in the mind. This kind of dissonance, he says, would not be compatible with "well-ordered psychological functioning." There are experimental studies, however, which reveal that such errors can sometimes occur. One such case, he says, is that of "change blindness," in which subjects fail to notice significant shifts and changes in their visual field.

The last case of error in higher-order awareness that Rosenthal considers is the possibility that one can be consciously aware of a mental quality that doesn't exist at all. His example is of someone who is aware of themselves as having a red sensation, where in fact no such sensation exists. His reply is a clarification of the nature of higher-order awareness: HOAs do not simply make one aware of a mental quality, they make one aware of *oneself* as being in a state that has that mental quality. So the conscious state is the state that one is aware of oneself as being in, regardless of whether this state exists. This, he says, is no more mysterious than any other case of something being the object of a thought (e.g., a unicorn) despite not existing.

The Problems of Qualia

In the final five paragraphs of the article, Rosenthal reviews the four main arguments for irreducible qualia: the two thought experiments of an inverted spectrum and of zombies lacking any conscious experience, and the closely related issues of the "hard problem" and the "explanatory gap." How do the quality space theory of mental qualities and the higher-order awareness theory of consciousness fare together in responding to these arguments?

First, color inversion: According to the higher-order theory of consciousness, we are consciously aware of mental qualities with respect to their relative locations within the relevant quality spaces. For example, a quality space for color reflects the discriminations people make among hues across the spectrum, and, according to HOA, we are consciously aware of differences in hue to the extent that we make such discriminations. It follows that, to the extent that there is a lack of symmetry between two regions of a quality space, we will be aware of that difference in our perceptions of the two qualities. So if our concept of mental qualities is reflected in QST and the HOA theory, we cannot actually conceive of the two as inverted without our being capable of noticing.

The thought experiment of zombies involves creatures that behave exactly like normally conscious people, while lacking any conscious experience at all. But QST makes no distinction between conscious and unconscious perceptions, in terms of their qualitative properties. Accordingly, it allows that subliminal perceptions of perceptible properties can guide behavior just as conscious perceptions can. So a zombie, with no conscious awareness of perception, might exhibit many of the capacities for action as a normally conscious person. It will not, however, exhibit the same capacity for being aware of what mental states it is in without the aid of conscious inference or observation—this requires HOAs. A subject that lacks higher-order awareness will not, therefore, exhibit identical behavior to that of a normally conscious person. If QST and the HOA theory of consciousness are right, then zombies are not conceivable.

Finally, we come to the so-called hard problem and the explanatory gap. The issue here, as Rosenthal sees it, is whether a theory of consciousness can explain why particular neural or cognitive processes subserve particular conscious mental qualities. Why is a certain kind of neural activity of a certain region of the brain associated with experiences of blueness, for example, rather than of greenness, or no experience at all? According to QST, we search for the neural structures that render possible the kinds of discriminations that people make between perceptible properties. That is, we look for relations of cause and effect between neural activity and the quality spaces for the various perceptible properties. There are, then, perfectly good neural or cognitive explanations of mental qualities, as they are mapped by QST. But, as noted, these explanations do not aim to capture what it is that explains which mental qualities are conscious; that is solely a matter of whether or not there is a higher-order awareness of them.

So, together with the HOA theory of consciousness, QST can just as easily explain conscious perception of mental qualities as it can any other perceptual capacities. Any explanation of the neural activity that can generate the kinds of perceptual discriminations that people make is capable of explaining why we have the kinds of quality spaces we do. And, Rosenthal maintains, if some neural activity is capable of subserving higher-order awareness, this explains why it subserves conscious mental qualities. There is, then, no explanatory gap between theories of neural activity and theories of conscious perception, as the proponents of irreducible qualia contend.

What Is It Like to Be a Bat?

Our final author in this chapter is Kathleen A. Akins. Akins is Professor of Philosophy and Cognitive Science at Simon Fraser University, and James S. McDonnell Centennial Fellow in Philosophy of Science. Her studies attempt to understand how results in neuroscience can resolve issues about the nature of the mind. Like Rosenthal, Akins wishes to examine what she calls the "intuitive pull" of the view, shared by Nagel, Jackson, and others, that qualia are properties of mental states that can only be accessed via consciousness, that is, from the first-person perspective.

Akins starts by considering our everyday experience of finding it difficult to communicate the nature of some subjective experience to someone who has never had it. This experience, she claims, likely serves as a major source of our intuitions that phenomenology is forever inaccessible from the third-person point of view. She uses the example of trying to express, with considerable frustration, one's experience of a migraine headache to someone who has never suffered from one. The best we can do in such cases, she says, is often to abandon the futile hope of describing the *feeling* itself, and instead turning to describing the beliefs and desires that accompany it.

This "epistemic difficulty" is only compounded in the case of an alien creature, like Nagel's bat, with a sensory apparatus that gives rise to experiences that are completely different from our own. If, without ever having had a migraine, we are hopeless to understand the experience of a migraine sufferer, we are sure to be hopeless to understand what an experience that we are not even capable of having might be like.

Of course, Nagel's own claim, Akins is quick to point out, is about scientific explanation, not everyday explanation. But here the seemingly ineffable nature of our everyday sensations just gives rise to closely related feelings about the inability of science to aid in solving the problem. If we can't express, in everyday language, what feelings we are undergoing to someone who has never shared them, what could science possibly do to help? Suppose we had a completed neuroscience, with a full account of the neurological facts underlying a migraine experience or a broken toe. The idea that this would somehow help us understand what it feels like to experience these things is intuitively quite puzzling. Even such a full scientific account must necessarily "leave something out."

But what exactly is it that science is thought to leave out? Here Akins invokes the difference between a child's coloring book, with only the black outlines of the pictures, and the same coloring book with all the pictures colored in. If we have access only to the first coloring book, we might ask questions pertaining to the colors of the various objects depicted: "It is questions analogous to these, then," Akins writes, "that are allegedly left unanswered given only the neurological/ computational facts about another organism's brain process." Intuitively, science may one day give us a solid grip on the structural and representational properties of an experience—analogous to the "empty" outlines in the pre-filled-in coloring book and the objects they depict—but we'd still have no idea how the experiences are "filled in."

Phenomenal and Representational Properties

This picture may be tempting, but next, Akins goes on to argue that it is actually deeply misleading when it comes to understanding the relationship between the phenomenal and representational properties of our mental states. To help us see why, Akins has us imagine that she travels here from the future, when neuroscience is complete, and reports having what she calls a "sen-surround" film of what it is like to be a bat. The film depicts a sequence on repeat of a bat using echolocation to hunt down a mealworm. The film is taken from the bat's "auditory point of view," as it uses acoustic properties of objects in order to construct representations of their spatial properties and relations, much like we use visual properties of objects for similar purposes.

Now, what the film looks like to a human observer is a series of swirling color forms spinning and vibrating across the screen. But of course, in this case, since the color properties of the forms are standing in for acoustic properties, what they mean for the bat is something very different from what they mean for us—the viewers of the film. The problem though is that without understanding what role these color sensations play in the bat's perceptual system, we can't begin to understand the point of view of the bat. That is, it is not for lack of access to the phenomenal qualities that we fail to access the bat's point of view, but for lack of access to the *representational* properties of the bat's experience. For we don't know what the bat takes the acoustic properties to represent.

Moreover, there is a deeper mistake residing in this picture. This mistake lies in presupposing that phenomenal properties can be separated from representational properties *at all*—that somehow we could have one without the other—and that what's missing from our understanding of the bat's point of view is simply the phenomenal component of this pair. Akins maintains that we have no idea how to comply with the instruction to imagine that what the bat hears is just like color except that the colors represent different things than they do for us. To do this we would have to separate the phenomenal property from what it represents. But teasing these two properties apart, she says, "is not something we have any idea how to do: we do not know what the two 'parts' would be like, of and by themselves, so we have no inkling how to pull them apart or put them together."

Here one might reply that we do just that when we imagine the bat film. After all, doesn't imagining the film involve an understanding of the separation between phenomenal and representational properties? Isn't it just like what happens when one goes to an art gallery and views an abstract painting, devoid of any meaning or content, but vibrant with colors and shapes? But Akins points out that this is not an apt analogy. This is because, in these cases, the colored shapes and forms *do* have meaning for us; we see them *as* colored shapes on a canvas in front of us. So we do not have a separation of content from color in the case of abstract art, and likewise we do not achieve a separation of representational and phenomenal properties in imagining the bat film. We imagine ourselves viewing a film of swirling colors, not experiencing phenomenal properties in isolation.

The upshot, according to Akins, is that we have no clear idea what these properties are like isolated from the representational properties of our experiences. And that means we cannot trust our intuitions regarding whether science will one day uncover the nature of phenomenal properties. She concludes that this gives us "good reason to continue with our empirical investigations of mental representation," despite any intuitive sense we might have that such investigations must arrive at limited results.

Knowing Ourselves

Akins closes her paper by highlighting an important implication of the picture she has been presenting, which yokes together representational and phenomenal properties. This is that, even our own subjective experiences are the proper targets of empirical enquiry, just as much as are those of a bat. We can find out things about ourselves, and even our own point of view, through science and what it uncovers about the nature of representational systems like our minds.

Akins recognizes that this is a counterintuitive view. The traditional view of qualia has always had it that we have privileged access to them and that, as she puts it, "[i]f anyone knows about my subjective experience, it is certainly me…" Nonetheless, she urges that perhaps science can sometimes reveal that our intuitive picture of ourselves is mistaken.

By way of illustration, she calls up an example of eagles with which she began her article. Unlike humans, eagles have two foveal regions in each eye. In an attempt to imagine what the experience of the eagle is like, we might incorporate our *own* experience of shifting from one focal region to another in sequence. But, she points out, there is no reason to think that an *eagle* shifts attention sequentially in the way that we would have to. If we can get things wrong in our attempt to understand the experience of the eagle, however, why not also think that we sometimes get things wrong with respect to ourselves?

Akins suggests that our intuitive picture of conscious attention as a "spotlight" that moves its focus from object to object might be just the kind of thing that future science challenges.[12] After all, the metaphor of the "spotlight" clearly derives from the way we experience our conscious vision working—and since vision is such a dominant sense for humans we are tempted to understand internal attention and focus as working in the same way. But science may eventually help us see that "the way our own attentional mechanisms seem could diverge from how in fact they are."

Looking Ahead

In this chapter, we have reviewed various positions on how to understand the qualitative character of conscious experience. We have seen that for many theorists, the hope that science will one day be able to uncover all aspects of such character is not a vain one, whereas for others it is just that. In the next chapter, we turn to look more closely at the relationship between consciousness and scientific investigations of it. Such investigations rely on there being some sort of reliable third-person access to the presence of conscious states. And this, in turn, requires that conscious properties of mental states be, at least in part, functional properties that make a difference to behavior. But is this always the case? Can consciousness sometimes be separated from function? We turn next to look at various ways of responding to these questions.

Notes

1. *Consciousness Explained* (Boston: Little, Brown and Company, 1991). Dennett's more recent books on the philosophy of mind are *Kinds of Minds: Toward an Understanding of Consciousness* (New York: Basic Books, 1996) and *Sweet Dreams: Philosophical Obstacles to a Science of Consciousness* (Cambridge MA: MIT Press, 2005), *From Bacteria to Bach and Back: The Evolution of Minds* (New York: W.W. Norton & Co. 2017).
2. See page 275 above.
3. For other such cases, see the works of the neurologist, Oliver Sacks, especially *An Anthropologist on Mars* (Toronto: Alfred A. Knopf, 1995).
4. *A Theory of Sentience* (Oxford: Oxford University Press, 2000), pp. 4–6.
5. The perception of yellow, for which there is no receptor, is the product of simultaneous stimulation of red and green receptors, which inhibits the blue signal.
6. Allisa D. Winkler, Lothar Spillmann, John S. Werner, and Michael A. Webster, "Asymmetries in Blue-Yellow Color Perception and in the 'Color of the Dress,'" *Current Biology* 25 (2015): pp. R547–R548.
7. More recently, a similar phenomenon has gripped the internet, but related to sound rather than color. A certain audio clip is heard by some as "Yanny" and by others as "Laurel."
8. Clark (pp. 5–6) makes the point, then, that a quality space is a mapping from what he calls "phenomenal properties," which are the ways things in the world appear to us, to what he

calls "qualitative properties," which are the properties of our mental states in virtue of which the things in the world appear to us as they do.

9. Shoemaker, Sydney, "The Inverted Spectrum," *Journal of Philosophy* LXXIX (1982): p. 7.

10. There is a point here that an astute reader might notice: If two quality spaces are identical in their structure (the same number of points, related to one another in all the same ways), then QST would not distinguish them, even if they are of different modalities. Technically, we express this by saying that, in QST, isomorphic quality spaces are indistinguishable.

11. Unfortunately, the word 'intrinsic' is being used here in a different sense from the way it has been used before this.

12. The spotlight metaphor of consciousness is one that is used by psychologists in studying the function of consciousness. We will examine such a metaphor in the next chapter.

THOMAS NAGEL

"What Is It Like to Be a Bat?"

Consciousness is what makes the mind-body problem really intractable. Perhaps that is why current discussions of the problem give it little attention or get it obviously wrong. The recent wave of reductionist euphoria has produced several analyses of mental phenomena and mental concepts designed to explain the possibility of some variety of materialism, psychophysical identification, or reduction.[1] But the problems dealt with are those common to this type of reduction and other types, and what makes the mind-body problem unique, and unlike the water-H_2O problem or the Turing machine-IBM machine problem or the lightning-electrical discharge problem or the gene-DNA problem or the oak tree-hydrocarbon problem, is ignored.

Every reductionist has his favorite analogy from modern science. It is most unlikely that any of these unrelated examples of successful reduction will shed light on the relation of mind to brain. But philosophers share the general human weakness for explanations of what is incomprehensible in terms suited for what is familiar and well understood, though entirely different. This has led to the acceptance of implausible accounts of the mental largely because they would permit familiar kinds of reduction. I shall try to explain why the usual examples do not help us to understand the relation between mind and body—why, indeed, we have at present no conception of what an explanation of the physical nature of a mental phenomenon would be. Without consciousness the mind-body problem would be much less interesting. With consciousness it seems hopeless. The most important and characteristic feature of conscious mental phenomena is very poorly understood. Most reductionist theories do not even try to explain it. And careful examination will show that no currently available concept of reduction is applicable to it. Perhaps a new theoretical form can be devised for the purpose, but such a solution, if it exists, lies in the distant intellectual future.

Conscious experience is a widespread phenomenon. It occurs at many levels of animal life, though we cannot be sure of its presence in the simpler organisms, and it is very difficult to say in general what provides evidence of it. (Some extremists have been prepared to deny it even of mammals other than man.) No doubt it occurs in countless forms totally unimaginable to us, on other planets in other solar systems throughout the universe. But no matter how the form may vary, the fact that an organism has conscious experience *at all* means, basically, that there is something it is like to *be* that organism. There may be further implications about the form of the experience; there may even (though I doubt it) be implications about the behavior of the organism. But fundamentally an organism has conscious mental states if and only if there is something that it is like to *be* that organism—something it is like *for* the organism.

We may call this the subjective character of experience. It is not captured by any of the familiar, recently devised reductive analyses of the mental, for all of them are logically compatible with its absence. It is not analyzable in terms of any explanatory system of functional states, or intentional states, since these could be ascribed to robots or automata that behaved like people though they experienced nothing.[2] It is not analyzable in terms of the causal role of experiences in relation to typical human behavior—for similar reasons.[3] I do not deny that conscious mental states and events cause behavior, nor that they may be given functional characterizations. I deny only that this kind of thing exhausts their analysis. Any reductionist program has to be based on an analysis of what is to be reduced. If the analysis leaves something out, the problem will be falsely posed. It is useless to base the defense of materialism on any analysis of mental phenomena that fails to deal explicitly with their subjective character.

For there is no reason to suppose that a reduction which seems plausible when no attempt is made to account for consciousness can be extended to include consciousness. Without some idea, therefore, of what the subjective character of experience is, we cannot know what is required of a physicalist theory.

While an account of the physical basis of mind must explain many things, this appears to be the most difficult. It is impossible to exclude the phenomenological features of experience from a reduction in the same way that one excludes the phenomenal features of an ordinary substance from a physical or chemical reduction of it—namely, by explaining them as effects on the minds of human observers.[4] If physicalism is to be defended, the phenomenological features must themselves be given a physical account. But when we examine their subjective character it seems that such a result is impossible. The reason is that every subjective phenomenon is essentially connected with a single point of view, and it seems inevitable that an objective, physical theory will abandon that point of view.

Let me first try to state the issue somewhat more fully than by referring to the relation between the subjective and the objective, or between the *pour-soi* and the *en-soi*. This is far from easy. Facts about what it is like to be an X are very peculiar, so peculiar that some may be inclined to doubt their reality, or the significance of claims about them. To illustrate the connection between subjectivity and a point of view, and to make evident the importance of subjective features, it will help to explore the matter in relation to an example that brings out clearly the divergence between the two types of conception, subjective and objective.

I assume we all believe that bats have experience. After all, they are mammals, and there is no more doubt that they have experience than that mice or pigeons or whales have experience.

I have chosen bats instead of wasps or flounders because if one travels too far down the phylogenetic tree, people gradually shed their faith that there is experience there at all. Bats, although more closely related to us than those other species, nevertheless present a range of activity and a sensory apparatus so different from ours that the problem I want to pose is exceptionally vivid (though it certainly could be raised with other species). Even without the benefit of philosophical reflection, anyone who has spent some time in an enclosed space with an excited bat knows what it is to encounter a fundamentally *alien* form of life.

I have said that the essence of the belief that bats have experience is that there is something that it is like to be a bat. Now we know that most bats (the microchiroptera, to be precise) perceive the external world primarily by sonar, or echolocation, detecting the reflections, from objects within range, of their own rapid, subtly modulated, high-frequency shrieks. Their brains are designed to correlate the outgoing impulses with the subsequent echoes, and the information thus acquired enables bats to make precise discriminations of distance, size, shape, motion, and texture comparable to those we make by vision. But bat sonar, though clearly a form of perception, is not similar in its operation to any sense that we possess, and there is no reason to suppose that it is subjectively like anything we can experience or imagine. This appears to create difficulties for the notion of what it is like to be a bat. We must consider whether any method will permit us to extrapolate to the inner life of the bat from our own case,[5] and if not, what alternative methods there may be for understanding the notion.

Our own experience provides the basic material for our imagination, whose range is therefore limited. It will not help to try to imagine that one has webbing on one's arms, which enables one to fly around at dusk and dawn

catching insects in one's mouth, that one has very poor vision, and perceives the surrounding world by a system of reflected high-frequency sound signals, and that one spends the day hanging upside down by one's feet in an attic. In so far as I can imagine this (which is not very far), it tells me only what it would be like for *me* to behave as a bat behaves. But that is not the question. I want to know what it is like for a *bat* to be a bat. Yet if I try to imagine this, I am restricted to the resources of my own mind, and those resources are inadequate to the task. I cannot perform it either by imagining additions to my present experience, or by imagining segments gradually subtracted from it, or by imagining some combination of additions, subtractions, and modifications.

To the extent that I could look and behave like a wasp or a bat without changing my fundamental structure, my experiences would not be anything like the experiences of those animals. On the other hand, it is doubtful that any meaning can be attached to the supposition that I should possess the internal neurophysiological constitution of a bat. Even if I could by gradual degrees be transformed into a bat, nothing in my present constitution enables me to imagine what the experiences of such a future stage of myself thus metamorphosed would be like. The best evidence would come from the experiences of bats, if we only knew what they were like.

So if extrapolation from our own case is involved in the idea of what it is like to be a bat, the extrapolation must be incompletable. We cannot form more than a schematic conception of what it *is* like. For example, we may ascribe general *types* of experience on the basis of the animal's structure and behavior. Thus we describe bat sonar as a form of three-dimensional forward perception; we believe that bats feel some versions of pain, fear, hunger, and lust, and that they have other, more familiar types of perception besides sonar. But we believe that these experiences also have in each case a specific subjective character, which it is beyond our ability to conceive. And if there is conscious life elsewhere in the universe, it is likely that some of it will not be describable even in the most general experiential terms available to us.[6] (The problem is not confined to exotic cases, however, for it exists between one person and another. The subjective character of the experience of a person deaf and blind from birth is not accessible to me, for example, nor presumably is mine to him. This does not prevent us each from believing that the other's experience has such a subjective character.)

If anyone is inclined to deny that we can believe in the existence of facts like this whose exact nature we cannot possibly conceive, he should reflect that in contemplating the bats we are in much the same position that intelligent bats or Martians[7] would occupy if they tried to form a conception of what it was like to be us. The structure of their own minds might make it impossible for them to succeed, but we know they would be wrong to conclude that there is not anything precise that it is like to be us: that only certain general types of mental state could be ascribed to us (perhaps perception and appetite would be concepts common to us both; perhaps not). We know they would be wrong to draw such a skeptical conclusion because we know what it is like to be us. And we know that while it includes an enormous amount of variation and complexity, and while we do not possess the vocabulary to describe it adequately, its subjective character is highly specific, and in some respects describable in terms that can be understood only by creatures like us. The fact that we cannot expect ever to accommodate in our language a detailed description of Martian or bat phenomenology should not lead us to dismiss as meaningless the claim that bats and Martians have experiences fully comparable in richness of detail to our own. It would be fine if someone were to develop concepts and a theory that enabled us to think about those things; but such an understanding may be permanently denied to us by the limits of our nature. And to deny the reality or logical significance of what we can never describe or understand is the crudest form of cognitive dissonance.

This brings us to the edge of a topic that requires much more discussion than I can give it here: namely, the relation between facts on the one hand and conceptual schemes or systems of representation on the other. My realism about the subjective domain in all its forms implies a belief in the existence of facts beyond the reach of human concepts. Certainly it is possible for a human being to believe that there are facts which humans never *will* possess the requisite concepts to represent or comprehend. Indeed, it would be foolish to doubt this, given the finiteness of humanity's expectations. After all, there would have been transfinite numbers even if everyone had been wiped out by the Black Death before Cantor discovered them. But one might also believe that there are facts which *could* not ever be represented or comprehended by human beings, even if the species lasted forever—simply because our structure does not permit us to operate with concepts of the requisite type. This impossibility might even be observed by other beings, but it is not clear that the existence of such beings, or the possibility of their existence, is a precondition of the significance of the hypothesis that there are humanly inaccessible facts. (After all, the nature of beings with access to humanly inaccessible facts is presumably itself a humanly inaccessible fact.) Reflection on what it is like to be a bat seems to lead us, therefore, to the conclusion that there are facts that do not consist in the truth of propositions expressible in a human language. We can be compelled to recognize the existence of such facts without being able to state or comprehend them.

I shall not pursue this subject, however. Its bearing on the topic before us (namely, the mind-body problem) is that it enables us to make a general observation about the subjective character of experience. Whatever may be the status of facts about what it is like to be a human being, or a bat, or a Martian, these appear to be facts that embody a particular point of view.

I am not adverting here to the alleged privacy of experience to its possessor. The point of view in question is not one accessible only to a single individual. Rather it is a *type*. It is often possible to take up a point of view other than one's own, so the comprehension of such facts is not limited to one's own case. There is a sense in which phenomenological facts are perfectly objective: one person can know or say of another what the quality of the other's experience is. They are subjective, however, in the sense that even this objective ascription of experience is possible only for someone sufficiently similar to the object of ascription to be able to adopt his point of view—to understand the ascription in the first person as well as in the third, so to speak. The more different from oneself the other experiencer is, the less success one can expect with this enterprise. In our own case we occupy the relevant point of view, but we will have as much difficulty understanding our own experience properly if we approach it from another point of view as we would if we tried to understand the experience of another species without taking up *its* point of view.[8]

This bears directly on the mind-body problem. For if the facts of experience—facts about what it is like *for* the experiencing organism— are accessible only from one point of view, then it is a mystery how the true character of experiences could be revealed in the physical operation of that organism. The latter is a domain of objective facts *par excellence*—the kind that can be observed and understood from many points of view and by individuals with differing perceptual systems. There are no comparable imaginative obstacles to the acquisition of knowledge about bat neurophysiology by human scientists, and intelligent bats or Martians might learn more about the human brain than we ever will.

This is not by itself an argument against reduction. A Martian scientist with no understanding of visual perception could understand the rainbow, or lightning, or clouds as physical phenomena, though he would never be able to understand the human concepts of rainbow, lightning, or cloud, or the place these things occupy in our phenomenal world. The objective nature of the things picked out by these concepts could be apprehended by him because, although the concepts themselves are connected with a particular point of view and a particular visual phenomenology, the things apprehended from that point of view are not: they are observable from the point of view but external to it; hence they can be comprehended from other points of view also, either by the same organisms or by others. Lightning has an objective character that is not exhausted by its visual appearance, and this can be investigated by a Martian without vision. To be precise, it has a *more* objective character than is revealed in its visual appearance. In speaking of the move from subjective to objective characterization, I wish to remain noncommittal about the existence of an end point, the completely objective intrinsic nature of the thing, which one might or might not be able to reach. It may be more accurate to think of objectivity as a direction in which the understanding can travel. And in understanding a phenomenon like lightning, it is legitimate to go as far away as one can from a strictly human viewpoint.[9]

In the case of experience, on the other hand, the connection with a particular point of view seems much closer. It is difficult to understand what could be meant by the *objective* character of an experience, apart from the particular point of view from which its subject apprehends it. After all, what would be left of what it was like to be a bat if one removed the viewpoint of the bat? But if experience does not have, in addition to its subjective character, an objective nature that can be apprehended from many different points of view, then how can it be supposed that a Martian investigating my brain might be observing physical processes which were my mental processes (as he might observe physical processes which were bolts of lightning), only from a different point of view? How, for that matter, could a human physiologist observe them from another point of view?[10]

We appear to be faced with a general difficulty about psychophysical reduction. In other areas the process of reduction is a move in the direction of greater objectivity, toward a more accurate view of the real nature of things. This is accomplished by reducing our dependence on individual or species-specific points of view toward the object of investigation. We describe it not in terms of the impressions it makes on our senses, but in terms of its more general effects and of properties detectable by means other than the human senses. The less it depends on a specifically human viewpoint, the more objective is our description. It is possible to follow this path because although the concepts and ideas we employ in thinking about the external world are initially applied from a point of view that involves our perceptual apparatus, they are used by us to refer to things beyond themselves—toward which we *have* the phenomenal point of view. Therefore we can abandon it in favor of another, and still be thinking about the same things.

Experience itself, however, does not seem to fit the pattern. The idea of moving from appearance to reality seems to make no sense here. What is the analogue in this case to pursuing a more objective understanding of the same phenomena by abandoning the initial subjective viewpoint toward them in favor of another that is more objective but concerns the same thing? Certainly it *appears* unlikely that we will get closer to the real nature of human experience by leaving behind the particularity of our human point of view and striving for a description in terms accessible to beings that could not imagine what it was like to be us. If the subjective character of experience is fully comprehensible only from one point of view, then any shift to greater objectivity—that is, less attachment to a specific viewpoint—does not take us nearer to the real nature of the phenomenon: it takes us farther away from it.

In a sense, the seeds of this objection to the reducibility of experience are already detectable in successful cases of reduction, for in discovering sound to be, in reality, a wave phenomenon in air or other media, we leave behind one viewpoint to take up another, and the auditory, human or animal viewpoint that we leave behind remains unreduced. Members of radically different species may both understand the same physical events in objective terms, and this does not require that they understand the phenomenal forms in which those events appear to the senses of members of the other species. Thus it is a condition of their referring to a common reality that their more particular viewpoints are not part of the common reality that they both apprehend. The reduction can succeed only if the species-specific viewpoint is omitted from what is to be reduced.

But while we are right to leave this point of view aside in seeking a fuller understanding of the external world, we cannot ignore it permanently, since it is the essence of the internal world, and not merely a point of view on it. Most of the neobehaviorism of recent philosophical psychology results from the effort to substitute an objective concept of mind for the real thing, in order to have nothing left over which cannot be reduced. If we acknowledge that a physical theory of mind must account for the subjective character of experience, we must admit that no presently available conception gives us a clue how this could be done. The problem is unique. If mental processes are indeed physical processes, then there is something it is like, intrinsically,[11] to undergo certain physical processes. What it is for such a thing to be the case remains a mystery.

What moral should be drawn from these reflections, and what should be done next? It would be a mistake to conclude that physicalism must be false. Nothing is proved by the inadequacy of physicalist hypotheses that assume a faulty objective analysis of mind. It would be truer to say that physicalism is a position we cannot understand because we do not at present have any conception of how it might be true. Perhaps it will be thought unreasonable to require such a conception as a condition of understanding. After all, it might be said, the meaning of physicalism is clear enough: mental states are states of the body; mental events are physical events. We do not know *which* physical states and events they are, but that should not prevent us from understanding the hypothesis. What could be clearer than the words "is" and "are"?

But I believe it is precisely this apparent clarity of the word "is" that is deceptive. Usually, when we are told that *X* is *Y* we know *how* it is supposed to be true, but that depends on a conceptual or theoretical background and is not conveyed by the "is" alone. We know how both "*X*" and "*Y*" refer, and the kinds of things to which they refer, and we have a rough idea how the two referential paths might converge on a single thing, be it an object, a person, a process, an event, or whatever. But when the two terms of the identification are very disparate it may not be so clear how it could be true.

We may not have even a rough idea of how the two referential paths could converge, or what kind of things they might converge on, and a theoretical framework may have to be supplied to enable us to understand this. Without the framework, an air of mysticism surrounds the identification.

This explains the magical flavor of popular presentations of fundamental scientific discoveries, given out as propositions to which one must subscribe without really understanding them. For example, people are now told at an early age that all matter is really energy. But despite the fact that they know what "is" means, most of them never form a conception of what makes this claim true, because they lack the theoretical background.

At the present time the status of physicalism is similar to that which the hypothesis that matter is energy would have had if uttered by a pre-Socratic philosopher. We do not have the beginnings of a conception of how it might be true. In order to understand the hypothesis that a mental event is a physical event, we require more than an understanding of the word "is." The idea of how a mental and a physical term might refer to the same thing is lacking, and the usual analogies with theoretical identification in other fields fail to supply it. They fail because if we construe the reference of mental terms to physical events on the usual model, we either get a reappearance of separate subjective events as the effects through which mental reference to physical events is secured, or else we get a false account of how mental terms refer (for example, a causal behaviorist one).

Strangely enough, we may have evidence for the truth of something we cannot really understand. Suppose a caterpillar is locked in a sterile safe by someone unfamiliar with insect metamorphosis, and weeks later the safe is reopened, revealing a butterfly. If the person knows that the safe has been shut the whole time, he has reason to believe that the butterfly is or was once the caterpillar, without having any idea in what sense this might be so. (One possibility is that the caterpillar contained a tiny winged parasite that devoured it and grew into the butterfly.)

It is conceivable that we are in such a position with regard to physicalism. Donald Davidson has argued that if mental events have physical causes and effects, they must have physical descriptions. He holds that we have reason to believe this even though we do not—and in fact *could* not—have a general psychophysical theory.[12] His argument applies to intentional mental events, but I think we also have some reason to believe that sensations are physical processes, without being in a position to understand how. Davidson's position is that certain physical events have irreducibly mental properties, and perhaps some view describable in this way is correct. But nothing of which we can now form a conception corresponds to it; nor have we any idea what a theory would be like that enabled us to conceive of it.[13]

Very little work has been done on the basic question (from which mention of the brain can be entirely omitted) whether any sense can be made of experiences having an objective character at all. Does it make sense, in other words, to ask what my experiences are *really* like, as opposed to how they appear to me? We cannot genuinely understand the hypothesis that their nature is captured in a physical description unless we understand the more fundamental idea that they *have* an objective nature (or that objective processes can have a subjective nature).[14] I should like to close with a speculative proposal. It may be possible to approach the gap between subjective and objective from another direction. Setting aside temporarily the relation between the mind and the brain, we can pursue a more objective understanding of the mental in its own right. At present we

are completely unequipped to think about the subjective character of experience without relying on the imagination—without taking up the point of view of the experiential subject. This should be regarded as a challenge to form new concepts and devise a new method—an objective phenomenology not dependent on empathy or the imagination. Though presumably it would not capture everything, its goal would be to describe, at least in part, the subjective character of experiences in a form comprehensible to beings incapable of having those experiences.

We would have to develop such a phenomenology to describe the sonar experiences of bats; but it would also be possible to begin with humans. One might try, for example, to develop concepts that could be used to explain to a person blind from birth what it was like to see. One would reach a blank wall eventually, but it should be possible to devise a method of expressing in objective terms much more than we can at present, and with much greater precision.

The loose intermodal analogies—for example, "Red is like the sound of a trumpet"—which crop up in discussions of this subject are of little use. That should be clear to anyone who has both heard a trumpet and seen red. But structural features of perception might be more accessible to objective description, even though something would be left out. And concepts alternative to those we learn in the first person may enable us to arrive at a kind of understanding even of our own experience which is denied us by the very ease of description and lack of distance that subjective concepts afford.

Apart from its own interest, a phenomenology that is in this sense objective may permit questions about the physical[15] basis of experience to assume a more intelligible form. Aspects of subjective experience that admitted this kind of objective description might be better candidates for objective explanations of a more familiar sort. But whether or not this guess is correct, it seems unlikely that any physical theory of mind can be contemplated until more thought has been given to the general problem of subjective and objective. Otherwise we cannot even pose the mind-body problem without sidestepping it.[16]

Notes

1. Examples are J.J.C. Smart, *Philosophy and Scientific Realism* (London, 1963); David K. Lewis, "An Argument for the Identity Theory," *Journal of Philosophy*, LXIII (1966), reprinted with addenda in David M. Rosenthal, *Materialism & the Mind-Body Problem* (Englewood Cliffs, NJ, 1971); Hilary Putnam, "Psychological Predicates" in Capitan and Merrill, *Art, Mind, & Religion* (Pittsburgh, 1967), reprinted in Rosenthal, op. cit., as "The Nature of Mental States"; D.M. Armstrong, *A Materialist Theory of the Mind* (London, 1968); D.C. Dennett, *Content and Consciousness* (London, 1969). I have expressed earlier doubts in "Armstrong on the Mind," *Philosophical Review*, LXXIX (1970), 394–403; "Brain Bisection and the Unity of Consciousness," *Synthese*, 22 (1971); and a review of Dennett, *Journal of Philosophy*, LXIX (1972). See also Saul Kripke, "Naming and Necessity" in Davidson and Hannan, *Semantics of Natural Language* (Dordrecht, 1972), esp. pp. 334–42; and M.T. Thornton, "Ostensive Terms and Materialism," *The Monist*, 56 (1972).

2. Perhaps there could not actually be such robots. Perhaps anything complex enough to behave like a person would have experiences. But that, if true, is a fact which cannot be discovered merely by analyzing the concept of experience.

3. It is not equivalent to that about which we are incorrigible, both because we are not incorrigible about experience and because experience is present in animals lacking language and thought, who have no beliefs at all about their experiences.

4. Cf. Richard Rorty, "Mind-Body Identity, Privacy, and Categories," *The Review of Metaphysics*, XIX (1965), esp. 37–38.

5. By "our own case" I do not mean just "my own case," but rather the mentalistic ideas that we apply unproblematically to ourselves and other human beings.

6. Therefore the analogical form of the English expression "what it is *like*" is misleading. It does not mean "what (in our experience) it *resembles*," but rather "how it is for the subject himself."

7. Any intelligent extraterrestrial beings totally different from us.

8. It may be easier than I suppose to transcend inter-species barriers with the aid of the imagination. For example, blind people are able to detect objects near them by a form of sonar, using vocal clicks or taps of a cane. Perhaps if one knew what that was like, one could by extension imagine roughly what it was like to possess the much more refined sonar of a bat. The distance between oneself and other persons and other species can fall anywhere on a continuum. Even for other persons the understanding of what it is like to be them is only partial, and when one moves to species very different from oneself, a lesser degree of partial understanding may still be available. The imagination is remarkably flexible. My point, however, is not that we cannot *know* what it is like to be a bat. I am not raising that epistemological problem. My point is rather that even to form a *conception* of what it is like to be a bat (and a fortiori to know what it is like to be a bat) one must take up the bat's point of view. If one can take it up roughly, or partially, then one's conception will also be rough or partial. Or so it seems in our present state of understanding.

9. The problem I am going to raise can therefore be posed even if the distinction between more subjective and more objective descriptions or viewpoints can itself be made only within a larger human point of view. I do not accept this kind of conceptual relativism, but it need not be refuted to make the point that psychophysical reduction cannot be accommodated by the subjective-to-objective model familiar from other cases.

10. The problem is not just that when I look at the "Mona Lisa," my visual experience has a certain quality, no trace of which is to be found by someone looking into my brain. For even if he did observe there a tiny image of the "Mona Lisa," he would have no reason to identify it with the experience.

11. The relation would therefore not be a contingent one, like that of a cause and its distinct effect. It would be necessarily true that a certain physical state felt a certain way. Saul Kripke (op. cit.) argues that causal behaviorist and related analyses of the mental fail because they construe, e.g., "pain" as a merely contingent name of pains. The subjective character of an experience ("its immediate phenomenological quality" Kripke calls it [p. 340]) is the essential property left out by such analyses, and the one in virtue of which it is, necessarily, the experience it is. My view is closely related to his. Like Kripke, I find the hypothesis that a certain brain state should *necessarily* have a certain subjective character incomprehensible without further explanation. No such explanation emerges from theories which view the mind-brain relation as contingent, but perhaps there are other alternatives, not yet discovered. A theory that explained how the mind-brain relation was necessary would still leave us with Kripke's problem of explaining why it nevertheless appears contingent. That difficulty seems to me surmountable, in the following way. We may imagine something by representing it to ourselves either perceptually, sympathetically, or symbolically. I shall not try to say how symbolic imagination works, but part of what happens in the other two cases is this. To imagine something perceptually, we put ourselves in a conscious state resembling the state we would be in if we perceived it. To imagine something sympathetically, we put ourselves in a conscious state resembling the thing itself. (This method can be used only to imagine mental events and states—our own or another's.) When we try to imagine a mental state occurring without its associated brain state, we first sympathetically imagine the occurrence of the mental state: that is, we put ourselves into a state that resembles it mentally. At the same time, we attempt to perceptually imagine the non-occurrence of the associated physical state, by putting ourselves into another state unconnected with the first: one resembling that which we would be in if we perceived the non-occurrence of the physical state. Where the imagination of physical features is perceptual and the imagination of mental features is sympathetic, it appears to us that we can imagine any experience occurring without its associated brain state, and vice versa. The relation between them will appear contingent even if it is necessary, because of the independence of the disparate types of imagination. (Solipsism, incidentally, results if one misinterprets sympathetic imagination as if it worked like perceptual imagination: it then seems impossible to imagine any experience that is not one's own.)

12. See "Mental Events" in Foster and Swanson, *Experience and Theory* (Amherst, 1970);

though I don't understand the argument against psychophysical laws.

13. Similar remarks apply to my paper "Physicalism," *Philosophical Review*, LXXIV (1965), 339–56, reprinted with postscript in John O'Connor, *Modern Materialism* (New York, 1969).

14. This question also lies at the heart of the problem of other minds, whose close connection with the mind-body problem is often overlooked. If one understood how subjective experience could have an objective nature, one would understand the existence of subjects other than oneself.

15. I have not defined the term "physical." Obviously it does not apply just to what can be described by the concepts of contemporary physics, since we expect further developments. Some may think there is nothing to prevent mental phenomena from eventually being recognized as physical in their own right. But whatever else may be said of the physical, it has to be objective. So if our idea of the physical ever expands to include mental phenomena, it will have to assign them an objective character—whether or not this is done by analyzing them in terms of other phenomena already regarded as physical. It seems to me more likely, however, that mental-physical relations will eventually be expressed in a theory whose fundamental terms cannot be placed clearly in either category.

16. I have read versions of this paper to a number of audiences, and am indebted to many people for their comments.

FRANK JACKSON

"Epiphenomenal Qualia"

It is undeniable that the physical, chemical and biological sciences have provided a great deal of information about the world we live in and about ourselves. I will use the label 'physical information' for this kind of information, and also for information that automatically comes along with it. For example, if a medical scientist tells me enough about the processes that go on in my nervous system, and about how they relate to happenings in the world around me, to what has happened in the past and is likely to happen in the future, to what happens to other similar and dissimilar organisms, and the like, he or she tells me—if I am clever enough to fit it together appropriately—about what is often called the functional role of those states in me (and in organisms in general in similar cases). This information, and its kin, I also label 'physical.'

I do not mean these sketchy remarks to constitute a definition of 'physical information,' and of the correlative notions of physical property, process, and so on, but to indicate what I have in mind here. It is well known that there are problems with giving a precise definition of these notions, and so of the thesis of Physicalism that all (correct) information is physical information.[1] But—unlike some—I take the question of definition to cut across the central problems I want to discuss in this paper.

I am what is sometimes known as a "qualia freak." I think that there are certain features of the bodily sensations especially, but also of certain perceptual experiences, which no amount of purely physical information includes. Tell me everything physical there is to tell about what is going on in a living brain, the kind of states, their functional role, their relation to what goes on at other times and in other brains, and so on and so forth and be I as clever as can be in fitting it all together, you won't have told me about the hurtfulness of pains, the itchiness of itches, pangs of jealousy, or about the characteristic experience of tasting a lemon, smelling a rose, hearing a loud noise or seeing the sky.

There are many qualia freaks, and some of them say that their rejection of Physicalism is an unargued intuition.[2] I think that they are being unfair to themselves. They have the following argument. Nothing you could tell of a physical sort captures the smell of a rose, for instance. Therefore, Physicalism is false. By our lights this is a perfectly good argument. It is obviously not to the point to question its validity, and the premise is intuitively obviously true both to them and to me.

I must, however, admit that it is weak from a polemical point of view. There are, unfortunately for us, many who do not find the premise intuitively obvious. The task then is to present an argument whose premises are obvious to all, or at least to as many as possible. This I try to do in §I with what I will call "the Knowledge argument." In §II I contrast the Knowledge argument with the Modal argument and in §III with the "What is it like to be" argument. In §IV I tackle the question of the causal role of qualia. The major factor in stopping people from admitting qualia is the belief that they would have to be given a causal role with respect to the physical world and especially the brain;[3] and it is hard to do this without sounding like someone who believes in fairies. I seek in §IV

to turn this objection by arguing that the view that qualia are epiphenomenal is a perfectly possible one.

I. The Knowledge Argument for Qualia

People vary considerably in their ability to discriminate colours. Suppose that in an experiment to catalogue this variation Fred is discovered. Fred has better colour vision than anyone else on record; he makes every discrimination that anyone has ever made, and moreover he makes one that we cannot even begin to make. Show him a batch of ripe tomatoes and he sorts them into two roughly equal groups and does so with complete consistency. That is, if you blindfold him, shuffle the tomatoes up, and then remove the blindfold and ask him to sort them out again, he sorts them into exactly the same two groups.

We ask Fred how he does it. He explains that all ripe tomatoes do not look the same colour to him, and in fact that this is true of a great many objects that we classify together as red. He sees two colours where we see one, and he has in consequence developed for his own use two words 'red$_1$' and 'red$_2$' to mark the difference. Perhaps he tells us that he has often tried to teach the difference between red$_1$ and red$_2$ to his friends but has got nowhere and has concluded that the rest of the world is red$_1$-red$_2$ colour-blind—or perhaps he has had partial success with his children, it doesn't matter.

In any case he explains to us that it would be quite wrong to think that because 'red' appears in both 'red$_1$' and 'red$_2$' that the two colours are shades of the one colour. He only uses the common term 'red' to fit more easily into our restricted usage. To him red$_1$ and red$_2$ are as different from each other and all the other colours as yellow is from blue. And his discriminatory behaviour bears this out: he sorts red$_1$ from red$_2$ tomatoes with the greatest of ease in a wide variety of viewing circumstances. Moreover, an investigation of the physiological basis of Fred's exceptional ability reveals that Fred's optical system is able to separate out two groups of wave lengths in the red spectrum as sharply as we are able to sort out yellow from blue.[4]

I think that we should admit that Fred can see, really see, at least one more colour than we can; red_1 is a different colour from red_2. We are to Fred as a totally red-green colour-blind person is to us. H.G. Wells's story "The Country of the Blind" is about a sighted person in a totally blind community.[5] This person never manages to convince them that he can see, that he has an extra sense. They ridicule this sense as quite inconceivable, and treat his capacity to avoid falling into ditches, to win fights and so on as precisely that capacity and nothing more. We would be making their mistake if we refused to allow that Fred can see one more colour than we can.

What kind of experience does Fred have when he sees red_1 and red_2? What is the new colour or colours like? We would dearly like to know but do not; and it seems that no amount of physical information about Fred's brain and optical system tells us. We find out perhaps Fred's cones respond differentially to certain light waves in the red section of the spectrum that make no difference to ours (or perhaps he has an extra cone) and that this leads in Fred to a wider range of those brain states responsible for visual discriminatory behaviour. But none of this tells us what we really want to know about his colour experience. There is something about it we don't know. But we know, we may suppose, everything about Fred's body, his behaviour and dispositions to behaviour and about his internal physiology, and everything about his history and relation to others that can be given in physical accounts of persons. We have all the physical information. Therefore, knowing all this is *not* knowing everything

about Fred. It follows that Physicalism leaves something out.

To reinforce this conclusion, imagine that as a result of our investigations into the internal workings of Fred we find out how to make everyone's physiology like Fred's in the relevant respects; or perhaps Fred donates his body to science and on his death we are able to transplant his optical system into someone else—again the fine detail doesn't matter. The important point is that such a happening would create enormous interest. People would say, "At last we will know what it is like to see the extra colour, at last we will know how Fred has differed from us in the way he has struggled to tell us about for so long." Then it cannot be that we knew all along all about Fred. But *ex hypothesi* we did know all along everything about Fred that features in the physicalist scheme; hence the physicalist scheme leaves something out.

Put it this way. *After* the operation, we will know *more* about Fred and especially about his colour experiences. But beforehand we had all the physical information we could desire about his body and brain, and indeed everything that has ever featured in physicalist accounts of mind and consciousness. Hence there is more to know than all that. Hence Physicalism is incomplete. Fred and the new colour(s) are of course essentially rhetorical devices. The same point can be made with normal people and familiar colours. Mary is a brilliant scientist who is, for whatever reason, forced to investigate the world from a black and white room *via* a black and white television monitor. She specialises in the neurophysiology of vision and acquires, let us suppose, all the physical information there is to obtain about what goes on when we see ripe tomatoes, or the sky, and use terms like 'red,' 'blue,' and so on. She discovers, for example, just which wave-length combinations from the sky stimulate the retina, and exactly how this produces *via* the central nervous system the contraction of the vocal chords and expulsion of air from the lungs that result in the uttering of the sentence 'The sky is blue.' (It can hardly be denied that it is in principle possible to obtain all this physical information from black and white television, otherwise the Open University would *of necessity* need to use colour television.) What will happen when Mary is released from her black and white room or is given a colour television monitor? Will she *learn* anything or not? It seems just obvious that she will learn something about the world and our visual experience of it. But then it is inescapable that her previous knowledge was incomplete. But she had *all* the physical information. *Ergo* there is more to have than that, and Physicalism is false. Clearly the same style of Knowledge argument could be deployed for taste, hearing, the bodily sensations and generally speaking for the various mental states which are said to have (as it is variously put) raw feels, phenomenal features or qualia. The conclusion in each case is that the qualia are left out of the physicalist story. And the polemical strength of the Knowledge argument is that it is so hard to deny the central claim that one can have all the physical information without having all the information there is to have.

II. The Modal Argument

By the Modal Argument I mean an argument of the following style.[6] Sceptics about other minds are not making a mistake in deductive logic, whatever else may be wrong with their position. No amount of physical information about another *logically entails* that he or she is conscious or feels anything at all. Consequently there is a possible world with organisms exactly like us in every physical respect (and remember that includes functional states, physical history, *et al.*) but which differ from us pro-

foundly in that they have no conscious mental life at all. But then what is it that we have and they lack? Not anything physical *ex hypothesi*. In all physical regards we and they are exactly alike. Consequently there is more to us than the purely physical. Thus Physicalism is false.[7]

It is sometimes objected that the Modal argument misconceives Physicalism on the ground that that doctrine is advanced as a *contingent* truth.[8] But say this is only to say that physicalists restrict their claim to *some* possible worlds, including especially ours; and the Modal argument is only directed against this lesser claim. If we in *our* world, let alone beings in any others, have features additional to those of our physical replicas in other possible worlds, then we have non-physical features or qualia.

The trouble rather with the Modal argument is that it rests on a disputable modal intuition. Disputable because it is disputed. Some sincerely deny that there can be physical replicas of us in other possible worlds which nevertheless lack consciousness. Moreover, at least one person who once had the intuition now has doubts.[9]

Head-counting may seem a poor approach to a discussion of the Modal argument. But frequently we can do no better when modal intuitions are in question, and remember our initial goal was to find the argument with the greatest polemical utility.

Of course, *qua* protagonists of the Knowledge argument we may well accept the modal intuition in question; but this will be a *consequence* of our already having an argument to the conclusion that qualia are left out of the physicalist story, not our ground for that conclusion. Moreover, the matter is complicated by the possibility that the connection between matters physical and qualia is like that sometimes held to obtain between aesthetic qualities and natural ones. Two possible worlds which agree in all "natural" respects (including the experiences of sentient creatures) must agree in all aesthetic qualities also, but it is plausibly held that the aesthetic qualities cannot be reduced to the natural.

III. The "What Is It Like to Be" Argument

In "What is it like to be a bat?" Thomas Nagel argues that no amount of physical information can tell us what it is like to be a bat, and indeed that we, human beings, cannot imagine what it is like to be a bat.[10] His reason is that what this is like can only be understood from a bat's point of view, which is not our point of view and is not something capturable in physical terms which are essentially terms understandable equally from many points of view.

It is important to distinguish this argument from the Knowledge argument. When I complained that all the physical knowledge about Fred was not enough to tell us what his special colour experience was like, I was not complaining that we weren't finding out what it is like to *be* Fred. I was complaining that there is something *about* his experience, a property of it, of which we were left ignorant. And if and when we come to know what this property is we still will not know what it is like to *be* Fred, but we will know more *about* him. No amount of knowledge about Fred, be it physical or not, amounts to knowledge "from the inside" concerning Fred. We are not Fred. There is thus a whole set of items of knowledge expressed by forms of words like 'that it is *I myself* who is …' which Fred has and we simply cannot have because we are not him.[11]

When Fred sees the colour he alone can see, one thing he knows is the way his experience of it differs from his experience of seeing red and so on, *another* is that he himself is seeing it. Physicalist and qualia freaks alike should acknowledge that no amount of information of whatever kind that *others* have *about*

Fred amounts to knowledge of the second. My complaint though concerned the first and was that the special quality of his experience is certainly a fact about it, and one which Physicalism leaves out because no amount of physical information told us what it is.

Nagel speaks as if the problem he is raising is one of extrapolating from knowledge of one experience to another, of imagining what an unfamiliar experience would be like on the basis of familiar ones. In terms of Hume's example, from knowledge of some shades of blue we can work out what it would be like to see other shades of blue. Nagel argues that the trouble with bats *et al.* is that they are too unlike us. It is hard to see an objection to Physicalism here. Physicalism makes no special claims about the imaginative or extrapolative powers of human beings, and it is hard to see why it need do so.[12]

Anyway, our Knowledge argument makes no assumptions on this point. If Physicalism were true, enough physical information about Fred would obviate any need to extrapolate or to perform special feats of imagination or understanding in order to know all about his special colour experience. *The information would already be in our possession.* But it clearly isn't. That was the nub of the argument.

IV. The Bogey of Epiphenomenalism

Is there any really *good* reason for refusing to countenance the idea that qualia are causally impotent with respect to the physical world? I will argue for the answer no, but in doing this I will say nothing about two views associated with the classical epiphenomenalist position. The first is that mental *states* are inefficacious with respect to the physical world. All I will be concerned to defend is that it is possible to hold that certain *properties* of certain mental states, namely those I've called qualia, are such that their possession or absence makes no differ-ence to the physical world. The second is that the mental is *totally* causally inefficacious. For all I will say it may be that you have to hold that the instantiation of *qualia* makes a difference to *other mental states* though not to anything physical. Indeed general considerations to do with how you could come to be aware of the instantiation of qualia suggest such a position.[13]

Three reasons are standardly given for hold-ing that a quale like the hurtfulness of a pain must be causally efficacious in the physical world, and so, for instance, that its instantiation must sometimes make a difference to what hap-pens in the brain. None, I will argue, has any real force. (I am much indebted to Alec Hyslop and John Lucas for convincing me of this.)

(i) It is supposed to be just obvious that the hurtfulness of pain is partly responsible for the subject seeking to avoid pain, saying 'It hurts' and so on. But, to reverse Hume, anything can fail to cause anything. No matter how often *B* follows *A*, and no matter how initially obvi-ous the causality of the connection seems, the hypothesis that *A* causes *B* can be overturned by an over-arching theory which shows the two as distinct effects of a common underly-ing causal process.

To the untutored the image on the screen of Lee Marvin's fist moving from left to right immediately followed by the image of John Wayne's head moving in the same general direction looks as causal as anything.[14] And of course throughout countless Westerns images similar to the first are followed by images simi-lar to the second. All this counts for precisely nothing when we know the over-arching theory concerning how the relevant images are both effects of an underlying causal process involv-ing the projector and the film. The epiphe-nomenalist can say exactly the same about the connection between, for example, hurtfulness and behaviour. It is simply a consequence of the fact that certain happenings in the brain cause both.

(ii) The second objection relates to Darwin's Theory of Evolution. According to natural selection the traits that evolve over time are those conducive to physical survival. We may assume that qualia evolved over time—we have them, the earliest forms of life do not—and so we should expect qualia to be conducive to sur-vival. The objection is that they could hardly help us to survive if they do nothing to the physical world.

The appeal of this argument is undeniable, but there is a good reply to it. Polar bears have particularly thick, warm coats. The Theory of Evolution explains this (we suppose) by point-ing out that having a thick, warm coat is con-ducive to survival in the Arctic. But having a thick coat goes along with having a heavy coat, and having a heavy coat is *not* conducive to sur-vival. It slows the animal down.

Does this mean that we have refuted Dar-win because we have found an evolved trait—having a heavy coat—which is not conducive to survival? Clearly not. Having a heavy coat is an unavoidable concomitant of having a warm coat (in the context, modern insulation was not available), and the advantages for survival of having a warm coat outweighed the disadvan-tages of having a heavy one. The point is that all we can extract from Darwin's theory is that we should expect any evolved characteristic to be *either* conducive to survival *or* a by-product of one that is so conducive. The epiphenomenalist holds that qualia fall into the latter category. They are a by-product of certain brain processes that are highly conducive to survival.

(iii) The third objection is based on a point about how we come to know about other minds. We know about other minds by knowing about other behaviour, at least in part. The nature of the inference is a matter of some controversy, but it is not a matter of controversy that it proceeds from behaviour. That is why we think that stones do not feel and dogs do feel. But, runs the objection, how can a person's behaviour provide any reason for believing he has qualia like mine, or indeed any qualia at all, unless this behaviour can be regarded as the *outcome* of the qualia. Man Friday's footprint was evidence of Man Friday because footprints are causal outcomes of feet attached to people. And an epiphenomenalist cannot regard behaviour, or indeed anything physical, as an outcome of qualia.

But consider my reading in *The Times* that Spurs won. This provides excellent evidence that *The Telegraph* has also reported that Spurs won, despite the fact that (I trust) *The Telegraph* does not get the results from *The Times*. They each send their own reporters to the game. *The Telegraph's* report is in no sense an outcome of *The Times'*, but the latter provides good evidence for the former nevertheless.

The reasoning involved can be reconstructed thus. I read in *The Times* that Spurs won. This gives me reason to think that Spurs won because I know that Spurs' winning is the most likely candidate to be what caused the report in *The Times*. But I also know that Spurs' winning would have had many effects, including almost certainly a report in *The Telegraph*.

I am arguing from one effect back to its cause and out again to another effect. The fact that neither effect causes the other is irrelevant. Now the epiphenomenalist allows that qualia are effects of what goes on in the brain. Qualia cause nothing physical but are caused by something physical. Hence the epiphenomenalist can argue from the behaviour of others to the qualia of others by arguing from the behaviour of others back to its causes in the brains of others and out again to their qualia.

You may well feel for one reason or another that this is a more dubious chain of reasoning than its model in the case of newspaper reports.

You are right. The problem of other minds is a major philosophical problem, the problem of other newspaper reports is not. But there is no special problem of Epiphenomenalism as opposed to, say, Interactionism here.

There is a very understandable response to the three replies I have just made. "All right, there is no knockdown refutation of the existence of epiphenomenal qualia. But the fact remains that they are an excrescence. They *do* nothing, they *explain* nothing, they serve merely to soothe the intuitions of dualists, and it is left a total mystery how they fit into the world view of science. In short we do not and cannot understand the how and why of them."

This is perfectly true; but is no objection to qualia, for it rests on an overly optimistic view of the human animal, and its powers. We are the products of Evolution. We understand and sense what we need to understand and sense in order to survive. Epiphenomenal qualia are totally irrelevant to survival. At no stage of our evolution did natural selection favour those who could make sense of how they are caused and the laws governing them, or in fact why they exist at all. And that is why we can't.

It is not sufficiently appreciated that Physicalism is an extremely optimistic view of our powers. If it is true, we have, in very broad outline admittedly, a grasp of our place in the scheme of things. Certain matters of sheer complexity defeat us—there are an awful lot of neurons—but in principle we have it all. But consider the antecedent probability that everything in the Universe be of a kind that is relevant in some way or other to the survival of *Homo sapiens*. It is very low surely. But then one must admit that it is very likely that there is a part of the whole scheme of things, maybe a big part, which no amount of evolution will ever bring us near to knowledge about or understanding. For the simple reason that such knowledge and understanding is irrelevant to survival.

Physicalists typically emphasise that we are a part of nature on their view, which is fair enough. But if we are a part of nature, we are as nature has left us after however many years of evolution it is, and each step in that evolutionary progression has been a matter of chance constrained just by the need to preserve or increase survival value. The wonder is that we understand as much as we do, and there is no wonder that there should be matters which fall quite outside our comprehension. Perhaps exactly how epiphenomenal qualia fit into the scheme of things is one such.

This may seem an unduly pessimistic view of our capacity to articulate a truly comprehensive picture of our world and our place in it. But suppose we discovered living on the bottom of the deepest oceans a sort of sea slug which manifested intelligence. Perhaps survival in the conditions required rational powers. Despite their intelligence, these sea slugs have only a very restricted conception of the world by comparison with ours, the explanation for this being the nature of their immediate environment. Nevertheless they have developed sciences which work surprisingly well in these restricted terms. They also have philosophers, called slugists. Some call themselves tough-minded slugists, others confess to being soft-minded slugists.

The tough-minded slugists hold that the restricted terms (or ones pretty much like them which may be introduced as their sciences progress) suffice in principle to describe everything without remainder. These tough-minded slugists admit in moments of weakness to a feeling that their theory leaves something out. They resist this feeling and their opponents, the soft-minded slugists, by pointing out—absolutely correctly—that no slugist has ever succeeded in spelling out how this mysterious residue fits into the highly successful view that their sciences have and are developing of how their world works.

Our sea slugs don't exist, but they might. And there might also exist super beings which stand to us as we stand to the sea slugs. We cannot adopt the perspective of these super beings, because we are not them, but the possibility of such a perspective is, I think, an antidote to excessive optimism.[15]

Notes

1. See, e.g., D.H. Mellor, "Materialism and Phenomenal Qualities," *Aristotelian Society Supp.* Vol. 47 (1973), 107–19; and J.W. Cornman, *Materialism and Sensations* (New Haven and London, 1971).

2. Particularly in discussion, but see, e.g., Keith Campbell, *Metaphysics* (Belmont, 1976), p. 67.

3. See, e.g., D.C. Dennett, "Current Issues in the Philosophy of Mind," *American Philosophical Quarterly*, 15 (1978), 249–61.

4. Put this, and similar simplifications below, in terms of Land's theory if you prefer. See, e.g., Edwin H. Land, "Experiments in Color Vision," *Scientific American*, 200 (5 May 1959), 54–99.

5. H.G. Wells, *The Country of the Blind and Other Stories* (London, n.d.).

6. See, e.g., Keith Campbell, *Body and Mind* (New York, 1970); and Robert Kirk, "Sentience and Behaviour," *Mind*, 83 (1974), 43–60.

7. I have presented the argument in an interworld rather than the more usual intraworld fashion to avoid inessential complications to do with supervenience, causal anomalies and the like.

8. See, e.g., W.G. Lycan, "A New Lilliputian Argument Against Machine Functionalism," *Philosophical Studies*, 35 (1979), 279–87, p. 280; and Don Locke, "Zombies, Schizophrenics and Purely Physical Objects," *Mind*, 85 (1976), 97–99.

9. See R. Kirk, "From Physical Explicability to Full-Blooded Materialism," *The Philosophical Quarterly*, 29 (1979), 229–37. See also the arguments against the modal intuition in, e.g., Sydney Shoemaker, "Functionalism and Qualia," *Philosophical Studies*, 27 (1975), 291–315.

10. *The Philosophical Review*, 83 (1974), 435–50. Two things need to be said about this article. One is that, despite my dissociations to come, I am much indebted to it. The other is that the emphasis changes through the article, and by the end Nagel is objecting not so much to Physicalism as to all extant theories of mind for ignoring points of view, including those that admit (irreducible) qualia.

11. Knowledge *de se* in the terms of David Lewis, "Attitudes De Dicto and De Se," *The Philosophical Review*, 88 (1979), 513–43.

12. See Laurence Nemirow's comments on "What is it…" in his review of T. Nagel, *Mortal Questions in The Philosophical Review*, 89 (1980), 473–77. I am indebted here in particular to a discussion with David Lewis.

13. See my review of K. Campbell, *Body and Mind*, in *Australasian Journal of Philosophy*, 50 (1972), 77–80.

14. Cf. Jean Piaget, "The Child's Conception of Physical Causality," reprinted in *The Essential Piaget* (London, 1977).

15. I am indebted to Robert Pargetter for a number of comments and, despite his dissent, to §IV of Paul E. Meehl, "The Compleat Autocerebroscopist" in *Mind, Matter, and Method*, ed. Paul Feyerabend and Grover Maxwell (Minneapolis, 1966).

DANIEL C. DENNETT

"Quining Qualia"

1. Corralling the Quicksilver

"Qualia" is an unfamiliar term for something that could not be more familiar to each of us: the *ways things seem to us*. As is so often the case with philosophical jargon, it is easier to give examples than to give a definition of the term. Look at a glass of milk at sunset; *the way it looks to you*—the particular, personal, subjective visual quality of the glass of milk is the *quale* of your visual experience at the moment. The *way the milk tastes to you then* is another, gustatory, *quale*, and *how it sounds to you* as you swallow is an auditory *quale*. These various

"properties of conscious experience" are prime examples of *qualia*. Nothing, it seems, could you know more intimately than your own qualia; let the entire universe be some vast illusion, some mere figment of Descartes's evil demon, and yet what the figment is *made of* (for you) will be the *qualia* of your hallucinatory experiences. Descartes claimed to doubt everything that could be doubted, but he never doubted that his conscious experiences had qualia, the properties by which he knew or apprehended them.

The verb "to quine" is even more esoteric. It comes from *The Philosophical Lexicon* (Dennett 1978c, 8th edn 1987), a satirical dictionary of eponyms: "quine, v. To deny resolutely the existence or importance of something real or significant." At first blush it would be hard to imagine a more quixotic quest than trying to convince people that there are no such properties as qualia; hence the ironic title of this chapter. But I am not kidding.

My goal is subversive. I am out to overthrow an idea that, in one form or another, is "obvious" to most people—to scientists, philosophers, lay people. My quarry is frustratingly elusive; no sooner does it retreat in the face of one argument than "it" reappears, apparently innocent of all charges, in a new guise.

Which idea of qualia am I trying to extirpate? Everything real has properties, and since I don't deny the reality of conscious experience, I grant that conscious experience has properties. I grant moreover that each person's states of consciousness have properties in virtue of which those states have the experiential content that they do. That is to say, whenever someone experiences something as being one way rather than another, this is true in virtue of some property of something happening in them at the time, but these properties are so unlike the properties traditionally imputed to consciousness that it would be grossly misleading to call any of them the long-sought qualia. Qualia are supposed to be *special* properties, in some hard-to-define way. My claim—which can only come into focus as we proceed—is that conscious experience has *no* properties that are special in *any* of the ways qualia have been supposed to be special.

The standard reaction to this claim is the complacent acknowledgment that while some people may indeed have succumbed to one confusion or fanaticism or another, one's own appeal to a modest, innocent notion of properties of subjective experience is surely safe. It is just that presumption of innocence I want to overthrow. I want to shift the burden of proof, so that anyone who wants to appeal to private, subjective properties has to prove first that in so doing they are *not* making a mistake. This status of *guilty until proven innocent* is neither unprecedented nor indefensible (so long as we restrict ourselves to concepts). Today, no biologist would dream of supposing that it was quite all right to appeal to some innocent concept of *élan vital*. Of course one *could* use the term to mean something in good standing; one could use *élan vital* as one's name for DNA, for instance, but this would be foolish nomenclature, considering the deserved suspicion with which the term is nowadays burdened. I want to make it just as uncomfortable for anyone to talk of qualia—or "raw feels" or "phenomenal properties" or "subjective and intrinsic properties" or "the qualitative character" of experience—with the standard presumption that they, and everyone else, knows what on earth they are talking about.[1]

What are qualia, *exactly*? This obstreperous query is dismissed by one author ("only half in jest") by invoking Louis Armstrong's legendary reply when asked what jazz was: "If you got to ask, you ain't never gonna get to know" (Block 1978 p. 281). This amusing tactic perfectly illustrates the presumption that is my target. If I succeed in my task, this move, which passes muster in most circles today, will look as quaint and insupportable as a jocular appeal to the ludicrousness of a living thing—a living thing, mind you!—doubting the existence of *élan vital*.

My claim, then, is not just that the various technical or theoretical concepts of qualia are vague or equivocal, but that the source concept, the "pretheoretical" notion of which the former are presumed to be refinements, is so thoroughly confused that even if we undertook to salvage some "lowest common denominator" from the theoreticians' proposals, any acceptable version would have to be so radically unlike the ill-formed notions that are commonly appealed to that it would be tactically obtuse—not to say Pickwickian—to cling to the term. Far better, tactically, to declare that there simply are no qualia at all.[2]

Rigorous arguments only work on well-defined materials, and since my goal is to destroy our faith in the pretheoretical or "intuitive" concept, the right tools for my task are intuition pumps, not formal arguments. What follows is a series of fifteen intuition pumps, posed in a sequence designed to flush out—and then flush away—the offending intuitions. In section 2, I will use the first two intuition pumps to focus attention on the traditional notion. It will be the burden of the rest of the paper to convince you that these two pumps, for all their effectiveness, mislead us and should be discarded. In section 3, the next four intuition pumps create and refine a "paradox" lurking in the tradition. This is not a formal paradox, but only a very powerful argument pitted against some almost irresistibly attractive ideas. In section 4, six more intuition pumps are arrayed in order to dissipate the attractiveness of those ideas, and section 5 drives this point home by showing how hapless those ideas prove to be when confronted with some real cases of anomalous experience. This will leave something of a vacuum, and in the final section three more intuition pumps are used to introduce and motivate some suitable replacements for the banished notions.

2. The Special Properties of Qualia

Intuition pump #1: watching you eat cauliflower. I see you tucking eagerly into a helping of steaming cauliflower, the merest whiff of which makes me faintly nauseated, and I find myself wondering how you could possibly relish *that taste,* and then it occurs to me that to you, cauliflower probably tastes (must taste?) different.

A plausible hypothesis, it seems, especially since I know that the very same food often tastes different to me at different times. For instance, my first sip of breakfast orange juice tastes much sweeter than my second sip if I interpose a bit of pancakes and maple syrup, but after a swallow or two of coffee, the orange juice goes back to tasting (roughly? exactly?) the way it did the first sip. Surely we want to say (or think about) such things, and surely we are not wildly wrong when we do, so…surely it is quite OK to talk of *the way the juice tastes to Dennett at time t,* and ask whether it is just the same as or different from the way the juice tastes to Dennett at time t′ or the way the juice tastes to Jones at time t.

This "conclusion" seems innocent, but right here we have already made the big mistake. The final step presumes that we can isolate the qualia from everything else that is going on—at least in principle or for the sake of argument. What counts as *the way the juice tastes to x* can be distinguished, one supposes, from what is a mere accompaniment, contributory cause, or by-product of this "central" way. One dimly imagines taking such cases and stripping them down gradually to the essentials, leaving their common residuum, the way things look, sound, feel, taste, smell to various individuals at various times, independently of how those individuals are stimulated or non-perceptually affected, and independently of how they are subsequently disposed to behave or believe. The mistake is not in supposing that we can in practice ever or always perform this act of purification with certainty, but the more fundamental mistake of supposing that there is such a residual property to take seriously, however uncertain our actual attempts at isolation of instances might be.

The examples that seduce us are abundant in every modality. I cannot imagine, will never know, could never know, it seems, how Bach sounded to Glenn Gould. (I can barely recover in my memory the way Bach sounded to me when I was a child.) And I cannot know, it seems, what it is like to be a bat (Nagel 1974), or whether you see what I see, colorwise, when we look up at a clear "blue" sky. The homely cases convince us of the reality of these special properties—those subjective tastes, looks, aromas, sounds—that we then apparently isolate for definition by this philosophical distillation. The specialness of these properties is hard to pin down, but can be seen at work in *intuition pump #2: the wine-tasting machine.* Could Gallo Brothers replace their human wine tasters with a machine? A computer-based "expert system" for quality control and classification is probably within the bounds of existing technology. We now know enough about the relevant chemistry to make the transducers that would replace taste buds and olfactory organs (delicate color vision would perhaps be more problematic), and we can imagine using the output of such transducers as the raw material—the "sense data" in effect—for elaborate evaluations, descriptions, classifications. Pour the sample in the funnel and, in a few minutes or hours, the system would type out a chemical assay, along with commentary: "a flamboyant and velvety Pinot, though lacking in stamina"—or words to such effect. Such a machine might well perform better than human wine tasters on all reasonable tests of accuracy and consistency the winemakers could devise,[3] but *surely* no matter how "sensitive" and "discriminating" such a system becomes, it will never have, and enjoy, what *we* do when we taste a wine: the qualia of conscious experience! Whatever informational, dispositional, functional properties its internal states have, none of them will be special in the way qualia are. If you share that intuition, you believe that there are qualia in the sense I am targeting for demolition.

What is special about qualia? Traditional analyses suggest some fascinating second-order properties of these properties. First, since one *cannot say* to another, no matter how eloquent one is and no matter how cooperative and imaginative one's audience is, exactly what way one is currently seeing, tasting, smelling and so forth, qualia are *ineffable*—in fact the paradigm cases of ineffable items. According to tradition, at least part of the reason why qualia are ineffable is that they are *intrinsic* properties—which seems to imply *inter alia* that they are somehow atomic and unanalyzable. Since they are "simple" or "homogeneous" there is nothing to get hold of when trying to describe such a property to one unacquainted with the particular instance in question.

Moreover, verbal comparisons are not the only cross-checks ruled out. *Any* objective, physiological or "merely behavioral" test—such as those passed by the imaginary wine-tasting system—would of necessity miss the target (one can plausibly argue), so all interpersonal comparisons of these ways-of-appearing are (apparently) systematically impossible. In other words, qualia are essentially *private* properties. And, finally, since they *are* properties of *my experiences* (they're not chopped liver, and they're not properties of, say, my cerebral blood flow—or haven't you been paying attention?), qualia are essentially directly accessible to the consciousness of their experiencer (whatever that means) or qualia are properties of one's experience with which one is intimately or directly acquainted (whatever that means) or "immediate phenomenological qualities" (Block 1978) (whatever that means). They are, after all, the very properties the appreciation of which permits us to identify our conscious states. So, to summarize the tradition, qualia are supposed to be properties of a subject's mental states that are

1 ineffable
2 intrinsic
3 private
4 directly or immediately apprehensible in consciousness.

Thus are qualia introduced onto the philosophical stage. They have seemed to be very significant properties to some theorists because they have seemed to provide an insurmountable and unavoidable stumbling block to functionalism, or more broadly, to materialism, or more broadly still, to any purely "third-person" objective viewpoint or approach to the world (Nagel 1986). Theorists of the contrary persuasion have patiently and ingeniously knocked down all the arguments, and said most of the right things, but they have made a tactical error, I am claiming, of saying in one way or another: "We theorists can handle *those qualia* you talk about just fine; we will show that you are just slightly in error about the nature of qualia." What they ought to have said is: "What qualia?"

My challenge strikes some theorists as outrageous or misguided because they think they have a much blander and hence less vulnerable notion of qualia to begin with. They think I am setting up and knocking down a strawman, and ask, in effect: "Who said qualia are ineffable, intrinsic, private, directly apprehensible ways things seem to one?" Since my suggested fourfold essence of qualia may strike many readers as tendentious, it may be instructive to consider, briefly, an apparently milder alternative: qualia are simply "the qualitative or phenomenal features of sense experience[s], in virtue of having which they resemble and differ from each other, qualitatively, in the ways they do" (Shoemaker 1982, p. 367). Surely I do not mean to deny *those* features!

I reply: it all depends on what "qualitative or phenomenal" comes to. Shoemaker contrasts *qualitative* similarity and difference with "intentional" similarity and difference—similarity and difference of the properties an experience represents or is "of." That is clear enough, but what then of "phenomenal"? Among the non-intentional (and hence qualitative?) properties of my visual states are their physiological properties. Might these very properties be the qualia Shoemaker speaks of? It is supposed to be obvious, I take it, that these sorts of features are ruled out, because they are not "accessible to introspection" (Shoemaker, private correspondence). These are features of my visual *state*, perhaps, but not of my visual *experience*. They are not *phenomenal* properties.

But then another non-intentional similarity some of my visual states share is that they tend to make me think about going to bed. I think this feature of them *is* accessible to introspection—on any ordinary, pretheoretical construal. Is that a phenomenal property or not? The term "phenomenal" means nothing obvious and untendentious to me, and looks suspiciously like a gesture in the direction leading back to ineffable, private, directly apprehensible ways things seem to one.[4]

I suspect, in fact, that many are unwilling to take my radical challenge seriously largely because they want so much for qualia to be acknowledged. Qualia seem to many people to be the last ditch defense of the inwardness and elusiveness of our minds, a bulwark against creeping mechanism. They are sure there must be *some* sound path from the homely cases to the redoubtable category of the philosophers, since otherwise their last bastion of specialness will be stormed by science.

This special status for these presumed properties has a long and eminent tradition. I believe it was Einstein who once advised us that science could not give us the *taste* of the soup. Could such a wise man have been wrong? Yes, if he is taken to have been trying to remind us of the qualia that hide forever from objective science in the subjective inner sancta of our minds. There are no such things. Another wise man said so—Wittgenstein (1958, esp. pp. 91–100). Actually, what he said was:

> The thing in the box has no place in the language-game at all; not even as a *something*; for the box might even be empty.—No, one can "divide through" by the thing in the box; it cancels out, whatever it is. (p. 100)

and then he went on to hedge his bets by saying "It is not a *something*, but not a *nothing* either! The conclusion was only that a nothing would serve just as well as a something about which nothing could be said" (p. 102). Both Einstein's and Wittgenstein's remarks are endlessly amenable to exegesis, but rather than undertaking to referee this War of the Titans, I choose to take what may well be a more radical stand than Wittgenstein's.[5] Qualia are not even "something about which nothing can be said"; "qualia" is a philosophers' term which fosters[6] nothing but confusion, and refers in the end to no properties or features at all.

3. The Traditional Paradox Regained

Qualia have not always been in good odor among philosophers. Although many have thought, along with Descartes and Locke, that it made sense to talk about private, ineffable properties of minds, others have argued that this is strictly nonsense—however naturally it trips off the tongue. It is worth recalling how qualia were presumably rehabilitated as properties to be taken seriously in the wake of Wittgensteinian and verificationist attacks on them as pseudo-hypotheses. The original version of *intuition pump #3: the inverted spectrum* (Locke 1690: II, xxxii, 15) is a speculation about two people: how do I know that you and I see the same subjective color when we look at something? Since we both learned color words by being shown public colored objects, our verbal behavior will match *even if we experience entirely different subjective colors*. The intuition that this hypothesis is systematically unconfirmable (and undisconfirmable, of course) has always been quite robust, but some people have always been tempted to think technology could (in principle) bridge the gap.

Suppose, in *intuition pump #4: the Brainstorm machine*, there were some neuroscientific apparatus that fits on your head and feeds your visual experience into my brain (as in the movie, *Brainstorm*, which is not to be confused with the book, *Brainstorms*). With eyes closed I accurately report everything you are looking at, except that I marvel at how the sky is yellow, the grass red, and so forth. Would this not confirm, empirically, that our qualia were different? But suppose the technician then pulls the plug on the connecting cable, inverts it 180 degrees and reinserts it in the socket. Now I report the sky is blue, the grass green, and so forth. Which is the "right" orientation of the plug? Designing and building such a device would require that its "fidelity" be tuned or calibrated by the normalization of the two subjects' reports—so we would be right back at our evidential starting point. The moral of this intuition pump is that no intersubjective comparison of qualia is possible, even with perfect technology.

So matters stood until someone dreamt up the presumably improved version of the thought experiment: the *intra*personal inverted spectrum. The idea seems to have occurred to several people independently (Gert 1965; Putnam 1965; Taylor 1966; Shoemaker 1969, 1975; Lycan 1973). Probably Block and Fodor (1972) have it in mind when they say "It seems to us that the standard verificationist counterarguments against the view that the 'inverted spectrum' hypothesis is conceptually incoherent are not persuasive" (p. 172). In this version, *intuition pump #5: the neurosurgical prank*, the experiences to be compared are all in one mind. You wake up one morning to find that the grass has turned red, the sky yellow, and so forth. No one else notices any color anomalies in the world, so the problem must be in you. You are entitled, it seems, to conclude that you have undergone visual color qualia inversion (and we later discover, if you like, just how the evil neurophysiologists tampered with your neurons to accomplish this).

Here it seems at first—and indeed for quite a while—that qualia are acceptable properties after all, because propositions about them can be justifiably asserted, empirically verified and even explained. After all, in the imagined case, we can tell a tale in which we confirm a detailed neurophysiological account of the precise etiology of the dramatic change you undergo. It is tempting to suppose, then, that neurophysiological evidence, incorporated into a robust and ramifying theory, would have all the resolving power we could ever need for determining whether or not someone's qualia have actually shifted.

But this is a mistake. It will take some patient exploration to reveal the mistake in depth, but the conclusion can be reached—if not secured—quickly with the help of *intuition pump #6: alternative neurosurgery*. There are (at least) two different ways the evil neurosurgeon might create the inversion effect described in intuition pump #5:

I Invert one of the "early" qualia-producing channels, e.g., in the optic nerve, so that all relevant neural events "downstream" are the "opposite" of their original and normal values. *Ex hypothesi* this inverts your qualia.

II Leave all those early pathways intact and simply invert certain memory-access links—whatever it is that accomplishes

your tacit (and even unconscious!) comparison of today's hues with those of yore. *Ex hypothesi* this does *not* invert your qualia at all, but just your memory-anchored dispositions to react to them.

On waking up and finding your visual world highly anomalous, you should exclaim "Egad! *Something* has happened! Either my qualia have been inverted or my memory-linked qualia-reactions have been inverted. I wonder which!"

The intrapersonal inverted spectrum thought experiment was widely supposed to be an improvement, since it moved the needed comparison into one subject's head. But now we can see that this is an illusion, since the link to earlier experiences, the link via memory, is analogous to the imaginary cable that might link two subjects in the original version.

This point is routinely—one might say traditionally—missed by the constructors of "intrasubjective inverted spectrum" thought experiments, who suppose that the subject's *noticing the difference*—surely a vivid experience of discovery by the subject—would have to be an instance of (directly? incorrigibly?) recognizing the difference as *a shift in qualia*. But as my example shows, we could achieve the same startling effect in a subject without tampering with his presumed qualia at all. Since *ex hypothesi* the two different surgical invasions can produce exactly the same introspective effects while only one operation inverts the qualia, nothing in the subject's experience can favor one of the hypotheses over the other. So unless he seeks outside help, the state of his own qualia must be as unknowable to him as the state of anyone else's qualia. Hardly the privileged access or immediate acquaintance or direct apprehension the friends of qualia had supposed "phenomenal features" to enjoy!

The outcome of this series of thought experiments is an intensification of the "verificationist" argument against qualia. *If* there are qualia, they are even less accessible to our ken than we had thought. Not only are the classical intersubjective comparisons impossible (as the Brainstorm machine shows), but we cannot tell in our own cases whether our qualia have been inverted—at least not by introspection. It is surely tempting at this point—especially to non-philosophers—to decide that this paradoxical result must be an artifact of some philosophical misanalysis or other, the sort of thing that might well happen if you took a perfectly good pretheoretical notion—our everyday notion of qualia—and illicitly stretched it beyond the breaking point. The philosophers have made a mess; let them clean it up; meanwhile we others can get back to work, relying as always on our sober and unmetaphysical acquaintance with qualia.

Overcoming this ubiquitous temptation is the task of the next section, which will seek to establish the unsalvageable incoherence of the hunches that lead to the paradox by looking more closely at their sources and their motivation.

4. Making Mistakes about Qualia

The idea that people might be mistaken about their own qualia is at the heart of the ongoing confusion, and must be explored in more detail, and with somewhat more realistic examples, if we are to see the delicate role it plays.

Intuition pump #7: Chase and Sanborn. Once upon a time there were two coffee tasters, Mr. Chase and Mr. Sanborn, who worked for Maxwell House.[7] Along with half a dozen other coffee tasters, their job was to ensure that the taste of Maxwell House stayed constant, year after year. One day, about six years after Mr. Chase had come to work for Maxwell House, he confessed to Mr. Sanborn:

I hate to admit it, but I'm not enjoying this work anymore. When I came to Maxwell House six years ago, I thought Maxwell House coffee was the best-tasting coffee in the world. I was proud to have a share in the responsibility for preserving that flavor over the years. And we've done our job well; the coffee tastes just the same today as it tasted when I arrived. But, you know, I no longer like it! My tastes have changed. I've become a more sophisticated coffee drinker. I no longer like *that taste* at all.

Sanborn greeted this revelation with considerable interest. "It's funny you should mention it," he replied, "for something rather similar has happened to me." He went on:

When I arrived here shortly before you did, I, like you, thought Maxwell House coffee was tops in flavor. And now I, like you, really don't care for the coffee we're making. But *my* tastes haven't changed; my...*tasters* have changed. That is, I think something has gone wrong with my taste buds or some other part of my taste-analyzing perceptual machinery. Maxwell House coffee doesn't taste to me the way it used to taste; if only it did, I'd still love it, for I still think *that taste* is the best taste in coffee. Now I'm not saying we haven't done our job well. You other tasters all agree that the taste is the same, and I must admit that on a day-to-day basis I can detect no change either. So it must be my problem alone. I guess I'm no longer cut out for this work.

Chase and Sanborn are alike in one way at least: they both used to like Maxwell House coffee, and now neither likes it. But they claim to be different in another way. Maxwell House tastes to Chase just the way it always did, but not so for Sanborn. But can we take their protestations at face value? Must we? Might one or both of them simply be wrong? Might their predicaments be importantly the same and their apparent disagreement more a difference in manner of expression than in experiential or psychological state? Since both of them make claims that depend on the reliability of their memories, is there any way to check on this reliability?

My reason for introducing two characters in the example is not to set up an interpersonal comparison between how the coffee tastes to Chase and how it tastes to Sanborn, but just to exhibit, side-by-side, two poles between which cases of intrapersonal experiential shift can wander. Such cases of intrapersonal experiential shift, and the possibility of adaptation to them, or interference with memory in them, have often been discussed in the literature on qualia, but without sufficient attention to the details, in my opinion. Let us look at Chase first. Falling in for the nonce with the received manner of speaking, it appears at first that there are the following possibilities:

(a) Chase's coffee-taste-qualia have stayed constant, while his reactive attitudes to those qualia, devolving on his canons of aesthetic judgment, etc., have shifted—which is what he seems, in his informal, casual way, to be asserting.
(b) Chase is simply wrong about the constancy of his qualia; they have shifted gradually and imperceptibly over the years, while his standards of taste haven't budged—in spite of his delusions about having become more sophisticated. He is in the state Sanborn claims to be in, but just lacks Sanborn's self-knowledge.
(c) Chase is in some predicament intermediate between (a) and (b); his qualia have shifted some *and* his standards of judgment have also slipped.

Sanborn's case seems amenable to three counterpart versions:

(a) Sanborn is right; his qualia have shifted, due to some sort of derangement in his perceptual machinery, but his standards have indeed remained constant.
(b) Sanborn's standards have shifted unbeknownst to him. He is thus misremembering his past experiences, in what we might call a nostalgia effect. Think of the familiar experience of returning to some object from your childhood (a classroom desk, a tree-house) and finding it much smaller than you remember it to have been. Presumably as you grew larger your internal standard for what was large grew with you somehow, but your memories (which are stored as fractions or multiples of that standard) didn't compensate, and hence when you consult your memory, it returns a distorted judgment. Sanborn's nostalgia-tinged memory of good old Maxwell House is similarly distorted. (There are obviously many different ways this impressionistic sketch of a memory mechanism could be implemented, and there is considerable experimental work in cognitive psychology that suggests how different hypotheses about such mechanisms could be tested.)
(c) As before, Sanborn's state is some combination of (a) and (b).

I think that everyone writing about qualia today would agree that there are all these possibilities for Chase and Sanborn. I know of no one these days who is tempted to defend the high line on infallibility or incorrigibility that would declare that alternative (a) is—and must be—the truth in each case, since people just cannot be wrong about such private, subjective matters.[8]

Since quandaries are about to arise, however, it might be wise to review in outline why the attractiveness of the infallibilist position is only superficial, so it won't recover its erstwhile allure when the going gets tough. First, in the wake of Wittgenstein (1958) and Malcolm (1956, 1959) we have seen that one way to buy such infallibility is to acquiesce in the complete evaporation of content (Dennett 1976). "Imagine someone saying: 'But I know how tall I am!' and laying his hand on top of his head to prove it" (Wittgenstein 1958, p. 96). By diminishing one's claim until there is nothing left to be right or wrong about, one can achieve a certain empty invincibility, but that will not do in this case. One of the things we want Chase to be right about (if he is right) is that he is not in Sanborn's predicament, so if the claim is to be viewed as infallible, it can hardly be because it declines to assert anything.

There is a strong temptation, I have found, to respond to my claims in this paper more or less as follows: "But after all is said and done, there is still something I know in a special way: I know *how it is with me right now.*" But if absolutely nothing follows from this presumed knowledge—nothing, for instance, that would shed any light on the different psychological claims that might be true of Chase or Sanborn—what is the point of asserting that one has it? Perhaps people just want to reaffirm their sense of proprietorship over their own conscious states.

The infallibilist line on qualia treats them as properties of one's experience one cannot in principle misdiscover, and this is a mysterious doctrine (at least as mysterious as papal infallibility) unless we shift the emphasis a little and treat qualia as logical constructs out of subjects' qualia-judgments: a subject's experience has the quale F if and only if the subject judges his experience to have quale F. We can then treat such judgings as constitutive acts, in effect, bringing the quale into existence by the same sort of license as novelists have to determine the hair color of their characters by fiat. We do not ask how Dostoevski knows that Raskolnikov's hair is light brown.

It seems easy enough, then, to dream up empirical tests that would tend to confirm Chase and Sanborn's different tales, but if passing such tests could support their authority (that is to say, their reliability), failing the tests would have to undermine it. The price you pay for the possibility of empirically confirming your assertions is the outside chance of being discredited. The friends of qualia are prepared, today, to pay that price, but perhaps only because they haven't reckoned how the bargain they have struck will subvert the concept they want to defend.

Consider how we could shed light on the question of where the truth lies in the particular cases of Chase and Sanborn, even if we might not be able to settle the matter definitively. It is obvious that there might be telling objective support for one extreme version or another of their stories. Thus if Chase is unable to reidentify coffees, teas, and wines in blind tastings in which only minutes intervene between first and second sips, his claim to *know* that Maxwell House tastes just the same to him now as it did six years ago will be seriously undercut. Alternatively, if he does excellently in blind tastings, and exhibits considerable knowledge about the canons of coffee style (if such there be), his claim to have become a more sophisticated taster will be supported. Exploitation of the standard principles of inductive testing—basically Mill's method of differences—can go a long way toward indicating what sort of change has occurred in Chase or Sanborn—a change near the brute perceptual processing end of the spectrum or a change near the ultimate reactive judgment end of the spectrum. [...]

But let us not overestimate the resolving power of such empirical testing. The space in each case between the two poles represented by possibility (a) and possibility (b) would be occupied by phenomena that were the product, somehow, of two factors in varying proportion: roughly, dispositions to generate or produce qualia and dispositions to react to the qualia once they are produced. (That is how our intuitive picture of qualia would envisage it.) Qualia are supposed to affect our action or behavior only via the intermediary of our judgments about them, so any behavioral test, such as a discrimination or memory test, since it takes acts based on judgments as its primary data, can give us direct evidence only about the *resultant* of our two factors. In extreme cases we can have indirect evidence to suggest that one factor has varied a great deal, the other factor hardly at all, and we can test the hypothesis further by checking the relative sensitivity of the subject to variations in the conditions that presumably alter the two component factors. But such indirect testing cannot be expected to resolve the issue when the effects are relatively small—when, for instance, our rival hypotheses are Chase's preferred hypothesis (a) and the minor variant to the effect that his qualia have shifted *a little* and his standards *less than he thinks*. This will be true even when we include in our data any unintended or unconscious behavioral effects, for their import will be ambiguous. (Would a longer response latency in Chase today be indicative of a process of "attempted qualia renormalization" or "extended aesthetic evaluation"?)

The limited evidential power of neurophysiology comes out particularly clearly if we imagine a case of adaptation. Suppose, in *intuition pump #8: the gradual post-operative recovery*, that we have somehow "surgically inverted" Chase's taste bud connections in the standard imaginary way: post-operatively, sugar tastes salty, salt tastes sour, etc. But suppose further—and this is as realistic a supposition as its denial—that Chase has subsequently compensated—as revealed by his behavior. He now *says* that the sugary substance we place on his tongue is sweet, and no longer favors gravy on his ice cream. Let us suppose the compensation is so thorough that on all behavioral and verbal tests his performance is indistinguishable from that of normal subjects—and from his own pre-surgical performance.

If all the internal compensatory adjustment has been accomplished early in the process—intuitively, pre-qualia—then his qualia today are restored to just as they were (relative to external sources of stimulation) before the surgery. If on the other hand some or all of the internal compensatory adjustment is post-qualia, then his qualia have not been renormalized *even if he thinks they have.* But the physiological facts will not in themselves shed any light on where in the stream of physiological process twixt tasting and telling to draw the line at which the putative qualia appear as properties of that phase of the process. The qualia are the "immediate or phenomenal" properties, of course, but this description will not serve to locate the right phase in the physiological stream, for, echoing intuition pump #6, there will always be at least two possible ways of interpreting the neurophysiological theory, however it comes out. Suppose our physiological theory tells us (in as much detail as you like) that the compensatory effect in him has been achieved by an *adjustment in the memory-accessing process* that is required for our victim to compare today's hues to those of yore. There are *still* two stories that might be told:

I Chase's current qualia are still abnormal, but thanks to the revision in his memory-accessing process, he has in effect adjusted his memories of how things used to taste, so he no longer notices any anomaly.

II The memory-comparison step occurs just prior to the qualia phase in taste perception; thanks to the revision, it now *yields* the same old qualia for the same stimulation.

In (I) the qualia contribute to the input, in effect, to the memory-comparator. In (II) they are part of the output of the memory-comparator. These seem to be two substantially different hypotheses, but the physiological evidence, no matter how well developed, will not tell us on which side of memory to put the qualia. Chase's introspective evidence will not settle the issue between (I) and (II) either, since *ex hypothesi* those stories are not reliably distinguishable by him. Remember that it was in order to confirm or disconfirm Chase's opinion that we turned to the neurophysiological evidence in the first place. We can hardly use his opinion in the end to settle the matter between our rival neurophysiological theories. Chase may think that he thinks his experiences are the same as before *because* they really are (and he remembers accurately how it used to be), but he must admit that he has no introspective resources for distinguishing that possibility from alternative (I), on which he thinks things are as they used to be *because* his memory of how they used to be has been distorted by his new compensatory habits.

Faced with their subject's systematic neutrality, the physiologists may have their own reasons for preferring (I) to (II) or vice versa, for they may have *appropriated* the term "qualia" to their own theoretical ends, to denote some family of detectable properties that strike them as playing an important role in their neurophysiological theory of perceptual recognition and memory. Chase or Sanborn might complain—in the company of more than a few philosophical spokesmen—that these proper-

ties the neurophysiologists choose to call "qualia" are not the qualia they are speaking of. The scientists' retort is: "If we cannot distinguish (I) from (II), we certainly cannot support either of your claims. If you want our support, you must relinquish your concept of qualia."

[…]

5. Some Puzzling Real Cases

It is not enough to withhold our theoretical allegiances until the sunny day when the philosophers complete the tricky task of purifying the everyday concept of qualia. Unless we take active steps to shed this source concept, and replace it with better ideas, it will continue to cripple our imaginations and systematically distort our attempts to understand the phenomena already encountered.

What we find, if we look at the actual phenomena of anomalies of color perception, for instance, amply bears out our suspicions about the inadequacy of the traditional notion of qualia. Several varieties of *cerebral achromatopsia* (brain based impairment of color vision) have been reported, and while there remains much that is unsettled about their analysis, there is little doubt that the philosophical thought experiments have underestimated or overlooked the possibilities for counter-intuitive collections of symptoms, as a few very brief excerpts from case histories will reveal.

> Objects to the right of the vertical meridian appeared to be of normal hue, while to the left they were perceived only in shades of gray, though without distortions of form…. He was unable to recognize or name any color in any portion of the left field of either eye, including bright reds, blues, greens and yellows. As soon as any portion of the colored

object crossed the vertical meridian, he was able to instantly recognize and accurately name its color. (Damasio et al. 1980)

This patient would seem at first to be unproblematically describable as suffering a shift or loss of color qualia in the left hemifield, but there is a problem of interpretation here, brought about by another case:

> The patient failed in all tasks in which he was required to match the seen color with its spoken name. Thus, the patient failed to give the names of colors and failed to choose a color in response to its name. By contrast, he succeeded on all tasks where the matching was either purely verbal or purely nonverbal. Thus, he could give verbally the names of colors corresponding to named objects and vice versa. He could match seen colors to each other and to pictures of objects and could sort colors without error. (Geschwind and Fusillo 1966)

This second patient was quite unaware of any deficit. He "never replied with a simple 'I don't know' to the demand for naming a color" (Geschwind and Fusillo 1966, p. 140). There is a striking contrast between these two patients; both have impaired ability to name the colors of things in at least part of their visual field, but whereas the former is acutely aware of his deficit, the latter is not. Does this difference make all the difference about qualia? If so, what on earth should we say about this third patient?

> His other main complaint was that "everything looked black or grey" and this caused him some difficulty in everyday life...He had considerable difficulty recognizing and naming colours. He

would, for example, usually describe bright red objects as either red or black, bright green objects as either green, blue or black, and bright blue objects as black. The difficulty appeared to be perceptual and he would make remarks suggesting this; for example when shown a bright red object he said "a dirty smudgy red, not as red as you would normally see red." Colours of lesser saturation or brightness were described in such terms as "grey," "off-white" or "black," but if told to guess at the colour, he would be correct on about 50 per cent of occasions, being notably less successful with blues and greens than reds. (Meadows 1974)

This man's awareness of his deficit is problematic to say the least. It contrasts rather sharply with yet another case:

> One morning in November 1977, upon awakening, she noted that although she was able to see details of objects and people, colors appeared "drained out" and "not true." She had no other complaint...her vision was good, 20/20 in each eye...The difficulty in color perception persisted, and she had to seek the advice of her husband to choose what to wear. Eight weeks later she noted that she could no longer recognize the faces of her husband and daughter...[So in] addition to achromatopsia, the patient had prosopagnosia, but her linguistic and cognitive performances were otherwise unaffected. The patient was able to tell her story cogently and to have remarkable insight about her defects. (Damasio et al. 1980)

As Meadows notes, "Some patients thus complain that their vision for colours is defective while others have no spontaneous complaint but show striking abnormalities on testing."

What should one say in these cases? When no complaint is volunteered but the patient shows an impairment in color vision, is this a sign that his qualia are unaffected? ("His capacities to discriminate are terribly impaired, but luckily for him, his inner life is untouched by this merely public loss!") We could line up the qualia this way, but equally we could claim that the patient has simply not noticed the perhaps gradual draining away or inversion or merging of his qualia revealed by his poor performance. ("So slowly did his inner life lose its complexity and variety that he never noticed how impoverished it had become!") What if our last patient described her complaint just as she did above, but performed normally on testing? One hypothesis would be that her qualia had indeed, as she suggested, become washed out. Another would be that in the light of her sterling performance on the color discrimination tests, her qualia were fine; she was suffering from some hysterical or depressive anomaly, a sort of color-vision hypochondria that makes her complain about a loss of color perception. Or perhaps one could claim that her qualia were untouched; her disorder was purely verbal: an anomalous understanding of the words she uses to describe her experience. (Other, startlingly specific color-*word* disorders have been reported in the literature.)

The traditional concept leads us to overlook genuine possibilities. Once we have learned of the curious deficit reported by Geschwind and Fusillo, for instance, we realize that our first patient was never tested to see if he could still sort colors seen on the left or pass other non-naming, non-verbal color-blindness tests. Those tests are by no means superfluous. Perhaps he would have passed them; perhaps, *in spite of what he says* his qualia are as intact for the left field as for the right!—if we take the

capacity to pass such tests as "criterial." Perhaps his problem is "purely verbal." If your reaction to this hypothesis is that this is impossible, that must mean you are making his verbal, reporting behavior sovereign in settling the issue—but then you must rule out a priori the possibility of the condition I described as color-vision hypochondria.

There is no prospect of *finding* the answers to these brain-teasers in our everyday usage or the intuitions it arouses, but it is of course open to the philosopher to *create* an edifice of theory defending a particular set of interlocking proposals. The problem is that although normally a certain family of stimulus and bodily conditions yields a certain family of effects, any particular effect can be disconnected, and our intuitions do not tell us which effects are "essential" to quale identity or qualia constancy (cf. Dennett 1978a, ch. 11). It seems fairly obvious to me that none of the real problems of interpretation that face us in these curious cases is advanced by any analysis of how the concept of *qualia* is to be applied—unless we wish to propose a novel, technical sense for which the traditional term might be appropriated. But that would be at least a tactical error: the intuitions that surround and *purport* to anchor the current understanding of the term are revealed to be in utter disarray when confronted with these cases.

My informal sampling shows that some philosophers have strong opinions about each case and how it should be described in terms of qualia, but they find they are in strident (and ultimately comic) disagreement with other philosophers about how these "obvious" descriptions should go. Other philosophers discover they really don't know what to say—not because there aren't enough facts presented in the descriptions of the cases, but because it begins to dawn on them that they haven't really known what they were talking about over the years.

6. Filling the Vacuum

If qualia are such a bad idea, why have they seemed to be such a good idea? Why does it seem as if there are these intrinsic, ineffable, private, "qualitative" properties in our experience? A review of the presumptive second-order properties of the properties of our conscious experiences will permit us to diagnose their attractiveness and find suitable substitutes. (For a similar exercise see Kitcher 1979.)

Consider "intrinsic" first. It is far from clear what an intrinsic property would be. Although the term has had a certain vogue in philosophy, and often seems to secure an important contrast, there has never been an accepted definition of the second-order property of intrinsicality. If even such a brilliant theory-monger as David Lewis can try and fail, by his own admission, to define the extrinsic/intrinsic distinction coherently, we can begin to wonder if the concept deserves our further attention after all. In fact Lewis (1983) begins his survey of versions of the distinction by listing as one option: "We could Quine the lot, give over the entire family as unintelligible and dispensable," but he dismisses the suggestion immediately: "That would be absurd" (p. 197). In the end, however, his effort to salvage the accounts of Chisholm (1976) and Kim (1982) are stymied, and he conjectures that "if we still want to break in we had best try another window" (p. 200).

Even if we are as loath as Lewis is to abandon the distinction, shouldn't we be suspicious of the following curious fact? If challenged to explain the idea of an intrinsic property to a neophyte, many people would hit on the following sort of example: consider Tom's ball; it has many properties, such as its being made of rubber from India, its belonging to Tom, its having spent the last week in the closet, and its redness. All but the last of these are clearly *relational* or *extrinsic* properties of the ball.

Its redness, however, is an intrinsic property. Except this isn't so. Ever since Boyle and Locke we have known better. Redness—public redness—is a quintessentially relational property, as many thought experiments about "secondary qualities" show. (One of the first was Berkeley's [1713] pail of lukewarm water, and one of the best is Bennett's [1965] phenol-thio-urea.) The seductive step, on learning that public redness (like public bitterness, etc.) is a relational property after all, is to cling to intrinsicality ("*something* has to be intrinsic!") and move it into the subject's head. It is often thought, in fact, that if we take a Lockean, relational position on objective bitterness, redness, etc., we *must* complete our account of the relations in question by appeal to non-relational, intrinsic properties. If what it is to be objectively bitter is to produce a certain effect in the members of the class of normal observers, we must be able to specify that effect, and distinguish it from the effect produced by objective sourness and so forth.

What else could distinguish this effect but some intrinsic property? Why not another relational or extrinsic property? The relational treatment of monetary value does not require, for its completion, the supposition of items of intrinsic value (value independent of the valuers' dispositions to react behaviorally). The claim that certain perceptual properties are different is, in the absence of any supporting argument, just question-begging. It will not do to say that it is just obvious that they are intrinsic. It may have seemed obvious to some, but the considerations raised by Chase's quandary show that it is far from obvious that any intrinsic property (whatever that comes to) could play the role of anchor for the Lockean relational treatment of the public perceptual properties.

Why not give up intrinsicality as a second-order property altogether, at least pending resolution of the disarray of philosophical opinion about what intrinsicality might be? Until such time the insistence that qualia are the intrinsic properties of experience is an empty gesture at best; no one could claim that it provides a clear, coherent, understood prerequisite for theory.[11] What, then, of ineffability? Why does it seem that our conscious experiences have ineffable properties? Because they do have *practically* ineffable properties. Suppose, in *intuition pump #13: the osprey cry*, that I have never heard the cry of an osprey, even in a recording, but know roughly, from reading my bird books, what to listen for: "a series of short, sharp, cheeping whistles, *cheep cheep* or *chewk chewk*, etc.; sounds annoyed" (Peterson 1947) (or words to that effect or better). The verbal description gives me a partial confinement of the logical space of possible bird cries. On its basis I can rule out many bird calls I have heard or might hear, but there is still a broad range of discriminable-by-me possibilities within which the actuality lies hidden from me like a needle in a haystack.

Then one day, armed with both my verbal description and my binoculars, I identify an osprey visually, and then hear its cry. So *that's* what it sounds like, I say to myself, ostending—it seems—a particular mental complex of intrinsic, ineffable qualia. I dub the complex "S" (*pace* Wittgenstein), rehearse it in short term memory, check it against the bird book descriptions, and see that while the verbal descriptions are true, accurate and even poetically evocative—I decide I could not do better with a thousand words—they still fall short of *capturing* the qualia-complex I have called S. In fact, that is why I need the neologism "S" to refer directly to the ineffable property I cannot pick out by description. My perceptual experience has pinpointed for me the location of the osprey cry in the logical space of possibilities in a way verbal description could not.

But tempting as this view of matters is, it is overstated. First of all, it is obvious that from

a single experience of this sort I don't—can't—know how to generalize to other osprey calls. Would a cry that differed only in being half an octave higher also be an osprey call? That is an empirical, ornithological question for which my experience provides scant evidence. But moreover—and this is a psychological, not ornithological, matter—I don't and can't know, from a single such experience, which physical variations and constancies in stimuli would produce an indistinguishable experience in me. Nor can I know whether I would react the same (have the same experience) if I were presented with what was, by all physical measures, a re-stimulation identical to the first. I cannot know the modulating effect, if any, of variations in my body (or psyche).

This inscrutability of projection is surely one of the sources of plausibility for Wittgenstein's skepticism regarding the possibility of a private language.

> Wittgenstein emphasizes that ostensive definitions are always in principle capable of being misunderstood, even the ostensive definition of a color word such as "sepia." How someone understands the word is exhibited in the way someone goes on, "the use that he makes of the word defined." One may go on in the right way given a purely minimal explanation, while on the other hand one may go on in another way no matter how many clarifications are added, since these too can be misunderstood...(Kripke 1982, p. 83; see also pp. 40–46)

But what is inscrutable in a single glance, and somewhat ambiguous after limited testing, can come to be justifiably seen as the deliverance of a highly specific, reliable, and projectible property-detector, once it has been field-tested under a suitably wide variety of circumstances. In other words, when first I hear the osprey cry, I may have identified a property-detector in myself, but I have no idea (yet) what property my new-found property-detector detects. It might seem then that I know nothing new at all—that my novel experience has not improved my epistemic predicament in the slightest. But of course this is not so. I may not be able to describe the property or identify it relative to any readily usable public landmarks (yet), but I am acquainted with it in a modest way: I can refer to the property I detected: it is the property I detected in *that* event. My experience of the osprey cry has given me a new way of thinking about osprey cries (an unavoidably inflated way of saying something very simple) which is practically ineffable both because it has (as yet for me) an untested profile in response to perceptual circumstances, and because it is—as the poverty of the bird-book description attests—such a highly informative way of thinking: a deliverance of an informationally very sensitive portion of my nervous system.

In this instance I mean information in the formal information theory sense of the term. Consider (*intuition pump #14: the Jello box*) the old spy trick, most famously encountered in the case of Julius and Ethel Rosenberg, of improving on a password system by tearing something in two (a Jello box, in the Rosenberg's case), and giving half to each of the two parties who must be careful about identifying each other. Why does it work? Because tearing the paper in two produces an edge of such informational complexity that it would be virtually impossible to reproduce by deliberate construction.

[...]

#15: the guitar string. Pluck the bass or low E string open, and listen carefully to the sound. Does it have describable parts or is it one and whole and ineffably guitarish? Many will opt for the latter way of talking. Now pluck the open string again and carefully bring a finger down lightly over the octave fret to create a high "harmonic." Suddenly a new sound is heard: "purer" somehow and of course an octave higher. Some people insist that this is an entirely novel sound, while others will describe the experience by saying "the bottom fell out of the note"—leaving just the top. But then on a third open plucking one can hear, with surprising distinctness, the harmonic overtone that was isolated in the second plucking. The homogeneity and ineffability of the first experience is gone, replaced by a duality as "directly apprehensible" and clearly describable as that of any chord.

The difference in experience is striking, but the complexity apprehended on the third plucking was there all along (being responded to or discriminated). After all, it was by the complex pattern of overtones that you were able to recognize the sound as that of a guitar rather than a lute or harpsichord. In other words, although the subjective experience has changed dramatically, the pip hasn't changed; you are still responding, as before, to a complex property so highly informative that it practically defies verbal description.

There is nothing to stop further refinement of one's capacity to describe this heretofore ineffable complexity. At any time, of course, there is one's current horizon of distinguishability—and that horizon is what sets, if anything does, what we should call the primary or atomic properties of what one consciously experiences (Farrell 1950). But it would be a mistake to transform the fact that inevitably there is a limit to our capacity to describe things we experience into the supposition that there are absolutely indescribable properties in our experience.

So when we look one last time at our original characterization of qualia, as ineffable, intrinsic, private, directly apprehensible properties of experience, we find that there is nothing to fill the bill. In their place are relatively or practically ineffable public properties we can refer to indirectly via reference to our private property-detectors—private only in the sense of idiosyncratic. And in so far as we wish to cling to our subjective authority about the occurrence within us of states of certain types or with certain properties, we can have some authority—not infallibility or incorrigibility, but something better than sheer guessing—but only if we restrict ourselves to relational, extrinsic properties like the power of certain internal states of ours to provoke acts of apparent re-identification. So contrary to what seems obvious at first blush, there simply are no qualia at all.[14]

Notes

1. A representative sample of the most recent literature on qualia would include Block 1980; Shoemaker 1981, 1982; Davis 1982; White 1985; Armstrong and Malcolm 1984; Churchland 1985; and Conee 1985.

2. The difference between "eliminative materialism"—of which my position on qualia is an instance—and a "reductive" materialism that takes on the burden of identifying the problematic item in terms of the foundational materialistic theory is thus often best seen not so much as a doctrinal issue as a tactical issue: how might we most gracefully or effectively enlighten the confused in this instance? See my discussion of "fatigues" in the Introduction to *Brainstorms* (Dennett 1978a), and earlier, my discussion of what the enlightened ought to say about the metaphysical status of *sakes* and *voices* in *Content and Consciousness* (Dennett 1969), ch. 1.

3. The plausibility of this concession depends less on a high regard for the technology,

than on a proper skepticism about human powers, now documented in a fascinating study by Lehrer (1983).

4. Shoemaker (1984) seems to be moving reluctantly towards agreement with this conclusion: "So unless we can find some grounds on which we can deny the possibility of the sort of situation envisaged...we must apparently choose between rejecting the functionalist account of qualitative similarity and rejecting the standard conception of qualia. I would prefer not to have to make this choice; but if I am forced to make it, I reject the standard conception of qualia" (p. 356).

5. Shoemaker (1982) attributes a view to Wittgenstein (acknowledging that "it is none too clear" that this is actually what Wittgenstein held) which is very close to the view I defend here. But to Shoemaker, "it would seem offhand that Wittgenstein was mistaken" (p. 360), a claim Shoemaker supports with a far from offhand thought experiment—which Shoemaker misanalyzes if the present paper is correct. (There is no good reason, contrary to Shoemaker's declaration, to believe that his subject's *experience* is systematically different from what it was before the inversion.) Smart (1959) expresses guarded and partial approval of Wittgenstein's hard line, but cannot see his way clear to as uncompromising an eliminativism as I maintain here.

6. In 1979, I read an earlier version of this paper in Oxford, with a commentary, by John Foster, who defended qualia to the last breath, which was: "qualia should not be quined but fostered!" Symmetry demands, of course, the following definition for the eighth edition of *The Philosophical Lexicon*: "foster, *v.* To acclaim resolutely the existence or importance of something chimerical or insignificant."

7. This example first appeared in print in my "Reflections on Smullyan" in *The Mind's I* (Hofstadter and Dennett 1981), p. 427–28.

8. Kripke (1982) comes close, when he asks rhetorically "Do I not know, directly, and *with a fair degree of certainty* [emphasis added], that I mean plus [by the function I call "plus"]?" (p. 40) Kripke does not tell us what is implied by "a fair degree of certainty," but presumably he means by this remark to declare his allegiance to what Millikan (1984) attacks under the name of "meaning rationalism."

[…]

11. A heroic (and, to me, baffling) refusal to abandon intrinsicality is Wilfrid Sellars's contemplation over the years of his famous pink ice cube, which leads him to postulate a revolution in microphysics, restoring objective "absolute sensory processes" in the face of Boyle and Locke and almost everybody since them. See Sellars (1981) and my commentary (Dennett 1981).

[…]

14. The first version of this paper was presented at University College London, in November 1978, and in various revisions at a dozen other universities in 1979 and 1980. It was never published, but was circulated widely as Tufts University Cognitive Science Working Paper #7, December 1979. A second version was presented at the Universities of Adelaide and Sydney in 1984, and in 1985 to psychology department colloquia at Harvard and Brown under the title "Properties of conscious experience." The second version was the basis for my presentation at the workshop on consciousness in modern science, Villa Olmo, Como, Italy, April 1985, and circulated in preprint in 1985, again under the title "Quining qualia." The present version, the fourth, is a substantial revision, thanks to the helpful comments of many people, including Kathleen Akins, Ned Block, Alan Cowey, Sydney Shoemaker, Peter Bieri, William Lycan, Paul Churchland, Gilbert Harman and the participants at Villa Olmo.

References

Akins, K. (1987) *Information and Organisms: Or, Why Nature Doesn't Build Epistemic Engines*, PhD dissertation, Univ. of Michigan Dept. of Philosophy.

Armstrong, D. and Malcolm, N. (eds) (1984) *Consciousness and Causality*. Oxford: Basil Blackwell.

Bennett, J. (1965) "Substance, Reality and Primary Qualities." *American Philosophical Quarterly* 2, 1–17.

Berkeley, G. (1713) *Three Dialogues between Hylas and Philonous*.

Block, N. (1978) "Troubles with Functionalism," in W. Savage (ed.) *Perception and Cognition: Minnesota Studies in the Philosophy of Science, Vol. IX*. Minneapolis: University of Minnesota Press.

Block, N. (1980) "Are Absent Qualia Impossible?," *Philosophical Review* 89, 257.

Block, N. and Fodor, J. (1972) "What Psychological States Are Not," *Philosophical Review* 81, 159–81.

Chisholm, R. (1976) *Person and Object*. La Salle, Illinois: Open Court Press.

Churchland, P.M. (1979) *Scientific Realism and the Plasticity of Mind*. Cambridge, MA: Cambridge University Press.

Churchland, P.M. (1985) "Reduction, Qualia and the Direct Inspection of Brain States," *Journal of Philosophy*, LXXXII, 8–28.

Conee, E. (1985) "The Possibility of Absent Qualia," *Philosophical Review* 94, 345–66.

Damasio, A. et al. (1980) "Central Achromatopsia: Behavioral, Anatomic, and Physiological Aspects," *Neurology* 30, 1064–71.

Danto, A. (1963) "What We Can Do," *Journal of Philosophy*, LX, 435–45.

Danto, A. (1965) "Basic Actions," *American Philosophical Quarterly*, 141–48.

Davis, L. (1982) "Functionalism and Absent Qualia," *Philosophical Studies* 41, 231–51.

Dennett, D.C. (1969) *Content and Consciousness*. London: Routledge & Kegan Paul.

Dennett, D.C. (1976) "Are Dreams Experiences?," *Philosophical Review* 85, 151–71. (Reprinted in Dennett 1978a.)

Dennett, D.C. (1978a) *Brainstorms*. Bradford Books/MIT Press.

Dennett, D.C. (1978b) "Two Approaches to Mental Images," in Dennett 1978a.

Dennett, D.C. (1978c) *The Philosophical Lexicon* (privately printed, available from the American Philosophical Association, University of Delaware), 8th edn.

Dennett, D.C. (1979) "On the Absence of Phenomenology," in D.F. Gustafson and B.L. Tapscott (eds) *Body, Mind, and Method* (Festschrift for Virgil Aldrich). Dordrecht: Reidel, pp. 93–114.

Dennett, D.C. (1981) "Wondering Where the Yellow Went," *Monist* 64, 102–08.

Dennett, D.C. (1982) "How to Study Human Consciousness Empirically: Or Nothing Comes to Mind," *Synthese* 53, 159–80.

Dennett, D.C. (1987) *The Intentional Stance*. Cambridge, MA: Bradford/MIT.

Dretske, F. (1981) *Knowledge and the Flow of Information*. Cambridge, MA: Bradford/MIT.

Elster, J. (1985) *Making Sense of Marx*. Cambridge, England: Cambridge University Press.

Farrell B. (1950) "Experience," *Mind* 59, 170–98.

Gert, B. (1965) "Imagination and Verifiability," *Philosophical Studies* 16, 44–47.

Geschwind, N. and Fusillo, M. (1966) "Color-naming Defects in Association with Alexia," *Archives of Neurology* 15, 137–46.

Goldman, A. (1970) *A Theory of Human Action*. Englewood Cliffs, NJ: Prentice Hall.

Gregory, R. (1977) *Eye and Brain*, 3rd edn. London: Weidenfeld & Nicolson.

Hofstadter, D. and Dennett, D.C. (1981) *The Mind's I: Fantasies and Reflections on Mind and Soul*. New York: Basic Books.

Kim, J. (1982) "Psychophysical Supervenience," *Philosophical Studies* 41, 51–70.

Kitcher, P. (1979) "Phenomenal Qualities," *American Philosophical Quarterly* 16, 123–29.

Kripke, S. (1982) *Wittgenstein on Rules and Private Language*. Cambridge, MA: Harvard University Press.

Lehrer, A. (1983) *Wine and Conversation*. Bloomington, Indiana: Univ. of Indiana Press.

Lewis, D. (1983) "Extrinsic Properties," *Philosophical Studies* 44, 197–200.

Locke, J. (1690) *An Essay Concerning Human Understanding* (A.C. Fraser edition). New York: Dover, 1959.

Lycan, W. (1973) "Inverted Spectrum," *Ratio* XV, 315–19.

Malcolm, N. (1956) "Dreaming and Skepticism," *Philosophical Review* 64, 14–37.

Malcolm, N. (1959) *Dreaming*. London: Routledge & Kegan Paul.

Meadows, J.C. (1974) "Disturbed Perception of Colours Associated with Localized Cerebral Lesions," *Brain* 97, 615–32.

Millikan, R. (1984) *Language, Thought and Other Biological Categories*. Cambridge, MA: Bradford/MIT.

Nagel, T. (1974) "What Is It Like to Be a Bat?," *Philosophical Review* 83, 435–51.

Nagel, T. (1986) *The View from Nowhere*. Oxford: Oxford University Press.

Peirce, C. (1931–58), C. Hartshorne and P. Weiss (eds), *Collected Works*. Cambridge, MA: Harvard University Press.

Peterson, R.T. (1947) *A Field Guide to the Birds*. Boston: Houghton Mifflin.

Putnam, H. (1965) "Brains and Behavior," in J. Butler (ed.) *Analytical Philosophy* (second series). Oxford: Basil Blackwell.

Pylyshyn, Z. (1980) "Computation and Cognition: Issues in the Foundation of Cognitive Science," *Behavioral and Brain Sciences* 3, 111–32.

Pylyshyn, Z. (1984) *Computation and Cognition: Toward a Foundation for Cognitive Science*. Cambridge, MA: Bradford/MIT Press.

Sellars, W. (1981) "Foundations for a Metaphysics of Pure Process" (the Carus Lectures), *Monist* 64, 3–90.

Shoemaker, S. (1969) "Time without Change," *Journal of Philosophy* 66, 363–81.

Shoemaker, S. (1975) "Functionalism and Qualia," *Philosophical Studies* 27, 291–315.

Shoemaker, S. (1981) "Absent Qualia Are Impossible—A Reply to Block," *Philosophical Review* 90, 581–99.

Shoemaker, S. (1982) "The Inverted Spectrum," *Journal of Philosophy* 79, 357–81.

Shoemaker, S. (1984) "Postscript (1983)," in *Identity, Cause, and Mind*. Cambridge, England: Cambridge Univ. Press, pp. 351–57.

Smart, J.J.C. (1959) "Sensations and Brain Processes," *Philosophical Review* 68, 141–56. (Reprinted in Chappell 1962.)

Stich, S. (1983) *From Folk Psychology to Cognitive Science: The Case Against Belief*. Cambridge, MA: Bradford/MIT.

Taylor, D.M. (1966) "The Incommunicability of Content," *Mind* 75, 527–41.

Von der Heydt, R., Peterhans, F., and Baumgartner, G. (1984) "Illusory Contours and Cortical Neuron Response," *Science* 224, 1260–62.

Walzer, M. (1985) "What's Left of Marx," *New York Review of Books*, Nov. 21, pp. 43–46.

White, S. (1985) "Professor Shoemaker and So-Called 'Qualia' of Experience," *Philosophical Studies* 47, 369–83.

Wittgenstein, L. (1958), G.E.M. Anscombe (ed.), *Philosophical Investigations*. Oxford: Basil Blackwell.

DAVID ROSENTHAL

"How to Think about Mental Qualities"

I. Intuitions about Mental Qualities

It's often held that undetectable inversion of mental qualities is, if not possible, at least conceivable. It's thought to be conceivable that the mental quality your visual states exhibit when you see something red in standard conditions is literally of the same type as the mental quality my visual states exhibit when I see something green in such circumstances. It's thought, moreover, to be conceivable that such inversion of mental qualities could be wholly undetectable by any third-person means. And since first-person access is limited to a single individual, and so could not reveal a disparity in mental quality between us, third-person undetectability means undetectability *tout court*.

There is an extensive literature about whether such inversion is conceivable, and whether it's even possible. But my concern here will not be with the details of such discussions, but with the status of intuitions about undetectable quality inversion and what if any implications it has for theorizing about mental qualities.

It's important that the relevant quality inversion is undetectable. Humans do sometimes differ in what mental qualities occur when perceiving the same stimuli in the same perceptual circumstances. Some people, for example, are red-green color blind. And there are slight variations among individuals as to what color stimuli they can distinguish, which probably reflect slight variation in mental color qualities. These differences are all detectable by appeal to the physical stimuli people can discriminate. By contrast, the inversion of mental qualities that many take to be conceivable is hypothesized to be undetectable by any such means. And it's such undetectable inversion that will likely affect the way we theorize about mental qualities.

It's widely recognized that the quality space that defines the human ability to discriminate among perceptible physical color properties is asymmetric. So many theorists have retreated from the claim that inversion of mental qualities is possible to an ostensibly weaker claim that it's merely conceivable.[1] And it's arguable that since we can coherently describe such undetectable inversion, it must at least be conceivable.

I'll argue in what follows that undetectable inversion is not even conceivable. But as already noted, my concern with undetectable inversion is mainly with the status of claims about it and their implications for theorizing about mental qualities.

Why would the mere conceivability of undetectable inversion matter? Indeed, why would it matter if such inversion were also possible? We can't theorize in a vacuum; we always need data to theorize from and to test our theories' predictions. And it's often assumed that pretheoretic folk intuitions serve as data for theorizing in philosophy. What else, one may wonder, could serve as data for philosophy if that field is distinct from the empirical sciences? Also, it's often assumed that many of these pretheoretic folk intuitions in theorizing in philosophy will concern what's possible and what's conceivable, rather than what's actually the case.

The conceivability of quality inversion is often taken to serve as just such a datum for a theory of mental qualities; any satisfactory theory would then have to accommodate such conceivability. And it turns out that this imposes a remarkably strong condition on any theorizing about mental qualities. Such conceivable inversion would be undetectable. But if we could access or find out about mental qualities in any way that's independent of first-person, subjective access, any inversion would be readily detectable. So the mere conceivability of undetectable quality inversion implies that it's inconceivable that we have any third-person, intersubjective access to mental qualities. This striking consequence is seldom noted, perhaps because those who take undetectable quality inversion at all seriously to begin with also simply take for granted that mental qualities allow only for first-person access. And if one builds the restriction to first-person access into one's conception of mental qualities, the conceivability of inversion is a straightforward consequence.

It's not obvious that there is any independent reason to suppose that undetectable inversion actually is conceivable. One could urge that it's conceivable in that one can describe such inversion and simply stipulate that it's undetectable. It's also often said that such inversion is part of our folk theory about mental qualities; many people, especially children, will say when presented with the inversion scenario that undetectable inversion is conceivable or even possible. Intuitions, moreover, arguably encapsulate aspects of our folk theories about things. So locating the conceivability of undetectable inversion as a plank in our folk theory of the mental arguably does justice to its alleged status as a pretheoretic intuition.

But these cases for conceivability are very weak. Consider the claim that it's conceivable that water is a simple, basic physical substance. Anybody who advanced that claim would be operating with too impoverished a concept of water, for example, a concept of something that simply looks and behaves like water in a relatively narrow range of common conditions. Given what water actually is and given anything like a satisfactory concept of water, it is simply not conceivable that water is a simple, basic substance.

The mere appearance that undetectable quality inversion is conceivable may in just that way mislead about what is actually conceivable. I'll argue in what follows that a satisfactory conception of mental qualities precludes the conceivability of undetectable inversion. But the paucity of substantive reasons for thinking that undetectable inversion is actually conceivable encourages the hypothesis that it seems conceivable only on the assumption that we can know about mental qualities solely by way of first-person access. The view that we can conceive of undetectable inversion is in effect simply an expression of the theory that consciousness is both the first and last word about mental qualities.

Similar considerations apply to several other intuitively inviting claims about mental qualities. It's often said to be conceivable that a creature physically and behaviorally indis-

tinguishable from an ordinary human might nonetheless be in no states with qualitative character. Again, there is little to be said in support of the conceivability of such a creature, often referred to, following David Chalmers,[2] as a zombie. As with undetectable inversion, the conceivability of zombies is often taken simply to be a pretheoretic intuition that any satisfactory theory must accommodate.

Suppose, however, that we can know about mental qualities independent of consciousness, independent, that is, of any first-person access to them. That would have to be due to some difference mental qualities make to the physical makeup or behavior of the relevant creature; there's no other way to get knowledge of their presence independent of consciousness. So if the same physical makeup and behavior can occur sometimes with mental qualities and sometimes without, we cannot have third-person access to mental qualities. The possibility or conceivability of zombies rests on the view that mental qualities are accessible only in a first-person way.

The same considerations apply also to Joseph Levine's explanatory gap and Chalmers's hard problem. Levine, Chalmers, and others hold that a special difficulty affects any effort to explain why any particular physical process should subserve a particular conscious qualitative state rather than some other. Why should a particular brain state result in an experience of red rather than an experience of green? Indeed why it would result in any experience at all? Levine accordingly urges that an explanatory gap separates conscious qualitative states from whatever physical states underlie them;[3] Chalmers calls this the hard problem of consciousness.[4]

Levine argues for such an explanatory gap by urging a difference in what's conceivable about the mental quality of pain and what's conceivable about water. He writes:

While it is conceivable that something other than H_2O should manifest the superficial macro properties of water,…it is not conceivable…that H_2O should fail to manifest those properties (assuming, of course, that we keep the rest of chemistry constant).

By contrast, he maintains, "it is…conceivable that there should exist a pain without the firing of C-fibers, and the firing of C-fibers without pain" (548).

Since chemistry is needed for it to be inconceivable "that H_2O should fail to manifest" the relevant properties, it's unclear why a satisfactory neuropsychological theory would not yield parallel results for pain. But put that aside for now. The idea that an explanatory gap separates conscious mental qualities from their physical underpinnings is again not a pretheoretic intuition that any satisfactory theory must honor. Rather, whatever plausibility there may be to an explanatory gap rests again on the tacit claim that mental qualities are accessible only by way of consciousness. Third-person access to mental qualities would provide the resources needed to build an explanatory bridge from physical makeup to mental qualities. We would encounter difficulties in bridging that gap only if mental qualities are accessible solely by way of consciousness.[5]

Chalmers's hard problem and Levine's explanatory gap both echo Leibniz's well-known mill argument, according to which "perception, and anything that depends upon it, cannot be explained in terms of mechanistic causation, that is, in terms of shapes and motions." Leibniz invites us to imagine "a machine, which was constructed in such a way as to give rise to thinking, sensing, and having perceptions." If the machine were expanded so that one could go inside, "like going into a mill," one would not, he maintains, see "anything which would explain a perception."[6]

Leibniz uses this intuition pump to argue that perceiving occurs only in simple substances. But that Cartesian claim to one side, the thought experiment encourages thinking that we can never explain how anything about physical makeup could result in any qualitative state, let alone result in one mental quality rather than another. But Leibniz's claim that we would see nothing inside the machine that explains perception simply captures in an especially memorable way the view that the mental qualities that occur in perceiving are accessible only by way of consciousness.

The same holds for Frank Jackson's well-known thought experiment about Mary, the scientist who knows everything there is to know from a third-person point of view about visual mental qualities, but has never consciously experienced red.[7] According to Jackson, when Mary first consciously sees red, she learns something new, namely, what it's like for her to see red. If so, that new knowledge is presumably something about the mental quality that figures in her consciously seeing red, something she can, by hypothesis, know about only by way of consciousness.[8]

The ostensibly pretheoretic intuitions surveyed above all rest on the view, seldom explicitly articulated, that consciousness is our only source of knowledge about mental qualities. But that's not a pretheoretic intuition, but a theoretical claim about mental qualities, a claim that one might well contest. So the intuitions about quality inversion, zombies, the explanatory gap, and the hard problem, though at first sight they may seem independent of theory, all rest on a theoretical claim about mental qualities. Unless there is no alternative to theorizing about mental qualities in that way, those alleged intuitions cannot serve as data that any satisfactory theory must accommodate.

Recent work in so-called experimental philosophy has raised questions about the reliability of many ostensibly pretheoretic intuitions used to guide theorizing in philosophy, some relevant to issues about qualitative consciousness.[9] Much of this work convincingly suggests that these alleged intuitions are not actually endorsed by people who lack the relevant training in philosophy. And that suggests in turn that the alleged intuitions are often, or even always, induced by the adoption of a theoretical position.

It's not surprising that those of the folk innocent of philosophical debate fail to share many of the intuitions most cherished by those in philosophy and often regarded by them as beyond serious dispute. After all, there is substantial disparity even among those in philosophy about which intuitions to credit. And though endorsement of alleged intuitions typically matches theoretical proclivities, it's unclear whether intuitions influence theory or conversely. So it's likely that intuitions often follow substantive theoretical commitments, and are not theoretically neutral.

Perhaps the most significant contribution of experimental philosophy, then, is to underscore the likelihood that various intuitions are not theory neutral, but products of such theoretical commitments. If intuitions aren't widely shared by the folk and fit conveniently with theories espoused by those who invoke the intuitions, it's natural to ask whether the intuitions encapsulate those theories, rather than providing independent support.

But simply showing that the folk don't widely endorse those intuitions cannot by itself isolate the theoretical presuppositions that are likely to figure in forming the alleged folk intuitions. Nor can it settle whether the intuitions result from theoretical commitments or conversely. For that, we must examine the relation between intuitions and theory. It is that kind of consideration that provides reason to conclude that the intuitions most frequently invoked

in recent discussions of mental qualities and qualitative consciousness are not neutral data, but stem from positions taken in those debates. Those intuitions rest on an unsupported and optional theoretical position about how it's possible to know about mental qualities.

In what follows, I examine whether there is any alternative to the theoretical position that underlies those intuitions. I argue in §II that an alternative theoretical approach is available, and in §III I sketch a specific development of that approach. And in §IV I argue that the theory advanced in §III fits comfortably with an independently supported explanation of the way mental qualities occur in conscious qualitative states.

II. Two Concepts of Mental Quality

If we know about mental qualities only, or in the last instance, by way of first-person access, such knowledge will be immune to challenge. And there can then be no reason to think there's anything about mental qualities that we cannot know in that way. Holding that consciousness is the last word about mental qualities leads to what C.D. Broad aptly called the "curious superstition," that introspection "must give exhaustive and infallible information."[10]

Another consequence of adopting this view is that we will be able to say relatively little that's informative about the nature of mental qualities. Thus Ned Block's appeal, in saying what qualitative mental states are, to Louis Armstrong's remark about jazz: "If you gotta ask, you ain't never gonna get to know."[11] This echoes Justice Potter Stewart's famously uninformative remark about defining hard-core pornography: "I know it when I see it."[12]

Such epigrams are appealing in this context, since they vividly capture the idea that there's nothing more to know than what consciousness reveals.[13] But it raises a concern about whether it's all that clear what is being talked about, and the question of whether there might after all be something more informative to say about mental qualities. The conception of mental qualities that results from holding that consciousness is the only way we know about them is simply too thin to operate with.

One might suppose that we have no choice but to tolerate these uncomfortable consequences; after all, mental qualities are indisputably properties accessible by way of consciousness. But being accessible by way of consciousness does not by itself imply being accessible in that way only. And there is an alternative way of conceiving of mental qualities, based on another kind of access we have to them. We have access to mental qualities not only by way of consciousness, but also by way of their intimate and arguably essential role in perception. This second way of thinking about mental qualities provides an alternative to conceiving of them as accessible solely by way of consciousness.

I'll refer to theories on which we know about mental qualities only by way of consciousness as *consciousness based*, in contrast to *perceptual-role theories*, which appeal to the connection mental qualities have with perceiving. Perceptual-role theories don't deny the access consciousness gives us to mental qualities, but only that consciousness is the first and last word about their nature. The role mental qualities play in perceiving gives us, according to those theories, an alternative, independent route to learn about mental qualities.

On a perceptual-role theory, mental qualities are the properties in virtue of which we make perceptual discriminations. So independent of anything that consciousness tells us, if an individual's perceiving involves such discriminations, that individual is in mental states that have mental qualities that pertain to those discriminations. Perceiving provides a third-person way of determining what mental qualities occur, independent of the first-person access that consciousness delivers.

Might perceptual role and consciousness conflict about what mental qualities an individual's perceptual states exhibit? There is no guarantee that this would never happen. But that's the situation with all knowledge about things; we have alternative ways of knowing about things, which may sometimes conflict. The job of a good theory is in part to help adjudicate such conflicts when they arise.

I'll say more in §IV about possible conflicts between consciousness and perceptual role. For now it's worth noting a striking way in which the two types of theory differ. Perceiving is not always conscious. Perceiving can occur subliminally, as demonstrated in masked-priming experiments, in which an individual reports not seeing a stimulus that nonetheless affects that individual's subsequent mental processing. This effect on mental processing is taken to show that perceiving did occur, and the individual's denial of seeing the stimulus as evidence that the perceiving was not conscious.[14]

Perceiving that isn't conscious also occurs in blindsight, in which cortical damage to a region of primary visual cortex, area V1, results again in visual input that the affected individual denies any awareness of.[15] Visual acuity in blindsight is impaired, since it relies on neural pathways that bypass area V1. But there is strong reason to think that mental qualities occur in blindsight as well as in subliminal vision in intact individuals.[16] Some partial blindsight patients can spontaneously respond or attend to input in the affected field,[17] and an individual with complete destruction of area V1 can spontaneously navigate relying solely on visual input.[18]

Nonconscious mental qualities likely occur also in commonsense contexts. One may be awaiting somebody's arrival in a crowded room and, without having consciously noticed the person, suddenly cast one's gaze straight to where the person is standing. There must have been visual input that enables one to shift one's gaze straight to the person, and hence mental qualities relevant to perceiving that person. But since one didn't previously notice the person consciously, the mental qualities occurred without being conscious.

So if mental qualities are properties essential to perceptual discrimination, they sometimes occur without being conscious. Perceptual-role theories not only rely on access to mental qualities that's independent of consciousness; they rely on access to mental qualities in the absence of any consciousness of those qualities at all. On a consciousness-based theory, mental qualities have an essential tie to consciousness but not to perception; the opposite holds for perceptual-role theories, on which mental qualities have an essential tie to perception, but not consciousness.

One could simply dig one's heels in at this point and insist that if a mental state is not conscious, none of its mental properties are qualitative. It's now widely acknowledged that intentional states, such as thoughts, desires, expectations, wishes, and the like can occur without being conscious. But none of these states exhibits mental qualities. So one might maintain that mental states with only intentional properties can occur without being conscious, but not states with qualitative properties. Even Freud, who soundly rejected the traditional "equation . . . of what is conscious with what is mental,"[19] nonetheless insisted that "emotions, feelings and affects," that is, states with qualitative character, cannot occur without being conscious.[20]

But it's unclear what non-question-begging reason there could be to insist that states with mental quality cannot occur without being conscious. We count states that aren't conscious as nonetheless being intentional if there's good reason to describe them, as we do conscious intentional states, as having intentional properties, that is, content and mental attitude.[21] And perceptual role provides reason to describe the states that occur in perceiving as having mental quality whether or not the perceiving is conscious.

The mental quality of red occurs when one consciously sees something red under suitably standard conditions; so we can assume that the very same mental quality occurs when an individual subliminally sees a stimulus as being red. Indeed, priming evidence in laboratory settings often shows that an individual's nonconscious psychological processing distinguishes colors and other qualitative features of stimuli just as in conscious perceiving. There is every reason to conclude that mental qualities occur even when perceiving fails to be conscious.

Some might express puzzlement about what mental qualities could possibly be if they were to occur without being conscious. But this is just an expression of the consciousness-based view that access to mental qualities is solely by way of consciousness. On that view, we could in principle have no access to nonconscious mental qualities, and so no conception of them. But we cannot adopt the consciousness-based approach to mental qualities in evaluating the competing perceptual-role approach. We must evaluate each approach independent of any assumptions that rely on the other.

[. . .]

Consciousness-based objections to the perceptual-role approach to mental qualities will have no force without independent support. And we can't derive support for such objections from intuitions, such as the conceivability of inversion or zombies or the hard problem or explanatory gap, since they rely themselves on the consciousness-based approach to mental qualities. Nonetheless, there are reasonable concerns to raise about a perceptual-role theory. Is there any developed perceptual-role theory that taxonomizes mental qualities as well as a consciousness-based theory? And is such a theory independently defensible? In §III I'll sketch a perceptual-role theory that does taxonomize mental qualities in as accurate and fine-grained a way as any appeal to consciousness. And I'll argue that that theory fits comfortably with both empirical findings and our commonsense views about mental qualities and perceiving.

[…]

A perceptual-role theory need not do justice to the intuitions discussed in §I, since they rely on a consciousness-based approach. Still, a perceptual-role theory must in some way account for the way mental qualities do occur in conscious perceiving.

This is crucial. On a perceptual-role theory, mental qualities occur in both conscious and nonconscious perceiving, and they cannot on such a theory be intrinsically conscious. So a perceptual-role theory is unlikely by itself to be able to explain how it is that mental qualities sometimes occur consciously—why there is sometimes something it's like for one to be in states that exhibit mental qualities. But we can, it turns out, explain that by supplementing a perceptual-role theory with an independent theory of consciousness; that is the task of §IV.

III. Quality-Space Theory

In perceiving things, we discriminate among various perceptible properties. As already noted, such discriminations occur both consciously and not. We use vision to discriminate among colors and the spatial properties of visible size, shape, and location, audition to discriminate among pitches, timbres, and origins of sounds, and other sense modalities for perceptible properties special to those senses.

To discriminate among perceptible properties, a creature must be able to be in states that differ at least as finely as the perceptible properties being discriminated. And the relative differences among those states must reflect those among the perceptible properties. We can determine for any two properties a creature can perceive whether the creature can discriminate between them. And this allows us to construct a quality space in which the distance between any two perceptible properties is a function of how many properties between the two the creature can discriminate.[23]

The differences among the states in virtue of which the creature can perform these discriminations must reflect the differences among perceptible properties that the creature can discern. So the quality space that reflects the perceptible properties a creature can discriminate by a particular sense modality will also determine the perceptual states that make such discriminations possible. And if mental qualities play a role in perceiving, it's natural to identify them with the properties in virtue of which perceptual states differ. The quality space that captures the similarities and differences among the perceptible properties a creature can discriminate will also describe the mental qualities that figure in such discrimination. And this gives us an account of mental qualities in terms of the quality space that describes a creature's ability to discriminate.

Discrimination among the properties perceptible by a modality occurs even when the relevant perceptual states aren't conscious. So an account of mental qualities based on the quality spaces such discrimination determines does not require that the qualities occur consciously, and it does not therefore appeal in any way to first-person access to the qualities. Even when the mental qualities that figure in such discrimination are conscious, it is not their being conscious that enables such discrimination, but only the qualitative differences among them. And there is extensive evidence that individuals respond differentially to stimuli they're not consciously aware of.[24]

The use of such a quality space to describe the color properties perceptible by humans is standard, but the foregoing approach applies to every sensory modality. For any sense modality that discriminates among a range of perceptible properties, we can use matching or just noticeable differences to construct a quality space of all the discriminable properties in respect of how distant each is from every other. And that quality space of perceptible properties will also determine the mental qualities that enable such perceptual discriminations to be made.[25] This quality-space theory can account for the mental qualities special to any perceptual modality.

The quality spaces that describe the properties perceptible by each of the exteroceptive modalities, vision, audition, olfaction, gustation, and tactition, determine the corresponding mental qualities. But quality-space theory also applies to the spatial properties of size, shape, and location within a perceptual field that are accessible by each modality.[26] The position of each perceptible spatial property in a quality space is determined by its perceptual discriminability from similar properties, just as with color and the other so-called proper sensibles.[27] And because quality-space theory describes these spatial perceptible properties, it can do so for proprioception and kinesthetic sensation as well.

The spatial properties perceptible by different sensory modalities are of course the same; the physical shapes, sizes, and locations we perceive by sight are the same as those we perceive by touch. But the corresponding mental qualities are not. Vision determines spatial perceptible properties as boundaries of color, whereas tactition determines them as boundaries pertaining to perceptible pressure and texture. The mental qualities that pertain to spatial properties are special to each of the sense modalities.[28] Cross-modal calibration of the spatial properties discerned by each modality must be learned.[29]

Quality-space theory also handles the mental qualities that figure in bodily sensations, such as pain. Pains are distinguishable in respect of intensity, bodily location,[30] and whether they are burning, throbbing, dull, sharp, and so forth. All these variations correspond to differences in stimuli that standardly cause pains. So we can locate the mental qualities in virtue of which we discriminate among pains in a quality space constructed from matching or just noticeable differences among the relevant stimuli.

It's important to forestall a particular misunderstanding about quality-space theory. The consciousness-based approach to mental qualities holds that our only route to mental qualities is the way they are conscious. If that were so, the only way to establish a correspondence between a quality space of perceptible properties and that of mental qualities would be to compare the two spaces and note that they correspond.

But quality-space theory adopts instead the perceptual-role approach to mental qualities, and rejects the claim that we have only first-person access to mental qualities. So quality-space theory does not establish correspondence between the two spaces by comparing them. Rather, it extrapolates from the quality space of perceptible properties to determine the space of the corresponding mental qualities. The two spaces match because mental qualities are the properties of perceptions in virtue of which an individual can discriminate among the relevant perceptible properties.

The quality spaces relevant here don't rely on the physical properties of the stimuli, for example, on the wave-mechanical properties of light or sound. Such a space for color would be one-dimensional along the single parameter of wave length or, equivalently, frequency. The quality spaces that figure here reflect instead only the relative discriminability of the stimuli for a particular individual, perhaps averaged over members of a species, as in a quality space for humans generally. That requires for color a two-dimension space just to accommodate all perceptible chromaticities, that is, hues and saturations, and a three-dimensional space to accommodate brightness as well.[31]

Nor must the quality spaces for mental qualities reflect properties of the neural processes that subserve, or may even be identical with, those mental qualities. The relevant quality spaces reflect only the similarities and differences among mental qualities determined by a creature's ability to discriminate among various perceptible properties.

[...]

Quality-space theory taxonomizes mental qualities by their role in such discriminations. So the theory taxonomizes mental qualities at least as finely as any consciousness-based approach can. Consider distinguishing two mental qualities by the way they appear to consciousness. Whatever difference consciousness reveals will correspond to a difference between stimuli that those mental qualities could result from. Consciousness reveals no difference among mental qualities that doesn't correspond to a difference among perceptible stimuli.[36]

Indeed, quality-space theory taxonomizes mental qualities more finely than consciousness often does. On quality-space theory, the mental qualities that occur in perception differ in respect of the most fine-grained discrimina-tions an individual can make. Consciousness, by contrast, often fails to reveal such fine-grained differences; we seldom consciously discriminate between mental qualities as finely as we can.[37]

Quality-space theory taxonomizes mental qualities by relative location in a space constructed from an individual's ability to discriminate the corresponding perceptible properties. So if there were an axis with respect to which that quality space is symmetrical, it would be impossible to distinguish stimuli on one side of that axis from stimuli on the other. Quality-space theory would represent the properties on the two sides of the axis as indistinguishable. The qualities on one side of the axis would be redundant with respect to those on the other. But inversion around an axis would be undetectable only if that inversion preserved the relative locations of qualities on each side of the axis, and that could happen only if the space were symmetrical around the axis. So quality-space theory precludes undetectable inversion of mental qualities.

This is not surprising. The possibility of undetectable inversion rests on the consciousness-based approach to mental qualities, on which such qualities are accessible only by way of consciousness. A perceptual-role theory, by contrast, accommodates the occurrence of mental qualities in nonconscious perceiving, and thereby undermines any consciousness-based approach. So we can expect that no perceptual-role theory, such as quality-space theory, will accommodate undetectable inversion. And quality-space theory goes a step further in giving concrete reasons why such inversion is impossible.

But even if it's impossible, is it nonetheless conceivable? We can, it seems, conceive of many things that are not possible. But as noted in §I, the case for conceivability is weak. What's conceivable about some type of thing depends on what concept of that thing we're operating with. If our concept of mental qualities dictated accessibility only by way of consciousness, undetectable inversion would be conceivable, but not if that concept involves an essential tie with perceptual role, and hence a quality-space way of taxonomizing.

We can conceive of water's being a basic physical substance only given a highly impoverished concept of water. Similarly, undetectable inversion is conceivable only given a concept of mental qualities on which they have an essential tie to consciousness, but not to perceiving. Since mental qualities plainly do play a pivotal role in perceiving, that is arguably an impoverished concept of mental qualities. Indeed, the impoverished character of that concept is evident in the uninformative characterization, evoked by the Louis Armstrong's epigram, which a consciousness-based approach must give of mental qualities. There is little on such an approach to say about their nature. Undetectable inversion is conceivable only on such an impoverished concept.

Though undetectable inversion is precluded on quality-space theory, a related issue arises, which seems to present a problem. Quality-space theory describes mental qualities by location in a particular quality space. But suppose there are two types of perceptible property a creature can discriminate among, and the discriminations the creature can make among qualities of each type define indistinguishable quality spaces. Suppose, for example, that the perceptible colors and sounds a creature can distinguish determined indistinguishable quality spaces. If there is nothing to mental qualities but location in a quality space, the mental qualities in the visual space would be identical with those in the auditory space.

One way out would be to stipulate that quality-space theory precludes a creature from having two indistinguishable quality spaces.

That's not altogether unreasonable; it seems independently unlikely that the perceptible differences among distinct types of stimulus would be the same. And perhaps that's good enough.[38] But rather than let the theory be held hostage to empirical findings, we can just add a condition for taxonomizing mental qualities. We can supplement location in a quality space by the dependence of the mental qualities in question on the operation of a particular sensory modality. Since quality-space theory is a type of perceptual-role theory, appeal to role in a particular modality is wholly within the spirit of the theory.

The appeal to perceptual role not only undermines the intuition about undetectable quality inversion; it also undercuts the conceivability of zombies and claims of an explanatory gap or a hard problem. Quality-space theory helps take that a step further. If mental qualities are defined by a quality-space constructed from a creature's discriminative ability with a range of perceptible properties, zombies are neither possible nor conceivable. Any creature that can discriminate in the relevant ways will be in states that exhibit mental qualities.

The hard problem concerns the apparent difficulty in saying why a particular neural occurrence should subserve the mental qualities it does, or indeed any at all. The difficulty in explaining these things allegedly results in an explanatory gap. But on quality-space theory, there is no difficulty. Each neural occurrence subserves the mental quality it does because of its role in the discrimination of the relevant perceptible properties.

But these consequences of quality-space theory arguably miss the point. The mental qualities that quality-space theory determines occur without being conscious. And all the intuitions about inversion, zombies, the hard problem, and the explanatory gap pertain just to conscious mental qualities. So to see whether quality-space theory tells against those intuitions, we must consider mental qualities in their conscious form. And that requires addressing the more general concern about whether quality-space theory can, supplemented by another theory, account for there being something it's like for one to be in conscious qualitative states.

IV. Higher-Order Awareness

Arguments for theories of consciousness typically appeal to the phenomenological appearances. Any theory of consciousness must of course save those appearances, but saving the appearances need not involve taking those appearances to exhaust the relevant mental reality.

The consciousness of mental states is mental appearance; it is the way one's mental life subjectively appears to one. But appearances can be inaccurate, no less with the mental than in any other realm. A consciousness-based theory suggests otherwise; if we know about mental qualities only by way of what consciousness reveals, perhaps there is after all nothing to mental reality beyond mental appearance.[39] But we need not acquiesce in the dictates of consciousness-based theories, since a tenable perceptual-role alternative is available.

There are, moreover, disadvantages to consciousness-based theories when it comes to explaining consciousness. Identifying mental reality with the mental appearance that consciousness delivers results in a stipulative exclusion of the nonconscious mental states that occur, for example, in subliminal perception and blindsight. And by ruling that mental states are all conscious, it likely precludes explaining what that consciousness consists in and why mental states are sometimes conscious, since an explanation that appeals only to conscious mentality would be uninformative.

[...]

When a mental state is conscious, one is aware of being in that state. One can report that one is in the state, and say something about its mental character. By contrast, when we have evidence that somebody is in a mental state but that individual is unaware of being in it and denies that it occurs, we have evidence that the mental state that individual is in is not conscious. No state of which an individual is wholly unaware, and so cannot report, is conscious.

These considerations provide a necessary condition for a state to be conscious: A mental state is conscious if one is aware of that state, more precisely, if one is aware of oneself as being in the state. The more precise formulation is important, since it's unclear what it would be simply to be aware of a token state independently being aware of it as a state of some individual. And the individual that figures in a mental state's being conscious is plainly oneself. The more precise formulation will, moreover, turn out to be useful in what follows.

I've argued elsewhere[40] that the way one is aware of a state when that state is conscious consists in having a thought to the effect that one is in that state. Our awareness of conscious states seems subjectively to be unmediated and direct, and we can explain that by stipulating that these higher-order thoughts do not themselves seem subjectively to rely on any conscious inference or observation. And we can explain why we are rarely aware of these higher-order thoughts; that would require a third-order thought about a second-order thought, and we can assume that these seldom occur. Invoking higher-order thoughts explains, moreover, the connection between consciousness and reportability, since reporting a state means verbally expressing a thought that one is in that state. Still, the specific way we are aware of our conscious states will not matter in what follows; so I won't speak in what follows of higher-order thoughts, but in a more generic way of *higher-order awarenesses* (*HOAs*).

If one is not in any way aware of a mental quality, there is nothing it's like for one to be in a state that exhibits that mental quality. There being something it's like for one to be in a qualitative state is due to the HOA in virtue of which one is aware of that state. Qualitative states, moreover, are conscious in respect of the mental qualities they exhibit. So the HOA in virtue of which one is aware of a qualitative state must represent that state as having the relevant mental qualities. And since mental qualities are taxonomized by location in a suitable quality space, HOAs must represent them in respect of such locations. When qualitative states are conscious, one is aware of their distinctive mental qualities in terms of the location those qualities have in a suitable quality space.

There is evidence, independent of quality-space theory and a higher-order theory of consciousness, that this is so. It's well-known that we can identify and distinguish mental qualities that occur together much more finely than we can when the mental qualities occur in temporal succession.[41] This finding is commonly presented in connection with color qualities; one can discriminate mental qualities of similar shades in far finer grain if they occur together than one after the other. But the effect occurs with other modalities as well.[42]

[...]

The result about simultaneous and successive occurrence will seem odd if one assumes that mental qualities are intrinsic properties of qualitative states; comparing the qualities would then make no difference to how they seem to one. But if quality-space theory is right, and mental qualities are taxonomized in respect not of their intrinsic nature, but rather their relative location in a quality space,

the result is to be expected. Fine-grained differences among mental qualities will then be a relative matter, and our awareness of them will follow suit. The effect about simultaneous and successive occurrence follows from the comparative nature of mental qualities and our awareness of them.[44]

[...]

Many theorists have held that consciousness is intrinsic to mental qualities, and that it can't be wrong. These claims are natural on a consciousness-based theory. The best explanation of our having access to mental qualities only by way of consciousness is that consciousness is intrinsic to those qualities, and nothing could then contest what consciousness tells us about them.

But we can readily explain the subjective appearance that consciousness is intrinsic to mental qualities and the last word about them on a HOA theory of consciousness. The HOA is seldom itself a conscious state; to be so, there would have to be a third-order awareness of the HOA. So when a qualitative state is conscious, one is subjectively aware only of a single state, and one's awareness of it seems not to be a matter of a distinct state, but to be intrinsic to the state one is aware of. And even though there are third-person considerations that may force an adjustment of what consciousness tells one about one's mental qualities, there are no first-person considerations apart from consciousness itself. So it seems subjectively as though consciousness is the last word about mental qualities.

The HOA in virtue of which one is aware of a qualitative state when it's conscious is independent of that qualitative state. Otherwise it would be difficult to explain how qualitative states can occur consciously at one time and at another time not.[45] So the combined HOA and quality-space theory allows for one to be aware of a qualitative state inaccurately, as exhibiting a mental quality distinct from the quality it actually has. Indeed, the HOA might even make one aware of oneself as being in a qualitative state that one isn't in at all.

There are mundane types of inaccuracy, as when one is aware of a mental color quality simply as a generic red, for example, and not as the specific shade of red that it is. But more dramatic inaccuracy will presumably be rare, since inaccurate awareness of one's own mental states would occasion a measure of cognitive dissonance. If a HOA awareness of a green sensation occurs in connection with a sensation of red, the sensations and HOA will exert conflicting psychological pulls, and we can expect well-ordered psychological functioning to make such occurrences rare.

Subjectively, it seems as though an inaccurate HOA never occurs. But we have nothing to go on subjectively except the way we're aware of mental qualities; so subjective phenomenological appearances can't help in determining whether those appearances themselves are occasionally inaccurate.

And there is evidence that inaccurate HOAs do sometimes occur. Change blindness is the somewhat surprising tendency of people not to consciously notice salient changes in their visual fields. John Grimes demonstrated change blindness by relying on changes that occur during the eyes' saccadic movements. No retinal signal reaches primary visual cortex during saccades, and using eye trackers Grimes had changes occur during saccades. One particular striking result involved a salient shift in the color of a parrot between red and green, which 18% of participants failed to detect. Attention doesn't figure, since the parrot is the central object in the presentation, occupying over 25% of the screen. Similarly for many other switches of visible properties.[46]

What occurs subjectively for participants that fail to detect the change? The parrot starts being red, and changes to green. Since the stimulus is green, green is projecting from the retina to primary visual cortex. So we can assume that a mental quality of green occurs in the participant. But when that change isn't detected, the subjective experience of such a participant continues to be that of seeing red. So the HOA is unchanged from the initial HOA, when the awareness was of a mental quality of red; otherwise the participant would consciously detect the change in color. So when a participant fails consciously to detect that the parrot has changed to green, there is a mental quality of green but a HOA of the relevant mental color quality as being of red. Subjective consciousness cannot reveal such a disparity between mental quality and HOA, but experimental tests can.

How about the possibility of a HOA without any relevant mental quality at all?[47] It's sometimes urged that such a case would pose a problem about what the conscious state is. Suppose I have a HOA of a red sensation and there's no relevant sensation. On the HOA theory, the conscious state is the state I'm conscious of; but that state doesn't exist. And the HOA can't, in most cases at least, be the conscious state, since we're rarely aware of our HOAs. There seems at first sight to be nothing reasonable to say about what the conscious state would be in such a case.

But as noted earlier, the HOA is not simply an awareness of a state; it's an awareness of oneself as being in a state. When one isn't actually in the relevant state, that's still the way it seems to one subjectively; one's phenomenological appearance is that one is in that state. The conscious state is the state one is subjectively aware of oneself as being in, whether or not that state actually occurs. Just as something need not exist for it to be an object of one's thoughts, so a state need not occur in order to be a conscious state, that is, a state one is conscious of oneself as being in.

Consciousness is mental appearance; it is the way one's mental life appears to one. So it is natural to regard as conscious a state one appears phenomenologically to be in, whether or not one is actually in that state. There is no special problem about a HOA that occurs without any relevant mental target.

As noted at the end of §III, quality inversion, zombies, the hard problem, and the explanatory gap all concern mental qualities when they occur consciously, not when they occur without being conscious. How do those things fare given quality-space theory supplemented by a HOA theory of consciousness?

Quality spaces cannot be symmetrical around any axis without making it impossible to distinguish qualities on one side of the axis from qualities on the other. And HOAs make one aware of mental qualities in respect of their relative position in the relevant quality space. So that lack of symmetry carries over to the way the HOAs make us aware of mental qualities. Undetectable quality inversion is accordingly no more possible for conscious than for nonconscious mental qualities. Since a consciousness-based concept of mental qualities cannot accommodate subliminal perceiving, quality-space theory and a HOA theory of consciousness likely reflect our commonsense, folk concept of conscious qualities. So on that concept, undetectable inversion of conscious mental qualities is also not conceivable.

Mental qualities are detectable by way of their role in perceiving, though it's not obvious that there need be any perceptual impairment due simply to mental qualities' not being conscious.[48] But if an individual reports mental qualities in a way that does not so far as we can determine rely on conscious inference or self-observation, that indicates that the individual has HOAs in virtue of which those mental qualities are conscious. So the undetectable absence of conscious mental qualities characteristic of zombies is not possible. And if quality-space theory and a HOA theory of consciousness does capture our commonsense, folk concept of conscious mental qualities, undetectable absence of conscious qualities will not even be conceivable.

Can we explain why a particular neural state should subserve one conscious quality rather than another, or any at all? The roles the neural states play in perceiving enable us to explain why particular neural states subserve the mental qualities they do independent of consciousness. Similarly, the neural states that subserve HOAs result in there being something it's like for one to be in particular types of qualitative state because those neural states subserve awareness of being in those states. Contrary to claims of a hard problem and an explanatory gap, there is no difficulty explaining why particular neural states subserve the conscious mental qualities they do.

Rejecting the unargued and unwarranted assumption that we have access to mental qualities only by way of consciousness makes room for an informative quality-space theory of mental qualities. Combining that theory with a HOA theory of consciousness explains how some mental qualities come to be conscious, and does justice to both our folk conceptions of conscious mental qualities and relevant experimental findings.

Notes

1. E.g., Sydney Shoemaker: "The Inverted Spectrum," in Shoemaker, *Identity, Cause, and Mind: Philosophical Essays*, 2nd edn., Oxford: Clarendon Press, 2003, 327–57, p. 336, and "Intrasubjective/Intersubjective," in Shoemaker, *The First-Person Perspective and Other Essays*, Cambridge and New York: Cambridge University Press, 1996, 141–54, p. 150.

There is debate about whether conceivability is weaker than possibility, or perhaps coincides with it. See, e.g., David J. Chalmers, "Does Conceivability Entail Possibility?," in *Conceivability and Possibility*, ed. Tamar Szabó Gendler and John Hawthorne, Oxford: Clarendon Press, 2002, 145–200. I'll assume for present purposes that conceivability is indeed weaker.

2. *The Conscious Mind: In Search of a Fundamental Theory*, New York: Oxford University Press, 1996, 94.

3. "On Leaving Our What It's Like," in *Consciousness: Psychological and Philosophical Essays*, ed. Martin Davies and Glyn W. Humphreys (Oxford: Basil Blackwell, 1993), pp. 121–36; reprinted in Ned Block, Owen Flanagan, and Güven Güzeldere, eds., *The Nature of Consciousness: Philosophical Debates*, Cambridge, Massachusetts: MIT Press/Bradford Books, 1997, pp. 543–55, 548; page references below are to Block et al.

4. "Facing Up to the Problem of Consciousness," *Journal of Consciousness Studies*, 2, 3 (1995): 200–19; "The Puzzle of Conscious Experience," *Scientific American*, 237, 6 (December 1995): 62–68; *The Conscious Mind*, xii.

5. Indeed, Levine himself notes that the explanatory gap is of a piece with the conceivability of zombies, something he also endorses. *Purple Haze: The Puzzle of Consciousness*, New York: Oxford University Press, 2001, 79.

6. Gottfried Wilhelm Leibniz, Monadology, tr. George MacDonald Ross, available at http://www.philosophy.leeds.ac.uk/GMR/moneth/monadology.html, §17.

7. "What Mary Didn't Know," *The Journal of Philosophy* LXXXIII, 5 (May 1986): 291–95.

8. It's arguable that whenever there is knowledge that we describe using a 'wh' nominal, such as 'what it's like for one,' that knowledge must be sustained by specific knowledge that something is the case. We can't know what or where something is, e.g., unless we know that it is a particular thing or at a particular place. Even learning who somebody is by acquaintance yields some new descriptive information. But it's unclear what new knowledge Mary could gain that would be describable with a 'that' clause. And if there is none, her new knowledge might be nothing more than the circumstance of Mary's first consciously experiencing something that's red.

9. Among the work that is relevant to mental qualities, see Justin Sytsma and Edouard Machery, "How to Study Folk Intuitions about Phenomenal Consciousness," *Philosophical Psychology*, 22, 1 (2009): 21–35; Bryce Huebner, Michael Bruno, and Hagop Sarkissian, "What Does the Nation of China Think about Phenomenal States?," *Review of Philosophy and Psychology*, [1(2) (2009): 225–43]; Justin Sytsma and Edouard Machery, "Two Conceptions of Subjective Experience," *Philosophical Studies*, [151 (2): (2010) 299–327]; and Bryce Huebner, "Commonsense Concepts of Phenomenal Consciousness: Does Anyone Care about Functional Zombies?," *Phenomenology and the Cognitive Sciences*, [9 (1) (2010): 133–55].

10. *The Mind and Its Place in Nature*, London: Routledge & Kegan Paul, 1925, p. 284.

11. Block writes: "You ask: What is it that philosophers have called qualitative states? I answer, only half in jest: As Louis Armstrong said when asked what jazz is, 'If you got to ask, you ain't never gonna get to know.'" "Troubles with functionalism," in *Minnesota Studies in the Philosophy of Science*, IX, ed. C. Wade Savage, Minneapolis: University of Minnesota Press, 1978, widely reprinted, §1.3.

Block's move is endorsed, without the quasi-qualification, by Galen Strawson, "Realistic Monism: Why Physicalism Entails Panpsychism," *Journal of Consciousness Studies*, 13, 10–11 (October–November 2006): 117–28, n. 6; reprinted in *Consciousness and Its Place in Nature: Why Physicalism Entails Panpsychism*, Galen Strawson et al., ed. Anthony Freeman, Thorverton, UK: Imprint Academic, 2006, pp. 117–28.

12. *Jacobellis v. Ohio*, 378 U.S. 184 (1964) (Stewart, J., concurring) (discussing possible obscenity in "The Lovers").

13. Recall the difficulty (n. 8) in saying just what it is that Jackson's Mary might learn on first consciously seeing red. Presumably she learns what it's like for her consciously to see red. But learning 'wh' implies learning that something is the case, and it's unclear how Mary could indicate descriptively what new thing she has learned.

14. E.g., Anthony J. Marcel, "Conscious and Unconscious Perception: Experiments on Visual Masking and Word Recognition," *Cognitive Psychology* 15, 2 (April 1983): 197–237, and "Conscious and Unconscious Perception: An Approach to the Relations between Phenomenal Experience and Perceptual Processes," *Cognitive Psychology* 15, 2 (April 1983): 238–300; Bruno G. Breitmeyer and Haluk Öğmen, *Visual Masking: Time Slices through Conscious and Unconscious Vision*, 2nd edn., New York: Oxford University Press, 2006; and Haluk Öğmen and Bruno G. Breitmeyer, eds., *The First Half Second: The Microgenesis and Temporal Dynamics of Unconscious and Conscious Visual Processes*, Cambridge, Massachusetts: MIT Press, 2006.

15. E.g., Lawrence Weiskrantz, *Blindsight: A Case Study and Implications*, new edition, Oxford: Clarendon Press, 1998; *Consciousness Lost and Found: A Neuropsychological Exploration*, Oxford: Oxford University Press, 1997; and "Unconscious Vision: The Strange Phenomenon of Blindsight," *The Sciences* 32, 5 (September/October 1992): 22–28.

16. See, e.g., Weiskrantz, "Pupillary Responses With and Without Awareness in Blindsight," *Consciousness and Cognition* 7, 3 (September 1998): 324–26.

17. James Danckert and Yves Rossetti, "Blindsight in Action: What Does Blindsight Tell Us about the Control of Visually Guided Actions?," *Neuroscience and Biobehavioural Reviews*, 29, 7 (2005): 1035–46.

18. Beatrice de Gelder, Marco Tamietto, Geert van Boxtel, Rainer Goebel, Arash Sahraie, Jan van den Stock, Bernard M.C. Stienen, Lawrence Weiskrantz, and Alan Pegna, "Intact Navigation Skills after Bilateral Loss of Striate Cortex," Current Biology, 18, 24 (December 23, 2008): R1128–R1129. It's likely that total blindsight results in pressure to make us aware of blindsight input, as in the prodigious vision-based behavior of an early blindsight monkey (Nicholas Humphrey, Consciousness Regained, Oxford: Oxford University Press, 1983, 38, 19–20).

Also of considerable interest in this connection is Petra Stoerig, "Cueless Blindsight," *Frontiers in Human Neuroscience*, 3, 74 (January 2010): 1–8.

19. "The Unconscious" in *The Complete Psychological Works of Sigmund Freud* (henceforth S.E.), tr. and ed. James Strachey, London: The Hogarth Press, 1966–74, XIV: 166–215, p. 167.

20. "The Unconscious," 177–78; also, e.g., *The Ego and the Id*, S.E., XIX: 3–68, pp. 22–23, and *An Outline of Psychoanalysis*, S.E., XXIII, p. 197. To describe feelings as unconscious, he maintained, is to "speak in

a condensed and not entirely correct manner" (*The Ego and the Id*, 22) about cases in which the representational character of the feelings is repressed or misrepresented.

21. Again Freud: "[A]ll the categories which we employ to describe conscious mental acts [i.e., intentional states]...can be applied" equally well to various states that aren't conscious ("The Unconscious," 168).

[...]

23. Even apart from masked priming, nonconscious discrimination occurs in so-called statistical learning (e.g., Nicholas B. Turk-Browne, Justin Jungé, and Brian J. Scholl, "The Automaticity of Visual Statistical Learning," *Journal of Experimental Psychology*: General, 134, 4 [November 2005]: 552–64, and Gustav Kuhn and Zoltán Dienes, "Learning Non-local Dependencies," *The Quarterly Journal of Experimental Psychology*, 61, 4 [April 2008]: 601–24), as well other paradigms (e.g., Bruno Berberian, Stephanie Chambaron-Ginhaca, and Axel Cleeremans, "Action Blindness in Response to Gradual Changes," *Consciousness and Cognition*, 19, 1 [March 2010]: 152–71).

24. For an example of empirical work that sustains such a quality-space approach for olfaction, see James D. Howard, Jane Plailly, Marcus Grueschow, John-Dylan Haynes, and Jay A. Gottfried, "Odor Quality Coding and Categorization in Human Posterior Piriform Cortex," *Nature Neuroscience*, 12, 7 (July 2009): 932–38.

25. See, e.g., my *Consciousness and Mind*, Oxford: Clarendon Press, 2005, pp. 198–201, 206, and 222, and "Color, Mental Location, and the Visual Field," *Consciousness and Cognition*, 10, 1 (March 2001): 85–93; and Douglas B. Meehan, "Spatial Experience, Sensory Qualities, and the Visual

Field," in *Proceedings of the Twenty-Third Annual Conference of the Cognitive Science Society*, ed. Johanna D. Moore and Keith Stenning, Mahwah, NJ: Erlbaum, 2001, 623–27, and "Qualitative Character and Sensory Representation," *Consciousness and Cognition*, 11, 4 (December 2002): 630–41.

26. I.e., perceptible properties accessible only by one modality; Aristotle, e.g., *de Anima*, II.6, 418a11.

27. Aristotle held that they are the same. But he inferred that because he held that perceiving consists of the organism's literally taking on the perceptible properties of the object (*de Anima* II.5 418a4, II.11 423b31, II.12 424a18, III.2 425b23). On that view, mental qualities are literally identical with the corresponding perceptible properties; so since perceived spatial properties are the same across modalities, the corresponding mental qualities would be as well.

28. Most experimental work is done with older infants, in which some learning may already have occurred; for work on very young infants, see Kathleen W. Brown and Allen W. Gottfried, "Cross-model Transfer of Shape in Early Infancy: Is There Reliable Evidence?," *Advances in Infancy Research*, 4, 1986: 163–70, 240–45. But see also Susan A. Rose and Esther K. Orlian, "Asymmetries in Infant Cross-Modal Transfer," *Child Development*, 62, 4 (August 1991): 706–18.

Andrew N. Meltzoff tested one-month-old infants on two types of pacifiers, both spherical in shape but one with eight or so small protuberances, and concluded that they already associate tactile with visible shapes without prior learning. "Molyneux's Babies: Cross-Modal Perception, Imitation and the Mind of the Preverbal Infant," in *Spatial Representation: Problems in Philosophy and Psychology*, ed. Naomi Eilan, Rosaleen McCarthy, and Bill Brewer, Oxford: Blackwell Publishers, 1993, pp. 219–35. But Meltzoff's dismissal of prior learning at one month is unfounded, since the small protuberances have roughly the shape of tiny nipples, with which one-month-olds will have had extensive, salient experience, both visual and tactile.

29. See my "Consciousness, the Self, and Bodily Location," *Analysis*, 70, 1 (April 2010).

30. The 1931 International Commission on Illumination (CIE) chromaticity diagram, widely available online, is still relatively standard for the former; there are a variety of ways to incorporate brightness into a three-dimensional space.

31. "The Intrinsic Quality of Experience," *Philosophical Perspectives* IV (1990): 31–52, p. 39. Harman also argues there that such experiences have no qualitative properties that we're aware of, which I'll contest in §IV.

    Block uses the idea of mental paint to argue for his view that there is an aspect of phenomenal character that outstrips representational content ("Mental Paint"; see also Block, "Attention and Mental Paint," *Philosophical Issues*, [20 1 (2010): 23–63]).

[...]

36. Indeed, it's likely that quality-space theory will individuate mental qualities even more finely than a consciousness-based theory could, since it's likely that subliminal perception sometimes draws qualitative distinctions unavailable to conscious perception.

37. It's even possible that subliminal perception sometimes draws qualitative distinctions that outstrip an individual's ability to discriminate consciously among mental quali-

ties. But it's difficult to test the fineness of subliminal discrimination, since subliminal perceiving typically results from somewhat weaker neural signal strength. Still, there is some evidence of exceptionally fine-grained nonconscious vision; see Bruno G. Breitmeyer, Tony Ro, Neel S. Singhal, "Unconscious Color Priming Occurs at Stimulus—Not Percept-Dependent Levels of Processing," *Psychological Science*, 15, 3 (May 2004): 198–202; Bruno G. Breitmeyer, Tony Ro, Haluk Öğmen, Steven Todd, "Unconscious, Stimulus-Dependent Priming and Conscious, Percept-Dependent Priming with Chromatic Stimuli," *Perception and Psychophysics*, 69, 4 (May 2007): 550–57.

    Still, see Tony Ro, Neel S. Singhal, Bruno G. Breitmeyer, and Javier O. Garcia, "Unconscious Processing of Color and Form in Metacontrast Masking," *Attention, Perception, and Psychophysics*, 71, 1 (January 2009): 95–103, and Bruno Berberian, Stephanie Chambaron-Ginhaca, and Axel Cleeremans, "Action Blindness in Response to Gradual Changes," *Consciousness and Cognition*, 19, 1 (March 2010): 152–71, for suggestive findings.

38. The mental qualities that pertain to spatial perceptible properties would not tell against that move. Even though the quality spaces for spatial mental qualities might be the same for distinct modalities, spatial mental qualities are tied to nonspatial mental qualities, such as those that pertain to color and pressure. And the connection with quality spaces that define those nonspatial mental qualities would differentiate the spatial qualities.

39. As Thomas Nagel, e.g., maintains; "What Is It Like to Be a Bat?," *The Philosophical Review* LXXXIII, 4 (October 1974): 435–50, p. 444.

40. E.g., *Consciousness and Mind.*

41. E.g., Rita M. Halsey and Alphonse Chapanis, "On the Number of Absolutely Identifiable Spectral Hues," *Journal of the Optical Society of America*, 41 (1951): 1057–58, and Joaquín Pérez-Carpinell, Rosa Baldoví, M. Dolores de Fez, José Castro, "Color Memory Matching: Time Effect and Other Factors," *Color Research and Application*, 23, 4 (August 1998): 234–47. For additional references and discussion, see Diana Raffman, "On the Persistence of Phenomenology," in *Conscious Experience*, ed. Thomas Metzinger, Exeter, UK: Imprint Academic, 1995, pp. 293–308.

42. Edward M. Burns and W. Dixon Ward, "Intervals, Scales, and Tuning," in *The Psychology of Music*, ed. Diana Deutsch, New York: Academic Press, 1982. See Raffman for other results.

[...]

44. Thomas Metzinger has argued that the memory constraint undermines any version of a HOA theory on which the HOA is conceptual, as on my higher-order-thought theory. He infers that if memory can't capture the fine-grained differences among mental qualities, those differences can't be captured conceptually. *Being No One: The Self-Model Theory of Subjectivity*, Cambridge, MA: The MIT Press/A Bradford Book, 2003, 70.

It's not obvious that limitations of memory reflect conceptual limitations. But that aside, there need not be concepts for every distinct mental quality, since individuating them often depends on comparative concepts.

45. Uriah Kriegel (e.g., *Subjective Consciousness: A Self-Representational Theory*, Oxford: Oxford University Press, 2009) and Rocco Gennaro (e.g., *Consciousness and Self-Consciousness: A Defense of the Higher-Order Thought Theory of Consciousness*, John Benjamins Publishers, 1996) have advanced higher-order theories on which the higher-order content is intrinsic to the conscious states themselves. Such theories face difficulties, such as evidence that the onset of qualitative states occurs before they become conscious (e.g., Benjamin Libet, *Mind Time: The Temporal Factor in Consciousness*, Cambridge, MA: Harvard University Press, 2004, ch. 2, and "Neuronal vs. Subjective Timing, for a Conscious Sensory Experience," in *Cerebral Correlates of Conscious Experience*, ed. Pierre A. Buser and Arlette Rougeul-Buser, Amsterdam and New York: North Holland, 1978, 69–82).

In any case, the issues discussed here arguably also arise for such intrinsicalist higher-order theories.

46. "On the Failure to Detect Changes in Scenes across Saccades," *Perception*, ed. Kathleen Akins, New York: Oxford University Press, 1996, pp. 89–110.

47. The line separating disparity between HOA and mental quality and HOA without any relevant mental quality is somewhat arbitrary. If one has a sensation of red and is aware of oneself as having a sensation of green, is one aware inaccurately of that sensation of red? Or is one aware of oneself as having a sensation of green that one does not actually have? But that issue won't matter for present purposes.

48. Perceptual states that fail to be conscious often are also perceptually impaired, but not always (see n. 37). When perceptual impairment and failure to be conscious do co-occur, they likely aren't directly connected, but rather result from a single cause, such as low neural signal strength.

So even when perceptual acuity is unimpaired, other factors may prevent formation of a HOA, and so block consciousness.

This raises the question whether there is any utility to a qualitative state's being conscious. For parallel doubts about the utility of intentional states' being conscious, see my "Consciousness and Its Function," *Neuropsychologia* 46, 3 (2008): 829–40.

KATHLEEN A. AKINS

"A Bat without Qualities?"

The Bird's Eye View

The other day in a physiology seminar we were discussing the effect of retinal foveation on visual perception. The fovea is a small portion of the retina densely packed with receptor cells—a density that makes possible those visual tasks that require high spatial resolution, the identification of shape and texture, accurate depth perception and so on. The fovea, however, can 'see' only a small part of the entire visual field. So, much like directing a telescope across the night sky, foveated creatures move their eyes—shifting the 'interesting' parts of the scene in and out of the foveal area. This is why we, but not rabbits, move our eyes about.

Enter the eagle—or, rather, birds of prey in general. They too have foveated eyes, but eyes with even better spatial resolution than our own. The African vulture, for example, can discern live prey from dead at an elevation of 3,000–4,000 metres, an elevation at which it is difficult for us even to sight the bird (Duke-Elder, 1958). Eagles, too, have high resolution foveae. Because they dive for the ground at speeds greater than 200 mph, their eyes must be capable of extremely accurate depth perception. Indeed, given the broad range of visual information that an eagle makes use of in its behaviour, the evolutionary 'solution' was the development of *two* circular foveae connected together by a horizontal band of densely packed receptor cells (think here of the shape of a barbell). The horizontal band serves to scan the horizon. The central fovea, like those of most birds, looks to either side, each one (in the left and right eyes) taking in a different part of the world. Finally, the eagle has an extra pair of (temporal) foveae pointing forward, converging on a shared field—a foveal pair much the same as our own except with three times the density of receptor cells (Duke-Elder, 1958). It is this forward-looking foveal region that provides the high spatial resolution. Attending to the scene below via the temporal fovea, eagles spot their prey and dive at fantastic speeds, pulling up at exactly the right instant.

But therein lies a mystery, I thought, the mystery of the 'eagle's eye' view. Given two foveal areas and a horizontal band, how does an eagle 'attend to' a scene, look at the world? What does that mean and, more interestingly, what would that be like? Here, in my mind's eye, I imagined myself perched high in the top of a dead tree sporting a pair of very peculiar bifocal spectacles. More precisely, I pictured myself in a pair of quadra-focals, with different lenses corresponding to the horizontal band, foveal and peripheral regions of the eagle's eye. I wonder whether it is just like that, I thought, like peering successively through each lens, watching the world move in and out of focus depending upon where I look. First I stare through the horizontal section and scan the horizon for other predators; then I switch to my left central lens and make sure no one is approaching from behind; then I use the high-powered temporal lens to scrutinize the water below for the shadows of some dinner. Is that how the world looks to an eagle?, I wondered. Is that what it is like to have two foveae?

The Problem: Nagel's Claim and Its Intuitive Basis

In 'What Is It Like to Be a Bat?' (1974), Thomas Nagel made the claim that science would not, and indeed, could not, give us an answer to these kinds of questions. When all of science is done and said—when a completed neuroscience has told us 'everything physical there is to tell' Oackson, 1982, p. 127)—we will still not understand the experiences of an 'essentially alien' organism. It will not matter that we have in hand the finer and grosser details of neuroanatomy, neurophysiology and hence, the functional characterization of the system at various levels of complexity—nor will the 'completed' set of psychophysics provide us with the essential interpretative tool. For all of neuroscience, something would be missed—what it is like to be a particular creature, what it is like *for* the bat or the eagle.

There are many reasons, I think, both intuitive and theoretical, why Nagel's claims about the limits of scientific explanation have seemed so plausible. Nagel himself, for example, argued for this conclusion by appeal to a theoretic notion, that of a point of view. Phenomenal experience, he said, is necessarily an experience from a particular point of view, hence the facts of experience are essentially subjective in nature. On the other hand, the kinds of phenomena that science seeks to explain are essentially objective, or viewer independent—'the kind [of facts] that can be observed and understood from many points of view and by individuals with differing perceptual systems' (Nagel, 1974, p. 145). So any attempt to understand the experience of an alien creature by appeal to scientific facts (facts about his behaviour and internal computational/physiological processes) will only serve to distance us from the very property we seek to explain: the subjectivity of phenomenal experience. Or so Nagel argued. Nagel's conclusion was that the only possible access one could have to the phenomenal experience of another organism is by means of a kind of empathetic projection—by extrapolation from one's case, we can ascribe similar experiences to other subjects. Needless to say, this is a process that will work well enough given a suitably 'like-minded' organism (such as another person) but which will be entirely inadequate for understanding the point of view of more alien creatures. Hence, given only empathetic means, said Nagel, we cannot know the nature of a bat's phenomenal experience.

Nagel's argument, like those of a number of other philosophers (for example, see McGinn, 1983), makes use of a variety of theoretic tenets—about the objectivity of scientific facts, the subjectivity of experience and about the nature of a point of view. In the usual case, such arguments hinge upon a claim that 'you can't get from there to here'—that there is no route from the objective to the subjective, from the non-intentional to the intentional, from the sub-personal to the personal, and so on—even given all of the resources of the natural sciences. These are views that must be addressed,

I think, by argument, each in its own right or, better, met by a demonstration that the dichotomy at issue can in fact be bridged by scientific insight. Rather than address here these theoretic concerns, about subjectivity, point of view and so on, I want to look instead at the *intuitive* pull towards Nagel's conclusion—why most of us harbour that nagging suspicion that science must fail, that it cannot tell us what we want to know. This is the intuition that science will necessarily omit the one essential element of phenomenal experience, namely its very 'feel.'

The unfortunate fact of the matter, I think, is that these negative intuitions are well grounded in our everyday experiences. We have all faced the difficulty of trying to communicate the nature of a particular phenomenal experience, good or bad. 'It was awful, absolutely horrible!!' you might recount, speaking of a bad migraine headache—but, apart from a fellow migraine sufferer, no one seems the wiser for your description. Frustratingly, despite the listener's own extensive catalogue of aches and pains, any elaboration on the 'horribleness' of a migraine seems to do little good. 'Yes, it's a bit like that but....' one will hedge, when asked how a migraine compares to an ordinary headache, one caused by tension or by sinus inflammation. Or is it like having a nasty hangover, a bad case of the flu, or like the stabbing pain one feels when the lights are suddenly switched on in a darkened room? 'It's sort of like that, except, only, um...well...much, much *worse!*' This is what a sufferer will typically reply, unsure, even in his own mind, what to make of such comparisons. (Does a migraine differ from a bad hangover only in intensity or is there in fact a difference in kind? Or does the difference in intensity *constitute* a difference in kind?) Ironically, the best descriptions one can give, the descriptions that elicit the most empathetic sounds and nods, are usually not descriptions of the pain at all, but of the beliefs

and desires that go along with the migraine. 'If I knew the migraine wasn't going to end, I'd seriously wonder whether life was worth living' or 'the pain is so intense, you don't even want to roll over, to find a more comfortable position in which to lie'—it is such thoughts that make clear the severity of the experience. Describing the feelings *per se* just does not seem possible. You simply have to have a migraine.

Extend, then, this epistemic difficulty to the phenomenal experience of an alien creature. Suppose that an organism has sense organs of a completely unfamiliar kind and, further, that it processes the information gathered from these strange sense organs in a manner unique to its species (or at least, in a manner unknown to ours). This is an organism that, undoubtedly, will have experiences that we do not: some of its sensations will be nothing like our sensations. So if we think of an organism's phenomenological experience as constituted by the set of all those alien 'qualia,' the problem of understanding seems insuperable. Given that we cannot comprehend by description the relatively familiar and circumscribed sensations of the migraine sufferer, what could we possibly know about an alien creature's point of view—about an entirely foreign phenomenological repertoire? If we can comprehend only those sensations that we have experienced, and if our own sensations are very unlike those of the bat, then we will be unable to understand a bat's phenomenology. This is the intuitive conclusion grounded in everyday experience.

The problem about the experience of bats, however, was, as Nagel described it, a problem about scientific description—whether science, not everyday conversation, could buy us any leverage on the bat's point of view. So what does common sense tell us here? The answer, I think, is that our conclusions about the ineffable nature of sensations fit hand in glove with another common feeling about the efficacy of science: to the average person, the suggestion that science might resolve these communicative difficulties seems quite strange, if not downright puzzling. How could science possibly help us in this respect?

Suppose, for example, that I am trying to describe to you a certain kind of feeling, say the pain of my broken toe. I might say something like this:

> Well, at first, when I tripped over the broom handle, there was a sharp, intense pain—a blinding flash of 'white' that occurred behind my eyes. Then the pain evened out to a dull throbbing in the toe—and, later, by that night, it had turned into what I think of as 'pain somewhere.' You know, that's the pain of a deep injury—when the pain is clearly where it should be, in this case, in the *toe*, but it's also nowhere in particular. Your whole body feels, well, dragged out.

If you have actually had a broken toe or another injury of this sort, these sensations might sound quite familiar. You know, for example, exactly what I mean by the phrase 'a blinding pain.' But if you have been fortunate enough to have avoided such traumas, certain parts of the description will seem quite peculiar. (A 'throbbing' pain you can understand, but what is it to have a pain that is 'blinding' or felt 'nowhere in particular'? Surely this is just a figure of speech?) One can, of course, on the basis of the description, obtain *some* understanding of the phenomenological properties at issue (after all, if asked about the pain of a broken toe, you could simply paraphrase the above description!). But it does little to help you understand how the pain actually *feels*. That is the part you cannot grasp given the description alone. Imagine, now, that you are given a completed model of human nociception, a model of all the neurophysiological/computational processes that underlie the production of pain, including, of course, the pain of a broken toe. That this model could in any way help seems entirely dubious. Why would you understand the pain of a broken toe any better if presented with a corpus of facts about C-fibres and A-fibres, conductance times, cortical and sub-cortical pathways, transmitter release, the function of endogenous opiates and so on? How could these statements about brain function possibly tell you about the feeling of a broken toe?

It is this intuitive sense of puzzlement, I think, that lies behind the more theoretical philosophical arguments of Nagel (1974), Block (1978), Jackson (1982), McGinn (1989) and Levine (chapter 6, this volume)—behind philosophical arguments that 'you can't get from here to there,' that there is an unbridgeable explanatory gap between the facts of science and those of subjective experience. In this sophisticated guise, the puzzlement is not given a naive dualist expression: most philosophers do not hold that science must fail to explain phenomenological events because those events occur in a 'realm' beyond the physical world. Rather, the materialistic tenets are upheld: descriptions of neurological processes, it is generally agreed, are descriptions of inner sensations *in some sense of the phrase*. Moreover, given that sensations *are* brain processes, most Nagelians admit that science could not be entirely irrelevant to our understanding of an alien creature's experience. Neurophysiology, psychology and psychophysics will illuminate (no doubt) some aspects of an alien point of view. Still—and this is where the intuitive puzzlement resurfaces—no matter how much we come to understand about a brain's representational or computational capacities (the nature of its functional states at various levels of description, plus their structural and relational properties), the qualitative properties of that organism's point of view will still be missing. Again, it is the 'very feel' of the experience that science is said to leave out. But what exactly does this mean? What is given and what is not by science?

Think here of the difference between, say, a pristine page in a child's colouring book, with only the thick black outlines of the picture drawn in, and that same page alive with colour, the trees and flowers and birds given hue according to the whims and palette of a particular individual. In one we have the 'basic outline' of the image, the two-dimensional form; in the other, we have that outline plus the hues of the forms—colours that might have been different had the artist chosen otherwise. Now if we were given only the pristine page, various questions about the scene would remain unanswered. 'But is the sky blue or is it really grey?' 'Is the flower on the left yellow or is it actually white?' Without the completed picture, it is impossible to tell. It is questions analogous to these, then, that are allegedly left unanswered given only the neurological/computational facts about another organism's brain processes. Even if we knew the basic outline or, in Nagel's terms (1974, p. 179) the 'structural properties' of an alien creature's representational scheme, the very 'colour' of the experiences, the qualia, would still be missing. Like the missing colours of the outlined page, there are any number of ways, consistent with the structural properties of the representations, that those subjective experiences could be. What science can give us, at best, are boundaries on the space of possible qualia, on the pure 'colours' yet to be filled in. In this way, our everyday intuitions cast the problem of consciousness, both in its naive and philosophical forms, as largely a problem about the intrinsic or qualitative nature of sensations, about the 'greens, reds and blues' of phenomenal experience.

The Film

Imagine, then, that I, having dropped in from some future time towards the end of neuroscience, claim to have a film of 'what it is like.' I have, that is, a film of the phenomenology of the bat. While such a suggestion might at first seem unlikely, let me assure you that this film carries the stamp of approval of future science. For what science has found out, in the fullness of time, is that just as some people have suspected (Dawkins, 1986), the bat's sonar echo is used to solve the very same informational problems for which we humans use light. The bat uses the informational properties of sound to construct a representation of objects and their spatial relations. This is why the bat's experience can be presented on film to us, the human observers—why it has, I claim, a strangely 'visual' quality. Needless to say, this film was made in the appropriate Disney style: a 'cinerama' or 'sen-surround' film projected on a curved screen, 180 degrees around the theatre, presented to an audience outfitted in '3-D glasses,' for the sake of stereo vision. And, of course, the film is in colour.

What, then, does the bat film look like? First, the plot is simple. It shows, from the bat's auditory viewpoint, a boring sort of chase scene: the bat, flying about, uses sonar signals to catch mealworms that have been thrown into the air by an experimenter. (Bats, of course, are not blind—they see as well as hear. For the purposes of this thought experiment, however, I am considering only their auditory sensations.) This feat is accomplished with a manoeuvre characteristic of the Little Brown bat. First the bat flaps around, emitting his Fm sonar signal (a cry that begins at about 60 khz and sweeps downward, through the intermediate frequencies, to a cry of about 20 khz) and waiting for something edible to appear; then when he sights a meal worm, he flies over and manoeuvres until he can swat the mealworm with his wing; performing a somersault, the bat then secures the prey in his tail pouch; finally, he reaches down to grab it, eating the mealworm from his pouch.... (Why bother with the pouch? As someone recently pointed out, 'Every good meal deserves to be eaten sitting down.'[1]) This is the basic scenario, one that is repeated several times. Now, what the film actually shows to the human observer is a kaleidoscopic display of vibrant colour forms. Swirling and pulsating in three-dimensions, the coloured forms dance across the screen, colliding and dispersing, suddenly appearing or vanishing. That's all. That, I claim, is what it's like. It is not, of course, what we humans would see, if we were acting the part of the bat—if we, with our human visual systems, were trying to catch a mealworm (Nagel, 1974). It is not 'visual' in the human sense. On the other hand, this is not a film from our point of view, but from the point of view of a bat.

As you, the reader, will no doubt object, something is clearly wrong with this story. That is, whether or not the film 'accurately depicts' some part of the bat's phenomenology—the sensory 'colours'—watching the swirling display seems to leave out much of what is surely important to the bat's point of view. First, unlike our experiences during a film of a roller-coaster ride or a hang-glider's flight, we do not feel any of the additional 'sympathetic' sensations appropriate to the moment. It does not seem to us that we are making any of the swooping and diving movements that are made by the bat. Nor do we understand the significance of the coloured images. Barring any subtitles of the form 'now the somersault begins' or 'now you've got the mealworm in your pouch,' you will not know what is happening—what you, as a bat, are doing. When the bright red image swirls across your left 'auditory' field, is something (the mealworm? a background

object?) moving past you or are you moving relative to it (maybe this is a somersault?)? Then again, is anything even moving at all? Can you infer that the movement of the colours stands for movement in the world? Probably not. And what does the three-dimensional nature of the film buy you? What does it mean when one coloured patch appears behind or in front of another? Is this a spatial relation or....? All in all, the coloured images hold little insight for the human observer.

As a first pass at explaining what is wrong with this story—why a cineramic film could not tell us what we want to know about the bat—note that, while not particularly helpful in this instance, such 'sen-surround' films are extremely useful in understanding the human point of view. When we watch a film of, say, the hang-glider's flight, the pictures go proxy for the real world. The brain interprets the intensity, frequency and spatial cues of the film in much the same way as it would interpret these same properties of light, reflected by real objects in the three-dimensional world. Hence, we really do see (more or less) what is seen during a hang-glider's flight. Indeed, because the visual system informs both the vestibular and the sympathetic nervous systems, we even feel the non-visual sensations—the terror before the leap, the drop in the stomach that follows. Through watching the film, seeing from this novel perspective the world rush by and feeling the sympathetic sensations of movement, a good deal about the experience of hang-gliding is communicated. In other words, we can simulate another person's point of view just because (a) we share a similar visual system, and (b) we can artificially create the hang-glider's visual input.

Similarly, when we watch the film of the 'bat experience,' we use the spectral cues in ways typical of human vision (what other choice could there be?). But what exactly does that mean? Unfortunately, we do not really know how colour vision works, in what 'typical' ways spectral cues are employed. What we do know is that the colours we see depend upon the current ambient light plus the profile of wavelengths that specific materials are disposed to reflect. Further, we suspect that spectral signals are involved in just those visual tasks for which intensity cues prove inadequate. For example, it is often postulated that such cues are used to define equiluminescent borders, highlight the contrast between object and background, and to differentiate objects that are similar in all other respects (e.g., the ripe and unripe pear). (For a short explanation of colour pathways, see De Yoe and Van Essen, 1988; for a more thorough review of colour vision, see Gouras, 1984.) In other words, while we may think of the colour system as whatever neural machinery produces colour sensations, the colour system is more than that: it is that part(s) of the visual system that responds to; discriminates and utilizes spectral cues. It is this system, then, whatever it might be, that is activated when we see the film of the 'bat experience.'

Needless to say, a bat's colour sensations of acoustic stimuli would be quite another matter. Its sensations would not be tied to the ways in which external objects reflect ambient light nor would its sensations be a part of a system that uses the spectral composition of light for various information processing tasks. The bat's colour sensations would be linked to properties of acoustic stimuli and to its auditory processes involved in spatial processing. As it turns out, although the bat film was presented as consisting of seemingly random coloured patches, I had in mind a specific process for the generation of those images. There was an informational relation between the properties of the visual image and those of the acoustic stimuli about which you, the 'viewer,' were not told. That relation was as follows. First, the hue of the sensations (red, green, blue, etc.) encoded

the frequency of the sound waves; second, the brightness of the colours gave the volume or intensity of the sound; and, third, the configuration of the patches showed, straightforwardly, the spatial properties of the sound waves. Finally, the film encoded the time delay of the echo or the bat's distance from surrounding objects. By making the coloured patches appear at different depths, spatial disparity mimicked a disparity in time—the amount of time it takes for the bat's outgoing cry to bounce off a distant object and return. The longer the delay between the cry and the echo, the further 'back' the coloured patches appeared in the 'visual' field. In this way, distance was represented by stereoscopic display.[2] Now, such an image of the sound field, in itself, would not buy the bat a sensory system for spatial perception. In order for the bat to perceive spatial relations in the world, something more would be needed: the visual images would have to be hooked up with various other neural processes 'further down the line'—with the bat's cortical pattern analysers that decode object shape, texture and identity, with the bat's vestibular and motor systems, and with, well, who knows what else? The fiction of the bat film, however, is that these colour sensations are what the bat experiences, qualitatively—a coloured image of the sound field, over time, as the bat pursues a mealworm.

One problem with the bat film now looks relatively clear: as a result of the differences between the human visual system and the bat auditory system, we cannot expect that by inducing colour sensations in ourselves we will understand the role that such sensations play in the bat's phenomenal world.[3] Because a 'sensurround' film produces our visual experience through the usual means, we see the colours as we normally do, as the projection of moving coloured images upon a curved screen. Lacking the auditory/representational capacities of the bat, we do not experience the colours as does the bat, however that might be. All a film can show us are meaningless (albeit coloured!) visual events. Put another way, what the bat film seems to prove is that it is not for lack of the 'quality' of the bat's experience that his world eludes us. Even if, *ex hypothesi*, we were able to produce in ourselves the 'very feel' of the bat's experience, its 'qualitative' aspect, we would not understand the bat's point of view. Watching the swirl of colours, those sensations lack their proper representational content. We cannot expect to understand the bat's point of view, In other words, without access to both the representational and qualitative parts of its experience. And here we are given but one aspect, the phenomenological 'feel' of the bat's world.

Unfortunately, this way of putting things is not quite right, for it does not get to the root of the problem, does not fully explain why a film cannot give us the point of view of the bat. Let me try a different path. Both the description of the bat film as initially given and the conclusions drawn from it above presupposed that there could be a separation of the 'qualitative' and 'representational' aspects of phenomenal experience. 'What the bat hears is just like colour' the reader is told, 'except, of course, the colours mean something quite different. Imagine that!' This was how the thought experiment got off the ground. Yet sensible as that request might have seemed, we have no idea how to comply with it, what such a separation could be. As Daniel Dennett has often pointed out (see, for example, Dennett, 1988), what one is asked to imagine, what one can imagine and what one actually imagines are three distinct things. It is not clear that we do know how to separate our conscious experiences into two parts, the representational and qualitative aspects, or whether, indeed, this notion even makes sense. To illustrate this point, suppose that, instead of referring to the bat film, I had requested that you do the following:

Open your eyes and look around your office (it's the end of term)—at the stacks of books and papers, at the piles of articles, unopened mail and ungraded papers. Note the way the scene looks to you, the inner phenomenology of the event. Now, a bat's consciousness is just like that—the feel of the scene is exactly the same—except, of course, all those visual sensations *mean* something very different to the bat. They represent quite different properties. Imagine that!

The problem is that you cannot imagine that, no matter how sincerely or hard you try. First, it would require that you 'strip away' the representational content of the entire office scene (say, by erasing the 'black lines' of the image, leaving only the 'crayoned' parts?). Then, by some other process, the intentional content of the bat's representations must be 'overlaid' upon the remaining bare sensory qualities (by a process akin to drawing in new lines or attaching new labels?). This, I contend, is not something we have any idea how to do: we do not know what the two 'parts' would be like, of and by themselves, so we have no inkling how to pull them apart or put them together. Our intuitions do not provide a concrete distinction between the qualitative and representational aspects of perceptions.

Still, you might well ask, why then, if there is no such distinction, did the bat example work at all? That is, in the bat film, we were asked to imagine meaningless coloured patches swirling across the screen—and we did. It also seemed perfectly reasonable to imagine that those colours played a representational role in the bat's experience, one that was different from the role they play in our conceptual scheme. But if there is no distinction between the qualitative and representational parts of experience, how could this be so? Certainly it seemed to us that we could imagine such a distinction.

The answer here is that the description of the film was intentionally misleading: it was designed to play upon a common experience, that of seeing images or pictures we can not identify. Staring at an abstract painting perplexedly, we scan the blobs of colour for form—what could that possibly be a picture of?—when, suddenly, the figure of a man emerges. The apparently meaningless blobs of paint are transformed into a comprehensible image. These are the cases in which we legitimately regard content and 'mere colour' as distinct: at first the canvas contains only formless coloured blobs; after the 'aha!' experience, the painting has meaning—and this despite the fact that the canvas remains physically unchanged. It was this kind of event that set the stage for the original bat film. Given our familiarity with pictures and drawings, we tried to imagine a similar kind of thing—a film of 'meaningless' coloured shapes, non-intentional and non-representational sensory qualities, such that, if only we knew the proper 'squint' of the bat, those images would have content for us as well. We imagined, or at least we thought we could imagine, an unchanging substrate of pure sensation—a substrate analogous to the physical paint upon the canvas—onto which the bat's meaning could be affixed. The problem, however, is that our experience of abstract art does not provide a genuine example of what we need, the separation of content from 'mere colour.' Viewing an abstract painting does not involve an experience of a 'meaningless' image in the proper sense, that is, because the sudden emergence of a form in an abstract artwork is not the experience of having sensory stimuli, devoid of content, instantaneously gain representational properties. Even if we do not initially see the coloured shapes as the ghostly portrait of a man, we do see the colours as something—as coloured shapes upon a canvas, external to us, 3 ft dead ahead. The same is true for the patches

of colour in the bat film. Perceiving (or imagining) moving coloured patches on a screen is an intentional—or at least, quasi-intentional—event, an experience of coloured patches as coloured patches. So when we imagined the bat film, we did not thereby imagine pure sensory qualities, colour qualia devoid of content. Our understanding of abstract art forms was misleading because it fostered the illusion that we could imagine exactly that.

Where does this leave us with respect to Nagel's original question and its intuitive basis? In questioning whether we could ever understand an alien organism's point of view, we intuitively construe this problem as analogous to the everyday task of understanding the phenomenal experiences of each other. Here, because our own difficulties turn around individual sensations, around the 'feel' of sensory events—the pain of a migraine headache, the azure blue of the Mediterranean, the 'essence' of flamingo pink—we infer that the main stumbling block to understanding an alien creature must be the inaccessibility of those qualia. We treat a conscious experience, in other words, as a mere collection of qualia, as a bunch of individual sense data that have somehow come together to form a phenomenological whole. (Certainly, this is the route that most analytic philosophical debates have also taken. In the 'inverted spectrum' problem, for example, the question is asked whether it would be possible for two people to have exactly the same neural structures and functions and yet have their colour experiences be 'spectral inversions,' one of the other. Could you, my neurological equivalent, see the sky as red even though I see it as blue? In the 'absent qualia' problem [Block, 1978], the question is whether an artificial system functionally identical to one's own brain could be entirely devoid of qualitative experience. If, given a Turing-machine table that described the functional states of my brain, the entire population of China could be talked into instantiating, for one hour, the state types specified by that table, would my aches, tickles and pains be somehow 'experienced' [collectively?] by all the citizens of China? These are the kinds of questions—questions phrased in terms of individual sensations—that are currently asked.)

What is overlooked by the intuitive construal of the problem are the following two points. First, because we are able to individuate, identify and catalogue some of our phenomenological experiences and to converse with other people about such perceptual experiences as 'that very colour' (referring, say, to the intense blue-green of the Mediterranean), it does not follow that these sensations come to exist *in vacuo*. This 'isolation' of those sensations (whether as a result of some internal process of individuation or merely in virtue of linguistic convention) does not thereby produce sensations that stand apart from our representational/conceptual schemes. What the intuitive view conflates, in other words, is an ability to refer to certain parts of conscious intentional experience with an ability to pick out its purely qualitative aspects. Isolation does not distil qualia from content. So, whatever the root of our everyday problems in communication, it is not the intrinsic nature of sensations per se that makes for trouble—or, rather, there is no reason to think that this is the case given our communicative problems. If our utterances do not refer to pure sensation, one sees that the problems of communicating our phenomenological experience are equally a problem about representational states.

Second, a point of view, as we know from our own—paradigmatic—case, is not a jumble of qualia. In the normal non-pathological subject, consciousness is systematic, representational and intentional (e.g., we represent objects as being a certain way or of a certain type).

Moreover, such properties are not 'optional' parts of our conscious experience, merely accidental or inconsequential aspects, if they can be considered 'parts' at all. Rather, these properties are constitutive of a point of view. That we experience the world in any way at all—that it is like anything to be me—is made possible by exactly these properties. So, given that our own phenomenal experience is the starting point for an explanation of the very notion of a point of view, and that our own experience is not a mere collection of qualia, we must assume that the same holds for the bat. If there is anything it is like to be bat, we have no reason to think—indeed, there is no sense to the suggestion—that that bat's experience is but a collection of pure qualia.

The mistake of the intuitive view, then, was first to think that our problem of communication was one about pure qualitative states, and then, second, to import this interpretation of the problem into the task of understanding an alien point of view. If we construe our communicative failures to hinge upon pure qualitative states of which the speakers do not have a common experience, then what we face in understanding a foreign phenomenology is simply 'much more of the same'—for the bat will have more and more purely qualitative states of which we ourselves have had no experience. By misconstruing the nature of an interpersonal problem, the puzzle about another creature's point of view becomes a problem about pure qualia.

The upshot of the bat film, then, is this. Nagel has claimed that we will never understand the point of view of an alien creature. This is a claim that our intuitions support with a nod towards 'that something,' pure phenomenal experience, which cannot be known merely by description, without personal experience. But if introspection does not yield any clear distinction between the representational and qualitative properties of experience, then we do not know, *a priori*, what insights or even what kinds of insights will result from empirical investigation. Certainly we cannot confidently declare that science must fail to unearth 'that something,' for we have no clear idea to what this amounts; nor can one say what the scientific approach will necessarily leave out, if it must leave out anything at all. This gives us, I think, good reason to continue on with our empirical investigations of mental representation—to look towards the disciplines of neurophysiology, psychology and artificial intelligence—without undue pessimism about the relevance of their experimental results.

Ourselves as Subject

One consequence of tying together sensation and representational experience is that the nature of our own subjective experience is opened to investigation (Sellars, 1963; Dennett, 1978a; Churchland, 1983). It is as legitimate a subject of inquiry as the experience of other creatures. Because the questions about phenomenology are no longer focused on the intrinsic quality of particular sensations but on a phenomenology as a whole—complete with its representational/intentional nature—our ignorance extends to ourselves as well. We, as the 'owners' of our point of view, do not thereby understand its representational character. Hence, our study of representational systems is also an investigation into our own point of view.

This consequence is, I suspect, somewhat counter-intuitive. If anyone knows about my subjective experience, it is certainly me, or at least that is what we have always thought about the matter. By way of lending some small amount of plausibility to this result, then, I want to end this chapter by going back to the example at the beginning, that of the eagle. What did learning a simple anatomical fact about the eagle, about the foveation of the eye, tell us about that creature's experience? More importantly, how would a fact about an eagle nudge our sense of self, reflect upon the human experience?

In learning that the eye of the eagle has two separate foveal regions, it suddenly seemed clear that the experience of the eagle must be different from our own. On the other hand, when I tried to imagine *how* the experience of an eagle would differ from my own, I immediately adopted a hypothesis that incorporated my own visual system into the experience. I wondered, that is, whether being an eagle might not be akin to the experience I would have while wearing strange quadra-focals—whether it wouldn't be like shifting my own gaze from lens to lens sequentially. In essence, I incorporated my own foveal field into the experience of being an eagle. (This would give me, in effect, eight different levels of visual acuity: four lenses imposed upon my foveal and non-foveal regions.) Of course, nothing we know about the visual system of the bird of prey constrains its visual 'attention' in a similar way. Although my foveae must move from lens to lens sequentially, the bird need not have any analogous 'inner' eye that receives, serially, the information from the two foveae and the horizontal band. Because there are parallel lines from all regions of the retina, there is no reason why the brain must process the information sequentially—no reason why, say, the eagle must first attend to the left, then forward, then to the horizon just as I would. The eagle might 'attend' simultaneously to all this information at once, no matter how this might conflict with our intuitive notion of visual attention. This is a possibility that the anatomical data reveals.

Note that once we see how a notion of 'foveal' processing has been misapplied to the eagle's point of view, it is an interesting question whether or not we have also 'moved the eye inward' not merely in thinking about the eagle, but alas in thinking about ourselves. Here, I am referring to the many models of conscious attention that utilize, in one form or another, the 'spotlight' metaphor: the 'inner eye' of consciousness shifts like a searchlight from one neural event to another, successively attending to different mental events. This, too, is a 'foveal' theory of attention, not of another organism's consciousness but of our own. We apply the foveal metaphor to our conscious experience as a whole. Certainly, this is a model with intuitive plausibility. Something about it seems just right. The question that the eagle's eye raises, however, is about the basis of this appeal. Is it appealing because this is, in fact, how our inner experience is, or does it seem right just because the foveated nature of our visual experience colours our understanding of conscious attentive processes as a whole?

First, the former alternative could be true. The spotlight theory might seem plausible because, on looking inwardly at ourselves, we can see by introspection that our consciousness is sequentially focused on single events. That is, the introspective evidence coheres with the metaphor. But is this really so? Recall what it is like to struggle through a recalcitrant screen door weighed down by several bags of groceries. First, you juggle the groceries and grasp the door handle; then you feel a mosquito land on your ankle; then you hear the creaking door hinge and the rip of a paper bag; then the mosquito makes a stab with his proboscis; then you loose your grip on the handle; then the screen slams shut on your shin; then a tin can bounces off your thigh...Somehow, this strictly sequential narrative does not quite capture the experience, even if it does record the objective order of the external events. The very problem with such experiences is that 'everything happens at once.' In the midst of the calamity, what happens first—the bag ripping or the mosquito bit-

ing or the screen door slamming—is not always clear. On the basis of experience alone, there is no distinct ordering of all of the events, no clear sequence of this event, then this one, then this and finally that.

Perhaps, then, the explanation goes the other way about: perhaps the searchlight metaphor, combined with our story-telling practices and our understanding of the relevant causal chain of events, confer order upon the conscious events only in retrospect. What I am suggesting is that the spot-light metaphor may be adopted just because (a) we are foveated animals and (b) we do not actually perceive any firm order in the events (i.e., such events are not 'tagged' for time). Because we are such strongly visual organisms and because eye movements are required for our perception of the world, the metaphor seems plausible. Needing an explanation, we mistake our intuitive grasp of the visual perception of external events for an accurate description of internal attentional processes. We co-opt the visual notions of 'searching,' 'focusing' and 'watching' and apply them to all of conscious experience. This, I think, is possible. What the eye of the eagle should make us wonder is whether our conception of ourselves might not be 'tainted' with the same foveal metaphors we naturally apply to other creatures. The above example is not meant as a serious criticism of spotlight theories of conscious attention. Rather, it is given as a suggestive example of how it could come about that we are mistaken about our own inner events—how the way our own attentional mechanisms seem to us could diverge from how in fact they are. It offers a small glimpse of the ways a possible reconception of ourselves, and our point of view, could come about in the light of physiological/computational discoveries.

Still, the central idea of this chapter has been that we do not know what science will explain, just because we lack a firm grasp on the subject matter: the nature of conscious events. If so, we are in a funny position. We will know what science can tell us only after it has done so. Hence, only suggestive examples are now possible. What we can provide, however, are good reasons to wait—to see what science will do. In effect, this is what I have been attempting to show in this chapter.

Acknowledgements

This chapter began as an introduction to a paper, 'What Is It Like to Be Boring and Myopic?' (Akins, 1993) where it served, in a much abbreviated form, to motivate the neuroscientific approach to the problem of consciousness used there. An earlier version appeared under the title 'Science and Our Inner Lives: Birds of Prey, Bats and the Common (Featherless) Bi-ped' in a collection edited by Marc Beckoff and Dale Jamieson (1990). For their generous comments on and discussion of the manuscript, I would like to thank Marc Beckoff, Daniel C. Dennett, Dale Jamieson, Joseph Malpeli, Wright Neely, Brian C. Smith, Tony Stone, Tom Stoneham and Mary Windham. I would also like to thank Martin Davies for his extensive comments on the final draft.

Notes

1. That someone being Jeremy Butterfield.
2. This way of generating the film was given only for the sake of example, not because I think that this is what a bat's experience is really like. That is, assuming that a bat does have a point of view (and I doubt that it has), the film represents the properties of the sound field before the sound waves are transduced, processed and filtered by the basilar membrane, midbrain and auditory cortex of the bat. At the level of the auditory cortex (surely the first neural level at which conscious experience would be possible), the informational characteristics of the signal have been significantly changed.
3. It is an interesting question, however, whether, given the addition of doppler-shift or velocity information to the visual display, our own visual systems could act as a spatial pattern analyser of some sort—that is, whether if we, given the intellectual knowledge of how the image is produced, were to look at the screen we could learn to use that information to guide our actions, say to walk around a room filled with objects.

Study Questions

1. What, precisely, is it about bats that Nagel argues we can't know, despite all the physical information about them we could wish?
2. Is Nagel really arguing against physicalism or against reductionism? What is the difference?
3. Compare the "Modal Argument" Jackson considers with Kripke's argument against physicalism.
4. Consider Jackson's response to Nagel. State his objections to Nagel's arguments in your own terms. Has Jackson got Nagel right? Are his objections correct?

5. What is epiphenomenalism? Why, according to Jackson, does this position entail that qualia are irrelevant to survival?

6. Dennett argues that sometimes empirical methods (from "outside") provide better evidence about experience-claims than the subject's own introspective convictions. Which of his examples are supposed to make this plausible? If he's right, then how does this fit into his overall argument that qualia, as traditionally understood, do not exist?

7. Outline Dennett's osprey-call detection example in Section 6. What main points does he draw from this example? What is the *inscrutability of projection*? Dennett quotes Wittgenstein here: how does his argument connect with Wittgenstein's? How does the "inscrutability of projection" figure in his overall argument against qualia?

8. Explain what Dennett means when he says, "We don't have to know how we identify or re-identify or gain access to such internal response types in order to be able so to identify them." Have a look at Smart's reply to Objection 3 on page 245; explain how this is an example of that point. Show how Dennett's point might be used against arguments produced by Nagel and Jackson.

9. Rosenthal relies on "perceptual-role" theory for understanding mental qualities. What is a perceptual role? How is this way of understanding mental qualities supposed to be an account, for example, of the mental quality of tasting a peach? Compare this sort of approach to mentality to the functionalism advocated by Fodor. Is this a form of functionalism?

10. In Chapter Nine we saw that Armstrong claims, against J.J.C. Smart, that perceptual states can be defined behaviorally. He says, "We can then think of the animal's perception [of red and green] as a state within the animal apt, if the animal is so impelled, for selective behaviour between the red- and green-lighted pathways." Compare this claim to David Rosenthal's description of "mental qualities." Would Armstrong accept the conclusions of Rosenthal's argument in this chapter as an extension of his own position?

11. Explain Rosenthal's view of consciousness as awareness of oneself as being in some mental state. Fred Dretske elsewhere argues that a state's being conscious does not consist in one's being conscious of the state; rather, it consists in being conscious of something. For instance, when one is looking at an apple, one might not be aware that one is perceiving an apple, so on Rosenthal's view, this is not a conscious state. But on Dretske's view, one is conscious of the apple, so it is a conscious state. Who is right? Explain why Rosenthal's view, but not Dretske's, makes for the possibility of unconscious mental states.

12. Akins argues that even if we could "produce in ourselves the 'very feel' of the bat's experience, its 'qualitative' aspect, we would not understand the bat's point of view." Why does she think this? What would be missing from our understanding? Explain how this supports her further contention that "what it's like" to be some organism may be amenable to scientific ("objective") investigation.

13. Akins argues that it is possible that we are mistaken to use the "spotlight metaphor" in order to understand how conscious attention works. Explain why she thinks that this "offers a small glimpse" of how scientific discoveries may help us reconceive of ourselves and our subjective point of view.

Suggested Readings

Nagel on what it's like to be a bat has been widely discussed. Here are some relevant sources:

William G. Lycan, "Subjectivity," in his *Consciousness*. (Cambridge, MA: MIT Press, 1987); and "What Is the 'Subjectivity' of the Mental?," *Philosophical Perspectives* 4 (1990): pp. 109–30.

Ned Block and Robert Stalnaker, "Conceptual Analysis, Dualism, and the Explanatory Gap," *Philosophical Review* 108 (1999): pp. 1–46.

Rom Harré, "Nagel's Challenge and the Mind-Body Problem," *Philosophy* 74 (1999): pp. 247–70.

Gregory McCulloch, "What It Is Like," *Philosophical Quarterly* 38 (1988): pp. 1–19.

Norman Malcolm, "Subjectivity," *Philosophy* 63 (1988): pp. 147–60.

Paul R. Teller, "Subjectivity and Knowing What It's Like," in *Emergence or Reduction? Essays on the Prospects of Nonreductive Physicalism*. Ansgar Beckermann, Hans Flohr, and Jaegwon Kim (eds.). (Berlin: De Grutyer, 1992).

Another influential article by Jackson is "What Mary Didn't Know," *Journal of Philosophy* 83 (1986): pp. 291–95. Reprinted in *The Nature of Consciousness*, Ned Block *et al.*, (eds). (Cambridge MA: MIT Press (1997); and in *The Nature of the Mind*, David Rosenthal (ed.). (Oxford: Oxford University Press, 1991).

For discussion of Jackson's argument see:

Jeffrey E. Foss, "On the Logic of What It Is Like to Be a Conscious Subject," *Australasian Journal of Philosophy* 67 (1989): pp. 305–20.

John C. Bigelow and Robert Pargetter, "Acquaintance with Qualia," *Theoria* 61 (1990): pp. 129–47.

Brie Gertler, "A Defense of the Knowledge Argument," *Philosophical Studies* 93 (1999): pp. 317–36.

Dennett's arguments are considered in:

Edmond L. Wright, "Querying Quining Qualia," *Acta Analytica* 4 (1989): pp. 9–32.

Don Ross, "Quining Qualia Quine's Way," *Dialogue* 32 (1993): pp. 439–59.

Danielle Mason, "Demystifying without Quining: Wittgenstein and Dennett on Qualitative States," *South African Journal of Philosophy* 24 (2005): pp. 33–43.

Some more recent treatments of the relation between qualia and representation:

Jacob Berger, "A Defense of Holistic Representationalism," *Mind & Language* 33(2) (2018): pp. 161–76.

Todd Ganson, "Are Color Experiences Representational?," *Philosophical Studies* 166 (2013): pp. 1–20.

John Morrison, "Anti-Atomism about Color Representation," *Noûs* 49 (2015): pp. 94–122.

12

 # WHAT IS CONSCIOUSNESS FOR?

Determining the Functions of Consciousness

For most people, the arguments of the previous chapter demonstrate the existence of a certain phenomenon in the natural world: Human beings, and many other animal species as well, possess what we have been calling "phenomenal consciousness." While there is a dispute about whether there are facts about the properties of qualia, there is no doubt that conscious experience is something that occurs across the animal world. It seems unlikely that a phenomenon as complex and as widespread as conscious experience would exist without some biological purpose. If we assume, as virtually all psychologists working today do, that most biological capacities have come about through evolution, then it seems likely that consciousness has evolved in living things as the result of some biological advantage it confers. The inference that consciousness *itself* has a function isn't direct, even if it is true that it has emerged through evolution. For it might be an epiphenomenon, a by-product, of certain mental processes that do confer an evolutionary advantage. Yet even in such a case, we would want to know what those processes are that yield conscious experience. Where some psychologists are interested in mapping the qualitative character of experiences, others have attempted to determine the mental functions that are made possible through conscious experience.

An Example of Explaining the Functions of Consciousness

There are numerous theories about the functions of consciousness, and the research is not at a stage where the evidence supports any one theory clearly over the others. One of the strongest contenders is called **global workspace theory** (**GWT**).[1] According to GWT, the principal function of consciousness is to make available a vast amount of information that is needed for very demanding tasks, such as driving a car through difficult traffic, or interpreting sentences of natural language and understanding the implications of what is being said. The idea is that when we attend to information in the world, that information is brought into working memory and thereby made available to a large number of unconscious information-processing systems across the brain. These systems then perform operations on the items made available to them, and send the results back to working memory. Information made available in this way is said to be conscious information.

This process can be illustrated by the manner in which the mind determines the appropriate meaning of an ambiguous word. The word 'set,' for example, has multiple meanings. But when we see it together with another word that provides context (as in 'tennis set' or 'stage-set'), its meaning in that context is *immediately* fixed. The task is carried out instantly without any consciousness awareness of its occurrence. Another example is drawn from the use of memory of past experiences (what we call autobiographical memory). When we consciously view a very large number of pictures (even up to 10,000), we are able to recognize them again without having to memorize them consciously. In both of these cases, when something is brought to conscious attention, unconscious processes are immediately brought into play, and the results are then delivered back to working memory.

GWT presents a picture of how the mind works that is contrary to our intuitive understanding. According to this theory, most of the "real work" of the mind is done unconsciously by small, local processors. There is "executive control" in some sense, but it operates through specialized unconscious mechanisms. These unconscious processes, which have access to the items illuminated by consciousness, in fact do most of the work in cognition. While working memory provides a kind of "communal blackboard" (as David Chalmers describes it), it is the specialized processes in the unconscious background, which act on the items that are written there, that perform most of the cognitive functions. The function of consciousness is to make the items available to those specialized processes.

In this picture of cognition there is a direct trade-off between the slow, one-at-a-time processes of conscious thought and the speed and efficiency of unconscious processes that run in parallel. Consciousness makes possible the carrying out of complex tasks and responses to novel situations by organizing the information supplied by unconscious processes. Those unconscious routines, on the other hand, are effective and fast because they are specialized to the tasks for which they have evolved. According to GWT, then, the operation of consciousness combines the virtues of flexible problem-solving with the speed and effectiveness of highly specialized functions.

A Confusion about Consciousness

According to theories like GWT, consciousness serves a vital function in mental life: making items in working memory available to the vast array of unconscious subsystems. It would seem that if this theory were true, it would offer an *explanation* of consciousness. When we ask the questions why and in what manner consciousness arises, we can point to global workspace theory. In the language we introduced in Chapter Eleven, what we seem to have here, then, is a *reduction* of consciousness to a certain cognitive function, namely, global access. When we ask what conscious experience is, there is now a ready answer: Conscious experience is global access to the contents of working memory.

There are, however, grounds to deny that conscious experience can be reduced to cognitive function in this way, for there are the qualitative properties of conscious experience that we considered in the previous chapter. We can ask whether these properties too are reducible to the function of global access. This is in fact the criticism that Ned Block raised against the functionalist theory of mind that we reviewed in Chapter Nine. The argument there was that describing the functional properties of a mental state does not explain the occurrence of qualia. In his 1995 article excerpted below, Block raises a similar question about theories such as GWT: What exactly is being explained? By using the term 'consciousness,' researchers in GWT, like Bernard Baars, might appear to be offering an explanation of the qualitative character of experience. But Block claims that this appearance is an illusion. Global workspace theory, and others like it, explain something quite different from what the term 'consciousness' commonly refers to.

The reason for this illusion, Block argues, is that there is an ambiguity in the term 'consciousness.' There are actually several different concepts at play here, only one of which is that of conscious experience. Consciousness, he says, is a mongrel concept. As a result, he claims, studies of consciousness have been hampered by a fundamental confusion about what is being explained by so-called "theories of consciousness." This confusion, he says, is similar to confusions among seventeenth century physicists about the meaning of the word 'heat,' by which a single word denoted two quite different subject matters. A satisfactory theory of heat required the resolution of this confusion of meanings, and a similar resolution is required in the study of consciousness.

Blindsight

To illustrate this confusion, Block turns to a striking phenomenon, called **blindsight**, which occurs in subjects who have suffered damage to their visual cortex. Certain kinds of neural damage can result in a "blind" area in the visual field, in which the subjects experience no sensations at all. When presented with a visual stimulus they report seeing "nothing at all" in the affected region of their field of vision. Studies of the perceptual and cognitive abilities of subjects with blindsight yield interesting results. First, while blind-sighted patients do not experience any conscious perception in the "blind" portion of their visual field, information about the stimulus that is not experienced reaches the mind in other ways. For example, when asked whether a grid they do not see is oriented vertically or horizontally, the subjects' answers are remarkable accurate, well beyond what might be lucky guesses. They can also shape their hand appropriately for grasping an object they do not consciously see. At the same time, however, experimenters report that the subjects cannot use that same information in their deliberate control of action.

Similar results are obtained from subjects with other kinds of neural impairment. Block refers to studies of patients with epilepsy who, during a seizure, can maintain routine or automatic functions, such as walking, driving, or playing piano, despite a total lack of consciousness that prevents them from any kind of flexible or creative behavior. In his second section, Block discusses cases of prosopagnosia, the inability to recognize faces. Despite this inability, subjects can successfully "guess" at other aspects of faces such as expressions, which suggests that visual information they cannot access consciously is somehow accessed in other ways. Moreover, there is similar evidence from people who do not suffer from any loss of sensory experience. For example, regular subjects can be made to count the vowels in a string of words in such a way that they have no memory or recognition of the words, and yet those same words appear to influence their subsequent guesses about word-completion.

In each of these studies, it appears that information about sensory stimuli reaches certain parts of the cognitive system even though the subjects of the studies have no conscious experience of that information. On the other hand, the lack of conscious experience appears to render impossible the use of that same information in deliberative or rational action. From these studies, cognitive scientists have constructed models of how conscious experience is deployed in the operations of the mind. Baars's theory would fall into this group, for it would imply that the global access needed for deliberative action is impaired through the neural damage, even though a certain amount of visual information reaches certain sub-systems. It is in these models that Block claims the confusion about different meanings of the word 'consciousness' arises.

The Schacter Model

To illustrate the reasoning concerning the functions of consciousness he wishes to criticize, Block uses a very simplified model of the cognitive system put forward by D.L. Schacter, illustrated in Figure 1 of Block's article. In the illustration are various boxes representing modules in the operation of the cognitive system, with arrows showing the flow of information between the modules. There are boxes labeled 'Response Modules,' which represent modules controlling movement of the limbs, and boxes labeled 'Specialized Modules,' which represent the modules that provide sensory information. Think of these as output and input respectively. (There are two boxes labeled 'Procedural Habit Module' and 'Declarative/Episodic Memory,' which we can ignore.) The sets of input and output boxes are connected to two information-processing modules, labeled 'Phenomenal Consciousness' and the 'Executive System.' The latter is the part of the system that carries out deliberative reasoning and action control. According to this model, the module responsible for phenomenal consciousness carries out certain kinds of information processing, receiving information from the "input" modules, and delivering its "output" to the Executive System. (The arrows run in both directions, indicating feed-back loops passing information back and forth.)

The Schacter model is significant for Block because it can be used to explain the kinds of abilities exhibited in subjects with blindsight and similar kinds of cognitive impairment. According to the Schacter model, the neural damage impairs the flow of information between one of the sensory modules and the module for conscious experience. There are two results from this damage. First, the subject has no conscious experience of the information delivered by the sensory module, and, second, that information does not reach the Executive System, so that it cannot be deployed in deliberative control of action. However, according to the model, there is nonetheless a direct connection between the sensory module and response module, so that that information can affect behavior despite the fact that the subject has no experience of it.

The point that Block wants to make about the Schacter model is that it postulates a single module that is responsible *both* for the conscious experience of sensory information *and* for processing and delivery of that information to the Executive System for use in deliberative control of action. Conscious experience, then, is something occurring in an information-processing module, and it has both qualitative properties *and* a cognitive function. This form of explanation is what Block refers to as the "target reasoning," the reasoning that he wishes to criticize in this article. The mistake Block claims is made is that the reasoning fails to recognize that phenomenological properties and functional role are two quite distinct *kinds of consciousness* that can exist independently of one another, even though they commonly occur together. The result is that, in many models of consciousness, it is unclear which of these two is being explained. Block calls these two kinds, *phenomenal*-consciousness and *access*-consciousness.

Two Kinds of Consciousness

Block treats the distinction between phenomenal-consciousness (or P-consciousness) and access-consciousness (or A-consciousness) as a difference between two different kinds of mental *states*, and so his definitions give the distinguishing characteristics of these states. First, a state is **P-conscious** if it has *experiential properties*, which Block explains as *there being something it is like* to be in that state. P-consciousness, then, is the kind of consciousness emphasized by Nagel and Jackson. Block says that P-conscious states have *perceptual content*, but that this content need not be intentional or propositional. When I gaze at a red rose, the qualitative or experiential character of my experience (its redness) is the *content* of my conscious state; the content of the visual experience is simply its redness. Block also allows that the qualitative or phenomenal character of P-conscious states can also have intentional content. There is, for example, a difference between what it is like to hear a sound as coming from the left and what it is like to hear a sound as coming from the right. But P-conscious states can also have purely experiential content.

The concept of A-consciousness, on the other hand, derives from the observation that consciousness is often involved in reasoning and in deliberative control of action. So A-consciousness does not involve experiential properties, but instead involves the role that a state plays in thought and action. A state is **A-conscious** if its content meets three conditions:

1. It is informationally promiscuous.
2. It is poised for rational control of action.
3. It is poised for rational control of speech.

Actually, only the first two are necessary for A-consciousness, since Block allows that creatures without speech (such as chimpanzees) can nonetheless have A-conscious states. So we need to explain the first two conditions.

To say that the content of a state is **informationally promiscuous** means that the information it carries is available to a wide range of mental processes. The term was introduced by Stephen Stich, and it expresses a common feature of reasoning. For example, suppose Sarah knows that her bank stays open until 7 pm. She can use that knowledge in all kinds of ways. On the way to the bank at 6:55, she may use it to realize she has to hurry. She may use it to decide not to switch to a bank that is open only until 5 pm. She may use it to decide she has time for an early dinner before going to the bank. And on and on. This is characteristic of how we use information in reasoning: Information is not encapsulated for certain uses, it is "promiscuous" across the whole range of rational cognition.

When Block says that the content of an A-conscious state is "*poised* for rational control of action," he means that the content is *available* to be used in rational decision-making. Consider Sarah again. Her knowledge of the bank's closing hour may not be something she is consciously thinking about at one moment, but then at a later moment, when she suddenly wonders whether there is still time to get to the bank, it becomes available to her for making her decision. She can then use that information in her reasoning. The contrast that Block has in mind here is with the kind of unconscious information about the stimulus in situations like blind sight. In the blind sight experiments, the information that a grid is horizontal rather than vertical may be used by a subject's cognitive system in certain, limited ways, yet because that information is not the content of an A-conscious state, it is not available to the subject in her rational decision-making. When the subject correctly says that the grid is horizontal, she cannot say *how* she knows that, it feels like just a lucky guess.

Another form of informational access is found in global workspace theory. According to GWT, items in working memory that become conscious are accessible to unconscious distributed processes throughout the brain. So we get a different kind of informational promiscuity: rather than information shared across rational decision-making processes, information is shared with the vast array of unconscious sub-systems that perform various kinds of analysis or memory search and deliver the results back to conscious experience. According to Block's definition, information that is A-conscious is accessible to rational decision-making, and he makes no mention there of unconscious distributed sub-systems. Yet Block himself describes GWT as a "global workspace model of A-consciousness," and he cites Bernard Baars's reasoning as an instance of the common mistake of conflating phenomenal and access consciousness. So it is clear that he intends A-consciousness to include any state that is accessible to the processes that influence action and decision-making, whether those processes are high-level rational functions or low-level unconscious processes.

Differences between P-consciousness and A-consciousness

Block contends that there are three principal differences between these two kinds of consciousness. We will look only at the first of these, which is derived from the definitions of the two kinds of states. The *content* of a P-conscious state is always *phenomenal*, that is, it always involves what being in the state is like for the subject. In contrast, the content of an A-conscious state is always *representational*, that is, it always carries a certain propositional content. Another way Block puts this is to say that A-conscious states are always *transitive*, which means that the information carried by the content of an A-conscious state is always information *about* something. The content of an A-conscious state always has an object. This is not always the case with P-consciousness. For example, Block argues that pains and other bodily sensations can occur without there being consciousness of any object. But A-consciousness is always consciousness *of* something.

A few paragraphs further on, Block says that it is easy to mistakenly infer from this last point that the difference between P-conscious and A-conscious states is whether or not they are transitive, that is, whether or not their content conveys information about something. This impression is mistaken, however, because P-conscious states can also have representational content. The error derives from the paradigmatic examples of the two kinds of consciousness. The paradigm cases of P-conscious states are sensations, which bear only their qualitative properties, and the paradigm cases of A-conscious states are propositional attitudes, which carry only intentional content. Typically, however, perceptual experiences are perceptions of objects (a red square) or of their bodily causes (an injury). They do, then, normally carry representational content. In such cases, though, if the content is informationally promiscuous, then the state is both P-conscious and A-conscious. He argues later on that this is in fact the most common case.

A-consciousness without P-consciousness

Since states can be both P-conscious and A-conscious, on what grounds does Block argue that these are two different kinds of consciousness, rather than one kind with two characteristics, corresponding to phenomenality and access? To this end he constructs certain thought experiments within which a state is A-conscious without being P-conscious, and vice versa. This is taken to reveal a difference between the two concepts. In his first such thought experiment he presents the possibility of a mental state with representational content that is informationally promiscuous (i.e., is A-conscious), but without any accompanying phenomenal consciousness. Such a possibility is what some philosophers have argued for on the grounds of the conceivability of so-called zombies: creatures who behave in every way as do normal humans, but who lack any phenomenal consciousness at all.

Block argues for the possibility of something like the zombie scenario by extending the case of blindsighted subjects. A blindsighted subject will typically report no conscious experience of an object before them, for example a large X. They have no P-consciousness of the presence of the X. They have no A-consciousness of the X either, because that information is not available to them in their deliberative reasoning, rational action, or speech. Although they have no conscious perception of the X, psychologists believe that perceptual information about the X is still available in some other way, because they can successfully "guess" at its presence. So in cases of blindsight, there is information that is somehow represented, but that is neither P-conscious nor A-conscious. Now Block asks us to extend that situation in our imagination to what he calls "superblindsightedness." This is a situation in which a subject can somehow cause the information, the presence of an X, to pop into their A-consciousness without the accompanying visual experience. The information would suddenly become known to the subject in their deliberative reasoning and verbal reporting, yet they still have no visual experience of the information. Block says the phenomenon would be similar to the way that the solution to a puzzle can suddenly pop into one's head. If such a case were possible, Block contends, there would be A-consciousness of the information without any P-consciousness of it. There are, in fact, no known cases of this superblindsightedness, but Block believes that the thought experiment demonstrates its possibility.

P-consciousness without A-consciousness

Block begins here with another thought experiment: One can imagine an animal that has suffered severe brain damage such that it has lost all forms of reasoning and deliberative control of action. Yet as it is still alive, it experiences sensations of color, sound, taste, pain, etc., just as before. If we find that thought experiment implausible (or maybe just too depressing), he offers another argument based on our own common experiences.

When we are engaged in deep thought or conversation, there can be very loud sounds going on in the background that one doesn't consciously notice. Block asks us to imagine an intense conversation while a loud pneumatic drill is operating in the street. During a lull in the conversation, you become suddenly aware of the noise, and you realize that you had been aware of the sound all along, but you were not *consciously* aware of it. Block's explanation of such cases is that during the conversation one is P-conscious of the noise, but when the conversation ends one also becomes A-conscious of it. Before the lull in the conversation, P-consciousness existed without any corresponding A-consciousness. That is, there were mental states that carried the qualitative character of the sound of a concrete drill, yet there was no *awareness* of the state because it was not made available to the higher systems that control reasoning and action. When the conversation paused, suddenly the qualitative character of the sound was made available to these higher systems, and so was available to conscious awareness.

In the remainder of the section Block considers and replies to a number of objections to the reasoning in the argument. We will comment only on one: Block concedes that the argument relies entirely on introspection, specifically one's purely introspective belief that one was aware of the sound throughout the conversation. He contends, however, that introspection is indispensable in explaining the nature of P-consciousness. As he puts it, "introspection is not the last word, but it is the first word, when it comes to P-consciousness." This means that the burden of proof is on someone who can put forward empirical evidence that this introspective impression is not correct.

The Conflation of P-consciousness with A-consciousness

In Section 5, Block presents several cases of how the confusion of P-consciousness and A-consciousness occurs in the inferences made from experimental evidence and in philosophical reasoning about consciousness.[2] The first that he mentions—as we highlighted earlier—is the reasoning that Bernard Baars offers for the global workspace model of consciousness. According to Block, Baars presents GWT as an account of P-consciousness, since he says it is "a theory of the nature of experience. The reader's private experience of this word, his or her mental image of yesterday's breakfast, or the feeling of a toothache."[3] Yet what he offers, Block says, is a global workspace theory of *A-consciousness*, that is, of how conscious awareness of information in working memory is made accessible to the unconscious distributed processes that shape and inform our experiences and actions. Block identifies the same conflation in the arguments of several other prominent theories of consciousness. There are too many of these arguments to survey them here.

In each case, Block's critique is similar: Theorists claim to be providing an explanation of P-consciousness, that is, of the reason for the existence of, as well as the nature of, the qualitative properties of mental states. But what they offer turns out instead to be an explanation of A-consciousness, of how information is made available for reasoning and control of action. Since the two kinds of consciousness are independent of one another, the reasoning is a form of bait-and-switch, offering one thing and delivering another.

The Fallacy of the Target Reasoning

In Section 6 Block turns to "the denouement of the paper," which is to show the mistake in reasoning that results from failing to recognize the distinction between P-consciousness and A-consciousness. At the end of the first paragraph of the section, Block quotes John Searle's argument that consciousness plays an important role in the flexibility and creativity of action. The argument uses as its illustration the abilities of people who suffer loss of consciousness as a result of an epileptic seizure. The argument quoted is as follows.

1. The epileptic seizure rendered the patient totally unconscious.
2. The patient continued to exhibit what would normally be called goal-directed behavior.

3. The patient was performing types of actions that were habitual, routine, and memorized.
4. Normal, human, conscious behavior has a degree of flexibility and creativity that was absent.
5. Therefore, consciousness adds powers of discrimination and flexibility even to memorized routine activities.

So the premises are intended to show that an absence of consciousness allows habitual or routine goal-directed actions, but not the kind of flexibility and creativity found in conscious subjects.

According to Block's analysis, the kind of consciousness Searle is referring to is P-consciousness, and the objective of the argument is to show that an absence of *P-consciousness* results in diminished capacity for action. Block's response is that if the first premise *does* concern P-consciousness, then no evidence is offered for it. In fact, Block argues, the descriptions of the subjects' behavior suggest that there *is* some degree of P-consciousness, for the kinds of routine behaviors the subjects exhibit require some degree of sensory perception of their surroundings. The kind of sensory perception Block thinks is involved is the kind described in the previous section, cases where we suddenly become aware of a loud sound that we were earlier not paying attention to. In these situations, he argues, before the awareness of the sound there is P-consciousness without A-consciousness. This is a kind of consciousness that Block claims cannot be ruled out from the studies of epileptics on which Searle draws. The limitations on the subjects' actions described in premises 2 to 4 of Searle's argument are evidence of limited *A-consciousness*, which does not preclude the possibility that the subjects have full and vivid P-consciousness, even if that same content is not available for use in deliberative action. So the argument does not show that a lack of P-consciousness results in diminished capacity for action.

At the end of the section Block turns to the cases of blindsight with which he began the article. Here he addresses arguments from A.J. Marcel and Owen Flanagan that are nearly identical to Searle's. These arguments address a blindsight subject who is thirsty but does not reach for a glass of water. These arguments, just as in Searle's, are that the information must be presented to phenomenal consciousness before it can be accessed for voluntary action. And again Block's reply is that it is the absence of *A-consciousness*, not P-consciousness, that is affecting the subject's behavior.

There is one difference in the blindsight cases from Searle's epilepsy cases: the blindsight subjects report that they have no conscious perception of the stimulus. If the subjects are somehow mistaken, then the situation reverts to Searle's case in which there might be P-consciousness but not A-consciousness. But Block says he is willing to take the subjects' introspective word on this. This means that in the blindsight cases there is neither A-consciousness nor P-consciousness, whereas in the typical subject both are present.

To this Block adds a point he acknowledged earlier: that there are no known cases of super-blindsightedness, in which a subject is clearly lacking P-consciousness but in possession of full A-consciousness. In fact, P-consciousness and A-consciousness are "almost always present or absent together, or rather this seems plausible." This is the reason, he argues, that the two are so often confused. A question Block does consider, however, is why is it necessary to keep them apart, if they rarely or never occur apart. His answer to this is that without drawing this distinction one can make the mistake of inferring that P-consciousness has a functional role in cognition. He says,

The fallacy, then, is jumping from the premise that "consciousness" is missing—without being clear about what kind of consciousness is missing—to the conclusion that P-consciousness has a certain function.

The point of the distinction, then, is to avoid erroneous inferences.

A Model of P-consciousness and A-consciousness

Block's arguments for the distinction between P-consciousness and A-consciousness are philosophical, although his claims are supported by certain empirical results. We can, however, review a theory that puts forward a neurological account of visual perception that supposes the existence of P-consciousness prior to and separate from any A-consciousness. This is represented by the recurrent processing model of vision advanced by Victor Lamme at the University of Amsterdam.[4] Lamme is often cited along with Block as an advocate of the distinctness of the two forms of consciousness.

According to Lamme, when information from the optical nerves reaches the visual cortex it is passed through a series of subsections of the cortex, labeled V1 through V5. This sequence Lamme calls "feedforward sweep." Feedforward connections extract high-level information from the receptive field of the retinas, and they can also produce behavioral responses to bright lights or moving stimuli. Evidence indicates, however, that no cognitive effects are generated from this process. As soon as information is passed to higher cortical levels, a second process occurs, which Lamme calls "recurrent processing." Information that has reached higher cortical subsections, and which has already undergone a degree of analysis, is passed back to the lower levels and is used to fine-tune the information there. Information thus becomes increasingly refined through the interactions between sub-systems. According to Lamme, this recurrent processing generates rich representations of the visual scene, and this is what produces P-consciousness. But as long as the processes remain local, within small regions of the cortex, the information is not globally available. There is, then, no A-consciousness.

However, as the recurrent interactions spread and the representations become richer, two things happen. First, the interactions reach the executive and memory regions of the brain. At this point, the information becomes globally accessible, and the information about the scene is put into the context of the system's needs and goals. Second, given the larger amount of information, there is less space for concurrent analyses of different items of information, so only certain items from the visual scene are selected. This is the function of attention, of which Lamme says, "It seems that attention guards the gate towards a representation that can be consciously reported or remembered." There is, at this later stage of information processing, A-consciousness of the visual scene in the two senses advocated by Block: informational promiscuity, and availability for action and reporting.

Consciousness and Awareness

Our next reading is from David J. Chalmers. Chalmers is a University Professor of Philosophy and Neural Science at New York University. His theory of consciousness is defended in his book, *The Conscious Mind*, published in 1996. In this book Chalmers denies that conscious experience can be reduced to functional properties of neural processes in the manner suggested by GWT. But his argument for this conclusion is very different from Block's. Chalmers does not accept the distinction Block draws between P-consciousness and A-consciousness. Rather, his rejection of functional reduction is for the reason that it doesn't answer the right question about conscious experience. While functional theories like Baars's can solve what Chalmers calls the "easy problems of consciousness," they cannot answer the "hard problem." (We will discuss each of these terms further below.) This distinction has become quite famous in the literature on consciousness since Chalmers's book was published.

We will look first at Chalmers's view of the relationship between conscious experience and cognitive function. For this purpose we will turn to Sections 6.2 and 6.3 of Chalmers's book, *The Conscious Mind*. In these sections Chalmers distinguishes *consciousness*, by which he means qualitative character of conscious experience, from *awareness*. The term 'awareness' is most often used to refer to a state of consciousness, as something consciously before the mind. But awareness, as Chalmers defines it, is a *functional* state of the brain. It is "the psychological correlate of consciousness." By this he means that, where consciousness is information represented in experience, awareness is information represented in the systems that guide and control behavior. Awareness, Chalmers says, is "a state wherein some information is directly accessible, and available for the deliberate control of behavior and for verbal report."[5] Thus he defines this notion in a way very similar to how Block defines A-consciousness. Later on, in Section 6.3, Chalmers extends this definition of awareness. There he defines it as "direct availability for global control. That is, a subject is aware of some information when that information is directly available to bring to bear in the direction of a wide range of behavioral processes." The content of the judgments in awareness are made available to many different cognitive processes. Awareness, then, is the functional property that Baars calls global accessibility. Our question, then, concerns the relationship Chalmers sees between conscious experience and awareness.

Structural Coherence

Chalmers's first statement about the relations between consciousness and awareness is that they always co-occur: "where there is consciousness, there is awareness, and where there is (the right kind of) awareness, there is consciousness." Contrary to Block's assertion of phenomenal consciousness in the absence of global access, Chalmers claims that they always coincide. But Chalmers asserts a much closer relationship between consciousness and awareness than just their constant co-occurrence. In his view, the two always exactly mirror one another. To understand this properly, we need to unpack the idea of *structural coherence*.

'Structure' is a term that refers to the elements that make up a particular situation or state of affairs, as well as the relations that exist between those elements. For example, a family is a structure. The elements are the people that make up the family, and the relations are ones of parent, child, sibling, grandparent, cousin, and so on. A triangle is also a structure with vertices and sides. Chalmers argues that conscious experience has "a detailed internal structure." The visual field, for example, has many elements—e.g., patches of color—and these stand in many spatial relations to one another. The spatial relations give shape and depth to the different parts of the visual field. Chalmers describes the character of this structure in some detail.

In the middle of a long paragraph, where it might easily be missed, Chalmers asserts his central claim. He makes it first about the structure of visual perception: "It turns out that this three-dimensional *phenomenal* structure is mirrored by a three-dimensional structure in the color information processed *within our perceptual systems*" (our emphasis). That is, the structure that makes up the field of visual experience corresponds element-by-element and relation-by-relation with the structure of the information that is processed in the visual system of the brain. And Chalmers claims that the same kind of correspondence is found in the other areas of conscious experience, such as sound and taste: In general, what we experience in consciousness mirrors the information that is made available to the processing systems of the brain. Chalmers ends the section with the following summary:

> So alongside the general principle that where there is consciousness, there is awareness, and vice versa, we have a more specific principle: the structure of consciousness is mirrored by the structure of awareness, and the structure of awareness is mirrored by the structure of consciousness. I will call this the principle of structural coherence. This is a central and systematic relation between phenomenology and psychology, and ultimately can be cashed out into a relation between phenomenology and underlying physical processes.

Some Problem Cases and What They Reveal

In Section 6.3, Chalmers revises and fine-tunes the notion of awareness. First, he discusses the matter of global control, which we mentioned earlier, and makes some remarks about the application of the concept of awareness to non-human animals. Of interest to us in this section is his discussion of blindsight and other similar cases that appear to separate conscious experience from the global accessibility of information across the cognitive system.

With regard to blindsight, Chalmers says that it might at first appear that in such cases consciousness and functional role come apart, because the subjects report no conscious experience of the objects in their blind spot while they seem to extract information about those objects nonetheless. But to this Chalmers points out that the information about the objects of which the subjects are unaware is not *globally* accessible. It is not accessible for deliberate control of action nor for reporting. Precisely the kind of access required for awareness is lacking in these cases. Such cases, he says, "cannot damage the principle of coherence; they can only bolster and refine it."

Notice the difference between this claim and Block's argument that conscious experience—P-consciousness—has no relation to global accessibility. Therefore, in order to defend the principle of structural coherence, Chalmers has to deal with Block's examples of cases where P-consciousness and A-consciousness can occur independently. To the possibility of A-consciousness and P-consciousness, Chalmers responds that the only cases Block offers are thought experiments involving zombies and super-blindsight. Such cases, Chalmers admits, are conceivable. In fact, he himself embraces the possibility that cognitive functions could occur independently of conscious experience. But in fact such possibilities do not occur in human mental life, as the principle of structural coherence states. By this principle there are no cases of global accessibility independently of conscious experience.

P-consciousness without A-consciousness is a different matter, since Block describes situations in which he says this does occur. First, recall that he gives his example of a person suddenly becoming aware, during a lull in a conversation, of a loud noise that had been going on unnoticed for some time. Block argues that during the conversation the person was phenomenally conscious of the noise, but there was no access consciousness of it. In another example, Block refers to experiments in which people report seeing all nine letters of an array on a screen (that is, being conscious of them), but they are able to report only one row of letters at a time. To these examples Chalmers responds with a concept of information of which a subject is aware, but that information is not *accessed*. On his definition, awareness is defined in terms of what is *potentially accessible*, rather than what is *actually* accessed. When awareness is defined in this way (dispositionally), then it is straightforward to say that the subjects were conscious of the information (as Block says), *and* they were aware of it (the information was potentially accessible), but they had not actually accessed it. In both cases, information that is potentially accessible (the loud noise, the nine letters) is blocked from access by what the subject is actually attending to (the conversation, the three letters that are focused on).

The Easy Problems and the Hard Problem

At this point, let's take stock of Chalmers's position. He argues, contra Block, that there is only one kind of consciousness, and that is conscious experience, Block's P-consciousness. Second, he argues that this consciousness coincides with, and exactly mirrors, the information that is globally accessible for deliberate control of action and speech. Notice that this much is in complete agreement with Baars's functional reductionism. For it would seem that the reason conscious experience has such a close relationship with global accessibility is that conscious experience *is* global accessibility. (Compare: Why does Alecia Beth Moore spend so much time with Pink?) Thus Chalmers's principle of structural coherence seems to offer evidence for the identity of consciousness and a certain functional state of the brain. But Chalmers does not take this avenue. Despite the close relationship between consciousness and awareness, he argues that they are two entirely different states. It is to make this claim that Chalmers introduces his distinction between the easy problems and the hard problem of consciousness. The most concise statement of this argument is in an article, "Facing Up to the Problem of Consciousness," which Chalmers published just before the release of his book.

In the second paragraph of "Facing Up to the Problem of Consciousness," Chalmers makes a point that is similar to one made by Ned Block. Like Block, Chalmers argues that the word 'consciousness' is used to refer to several aspects of the mind; it is, as Block says, a mongrel concept. Chalmers also agrees with Block that there is an important distinction to be drawn between the phenomenology of consciousness and cognitive functioning. Despite these agreements with Block, Chalmers denies that the difference between phenomenology and function indicates a distinction between two *types* of consciousness. Instead, it reveals the fact that entirely different explanations have to be given of the qualitative character of consciousness and of the cognitive functions that conscious processes perform. According to Chalmers, functional theories, like Baars's global workspace theory, solve what he calls the "easy problems" of consciousness, but ignore the "hard problem." The so-called easy problems involve giving functional explanations of the mental processes associated with consciousness. The hard problem is to explain how such cognitive functions can give rise to conscious experience.

Let's look first at the **"easy" problems**. He offers a list of such problems in the second section of his article. Two of them are the ability to "discriminate, categorize, and react to environmental stimuli, and the ability of a system to access its own inner states." What these problems all have in common is that they are all aspects of the mind that lend themselves to explanation in terms of functional processes or neural processes. For example, a theory might explain how a cognitive system can recognize objects in the environment in terms of the computations involved in performing the task. Indeed cognitive scientists have constructed many such theories of various perceptual abilities. Chalmers calls these the "easy" problems, not because their solutions are obvious, but rather because we understand what is involved in constructing a solution. They are familiar problems, even if their solutions are complex.

The **"hard" problem**, Chalmers says, is the problem of explaining how it is that there is such a phenomenon as the qualitative character of experience at all. Thus he says,

> It is widely agreed that experience arises from a physical basis, but we have no good explanation of why and how it arises. Why should physical processing give rise to a rich inner life at all? It seems objectively unreasonable that it should, and yet it does.

Why the Hard Problem Is Hard

The reason we know how to go about constructing solutions to the easy problems, Chalmers argues, is that in each case what needs explaining is an ability of the mind or a function that some part of the mind performs. For example, the mind is capable of discriminating between objects in its environment; how is that possible? To answer a question like that it is necessary to describe a mechanism that has that ability, and then to show how such a mechanism is embedded in the neural processes of the brain. A very well-known example of this kind of task is the set of explanations of visual processing constructed by David Marr and his colleagues in the 1980s. Marr divided the stages of vision into a set of computational tasks, worked out how these tasks could be carried out by a computational mechanism, and then looked for evidence that the brain uses a process that realizes such a mechanism. The field of cognitive science is to a large extent the construction of theories of this sort to give explanations of the information-processing abilities of the mind.

As Chalmers points out, the same type of explanation is offered throughout the sciences. He compares this with the mechanical explanation of how hereditary information is carried in DNA. The DNA molecule is a mechanism that performs the task of passing information from the parent cells to the offspring. Functional explanations are an extension of the mechanical sciences that were introduced in the seventeenth century. But, as we have seen, it is the qualitative character of consciousness that the introduction of the mechanical sciences made so problematic. So much so that it led early mechanical scientists such as Descartes to dualism.

Chalmers argues, then, that explaining the existence of conscious experience is hard precisely because it is not a call to explain a mechanical function or ability. Consciousness may well have a function, he admits. But when we ask, why and how is there conscious experience, we are not asking a question about any specific function, but rather why the performance of certain mental functions (like perceptual discrimination) is accompanied by conscious states that have a qualitative character.

Giving the Wrong Explanations

Chalmers claims that it is common to confuse the easy problems of giving functional explanations of mental abilities with the hard problem. In the fourth section of his paper Chalmers presents examples of cases where a solution is given to one of the functional problems with the implication that a solution has been given to the problem of consciousness generally, including the hard problem. One of his examples is the hypothesis that consciousness is a neural activity, called binding, whereby separate pieces of information are brought together for use by other mental processes. His other example is Baars's global workspace theory, which we reviewed earlier. According to Chalmers, these two theories are examples of the nature of nearly all the explanations of consciousness currently on offer. In each case, an explanation is given of a functional process of the mind, such as exchanging or facilitating communication between mental processes. In the case of global workspace theory, the theory states that items in working memory are highlighted and thus accessible across the system. The issue, Chalmers says, is understanding how theories such as these help in answering the hard question. Even if consciousness does make global accessibility possible, there remains the question, "why should global accessibility give rise to conscious experience?"

On this issue Chalmers claims that several answers are given. Some researchers assert that the hard problem is simply too difficult, and offer their theories as answers to questions that can be more easily addressed. Others, like Daniel Dennett, assert that once the easy problems are all solved there is nothing left to explain—there simply is no hard problem at all. Still others assert that their theories are explanations of consciousness in the full sense, while the important step of explaining the existence of qualitative experience is "passed over quickly,...and usually ends up looking like magic." A fourth strategy is to take the existence of conscious experience as given, and to offer instead an explanation of the relations between different aspects of experience (between color experiences, for example) in terms of the processing abilities of the mind (to make discriminations within the visual environment, for example). Finally, some theorists attempt to find the "neural correlates" of consciousness, that is, the neural processes that underlie aspects of conscious experience. Each of these five different strategies, Chalmers argues, fails to provide a solution to the hard problem; none of them explains why conscious experience occurs and how.

The Failure of Reduction

Chalmers contends, then, that something must be added to these explanations of the functional abilities of the mind—an "extra ingredient" that will tell us how consciousness arises. There are, he says, a number of theories that have attempted to do this. They each appeal to some novel property that might account for the unique features of consciousness. Some suggest nonalgorithmic processing; others nonlinear dynamics; and yet others quantum mechanics. Yet the same problem arises here as with the functional explanations. One must still ask the question, how do these processes give rise to conscious experience? For we can always suppose that these same processes could occur in the absence of conscious experience.

Here Chalmers makes a point very similar to Nagel's. Each of these attempts at explaining consciousness, both the functional explanations and the appeals to some novel processes, are attempts at reducing conscious experience to some more basic or fundamental processes. They want to say that conscious experience is really X, where X is some functional or physical process of the brain. But reduction of this kind, Chalmers argues, is impossible in the case of consciousness. Reduction works when an explanation is sought of a function or process in terms of more fundamental functions and processes. For example, we can reduce genes to elements of DNA because the function of genes in inheritance can be carried out by the molecular structure of

DNA. But the question how conscious experience arises is not a request for a reduction of one process to more fundamental ones, so it cannot be answered in those terms.

Nonreductive Explanation and Naturalistic Dualism

Chalmers's solution to this situation is to argue that consciousness is a fundamental phenomenon, one that cannot be explained in terms of, or reduced to, anything more basic. Such a solution, he argues, was adopted in the nineteenth century to explain electromagnetism. When it became apparent that mechanical properties of matter, motion or gravitational attraction for example, could not explain electromagnetic phenomena, James Clerk Maxwell and other physicists concluded that electromagnetic charge and electromagnetic forces are fundamental properties of matter. They expanded the number of basic properties and basic laws in physics. Newton did something similar in postulating the existence of mass and gravitational attraction to explain the motion of the planets and tides. According to Chalmers, the same step must be taken in the case of consciousness. We need to admit conscious experience into our ontology as a new fundamental property with its own fundamental laws.

Here Chalmers makes a general point that underlies his overall position. He says that we must admit consciousness as fundamental because, "everything in physics is compatible with the absence of consciousness." This statement draws out an element of Chalmers's argument that is implicit in what we have looked at so far. Whenever a functional or physical aspect of the mind or the brain is postulated as an explanation of consciousness, Chalmers says that we can always ask the question, "Why should that process be accompanied by conscious experience?" Notice the fact that in cases of reduction such a question cannot be asked. We cannot ask why H_2O is accompanied by water, or why DNA is accompanied by genes. This is why Chalmers believes there cannot be a reductive explanation of conscious experience.

Chalmers is thus arguing for a version of property dualism. There are, he says, "basic properties over and above the properties invoked in physics." But he defends his thesis as an "innocent" version of dualism. It does not contradict anything in physics or introduce anything spiritual or mystical. It is nothing more than an expansion of the fundamental properties of the world in a manner similar to what Maxwell and other physicists have done in the past. In the end, the world will still be seen as the product of a certain set of fundamental properties and laws. Chalmers gives his position the name **naturalistic dualism**. This position makes consciousness more akin to physics than to biology, he says, because biology is fully reducible to physics and requires no fundamental biological properties. In physics, however, there are properties that cannot be reduced to anything more fundamental. They are what philosophers sometimes call "**brute facts**." Conscious experience, in Chalmers's view, is similarly a brute fact.

What's Really at Issue?

Let's review again the relationship between Chalmers's position and that of a global workspace theorist like Bernard Baars. According to the global workspace theorist, global access is the very same property as consciousness in Chalmers's sense. Our conscious experience of objects in our perceptual field is *one and the same state as* the accessibility of the information about those objects to processing systems across the brain. According to global workspace theory, this identity means that descriptions of the functioning of awareness explain the nature and occurrence of consciousness. Chalmers agrees with Baars that consciousness always accompanies, and precisely mirrors, the information made globally accessible. But this is not because consciousness is numerically identical to global accessibility, but because of the principle of structural coherence, which is a metaphysical principle relating two fundamentally different sets of states. Given his dualism, Chalmers claims that conscious experience, which is one side of the relationship of structural coherence, is a fundamental property of the world, irreducible to any functional or physical properties. So the principle of structural coherence says that the purely experiential, irreducible content of consciousness is exactly mirrored in the strictly functional, reducible content of cognitive states.

Interestingly, there is a sense in which Chalmers's theory is the same as the functionalist account, but with the addition of conscious experience as a distinct property of functional states. Thus, Chalmers says, "This project can be seen as a search for a sort of functionalist account of consciousness."[6] The task is to identify all the functional processes of the brain that are associated with consciousness. Yet he continues,

> It is not a *reductive* functionalist account—it does not say that the playing of some functional role is all there is to consciousness, or all there is to be explained. Rather, it is a nonreductive account, one that gives functional criteria for when consciousness arises. All the same, there is a sense in which it is playing in the same ballpark as reductive functionalist accounts; these also give functional criteria for when consciousness arises, alongside their more ambitious metaphysical claims.[7]

The "metaphysical claims" he is referring to here are statements of identity between functional states and consciousness—that playing a certain functional role is all there is to consciousness. The difference between Chalmers's theory and functionalist theories is his denial of this claim.

What lies behind Chalmers's insistence that conscious experience is not reducible to functional states or processes of the brain is that such a reduction does not solve the hard problem: Why should such functions or processes give rise to conscious experience? His answer is that no functional (or neural) reductionist answer can be given to this question. In this manner, Chalmers's position is akin to that of Thomas Nagel. What is common to both Nagel and Chalmers is the view that giving a functional description of a cognitive system can never capture or explain the qualitative character of consciousness in that system. It is thus impossible ever to have a true statement of the form, "Consciousness is identical to X," where X is some functional description of the system. Others argue that it is perfectly possible that we will find a true identity statement of that kind that will yield a scientific explanation of the nature of consciousness. For example, while Daniel Dennett denies that there are qualia, he does hold that the features that conscious experience does have can all be explained in terms of various functional features of systems that have consciousness. Whatever facts there are about consciousness, they are functional facts. Since these positions were formulated and sharpened neither side has yielded to the other.

Brute Facts Again

Valerie Gray Hardcastle explains the impasse in this debate by arguing that the differences between those who hold these opposing positions are in fact impossible to bridge. Hardcastle is Professor of Philosophy, Psychology, and Psychiatry & Behavioral Neuroscience at The University of Cincinnati. As well as work on consciousness and neuroscience, she studies the neuroscience of violence and the implications of embodied cognition. In her article, "The Why of Consciousness: A Non-Issue for Materialists" she refers to the two principal groups in the debate over consciousness as *naturalists* and *sceptics*. The former are those who claim that consciousness is not fundamentally different from any other phenomenon in the natural world, and will eventually yield to reduction in the same manner as other natural phenomena. The latter emphasize the mystery of consciousness, and are skeptical of any functional or biological explanation of consciousness. According to Hardcastle, this divide is not about the correctness of one or another theory, but rather a difference in opinion about what explanation really is. Hence, their arguments talk past one another, and no amount of further argumentation will resolve the disagreement.

According to Hardcastle, the basis of the skeptical argument is that assertions of the form, "Consciousness is simply X," fail to explain *why* such an identity statement should be true. It doesn't make the assertion "intelligible, plausible, or reasonable." This is what the sceptics are looking for in an explanation of consciousness. Therefore, no identity statement of the kind that naturalists could propose will ever explain consciousness in *this* sense.

Because we cannot explain why a mind-brain identity statement should be true, Hardcastle argues, Chalmers sees consciousness as a brute fact—a basic fact that simply has no explanation, such as the existence of gravitational attraction. Scientists do not try to explain why it is reasonable that gravitation exists; such an explanation, we now assume, is simply impossible. Similarly, because we cannot explain why it is reasonable that consciousness should exist, Chalmers contends that it too should be taken as a brute fact.

Hardcastle gives an argument for thinking that consciousness is not a brute fact. Her point is similar to one that Armstrong makes in "The Nature of Mind." He says that it is simply implausible that a brute fact about the world should exist only in highly complex organisms; in all other cases, brute facts are features of the basic parts of the physical world. Properties such as mass and electromagnetic charge are properties of the most elementary components of the world and exist in all things. Consciousness, however, exists only in the higher animal kingdom. Hardcastle gives a reason why such a scenario is unlikely. If (a) consciousness is a biological phenomenon, and (b) every other biological phenomenon is explained in terms of more fundamental facts such as chemistry, then it would be "perverse" to think that a single biological fact—consciousness—is fundamental, independent of chemistry.

According to Hardcastle, Chalmers avoids that awkward situation by denying that consciousness is a biological phenomenon. As we recall, he claims that consciousness is a separate aspect of information from the physical aspect. It is a brute fact about information, not a biological fact about higher organisms. The basis for this claim in turn is the assertion of a coherence between the structure of consciousness and that of the physical processes of the brain. But Hardcastle argues that this only makes matters worse for Chalmers's position. For commonly the existence of the parallel between consciousness and physical processes of the brain is given as a reason for believing that the two are numerically identical. This is a standard argument that identity theorists offer: The many parallels between consciousness and the brain are strong evidence for their identity. One simple way of explaining a structural coherence between system A and system B is that A and B are the same thing—every system is structurally coherent with itself!

Mysterians

So the question then is, why does Chalmers reject the identity of consciousness and brain processes, which the structural coherence of the two would normally support? Hardcastle's answer to this question, in Section II, is that Chalmers is one of the **mysterians**. These are people who argue that consciousness is an impenetrable mystery. No identity statement can ever tell us why a particular biological or functional process is identical to the remarkable fact of consciousness. A bald statement of identity, "Consciousness is simply X," does not satisfy our need to know how this identity is *possible*.

Hardcastle's response to this argument is that the same question could be asked, with the same lack of a clear answer, for any other identity statement in the sciences. So consciousness does not stand out as a phenomenon radically different from others in the natural world. For example, Hardcastle says that there could just as easily be "water-mysterians." Such people are fascinated by the mystery of water—the "wateriness of water." They would agree that water and H_2O are *correlated*. But they would argue that we can't simply identify the one with other, because that would leave the question, why is water H_2O rather than something else? Why is *this* chemical combination the origin of the wateriness of water? The bald statement of identity doesn't tell us why it is reasonable that water is H_2O. A similar comparison, Hardcastle argues, would be "life-mysterians," who are fascinated by the mystery of life. No reduction to any biological facts would ever explain why those facts and not others constitute life, or would explain the aliveness of life.

Here Chalmers follows Saul Kripke, whose arguments we considered in Chapter Eight. Kripke argues that the identity of water and H_2O is a conceptual truth—whatever is *not* H_2O simply isn't water. We couldn't imagine a world in which there is water that isn't H_2O; such a world is conceptually impossible. The same, however, is not true of consciousness. We could not argue that whatever doesn't have a certain biological or functional description simply isn't consciousness. For we can imagine consciousness occurring in the absence of any given biological or functional properties. Therefore, the occurrence of consciousness will remain a mystery—a brute fact that has no reduction to any other facts.

According to Hardcastle, however, there is no difference whatsoever in the arguments of the consciousness-mysterians and those of the water- and life-mysterians. In each case, the mysterians will insist that the phenomenon in question (the wateriness of water, the aliveness of life, or the qualitative character of consciousness) can be conceived to exist in the absence of any given physical, biological, or functional facts. The phenomenon would then have to be taken as a mysterious brute fact, irreducible to any others. What can we say to such mysterians? According to Hardcastle, nothing. As long as mysterians remain determined that the phenomenon cannot be reduced, there is nothing we can say to convince them otherwise. The naturalists and the mysterians are stuck at an impasse.

Reduction and the Scientific Enterprise

In Section III Hardcastle considers one final way of arguing that consciousness really is different from cases of successful scientific reduction. In the case of the reduction of water to H_2O we have more than simply an identity claim that has empirical support. The identity statement is embedded in (forms a part of) a much larger set of scientific theories, what Hardcastle calls a "scientific framework." This includes molecular chemistry, based on the table of the elements, and sub-atomic physics, which describes the composition and behavior of sub-atomic particles. So the identity of water with H_2O can be explained as part of our general scientific understanding of the physical world. The skeptic can then argue that no such framework exists for consciousness. We have no idea how the reduction of consciousness to any biological or functional processes of the brain would fit in with a larger set of theories. At present, the phenomenon of consciousness lies outside our scientific framework altogether. A crucial phrase in the preceding paragraph, however, is "at present." According to Hardcastle, Chalmers cannot conclude from this argument that consciousness *cannot ever* be embedded in a larger scientific framework, but only that at the present time we don't know what such a framework might look like. So the issue, as Hardcastle sees it, is a matter of confidence in the naturalist project. Naturalists are committed to the goal of eventually finding a satisfactory reduction of consciousness that forms a part of an overall understanding of the biological and physical world. The lack of such a reduction at present is no reason to abandon the project. The skeptic, however, is committed to the view that that project is ultimately impossible. The question which of these commitments will prove justified will have to wait for the future development of the field.

Yet Hardcastle is doubtful that the skeptic will yield to such an outcome. For at bottom she believes that the difference of view between the naturalist and the skeptic is not about the possibility of success or failure; it is about the goal itself. The goal, both for the naturalist and the skeptic, is some form of explanation. But Hardcastle argues that the two sides disagree on what a successful explanation should do. The skeptic is seeking an explanation that will account for the mystery of consciousness, whereas the naturalist accepts the mystery of consciousness in the same manner as the mysteries of water and life. Hardcastle draws on the work of Bas van Fraassen on the nature of scientific explanation. He argues that there is no such thing as *the* explanation of a given phenomenon. Requests for explanation are requests for answers to questions, and what counts as a satisfactory answer will depend on what the question is. The skeptic simply does not accept the kinds of questions that naturalists are asking as satisfactory. As Hardcastle puts it, skeptics and naturalists are playing by different rules.

There is, then, no solution to the impasse. Participants in the debate can only attempt to gain converts to their side, but the question "Can there be a reductive explanation of consciousness?" is one on which there are no common grounds for resolution.

Against Dissociative Theories

The final article in this chapter is by Michael A. Cohen and Daniel C. Dennett. We met Dennett already in Chapter Eleven in the context of the debates about qualia. Cohen is Assistant Professor of Psychology and Neuroscience at Amherst College, and also a Research Scientist in the McGovern Institute for Brain Research at MIT. Before doing his PhD at Harvard, Cohen was a student of Dennett's at Tufts University. Their arguments are directed against what they call "dissociative" theories of consciousness, by which they mean theories based on the assertion that phenomenal consciousness and access consciousness are distinct mental states. Within this group of theories they include both Block's distinction between P-consciousness and A-consciousness, and Lamme's recurrent processing theory.

The position the authors take in this article is closely related to Dennett's skepticism regarding qualia. They argue that any distinction between phenomenal consciousness and access consciousness can be neither confirmed nor falsified by any evidence, and therefore the distinction lies outside the scope of science. The same point, they argue, applies to Chalmers's hard problem of consciousness. They conclude that adequate theories of consciousness must explain the formation of representations in the brain, but they must also "explain *in functional terms* how those representations are experienced and accessed by the multiple functions constituting an observer" (our emphasis). To demand a search for consciousness outside of these cognitive functions will only block further research. For this reason, Cohen and Dennett argue that Chalmers's hard question is unanswerable for precisely the same reason that dissociative theories fail: The attempt to separate consciousness from cognitive function.

Cohen and Dennett's article has two parts. The first considers an argument in support of the existence of phenomenal consciousness independent of access consciousness. The authors argue that the evidence cited in this argument can also be explained without the necessity of conscious experience without access. To this, they add additional evidence that supports their explanation. In the second part of their article they describe what they refer to as a "perfect experiment" for establishing conscious experience divorced from any cognitive functions. They argue that such an experiment would lack any means of obtaining results at all.

Does Phenomenology Overflow Access?

Cohen and Dennett first cite an argument by Ned Block that we experience more than is accessed by the cognitive functions of the brain, and that this demonstrates that there is P-consciousness outside of A-consciousness. Block offers two experimental results that support this claim. One of these is an experiment by George Sperling, in which subjects were shown three rows of four characters followed by a blank field. The subjects reported that they could see all of the characters, but when asked to identify them, they could name only about four. To test whether their report that they saw all the characters was true, Sperling introduced a wrinkle in the procedure. He played a tone after the display, and told subjects to report the top row if the tone was high, the bottom row if the tone was low, and the middle row if the tone was intermediate. Since subjects could successfully report any row following the tone, the evidence suggested that there was experience of all of the rows, despite the fact that only one row persisted in working memory.

To this argument, Cohen and Dennett reply that it is not necessary to postulate consciousness outside of access to explain this result. It is possible that the identities of the characters are stored in unconscious memory until the tone brings them into the focus of attention. They argue that before the tone subjects are aware only of the row they are attending to, together with an impression that there are other characters. To support this claim they cite a further experiment in which subjects are given an array of characters similar to those in Sperling's experiment. But in this case the subjects do not notice when all but the attended characters are replaced by uniform Xs. They do notice, however, when there are no other characters at all.

Cohen and Dennett argue that their interpretation of the Sperling result is also supported by a phenomenon known as *change blindness*. For example, in one experiment subjects are shown two nearly identical pictures in succession, with a blank image between them. The images are identical except that in the second image the area outside the center of attention is severely degraded. When the succession of images is fairly rapid, subjects do not notice the degradation in the second image. This suggests that people do not experience all the details of a visual scene, even though it seems to them that they do. The explanation Cohen and Dennett give for the false impression is that normally we can move our focal attention around a scene very quickly and easily, giving the false impression we see all of it at once.

A Perfect Experiment

The second part of Cohen and Dennett's article makes a more general claim. They argue that it is simply impossible to empirically confirm (or disconfirm) the existence of conscious experience outside of function. Any claim that there is such experience is thus unscientific. For this they present a thought experiment in which we are to consider what they call a "perfect experiment" for testing the possibility of conscious experience without cognitive access. They ask us to imagine that surgeons could surgically separate the portions of the visual cortex that represent color from all other visual representations, such as motion, luminance, or object recognition. These other representations are all connected to higher-level processes in the normal way. When presented with an object like an apple, the subjects would report seeing no color, because the area responsible for color would be separated from all other functions, including speech. It would be as if the subjects have blindsight for color only. Yet they would nonetheless recognize the object as an apple, and otherwise respond normally to it. Despite the subjects' insistence that they experience no color, we would know that all the *neurological* conditions for experience of color are in place. Those conditions would thus indicate that the subject does have experience of color, but has no access to that experience.

An argument that neurological evidence for conscious experience must be accepted, even in the absence of behavioral or functional evidence, is made by Victor Lamme, whom we introduced earlier. Lamme calls this approach "taking the neural stance." According to this model, recurrent processing generates experience of a visual scene, even though the content of that experience is not accessible to any executive or memory functions. He argues that the scientific study of consciousness must adopt the neural stance in order to accommodate all the evidence available. Lamme contends that dissociating conscious experience from other cognitive functions is "a prerequisite for using the term at all."[8]

Cohen and Dennett argue that such a position takes the distinctness of conscious experience outside of the domain of science altogether. For if the "perfect experiment" doesn't disprove the distinctness of phenomenal and access consciousness, then nothing else *could*. The dissociative hypothesis is unfalsifiable by any evidence whatsoever. So the claim that there is conscious experience independent of any cognitive function, based on neurological evidence alone, is an untestable and therefore unscientific hypothesis.

What Should a Science of Consciousness Study?

The final two sections of Cohen and Dennett's article look at the question of what their argument reveals about the character of the scientific study of conscious experience. They maintain that "proper scientific theories of consciousness are those that specify which functions are necessary for consciousness to arise." Evidence for conscious experience in neural activity has a functional basis, or else no basis at all. This claim goes against dissociative theories like those of Block and Lamme, and also against Chalmers's naturalistic dualism. According to Chalmers, conscious experience is a property of the mind that exists alongside of, and parallel to, cognitive function, and yet it is an entirely distinct property. His dualism is thus committed to the claim that the cognitive functions that are always *in fact* accompanied by consciousness could *in principle* operate without such accompaniment. But Cohen and Dennett argue that this hypothesis too is entirely untestable, and hence unscientific. This is because Chalmers, like Block, has severed the connection between consciousness and function, the only basis on which conscious experience can be empirically studied. "Any theory," they say, "wherein the neural correlates of conscious experience are separate from the neural correlates of cognitive function is ultimately doomed."

Notes

1. A leading developer of the theory is Bernard Baars, of The Neurosciences Institute in California. The description of GWT in this section is drawn principally from two of his articles: "A Thoroughly Empirical Approach to Consciousness," *Psyche: An Interdisciplinary Journal of Research On Consciousness* 1 (1994), http://psyche.cs.monash.edu.au/v2/psyche-1-6-baars.html, and "In the Theatre of Consciousness," *Journal of Consciousness Studies* 4 (1997), pp. 292–309.

2. Section 5 of Block's article is not reproduced in the readings. Here we offer a synopsis of some main points of the section.

3. Bernard Baars, *A Cognitive Theory of Consciousness* (Cambridge: Cambridge University Press, 1988), p. 14.

4. See, for example, Victor A.F. Lamme, "Towards a True Neural Stance on Consciousness," *Trends in Cognitive Science* 10 (2006): pp. 494–501.

5. The content of these states, he says, correspond to the contents of "first-order phenomenal judgments," an example of which would be judgments about the appearances of things in the world, such as the visual appearance of a red book on a table.

6. David Chalmers, *The Conscious Mind: In Search of a Fundamental Theory* (Oxford: Oxford University Press, 1996), p. 229.

7. Ibid., emphasis added.

8. Lamme, V.A., "Towards a True Neural Stance on Consciousness," *Trends in Cognitive Sciences* 10 (11) (2006): pp. 494–501.

NED BLOCK

"On a Confusion about a Function of Consciousness"

Abstract

Consciousness is a mongrel concept: there are a number of very different "consciousnesses." Phenomenal consciousness is experience; the phenomenally conscious aspect of a state is what it is like to be in that state. The mark of access-consciousness, by contrast, is availability for use in reasoning and rationally guiding speech and action. These concepts are often partly or totally conflated, with bad results. This target article uses as an example a form of reasoning about a function of "consciousness" based on the phenomenon of blindsight. Some information about stimuli in the blind field is represented in the brains of blindsight patients, as shown by their correct "guesses." They cannot harness this information in the service of action, however, and this is said to show that a function of phenomenal consciousness is somehow to enable information represented in the brain to guide action. But stimuli in the blind field are both access-unconscious and phenomenally unconscious. The fallacy is: an obvious function of the machinery of access consciousness is illicitly transferred to phenomenal consciousness.

1. Introduction

The concept of consciousness is a hybrid, or better, a mongrel concept: the word "consciousness" connotes a number of different concepts and denotes a number of different phenomena. We reason about "consciousness" using some premises that apply to one of the phenomena that fall under "consciousness," other premises that apply to other "consciousnesses," and we end up with trouble. There are many parallels in the history of science. Aristotle used "velocity" sometimes to mean average velocity and sometimes to mean instantaneous velocity; his failure to see the distinction caused confusion (Kuhn 1964). The Florentine Experimenters of the seventeenth century used a single word (roughly translatable as "degree of heat") for temperature and for heat, generating paradoxes. For example, when they measured "degree of heat" by whether various heat sources could melt paraffin, heat source *A* came out hotter than *B*, but when they measured "degree of heat" by how much ice a heat source could melt in a given time, *B* was hotter than *A* (Wiser & Carey 1983). These are very different cases, but there is a similarity, one that they share with the case of "consciousness." The similarity is: very different concepts are treated as a single concept. I think we all have some tendency to make this mistake in the case of "consciousness."

[…]

Patients with damage in primary visual cortex typically have "blind" areas in their visual fields. If the experimenter flashes a stimulus in one of these blind areas and asks the patient what he saw, the patient answers "nothing." The striking phenomenon is that some (but not all) of these patients are able to "guess" reliably about certain features of the stimulus, features having to do with motion, location, direction (e.g., whether a grid is horizontal or vertical). In "guessing," they are able to discriminate some simple forms. If they are asked to grasp an object in the blind field (which they say they cannot see), they can shape their hands in a way appropriate to grasping it, and there are some signs of color discrimination. It is interesting that visual acuity (as measured, e.g., by how fine a grating can be detected) increases further from where the patient is looking in blindsight, the opposite of normal sight. (Blindsight was first noticed by Poppel et al., 1973; there is now a huge body of literature on this and related phenomena. See Bornstein & Pittman 1992; Milner & Rugg 1992.) [See also Campion et al.: "Is Blindsight an Effect of Scattered Light, Spared Cortex, and Near-threshold Vision?" *BBS* 6(3) 1983.]

Consciousness in some sense is apparently missing (though see McGinn, 1991, p. 112, for an argument to the contrary), and with it the ability to deploy information in reasoning and rational control of action. For example, Marcel (1986) observed that a thirsty blindsight patient would not reach for a glass of water in his blind field (one must grant Marcel some "poetic license" in this influential example;

blindsight patients appear to have insufficient form perception in their blind fields to pick out a glass of water). It is tempting to argue (Barrs 1988; Flanagan 1991; 1992; Marcel 1986; 1988; van Gulick 1989) that because consciousness is missing in blindsight, consciousness must have a function of somehow enabling information represented in the brain to be used in reasoning, reporting, and rationally guiding action. I mean the "rationally" to exclude the "guessing" kind of guidance of action that blindsight patients *are* capable of in the case of stimuli presented to the blind field. The idea is that when a content is not conscious—as in the blindsight patient's blind field perceptual contents, it can influence behavior in various ways, but only when the content is conscious does it play a *rational* role; and so consciousness must be involved in promoting this rational role.

A related argument is also tempting: van Gulick (1989) and Searle (1992) discuss Penfield's (1975) observations of epileptics who have a seizure while walking, driving, or playing the piano. The epileptics continue their activities in a routinized, mechanical way despite, it is said, a total lack of consciousness. Searle says that because consciousness as well as flexibility and creativity of behavior are missing, we can conclude that a function of consciousness is somehow to promote flexibility and creativity. These two arguments are the springboard for this target article. Although some variants of this sort of reasoning have some merit, they are often given more weight than they deserve, because of a persistent fallacy involving a conflation of two very different concepts of consciousness.

The plan of the paper is as follows: in the following section I will briefly discuss some other syndromes much like blindsight, sketching one model that has been offered for explaining them. Then, in the longest part of the paper, I will distinguish the two concepts of con-

sciousness whose conflation is the root of the fallacious arguments. Once that is done, I will sketch what is wrong with the target reasoning and also what is right about it, concluding with some remarks on how it is possible to investigate the function of consciousness empirically without having much of an idea about the scientific nature of consciousness.

2. Other Syndromes and Schacter's Model

To introduce a second blindsight-like syndrome, I want first to explain a syndrome that is not like blindsight: prosopagnosia (*prosop* = face, *agnosia* = neurological deficit in recognizing). Prosopagnosics are unable to recognize visually their closest relatives—even pictures of themselves, though usually they have no trouble recognizing their friends by their voices or, according to anecdotal reports, visually recognizing people by recognizing characteristic motions of their bodies. Although there is wide variation from case to case, prosopagnosia is compatible with a high degree of visual ability, even in tasks involving faces.

One patient who has been studied by my colleagues in the Boston area is LH, a Harvard undergraduate who emerged from a car accident with very localized brain damage that left him unable to recognize even his mother. His girl friend began to wear a special ribbon so that he would know who she was. Now, years later, he still cannot identify his mother or his wife and children from photographs (Etcoff et al. 1991). Still, if shown a photo and asked to choose another photo of the same person from a set of, say, five photos presented simultaneously with the original, LH can do almost as well as normal people despite differences between the target and matching photos in lighting, angle, and expression.

Now we are ready for the analog of blindsight. The phenomenon is exhibited in many experimental paradigms, but I will mention only this: it has recently been discovered (by Sergent & Poncet 1990) that some prosopagnosics are very good at "guessing" between two names in the same occupational category ("Reagan" and "Bush") for a person whose face they claim is unfamiliar (see Young 1994a, 1994b; Young & de Haan 1993, for a description of these phenomenon). Interestingly, LH does not appear to have "covert knowledge" of the people whose faces he sees, but he does appear to have "covert knowledge" of their facial expressions (Etcoff et al. 1992). Many such phenomena in brain-damaged patients have now been explored using the techniques of cognitive and physiological psychology. Further, there are a variety of phenomena that occur in normal people like you and me. For example, suppose that you are given a string of words and asked to count the vowels. This can be done so that you will have no conscious recollection or even recognition of the words, and you will be unable to "guess" at a level above chance which words you have seen. However, if I give you a series of word stems to complete according to your whim, the likelihood of your completing "rea-" as "reason" is greater if "reason" is one of the words that you saw, even if you do not recall or recognize it as one of the words you saw (see Bowers & Schacter 1990; Reingold & Merikle 1993).[1]

Recall that the target reasoning (the reasoning I will be saying is substantially confused but also substantially right) is that when consciousness is missing subjects cannot report or reason about nonconscious contents or use them to guide action; we can conclude that a function of consciousness is to facilitate reasoning, reporting, and guiding action. This reasoning is partially captured in a model suggested by Schacter (1989, see also Schacter et al. 1988) in a paper reviewing phenomena such as the ones described above. Figure 1 is derived from Schacter's model.

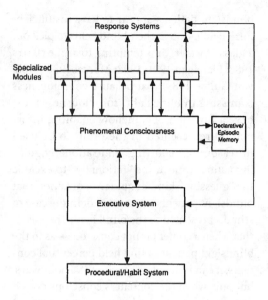

Figure 1 Schacter's Model

The model is only partial (that is, it models some aspects of the mind but not others), and so may be a bit hard to grasp for those who are used to seeing inputs and outputs. Think of the hands and feet as connected to the Response Systems box, and the eyes and ears as connected to the specialized modules. (See Schacter, 1989, for some indication of how these suggestions are oversimplified.) The key feature of the model is that it contains a box for something called "phenomenal consciousness." I'll address this in more detail later, but for now let me just say that phenomenal consciousness is experience; what makes a state phenomenally conscious is that there is something "it is like" (Nagel 1974) to be in that state. The model dictates that the phenomenal consciousness module has a function: it is the gateway between the special purpose "knowledge" modules and the central Executive System that is in charge of direct control of reasoning, reporting, and guiding action. So, a function of consciousness according to this model includes integrating the outputs of the specialized modules and transmitting the integrated contents to mechanisms of reasoning and control of action and reporting.

[…]

The information-processing function of phenomenal consciousness in Schacter's model is the ground of the concept of consciousness that I will mainly be contrasting with phenomenal consciousness, what I call "access consciousness." A perceptual state is access-conscious, roughly speaking, if its content—what is represented by the perceptual state—is processed via that information processing function, that is, if its content gets to the Executive System, whereby it can be used to control reasoning and behavior.

Schacter's model is useful for my purposes both because it can be used to illustrate the contrast between phenomenal and access-consciousness, and because it allows us to see one possible explanation of the "covert knowledge" syndromes just described. This explanation (and also Schacter's model) are certainly incomplete and no doubt oversimplified at best, but it is nonetheless useful to see the outlines of how an account might go. In addition, there is an association between Schacter's model and the target reasoning—though as we shall see there is another processing model that perhaps better embodies the target reasoning.

Consider a blindsight patient who has just had a vertical line displayed in his blind field. "What did you see?" "Nothing," says the patient. "Take a guess between a vertical and a horizontal line," says the experimenter. "Vertical," says the patient, correctly. Here's a possible explanation of what happened. One of the modules is specialized for spatial information; it has some information about the verticality of the stimulus. The pathways between

this specialized module and the phenomenal consciousness system have been damaged, creating the "blind field," so the patient has no phenomenally conscious experience of the line, and hence his Executive System has no information about whether the line is vertical or horizontal. The specialized module has a direct connection to the response system, however, so when the subject is given a binary choice, the specialized module can somehow directly affect the response.

[…]

3. Two Concepts of Consciousness

First, consider phenomenal consciousness, or P-consciousness, as I will call it. Let me acknowledge at the outset that I cannot define P-consciousness in any remotely noncircular way. I don't consider this an embarrassment. The history of reductive definitions in philosophy should lead one not to expect a reductive definition of anything. The best one can do for P-consciousness is in some respects worse than for many other concepts, though, because really all one can do is *point* to the phenomenon (cf. Goldman 1993a). Nonetheless, it is important to point properly. Searle, acknowledging that consciousness cannot be defined noncircularly, defines it as follows:

> By consciousness I simply mean those subjective states of awareness or sentience that begin when one wakes in the morning and continue throughout the period that one is awake until one falls into a dreamless sleep, into a coma, or dies or is otherwise, as they say, unconscious. (Searle 1990; there is a much longer attempt along the same lines in Searle 1992, p. 83ff.)

I will argue that this sort of pointing is flawed, because it points to too many things, too many different consciousnesses.

So how should we point to P-consciousness? One way is with rough synonyms. As I said, P-consciousness is experience. P-consciousness properties are experiential ones. P-conscious states are experiential, that is, a state is P-conscious if it has experiential properties. The totality of the experiential properties of a state are "what it is like" to have it. Moving from synonyms to examples, we have P-conscious states when we see, hear, smell, taste, and have pains. P-conscious properties include the experiential properties of sensations, feelings, and perceptions, but I would also include thoughts, desires, and emotions.[3] A feature of P-consciousness that is often missed is that differences in intentional content often make a P-conscious difference. What it is like to hear a sound as coming from the left differs from what it is like to hear a sound as coming from the right. P-consciousness is often representational (see Flanagan 1992, Chap. 4; Goldman 1993b; Jackendoff 1987; McGinn 1991, Chap. 2; van Gulick 1989). So far, I don't take myself to have said anything terribly controversial. The controversial part is that I take P-conscious properties to be distinct from any cognitive, intentional, or functional property. (Cognitive = essentially involving thought; intentional properties = properties in virtue of which a representation or state is about something; functional properties = properties definable (for example) in terms of a computer program. See Searle 1983, on intentionality; see Block 1980; 1994, for better characterizations of a functional property.) Still, I am trying hard to limit the controversiality of my assumptions. Although I will be assuming that functionalism about P-consciousness is false, I will be pointing out that limited versions of many of the points I make can be acceptable to the functionalist.[4]

It is of course P-consciousness rather than access consciousness or self-consciousness that has seemed such a scientific mystery. The magazine *Discover* (November 1992) devoted an issue to the ten great unanswered questions of science, such as What Is Consciousness?; Does Chaos Rule the Cosmos?; and How Big Is the Universe?—The topic was P-consciousness, not, for example, self-consciousness. By way of homing in on P-consciousness, it is useful to appeal to what may be a contingent property of it, namely, the famous "explanatory gap." To quote T.H. Huxley (1866), "How it is that anything so remarkable as a state of consciousness comes about as a result of irritating nervous tissue, is just as unaccountable as the appearance of Djin when Aladdin rubbed his lamp."

[...]

The explanatory gap in the case of P-consciousness contrasts with our relatively good understanding of cognition. We have two serious research programs into the nature of cognition, the classical "language of thought" paradigm, and the connectionist research program. Though no doubt there are many ideas missing in our understanding of cognition, we have no difficulty seeing how pursuing one or both of these research programs could lead to an adequate theoretical perspective on cognition. It is not easy, however, to see how current approaches to P-consciousness *could* yield an account of it. Indeed, what passes for research programs on consciousness just is a combination of cognitive psychology and explorations of neuropsychological syndromes that contain no theoretical perspective on what P-consciousness actually is.

I mentioned the explanatory gap partly by way of pointing at P-consciousness: *that* is the entity to which the mentioned explanatory gap applies. Perhaps this identification is contingent; at some time in the future, when we have the concepts to conceive of much more about the explanation of P-consciousness, there may be no explanatory gap to use in picking out P-consciousness (see McGinn, 1991, for a more pessimistic view).

What I have been saying about P-consciousness is of course controversial in a variety of ways, both for some advocates and some opponents of some notion of P-consciousness. I have tried to steer clear of certain controversies, for example, over inverted and absent qualia; over Jackson's (1986) Mary (the woman raised in a black and white room, learning all the physiological and functional facts about the brain and color vision, but nonetheless discovers a new fact when she goes outside the room for the first time and learns what it is like to see red); and even over Nagel's (1974) view that we cannot know what it is like to be a bat.[6] Even if you think that P-consciousness as I have described it is an incoherent notion, you may be able to agree with the main point of this article, that a great deal of misunderstanding arises as a result of confusing P-consciousness with something else. Not even the concept of what time it is now on the sun is so confused that it cannot itself be mistaken for something else.

4. Access-Consciousness

I now turn to the nonphenomenal notion of consciousness that is most easily and dangerously conflated with P-consciousness: access-consciousness. A state is access conscious (A-conscious) if, in virtue of one's having the state, a representation of its content is (1) inferentially promiscuous (Stich 1978), that is, poised for use as a premise in reasoning, (2) poised for rational control of action, and (3) poised for rational control of speech. (I will speak of both states and their contents as A-conscious.) These three conditions are together sufficient, but

not all necessary. I regard (3) as not necessary (and not independent of the others), because I want to allow that nonlinguistic animals, for example chimps, have A-conscious states. I see A-consciousness as a cluster concept, in which (3)—roughly, reportability—is the element of the cluster with the smallest weight, though (3) is often the best practical guide to A-consciousness.[7]

Although I make a firm distinction between A-consciousness and P-consciousness, I also want to insist that they interact. What perceptual information is being accessed can change figure to ground and vice versa, and a figure-ground switch can affect one's phenomenal state. For example, attending to the feel of the shirt on your neck—accessing those perceptual contents—switches what was in the background to the foreground, thereby changing one's phenomenal state (see Hill 1991, pp. 118–26; Searle 1992).

[...]

There are three main differences between P-consciousness and A-consciousness. The first point, put crudely, is that P-conscious content is phenomenal, whereas A-conscious content is representational. It is of the essence of A-conscious content to play a role in reasoning, and only representational content can figure in reasoning. Many phenomenal contents are *also* representational, however, so it would be better to say that it is in virtue of its phenomenal content or the phenomenal aspect of its content that a state is P-conscious, whereas it is in virtue of its representational content, or the representational aspect of its content, that a state is A-conscious.[9]

The last paragraph referred to P-conscious *content*. The P-conscious content of a state is the totality of the state's experiential properties, what it is like to be in that state. One can think of the P-conscious content of a state as the state's experiential "value" by analogy with the representational content as the state's representational "value."

In my view, the content of an experience can be both P-conscious and A-conscious, the former in virtue of its phenomenal feel and the latter in virtue of its representational properties. A closely related point: A-conscious states are necessarily transitive: A-conscious states must always be states of consciousness of P-conscious states, by contrast, sometimes are and sometimes are not transitive. P-consciousness, as such, is not consciousness of.

A second difference is that A-consciousness is a functional notion, so A-conscious content is system-relative: what makes a state A-conscious is what a representation of its content does in a system. P-consciousness is not a functional notion.[10] In terms of Schacter's model, content gets to be P-conscious because of what happens *inside* the P-consciousness module. But what makes content A-conscious is not something that could go on inside a module, but rather informational relations *among* modules. Content is A-conscious in virtue of (a representation with that content) reaching the Executive System, the system in charge of rational control of action and speech; to this extent we could regard the Executive System as the A-consciousness module; but to regard *anything* as an A-consciousness module is misleading, because what makes content A-conscious depends on what the Executive System is disposed to do with the representation.

A third difference is that there is such a thing as a P-conscious *type* or *kind* of state. For example, the feel of pain is a P-conscious type—every pain must have that feel. But any particular thought that is A-conscious at a given time could fail to be accessible at some other time, just as my car is accessible now but will not be so later when my wife has it. A state whose content is informationally promiscuous now may not be so later.

The paradigm P-conscious states are sensations, whereas the paradigm A-conscious states are "propositional attitude" states such as thoughts, beliefs, and desires, states with representational content expressed by "that" clauses (e.g., the thought that grass is green). As noted, however, thoughts are often P-conscious and perceptual experiences often have representational content. For example, a perceptual experience may have the representational content *that there is a red square in front of me*. Even pain typically has some kind of representational content. Pains often represent something (the cause of the pain? the pain itself?) as somewhere (in the leg). A number of philosophers have taken the view that the content of pain is *entirely* representational (see Dretske 1993; Shoemaker 1944; Tye, forthcoming). I don't agree with this view, so I certainly don't want to rely on it here, but I also don't want to suggest that the existence of cases of P-consciousness without A-consciousness is a trivial consequence of an idiosyncratic set of definitions. To the extent that representationalism of the sort just mentioned is plausible, one can regard a pain as A-conscious if its representational content is inferentially promiscuous, and so on. Alternatively, we could take the A-conscious content of pain to consist in the content that one has a pain or that one has a state with a certain phenomenal content.[11]

[...]

4.1. A-consciousness without P-consciousness

The main point of this target article is that these two concepts of consciousness are easily confused, so it will pay us to consider conceptually possible cases of one without the other. Actual cases will be more controversial. As an example of A-consciousness without P-consciousness, imagine a full-fledged phenomenal zombie, say, a robot computationally identical to a person, but one whose silicon brain does not support P-consciousness. I think such cases are conceptually possible, but this is very controversial, and I am trying to avoid controversy (see Shoemaker 1975, 1981a).

There is a less controversial kind of case, however—that is a very limited sort of partial zombie. Consider the blindsight patient who "guesses" that there is an X rather than an O in his blind field. Temporarily taking his word for it, I am assuming that he has no P-consciousness of the X. As mentioned, I am following the target reasoning here, but my own argument does not depend on this assumption. I am certainly not assuming that lack of A-consciousness guarantees lack of P-consciousness—that is, I am not assuming that if you don't say it you haven't got it.

The blindsight patient also has no X representing A-consciousness content, because although the information that there is an X affects his "guess," it is not available as a premise in reasoning (until he has the quite distinct state of hearing and believing his own guess), or for rational control of action or speech. Recall Marcel's (1986) point that the thirsty blindsight patient would not reach for a glass of water in the blind field. So the blindsight patient's perceptual or quasi-perceptual state is unconscious in the phenomenal *and* access senses (*and* in the monitoring senses to be discussed later).

Now imagine something that may not exist, what we might call *superblindsight*. A real blindsight patient can only guess when given a choice from a small set of alternatives (X/0; horizontal/vertical, etc.). But suppose—contrary to fact apparently—that a blindsight patient could be trained to prompt himself at will, guessing what is in the blind field without being told to guess. The superblindsighter

spontaneously says, "Now I know there is a horizontal line in my blind field even though I don't actually see it." Visual information from his blind field simply pops into his thoughts in the way that solutions to problems we've been worrying about pop into our thoughts, or in the way some people just know the time or which way is North without having any perceptual experience of it. The superblindsighter himself contrasts what it is like to know visually about an X in his blind field and an X in his sighted field. There is something it is like to experience the latter, but not the former, he says. It is the difference between *just knowing* and knowing via a visual experience. Let us take his word for it; here is the point: the content that there is an X in his visual field is A-conscious but not P-conscious. The superblindsight case is a very limited partial zombie.[14]

Of course, the superblindsighter has a thought that there is an X in his blind field that is *both* A-conscious and P-conscious. I am not talking about the thought, however, but about the state of his perceptual system that gives rise to the thought. It is this state that is A-conscious without being P-conscious.[15]

Is there actually such a thing as superblindsight? Humphrey (1992) describes a monkey (Helen) who despite near-total loss of the visual cortex could nonetheless act in a somewhat normal way (as if seeing) in certain circumstances, without any "prompting." One reason to doubt that Helen is a case of superblindsight is that Helen may be a case of sight. There was some visual cortex left, and the situations in which she showed unprompted visual discrimination were natural ones in which there was no control of where the stimuli engaged her retina. Another possibility mentioned by Cowie and Stoerig (1992, attributed to an unpublished paper by Humphrey) is that there were P-conscious sensory events, though perhaps auditory in nature. Helen appeared to confuse brief tones with visual stimuli. Cowie and Stoerig propose a number of ways of getting out of monkeys information that is close to what we get out of blindsighted humans. Weiskrantz (1992) mentions that a patient GY sometimes knows there is a stimulus (though not what it is) while claiming to see nothing. GY also seems to be having some kind of P-conscious sensation, however (see Cowie & Stoerig 1992).

The (apparent) nonexistence of superblindsight is a striking fact, one that a number of writers have noticed. Indeed, it is the basis for the target reasoning. After all, what Marcel was in effect pointing out was that the blindsight patients, in not reaching for a glass of water, are not superblindsighters. Farah (1994) notes that blindsight (and blind perception generally) turns out always to be degraded. In other words, blind perception is never superblind perception.[16]

I don't know whether there are any actual cases of A-consciousness without P-consciousness, but I hope I have illustrated their conceptual possibility.

4.2. P-consciousness without A-consciousness

Consider an animal you are happy to think of as having P-consciousness, for which brain damage has destroyed centers of reasoning and rational control of action, thus preventing A-consciousness. It certainly seems *conceptually possible* that the neural bases of P-consciousness systems and A-consciousness systems are distinct; if so, then it is possible, at least conceptually, for one to be damaged while the other is working well. Evidence has been accumulating for 25 years that the primate visual system has distinct dorsal and ventral subsystems. Though there is much disagreement about the specializations of the two systems, it does appear that much of the information in the ventral system is much more closely connected to P-consciousness than

that in the dorsal system (Goodale & Milner 1992). So it may actually be possible to damage A-consciousness without P-consciousness and vice versa.[17]

One might suppose (Rey 1983, 1988; White 1987) that some of our own subsystems—say, each of the hemispheres of the brain—could themselves be separately P-conscious. [See Puccetti, "The Case for Mental Duality," *Behavioral and Brain Sciences* 4(1) 1981.] Some of these subsystems might also be A-conscious, but other subsystems might not have enough machinery for reasoning or reporting or rational control of action to allow their P-conscious states to be A-conscious; so if those states are not accessible to another system that does have adequate machinery, they will be P-conscious but not A-conscious.

Here is another reason to believe in P-consciousness without A-consciousness: suppose you are engaged in intense conversation when suddenly at noon you realize that right outside your window there is—and has been for some time—a deafening pneumatic drill digging up the street. You were aware of the noise all along, but only at noon are you *consciously* aware of it. That is, you were P-conscious of the noise all along, but at noon you are both P-conscious *and* A-conscious of it. Of course, there is a very similar string of events in which the crucial event at noon is a bit more intellectual. In this alternative scenario, at noon you realize not just that there is and has been a noise, but also that you are now and have been experiencing the noise. In this alternative scenario, you get "higher order thought" as well as A-consciousness at noon. So, on the first scenario, the belief that is acquired at noon is that there is and has been a noise, and on the second scenario, the beliefs that are acquired at noon are the first one plus the belief that you are and have been experiencing the noise. But it is the first scenario, not the second, that interests me, for it is a pure case of P-consciousness without A-consciousness. Note that this case involves a natural use of "conscious" and "aware" for A-consciousness and P-consciousness, respectively. "Conscious" and "aware" are more or less synonymous, so calling the initial P-consciousness "awareness" makes it natural to call the later P-consciousness plus A-consciousness "conscious awareness." Of course I rely here on introspection, but when it comes to P-consciousness, introspection is an important source of insight.[18] This case of P-consciousness without A-consciousness exploits what William James (1890) called "secondary consciousness," a category in which he meant to include cases of P-consciousness without attention.[19]

[...]

6. The Fallacy of the Target Reasoning

We now come to the denouement of the paper, the application of the P-consciousness/A-consciousness distinction to the fallacy of the target reasoning. Let me begin with the Penfield/van Gulick/Searle reasoning. Searle (1992) adopts Penfield's (1975) claim that during petit mal seizures patients are "totally unconscious." Quoting Penfield at length, Searle describes three patients who, despite being "totally unconscious" continue walking or driving home or playing the piano, but in a mechanical way. Van Gulick (1989, p. 220) gives a briefer treatment, also quoting Penfield. He says, "The importance of conscious experience for the construction and control of action plans is nicely illustrated by the phenomenon of automatism associated with some petit mal epileptic seizures. In such cases, electrical disorder leads to a loss of function in the higher brain stem.... As a result the patient suffers a loss of conscious experience in the phenomenal sense although he can continue to react selectively to environmental stim-

uli." Because van Gulick's treatment is more equivocal and less detailed, and because Searle also comments on my accusations of conflating A-consciousness with P-consciousness, I will focus on Searle. Searle says:

> The epileptic seizure rendered the patient *totally unconscious*, yet the patient continued to exhibit what would normally be called goal-directed behavior.... In all these cases, we have complex forms of apparently goal-directed behavior without any consciousness. Now why could all behavior not be like that? Notice that in the cases, the patients were performing types of actions that were habitual, routine and memorized...normal, human, conscious behavior has a degree of flexibility and creativity that is absent from the Penfield cases of the unconscious driver and the unconscious pianist. *Consciousness adds powers of discrimination and flexibility* even to memorized routine activities.... One of the evolutionary advantages conferred on us by consciousness is the much greater *flexibility, sensitivity*, and *creativity* we derive from being conscious. (1992, pp. 108–09; italics mine)

Searle's reasoning is that consciousness is missing, and with it flexibility, sensitivity, and creativity, so this is an indication that a function of consciousness is to add these qualities. Now it is completely clear that the concept of consciousness invoked by both Searle and van Gulick is P-consciousness. Van Gulick speaks of "conscious experience in the phenomenal sense," and Searle criticizes me for supposing that there is a legitimate use of "conscious" to mean A-conscious: "Some philosophers (e.g., Block, "Two Concepts of Consciousness") claim that there is a sense of this word that implies no sentience whatever, a sense in which a total zombie could be 'conscious.' I know of no such sense, but in any case, that is not the sense in which I am using the word" (Searle 1992, p. 84). But neither Searle nor van Gulick nor Penfield give any reason to believe that P-consciousness is missing or even diminished in the epileptics they describe. The piano player, the walker, and the driver don't cope with new situations very well, but they do show every sign of *normal sensation*. For example, Searle, quoting Penfield, describes the epileptic walker as "thread[ing] his way" through the crowd. Doesn't he *see* the obstacles he avoids? Suppose he gets home by turning right at a red wall. Isn't there something it is like for him to see the red wall—and isn't it different from what it is like for him to see a green wall? Searle gives no reason to think the answer is no. Because of the very inflexibility and lack of creativity of the behavior they exhibit, it is the *thought processes* of these patients (including A-consciousness) that are most obviously deficient; no reason at all is given to think that their P-conscious states lack vivacity or intensity. Of course, I don't claim to know what it is really like for these epileptics; my point is rather that for the argument for the function of P-consciousness to have any force, a case would have to be made that P-consciousness is actually missing, or at least diminished. Searle argues: P-consciousness is missing; so is creativity; therefore the former lack explains the latter lack. But no support at all is given for the first premise, and as we shall see, it is no stretch to suppose that what has gone wrong is that the ordinary mongrel notion of consciousness is being used; it wraps P-consciousness and A-consciousness together, and so an obvious function of A-consciousness is illicitly transferred to P-consciousness.

This difficulty in the reasoning is highlighted if we assume Schacter's model. In terms of Schacter's model, there is no reason to doubt

that the information from the epileptic's senses reaches the P-conscious module, but there is reason to doubt that the Executive System processes this information in the normal way. So there is reason to blame their inflexibility and lack of creativity on problems in the Executive System or the link between P-consciousness module and the Executive System.[25]

[...]

Let us now move to the line of thought mentioned at the outset about why the thirsty blindsight patient doesn't reach for the glass of water in the blind field.[27] The reasoning is that (1) consciousness is missing, and (2) information that the patient in some sense possesses is not used in reasoning, guiding action or reporting, hence (3) the function of consciousness must be somehow to allow information from the senses to be so used in guiding action (Marcel 1986; 1988). Flanagan (1992) agrees with Marcel: "Conscious awareness of a water fountain to my right will lead me to drink from it if I am thirsty. But the thirsty blindsighted person will make no move towards the fountain unless pressed to do so. The inference to the best explanation is that conscious awareness of the environment facilitates semantic comprehension and adaptive motor actions in creatures like us." And: "Blindsighted patients never initiate activity toward the blindfield because they lack subjective awareness of things in that field" (Flanagan 1992, pp. 141–42; the same reasoning occurs in his 1991, p. 349). Van Gulick (1989, p. 220) agrees with Marcel, saying, "subjects never initiate on their own any actions informed by perceptions from the blindfield. The moral to be drawn from this is that information must normally be represented in phenomenal consciousness if it is to play any role in guiding voluntary action."

Schacter (1989) quotes Marcel approvingly, using this reasoning (about why the thirsty blindsight patient doesn't reach) to some extent in formulating the model of Figure 1. The P-consciousness module has the function of integrating information from the specialized modules, injecting them with P-conscious content, and of sending these contents to the system in charge of reasoning and rational control of action and reporting.

Baars (1988, p. 356) argues for eighteen different functions of consciousness on the same ground. He says that the argument for these functions is "that loss of consciousness—through habituation, automaticity, distraction, masking, anesthesia, and the like—inhibits or destroys the functions listed here."[28]

This is the fallacy: in the blindsight patient, both P-consciousness and A-consciousness of the glass of water are missing. There is an obvious explanation of why the patient doesn't reach for the glass in terms of the information about it not reaching mechanisms of reasoning and rational control of speech and action, the machinery of A-consciousness. (If we believe in an Executive System, we can explain why the blindsight patient does not reach for the water by appealing to the claim that the information about the water does not reach the Executive System.) More generally, A-consciousness and P-consciousness are almost always present or absent together, or rather this seems plausible. This is, after all, why they are folded together in a mongrel concept. A function of the mechanisms underlying A-consciousness is completely obvious. If information from the senses did not get to mechanisms of control of reasoning and of rational control of action and reporting, we would not be able to use our senses to guide our action and reporting. But it is a mistake to slide from a function of the machinery of A-consciousness to any function at all of P-consciousness.

Of course, it could be that the lack of P-consciousness is itself responsible for the lack of A-consciousness. If that is the argument in any of these cases, I do not say "fallacy." The idea that the lack of P-consciousness is responsible for the lack of A-consciousness is a bold hypothesis, not a fallacy. Recall, however, that there is some reason to ascribe the opposite view to the field as a whole. The discussion in section 5 of Baars, Shallice, Kosslyn and Koenig, Edelman, Johnson-Laird, Andrade, and Kihlstrom et al. suggested that to the extent that the different types of consciousness are distinguished from one another, it is often thought that P-consciousness is a product of (or is identical to) cognitive processing. In this climate of opinion, if P-consciousness and A-consciousness were clearly distinguished, and something like the opposite of the usual view of their relation advanced, we would expect some comment on this fact, something that does not appear in any of the works cited.

The fallacy, then, is jumping from the premise that "consciousness" is missing—without being clear about what kind of consciousness is missing—to the conclusion that P-consciousness has a certain function. If the distinction were seen clearly, the relevant possibilities could be reasoned about. Perhaps the lack of P-consciousness causes the lack of A-consciousness. Or perhaps the converse is the case: P-consciousness is somehow a product of A-consciousness, or both could be the result of something else. If the distinction were clearly made, these alternatives would come to the fore. The fallacy is failing to make the distinction, rendering the alternatives invisible.

Note that the claim that P-consciousness is missing in blindsight is just an assumption. I decided to take the blindsight patient's word for his lack of P-consciousness of stimuli in the blind field. Maybe this assumption is mistaken; but if it is, then the fallacy now under discussion reduces to the fallacy of the Searle-Penfield reasoning: if the assumption is wrong, if the blindsight patient *does* have P-consciousness of stimuli in the blind field, then *only* A-consciousness of the stimuli in the blind field is missing, so of course we cannot draw the aforementioned conclusion about the function of P-consciousness from blindsight.

I said at the outset that although there is a serious fallacy in the target reasoning, something important is also right about it: in blindsight, both A-consciousness and (I assume) P-consciousness are gone, just as in normal perception both are present. So blindsight is yet another case in which P-consciousness and A-consciousness are both present or both absent. In addition, as mentioned earlier, cases of A-consciousness without P-consciousness, such as my "superblindsight patient," do not appear to exist. Training of blindsight patients has produced a number of phenomena that look a bit like superblindsight, but each such lead I have pursued has failed. This suggests an intimate relation between A-consciousness and P-consciousness. Perhaps there is something about P-consciousness that greases the wheels of accessibility. Perhaps P-consciousness is like the liquid in a hydraulic computer, the means by which A-consciousness operates. Alternatively, perhaps P-consciousness is the gateway to mechanisms of access as in Schacter's (1989) model, in which case P-consciousness would have the function Marcel and the others mention. Or perhaps P-consciousness and A-consciousness amount to much the same thing empirically even though they differ conceptually, in which case P-consciousness would also have the aforementioned function. Perhaps the two are so intertwined that there is no empirical sense to the idea of one without the other.

[...]

7.1. Conclusions

The form of the target reasoning discussed misses the distinction between P-consciousness and A-consciousness and thus jumps from the fact that consciousness in some sense or other is missing simultaneously with missing creativity or voluntary action to the conclusion that P-consciousness functions to promote the missing qualities in normal people. If we make the right distinctions, however, we can investigate nonfallaciously whether any such conclusion can be drawn. [...]

My purpose in this target article has been to expose a confusion about consciousness. But in reasoning about it I raised the possibility that it may be possible to find out something about the function of P-consciousness without knowing very much about what it is. Indeed, learning something about the function of P-consciousness may help us in finding out what it is.

Acknowledgements

I would like to thank Tyler Burge, Susan Carey, David Chalmers, Martin Davies, Wayne Davis, Bert Dreyfus, Paul Horwich, Jerry Katz, Leonard Katz, Joe Levine, David Rosenthal, Jerome Shaffer, Sydney Shoemaker, Stephen White, and Andrew Young for their very helpful comments on earlier versions of this paper. I am grateful to Kathleen Akins for her presentation as Commentator when this paper was given at a conference at the University of Washington in 1991. I am also grateful to many audiences at talks on this material for their criticisms, especially the audience at the conference on my work at the University of Barcelona in June 1993.

Notes

1. The phenomenon just mentioned is very similar to phenomena involving "subliminal perception," in which stimuli are degraded or presented very briefly. Holender (1986) harshly criticizes a variety of "subliminal perception" experiments, but the experimental paradigm just mentioned and many

others are, in my judgment, free of the problems of certain other studies. Another such experimental paradigm is the familiar dichotic listening experiment in which subjects wear headphones that present different stimuli to different ears. If subjects are asked to pay attention to the stimuli in one ear, they can report only superficial features of the unattended stimuli, but the latter influences the interpretation of ambiguous sentences presented to the attended ear (see Lackner & Garrett 1973).

[...]

3. But what is it about thoughts that makes them P-conscious? One possibility is that it is just a series of mental images or subvocalizations that make thoughts P-conscious. Another possibility is that the contents themselves have a P-conscious aspect independently of their vehicles (see Lormand, forthcoming).

4. I say both that P-consciousness is not an intentional property and that intentional differences can make a P-conscious difference. My view is that although P-conscious content cannot be reduced to intentional content, P-conscious contents often have an intentional aspect, and also that P-conscious contents often represent in a primitive, nonintentional way. A perceptual experience can represent space as being filled in certain ways without representing the object perceived as falling under any concept. Thus, the experiences of a creature that does not possess the concept of a donut could represent space as being filled in a donutlike way (see Davies [1992, in press]; Peacocke [1992]; and finally Evans [1982] in which the distinction between conceptualized and nonconceptualized content is first introduced).

[...]

6. I know some will think that I invoked inverted and absent qualia a few paragraphs ago when I described the explanatory gap as involving the question of why a creature possessing a brain with a physiological and functional nature like ours couldn't have different experience or none at all. But the spirit of the question as I asked it allows for an answer that explains why such creatures cannot exist, and thus there is no presupposition that these are real possibilities. Levine (1983, 1993) stresses that the relevant modality is epistemic possibility.

[...]

7. Poised = ready and waiting. To be poised to attack is to be on the verge of attacking. What if an A-unconscious state causes an A-conscious state with the same content? Then it could be said that the first state must be A-conscious because it is in virtue of having that state that the content it shares with the other state satisfies the three conditions. So the state is A-unconscious by hypothesis, but A-conscious by my definition (I am indebted to Paul Hoiwich). What this case points to is a refinement needed in the notion of "in virtue of." One does not want to count the inferential promiscuity of a content as being in virtue of having a state if that state can only cause this inferential promiscuity via another state. I will not try to produce an analysis of "in virtue of" here.

[...]

9. Some may say that only fully conceptualized content can play a role in reasoning, be reportable, and rationally control action. If

so, then nonconceptualized content is not A-conscious.

10. However, I acknowledge the empirical possibility that the scientific nature of P-consciousness has something to do with information processing. We can ill afford to close off empirical possibilities given the difficulty of solving the mystery of P-consciousness (cf. Loar 1990).

11. In my view, there are a number of problems with the first of these suggestions. One of them is that perhaps the representational content of pain is too primitive for a role in inference. Arguably, the representational content of pain is nonconceptualized. After all, dogs can have pain and one can reasonably wonder whether dogs have the relevant concepts at all. Davies and Humphreys (1993) discuss a related issue. Applying a suggestion of theirs about the higher-order thought notion of consciousness to A-consciousness, we could characterize A-consciousness of a state with nonconceptualized content as follows: such a state is A-conscious if, in virtue of one's having the state, its content would be inferentially promiscuous and available for rational control of action and speech if the subject were to have had the concepts required for that content to be a conceptualized content. The idea is to bypass the inferential disadvantage of nonconceptualized content by thinking of its accessibility counterfactually—in terms of the rational relations it would have if the subject were to have the relevant concepts (see Lormand, forthcoming, on the self-representing nature of pain).

[...]

14. Tye (1993b) argues (on the basis of a neuro-psychological claim) that the visual information processing in blindsight includes no processing by the object recognition system or the spatial attention system, and so is very different from the processing of normal vision. This does not challenge my claim that the superblindsight case is a very limited partial zombie. Note that superblindsight, as I describe it, does not require object recognition or spatial attention. Whatever it is that allows the blindsight patient to discriminate an X from an O and a horizontal from a vertical line, will do. I will argue later that the fact that such cases do not exist, if it is a fact, is important. Humphrey (1992) suggests that blindsight is mainly a motor phenomenon—the patient is perceptually influenced by his own motor tendencies.

15. If you are tempted to deny the existence of these states of the perceptual system, you should think back to the total zombie just mentioned. Putting aside the issue of the possibility of this zombie, note that on a computational notion of cognition, the zombie has all the same A-conscious contents that you have (if he is your computational duplicate). A-consciousness is an informational notion. The states of the superblindsighter's perceptual system are A-conscious for the same reason as the zombie's.

16. Actually, my notion of A-consciousness seems to fit the data better than the conceptual apparatus she uses. Blindsight isn't always more degraded in any normal sense than sight. Weiskrantz (1988) notes that his patient DB had better acuity in some areas of the blind field (in some circumstances) than in his sighted field. It would be better to understand her use of "degraded" in terms of lack of access. Notice that the superblindsighter I have described is just a little bit different (though in a crucial way) from the ordinary blindsight

patient. In particular, I am not relying on what might be thought of as a full-fledged quasi-zombie, a super-duper-blindsighter whose blindsight is every bit as good, functionally speaking, as his sight. In the case of the super-duper-blindsighter, the only difference between vision in the blind and sighted fields, functionally speaking, is that the quasi-zombie himself regards them differently. Such an example will be regarded by some (although not by me) as incoherent—see Dennett (1991) for example. But we can avoid disagreement about the super-duper-blindsighter by illustrating the idea of A-consciousness without P-consciousness by appealing only to the superblindsighter. Functionalists may want to know why the superblindsight case counts as A-consciousness without P-consciousness. After all, they may say, if we have really high-quality access in mind, the superblindsighter that I have described does not have it, so he lacks both P-consciousness and truly high-quality A-consciousness. The super-duper-blindsighter, on the other hand, has both, according to the functionalist, so in neither case, the objection goes, is there A-consciousness without P-consciousness. But the disagreement about the super-duper-blindsighter is irrelevant to the issue about the superblindsighter, and the issue about the superblindsighter is merely verbal. I have chosen a notion of A-consciousness whose standards are lower in part to avoid conflict with the functionalist. One could put the point by distinguishing three types of access: (1) truly high-quality access, (2) medium access, and (3) poor access. The actual blindsight patient has poor access, the superblindsight patient has medium access, and the super-duper-blindsight patient—as well as most of us—has really high-quality access. The

functionalist identifies P-consciousness with A-consciousness of the truly high-quality kind. Although functionalists should agree with me that there can be A-consciousness without P-consciousness, some functionalists will see the significance of such cases very differently from the way I see them. Some functionalists will see the distinction between A-consciousness and P-consciousness primarily as a difference in degree rather than in kind, as is suggested by the contrast between truly high-quality access and medium access. So all that A-consciousness without P-consciousness illustrates, on this functionalist view, is some access without more access. Other functionalists will stress kind rather than degree of information processing. The idea behind this approach is that there is no reason to think that the P-consciousness of animals whose capacities for reasoning, reporting, and rational guidance of action are more limited than ours thereby have anything less in the way of P-consciousness. The functionalist can concede that this thought is correct, and thereby treat the difference between A-consciousness and P-consciousness as a difference of kind, albeit kind of information processing.

17. Thus, there is a conflict between this psychological claim and the Schacter model, which dictates that destroying the P-consciousness module will prevent A-consciousness.

18. There is a misleading aspect to this example—namely, that to the extent that "conscious" and "aware" differ in ordinary talk, the difference goes in the opposite direction.

19. Of course, even those who do not believe in P-consciousness at all, as distinct from A-consciousness, can accept the distinction between a noise that is A-conscious

and a noise that is not A-conscious. There is a more familiar situation that illustrates the same points. Think back to all those times you have been sitting in the kitchen when suddenly the compressor in the refrigerator goes off. Again, one might naturally say that one was aware of the noise, but only at the moment when it went off was one consciously aware of it. I didn't use this example because I am not sure that one really has P-consciousness of the noise of the compressor all along; habituation would perhaps prevent it. Perhaps what happens at the moment it goes off is that one is P-conscious of the change only.

[...]

25. There is an additional problem in the reasoning that I will not go into except here. There is a well-known difficulty in reasoning of the form: X is missing; the patient has lost the ability to do such and such; therefore a function of X is to facilitate such and such. In a complex system, a loss may reverberate through the system, triggering a variety of malfunctions that are not connected in any serious way with the function of the missing item. An imperfect but memorable example (that I heard from Tom Bever) will illustrate: the Martians want to find out about the function of various Earthly items. They begin with the Pentagon, and focus in on a particular drinking fountain in a hall on the third floor of the north side of the building. "If we can figure out what that is for," they think, "we can move on to something more complex." So they vaporize the drinking fountain, causing noise and spurting pipes. Everyone comes out of their offices to see what happened and the Martians conclude that the function of the fountain was to

keep people in their offices. The application of this point to the petit mal case is that even if I am right that it is A-consciousness, not P-consciousness, that is diminished or missing, I would not jump to the conclusion that A-consciousness has a function of adding powers of discrimination, flexibility, and creativity. Creativity, for example, may have its sources in the A-unconscious, requiring powers of reasoning and control of action and reporting only for its expression.

[...]

27. A similar line of reasoning appears in Shevrin (1992); he notes that in subliminal perception we don't fix the source of a mental content. Subliminal percepts aren't conscious, so consciousness must have the function of fixing the source of mental contents.

28. Although Baars is talking about the function of "conscious experience," he does have a tendency to combine P-consciousness with A-consciousness under this heading.

[...]

References

Akins, K. (1993) A bat without qualities. In: *Consciousness: Psychological and philosophical essays*, ed. M. Davies & G. Humphreys. Blackwell.

Alston, W. (1967) Religion. In: *The encyclopedia of philosophy*. Macmillan/Free Press.

Anderson, J. (1993) To see ourselves as others see us: A response to Mitchell. *New Ideas in Psychology* 11(3):339–34.

Andrade, J. (1993) Consciousness: Current views. In: *Depth of anesthesia*, ed. J.G. Jones. Little Brown.

Armstrong, D.M. (1968) *A materialist theory of mind*. Humanities Press.

Armstrong, D.M. (1980) What is consciousness? In: *The nature of mind*. Cornell University Press.

Baars, B.J. (1988) *A cognitive theory of consciousness*. Cambridge University Press.

Block, N. (1980) What is functionalism? In: *Readings in the philosophy of psychology*, vol. I, ed. N. Block. Harvard University Press.

Block, N. (1990a) Inverted earth. In: *Philosophical perspectives*, vol. 4, ed. J. Tomberlin. Ridgeview.

Block, N. (1990b) Consciousness and accessibility. *Behavioral and Brain Sciences* 13:596–59.

Block, N. (1991) Evidence against epiphenomenalism. *Behavioral and Brain Sciences* 14:670–67.

Block, N. (1992) Begging the question against phenomenal consciousness. *Behavioral and Brain Sciences* 15:205–07.

Block, N. (1993) Review of Dennett: Consciousness explained. *The Journal of Philosophy* 4:181–19.

Block, N. (1994) "Functionalism," "Qualia." In: *A companion to philosophy of mind*, ed. S. Guttenplan. Blackwell.

Bornstein, R. & Pittman. T. (1992) *Perception without awareness*. Guilford Press.

Bowers, J. & Schacter, D. (1990) Implicit memory and test awareness. *Journal of Experimental Psychology: Learning, Memory and Cognition* 16(3):404–41.

Byrne, A. (1993) *The emergent mind*. Princeton University, PhD dissertation. [aNB]

Byrne, R.W. (1993) The meaning of 'awareness': A response to Mitchell. *New Ideas in Psychology* 11(3):347–35.

Carruthers, P. (1989) Brute experience. *Journal of Philosophy* 86.

Carruthers, P. (1992) Consciousness and concepts. *Proceedings of the Aristotelian Society* (Supplement) 66:40–45.

Chalmers, D.J. (1993) *Toward a theory of consciousness*. University of Indiana PhD thesis.

Churchland, P.S. (1983) Consciousness: The transmutation of a concept. *Pacific Philosophical Quarterly* 64:80–93.

Churchland, P.S. (1986) Reduction and the neurobiological basis of consciousness. In: *Consciousness in contemporary society*, ed. A.J. Marcel & E. Bisiach. Oxford University Press.

Coslett, H. & Saffron, E. (1994) Mechanisms of implicit reading in alexia. In: *The neuropsychology of high-level vision*, ed. M. Farah & G. Ratcliff. Erlbaum.

Cowie, A. & Stoerig, P. (1992) Reflections on blindsight. In: *The neuropsychology of consciousness*, ed. B. Milner & M. Rugg. Academic Press.

Crick, F. & Koch, C. (1990) Towards a neurobiological theory of consciousness. *Seminars in the Neurosciences* 2:263–75.

Davies, M. (1992) Perceptual content and local supervenience. *Proceedings of the Aristotelian Society* 92:21–45.

Davies, M. (forthcoming) Externalism and experience. In: *Categories, consciousness and reasoning*, ed. A. Clark, J. Exquerro, J. Larrazabal. Dordrecht.

Davies, M. & Humphreys, G. (1993a) *Consciousness: Psychological and philosophical essays*. Blackwell. [aNB, APA, CG]

Davies, M. & Humphreys, G. (1993b) Introduction. In: *Consciousness*, ed. M. Davies & G. Humphreys. Blackwell.

de Lannoy, J. Two theories of a mental model of mirror self-recognition: A response to Mitchell. *New Ideas in Psychology* 11(3):337–33.

Dennett, D. (1986) Julian Jaynes' software archeology. *Canadian Psychology* 27(2):149–15.

Dennett, D. (1991) *Consciousness explained.* Little Brown. [aNB, DCD, AM, rNB]

Dennett, D. (1993) The message is: There is no medium. In: *Philosophy and Phenomenological Research* 111.

Dennett, D. & Kinsboume, M. (1992a) Time and the observer: The where and when of consciousness in the brain. *Behavioral and Brain Sciences* 15:183–20.

Dennett, D. & Kinsboume, M. (1992b) Escape from the Cartesian theater. *Behavioral and Brain Sciences* 15:234–24.

Dimond, S. (1976) Brain circuits for consciousness. *Brain, Behavior and Evolution* 13:376–95.

Dretske, F. (1993) Conscious experience. *Mind* 102 406:263–84.

Dupre, J. (1981) Natural kinds and biological taxa. *Philosophical Review* 90:66–69.

Edelman, G. (1989) *The remembered present: A biological theory of consciousness.* Basic Books.

Etcoff, N.L., Freeman, R. & Cave, K. Can we lose memories of faces? Content specificity and awareness in a prosopagnosic. *Journal of Cognitive Neuroscience* 3.

Etcoff, N.L. & Magee, J.J. (1992) Covert recognition of emotional expressions. *Journal of Clinical and Experimental Neuropsychology* 14:95–99.

Evans. C. (1982) *The varieties of reference.* Oxford University Press.

Farah, M. (1994) Visual perception and visual awareness after brain damage: A tutorial overview. In: *Attention and performance* 15, ed. C. Umilá & M. Moskovitch. MIT Press.

Flanagan, O. (1991) *The science of the mind,* 2d ed. MIT Press.

Flanagan, O. (1992) *Consciousness reconsidered.* MIT Press.

Gallup, G. (1982) Self-awareness and the emergence of mind in primates. *American Journal of Primatology* 2:237–48.

Gallup, G. & Povinelli, D. Mirror, mirror on the wall, which is the most heuristic theory of them all? A response to Mitchell. *New Ideas in Psychology* 11:327–3.

Ghoneim, M. & Block, R. (1993) Learning during anesthesia. In: *Depth of anesthesia,* ed. J.G. Jones. Little Brown.

Ghoneim, M., Hinrichs, J. & Mewaldt, S. (1984) Dose-response analysis of the behavioral effects of diazepam: I. Learning and memory. *Psychopharmacology* 82:291–95.

Goldman, A. (1993a) The psychology of folk psychology. *Behavioral and Brain Sciences* 16:15–82.

Goldman, A. (1993b) Consciousness, folk psychology and cognitive science. *Consciousness and Cognition* 11. [aNB]

Goodale, M.A. & Milner, A.D. (1992) Separate visual pathways for perception and action. *Trends in Neurosciences* 15:20–25.

Harman, G. (1990) The intrinsic quality of experience. In: *Philosophical perspectives,* vol. 4, ed. J. Tomberlin. Ridgeview.

Heyes, C. (1986) *Divided consciousness,* 2d ed. Wiley.

Heyes, C. (1993) Reflections on self-recognition in primates. *Animal Behavior.*

Hill, C. (1991) *Sensations: A defense of type materialism.* Cambridge University Press.

Holender, D. (1986) Semantic activation without conscious identification in dichotic listening, parafoveal vision, and visual masking: A survey and appraisal. *Behavioral and Brain Sciences* 9:1–66.

Humphrey, N. (1992) *A history of the mind.* Simon & Schuster.

Huxley, T.H. (1866) *Lessons in elementary psychology.* Quoted in Humphrey, 1992.

Jackendoff, R. (1987) *Consciousness and the computational mind.* MIT Press.

Jackson, F. (1977) *Perception.* Cambridge University Press.

Jackson, F. (1986) What Mary didn't know. *Journal of Philosophy* 83:291–99.

Jackson, F. (1993a) Appendix A (for philosophers). In: *Philosophy and phenomenological research* 111.

Jackson, F. (1993b) Armchair metaphysics. In: *Philosophy in mind*, ed. J. O'Leary-Hawthorne & M. Michael. Kluwer.

Jacoby, L., Toth, J., Lindsay, D. & Debner, J. (1992) Lectures for a layperson: Methods for revealing unconscious processes. In: *Perception without awareness*, ed. R. Bornstein & T. Pittman. Guilford Press.

James, W. (1890) *The principles of psychology.* Dover, 1950.

Jaynes, J. (1976) *The origin of consciousness in the breakdown of the bicameral mind.* Houghton-Mifflin.

Jones, J.G. (1993) *Depth of anesthesia.* Little Brown.

Kihlstrom, J. (1987) The cognitive unconscious. *Science* 237:1445–45.

Kihlstrom, J. & Barnhardt, T. & Tataryn, D. (1992) Implicit perception. In: *Perception without awareness*, ed. R. Bornstein & T. Pittman. Guilford Press.

Kihlstrom, J. & Couture, L. (1992) Awareness and information processing in general anesthesia. *Journal of Psychopharmacology* 6(3):410–41.

Kihlstrom, J. & Schacter, D. (1990) Anaesthesia, amnesia, and the cognitive unconscious. In: *Memory and awareness in anaesthesia*, ed. B. Bonke. Swets & Zeitlinger.

Kirk, R. (1992) Consciousness and concepts. *Proceedings of the Aristotelian Society* (Supplement) 66:23–24.

Kuhn, T. (1964) A function for thought experiments. In: *Melanges Alexandre Koyré*, vol 1. Hermann.

Lackner, J. & Garrett, M. (1973) Resolving ambiguity: Effects of biasing context in the unattended ear. *Cognition* 1:359–37.

Landis, T., Regard, M. & Serral, A. (1980) Iconic reading in a case of alexia without agraphia caused by a brain tumour: A tachistoscopic study. *Brain and Language* 11:45–53.

Levine, J. (1983) Materialism and qualia: The explanatory gap. *Pacific Philosophical Quarterly* 64:354–36.

Levine, J. (1993) On leaving out what it is like. In: *Consciousness: Psychological and philosophical essays*, ed. M. Davies & G. Humphreys. Blackwell.

Levine, J. (1994) Review of Owen Flanagan: *Consciousness reconsidered. Philosophical Review.*

Loar, B. (1990) Phenomenal properties. In: *Philosophical perspectives: Action theory and philosophy of mind*, ed. J. Tomberlin. Ridgeview.

Lormand, E. (forthcoming) What qualitative consciousness is like.

Lycan, W.G. (1987) *Consciousness.* MIT Press.

Mandler, G. (1985) *Cognitive psychology.* Erlbaum.

Marcel, A.J. (1983) Conscious and unconscious perception: An approach to relations between phenomenal experience and perceptual processes. *Cognitive Psychology* 15:238–300.

Marcel, A.J. (1986) Consciousness and processing: Choosing and testing a null hypothesis. *Behavioral and Brain Sciences* 9:40–44.

Marcel, A.J. (1988) Phenomenal experience and functionalism. In: *Consciousness in contemporary science*, ed. A.J. Marcel & E. Bisiach. Oxford University Press.

Marcel, A.J. & Bisiach, E., eds. (1988) *Consciousness in contemporary science.* Oxford University Press.

McCullough, G. (1993) The very idea of the phenomenological. *Proceedings of the Aristotelian Society* 93:39–58.

McGinn, C. (1991) *The problem of consciousness*. Blackwell.

McGinn, C. (1993) Consciousness and cosmology: Hyperdualism ventilated. In: *Consciousness: Psychological and philosophical essays*, ed. M. Davies & G. Humphreys. Blackwell.

Melzack, R. & Wall, P. (1988) *The challenge of pain*, 2d ed. Penguin.

Menzel, E., Savage-Rumbaugh, E. & Lawson, J. (1985) Chimpanzee (Pan troglogdytes) spatial problem solving with the use of mirrors and televised equivalents of mirrors. *Journal of Comparative Psychology* 99:211–17.

Milner, B. & Rugg, M., eds. (1992) *The neuropsychology of consciousness*. Academic Press.

Mitchell, R.W. (1993a) Mental models of mirror self-recognition: Two theories. *New Ideas in Psychology* 11:295–32.

Mitchell, R.W. (1993b) Recognizing one's self in a mirror? A reply to Gallup and Povinelli, de Lannoy, Anderson, and Byrne. *New Ideas in Psychology* 11:351–77.

Moscovitch, M., Goshen-Gottstein, Y. & Vriezen, E. (1994) Memory without conscious recollection: A tutorial review from a neuropsychological perspective. In: *Attention and performance* 15, ed. C. Umiltá & M. Moscovitch. MIT Press.

Nagel T. (1979) *Mortal questions*. Cambridge University Press.

Nagel T. (1986) *The view from nowhere*. Oxford University Press.

Nathan, P. (1985) Pain and nociception in the clinical context. *Philosophical Transactions of the Royal Society* London B 308:219–22.

Natsoulas, T. (1993) What is wrong with the appendage theory of consciousness? *Philosophical Psychology* 6(2):137–15.

Nelkin, N. (1993) The connection between intentionality and consciousness. In: *Consciousness: Psychological and philosophical essays*, ed. M. Davies & G. Humphreys. Blackwell.

Nisbett, R. & Wilson, T. (1977) Telling more than we can know: Verbal reports on mental processes. *Psychological Review* 84:231–59.

Paley, W. (1964) *Natural theology*, ed. F. Ferre. Indiana University Press.

Parkin, D. (1985) Reason, emotion, and the embodiment of power. In: *Reason and morality*, ed. J. Overing. Tavistock.

Peacocke, C. (1983) *Sense and content*. Oxford University Press.

Peacocke, C. (1992) *A study of concepts*. MIT Press.

Pendlebury, M. (1992) Theories of experience. In: *A companion to epistemology*, ed. J. Dancy & E. Sosa. Blackwell.

Penfield, W. (1975) *The mystery of the mind: A critical study of consciousness and the human brain*. Princeton University Press.

Plourde, G. (1993) Clinical use of the 40-Hz auditory steady state response. In: *Depth of anesthesia*, ed. J.G. Jones. Little Brown.

Povinelli, D. (1994) What chimpanzees know about the mind. In: *Behavioral diversity in chimpanzees*. Harvard University Press.

Putnam, H. (1975) The meaning of 'meaning.' In: *Mind, language and reality*, ed. H. Putnam. Cambridge University Press.

Reingold, E. & Merikle, P. (1993) Theory and measurement in the study of unconscious processes. In: *Consciousness: Psychological and philosophical essays*, ed. M. Davies & G. Humphreys. Blackwell.

Rey, G. (1983) A reason for doubting the existence of consciousness. In: *Consciousness and self-regulation*, vol 3., ed. R. Davidson, G. Schwartz & D. Shapiro. Plenum.

Rey, G. (1988) A question about consciousness. In: *Perspectives on mind*, ed. H. Otto & J. Tuedio. Reidel.

Rosenthal, D. (1986) Two concepts of consciousness. *Philosophical Studies* 49:329–35.

Rosenthal, D. (1993) Thinking that one thinks. In: *Consciousness: Psychological and philosophical essays*, ed. M. Davies & G. Humphreys. Blackwell.

Schacter, D.L. (1989) On the relation between memory and consciousness: Dissociable interactions and conscious experience. In: *Varieties of memory and consciousness: Essays in honour of Endel Tulving*, ed. H. Roediger & F. Craik. Erlbaum.

Searle, J.R. (1983) *Intentionality*. Cambridge University Press.

Searle, J.R. (1990a) Consciousness, explanatory inversion and cognitive science. *Behavioral and Brain Sciences* 13:4:585–95.

Searle, J.R. (1990b) Who is computing with the brain? *Behavioral and Brain Sciences* 13:4:632–64.

Searle, J.R. (1992) *The rediscovery of the mind*. MIT Press.

Sergent, J. & Poncet, M. (1990) From covert to overt recognition of faces in a prosopagnosic patient. *Brain* 113:989–1004.

Shallice, T. (1988a) *From neuropsychology to mental structure*. Cambridge University Press.

Shallice, T. (1988b) Information-processing models of consciousness: Possibilities and problems. In: *Consciousness in contemporary science*, ed. A.J. Marcel & E. Bisiach. Oxford University Press.

Shepard, R.N. (1993) On the physical basis, linguistic representation, and conscious experience of colors. In: *Conceptions of the human mind: Essays in honor of George A. Miller*, ed. G. Harman. Erlbaum. [RNS]

Shevrin, H. (1992) Subliminal perception, memory and consciousness: Cognitive and dynamic perspectives. In: *Perception without awareness*, ed. R. Bornstein & T. Pittman. Guilford Press.

Shoemaker, S. (1975) Functionalism and qualia. *Philosophical Studies* 27:291–315.

Shoemaker, S. (1981a) Absent qualia are impossible—a reply to Block. *Philosophical Review* 90(4):581–59.

Shoemaker, S. (1981b) The inverted spectrum. *Journal of Philosophy* 74(7):357–38.

Shoemaker, S. (1993) Lovely and suspect ideas. *Philosophy and Phenomenological Research* 3(4):905–91.

Shoemaker, S. (1994) Phenomenal character. *Nous.* 28(1): 21–38.

Sperling, G. (1960) The information available in brief visual presentations. *Psychological Monographs* 74:11.

Stich, S. (1978) Beliefs and sub-doxastic states. *Philosophy of Science* 45:499–58.

Tye, M. (1991) *The imagery debate*. MIT Press.

Tye, M. (1993a) Reflections on Dennett and consciousness. *Philosophy and Phenomenological Research* 34:893–98.

Tye, M. (1993b) Blindsight, the absent qualia hypothesis and the mystery of consciousness. *Royal Institute of Philosophy Supplements* 34:19–40.

Tye, M. (forthcoming) Does pain lie within the domain of cognitive psychology? In: *Philosophical perspectives*, ed. J. Tomberlin. Northridge CA: Ridgeview. [NOTE: We find no record of this publication. It (or a revision) may have been published as (1995) A representational theory of pains and their phenomenal character, *Philosophical Perspectives* 9: 223–39. —Eds.]

Umiltá, C. & Moscovitch, M. (1994) *Attention and performance 15*. MIT Press.

Van Gulick, R. (1989) What difference does consciousness make? *Philosophical Topics* 17(1):211–23.

Van Gulick, R. (1993) Understanding the phenomenal mind: Are we all just armadillos? In: *Consciousness: Psychological and philosophical essays*, ed. M. Davies & G. Humphreys. Blackwell.

Weiskrantz, L. (1986) *Blindsight*. Oxford University Press.

Weiskrantz, L. (1988) Some contributions of neuropsychology of vision and memory to the problem of consciousness. In: *Consciousness in contemporary science*, ed. A.J. Marcel & E. Bisiach. Oxford University Press.

Weiskrantz, L. (1992) Introduction: Dissociated issues. In: *The neuropsychology of consciousness*, ed. B. Milner & M. Rugg. Academic Press.

White, S.L. (1987) What is it like to be an homunculus. *Pacific Philosophical Quarterly* 68:148–17.

White, S.L. (1991) Transcendentalism and its discontents. In: *The unity of the self*. ed. S.L. White. MIT Press.

Wiser, M. & Carey, S. (1983) When heat and temperature were one. In: *Mental models*, ed. D. Gentner & A. Stevens. Erlbaum.

Young, A.W. (1994a) Covert recognition. In: *The neuropsychology of higher vision: Collected tutorial essays*, ed. M. Farah & G. Ratcliff. Erlbaum.

Young, A.W. (1994b) Neuropsychology of awareness. In: *Consciousness in philosophy and cognitive neuroscience*, ed. M. Kappinen & A. Revonsuo. Erlbaum.

Young, A.W. & De Haan, E. (1993) Impairments of visual awareness. In: *Consciousness: Psychological and philosophical essays*, ed. M. Davies & G. Humphreys. Blackwell.

DAVID J. CHALMERS

Selection from *The Conscious Mind: In Search of a Theory of Conscious Experience*

[...]

6.2 Principles of Coherence

The most promising way to get started in developing a theory of consciousness is to focus on the remarkable coherence between conscious experience and cognitive structure. The phenomenology and the psychology of mind do not float free of each other; they are systematically related. The many lawful relations between consciousness and cognition can provide much of what we need to get a theory of consciousness off the ground.

The Coherence between Consciousness and Awareness

The most fundamental coherence principle between consciousness and cognition [...] concerns the relationship between consciousness and first-order judgments. The principles with which we will deal here concern the coherence between consciousness and awareness. Recall that awareness is the psychological correlate of consciousness, roughly explicable as a state wherein some information is directly accessible, and available for the deliberate control of behavior and for verbal report. The contents of awareness correspond to the contents of first-order phenomenal judgments (with a caveat to be mentioned), the contentful states that are not about consciousness but parallel to it.

Where there is consciousness, there is awareness. My visual experience of a red book upon my table is accompanied by a functional perception of the book. Optical stimulation is processed and transformed, and my perceptual systems register that there is an object of such-and-such shape and color on the table, with this information available in the control of behavior. The same goes for the specific details in what is experienced. Each detail is cognitively represented. To see that each detail must be so represented, simply observe that I am able to comment on those details and to direct my behavior in ways that depend on them; for instance, I can point to appropriate parts of the book. Such systematic availability of information implies the existence of an internal state carrying that content.

This internal state is a first-order phenomenal judgment—at least to a first approximation. I include the qualification because one might question whether this state should be strictly called a "judgment" at all. The content of this state need not be something that the subject would endorse on reflection, and indeed it might not be conceptualized by the subject at all. Such a state might qualify as a judgment only in a weak sense; it may be better to speak of it as a sort of informational registration, or an implicit or subpersonal judgment at best. I will discuss this issue in more depth later in this chapter, but for now, when I speak of these states as judgments, this talk should be understood broadly as picking out a class of representational states that need not be reflectively endorsed by the subject, and which need not have conceptualized content.

What goes for visual experience here goes equally for any sensory experience. What is experienced in audition is represented in our auditory system, in such a way that later processes have access to it in the control of behavior; in particular, the contents are available for verbal report. In principle, somebody who knew nothing about consciousness might examine our cognitive processes and ascertain these contents of awareness by observing the role that information plays in directing later processes. In the same sort of way we can handle hallucinations and other cases of sensations without a real object being sensed. Although there is no real object for the contents of perception to concern, there is still representation in our perceptual system. Macbeth had a first-order cognitive state with the content "dagger there" to accompany his experience of a dagger, despite the fact that there was no dagger to be perceived or experienced.

Even non-perceptual experience falls under this umbrella. Although there may be no object of a pain experience, contents along the line of "something hurts"—or perhaps better, "something bad"—are still cognitively represented. The very fact that we can comment on the pain and direct our behavior appropriately brings out this fact. There is awareness here just as there is awareness in visual perception, even though the object of the awareness is not so clear-cut. A similar story goes for our experience of emotion, and other "internal" experiences. In all these cases, there are cognitive states corresponding to the experiences; if there were not, then the content of the experience could not be reflected in behavior at all. Note that the principle is not that whenever we have a conscious experience we are aware of the experience. It is first-order judgments that are central here, not second-order judgments. The principle is that when we have an experience, we are aware of the contents of the experience. When we experience a book, we are aware of the book; when we experience a pain, we are aware of something hurtful; when we experience a thought, we are aware of whatever it is that the thought is about. It is not a matter of an experience followed by a separate judgment, as might be the case for second-order judgments; these first-order judgments are concomitants of experiences, existing alongside them.

[...]

Thus it is plausible that with awareness appropriately defined, consciousness is always accompanied by awareness, and vice versa. There is more than can be said about characterizing the relevant sort of awareness; I will refine it further in what follows, based in part on the consideration of various interesting cases. Even at the coarse level, however, we can see that this relationship provides a useful focal point in understanding the coherence between consciousness and cognition.

The Principle of Structural Coherence

So far we have a hypothesis: where there is consciousness, there is awareness, and where there is (the right kind of) awareness, there is consciousness. The correlation between these can be made more detailed than this. In particular, various structural features of consciousness correspond directly to structural features that are represented in awareness.

An individual's conscious experience is not in general a homogeneous blob; it has a detailed internal structure. My visual field, for example, has a definite geometry to it. There is a large red patch here, with a small yellow patch in close proximity, with some white in between; there are patterns of stripes, squares, and triangles; and so on. In three dimensions, I have experiences of shapes such as cubes, experiences of one thing as being behind another thing, and other manifestations of the geometry of

depth. My visual field consists in a vast mass of details, which fit together into an encompassing structure.

Crucially, all of these details are cognitively represented, within what we can think of as the structure of awareness. The size and shape of various patches is represented in my visual system for example: perhaps in a fairly direct topographic map, but even if not, we know that it is represented somehow. It must be, as witnessed by the fact that the relevant information is available to guide the control of behavior. The same goes for perceptual representation of the stripes, and of cubical shapes, and so on. Each of these structural details is accessible to the cognitive system, and available for use in the control of behavior, so each is represented in the contents of awareness.

In principle, someone with complete knowledge of my cognitive processes would be able to recover all of these structural details. The geometry of the visual field can be recovered by an analysis of the information that the visual system makes available for later control processes; the very fact that each of these details can be reflected in the behavioral capacities of the subject—a subject might trace the various structural details with arm movements, for example, or comment on them in verbal reports—implies that the information must be present somewhere. Of course the details of the analysis would be very tricky, and far beyond present-day methods, but we know that the information must be there. In this way we can see that the structure of consciousness is mirrored in the structure of awareness. The same goes for implicit structure in the phenomenal field, such as relations between colors. Even if I am only seeing one color at a given time, there are a host of colors I could have been seeing, colors to which this color bears a structural relation. One color is very similar to another color, and quite different from another. Two colors can seem complementary, or one color group can seem "warm" and another "cold." On a close analysis, our phenomenal colors turn out to fall into a three-dimensional structure, ordered along a red-green dimension, a yellow-blue dimension, and an white-black dimension (the choice of axes is somewhat arbitrary, but there will always be three of them). It turns out that this three-dimensional phenomenal structure is mirrored by a three-dimensional structure in the color information processed within our perceptual systems. Of course it is predictable that it would be, as we know the relevant information is available in the control of behavior, but it is interesting to see that the structure is currently being worked out in detail in studies of the visual system (see Hardin 1988 for discussion). We might say that in this case there is a difference-structure in our conscious experience (a space of differences between possible experiences) that is mirrored by a difference-structure in awareness: to the manifold of color experiences and relations among them, there corresponds a manifold of color representations and corresponding relations among them.

We can find similar sorts of implicit structure in other phenomenal domains, and a similar correspondence to implicit structures at the processing level. The phenomenological structure in a musical chord must be mirrored by structure in what is represented, for example, in order that it can be reported and reflected in other processes of control. The same holds for the implicit structure of tastes. Such correspondences are found in empirical studies of the relevant processes with considerable frequency; but even without such studies, one can see that there must be some sort of correspondence, by reflecting on the fact that these structural details are available to play a control role. In general, this sort of reasoning leads us to the conclusion that any detailed structure that one might find in a phenomenal field will be mirrored in the structures represented in awareness.

There are various more specific features of experience that are also mirrored within awareness. The most obvious of these is intensity of experience. It is clear that intensity makes a difference to later processes, so it must somehow be represented in the structure of awareness. Indeed, it is plausible that the intensity of an experience corresponds directly to the extent to which an underlying representation tends to play a control role, occupying the resources of later processes (think of the difference between an intense pain and a faint one, or between an all-consuming emotion and a background emotion). Another example is the resolution of experiences, as found for example in the difference between the high resolution at the center of a visual field and the low resolution at the fringes. This resolution is something that we would expect to find to be mirrored in the resolution of underlying representations, and indeed that is what we find.

In general, even if experiences are in some sense "ineffable," relations between experiences are not; we have no trouble discussing these relations, whether they be relations of similarity and difference, geometric relations, relations of intensity, and so on. As Schlick (1938) pointed out, the form of experience seems to be straightforwardly communicable, even if the content (intrinsic quality) is not.[3] So we should expect that these relations will be cognitively represented, and this is indeed what we find. Similarities and differences between experiences correspond to similarities and differences represented in awareness; the geometry of experience corresponds to the geometry of awareness; and so on. If we refine the notion of awareness as suggested above, so that states of awareness are always accompanied by states of experience, then a structural correspondence in the other direction will also be plausible: the structure represented in awareness is mirrored in the structure of experience.

So alongside the general principle that where there is consciousness, there is awareness, and vice versa, we have a more specific principle: the structure of consciousness is mirrored by the structure of awareness, and the structure of awareness is mirrored by the structure of consciousness. I will call this the principle of structural coherence.[4] This is a central and systematic relation between phenomenology and psychology, and ultimately can be cashed out into a relation between phenomenology and underlying physical processes. As we will see, it is useful in a number of ways.

6.3 More on the Notion of Awareness

One of the most interesting philosophical projects in the study of consciousness is that of refining the notion of awareness so that it becomes a more perfect psychological correlate of consciousness. On an initial definition, awareness corresponds only imperfectly to consciousness, but the notion can be refined to handle problem cases. Ultimately we would like to characterize a psychological state that plausibly correlates with conscious experience across the board, at least in a range of cases with which we are familiar. I defined awareness initially as the state wherein some information is directly accessible and available for verbal report and the deliberate control of behavior. Considerations about propositional awareness in the absence of experience suggested modifying this to require direct access. Other modifications are possible. The most obvious is that availability for verbal report is not strictly required for conscious experience, as considerations about experience in mammals suggest, although it is a good heuristic in cases where language is present. A natural suggestion is to modify the definition of awareness to something like direct availability for global control. That is, a subject is aware of some information when that information is directly available to bring to bear in the direction of a wide range of behavioral processes. This allows for the possibility of experience in non-human animals, and also squares nicely with the reportability criterion. In cases where information is reportable, it is generally available for global control (for example, in the deliberate direction of a wide range of behaviors). The reverse implication does not always hold (as witnessed by the animal case), but at least in subjects that have the capacity to report, availability of information for global control generally implies its availability for report.

Of course this project of refinement can only go so far, as we lack an experience meter with which to confirm and refine these hypotheses empirically. Still, we have a good idea from the first-person case about states in which we have experiences and states in which we do not, and an analysis of what is going on in these cases usually allows us to characterize those states in functional terms. So reflection on the relationship between experience and function in familiar cases gives us considerable leverage. We might also think of empirically refining these hypotheses here via first-person experimentation—we can place ourselves into a given functional state, and see what sort of experience we have—and with a little help from principles of homogeneity and reliability, we can draw conclusions from the investigation of corresponding situations in others.

There is also a role for the empirical consideration of cases farther from home, for example by considering what sorts of experiences are plausibly had by subjects suffering from certain pathologies, or (as above) by non-human animals. Of course, we can never be completely certain about what experiences are present in these cases, but some conclusions are much more plausible than others. In effect, these cases act as a focus for our reasoning and an aid to the imagination in distilling plausible principles on the connection between experience and function. The principles may be ultimately grounded in non-empirical analysis, but focus on empirical cases at least ties this sort of reasoning to the real world. For example, reflection on the attribution of experience to mammals squares with the refined criterion I have suggested above. We are generally prepared to attribute perceptual experience of a stimulus to mammals in cases where the direction of behavior can be made to depend on that stimulus, especially if this is exhibited in a number of different sorts of behavior. If we found that information about a stimulus could only be exhibited in a single, relatively minor behavioral reaction, we might suppose that the information is entirely unconscious.

As its availability for use becomes more widespread, it becomes more plausible to suppose that it is experienced. So the coherence between consciousness and this notion of awareness is compatible both with the first-person data and with the natural reasoning concerning non-human cases.

There are a number of other interesting problem cases for analysis. One example is blindsight (described in Weiskrantz 1986). This is a pathology arising from damage to the visual cortex, in which the usual route for visual information-processing is damaged, but in which visual information nevertheless seems to be processed in a limited way. Subjects with blindsight can see nothing in certain areas of their visual field, or so they say. If one puts a red or green light in their "blind area" they claim to see nothing. But when one forces them to make a choice about what is in that area—on whether a red or green light is present, for example— it turns out that they are right far more often

than they are wrong. Somehow they are "seeing" what is in the area without really seeing it.

Blindsight is sometimes put forward as a case in which consciousness and the associated functional role comes apart. After all, in blindsight there is discrimination, categorization, and even verbal report of a sort, but it seems that there is no conscious experience. If this were truly a case in which functional role and experience where dissociated, it would clearly raise problems for the coherence principle. Fortunately, the conclusion that this is an example of awareness without consciousness is ungrounded. For a start, it is not obvious that there is no experience in these cases; perhaps there is a faint experience that bears an unusual relation to verbal report. More to the point, however, this is far from a standard case of awareness. Clearly there is a vast difference between the functional roles played here and those played in the usual case—it is precisely because of this difference in functional roles that we notice something amiss in the first place.[5]

In particular, subjects with blindsight seem to lack the usual sort of access to the information at hand. Their access is curiously indirect, as witnessed by the fact that it is not straightforwardly available for verbal report, and in the deliberate control of behavior. The information is available to many fewer control processes than is standard perceptual information; it can be made available to other processes, but only by unusual methods such as prompting and forced choice. So this information does not qualify as directly available for global control, and the subjects are not truly aware of the information in the relevant sense. The lack of experience corresponds directly to a lack of awareness. It is also possible, perhaps, that blindsight subjects have a weak sort of experience, in which case one might also want to say that they have a weak sort of awareness, by drawing the standards of directness and globality appropriately. The description of the situation is somewhat underdetermined given our lack of access to the facts of the matter, but either way it is compatible with the coherence between consciousness and awareness.

In general, this sort of case cannot provide evidence against a link between functional organization and conscious experience, as our conclusions about the presence or absence of consciousness in these cases are drawn precisely on functional grounds. In particular, the evidence for unusual states of consciousness in these pathological cases usually relies entirely on evidence for unusual states of awareness. Such cases therefore cannot damage the principle of coherence; they can only bolster and refine it.

A tricky problem case is provided by experiences during sleep. It is plausible that we have experiences when we dream (although see Dennett 1978b), but reportability and any role in the control of action are missing, as action is missing entirely. Still, these cases might plausibly be analyzed in terms of availability for global control; it is just that the relevant control processes themselves are mostly shut down. Perhaps the information makes it into the sort of position from which it can usually be used for control purposes; this suggestion is supported by the accessibility of current dream content in a half-waking state. We could then still run the counterfactual: if reportability and control had been enabled (e.g., if the motor cortex had been functioning normally), then the information could have played a role. But this deserves a more careful analysis, along with empirical investigation of what is really going on during sleep.

Some interesting cases are presented by Block (1995) in his extended discussion of the distinction between phenomenal consciousness and "access consciousness." On Block's account, a state is access-conscious if its content is poised to be used as a premise in reasoning, poised for rational control of action, and poised for rational control of speech. So access consciousness corresponds roughly to my initial definition of awareness, although my definition gives less of a role to rationality. Block presents some cases where the two varieties of consciousness might come apart. It is instructive to see how a coherence principle might handle them.

On the possibility of access consciousness without phenomenal consciousness, Block appeals only to cases that are conceptually possible, such as zombies; these non-actual cases clearly cannot threaten the coherence principle. He mentions blindsight, but notes that blindsight only yields access consciousness in a weak sense. He also discusses cases such as "super-blindsight," which is like blindsight except that a subject is trained to have much better access to the information in the blind field. There are clearly conceivable cases of awareness without consciousness in the vicinity, but Block himself notes that there is no reason to believe such cases are actual. Interestingly, he notes that in the closest thing to empirical examples of such a case (a monkey described in Humphrey 1992, and a human patient described in Weiskrantz 1992), there is reason to believe that phenomenal consciousness is actually present.[6]

On phenomenal consciousness without access consciousness, Block mentions some actual cases. One is a situation in which a subject suddenly becomes aware of the fact that there has been a loud drill in the background for some time. Block suggests that before realizing this, the subject was phenomenally conscious but not access conscious of the drilling noise. On the account of awareness I have given, however, it seems reasonable to say that the subject was aware of the drill all along. It is plausible that relevant information about the drill was available the whole time; it simply was not accessed. So if access consciousness or awareness is defined dispositionally, this case is no problem for a coherence principle. Block also mentions a case in which a three-by-three array of letters is flashed briefly at a subject (Sperling 1960). If asked to name the letters in the top row, subjects can name those but then cannot name the others; the same for the other rows. Block argues that a subject is phenomenally conscious of all nine of the letters, but is access-conscious of only three at a time. But once again it is plausible that information about all nine letters was initially available; it is just that information about only three letters was accessed, and the very process of access destroyed the accessibility of the other information. So this case is also compatible with the coherence principle, on a dispositional account of awareness.

There are many other cases that might be considered. All I have done here is to present some cases and some brief analysis as illustration, to give some idea of the shape of an interesting philosophical project. In a more careful analysis, one might seek to put stronger constraints on just what kind of accessibility goes along with conscious experience, and just what kind of global control role is relevant. The account of awareness in terms of direct availability for global control is just a start. This is a fertile area for further analysis.

[...]

Notes

[...]

3. Compare also the observation by Nagel (1974) that "structural features of perception might be more accessible to objective description, even though something would be left out."

4. This is closely related to Jackendoff's Hypothesis of Computational Sufficiency: "Every phenomenological distinction is caused by/supported by/projected from a corresponding computational distinction" (Jackendoff 1987, p. 24).

5. For related discussions of blindsight, see Tye 1993, Block 1995, and especially Dennett 1991.

6. See also Cowey and Stoerig 1992.

[...]

References [Eds.: References for the reproduced pages only.]

Block, N. 1995. On a confusion about the function of consciousness. *Behavioral and Brain Sciences* 18, 227–87.

Cowey, A. & Stoerig, P. 1992. Reflections on blindsight. In (D. Milner & M. Rugg, eds.) *The Neuropsychology of Consciousness*. London: Academic Press.

Dennett, D.C. 1978b. Why you can't make a computer that feels pain. In Dennett, D.C. 1978a. *Brainstorms*. Cambridge, MA: MIT Press.

Dennett, D.C. 1991. *Consciousness Explained*. New York: Little, Brown.

Humphrey, N. 1992. *A History of the Mind: Evolution and the Birth of Consciousness*. New York: Simon and Schuster.

Jackendoff, R. 1987. *Consciousness and the Computational Mind*. Cambridge, MA: MIT Press.

Nagel, T. 1974. What is it like to be a bat? *Philosophical Review* 4, 435–50.

Schlick, M. 1938. *Form and Content: An Introduction to Philosophical Thinking*. In Gesammelte Aufsätze 1926–1936. Vienna: Gerold & Co. *Reprinted in Philosophical Papers*, volume II (H.L Mulder & B. van de Velde-Schlick, eds.). Dordrecht: D. Reidel, 1979.

Sperling, G. 1960. The information available in brief visual presentations. *Psychological Monographs* 74.

Tye, M. 1993. Blindsight, the absent qualia hypothesis, and the mystery of consciousness. In *Philosophy and the Cognitive Sciences*. C. Hookway, ed. Cambridge, UK: Cambridge University Press.

Weiskrantz, L. 1986. *Blindsight: A Case Study and Implications*. Oxford: Oxford University Press.

Weiskrantz, L. 1992. Introduction: Dissociated issues. In (D. Milner, & M. Rugg, eds.) *The Neuropsychology of Consciousness*. London: Academic Press.

DAVID J. CHALMERS

Selection from "Facing Up to the Problem of Consciousness"

I: Introduction

Consciousness poses the most baffling problems in the science of the mind. There is nothing that we know more intimately than conscious experience, but there is nothing that is harder to explain. All sorts of mental phenomena have yielded to scientific investigation in recent years, but consciousness has stubbornly resisted. Many have tried to explain it, but the explanations always seem to fall short of the target. Some have been led to suppose that the problem is intractable, and that no good explanation can be given.

To make progress on the problem of consciousness, we have to confront it directly. In this paper, I first isolate the truly hard part of the problem, separating it from more tractable parts and giving an account of why it is so difficult to explain. I critique some recent work that uses reductive methods to address consciousness, and argue that these methods inevitably fail to come to grips with the hardest part of the problem. Once this failure is recognized, the door to further progress is opened. In the second half of the paper, I argue that if we move to a new kind of nonreductive explanation, a naturalistic account of consciousness can be given. I put forward my own candidate for such an account: a nonreductive theory based on principles of structural coherence and organizational invariance and a double-aspect view of information.

II: The Easy Problems and the Hard Problem

There is not just one problem of consciousness. 'Consciousness' is an ambiguous term, referring to many different phenomena. Each of these phenomena needs to be explained, but some are easier to explain than others. At the start, it is useful to divide the associated problems of consciousness into 'hard' and 'easy' problems. The easy problems of consciousness are those that seem directly susceptible to the standard methods of cognitive science, whereby a phenomenon is explained in terms of computational or neural mechanisms. The hard problems are those that seem to resist those methods.

The easy problems of consciousness include those of explaining the following phenomena:

- the ability to discriminate, categorize, and react to environmental stimuli;
- the integration of information by a cognitive system;
- the reportability of mental states;
- the ability of a system to access its own internal states;
- the focus of attention;
- the deliberate control of behaviour;
- the difference between wakefulness and sleep.

All of these phenomena are associated with the notion of consciousness. For example, one sometimes says that a mental state is conscious when it is verbally reportable, or when it is internally accessible. Sometimes a system is said to be conscious of some information when it has the ability to react on the basis of that information, or, more strongly, when it attends to that information, or when it can integrate that information and exploit it in the sophisticated control of behaviour. We sometimes say that an action is conscious precisely when it is deliberate. Often, we say that an organism is conscious as another way of saying that it is awake.

There is no real issue about whether *these* phenomena can be explained scientifically. All of them are straightforwardly vulnerable to explanation in terms of computational or neural mechanisms. To explain access and reportability, for example, we need only specify the mechanism by which information about internal states is retrieved and made available for verbal report. To explain the integration of information, we need only exhibit mechanisms by which information is brought together and exploited by later processes. For an account of sleep and wakefulness, an appropriate neurophysiological account of the processes responsible for organisms' contrasting behaviour in those states will suffice. In each case, an appropriate cognitive or neurophysiological model can clearly do the explanatory work.

If these phenomena were all there was to consciousness, then consciousness would not be much of a problem. Although we do not yet have anything close to a complete explanation of these phenomena, we have a clear idea of how we might go about explaining them. This is why I call these problems the easy problems. Of course, 'easy' is a relative term. Getting the details right will probably take a century or two of difficult empirical work. Still, there is every reason to believe that the methods of cognitive science and neuroscience will succeed.

The really hard problem of consciousness is the problem of *experience*. When we think and perceive, there is a whir of information-processing, but there is also a subjective aspect. As Nagel (1974) has put it, there is *something it is like* to be a conscious organism. This subjective aspect is experience. When we see, for example, we *experience* visual sensations: the felt quality of redness, the experience of dark and light, the quality of depth in a visual field. Other experiences go along with perception in different modalities: the sound of a clarinet, the smell of mothballs. Then there are bodily sensations, from pains to orgasms; mental images that are conjured up internally; the felt quality of emotion, and the experience of a stream of conscious thought. What unites all of these states is that there is something it is like to be in them. All of them are states of experience.

It is undeniable that some organisms are subjects of experience. But the question of how it is that these systems are subjects of experience is perplexing. Why is it that when our cognitive systems engage in visual and auditory information-processing, we have visual or auditory experience: the quality of deep blue, the sensation of middle C? How can we explain why there is something it is like to entertain a mental image, or to experience an emotion? It is widely agreed that experience arises from a physical basis, but we have no good explanation of why and how it so arises. Why should physical processing give rise to a rich inner life at all? It seems objectively unreasonable that it should, and yet it does.

If any problem qualifies as *the* problem of consciousness, it is this one. In this central sense of 'consciousness,' an organism is conscious if there is something it is like to be that organism, and a mental state is conscious if there is something it is like to be in that state. Sometimes terms such as 'phenomenal consciousness' and 'qualia' are also used here, but I find it more natural to speak of 'conscious experience' or simply 'experience.' Another useful way to avoid confusion (used by e.g., Newell 1990, Chalmers 1996) is to reserve the term 'consciousness' for the phenomena of experience, using the less loaded term 'awareness' for the more straightforward phenomena described earlier. If such a convention were widely adopted, communication would be much easier. As things stand, those who talk about 'consciousness' are frequently talking past each other.

The ambiguity of the term 'consciousness' is often exploited by both philosophers and scientists writing on the subject. It is common to see a paper on consciousness begin with an invocation of the mystery of consciousness, noting the strange intangibility and ineffability of subjectivity, and worrying that so far we have no theory of the phenomenon. Here, the topic is clearly the hard problem—the problem of experience. In the second half of the paper, the tone becomes more optimistic, and the author's own theory of consciousness is outlined. Upon examination, this theory turns out to be a theory of one of the more straightforward phenomena—of reportability, of intro-

spective access, or whatever. At the close, the author declares that consciousness has turned out to be tractable after all, but the reader is left feeling like the victim of a bait-and-switch. The hard problem remains untouched.

III: Functional Explanation

Why are the easy problems easy, and why is the hard problem hard? The easy problems are easy precisely because they concern the explanation of cognitive *abilities* and *functions*. To explain a cognitive function, we need only specify a mechanism that can perform the function. The methods of cognitive science are well-suited for this sort of explanation, and so are well-suited to the easy problems of consciousness. By contrast, the hard problem is hard precisely because it is not a problem about the performance of functions. The problem persists even when the performance of all the relevant functions is explained.[1]

To explain reportability, for instance, is just to explain how a system could perform the function of producing reports on internal states. To explain internal access, we need to explain how a system could be appropriately affected by its internal states and use information about those states in directing later processes. To explain integration and control, we need to explain how a system's central processes can bring information contents together and use them in the facilitation of various behaviours. These are all problems about the explanation of functions.

How do we explain the performance of a function? By specifying a *mechanism* that performs the function. Here, neurophysiological and cognitive modelling are perfect for the task. If we want a detailed low-level explanation, we can specify the neural mechanism that is responsible for the function. If we want a more abstract explanation, we can specify a mechanism in computational terms. Either way, a full and satisfying explanation will result. Once we have specified the neural or computational mechanism that performs the function of verbal report, for example, the bulk of our work in explaining reportability is over.

In a way, the point is trivial. It is a *conceptual* fact about these phenomena that their explanation only involves the explanation of various functions, as the phenomena are *functionally definable*. All it *means* for reportability to be instantiated in a system is that the system has the capacity for verbal reports of internal information. All it means for a system to be awake is for it to be appropriately receptive to information from the environment and for it to be able to use this information in directing behaviour in an appropriate way. To see that this sort of thing is a conceptual fact, note that someone who says 'you have explained the performance of the verbal report function, but you have not explained reportability' is making a trivial conceptual mistake about reportability. All it could *possibly* take to explain reportability is an explanation of how the relevant function is performed; the same goes for the other phenomena in question.

Throughout the higher-level sciences, reductive explanation works in just this way. To explain the gene, for instance, we needed to specify the mechanism that stores and transmits hereditary information from one generation to the next. It turns out that DNA performs this function; once we explain how the function is performed, we have explained the gene. To explain life, we ultimately need to explain how a system can reproduce, adapt to its environment, metabolize, and so on. All of these are questions about the performance of functions, and so are well-suited to reductive explanation. The same holds for most problems in cognitive science. To explain learning, we need to explain the way in which a system's behavioural capacities are modified in light of environmental information, and the way in which new information can be brought to bear in adapting a system's actions to its environment. If we show how a neural or computational mechanism does the job, we have explained learning. We can say the same for other cognitive phenomena, such as perception, memory, and language. Sometimes the relevant functions need to be characterized quite subtly, but it is clear that insofar as cognitive science explains these phenomena at all, it does so by explaining the performance of functions.

When it comes to conscious experience, this sort of explanation fails. What makes the hard problem hard and almost unique is that it goes *beyond* problems about the performance of functions. To see this, note that even when we have explained the performance of all the cognitive and behavioural functions in the vicinity of experience—perceptual discrimination, categorization, internal access, verbal report—there may still remain a further unanswered question: *Why is the performance of these functions accompanied by experience?* A simple explanation of the functions leaves this question open.

There is no analogous further question in the explanation of genes, or of life, or of learning. If someone says 'I can see that you have explained how DNA stores and transmits hereditary information from one generation to the next, but you have not explained how it is a *gene*,' then they are making a conceptual mistake. All it means to be a gene is to be an entity that performs the relevant storage and transmission function. But if someone says 'I can see that you have explained how information is discriminated, integrated, and reported, but you have not explained how it is *experienced*,' they are not making a conceptual mistake. This is a nontrivial further question.

This further question is the key question in the problem of consciousness. Why doesn't all this information-processing go on 'in the dark,' free of any inner feel? Why is it that when electromagnetic waveforms impinge on a retina and are discriminated and categorized by a visual system, this discrimination and categorization is experienced as a sensation of vivid red? We know that conscious experience *does* arise when these functions are performed, but the very fact that it arises is the central mystery. There is an *explanatory gap* (a term due to Levine 1983) between the functions and experience, and we need an explanatory bridge to cross it. A mere account of the functions stays on one side of the gap, so the materials for the bridge must be found elsewhere.

This is not to say that experience *has* no function. Perhaps it will turn out to play an important cognitive role. But for any role it might play, there will be more to the explanation of experience than a simple explanation of the function. Perhaps it will even turn out that in the course of explaining a function, we will be led to the key insight that allows an explanation of experience. If this happens, though, the discovery will be an *extra* explanatory reward. There is no cognitive function such that we can say in advance that explanation of that function will *automatically* explain experience.

To explain experience, we need a new approach. The usual explanatory methods of cognitive science and neuroscience do not suffice. These methods have been developed precisely to explain the performance of cognitive functions, and they do a good job of it. But as these methods stand, they are *only* equipped to explain the performance of functions. When it comes to the hard problem, the standard approach has nothing to say.

IV: Some Case-Studies

In the last few years, a number of works have addressed the problems of consciousness within the framework of cognitive science and neuroscience. This might suggest that the analysis above is faulty, but in fact a close examination of the relevant work only lends the analysis further support. When we investigate just which aspects of consciousness these studies are aimed at, and which aspects they end up explaining, we find that the ultimate target of explanation is always one of the easy problems. I will illustrate this with two, representative examples.

The first is the 'neurobiological theory of consciousness' outlined by Francis Crick and Christof Koch (1990; see also Crick 1994). This theory centers on certain 35–75 hertz neural oscillations in the cerebral cortex; Crick and Koch hypothesize that these oscillations are the basis of consciousness. This is partly because the oscillations seem to be correlated with awareness in a number of different modalities—within the visual and olfactory systems, for example—and also because they suggest a mechanism by which the *binding* of information contents might be achieved. Binding is the process whereby separately represented pieces of information about a single entity are brought together to be used by later processing, as when information about the colour and shape of a perceived object is integrated from separate visual pathways. Following others (e.g., Eckhorn *et al.* 1988), Crick and Koch hypothesize that binding may be achieved by the synchronized oscillations of neuronal groups representing the relevant contents. When two pieces of information are to be bound together, the relevant neural groups will oscillate with the same frequency and phase.

The details of how this binding might be achieved are still poorly understood, but suppose that they can be worked out. What might the resulting theory explain? Clearly it might explain the binding of information contents, and perhaps it might yield a more general account of the integration of information in the brain. Crick and Koch also suggest that these oscillations activate the mechanisms of working memory, so that there may be an account of this and perhaps other forms of memory in the distance. The theory might eventually lead to a general account of how perceived information is bound and stored in memory, for use by later processing.

Such a theory would be valuable, but it would tell us nothing about why the relevant contents are experienced. Crick and Koch suggest that these oscillations are the neural *correlates* of experience. This claim is arguable—does not binding also take place in the processing of unconscious information?—but even if it is accepted, the *explanatory* question remains: Why do the oscillations give rise to experience? The only basis for an explanatory connection is the role they play in binding and storage, but the question of why binding and storage should themselves be accompanied by experience is never addressed. If we do not know why binding and storage should give rise to experience, telling a story about the oscillations cannot help us. Conversely, if we *knew* why binding and storage gave rise to experience, the neurophysiological details would be just the icing on the cake. Crick and Koch's theory gains its purchase by *assuming* a connection between binding and experience, and so can do nothing to explain that link.

I do not think that Crick and Koch are ultimately claiming to address the hard problem, although some have interpreted them otherwise. A published interview with Koch gives a clear statement of the limitations on the theory's ambitions.

> Well, let's first forget about the really difficult aspects, like subjective feelings, for they may not have a scientific solution. The subjective state of play, of pain, of pleasure, of seeing blue, of smelling a rose—there seems to be a huge jump between the materialistic level, of explaining molecules and neurons, and the subjective level. Let's focus on things that are easier to study—like visual awareness. You're now talking to me, but you're not looking at me, you're looking at the cappuccino, and so you are aware of it. You can say, 'It's a cup and there's some liquid in it.' If I give it to you, you'll move your arm and you'll take it—you'll respond in a meaningful manner. That's what I call awareness. ("What is Consciousness?," *Discover*, November 1992, p. 96)

The second example is an approach at the level of cognitive psychology. This is Bernard Baars' global workspace theory of consciousness, presented in his book *A Cognitive Theory of Consciousness* (1988). According to this theory, the contents of consciousness are contained in a *global workspace*, a central processor used to mediate communication between a host of specialized nonconscious processors. When these specialized processors need to broadcast information to the rest of the system, they do so by sending this information to the workspace, which acts as a kind of communal blackboard for the rest of the system, accessible to all the other processors.

Baars uses this model to address many aspects of human cognition, and to explain a number of contrasts between conscious and unconscious cognitive functioning. Ultimately, however, it is a theory of *cognitive accessibility*, explaining how it is that certain information contents are widely accessible within a system, as well as a theory of informational integration and reportability. The theory shows promise as a theory of awareness, the functional correlate of conscious experience, but an explanation of experience itself is not on offer.

One might suppose that according to this theory, the contents of experience are precisely the contents of the workspace. But even if this is so, nothing internal to the theory *explains* why the information within the global workspace is experienced. The best the theory can do is to say that the information is experienced because it is *globally accessible*. But now the question arises in a different form: why should global accessibility give rise to conscious experience? As always, this bridging question is unanswered.

Researchers using these methods are often inexplicit about their attitudes to the problem of conscious experience, although sometimes they take a clear stand. Even among those who are clear about it, attitudes differ widely. In placing this sort of work with respect to the problem of experience, a number of different strategies are available. It would be useful if these strategic choices were more often made explicit.

The first strategy is simply to *explain something else*. Some researchers are explicit that the problem of experience is too difficult for now, and perhaps even outside the domain of science altogether. These researchers instead choose to address one of the more tractable problems such as reportability or the self-concept. Although I have called these problems the 'easy' problems, they are among the most interesting unsolved problems in cognitive science, so this work is certainly worthwhile. The worst that can be said of this choice is that in the context of research on consciousness it is relatively unambitious, and the work can sometimes be misinterpreted. The second choice is to take a harder line and *deny the phenomenon*. (Variations on this approach are taken by Allport 1988; Dennett 1991; Wilkes 1988.) According to this line, once we have explained the functions such as accessibility, reportability, and the like, there is no further phenomenon called 'experience' to explain. Some explicitly deny the phenomenon, holding for example

that what is not externally verifiable cannot be real. Others achieve the same effect by allowing that experience exists, but only if we equate 'experience' with something like the capacity to discriminate and report. These approaches lead to a simpler theory, but are ultimately unsatisfactory. Experience is the most central and manifest aspect of our mental lives, and indeed is perhaps the key explanandum in the science of the mind. Because of this status as an explanandum, experience cannot be discarded like the vital spirit when a new theory comes along. Rather, it is the central fact that any theory of consciousness must explain. A theory that denies the phenomenon 'solves' the problem by ducking the question.

In a third option, some researchers *claim to be explaining experience* in the full sense. These researchers (unlike those above) wish to take experience very seriously; they lay out their functional model or theory, and claim that it explains the full subjective quality of experience (e.g., Flohr 1992; Humphrey 1992). The relevant step in the explanation is usually passed over quickly, however, and usually ends up looking something like magic. After some details about information processing are given, experience suddenly enters the picture, but it is left obscure *how* these processes should suddenly give rise to experience. Perhaps it is simply taken for granted that it does, but then we have an incomplete explanation and a version of the fifth strategy below.

A fourth, more promising approach appeals to these methods to *explain the structure of experience*. For example, it is arguable that an account of the discriminations made by the visual system can account for the structural relations between different colour experiences, as well as for the geometric structure of the visual field (see e.g., Clark 1992; Hardin 1992). In general, certain facts about structures found in processing will correspond to and arguably explain facts about the structure of experience. This strategy is plausible but limited. At best, it takes the existence of experience for granted and accounts for some facts about its structure, providing a sort of nonreductive explanation of the structural aspects of experience (I will say more on this later). This is useful for many purposes, but it tells us nothing about why there should be experience in the first place.

A fifth and reasonable strategy is to *isolate the substrate of experience.* After all, almost everyone allows that experience *arises* one way or another from brain processes, and it makes sense to identify the sort of process from which it arises: Crick and Koch put their work forward as isolating the neural correlate of consciousness, for example, and Edelman (1989) and Jackendoff (1987) make related claims. Justification of these claims requires a careful theoretical analysis, especially as experience is not directly observable in experimental contexts, but when applied judiciously this strategy can shed indirect light on the problem of experience. Nevertheless, the strategy is clearly incomplete. For a satisfactory theory, we need to know more than *which* processes give rise to experience; we need an account of why and how. A full theory of consciousness must build an explanatory bridge.

V: The Extra Ingredient

We have seen that there are systematic reasons why the usual methods of cognitive science and neuroscience fail to account for conscious experience. These are simply the wrong sort of methods: nothing that they give to us can yield an explanation. To account for conscious experience, we need an *extra ingredient* in the explanation. This makes for a challenge to those who are serious about the hard problem of consciousness: What is your extra ingredient, and why should *that* account for conscious experience?

[. . .]

Perhaps the most popular 'extra ingredient' of all is quantum mechanics (e.g., Hameroff 1994). The attractiveness of quantum theories of consciousness may stem from a Law of Minimization of Mystery: consciousness is mysterious and quantum mechanics is mysterious, so maybe the two mysteries have a common source. Nevertheless, quantum theories of consciousness suffer from the same difficulties as neural or computational theories. Quantum phenomena have some remarkable functional properties, such as nondeterminism and nonlocality. It is natural to speculate that these properties may play some role in the explanation of cognitive functions, such as random choice and the integration of information, and this hypothesis cannot be ruled out *a priori.* But when it comes to the explanation of experience, quantum processes are in the same boat as any other. The question of why these processes should give rise to experience is entirely unanswered.[2]

At the end of the day, the same criticism applies to any purely physical account of consciousness. For any physical process we specify there will be an unanswered question: Why should this process give rise to experience? Given any such process, it is conceptually coherent that it could be instantiated in the absence of experience. It follows that no mere account of the physical process will tell us why experience arises. The emergence of experience goes beyond what can be derived from physical theory.

Purely physical explanation is well-suited to the explanation of physical *structures,* explaining macroscopic structures in terms of detailed microstructural constituents; and it provides a satisfying explanation of the performance of *functions,* accounting for these functions in terms of the physical mechanisms that perform them. This is because: a physical account can *entail* the facts about structures and functions: once the internal details of the physical account are given, the structural and functional properties fall out as an automatic consequence. But the structure and dynamics of physical processes yield only more structure and dynamics, so structures and functions are all we can expect these processes to explain. The facts about experience cannot be an automatic consequence of any physical account, as it is conceptually coherent that any given process could exist without experience. Experience may *arise* from the physical, but it is not *entailed* by the physical.

The moral of all this is that *you can't explain conscious experience on the cheap*. It is a remarkable fact that reductive methods—methods that explain a high-level phenomenon wholly in terms of more basic physical processes—work well in so many domains. In a sense, one *can* explain most biological and cognitive phenomena on the cheap, in that these phenomena are seen as automatic consequences of more fundamental processes. It would be wonderful if reductive methods could explain experience, too; I hoped for a long time that they might. Unfortunately, there are systematic reasons why these methods must fail. Reductive methods are successful in most domains because what needs explaining in those domains are structures and functions, and these are the kind of thing that a physical account can entail. When it comes to a problem over and above the explanation of structures and functions, these methods are impotent.

This might seem reminiscent of the vitalist claim that no physical account could explain life, but the cases are disanalogous. What drove vitalist skepticism was doubt about whether physical mechanisms could perform the many remarkable functions associated with life, such as complex adaptive behaviour and reproduction. The conceptual claim that explanation of functions is what is needed was implicitly accepted, but lacking detailed knowledge of biochemical mechanisms, vitalists doubted whether any physical process could do the job and put forward the hypothesis of the vital spirit as an alternative explanation. Once it turned out that physical processes could perform the relevant functions, vitalist doubts melted away.

With experience, on the other hand, physical explanation of the functions is not in question. The key is instead the *conceptual* point that the explanation of functions does not suffice for the explanation of experience. This basic conceptual point is not something that further neuroscientific investigation will affect. In a similar way, experience is disanalogous to the élan vital. The vital spirit was put forward as an explanatory posit, in order to explain the relevant functions, and could therefore be discarded when those functions were explained without it. Experience is not an explanatory posit but an explanandum in its own right, and so is not a candidate for this sort of elimination.

It is tempting to note that all sorts of puzzling phenomena have eventually turned out to be explainable in physical terms. But each of these were problems about the observable behaviour of physical objects, coming down to problems in the explanation of structures and functions. Because of this, these phenomena have always been the kind of thing that a physical account *might* explain, even if at some points there have been good reasons to suspect that no such explanation would be forthcoming. The tempting induction from these cases fails in the case of consciousness, which is not a problem about physical structures and functions. The problem of consciousness is puzzling in an entirely different way. An analysis of the problem shows us that conscious experience is just not the kind of thing that a wholly reductive account could succeed in explaining.

VI: Nonreductive Explanation

At this point some are tempted to give up, holding that we will never have a theory of conscious experience. McGinn (1989), for example, argues that the problem is too hard for our limited minds; we are "cognitively closed" with respect to the phenomenon. Others have argued that conscious experience lies outside the domain of scientific theory altogether.

I think this pessimism is premature. This is not the place to give up; it is the place where things get interesting. When simple methods of explanation are ruled out, we need to investigate the alternatives. Given that reductive explanation fails, *nonreductive* explanation is the natural choice.

Although a remarkable number of phenomena have turned out to be explicable wholly in terms of entities simpler than themselves, this is not universal. In physics, it occasionally happens that an entity has to be taken as *fundamental.* Fundamental entities are not explained in terms of anything simpler. Instead, one takes them as basic, and gives a theory of how they relate to everything else in the world. For example, in the nineteenth century it turned out that electromagnetic processes could not be explained in terms of the wholly mechanical processes that previous physical theories appealed to, so Maxwell and others introduced electromagnetic charge and electromagnetic forces as new fundamental components of a physical theory. To explain electromagnetism, the ontology of physics had to be expanded. New basic properties and basic laws were needed to give a satisfactory account of the phenomena.

Other features that physical theory takes as fundamental include mass and space-time. No attempt is made to explain these features in terms of anything simpler. But this does not rule out the possibility of a theory of mass or of space-time. There is an intricate theory of how these features interrelate, and of the basic laws they enter into. These basic principles are used to explain many familiar phenomena concerning mass, space, and time at a higher level.

I suggest that a theory of consciousness should take experience as fundamental. We know that a theory of consciousness requires the addition of *something* fundamental to our ontology, as everything in physical theory is compatible with the absence of consciousness. We might add some entirely new nonphysical feature, from which experience can be derived, but it is hard to see what such a feature would be like. More likely, we will take experience itself as a fundamental feature of the world, alongside mass, charge, and space-time. If we take experience as fundamental, then we can go about the business of constructing a theory of experience.

Where there is a fundamental property, there are fundamental laws. A nonreductive theory of experience will add new principles to the furniture of the basic laws of nature. These basic principles will ultimately carry the explanatory burden in a theory of consciousness. Just as we explain familiar high-level phenomena involving mass in terms of more basic principles involving mass and other entities, we might explain familiar phenomena involving experience in terms of more basic principles involving experience and other entities.

In particular, a nonreductive theory of experience will specify basic principles telling us how experience depends on physical features of the world. These *psychophysical* principles will not interfere with physical laws, as it seems that physical laws already form a closed system. Rather, they will be a supplement to a physical theory. A physical theory gives a theory of physical processes, and a psychophysical theory tells us how those processes give rise to experience. We know that experience depends on physical processes, but we also know that this dependence cannot be derived from physical laws alone. The new basic principles postulated by a nonreductive theory give us the extra ingredient that we need to build an explanatory bridge.

Of course, by taking experience as fundamental, there is a sense in which this approach does not tell us why there is experience in the first place. But this is the same for any fundamental theory. Nothing in physics tells us why there is matter in the first place, but we do not count this against theories of matter. Certain features of the world need to be taken as fundamental by any scientific theory. A theory of matter can still explain all sorts of facts about matter, by showing how they are consequences of the basic laws. The same goes for a theory of experience.

This position qualifies as a variety of dualism, as it postulates basic properties over and above the properties invoked by physics. But it is an innocent version of dualism, entirely compatible with the scientific view of the world. Nothing in this approach contradicts anything in physical theory; we simply need to add further *bridging* principles to explain how experience arises from physical processes. There is nothing particularly spiritual or mystical about this theory—its overall shape is like that of a physical theory, with a few fundamental entities connected by fundamental laws. It expands the ontology slightly, to be sure, but Maxwell did the same thing. Indeed, the overall structure of this position is entirely naturalistic, allowing that ultimately the universe comes down to a network of basic entities obeying simple laws, and allowing that there may ultimately be a theory of consciousness cast in terms of such laws. If the position is to have a name, a good choice might be *naturalistic dualism*.

If this view is right, then in some ways a theory of consciousness will have more in common with a theory in physics than a theory in biology. Biological theories involve no principles that are fundamental in this way, so biological theory has a certain complexity and messiness to it; but theories in physics, insofar as they deal with fundamental principles, aspire to simplicity and elegance. The fundamental laws of nature are part of the basic furniture of the world, and physical theories are telling us that this basic furniture is remarkably simple. If a theory of consciousness also involves fundamental principles, then we should expect the same. The principles of simplicity, elegance, and even beauty that drive physicists' search for a fundamental theory will also apply to a theory of consciousness.[3]

[...]

Notes

1. Here 'function' is not used in the narrow teleological sense of something that a system is designed to do, but in the broader sense of any causal role in the production of behaviour that a system might perform.

2. One special attraction of quantum theories is the fact that on some interpretations of quantum mechanics, consciousness plays an active role in 'collapsing' the quantum wave function. Such interpretations are controversial, but in any case they offer no hope of explaining consciousness in terms of quantum processes. Rather, these theories assume the existence of consciousness, and use it in the explanation of quantum processes. At best, these theories tell us something about a physical role that consciousness may play. They tell us nothing about how it arises.

3. Some philosophers argue that even though there is a conceptual gap between physical processes and experience, there need be no metaphysical gap, so that experience might in a certain sense still be physical (e.g., Hill 1991; Levine 1983; Loar 1990). Usually this

line of argument is supported by an appeal to the notion of a posteriori necessity (Kripke 1980). I think that this position rests on a misunderstanding of a posteriori necessity, however, or else requires an entirely new sort of necessity that we have no reason to believe in; see Chalmers 1996 (also Jackson 1994; Lewis 1994) for details. In any case, this position still concedes an explanatory gap between physical processes and experience. For example, the principles connecting the physical and the experiential will not be derivable from the laws of physics, so such principles must be taken as explanatorily fundamental. So even on this sort of view, the explanatory structure of a theory of consciousness will be much as I have described.

References

Akins, K. (1993), "What Is It Like to Be Boring and Myopic?" in *Dennett and His Critics*, ed. B. Dahlbom (Oxford: Blackwell).

Allport, A. (1988), "What Concept of Consciousness?" in *Consciousness in Contemporary Science*, ed. A. Marcel and E. Bisiach (Oxford: Oxford UP).

Baars, B.J. (1988), *A Cognitive Theory of Consciousness* (Cambridge: Cambridge UP).

Bateson, G. (1972), *Steps to an Ecology of Mind* (Chandler Publishing).

Block, N. (1995), "On a Confusion about the Function of Consciousness," *Behavioral and Brain Sciences*, in press.

Block, N., Flanagan, O. and Güzeldere, G. (eds. 1996), *The Nature of Consciousness: Philosophical and Scientific Debates* (Cambridge, MA: MIT P).

Chalmers, D.J. (1996), *The Conscious Mind* (New York: Oxford UP).

Churchland, P.M. (1995), *The Engine of Reason, The Seat of the Soul: A Philosophical Journey into the Brain* (Cambridge, MA: MIT P).

Clark, A. (1992), *Sensory Qualities* (Oxford: Oxford UP).

Crick, F. and Koch, C. (1990), "Toward a Neurobiological Theory of Consciousness," *Seminars in the Neurosciences*, 2, pp. 263–75.

Crick, F. (1994), *The Astonishing Hypothesis: The Scientific Search for the Soul* (New York: Scribners).

Dennett, D.C. (1991), *Consciousness Explained* (Boston: Little, Brown).

Dretske, F.I. (1995), *Naturalizing the Mind* (Cambridge, MA: MIT P).

Edelman, G. (1989), *The Remembered Present: A Biological Theory of Consciousness* (New York: Basic Books).

Farah, M.J. (1994), "Visual Perception and Visual Awareness after Brain Damage: A Tutorial Overview," in *Consciousness and Unconscious Information Processing: Attention and Performance Vol. XV*, ed. C. Umiltá and M. Moscovitch (Cambridge, MA: MIT P).

Flohr, H. (1992), "Qualia and Brain Processes," in *Emergence or Reduction?: Prospects for Nonreductive Physicalism*, ed. A. Beckermann, H. Flohr, and J. Kim (Berlin: De Gruyter).

Hameroff, S.R. (1994), "Quantum Coherence in Microtubules: A Neural Basis for Emergent Consciousness?," *Journal of Consciousness Studies*, 1, pp. 91–118.

Hardin, C.L. (1992), "Physiology, Phenomenology, and Spinoza's True Colors," in *Emergence or Reduction?: Prospects for Nonreductive Physicalism*, ed. A. Beckermann, H. Flohr, and J. Kim (Berlin: De Gruyter).

Hill, C.S. (1991), *Sensations: A Defense of Type Materialism* (Cambridge: Cambridge UP).

Hodgson, D. (1988), *The Mind Matters: Consciousness and Choice in a Quantum World* (Oxford: Oxford UP).

Humphrey, N. (1992), *A History of the Mind* (New York: Simon and Schuster).

Jackendoff, R. (1987), *Consciousness and the Computational Mind* (Cambridge, MA: MIT P).

Jackson, F. (1982), "Epiphenomenal Qualia," *Philosophical Quarterly*, 32, pp. 127–36.

Jackson, F. (1994), "Finding the Mind in the Natural World," in *Philosophy and the Cognitive Sciences*, ed. R. Casati, B. Smith, and S. White (Vienna: Hölder-Pichler-Tempsky).

Kirk, R. (1994), *Raw Feeling: A Philosophical Account of the Essence of Consciousness* (Oxford: Oxford UP).

Kripke, S. (1980), *Naming and Necessity* (Cambridge, MA: Harvard UP).

Levine, J. (1983), "Materialism and Qualia: The Explanatory Gap," *Pacific PhilosophicalQuarterly*, 64, pp. 354–61.

Lewis, D. (1994), "Reduction of Mind," in *A Companion to the Philosophy of Mind*, ed. S. Guttenplan (Oxford: Blackwell).

Libet, B. (1993), "The Neural Time Factor in Conscious and Unconscious Events," in *Experimental and Theoretical Studies of Consciousness* (Ciba Foundation Symposium 174), ed. G.R. Block and J. Marsh (Chichester: John Wiley and Sons).

Loar, B. (1990), "Phenomenal States," *Philosophical Perspectives*, 4, pp. 81–108.

Lockwood, M. (1989), *Mind, Brain, and the Quantum* (Oxford: Blackwell).

McGinn, C. (1989), "Can We Solve the Mind-Body Problem?," *Mind*, 98, pp. 349–66.

Metzinger, T. (ed. 1995), *Conscious Experience* (Exeter: Imprint Academic).

Nagel, T. (1974), "What Is It Like to Be a Bat?," *Philosophical Review*, 4, pp. 435–50.

Nelkin, N. (1993), "What Is Consciousness?," *Philosophy of Science*, 60, pp. 419–34.

Newell, A. (1990), *Unified Theories of Cognition* (Cambridge, MA: Harvard UP).

Penrose, R. (1989), *The Emperor's New Mind* (Oxford: Oxford UP).

Penrose, R. (1994), *Shadows of the Mind* (Oxford: Oxford UP).

Rosenthal, D.M. (1996), "A Theory of Consciousness," in *The Nature of Consciousness*, ed. N. Block, O. Flanagan, and G. Güzeldere (Cambridge, MA: MIT P).

Seager, W.E. (1991), *Metaphysics of Consciousness* (London: Routledge).

Searle, J.R. (1980), "Minds, Brains and Programs," *Behavioral and Brain Sciences*, 3, pp. 417–57.

Searle, J.R. (1992), *The Rediscovery of the Mind* (Cambridge, MA: MIT P).

Shallice, T. (1972), "Dual Functions of Consciousness," *Psychological Review*, 79, pp. 383–93.

Shannon, C.E. (1948), "A Mathematical Theory of Communication," *Bell Systems Technical Journal*, 27, pp. 379–423.

Strawson, G. (1994), *Mental Reality* (Cambridge, MA: MIT P).

Tye, M. (1995), *Ten Problems of Consciousness* (Cambridge, MA: MIT P).

Velmans, M. (1991), "Is Human Information-Processing Conscious?," *Behavioral and Brain Sciences*, 14, pp. 651–69.

Wheeler, J.A. (1990), "Information, Physics, Quantum: The Search for Links," in *Complexity, Entropy, and the Physics of Information*, ed. W. Zurek (Redwood City, CA: Addison-Wesley).

Wilkes, K.V. (1988), "—, Yíshí, Duh, Um and Consciousness," in *Consciousness in Contemporary Science*, ed. A. Marcel and E. Bisiach (Oxford: Oxford UP).

VALERIE GRAY HARDCASTLE

"The Why of Consciousness: A Non-Issue for Materialists"

In my (albeit limited) experience of these matters, I have discovered that there are two sorts of people engaged in the study of consciousness. There are those who are committed naturalists; they believe that consciousness is part of the physical world, just as kings and queens and sealing wax are. It is completely nonmysterious (though it is poorly understood). They have total and absolute faith that science as it is construed today will someday explain this as it has explained the other so-called mysteries of our age.

Others are not as convinced. They might believe that consciousness is part of the natural world, but surely it is completely mysterious (and maybe not physical after all). Thus far, science has little to say about conscious experience because it has made absolutely no progress in explaining *why* we are conscious at all.

Different sceptics draw different morals from their observation. Some conclude that a scientific theory of consciousness is well-nigh impossible; others believe that it is possible, but do not expect anything of value to be immediately forthcoming; still others remain confused and are not sure what to think. (Perhaps unfairly, I put David Chalmers in the last category, as he remarks, 'Why should physical processing give rise to a rich inner life at all? It seems objectively unreasonable that it should, and yet it does' [Chalmers, 1995, p. 201]. His intuition that consciousness is too bizarre to be real, yet still exists anyway illustrates the sentiments of the third category quite nicely. Further, as I discuss below, I think his tentative programme of redoing our basic scientific

ontology reflects some basic confusions on his part.)

I have also noticed that these two camps have little to say to one another, for their differences are deep and deeply entrenched. I can't say that I expect to change that fact here. I fall into the former camp. I am a committed materialist and believe absolutely and certainly that empirical investigation is the proper approach in explaining consciousness. I also recognize that I have little convincing to say to those opposed to me. There are few useful conversations; there are even fewer converts.

In this brief essay, I hope to make clearer where the points of division lay. In the first section, I highlight the disagreements between Chalmers and me, arguing that consciousness is not a brute fact about the world. In section II, I point out the fundamental difference between the materialists and the sceptics, suggesting that this difference is not something that further discussion or argumentation can overcome. In the final section, I outline one view of scientific explanation and conclude that the source of conflict really turns on a difference in the rules each side has adopted in playing the game.

I

In large part, these divergent reactions turn on antecedent views about what counts as explanatory. There are those who are sold on the programme of science. They believe that the way to explain something is to build a model of it that captures at least some of its etiologic history and some of its causal powers. Their approach to explaining consciousness is the same as mine: isolate the causal influences with respect to consciousness and model them (cf. Churchland, 1984; Flanagan, 1992; Hardcastle, 1995; Hardin, 1988).

In contrast, others (e.g., Block, 1995; Chalmers, 1995; McGinn, 1991; Nagel, 1974; Searle, 1992) do not believe that science and its commitment to modelling causal interactions are necessarily the end-all and be-all of explanation. They believe that some things—many things—are explained in terms of physical causes, but qualia may not be. Isolating the causal relations associated with conscious phenomena would simply miss the boat, for there is no way that doing that ever captures the qualitative aspects of awareness. What the naturalists might do is illustrate *when* we are conscious, but that won't explain the *why* of consciousness. The naturalists would not have explained why it is neuronal oscillations (cf. Crick and Koch, 1990), or the activation of episodic memory (cf. Hardcastle, 1995), or an executive processor (cf. Baars, 1988), or whatever, should have a qualitative aspect, and until they do that, they cannot claim to have done anything particularly interesting with consciousness.

To them, I have little to say in defence of naturalism, for I think nothing that I as an already committed naturalist could say would suffice, for we don't agree on the terms of the argument in the first place. Nevertheless, I shall try to say something, if for no other reason than to make the points of disagreement clearer so that informed buyers can choose all the more wisely. Let me sketch in particular the point of conflict between Chalmers and me.

Let us assume a prior and fundamental commitment to materialism. I say that if we are materialists, then we have to believe that consciousness is something physical. Presum-ably it is something in the brain. If we believe this and we want to know what consciousness is exactly, then we need to isolate the components of the brain or of brain activity that are necessary and sufficient for consciousness. If I understand Chalmers' taxonomy of research programmes correctly, then I am advocating following option five: 'isolate the substrate of experience.' Indeed, it is my contention that pointing out the relevant brain activity conjoined with explaining the structure of experience (his option four) and some functional story about what being conscious buys us biologically (not one of Chalmers' options) would be a complete theory of consciousness. Let us pretend though that I have only completed the first step in this programme and have isolated the substrate of experience. Call this component of the brain C.

Chalmers would reply that though I might have been successful in isolating the causal etiology of consciousness, I have not explained why it is that C should be conscious. Why this? For that matter, why anything? Part of a good explanation, he maintains, is making the identity statement (or whatever) intelligible, plausible, reasonable. I have not done that. Hence, I have not explained the most basic, most puzzling, most difficult question of consciousness. I haven't removed the curiousness of the connection between mind and body. I haven't closed the explanatory gap.

How should I respond? He is, of course, exactly right: scientific theories of consciousness won't explain the weirdness of consciousness to those who find the identity weird. One possible move is to claim that consciousness just being C (or whatever theory you happen to believe) is just a brute fact about the world. That is just the way our universe works. At times, I am sure, it appears that this is what the naturalists are assuming, especially when they dismiss out of hand those overcome by the eeriness of consciousness. This, too, is what Chalmers wants to do with his dual aspect theory: phenomenal qualities are just part and parcel of information. No further explanation needed.

However, this response is too facile. It is true that we accept brute facts about our universe. We believe in things like gravitational attraction and the electromagnetic forces without question. We waste little energy wondering why our universe contains gravity. It just does, and we reason from there. On the other hand, there are other facts about the world that we do not accept as brute. We feel perfectly comfortable expecting an answer to why water is wet. That is not a brute fact. We explain the liquidity of water by appeal to other facts about the world, the molecular structure of water and its concomitant microphysical properties, for example. And these facts are explained in turn by other facts, such as the quantum mechanical structure of the world. Now *these* might be brute facts, but so it goes. (At least this is one popular and rosy view of scientific unity. I shan't defend that here.)

Notice two things. First, the facts we accept as brute are few and basic. Essentially, we accept the most fundamental elements and relations of the universe as given. The rest then depend upon these key ingredients in some fashion. Second, and following from the first observation, it seems highly unlikely that some relatively chauvinistic *biological* fact should ever be brute. For those facts turn on the more fundamental items in the universe. Hence, if one is to claim that consciousness being C is simply a brute fact about the universe, then one is *prima facie* operating with a perverse metaphysics.

Chalmers tries to overcome the latter difficulty by denying that consciousness is biological. However, he has no reason to claim this except that it saves his theory. Considerations of structural coherence and organizational invariance aren't telling because they are generally taken to support material identity. That

is, if you find structural isomorphisms between our perceptions and twitches in the brain, then that is taken to be good reason to think that the mind is nothing more than activity in the brain. (What other sort of evidence could you use?) And if you hypothesize that the same 'fine-grained' functional organization supports the same phenomenal experiences, then you are advocating some sort of materialistic functional theory; otherwise the perceptions can diverge even though the functional organization remains the same (cf. Shoemaker, 1975; 1981; see also Lycan, 1987).[1]

The only consideration he brings to bear is the putative 'elegance' of a dual aspect theory. However, when we weigh a suggestion's simplicity and elegance against countervailing data, the data have to win. We already know that not all information has a phenomenal edge to it, insofar as we know quite a bit of our information processing is carried out unconsciously. Documenting subliminal effects, implicit priming, and repressed but effective memories are all cottage industries in psychology, and have been since Freud.[2] Chalmers is either going to have to deny some of the most robust psychological results we have and claim that no information processing is occurring in those cases, or do a 'bait-and-switch' and claim that, contrary to introspective verbal reports, we are conscious of all of those things (we just don't realize it). Neither option is plausible. Chalmers gives us no counter-examples to the mass of psychological evidence, and denying that first person viewpoints can tell us whether we are conscious denies exactly what Chalmers wants to defend. Hence, we are left with the *prima facie* plausible claim that for all cases of consciousness of which we are aware, consciousness is biological.

In any event, I don't want to make the claim consciousness is brute. So what do I say if I think that consciousness is a biological phenomenon?[3]

How do I make my identification of consciousness with some neural activity intelligible to those who find it mysterious? My answer is that I don't. The 'solution' to this vexing difficulty, such as it is, is all a matter of attitude. That is, the problem itself depends on the spirit in which we approach an examination of consciousness.

II

Let us return to the example of water being wet. Consider the following exchange. A water-mysterian wonders why water has this peculiar property. She inquires and you give an explanation of the molecular composition of water and a brief story about the connection between micro-chemical properties and macro-phenomena. Ah, she says, I am a materialist, so I am convinced that you have properly correlated water with its underlying molecular composition. I also have no reason to doubt that your story about the macro-effects of chemical properties to be wrong. But I still am not satisfied, for you have left off in your explanation what I find most puzzling. Why *is* water H_2O? Why couldn't it be XYZ? Why couldn't it have some other radically different chemical story behind it? I can imagine a possible world in which water has all the macro-properties that it has now, but is not composed of H_2O.

Of course, people like Kripke have a ready response to the water-mysterians. 'Water = H_2O' is an identity statement. Hence, you can't really imagine possible worlds in which water is not H_2O because you aren't imagining *water* in those cases (or, you aren't *imagining* properly).

As Chalmers would claim, it is a *conceptual truth* about water that it is H_2O. But, to the sceptical and unconvinced, to those who insist that they can imagine honest-to-goodness water not being H_2O, what *can* one say? I think nothing. Water-mysterians are antecedently convinced

of the mysteriousness of water and no amount of scientific data is going to change that perspective. Either you already believe that science is going to give you a correct identity statement, or you don't and you think that there is always going to be something left over, the wateriness of water.

I doubt there are any such mysterians, so perhaps this is a silly example. Let us now turn to life-mysterians. Consider the following exchange. A life-mysterian wonders why living things have the peculiar property of being alive.

She inquires and you give a just-so story about the origin of replicating molecules in primordial soup and wave your hands in the direction of increasing complexity. Ah, she says, I am an evolutionist, so I am convinced that you have properly correlated the history of living things with their underlying molecular composition. I also have no reason to doubt that your story about increasing complexity to be wrong. But I still am not satisfied, for you have left off in your explanation what I find most puzzling, the *aliveness* of life. Why couldn't that be a soul? Why couldn't it have some other radically different evolutionary story behind it, namely, one with God in it? I can imagine a possible world in which living things have all the macro-properties that they have now, but are not comprised of DNA or RNA.

Of course, as Chalmers indicates, we too have a ready response to the life-mysterians. We presume that there is some sort of identity statement for biological life. (Of course, we don't actually have one yet, but for those of us who are not life-mysterians, we feel certain that one is in the offing.) Hence, they can't really imagine possible worlds in which life is not whatever we ultimately discover it to be because they aren't imagining *life* in those cases (or, they aren't *imagining* properly). But, that aside, what *can* we say to those who insist that they can imagine life as requiring an animator? I think nothing.

Just getting on with the biological enterprise is perhaps appropriate. Life-mysterians are antecedently convinced of the mysteriousness of life and no amount of scientific data is going to change that perspective. Either you already believe that science is going to give you a correct identity statement, or you don't and you think that there is always going to be something left over, the aliveness of living things.

So what about Chalmers and other consciousness-mysterians? They are no different. They are antecedently convinced of the mysteriousness of consciousness and no amount of scientific data is going to change that perspective. Either you already believe that science is going to give you a correct identity statement, or you don't and you think that there is always going to be something left over, the phenomenal aspects of conscious experience. 'Experience…is not *entailed* by the physical.' Chalmers wants to know: 'Why is the performance of these [cognitive] functions *accompanied* by experience?' (p. 203; emphasis mine). Though he does believe that 'experience *arises* one way or another from brain processes,' he thinks that it is a 'conceptual point' that consciousness is not identical to C.

In some sense, of course, I have a ready response to the consciousness-mysterians. Like the water-mysterian and the life-mysterian, consciousness-mysterians need to alter their concepts. To put it bluntly: their failure to appreciate the world as it really is cuts no ice with science. Their ideas are at fault, not the scientific method. Materialists presume that there is some sort of identity statement for consciousness. (Of course, we don't actually have one yet, but for those of us who are not consciousness-mysterians, we feel certain that one is in the offing.) Hence, the sceptics can't really imagine possible worlds in which consciousness is not whatever we ultimately discover it to be because they aren't imagining *consciousness*

in those cases (or, they aren't *imagining* properly). But nevertheless, what *can* I say to those who insist that they can imagine consciousness as beyond science's current explanatory capacities? I think nothing, for they can claim that I am conceptually confused as well. Agreeing to disagree is perhaps appropriate. I suppose we have reached a stand-off of sorts. I say materialism and mechanism entail an identity statement for consciousness, just as we get one for water and we expect one for life. Consciousness is no more mysterious to me than the wetness of water or the aliveness of life. That is to say, I find all of the phenomena interestingly weird, and the identity statements that science produces marvelously curious. But all are on a par. The sceptics do not share my intuitions. So be it. However, I feel no more inclined to try to convince them otherwise than I do trying to convince the religious that souls don't exist. I recognize hopeless projects. Our antecedent intuitions simply diverge too much to engage in a productive dialogue.

III

But perhaps again I am not being fair. The reason water-mysterianism seems implausible is that we are able to embed our understanding of water and H_2O in the sophisticated larger framework of molecular chemistry and subatomic physics. We just know an awful lot about how atoms and molecules interact with one another and the corresponding micro- and macro-properties. Life-mysterianism seems implausible to those for whom it seems implausible for similar reasons. We don't know as much about biological history as we do about molecular chemistry, but we do know enough at least to gesture toward a suitable framework in which to embed a decomposition of life. But consciousness might be different. We have far, far to go before we can claim to understand either cognitive or brain processes with any surety. Perhaps there just isn't a suitable larger framework in which to embed an understanding of consciousness; hence, any scientific model we try to construct will appear strained and stilted at best. And perhaps this is what really drives the explanatory gap—we don't yet know what we are talking about when we claim that consciousness is a natural phenomenon.

Suppose this argument is correct (though I am not sure that it is, for reasons I explain below). What follows from it? It can't be that a theory of consciousness is not possible, nor even that consciousness is fundamentally odd. Rather, all we can say is that we have to wait and see what else we learn about the mind and brain before a decomposition and localization of consciousness can be intuitively satisfying. Consciousness might very well be C, but our informed intuitions lag behind.

(An aside: Can we *really* say what would happen if my neural circuits are replaced by silicon isomorphs? Maybe it is reasonable to think that your experiences would not be affected. But, in the same vein, it is reasonable to believe that the world is Euclidean—though it isn't, of course—and it used to be reasonable to burn witches at the stake—though it is no longer. What seems reasonable at first blush often isn't once the parameters of the problem are made sufficiently clear; moreover, our intuitions change as our perspective on the world changes. At present, we simply don't know enough about the explanatory currency of the brain to hypothesize *intelligently* about what will happen if we push on it in various ways. Intuition pumps only work if we have robust and well-founded intuitions in the first place.)

All we can say at this point is that an antecedent commitment to materialism means that an understanding of consciousness will someday be embedded in some larger mind-brain framework. We are just going to have to wait

until that time before our intuitions concerning what counts as a satisfactory identification for phenomenal experience will be useful (or even usable).

Nevertheless, though there is a great deal we don't know about the mind and the brain, there is still a lot that we do. Indeed, within the broader framework of currently accepted psychological and neurophysiological theories, we have found striking parallels between our phenomenal experiences and activities in the brain. Chalmers points to some in his paper; others are more basic. E.g., removing area MT is correlated with phenomenal blindness; ablations in various regions of cortex are correlated with inabilities to perceive shapes, colours, motion, objects; lesions surrounding the hippocampus are correlated with the loss of episodic memory.[4] Or, for less invasive results, consider what happens when various chemicals are added to our brains. We decrease pain, increase sensitivity, induce hallucinations, alter moods, and so on. Data such as these should (someday) allow us to locate conscious experiences both within our information processing stream and within the head.

Perhaps more data, better constructed scientific models, and more agreement among the scientists themselves about the details, would alter the intuitions of the sceptics, but I doubt it. For the difference between someone like Chalmers and me is not in the details; it is in how we understand the project of explaining consciousness itself. It is a difference in how we think of scientific inquiry and what we think explanations of consciousness are supposed to do.

Explanations are social creatures. They are designed for particular audiences asking particular questions within a particular historically determined framework. (See van Fraassen, 1980, for more discussion of this point.) Materialists are trying to explain to each other what consciousness is within current scientific frameworks. Their explanations are designed for them. If you don't antecedently buy into this project, including its biases, history, context, central questions, possible answers, and relevant actors, then a naturalist's explanation probably won't satisfy you. It shouldn't. But that is not the fault of the explanation, nor is it the fault of the materialists. If you don't accept the rules, the game won't make any sense. If you do accept the rules, then the explanations will follow because they are designed for you as a member of the relevant community. (This is not to say that you will *agree* with explanations, just that they will seem to be of the right sort of thing required for an answer.) Who's in and who's out is a matter of antecedent self-selection. I opt in; the sceptics opt out. Because we don't agree on the rules, my explanations don't make sense to them, and their explanations don't make sense to me.

Explanation for the cognitive and biological sciences just *is* a matter of uncovering the appropriate parallels between the phenomena and the physical system. Huntington's chorea is explained by a disruption in the GABA-ergic loop. Equilibrium in neurons is explained in terms of the influx and efflux of ions across the cell membrane. Perceptual binding is explained (maybe) in terms of 40 Hz neuronal oscillations. The withdrawal reflex in *Aplysia* is explained in terms of patterns of activation across the motor system. Echolocation is explained in terms of deformed tensor networks. So: find the parallels between brain activity and phenomenal experience and you will have found a naturalistic account of consciousness.

Denying the project and devising different criteria for explanation is a perfectly legitimate move to make, of course. There is always room for more. Winning converts though is something else. I wish Chalmers well in that enterprise, for how to do that truly is the gap that remains.

Notes

1. I find it strange (though not inconsistent) that in the first portion of the paper, Chalmers uses the putative imaginability of inverted qualia as an argument against what he calls 'reductionism' (though to me it is simply a good old fashioned identity theory), yet in discussing constraints on possible theories he argues against the possibility of inverted qualia in support of his prototheory. He should recognize that if the fine-grainedness of his functional organization is fine-grained enough, then we would be discussing the functional organization of neurons (or action potentials, IPSPs, EPSPs, or what have you), which is all one needs to muster a claim for mind-brain identity.

2. I take it that these facts are well known. I summarize quite a bit of this research in Hardcastle (1995). Aside from Freud, other important players include Endel Tulving, George Mandler, Anthony Marcel and Daniel Schacter.

3. Note that claiming that consciousness is biological does not mean that we could not create consciousness artificially. Life is a biological phenomenon too, but that doesn't rule out creating life in test-tubes.

4. I note that in each of these cases, there is evidence that such patients still process at least some of the information unconsciously. For example, prosopagnosics claim that they can no longer recognize faces upon visual inspection. However, their galvanic skin response changes in the presence of caretakers or loved ones in a manner consistent with their in fact knowing and recognizing the people. For a review of this literature, see Hardcastle (1995).

References

Baars, B.J. (1988), *A Cognitive Theory of Consciousness* (Cambridge: Cambridge UP).

Block, N. (1995), "On a Confusion about a Function of Consciousness," *Behavioral and Brain Sciences*, 18 (2), pp. 227–47.

Chalmers, D.J. (1995), "Facing Up to the Problem of Consciousness," *Journal of Consciousness Studies*, 2 (3), pp. 200–19.

Churchland, P.M. (1984), *Matter and Consciousness* (Cambridge, MA: MIT P).

Crick, F. and Koch, C. (1990), "Toward a Neurobiological Theory of Consciousness," *Seminars in the Neurosciences*, 2, pp. 263–75.

Flanagan, O. (1992), *Consciousness Reconsidered* (Cambridge, MA: MIT P).

Hardcastle, V.G. (1995), *Locating Consciousness* (Amsterdam and Philadelphia: John Benjamins).

Hardin, C.L. (1988), *Color for Philosophers: Unweaving the Rainbow* (New York: Hackett).

Lycan, W.G. (1987), *Consciousness* (Cambridge, MA: MIT P).

McGinn, C. (1991), *The Problem of Consciousness* (Oxford: Blackwell).

Nagel, T. (1974), "What Is It Like to Be a Bat?" *Philosophical Review*, 83, pp. 435–50.

Searle, J. (1992), *The Rediscovery of Mind* (Cambridge, MA: MIT P).

Shoemaker, S. (1975), "Functionalism and Qualia," *Philosophical Studies*, 27, pp. 291–315.

Shoemaker, S. (1981), "Absent Qualia Are Not Possible—A Reply to Block," *Philosophical Review*, 90, pp. 581–99.

van Fraassen, B. (1980), *The Scientific Image* (Cambridge, MA: MIT P).

MICHAEL A. COHEN AND DANIEL C. DENNETT

"Consciousness Cannot Be Separated from Function"

The Hard Problem of Consciousness Is an Impossible Problem

A goal of neuroscience is to locate the neural correlates of consciousness: the minimal set of neuronal events leading to subjective awareness.... Numerous influential theories hold that conscious experience has its own neural underpinnings that can be separated from all cognitive functions (i.e., attention, working memory, language, decision making, motivation etc.). Different theories equate consciousness with different correlates: recurrent activation between cortical areas [4–7], coalitions of 'winning' neurons [8–10], special microactivations distributed throughout the brain [11–13] or activity in the ventral stream [14]. Although the details of these theories vary, they all assert that conscious experience and cognitive functions have distinct neural correlates (Box 1).

Box 1. Example Dissociative Theories

The partitioning of conscious experience from cognitive function is common in neuro-biological theories of consciousness. Three representative theories are described below.

Local recurrency. The best-known theory that embraces the separation between experience and function is the local recurrency theory put forth by Lamme [4,5] and Block [6,7]. According to this theory, visual information is processed in the cortex by an initial feedforward sweep in which representations of motion, color and shape are formed [61,62]. Although representations at this stage can be rather detailed, no conscious experience accompanies this processing. Such experiences only arise as a result of sustained RP between visual areas. However, the experiences that accompany RP are independent of all cognitive functions, especially attention [4]. Indeed, this theory explicitly maintains that local recurrency is the neural correlate of one and only one form of consciousness: phenomenal consciousness [28]. Access consciousness, which comprises functions such as working memory, language production and so on, is achieved when RP extends into the frontal cortex and engages higher-level functions.

Microconsciousness. Zeki's theory of microconsciousness states that consciousness is not a unified state but is instead distributed in space and time [11–13]. Rather than emphasizing the flow of information between regions, like the local recurrency theory, this theory focuses on the activation of 'essential nodes' throughout the cortex. Each node represents different bits of information (e.g., color or motion) and the activation of each node generates its own microconsciousness. We have the impression of a unified consciousness because each of these individual representations is bound to others, post-experientially, to form an accessed macroconsciousness [13]. It is at this macrolevel that functions such as language and decision making operate on the distributed experiences and lead to subjective reports. Thus, the micro/macro distinction again dissociates conscious experience and cognitive function [29].

Coalitions of neurons. Crick and Koch proposed that consciousness stems from 'winning' coalitions of neurons (sustained activation of a collection of neurons that are dedicated to the processing and representation of a particular stimulus or event) [8].Under this view, coalitions supporting one representation compete with coalitions supporting other representations [9]. Only after a winning coalition becomes conscious can attention be diverted to it. Oftentimes, only one coalition 'wins' at a time, leading to a relatively tight correlation between consciousness and attention. However, this correlation is not perfect. Koch and colleagues have written extensively about the existence of consciousness without attention [63,64,69,70], recently claiming that consciousness without attention is a form of phenomenal consciousness as described by Block and Lamme [10].

All of these theories have distinctive strengths, and some plausibility, but they also share a fundamental flaw: they posit the existence of conscious states that even the individual him or herself does not realize he or she is having. Highlighting this flaw might provide impetus for revision and improvement of these theories: rejecting the one shared feature of them all and leaving the other features to be sorted out empirically.

This alleged division between experience and function is often mapped onto the distinction between the 'hard' and 'easy' problems of consciousness [3]. Under this view, the hard problem is answering the question of how phenomenal experience arises from physical events in the brain, whereas the easy problems are characterizing the mechanisms supporting cognitive functions. In this article we argue that, from an empirical perspective, the 'hard problem' is actually an impossible problem that inherently isolates consciousness from all current and future avenues of scientific investigation. All theories of consciousness based on the assumption that there are hard and easy problems can never be verified or falsified because it is the products of cognitive functions (i.e., verbal report, button pressing etc.) that allow consciousness to be empirically studied at all. A proper neurobiological theory of consciousness must utilize these functions in order to accurately identify which particular neural activations correlate with conscious awareness.

A motivation behind dissociative theories is the belief that theories associating awareness with access [15–17] cannot explain the richness of phenomenology. In other words, it is claimed that 'phenomenology overflows access' ([7], p. 487): we experience more than can possibly be captured by cognitive mechanisms that are known to have strict limits. Visual attention [18,19], working memory [20,21], dynamic tracking [22,23] and many other such processes have well-established capacity limits. Phenomenology, however, is claimed to have no such limitations. It is thought that when we look out onto the world we do not only see a few attended items; we see the whole world. Thus it is argued that although we are conscious of a variety of inputs we have access to only a small subset of these experiences [4,7,10,13].

Here, we analyze the data used to support the claim that phenomenology overflows access and show how these results can be accounted for under a pure access/functional view of consciousness. We then argue that dissociative theories are inherently unfalsifiable and beyond the scope of science, because inaccessible conscious states are intrinsically off-limits to investigation. With this in mind we end by describing the necessary components of a proper scientific theory of consciousness.

Evidence Supporting the Dissociation

What data support the view that consciousness occurs independently of, and can be experimentally dissociated from, higher-level functions (i.e., access)? The most frequently cited experiments use Sperling's partial report paradigm [24–27]. After being briefly shown a display of 9–12 letters, participants can only report some of the items through free recall. However, if cued to report a subset of the letters, they can report the entire subset and thus seem to have consciously perceived all of the items. According to dissociative theories, these results demonstrate that although we have access to only a few items we are nonetheless conscious of the identities of them all [4–7].

Although the partial report results are crucial to arguments for dissociating consciousness and function, they can be explained without this separation [27]. Participants can identify cued items because their identities are stored unconsciously until the cue brings them to the focus of attention. Before the cue, participants are conscious only of the few letters they attend to and the impression that there are other items on the display whose identities they do not know (Figure 1). Once the cue is presented, they are able to access an unconscious representation before it decays and successfully recall the letters presented.

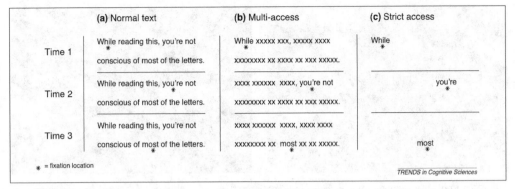

Figure 1   How much is consciously perceived at a given psychological moment? Those who argue for dissociating consciousness and function do so because they claim that awareness overflows conscious access. (a) In this case, the identities of all the letters on the screen are perceived. (b) However, McConkie and Rayner have shown that when uniform Xs replace the nonfixated words of text, participants do not realize this has happened [65,66]. (c) If there is no other text on the screen besides the fixated word, then participants will notice this instantly. This elegantly demonstrates that although people are aware of the 'presence' of nonattended items in this case, they are actually not aware of the 'identities' of those items.

Although Sperling's results can be explained by appealing to consciousness without access, this is not the only explanation or the clearest. Indeed a more nuanced notion of access and cognitive function can readily explain both the phenomenology and the results of these experiments.

A Multi-Access Model

Those who argue for experience without access [4–14, 28,29] emphasize the introspective experience of seeing a more vivid, detailed world than can be reported. The world beyond focused attention is not in total 'darkness': when staring intently at a single item, one is still aware of some aspects of the scene around it [30,31]. Such a claim is obviously true. Dissociative theorists cite this fact as the primary example of phenomenology overflowing access. However, this is not a problem for theories that identify consciousness with function.

The world beyond focal attention is not in darkness because when attention is not entirely engaged by a primary task, and it is unclear if attention can ever be entirely engaged using psychophysical techniques, excess attentional resources are automatically deployed elsewhere [32–35]. Thus, certain items are processed through focal attention, whereas others are processed via distributed attention [36,37]. Focal attention often leads to high resolution percepts whereas the percepts from distributed attention are at a lower resolution but with certain basic elements preserved [36–48] (Figure 2). It is inaccurate to say that information outside the focus of attention receives zero attention. Information not processed by focal attention can nevertheless be the target of other types of attention: distributed, featural, spatial, internal and so on [49].

Is this degraded visual information an example of phenomenology overflowing access? Indeed, the degraded information is consciously perceived. However, the function

Figure 2   Only foveated items are perceived in full color and at high resolution. As stimuli move further into the periphery, they gradually lose their color and fidelity [67–70]. However, although the quality of unattended or unfoveated stimuli is severely degraded, certain basic features and statistics are preserved. In the above example, a natural scene is presented (left) next to an image in which the quality of the image is systematically degraded from the center of the image (the [middle] fish) towards the periphery. When these two images are presented in rapid succession and with a blank gap in between, observers fixating at the center of the image are unable to detect the differences between the images and claim that they are identical. Observers do not notice that a single isolated percept is so degraded because they are able to move their eyes throughout a scene with so little effort that this behavior is often overlooked [31].

supporting this perception is simply distributed, rather than focal, attention. In fact, when attention is engaged in a sufficiently difficult task, observers can fail to perceive even coarse and degraded information, such as the gist of a scene, because of inattentional blindness [50]. This information is undoubtedly accessed because observers explicitly report seeing more than what is focally attended (the idea that such information is indeed accessed has been recognized by Block, see [7], p. 487).

Once it is recognized that distributed attention leads to degraded but accessed percepts, the motivation for claiming that this degraded information is an example of inaccessible conscious states disappears. The world beyond focused attention is not in darkness because there are functional resources (in this case, multiple forms of attention) dedicated to processing that information (Figure 1c).

Is There More to Phenomenology?

Dissociative theories claim that there is phenomenology over and above the accessed information previously described. However, various empirical results cast doubt upon this claim. In a modified version of the Sperling paradigm, where letters are sometimes unexpectedly replaced with pseudo-letters, participants still claim to see only letters [51]. Another example of this phenomenon can be seen in Figure 2. When participants are instructed to fixate at the center of a screen, two images can be successively presented in the same location, with a blank image briefly separating the two, and the drastic changes between the images go unnoticed (a phenomenon known as change blindness). If participants are conscious of the identities of all elements in the scene, as has been repeatedly claimed by dissociative theorists, then participants should instantly notice the pseudo-letters or the scrambled image. The fact that they do not suggests that participants are overestimating the contents of their own experience.

Even though people do not notice these changes, the illusion of seeing more still needs to be explained. Why is it that people overestimate the richness of their conscious perceptions [52]? The nature of this illusory experience still needs to be explained and should be the focus of future empirical work. Functionalist accounts can study this by varying the prior expectations and confidence levels of participants in a variety of paradigms [27,51]. Dissociative theories, meanwhile, 'explain' this illusion by relying on inaccessible conscious states that, as the next section describes, inherently prevent the possibility of confirmation or falsification.

The Perfect Experiment

Currently, no experimental results uniquely support the existence of consciousness independent of function and access. Could future experiments accomplish this? We argue that all theories of consciousness that are not based on functions and access [4–14] are not scientific theories. Consider perhaps the most drastic experiment possible, the 'perfect' experiment: imagine that, in the future, surgeons are able to isolate the parts of the visual cortex that represent color while wholly preserving their activation patterns. After this surgery, the areas involved in color perception (visual area V4, inferotemporal cortex etc.) behave normally but are simply unable to project to higher brain areas [53–57]: perfect isolation. Although the color areas are isolated, all other visual areas (e.g., motion, luminance, object recognition etc.) are untouched and project to higher-level regions in a normal manner (Figure 3). Such a clean separation of one aspect, color, of visual perception is profoundly unrealistic but this idealization provides a simplification that is revealing of the key flaw in theories that dissociate function from consciousness.

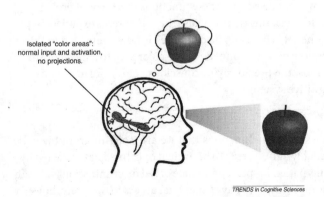

Isolated "color areas": normal input and activation, no projections.

TRENDS in Cognitive Sciences

Figure 3   A graphic depiction of the perfect experiment. When presented with a red apple there will be normal activation of the color areas of the brain but without projections to higher–level areas. Other areas of the brain (e.g., object representation and identification, language production etc.) will function normally, so the patient will be able to report that he or she sees an apple but an apple that has no colors. [—Ed. In the original published version of this image, the apple on right is red, while the apple at top is black and white.]

According to all the theories discussed above, or possible theories based on the experience/function divide, whatever is necessary for color consciousness will be preserved in these color areas. If these theories are mutually exclusive, then we can imagine a different participant for each particular theory. All that matters is that we do not allow these isolated areas of a supposed type of phenomenal consciousness to interact with other cognitive functions.

When shown a colored apple what will our hypothetical participants say? They will surely not say that they see any colors because the areas responsible for processing color have been isolated from higher-level areas, including language production. They will be able to identify the object as an apple because visual areas responsible for all other aspects of visual cognition are intact and connected to these higher-level regions. Thus, they are simply colorblind. We can imagine them saying, 'I know you say my color areas are activated in a unique way, and I know you believe this means I am consciously experiencing color but I'm looking at the apple, I'm focused on it, and I'm just not having any experience of color whatsoever' (Box 2).

Box 2. What If We Gave the Isolated Color Area the Ability to Communicate?

Is it possible that even though the subject is not conscious of red, the isolated color area itself is experiencing color (similar to the way the right hemisphere of split-brain patients is often described) [11]? What would happen if we supplied a reporting mechanism for the isolated color area? Imagine the reporting mechanism is nothing more than the simple hardware needed to actually transmit a message (e.g., a speaker). If this device were connected to the color area, then it seems clear that there would be no reports of color consciousness. The cognitive functions needed to select a particular thought, decide how best to describe it, and to execute that action are still absent, preventing any type of response from being formed or conveyed. Whereas if the color area were connected to a more sophisticated reporting mechanism that was endowed with these functions there would probably be reports of color consciousness. However, this is not because the color area is experiencing its own isolated consciousness; rather, it is because the color area is now connected to the functions that are crucial for consciousness. By connecting the color area to a mechanism endowed with the relevant functions, the previously unconscious color information can now be accessed by a broader cognitive system.

Moreover, imagine that, before the surgery, that particular shade of red would reliably agitate or excite the patient. Would the patient have such feelings now and say something like, 'I don't see red but I notice that I've gotten a little tense'? As described here, the patient would not because such affective, emotional or 'limbic' reactions are themselves the types of functions that we are isolating from the color area. To be excited or calmed or distracted by a perceptual state of red discrimination is already to have functional access to that state, however coarse-grained or incomplete, because such a reaction can obviously affect decision making or motivation (Box 3).

Box 3. Access When There Is No Behavioral Output

How does the relationship between access, function and consciousness apply if a person cannot move or give any type of behavioral response? Consider patients with locked-in syndrome. Patients with this condition are conscious but cannot move due to paralysis of all muscles except (usually) the eyes and eyelids. This small volitional movement is the only means by which they can communicate. Imagine, however, that even this behavior is disabled so the patient is still fully conscious but completely paralyzed: perfectly locked-in.

This is an important case for understanding the functional view: behavioral outcomes are not its defining component. People can still consciously experience the world without there ever being any behavioral result that follows from those experiences. What is important is that there are enough high-level functions engaged with that information such that the patient could volitionally act upon those experiences if he or she so desired and was not paralyzed. In this case, even though the patient cannot move, the patient can do things such as attend to what he or she is hearing or store selected bits of information in working memory. This patient being conscious is perfectly consistent with the functional account of consciousness because those functions are fully preserved.

In spite of this frank denial by subjects, theories that posit dissociation between consciousness and function would necessarily assume that participants of the 'perfect experiment' are conscious of the apple's color but simply cannot access that experience. After all, the conditions these theories stipulate for phenomenal consciousness of color are all met, so this experiment does not disprove the existence of isolated consciousness; it merely provides another particularly crisp example of consciousness without access.

However, there is a crucial problem with this logic. If this 'perfect experiment' could not definitively disprove dissociative theories, then what could? The subject manifests all the functional criteria for not being conscious of color so what would ground the claim that the subject nevertheless enjoys a special kind of consciousness: phenomenal consciousness without access consciousness?

The Domain of a Science of Consciousness

What the perfect experiment demonstrates is that science necessarily relies on cognitive functions in order to investigate consciousness. Without input from subjects, input that is the product of such functions, theorists are left to define consciousness based on certain types of activation that are independent of a subject's own experience. It has been claimed that separating consciousness from other cognitive functions is required because it 'is a prerequisite for using the term [consciousness] at all' ([5], p. 500). What does it mean to study consciousness without function? Inevitably, theories motivated by this view will define consciousness in their own way (local recurrency, microconsciousness, coalitions of neurons etc.) and say that whenever that criterion is met, consciousness must occur. But how do we set this criterion?

For example, what reason is there to think that local recurrency is conscious experience?

Could local recurrency simply be a form of unconscious processing? It cannot be based on subjective reports because these reports are the direct result of cognitive functions. When an observer says, 'But in the Sperling display I don't just see a few letters on the screen, I see all the letters,' there is no reason to believe that such an experience occurs independent of function.

The fact that the observer is reporting on this visual experience proves that the experience has been accessed by the broader cognitive system as a whole. Lamme writes, 'You cannot know whether you have a conscious experience without resorting to cognitive functions such as attention, memory or inner speech' ([5], p. 499). If this is true, then what reason is there to think this particular type of activation should be classified as correlating with conscious experience? What does it mean to have a conscious experience that you yourself do not realize you are having? In the face of such clear grounds for doubting such a conscious experience, dissociative theories need to provide a reason for claiming that these isolated types of activation involve any kind of consciousness.

The Future of Scientific Theories of Consciousness

It is clear, then, that proper scientific theories of consciousness are those that specify which functions are necessary for consciousness to arise. A true scientific theory will say how functions such as attention, working memory and decision making interact and come together to form a conscious experience. Any such theory will need to have clear and testable predictions that can in principle be verified or falsified. Most importantly, such theories will not claim that consciousness is a unique brain state that occurs independently of function; instead, the focus will be placed on the functions themselves and how they interact and come together to form consciousness.

There are several theorists who have already realized the need for functions in developing theories of consciousness. Dehaene and colleagues [16] have put forth a global neuronal workspace model that claims consciousness is defined by the orientation of top-down attention, long distance feedback loops that extend into parietofrontal networks, and conscious reportability. Similarly, Kouider and colleagues [27] have discussed at great length how information that is in consciousness relies on a hierarchy of representational levels. Under this view, each level corresponds to different cognitive mechanisms responsible for different units of representation.

It is important to stress that both of these theories are merely the beginning, rather than the end, of the study of consciousness. There is still much work to be done in regards to how these functions and mechanisms interact. In Dehaene et al.'s theory, for example, a more thorough and specific understanding of the type of parietofrontal activation [16] and how it relates to the formation of memories and decisions is still necessary. The upshot of function-based theories is that they make claims about consciousness that can be tested and examined scientifically.

Although there are certainly those who disagree with the specifics of the theories put forth by Dehaene et al. and Kouider et al. [4–14], these are disagreements that can eventually be settled through more rigorous examination and testing. The same cannot be said of theories that maintaining that consciousness occurs independent of function. As the perfect experiment illustrates, such theories inherently prevent any future avenue for scientific research.

Concluding Remarks

Understanding the necessary relation between function and experience reveals that the so-called hard problem of consciousness should be reclassified. Far from being a formidable obstacle to science, it achieves its apparent hardness by being systematically outside of science, not only today's science but any science of the future that insists on dissociating consciousness from the set of phenomena that alone could shed light on it. This is not to suggest that consciousness is a mystery that the human mind cannot comprehend [58]. It is simply that whatever mysteries and puzzles might continue to baffle us, we should not cripple our attempts at understanding by adopting a concept of consciousness that systematically blocks all avenues of further research.

The issues raised here generalize beyond the specific theories discussed [4–14]. Any theory wherein the neural correlates of conscious experience are separate from the neural correlates of cognitive function is ultimately doomed. No matter the specifics of the theory—C-fibers firing, grandmother cells, winning coalitions, microconsciousness, recurrent processing (RP) and so on—it is always possible in principle to isolate this activation. Such imagined isolation, however, actually removes the experience in question from further testing, scrutiny and verification. Although these theories might provide considerable insight into the formation of internal representations of the sensory and perceptual world, that is not enough to explain one's personal awareness. A proper theory of consciousness cannot exclusively focus on how the brain forms and maintains representations.

Such a theory must also explain in functional terms how those representations are experienced and accessed by the multiple functions constituting an observer [59]. Theories that do not acknowledge this are fundamentally incapable of explaining the full scope of consciousness.

Acknowledgments

This work was supported by a National Science Foundation Graduate Research Fellowship (M.A.C.). Special thanks to Justin Junge for extensive discussion and comments on the project. Thanks to Arash Afraz and Maryam Vaziri Pashkam for helpful discussions, and to Ray Jackendoff, Sid Kouider, Ken Nakayama, Jordan Suchow, and two anonymous reviewers for comments on the manuscript. Thanks to Jeremy Freeman for providing the images for Figure 2.

References

1. Crick, F. and Koch, C. (1995) Are we aware of neural activity in primary visual cortex. *Nature* 375, 121–23

2. Crick, F. and Koch, C. (1990) Towards a neurobiological theory of consciousness. *Semin. Neurosci.* 2, 263–75

3. Chalmers, D.J. (2000) What is a neural correlate of consciousness? In *Neural Correlates of Consciousness: Empirical and Conceptual Questions* (Metzinger, T., ed.), pp. 17–39, MIT Press

4. Lamme, V.A. (2003) Why visual attention and awareness are different. *Trends Cogn. Sci.* 7, 12–18

5. Lamme, V.A. (2006) Towards a true neural stance on consciousness. *Trends Cogn. Sci.* 10, 494–501

6. Block, N. (2005) Two neural correlates of consciousness. *Trends Cogn. Sci.* 9, 46–52

7. Block, N. (2007) Consciousness, accessibility, and the mesh between psychology and neuroscience. *Behav. Brain Sci.* 30, 481–99

8. Crick, F. and Koch, C. (2003) A framework for consciousness. *Nat. Neurosci.* 6, 119–26

9. Koch, C. (2004) *The Quest for Consciousness: A Neurobiological Approach*, Roberts & Company

10. Koch, C. and Tsuchiya, N. (2007) Phenomenology without conscious access is a form of consciousness without top-down attention. *Behav. Brain Sci.* 30, 509–10

11. Zeki, S. (2003) The disunity of consciousness. *Trends Cogn. Sci.* 7, 214–18

12. Zeki, S. and Bartels, A. (1999) Toward a theory of visual consciousness. *Conscious. Cogn.* 8, 225–59

13. Zeki, S. (2001) Localization and globalization in conscious vision. *Annu. Rev. Neurosci.* 24, 57–86

14. Goodale, M. (2007) Duplex vision: separate cortical pathways for conscious perception and the control of action. In *The Blackwell Companion to Consciousness* (Velmans, M. and Schneider, S., eds), pp. 580–88, Blackwell

15. Baars, B.J. (1989) *A Cognitive Theory of Consciousness*, Cambridge Univ. Press

16. Dehaene, S. et al. (2006) Conscious, preconscious, and subliminal processing: a testable taxonomy. *Trends Cogn. Sci.* 10, 204–11

17. Dennett, D.C. (1991) *Consciousness Explained*, Little Brown

18. Awh, E. and Pashler, H. (2000) Evidence for split attentional foci. *J. Exp. Psychol. Hum. Percept. Perform.* 26, 834–46

19. McMains, S.A. and Somers, D.C. (2004) Multiple spotlights of attentional selection in human visual cortex. *Neuron* 42, 677–86

20. Luck, S.J. and Vogel, E.K. (1997) The capacity of visual working memory for features and conjunctions. *Nature* 390, 279–81

21. Alvarez, G.A. and Cavanagh, P. (2004) The capacity of visual short-term memory is set both by visual information load and by number of objects. *Psychol. Sci.* 15, 106–11

22. Pylyshyn, Z.W. and Storm, R.W. (1988) Tracking multiple independent targets: evidence for a parallel tracking mechanism. *Spat. Vis.* 3, 179–97

23. Cavanagh, P. and Alvarez, G.A. (2005) Tracking multiple targets with multifocal attention. *Trends Cogn. Sci.* 9, 349–54

24. Sperling, G. (1960) The information available in brief visual presentation. *Psychol. Monogr.* 74, 1–29

25. Landman, R. et al. (2003) Large capacity storage of integrated objects before change blindness. *Vision Res.* 43, 149–64

26. Sligte, I. et al. (2008) Are there multiple visual short-term memory stores? *PLoS ONE* 3, 1–9

27. Kouider, S. et al. (2010) How rich is consciousness? The partial awareness hypothesis. *Trends Cogn. Sci.* 14, 301–07

28. Block, N. (1995) On a confusion about the function of consciousness. *Behav. Brain Sci.* 18, 227–87

29. Zeki, S. (2007) A theory of microconsciousness. In *The Blackwell Companion to Consciousness* (Velmans, M. and Schneider, S., eds), pp. 580–88, Blackwell

30. Wolfe, J.M. (1999) Inattentional amnesia. In *Fleeting Memories: Cognition of Brief Visual Stimuli* (Coltheart, M., ed.), pp. 71–94, MIT Press

31. O'Regan, J.K. and Noe, A. (2001) A sensorimotor account of vision and visual consciousness. *Behav. Brain Sci.* 24, 939–1031

32. Yi, D.J. et al. (2004) Neural fate of ignored stimuli: dissociable effects of perceptual and working memory load. *Nat. Neurosci.* 7, 992–96

33. Lavie, N. (1995) Perceptual load as a necessary condition for selective attention. *J. Exp. Psychol. Hum. Percept. Perform.* 21, 451–68

34. Cartwright-Finch, U. and Lavie, N. (2006) The role of perceptual load in inattentional blindness. *Cognition* 102, 321–40

35. Schwartz, S. et al. (2005) Attentional load and sensory competition in human vision: modulation of fMRI responses by load at

fixation during task-irrelevant stimulation in the peripheral visual field. *Cereb. Cortex* 15, 770–86

36. Chong, S.C. and Treisman, A. (2003) Representation of statistical properties. *Vision Res.* 43, 393–404

37. Alvarez, G.A. (2011) Representing multiple objects as an ensemble enhances visual cognition. *Trends Cogn. Sci.* 15, 122–31

38. Oliva, A. and Schyns, P.S. (2000) Diagnostic colors mediate scene recognition. *Cogn. Psychol.* 41, 176–210

39. Alvarez, G.A. and Oliva, A. (2008) The representation of ensemble visual features outside the focus of attention. *Psychol. Sci.* 19, 678–85

40. Alvarez, G. and Oliva, A. (2009) Spatial ensemble statistics: efficient codes that can be represented with reduced attention. *Proc. Natl. Acad. Sci. U.S.A.* 106, 7345–50

41. Ariely, D. (2001) Seeing sets: representation by statistical properties. *Psychol. Sci.* 12, 157–62

42. Chong, S.C. and Treisman, A. (2005) Statistical processing: computing the average size in perceptual groups. *Vision Res.* 45, 891–900

43. Halberda, J. et al. (2006) Multiple spatially overlapping sets can be enumerated in parallel. *Psychol. Sci.* 17, 572–76

44. Dakin, S. and Watt, R. (1997) The computation of orientation statistics from visual texture. *Vision Res.* 37, 3181–92

45. Parkes, L. et al. (2001) Compulsory averaging of crowded orientation signals in human vision. *Nat. Neurosci.* 4, 739–44

46. Atchley, P. and Andersen, G. (1995) Discrimination of speed distributions: sensitivity to statistical properties. *Vision Res.* 35, 3131–44

47. Watamaniuk, S. and Duchon, A. (1992) The human visual system averages speed information. *Vision Res.* 32, 931–41

48. Haberman, J. and Whitney, D. (2007) Rapid extraction of mean emotion and gender from sets of faces. *Curr. Biol.* 17, R751–R753

49. Chun, M.M. et al. (2011) A taxonomy of external and internal attention. *Annu. Rev. Psychol.* 62, 73–101

50. Cohen, M.A. et al. Natural scene perception requires attention. *Psychol. Sci.* (in press)

51. De Gardelle, V. et al. (2009) Perceptual illusions in brief visual presentations. *Conscious. Cogn.* 18, 569–77

52. Levin, D.T. et al. (2000) Change blindness: the metacognitive error of overestimating change-detection ability. *Vis. Cogn.* 7, 397–412

53. Pascual-Leone, A. et al. (2001) Fast back-projections from the motion to the primary visual area necessary for visual awareness. *Science* 292, 510–12

54. Haynes, J. et al. (2005) Visibility reflects dynamic changes of effective connectivity between V1 and fusiform cortex. *Neuron* 46, 811–21

55. Boehler, C.N. et al. (2008) Rapid recurrent processing gates awareness in primary visual cortex. *Proc. Natl. Acad. Sci. U.S.A.* 105, 8742–47

56. Super, H. et al. (2001) Two distinct modes of sensory processing observed in monkey primary visual cortex (V1). *Nat. Neurosci.* 4, 304–10

57. Bullier, J. (2001) Feedback connections and conscious vision. *Trends Cogn. Sci.* 5, 369–70

58. McGinn, C. (1999) *The Mysterious Flame: Conscious Minds in a Material World*, Basic Books

59. Jackendoff, R. (1987) *Consciousness and the Computational Mind*, MIT Press

60. Nagel, T. (1974) What is it like to be a bat? *Philos. Rev.* 4, 435–50

61. Lamme, V.A. and Roelfsema, P.R. (2000) The distinct modes of vision offered by feedforward and recurrent processing. *Trends Neurosci.* 23, 571–79

62. Lamme, V.A. (2000) Neural mechanisms of visual awareness: a linking proposition. *Brain Mind* 1, 385–406

63. Koch, C. and Tsuchiya, N. (2007) Attention and consciousness: two distinct brain processes. *Trends Cogn. Sci.* 11, 16–22

64. Tononi, G. and Koch, C. (2008) The neural correlates of consciousness—an update. *Ann. N. Y. Acad. Sci.* 1124, 239–61

65. McConkie, G.W. and Rayner, K. (1975) The span of effective stimulus during a fixation in reading. *Percept. Psychophys.* 17, 578–86

66. Rayner, K. (1975) The perceptual span and peripheral cues in reading. *Cogn. Psychol.* 7, 65–81

67. Newton, J.R. and Eskew, R.T., Jr (2003) Chromatic detection and discrimination in the periphery: a postreceptoral loss of color sensitivity. *Vis. Neurosci.* 20, 511–21

68. Hecht, E. (1987) *Optics*, Addison Wesley

69. Wandell, B.A. (1995) *Foundations of Vision*, Sinauer

70. Azzopardi, P. and Cowey, A. (1993) Preferential representation of the fovea in the primary visual cortex. *Nature* 361, 719–21

Study Questions

1. Carefully distinguish the two kinds of consciousness (access and phenomenal) that Block talks about. What's the difference between his view and the other theories of consciousness he discusses?

2. What is blindsight? How is this relevant to Block's distinction between access and phenomenal consciousness?

3. Chalmers calls his view "naturalistic" dualism, and says that it's dualism about properties, not about substances. Explain. Think about the property of *being a clock*: is this property not reducible to a physical property? Is this property a functional property? Why are functional properties non-reducible? Explain why Chalmers and Block agree that the non-reducibility of consciousness is not a matter of its being a functional property.

4. What is the "bait and switch" strategy Chalmers accuses some philosophers of practicing? What does "bait and switch" mean here? Do you think that he'd argue that Dennett's article provides an example? Explain.

5. What is the "explanatory gap" that Chalmers thinks functionalist views of consciousness suffer from?

6. According to Chalmers, physical processes could not possibly explain consciousness. Summarize his argument for this conclusion, which is given near the end of section V. Challenge or defend his reasoning.

7. What's the difference, according to Chalmers, between a reductive and a non-reductive theory? Why does he think that the latter sort might be possible for consciousness?

8. Hardcastle imagines a time when brain-science has isolated the substrate of experience in the brain. Chalmers allows this might happen. But Hardcastle argues, and Chalmers denies, that this would provide a reductive explanation. Explain her reasoning. How might Chalmers reply?

9. Hardcastle argues that her willingness to accept a future biological reduction of consciousness, and others' unwillingness, is really a matter of difference in "attitude"—in "the spirit in which we approach an examination of consciousness." Explain what she means.

10. Hardcastle speaks of Chalmers and others as "mysterians." What does she mean? Explain her analogy about "water mysterians"—what's her point? Whom among the philosophers we've read in Chapters 8, 9, 10, and 11 might this label be applied to? Explain why.

11. Cohen and Dennett argue that the belief in non-functional characteristics of consciousness could never be demonstrated by science. Why do they think this? If it is true, why don't they agree with Chalmers that the investigation of this kind of consciousness is a hard problem indeed?

Suggested Readings

For more recent discussion of Block's (somewhat updated) distinction between A- and P-consciousness, see:

Ned Block (2007), "Consciousness, Accessibility, and the Mesh between Psychology and Neuroscience," *Behavioural and Brain Sciences* 30(5): pp. 481–548.

Having run Chalmers's article (excerpted above) in Volume 2 Number 3 (1995), the *Journal of Consciousness Studies* followed this by a large number of articles by well-known contributors to the field, discussing the issues Chalmers raised. See the rest of Number 3, and the following two issues: Volume 3, Numbers 1 and 2. Chalmers replies to a number of them in Volume 4, Number 1 (1997).

For a short reply to Cohen/Dennett see: "A True Science of Consciousness Explains Phenomenology: Comment on Cohen and Dennett," Johannes J. Fahrenfort and Victor A.F. Lamme, *Trends in Cognitive Sciences*, 16 (2012): pp. 138–39. Cohen and Dennett respond equally briefly in the same journal issue.

13

 # WHAT IS AN ACTION?

A central feature of persons is that they are **agents**. And agents are, in turn, things that are capable of **acting**. But what exactly does this ability consist in? And how exactly do bodily movements that are actions differ from those that are not? To see the puzzle that this second question raises, consider the items on the following list: Digesting your lunch, sneezing, daydreaming, blinking, keeping a secret, misremembering a date, and paying attention. Which of the items on this list are actions, or things that you *do*? And which of them are things that merely *happen to you*? To answer these questions, we need some principled way of classifying certain things as actions, and others as not.

A dominant view, going back at least to the time of Aristotle, is that something is an action in virtue of being caused in the right way by an agent's psychological states. For example, one's arm going up might be an action in virtue of being caused by a desire to get someone's attention, and a belief that raising one's arm will achieve this result. This is, in broad strokes, the **causal theory of action**, which is also sometimes referred to as "the standard story." because it is so commonly accepted.

In his 1963 article, "Actions, Reasons, and Causes," Donald Davidson develops what is often viewed as a contemporary defense of the causal theory of action. Davidson himself was one of the most influential philosophers of the twentieth century, whose work had wide-ranging impact on the philosophy of mind, language, action, ethics, and epistemology. He spent most of his career as Slusser Professor of Philosophy at UC Berkeley. Davidson's central claim in this paper is that when we explain an agent's action in terms of their reasons—what is known as a **rationalization**—what we are doing is actually giving a type of **causal explanation**. Why is this claim—that reasons are causes of action—significant? For one thing, it brings reasons and rationalization into the natural causal order. If rationalizations are not causal explanations, then it is hard to see how we can square them with a scientific understanding of human actions, since science works on the assumption that all events have a cause. It is therefore important, in order to reconcile a scientific picture of the world with our commonsense picture of agency, to see how reasons can be causes of action.

Before we look at this claim in more detail, it will be useful to have some background on how Davidson understands rationality more generally. Davidson takes the assumption of rationality to be the fundamental law of psychology. Here is a useful quotation of his for illustrating this point:

> There is no assigning beliefs to a person one by one on the basis of his verbal behavior, his choices, or other local signs no matter how plain and evident, for we make sense of particular beliefs only as they cohere with other beliefs, with preferences, with intentions, hopes, fears, expectations, and the rest.[1]

There are two points alluded to here. The first is that we can only make sense of a person's behavior in psychological terms by appeal to a large number of propositional attitudes. Determining from their behavior whether a person has this belief or that belief is a matter of placing the person's beliefs in a network of inter-related propositional attitudes. For a simple example, predicting whether and when a person will drink water will depend, not only on their thirst, but also on their beliefs about when it is safe and appropriate to drink. The second point is that a person's particular beliefs have to *cohere* with their other beliefs and attitudes. This means that the person's system of beliefs, desires, etc., is assumed to be *consistent*. If, for example, someone is thirsty and believes that drinking a glass of water will quench her thirst, then to explain why she *doesn't* drink it requires attributing to her some other beliefs or desires to eliminate the apparent contradiction. Perhaps she believes the water is poisoned, or she doesn't want to reveal her thirst to others. So we understand and predict people's behavior only by assuming rationality and consistency in the set of propositional attitudes we attribute to them. To do this is to provide a rationalization of their behavior.

The assumption of rationality is not always binding. We could explain the thirsty person's not drinking by saying, "Gee, I guess she's just not behaving rationally." Yet, as Davidson often points out, this is always a last resort. For if we do not assume rationality as a basic property of human beings it would be impossible to assign to them any beliefs or desires whatsoever. The assumption of rationality is a pre-condition for attributing propositional attitudes at all. Specific instances of occasional irrationality still require a background of consistent belief. Even the insane have their own logic.

Primary Reasons and Intentional Action

Let's return now to Davidson's claim that rationalization is just one kind of causal explanation, that is, explanation of an event by giving its causes. From this basis, Davidson constructed a detailed theory of what it is to act that is in keeping with the causal theory of action. It goes like this. When we rationalize an action we do so by citing its **primary reason**. The primary reason for an action consists of two propositional attitudes:

1. a pro-attitude (desire, wanting, wishing, etc.) towards a certain kind of action
2. a belief that a certain action is of that kind

To illustrate, suppose that a young girl, Janine, is playing in her back garden when she sees her cat, Whiskers, sneaking up on a robin that is standing on the lawn. Janine saves the bird by throwing a stone to alarm Whiskers so that he runs off. But the stone doesn't only alarm Whiskers; it also breaks the window of the greenhouse. When Janine's mother discovers the broken window, she asks "Why did you throw the rock at the window?" "I didn't mean to throw it at the window," says Janine, "I only wanted to frighten Whiskers to save the bird."

Here we can say that Janine had a desire to alarm the cat (to save the bird) and a belief that throwing the rock would alarm the cat. Together, this belief and desire make up Janine's primary reason for throwing the stone. As Davidson notes, when we give the primary reason for an action, we do not usually spell out both the desire and the belief but only one or the other—just as Janine only mentions her desire to frighten Whiskers, but not her belief that throwing the rock is a way of doing so.

Now, Janine's action had another consequence beyond alarming the cat—it also broke the window. Janine's protest to her mother was that a desire to break the window was not part of her primary reason for throwing the stone. When we explain an action in terms of its primary reason, we describe the **intention** with which it was done. So here we would say that Janine threw the stone with the intention of alarming the cat, but not with the intention of breaking the window. Davidson remarks here that an intention is not an entity, state, disposition, or event. According to Davidson, when we say "Janine threw the rock with the intention of alarming the cat," we are not describing a state of Janine or a property of Janine's action; we are giving a fuller description of Janine's action. (In a later paper[2] Davidson changed his mind about this, allowing that intentions are distinct mental states, a special type of judgement.) This point will come up later when we read Harry Frankfurt's article.

Davidson points out an interesting aspect of explanations of actions in terms of their primary reasons. Such explanations have a *normative character*. That is, they indicate that a certain action *ought* to be done, or that it ought not to be done, in light of some standard of rationality. Given Janine's desire to alarm the cat, throwing the rock was rationally a *good* thing to do. That is how she justifies her action to her mother: "I wanted to alarm the cat, in order to save the bird." And we also reference reasons when we are trying to understand someone's behavior that we find strange or puzzling. We say, "Oh, that's why she did it." So explanations in terms of primary reasons are rational justifications of actions, which is a form of normative evaluation. And this is why, Davidson says, many philosophers do not like to think of primary reasons as *causes* of actions. We are not giving the cause of Janine's action in saying it was to alarm the cat, they say, but rather we are describing her action in light of a rational justification. By contrast, when we say that the lightning striking the ground was the explanation for the forest fire, we are giving its cause. Causes are what explain events in the natural world where there are no primary reasons. Reasons, the argument goes, are not causes.

Some people have also denied that reasons are causes due to the fact that, when we explain someone's action by giving the reason for why they did it, we merely *redescribe* the action. But causes must be *distinct* from their effects, not mere redescriptions of them. And so reasons cannot, on this view, be causes.

In reply, Davidson points out that explaining an event by redescribing it is sometimes a way of giving a causal explanation of that event. We may say, for example, that Janine's throwing the stone was an event caused by her wanting to alarm the cat. Here we have a redescription of the event of Janine's throwing the stone that explains it in terms of its cause, which is itself a distinct event. So to allow that actions are sometimes redescribed in terms of the reasons that make them intelligible is *not* to deny that those reasons are their causes.

Davidson's argument against denying that reasons are causes of our actions is that, unless they are, we cannot explain the force of the word 'because' in action explanation. This becomes evident in cases in which there are multiple rationalizations available for the same action. Suppose that Janine, in addition to having a desire to alarm the cat, also wants to break the greenhouse window. In the case as we described it, however, it is her desire to alarm the cat that lies behind her throwing the rock. In that case, we can accurately say that Janine threw the rock *because* she wanted to alarm the cat, but we cannot accurately say that Janine threw the rock because she wanted to shatter the greenhouse window. Why not? Though both explanations succeed in identifying a reason Janine has for throwing the rock, only one picks out the reason that actually *caused* her action on that occasion. As Davidson puts it, "a person can have a reason for an action, and perform the action, and yet this reason not be the reason why he did it. Central to the relation between a reason and an action it explains is the idea that the agent performed the action because he had the reason." Note that this is still the case even in explanations where the desired consequence of the action is not a distinct event from the act itself. A person's raising her arm is not a distinct event from her saluting the flag, and yet we still want to say that she is raising her arm because she wants to salute the flag. The cause of her raising her arm is her desire to salute the flag, and this *desire* is a distinct event that is the cause of her arm raising. The causation, then, is not between the act and its consequences, but between the primary reason and the act. There is, then, a sequence of events, from belief and desire to action, which stand in a relation of cause and effect.

The Problem of Action

When we identify a piece of behavior as an action in accordance with the causal theory, we cite its causal history: An agent's behavior is an action if and only if it is suitably caused by the agent's psychological states. According to Harry Frankfurt, who is Professor Emeritus of Philosophy at Princeton University in his article reproduced in this chapter, this account fails as a solution to what he calls "the problem of action." This is the problem of explaining "the contrast between what an agent does and what merely happens to him, or between the bodily movements he makes, and those that occur without his making them." Causal theories, he argues, are "inherently implausible" and cannot provide a "satisfactory analysis of the nature of action." According to Frankfurt, "it is no part of the nature of an action to have a prior causal history of any particular kind."

This is shown in part, he argues, by a set of counter-examples with a common pattern. In these examples, there is a bodily movement that is caused by a person's beliefs and desires, but nonetheless is not plausibly seen as an action that the person performed as an agent. In his own example, a person wants to spill what is in his glass in order to commence a robbery. In terms of the causal theory, he has a primary reason for spilling the contents of the glass: a desire to commence a robbery and a belief that spilling the contents of the glass will produce that effect. But before this can happen, he spills the contents of his glass out of nervousness over the impending robbery. The person's belief and his desire were in a certain way causes of the spilling, but the spilling was nonetheless not an action of the person as agent—it was an accident. With some imagination one can concoct endless such counter-examples to the simple causal theory of action as Davidson defends it. Philosophers now refer to these as cases of **deviant causes**.

Frankfurt maintains that the reason that causal theories are vulnerable to such counterexamples is that, in focusing on the causes of action, which must occur *prior* to the action itself, "they direct attention exclusively away from the events whose natures are at issue, and away from the times at which they occur." The result is that they cannot require that if a person is performing an action, then they are "in some particular relation" to their bodily movements at the time that the action is unfolding. But according to Frankfurt, it is precisely the way in which a person is "in touch" with their movements *as they are making them* that distinguishes actions from non-actions.

Frankfurt breaks down this idea of an agent's being "in touch" with their movements in terms of the notion of **guidance**. What it is, on Frankfurt's view, for a person to be performing an action is for their movements to be under their guidance. And such guidance is importantly not, on Frankfurt's picture, a matter of being caused by appropriate events, since "an event cannot be guided through the course of its occurrence at a temporal distance." In other words, a psychological event that occurs *prior* to the start of a bodily movement cannot, on his view, contribute to the guidance of that later movement as it unfolds.

When a movement is guided by an agent, Frankfurt calls this an 'intentional movement.' He contrasts the case of a movement's being guided by an agent with that of being guided by some causal mechanism, where the activity of that mechanism does not constitute something that an *agent* does. Consider one's pupils dilating in response to the light dimming. Certainly, one's dilating pupils are guided by a causal mechanism in this case. But we do not say that an *agent* dilates their pupils.

Frankfurt reserves the term 'intentional action' for intentional movements that are performed by an agent "more or less deliberately or self-consciously." In other words, he says, these are movements that are *intended* by an agent. Now, as we mentioned in our discussion of Davidson, intentions have not always been viewed as distinct psychological states, alongside beliefs and desires. Sometimes, as in Davidson's "Actions, Reasons, and Causes," talk of intentions is simply analyzed in terms of the beliefs and desires that initiate an action. But Frankfurt here appears to be treating intentions as distinct psychological states, whose role goes beyond that of action initiation, and extends to action planning and guidance. In virtue of this richer role, we can say that they cannot be simply reduced to beliefs and desires.

Purposive Movement

Frankfurt maintains that a movement's being guided is synonymous with its being **purposive**. When exactly is a movement purposive, or guided, on Frankfurt's view? Frankfurt's answer here is that a movement is purposive when two conditions are met. First, the course of the movement must be such that it is available for adjustments "which compensate for the effects of forces which would otherwise interfere" with it. Second, if these adjustments take place, their occurrence must not be "explainable by what explains the state of affairs that elicited them." To help illustrate what this means, consider a case of a toy vehicle being guided by remote control in a straight line towards a target location. Suppose that at some point, it veers off its course due to a heavy gust of wind. Now consider two ways in which it might return to its course after this interference. One way is if the wind suddenly reversed direction, and another gust pushed it back onto its original trajectory. This would clearly not be a case of the behavior of the vehicle being guided or purposive, since the very factor that is responsible for the interference is also responsible for the subsequent adjustment. If it is brought back on its course by way of the causal operations of the remote control, however, we can say that its course is guided. This is because, as Frankfurt puts it, "the behavior is in that case under the guidance of an independent causal mechanism," that is, independent of the mechanism that caused it to go off course, and it is the readiness of this causal mechanism to adjust for any interference in the unfolding of some movement that allows us to say that the movement is guided by it.

Frankfurt is clear that movements need not *actually* be causally affected by the relevant adjusting mechanisms in order for them to be guided. He offers an illustration of this point by way of a driver who wants to coast down a hill at a certain speed, and who happens to be doing so by way of the pull of gravity on their car. Now suppose that, since the driver is going in their desired direction and at their desired speed, they do not adjust the steering wheel or press on the gas pedal. That is, they do not causally intervene with respect to the direction or speed of the car. Nonetheless, Frankfurt says, they guide the car because they are "prepared to intervene if necessary" and are "in a position to do so more or less effectively." So, if the vehicle were to go off course, or start to go too fast, the driver would then be able to effectively compensate for these changes, and it is due to this fact that the car's trajectory is guided.

In the final section of his paper, Frankfurt makes a case for attributing agency to creatures other than human beings. The implication of this is that an appeal to "higher faculties," like self-consciousness and deliberation, are not required in order to draw a general distinction between what an agent does and what merely happens to them. Frankfurt points out that "[t]here are numerous agents besides ourselves, who may be active as well as passive with respect to the movements of their bodies." He asks us to consider the contrast between a spider moving its legs as it walks and its legs being moved by someone who has tied strings to them. In the first case, not only are the movements purposive, but they are also attributable to the spider, who makes them. In the second case, the same movements take place, but they are not so attributable. Frankfurt does not specify the conditions under which we are to attribute behavior to a creature as an agent. Indeed, he allows that, understood in this way, "the general conditions of agency are unclear." Still, we must not assume that these conditions cannot by satisfied by creatures other than human beings, and thus we ought to take care not to analyze the notion of agency in ways that rule out the possibility of other creatures achieving instances of it.

The Role of Consciousness in Action

Our next author is Élisabeth Pacherie, who is a philosopher of mind, action, and cognitive science at the Jean Nicod Institute/École Normale Supérieure in Paris, France. Pacherie's paper, "Can Conscious Agency Be Saved?," deals with the role of consciousness in the control of human action. Reasons, intentions, and sensory states, all of which are involved in the control of action, can occur both consciously and non-consciously. This raises the following question: what difference does it make to the control of action whether or not the relevant psychological states are conscious?

One might think that it is indisputable that consciousness plays an important role in action control. But recently, on the basis of empirical evidence, some have put forth so-called *zombie challenges* to this seemingly obvious claim. In particular, zombie challenges *purport* to show that some feature of action control that seems to be under the guidance of conscious states and processes is actually driven by nonconscious states and processes. Perhaps the most widely discussed zombie challenge is based on now-famous results from the studies of neuroscientist Benjamin Libet in the 1980s. Libet aimed to uncover how our conscious decisions to act relate to underlying brain activity surrounding the time of action.

In Libet's experiments, participants were seated facing an analog clock, around which a dot would revolve very quickly. At the same time, they were hooked up to an EEG machine which measured their brain activity, and an EMG machine which measured their muscle activity. Their task was simple: they were to perform a spontaneous movement without any preplanning—either a flexing of the finger or wrist—and report the time at which they were aware of having decided to move by reference to the clock. The striking finding was that brain activity thought to indicate the initiation of action—the so-called Readiness Potential or RP—preceded the timing of the conscious decision to act by about 350 milliseconds.

Some have thought that this gap between the awareness of a decision to act, and the decision itself as reflected in neural activity suggests that consciousness cannot be operative in the making of that decision. And if this were to generalize to *all* of our decisions, this would be rather unsettling. By way of illustration, consider the following scenario: You've been offered a job, but you're not sure whether you want to take it. It would mean a long commute, and working extended hours. On the other hand, it would provide a good salary and benefits, and you think you might enjoy the challenge it would offer you. You engage in lengthy conscious deliberation, carefully weighing the various pros and cons. Eventually, at time t, you arrive at a decision: you will accept the job. Now what if the picture that neuroscience reveals is that, prior to time t, unconscious processes in the brain indicated that you had already made your decision to accept the job. Is it really *you* that ultimately decided then?

Some have taken this worry to support a view that has been dubbed "will skepticism," according to which the fact that our conscious intentions are reliably preceded by unconscious brain activity spells trouble for the belief that we are capable of free action. Before seeing how Pacherie responds to this skepticism, it will be helpful to visit the main positions in the free will debate in order to get a better handle on the challenge.

What Is Free Will?

According to some the term '**free will**' is best understood as referring to the ability to act freely. The question then becomes what this ability consists in. Traditionally, answers to this question have fallen into two broad camps, each of which takes a stance on the relationship between free will and *determinism*. The thesis of **determinism** can be understood intuitively as the claim that whatever happens is necessitated by what came before. Think of a chain of domino tiles that are perfectly spaced apart. Once the first tile in the chain is tipped over, the rest will inevitably follow. Barring any external influence, this chain reaction will continue on its course until the last domino has dropped. Put in more technical terms, the thesis of determinism is that a complete statement of the laws of nature governing the universe, along with a statement describing the complete state of the universe at some time, together entail a statement describing the complete state of the universe at any other time.

Those who believe that there is no room for free will in a deterministic universe are referred to as **incompatibilists**. On this view, if determinism is true, then no one has the ability to act freely, since every decision and action is entailed by what came before and the laws of the physical universe. Among incompatibilists, **libertarians** are the optimists. They hold that there is enough *in*determinism in the universe to ground the existence of free will. So-called **hard determinists**, on the other hand, are the pessimists. They affirm the truth of determinism and thereby deny that free will exists. By contrast to both libertarians and hard determinists, **compatibilists** believe that there is no clash or conflict between determinism and the ability to act freely. On their view, even if determinism is true, we can still have free will. Why is this? Compatibilists maintain that the real threats to free will are compulsion and coercion, not determinism. A compatibilist might argue as follows: Consider two cases of deterministic causation. In one case, a kleptomaniac has an irresistible urge, born out of compulsion, to steal a t-shirt from a clothing store, despite their not wanting to give in to the urge, and having decided that, all things considered, stealing is not the best course of action to take. They steal the shirt. In a second case, someone steals the t-shirt, not out of a compulsive desire to do so, but because they find it stylish and they recognize that they will never be able to afford it. Now, if determinism is true, both actions of stealing under consideration here are determined. Neither person could have done otherwise than they actually did. Still, it doesn't seem unreasonable to suppose that we might hold the second person morally responsible for their behavior, while either refraining from doing so in the case of the kleptomaniac, or at least holding them responsible to a lesser degree. Similarly, we might say that, given their compulsive desire, the kleptomaniac was not free to refrain from stealing the shirt. Someone could have offered them $1000 not to go ahead with the action, and they would have done so anyway, out of compulsion. The second person, on the other hand, would have gladly accepted this offer, and recognized it as a reason not to steal the shirt. So the action of the kleptomaniac does not seem to be in their control in the way that the second person's action is, and thereby seems not to be free in an important sense. According to compatibilists, then, our ordinary notions of free will and moral responsibility are not tracking whether or not an agent is determined to act as they do, but whether or not their action is an expression of their rational agency, that is, the result of one's capacity to recognize and act upon reasons.

The Libet Results and "Will Skepticism"

In light of this background, let's now consider the claim that Libet's results pose a challenge to free will, and support will skepticism. Pacherie takes issue with this conclusion on the grounds that further premises are needed in order to support it. Her strategy in Section 2 of her paper is to go through candidate premises that would help to fill in the argument, and show that they should not be accepted.

What are the candidates? First, one might think that *an action is performed freely only if the conscious decision that produced it was itself uncaused.* This is in keeping with the libertarian approach to free will. This suggestion relies on a view on which an agent cannot act freely unless they are the uncaused cause of their action: one might read this as entailing that their decision itself must not be caused. But Pacherie points out that the notion of an uncaused cause is rather difficult to square with what she calls a "naturalistic" stance. What she means by this is that this notion does not seem to fit within our current scientific framework, since that framework presupposes that every physical event has a cause. She writes that, "[o]nly hardcore mind–body dualists would contend that conscious intentions do not arise as a result of brain activity." And this would be a high price to pay in order to save the possibility of an uncaused cause.

Next, one might take Libet's results to suggest that *determinism is true.* Now this would be a bold claim in and of itself. For the fact that the RP reliably precedes a conscious decision to act does not entail that the decision is determined. Instead, it might merely suggest that the occurrence of the decision takes place with a certain degree of probability that falls short of 100%. Even if we accept, though, that the results indicate that determinism is true, this would not be bothersome to a compatibilist, for reasons introduced earlier.

Pacherie considers a third way in which one might take the Libet results to support will skepticism. She notes that this option has the least theoretical baggage, since it does not require that one endorse the truth of substance dualism, determinism, or incompatibilism. The strategy is to argue *in favor of epiphenomenalism*—the idea we introduced in Chapter Eleven—by arguing that the Libet results are evidence for two causal paths stemming from the RP. The first leading from the RP to the action itself, and the second leading to the conscious experience of intending, or willing. (See Figure 1.)

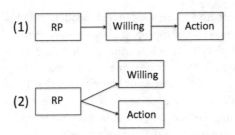

Figure 1   Two possible interpretations of the Libet results.

If true, this would be problematic, since the conscious intention (the willing) would not serve as a causal intermediary between unconscious brain activity and action, but rather as part of a divergent causal pathway. In response, Pacherie points out that we would need good reason to accept that this is the better interpretation versus one on which the unconscious brain activity causes a conscious decision, which *then* causes the action. Both interpretations are equally compatible with the available data, since the results, if reliable, only establish that unconscious brain activity that is thought to initiate action precedes a conscious decision to act, but are silent as to whether that brain activity goes on to cause the conscious decision alone (or is even to be identified with it), or whether it goes on to cause the conscious decision *as well as* the subsequent action. The burden of proof here lies on the skeptic to establish that the second interpretation is correct.

Finally, Pacherie articulates what will skeptics have taken to be the central challenge posed by the Libet results. This is that the results seem to suggest that conscious deliberation (vs. conscious intention considered in the previous paragraph) is merely epiphenomenal. But given that our purportedly free decisions (e.g., to accept a job offer) and the actions that those decisions cause (e.g., accepting the job) are precisely those that appear to be arrived at through such deliberation, this would seem to be a serious problem. Pacherie offers us two ways for pushing back on this worry.

First, she points out that it only succeeds if Libet's data are actually reliable to begin with. But many have argued on the basis of empirical and methodological considerations that the dominant interpretation of the results is unwarranted given either biases in measuring the onset of conscious decision or movement, or a mistaken view of the significance of the RP. Going into these criticisms will take us deep into technical territory, so we set them aside here.

Action Guidance and Internal Models

Instead, we take up the second way of pushing back on this final worry, and the central challenge that Pacherie mounts against the significance of the Libet results for conscious agency. This challenge is that the results reflect an overly narrow focus on the initiation of the action, and thereby ignore other aspects of action production and control, such as action guidance, wherein consciousness might play a more critical role. Pacherie notes how this echoes Frankfurt's critique of the causal theory more generally, and then goes on to update this idea by appeal to an influential strand in motor cognition research, which seeks to explain action guidance in terms of monitoring and control mechanisms, and to explain these mechanisms in terms of internal models. Within this research, an **internal model** is a process that models the behavior of the motor system and its results, in order to generate motor commands and calculate the effects of external disturbances.

Two kinds of internal model are relevant here. First, there are so-called **inverse models**, which take as input an agent's intention, as well as the current state of the agent's body and environment, and output the relevant motor commands for satisfying that intention. For instance, the inverse model might take as input one's intention to reach for one's coffee mug, and output motor commands specifying aspects of the movement like force, direction, and velocity, such that the sequence of behavior that results will satisfy that intention. Second, there are so-called **forward models**, which take as input a "copy" of the motor command output by the inverse model and output predictions of what the sensory consequences of executing that motor command would be. For instance, the forward model would take as input the motor command for the reaching and grasping movement and determine what position the body would end up in were that command to be executed. The outputted predictions of the forward model are then compared against the intention and the actual sensory feedback in order to correct for any errors that arise during the programming or execution of the action. Control of action, on this theory, is performed by a series of inverse and forward models that compare the desired, predicted, and actual states. Such a series is called a **comparator mechanism**.

Importantly, Pacherie points out that while internal model theory was originally developed to account for the fine-grained aspects of movement control, more recent versions hold that inverse and forward models are *hierarchically organized* such that there are several levels at which an action can be controlled by them, ranging from the very general to the very specific. At the highest level, the action is represented as a whole in terms of its main goal (e.g., reach for the coffee cup in order to pick it up). At the next level down, a motor program is selected so that the action can be implemented in the particular context that the agent finds herself in. So here factors like the orientation of the mug, its distance from the agent, and its shape will all be taken into account in order for a proper motor program to be selected. It will need to specify, for example, the appropriate type of hand grip for grasping the mug, and this will depend on whether the mug has one handle or two, and whether the handle is square or round, narrow or wide. Finally, the exact values of the parameters of the motor program must be set, including the precise trajectory and speed of the movement.

An important feature of this hierarchical model is that if one level of action control is unable to compensate for something's going wrong all on its own, an error signal is sent to the next level up, and the action is corrected there. So, for example, if you are reaching for your coffee mug when suddenly someone moves it out of your reach, the motor program that is guiding your action must be revised. In this case an error signal will be passed up to the level that involves the initial selection of a motor program, so that a new motor program that is sensitive to the mug's new location can be selected.

Once we understand the hierarchical nature of action guidance and control, and move our focus away from action initiation, new possibilities open up for how to understand the contribution of *both* conscious and unconscious control processes. As Pacherie points out, the question is not whether action guidance *can* proceed outside awareness, or whether it sometimes does, but whether it *always* does. If action guidance involves interactions across multiple levels, there are many more junctures at which conscious states may exert their role.

Consciousness and Action Guidance

Pacherie points to certain experimental results that serve to illustrate her point. The experiments in question required participants to move a stylus across a graphic tablet towards a target, with their arms hidden from view. A line on a computer screen represented the trajectory of their arm. Unbeknownst to the participants, on some trials the experimenters would introduce a bias in the visual feedback they received. For example if the trajectory of their actual movements were 15 degrees off the target, they might receive feedback indicating that it was 20 degrees off. When the introduced biases were small, participants made automatic adjustments to compensate for them, but they were not aware of doing so. For instance, in the example just given, they might adjust their movement 5 degrees in the direction opposite the bias, to make up for it. This is a case of unconscious guidance at work. The interesting finding is that when the perturbation was greater than 7 degrees, participants became aware of making the necessary corrections. As Pacherie puts it, "when discrepancies become too large to be automatically compensated, we become aware of them and shift to a conscious compensation strategy."

This set of experiments suggests an interesting picture of action guidance—one consistent with the picture that Frankfurt presents—such that control mechanisms need only be *available* to intervene if needed for an action to be guided by them; it needn't be the case that they actually intervene. Thus, on Pacherie's view, even when automatic mechanisms are responsible for action guidance, so long as conscious control mechanisms *could* intervene if needed—just as in the case of Frankfurt's downhill driver—then the action is consciously controlled by them.

Consciousness and Action Planning

Having looked at the potential role for consciousness *after* an action is initiated, Pacherie next looks *prior* to action initiation, to the role of prospective intentions in action control, and the contributions that consciousness might make here. She adopts a model of such intentions put forth by Michael Bratman.[3] According to Bratman, the ability to plan is a central human capacity, and one that is supported by our ability to form prospective intentions. Forming prospective intentions in advance of action saves us time and precious cognitive resources, and also helps us to coordinate future plans and activities both with respect to ourselves and other agents. If you intend to meet a friend at the movies at 6pm, for example, this will help ensure that you do not also form the intention to eat dinner then, but plan to do so earlier so as to give you enough time to get to the movies. It will also help ensure that your friend makes corresponding adjustments to *their* overall activities for the evening in order that the two of you may successfully meet up at the planned time.

A core feature of prospective intentions is that they involve commitment to a course of action. And one important dimension of such commitment is the fact that it prompts an agent to start reasoning about the means that they will use to arrive at their committed goal. In other words, one role of prospective intention is to initiate a process of *advance planning*. Pacherie identifies two kinds of cognitive process that go into such planning. The first is instrumental reasoning (IR) and the second is mental time travel (MTT). Instrumental reasoning is the reasoning we engage in to establish the means we will take to achieve our goals. For instance, if a person has the goal of taking a trip from Ontario to British Columbia, she might engage in instrumental reasoning to determine how best to save money for the trip, what travel dates will work best, what airline to fly, where she will stay, and so on. Mental time travel refers to the ability to mentally project oneself, by way of mental imagery, forward into the future in order to arrive at a plan of action. For example, in the case that Pacherie uses to illustrate it, one might mentally simulate various possible ways to get to their new dentist's office. Importantly, Pacherie argues on the basis of various empirical considerations that both instrumental reasoning and MTT require consciousness. If this is right, then a role is secured prior to action initiation for conscious states and processes.

Looking Ahead

We said at the outset of this chapter that an agent is someone who acts. We have now seen some influential ways of understanding what it is to act, and how to distinguish between what an agent *does* and what merely happens to them. But it might be wondered whether this is sufficient for a *full* understanding of what it is to act *as an agent*? Perhaps the capacity to act is *part* of what it is to be an agent, but not the whole story. In the next chapter, we take a closer look at what this fuller concept of agency may amount to.

Notes

1. Donald Davidson, "Mental Events," in *Essays on Actions and Events* (New York: Oxford University Press, 2001), p. 221.
2. "Intending," in *Philosophy of History and Action*, Yirmiahu Yovel (ed.) (Dordrecht: D. Reidel, 1978).
3. Michael Bratman, *Intention, Plans, and Practical Reason* (Cambridge, MA: Harvard University Press, 1987).

DONALD DAVIDSON

"Actions, Reasons, and Causes"

What is the relation between a reason and an action when the reason explains the action by giving the agent's reason for doing what he did? We may call such explanations *rationalizations*, and say that the reason *rationalizes* the action.

In this paper I want to defend the ancient—and common-sense—position that rationalization is a species of ordinary causal explanation. The defense no doubt requires some redeployment, but not more or less complete abandonment of the position, as urged by many recent writers.[1]

I

A reason rationalizes an action only if it leads us to see something the agent saw, or thought he saw, in his action—some feature, consequence, or aspect of the action the agent wanted, desired, prized, held dear, thought dutiful, beneficial, obligatory, or agreeable. We cannot explain why someone did what he did simply by saying the particular action appealed to him; we must indicate what it was about the action that appealed. Whenever someone does something for a reason, therefore, he can be characterized as (a) having some sort of pro attitude toward actions of a certain kind, and (b) believing (or knowing, perceiving, noticing, remembering) that his action is of that kind. Under (a) are to be included desires, wantings, urges, promptings, and a great variety of moral views, aesthetic principles, economic prejudices, social conventions, and public and private goals and values in so far as these can be interpreted as attitudes of an agent directed toward actions of a certain kind. The word 'attitude' does yeoman service here, for it must cover not only permanent character traits that show themselves in a lifetime of behavior, like love of children or a taste for loud company, but also the most passing fancy that prompts a unique action, like a sudden desire to touch a woman's elbow. In general, pro attitudes must not be taken for convictions, however temporary, that every action of a certain kind ought to be performed, is worth performing, or is, all things considered, desirable. On the contrary, a man may all his life have a yen, say, to drink a can of paint, without ever, even at the moment he yields, believing it would be worth doing.

Giving the reason why an agent did something is often a matter of naming the pro attitude (a) or the related belief (b) or both; let me call this pair the *primary reason* why the agent performed the action. Now it is possible to reformulate the claim that rationalizations are causal explanations, and give structure to the argument as well, by stating two theses about primary reasons:

1. For us to understand how a reason of any kind rationalizes an action it is necessary and sufficient that we see, at least in essential outline, how to construct a primary reason.
2. The primary reason for an action is its cause.

I shall argue for these points in turn.

II

I flip the switch, turn on the light, and illuminate the room. Unbeknownst to me I also alert a prowler to the fact that I am home. Here I do not do four things, but only one, of which four descriptions have been given.[2] I flipped the switch because I wanted to turn on the light, and by saying I wanted to turn on the light I explain (give my reason for, rationalize) the flipping. But I do not, by giving this reason, rationalize my alerting of the prowler nor my illuminating of the room. Since reasons may rationalize what someone does when it is described in one way and not when it is described in another, we cannot treat what was done simply as a term in sentences like 'My reason for flipping the switch was that I wanted to turn on the light'; otherwise we would be forced to conclude, from the fact that flipping the switch was identical with alerting the prowler, that my reason for alerting the prowler was that I wanted to turn on the light. Let us mark this quasi-intensional[3] character of action descriptions in rationalizations by stating a bit more precisely a necessary condition for primary reasons:

> C1. R is a primary reason why an agent performed the action A under the description d only if R consists of a pro attitude of the agent toward actions with a certain property, and a belief of the agent that A, under the description d, has that property.

How can my wanting to turn on the light be (part of) a primary reason, since it appears to lack the required element of generality? We may be taken in by the verbal parallel between 'I turned on the light' and 'I wanted to turn on the light.' The first clearly refers to a particular event, so we conclude that the second has this same event as its object. Of course it is obvious that the event of my turning on the light can't be referred to in the same way by both sentences, since the existence of the event is required by the truth of 'I turned on the light' but not by the truth of 'I wanted to turn on the light.' If the reference were the same in both cases, the second sentence would entail the first; but in fact the sentences are logically independent. What is less obvious, at least until we attend to it, is that the event whose occurrence makes 'I turned on the light' true cannot be called the object, however intensional, of 'I wanted to turn on the light.' If I turned on the light, then I must have done it at a precise moment, in a particular way—every detail is fixed. But it makes no sense to demand that my want be directed at an action performed at any one moment or done in some unique manner. Any one of an indefinitely large number of actions would satisfy the want, and can be considered equally eligible as its object. Wants and desires often are trained on physical objects. However, 'I want that gold watch in the window' is not a primary reason, and explains why I went into the store only because it suggests a primary reason—for example, that I wanted to buy the watch.

Because 'I wanted to turn on the light' and 'I turned on the light' are logically independent, the first can be used to give a reason why the second is true. Such a reason gives minimal information: it implies that the action was intentional, and wanting tends to exclude some other pro attitudes, such as a sense of duty or obligation. But the exclusion depends very much on the action and the context of explanation. Wanting seems pallid beside lusting, but it would be odd to deny that someone who lusted after a woman or a cup of coffee wanted her or it. It is not unnatural, in fact, to treat wanting as a genus including all pro attitudes as species. When we do this and when we know some action is intentional, it is empty to add that the agent wanted to do it. In such cases, it is easy to answer the question 'Why did you do it?' with 'For no reason,' meaning not that there is no reason but that there is no *further* reason, no reason that cannot be inferred from the fact that the action was done intentionally; no reason, in other words, besides wanting to do it. This last point is not essential to the present argument, but it is of interest because it defends the possibility of defining an intentional action as one done for a reason.

A primary reason consists of a belief and an attitude, but it is generally otiose to mention both. If you tell me you are easing the jib because you think that will stop the main from backing, I don't need to be told that you want to stop the main from backing; and if you say you are biting your thumb at me because you want to insult me, there is no point in adding that you think that by biting your thumb at me you will insult me. Similarly, many explanations of actions in terms of reasons that are not primary do not require mention of the primary reason to complete the story. If I say I am pulling weeds because I want a beautiful lawn, it would be fatuous to eke out the account with 'And so I see something desirable in any action that does, or has a good chance of, making the lawn beautiful.' Why insist that there is any *step*, logical or psychological, in the transfer of desire from an end that is not an action to the actions one conceives as means? It serves the argument as well that the desired end explains the action only if what are believed by the agent to be means are desired.

Fortunately, it is not necessary to classify and analyze the many varieties of emotions, sentiments, moods, motives, passions, and hungers whose mention may answer the question 'Why did you do it?' in order to see how, when such mention rationalizes the action, a primary reason is involved. Claustrophobia gives a man's reason for leaving a cocktail party because we know people want to avoid,

escape from, be safe from, put distance between themselves and, what they fear. Jealousy is the motive in a poisoning because, among other things, the poisoner believes his action will harm his rival, remove the cause of his agony, or redress an injustice, and these are the sorts of things a jealous man wants to do. When we learn a man cheated his son out of greed, we do not necessarily know what the primary reason was, but we know there was one, and its general nature. Ryle analyzes 'he boasted from vanity' into "he boasted on meeting the stranger and his doing so satisfies the lawlike proposition that whenever he finds a chance of securing the admiration and envy of others, he does whatever he thinks will produce this admiration and envy" (*The Concept of Mind*, 89). This analysis is often, and perhaps justly, criticized on the ground that a man may boast from vanity just once. But if Ryle's boaster did what he did from vanity, then something entailed by Ryle's analysis is true: the boaster wanted to secure the admiration and envy of others, and he believed that his action would produce this admiration and envy; true or false, Ryle's analysis does not dispense with primary reasons, but depends upon them.

To know a primary reason why someone acted as he did is to know an intention with which the action was done. If I turn left at the fork because I want to get to Katmandu, my intention in turning left is to get to Katmandu. But to know the intention is not necessarily to know the primary reason in full detail. If James goes to church with the intention of pleasing his mother, then he must have some pro attitude toward pleasing his mother, but it needs more information to tell whether his reason is that he enjoys pleasing his mother, or thinks it right, his duty, or an obligation. The expression 'the intention with which James went to church' has the outward form of a description, but in fact it is syncategorematic and cannot be taken to refer to an entity, state, disposition, or event. Its function in context is to generate new descriptions of actions in terms of their reasons; thus 'James went to church with the intention of pleasing his mother' yields a new, and fuller, description of the action described in 'James went to church.' Essentially the same process goes on when I answer the question 'Why are you bobbing around that way?' with 'I'm knitting, weaving, exercising, sculling, cuddling, training fleas.'

Straight description of an intended result often explains an action better than stating that the result was intended or desired. 'It will soothe your nerves' explains why I pour you a shot as efficiently as 'I want to do something to soothe your nerves,' since the first in the context of explanation implies the second; but the first does better, because, if it is true, the facts will justify my choice of action. Because justifying and explaining an action so often go hand in hand, we frequently indicate the primary reason for an action by making a claim which, if true, would also verify, vindicate, or support the relevant belief or attitude of the agent. 'I knew I ought to return it,' 'The paper said it was going to snow,' 'You stepped on my toes,' all, in appropriate reason-giving contexts, perform this familiar dual function.

The justifying role of a reason, given this interpretation, depends upon the explanatory role, but the converse does not hold. Your stepping on my toes neither explains nor justifies my stepping on your toes unless I believe you stepped on *my* toes, but the belief alone, true or false, explains my action.

III

In the light of a primary reason, an action is revealed as coherent with certain traits, long- or short-termed, characteristic or not, of the agent, and the agent is shown in his role of Rational Animal. Corresponding to the belief and attitude of a primary reason for an action, we can always construct (with a little ingenuity) the premises of a syllogism from which it follows that the action has some (as Miss Anscombe calls it) "desirability characteristic."[4] Thus there is a certain irreducible—though somewhat anemic—sense in which every rationalization justifies: from the agent's point of view there was, when he acted, something to be said for the action.

Noting that nonteleological causal explanations do not display the element of justification provided by reasons, some philosophers have concluded that the concept of cause that applies elsewhere cannot apply to the relation between reasons and actions, and that the pattern of justification provides, in the case of reasons, the required explanation. But suppose we grant that reasons alone justify in explaining actions; it does not follow that the explanation is not also—and necessarily—causal. Indeed our first condition for primary reasons (Cl) is designed to help set rationalizations apart from other sorts of explanation. If rationalization is, as I want to argue, a species of causal explanation, then justification, in the sense given by C1, is at least one differentiating property. How about the other claim: that justifying is a kind of explaining, so that the ordinary notion of cause need not be brought in? Here it is necessary to decide what is being included under justification. Perhaps it means only what is given by C1: that the agent has certain beliefs and attitudes in the light of which the action is reasonable. But then something essential has certainly been left out, for a person can have a reason for an action, and perform the action, and yet this reason not be the reason why he did it. Central to the relation between a reason and an action it explains is the idea that the agent performed the action because he had the reason. Of course, we can include this idea too in justification; but then the notion of justification becomes as dark as the notion of reason until we can account for the force of that 'because.'

When we ask why someone acted as he did, we want to be provided with an interpretation. His behavior seems strange, alien, outré, pointless, out of character, disconnected; or perhaps we cannot even recognize an action in it. When we learn his reason, we have an interpretation, a new description of what he did which fits it into a familiar picture. The picture certainly includes some of the agent's beliefs and attitudes; perhaps also goals, ends, principles, general character traits, virtues or vices. Beyond this, the redescription of an action afforded by a reason may place the action in a wider social, economic, linguistic, or evaluative context. To learn, through learning the reason, that the agent conceived his action as a lie, a repayment of a debt, an insult, the fulfillment of an avuncular obligation, or a knight's gambit is to grasp the point of the action in its setting of rules, practices, conventions, and expectations.

Remarks like these, inspired by the later Wittgenstein, have been elaborated with subtlety and insight by a number of philosophers. And there is no denying that this is true: when we explain an action, by giving the reason, we do redescribe the action; redescribing the action gives the action a place in a pattern, and in this way the action is explained. Here it is tempting to draw two conclusions that do not follow. First, we can't infer, from the fact that giving reasons merely redescribes the action and that causes are separate from effects, that therefore reasons are not causes. Reasons, being beliefs and attitudes, are certainly not identical with actions; but, more important, events are often redescribed in terms of their causes. (Suppose someone was burned. We could redescribe this event "in terms of a cause" by saying he was burned.) Second, it is an error to think that, because placing the action in a larger pattern

explains it, therefore we now understand the sort of explanation involved. Talk of patterns and contexts does not answer the question of how reasons explain actions, since the relevant pattern or context contains both reason and action. One way we can explain an event is by placing it in the context of its cause; cause and effect form the sort of pattern that explains the effect, in a sense of 'explain' that we understand as well as any. If reason and action illustrate a different pattern of explanation, that pattern must be identified.

Let me urge the point in connection with an example of Melden's. A man driving an automobile raises his arm in order to signal. His intention, to signal, explains his action, raising his arm, by redescribing it as signaling. What is the pattern that explains the action? Is it the familiar pattern of an action done for a reason? Then it does indeed explain the action, but only because it assumes the relation of reason and action that we want to analyze. Or is the pattern rather this: the man is driving, he is approaching a turn; he knows he ought to signal; he knows how to signal, by raising his arm. And now, in this context, he raises his arm. Perhaps, as Melden suggests, if all this happens, he does signal. And the explanation would then be this: if, under these conditions, a man raises his arm, then he signals. The difficulty is, of course, that this explanation does not touch the question of why he raised his arm. He had a reason to raise his arm, but this has not been shown to be the reason why he did it. If the description "signaling" explains his action by giving his reason, then the signaling must be intentional; but, on the account just given, it may not be.

If, as Melden claims, causal explanations are "wholly irrelevant to the understanding we seek" of human actions (184) then we are without an analysis of the 'because' in 'He did it because...,' where we go on to name a reason. Hampshire remarks, of the relation between reasons and action, "In philosophy one ought surely to find this...connection altogether mysterious" (166). Hampshire rejects Aristotle's attempt to solve the mystery by introducing the concept of wanting as a causal factor, on the grounds that the resulting theory is too clear and definite to fit all cases and that "There is still no compelling ground for insisting that the word 'want' *must* enter into every full statement of reasons for acting" (168). I agree that the concept of wanting is too narrow, but I have argued that, at least in a vast number of typical cases, some pro attitude must be assumed to be present if a statement of an agent's reasons in acting is to be intelligible. Hampshire does not see how Aristotle's scheme can be appraised as true or false, "for it is not clear what could be the basis of assessment, or what kind of evidence could be decisive" (167). Failing a satisfactory alternative, the best argument for a scheme like Aristotle's is that it alone promises to give an account of the "mysterious connection" between reasons and actions.

IV

In order to turn the first 'and' to 'because' in 'He exercised and he wanted to reduce and thought exercise would do it,' we must, as the basic move,[5] augment condition C1 with:

> C2. A primary reason for an action is its cause.

The considerations in favor of C2 are by now, I hope, obvious; in the remainder of this paper I wish to defend C2 against various lines of attack and, in the process, to clarify the notion of causal explanation involved.

A. The first line of attack is this. Primary reasons consist of attitudes and beliefs, which are states or dispositions, not events; therefore they cannot be causes.

It is easy to reply that states, dispositions, and conditions are frequently named as the causes of events: the bridge collapsed because of a structural defect; the plane crashed on takeoff because the air temperature was abnormally high; the plate broke because it had a crack. This reply does not, however, meet a closely related point. Mention of a causal condition for an event gives a cause only on the assumption that there was also a preceding event. But what is the preceding event that causes an action?

In many cases it is not difficult at all to find events very closely associated with the primary reason. States and dispositions are not events, but the onslaught of a state or disposition is. A desire to hurt your feelings may spring up at the moment you anger me; I may start wanting to eat a melon just when I see one; and beliefs may begin at the moment we notice, perceive, learn, or remember something. Those who have argued that there are no mental events to qualify as causes of actions have often missed the obvious because they have insisted that a mental event be observed or noticed (rather than an observing or a noticing) or that it be like a stab, a qualm, a prick or a quiver, a mysterious prod of conscience or act of the will. Melden, in discussing the driver who signals a turn by raising his arm, challenges those who want to explain actions causally to identify "an event which is common and peculiar to all such cases" (87), perhaps a motive or an intention, anyway "some particular feeling or experience" (95). But of course there is a mental event; at some moment the driver noticed (or thought he noticed) his turn coming up, and that is the moment he signaled. During any continuing activity, like driving, or elaborate performance, like swimming the Hellespont, there are more or less fixed purposes, standards, desires, and habits that give direction and form to the entire enterprise, and there is the continuing input of information about what we are doing, about changes in the environment, in terms of which we regulate and adjust our actions. To dignify a driver's awareness that his turn has come by calling it an experience, much less a feeling, is no doubt exaggerated, but whether it deserves a name or not, it had better be the reason why he raises his arm. In this case, and typically, there may not be anything we would call a motive, but if we mention such a general purpose as wanting to get to one's destination safely, it is clear that the motive is not an event. The intention with which the driver raises his arm is also not an event, for it is no thing at all, neither event, attitude, disposition, nor object. Finally, Melden asks the causal theorist to find an event that is common and peculiar to all cases where a man intentionally raises his arm, and this, it must be admitted, cannot be produced. But then neither can a common and unique cause of bridge failures, plane crashes, or plate breakings be produced.

The signaling driver can answer the question 'Why did you raise your arm when you did?,' and from the answer we learn the event that caused the action. But can an actor always answer such a question? Sometimes the answer will mention a mental event that does not give a reason: 'Finally I made up my mind.' However, there also seem to be cases of intentional action where we cannot explain at all why we acted when we did. In such cases, explanation in terms of primary reasons parallels the explanation of the collapse of the bridge from a structural defect: we are ignorant of the event or sequence of events that led up to (caused) the collapse, but we are sure there was such an event or sequence of events.

B. According to Melden, a cause must be "logically distinct from the alleged effect" (52); but a reason for an action is not logically distinct from the action; therefore, reasons are not causes of actions.[6]

One possible form of this argument has already been suggested. Since a reason makes an action intelligible by redescribing it, we do not have two events, but only one under different descriptions. Causal relations, however, demand distinct events.

Someone might be tempted into the mistake of thinking that my flipping of the switch caused my turning on of the light (in fact it caused the light to go on). But it does not follow that it is a mistake to take 'My reason for flipping the switch was that I wanted to turn on the light' as entailing, in part, 'I flipped the switch, and this action is further describable as having been caused by my wanting to turn on the light.' To describe an event in terms of its cause is not to identify the event with its cause, nor does explanation by redescription exclude causal explanation. The example serves also to refute the claim that we cannot describe the action without using words that link it to the alleged cause. Here the action is to be explained under the description: 'my flipping the switch,' and the alleged cause is 'my wanting to turn on the light.' What possible logical relation is supposed to hold between these phrases? It seems more plausible to urge a logical link between 'my turning on the light' and 'my wanting to turn on the light,' but even here the link turned out, on inspection, to be grammatical rather than logical.

In any case there is something very odd in the idea that causal relations are empirical rather than logical. What can this mean? Surely not that every true causal statement is empirical. For suppose '*A* caused *B*' is true. Then the cause of $B = A$; so, substituting, we have 'The cause of *B* caused *B*,' which is analytic. The truth of a causal statement depends on *what* events are described; its status as analytic or synthetic depends on *how* the events are described. Still, it may be maintained that a reason rationalizes an action only when the descriptions are appropriately fixed, and the appropriate descriptions are not logically independent.

Suppose that to say a man wanted to turn on the light *meant* that he would perform any action he believed would accomplish his end. Then the statement of his primary reason for flipping the switch would entail that he flipped the switch—"straightway he acts," as Aristotle says. In this case there would certainly be a logical connection between reason and action, the same sort of connection as that between 'It's water-soluble and was placed in water' and 'It dissolved.' Since the implication runs from description of cause to description of effect but not conversely, naming the cause still gives information. And, though the point is often overlooked, 'Placing it in water caused it to dissolve' does not entail 'It's water-soluble'; so the latter has additional explanatory force. Nevertheless, the explanation would be far more interesting if, in place of solubility, with its obvious definitional connection with the event to be explained, we could refer to some property, say a particular crystalline structure, whose connection with dissolution in water was known only through experiment. Now it is clear why primary reasons like desires and wants do not explain actions in the relatively trivial way solubility explains dissolvings. Solubility, we are assuming, is a pure disposition property: it is defined in terms of a single test. But desires cannot be defined in terms of the actions they may rationalize, even though the relation between desire and action is not simply empirical; there are other, equally essential criteria for desires—their expression in feelings and in actions that they do not rationalize, for example. The person who has a desire (or want or belief) does not normally need criteria at all—he generally knows, even in the absence of any clues available to others, what he wants, desires, and believes. These logical features of primary reasons show that it is not just lack of ingenuity that keeps us from defining them as dispositions to act for these reasons.

C. According to Hume, "we may define a cause to be an object, followed by another, and where all the objects similar to the first are followed by objects similar to the second." But, Hart and Honoré claim, "The statement that one person did something because, for example, another threatened him, carries no implication or covert assertion that if the circumstances were repeated the same action would follow" (52). Hart and Honoré allow that Hume is right in saying that ordinary singular causal statements imply generalizations, but wrong for this very reason in supposing that motives and desires are ordinary causes of actions. In brief, laws are involved essentially in ordinary causal explanations, but not in rationalizations.

It is common to try to meet this argument by suggesting that we do have rough laws connecting reasons and actions, and these can, in theory, be improved. True, threatened people do not always respond in the same way; but we may distinguish between threats and also between agents, in terms of their beliefs and attitudes.

The suggestion is delusive, however, because generalizations connecting reasons and actions are not—and cannot be sharpened into—the kind of law on the basis of which accurate predictions can reliably be made. If we reflect on the way in which reasons determine choice, decision, and behavior, it is easy to see why this is so. What emerges, in the *ex post facto* atmosphere of explanation and justification, as *the* reason frequently was, to the agent at the time of action, one consideration among many, *a* reason. Any serious theory for predicting action on the basis of reasons must find a way of evaluating the relative force of various desires and beliefs in the matrix of decision; it cannot take as its starting point the refinement of what is to be expected from a single desire. The practical syllogism exhausts its role in displaying an action as falling under one reason; so it cannot be subtilized into a reconstruction of practical reasoning, which involves the weighing of competing reasons. The practical syllogism provides a model neither for a predictive science of action nor for a normative account of evaluative reasoning.

Ignorance of competent predictive laws does not inhibit valid causal explanation, or few causal explanations could be made. I am certain the window broke because it was struck by a rock—I saw it all happen; but I am not (is anyone?) in command of laws on the basis of which I can predict what blows will break which windows. A generalization like 'Windows are fragile, and fragile things tend to break when struck hard enough, other conditions being right' is not a predictive law in the rough—the predictive law, if we had it, would be quantitative and would use very different concepts. The generalization, like our generalizations about behavior, serves a different function: it provides evidence for the existence of a causal law covering the case at hand.

We are usually far more certain of a singular causal connection than we are of any causal law governing the case; does this show that Hume was wrong in claiming that singular causal statements entail laws? Not necessarily, for Hume's claim, as quoted above, is ambiguous. It may mean that 'A caused B' entails some particular law involving the predicates used in the descriptions 'A' and 'B,' or it may mean that 'A caused B' entails that there exists a causal law instantiated by some true descriptions of A and B.[7] Obviously, both versions of Hume's doctrine give a sense to the claim that singular causal statements entail laws, and both sustain the view that causal explanations "involve laws." But the second version is far weaker, in that no particular law is entailed by a singular causal claim, and a singular causal claim can be defended, if it needs defense, without defending any law. Only the second version of Hume's doctrine can be made to fit with most

causal explanations; it suits rationalizations equally well.

The most primitive explanation of an event gives its cause; more elaborate explanations may tell more of the story, or defend the singular causal claim by producing a relevant law or by giving reasons for believing such exists. But it is an error to think no explanation has been given until a law has been produced. Linked with these errors is the idea that singular causal statements necessarily indicate, by the concepts they employ, the concepts that will occur in the entailed law. Suppose a hurricane, which is reported on page 5 of Tuesday's *Times*, causes a catastrophe, which is reported on page 13 of Wednesday's *Tribune*. Then the event reported on page 5 of Tuesday's *Times* caused the event reported on page 13 of Wednesday's *Tribune*. Should we look for a law relating events of these *kinds*? It is only slightly less ridiculous to look for a law relating hurricanes and catastrophes. The laws needed to predict the catastrophe with precision would, of course, have no use for concepts like hurricane and catastrophe. The trouble with predicting the weather is that the descriptions under which events interest us—'a cool, cloudy day with rain in the afternoon'—have only remote connections with the concepts employed by the more precise known laws.

The laws whose existence is required if reasons are causes of actions do not, we may be sure, deal in the concepts in which rationalizations must deal. If the causes of a class of events (actions) fall in a certain class (reasons) and there is a law to back each singular causal statement, it does not follow that there is any law connecting events classified as reasons with events classified as actions—the classifications may even be neurological, chemical, or physical.

D. It is said that the kind of knowledge one has of one's own reasons in acting is not compatible with the existence of a causal relation between reasons and actions: a person knows his own intentions in acting infallibly, without induction or observation, and no ordinary causal relation can be known in this way. No doubt our knowledge of our own intentions in acting will show many of the oddities peculiar to first-person knowledge of one's own pains, beliefs, desires, and so on; the only question is whether these oddities prove that reasons do not cause, in any ordinary sense at least, the actions that they rationalize.

You may easily be wrong about the truth of a statement of the form 'I am poisoning Charles because I want to save him pain,' because you may be wrong about whether you are poisoning Charles—you may yourself be drinking the poisoned cup by mistake. But it also seems that you may err about your reasons, particularly when you have two reasons for an action, one of which pleases you and one which does not. For example, you do want to save Charles pain; you also want him out of the way. You may be wrong about which motive made you do it.

The fact that you may be wrong does not show that in general it makes sense to ask you how you know what your reasons were or to ask for your evidence. Though you may, on rare occasions, accept public or private evidence as showing you are wrong about your reasons, you usually have no evidence and make no observations. Then your knowledge of your own reasons for your actions is not generally inductive, for where there is induction, there is evidence. Does this show the knowledge is not causal? I cannot see that it does.

Causal laws differ from true but non-lawlike generalizations in that their instances confirm them; induction is, therefore, certainly a good way to learn the truth of a law. It does not follow that it is the only way to learn the truth of a law. In any case, in order to know that a singular causal statement is true, it is not necessary to know the truth of a law; it is necessary only to know that some law covering the events at hand exists. And it is far from evident that induction, and induction alone, yields the knowledge that a causal law satisfying certain conditions exists. Or, to put it differently, one case is often enough, as Hume admitted, to persuade us that a law exists, and this amounts to saying that we are persuaded, without direct inductive evidence, that a causal relation exists.

E. Finally I should like to say something about a certain uneasiness some philosophers feel in speaking of causes of actions at all. Melden, for example, says that actions are often identical with bodily movements, and that bodily movements have causes; yet he denies that the causes are causes of the actions. This is, I think, a contradiction. He is led to it by the following sort of consideration: "It is futile to attempt to explain conduct through the causal efficacy of desire—all *that* can explain is further happenings, not actions performed by agents. The agent confronting the causal nexus in which such happenings occur is a helpless victim of all that occurs in and to him" (128, 129). Unless I am mistaken, this argument, if it were valid, would show that actions cannot have causes at all. I shall not point out the obvious difficulties in removing actions from the realm of causality entirely.

But perhaps it is worth trying to uncover the source of the trouble. Why on earth should a cause turn an action into a mere happening and a person into a helpless victim? Is it because we tend to assume, at least in the arena of action, that a cause demands a causer, agency an agent? So we press the question; if my action is caused, what caused it? If I did, then there is the absurdity of infinite regress; if I did not, I am a victim. But of course the alternatives are not exhaustive. Some causes have no agents. Primary among these are those states and changes of state in persons which, because they are reasons as well as causes, make persons voluntary agents.

Notes

1. Some examples: G.E.M. Anscombe, *Intention*, Oxford, 1959; Stuart Hampshire, *Thought and Action*, London, 1959; H L.A. Hart and A.M. Honoré, *Causation in the Law*, Oxford, 1959; William Dray, *Laws and Explanation in History*, Oxford, 1957; and most of the books in the series edited by R.F. Holland, *Studies in Philosophical Psychology*, including Anthony Kenny, *Action, Emotion and Will*, London, 1963, and A.I. Melden, *Free Action*, London, 1961. Page references in parentheses will all be to these works.

2. We would not call my unintentional alerting of the prowler an action, but it should not be inferred from this that alerting the prowler is therefore something different from flipping the switch, say just its consequence. Actions, performances, and events not involving intention are alike in that they are often referred to or defined partly in terms of some terminal stage, outcome, or consequence.

    The word 'action' does not very often occur in ordinary speech, and when it does it is usually reserved for fairly portentous occasions. I follow a useful philosophical practice in calling anything an agent does intentionally an action, including intentional suppose 'A' is a description of an action, 'B' is a description of something done voluntarily, though not intentionally, and 'C' is a description of something done involuntarily and unintentionally; finally, suppose A = B = C. Then A, B, and C are the same—what? 'Action,' 'event,' 'thing done,' each have, at least in some contexts, a strange ring when coupled with the wrong sort of description. Only the question "Why did you (he) do A?" has the true generality required. Obviously, the problem is greatly aggravated if we assume, as Melden does (*Free Action*, 85), that an action (raising one's arm) can be identical with a bodily movement ("one's arm going up").

3. "Quasi-intentional" because, besides its intentional aspect, the description of the action must also refer in rationalizations; otherwise it could be true that an action was done for a certain reason and yet the action not have been performed. Compare 'the author of *Waverley*' in 'George IV knew the author of *Waverley* wrote *Waverley*.'

4. Miss Anscombe denies that the practical syllogism is deductive. This she does partly because she thinks of the practical syllogism, as Aristotle does, as corresponding to a piece of practical reasoning (whereas for me it is only part of the analysis of the concept of a reason with which someone acted), and therefore she is bound, again following Aristotle, to think of the conclusion of a practical syllogism as corresponding to a judgment, not merely that the action has a desirable characteristic, but that the action is desirable (reasonable, worth doing, etc.).

5. I say "as the basic move" to cancel the suggestion that C1 and C2 are jointly *sufficient* to define the relation of reasons to the actions they explain. I believe C2 can be strengthened to make C1 and C2 sufficient as well as necessary conditions, but here I am concerned only with the claim that both are, as they stand, necessary.

6. This argument can be found, in one or more versions, in Kenny, Hampshire, and Melden, as well as in P. Winch, *The Idea of a Social Science*, London, 1958, and R.S. Peters, *The Concept of Motivation*, London, 1958. In one of its forms, the argument was of course inspired by Ryle's treatment of motives in *The Concept of Mind*.

7. We could roughly characterize the analysis of singular causal statements hinted at here

as follows: 'A caused B' is true if and only if there are descriptions of A and B such that the sentence obtained by putting these descriptions for 'A' and 'B' in 'A caused B' follows from a true causal law. This analysis is saved from triviality by the fact that not all true generalizations are causal laws; causal laws are distinguished (though of course this is no analysis) by the fact that they are inductively confirmed by their instances and by the fact that they support counterfactual and subjunctive singular causal statements.

HARRY G. FRANKFURT

"The Problem of Action"

I

The problem of action is to explicate the contrast between what an agent does and what merely happens to him, or between the bodily movements that he makes and those that occur without his making them. According to causal theories of the nature of action, which currently represent the most widely followed approach to the understanding of this contrast, the essential difference between events of the two types is to be found in their prior causal histories: a bodily movement is an action if and only if it results from antecedents of a certain kind. Different versions of the causal approach may provide differing accounts of the sorts of events or states which must figure causally in the production of actions. The tenet they characteristically share is that it is both necessary and sufficient, in order to determine whether an event is an action, to consider how it was brought about.

Despite its popularity, I believe that the causal approach is inherently implausible and that it cannot provide a satisfactory analysis of the nature of action. I do not mean to suggest that actions have no causes; they are as likely to have causes, I suppose, as other events are. My claim is rather that it is no part of the nature of an action to have a prior causal history of any particular kind. From the fact that an event is an action, in my view, it does not follow even that it has a cause or causes at all, much less that it has causal antecedents of any specific type.

In asserting that the essential difference between actions and mere happenings lies in their prior causal histories, causal theories imply that actions and mere happenings do not differ essentially in themselves at all. These theories hold that the causal sequences producing actions are necessarily of a different type than those producing mere happenings, but that the effects produced by sequences of the two types are inherently indistinguishable. They are therefore committed to supposing that a person who knows he is in the midst of performing an action cannot have derived this knowledge from any awareness of what is currently happening, but that he must have derived it instead from his understanding of how what is happening was caused to happen by certain earlier conditions. It is integral to the causal approach to regard actions and mere happenings as being differentiated by nothing that exists or that is going on at the time those events occur, but by something quite extrinsic to them—a difference at an earlier time among another set of events entirely.

This is what makes causal theories implausible. They direct attention exclusively away from the events whose natures are at issue, and away from the times at which they occur. The result is that it is beyond their scope to stipulate that a person must be in some particular relation to the movements of his body *during* the period of time in which he is presumed to be performing an action. The only conditions they insist upon as distinctively constitutive of action may cease to obtain, for all the causal accounts demand, at precisely the moment when the agent commences to act. They require nothing of an agent, once the specified causal antecedents of his performing an action have occurred, except that his body move as their effect.

It is no wonder that such theories characteristically run up against counterexamples of a well-known type. For example: a man at a party intends to spill what is in his glass because he wants to signal his confederates to begin a robbery and he believes, in virtue of their prearrangements, that spilling what is in his glass will accomplish that; but all this leads the man to be very anxious, his anxiety makes his hand tremble, and so his glass spills. No matter what kinds of causal antecedents are designated as necessary and sufficient for the occurrence of an action, it is easy to show that causal antecedents of that kind may have as their effect an event that is manifestly not an action but a mere bodily movement. The spilling in the example given has among its causes a desire and a belief, which rationalise the man's spilling what is in his glass, but the spilling as it occurs is not an action. That example makes trouble particularly for a causal theory in which actions are construed as essentially movements whose

causes are desires and beliefs by which they are rationalized. Similar counterexamples can readily be generated to make similar trouble for other variants of the causal approach.

I shall not examine the various maneuvers by means of which causal theorists have attempted to cope with these counterexamples.[1] In my judgment causal theories are unavoidably vulnerable to such counterexamples, because they locate the distinctively essential features of action exclusively in states of affairs which may be past by the time the action is supposed to occur. This makes it impossible for them to give any account whatever of the most salient differentiating characteristic of action: during the time a person is performing an action he is necessarily in touch with the movements of his body in a certain way, whereas he is necessarily not in touch with them in that way when movements of his body are occurring without his making them. A theory that is limited to describing causes prior to the occurrences of actions and of mere bodily movements cannot possibly include an analysis of these two ways in which a person may be related to the movements of his body. It must inevitably leave open the possibility that a person, whatever his involvement in the events from which his action arises, loses all connection with the movements of his body at the moment when his action begins.

II

In order to develop a more promising way of thinking about action, let us consider the notion that actions and mere happenings are indistinguishable in themselves. This notion is an important element in the motivation for causal theories. If it were thought that actions and mere happenings differ inherently, then it would be obvious that the way to explicate how they differ would be by identifying this inherent difference between them. It is because causal theorists think that there is no other way to differentiate between actions and mere happenings that they seek a differentiating difference among the events that precede them.

David Pears, who believes that desires play an essential causal role in the production of actions, makes this explicit:

> We simply do not possess the general ability to distinguish between those bodily movements which are actions and those which are mere bodily movements without using as a criterion the presence or absence of the relevant desire.... It is true that there are various intrinsic characteristics of bodily movements which do give some indication of their classification. For example, a very complicated movement was probably produced by a desire. But...the simplicity of a movement does not even make it probable that it was not produced by a desire.

Because we cannot find any inherent characteristic of action which permits us to distinguish it reliably from mere bodily movement, we must therefore, in Pears' view, "classify some bodily movements as actions solely by virtue of their origins."[2]

Pears observes correctly that the movements of a person's body do not definitively reveal whether he is performing an action: the very same movements may occur when an action is being performed or when a mere happening is occurring. It does not follow from this, however, that the only way to discover whether or not a person is acting is by considering what was going on *before* his movements began—that is, by considering the causes from which they originated. In fact, the state of affairs *while* the movements are occurring is far more pertinent. What is not merely pertinent but decisive, indeed, is to

consider whether or not the movements as they occur are *under the person's guidance*. It is this that determines whether he is performing an action. Moreover, the question of whether or not movements occur under a person's guidance is not a matter of their antecedents. Events are caused to occur by preceding states of affairs, but an event cannot be guided through the course of its occurrence at a temporal distance.

It is worth noticing that Pears is mistaken when he concedes that very complicated movements, though they may possibly be mere happenings, are probably to be classified as actions. The complicated movements of a pianist's hands and fingers do, to be sure, compellingly suggest that they are not mere happenings. Sometimes, however, complexity may quite as compellingly suggest the likelihood of mere bodily movement. The thrashings about of a person's body during an epileptic seizure, for example, are very complicated movements. But their complexity is of a kind which makes it appear unlikely to us that the person is performing an action.

When does complexity of movement suggest action, and when does it suggest its absence? This depends, roughly speaking, upon whether the movements in question cohere in creating a pattern which strikes us as meaningful. When they do, as in the case of the pianist, we find it difficult to imagine that the movements would have occurred, in just those complicated ways required by the meaningful pattern they have created, unless the pianist had been guiding his hands and fingers as they moved. In the epileptic's case, on the other hand, we find it unlikely that a person would have created such an incoherently complicated pattern if he had been guiding his body through its movements. A person's simple movements, as Pears notes, generally suggest neither an action nor a mere happening. This is because their patterns do not ordinarily strike us as being in themselves either meaningful or incoherent. They do not present us on their faces with any indication of whether or not they are being guided by the person as they occur.

Complexity of body movement suggests action only when it leads us to think that the body, during the course of its movement, is under the agent's guidance. The performance of an action is accordingly a complex event, which is comprised by a bodily movement and by whatever state of affairs or activity constitutes the agent's guidance of it. Given a bodily movement which occurs under a person's guidance, the person is performing an action regardless of what features of his prior causal history account for the fact that this is occurring. He is performing an action even if its occurrence is due to chance. And he is not performing an action if the movements are not under his guidance as they proceed, even if he himself provided the antecedent causes—in the form of beliefs, desires, intentions, decisions, volitions, or whatever—from which the movement has resulted.

III

When we act, our movements are purposive. This is merely another way of saying that their course is guided. Many instances of purposive movement are not, of course, instances of action. The dilation of the pupils of a person's eyes when the light fades, for example, is a purposive movement; there are mechanisms which guide its course. But the occurrence of this movement does not mark the performance of an action by the person; his pupils dilate, but he does not dilate them. This is because the course of the movement is not under *his* guidance. The guidance in this case is attributable only to the operation of some mechanism with which he cannot be identified.

Let us employ the term "intentional" for referring to instances of purposive movement

in which the guidance is provided by the agent. We may say, then, that action is intentional movement. The notion of intentional movement must not be confused with that of intentional action. The term "intentional action" may be used, or rather mis-used, simply to convey that an action is necessarily a movement whose course is under an agent's guidance. When it is used in this way, the term is pleonastic. In a more appropriate usage, it refers to actions which are undertaken more or less deliberately or self-consciously—that is, to actions which the agent intends to perform. In this sense, actions are not necessarily intentional.

When a person intends to perform an action, what he intends is that certain intentional movements of his body should occur. When these movements do occur, the person is performing an intentional action. It might be said that he is then guiding the movements of his body in a certain way (thus, he is acting), and that in doing so he is guided by and fulfilling his intention to do just that (thus, he is acting intentionally). There appears to be nothing in the notion of an intentional movement which implies that its occurrence must be intended by the agent, either by way of forethought or by way of self-conscious assent. If this is correct, then actions (i.e., intentional movements) may be performed either intentionally or not.

Since action is intentional movement, or behavior whose course is under the guidance of an agent, an explication of the nature of action must deal with two distinct problems. One is to explain the notion of guided behavior. The other is to specify when the guidance of behavior is attributable to an agent and not simply, as when a person's pupils dilate because the light fades, to some local process going on within the agent's body. The first problem concerns the conditions under which behavior is purposive, while the second concerns the conditions under which purposive behavior is intentional.

The driver of an automobile guides the movement of his vehicle by acting: he turns the steering wheel, he depresses the accelerator, he applies the brakes, and so on. Our guidance of our movements, while we are acting, does not similarly require that we perform various actions. We are not at the controls of our bodies in the way a driver is at the controls of his automobile. Otherwise action could not be conceived, upon pain of generating an infinite regress, as a matter of the occurrence of movements which are under an agent's guidance. The fact that our movements when we are acting are purposive is not the effect of something we do. It is a characteristic of the operation at that time of the systems we are.

Behavior is purposive when its course is subject to adjustments which compensate for the effects of forces which would otherwise interfere with the course of the behavior, and when the occurrence of these adjustments is not explainable by what explains the state of affairs that elicits them. The behavior is in that case under the guidance of an independent causal mechanism, whose readiness to bring about compensatory adjustments tends to ensure that the behavior is accomplished.[3] The activity of such a mechanism is normally not, of course, guided by us. Rather it is, when we are performing an action, our guidance of our behavior. Our sense of our own agency when we act is nothing more than the way it feels to us when we are somehow in touch with the operation of mechanisms of this kind, by which our movements are guided and their course guaranteed.

Explaining purposive behavior in terms of causal mechanisms is not tantamount to propounding a causal theory of action. For one thing, the pertinent activity of these mechanisms is not prior to but concurrent with the movements they guide. But in any case it is not essential to the purposiveness of a movement that it actually be causally affected by the mechanism under whose guidance the movement proceeds. A driver whose automobile is coasting downhill in virtue of gravitational forces alone may be entirely satisfied with its speed and direction, and so he may never intervene to adjust its movement in any way. This would not show that the movement of the automobile did not occur under his guidance. What counts is that he was prepared to intervene if necessary, and that he was in a position to do so more or less effectively. Similarly, the causal mechanisms which stand ready to affect the course of a bodily movement may never have occasion to do so; for no negative feedback of the sort that would trigger their compensatory activity may occur. The behavior is purposive not because it results from causes of a certain kind, but because it would be affected by certain causes if the accomplishment of its course were to be jeopardised.

IV

Since the fact that certain causes originate an action is distinct from the considerations in virtue of which it is an action, there is no reason in principle why a person may not be caused in a variety of different ways to perform the same action. This is important in the analysis of freedom. It is widely accepted that a person acts freely only if he could have acted otherwise. Apparent counterexamples to this principle—"the principle of alternate possibilities"—are provided, however, by cases that involve a certain kind of overdetermination. In these cases a person performs an action entirely for his own reasons, which inclines us to regard him as having performed it freely; but he would otherwise have been caused to perform it by forces alien to his will, so that he cannot actually avoid acting as he does.[4]

Thus, suppose a man takes heroin because he enjoys its effects and considers them to be beneficial. But suppose further that he is unknowingly addicted to the drug, and hence that he will be driven to take it in any event, even if he is not led to do so by his own beliefs and attitudes. Then it seems that he takes the drug freely, that he could not have done otherwise than to take it, and that the principle of alternate possibilities is therefore false.

Donald Davidson argues to the contrary that whereas a person does intentionally what he does for his own reasons, he does not do intentionally what alien forces cause him to do. While the movements of his body may be the same in both cases, Davidson maintains that the person is not performing an action when the movements occur apart from pertinent attitudes and beliefs. Someone who has acted freely might have done the same thing even if he had not been moved on his own to do it, but only in the sense that his body might have made the same movements: "he would not have acted intentionally had the attitudinal conditions been absent." Even in the "overdetermined" cases, then, something rests with the agent: "not...what he does (when described in a way that leaves open whether it was intentional), but whether he does it intentionally."[5]

The issue here is not, as Davidson suggests at one point, whether a person's *action* can be intentional when alien forces rather than his own attitudes account for what he does. It is whether his *behavior* can be intentional in those circumstances. Now the behavior of the unknowing addict is plainly as intentional when he is caused to take the drug by the compulsive force of his addiction, as it is when he takes it as a matter of free choice. His movements are not mere happenings, when he takes the drug because he cannot help himself. He is then performing the very same action that he would have performed had he taken the drug freely and with the illusion that he might have done otherwise.

This example is not designed to show that Davidson is mistaken in insisting that there can be no action without intentionality, or in the absence of pertinent attitudinal conditions. Even when the addict is driven to do what he does, after all, his behavior is presumably affected both by his craving for the drug and by his belief that the procedure he follows in taking it will bring him relief. His movements, as he sticks the syringe into his arm and pushes the plunger, are certainly intentional. However, the relevant problem is not whether an action can occur apart from attitudinal conditions. It is whether it is possible that an action should be caused by alien forces alone.

This will seem to be impossible only if it is thought that an action must have attitudinal conditions among its causes. But it is not essential to an action that it have an antecedent causal history of any particular kind. Even if there can be no action in the absence of certain attitudinal conditions, therefore, it is not as prior causes that these conditions are essential. The example bears upon the point that is actually at issue, by illustrating how an action (including, of course, any requisite attitudinal constituents) may have no causes other than nonattitudinal or alien ones. Thus it confirms the falsity of the principle of alternate possibilities, by showing that a person may be caused by alien forces alone to perform an action which he might also perform on his own.

The example also suggests, by the way, that the attitudinal conditions of a person's action may themselves be alien to him. There is no reason to assume that an addict who succumbs unwillingly to his craving finally adopts as his own the desire he has tried to resist. He may in the end merely submit to it with resignation, like a man who knows he is beaten and who therefore despairingly accepts the consequences defeat must bring him, rather than like someone who decides to join with or to incorporate forces which he had formerly opposed. There are also obsessional and delusional beliefs—e.g., "If I step on a crack it will break my mother's back"—which a person may know to be false but whose influence he cannot escape. So even if it were true (which it is not) that every action necessarily has attitudinal conditions among its antecedent causes, it might nonetheless be alien forces alone which bring it about that a person performs an action.

The assertion that someone has performed an action entails that his movements occurred under his guidance, but not that he was able to keep himself from guiding his movements as he did. There are occasions when we act against or independently of our wills. On other occasions, the guiding principle of our movements is one to which we are not merely resigned; rather we have embraced it as our own. In such cases, we will ordinarily have a reason for embracing it. Perhaps, as certain philosophers would claim, our having a reason for acting may sometimes cause it to be the case that movements of our bodies are guided by us in a manner which reflects that reason. It is indisputable that a person's beliefs and attitudes often have an important bearing upon how what he is doing is to be interpreted and understood; and it may be that they also figure at times in the causal explanations of his actions. The facts that we are rational and self-conscious substantially affect the character of our behavior and the ways in which our actions are integrated into our lives.

V

The significance to *our* actions of states and events which depend upon the exercise of our higher capacities should not lead us, however, to exaggerate the peculiarity of what human beings do. We are far from being unique either in the purposiveness of our behavior or in its intentionality. There is a tendency among philosophers to discuss the nature of action as though agency presupposes characteristics which cannot plausibly be attributed to members of species other than our own. But in fact the contrast between actions and mere happenings can readily be discerned elsewhere than in the lives of people. There are numerous agents besides ourselves, who may be active as well as passive with respect to the movements of their bodies.

Consider the difference between what goes on when a spider moves its legs in making its way along the ground, and what goes on when its legs move in similar patterns and with similar effect because they are manipulated by a boy who has managed to tie strings to them. In the first case the movements are not simply purposive, as the spider's digestive processes doubtless are. They are also attributable to the spider, who makes them. In the second case the same movements occur but they are not made by the spider, to whom they merely happen.

This contrast between two sorts of events in the lives of spiders, which can be observed in the histories of creatures even more benighted, parallels the more familiar contrast between the sort of event that occurs when a person raises his arm and the sort that occurs when his arm goes up without his raising it. Indeed, the two contrasts are the same. The differences they respectively distinguish are alike; and they have, as it were, the same point. Each contrasts instances in which purposive behavior is attributable to a creature as agent and instances in which this is not the case.

This generic contrast cannot be explicated in terms of any of the distinctive higher faculties which characteristically come into play when a person acts. The conditions for attributing the guidance of bodily movements to a whole creature, rather than only to some local mechanism within a creature, evidently obtain outside of human life. Hence they cannot be satisfactorily understood by relying upon concepts which are inapplicable to spiders and their ilk. This does not mean that it must be illegitimate for an analysis of human agency to invoke concepts of more limited scope. While the general conditions of agency are unclear, it may well be that the satisfaction of these conditions by human beings depends upon the occurrence of events or states which do not occur in the histories of other creatures. But we must be careful that the ways in which we construe agency and define its nature do not conceal a parochial bias, which causes us to neglect the extent to which the concept of human action is no more than a special case of another concept whose range is much wider.

Notes

1. For discussion of the problem by adherents to the causal approach, cf. Alvin Goldman, *A Theory of Human Action* (Princeton, 1970), pp. 61–63; Donald Davidson, "Freedom to Act," in T. Honderich (ed.), *Essays on Freedom of Action* (London, 1973), pp. 153–54; Richard Foley, "Deliberate Action," *The Philosophical Review*, vol. 86 (1977), pp. 58–69. Goldman and Davidson evidently believe that the problem of avoiding the counterexamples is an empirical one, which is appropriately to be passed on to scientists. Foley's "solution" renounces the obligation to provide suitable analysis in another way: he specifies conditions for acting and, when he recognises that they may be met by spasms and twitches, he simply declares that such movements are nonetheless actions if they satisfy his conditions.

2. David Pears, "Two Problems about Reasons for Actions," in R. Binkley, R. Bronaugh, A. Marras (eds.), *Agent, Action and Reason* (Oxford, 1971), pp. 136–37, 139.

3. A useful discussion of this way of understanding purposive behavior is provided by Ernest Nagel, "Goal-Directed Processes in Biology," *The Journal of Philosophy*, vol. 74 (1977), pp. 271ff. The details of the mechanisms in virtue of which some item of behavior is purposive can be discovered, of course, only by empirical investigation. But specifying the conditions which any such mechanism must meet is a philosophical problem, belonging to the analysis of the notion of purposive behavior.

4. Cf. my "Alternate Possibilities and Moral Responsibilities," *The Journal of Philosophy*, vol. 66 (1969), pp. 829–39; and "Freedom of the Will and the Concept of a Person," *The Journal of Philosophy*, vol. 68 (1971), pp. 5–20.

5. Op. cit.; pp. 149–50.

ÉLISABETH PACHERIE

"Can Conscious Agency Be Saved?"

Abstract

This paper is concerned with the role of conscious agency in human action. On a folk-psychological view of the structure of agency, intentions, conceived as conscious mental states, are the causes of actions. In the last decades, the development of new psychological and neuroscientific methods has made conscious agency an object of empirical investigation and yielded results that challenge the received wisdom. Most famously, the results of Libet's studies on the 'readiness potential' have been interpreted by many as evidence in favor of a skeptical attitude towards conscious agency. It is questionable, however, whether action initiation should be regarded as the touchstone of conscious agency. I shall argue that the traditional folk-psychological view, but also some of the objections leveled against it, rest in part on an over-simplified conception of the structure of agency, that neglects both the role of control processes after action initiation and the role of planning processes before action initiation. Taking these processes into account can lead to a reassessment of the relation between intentions and action and of the role of conscious agency in action production.

1. Introduction

Libet's studies on the timing of conscious intentions have been hailed in some quarters as one of the most important psychological experiments ever. Libet's results have been claimed to undermine folk-psychological conceptions and traditional philosophical views of free will, of the role of conscious agency in human behavior and of conscious mental causation more generally. In response to these attacks, a number of philosophers have countered that these skeptical claims, at least in their more radical forms, are largely overblown, being both ill supported by the empirical data and premised on dubious metaphysical assumptions regarding the nature of free will and the nature of the relation between the mental and the physical.

Thirty years after its inception, the lively debate started by Libet's studies still hasn't lost steam. On the one hand, additional empirical findings have further highlighted the role of unconscious processes in action production and thus tended to further fuel what Bayne and Levy (2006) aptly termed 'will-skepticism.' On the other hand, both philosophers and cognitive scientists have contributed to the development of more sophisticated models of the structure of human agency, emphasizing both the hierarchical nature of intentions and action representations and the crucial importance of control and monitoring processes in action production.

In this paper, I shall concentrate on the role of conscious agency in action production. I shall argue that taking into account the hierarchical nature of intentions and control processes can lead to a reassessment of the relation between intentions and action and of the role of conscious agency in action production. Apart from a brief discussion in the next section of why Libet thought his results should undermine beliefs in free will and why others have resisted this conclusion, I will set aside issues regarding free will. Importantly, I will also keep away from issues in the metaphysics of consciousness. If we accept Chalmers' distinction between easy and hard problems of consciousness, the problem I am concerned with falls squarely on the easy side of the divide. As Chalmers (1995) explains, the easy problems of consciousness are easy because they concern the explanation of cognitive abilities and functions, explanations that can be given by specifying a mechanism that can perform the function, a task to which the methods of cognitive science are well suited.

In my view, the specific challenge posed by Libet's results and other recent empirical results is not, as is often assumed, a metaphysical challenge. Rather, these results seem to cast doubt on traditional functional characterizations of conscious intentions by providing evidence that the roles these accounts assign to conscious intentions can be fulfilled by unconscious states and processes. The risk then is not so much that conscious intentions be cast aside as being metaphysically untenable but as being useless. Some have tried to save conscious intentions from functional obsolescence by arguing that their primary function is not pragmatic but epistemic (i.e., that their role is to contribute to self-awareness rather than to action production).[1] While I certainly agree that conscious intentions can serve epistemic functions, I don't think we should give up on intentions' pragmatic functions too easily. But to see conscious agency in action, one should look for it in the right places and these are not always the most obvious ones or those most brightly lit up by the lampposts of either philosophy or empirical research. In search of a function for conscious intentions, philosophers and cognitive scientists have largely concentrated on action initiation. If, as causal theories of actions have claimed, the role of intentions is to cause action, it was indeed not unreasonable

to expect this to be where conscious intentions are at work. These expectations seem to have met with disappointment. What I propose to do here is to look at what happens both before action initiation and after action initiation.

I will start in Sect. 2 with a brief review of Libet's experiments, the ways in which their results have been interpreted and the debates these interpretations have provoked. In Sect. 3, I shall concentrate on what happens after action initiation. I will discuss Frankfurt's early critique of the standard causal theory of action and his proposal that the essential function of intentions is not so much action initiation as action guidance. I will also consider how empirical work on motor control and the forms it can take can help us both flesh out this proposal and assess more precisely the respective roles of automatic and conscious processes of action control and their complement. In Sect. 4, I will be concerned with what happens before action initiation, when prospective intentions are formed and advance planning intervenes in order to flesh out these prospective intentions to the point where they can eventuate into corresponding actions. In particular, I will distinguish two main ways in which advance planning can proceed. I will also discuss the implications these different modes of action planning can have for the role of conscious intentions at the moment of action initiation.

2. Action Initiation

In Libet's famous studies on the 'readiness potential' (Libet *et al.* 1983; Libet 1985), subjects were asked to flex their wrist at will and to note when they felt the urge to move by observing the position of a dot on a special clock. While subjects were both acting and monitoring their urges (intentions, decisions) to act, Libet used an EEG to record the activity of prefrontal motor areas. On average, participants reported the conscious intention to act, what Libet called the W-judgement, about 200 ms before the onset of muscle activity. By contrast, the EEG revealed that preparatory brain activity, termed by Libet type II readiness potential (RP), preceded action onset by about 550 ms. In other words, their brain started preparing the action at least 350 ms before the participants became aware of the intention to act.

Libet and others have claimed that these results provide evidence in favor of a skeptical attitude towards freely willed actions. While Libet himself fell short of endorsing full-blown will-skepticism and suggested that in the interval separating the agent's conscious decision from the onset of the action a kind of free will could still intervene in the form of conscious veto of the unconsciously initiated action, many have been more radical and have taken his work as a death blow to free will.[2]

It is far from obvious, however, why the fact, if it is one, that conscious intentions are reliably preceded by unconscious brain activity in the form of a readiness potential should lead us to conclude that our actions are not freely willed. It seems that one or several further premises are needed to reach this conclusion. One of the main lines of objection to the will-skeptic interpretations of Libet's results concern the conception(s) of free will these interpretations must work with. Libet and others sometimes make it sound as though the fact that the volitional process is initiated by unconscious brain activity is enough to undermine free will. This suggests a conception of free will requiring that the conscious decision or intention to act be the ultimate cause of the action, that is, a cause that is itself uncaused. However, as several critiques have pointed out (Bayne 2011; Mele 2007), the notion of an uncaused cause is, to put it euphemistically, hard to square with a naturalistic stance. Only hardcore mind–body dualists would contend

that conscious intentions do not arise as a result of brain activity.

It can also be argued that what makes Libet's data a threat to free willed action is not the mere fact that unconscious brain activity contributes to the arising of conscious intentions, but the fact that these conscious intentions are fully determined by this unconscious brain activity. Here the argument would rest on a conception of free will according to which free will is incompatible with determinism. However, incompatibilism isn't the only option. Indeed, the majority of contemporary philosophers are compatibilists,[3] that is, they believe that even if determinism were true, we would still be able to act freely.

Another route to will-skepticism involves interpreting Libet's data as showing that the RP is causing two independent effects: on the one hand it causes the action itself; on the other it causes the conscious experience of intending. On this reading, the conscious intention isn't an intermediary step in the causal path leading from unconscious brain activity to action but is actually part of a different causal path. On this interpretation of Libet's data, conscious intentions do not causally contribute to action initiation and in thinking that they do, we fall prey to an illusion.[4] This route to will-skepticism is metaphysically less loaded than the previous ones, since it does not require one to subscribe to substance dualism, to accept the truth of determinism or to take an incompatibilist stance on free will. It simply takes conscious intentions to be epiphenomenal with respect to action initiation, because they lie on a different causal pathway.[5] However, one may wonder what warrants this interpretation of Libet's data. These data simply give us a time line with unconscious brain activity (RP) coming first, then conscious intentions (W) and finally action onset (A). This time line is equally compatible with two causal stories, one on which unconscious brain activity causes conscious intentions that in turn more proximally cause action onset and the other on which unconscious brain activity causes both conscious intentions and action initiation as independent effects. To follow this route to will skepticism, we would need evidence that the second story is the correct one, but Libet's data themselves simply do not provide this evidence.

However, what many philosophers have taken to be the central worry raised by Libet's data is that if consciousness lags behind-decision making, then our deliberative activity is merely epiphenomenal. If we take the exercise of deliberation to be the hallmark of freely willed actions, the worry raised by Libet's data is that the conscious decision to act is arrived at through unconscious brain processes rather than through conscious deliberative processes. How serious this threat is depends, first, on how robust Libet's data are and, second, on whether the processes he studies and the time-window he focuses on are the only relevant ones.

One group of objections raised against Libet's experiments have questioned the empirical validity of their results. Do his data really show that the actions he studied were initiated not by conscious decisions but by the RP instead? Some of these objections have targeted the methodology of the experiment (see, e.g., the commentaries on Libet 1985). One line of objection emphasizes potential inaccuracies and biases in the measurement of the onset of conscious experience and of the onset of movement (Glynn 1990; Gomes 1998, 1999; Joordens et al. 2002; Miller et al. 2010; van de Grind 2002). For instance, in a recent study, Miller et al. (2011) found that clock monitoring had an effect on electroencephalographic activity. The participants' task was to make spontaneous key-press movements and in one condition they also had to report the position of the dot on a clock when they decided to move. Average EEG

activity preceding key presses was substantially different when participants had to monitor the clock than when they did not. The authors suggest that the effects of clock monitoring on EEG activity could be responsible for Libet's findings that movement-related brain activity begins before participants have consciously decided to move.

Another important line of objection, raised for instance by Mele (2009) and Roskies (2011), points to a fundamental limitation of the back-averaging techniques used to extract signals from EEG recordings. Because EEG recordings are typically noisy, to extract signals from noise, one has to average the data collected on a large number of trials. In order to compute this average, the EEG recordings on different trials need to be aligned, and this requires some fixed point that can be identified across trials. In Libet's experiment, to extract the RP data, EEG recordings had to be aligned using the onset of muscular activity as a fixed point. As a result, RPs that are not followed by an action would not be measured. This means that we don't know whether the correlation between the RP and Libet-actions is sufficiently robust to make it plausible that the RP is what initiates the action.[6]

In a recent experiment, Schurger et al. (2012) used a modified Libet task to circumvent the limitations due to back-averaging techniques. Their aim was to test the proposal that RPs correlate with predecision activity rather than, as Libet proposed, with activity that coincides with, or is subsequent to, the agent's decision. Schurger et al. proceeded on the assumption that the decisions of the participants in Libet's experiment can be modelled—as neural decision tasks typically are—in terms of an accumulator-plus-threshold mechanism: decisions are made when relevant evidence accumulated over time reaches a certain threshold. What is unique to Libet's task is that subjects are explicitly instructed not to base their decision on any specific evidence. Schurger *et al.* propose that the motor system constantly undergoes random fluctuations of RPs and that this random premotor activity is used as a substitute for actual evidence. According to their stochastic decision model, the decision process, given Libet's instructions, amounts to simply shifting premotor activation up closer to the threshold for initiation of the movement and waiting for a random threshold-crossing fluctuation in RP. Time-locking to movement onset ensures that these fluctuations appear in the average as a gradual increase of neuronal activity, when in fact what is measured are simply random fluctuations of RPs that happened to cross a decision threshold.

Thus Schurger *et al.* predict the same premotor activation buildup that Libet does when a movement is produced. However, whereas on Libet's postdecision interpretation of this buildup there should be no premotor activity (and hence no RPs) when no movement is produced, on their predecision interpretation there should be continuous random fluctuations in RPs even when no movement is produced. Schurger *et al.* reasoned that it should be possible to capture these fluctuations by interrupting subjects in a Libet task with a compulsory response cue and sorting trials by their reaction times. On the assumption that the interrupted responses arise from the same decision accumulator as the self-initiated ones, response times should be shorter in trials in which the spontaneous fluctuations of RPs happened to be already close to threshold at the time of the interruption. On the assumption that close to threshold activity reflects spontaneous fluctuations of RPs rather than mounting preparation to move building over the course of the entire trial, slow and fast reaction times should be distributed equally across time within trials. To test these predictions, they therefore devised what they called a *Libetus Interruptus* task,

where they added random interruptions to trials. They found, as they had predicted, that slow and fast responses to interruptions were distributed equally throughout the time span of the trial.

According to the predecision model, Libet's contention that the neural decision to move happens much before we are aware of an intention or urge to move is unfounded. The neural decision to move isn't made when a RP starts building up, since spontaneous fluctuations of RPs happen all the time, but when a random fluctuation in RP crosses a threshold. The reason we do not experience the urge to move earlier is simply that the decision threshold has not yet been crossed and thus the decision has not yet been made. While Schurger *et al.* take no stand on the exact temporal relation between the conscious urge to move and the neural decision to move, their results cast serious doubt on Libet's claim that the neural decision to move coincides with the onset of the RP and thus on his further claim that since RP onset precedes the urge to move by 350 ms or more, conscious intentions play no role in the initiation of the movement. If instead the neural decision to move coincides with a much later threshold-crossing event, it remains at least an open possibility that this event coincides with and constitutes the neural basis of a conscious urge to move. In any case, Schurger *et al.* also insist that this threshold-crossing event should not be interpreted as the cause of the movement but rather as simply one of the many factors involved in the causation of self-initiated movements.

These considerations have given heart to philosophers hoping to preserve a role for conscious intentions in the initiation of action. They suggest that the correlations between RPs and actions are not robust enough to warrant the claim that the apparition of a RP 550 ms before action onset corresponds to the brain decision to initiate an action. According to

Mele (2007), it might be more credible to associate RPs with desires, wants, wishes or urges than with intentions or decisions. This would leave it open that at -550 ms, the person instead acquires an unconscious urge or desire and that what happens at -200 ms is that the person becomes conscious of this desire or urge. If so, no one should be surprised to find that desires or urges precede conscious intentions. In addition, finding that we have such desires does not commit us to acting upon them. For all Libet has shown, it might still be that a further conscious decision is necessary for action initiation.[7]

[...]

3. Action Control

The objections reviewed in the previous section suggest that neither Libet's data nor more recent empirical results from psychology and neuroscience provide incontrovertible evidence that conscious intentions play no role in the initiation of action. But even if they did, would we thereby be forced to conclude that conscious agency is an illusion? The temptation to think this conclusion inevitable depends on our taking action initiation to be the touchstone of conscious agency. While this assumption appears widespread among both scientists and philosophers, should we really accept it?

The idea that action initiation is the touchstone of agency certainly seemed to play a central role in early versions of the causal theory of action. The causal theory of action, first made popular by Davidson (1980, Essay 1) and Goldman (1970), holds that behavior qualifies as action just in case it has psychological antecedents of a certain kind. While different philosophers offered different accounts of what these psychological antecedents must be, disagreeing among other things on whether intentions are

reducible to belief and desire complexes, they all agreed that the role of these psychological antecedents is to cause the ensuing action. In an early and powerful critique of these causal theories, Frankfurt (1978) claimed that their main flaw was to direct attention away from the actions themselves and away from the time at which they occur. As a result, Frankfurt argued, causal theories fail to acknowledge that: "a person must be in some particular relation to the movements of his body *during* the period of time in which he is presumed to be performing an action" (1978: 157).

Frankfurt characterized this relation as one of guidance and pointed out that while guidance must appeal to causal mechanisms, a guidance theory of action differs in two crucial ways from a causal theory of action.[8] First, the activity of these causal mechanisms is not prior to but concurrent with the movements they guide. Second, and perhaps even more importantly, it is not essential to the purposefulness of these movements that the mechanism under whose guidance they proceed causally affect them. Frankfurt illustrates his point with the following analogy:

A driver whose automobile is coasting downhill in virtue of gravitational forces alone may be entirely satisfied with its speed and direction, and so he may never intervene to adjust its movement in any way. This would not show that the movement of the automobile did not occur under his guidance. What counts is that he was prepared to intervene if necessary and that he was in a position to do so more or less effectively. Similarly, the causal mechanisms which stand ready to affect the course of a bodily movement may never have occasion to do so; for no negative feedback of the sort that would trigger their compensatory activity may occur. The behavior is purposive not because it results from causes of a certain kind, but because it could be affected by certain causes if the accomplishment of its course were to be jeopardized. (1978: 160)

The central role assigned by Frankfurt to guidance mechanisms in the characterization of agency finds a strong echo in the literature on motor cognition with its emphasis on monitoring and control mechanisms.[9] According to the very influential internal model theory of motor control, motor control strategies are based on the coupling of two types of internal models: inverse models and forward models (Frith *et al.* 2000; Jordan and Wolpert 1999; Wolpert 1997; Wolpert and Ghahramani 2000; Wolpert *et al.* 1995). Inverse models compute the motor commands needed for achieving a desired state given the current state of the system and of the environment. An efference copy of these commands is fed to forward models, whose role is to make predictions about the consequences of the execution of these commands. The control of action is thought to depend on the coupling of inverse and forward models through a series of comparators: error signals arising from the comparison of desired, predicted, and actual states (monitoring) are used for various kinds of regulation (control). In particular, they can be used to correct and adjust the ongoing action in the face of perturbations, as well as to update both inverse and forward models to improve their future functioning.

While both Frankfurt's critique of causal theories and recent work in motor cognition stress the crucial role of action control and not just action initiation in agency, one may still wonder what this has to do with conscious agency. After all, it seems that action control could well proceed independently of conscious awareness. The real issue, however, isn't whether some or much of action control can operate automatically and outside of conscious awareness, but whether action control always takes this form. While the internal model theory of motor control was initially introduced to account for fine-grained aspects of motor control (such as joint angles, torque, limb positions and trajectories), more recent versions of the theory emphasize the hierarchical nature of motor control (Jeannerod 1997; Fletcher and Frith 2009). They propose that internal inverse and forward models are arranged in a hierarchy and that error signals generated at one level of the hierarchy can propagate to the next level when correction mechanisms at this level are not able to make the necessary compensations. As a first approximation, one can distinguish three main levels in this action specification and control hierarchy (Pacherie 2008). At the highest level, action representations represent the whole action as a unit, in terms of its overarching goal and of the sequence of steps or subgoals needed to achieve that goal. At this level, the action may still be represented in a rather abstract format. The second level is concerned with the implementation of each step in the action plan and involves selecting an appropriate motor program given the immediate goal and contextual information about the current state of the agent and the current state of its environment. In other words, processes at this level are in charge of anchoring the successive steps of the action plan in the current situation and of selecting appropriate motor programs. Finally, once a motor program has been selected, the exact values of its parameters must still be set. This is done at the third level, where incoming sensory information about external constraints is used to specify these values.

This distinction of three levels is an oversimplification and should be qualified in several ways. First, the organization within each level can itself be decomposed into hierarchical stages. Second, the distinction between levels is not always sharp. In particular, a given action may be planned to a greater or a lesser extent, depending on the agent's expertise. Third, talk of a hierarchical organization and of a series of levels may give the impression that the processing steps must be ordered serially; that planning must be over before programming starts, and that programming in turn must be over before the execution starts.

As Jeannerod (1997) points out, however, activation in the cortical areas thought to correspond to the various levels of organization occurs simultaneously and the existence of a sequence can only be detected statistically. Yet, the existence of parallel processing in the motor system does not contradict the idea of hierarchy of levels. A hierarchy between levels implies degrees of specialization for each level but it does not imply a sequential order of activation. Acknowledging the existence of different levels of action control may allow us to accommodate both unconscious and conscious action control processes. Indeed, direct evidence for this duality of control processes comes from a set of experiments (Fourneret and Jeannerod 1998; Fourneret *et al.* 2001, 2002) in which participants were instructed to move a stylus on a graphic tablet along a straight line to a visual target. Participants could not see their drawing hand, but its trajectory was visible as a line on a computer screen. On some trials, the experimenter introduced a directional bias electronically so that the visible trajectory no longer corresponded to that of the hand. When the bias was small (<7°) participants made automatic adjustments of their hand movements to reach the target but remained unaware that they were making these corrections. It is only with larger biases that participants became aware of a discrepancy and began to use conscious correction strategies to compensate for the bias and reach the target. For instance, in

trials with a 15° perturbation to the right, participants explicitly reported a strategy of moving their hand to the left so as to be able to join the starting point and the target with a straight line. These results suggest that although small discrepancies between predicted and actual sensory feedback are detected at some level since they are used to make appropriate corrections of the hand movement, they are not normally consciously monitored and the corrections are automatic. However, when discrepancies become too large to be automatically compensated, we become aware of them and shift to a conscious compensation strategy.

Thus far, I have suggested in this section that we should heed Frankfurt's insight and take agency to have more to do with the guidance and control than with the initiation of movement. Importantly, and following Frankfurt again, it is not essential for movements to be controlled that control mechanisms actually affect their course, but that these control mechanisms would intervene to adjust the movements if the need arose. In addition, there is evidence that action control operates at several levels in parallel and that while low-level motor control may be automatic and unconscious, control at higher-level may be conscious. In other words, an action may be consciously controlled even though unconscious rather than conscious control mechanisms intervene to adjust movements, provided conscious control mechanisms would have kicked in, had automatic movement corrections proved insufficient.

[…]

4. Advance Action Planning

At the end of Sect. 2, I suggested that even if we had overwhelming evidence that actions are initiated unconsciously, we should look at what happens both before and after action initiation before concluding that conscious agency is an illusion. In Sect. 3, I discussed the role conscious agency could play in the control of action after its initiation. I now turn to what happens before action initiation and to the role of prospective intentions.

Bratman's theory of human planning agency (Bratman 1987) probably offers the most detailed and influential philosophical account of prospective intentions, or as he calls them, future-directed intentions. I start with a brief review of his account of prospective intentions, of what functions they serve and what makes it useful to have them. I then turn to the issue what kind of cognitive processes are engaged in advance planning and how these relate to the processes involved in immediate intentions.

We are, in Bratman's words, planning agents regularly making more or less complex plans for the future and guiding our later conduct by these plans. This planning ability appears to be if not unique to humans at least uniquely developed in the human species. People can, and frequently do, form intentions concerning actions not just in the near but also in the distant future (e.g., to take a 6-month trip to Asia after retirement). Why should we bother forming today an intention to do something tomorrow, or next week or 10 years from now? What purposes can forming prospective intentions serve? What benefits does it bring us?

Bratman offers two complementary answers to that challenge. The first stems from the fact that we are epistemically limited creatures: our cognitive resources for use in attending to problems, gathering information, deliberating about options and determining likely consequences are limited and these processes are time consuming.

As a result, if our actions were influenced by deliberation only at the time of action, this influence would be minimal as time pressure isn't conducive to careful deliberation. Forming prospective intentions makes advance planning possible, freeing us from that time pressure and allowing us to deploy the cognitive resources needed for successful deliberation. Second, intentions once formed commit us to future courses of action, thus making the future more predictable and making it possible for agents to coordinate their activities over time and to coordinate them with the activities of other agents. Making deliberation and coordination possible are thus the two main benefits that accrue from a capacity to form prospective intentions.

What makes it possible for prospective intentions to yield these benefits is, according to Bratman, the fact that intentions essentially involve commitments to action. Bratman distinguishes two dimensions of commitments: a volitional dimension and a reasoning-centered dimension. The volitional dimension concerns the relation of intention to action and can be characterized by saying that intentions are "conduct-controlling pro-attitudes" (1987: 16). In other words, unless something unexpected happens that forces me to revise my intention, my intention today to go shopping tomorrow will control my conduct tomorrow. The reasoning-centered dimension of commitment is a commitment to norms of practical rationality and is most directly linked to planning. What is at stake here are the roles played by intentions in the period between their initial formation and their eventual execution. First, intentions have what Bratman calls a characteristic stability or inertia: once we have formed an intention to A, we will not normally continue to deliberate whether to A or not. In the absence of relevant new information, the intention is rationally required to resist reconsideration: we will see the matter as settled and continue to so intend until the time of action. Intentions are thus terminators of practical reasoning about ends or goals. Second, during this period between the formation of an intention and action, we will frequently reason from such an intention to further intentions, reasoning for instance from intended ends to intended means or preliminary steps. When we first form an intention, our plans are typically only partial, but if they are to eventuate into action, they will need to be filled in. Thus intentions are also prompters of practical reasoning about means.

In the remainder of this section, I will concentrate on this last function of prospective intentions.[11] What kind of cognitive processes are engaged in advance planning? To what extent can we and do we actually plan our actions in advance? How is the gap bridged between prospective intentions that may initially remain unspecific in many ways and immediate intentions specific enough to ensure that the action is actually produced?

Let me consider first the cognitive processes that can support advance planning. On a traditional philosophical picture, action planning is often, implicitly if not explicitly, taken to involve *instrumental reasoning* exploiting semantic knowledge. We have instrumental beliefs about means-ends relations as well as various beliefs about how the world is and we use a relevant subset of these beliefs as premises in our reasoning from intended ends to intended means. Another way in which advance planning could be carried out is by using what has now become known as mental time travel, the faculty that allows a person to mentally project herself backward in time to relive past events or forwards to pre-live events (Klein 2013; Klein *et al.* 2010; Suddendorf *et al.* 2009; Suddendorf and Corballis 1997, 2007; Suddendorf and Busby 2005; Szpunar 2010; Wheeler *et al.* 1997). Mental time travel exploits episodic information and involves processes of mental simulation. Mental time travel in the past, the conscious reliving of past events known as episodic memory, has been intensively studied (e.g., Tulving 1983, 2005).

Mental travel into the future, in contrast, has only recently begun to draw attention. However, recent work indicates that mental travel into the past and mental travel into the future are closely related, involving similar cognitive processes and recruiting strongly overlapping neural systems (D'Argembeau and Van der Linden 2006; Hassabis *et al.* 2007; Klein 2002).[12]

Planning using instrumental reasoning (IR planning, for short) and planning using mental time travel (MTT planning) should not be seen as mutually exclusive conceptions of what action planning is about, rather they may often function as complementary processes. Nor should we think that instrumental reasoning exploits only semantic information while mental time travel is concerned only with episodic information. For one thing, semantic and episodic information are not without links. The encoding of episodic information often relies on semantic information we already have and, conversely, semantic information is often extracted from episodic information.

A further important communality between IR planning and MTT planning is that conscious thought appears to be needed for both. In their discussion of the functions of conscious thought, Baumeister and Masicampo (2010) argue that human consciousness enables, among other things, the construction of meaningful, sequential thought, as in narratives and logical reasoning, the simulation of hypothetical scenarios and the exploration of options in complex decisions. As they point out, evidence has accumulated that automatic, non-conscious systems do not properly engage in logical reasoning (Lieberman *et al.* 2002; Smith and DeCoster 1999, 2000). There is also direct evidence that logical reasoning is the province of conscious thought. In particular, studies have shown that manipulations of conscious processes (e.g., hampering conscious processes by cognitive load or increasing conscious involvement by setting up conscious goals) affects performance in logical reasoning tasks but that corresponding manipulations of unconscious processes have no effect on reasoning performance (De Neys 2006; DeWall *et al.* 2008). Similarly, while there is evidence that mental time travel into the past or into the future can often take place in an involuntary or spontaneous mode (Berntsen and Jacobsen 2008), theorists have argued that mental time travel in the service of planning is a goal-directed and intentional process that requires the engagement of higher order executive mental functions (e.g., Suddendorf and Corballis 1997, 2007; Wheeler *et al.* 1997). This claim is supported by neuroimaging evidence indicating that MTT planning engages the neural substrates of working memory, including the dorsolateral prefrontal cortex (Gerlach *et al.* 2011; Spreng *et al.* 2010). As the engagement of working memory resources is generally considered as the hallmark of consciously controlled processes as opposed to automatic processes, that are independent of working memory (e.g., Evans 2008; Baars and Franklin 2003), this strongly suggests that MTT planning is a form of conscious thought, involving the cooperation of the autobiographical memory system and of executive control processes.

While IR planning and MTT planning share important properties, what is distinctive of MTT planning is that the representations it yields inherit some of the central characteristics of episodic memories. First, MTT planning involves imagining or mentally constructing specific future events, including at least some of their particularities. Second, these events are not just thought about, they are experienced. This experiential quality is manifested first by the multimodal content of these simulations that bind information from diverse systems (perceptual, motor, emotional) into a unitary episode representation and second by their autonoetic dimension, that is, these events are

mentally experienced from a first-person perspective. The construction of plans for future actions depends in part on semantic memory since it is crucial to their success that the plans we come up with be consistent with our general knowledge about the world. Yet, filling in the details of a plan may depend on our ability to imagine future episodes, since they provide the particularities that will help fine-tune the plan to the particular occasion. However, a number of factors may modulate the extent to which we rely on advance planning and the extent to which this planning takes the form of IR as opposed to MTT planning. As an illustration, let me contrast three cases. As a first case, suppose that I form the prospective intention to go to my office tomorrow as I normally do on weekdays. In such a case, it seems that I don't need to engage in explicit planning as to how to get to my office. I already have a well worked out plan stored in memory and the route is familiar enough that I can trust myself to do the right thing when the time comes. Now, consider instead the case where I have my first appointment tomorrow with a new dentist. I have never been to this particular dental office before but I have been living in Paris for many years and I know my way around the city. In that case, it may be worthwhile for me not just to rely on semantic information (e.g., public transportation maps) but also to engage in the mental simulation of different ways of getting there, using stored episodic information I have. For instance, I may remember that changing lines at this station takes forever and involves walking along endless, badly lit, corridors or I may remember getting stuck in heavy traffic on a given bus line. Mentally simulating these scenarios may not just help me decide among various options but also facilitate the future implementation of the chosen scenario through the anticipation of relevant situational cues. Finally, consider a third case where I am setting foot in a given city, say Budapest, for the first time in my life. In deciding how to get from one place to another, I have no relevant episodic information I could rely on. All I have to get by is semantic information in the form of maps or instructions from guidebooks. What these examples suggest is that the extent to which we rely on MTT or on IR in planning our actions depends on the degree of novelty of the prospective action and on whether the information at our disposal is mostly semantic or episodic in form. In addition, whether we engage in MTT planning may also depend on whether we think we need to reinforce our motivation. For instance, while on a diet, I may be aware that it will be difficult for me to resist ordering chocolate cake tonight at the restaurant; rehearsing a scenario where I virtuously order fruit salad instead may help me abide by my resolution to limit my calorie intake.[13]

[…]

So far, I have concentrated on the role of conscious agency prior to action initiation and more specifically on the advance planning processes that take place once one has formed a prospective intention to pursue a certain goal. However, understanding what happens prior to action initiation may also help us understand what happens at the time of action initiation. In particular, it could help us answer the following question: what additional contribution, if any, could conscious immediate intentions make to the production of actions that are already preceded by prospective intentions?

In this section, I distinguished three types of scenarios involving prospective intentions. The answer to the present question could depend, I suggest, on what scenario is exemplified. When we form a prospective intention to perform an action for which we have a well-established routine, we don't need to engage in advance planning. We can rely on situational cues to trigger the appropriate pattern of behavior at the appropriate time. Alternatively, if the prospective action is not habitual but we have relevant episodic information we can exploit, we can use MTT planning to form relevant implementation intentions and thus strategically delegate the initiation of goal-directed responses to anticipated situational cues. In both types of scenarios, the conscious formation of immediate intentions does not appear to be needed to ensure action initiation. This contrasts with the third type of scenario where either for lack of relevant episodic information or for lack of sufficient motivation to engage in MTT planning, the action plan we have formed consists solely or mainly in a hierarchical structure of goal-intentions. Goal-intentions, even if they specify goals in a detailed manner, do not specify how the intended action is to be weaved into the ongoing flow of behavior and experience. To bridge this gap between her goal intentions and action initiation, the agent must retain some endogenous control over action initiation. She cannot delegate it to automatic responses to environmental triggers, but must form immediate intentions specifying how the intended action it to be contextually modulated. In such cases, I surmise, action initiation would depend on the formation of conscious immediate intentions.

5. Concluding Remarks

In this paper, I have tried to argue that the debate on the role of conscious agency in action production started by Libet's experiments was too narrowly focused on action initiation. I suggested that if we widened our temporal horizons and considered the potential role of conscious agency both prior to and after action initiation, we might be less tempted to succumb to will-skepticism. In Sect. 3, I argued that conscious action control during action execution constitutes an important facet of conscious agency. In particular, I emphasized the fact that conscious control does not necessarily mean causal intervention: action may be consciously controlled even though unconscious rather than conscious control mechanisms intervene to adjust movements, provided conscious control mechanisms would have kicked in, had automatic control proved insufficient. In Sect. 4, I argued that conscious agency could also be manifested in the form of advance action planning and that such planning can, when it takes a particular form, induce strategic automaticity. While, for the sake of exposition, I distinguished three routes that may lead from an initially underspecified prospective intentions to action initiation—reliance on action routines, IR planning and MTT planning—, it should be expected that in most cases we will use mixed strategies.

My parting message is that we shouldn't see automaticity as an unbearable affront to our vanity as conscious agents. Rather than picturing automaticity and conscious agency as fiends vying for the same territory, one army being supported by cognitive scientists in an all-conquering mood, the other by philosophers fighting a rear-guard action, it may be more fruitful to see them as complementary forces, even if their cooperation isn't always easy and straightforward. If anything, what makes human agency unique is the richness and the complexity of their interactions and the flexible ways in which control can be passed up to conscious processes or down to automatic processes as the need arises.

Acknowledgments

Preliminary versions of this paper were presented at the Topoi Conference "Intentions: Philosophical and Empirical Issues" in Rome in November 2012 and at the Colloquium series of the Department of Philosophy at the Central European University in Budapest in February 2013. I would like to thank both audiences for their questions and comments. I am also grateful to two anonymous reviewers for this journal for their insightful comments and suggestions. I completed this paper while a Fellow at the Institute of Advanced Studies at the Central European University in Budapest and am grateful to this institution for its support.

Notes

1. This possibility is discussed by Velleman (2007), who does not really endorse it but rather uses it as an antidote to the assumption that the raison d'être of intentions is to support pragmatic functions. Dennett (Dennett 1991, 2003) and Wegner (2002) seem closer to endorsing this view.

2. Examples of free will skepticism that appeal to Libet's work include Banks and Isham (2011), Hallett (2007), Pockett (2004), Roediger *et al.* (2008), Spence (2009) and Wegner (2002).

   Contemporary defenses of compatibilism include, among many others, Frankfurt (1988), McKenna (2005), Scanlon (2008) and Smith (2003).

3. This is the interpretation of Libet's data Wegner appears to favor: "The position of conscious will in the time line suggests perhaps that the experience of will is a link in a causal chain leading to action, but in fact it might not even be that. It might just be a loose end—one of those things, like the action, that is caused by prior brain and mental events" (Wegner 2002: 55). On Wegner's account of how the experience of conscious will is generated, what he calls the theory of apparent mental causation, conscious will is experienced when we infer that our thought has caused our action and

we draw such an inference when we have thoughts that occur just before the actions, when these thoughts are consistent with the actions, and when other potential causes of the actions are not present. However, according to Wegner, our actions spring from unconscious causal processes and the conscious ideas we mistakenly experience as their causes are themselves caused by unconscious processes whose links to the unconscious processes causing the action, when they exist, are often at best indirect.

4. This is the interpretation of Libet's data Wegner appears to favor: "The position of conscious will in the time line suggests perhaps that the experience of will is a link in a causal chain leading to action, but in fact it might not even be that. It might just be a loose end—one of those things, like the action, that is caused by prior brain and mental events" (Wegner 2002: 55). On Wegner's account of how the experience of conscious will is generated, what he calls the theory of apparent mental causation, conscious will is experienced when we infer that our thought has caused our action and we draw such an inference when we have thoughts that occur just before the actions, when these thoughts are consistent with the actions, and when other potential causes of the actions are not present. However, according to Wegner, our actions spring from unconscious causal processes and the conscious ideas we mistakenly experience as their causes are themselves caused by unconscious processes whose links to the unconscious processes causing the action, when they exist, are often at best indirect.

5. This "local" epiphenomenalism should be distinguished from global epiphenomenalist claims stemming from the causal

exclusion problem, where the argument is that the causal efficacy of mental properties is excluded by the causal efficacy of the physical properties on which they supervene (Kim 1993). This challenge applies to mental causation in general and is much broader than the challenge raised by Libet's data. The causal exclusion problem has given rise to a huge literature and there is no clear consensus as to how it can be solved. However, I won't engage with this debate here; rather my focus here will be on Libet's more specific challenge.

6. In addition, even limiting ourselves to cases where RPs are followed by actions, RPs and W-judgments do not appear to be sufficiently coupled to warrant a causal claim. Haggard and Eimer (1999) found no correlation between the onset of the RP and W-judgments, but did find a positive correlation between the onset of a later phase of the readiness potential, the lateralized readiness potential (LRP), and W-judgments, suggesting that the RP does not reflect processes causal of W but that the LRP might. However, a recent study by Schlegel *et al.* (2013) failed to replicate their results and found no within-subject covariation between LRP onset and W judgment, leading them to conclude that neither RP onset nor LRP onset cause W.

7. One can offer a similar deflationary interpretation of a more recent experiment (Soon *et al.* 2008) that found that while subjects who had to decide between two actions reported having made a conscious decision on average 1,000 ms before action onset, the outcome of their decision could be predicted from brain activity in prefrontal and parietal cortex up to 10 s before it entered awareness. These results have been claimed to show that decisions about what to do and not just about when to act are

made unconsciously. However, in view of the fact that the accuracy with which the conscious decisions could be predicted from prior unconscious brain activity in these areas was less than 60% (50% corresponding to chance), a more reasonable conclusion might be that the decision was causally influenced to some degree by these unconscious brain processes rather than determined by them (see, for instance, section 3 in Mele 2012 for further discussion of this point).

8. While I am focusing here on Frankfurt's guidance theory of action, it is important to note that other philosophers also criticized the oversimplistic view of the relation between intention and action found in early causal theories of action. For instance, Brand (1984), Bishop (1989) and Mele (1992) all insist that a full-blown causal theory should incorporate the guiding and monitoring roles of intentions in the production of intentional action. The notion of an intention-inaction proposed by Searle (1983) was also aimed at capturing the close and continuous connection between intention and ongoing action (see, for instance, the discussion in Pacherie (2000)).

9. Useful entry points into the literature on motor cognition are provided by Jeannerod (1997, 2006).

[…]

11. For reasons of space, I decided to limit my discussion to action planning after the formation of an initial prospective intention. I am not assuming that the formation of prospective intentions always involves explicit conscious deliberation. When it does, however, deliberation could involve classical forms of practical reasoning, but also what I describe below as mental time travel processes. For instance, we may mentally simulate various potential future situations and use our emotional responses to these imagined scenarios as guides to our decisions (Boyer 2008).

12. Indeed, several researchers have argued that mental time travel into the future is a crucial cognitive adaptation, enhancing planning and deliberation by allowing a subject to mentally simulate and evaluate contingencies, and thus enhancing fitness, and that mental time travel into the past is subsidiary to our ability to imagine future scenarios (Dudai and Carruthers 2005; Suddendorf and Corballis 2007).

13. In addition, there appear to be important individual differences in the ability to project oneself into possible future events. A recent study (D'Argembeau and Van der Linden 2006) provides evidence that the individual differences in dimensions known to affect memory for past events similarly influence the experience of projecting oneself into the future. People less adept at recalling in vivid detail past episodes of their life, are also less able to simulate specific future events.

References

Aarts, H, Dijksterhuis, A P, & Midden, C (1999) To plan or not to plan? Goal achievement or interrupting the performance of mundane behaviors. *European Journal of Social Psychology*, 29(8): 971–79.

Baars, B J, & Franklin, S (2003) How conscious experience and working memory interact. *Trends in Cognitive Sciences*, 7(4): 166–72.

Banks, WP and Isham, E A (2011) Do we really know what we are doing? Implications of reported time of decision for theories of volition. In W Sinnott–Armstrong and L Nadel (eds) *Conscious will and responsibility*. New York: Oxford University Press, pp. 47–60.

Baumeister, R F, & Masicampo, E J (2010) Conscious thought is for facilitating social and cultural interactions: How mental simulations serve the animal–culture interface. *Psychological Review*, 117(3): 945–71.

Bayne, T J & Levy, N (2006) The feeling of doing: Deconstructing the Phenomenology of Agency. In N Sebanz & W Prinz (eds), *Disorders of volition*. Cambridge, Mass: MIT Press, pp. 49–68.

Bayne, T (2011) Libet and the case for free will scepticism. In R Swinburne (ed), *Free will and modern science*. Oxford: Oxford University Press, pp. 25–46.

Berntsen, D, & Jacobsen, A S (2008) Involuntary (spontaneous) mental time travel into the past and future. *Consciousness and Cognition*, 17(4): 1093–1104.

Bishop, J C (1989) *Natural agency: an essay on the causal theory of action*. Cambridge University Press.

Boyer, P (2008) Evolutionary economics of mental time travel? *Trends in Cognitive Sciences*, 12(6): 219–24.

Brand, M (1984) *Intending and acting: toward a naturalized action theory*. Cambridge, Mass: MIT Press.

Brass, M & Haggard, P (2007) To do or not to do: the neural signature of self–control. *Journal of Neuroscience*, 27: 9141–45.

Bratman, M E (1987) *Intention, plans, and practical reason*. Cambridge, MA: Harvard University Press.

Chalmers, D (1995) Facing up to the problem of consciousness. *Journal of Consciousness Studies*, 2, 3: 200–19.

D'Argembeau, A & Van der Linden, M (2006) Individual differences in the phenomenology of mental time travel: The effect of vivid visual imagery and emotion regulation strategies. *Consciousness and Cognition*, 15: 342–50.

Davidson, D (1980) *Essays on actions and events*. Oxford: Oxford University Press.

De Neys, W (2006) Dual processing in reasoning: two systems but one reasoner. *Psychological Science*, 17: 428–33.

Dennett, D C (1991) *Consciousness explained*. Boston, MA: Little Brown.

Dennett, D C (2003) *Freedom evolves*. New York: Viking.

DeWall, C N, Baumeister, R F, & Masicampo, E J (2008) Evidence that logical reasoning depends on conscious processing. *Consciousness and Cognition*, 17: 628–45.

Dudai, Y & Carruthers, M (2005) The Janus face of Mnemosyne. *Nature*, 434: 567.

Evans, J S B (2008) Dual–processing accounts of reasoning, judgment, and social cognition. *Annual Review of Psychology*, 59: 255–78.

Filevich E, Kühn S, Haggard P (2013) There Is No Free Won't: Antecedent Brain Activity Predicts Decisions to Inhibit. *PLoS One*, 8(2): e53053. doi:10.1371*f*journal. pone.0053053

Fischer, J M (1994) *The metaphysics of free will*. Oxford: Blackwell Publishers.

Fourneret, P, & Jeannerod, M (1998) Limited conscious monitoring of motor performance in normal subjects. *Neuropsychologia*, 36, 11: 1133–40.

Fourneret, P, Franck, N, Slachevsky, A, & Jeannerod, M (2001) Self–monitoring in schizophrenia revisited. *Neuroreport*, 12(6): 1203–08.

Fourneret, P, Vignemont, F D, Franck, N, Slachevsky, A, Dubois, B, & Jeannerod, M (2002) Perception of self–generated action in schizophrenia. *Cognitive Neuropsychiatry*, 7(2): 139–56.

Flanagan, O (1996) Neuroscience, agency, and the meaning of life. In *Self–Expressions*. Oxford: Oxford University Press, pp. 53–64.

Fleming, S M, Mars, R J, Gladwin, T E, & Haggard, P (2009) When the brain changes its mind: Flexibility of action selection in instructed and free choices. *Cerebral Cortex*, 19(10): 2352–60.

Fletcher, P C, & Frith, C D (2009) Perceiving is believing: a Bayesian approach to explaining the positive symptoms of schizophrenia. *Nature Neuroscience*, 16: 48–58.

Frankfurt, H (1978) The problem of action. *American Philosophical Quarterly*, 15, 2: 157–62.

Frankfurt, H (1988) *The importance of what we care about*. Cambridge: Cambridge University Press.

Frith, C D, Blakemore, S–J, & Wolpert, D M (2000) Abnormalities in the awareness and control of action. *Philosophical Transactions of the Royal Society of London B*, 355: 1771–88.

Gallagher, S (2006) Where's the action? Epiphenomenalism and the problem of free will. In W Banks, S Pockett, & S Gallagher (eds), *Does consciousness cause behavior? An investigation of the nature of volition*, Cambridge, MA: MIT Press, pp. 109–24.

Gerlach, K D, Spreng, R N, Gilmore, A W, & Schacter, D L (2011) Solving future problems: Default network and executive activity associated with goal directed mental simulations. *Neuroimage*, 55(4): 1816–24.

Glynn, I M (1990) Consciousness and time. *Nature*, 348, 6301: 477–79.

Goldman, A (1970) *A theory of human action*. Englewood Cliffs, NJ: Prentice–Hall.

Gollwitzer, P M (1999) Implementation intentions: Strong effects of simple plans. *American Psychologist*, 54: 493–503.

Gollwitzer, P M, & Sheeran, P (2006) Implementation intentions and goal achievement: A meta–analysis of effects and processes. *Advances in Experimental Social Psychology*, 38: 69–119.

Gomes, G (1998) The Timing of Conscious Experience: A Critical Review and Reinterpretation of Libet's Research. *Consciousness and Cognition*, 7, 4: 559–95.

Gomes, G (1999) Volition and the readiness potential. *Journal of Consciousness Studies*, 6ƒ8–9: 59–76.

Haggard, P (2006) Conscious intention and the sense of agency. In N Sebanz and W Prinz (eds) *Disorders of volition*. Cambridge, MA: MIT Press, 69–86.

Haggard, P (2008) Human volition: Towards a neuroscience of will. *Nature Reviews Neuroscience*, 9: 934–46.

Haggard, P, & Eimer, M (1999) On the relation between brain potentials and the awareness of voluntary movements. *Experimental Brain Research* 126: 128–33.

Hallett, M (2007) Volitional control of movement: the physiology of free will. *Clinical Neurophysiology*, 118: 1179–92.

Hassabis, D K D, Vann, S D, & Maguire, E A (2007). Patients with hippocampal amnesia cannot imagine new experiences. *Proceedings of the National Academy of Sciences*, 104: 1726–31.

Jeannerod, M (1997) *The cognitive neuroscience of action*. Oxford: Blackwell.

Jeannerod, M (2006) *Motor cognition*. Oxford: Oxford University Press.

Joordens, S, van Duijn, M, & Spalek, T M (2002) When timing the mind one should also mind the timing: Biases in the measurement of voluntary actions. *Consciousness and Cognition*, 11, 2: 231–40.

Jordan, M I, & Wolpert, D M (1999) Computational motor control. In M Gazzaniga (ed), *The cognitive neurosciences*. Cambridge, MA: MIT Press.

Keller, I, & Heckhausen, H (1990) Readiness Potentials preceding spontaneous motor acts: voluntary vs. involuntary control. *Electroencephalography and Clinical Neurophysiology*, 76: 351–61.

Kim, J (1993) *Supervenience and mind*. Cambridge: Cambridge University Press.

Klein, S B (2002) Memory and temporal experience: The effects of episodic memory loss on an amnesic patient's ability to remember the past and imagine the future. *Social Cognition*, 20: 353–79.

Klein, S B (2013) The complex act of projecting oneself into the future. *Wiley Interdisciplinary Reviews: Cognitive Science*, 4(1): 63–79.

Klein, S B, Robertson, T E, & Delton, A W (2010) Facing the future: Memory as an evolved system for planning future acts. *Memory and Cognition*, 38(1): 13–22.

Libet, B (1985) Unconscious cerebral initiative and the role of conscious will in voluntary action. *Behavioral and Brain Sciences*, 8: 529–66.

Libet, B, Gleason, C A, Wright, E W, & Pearl, D K (1983) Time of conscious intention to act in relation to onset of cerebral activity (readiness–potential): the unconscious initiation of a freely voluntary act. *Brain*, 106: 623–42.

Lieberman, M D, Gaunt, R, Gilbert, D T, & Trope, Y (2002) Reflexion and reflection: A social cognitive neuroscience approach to attributional inference. In M P Zanna (ed), *Advances in experimental social psychology*. San Diego, CA: Academic Press, pp. 199–249.

McKenna, M (2005) Reasons Reactivity & Incompatibilist Intuitions. *Philosophical Explorations*, 8(2): 131–43.

Mele, A R (1992) *Springs of action: Understanding intentional behavior*. Oxford University Press.

Mele, A R (2007) Free will: action theory meets neuroscience. In C Lumer & S Nannini (eds), *Intentionality, deliberation and autonomy*. Bulington, VT: Ashgate, pp. 257–72.

Mele, A R (2009) *Effective intentions: the power of conscious will*. New York: Oxford University Press.

Mele, A R (2012) Another Scientific Threat to Free Will? *The Monist*, 95(3): 422–40.

Miller, J, Shepherdson, P, & Trevena, J (2011) Effects of Clock Monitoring on Electroencephalographic Activity Is Unconscious Movement Initiation an Artifact of the Clock? *Psychological Science*, 22(1): 103–09.

Miller, J O, Vieweg, P, Kruize, N, & McLea, B (2010) Subjective reports of stimulus, response, and decision times in speeded tasks: How accurate are decision time reports? *Consciousness and Cognition*, 19: 1013–36.

Nahmias, E (2002) When consciousness matters: A critical review of Daniel Wegner's The illusion of conscious will. *Philosophical Psychology*, 15: 527–41.

Pacherie, E (2000) The content of intentions. *Mind and Language*, 15, 4: 400–32.

Pacherie, E (2006) Towards a dynamic theory of intentions. In S Pockett, WP Banks, & S Gallagher (eds), *Does consciousness cause behavior? An investigation of the nature of volition*. Cambridge, MA: MIT Press, pp. 145–67.

Pacherie, E (2008) The phenomenology of action: A conceptual framework. *Cognition*, 107, 1: 179–217.

Pockett, S (2004) Does consciousness cause behaviour? *Journal of Consciousness Studies*, 11ƒ2: 23–40.

Rigoni, D, Kühn, S, Sartori, G, & Brass, M (2011) Inducing disbelief in free will alters brain correlates of preconscious motor preparation: The brain minds whether we believe in free will or not. *Psychological Science*, 22(5): 613–8.

Roediger, H K, Goode, MK, and Zaromb, FM (2008) Free will and the control of action. In J Baer, JC Kaufman and RF Baumeister (eds) *Are we free?* Oxford: Oxford University Press, pp. 205–25.

Roskies, A (2011) Why Libet's studies don't pose a threat to free will. In W Sinnott–Armstrong and L Nadel (eds) *Conscious will and responsibility*. New York: Oxford University Press, pp. 11–22.

Scanlon, TM (2008) *Moral dimensions: permissibility, meaning, blame*. Cambridge, Mass: Belknap Harvard Press.

Schlegel, A, Alexander, P, Sinnott–Armstrong, W, Roskies, A, Tse, P, & Wheatley, T (2013) Barking up the wrong free: readiness potentials reflect processes independent of conscious will. *Experimental Brain Research*. DOI 10.1007fs00221–013–3479–3

Schurger, A, Sitt, J D, & Dehaene, S (2012) An accumulator model for spontaneous neural activity prior to self–initiated movement. *Proceedings of the National Academy of Sciences*, 109(42): E2904–E2913.

Searle, J R (1983) *Intentionality: an essay in the philosophy of mind*. Cambridge University Press.

Searle, J R (2001) *Rationality in action*. Cambridge, Mass: MIT Press.

Sheeran, P, & Orbell, S (1999) Implementation intentions and repeated behaviour: Augmenting the predictive validity of the theory of planned behaviour. *European Journal of Social Psychology*, 29(2–3): 349–69.

Smith, E R, & DeCoster, J (1999) Associative and rule–based processing: A connectionist interpretation of dual–process models. In S Chaiken, & Y Trope (eds), *Dual–process theories in social psychology* (pp. 323–36). New York, NY: Guilford Press.

Smith, E R, & DeCoster, J (2000). Dual–process models in social and cognitive psychology: Conceptual integration and links to underlying memory systems. *Personality and Social Psychology Review*, 4: 108–31.

Smith, M (2003) Rational Capacities. In S Stroud and C Tappolet (eds), *Weakness of will and practical irrationality*. Oxford: Clarendon Press, pp. 17–38.

Soon, C S, Brass, M, Heinze, H–J, & Haynes, J–D (2008) Unconscious determinants of free decisions in the human brain. *Nature Neuroscience*, 11f5: 543–5.

Spence, S (2009) *The actor's brain: exploring the cognitive neuroscience of free will*. New York: Oxford University Press.

Spreng, R N, Stevens, W D, Chamberlain, J P, Gilmore, A W, & Schacter, D L (2010) Default network activity, coupled with the frontoparietal control network, supports goal–directed cognition. *Neuroimage*, 53(1): 303–17.

Suddendorf, T, Addis, D R, & Corballis, M C (2009) Mental time travel and the shaping of the human mind. *Philosophical Transactions of the Royal Society B: Biological Sciences*, 364(1521): 1317–24.

Suddendorf, T, & Busby, J (2005) Making decisions with the future in mind: Developmental and comparative identification of mental time travel. *Learning and Motivation*, 3: 110–25.

Suddendorf, T, & Corballis, M C (1997) Mental time travel and the evolution of the human mind. *Genetic, Social, and General Psychology Monographs*, 123: 133–67.

Suddendorf, T, & Corballis, M C (2007) The evolution of foresight: What is mental time travel, and is it unique to humans? *Behavioral and Brain Sciences*, 30: 299–351.

Szpunar, K K (2010) Episodic future thought an emerging concept. *Perspectives on Psychological Science*, 5(2): 142–62.

Tulving, E (1983) *Elements of episodic memory*. Oxford: Clarendon Press.

Tulving, E (2005) Episodic memory and autonoesis: Uniquely human? In H S Terrace & J Metcalfe (eds), *The missing link in cognition: origins of self–reflective consciousness*. Oxford: Oxford University Press, pp. 3–56.

Webb, T L, & Sheeran, P (2004) Identifying good opportunities to act: Implementation intentions and cue discrimination. *European Journal of Social Psychology*, 34(4): 407–19.

Webb, T L, & Sheeran, P (2007) How do implementation intentions promote goal attainment? A test of component processes. *Journal of Experimental Social Psychology*, 43: 295–302.

Wheeler, M A, Stuss, D T, & Tulving, E (1997) Toward a theory of episodic memory: The frontal lobes and autonoetic consciousness. *Psychological Bulletin*, 121: 331–54.

van de Grind, W (2002) Physical, neural, and mental timing. *Consciousness and Cognition*, 11: 241–64.

Velleman, D (2007) What good is a will? In A Leist & H Baumann (eds), *Action in context*, Berlin: de Gruyter, pp. 193–215.

Wegner, DM (2002) *The illusion of conscious will*. Cambridge, MA: MIT Press.

Wolpert, D M (1997) Computational approaches to motor control. *Trends in Cognitive Sciences*, 1(6): 209–16.

Wolpert, D M, & Ghahramani, Z (2000) Computational principles of movement neuroscience. *Nature Neuroscience Supplement*, 3: 1212–17.

Wolpert, D M, Ghahramani, Z, & Jordan, M I (1995) An internal model for sensorimotor integration. *Science*, 269: 1880–82.

Zhu, J (2003) Reclaiming Volition. *Consciousness and Cognition*, 10: 61–77.

Study Questions

1. Consider Frankfurt's example involving a spider. When its legs move, that's an action attributable to the spider: those movements are made by the spider. But if its legs move in the same way when a boy has attached strings to them and makes them move, then that's something that merely happens to the spider. This is supposed to provide a counter-example to Davidson's theory of the difference between intentional action and things that merely happen to one because, we assume, spiders are never capable of having reasons for their actions. The difference here according to Frankfurt is that in the first case, the movement is up to the spider—it's purposive and internally guided by "the whole creature." But now consider the case of the reflex movement of jerking your hand back when you touch something hot. That's not caused by a belief or a desire either, but it is internally guided and purposive (its purpose is to prevent you from

getting a serious burn). But this is clearly not intentional movement. What does this show about the Frankfurt/Davidson debate?

2. Consider Frankfurt's example about a car rolling down a hill. The driver does nothing, because the car's speed and direction are in accordance with the driver's desires, but if the car were to veer off course, she could intervene. So the movement of the car is guided by the driver, even though she does not *cause* it. But is he right that the driver does not cause the car to move that way because she does not move? Is her refraining from steering, braking, or accelerating a cause of the car's movement? If so, is it true that the driver does nothing?

3. Causes need not occur entirely prior to their effects. My desires and beliefs might still be causally contributing to my movement while it's happening. Show how Davidson might respond to one of Frankfurt's objections by modifying his view to make this continuing causation necessary.

4. Fred wants to kill Arnold, so he cuts the brake lines on Arnold's car, knowing that the next morning, when Arnold drives to work down that big hill, he won't be able to stop before a fatal crash. Can we redescribe Fred's actions as murder? It wouldn't be murder unless the car rolled out of control and crashed, killing Arnold; but by this time, Fred has gone home and isn't in control of—couldn't modify—what happens. Does this show that Frankfurt is wrong about actions being under the agent's guidance throughout?

5. What does Frankfurt mean when he says that a movement is under the agent's guidance? On a standard causal account of this (not Frankfurt's), it means roughly that a change in the agent's desires or beliefs will *cause* modification of the movements. What does Frankfurt mean, instead? Is he right?

6. Pacherie suggests that neuroscientific evidence might show that conscious decisions are just an epiphenomenon of intentional action. Explain why this is possible; and explain her reasons why the evidence might have alternative explanations.

7. Pacherie argues that the "folk psychology" of intentional action is overly simple. What is this "folk psychological" view? Outline the ways she thinks it's overly simple, and her arguments and evidence for these conclusions.

8. Pacherie argues that consciousness may indeed play a necessary role in the planning processes leading up to action initiation, and the guidance processes that occur downstream of such initiation. What are the main reasons she gives for this conclusion? Are they sufficient for showing that it is consciousness that is doing the relevant work?

Suggested Readings

For an introduction to the issues and positions in action theory, see the Introduction to, *Causing Human Actions: New Perspectives on the Causal Theory of Action*, Jesús H. Aguilar & Andrei A. Buckareff (eds.). (Cambridge, MA: Bradford, 2010).

A great deal of the action-theory literature of the last half-century consists in defenses or refinements of, or attacks on, the causal theory, the "standard story," presented in Davidson's 1963 article reprinted in this chapter. The articles in the anthology mentioned above are among the central ones in this area. Here are some more useful works on the causal theory:

John Bishop, *Natural Agency: An Essay on the Causal Theory of Action.* (Cambridge: Cambridge University Press, 1989).

Berent Enç, *How We Act: Causes, Reasons, and Intentions.* (Oxford: Oxford University Press, 2003).

Alfred R. Mele, *Springs of Action: Understanding Intentional Behavior.* (Oxford: Oxford University Press, 1992).

Alfred R. Mele, "Goal-Directed Action: Teleological Explanations, Causal Theories, and Deviance." *Noûs* 34 (2000): pp. 279–300.

Alfred R. Mele, *Motivation and Agency.* (Oxford: Oxford University Press, 2003).

14

 WHEN DO AGENTS ACT?

Some philosophers argue that the cases of deviant causes that we reviewed in the last chapter serve to highlight an even deeper problem for the causal theory of action that extends to non-deviant cases of causation as well. The problem that they allege is that the causal theory explains actions in terms of the mental events or psychological states *of* the agent, but these do not "add up" to the *agent*'s being involved in the action. As David Velleman, who is Professor of Philosophy at New York University, puts the worry below, "[w]hen reasons are described as directly causing an intention, and the intention as directly causing movements, not only has the agent been cut out of the story but so has any psychological item that might play his role." This is known as the **problem of the disappearing agent**. The problem, we might say, is to put the agent back into the causal story.

To get a better sense of the problem, consider a case in which someone is walking along a street and then crosses the road inconveniently and unnecessarily. Later they remember they had witnessed an accident at that place years ago and conclude that the memory had likely caused a desire in them to avoid the place where it occurred and a decision to cross over to the other side of the street. This type of case leads Velleman to conclude that when an agent "participates" in an action, they must be "adding something to the normal motivational influence of [their] desires, beliefs, and intentions." But the causal theory does not seem to have the resources, at least as it stands, to account for what this extra ingredient might be.

A possible reply here is that an agent's participation in their action is *implicit* insofar as they are the subject of the relevant mental states and events that lead up to their behavior, just as the ocean is implicit in a description of the causal interactions among its waves, and a clock is implicit in a description of the causal links among its various springs, wheels, hands, and dial. But Velleman rejects this move, maintaining that, "reflection on the phenomena of action reveals that being the subject of causally related attitudes and movements does not amount to participation of the sort appropriate to an agent." According to Velleman, then, the problem of the disappearing agent highlights an apparent weakness in causal theories: an inability to explain what we will call **agentive participation** in one's actions. The idea is that in order for behavior to be the action of an agent, it is not sufficient for it to be caused by the agent's psychological states—the beliefs, desires, and intentions leading up to the relevant behavior. Rather, it must involve the agent herself, in a way that goes beyond the involvement of these states.[1]

How can the causal theory account for the involvement of an agent in their actions? One potential answer to this question comes from Harry Frankfurt's 1971 article "Freedom of the Will and the Concept of a Person." Frankfurt begins by giving an analysis of the concept of a person. This concept, he thinks, is philosophically interesting, not because it serves to mark out membership in a certain biological species, but rather because it designates attributes which are central to "what interests us most in the human condition," and this may apply equally well to human beings and at least some non-human animals.

Frankfurt points out that many creatures act on desires, yet are not persons in the sense that they can be said to *choose* their actions. Frankfurt proposes that the difference lies in the "structure of a person's will." Specifically, he argues that only persons are capable of forming what he calls **second-order volitions** that are directed towards their **first-order desires**. A first-order desire is simply a desire to do something or not to do something. But what Frankfurt calls a second-order volition is a desire that a certain first-order desire should succeed over other, competing first-order desires.[2] Frankfurt says that when we have such a second-order volition, we **identify** with the first-order desire that we want to prevail, in the sense that we endorse it as agents. Consider the case of someone who is training for a marathon, which given her schedule requires that she go on a long run this coming Sunday morning. When Sunday morning comes along, she finds herself with a desire to spend it relaxing on the couch. At the same time, she has a competing desire to go on her long run and fulfill her goal for the day, as well as a second-order volition for this latter desire to be effective. Within Frankfurt's framework, we can say that our runner identifies with her first-order desire to go on a long run, but not with her competing first-order desire to relax on the couch.

In giving this account of personhood, Frankfurt articulates what it is for a person to "participate" in the activity of their will as an agent, as opposed to cases in which the person is alienated from the motives that drive their behavior. Insofar as our runner's desire to go on a long run is not effective, in relaxing on the couch, she fails to exercise agentive control over her behavior, and is instead alienated from it in an important way. Thus, Frankfurt can be seen here as giving a solution to the problem of the disappearing agent. On Frankfurt's view, the agent exerts their influence in the causal order leading up to their action by way of "throwing [their] weight" (as Velleman puts it) behind some of their motives rather than others.

Yet Velleman objects that, far from solving the problem, Frankfurt's proposal actually presupposes a solution to it. He notes that Frankfurt treats "self-identification" as a primitive mental act—that is, one that cannot be reduced to further mental acts—that always entails the involvement of the agent. Velleman refers to this involvement as "agent-causation." But if so, then agentive control has not been *explained*, it has simply been *re-described* in terms of self-identification, which itself is a mental act that requires a form of agentive control. Velleman argues that this strategy is thereby hopeless as a way of understanding the phenomenon at issue. What is needed, rather, is that agentive control be broken down into its components—"and surely," Velleman writes, "the principal component of agent-causation is the agent himself." But if so, then we should "look for events and states to play the role of the agent."

Velleman confesses that this might sound like a bizarre project, since an agent is not technically identical to a set of mental states or events. But he notes that often a person performs a function in virtue of there being some part of them that performs it. For example, a person carries out the function of digestion by way of the activities of their digestive system. Similarly, then, one might perform the function of an agent in virtue of the activities of some mental states or events.

What, then, is the function of an agent? Velleman says "[t]he functional role of the agent is that of a single party prepared to reflect on, and take sides with, potential determinants of behavior." In other words, what an agent does is to adjudicate among their motives for different courses of action, and "throw their weight" behind those that they deem to be strongest in light of their other motives, goals, commitments, values, and so on. Importantly, in order to play this role, the agent must be detached from, and therefore separate from, the motives that they evaluate, in the same way that "a contest cannot be adjudicated by the contestants themselves."

Velleman urges that "[w]hatever intervenes in these ways between motives and behaviour is thereby playing the role of the agent and consequently is the agent, functionally speaking." The only psychological state that can play this role, of reflecting on and selecting among alternative motives, Velleman thinks, is the "motive that drives practical thought itself," that is, the desire to act in accordance with reasons. This desire adds additional motivational force to the selected motive, in addition to the original force of the motive itself, in virtue of its being the motive with strongest rational force. This is what it means, according to Velleman, for an agent to throw their weight behind some particular motive—it is to desire to act in accordance with that motive *from* a desire to act in accordance with reasons.

To illustrate how this motive is manifested, consider the following scenario: John wants to go to the movies tonight. He also wants to do well on his calculus exam, which is tomorrow morning. He will engage in practical thinking to determine what to do. In doing so, he will not just reflect on his motive to go to the movies and his motive to do well on his exam and determine which he "likes better." He will reflect on which motive "provide[s] stronger reason for acting" and make sure it wins out over motives with weaker "rational force." Velleman does not specify what constitutes the strength of a reason, nor its rational force, but a natural way of unpacking these ideas is by appeal, at least in part, to the extent to which a reason coheres with an agent's other motives, commitments, values, and so on. Thus John's desire to go to the movies might cohere well with his desire to be up on the latest cinema, and his desire to have an enjoyable and relaxing evening, but his desire to do well on his calculus exam coheres with his desire to finish at the top of his class, his desire to get a good job after he graduates, and his desire to be studious and disciplined. The rational force of his latter desire thus far outstrips that of his desire to go to the movies. The motive for practical thought drives the critical evaluation of an agent's motives, accepting or rejecting them, and subsequently pursuing or avoiding the courses of action that they specify.

Velleman further argues that, unlike a first-order desire or second-order volition, the motive for practical thought cannot be "disowned" by the agent. Typically, motives can be suppressed. One can suppress the desire to stop working and take a nap for long enough to complete the task at hand. In doing so, one exercises one's rational capacity; one deems it best to be moved by some other motive, and acts accordingly. But notice that a motive for practical thought cannot *itself* be suppressed in *this* way, since this process clearly involves the exercise of *that very motive*. The only way it may be suppressed, Velleman argues, is if the individual suspends practical thought itself.

In this case, though, one thereby "suspend[s] the functions in virtue of which [one] qualifies as an agent." The motive for practical thought is thus not one from which an agent, *qua agent*, can become detached.

Rejecting the "Standard Story"

Both Frankfurt and Velleman aim to solve the problem of the disappearing agent by supplementing the causal theory of action with additional psychological states that, for them, constitute the involvement of the agent in their action. But not all think this is a viable route. In her chapter, "Agency and Actions," Jennifer Hornsby, a Professor of Philosophy at Birkbeck College, University of London, sets out to show that the causal theory of action, what she dubs "the standard story," is deeply defective as an account of human agency, such that it cannot be fixed simply by adding to it.

Hornsby starts out her chapter by identifying what she takes to be a central difference in the aims of philosophy of mind and ethics when it comes to human agency. Philosophy of mind primarily aims to situate the agent within the physical world, that is, within the causal order that is revealed to us by science. Ethics, on the other hand, primarily aims to explain the connection between normative facts, that is, facts about what is right and wrong, and facts pertaining to an agent's capacity to deliberate about what to do, and arrive at a practical conclusion about what course of action would be best. The key point, then, is that ethics is "involved with questions of moral psychology whose answers admit a kind of richness in the life of human beings from which the philosophy of mind may ordinarily prescind."

This preliminary observation motivates Hornsby to evaluate and critique the "standard story" when it comes to explaining human agency, i.e., the causal theory of action. The standard story, she thinks, falls short specifically with respect to capturing the ethical dimensions of human agency. This explains why it enjoys orthodox status within philosophy of mind, but not within ethics where these broader normative concerns are more central.

Against Events-Based Theories

Hornsby's specific concern with the causal theory is stated quite boldly, for she argues that despite its aiming to be so, it is not a story of human agency at all. Moreover, its defect in accounting for human agency cannot be addressed by supplementing it in some way, e.g., adding a role for further psychological states and processes to the story, as Frankfurt and Velleman attempt.

Why does Hornsby so forcefully dismiss the causal theory? Her first challenge to the account targets what she calls its "event-based character." What this means is that the causal theory assumes that all actions are events that exist in space and time, and that agency can be explained by explaining the relevant causal relations among the relevant events (e.g., the event of forming a desire to raise one's arm and the event of one's arm going up).

There are two lines of critique that Hornsby pursues in relation to this events-based character of the causal theory of action. The first is to note that someone can do something intentionally without there being any event that is their doing that thing, and so no action, on the standard story. For example, she tells us, someone can refrain from taking a chocolate from the box, refrain from answering a phone call, or refrain from paying attention to an irritating acquaintance. But in each of these cases, though it can credibly be said that what is done is done intentionally, and is caused in the right way by the beliefs and desires of the agent as the standard story would have it, there is no bodily movement, and thus no event, that we can identify with the relevant doing.

Hornsby goes on to consider that the causal theorist might reply that there are actually two types of action explanation in terms of an agent's beliefs and desires. The first type is used to explain the occurrence of a bodily movement that is an agent's action, and corresponds to a statement of the form 'The agent's desire that p caused her F-ing' (where 'F-ing' is understood as an event which is a bodily movement). The second type is used when such a statement is not available to construct, because there is no relevant bodily movement, but it nonetheless accounts for why the agent did what they did in terms of their beliefs and desires. Here Hornsby replies that when we do explain why an agent did what they did, we need not determine first whether they did what they did by way of a bodily movement, that is, whether we can construct a statement of the form just described. As she later sums up the point, action explanations do not ever seem focused on explaining why an event occurred. Rather, what we are interested in knowing, in every case, is why an *agent* did something.

Hornsby's next line of critique reveals more directly, she thinks, that the standard story cannot account for human agency. She starts by quoting Hume, who, given his commitment to an events-based account of human agency, she thinks is forced to say that we "have no power" to move our limbs, since our limb movements are caused by successive events that are linked along a causal path, including neural impulses and muscle movements, and we have direct control over only those events in the chain—on Hume's view the "animal spirits"—that can serve as "the direct object of volition." Similarly, in his book *The View from Nowhere*,[3] the philosopher Thomas Nagel expresses the worry that our agency is lost "in a world of neural impulses, chemical reactions, and bone and muscle movements."

Making Room for the Agent

Hornsby's diagnosis of the cause of Hume's "manifestly false" conclusion that we do not move our limbs and Nagel's "anxiety" is that both are the result of thinking of human agency in terms of a series of causally related events. Such a picture, she thinks, leaves no room for a human agent to make "any difference to anything." But human beings do make a difference—they do things. And the way that they do things is part of our ordinary, commonsense understanding of action.

Hornsby spells this out by drawing out a feature of the language we use to describe action, which she terms its "causative character." Central to this is the connection between someone's doing something and their bringing something about. The connection is that the event of something being brought about is usually the result of the event of someone's doing something. Consider the following action: S throws the ball in the basket. We can describe this action as follows: S's throwing the ball in the basket brings it about that the ball is in the basket. In other words, the ball's being in the basket is the effect of S's action of throwing the ball in the basket. Similarly, if S raises her arm, we say that S's raising her arm brings it about that her arm goes up. In other words, S's arm going up is the effect of S's action of raising her arm. When agents cause such effects by moving their bodies, they draw on causal knowledge about causal relations between events, including their bodily movements. Hence the "causative character" of action language.

What the foregoing illustrates is that actions are indeed events. But this does not commit us, Hornsby thinks, to an events-based characterization of agency, committed as it is to all events that are actions being bodily movements. This is because, as Hornsby points out, an agent can bring something about by way of doing something, without there being any bodily movement. For example, an agent can bring it about that there is silence in the room by not talking. Here, there being silence in the room is the effect of S's action of not talking. But no bodily movement has taken place. While the standard story struggles with such cases, on Hornsby's view, her own account does not.

An upshot of this picture is the surprising result that agents do not cause their actions. Rather, what they cause are the *effects* of their actions. Consider again the action of throwing the ball in the basket. Here what the agent causes (among other things) is the event of the ball's being in the basket. But she does not cause her throwing of the ball. This applies, too, in the case of the action of raising one's arm. Here what the agent causes (among other things) is the event of her arm's going up. But she does not cause her action of raising her arm. This has the implication that, on Hornsby's view, bodily movements are not, strictly speaking, themselves actions. Though we can talk of the action of *her* moving her arm, the arm movement on its own is not something the agent does, and so not an action of the agent's.

Agency Par Excellence vs. Basic Ownership

A very different line of argumentation against the views of Frankfurt and Velleman is provided by Markus Schlosser, a Professor of Philosophy at University College, Dublin, in Ireland, in his article "Agency, Ownership, and the Standard Theory." Schlosser argues that, although Frankfurt and Velleman may provide ways of understanding "higher" forms of agency and ownership—what Velleman dubs "agency par excellence"—they both overlook a more basic or minimal type of ownership over one's actions. To see this, let's revisit the case of the unwilling addict, who Frankfurt describes as "a passive bystander to the forces that move him." It's important to notice here, Schlosser says, that contrary to Frankfurt's description, the unwilling addict actually exercises a "good degree of control and agency" in the pursuit of his drugs, and must be an effective planner and practical reasoner.

Schlosser also maintains that the unwilling addict's desire for the drugs and his drug-pursuing behavior are his own in a basic or minimal sense, a sense that appears to be absent in certain cases of pathology or brain damage. For instance, in anarchic hand syndrome (AHS) a lesion to part of the motor cortex results in the limb on the side opposite the lesion moving in goal-oriented ways that the agent cannot directly control, and denies experiencing as their own. For instance, the affected limb may grab nearby objects, or even do things at cross-purposes with the agent's intentions. For example, one person found their limb making moves on a checker board that they did not intend to make. Another case in which actions are experienced as disowned is that of schizophrenic individuals with so-called delusions of control, in which they report that their behavior is caused by some external source or agent. Clearly, though the unwilling addict does not identify with the motives with which they act, neither do they experience their bodily movements as alien, or as the result of external forces in the same way that those with these conditions do. So, though Frankfurt and Velleman's strategies may offer ways to account for agency par excellence, they do not seem to give us a way of understanding a more basic type of ownership that we have over our actions.

Schlosser proposes that in "normal cases" of agency, an agent's psychological states and actions are expressions of their own agency "by default," and it is only when something goes wrong that this default ownership is disrupted. Therefore, he denies that the event-causal theory, as it stands, fails to include agents. It is a mistake, he urges, to think that event-causal theories must be refined and supplemented in order to bring the agent back into the picture: the agent is there all along. Indeed, he rejects the agent/non-agent distinction as a strict dichotomy, and argues instead for the usefulness of understanding agency hierarchically, going from lower or more basic forms to higher or more complex forms, and for treating ownership as corresponding to these different levels of agency.

What Is It Like to Be an Agent?

Of course, in order for this to be a viable response, we need some understanding of what these "normal" cases are. And here Schlosser shifts the debate in an important way. He takes "normal cases" to be those in which one has a *subjective sense of ownership* over an action, i.e., those cases in which one experiences oneself as the source of one's behavior, in the way that schizophrenic individuals sometimes do not. An agent's ownership over their action is not here a matter of second-order volitions or a desire to act on the strongest reasons, but of the agent's subjective awareness of their own agency.

In order to explain how this sense of ownership arises, Schlosser appeals to the sub-personal comparator mechanism outlined in the previous chapter in our discussion of Pacherie's paper. Recall that this mechanism is responsible for the online monitoring, control, and guidance of behavior as it unfolds. It follows that "normal cases" of agency are those in which the "feedback-comparison" mechanism is functioning as it should. In particular, the sense of ownership over one's action arises when there is a match between the sensory feedback predicted by the forward model on the basis of some motor command, and the sensory feedback itself. This seems natural, since a match here would indicate that the action was unfolding as predicted, and this could be taken as a marker of successful control and guidance by the agent. In this way, then, Schlosser provides us with an explanation of a more minimal and basic type of ownership than can be captured by either Frankfurt's endorsement strategy or Velleman's appeal to a special desire. Schlosser allows, however, that his account could be *supplemented* with Frankfurt's or Velleman's theories to give an account of higher-order aspects of agency, such as when one exercises second-order volitions or chooses the action that is the most rational.

Notice that in making the case for a default sense of ownership over one's actions, Schlosser has introduced a special class of what we can call **agentive experiences**, namely, *experiences of oneself as the source of one's own behavior.* But once we recognize this novel class of experiences, new questions arise about how best to understand their nature. For instance, we may ask the descriptive question about what these experiences are like, the explanatory question of *how* exactly these experiences arise, and the functional question of what, if anything, these experiences are for.

Agentive Experience as a Form of Perception

Perhaps the simplest answer to these questions is that, like many of our experiences, agentive experiences are types of *sensory* experience arising out of a distinctive mode of sensory perception, with the function of informing us about our own agency. This is precisely the view defended by Tim Bayne, a philosopher of mind and cognitive science at Monash University in Melbourne, Australia, in "The Sense of Agency." Thus Bayne says, "[j]ust as we have sensory systems that function to inform us about the distribution of objects in our immediate environment, damage to our limbs, and our need for food, so too we have a sensory system (or systems) whose function it is to inform us about facets of our own agency."

His overall argument in his article is one of elimination. He starts with the claim that the three best candidates for where agentive experiences lie are thought, perception, and action, proceeding to argue that neither the doxastic model (thought) nor the telic model (action) succeed in accounting for such experiences. This leaves the perceptual model, which he shows can deal with various objections.

Bayne starts out by articulating what he takes to be at the core of agentive experience, i.e., "the experience of a particular movement or mental event as realizing one's own agency." How might we make sense of these experiences in perceptual terms? For this, Bayne turns, like Pacherie and Schlosser, to the comparator model of motor control. And in the same way that they do, Bayne explicitly connects this model of action control to agentive experiences by positing that when there is a match between the forward model prediction and sensory feedback, agentive experiences are generated, and when there is a mismatch, by contrast, experiences of alienation from the movement occur.

One reaction to this proposal might be to protest that agentive experiences can be explained in simpler terms, by appeal to conscious thoughts to the effect that one is engaging in some action, rather than by appeal to a distinct sensory experience. This is the *doxastic model* of agentive self-awareness.

One of the main challenges Bayne offers against the doxastic model appeals to the notion of **cognitive penetration**. This concept concerns the information a system has access to when it produces outputs on the basis of the inputs that it receives and the computations it performs. In particular, it concerns the extent to which *propositional attitudes*, like beliefs and desires, influence those computations and outputs. The systems that generate genuine actions are cognitively penetrable because they are influenced by what we believe. For example, an action of taking milk out of the fridge will be halted by the memory that there is no milk left. Perceptual systems, on the other hand, generally do not display this feature. Such systems, we say, are **informationally encapsulated** to the extent that they *lack* access to information stored outside the system. For example, the visual system receives light energy as input and outputs perceptual representations. The representations it produces are not influenced by beliefs about the stimuli. This is illustrated by perceptual illusions. When a stick is half submerged in water, for example, it falsely appears bent at the location that it makes contact with the surface. Although one may realize that the stick is actually straight, this belief will not alter one's visual experience; the stick still *looks* bent. This suggests that the visual system does not have access to the information carried by this belief.

Bayne argues that if cases of alienated agency, like those involved in anarchic hand syndrome, were explicable in terms of belief or judgment, as the doxastic model would have it, then one would expect that the experience would be cognitively penetrable. A change in belief would therefore result in a change in one's experience of one's behavior as alien. But Bayne maintains that if an individual with anarchic hand syndrome were to come to believe that all the movements made by their anarchic limb were indeed their own actions, they would *not* thereby come to *experience* those actions as their own. The illusion of alien agency would still be present. He says that this tells "firmly against" the doxastic model of agentive experiences, because it suggests that agentive experiences are informationally encapsulated, and informational encapsulation is a mark of perception.

An alternative to the doxastic model is what Bayne calls the *telic model* of agentive experience. In order to understand this model, it is important to get a grip on the distinction between **telic** and **thetic states**. Thetic states have the function of representing the way the world is. Paradigmatically thetic states are beliefs and perceptions. Telic states, on the other hand, have the function of bringing about changes in the world. Desires are paradigm telic states. On the telic model of agentive experiences, these experiences are telic states of the motor system.

Bayne rejects the telic model partly on the grounds that agentive experiences appear to be thetic, rather than telic. He asks us to consider the case of a patient discussed by the pioneering psychologist William James, who has his eyes closed while his arm is anaesthetized, and is asked to raise it. Unbeknownst to him, his arm is being held down so that, when he tries to raise his arm, his arm does not go up. He is surprised to see that this is the case when he finally opens his eyes. Now it seems, as Bayne argues, that the correct thing to say about this case is that James's patient has an (erroneous) experience of raising his arm rather than an experience of merely trying to raise his arm. But if so, then we should view the patient's experience of raising his arm as misrepresenting the world, in just the same way that we would view a perceptual experience of raising his arm as misrepresenting it. This counterexample seems to tell in favor of a non-telic model of agentive experiences. Bayne's argument, then, is that agentive experience must be thetic states, but ones that are not cognitively penetrable. And this combination of requirements suggests that they are sensory states.

A Worry for the Perceptual Model

Despite Bayne's argument for the perceptual model, there are worries one might have for it as well. One of the main objections that Bayne considers is that, unlike other perceptual experiences, there does not seem to be any perceptual organ dedicated to those of the agentive variety. Bayne proposes that we understand a perceptual organ as "a dedicated mechanism that takes as input energy of some kind and generates representations in an appropriate format, at least some of which are experiential." This applies well to the visual system, for example, which takes as input energy in the form of light waves and generates visually formatted representations, which can be consciously experienced. But Bayne's characterization doesn't seem to work for agentive experiences, since the comparator mechanism, which Bayne argues generates these experiences, does not take raw energy as input as his definition requires; it takes motor representations. In reply to this concern, Bayne proposes treating the sense of agency as a non-basic perceptual system, in virtue of this difference in the inputs it receives, where systems that receive raw energy as input are basic.

Taking Stock

In this chapter, we have seen various attempts at articulating how it is that *agency* might be exercised within the causal theory of action, such that we can account for the difference between cases where an agent participates in, and exercises ownership over their action, and cases where they do not. We saw that, according to Velleman and Frankfurt, agency requires the involvement of a special kind of mental state—either a desire to act in accordance with reason, or a second-order volition—by way of which an agent identifies with and participates in her actions. Hornsby rejects these attempts to supplement the causal story with additional psychological states, and argues that the causal theory is defective at its core, due to its "events-based character." Schlosser, on the other hand, maintains that, while the accounts of Velleman and Frankfurt may help us understand what he calls *agency par excellence*, there is a more *basic* sense of action ownership that is reflected instead by the subjective experiences of action generated by the comparator model of motor control. We ended by exploring the potential nature of these experiences, and in particular Bayne's view of them as sensory experiences.

Notes

1. Note that, in this way, the notion of agentive participation introduced here goes beyond the notion of guidance by an agent that Frankfurt introduced in the last chapter.
2. Frankfurt refers to a second-order volition, rather than a second-order desire for the following reason: To meet his requirement for agentive control, it is not enough for an agent to desire to have a certain first-order desire. They must also desire that that first-order desire be effective, that it be the one on which the agent's actions are based. The first-order desire, he says, must become the agent's will.
3. Oxford: Oxford University Press, 1986.

J. DAVID VELLEMAN

"What Happens When Someone Acts?"[1]

I

What happens when someone acts?

A familiar answer goes like this. There is something that the agent wants, and there is an action that he believes conducive to its attainment. His desire for the end, and his belief in the action as a means, justify taking the action, and they jointly cause an intention to take it, which in turn causes the corresponding movements of the agent's body. Provided that these causal processes take their normal course, the agent's movements consummate an action, and his motivating desire and belief constitute his reasons for acting.

This story is widely accepted as a satisfactory account of human action—or at least, as an account that will be satisfactory once it is completed by a definition of what's normal in the relevant causal processes. The story is widely credited to Donald Davidson's *Essays on Actions and Events* (1980), but I do not wish to become embroiled in questions of exegesis.[2] I shall therefore refer to it simply as the standard story of human action.

I think that the standard story is flawed in several respects. The flaw that will concern me in this paper is that the story fails to include an agent—or, more precisely, fails to cast the agent in his proper role.[3] In this story, reasons cause an intention, and an intention causes bodily movements, but nobody—that is, no person—does anything. Psychological and physiological events take place inside a person, but the person serves merely as the arena for these events: he takes no active part.[4]

To be sure, a person often performs an action, in some sense, without taking an active part in it; examples of such actions will be discussed below.[5] But these examples lack that which distinguishes human action from other animal behaviour, in our conception of it if not in reality. I shall argue that the standard story describes an action from which the distinctively human feature is missing, and that it therefore tells us, not what happens when someone acts, but what happens when someone acts halfheartedly, or unwittingly, or in some equally defective way. What it describes is not a human action *par excellence*.

II

Those who believe the story will of course contend that the events recounted in it add up to the agent's participating in his action, as components add up to a composite. The story doesn't mention his participation, they will explain, simply because his participation isn't a component of itself. Complaining that the agent's participation in his action isn't mentioned in the story is, in their view, like complaining that a cake isn't listed in its own recipe.

But this response strikes me as inadequate, because I don't accept the claim that the events recounted in the story add up to a person's activity. Various roles that are actually played by the agent himself in the history of a full-blooded action are not played by anything in the story, or are played by psychological elements whose participation is not equivalent to his. In a full-blooded action, an intention is formed by the agent himself, not by his reasons for acting. Reasons affect his intention by influencing him to form it, but they thus affect his intention by affecting him first. And the agent then moves his limbs in execution

of his intention; his intention doesn't move his limbs by itself. The agent thus has at least two roles to play: he forms an intention under the influence of reasons for acting, and he produces behaviour pursuant to that intention.

Of course, the agent's performance of these roles probably consists in the occurrence of psychological states and events within him. To insist that the story mention only the agent himself as the object of rational influence, or as the author and executor of intentions, would be to assume a priori that there is no psychological reduction of what happens in rational action. One is surely entitled to hypothesize, on the contrary, that there are mental states and events within an agent whose causal interactions constitute his being influenced by a reason, or his forming and conforming to an intention.

True enough. But the states and events described in a psychological reduction of a fully human action must be such that their interactions amount to the participation of the agent. My objection to the standard story is not that it mentions mental occurrences in the agent instead of the agent himself; my objection is that the occurrences it mentions in the agent are no more than occurrences in him, because their involvement in an action does not add up to the agent's being involved.

How can I tell that the involvement of these mental states and events is not equivalent to the agent's? I can tell because, as I have already suggested, the agent's involvement is defined in terms of his interactions with these very states and events, and the agent's interactions with them are such as they couldn't have with themselves. His role is to intervene between reasons and intention, and between intention and bodily movements, in each case guided by the one to produce the other. And intervening between these items is not something that the items themselves can do. When reasons are described as directly causing an intention, and the intention as directly causing movements, not only has the agent been cut out of the story but so has any psychological item that might play his role.[6] At this point, defenders of the standard story might wish to respond that it includes the agent implicitly, as the subject of the mental and physiological occurrences that it explicitly describes.[7] The reasons, intention, and movements mentioned in the story are modifications of the agent, and so their causal relations necessarily pass through him. Complaining that the agent takes no part in causal relations posited between reasons and intention, they might claim, is like complaining that the ocean takes no part in causal relations posited between adjacent waves.

But reflection on the phenomena of action reveals that being the subject of causally related attitudes and movements does not amount to participation of the sort appropriate to an agent.[8] As Harry Frankfurt has pointed out, an agent's desires and beliefs can cause a corresponding intention despite him, and hence without his participation. When an addict's desire for a drug causes his decision to take it, Frankfurt reminds us, "he may meaningfully make the analytically puzzling [statement] that the force moving him to take the drug is a force other than his own" (1988, p. 18), and so he may be "a helpless bystander to the forces that move him" (p. 21). Similarly, an agent can fail to participate when his intention causes bodily movements. A frequently cited example is the assassin whose decision to fire on his target so unnerves him as to make his trigger-finger twitch, causing the gun to fire.[9] In such a case, the agent's intention has caused corresponding movements of his body, but it has done so without the agent's participation.

III

Proponents of the standard story believe that the agent's participation is lacking from these cases only because the train of causes leading from his motives to his intention, or from his intention to his behaviour, is somehow abnormal.[10] They therefore deny that these cases demonstrate the inadequacy of the standard story. The story is committed only to the claim that the causal sequence from motives to behaviour will involve the agent himself when it proceeds in the normal way.

In my view, however, the discussion of "deviant" causal chains has diverted attention from simpler counterexamples, which omit the agent without lapsing into causal deviance; and it has thereby engendered a false sense of confidence in the requirement of causal normality, as sufficient to protect the standard story from counterexamples. In reality, an agent can fail to participate in his behaviour even when it results from his motives in the normal way. Consequently, no definition of causal normality will fix what ails the standard story.

Suppose that I have a long-anticipated meeting with an old friend for the purpose of resolving some minor difference; but that as we talk, his offhand comments provoke me to raise my voice in progressively sharper replies, until we part in anger. Later reflection leads me to realize that accumulated grievances had crystallized in my mind, during the weeks before our meeting, into a resolution to sever our friendship over the matter at hand, and that this resolution is what gave the hurtful edge to my remarks.[11] In short, I may conclude that desires of mine caused a decision, which in turn caused the corresponding behaviour; and I may acknowledge that these mental states were thereby exerting their normal motivational force, unabetted by any strange perturbation or compulsion. But do I necessarily think that I made the decision or that I executed it? Surely, I can believe that the decision, though genuinely motivated by my desires, was thereby induced in me but not formed by me; and I can believe that it was genuinely executed in my behaviour but executed, again, without my help. Indeed, viewing the decision as directly motivated by my desires, and my behaviour as directly governed by the decision, is precisely what leads to the thought that as my words became more shrill, it was my resentment speaking, not I.[12]

Of course, to say that I was not involved in the formation and execution of my intention is to concede that these processes were abnormal in some sense. My point, however, is that they were not abnormal in respect to the causal operation of the motives and intention involved. When my desires and beliefs engendered an intention to sever the friendship, and when that intention triggered my nasty tone, they were exercising the same causal powers that they exercise in ordinary cases, and yet they were doing so without any contribution from me. Hence what constitutes my contribution, in other cases, cannot be that these attitudes are manifesting their ordinary causal powers. When I participate in an action, I must be adding something to the normal motivational influence of my desires, beliefs, and intentions; and so a definition of when their influence is normal still won't enable the standard story to account for my participation.

IV

In omitting the agent's participation from the history of his action, the standard story falls victim to a fundamental problem in the philosophy of action—namely, that of finding a place for agents in the explanatory order of the world.[13] Our concept of full-blooded human action requires some event or state of affairs that owes its occurrence to an agent and hence has an explanation that traces back to him. As I have already noted, not all actions are full-blooded—witness the aforementioned raising of my voice, which owed its occurrence to my attitudes but not to me. Such an occurrence

may still count as the behavioural component of an action, as something that I did; but it lacks those features which seem to set human action apart from the rest of animal behaviour, and which thus provide the philosophy of action with its distinctive subject matter. What makes us agents rather than mere subjects of behaviour—in our conception of ourselves, at least, if not in reality—is our perceived capacity to interpose ourselves into the course of events in such a way that the behavioural outcome is traceable directly to us.

The question whether our practical nature is as we conceive it in this respect or in any other, for that matter—should be clearly distinguished from the question what we conceive our practical nature to be. Carl Ginet has recently argued (1990, pp. 11–15) that what happens when someone acts is that his behaviour is caused by a mental event whose intrinsic qualities include feeling as if it issues directly from him; but that this feeling corresponds to no actual feature of the event's causal history or structure. Even if Ginet's account correctly describes what actually happens in all or most of the episodes that we describe as actions, the question remains whether it correctly expresses what we mean to say about those episodes in so describing them.

Indeed, Ginet's account strongly suggests that what we mean to say about an event, in calling it an action, is unlikely to be what the account itself says, since it says that an action begins with a mental event that feels as if it were something that, according to this account, it is not—namely, a direct production of the agent. If our actions always begin with mental events that feel as if they are of agential origin, then one might expect the notion of agential origin to crop up in our commonsense concept of action; whereas one wouldn't expect a commonsense concept to include the philosophical critique of this notion, as having no realization in the history or structure of events. Ginet's account therefore suggests that we are likely to conceive actions as traceable to the agent in a sense in which, according to Ginet, they actually are not.[14]

Of course, if actions can fail to be as we conceive them, then the philosopher of action must specify whether his object of study is the concept or the reality. Does the philosopher seek to explain what we ordinarily mean when we call something an action, or does he seek to explain what something ordinarily is when so called?[15] My aim is to explain the former, at least in the first instance. For I suspect that our practices of deliberation, rationalizing explanation, and moral assessment are designed for action as we conceive it to be, and that any account of a reality substantially different from this conception will not help us to understand the logic of these practices.

In saying that my aim is to explicate our concept of action, as opposed to the reality, I do not mean to imply that I have given up hope of finding that the two are in accord. All I mean is that the concept has an antecedently fixed content that doesn't depend on what actually goes on in all or most or even a privileged few of the cases to which it's applied, and hence that correspondence between concept and reality will count as a cognitive achievement on our part. As for this cognitive achievement, however, I do hope to show that we need not despair of having attained it. For I hope to show that our concept of full-bloodied action, as involving behaviour that's ultimately traceable to an agent, can be understood in a way that may well be realized in the world, as we otherwise understand it.[16]

V

The obstacle to reconciling our conception of agency with the possible realities is that our scientific view of the world regards all events and states of affairs as caused, and hence explained, by other events and states, or by nothing at all. And this view would seem to leave no room for agents in the explanatory order. As Thomas Nagel puts it, "Everything I do or that anyone else does is part of a larger course of events that no one 'does,' but that happens, with or without explanation. Everything I do is part of something I don't do, because I am a part of the world" (1986, p. 114; cf. Bishop 1989, pp. 39ff.).

I implicitly endorsed this naturalistic conception of explanation when I conceded, earlier, that the standard story of action cannot be faulted merely for alluding to states and events occurring in the agent's mind. Any explanation of human action will speak in terms of some such occurrences, because occurrences are the basic elements of explanation in general.

Some philosophers have not been willing to concede this point. According to Roderick Chisholm (1976), for example, the explanatory order must include not only occurrences but also agents, conceived as additional primitive elements. The causation of occurrences by agents, rather than by other occurrences, is what Chisholm calls "agent-causation."

If the phrase "agent-causation" is understood in Chisholm's sense, then the naturalistic conception of explanation implies that agent-causation doesn't exist. Yet those who endorse the naturalistic conception of explanation, as I do, may still want to reconcile it with our commonsense conception of full-bloodied action, in which behaviour is traced to the agent himself rather than to occurrences within him. Such a reconciliation will have to show how the causal role assigned to the agent by common sense reduces to, or supervenes on, causal relations among events and states of affairs. And the agent's being a supervenient cause of this sort might also be called agent-causation, in a more relaxed sense of the phrase. If "agent-causation" is understood to encompass this possibility as well as the one envisioned by

Chisholm, then naturalists may want a theory of agent-causation, too.

This broader understanding of the phrase "agent-causation" is in fact endorsed by Chisholm himself, in a passage whose obscure provenance justifies extended quotation. Chisholm says:

> [T]he issues about "agent-causation"... have been misplaced. The philosophical question is not—or at least it shouldn't be—the question whether or not there is "agent-causation." The philosophical question should be, rather, the question whether "agent-causation" is reducible to "event causation." Thus, for example, if we have good reason for believing that Jones...kill[ed] his uncle, then the philosophical question about Jones as cause would be: Can we express the statement "Jones killed his uncle" without loss of meaning into a set of statements in which only events are said to be causes and in which Jones himself is not said to be the source of any activity? And can we do this without being left with any residue of agent-causation—that is, without being left with some such statement as "Jones raised his arm" wherein Jones once again plays the role of cause or partial cause of a certain event? (1978, pp. 622–23)

As the failings of the standard story reveal, we may have difficulty in meeting this challenge even if we help ourselves to a rich inventory of mental events and states. We could of course make the problem even harder, by asking how statements about Jones's action can be reexpressed, not just in terms of occurrences, but in terms of physical occurrences taking place among particles and fields. In that case, we would be worrying, in part, about the mind-body problem. But the problem of agent-causation lingers even if the mind-body problem can be made to disappear. For let there be mental states and events in abundance—motives, reasons, intentions, plans—and let them be connected, both to one another and to external behaviour, by robust causal relations; still, the question will remain how the existence and relations of these items can amount to a person's causing something rather than merely to something's happening in him, albeit something mental.[17] The problem of agency is thus independent of, though indeed parallel to, the mind-body problem. Just as the mind-body problem is that of finding a mind at work amid the workings of the body, so the problem of agency is that of finding an agent at work amid the workings of the mind.[18]

Now, Chisholm's non-reductionist solution to the problem of agency hasn't been taken seriously by many philosophers, nor do I intend to accord it serious attention here. However, I do sympathize with Chisholm's complaint that those who smirk at his solution do so unjustly, since they haven't taken seriously the problem that it is intended to solve. Chisholm says:

> Now if you can analyze such statements as "Jones killed his uncle" into event-causation statements, then you may have earned the right to make jokes about the agent as [a primitive] cause. But if you haven't done this, and if all the same you do believe such things as that I raised my arm and that Jones killed his uncle, and if moreover you still think it's a joke to talk about the agent as cause, then, I'm afraid, the joke is entirely on you. You are claiming the benefits of honest philosophical toil without even having a theory of human action. (ibid.)[19]

Here I think that Chisholm has come as close as anyone ever has to speaking frankly about a philosophical disagreement. And I hope that he would recognize it as a token of my respect for this accomplishment if I adopt his locution and declare that the proper goal for the philosophy of action is to earn the right to make jokes about primitive agent-causation, by explaining how an agent's causal role supervenes on the causal network of events and states.[20]

VI

The best sustained attempt at such an explanation, I think, is contained in a series of articles by Harry Frankfurt.[21] These articles begin with the question of what constitutes a person, but the focus quickly narrows to the person as an element in the causal order.[22] What primarily interests Frankfurt, as I have mentioned, is the difference between cases in which a person "participates" in the operation of his will and cases in which he becomes "a helpless bystander to the forces that move him."[23] And this distinction just is that between cases in which the person does and does not contribute to the production of his behaviour.

In attempting to draw this distinction, Frankfurt is working on the same problem as Chisholm, although he is seeking a reductive solution rather than a solution of the non-reductive sort that Chisholm favours. What's odd is that Frankfurt conceives of the problem in a way that initially appears destined to frustrate any reductive solution. In the following sections, I shall first explain why Frankfurt's project can thus appear hopeless; and I shall then suggest a conception of agency that might offer Frankfurt some hope.

VII

Frankfurt's strategy for identifying the elements of agent-causation is to identify what's missing from cases in which human behaviour proceeds without the agent as its cause. Frank-furt figures that if he can find what's missing from instances of less-than-full-blooded action, then he'll know what makes it the case, in other instances, that the agent gets into the act.

The cases of defective action that occupy Frankfurt's attention are cases in which the agent fails to participate because he is "alienated" from the motives that actuate him and which therefore constitute his will, or (as Frankfurt calls it) his "volition." And what's missing when an agent is alienated from his volition, according to Frankfurt, is his "identifying" or "being identified" with it.

Although Frankfurt draws this observation from cases in which the agent consciously dissociates himself from the motives actuating him— cases involving addiction or compulsion—it can equally be drawn from cases of the more familiar sort that I illustrated above. When my latent resentments against a friend yield an intention that causes my voice to rise, for example, I am not consciously alienated from that intention, perhaps, but I do not identify with it, either, since I am simply unaware of it. Hence Frankfurt might say that I do not participate in raising my voice because, being unaware of my intention, I cannot identify with it.

From this analysis of defective actions, Frankfurt draws the conclusion that what makes the difference between defective and full-blooded actions must be that, in the case of the latter, the agent identifies with the motives that actuate him (pp. 18 ff., 54). Here Frankfurt casts the agent in a role of the general sort that I envisioned in my critique of the standard story. That is, he doesn't think of the agent as entering the causal history of his action by displacing the motivational force of his desires or intentions; rather, he thinks of the agent as adding to the force of these attitudes, by intermediating among them. Specifically, the agent interacts with his motives, in Frankfurt's conception, by throwing his weight behind some of them rather than others, thereby determining which ones govern his behaviour.

VIII

Frankfurt thus arrives at the conclusion that if a causal account of action is to include the agent's contribution to his behaviour, it must include the agent's identifying himself with his operative motives. He therefore looks for mental events or states that might constitute the agent's self-identification.

Frankfurt's first candidate for the role is a second-order motive. The agent's identifying with the motive that actuates him, Frankfurt suggests, consists in his having a second-order desire to be actuated by that motive, whereas his being alienated from the motive consists in his having a desire not to be so actuated. These higher-order desires either reinforce or resist the influence of the agent's operative motive, and they thereby "constitute his activity"—that is, his throwing his weight behind, or withholding his weight from, the motive that actuates him, and thereby making or withholding a contribution to the resulting behaviour (p. 54).

As Gary Watson (1982) has pointed out and Frankfurt (pp. 65–66) has conceded, however, the same considerations that show the standard story to be incomplete can be applied to this enhanced version of it. For just as an agent can be alienated from his first-order motives, so he can be alienated from his second-order desires about them; and if his alienation from the former entails that they operate without his participation, then his alienation from the latter must entail similar consequences. Yet if the agent doesn't participate when a second-order desire reinforces his operative motive, then how can its doing so constitute his identifying with that motive and contributing to the resulting behaviour?

The occurrence that supposedly constitutes the agent's contributing to his behaviour seems itself to stand in need of some further contribution from him. Hence Frankfurt has failed to identify a mental item that necessarily implicates the agent in producing his behaviour.

Watson and Frankfurt have subsequently sought alternative candidates for the role. Watson argues that Frankfurt's references to second-order desires should be replaced with references to the agent's values. What is distinctive about behaviour in which the agent isn't fully involved, according to Watson, "is that the desires and emotions in question are more or less radically independent of [his] evaluational systems" (1982, p. 110).[24] Watson therefore suggests that the agent's contribution to an action is the contribution made by his system of values. But this suggestion solves nothing. A person can be alienated from his values, too; and he can be alienated from them even as they continue to grip him and to influence his behaviour—as, for instance, when someone recoils from his own materialism or his own sense of sin.[25] Hence the contribution of values to the production of someone's behaviour cannot by itself be sufficient to constitute his contribution, for the same reason that the contribution of his second-order desires proved insufficient.[26]

Frankfurt has made an attempt of his own to solve the problem, in subsequent papers, but with no more success.[27] Frankfurt now suggests that the agent's involvement in his behaviour can be provided by "decisions" or "decisive commitments" to his operative motives, since these mental items are indivisible from the agent himself. Frankfurt writes, "Decisions, unlike desires or attitudes, do not seem to be susceptible both to internality and to externality"—that is, to identification and alienation—and so "[i]nvoking them . . . would appear to avoid . . . the difficulty" (p. 68, n. 3). Yet the example of my unwitting decision to break off a friendship shows that even decisions and commitments can be foreign to the person in whom they arise.[28] How, then, can a decision's contribution to behaviour guarantee that the agent is involved?

One might wonder, of course, why Frankfurt and Watson assume that the agent's identifying with his operative motives must consist in a mental state or event specifiable in other terms, as a particular kind of desire, value, or decision. Perhaps identifying with one's motives is a mental state or event sui generis rather than a species of some other genus.

IX

Tempting though this suggestion may be, it is really just an invitation to beg the question of agent-causation. The question, after all, is how an agent causally contributes to the production of his behaviour; and to observe that he sometimes identifies with the motives producing that behaviour is to answer this question only if identifying with motives entails somehow making a causal contribution to their operation—throwing one's weight behind them, as I put it before. Other kinds of identification may not at all guarantee that the agent gets into the act. Frankfurt seems to think that an agent cannot fail to get into the act when he identifies with a motive. "It makes no sense," he says, "to ask whether someone identifies himself with his identification of himself, unless this is intended simply as asking whether his identification is wholehearted or complete" (p. 54). What this remark shows, however, is that Frankfurt is using the term "identification" in a specialized sense, since ordinary talk of identifying with something often denotes a mental event or state from which the subject can indeed be alienated. For example, you may find yourself identifying with some character in a trashy novel, even as you recoil from this identification. Identifying with the character may then seem like something that happens to you, or comes over you, without your participation.

One might think that such a case is what Frankfurt has in mind when he says that an agent's identification of himself may not be "wholehearted" or "complete," but I think not. For if it were, then Frankfurt would in effect be conceding that self-identification can sometimes occur without the agent's participation; and in that case, he could no longer claim that self-identification alone is what distinguishes the actions in which the agent participates from those in which he doesn't. An agent who identifies with a motive needn't be implicated in the behaviour that it produces if he can somehow dissociate himself from the identification. I think that what Frankfurt means, when he refuses to ask whether someone identifies with his self-identification, is that identifying oneself with a motive is unlike identifying with a character in a novel precisely in that it cannot happen at all without one's participation. Identifying with another person is, at most, a matter of imagining oneself in his skin, whereas identifying with a motive entails taking possession of it in fact, not just in imagination. Frankfurt therefore assumes, I think, that identifying with a motive is a mental phenomenon that simply doesn't occur unless one participates, although one may participate halfheartedly or incompletely.

Having put our finger on this assumption, however, we can see that for Frankfurt to posit self-identification as a primitive mental phenomenon would be to beg the question of agent-causation. For if self-identification is something that cannot occur without the agent's contributing to it, then it cannot occur without agent-causation, and we cannot assume that it occurs without assuming that agent-causation occurs—which is what we set out to show, in the first place. The question is whether there is such a thing as a person's participating in the causal order of events and states, and we can't settle this question simply by positing a primitive state or event that requires the person's participation.

Lest the question be begged, then, "self-identification" must not be understood as naming the primitive event or state that provides the needed reduction of agent-causation; it must be understood, instead, as redescribing agent-causation itself, the phenomenon to be reduced. When Frankfurt says that an agent participates in an action by identifying with its motives, he doesn't mean that self-identification is, among mere states and events, the one in virtue of which the agent gets into the act; rather, he is saying that if we want to know which are the mere states and events that constitute the agent's getting into the act, we should look for the ones that constitute his identifying with his motives. Frankfurt and Watson are therefore correct in trying to reduce self-identification to desires, values, or decisions—that is, to mental phenomena whose existence we can assume without presupposing that agent-causation occurs.

X

But how can such a reduction ever succeed? If we pick out mental states and events in terms that do not presuppose any causal contribution from the agent, then we shall have picked out states and events from which the agent can in principle dissociate himself. Since the occurrence of these items will be conceptually possible without any participation from the agent, we shall have no grounds for saying that their occurrence guarantees the agent's participation in the causal order.

The only way to guarantee that a mental state or event will bring the agent into the act is to define it in terms that mandate the agent's being in the act; but then we can't assume the occurrence of that state or event without already assuming the occurrence of agent-causation. Hence we seem to be confronted with a choice between begging the question and not answering it at all.

We may be tempted to slip between the horns of this dilemma, by characterizing some mental items in terms that are sufficiently vague to carry an assumption of agent-causation while keeping that assumption concealed. I suspect that Watson's appeals to "the agent's system of values," and Frankfurt's appeals to "decisive commitments" seem to succeed only insofar as they smuggle such an assumption into the story.[29] But a genuine resolution of the dilemma will require a more radical change of approach.

XI

The main flaw in Frankfurt's approach, I think, is that substituting one instance of agent-causation for another, as the target of reduction, does not advance the reductionist project. Since self-identification won't serve our purpose unless it's conceived as something to which the agent contributes, rather than something that happens to him, reducing self-identification to mere events and states is unlikely to be any easier than reducing action itself.

The way to advance the reductionist project is not to substitute one agent-causal phenomenon for another as the target of reduction, but to get the process of reduction going, by breaking agent-causation into its components. And surely, the principal component of agent-causation is the agent himself. Instead of looking for mental events and states to play the role of the agent's identifying with a motive, then, we should look for events and states to play the role of the agent. Something to play the role of agent is precisely what I earlier judged to be lacking from the standard story of human action. I pointed out that the agent intermediates in various ways between his reasons and intentions, or between his intentions and bodily movements; and I argued that the standard story omits the agent, not because it fails to mention him by name, but rather because it fails to mention anything that plays his intermediating role.

What plays the agent's role in a reductionist account of agent-causation will of course be events or states—most likely, events or states in the agent's mind. We must therefore look for mental events and states that are functionally identical to the agent, in the sense that they play the causal role that ordinary parlance attributes to him.

Looking for a mental event or state that's functionally identical to the agent is not as bizarre as it sounds. Of course, the agent is a whole person, who is not strictly identical with any subset of the mental states and events that occur within him. But a complete person qualifies as an agent by virtue of performing some rather specific functions, and he can still lay claim to those functions even if they are performed, strictly speaking, by some proper part of him. When we say that a person digests his dinner or fights an infection, we don't mean to deny that these functions actually belong to some of his parts. A person is a fighter of infections and a digester of food in the sense that his parts include infection-fighting and food-digesting systems. Similarly, a person may be an initiator of actions—and hence an agent—in the sense that there is an action initiating system within him, a system that performs the functions in virtue of which he qualifies as an agent and which are ordinarily attributed to him in that capacity. A reductionist philosophy of action must therefore locate a system of mental events and states that perform the functional role definitive of an agent.

I sometimes suspect that Frankfurt sees the necessity of this approach and may even think that he's taking it. My suspicion is based on the potential confusions that lurk in Frankfurt's talk of "identifying oneself with a motive" and thereby "making it one's own" (p. 18). The reader, and perhaps the writer, of these phrases may think that when a person identifies himself with motives, they become functionally identical to him, or that when motives become his, they do so by becoming him, in the sense that they occupy his functional role. But the psychological items that are functionally identical to the agent, in the sense that they play the causal role attributed to him in his capacity as agent, cannot be items with which he identifies in Frankfurt's sense, because identifying with something, in that sense, is a relation that one bears to something functionally distinct from oneself. The agent's identifying with an attitude requires, not only something to play the role of the attitude identified with, but also something else to play the role of the agent identifying with it; and the latter item, rather than the former, will be what plays the functional role of the agent and is therefore functionally identical to him.

XII

What, then, is the causal role that mental states and events must play if they are to perform the agent's function? I have already outlined what I take to be the causal role of an agent; but for the remainder of this paper, I want to confine my attention to that aspect of the role which interests Frankfurt, since my approach is simply a modification of his. Frankfurt doesn't think of the agent as having a function to play in implementing his own decisions, nor does he think of the agent as interacting with reasons *per se*. Frankfurt focuses instead on the agent's interactions with the motives in which his reasons for acting are ordinarily thought to consist. The agent's role, according to Frankfurt, is to reflect on the motives competing for governance of his behaviour, and to determine the outcome of the competition, by taking sides with some of his motives rather than others. For the moment, then, I shall adopt Frankfurt's assumption that the agent's role is to adjudicate conflicts of motives (though I shall subsequently argue that such adjudication is best understood as taking place among reasons instead).

Which mental items might play this role? Here, too, I want to begin by following Frankfurt. Frankfurt says that adjudicating the contest among one's motives entails occupying an "identity apart" from them (p. 18); and he says this, I assume, because a contest cannot be adjudicated by the contestants themselves. When an agent reflects on the motives vying to govern his behaviour, he occupies a position of critical detachment from those motives; and when he takes sides with some of those motives, he bolsters them with a force additional to, and hence other than, their own. His role must therefore be played by something other than the motives on which he reflects and with which he takes sides.

Indeed, the agent's role is closed, not only to the actual objects of his critical reflection, but to all potential objects of it as well. Even when the agent's reflections are confined to his first-order motives, for example, his second-order attitudes toward them cannot be what play his role; for he can sustain his role as agent while turning a critical eye on those second-order attitudes, whereas they cannot execute such a critical turn upon themselves. The functional role of agent is that of a single party prepared to reflect on, and take sides with, potential determinants of behaviour at any level in the hierarchy of attitudes; and this party cannot be identical with any of the items on which it must be prepared to reflect or with which it must be prepared to take sides.

Thus, the agent's role cannot be played by any mental states or events whose behavioural influence might come up for review in practical thought at any level. And the reason why it cannot be played by anything that might undergo the process of critical review is precisely that it must be played by whatever directs that process. The agent, in his capacity as agent, is that party who is always behind, and never in front of, the lens of critical reflection, no matter where in the hierarchy of motives it turns.

What mental event or state might play this role of always directing but never undergoing such scrutiny? It can only be a motive that drives practical thought itself. That is, there must be a motive that drives the agent's critical reflection on, and endorsement or rejection of, the potential determinants of his behaviour, always doing so from a position of independence from the objects of review. Only such a motive would occupy the agent's functional role, and only its contribution to his behaviour would constitute his own contribution.

What I'm positing here is an attitude that embodies the concerns of practical thought *per se*, concerns distinct from those embodied in any of the attitudes that practical thought might evaluate as possible springs of action. Frankfurt seems to assume that the concerns animating the agent's critical reflection on his first-order motives are embodied in his second-order desires about whether to be governed by those motives—such as the desire not to act out of anger, for example, or the desire to be actuated by compassion instead. Yet these second-order desires figure in critical reflection only with respect to a particular conflict of motives, and they can themselves become the objects of critical reflection one step further up the attitudinal hierarchy. Hence the concerns that they embody cannot qualify as the concerns directing practical thought as such, concerns that must be distinct from the objects of critical reflection and that must figure in such reflection whenever it occurs. If we want to find the concerns of practical thought *per se*, we must find motives that are at work not only when the agent steps back and asks whether to act out of anger but also when he steps back further and asks whether to restrain himself out of shame about his anger, and so on. Only attitudes that are at work in all such instances of reflection will be eligible to play the role of agent, who himself is at work whenever critical reflection takes place.

One is likely to balk at this proposal if one isn't accustomed to the idea that practical thought is propelled by a distinctive motive of its own. Agency is traditionally conceived as a neutral capacity for appraising and exercising motives—a capacity that's neutral just in the sense that it is not essentially animated by any motive in particular. This traditional conception is not hospitable to the idea that the deliberative processes constitutive of agency require a distinctive motive of their own. My point, however, is that anyone who wants to save our ordinary concept of full-bloodied action, as involving behaviour caused by the agent, had better grow accustomed to this idea, because the problem of agent-causation cannot be solved without it. Some motive must be behind the processes of practical thought— from the initial reflection on motives, to the eventual taking of sides; and from second-order reflection to reflection at any higher level— since only something that was always behind such processes would play the causal role that's ordinarily attributed to the agent.

XIII

Is there in fact such a motive? I believe so, though it is not evident in Frankfurt's account. Frankfurt's conception of critical reflection strikes me as omitting a concern that's common to reflection in all instances and at all levels.

The agent's concern in reflecting on his motives, I believe, is not just to see which ones he likes better; it's to see which ones provide stronger reasons for acting, and then to ensure

that they prevail over those whose rational force is weaker. What animates practical thought is a concern for acting in accordance with reasons. And I suggest that we think of this concern as embodied in a desire that drives practical thought.

When I speak of a desire to act in accordance with reasons, I don't have a particular desire in mind; any one of several different desires would fill the bill. On the one hand, it could be a desire to act in accordance with reasons so described; that is, the *de dicto* content of the desire might include the concept of reasons.[30] On the other hand, it could be a desire to act in accordance with considerations of some particular kind, which happened to be the kind of consideration that constituted a reason for acting. For example, I have argued elsewhere (1989) that rational agents have a desire to do what makes sense, or what's intelligible to them, in the sense that they could explain it; and I have argued that reasons for a particular action are considerations by which the action could be explained and in light of which it would therefore make sense. Thus, if someone wants to do what makes sense, then in my view he wants to act in accordance with reasons, though not under that description. In any of its forms, the desire to act in accordance with reasons can perform the functions that are attributed to its subject in his capacity as agent. We say that the agent turns his thoughts to the various motives that give him reason to act; but in fact, the agent's thoughts are turned in this direction by the desire to act in accordance with reasons. We say that the agent calculates the relative strengths of the reasons before him; but in fact, these calculations are driven by his desire to act in accordance with reasons. We say that the agent throws his weight behind the motives that provide the strongest reasons; but what is thrown behind those motives, in fact, is the additional motivating force of the desire to act in accordance with reasons. For when a desire appears to provide the strongest reason for acting, then the desire to act in accordance with reasons becomes a motive to act on that desire, and the desire's motivational influence is consequently reinforced. The agent is moved to his action, not only by his original motive for it, but also by his desire to act on that original motive, because of its superior rational force. This latter contribution to the agent's behaviour is the contribution of an attitude that performs the functions definitive of agency; it is therefore, functionally speaking, the agent's contribution to the causal order.

What really produces the bodily movements that you are said to produce, then, is a part of you that performs the characteristic functions of agency. That part, I claim, is your desire to act in accordance with reasons, a desire that produces behaviour, in your name, by adding its motivational force to that of whichever motives appear to provide the strongest reasons for acting, just as you are said to throw your weight behind them.

Note that the desire to act in accordance with reasons cannot be disowned by an agent, although it can be disowned by the person in whom agency is embodied. A person can perhaps suppress his desire to act in accordance with reasons; but in doing so, he will have to execute a psychic manoeuvre quite different from suppressing his anger or his addiction to drugs or his other substantive motives for acting. In suppressing his anger, the person operates in his capacity as agent, rejecting anger as a reason for acting; whereas in suppressing his desire to act in accordance with reasons, he cannot reject it as a reason for acting, or he will in fact be manifesting his concern for reasons rather than suppressing it, after all. The only way for a person truly to suppress his concern for reasons is to stop making rational assessments of his motives, including this one, thus

suspending the processes of practical thought. And in suspending the processes of practical thought, he will suspend the functions in virtue of which he qualifies as an agent. Thus, the sense in which an agent cannot disown his desire to act in accordance with reasons is that he cannot disown it while remaining an agent.

Conversely, a person's desire to act in accordance with reasons cannot operate in him without its operations being constitutive of his agency. What it is for this motive to operate is just this: for potential determinants of behaviour to be critically reviewed, to be embraced or rejected, and to be consequently reinforced or suppressed. Whatever intervenes in these ways between motives and behaviour is thereby playing the role of the agent and consequently is the agent, functionally speaking. Although the agent must possess an identity apart from the substantive motives competing for influence over his behaviour, he needn't possess an identity apart from the attitude that animates the activity of judging such competitions. If there is such an attitude, then its contribution to the competition's outcome can qualify as his—not because he identifies with it but rather because it is functionally identical to him.

XIV

Note, finally, that this reduction of agent-causation allows us to preserve some aspects of commonsense psychology about which we may have had philosophical qualms. What we would like to think, pre-philosophically, is that a person sometimes intervenes among his motives because the best reason for acting is associated with the intrinsically weaker motive, and he must therefore intervene in order to ensure that the weaker motive prevails. What inhibits us from saying this, however, is the philosophical realization that the weaker motive can never prevail, since an incapacity to prevail over other motives is precisely what constitutes motivational weakness. Every action, we are inclined to say, is the result of the strongest motive or the strongest combination of motives, by definition.

But my reduction of agent-causation enables us to say both that the agent makes the weaker motive prevail and that the contest always goes to the strongest combination of motives. The agent can make the weaker motive prevail, according to my story, in the sense that he can throw his weight behind the weaker of those motives which are vying to animate his behaviour and are therefore objects of his practical thought. But the agent's throwing his weight behind the weaker of these motives actually consists in its being reinforced by another motive, so that the two now form the strongest combination of motives. Thus, the weaker motive can prevail with the help of the agent simply because it can prevail with the help of another motive and because the agent is another motive, functionally speaking.

Come to think of it, what else could an agent be?

Notes

1. The material in this paper was originally presented to a seminar in the philosophy of action at the University of Michigan. I am grateful to the participants in that seminar for their comments and questions. A very different paper was presented under a similar title to the philosophy departments of Yale University and the University of Dayton; this paper shows the benefit of comments from those audiences as well. For comments on earlier drafts, I am grateful to Paul Boghossian, Sarah Buss, Daniel Cohen, John Martin Fischer, Harry Frankfurt, Carl Ginet, Brian Leiter, Connie Rosati, and several anonymous reviewers for this journal.

2. The story can be traced back at least as far as Hobbes, *Leviathan*, Part I, chapter vi.

3. I discuss another problem with the standard story in my (1992).

4. A critique along these lines, with special reference to Hobbes, appears in Dent (1984, Chapter 4). See, e.g., p. 99: "a weighty reason does not, like a weighty brick, fall upon one and impart a certain push to one's body."

5. Here I part company with some philosophers of action, who believe that nothing counts as an action unless the agent participates in it. (See, e.g., Bishop 1989, p. 41.) Of course, every action must be someone's doing and must therefore be such that an agent participates in it, in the sense that he does it. But this conception of agential participation doesn't require anything that is obviously missing from the standard story. What's missing from that story is agential participation of a more specific kind, which may indeed be missing from doings that count as cases—albeit defective or borderline cases—of action.

6. See Bishop (1989, p. 72): "Intuitively, we think of agents as carrying out their intentions or acting in accordance with their practical reasons, and this seems different from (simply) being caused to behave by those intentions or reasons."

7. See Goldman (1970, pp. 80ff).

8. See Ginet (1990, pp. 6–7): "For a person S to cause E, it is not enough for S to be the subject of just any sort of event that causes E."

9. The most recent discussion of such "deviant causal chains" appears in Bishop (1989, Chapters 4 and 5). See also Harman (1976, p. 445), Peacocke (1979, p. 124), Taylor (1966, p. 248), Goldman (1970, p. 54), and Davidson (1980, p. 79).

10. See, e.g., Davidson (1980, pp. xiii, 79, 87).

11. We can assume that this causal relation was mediated by any number of subconscious intentions—intentions to sever the friendship by alienating my friend, to alienate my friend by raising my voice, to raise my voice now... etc. So long as we assume that these intentions subconsciously crystallized as the conversation progressed (which is not hard to assume) we preserve the intuition that I'm currently trying to evoke—namely, that I did not participate in the resulting action. And surely, this intuition doesn't depend on the assumption that the causal links between these intentions and my behaviour weren't "sensitive" to counterfactual differences in them (in the sense defined by Bishop 1989, Chapter 5). Thus, we can conceive of cases in which reasons cause intentions, intentions cause behaviour in all the "right ways," and yet the agent doesn't participate.

12. I don't mean to suggest that these reflections absolve me of responsibility for my action. I have an obligation to be vigilant against unconsidered intentions and to keep my voice down, no matter what may be causing it to rise. The fact remains, however, that my responsibility for the action in question arises from my having failed to prevent or control it rather than from my having truly initiated it. And I am responsible for having failed to prevent or control the action because it would have yielded to various measures of self-scrutiny and self-restraint that I could have initiated. Thus, my responsibility depends on my capacity to intervene among events in a way in which I failed to intervene among my desires, intentions, and movements in this instance. If my behaviour could come about only in the manner described here— that is, springing directly from intentions that have simply come over me—nothing

would owe its occurrence to either my participating or failing to participate in events, and I might bear no responsibility for anything.

13. I believe that this problem is distinct from the problem of free-will, although the two are often treated together. For my views on the latter problem, see my (1990).

14. Ginet thinks that actions other than simple mental actions do issue from the agent in the sense that they involve the agent's causing something. But he thinks that something can be caused by an agent only insofar as it is caused by one of the agent's actions. And he thinks that the resulting regress, of actions in which things are caused by other actions, must terminate in a simple mental action—usually, the act of willing—which qualifies as an action only because it feels as if it was caused by the agent himself, although it hasn't in fact been caused by him in any sense. Thus, Ginet thinks that complex actions issue from the agent only in the sense that their component behaviour is ultimately caused by a mental event that misleadingly feels as if it issued from the agent. Since the agential ancestry of complex action is thus inherited from a simple mental act whose agential ancestry is itself illusory, the ancestry of all actions would seem to be tainted by illusion.

15. Here, of course, I assume that the term "action" does not function like the Kripkean name of a natural kind, referring to whatever shares the essential nature of all or most or a privileged few of the episodes to which it is applied. I assume that "action" has a de dicto meaning in virtue of which it may in fact fail to be a correct description of anything to which it is applied.

16. I therefore think that Ginet dismisses the causal conception of action too quickly. I do agree with Ginet that an agent, as a

persisting entity, is the wrong sort of thing to cause particular events. (Ginet cites Broad 1952, p. 215, as the source of this objection.) But this objection militates only against a non-reductive theory of agent-causation. It leaves open the possibility that the causation of events by the right sort of things—that is, by other events—may in some cases amount to, or deserve to be described as, their being caused by the agent himself. It therefore leaves open the possibility of agent-causation that's reducible to, or supervenient on, causation by events. (I discuss this possibility, and its implications, in the next section of the text.) Ginet argues against a conception that characterizes action in terms of event causation (pp. 11–13). But Ginet's argument suffers from two flaws. Ginet's argument is that we can conceive of a simple mental act, such as mentally saying a word, without conceiving of it as comprising a structure of distinct, causally related events. ("I mean that it is not conceptually required to have such a structure, under our concept of it as that kind of mental act" [p. 12].) Yet this point doesn't speak to the hypothesis that we conceive of the act in question as comprising behaviour caused by the agent, and that the behaviour's being caused by the agent supervenes on its causal relation to other events. Our concept of action may include agent-causation without including the supervenience base thereof. What's more, the illustrations that Ginet provides for his argument—pairs of mental causes and effects whose structure is clearly different from that of the mental act in question—are all cases in which the imagined cause is itself a mental act. But someone who thinks that a mental act consists in mental behaviour caused by the agent, in a sense that supervenes on it's being caused

by another event, is not likely to think that the causing event is yet another act.

17. Cf. Bishop (1989, p. 43).

18. The standard story of rational action has also illustrated that the problem is more than that of casting the agent in the role of cause. In explaining an action, we trace its history back to the agent who brought the action about; but then we trace back further, to the reasons that persuaded him to do so. And as Donald Davidson has argued (1980), the reasons cited in the explanation of an action must be, not just reasons that were available to the agent, but reasons for which he acted, the difference being precisely that the latter are the reasons that induced him to act. The reasons that explain an action are thus distinguished by their having exerted an influence upon the agent. In the explanation of an action, then, the agent must serve not only as an origin of activity, or cause, but also as an object of rational influence—and hence, in a sense, as an effect.

19. Note the need to insert the word "primitive" in Chisholm's phrase "the agent as cause," which illustrates that Chisholm has reverted to understanding agent-causation in a narrower sense.

20. See Bishop (1989, p. 69): "Of course action differs from other behaviour in that the agent brings it about, but the problem is how to accommodate such bringing about within a naturalist ontology."

21. "Freedom of the Will and the Concept of a Person," "Three Concepts of Free Action," "Identification and Externality," "The Problem of Action," "Identification and Wholeheartedness," all in Frankfurt's (1988). Frankfurt has recently returned to the topic, in his 1991 Presidential Address to the Eastern Division of the APA, entitled "The Faintest Passion." I shall not be dis-

cussing the new suggestions contained in this address.

22. Frankfurt says that the "essential difference between persons and other creatures" that he wishes to discuss "is to be found in the structure of a person's will" (1988, p.12). And he later suggests that if someone becomes unable to exercise his will in the relevant way, this inability "destroys him as a person" (p. 21).

23. 1988, p. 21. The same phrase appears on p. 22. In another essay Frankfurt formulates the distinction in terms of a person's "activity or passivity with respect to…states of affairs" (p. 54).

24. For a recent discussion of Watson's view, see Wolf (1990, Chapter 2).

25. I owe the latter example to Elizabeth Anderson (MS).

26. Of course, Watson refers not just to values lodged in the agent but to the agent's evaluational system; and he might argue that values are no longer integrated into that system once the agent becomes alienated from them. But in that case, Watson would simply be smuggling the concept of identification or association into his distinction between the agent's evaluational system and his other, unsystematized values. And just as Frankfurt faced the question how a volition becomes truly the agent's, Watson would face the question how a value becomes integrated into the agent's evaluational system.…

27. Again, the discussion that follows deals only with Frankfurt's published work on the subject, not his 1991 Presidential Address to the Eastern Division of the American Philosophical Association, in which he outlines a somewhat different solution.

28. I can of course imagine defining a phrase "decisive commitments" denoting only those commitments which an agent actively makes. In that case, decisive commitments indeed be such as cannot fail to have the agent's participation; but in what that participation consists will remain a mystery, and the claim that the agent participates in his actions by way of decisive commitments will be uninformative. A related criticism of Frankfurt's solution appears in Christman (1991, pp. 8–9)….

29. See notes 26 and 28, above.

30. This possibility may be ruled out by an argument in Bernard Williams' paper "Internal and External Reasons" (1981). In any case, Williams' argument does not rule out the alternative possibility, which is the one that I favour. I discuss Williams' argument in a manuscript tentatively entitled "External Reasons."

References

Anderson, E. (unpublished manuscript): "The Sources of Norms."

Bishop, J. 1989: *Natural Agency; an Essay on the Causal Theory of Action*. Cambridge: Cambridge University Press.

Broad, C.D. 1952: *Ethics and the History of Philosophy*. London: Routledge and Kegan Paul.

Chisholm, R. 1976: *Person and Object: a Metaphysical Study*. London: Allen and Unwin.

Chisholm, R. 1978: "Comments and Replies." *Philosophia*, 7, pp. 597–636.

Christman, J. 1991: "Autonomy and Personal History." *Canadian Journal of Philosophy*, 21, 1, pp. 1–24.

Davidson, D. 1980: *Essays on Actions and Events*. Oxford: Clarendon Press.

Dent, N.J.H. 1984: *The Moral Psychology of the Virtues*. Cambridge: Cambridge University Press.

Frankfurt, H. 1988: *The Importance of What We Care About*. Cambridge: Cambridge University Press.

Ginet, C. 1990: *On Action*. Cambridge: Cambridge University Press.

Goldman, A.I. 1970: *A Theory of Human Action*. Princeton: Princeton University Press.

Harman, G. 1976: "Practical Reasoning." *Review of Metaphysics*, 29, 3, pp. 431–63.

Nagel, T. 1986: *The View from Nowhere*. Oxford: Oxford University Press.

Peacocke, C. 1979: "Deviant Causal Chains." *Midwest Studies in Philosophy*, 4, pp. 123–56.

Taylor, R. 1966: *Action and Purpose*. Englewood Cliffs, NJ: Prentice-Hall.

Velleman, J.D. 1989: *Practical Reflection*. Princeton: Princeton University Press.

Velleman, J.D. 1990: "Epistemic Freedom." *Pacific Philosophical Quarterly*, 70, 1, pp. 73–97.

Velleman, J.D. 1992: "The Guise of the Good." *Nous*, 26, 1, pp. 3–26.

Watson, G. 1982: "Free Agency," in his *Free Will*. Oxford: Oxford University Press, pp. 205–20.

Williams, Bernard 1981: "Internal and External Reasons," in his *Moral Luck*. Cambridge: Cambridge University Press, pp. 101–13.

Wolf, S. 1990: *Freedom within Reason*. Oxford: Oxford University Press.

HARRY G. FRANKFURT

"Freedom of the Will and the Concept of a Person"

What philosophers have lately come to accept as analysis of the concept of a person is not actually analysis of *that* concept at all. Strawson, whose usage represents the current standard, identifies the concept of a person as "the concept of a type of entity such that *both* predicates ascribing states of consciousness *and* predicates ascribing corporeal characteristics...are equally applicable to a single individual of that single type."[1] But there are many entities besides persons that have both mental and physical properties. As it happens—though it seems extraordinary that this should be so—there is no common English word for the type of entity Strawson has in mind, a type that includes not only human beings but animals of various lesser species as well. Still, this hardly justifies the misappropriation of a valuable philosophical term.

Whether the members of some animal species are persons is surely not to be settled merely by determining whether it is correct to apply to them, in addition to predicates ascribing corporeal characteristics, predicates that ascribe states of consciousness. It does violence to our language to endorse the application of the term 'person' to those numerous creatures which do have both psychological and material properties but which are manifestly not persons in any normal sense of the word. This misuse of language is doubtless innocent of any theoretical error. But although the offense is "merely verbal," it does significant harm. For it gratuitously diminishes our philosophical vocabulary, and it increases the likelihood that we will overlook the important area of inquiry with which the term 'person' is most naturally associated. It might have been expected that no problem would be of more central and persistent concern to philosophers than that of understanding what we ourselves essentially are. Yet this problem is so generally neglected that it has been possible to make off with its very name almost without being noticed and, evidently, without evoking any widespread feeling of loss.

There is a sense in which the word 'person' is merely the singular form of 'people' and in which both terms connote no more than membership in a certain biological species. In those senses of the word which are of greater philosophical interest, however, the criteria for being a person do not serve primarily to distinguish the members of our own species from the members of other species. Rather, they are designed to capture those attributes which are the subject of our most humane concern with ourselves and the source of what we regard as most important and most problematical in our lives. Now these attributes would be of equal significance to us even if they were not in fact peculiar and common to the members of our own species. What interests us most in the human condition would not interest us less if it were also a feature of the condition of other creatures as well.

Our concept of ourselves as persons is not to be understood, therefore, as a concept of attributes that are necessarily species-specific. It is conceptually possible that members of novel or even of familiar nonhuman species should be persons; and it is also conceptually possible that some members of the human species are not persons. We do in fact assume, on the other hand, that no member of another species is a person. Accordingly, there is a presumption that what is essential to persons is a set of characteristics that we generally suppose—whether rightly or wrongly—to be uniquely human.

It is my view that one essential difference between persons and other creatures is to be found in the structure of a person's will. Human beings are not alone in having desires and motives, or in making choices. They share these things with the members of certain other species, some of whom even appear to engage in deliberation and to make decisions based upon prior thought. It seems to be peculiarly characteristic of humans, however, that they are able to form what I shall call "second-order desires" or "desires of the second order."

Besides wanting and choosing and being moved to do this or that, men may also want to have (or not to have) certain desires and motives. They are capable of wanting to be different, in their preferences and purposes, from what they are. Many animals appear to have the capacity for what I shall call "first-order desires" or "desires of the first order," which are simply desires to do or not to do one thing or another. No animal other than man, however, appears to have the capacity for reflective self-evaluation that is manifested in the formation of second-order desires.[2]

I

The concept designated by the verb 'to want' is extraordinarily elusive. A statement of the form "A wants to X"—taken by itself, apart from a context that serves to amplify or to specify its meaning—conveys remarkably little information. Such a statement may be consistent, for example, with each of the following statements: (a) the prospect of doing X elicits no sensation or introspectible emotional response in A; (b) A is unaware that he wants to X; (c) A believes that he does not want to X; (d) A wants to refrain from X-ing; (e) A wants to Y and believes that it is impossible for him both to Y and to X; (f) A does not "really" want to X; (g) A would rather die than X; and so on. It is therefore hardly sufficient to formulate the distinction between first-order and second-order desires, as I have done, by suggesting merely that someone has a first-order desire when he wants to do or not to do such-and-such, and that he has a second-order desire when he wants to have or not to have a certain desire of the first order.

As I shall understand them, statements of the form "A wants to X" cover a rather broad range of possibilities.[3] They may be true even when statements like (a) through (g) are true: when A is unaware of any feelings concerning X-ing, when he is unaware that he wants to X, when he deceives himself about what he wants and believes falsely that he does not want to X, when he also has other desires that conflict with his desire to X, or when he is ambivalent. The desires in question may be conscious or unconscious, they need not be univocal, and A may be mistaken about them. There is a further source of uncertainty with regard to statements that identify someone's desires, however, and here it is important for my purposes to be less permissive.

Consider first those statements of the form "A wants to X" which identify first-order desires—that is, statements in which the term 'to X' refers to an action. A statement of this kind does not, by itself, indicate the relative strength of A's desire to X. It does not make it clear whether this desire is at all likely to play a decisive role in what A actually does or tries to do. For it may correctly be said that A wants to X even when his desire to X is only one among his desires and when it is far from being paramount among them. Thus, it may be true that A wants to X when he strongly prefers to do something else instead; and it may be true that he wants to X despite the fact that, when he acts, it is not the desire to X that motivates him to do

what he does. On the other hand, someone who states that A wants to X may mean to convey that it is this desire that is motivating or moving A to do what he is actually doing or that A will in fact be moved by this desire (unless he changes his mind) when he acts.

It is only when it is used in the second of these ways that, given the special usage of 'will' that I propose to adopt, the statement identifies A's will. To identify an agent's will is either to identify the desire (or desires) by which he is motivated in some action he performs or to identify the desire (or desires) by which he will or would be motivated when or if he acts. An agent's will, then, is identical with one or more of his first-order desires. But the notion of the will, as I am employing it, is not coextensive with the notion of first-order desires. It is not the notion of something that merely inclines an agent in some degree to act in a certain way. Rather, it is the notion of an *effective* desire—one that moves (or will or would move) a person all the way to action. Thus the notion of the will is not coextensive with the notion of what an agent intends to do. For even though someone may have a settled intention to do X, he may nonetheless do something else instead of doing X because, despite his intention, his desire to do X proves to be weaker or less effective than some conflicting desire.

Now consider those statements of the form "A wants to X" which identify second-order desires—that is, statements in which the term 'to X' refers to a desire of the first order. There are also two kinds of situation in which it may be true that A wants to want to X. In the first place, it might be true of A that he wants to have a desire to X despite the fact that he has a univocal desire, altogether free of conflict and ambivalence, to refrain from X-ing. Someone might want to have a certain desire, in other words, but univocally want that desire to be unsatisfied.

Suppose that a physician engaged in psychotherapy with narcotics addicts believes that his ability to help his patients would be enhanced if he understood better what it is like for them to desire the drug to which they are addicted. Suppose that he is led in this way to want to have a desire for the drug. If it is a genuine desire that he wants, then what he wants is not merely to feel the sensations that addicts characteristically feel when they are gripped by their desires for the drug. What the physician wants, insofar as he wants to have a desire, is to be inclined or moved to some extent to take the drug.

It is entirely possible, however, that, although he wants to be moved by a desire to take the drug, he does not want this desire to be effective. He may not want it to move him all the way to action. He need not be interested in finding out what it is like to take the drug. And insofar as he now wants only to *want* to take it, and not to *take* it, there is nothing in what he now wants that would be satisfied by the drug itself. He may now have, in fact, an altogether univocal desire not to take the drug; and he may prudently arrange to make it impossible for him to satisfy the desire he would have if his desire to want the drug should in time be satisfied.

It would thus be incorrect to infer, from the fact that the physician now wants to desire to take the drug, that he already does desire to take it. His second-order desire to be moved to take the drug does not entail that he has a first-order desire to take it. If the drug were now to be administered to him, this might satisfy no desire that is implicit in his desire to want to take it. While he wants to want to take the drug, he may have *no* desire to take it; it may be that *all* he wants is to taste the desire for it. That is, his desire to have a certain desire that he does not have may not be a desire that his will should be at all different than it is.

Someone who wants only in this truncated way to want to X stands at the margin of pre-

ciosity, and the fact that he wants to want to X is not pertinent to the identification of his will. There is, however, a second kind of situation that may be described by 'A wants to want to X'; and when the statement is used to describe a situation of this second kind, then it does pertain to what A wants his will to be. In such cases the statement means that A wants the desire to X to be the desire that moves him effectively to act. It is not merely that he wants the desire to X to be among the desires by which, to one degree or another, he is moved or inclined to act. He wants this desire to be effective—that is, to provide the motive in what he actually does. Now when the statement that A wants to want to X is used in this way, it does entail that A already has a desire to X. It could not be true both that A wants the desire to X to move him into action and that he does not want to X. It is only if he does want to X that he can coherently want the desire to X not merely to be one of his desires but, more decisively, to be his will.[4]

Suppose a man wants to be motivated in what he does by the desire to concentrate on his work. It is necessarily true, if this supposition is correct, that he already wants to concentrate on his work. This desire is now among his desires. But the question of whether or not his second-order desire is fulfilled does not turn merely on whether the desire he wants is one of his desires. It turns on whether this desire is, as he wants it to be, his effective desire or will. If, when the chips are down, it is his desire to concentrate on his work that moves him to do what he does, then what he wants at that time is indeed (in the relevant sense) what he wants to want. If it is some other desire that actually moves him when he acts, on the other hand, then what he wants at that time is not (in the relevant sense) what he wants to want. This will be so despite the fact that the desire to concentrate on his work continues to be among his desires.

II

Someone has a desire of the second order either when he wants simply to have a certain desire or when he wants a certain desire to be his will. In situations of the latter kind, I shall call his second-order desires "second-order volitions" or "volitions of the second order." Now it is having second-order volitions, and not having second-order desires generally, that I regard as essential to being a person. It is logically possible, however unlikely, that there should be an agent with second-order desires but with no volitions of the second order. Such a creature, in my view, would not be a person. I shall use the term 'wanton' to refer to agents who have first-order desires but who are not persons because, whether or not they have desires of the second order, they have no second-order volitions.[5]

The essential characteristic of a wanton is that he does not care about his will. His desires move him to do certain things, without its being true of him either that he wants to be moved by those desires or that he prefers to be moved by other desires. The class of wantons includes all nonhuman animals that have desires and all very young children. Perhaps it also includes some adult human beings as well. In any case, adult humans may be more or less wanton; they may act wantonly, in response to first-order desires concerning which they have no volitions of the second order, more or less frequently.

The fact that a wanton has no second-order volitions does not mean that each of his first-order desires is translated heedlessly and at once into action. He may have no opportunity to act in accordance with some of his desires. Moreover, the translation of his desires into action may be delayed or precluded either by conflicting desires of the first order or by the intervention of deliberation. For a wanton may possess and employ rational faculties of a high

order. Nothing in the concept of a wanton implies that he cannot reason or that he cannot deliberate concerning how to do what he wants to do. What distinguishes the rational wanton from other rational agents is that he is not concerned with the desirability of his desires themselves. He ignores the question of what his will is to be. Not only does he pursue whatever course of action he is most strongly inclined to pursue, but he does not care which of his inclinations is the strongest.

Thus a rational creature, who reflects upon the suitability to his desires of one course of action or another, may nonetheless be a wanton. In maintaining that the essence of being a person lies not in reason but in will, I am far from suggesting that a creature without reason may be a person. For it is only in virtue of his rational capacities that a person is capable of becoming critically aware of his own will and of forming volitions of the second order. The structure of a person's will presupposes, accordingly, that he is a rational being.

The distinction between a person and a wanton may be illustrated by the difference between two narcotics addicts. Let us suppose that the physiological condition accounting for the addiction is the same in both men, and that both succumb inevitably to their periodic desires for the drug to which they are addicted. One of the addicts hates his addiction and always struggles desperately, although to no avail, against its thrust. He tries everything that he thinks might enable him to overcome his desires for the drug. But these desires are too powerful for him to withstand, and invariably, in the end, they conquer him. He is an unwilling addict, helplessly violated by his own desires.

The unwilling addict has conflicting first-order desires: he wants to take the drug, and he also wants to refrain from taking it. In addition to these first-order desires, however, he has a volition of the second order. He is not a neutral with regard to the conflict between his desire to take the drug and his desire to refrain from taking it. It is the latter desire, and not the former, that he wants to constitute his will; it is the latter desire, rather than the former, that he wants to be effective and to provide the purpose that he will seek to realize in what he actually does.

The other addict is a wanton. His actions reflect the economy of his first-order desires, without his being concerned whether the desires that move him to act are desires by which he wants to be moved to act. If he encounters problems in obtaining the drug or in administering it to himself, his responses to his urges to take it may involve deliberation. But it never occurs to him to consider whether he wants the relations among his desires to result in his having the will he has. The wanton addict may be an animal, and thus incapable of being concerned about his will. In any event he is, in respect of his wanton lack of concern, no different from an animal.

The second of these addicts may suffer a first-order conflict similar to the first-order conflict suffered by the first. Whether he is human or not, the wanton may (perhaps due to conditioning) both want to take the drug and want to refrain from taking it. Unlike the unwilling addict, however, he does not prefer that one of his conflicting desires should be paramount over the other; he does not prefer that one first-order desire rather than the other should constitute his will. It would be misleading to say that he is neutral as to the conflict between his desires, since this would suggest that he regards them as equally acceptable. Since he has no identity apart from his first-order desires, it is true neither that he prefers one to the other nor that he prefers not to take sides.

It makes a difference to the unwilling addict, who is a person, which of his conflicting first-order desires wins out. Both desires are his, to be sure; and whether he finally takes the drug or finally succeeds in refraining from taking it, he acts to satisfy what is in a literal sense his own desire. In either case he does something he himself wants to do, and he does it not because of some external influence whose aim happens to coincide with his own but because of his desire to do it. The unwilling addict identifies himself, however, through the formation of a second-order volition, with one rather than with the other of his conflicting first-order desires. He makes one of them more truly his own and, in so doing, he withdraws himself from the other. It is in virtue of this identification and withdrawal, accomplished through the formation of a second-order volition, that the unwilling addict may meaningfully make the analytically puzzling statements that the force moving him to take the drug is a force other than his own, and that it is not of his own free will but rather against his will that this force moves him to take it.

The wanton addict cannot or does not care which of his conflicting first-order desires wins out. His lack of concern is not due to his inability to find a convincing basis for preference. It is due either to his lack of the capacity for reflection or to his mindless indifference to the enterprise of evaluating his own desires and motives.[6] There is only one issue in the struggle to which his first-order conflict may lead: whether the one or the other of his conflicting desires is the stronger. Since he is moved by both desires, he will not be altogether satisfied by what he does no matter which of them is effective. But it makes no difference *to him* whether his craving or his aversion gets the upper hand. He has no stake in the conflict between them and so, unlike the unwilling addict, he can neither win nor lose the struggle in which he is engaged. When a person acts, the desire by which he is moved is either the will he wants or a will he wants to be without. When a *wanton* acts, it is neither.

III

There is a very close relationship between the capacity for forming second-order volitions and another capacity that is essential to persons—one that has often been considered a distinguishing mark of the human condition. It is only because a person has volitions of the second order that he is capable both of enjoying and of lacking freedom of the will. The concept of a person is not only, then, the concept of a type of entity that has both first-order desires and volitions of the second order. It can also be construed as the concept of a type of entity for whom the freedom of its will may be a problem. This concept excludes all wantons, both infrahuman and human, since they fail to satisfy an essential condition for the enjoyment of freedom of the will. And it excludes those suprahuman beings, if any, whose wills are necessarily free.

Just what kind of freedom is the freedom of the will? This question calls for an identification of the special area of human experience to which the concept of freedom of the will, as distinct from the concepts of other sorts of freedom, is particularly germane. In dealing with it, my aim will be primarily to locate the problem with which a person is most immediately concerned when he is concerned with the freedom of his will.

According to one familiar philosophical tradition, being free is fundamentally a matter of doing what one wants to do. Now the notion of an agent who does what he wants to do is by no means an altogether clear one: both the doing and the wanting, and the appropriate relation between them as well, require elucidation. But although its focus needs to be sharpened and its formulation refined, I believe that this notion does capture at least part of what is implicit in the idea of an agent who *acts* freely. It misses entirely, however, the peculiar content of the quite different idea of an agent whose *will* is free.

We do not suppose that animals enjoy freedom of the will, although we recognize that an animal may be free to run in whatever direction it wants. Thus, having the freedom to do what one wants to do is not a sufficient condition of having a free will. It is not a necessary condition either. For to deprive someone of his freedom of action is not necessarily to undermine the freedom of his will. When an agent is aware that there are certain things he is not free to do, this doubtless affects his desires and limits the range of choices he can make. But suppose that someone, without being aware of it, has in fact lost or been deprived of his freedom of action. Even though he is no longer free to do what he wants to do, his will may remain as free as it was before. Despite the fact that he is not free to translate his desires into actions or to act according to the determinations of his will, he may still form those desires and make those determinations as freely as if his freedom of action had not been impaired.

When we ask whether a person's will is free we are not asking whether he is in a position to translate his first-order desires into actions. That is the question of whether he is free to do as he pleases. The question of the freedom of his will does not concern the relation between what he does and what he wants to do. Rather, it concerns his desires themselves. But what question about them is it?

It seems to me both natural and useful to construe the question of whether a person's will is free in close analogy to the question of whether an agent enjoys freedom of action. Now freedom of action is (roughly, at least) the freedom to do what one wants to do. Analogously, then, the statement that a person enjoys freedom of the will means (also roughly) that he is free to want what he wants to want. More precisely, it means that he is free to will what he wants to will, or to have the will he wants. Just as the question about the freedom of an agent's action has to do with whether it is the action he wants to perform, so the question about the freedom of his will has to do with whether it is the will he wants to have.

It is in securing the conformity of his will to his second-order volitions, then, that a person exercises freedom of the will. And it is in the discrepancy between his will and his second-order volitions, or in his awareness that their coincidence is not his own doing but only a happy chance, that a person who does not have this freedom feels its lack. The unwilling addict's will is not free. This is shown by the fact that it is not the will he wants. It is also true, though in a different way, that the will of the wanton addict is not free. The wanton addict neither has the will he wants nor has a will that differs from the will he wants. Since he has no volitions of the second order, the freedom of his will cannot be a problem for him. He lacks it, so to speak, by default.

People are generally far more complicated than my sketchy account of the structure of a person's will may suggest. There is as much opportunity for ambivalence, conflict, and self-deception with regard to desires of the second order, for example, as there is with regard to first-order desires. If there is an unresolved conflict among someone's second-order desires, then he is in danger of having no second-order volition; for unless this conflict is resolved, he has no preference concerning which of his first-order desires is to be his will. This condition, if it is so severe that it prevents him from identifying himself in a sufficiently decisive way with any of his conflicting first-order desires, destroys him as a person. For it either tends to paralyze his will and to keep him from acting at all, or it tends to remove him from his will so that his will operates without his participation. In both cases he becomes, like the unwilling addict though in a different way, a helpless

bystander to the forces that move him.

Another complexity is that a person may have, especially if his second-order desires are in conflict, desires and volitions of a higher order than the second. There is no theoretical limit to the length of the series of desires of higher and higher orders; nothing except common sense and, perhaps, a saving fatigue prevents an individual from obsessively refusing to identify himself with any of his desires until he forms a desire of the next higher order. The tendency to generate such a series of acts of forming desires, which would be a case of humanization run wild, also leads toward the destruction of a person.

It is possible, however, to terminate such a series of acts without cutting it off arbitrarily. When a person identifies himself decisively with one of his first-order desires, this commitment "resounds" throughout the potentially endless array of higher orders. Consider a person who, without reservation or conflict, wants to be motivated by the desire to concentrate on his work. The fact that his second-order volition to be moved by this desire is a decisive one means that there is no room for questions concerning the pertinence of desires or volitions of higher orders. Suppose the person is asked whether he wants to want to want to concentrate on his work. He can properly insist that this question concerning a third-order desire does not arise. It would be a mistake to claim that, because he has not considered whether he wants the second-order volition he has formed, he is indifferent to the question of whether it is with this volition or with some other that he wants his will to accord. The decisiveness of the commitment he has made means that he has decided that no further question about his second-order volition, at any higher order, remains to be asked. It is relatively unimportant whether we explain this by saying that this commitment implicitly generates an endless series of confirming desires of higher orders, or by saying that the commitment is tantamount to a dissolution of the pointedness of all questions concerning higher orders of desire.

Examples such as the one concerning the unwilling addict may suggest that volitions of the second order, or of higher orders, must be formed deliberately and that a person characteristically struggles to ensure that they are satisfied. But the conformity of a person's will to his higher-order volitions may be far more thoughtless and spontaneous than this. Some people are naturally moved by kindness when they want to be kind, and by nastiness when they want to be nasty, without any explicit forethought and without any need for energetic self-control. Others are moved by nastiness when they want to be kind and by kindness when they intend to be nasty, equally without forethought and without active resistance to these violations of their higher-order desires. The enjoyment of freedom comes easily to some. Others must struggle to achieve it.

IV

My theory concerning the freedom of the will accounts easily for our disinclination to allow that this freedom is enjoyed by the members of any species inferior to our own. It also satisfies another condition that must be met by any such theory, by making it apparent why the freedom of the will should be regarded as desirable. The enjoyment of a free will means the satisfaction of certain desires—desires of the second or of higher orders—whereas its absence means their frustration. The satisfactions at stake are those which accrue to a person of whom it may be said that his will is his own. The corresponding frustrations are those suffered by a person of whom it may be said that he is estranged from himself, or that he finds himself a helpless or a passive bystander to the forces that move him.

A person who is free to do what he wants to do may yet not be in a position to have the will he wants. Suppose, however, that he enjoys both freedom of action and freedom of the will. Then he is not only free to do what he wants to do; he is also free to want what he wants to want. It seems to me that he has, in that case, all the freedom it is possible to desire or to conceive. There are other good things in life, and he may not possess some of them. But there is nothing in the way of freedom that he lacks.

It is far from clear that certain other theories of the freedom of the will meet these elementary but essential conditions: that it be understandable why we desire this freedom and why we refuse to ascribe it to animals. Consider, for example, Roderick Chisholm's quaint version of the doctrine that human freedom entails an absence of causal determination.[7] Whenever a person performs a free action, according to Chisholm, it's a miracle. The motion of a person's hand, when the person moves it, is the outcome of a series of physical causes; but some event in this series, "and presumably one of those that took place within the brain, was caused by the agent and not by any other events" (18). A free agent has, therefore, "a prerogative which some would attribute only to God: each of us, when we act, is a prime mover unmoved" (23).

This account fails to provide any basis for doubting that animals of subhuman species enjoy the freedom it defines. Chisholm says nothing that makes it seem less likely that a rabbit performs a miracle when it moves its leg than that a man does so when he moves his hand. But why, in any case, should anyone care whether he can interrupt the natural order of causes in the way Chisholm describes? Chisholm offers no reason for believing that there is a discernible difference between the experience of a man who miraculously initiates a series of causes when he moves his hand and a man who moves his hand without any such breach of the normal causal sequence. There appears to be no concrete basis for preferring to be involved in the one state of affairs rather than in the other.[8]

It is generally supposed that, in addition to satisfying the two conditions I have mentioned, a satisfactory theory of the freedom of the will necessarily provides an analysis of one of the conditions of moral responsibility. The most common recent approach to the problem of understanding the freedom of the will has been, indeed, to inquire what is entailed by the assumption that someone is morally responsible for what he has done. In my view, however, the relation between moral responsibility and the freedom of the will has been very widely misunderstood. It is not true that a person is morally responsible for what he has done only if his will was free when he did it. He may be morally responsible for having done it even though his will was not free at all.

A person's will is free only if he is free to have the will he wants. This means that, with regard to any of his first-order desires, he is free either to make that desire his will or to make some other first-order desire his will instead. Whatever his will, then, the will of the person whose will is free could have been otherwise; he could have done otherwise than to constitute his will as he did. It is a vexed question just how 'he could have done otherwise' is to be understood in contexts such as this one. But although this question is important to the theory of freedom, it has no bearing on the theory of moral responsibility. For the assumption that a person is morally responsible for what he has done does not entail that the person was in a position to have whatever will he wanted.

This assumption *does* entail that the person did what he did freely, or that he did it of his own free will. It is a mistake, however, to believe that someone acts freely only when he is free to do whatever he wants or that he acts of his own free will only if his will is free. Suppose that a person has done what he wanted to do, that he did it because he wanted to do it, and that the will by which he was moved when he did it was his will because it was the will he wanted. Then he did it freely and of his own free will. Even supposing that he could have done otherwise, he would not have done otherwise; and even supposing that he could have had a different will, he would not have wanted his will to differ from what it was. Moreover, since the will that moved him when he acted was his will because he wanted it to be, he cannot claim that his will was forced upon him or that he was a passive bystander to its constitution. Under these conditions, it is quite irrelevant to the evaluation of his moral responsibility to inquire whether the alternatives that he opted against were actually available to him.[9]

In illustration, consider a third kind of addict. Suppose that his addiction has the same physiological basis and the same irresistible thrust as the addictions of the unwilling and wanton addicts, but that he is altogether delighted with his condition. He is a willing addict, who would not have things any other way. If the grip of his addiction should somehow weaken, he would do whatever he could to reinstate it; if his desire for the drug should begin to fade, he would take steps to renew its intensity.

The willing addict's will is not free, for his desire to take the drug will be effective regardless of whether or not he wants this desire to constitute his will. But when he takes the drug, he takes it freely and of his own free will. I am inclined to understand his situation as involving the overdetermination of his first-order desire to take the drug. This desire is his effective desire because he is physiologically addicted. But it is his effective desire also because he wants it to be. His will is outside his control, but, by his second order desire that his desire for the drug should be effective, he has made this will his own. Given that it is therefore not only because of his addiction that his desire for the drug is effective, he may be morally responsible for taking the drug.

My conception of the freedom of the will appears to be neutral with regard to the problem of determinism. It seems conceivable that it should be causally determined that a person is free to want what he wants to want. If this is conceivable, then it might be causally determined that a person enjoys a free will. There is no more than an innocuous appearance of paradox in the proposition that it is determined, ineluctably and by forces beyond their control, that certain people have free wills and that others do not. There is no incoherence in the proposition that some agency other than a person's own is responsible (even *morally* responsible) for the fact that he enjoys or fails to enjoy freedom of the will. It is possible that a person should be morally responsible for what he does of his own free will and that some other person should also be morally responsible for his having done it.[10]

On the other hand, it seems conceivable that it should come about by chance that a person is free to have the will he wants. If this is conceivable, then it might be a matter of chance that certain people enjoy freedom of the will and that certain others do not. Perhaps it is also conceivable, as a number of philosophers believe, for states of affairs to come about in a way other than by chance or as the outcome of a sequence of natural causes. If it is indeed conceivable for the relevant states of affairs to come about in some third way, then it is also possible that a person should in that third way come to enjoy the freedom of the will.

Notes

1. P.F. Strawson, *Individuals* (London: Methuen, 1959), pp. 101–02. Ayer's usage of 'person' is similar: "it is characteristic of persons in this sense that besides having various physical properties...they are also credited with various forms of consciousness" [A.J. Ayer, *The Concept of a Person* (New York: St. Martin's, 1963), p. 82]. What concerns Strawson and Ayer is the problem of understanding the relation between mind and body, rather than the quite different problem of understanding what it is to be a creature that not only has a mind and a body but is also a person.

2. For the sake of simplicity, I shall deal only with what someone wants or desires, neglecting related phenomena such as choices and decisions. I propose to use the verbs 'to want' and 'to desire' interchangeably, although they are by no means perfect synonyms. My motive in forsaking the established nuances of these words arises from the fact that the verb 'to want,' which suits my purposes better so far as its meaning is concerned, does not lend itself so readily to the formation of nouns as does the verb 'to desire.' It is perhaps acceptable, albeit graceless, to speak in the plural of someone's "wants." But to speak in the singular of someone's "want" would be an abomination.

3. What I say in this paragraph applies not only to cases in which 'to X' refers to a possible action or inaction. It also applies to cases in which 'to X' refers to a first-order desire and in which the statement that 'A wants to X' is therefore a shortened version of a statement—"A wants to want to X"—that identifies a desire of the second order.

4. It is not so clear that the entailment relation described here holds in certain kinds of cases, which I think may fairly be regarded as nonstandard, where the essential difference between the standard and the nonstandard cases lies in the kind of description by which the first-order desire in question is identified. Thus, suppose that

A admires *B* so fulsomely that, even though he does not know what *B* wants to do, he wants to be effectively moved by whatever desire effectively moves *B*; without knowing what *B*'s will is, in other words, *A* wants his own will to be the same. It certainly does not follow that *A* already has, among his desires, a desire like the one that constitutes *B*'s will. I shall not pursue here the questions of whether there are genuine counterexamples to the claim made in the text or of how, if there are, that claim should be altered.

5. Creatures with second-order desires but no second-order volitions differ significantly from brute animals, and, for some purposes, it would be desirable to regard them as persons. My usage, which withholds the designation 'person' from them, is thus somewhat arbitrary. I adopt it largely because it facilitates the formulation of some of the points I wish to make. Hereafter, whenever I consider statements of the form "*A* wants to want to *X*," I shall have in mind statements identifying second-order volitions and not statements identifying second-order desires that are not second-order volitions.

6. In speaking of the evaluation of his own desires and motives as being characteristic of a person, I do not mean to suggest that a person's second-order volitions necessarily manifest a *moral* stance on his part toward his first-order desires. It may not be from the point of view of morality that the person evaluates his first-order desires. Moreover, a person may be capricious and irresponsible in forming his second-order volitions and give no serious consideration to what is at stake. Second-order volitions express evaluations only in the sense that they are preferences. There is no essential restriction on the kind of basis, if any, upon which they are formed.

7. "Freedom and Action," in K. Lehrer, ed., *Freedom and Determinism* (New York: Random House, 1966), pp. 11–44.

8. I am not suggesting that the alleged difference between these two states of affairs is unverifiable. On the contrary, physiologists might well be able to show that Chisholm's conditions for a free action are not satisfied, by establishing that there is no relevant brain event for which a sufficient physical cause cannot be found.

9. For another discussion of the considerations that cast doubt on the principle that a person is morally responsible for what he has done only if he could have done otherwise, see my "Alternate Possibilities and Moral Responsibility," [*Journal of Philosophy*], LXVI, 23 (Dec. 4, 1969): 829–39.

10. There is a difference between being *fully* responsible and being solely responsible. Suppose that the willing addict has been made an addict by the deliberate and calculated work of another. Then it may be that both the addict and this other person are fully responsible for the addict's taking the drug, while neither of them is solely responsible for it. That there is a distinction between full moral responsibility and sole moral responsibility is apparent in the following example. A certain light can be turned on or off by flicking either of two switches, and each of these switches is simultaneously flicked to the "on" position by a different person, neither of whom is aware of the other. Neither person is solely responsible for the light's going on, nor do they share the responsibility in the sense that each is partially responsible; rather, each of them is fully responsible.

JENNIFER HORNSBY

"Agency and Actions"

Among philosophical questions about human agency, one can distinguish in a rough and ready way between those that arise in philosophy of mind and those that arise in ethics. In philosophy of mind, one central aim has been to account for the place of agents in a world whose operations are supposedly 'physical.' In ethics, one central aim has been to account for the connexion between ethical species of normativity and the distinctive deliberative and practical capacities of human beings. Ethics then is involved with questions of moral psychology whose answers admit a kind of richness in the life of human beings from which the philosophy of mind may ordinarily prescind. Philosophy of mind, insofar as it treats the phenomenon of agency as one facet of the phenomenon of mentality, has been more concerned with how there can be 'mental causation' than with any details of a story of human motivation or of the place of evaluative commitments within such a story.

This little account of the different agenda of two philosophical approaches to human agency is intended only to speak to the state of play as we have it, and it is certainly somewhat artificial. I offer it here as a way to make sense of attitudes to what has come to be known as the *standard story of action*. The standard story is assumed to be the orthodoxy on which philosophers of mind, who deal with the broad metaphysical questions, have converged, but it is held to be deficient when it comes to specifically ethical questions. Michael Smith, for instance, asks: 'How do we turn the standard story of action into the story of "orthonomous action?,"' where

orthonomous action is action 'under the rule of the right as opposed to the wrong.'[1] [...]

The standard story is sometimes encapsulated in the slogan: 'Beliefs and desires cause actions.' In the version of Smith's that I shall consider here, it says:

> Actions are bodily movements that are caused and rationalized by an agent's desire for an end and a belief that moving her body in the relevant way will bring that end about.

Smith's unpacking of the slogan shows how reason is supposed to enter the story: the word 'rationalize' is used in conveying that that which causes an action constitutes the agent's reason for it.[2] For the purposes of the present paper, it need not matter very much exactly how the story is formulated. My objection to the standard story will be that—despite the fact that the word 'agent' appears in definitions like Smith's—*the story leaves agents out*. Human beings are ineliminable from any account of their agency, and, in any of its versions, the standard story is not a story of agency at all.

The claim I intend by saying that the story leaves agents out is not answered by adding states of mind of different sorts from beliefs and desires to the causes of bodily movements. For what concerns me is the fact, as I see it, that 'belief-desire psychology' as it is understood in the standard story can cover none of the ground where human agency is found, and cannot do so even when it is supplemented with further mental states.[3] The popularity of the standard story then seems very unfortunate. It is not merely that that which supplements it inherits its crucial flaw. It is worse than that. For when the standard story is the base line for questions in moral psychology, a shape is imposed on those questions that they should never have been allowed to take on. Meanwhile the orthodoxy in philosophy of mind is silently reinforced.

[…]

1

There are some ideas in the background of the standard causal story which I should start by spelling out. The basic idea is that there is a category of particulars called 'events,' and that some of the things in this category—spatiotemporal things that can happen only once—merit the title actions. Thus any of the following may on occasion apply to an event: 'a mosquito's biting me,' 'the chocolate's melting,' 'Don's falling from the cliff,' 'Jones's stealing the jewels,' 'Helen's waving her right arm.' And, very likely, the last two phrases here—but (*human action* being implicitly understood) only these two—apply to events that are actions. As we have seen, *bodily movements* (some of them) are said to be actions in the standard story. That is because such things as stealing the jewels are things that people do by moving their bodies; and if Jones stole the jewels by moving his body thus and so, then his stealing the jewels is (the same event as) his moving his body thus and so. 'His stealing the jewels' describes a bodily event by allusion to an effect that it had.[4]

[…]

An account of action which is *events-based*, as I shall mean this, assumes more than that actions are such redescribable bodily movements. It also assumes that the phenomenon of human agency, and not just a category of events, is delimited when it is said which events are actions. And it takes it that the causal truths about agency can be formulated as claims about causation of, or by, an action—as claims about particulars. (See Smith's version quoted above in which both of these assumptions are implicit.) An events-based account thus accords a very central role to events, having recourse to them both in marking out the phenomenon of agency, and in a causal depiction of it.

The events-based character of the standard story is what I shall criticize to begin with. One way to see the error of its first assumption is to think about failures to act (in a certain sense). One way to see the error of its second assumption is to think about how action-explanation works. I take each of these in turn now.

1.1 The key notion in much theory of action has been that of doing something *intentionally*. This is evidently the notion that has informed the standard story, which takes 'believe' 'desire' and 'do intentionally' to form a sort of conceptual trio. Behind the use of 'intentionally' is the thought that one keeps track of what is significant in someone's life as an agent if one attends to what they *intentionally* do. That was one of Davidson's principal claims in his paper 'Agency.'[5]

But someone can do something intentionally without there being any action that is their doing the thing. Consider A who decides she shouldn't take a chocolate, and refrains from moving her arm towards the box; or B who doesn't want to be disturbed by answering calls, and lets the telephone carry on ringing; or C who, being irritated by someone, pays that person no attention. Imagining that each of these things is intentionally done ensures that we have examples of agency in a sense that Davidson's claim brought out. But since in these cases, A, B and C don't move their bodies, we have examples which the standard story doesn't speak to.

[…]

1.2 [...]

Well, a proponent of the standard story might acknowledge that there are more explanations in the 'belief-desire' style than there are events [...] about which his story could be told, but respond by suggesting that action-explanation comes in two sorts. The suggestion would be that there are explanations in which the occurrence of an event—of a bodily movement—is explained and the standard story can straightforwardly be told; and there are, in addition, explanations in which the standard story cannot be told, although some other, related story, which also mentions 'beliefs and desires,' no doubt can. But the suggestion is actually not at all plausible. For when we ask why someone did something, expecting to learn about what they thought or wanted, we don't always need to consider whether or not there was a positive performance on their part; explanation can carry on in the same vein, whether there was or not. One might discover that it was because she wanted to wreak revenge on the producer that she spoiled the show, and it not matter very much whether, for example, she put a sleeping tablet into the principal performer's drink (so that her spoiling the show was an event that was her putting…) or she simply failed to turn up (so that there was no event, or at least no bodily movement of hers, that was her spoiling the show). Either way, we say that she spoiled the show because she wanted to wreak revenge; and it makes no odds here whether the case is of such a sort that we can construct a statement 'Her wanting to wreak revenge —— caused [an event which was whatever bodily movement was] her Φing.'

In the version of Smith's that we looked at, the standard story contains such causal statements as: 'Her wanting —— and her believing —— caused and rationalized a bodily move-

ment.' Simplifying a bit, we can say that the standard story's causal statements are on the following style and pattern:[8]

(SS) Her desire —— caused [an event which was] her bodily movement.

What we have just seen is that it is sometimes impossible to find a statement in this style, and implausible that we should be looking for statements in two different styles. That surely suggests that our focus should be on the sort of causal claim which comes naturally and which applies in every case:

(*) She did such and such because she desired ——.

Causal statements like this hardly need defence: they are statements of a kind that we commonly recognize to be true.[9]

[…]

It will have to suffice here to have questioned the conception of action-explanation that an events-based account characteristically leads to. First, a causal explanation of why someone did something could not always be the explanation of an event's occurrence (for want sometimes of a 'positive performance'). Secondly, an action-explanation doesn't ever seem to be focussed on saying why an event occurred. Once these points are appreciated, perhaps the habit of thinking that action-explanations mention items which combine with one another in the production of an event will start to be undermined.[13]

2

The foregoing is meant to indicate that agency is misconceived in an events-based account of it. Examples where there is no 'positive performance' suggest that the account leaves things out, and they point towards the impossibility of accommodating agency to its view about the operation of causality. Perhaps that view—of causality operating through items linked in causal chains—is the correct view of causal truths in some areas. But the truths that make up the phenomenon of agency seem not to belong in a world in which causality operates only in such a manner.[14]

I come now to a more direct way of showing that agency cannot be captured if one takes this view of causality's operation. I suggest that if one attempts to locate agency within the confines of such a view, one fails.

Consider Hume on the subject of bodily movements' production:

> We learn from anatomy, that the immediate object of power in voluntary motion, is not the member itself which is moved, but certain muscles, and nerves, and animal spirits, and, perhaps, something still more minute and more unknown, through which the motion is successively propagated, ere it reach the member itself whose motion is the immediate object of volition. [T]he power, by which this whole operation is performed is, to the last degree, mysterious and unintelligible.... [W]e have no power [to move our limbs]; but only that to move certain animal spirits, which, though they produce at last the motion of our limbs, yet operate in such a manner as is wholly beyond our comprehension.[15]

Hume's account of how limb movements come about provides one way of filling out one part of the standard story. But it is impossible to believe that Hume has succeeded in offering any part of any story of human agency. The lesson from anatomy, supposedly, is that the only effects we can produce are events in our brains, and thus, as Hume himself puts it, 'totally different from' the effects that we intend. But it is undeniable that among the effects we produce when we do something intentionally, there are some that we intend—whether bodily movements, or events in the region beyond our bodies. And if we do produce intended effects, then we can produce them. It is true, of course, that advances in neurophysiology have made the production of limb movements less incomprehensible than Hume took it to be. But the present point is not that Hume could not comprehend how our limbs come to move, but that, with an events-based account as his only resource, he finds himself saying that we cannot ('have no power to') move them.[16]

In Hume's story of agency, there is no place for beings who can move their bodies. Thomas Nagel has said that 'There seems no room for agency in a world of neural impulses, chemical reactions, and bone and muscle movements.' When he presented 'his problem of autonomy,' Nagel adopted an external perspective from which 'the agent and everything about him seems to be swallowed up by the circumstances of action; nothing of him is left to intervene in those circumstances.' If you try to imagine your actions as part of the flux of events, then you won't succeed, Nagel said. 'The essential source of the problem is a view of...the order of nature. That conception, if pressed, leads to the feeling that we are not agents at all.'[17]

Some commentators share Nagel's anxiety. Not everyone has gone along with it, however. Those who have got used to thinking that someone's doing something intentionally is constituted by states and events see no difficulty about discovering examples of human agency in the picture on show from Nagel's external perspective. But perhaps one can appreciate the source of some of Nagel's anxiety by thinking about where Hume was led by his assumption that instances of agency consist of items—volitions, and then movements of muscles, nerves, animal spirits and, eventually, limbs—linked on causal pathways. It is surely because there seems to be no place for a sort of being that can move itself in his account that Hume is led to the conclusion that we cannot move our limbs. Where Hume plumps for a manifestly false conclusion, Nagel tells us that we find problems.[18]

The problem now would seem to be that agency cannot be portrayed in a picture containing only psychological states and occurrences and no agent making any difference to anything. It is no wonder that some of those who share Nagel's worry take it to be a problem for the standard story of action.[19]

[...]

4

The idea that human beings make a difference—that they cause things, or bring them about—is surely a very ordinary and familiar one. Bratman tells us that 'it is difficult to know what it means to say that the agent, as distinct from relevant psychological events, processes and states, plays...a basic role in the aetiology and explanation of action.'[26] But I think that Bratman's difficulty must be a consequence of his espousal of an events-based account of agency. When one reflects upon what is present in that account, it can seem as if the only alternative to thinking of actions as 'embedded in an event causal order' were to treat agents as 'fundamentally separate and distinct elements in the metaphysics'[27]—as if any agent would have to encroach upon the causal chains that lead up to actions.

There is another view, however; and I think that it is a part of common sense. If we want to know what it means to say that an agent (as distinct from events and so on) brings things about,

then we need only to think about what is ordinarily meant when this is said. That is what I explore next (4.1). We shall discover that events-based accounts are ruled out when it is accepted that agents bring about the things that they actually do (4.2). When the actual causal role of agents is grasped, it becomes evident why the standard story is not a story of human agency (4.3).

4.1 An event of someone's doing something is usually an event of their bringing something about. A driver slams on the brakes and she brings it about that the car comes to a sudden stop; the event that is her slamming on the brakes brings it about that the car comes to a sudden stop. A tea drinker puts her cup on the table; the result of the event of her putting it there is that the cup is on the table. The thought here—that a person's doing something is typically that person's bringing something about—relies on the fact that typical action verbs are causatives of one or another sort. The causative character of action language reflects agents' abilities to affect things. When agents do things by moving their bodies, they draw on causal knowledge, some of which is knowledge of relations of event causation, including knowledge of what their bodies' movements cause. (A foot pressed against the appropriate pedal applies the brakes; braking causes stopping; and so on.) In taking up the language of events, then, one is able to recapitulate in an explicit way a kind of knowledge that agents exploit in affecting things beyond themselves.

The idea that actions are events that can be redescribed in terms of their effects or results was part of the background of events-based accounts. We see now that this idea fits in with a general way of spelling out the causative character of action language: something the driver did was to bring the car to a sudden stop, and the car's arriving at a sudden stop was an effect of the driver's action; something the tea drinker did was to put the cup on the table, and the cup's being on the table was a result of her putting it there. Although an event ontology is made explicit here, there is no call to import the two assumptions of an events-based account of agency. In the first place, to claim that there are events which merit the title 'actions' is not to adopt a conception of agency which confines examples of agency to the occurrence of events. For the upshot of agents' drawing on their causal knowledge can perfectly well be that they don't move their bodies. (So it was in the case of A, B and C, who, knowing that their moving would not have conduced to what they wanted, did things intentionally without there being any action.) Secondly, the claim that actions are events that are usually described in terms of their effects and results says nothing about the aetiology of actions. Taking a view about the language of action and its causative character can hardly settle the question of what kind of story to tell about the causation and explanation of action. Accepting that actions are events is one thing, endorsing an events-based account of agency quite another.

4.2 Advocates of events-based accounts are not alone in thinking that once events are on the scene, any causal question relating to human agency concerns the causation of the events that are actions. There are also the Agent Causationists who say that agents are causes of actions.[28] It is when this is said that it looks as though agents were intruders among events states and processes, encroaching there as 'fundamentally separate and distinct elements in the metaphysics.'

But in order to defend the causal role of agents, there is no need to say that they cause actions. Indeed there is every reason to say that agents do not cause actions. Consider again the examples of the driver and the tea drinker. What did they cause, or bring about? The driver caused (among other things) the car's coming to a halt; the tea drinker brought it about that

(among other things) her cup was on the table. These things, which they caused or brought about, are the effects or results of their actions. What agents cause, then, are not the events that are their actions, but the effects or results in terms of which their actions may be described.[29] And when we think of agents causing things, we don't think of them imposing themselves in causal chains that lead up to their actions.[30]

[. . .]

4.3 Before concluding, I should say something about *bodily movements*. (I indicated that I would postpone expression of my own disbelief in the standard story's accounting of these back at the start of §1.) What it will be important now to realize is that the agent's role—as cause of what her actions cause—still has application in connection with moving the body. Recognizing this will help to pinpoint where the standard story goes wrong. And it will also enable us to understand better why Hume should have been led to say that we can only produce effects totally different from any that we intend.

We move our bodies in order to effect changes beyond them. The driver, for instance, produced a movement of her foot for a purpose. Thanks to her causal knowledge, her moving her foot on the brake pedal belonged in a causal sequence that culminated in the car's coming to a halt. Her action then is describable as her moving her foot, as her slamming on the brakes, and as her bringing the car to a halt. But there is no possible reason to say that it is a foot's movement. Would anyone be inclined to think of someone's moving her foot as a foot's movement unless they imagined that a person's activity could be dissolved into the goings-on of states and events? The movement of a foot is not an action: it is not an agent's doing anything.

It is not a mere quibble to insist that someone's moving a bit of their body is their doing something, and that the movement they produce is not. For when the label 'action' is attached to bodily movements—to events which aren't actions—the events which *are* actions (to which 'action' had always been supposed to apply) are left out of account. Proponents of the standard story identify actions with bodily movements. And the identification gives their game away. Given that agents cause what their actions cause, an agent's place in any causal story must be the place of her actions. But then agents and the events that really are actions are obliterated with a single stroke when bodily movements are identified with actions. In the standard story no-one ever does anything.

When actions are removed from the scene, not only are agents removed, but also their capacities cannot be recorded. We saw that when one considers the teachings of anatomy as Hume relates these, human agents, with their usual powers of movement and abilities intentionally to do things, are not in sight. Hume denied us our normal capacities of movement. But if it is allowed, against Hume, that we can move our bodies, and can produce such effects as we know would be produced by moving them, then our actions will be thought of as exercises of our capacities. (When the driver, who is capable of moving her right foot [and knows how to put the brakes on etc.] exercises a capacity of movement, there is an event/action of her slamming on the brakes.) Agents then are seen as bodily beings who have a place in causal sequences which lead from influences upon them to the comprehensible effects that they have beyond them. It is only to be expected now that the facts about what we do are not recorded by speaking of items which operate 'in such a manner as is wholly beyond our comprehension.'

I hope to have elicited the force of my claim that human agents are ineliminable from any proper story of their agency. Nagel was right to think that the very idea of agency is threatened when we try to picture action from an objective or external standpoint. For in any picture of action, agents will be seen causing things. And since agents are not visible from the external standpoint, we must refuse the suggestion that we might account for agency from it. Some philosophers are inured to the external standpoint; others impose it as their own—for instance when they are led from the idea that actions are events to events-based accounts of agency. But we have established now that this was never the standpoint of anyone who had anything to say about people and what they do; and that treating actions as events incurs no commitment to any events-based account.

It may yet be thought that I exaggerate when I say that the standard story is not a story of human agency at all. Many people suppose that it is only a kind of shorthand that leads philosophers to favour a slogan like the summary version of the standard causal story—'beliefs and desires cause actions.' What this means, so these people say, is that 'a person's believing something and a person's desiring something causes that person's doing something.' According to this line, agents' mental states and their actions are really mentioned, even if agents themselves are not highlighted, in the language of the shorthand and of the standard story. Well, I think that what is represented now as shorthand is actually a way of talking that changes the subject. And I want to say something about why the change of subject should so frequently go unobserved.

Notice that even when what is alleged to be shorthand is given in its unabbreviated version, still the agent's role in action could not be conveyed. For when an account of the causal transaction in a case of agency is given in the claim that a person's believing something and a person's desiring something causes that person's doing something, it is assumed that the whole of the causal story is told in an action-explanation. The fact that the person exercises a capacity to bring something about is then suppressed. It is forgotten that the agent's causal part is taken for granted as soon as she is said to have done something. The species of causality that belongs with the relevant idea of a person's exercising her capacities is concealed.

There are many reasons why this should remain concealed, and why so many philosophers should have settled for a picture of agency like the one presented in the standard story's events-based account. There is the ease with which it is forgotten that 'action' is used in a semi-technical, philosophers' sense when the causal underpinnings of agency are in question (see §1.1). There is the readiness with which the very different uses of the word 'state' are confused (see §1.2). And perhaps there is a tendency simply (unreflectively) to equate a person's moving her body with the movement that she makes. But none of these slides and confusions is as powerful as the outlook which encourages them and which they encourage. From this outlook, the only possible reality is one in which any causal fact fits into an account in which everything that does any causal work is an event or state. Thus the correct and ordinary idea that to explain what human beings do is to give a kind of causal explanation is thought to be amenable to reconstruction as the idea that some events have causes belonging in a category of psychological occurrences.

Many philosophers with this outlook nod in the direction of the standard story, and offer it a sort of shallow endorsement. They assume that what they have to say about human agency is compatible with the story, without troubling to investigate it.

[…]

I suggest that a 'naturalistic' outlook engenders the story, and that the story sustains that outlook; we have an orthodoxy whose presuppositions aren't examined by most of those who perpetuate it. Peter Strawson once said that it takes a really great philosopher to make a really great mistake.[31] I can't help thinking that, these days, it takes a really great number of philosophers to contrive in the persistence of a really great mistake.

Notes

1. This is Smith's question in 'The Structure of Orthonomy,' the paper he presented to the conference on which the present volume is based. [Smith, D. 2004. The Structure of Orthonomy. In *Agency and Action*. eds. John Hyman and Helen Steward. Cambridge: Cambridge University Press, 165–193. —Eds.] The quotation from Smith below is taken from the handout he used at the conference. At the conference Michael Smith responded to my own paper by saying that the standard story could be retold so as to avoid my objections to it. The present, much revised, version is aimed at showing that that which I find objectionable in the standard story cannot simply be evaded. I thank Michael for his contribution to discussion there, Tom Pink and Miranda Fricker for comments they gave me.

2. This use of 'rationalize' is taken from Donald Davidson's 'Actions Reasons and Causes,' *Journal of Philosophy*, 60, (1967) 685–700, reprinted in his *Essays on Actions and Events* (Oxford University Press, 1980) 3–19, in which the seeds of the standard story were sown.

3. In 'The Possibility of Philosophy of Action,' in *Human Action, Deliberation and Causation*, ed. Jan Bransen and Stefaan Cuypers (Dordrecht: Kluwer Academic Publishers, 1998), 17–41, Michael Smith defends the standard story, which he there calls the

basic Humean story, to the hilt. He aims to show just how widely the story has application (however much one might need to embellish it in order to deal with all of the various cases). My present concern, one might say, is not with any of the particular claims in that paper, but with the general picture of agency that lies behind it.

4. For a defence of the idea that actions are described in terms of effects they have and the thesis about the individuation that underlies this claim, see Davidson's 'Agency,' reprinted in *Essays on Actions and Events*, cit. n.2, 43–61.

5. Cited in previous note. That paper begins with the question 'What events in the life of a person reveal agency?.' The question puts in place the assumption that the phenomenon of human agency will be delimited when it is said which events are actions.

[…]

8. The simplification assumes that *w* is a cause of that of which *d* and *b* are a cause. It is actually unclear how the 'and' of '*d* and *b* caused *m*' (a desire and a belief caused a movement) is supposed to work: cp. nn.13 and 15 *infra*. But I take it that those who tell the standard story will assent to 'Desires cause actions,' just as they assent to 'Desires and beliefs cause actions.'

9. I cannot defend the idea that action-explanation is causal in the present paper. About it, I would say what I say, in n.5 *supra* about the idea that actions are events.

[…]

13. A different way to undermine this habit is to show that there are no intelligible causal statements which mix together in a category of events with things in a category of conditions (where so-called 'token' states would need to be reckoned in the category of conditions). This is the conclusion of an argument of Davidson's 'Causal Relations' (reprinted in his *Essays on Actions and Events*, cit. n.10, 149–62). For a spelling out and endorsement of the relevant argument, see Helen Steward, 'On the notion of cause "philosophically speaking," Proceedings of the Aristotelian Society, XCVII (1997), 125–40. From the perspective of Steward's article, it must seem an irony that Davidson's writings about action should so much have influenced those who tell the standard story.

14. I hope that it will be evident now that the view about the operation of causality that I put into question need not be founded in the standard story's conception of events. At the outset of §1, I noted that some philosophers draw on a different conception: an example would be Jaegwon Kim. The criticisms of the standard story in §1 have relied upon a specific conception of events (upon the only conception, I should say, which allows that they are genuinely particulars). But I believe that my claims against "events"–based accounts have application also when "events" is understood in different (but all of them philosophically familiar) ways.

15. *An Enquiry Concerning Human Understanding* (1748), §7.1.

16. Hume's denial of causal powers is well-known. But I think that its consequences for an account of human agency are insufficiently appreciated. (I take these consequences to be revealed in the particular passage, though no doubt there could be more argument about this. I don't suggest that Hume really thought that no one can move their limbs. His compatibilist arguments always take it quite for granted that human beings can take their place in the causal nexus.)

17. See *The View from Nowhere* (Oxford University Press, 1986) pp. 110–11.

18. In Ch. VII of op. cit. n.17, Nagel discusses a question which 'applies even to the activity of spiders' before he introduces two different problems relating specifically to human agency. I have not been careful to distinguish here between Nagel's various problems, thinking as I do that they should all be solved together. I have said more about the problem that Nagel calls the problem of autonomy in 'Agency and Causal Explanation,' in *Mental Causation*, eds. J. Heil and A. Mele (Oxford University Press, 1993) 129-53 (reprinted in *Philosophy of Action*, ed. A. Mele, Oxford Readings in Philosophy 1997).

19. David Velleman introduces his problem about agency by reference to Nagel's puzzle in 'What Happens When Someone Acts?,' *Mind* 101, 461–81 (reprinted at 123–43 in his *The Possibility of Practical Reason*, Oxford University Press, 2000); but he settles for the view that the standard story is adequate if someone's agency falls short of what is needed for a case of 'agency par excellence'. I think then that Velleman fails to address what Nagel had supposed to be a quite general puzzle. I discuss Velleman's treatment in this and subsequent of his papers in my 'Agency and Alienation,' in *Naturalism in Question*, ed. Mario De Caro and David Macarthur (Harvard University Press, 2004) 173–87.

[...]

26. See 'Reflection, Planning,' op. cit. n.20, p. 39.

27. Ibid.

28. I introduce the initial capitals in 'Agent Causation' in order to suggest a distinctive doctrine—that of e.g. Richard Taylor (see further, next n.). Robert Kane, in *The Oxford Handbook of Free Will* (2002) p. 23, talks about the common practice of introducing a hyphen in 'agent causation' in order to indicate that a special kind of relation is intended. Well, many philosophers have had particular theoretical intentions when they have defined notions of agent causation; save for that, I don't think that we'd be inclined to think that there's anything special about it. Others who are called agent causationists include Timothy O'Connor and John Bishop. There is much agreement between the view I put forward here and theirs. But O'Connor and Bishop both define actions as *relations* (and perhaps, then, they do introduce a notion which is 'special' in the sense meant by Kane). Thus they abandon the idea in the background of events-based accounts, which, as it seems to me, can be perfectly acceptable.

29. And that is why it is not an ordinary notion of agent causation which is used when Agents are said to Cause actions (see preceding n.). Bringing in an agent to do some of the causal work of the states and events of an events-based theory can be a consequence of confusing actions with their effects or results. One sees this confusion in the following passage from Richard Taylor's *Action and Purpose* (Prentice-Hall, Englewood Cliffs, 1966. The quotation is at p.111 of the 1973 edition reprinted by Humanities Press, New York; I have added the numbering): (1) In acting, I make something happen, I cause it...(2) It seem[s] odd that philosophers should construe this as really meaning, not that I, but rather some event process or state not identical with myself should be the cause of that which is represented as my act. (3) It is plain that...I am not identical with any such event process or state as is usually proposed as the 'real cause' of my act. (4) Hence, if...I sometimes cause something

to happen, ... it is false that an event process or state not identical with my self should be the real cause of it. The philosophers, the oddness of whose construal Taylor points out at (2), claim that an event, state or process causes his action. But in order to arrive at their claim, one has to confuse 'acting' with the 'something' that he makes happen, or causes, in acting. In putting the cup on the table (say) that which he makes happen, or causes, is that the cup is on the table. His action, however, is his putting the cup on the table. Thus to represent that some event process or state caused the cup to be on the table is not to represent that some event state or process caused his putting it there. Nothing is said about the cause of his putting it there. Thus Taylor's assertion at (4) can be rejected. An event not identical with the agent (sc. an action) is a cause of that which an agent causes to happen. This does not conflict with Taylor's claims at (1) and (3), which are obviously true.

30. In Ch. VII of *Actions* (Routledge, 1980), I suggested that the question of the irreducibility of agent causation comes down to the question whether 'is an action of' can be analysed in terms of event-causal notions. It now seems to me that the principal thesis of that book—namely that actions are events that we always describe in terms of their effects—leads rather directly to the answer *No*. We don't know which events are *a*'s actions unless we know what *a*—the agent—caused. And we couldn't know what it is for something to be *a*'s action without knowing that things like *a* can cause things.

31. 'Self, Mind and Body' in *Freedom and Resentment and Other Essays* (Methuen & Co. Ltd., London, 1974).

MARKUS E. SCHLOSSER

"Agency, Ownership, and the Standard Theory"

[...]

1.3 Part 3: Disappearing Agency and Disappearing Agents

[...] I will offer a response to the challenge of disappearing agency. My response comes in two parts, which correspond to the following two versions of the challenge. According to the first, the event-causal theory altogether fails to capture the phenomenon of agency, as it reduces activity to mere happenings. Understood in this way, it is a fundamental challenge to the event-causal approach as such. Statements of this first challenge can be found in Melden (1961) and Nagel (1986), for instance. A weaker objection has been raised in the more recent debate. According to this second version, the standard event-causal theory fails to capture important aspects of human agency, because it fails to account for the proper role of the human agent in the performance or exercise of certain *kinds* of agency. This challenge grants that the event-causal theory can account for some basic kinds of human agency (and animal behaviour). But it calls for a substantial revision or supplementation of the view in order to account for the more refined or higher kinds of human agency. In this version, the challenge has been acknowledged even by many proponents of the event-causal approach, including Velleman (1992), Bratman (2001), Enç (2003), and Schroeter (2004). In the following, I will refer to the first challenge as the challenge of disappearing *agency*, indicating that it is a fundamental challenge to the event-causal approach to agency. And I will refer to the second challenge as the challenge of disappearing *agents*, indicating that it is a challenge concerning the role of agents in the performance of actions.

1.3.1 Disappearing Agency

Both challenges have been presented by means of spurious metaphors and rhetoric. According to the event-causal theory, it has been claimed, the agent is a *mere locus* in which events take place, a *mere bystander* or *victim* of causal pushes and pulls. Proponents of the fundamental challenge have sometimes used such metaphors in order to make the point that agency *disappears* within an ontology of events and event-causation.

One can acknowledge that this challenge has some intuitive force. But it is more important to note that its proponents have not produced a single *argument* to support their case, and they have certainly not identified a philosophical *problem*.[16] Their case is entirely based on intuition, and in some cases on mere metaphor and rhetoric.

However, having said this, and having acknowledged that the objection has some intuitive force, proponents of the event-causal theory should also be able to say something in response. It is not obvious that agency cannot

be understood in terms of event-causal processes. But it is also not obvious that agency can be understood in terms of event-causation. What can we say in response?

A first thing to point out is that some of the rhetoric is not just misleading, but false. The agent is certainly not a *victim* or a *helpless bystander* only in virtue of being a subject of events (in virtue of being a substance that is involved in events). Events may be called *happenings* in virtue of the fact that they *occur* in time. But the fact that events are occurrences does not entail or show that an agent's mental events and movements are things that *happen to* the agent, in the sense that they assail or befall the agent, or in the sense in which we say that a bad or unjust thing happened to us. When I remember something, for instance, I am a constitutive part of an event, but I am no victim or helpless bystander.

Secondly, we must remember that the event-causal theory is *intended* to be a reductive theory. Its proponents aim to provide necessary and sufficient conditions for agency, and they propose to do this without any kind of circularity by way of providing a reductive *explanation* of agency in terms of event-causal processes. But, as every proponent of a reductive explanation would insist, a reduction is a form of vindication rather than elimination. The theory does not eliminate agency, nor does it eliminate agents. Rather, it provides a vindication by giving an account of how agency can be minimally part of the event-causal order.

Thirdly, and most importantly, there is a constructive response to the challenge. The challenge says, basically, that the event-causal approach fails to capture agency. We can interpret this as saying that it fails to capture the fact that agents can exercise control over their behaviour. Construed in this way, proponents of the event-causal theory can respond by showing that the view has the resources to distinguish between event-causal processes that constitute agential control and event-causal processes that do not. If this can be achieved within the event-causal framework, then the challenge is mistaken.

1.3.2 Event-Causation and Agential Control

The event-causal theory construes control in terms of event-causation and rationalization. It says that an agent exercises control only if the behaviour in question is caused by mental states and events that rationalize its performance (we call such rationalizing attitudes reason-states). But causation by *reason-states* is not sufficient for control and agency. This is highlighted by examples involving deviant or wayward causal chains. In all standard examples of causal deviance, the causal chain that connects the agent's reason-states and the action runs through some state or event that undermines the agent's control. Typically, this is some state of nervousness or agitation.[17] Consider, for instance, Davidson's climber example.

> A climber might want to rid himself of the weight and danger of holding another man on a rope, and he might know that by loosening his hold on the rope he could rid himself of the weight and danger. This belief and want might so unnerve him as to cause him to loosen his hold.... (Davidson 1980, p. 79)

Examples of this kind raise a problem for the event-causal theory. The behaviour is caused and rationalized by mental states, but it seems clear that the agent is not performing an action at all. It is, rather, a sheer accident that the state of nervousness causes precisely that type of movement that is rationalized by the reason-states. In order to provide a satisfactory account of agency, the theory must exclude deviant causal chains in event-causal terms (in particular, without presupposing an irreducible notion of control or agency).

The interesting point for us here is that deviant causal chains are *control-undermining chains*. If the theory can exclude deviant causal chains, it can, *ipso facto*, exclude control-undermining chains. And if it can exclude control-undermining chains, it can distinguish between event-causal chains that constitute agential control and ones that do not.

I think that the problem of deviant causal chains can be solved, and I have proposed a solution elsewhere (Schlosser 2007b). In broad outline, I have argued that deviant causal chains are excluded if the theory requires that the agent's reason-states must be causally efficacious and explanatory *in virtue of their intentional contents*. This requirement is violated in the standard cases of causal deviance. Given this, we get a straightforward response to the challenge of disappearing agency. The event-causal theory can capture agency, because it has the resources to distinguish between event-causal chains that constitute agential control and ones that do not.

1.3.3 Ownership of Agency

In response, opponents might argue that the problem is not that causal chains can be deviant, but that the constituents of those chains are mere states and events. Let us assume, for the sake of argument, that actions are non-deviantly caused by the agent's mental states and events. The objection says that this still does not guarantee agency, because the agent may not identify with being moved by those states and events. Being non-deviantly caused by mental states and events, the resulting behaviour may still not be a true and proper expression of the *agent's own* agency. Let us call this the challenge from *ownership* (ownership of agency).

Many will associate this challenge with the issues raised by Harry Frankfurt's influential article on free will and personhood (1988, chap. 2, originally published in 1971). Following Frankfurt, one might be tempted to give a response to the objection by appealing to a notion of identification or endorsement within a so-called hierarchical theory of agency. This route has been taken by some philosophers in response to the problem of disappearing *agents*. The central idea here is to distinguish between desires or motives that *speak for* or *stand for* the agent by means of an account of identification or endorsement (compare Korsgaard 1996 and Bratman 2001, for instance). On this approach, an agent acts from desires that are truly his or her *own* just in case the agent *endorses* the desires as motives for action. Let us call this the *endorsement strategy*.

I shall not attempt here to assess the endorsement strategy as such. Nor will I go into the details of particular versions of this approach. I want to argue, rather, that the endorsement strategy would not give us a convincing response to the objection from ownership.

To begin with, let us consider Frankfurt's main example of the unwilling addict. He is moved by a desire to acquire and take drugs, but he does not want to be motivated in this way—he does not endorse being moved by those desires. We can agree with Frankfurt and his followers that cases of this kind highlight important and interesting aspects of human agency. But we must be careful to interpret them in the right way.

Frankfurt says that the unwilling addict is a "passive bystander to the forces that move him" (ibid. p. 22). Elsewhere he talks about desires that are "rejected" as "external" (1988, chap. 5, for instance). David Velleman and Michael Bratman have suggested that examples of this kind show that the event-causal theory "leaves out" the agent. The unwilling addict performs an action when he acts on the desire, but this falls short of "agency *par excellence*" (Velleman 1992) or "full-blooded" human agency (Bratman 2001). Construed in this way, the example can be used to raise the challenge of disappearing agents (to which we will turn below). But I think that this reading can and should be resisted here.

Firstly, it should be uncontroversial that the unwilling addict is not a mere bystander or locus in the flow of events. He is capable of a good degree of control and agency, and he exercises this ability in the pursuit of drugs, an endeavour which requires some planning and practical reason.

Secondly, it should also be uncontroversial that the addict's desire and the resulting behaviour is his *own* in some basic or minimal sense. In order to see this, compare the unwilling addict with serious cases of schizophrenia, where patients report that their actions are under the control of some external agent or force, or with cases of the "anarchic hand syndrome," where patients report that one of their hands moves on its own (compare Frith et al. 2000, for instance).

Third, proponents of the event-causal theory should seek to respond to the challenge at the most fundamental level. The endorsement strategy can be pursued in order to account for a *kind* of ownership that is characteristic of *autonomous* agency, for instance. But this would leave more basic kinds of agency unaccounted for. We can agree that the unwilling addict falls short of autonomous agency (or agency *par excellence*). But, on the other hand, he is not like the schizophrenic patient who feels as if alien forces are acting through him. What is required in order to meet the objection at the fundamental level is an account of the basic kind of ownership and agency that is exhibited even by the unwilling addict.

I propose the following response to the objection from ownership. In normal instances of human agency, including basic cases of minimally rational planning agency, actions that are non-deviantly caused by the agent's mental states and events are an expression of the agent's own agency *by default*: our agency springs from our mental states and events, unless defeating conditions obtain. Ownership of agency, in other words, does not have to be conferred by endorsement and it does not depend on it. It is a given, unless things go wrong.

But what are *normal* instances? In order to get a viable response, we must have an answer to this question. Fortunately, there is a computational model of the sense of agency that provides a good answer. In broad outline, the model is this. Whenever a motor command for the performance of a bodily movement is sent from premotor areas to the motor control system, a copy of this command is used to produce a prediction of the movement (a so-called *forward model*). This prediction is then sent to a comparator where it is compared with incoming visual and proprioceptive information concerning the actual movement. The main purpose of this sub-personal system is to monitor, correct, and fine-tune movements. But it is now widely assumed that this system is also responsible for a sense of the ownership of agency. This is the sense that the movements are our own doing, initiated and guided by us, and it is assumed that this sense or feeling is the result of a match between the prediction and the feedback (the match, of course, need not be perfect, as the function of the system is to correct and fine-tune).[18]

There is good empirical support for this model, and it is now widely deployed by psychologists and cognitive scientists working on human action. Given this model, we can say what normal instances are. They are cases in which the feedback-comparison system performs its function, producing a sense of the ownership of agency. This sub-personal mechanism may fail to produce a sense of agency for various reasons. It may be interfered with or break down in various ways that correspond to a variety of abnormal cases and defeating conditions. What the defeating conditions are is largely an empirical question. It has been argued that the model can explain a wide range of deficiencies and abnormalities, each highlighting ways in which the mechanism may break down or fail to perform its function (Frith et al. 2000).

It would be implausible, I think, to suggest that the ownership of agency is in all cases conferred by the agent's endorsement. The correct reading of Frankfurt's unwilling addict supports this. There is a basic or minimal sense in which the addict's desire for the drug is his own and in which his own agency springs from it (in combination with other mental states and events). It should be noted that the proposed default view is fully compatible with an endorsement theory, as I have argued only that the endorsement strategy should not be deployed in response to the challenge from ownership. So, the default view may well be supplemented with an endorsement theory of autonomous agency, for instance.

1.3.4 Disappearing Agents

Let us now turn to the challenge of disappearing *agents*, and let us assume that the outlined feedback-comparator model can account for a basic and default sense of the ownership of agency. What about the more refined and higher kinds of human agency, such as autonomous agency? Even *proponents* of the event-causal theory have conceded that the view fails to account for the agent's participation or proper role in the performance of higher kinds of agency.

I accept the point that the basic version of the event-causal theory has to be refined or supplemented in order to account for higher kinds of agency. But I do not accept all the claims made and implied by the challenge. In particular, I do not accept the suggestion that the event-causal theory fails to include the *agent* or fails to account for the *agent's* role and participation—a point that has been conceded even by some proponents of the event-causal approach.

Firstly, putting things in terms of the *agent's* role or participation creates a false dichotomy. Throughout this chapter, we distinguished between *more basic* and *higher* kinds of agency. It is very plausible to think that the aspects or kinds of human agency form a spectrum, or a hierarchy, from lower and basic to higher and more refined kinds of agency. At the bottom of this hierarchy one finds behaviour that is purposeful but to a high degree driven by environmental stimuli (such as instinctive, automatic or highly habitual reactions). Moving up the hierarchy we get intentional, rational, deliberative, reflective and self-controlled agency, and towards the top we find autonomous and free agency. For our purposes, the details and the exact order do not matter. The important point is that agency comes in shades of grey, as it were, not as an all-or-nothing phenomenon. Whenever human agency is exercised, some but not necessarily all kinds of human agency are instantiated.

This is why I find talk about the *agent's* role or participation unhelpful. If we say that the agent's participation is characteristic of autonomous agency, does that mean that the agent does not participate in lower kinds of behaviour? This would be rather odd, to say the least. If we want to capture the important aspects of human agency, we better begin with a framework of *kinds of agency*. Talk about the agent's role and the agent's participation creates a bipartition that does not match up with the varieties of human behaviour.

Secondly, as just pointed out, it is rather implausible to suggest that the agent does not participate in lower kinds of agency. The most natural thing to say, and the most natural assumption to begin with, is that all instances of agency involve an agent. Wherever there is agency, there is an agent participating, playing a role as the agent. As explained in part two, the event-causal theory provides a reductive explanation of the agent's role. It does not eliminate the agent. Given that, there is simply no room for an additional role of the agent in higher kinds of agency. The agent is already there, from the start, and the agent does play a role in all kinds of agency.

In other words, to ask for *further participation* of the agent is to miss the point of the reductive approach to agency. Higher kinds of agency do not spring from the participation of the agent. They spring, rather, from certain *features of the agent*. They spring from properties that are instantiated only in cases of autonomous agency, for instance. We may say that the agent participates more, or to a higher degree, in some instances of agency. But this is metaphorical. It should be taken to mean that the agent instantiates certain properties or exercises certain abilities, which are not instantiated or exercised in lower kinds of agency, and in virtue of which the agent exercises the higher kind of agency in question.

What should we make, then, of the challenge of disappearing *agents*? Is it an empty challenge? Construed, literally, as a challenge of disappearing agents it is an empty challenge, as I have just suggested. But that does not mean that it is empty altogether. I acknowledge that the event-causal theory must be supplemented and refined. But not by bringing the agent back into the picture. The agent was never absent. The right way to respond, rather, is to show how the theory can distinguish between the various kinds of agency within the event-causal framework (without, in particular, presupposing some kind of agent-causation). This task is beyond the scope of this chapter. But I shall briefly indicate two directions that proponents of the causal theory may take. One possible starting point for an account of higher kinds of agency is Frankfurt's (1988) hierarchical model. In order to solve the well-known regress problems that plague this approach, one may appeal to special types of mental attitudes, such as the motive to be governed by reasons (Velleman 1992) or higher-order policies that provide cross-temporal continuity and stability (Bratman 2001). Alternatively, one can appeal to historical conditions on the way in which agency-relevant attitudes, such as desires, beliefs and intentions, must have been formed or acquired (Mele 1995). I tend to favour this second approach, as I think that higher-order attitudes play a less significant role in human agency than Frankfurt and his followers assume.

More recently, François Schroeter (2004) argued that we must refer to the role of the *conscious self* in the initiation and guidance of autonomous action. In my view, this is not an option for the committed proponent of the event-causal approach. Schroeter insists that reference to the role of the conscious self is *not* a covert evocation of some kind of agent-causation, and he claims that the view is consistent with naturalism (p. 650). I understand Velleman's and Bratman's views, for instance, which account for the agent's role by reference to some of the agent's mental states. According to Schroeter, however, the conscious self cannot be reduced to conscious mental states and events, nor does he want to say that the self must therefore be a substance. But it seems clear that the self must be some kind of entity, in a metaphysically robust sense, as it is supposed to be causally relevant in the initiation and guidance of action. Schroeter does not say

what kind of thing it is, and I fail to see what it could possibly be.

Perhaps the role of the conscious self goes beyond the role of conscious mental states and events due to the *unity* of the self. The question of what this unity might consist in is, of course, also beyond the scope of this chapter. I should point out, though, that proponents of the event-causal approach are not restricted to explanations in terms of collections of mental states and [events]. They may, rather, refer to the agent's mental states, mental events, and the *relationships* that hold between them. Given this, it is, I think, far from obvious that the role of a conscious and unified self cannot be captured and reductively explained by an event-causal theory of agency.

Acknowledgements

I would like to thank John Bishop for very helpful comments on an earlier version of this chapter, which was written when I was a postdoc fellow at the University of Bristol with a research project on the causal theory of action. This project was funded by the Austrian Science Fund (FWF).

Notes

[...]

16. In contrast to that, the challenge from deviant causal chains does raise a genuine problem. Virtually all proponents of the event-causal approach have acknowledged this. Compare Davidson 1980, Bishop 1989, and Enç 2003, for instance.

17. I am restricting my considerations here to the most problematic type of causal deviance, which has been called basic or primary deviance. Compare Bishop 1989 and Schlosser 2007b.

18. This is the most basic version of the model. For more advanced and more detailed accounts see Frith et al. 2000 and Pacherie 2007, for instance. For an application of this model to the case of mental agency see Campbell 1999.

References

Bilgrami, A. (2006), *Self-Knowledge and Resentment*. Cambridge: Harvard University Press.

Bishop, J. (1989), *Natural Agency: An Essay on the Causal Theory of Action*. Cambridge: Cambridge University Press.

Brand, M. (1984), *Intending and Acting*. Cambridge: MIT Press.

Bratman, M.E. (1987), *Intention, Plans, and Practical Reason*. Cambridge: Harvard University Press.

Bratman, M.E. (2001), "Two Problems about Human Agency," *Proceedings of the Aristotelian Society* 2000–2001: 309–26.

Campbell, J. (1999), "Schizophrenia, the Space of Reasons, and Thinking as a Motor Process," *The Monist* 82: 609–25.

Child, W. (1994), *Causality, Interpretation and the Mind*. Oxford: Oxford University Press.

Chisholm, R. (1964), "Human Freedom and the Self," Reprinted in G. Watson (2003) (ed.), *Free Will*. Oxford: Oxford University Press, 26–37.

Clarke, R. (2003), *Libertarian Accounts of Free Will*. Oxford: Oxford University Press.

Crane, T. (1995), "The Mental Causation Debate," *Proceedings of the Aristotelian Society*, supplementary volume 69: 211–36.

Dancy, J. (2000), *Practical Reality*. Oxford: Oxford University Press.

Davidson, D. (1980), *Essays on Action and Events*. Oxford: Oxford University Press.

Enç, B. (2003), *How We Act: Causes, Reasons, and Intentions*. Oxford: Oxford University Press.

Frankfurt, H. (1988), *The Importance of What We Care About*. Cambridge: Cambridge University Press.

Frith, C.D., Blakemore, S. and Wolpert, D.M. (2000), "Abnormalities in the Awareness and Control of Action," *Philosophical Transactions of the Royal Society* 355: 1771–88.

Gibbons, J. (2006), "Mental Causation without Downward Causation," *Philosophical Review* 115: 79–103.

Ginet, C. (1990), *On Action*. Cambridge: Cambridge University Press.

Ginet, C. (2001), "Reasons Explanations of Action: Causalist versus Noncausalist Accounts," in R. Kane (ed.), *Oxford Handbook on Free Will*. Oxford: Oxford University Press, 386–405.

Korsgaard, Ch. (1996), *The Sources of Normativity*. Cambridge: Cambridge University Press.

Lowe, E.J. (1993), "The Causal Autonomy of the Mental," *Mind* 102: 629–44.

McCann, H. (1998), *The Works of Agency*. Ithaca: Cornell University Press.

Melden, A.I. (1961), *Free Action*. London: Routledge and Kegan Paul.

Mele, A.R. (1992), *Springs of Action*. Oxford: Oxford University Press.

Mele, A.R. (1995), *Autonomous Agents*. Oxford: Oxford University Press.

Mele, A.R. (1997), "Agency and Mental Action," *Philosophical Perspectives* 11: 231–49.

Nagel, T. (1986), *The View from Nowhere*. New York: Oxford University Press.

O'Connor, T. (2000), *Persons and Causes: The Metaphysics of Free Will*. Oxford: Oxford University Press.

Pacherie, E. (2007), "The Sense of Control and the Sense of Agency," *Psyche* 13: 1–30.

Pereboom, D. (2001), *Living Without Free Will*. Cambridge: Cambridge University Press.

Schlosser, M.E. (2007a), *The Metaphysics of Agency* (Doctoral dissertation, University of St. Andrews). Research Repository (http://hdl.handle.net/10023/163).

Schlosser, M.E. (2007b), "Basic Deviance Reconsidered," *Analysis* 67: 186–94.

Schlosser, M.E. (2008), "Agent-Causation and Agential Control," *Philosophical Explorations* 11: 3–21.

Schlosser, M.E. (2009), "Non-Reductive Physicalism, Mental Causation and the Nature of Actions," in H. Leitgeb and A. Hieke (eds), *Reduction: Between the Mind and the Brain*. Frankfurt: Ontos, pp. 73–89.

Schroeter, F. (2004), "Endorsement and Autonomous Agency," *Philosophy and Phenomenological Research* 69: 633–59.

Schueler, G.F. (2003), *Reasons and Purposes: Human Rationality and the Teleological Explanation of Action*. Oxford: Oxford University Press.

Sehon, S.R. (2000), "An Argument Against the Causal Theory of Action Explanation," *Philosophy and Phenomenological Research* 60: 67–85.

Velleman, D. (1992), "What Happens when Someone Acts?" Reprinted in his (2000) *The Possibility of Practical Reason*. Oxford: Oxford University Press, pp. 123–43.

Wilson, G.M. (1989), *The Intentionality of Human Action*. Stanford: Stanford University Press.

Yablo, S. (1997), "Wide Causation," *Philosophical Perspectives* 11: 251–81.

TIM BAYNE

"The Sense of Agency"

> *The motion of our body follows upon the command of our will.*
> *Of this we are at every moment conscious.*
> —David Hume, An Enquiry Concerning Human Understanding, 1748

1. Introduction

Hume was perhaps guilty of a certain degree of hyperbole in claiming that we are continually aware of ourselves as agents, but it is certainly true that agentive self-awareness is a frequent component of the stream of consciousness. The question with which I am concerned in this chapter is where we ought to locate states of agentive self-awareness—"experiences of agency," as I will also call them—in cognitive architecture.

To a first approximation, we can distinguish between three broad departments of the mind: perception, thought and action. Perception processes information about the world (where this can include the state of the subject's own body) and makes it available for cognitive consumption. Perceptual systems include among their number not only the five traditional senses but also those systems responsible for the various kinds of bodily sensations, such as experiences of joint position, pain, nausea, hunger, thirst and the need for oxygen. The department of thought is responsible for doing something with the information that it receives from perception—it is in the business of theoretical and practical reasoning. And the function of the department of agency is to implement the commands that it receives from thought. Its job is to plan and execute action in conjunction with the department of thought.

Where in this picture does agentive experience fall? I argue that agentive experiences are best thought of in perceptual terms—they are the products of a dedicated perceptual system (or perhaps systems). Just as we have sensory systems that function to inform us about the distribution of objects in our immediate environment, damage to our limbs, and our need for food, so, too, we have a sensory system (or systems), whose function it is to inform us about facets of our own agency.

The chapter unfolds as follows. The following section introduces the notion of agentive self-awareness and presents a sketch of the perceptual model; the remainder of the chapter provides an argument for the model, chiefly in the form of showing that its central rivals—the doxastic and telic models—are untenable. Section three examines the doxastic model of agentive self-awareness, according to which agentive self-awareness is solely a matter of judgment and is to be located within cognition. Section four examines the telic model of agentive self-awareness, according to which experiences of agency are located within the action system. Neither the doxastic nor the telic model provides us with a plausible analysis of agentive experience. Section five reinforces the intuitive case for the perceptual model of agentive experience by showing that a number of the most important objections to it can be met. My overall aim in this chapter is not to present a knockdown case for the perceptual model but

rather to show that it ought to be regarded as a viable option. On this view, talk of "the sense of agency" is no mere *façon de parler* but picks out a genuine sensory modality, at least in a fairly broad sense of the term.[1] Our conception of the senses ought to be wide enough to include room for the idea that there might be a system (or systems) that is in the business of representing one's own agency.

2. The Perceptual Model of Agentive Experience

Consider the following vignette:

> It's your first day as a waitperson, and you are pouring water into a glass from a jug. As you pour the water, you experience yourself as an agent. You experience yourself as someone who is doing something, rather than someone to whom things are merely happening. The experience of yourself as an agent is modulated in various ways. In pouring the water, you experience yourself as trying to avoid being distracted by the commotion in the kitchen. This attempt to control your attention is experienced as effortful—as difficult. You also experience yourself as having some degree of autonomy in controlling your attention. Having poured the water, you deliberate as to whether or not you should ask your customers whether they are ready to have their order taken. This act of deliberation has a distinctive experiential character; it too colors what it is like to be you during this episode.

This vignette contains reference to multiple forms of agentive self-awareness—states that I refer to as "agentive experiences."[2] There is no agreed taxonomy of such states.

Among the various terms in use are the following: "the experience of control," the "experience of free will," "the experience of acting," "the experience of volition," "the experience of conscious will," "the experience of efficacy," "the experience of mental causation," "the experience of effort," and "the feeling of doing." Some of these terms are best understood as synonyms of each other; others are best read as picking out distinct elements or aspects of agentive experience. Each of these labels refers to forms of experience that are individuated by reference to features of agency.

I take agentive experience to have as its core the experience of a particular movement or mental event as realizing one's own agency. Surrounding this core are a number of other experiential components, the precise nature and number of which is very much an open question. Actions are sometimes experienced as effortful and at other times as effortless. Actions are sometimes experienced as deliberate and at other times as spontaneous. More controversially, we often experience our actions as autonomous—as "up to us" in some way. There is debate about the content of such experiences—are they compatibilist or incompatibilist in nature?—but a strong case can be made for thinking that some form of free will is experientially encoded. One might add to this list the phenomenology of deliberating, and also that of deciding or choosing (Holton 2006).[3]

The existence of agentive self-awareness can be highlighted by drawing attention to pathologies of agency in which it is lost or disturbed. In the anarchic hand syndrome, patients will complain that they have lost control of a hand; that will report that one of their hands has acquired a "will of its own" (Banks et al 1989; Della Sala, Marchetti, and Spinnler 1991; Gasquoine 1993; Goldberg and Bloom 1990; Pacherie 2007). The hand in question might also appear to act in an anarchic fashion, by (say) grabbing food from a stranger's plate at a restaurant. Patients will deny that such actions are theirs, and may take steps to prevent the hand from moving by sitting on it or tying it down. Detailed reports of what it is like to have an anarchic hand are rare, but it is plausible to suppose that the syndrome involves an experience of alienated agency—an experience of one's hand as acting on its own accord.

Disturbances of agentive experience are also evident in the schizophrenic delusions of thought insertion and alien control (Mellors 1970; Frith et al 2000b). Patients suffering from these delusions complain that some of their thoughts and actions are no longer their own, or are at least no longer under their control. "My fingers pick up the pen, but I don't control them. What they do is nothing to do with me"; "The force moved my lips. I began to speak. The words were made for me" (Mellors 1970, 18). "My grandfather hypnotized me and now he moves my foot up and down." "They inserted a computer in my brain. It makes me turn to the left or right" (Frith et al 2000, 358). It is highly plausible to suppose that these delusions are at least partially grounded in abnormal experiences of agency (Pacherie et al 2006). And if these syndromes involve experiences of alienated agency, then there is some reason to suppose that unimpaired agency might be accompanied by experiences of intact or unimpaired agency. Of course, the fact that there are experiences of alienated agency does not entail that there are—or even could be—experience of [un]impaired agency, but it surely provides some support for that thesis.

Where in the cognitive architecture should we locate such experience? They are not located within the central cognition, nor are they located within the systems responsible for programming and executing actions, nor are they located within the high-level reaches of any of the standard perceptual modalities. Instead, such states are the products of a dedicated perceptual system (or systems). These systems involve forward models of action control, and operate along the following lines (Frith et al 2000a, 2000b; Blakemore and Frith, 2003). The forward models are fed a copy of the agent's motor commands, and are then put to the following uses. First, they are used to predict the sensory consequences of the agent's movement. These predictions are used to filter sensory information and to attenuate the component that is due to self-movement. Second, the copy of the motor commands is also sent to a comparator (or comparators), so-called because they compare the predicted sensory consequences of the movement with sensory feedback. When there is a match between predicted and actual state, the comparator sends a signal to the effect that the sensory changes are self-generated; when there is no match (or an insufficiently robust match), sensory changes are coded as externally caused. Crucial to the comparator approach is the notion that agentive awareness can be generated by mechanisms that need not—and typically will not—have access to fully-fledged intentions. It is very much an open question whether the comparator-based story can account for each and every one of the many components of agentive experience, but there is good reason to think that it lies at the heart of the phenomenon.[4]

Where in the cognitive architecture do these comparators fall? I take them to fall within perception, where that notion is very broadly construed. The representational states generated by these comparators play the role of perceptions. Like other perceptual systems, the function of the sense of agency is to generate representations of some domain—in this case, one's own agency—and make those representations available to the agent's cognitive systems in an experiential format.

It is important to note that the perceptual model of agentive experience is *not* committed to a perceptual account of introspection. The model is a model of agentive experiences themselves; it is not a model of our access to agentive experiences. Giving an account of agentive experience is one thing; giving an account of introspection is quite another. Perceptual approaches to introspection are decidedly unpopular, but that unpopularity should in no way be taken to discredit the perceptual model of agentive experience. Note also that the perceptual model is not intended to cover everything that might be subsumed by the term "agentive self-awareness." There is a broad sense of agentive self-awareness that includes the conceptually articulated awareness of what one is trying to do (tie one's shoelaces, look for a book, reach for the salt). A full account of agentive self-awareness needs to address these high-level, conceptually articulated forms of agentive awareness, but I do not take on that task here. The perceptual model is intended to apply only to fairly low-level forms of agentive awareness of the kind introduced earlier.[5]

That, in a nutshell, is the perceptual model. I will flesh the model out in more detail later (section five), but I turn now to its rivals.

3. The Doxastic Model of Agentive Experience

There will be those who think that the perceptual model gets off on the wrong foot by construing agentive self-awareness in experiential terms. According to what we might think of as the *doxastic model* of agentive self-awareness, such states are not really forms of experience at all; instead, they are states of thought. What it is to be aware of oneself as an agent is simply to have a conscious thought to that effect.

The doxastic model strikes me as intuitively implausible. Horgan, Tienson, and Graham's

(2003, 324) description of agentive experience as "an aspect of sensory-perceptual experience, broadly construed," and that seems right. The experience of acting is not exhausted by the conscious judgments one might have about what or how one is acting, if indeed one has any conscious judgments of that nature at all. Acting may frequently involve conscious judgment about what one is doing, but agentive self-awareness is not primarily a matter of judgment. Rather, it has the transparency, immediacy, and directness that characterizes our sensory engagement with the world. There might be good reasons to reject this view, but any such rejection would come at a significant cost to intuition.

Proponents of the doxastic model who are unmoved by the foregoing might find the following more convincing. If the doxastic view were right, then pathologies of agentive self-awareness would be pathologies of judgment rather than of experience. We should hold that the anarchic hand syndrome involves only a departure in the agentive judgments that the patient is prepared to make. Whereas a person whose hand has just taken food from a stranger's plate would normally be prepared to judge that they had performed the action (and perhaps confabulate a rationalization for it), anarchic hand patients are not prepared to make this judgment; instead, they insist that they did not move their hand—it moved of its own accord.

However this does not seem to capture the situation. Although it is certainly true that anarchic hand patients are not (typically) prepared to admit that the action was theirs, it seems plausible to appeal to agentive experience—or the lack thereof—in order to *explain* why they deny having performed the anarchic actions. Surely it is the fact that the normal and expected experience of *doing* has been replaced by an experience of *happening* that leads these patients to judge that the action is not theirs. Whether or not one's denial of agentive ownership of the action is erroneous—and there is room for debate about this—the patient's pathology appears to be primarily one of *experience* rather than *thought*.

This objection can be reinforced by noting that experiences of alienated agency are unlikely to be cognitively penetrable. Suppose that an anarchic hand patient *does* take herself to be the agent of "her" anarchic actions. After all, she might reason as follows: "The movements of my anarchic hand are not guided by anyone else. They are actions, and where are actions there must be an agent. So, these actions must be mine." Such a patient might form the belief that the movements of her anarchic hand realize her own actions, but it seems unlikely that the acquisition of this judgment will suffice to correct their agentive experience. The patient can no more restore the missing experience of agency by forming the belief that [her] anarchic actions are truly her own than you or I can correct our visual experiences of the Müller-Lyer illusion by forming the belief that the lines in question are equal in length. Cognitive impenetrability, one of the key markers of the perception-cognitive boundary, tells firmly against the doxastic analysis of agentive self-awareness.

The point generalizes. Patients suffering from depersonalization seem also to have lost the normal experience of themselves as agents. They "complain that they no longer have an ego, but are mechanisms, automatons, puppets; that what they do seems not done by them but happens mechanically" (Schilder 1953; Sierra & Berrios 1998). Nonetheless, they suffer from no delusions concerning agency: They know that their actions are their own. Phantom limb patients display what is in some sense the converse dissociation. They know that their "limb" is but a phantom, but they continue to experience themselves as acting with it. The history of philosophy provides us with additional examples of the cognitive impenetrability of agentive experience. Malebranche believed that God was the direct cause of his movements, but his commitment to occasionalism surely did not rob him of the experience of being the author of his deeds. Hard incompatibilists reject the reality of free will, but this has little impact on their experiences of freedom (see, e.g., Strawson 1986). Perhaps judgment can penetrate agentive experience under some conditions, but it seems clear that on the whole agentive experience exhibits the kind of doxastic impenetrability that is characteristic of perception. Agentive experiences are as distinct from the judgments to which they give rise as are visual experiences from the judgments to which they give rise. We might think of agentive experiences as "invitations to belief," but one should not confuse an invitation itself with that to which it is an invitation.

In response to this, the proponent of the doxastic model might hold that even if agentive experience is not a species of judgment strictly speaking, it does fall on the cognitive side of the perception-cognition divide. But what kind of cognitive state might agentive experience be if not a judgment? The only answer I know of is that it might be an entertaining of some kind. Suppose, when asked what the capital of Ethiopia is, the name "Addis Ababa" suddenly occurs to you. Do you judge that Addis Ababa is the capital of Ethiopia? Perhaps not. You might have no commitment whatsoever to the truth of that thought; it is merely that you "found yourself" with it when the question was put to you. Might agentive self-awareness involve states of this kind—thoughts that simply occur to one?

I think not. The difference between the case just discussed and agentive experience is as sharp as the difference between daydreaming about what it would be like to fly through the air unaided and actually experiencing oneself as being in this state. When it comes to daydreams and flights of fancy, one has no tendency to take oneself as being in touch with how things really are; perception, by contrast, does involve such a sense. And that is surely what agentive experience is like. It is, we might say, *committal*. The experience of raising one's arm does not leave open the question of whether one might really be raising one's arm, but instead has the force of an assertion: "I *am* raising my arm."

4. The Telic Model of Agentive Experience

Following Anscombe (1957) and Searle (1983), let us distinguish two ways in which mental states can be satisfied: in a thetic manner and in a telic manner. *Thetic* states are satisfied when they fit the world; they have a mind-to-world direction of fit. Judgments are paradigms of thetic states, for they are true (or veridical) when they fit the world and otherwise false (or nonveridical). Thetic states are in the business of responding to changes in the world. *Telic* states are satisfied when the world fits them; they have a world-to-mind direction of fit. Desires are the paradigms of telic states. They are in the business of bringing about a certain state of affairs. They are satisfied when they succeed; otherwise, they remain frustrated.

The perceptual model takes agentive experiences to have a thetic structure: They are representations (or "presentations") that matters are thus and so. By contrast, the telic model takes such states to have a telic structure. Searle himself endorses the telic model:

> As far as Intentionality is concerned, the differences between the visual experience and the experience of acting are in the direction of fit and in the direction of causation: the visual experience

711

stands to the table in the mind-to-world direction of fit. If the table isn't there, we say that I was mistaken, or was having a hallucination, or some such. And the direction of causation is from the object to the visual experience. If the Intentional component is satisfied it must be caused by the presence and features of the object. But in the case of the experience of acting, the Intention component has the world-to-mind direction of fit. If I have this experience but the event doesn't occur we say such things as that I *failed* to raise my arm, and that I *tried* to raise my arm but did not succeed. And the direction of causation is from the experience of acting to the event. Where the Intentional content is satisfied, that is, where I actually succeed in raising my arm, the experience of acting causes the arm to go up. If it didn't cause the arm to go up, but something else did, I didn't raise my arm: it just went up for some other reason. (1983, 88, emphasis in original; see also 1983, 123f.)

Although Searle is perhaps the most explicit advocate of the telic line, a number of other authors appear to have some sympathy for at least a limited version of the view (O'Shaughnessy 2003; Peacocke 2003).[6] Proponents of the telic model might agree with Horgan, Tienson, and Graham's (2003) description of agentive experience as "an aspect of sensory-perceptual experience, broadly construed," but they will insist that this description must be construed very broadly indeed if it is to be accurate, for on this account the structure of agentive experience is diametrically opposed to that of perceptual states.

There are multiple ways in which we might get a fix on the dispute between the thetic and telic analyses of agentive experience. It can be read as a dispute about how to read the "of" in the phrase "the phenomenology *of* agency," a phrase that is often used to refer to agentive experience. The thetic theorist reads this "of" intentionally: The phenomenology of agency involves experiences that are intentionally directed toward agency. By contrast, the telic theorist reads this "of" possessively. The phenomenology of agency is a matter of one's actions (or tryings) having experiential character. The dispute can also be captured by appeal to the contrast between transitive and intransitive conceptions of experience. The thetic theorist takes a transitive view of agentive experience (the phenomenology of agency is a matter of experiencing that certain things are the case), whereas the telic theorist takes an intransitive view of it (the phenomenology of agency is a matter of one's actions, intentions and the like having phenomenal properties).[7]

How might we determine whether agentive experience is thetic or telic? It is unclear whether introspection is competent to pronounce on this question. According to one widely endorsed view, introspection provides us with access only to the contents of experience. Since the debate between the thetic and telic accounts concerns the structure rather than the contents of experience, introspection may be impotent here. Of course, this view of introspection is highly contested, and many would argue that there are introspectively accessible differences between experiences that outrun their contents. (What it is like to see something as square is different from what it is like to feel it as square, but arguably the two states share the same content.) Whether or not the current debate falls within the domain in which introspection *could* deliver a verdict, it is clear that introspection has not proven particularly useful in resolving it. At best introspection is silent on the question of whether agentive experience has thetic or telic structure, at worst it inclines theorists in a telic direction and others in a thetic one.

We might hope to get more traction on this debate by asking how agentive experiences could fail. States with a mind-to-world direction of fit fail by being frustrated, whereas states with a world-to-mind direction of fit fail by misrepresenting how things are. In what way—or ways—do agentive experiences fail?

At least some forms of agentive experience fail (when they do) by misrepresenting. This is surely what we ought to say about experiences of free will. Whatever the exact content of experiences of free will, it is surely an open question whether we are free in the way(s) in which we experience ourselves as being free. Searle himself takes it to be very much an open question whether we actually possess the libertarian freedom that he thinks we experience ourselves as having (Searle 2001; see also Ginet 1997). Doubts about the veridicality of experiences of free will are most pressing for those attracted to an incompatibilist analysis of their content, but they can also be raised within the context of compatibilist analyses. Indeed, Searle himself takes it to be very much an open question whether we actually possess the libertarian freedom that he thinks we experience ourselves as having (Searle 2001).

Experiences of effort can also be nonveridical: in principle, it seems possible that one might experience effortful tasks as effortless and vice-versa. In fact, this possibility might not be merely theoretical. Naccache et al (2005) describe a patient who performed normally on measures of cognitive load but experienced tasks involving high cognitive load as no more effortful than tasks involving low cognitive load. It is natural to suppose that in experiencing these tasks as effortless this patient was misrepresenting her own cognitive processing—they were effortful, despite being experienced as effortless.

But what about the core components of agentive experience? Consider William James's case of a patient who is asked to raise his anesthetized arm. The patient's eyes are closed, and unbeknown to him his arm is prevented from moving. Upon opening his eyes he is surprised to discover that his arm has not moved. Although he tried to raise his arm, this attempt was a failure. What did James's patient *experience*? Searle describes his experience as one of '*trying* but *failing* to raise one's hand' (Searle 1983, 89; emphasis in original). I am not persuaded. Arguably, the patient was surprised to discover that his hand had not gone up because he experienced himself as raising it—the patient had an experience *as* of raising his arm. If this is right, then the experience of acting cannot be identified with acting "accompanied by certain phenomenal properties" (Searle 1983, 92), for in this case there was no action for phenomenal properties to accompany. The case appears to demand a thetic analysis. On discovering that his arm has not moved, James's patient ought to treat his experience of acting in just the way he treats his perceptual experience of illusions—that is, as misrepresenting some aspect of reality.

The proponent of the telic model might reply that the patient's experience misleads him only insofar as it represents the *movement* of his arm—and there is nothing agentive, as such, about that content. We can see the futility of this response by considering the following variant of James's case. Suppose that the patient is paralyzed; he can try to raise his arm, but his trying will not be causally efficacious. However, a mischievous scientist with brain-reading technology can detect the patient's tryings, and intervenes in his motor cortex so as to ensure that his tryings are successful. (This, of course, is the model that the occasionalists offered of all agency.) The patient will experience himself as raising his arm—after all, his arm goes up as and when he tries to raise it—but there is surely something non-veridical in his experience. This nonveridical element cannot be identified with the representation of the trajectory or location of his arm, for in this case these elements are veridical. Rather, it must concern his experience of *agency*—it must have something to do with the agent's role in producing the movement.[8]

Counterexamples aside, there is something rather odd with the thought that experiences (as) of acting successfully (unsuccessfully) could be identified with successful (failed) efforts. Why should agents have any first-person access to the success of their efforts, merely in virtue of having successful attempts? Consider, as a parallel, the proposal that we identify the experience of one's perceptions as veridical (nonveridical) with the veridicality (nonveridicality) of one's perceptions. Such a proposal is clearly a nonstarter: The veridicality of a perception is one thing, the experience of it as (non)veridical is another. Identifying the experience of one's intentions as satisfied or frustrated with the event of them being satisfied or frustrated is similarly implausible.[9]

In my view, the proponent of the telic model ought to restrict the scope of the model to experiences of trying. Perhaps the experience of trying to do something is not a state that represents oneself as trying to do something, but simply a trying "that possesses phenomenal character." In fact, there is some reason for taking Searle's phrase "the experience of acting" to refer to the experience of trying to act as opposed to the experience of acting, for it is this view that provides the most plausible reading of his position. At any rate, that is how I will understand his use of "the experience of acting."

Searle provides two arguments for the telic account of the experience of acting. First, he claims that it is part of the content of experi-ences of such experiences that they represent themselves as bringing about those actions with which they are associated: "If it [the experience of acting] didn't cause the arm to go up, but something else did, I didn't raise my arm: it just went up for some other reason" (1983, 88; see also 124). If this claim were true it would provide an attractive argument for the telic account, for as we saw in the case of the mischievous scientist, the satisfaction conditions of trying to raise one's arm appear to include a self-referential component. Arguably, it is part of the content of the trying that it itself plays a direct role in causing one's arm to go up. It is not implausible to identify experiences of trying with tryings *if* indeed they share the same self-referential content.

But do they share the same self-referential content? I doubt it. I can discern nothing in the phenomenology of the experience of trying to φ that represents that very experience as enabling me to φ. I am not convinced that experiences of trying contain any self-referential content, but, if they do, I am inclined to think that they represent themselves as being caused by tryings rather than representing themselves as causing actions. At any rate, I do not share Searle's intuition that in raising my arm I experience that experience as itself causing my arm to rise. In fact, I'm not sure that I experience *anything* as causing my arm to rise.

Searle's second argument for identifying experiences of tryings with tryings involves an appeal to failures of agency. He writes as follows: "[W]hen we have an experience [of acting] but the event doesn't occur we say such things as that I failed to raise my arm, and that I tried to raise my arm but did not succeed" (Searle 1983, 88). As I read it, the argument is that the telic account must be right because it correctly predicts that there is only a single "joint of intentionality" between experiences (as) of trying and actions. By contrast, the thetic account posits two such joints: one between experiences of trying and tryings themselves and another between tryings and their realization. If the thetic account were correct, it would follow that agents could experience themselves as trying to φ even when they did not φ for one of two reasons: Either their attempt at φ-ing was unsuccessful, or their experience as of attempting to φ was nonveridical. Searle's argument seems to be that experiences of tryings must be telic because we never countenance this second possibility.

I think that Searle is right to suggest that we do not generally recognize a gap between experiences of tryings and trying themselves, and in this sense he may also be right to suggest that our folk conception of experiences of trying is, in some sense, telic. But perhaps the folk model of experiences of trying is incorrect. Perhaps we should be open to the idea that experiences of trying—no less than experiences of actually acting—can lead us astray.[10]

We can create space for this possibility by considering anosognosia for hemiplegia, a condition in which one is unaware that one is paralyzed on one side of one's body. When requested to perform an action that involves the paralyzed limb (such as clapping one's hands together) patients will typically insist that they have performed the requested action, despite the fact that they have moved only one hand. Among the various accounts of anosognosia for hemiplegia is the feedforward account, according to which this condition involves a deficit in the motor effector system (Heilman 1991; Gold et al 1994; Adair et al 1997). Proponents of this account argue that damage to the motor effector system has resulted in the loss of the ability to form intentions to move. It is tempting to gloss this account by suggesting that patients no longer try to move. Nonetheless, there is every reason to think that patients retain the *experience* of trying to move their limb, for they insist that they are moving (or have just moved) the limb. In short, there is some reason to think that anosognosia for hemiplegia may involve a situation in which a person's experiences of trying to do something are nonveridical: There is no trying here, not even a frustrated one, only an experience thereof. This account of anosognosia for hemiplegia might not be correct but it does seem to be *coherent*, and its coherence suffices to undermine the claim that experiences of trying are, of conceptual necessity, telic.

The doxastic and telic models of agentive experience are the two leading competitors to the thetic model. If, as I have argued, these two models can be set to one side, then the intuitive case for the perceptual model that I sketched in §2 becomes all the more appealing. The next section reinforces the case for the perceptual model by responding to three lines of objection that might be leveled against it.[11]

5. Objections and Replies

The first objection concerns the relationship between agentive experiences and their intentional objects (that is, actions). The intentional object of a perceptual experience is typically independent of the experience itself. My visual experience of a dog is one thing while the dog itself is quite another; my auditory experience of a tree falling in the forest is one thing while the falling of the tree is quite another. One might take this independence—a fact that is arguably represented in the very contents of perception—to be a necessary feature of perceptual experience.

Are agentive experiences independent of their intentional objects? Some say "no." Mossel has recently rejected the perceptual model of what he calls "sensations of acting" on the grounds that such states are parts of actions, and hence are not independent of actions in the way in which they would need to be were they to qualify as perceptions of agency (Mossel 2005, 134). Mossel is not alone in suggesting that agentive experiences are in some way internal to actions themselves. Searle states that "if my arm goes up, but goes up [without the experience of acting], I didn't raise my arm, it just went up" (Searle 1983, 88, see also 95). Striking a similar note, Ginet claims that a simple mental event is an action "if and only if it has an intrinsic phenomenal quality," which he dubs "the actish quality" (1997, 89).[12]

There is *something* to this line of argument. Many people are reluctant to regard physical or mental happenings that are unaccompanied by a basic "experience of doing" as actions. This reluctance is manifest in our intuitive response to the anarchic hand syndrome—as we saw, there is some temptation to deny that anarchic actions really are actions of the patient in question. Arguably this intuitive resistance is best explained by supposing that agentive experience of some kind is essential to agency.

But there is another side to the story. If anarchic hand actions do not qualify as the patient's actions, whose actions are they? One might deny that they are actions at all, but that seems implausible. Anarchic hand movements certainly *look* like actions, for they can be evaluated for success. (The attempt to take food from a stranger's plate might be frustrated by the waitperson's intervention!) Peacocke (2003) has suggested that anarchic hand actions are "orphans"—actions without an agent. This position has something to recommend it but it comes at some intuitive cost, for we tend to think that actions must come attached to agents. So perhaps we should admit that anarchic hand actions belong to the patient despite the fact that the patient experiences no sense of agency towards them. Some support for the view that actions need not be accompanied by agentive experiences derives from what Bach (1978) calls "minimal actions," such as tapping

absentmindedly while listening to a lecture or walking to the shops while one's mind is on other matters. It is an open question whether minimal actions are always accompanied by an experience of agency. Would minimal actions that are not so-accompanied fail to qualify as bona fide actions? I do not see why they must.[13]

Although I reject the independence objection, I do not deny that agentive experiences of various stripes are often causally implicated in agency. Clearly, the experience of losing control of one's actions can lead one to attend more closely to what one is doing, which may in turn affect how (or indeed whether) one continues to act. Similarly, the experience of an action as effortful might lead one to either exert more effort or, alternatively, to abandon doing what one is trying to do. Indeed perhaps the experience of acting autonomously is in some way implicated in what it is to act autonomously. Just how agentive experience might be implicated in agency itself is a quite obscure issue, but it is not implausible to suppose agency of the kind that we ordinarily enjoy would be unrecognizable in the absence of agentive experience; perhaps we would not even have the tools to conceive of ourselves as agents in the absence of agentive experience. Granting all this, there remains enough independence between agentive experiences and their conditions of satisfaction for it to be possible, in principle if not in practice, that such states are nonveridical.[14]

A second objection to the perceptual model focuses on the question of whether agentive experience involves the operation of a perceptual organ of the requisite kind. On the face of things, there does not seem to be anything that stands to agentive experience as the eyes stand to seeing, the ears to hearing, or the skin to touch. Might this fact scuttle the perceptual model?

To address the question we need to consider how the notion of a perceptual organ is to be understood. O'Dea [2011] suggests that a perceptual organ is a mechanism over whose operation one has some degree of intentional control and whose mode of operation is implicitly represented in the very experiences it produces. On this proposal, perceptual experience involves some form of self-intimation of its own mode of acquisition. It is part of the content of visual experience that it is acquired via the deployment of the eyes, it is part of the content of tactile experience that it is acquired via the skin, and so on. O'Dea's account builds on a Gibsonian conception of perception, according to which perceptual organs are not mechanisms that passively register their input but tools by means of which we explore our environment.

O'Dea's analysis captures an important feature of the traditional senses—a feature that sets "the famous five" apart from other forms of sensory experience—but it is not the only viable notion of a perceptual organ. Consider proprioceptive, vestibular and nociceptive experience. The mechanisms that lie behind these forms of experience are not open to view and as a result of this they are not amenable to intentional control. There is nothing that one can do in order to get a better perspective on one's vestibular environment; there is no straightforward sense in which one can track the state of one's viscera. Nonetheless, there is a respectable sense in which these forms of experience do qualify as perceptual, for they are ways of gaining information about the state of the world (in this case, the state of the world that happens to coincide with one's own body). Furthermore, it is not clear that O'Dea's analysis even applies to each of the famous five without qualification. Perhaps animals and neonates can enjoy perceptual experience—they can see things, touch things, and so on—without any awareness of how they come by this information. O'Dea's

analysis does capture something important, but we should resist the suggestion that it gives us the only legitimate analysis of what it is to be a perceptual organ or, by extension, what it is to be a perceptual sense.

A more liberal view of what it is to be a perceptual organ thinks of organs as dedicated mechanisms that take as input energy of a distinctive kind and generate as outputs representations in an appropriate format, at least some of which are experiential. Does the mechanism responsible for agentive experience qualify as a perceptual organ even on this more relaxed conception of a sensory organ? Even here one might have qualms. On the comparator-based account introduced earlier, the sense of agency takes as input not raw energy but motor representations and representations drawn from the other perceptual modalities. So, there is a real difference between the mechanisms responsible for agentive experiences and those that generate (say) proprioceptive, vestibular, and nociceptive experiences: The latter involve sensory transducers whereas the former do not. Nonetheless, I am not inclined to regard this difference as particularly significant in the present context. The appropriate response to it is to draw a distinction between basic and nonbasic perceptual systems, where the former take as input forms of energy and the latter take as input representations. The five traditional senses (and various forms of proprioception and interoception) would qualify as basic perceptual systems, whereas the sense of agency would qualify as a nonbasic perceptual system. Nonetheless, a nonbasic perceptual system is still genuinely perceptual.

A third objection to the perceptual model is difficult to pin-down with any precision. Put most generally, the worry is the approach drains such experiences of their agentive nature. As Korsgaard puts it, "to experience something is (in part) to be passively receptive to it, and therefore we cannot have experiences of activity as such" (1996, 204). More enigmatically, O'Shaughnessy writes as follows:

> If one is to relate as observer to anything then one has to be "without it," whereas if one is intentionally to do anything then one has to be "within" the action we are attempting to observe, in which case we have an entirely empty and self-delusive experience of observation...or else we remain "without" in some less serious sense and genuinely seem to observe the action. But remaining "without," we lose the action as ours in gaining the observation: we lose any "withinness." (O'Shaughnessy 1980, 31)

I must admit that I fail to feel the force of the objection. There is no doubt some sense in which perception is passive, but it is surely a gross non sequitur to suppose that because a state is passive it cannot represent agency. After all, judgment is also passive, but there is no doubt that we can form judgments about our own agency. If it is possible for one's own agency to be represented in thought why should it not also be possible for it to be represented in experience? Why exactly would the perceptual representation of agency undermine its "withinness"?

I suspect that one of the worries behind this objection is the thought that on the perceptual model it must always be an open question whether the action being perceived as one's own really is one's own. Perceptual experience is not immune to error relative to the first person. For example, one can raise the question of whether the legs that appear to one in visual experience are one's own or those of another (Shoemaker 1968). But agentive *experience* does seem to be immune to error relative to the first person, for the question of whether the actions of which one is aware in experience are one's own or someone else's is puzzling at best and downright incoherent at worst. So, the objection runs, agentive experience is not perceptual. Engaging with this worry would lead us into deep waters that I cannot even begin to chart in this chapter, suffice it to say that the distinction between logical and de facto immunity to error might be of some help to us here. The objection requires that agentive experience be logically immune to error, but it may in fact be only de facto immune to error. We might compare agentive experiences to (say) proprioceptive experiences: we might be able to imagine scenarios in which these experiences track the states of another's body, but as things stand these experiences are restricted to states of oneself.

6. Conclusion: The Sense of Agency and the Famous Five

I have argued that there is much to be said on behalf of a perceptual model of agentive experience. The model does justice to its phenomenology; it receives some support from cognitive science; and it is able to meet the most pressing objections to it. Assuming that the perceptual model is on the right track, what lessons might we draw from it?

There are lessons to be drawn in two domains. First, the perceptual model opens up questions that are obscured by other analyses of agentive experience. How reliable is the sense of agency? Does agentive experience represent agency as it really is, or does the sense of agency lead us into error? To what degree is the manifest image of agency as encoded in agentive experience vindicated by the scientific image of agency? Versions of some of these questions can perhaps be posed from within the doxastic and telic models, but it is only the thetic model that brings them out into the clear light of day.

Secondly, the perceptual model encourages us to take a new look at perception's reach. If the sense of agency can be understood in perceptual terms how many *other* facets of human experience might also succumb to a perceptual treatment? Might it turn out that humans enjoy vomeronasal perception, as Keeley (2002, [2011]) has suggested? Might it turn out that we possess a sense of echolocation, as Schwitzgebel and Gordon (2000) have suggested? Might various forms of cognitive feelings—the experience of having a word on the tip of one's tongue, of taking oneself to know what the answer to a question is, of taking someone to be familiar—also qualify as perceptual?

If, as some theorists do, one begins one's analysis of perception with the assumption that there are only five senses, then each of the forgoing questions must be answered in the negative.[15] It seems to me that this would be a rather unwelcome result. In my view, the question of just how many senses we have is one that should be left open for now. Vision, audition, olfaction, taste and touch may be the paradigms of perception, but there is good reason to doubt whether they exhaust the category. We need a nuanced account of perception, one that does justice not only to the famous five but also to their less celebrated siblings.[16]

Notes

1. The "sense of agency" is sometimes used as a superordinate term for agentive experiences in general (e.g., Marcel 2003) and as a label for a particular component of agentive experience—roughly, the experience of authoring an action (see, e.g., Pacherie 2008). As should be clear from the foregoing, I use the term for a faculty (sensory system) that produces agentive experiences rather than as a term for (any species of) the experiences produced by this system.

2. "The phenomenology of first-person agency" is also used as a synonym for "agentive experience." I prefer the former label over the latter, for "phenomenology" has often been used to refer to a method for studying consciousness rather than as a term for the phenomenal character of experience.

3. See Bayne (2006, 2008), Bayne and Levy (2006), Hohwy (2004), Holton (2006), Horgan et al (2003), Marcel (2003), Nahmias et al. (2004), Pacherie (2008) and Siegel (2005) for further discussion of the contents of agentive experience.

4. For further details see Bayne and Pacherie (2007), David, Newen, and Vogeley (2008), Haggard (2005), Hallett (2007), and Pacherie (2008).

5. See Bayne and Pacherie (2007) for some discussion of how low-level and high-level agentive self-awareness might be related.

6. I find Peacocke's (2003, 2008) position difficult to pin down. On the one hand, Peacocke denies that agentive experience (what he calls "action-awareness") can be understood in perceptual terms. At the same time he grants that agentive experience is representational "[I]n the sense that in enjoying action-awareness, it seems to the subject that the world is a certain way" (2008, 247). I am unsure how to reconcile these two elements of Peacocke's account, and it may be that his view is not really a form of the telic model despite appearances to that effect.

7. We might note in passing that the telic model of agentive experience is at odds with standard representationalist conceptions of phenomenal character, for on such accounts the phenomenal character of a mental state is fixed by how it represents the world as being (see, e.g., Dretske 1995; Tye 1995). However, the telic model is consistent with the spirit of such

analyses, for it allows that facts about intentional content might fix facts about phenomenal character.

8. One can also arrive at this conclusion via a highly restrictive conception of actions, according to which actions are identified with attempts (Hornsby 1980). On this view, James's patient does in fact raise his arm, but it's just that the world fails to cooperate with his action. I assume here that this account of actions is incorrect, at least insofar as it is taken as an analysis of the content of the experience of acting.

9. Telic theorists could go disjunctive at this point. They could reject the "common factor" assumption, according to which agentive experiences belong to a single kind whether or not they occur in the context of successful intentions ('the good case') or unsuccessful intentions ('the bad case'). Wading into the murky waters of disjunctivism is beyond the scope of this chapter, but suffice it to say that, if the telic theorist needs to go disjunctivist, then I do not want to go telic.

10. Perhaps the representational nature of experiences of trying has been overlooked for the same reason that the representational nature of experiences of pain has been overlooked: In each case, having the experience of being in the target state provides by far the best evidence that we are in the target state.

11. Another alternative to the thetic account conceives of agentive experiences as pushmi-pullyu representations. See Bayne [2011] for discussion of this approach.

12. Searle does not seem to have a settled position on this issue, for certain passages in Intentionality appear to allow that actions need not be accompanied by the experience of acting (see, e.g., 1983, 92).

13. Although I have argued that the states of affairs represented by agentive experiences are independent of them, it may not be possible to give an analysis of what an action is that does not appeal in some way to agentive experience. However, even if this should turn out to be the case, it would still be possible for agentive experiences to be nonveridical. As a parallel, consider colors. Response-dependence conceptions of color hold that the analysis of colors must ultimately appeal to color experience, but such accounts allow that it is possible for an object to appear to be (say) green without being green. Similarly, a response-dependence conception of actions might allow that it is possible for something to appear to be an action without being an [action] (and vice-versa).

14. Perhaps the folk notion of action is not determinate enough for the question just examined to have an unequivocal answer. Our common-sense notion of action might simply have nothing to say about whether intentional goal-directed movement that fails to be accompanied by agentive experience qualifies as an action.

15. See, for example, O'Dea [2011] and Nudds (2003, [2011]).

16. I am very grateful to Frédérique de Vignemont, Elisabeth Pacherie, Michael Schmitz, Laura Schroeter, and especially Fiona Macpherson for comments on previous drafts of this chapter.

References

Adair, J.C., Schwartz, R.L., Na, D.L., Fennell, E., Gilmore, R.L., Heilman, K.M. 1997. Anosognosia: examining the disconnection hypothesis. *Journal of Neurology, Neurosurgery & Psychiatry*, 63: 798–800.

Anscombe, E. 1957. *Intention*. Oxford: Blackwell.

Bach, K. 1978. *A Representational Theory of Action*. Philosophical Studies 34: 361–79.

Banks, G., Short, P., Martinez, J., Latchaw, R., Ratcliff, G., Boller, F. 1989. The alien hand syndrome. *Archives of Neurology*, 46: 456–59.

Bayne, T. 2006. Phenomenology and the Feeling of Doing: Wegner on the Conscious Will. In S. Pockett, W.P. Banks and S. Gallagher (eds.), *Does Consciousness Cause Behavior?* Cambridge, MA: MIT Press, pp. 169–86.

Bayne, T. 2008. The Phenomenology of Agency. *Philosophy Compass*, 3: 1–21.

Bayne, T. 2011. Agentive Experiences as Pushmi-Pullyu Representations. In *New Waves in the Philosophy of Action*, ed. J. Aguilar, A. Buckareff and K. Frankish. Palgrave Macmillan.

Bayne, T. & Levy, N. 2006. The Feeling of Doing: Deconstructing the Phenomenology of Agency. In N. Sebanz and W. Prinz (eds.), *Disorders of Volition*. Cambridge, MA: MIT Press, pp. 49–68.

Bayne, T. & Pacherie, E. 2007. Narrators and comparators: the architecture of agentive self-awareness. *Synthese,* 159: 475–91.

Blakemore, S.-J. & Frith, C.D. 2003. Self-awareness and action. *Current Opinion in Neurobiology*, 13: 219–24.

David, N., Newen, A., and Vogeley, K. 2008. The "sense of agency" and its underlying cognitive and neural mechanisms. *Consciousness and Cognition*, 17: 523–34.

Della Sala S., Marchetti, C., Spinnler, H. 1991. Right-sided anarchic (alien) hand: A longitudinal study. *Neuropsychologia* 29(11): 1113–27.

Dretske, F. 1995. *Naturalizing the Mind*. Cambridge, MA: MIT Press.

Frith, C. 1992. *The Cognitive Neuropsychology of Schizophrenia*. Hove: Lawrence Erlblaum Associates.

Frith, C.D., Blakemore, S.-J. & Wolpert, D.M. 2000a. Abnormalities in the awareness and control of action. *Philosophical Transactions of the Royal Society of London*, Series B: Biological Sciences, 355 (1404): 1771–88.

Frith, C.D., Blakemore, S.-J. & Wolpert, D.M. 2000b. Explaining the symptoms of schizophrenia: Abnormalities in the awareness of action. *Brain Research Reviews*, 31: 357–63.

Gasquoine, P.G. 1993. Alien hand sign. *Journal of Clinical and Experimental Neuropsychology*, 15/5: 653–67.

Ginet, C. 1997. Freedom, responsibility and agency. *The Journal of Ethics*, 1: 85–98.

Gold, M., Adair, J.C., Jacobs, D.H., Heilman, K.M. 1994. Anosognosia for hemiplegia: an electrophysiologic investigation of the feed-forward hypothesis. *Neurology*, 44 (10): 1804–08.

Goldberg, G. & Bloom, K.K. 1990. The alien hand sign. Localization, lateralization and recovery. *American Journal of Physical Medicine and Rehabilitation*, 69: 228–38.

Haggard, P. 2005. Conscious intention and motor cognition. *Trends in Cognitive Science*, 9(6): 290–95.

Hallett, M. 2007. Volitional control of movement: The physiology of free will. *Clinical Neurophysiology*, 118: 1179–92.

Heilman, K.M. 1991. Anosognosia: Possible neuropsychological mechanisms. In *Awareness of deficit after brain injury. Clinical and theoretical issues*, G.P. Prigatano & D.L. Schacter (eds.), New York: Oxford University Press.

Hohwy, J. 2004. The experience of mental causation. *Behavior and Philosophy*, 32: 377–400.

Holton, R. 2006. The act of choice. *Philosophers' Imprint*, 6/3: 1–15.

Horgan, T., Tienson, J., & Graham, G. 2003. The phenomenology of first-person agency. In S. Walter and H.-D. Heckmann (eds.), *Physicalism and Mental Causation: The Metaphysics of Mind and Action*. Exeter, UK: Imprint Academic, pp. 323–40.

Hornsby, J. 1980. *Actions*. London: Routledge & Kegan Paul.

Keeley, B.L. 2002. Making sense of the senses. *The Journal of Philosophy*, 99: 5–28.

Korsgaard, C. 1996. Creating the kingdom of ends: Reciprocity and responsibility in personal relations. In *Creating the Kingdom of Ends*. Cambridge: Cambridge University Press.

Marcel, A. 2003. The sense of agency: Awareness and ownership of action. In J. Roessler & N. Eilan (eds.), *Agency and Self-Awareness*. Oxford: Oxford University Press, pp. 48–93.

Mellors, C.S. 1970. First rank symptoms of schizophrenia. *British Journal of Psychiatry*, 117: 15–23.

Mossel, B. 2005. Actions, control and sensations of acting. *Philosophical Studies*, 124/2: 129–80.

Naccache, L., Dehaene, S., Cohen, L., Habert, M-O., Guichart-Gomez., E., Galanaud, D., Willer, J.-C. 2003. Effortless control: executive attention and conscious feeling of mental effort are dissociable. *Neuropsychologia*, 43: 1318–28.

Nahmias, E., Morris, S. Nadelhoffer, T. & Turner, J. 2004. The phenomenology of free will. *Journal of Consciousness Studies*, 11/7–8: 162–79.

Nudds, M. 2003. The significance of the senses. *Proceedings of the Aristotelian Society*, 104/1: 31–51.

Nudds, M. 2011. The senses as psychological kinds. In F. Macpherson (ed.), *The Senses: Classic and Contemporary Philosophical Perspectives*. Oxford: OUP, pp. 311–40.

O'Dea, J. 2011. A proprioceptive account of the sensory modalities. In F. Macpherson (ed.), *The Senses: Classic and Contemporary Philosophical Perspectives*. Oxford: OUP, pp. 297–310.

O'Shaughnessy, B. 1980. *The Will* (Vol. II). Cambridge: Cambridge University Press.

O'Shaughnessy, B. 2003. The epistemology of physical action. In J. Roessler & N. Eilan (eds.), *Agency and Self-Awareness*. Oxford: Oxford University Press, pp. 345–57.

Pacherie, E., Green, M. & Bayne, T. 2006. Phenomenology and delusions: Who put the 'alien' in alien control?, *Consciousness and Cognition*, 15: 566–77.

Pacherie, E. 2007. The anarchic hand syndrome and utilization behaviour: A window onto agentive self-awareness. *Functional Neurology*, 22/4: 211–17.

Pacherie, E. 2008. The phenomenology of action: a conceptual framework. *Cognition*, 107: 179–217.

Peacocke, C. 2003. Awareness, ownership, and knowledge. In J. Roessler & N. Eilan (eds.), *Agency and Self-Awareness*. Oxford: Oxford University Press, pp. 94–110.

Peacocke, C. 2008. *Truly Understood*. Oxford: Oxford University Press.

Roessler, J. & Eilan, N. (eds.) 2003. *Agency and Self-Awareness*. Oxford: Oxford University Press.

Schilder P. 1953. *Medical Psychology*. New York: John Wiley & Sons.

Schwitzgebel, E. and Gordon, M.S. 2000. How well do we know our own conscious experience? The case of human echolocation. *Philosophical Topics*, 28/2: 235–46.

Searle, J. 1983. *Intentionality*. Cambridge: Cambridge University Press.

Searle, J. 2001. *Rationality in Action*. Cambridge, MA: MIT Press.

Shoemaker, S. 1968. Self-reference and self-awareness. *Journal of Philosophy*, 65(19): 555–67.

Siegel, S. 2005. The phenomenology of efficacy. *Philosophical Topics*, 33/1: 265–84.

Sierra, M. & Berrios, G.E. 1998. Depersonalization: Neurobiological Perspectives.
Biological Psychiatry, 44: 898–908.

Strawson, G. 1986. *Freedom and Belief.*
Oxford: OUP.

Tye, M. 1995. *Ten Problems of Consciousness:
A Representational Theory of the Phenomenal Mind.* Cambridge, MA: MIT Press.

Study Questions

1. Velleman argues (contra Davidson's account) that understanding intentional actions as those caused in the right way by beliefs and desires leaves out the agent. Consider this reply: that sort of account brings in the agent because it is *the agent's beliefs and desires*, not any other sort of cause, that results in such actions. How does (or would) Velleman respond?

2. Velleman agrees that events or states are the only things that can count as causes, but he also thinks that desires and beliefs (see Davidson), even second-order desires (see Frankfurt), leave out the agent in the account of intentional action. Give his proposal for what kinds of causes are necessary for intentional action. Are these causes actions or states? He says that this sort of cause is constitutive of an agent. Is he right? Are actions or states the sorts of things that can constitute an agent?

3. Velleman produces what he takes to be counter-examples to Davidson and Frankfurt: the drug addict who intentionally goes to his dealer and arranges a purchase, and the unconscious voice-raising which offends a friend. Explain how these two cases are sup-posed to be counter-examples to Davidson and/or Frankfurt. Do you agree that these are genuine counter-examples? Why/why not?

4. Do you find Velleman's account of being an agent in terms of the ability to act from a desire to act in accordance with reasons to be plausible? Could one be an agent despite not acting for *good* reasons? Could one be an agent despite not acting for reasons at all? Is he right that this is not an account like the others, in terms of a different sort of cause? Review his objections to the other causal accounts: does his fall prey to these as well?

5. Consider Frankfurt's imagined psychotherapist. He wants to desire to take drugs, but he doesn't desire to take drugs. Is this coherent? He wants to desire to take drugs and he wants this desire not to lead to action which would fulfil it. Is this a possible state? If you really desire X, can you at the same time desire that you not get X?

6. Frankfurt imagines a "rational wanton." He denies personhood to this human. Velle-man argues that rationality is what makes a human a person. Are these positions really in conflict? Explain clearly what each amounts to. Who (if either) is right?

7. Consider Frankfurt's contrast between the two addicts. The "wanton addict," he says, who has no second order desires, therefore doesn't care whether his desire to take drugs or his desire not to take them wins out. Is this possible? Suppose his desire to take drugs

wins out. Then his desire not to take drugs is frustrated. So he does care! (Is this criticism of Frankfurt sound?)

8. Is Frankfurt correct in characterizing a being with first-order, but no second-order, desires as unfree, a "helpless bystander to the forces that move him"?

9. It's usually assumed that a necessary condition for moral appraisal of someone's action is that they did it of their own free will. Frankfurt disagrees that this is a condition. Explain why. Do you think he's right?

10. One of Hornsby's objections to the causal account is that sometimes one can do something intentionally without there being any action that they performed. One of her examples: refraining from taking a chocolate. See Q. 2 in the Study Questions for Chapter 13 for a similar objection, and this reply: sometimes refraining itself is an action insofar as it figures in causal stories, caused in the right way by belief and desires. What is a refraining? (Remember that simply not doing something is not a refraining.) Might this answer Hornsby's objection?

11. Another of Hornsby's objections is that seeing bodily movements as effects of beliefs and desires "doesn't ever seem to be focussed on saying why an event occurred." But doesn't giving a redescription of that bodily movement in more salient terms, plus an account of the beliefs and desires that caused it, focus on why it occurred? (E.g., redescribe 'waving her arm' as 'signaling the taxi' and giving her desire that a taxi pick her up plus her beliefs that that was how to achieve this.) What would (or does) Hornsby reply? Who is right?

12. According to Hornsby, a foot-movement isn't an action. But if we allow that a foot-movement can be redescribed as a pushing of the brake, and as a stopping of the car, then it seems that it's exactly what action-theory is concerned with. Does she insist that these are not redescriptions of the same thing? Why?

13. Hornsby says that when the philosophers she criticizes say that it's *the agent's* beliefs and desires that cause *the agent's* actions, the agent is still missing from the story. Why does she say this? Is she right?

14. In what way does Schlosser think that the problem of the disappearing agent is an "empty challenge"? In what way does he think that it is "not altogether" empty? Is he right about this?

15. What is the challenge from ownership of agency and what is Schlosser's reply to it? What role does the experience of agency play in his reply?

16. Bayne distinguishes between the perceptual, doxastic, and telic models of the experience of agency. Explain the differences. What are his main arguments in favor of the perceptual model, and against the doxastic and telic models? Do you find anything in here to criticize?

Suggested Readings

For an excellent collection of contemporary essays on the philosophy of action (including the reading by Marcus Schlosser reproduced here) that further address some of the questions examined in this chapter, the reader may wish to consult *New Waves in Philosophy of Action* (Hampshire, UK: Palgrave MacMillan, 2011), edited by Jesús H. Aguilar, Andrei A. Buckareff, and Keith Frankish.

For more on agentive experiences, see Myrto Mylopoulos's critique of Bayne's view in her "Agentive Awareness Is Not Sensory Awareness," *Philosophical Studies* 172(3) (2015): 761–80, as well as Joshua Shepherd's "The Experience of Acting and the Structure of Consciousness," *Journal of Philosophy*, 114(8): 422–48, and Elisabeth Pacherie's "The Phenomenology of Action: A Conceptual Framework," *Cognition* 107 (2008): 179–217.

GLOSSARY

abstract ideas Ideas that are not ideas of any particular individual object, but that apply to a class of objects. For example, the abstract idea of a line is an idea that is not restricted to any particular line with any specific length or shape. Berkeley denies that there are any abstract ideas.

access consciousness (A-consciousness) According to Ned Block, a mental state is A-conscious if the information it contains is widely available for the control of action and speech. Contrasts with **phenomenal consciousness**.

act (verb) To do something, commonly with some form of purpose or **intention**.

action The event of someone or something **acting**.

agent Someone or something that **acts** or is capable of acting.

agentive experience The experience of oneself as the source of one's own behavior.

agentive participation This term refers to the involvement of an **agent** in their **action** that is thought to go beyond that of the beliefs, desires, and intentions leading up to it.

algorithm A set of rules that, if followed, will produce a particular result or accomplish a specific task. The rules should be written in such a way that they can be followed without knowing what result is to be accomplished. A computer program is an algorithm, where the rules specify operations to be carried out by the computer.

Artificial Intelligence (AI) The research discipline focusing on the development of machines that are capable of genuine intelligence. Sometimes the term is used to refer simply to the use of machines to perform complex tasks, or to the use of computers in modeling human intelligence.

artificial intelligence (AI) An artificial object that possesses a mind.

atomism The theory that the world consists entirely of minute particles of matter. Atoms are taken to be indestructible, and all objects are formed of collections of atoms. Atomism is a variety of **materialism**.

autonomy See **intertheoretic autonomy**.

behavioral disposition A tendency to exhibit certain specific kinds of behavior under certain conditions or in the presence of certain **stimuli**. A (simple) behavioral disposition can be expressed by a conditional sentence of the form 'If C then B,' where C is the condition or stimulus and B is the behavior.

behavioral plasticity The apparent ability of humans to respond to an indefinite number of different situations. Descartes uses this idea to argue that people cannot be merely material beings, because the behavior of human beings transcends what a purely mechanical being can produce. Behavioral plasticity is a topic of great interest in **Artificial Intelligence**.

behaviorism The position that the proper task of psychology is the study of human behavior. There are two varieties of behaviorism: **scientific behaviorism** and **logical behaviorism**.

blindsight A condition resulting from neural damage that causes a "blind spot" in the conscious visual field, where subjects report no sensation at all, while information contained in that region of the visual field remains available for certain unconscious functions.

brute fact A fact whose existence is not explained by, or due to, anything else.

category mistake A term used by Gilbert Ryle to refer to a particular kind of logical confusion, which he ascribes to Descartes. Two terms belong to the same "logical category" when meaningful conjunctions can be formed with them. The error arises when people mistakenly take two dissimilar terms to belong to a common logical category.

cause (noun) Generally, an object or event that brings something about, that produces an effect. In the sciences, causes bring about their effects as the result of the laws of nature.

causal explanation An explanation of an event or an occurrence in terms of its causes.

causal theory of action The theory that what makes a behavior an **action** is that it is caused in a certain way by certain of an agent's psychological states. According to Donald Davidson, an action is an event that is caused by **reasons**.

classical conditioning A change in behavior produced by forming new links between **stimulus** and **response**. This is done by associating a stimulus that already produces a particular response with a new stimulus. The most famous example of this effect is Pavlov's experiment with dogs, whereby he conditioned the dogs to salivate to the ringing of a bell by associating the bell with the arrival of food.

cognitive penetration This term refers to the degree to which a cognitive process is influenced by the agent's beliefs and knowledge. **Actions**, it is said, must be cognitively penetrable, that is, under the control of what the agent knows or believes. Contrasts with **informationally encapsulated**.

comparator mechanism A mechanism that guides bodily movement through a series of **inverse** and **forward models**.

compatibilism The thesis that free will and determinism are compatible with one another. Contrasts with **incompatibilism**.

complete thing Descartes's description of a **substance**.

conscious experience The subjective, experiential character of conscious mental states including thoughts, sensations, feelings, and memories. Described by Thomas Nagel as what thoughts, sensations, etc. are *like* for the creature that has them.

content See **intentional content**, **propositional content**, and **qualitative content**.

contingent facts Facts that are a result of how the world happens to be, and that might not have been facts were the world different than it is. Contrasts with **necessary facts**.

contingent identity A **numerical identity** that is a contingent fact. That is, it is an identity that depends on how the world happens to be. The identity of Mount Everest with the highest mountain peak is a contingent identity. Contrasts with **necessary identity**.

designator, nonrigid A word or expression that refers to some individual person or thing, where the object it refers to depends on some contingent facts. A nonrigid designator will refer to one individual in certain circumstances and to other individuals in different circumstances. Contrasts with **rigid designator**.

designator, rigid A word or expression that refers to some individual person or thing, where the object it refers to does not depend on any contingent facts. A rigid designator will refer to the same individual under any circumstances whatsoever. Contrasts with **nonrigid designator**.

determinism The thesis that the entire state of the universe at any time is entirely determined by its prior state together with the laws of nature.

deviant causes In the philosophy of action, deviant causes occur when an **agent**'s behavior is caused by their beliefs and desires and yet that behavior is not plausibly seen as an **action** of the agent.

digital computers An information-processing machine that operates according to an **algorithm**, and whose operation consists of reading and writing symbols.

discrete state machine A machine whose operation consists of jumps from one definite state to another, rather than in continuous motion.

dualism See **mind-body dualism**.

easy problems of consciousness The questions about consciousness that are amenable to answers in terms of functional or neural processes. According to David Chalmers, they are "easy" in the sense that we have an understanding of what a satisfactory answer would look like. Contrasts with the **hard problem of consciousness**.

environmental history The totality of the stimuli in a person's previous physical environment that have an effect on their behavior.

epiphenomenalism The position that mental states or mental properties are caused by activities of the brain, but do not in turn have any effect on the operation of the brain. Roughly speaking, then, mental phenomena are byproducts of nervous activity in the brain. Contrasts with **mind-body interactionism**.

essence See **form**.

first-order desires A desire to do something or not to do something. A second-order desire is then a desire to have or not to have a first-order desire.

form Aristotle defined form (or essence) as that which makes something the kind of thing it is. In living things the form is a principle of growth and movement that determines the species of a plant or animal. In this case, Aristotle claims that form is identical to soul.

formal properties See **syntactic properties**.

Forms, The The Forms constitute Plato's theory of **universals**. According to Plato, universals are independently existing objects that are both eternal and unchanging. Material objects have properties by imperfectly resembling the Forms. All genuine knowledge, according to Plato, is knowledge of the Forms. Sometimes the Forms are referred to as "Ideas."

forward model A form of **internal model** that takes motor commands as input and calculates the sensory consequences of performing those commands.

free will The ability to **act** freely. The term has been analyzed in several different ways.

function In science and mathematics, one variable y is said to be a function of another variable x when each value of x yields exactly one value for y.

functional organization A description of a system in terms of the functions performed by its states and processes rather than their physical construction.

functional reduction The idea that mental states and processes are reducible to **functional states** and processes. **Functionalism** is committed to this form of reduction. See **intertheoretic reduction**.

functional state Internal states of a system described in terms of their relations to input (or stimulus) and output (or behavior) and one another.

functionalism The theory of mind according to which mental states are defined in terms of what they do, rather than what they are made of. On this theory, mental states are characterized by their relations with stimuli, with behavior, and with one another.

global workspace theory (GWT) The theory that the function of consciousness is to make a large amount of information, contained in subconscious mechanisms, available to working memory. This facilitates the performance of highly complex tasks.

guidance According to Harry Frankfurt, a movement is under the guidance of an agent when the agent is capable of making adjustments to that movement that compensate for external interference. Such movements, according to Frankfurt, are **actions**.

hard determinism The thesis that both **determinism** and **incompatibilism** are true. Hard determinists deny the existence of free will.

hard problem of consciousness The problem of explaining why **phenomenal consciousness** exists, and why it has the **phenomenal properties** it does. It is a "hard" problem, according to David Chalmers, because it cannot be answered in terms of any functions of neural processes, and so it defies **reduction**.

higher-order awareness An awareness of oneself as being in a certain mental state. The idea is contrasted with a case wherein a person is aware of something by being in a certain mental state, without any awareness of being in that mental state, as in, e.g., subliminal perception. The term is used in David Rosenthal's theory of consciousness.

homunculus A little person inside a head that carries out mental functions, imagined in Block's **thought experiment**. (Plural: 'homunculi')

idealism The idea that nothing exists but immaterial minds. Idealists believe that material objects, such as apples and mountains, are collections of real or possible thoughts in the minds of thinking beings.

Ideas See **The Forms**.

identify with a desire According to Harry Frankfurt, to identify with a **first-order desire** is to want that desire to win out over competing desires. It is to endorse it or make it one's own.

identity See **numerical identity** and **qualitative identity.**

identity theory of mind The thesis that mental event **types** are **numerically identical** with physical event **types**—usually types of brain events (thus also the **mind-brain identity theory**). See also **type physicalism**.

incompatibilism The thesis that **free will** and **determinism** are not compatible, only one can be true.

informationally encapsulated A cognitive process is informationally encapsulated when its output is not affected by the agent's beliefs or knowledge. Optical illusions provide a good example: Their appearance is not altered when we discover the illusion.

informationally promiscuous The content of a mental state is informationally promiscuous when the information it carries is available to a wide range of mental processes.

innate ideas Ideas in the mind that do not come from sensory experience.

intellect That part of a person that is responsible for reason or rational thought. The intellect is often contrasted with the senses, the will, and the emotions.

intention In the theory of action, an intention is the determination to **act**. Some philosophers analyze intentions in terms of the beliefs and desires that initiate an **action**, while others take them as states that guide actions over periods of time.

intentional content The meaning that is carried by a mental state. This includes the **propositional content** of beliefs, desires, and other propositional attitudes. It can also include the information carried by a mental state. In its original use, the intentional content of a mental state was the manner in which the "intentional object" of the state is thought of.

intentionality The characteristic feature that mental states have of being *about* something. So a person's thought of Paris somehow involves a relationship between that person and the city that is Paris. The term derives from the Latin term *tendere* meaning "to aim at."

internal model In motor cognition research, an internal model is a process that models the behavior of the motor system and its results, in order to generate motor commands and calculate the effects of external disturbances.

intertheoretic autonomy Two theories are autonomous when understanding the entities and laws of one theory will not provide an explanation of the entities and laws of the other. Contrasted with **intertheoretic reduction**.

intertheoretic reduction When a phenomenon is identified with entities or processes belonging to a more basic or fundamental science, and that identification allows us to explain the phenomenon in terms of more basic entities or processes. An example is the reduction of lightning to electrical discharge.

introspection The reflection on, or study of, one's own thoughts and conscious experiences.

introspectionism A school of psychology based on the idea that introspection, when carefully and skillfully carried out, will reveal the true operations of the mind.

inverse models A form of **internal model** that determines the motor commands that will bring about an intended outcome.

inverted spectrum A **thought experiment** in which two people (or one person at different times) has color sensations opposite to one another, such as red and green reversed, or blue and yellow reversed.

language game The name given by Ludwig Wittgenstein for the social rules governing the use of a language.

Law of Effect A principle formulated by Edward Thorndike stating that the frequency with which a behavior is exhibited is related to the tendency it has to produce positive or negative effects. The law forms the basis of Skinner's concept of operant behavior.

libertarianism Within the subject of free will, libertarianism is the thesis that **incompatibilism** is true and yet **free will** exists. Hence, libertarians deny **determinism**.

logical behaviorism The theory of mind (or, more accurately, the analysis of psychology) produced by the logical positivists. It holds that the meaning of any psychological description of a person is given by a description of that person's actual or potential behavior. Contrasts with **scientific behaviorism**.

logical empiricism See **logical positivism**.

logical positivism A philosophical doctrine developed in Vienna in the early part of the twentieth century. Logical positivists reject all **metaphysical** theories as meaningless. Their view is based on the **verifiability theory of meaning**. According to logical positivists, the role of philosophy can be nothing more than the logical analysis of the meanings of scientific terms. Also called **logical empiricism**.

machine table A table that represents the behavior of a **discrete state machine**. It displays the relations between three elements: a set of inputs, a set of outputs, and a set of internal states connecting inputs with outputs.

materialism The idea that nothing exists but matter. Materialists deny that the mind consists of anything more than some part or attribute of the physical body. Also called **physicalism**.

matter Aristotle defined matter as that which an individual thing is made of. In this sense matter is contrasted with **form**. In Descartes's mechanical physics, matter possesses only one attribute: spatial extension. Since Descartes, other properties, such as mass, have been added to the mechanical description of matter.

mechanical theories Theories that explain change and motion in terms of external forces acting on objects that are otherwise inert. The mechanical sciences came to prominence with the rejection of Aristotelian **teleological theories**.

mental qualities David Rosenthal's term for the properties of mental states in virtue of which an individual is able to discriminate among perceptible properties of objects.

mental tokens/types A mental token is a mental state or activity of a particular person at a particular time. A mental type is a kind or category of mental state or activity.

metaphysics Roughly, the study of the ultimate nature of reality. The term originates with the title given to one of Aristotle's books, which concerned the principles and concepts (like that of **universals**) that form the basis of all of the sciences. **Dualism**, **idealism**, and **materialism** are metaphysical theories.

mind-body dualism The theory that the mind (or soul) is in some way nonphysical or immaterial. Dualists believe either that the mind is a distinct entity from the body (**substance dualism**) or that properties of the mind are not physical properties of the body (**property dualism**).

mind-body interactionism The position that states or properties of the mind are caused by states and properties of the physical body, particularly the brain, and in turn have an effect on the action of the body. Descartes's dualism is a variety of this position. It is contrasted with **epiphenomenalism**.

mind-brain identity theory See **identity theory of mind**.

monism The theory that there is only one kind of **substance** in the world. Generally, monists defend either **materialism** or **idealism**.

multi-dimensional scaling (MDS) A graphical technique for representing relations of similarity between objects.

multiple realizability A **type** is multiply realizable when there is no single physical property or characteristic that every **token** of that type must have in common. For example, *clock* is a multiply realizable type, as there are indefinitely many ways of physically constructing a device that tells the time. Functionalists claim that mental types are multiply realizable.

mysterians The name of a contemporary school of philosophers who hold that the nature of consciousness is a mystery which can never be explained, physically or otherwise. This name, applied by their philosophical opponents, is slightly derisive.

naturalism The view that the mind (or soul) is an integral part of the natural order of material objects, plants, and animals. It includes the view that the study of the mind is not separate from the study of the natural world.

naturalistic dualism David Chalmers's term for a **mind-body dualism** that denies any reduction of consciousness to more elementary properties, yet is still a **naturalist** theory.

necessary facts When we say that a fact is necessary, we mean that it could not have failed to be a fact, no matter how the world might have turned out. (Notice that this idea is not the same as saying that such a fact is necessary *for* anything, or that other things depend on these facts.) Contrasts with **contingent facts**.

necessary identity A **numerical identity** that is a necessary fact. When we say that *A* is necessarily identical to *B* we mean that *A* could not have been anything other than *B* no matter how the world might have turned out to be. The identity of three with the square root of nine is a necessary identity. Contrasts with **contingent identity**.

neurophysical reduction The idea that mental states and processes are reducible to neural states and processes. **Identity theory of mind** is committed to this form of reduction. See **inter-theoretic reduction**.

nomological dangler A phenomenon that is not explicable in terms of the laws of nature applicable everywhere else. According to Smart, physicalism makes mental phenomena into a nomological dangler. "Nomological" means "having to do with the law (of nature)."

numerical identity *X* and *Y* are numerically identical when *X is Y*, that is, when *X* and *Y* are the same thing.

nutritive soul In Aristotle, that part of the soul responsible for growth and nutrition. It is possessed by all living things.

objective facts This is a term that Thomas Nagel uses to refer to facts about the world that can be understood by creatures with very different forms of conscious experience (or "points of view"). Contrasts with **subjective facts**.

Ockham's Razor The principle that, whenever two theories are consistent with the same body of evidence, then the one that postulates the fewest entities and properties is more likely to be true. It is named for the medieval philosopher William of Ockham (whose name and principle are often spelled 'Occam'). It is sometimes referred to as the "Principle of Parsimony."

operant behavior Behavior that is a product of the Law of Effect. Roughly, it is behavior produced and maintained by its tendency to yield positive effects or avoid negative effects. Operant behavior forms the basis of the behavioral conditioning studied by B.F. Skinner.

ordinary language philosophy A school of philosophy that holds that the meanings of words are revealed by their everyday use. Most philosophical problems, on this view, are simply misunderstandings of ordinary linguistic practice. The school originated in England in the 1940s, and is represented by people such as Gilbert Ryle and some elements of Ludwig Wittgenstein's philosophy.

perceptible properties The apparent properties of objects as they appear to various kinds of creatures. The perceived colors of objects, for example, will depend on specific aspects of the visual system of a species.

perceptual mapping The application of **multi-dimensional scaling** for representing relations of perceived similarity.

phenomenal consciousness (P-consciousness) According to Ned Block, a mental state is P-conscious if it has **phenomenal properties**. It is contrasted with **access consciousness**.

phenomenal properties Properties of mental states, such as thoughts, sensations, and feelings that have to do with what the state is *like* for the person that has them. See **qualitative content, qualia**.

phenomenology The study of the intrinsic or qualitative character of conscious experience. It can be described as a study of what conscious experience is *like*. (Note: This term also names a philosophical discipline founded in the nineteenth century by Edmund Husserl.)

physical token/type A physical token is an individual physical object or event, such as a single flash of lightning or an individual drop of water. A physical type is a category of physical objects or events, such as lightning or H_2O.

physicalism A synonym for **materialism**.

primary qualities A term introduced by John Locke for qualities of physical objects that resemble the **sensations** that we have of them. They include size, shape, number, and motion. Contrasts with **secondary qualities**.

primary reason Donald Davidson's term for the **reasons** that **cause** an action. Citing a person's primary reason for an action is a description of their **intention** in performing the action.

private language This term refers to a certain understanding of the meaning of sensation words like 'pain.' It holds that such words receive their meaning by referring to private, inner experiences, and thus that such words have a private, subjective meaning for each person. Wittgenstein argues that this understanding of language is incoherent.

problem of the disappearing agent A problem for the causal theory action, whereby it is argued that explanations in terms of psychological states *of* the agent leave the agent herself out of the picture.

program The list of instructions that tell a computer (or a brain) what to do with the symbols in it. A *program state* is an internal state of a computer defined in terms of what the device will do with a given symbol or set of symbols.

property dualism The theory that, although the mind is not a distinct *entity* from the brain, there are mental properties of the brain that are distinct from any of its physical or neural properties. Contrasts with **substance dualism**.

proposition The content of a declarative sentence. When two sentences have the same meaning, as with 'It is snowing' and 'Il neige,' we say that the two sentences express the same proposition.

propositional attitude A psychological state characterized by a person's attitude toward a certain **proposition**. Beliefs and desires are paradigmatic examples of propositional attitudes. To say that someone believes that Paris is in France is to say that they hold a psychological attitude of *belief* toward the proposition *Paris is in France*.

propositional content The proposition to which a propositional attitude is directed. Wishing, hoping, fearing, doubting that the cat is on the mat all have the same propositional content; all are directed to the same content, the **proposition** that the cat is on the mat.

purposive movement According to Harry Frankfurt, a movement is purposive when it is under the **guidance** of an agent.

qualia The **phenomenal properties** of our sensations and conscious experiences. What coffee *tastes like*, and what the color red *looks like*, are the qualia of the experiences of the taste of coffee and the sensation of red. (The singular is 'quale.')

qualitative character The qualitative character of a mental state is the property of that state in virtue of which things in the world appear the way they do. For example, the sensation of a lemon has a yellow qualitative character in virtue of which the lemon looks yellow. See also **phenomenal properties**, **qualia**.

qualitative identity X and Y are qualitatively identical when X and Y are separate things, but are alike in every respect.

qualitative theories Theories that provide explanations in terms of certain fundamental qualities, such as warmth, coldness, dryness, and heat. Aristotle's science is qualitative. Contrasts with **quantitative theories**.

quality space theory (QST) The idea that relations of similarity between **mental qualities** of mental states can be represented using the techniques of **perceptual mapping**.

quantitative theories Theories that provide explanations in terms of mathematical relations between variables. The theories of the **mechanical** sciences are quantitative.

quine A humorous verb meaning "to deny resolutely the existence of something real or important." It is a satirical jab at the American philosopher, W.V.O. Quine.

rational soul In Aristotle, that part of the soul responsible for reason. See also **intellect**.

rationalization An explanation of behavior in terms of **reasons**.

reasons A motivation for an **action**. In the theory of action, a reason can consist of a desire that a certain state of affairs should come about, and a belief that a certain **action** will bring that state of affairs about.

reduction See **intertheoretical reduction**.

reflex A fixed and automatic or mechanical response to a **stimulus**. According to Descartes, all the actions of the physical body, as well as the activities of nonhuman animals, are simply collections of reflex actions.

response The behavior that a subject exhibits in the presence of a particular **stimulus**.

scientific behaviorism The position that the science of psychology should be restricted to the formulation of laws connecting **stimulus** and **response**. As a position solely concerned with the proper method of psychology, it makes no philosophical claims about the nature or existence of the mind. Contrasts with **logical behaviorism**.

secondary qualities A term introduced by John Locke for qualities of physical objects that have no resemblance to the sensations we have of them. They include color, fragrance, warmth, and taste. According to the **mechanical** philosophers, they consist of nothing but the movements of insensible particles of matter. Contrasts with **primary qualities**.

second-order volition According to Harry Frankfurt, a second-order volition is a desire that a certain **first-order desire** be *effective*, that it be the motivation for **action**.

semantic properties Any properties having to do with the meaning of a sentence, a mental state, or a computer state. Jerry Fodor refers to the **semantic content** of a sentence or mental state. Contrasts with **syntactic properties**.

semantics In general, semantics is the study of linguistic meaning. In computer theory, the **semantic properties** of a **symbolic** representation in a computer have to do with what the content of the representation is. For example, the symbols '10' might represent a number or a letter. In psychology and philosophy of mind, the semantics of mental states is a matter of their **intentional content**. Contrasts with **syntax**.

sensations The experiential effects produced in the mind by the sensory organs and the nerves of the body.

sensibility That part of a person or animal that makes them capable of perceiving the world through the sensory organs.

sensitive soul In Aristotle, that part of the soul responsible for sense perception and locomotion. It is possessed by all animals, but not by plants.

solipsism The idea that nothing exists but one's own mind. On this view, you who are reading this sentence are the only being that exists, and there is nothing in existence other than the contents of *your* thoughts and perceptions.

stimulus The name given to an aspect of a subject's environment that affects his or her behavior. According to behaviorists, human actions can be understood and predicted by studying the relations between stimulus and response. (The plural is 'stimuli.')

structure A structure consists of a set of objects or elements, and a set of relations between them. A family is a structure in this sense: The family members are the elements, and the relations are those of kinship. The numbers also comprise a structure, with relations of greater than, less than, square root of, etc.

subjective character of experience This is a term used by Thomas Nagel and others to describe the **phenomenal** character of conscious experience. It is intended to refer to such things as what coffee *tastes like* or what the color red *looks like*.

subjective facts This is a term used by Thomas Nagel to refer to facts about experience that can only be known by creatures with similar forms of consciousness experience (or "points of view"). Contrasts with **objective facts**.

substance This term has had several definitions, but in each case it is used to refer to the most basic elements that make up the world. Aristotle used the term to refer to the components that go together to make up an individual, namely, matter, form, and (for the individual itself) the combination of matter and form. Descartes defined substance as "that which depends on nothing else for its existence." He believed that the world contains only two kinds of substances, each of which possesses only one attribute: minds (which possess only thought) and matter (which possesses only spatial extension).

substance dualism The theory that the mind is a distinct entity from the body and any of its parts. Descartes's dualism is an example of this kind of dualism. Contrasts with **property dualism**.

symbols Characters such as letters or numerals, or physical states of a system, that can carry meaning. For example, most **digital computers** use a "binary symbol code," which means they recognize only the symbols 1 and 0.

syntactic properties The (physical) properties of the symbols of a system by which the system recognizes them. An example is the *shape* of the letter 'y'. Contrasts with **semantic properties**.

syntax The rules governing how **symbols** can occur in a computer representation, and the effect that their order of occurrence has on its operation. Contrasts with **semantics**.

teleological theories Theories that include reference to the ends, goals, or purposes toward which things are directed. Aristotle's notion of **form** is a teleological notion, according to which growth and movement are explained in terms of the natural end of each species or natural object. Contrasts with **mechanical theories**.

telic states Mental states that have the function of bringing about changes in the world. Desires are examples of telic states. Contrasts with **thetic states**.

Theoretician's Dilemma The argument that theoretical laws are unnecessary, if they accurately predict the relations between observable events, and useless, if they don't. It forms part of B.F. Skinner's argument against the study of inner psychological states.

thetic states Mental states that have the function of representing the way the world is. Thoughts and perceptions are examples of thetic states. Contrasts with **telic states**.

thought, thinking Most commonly, thought is the activity of the **intellect**. But Descartes uses this term to describe the activity of the mind in a way that includes conscious experience as well. In his view, sensory perception is a form of thinking.

thought experiment A fictional story, or imaginary situation, that is used to test and challenge the way we think about the world. According to some people (Descartes, for example), thought experiments can reveal substantial truths about the world. Others argue that they merely reveal to us the content of our own concepts.

tokens and types A **token** is an individual thing, such as a person or object. A **type** is a kind or category of thing. A type can have many tokens (although it might have none), and every token belongs to many different types.

token physicalism The position that every **mental token** is a **physical token**. Token physicalism says in essence that every individual thing is a physical thing, and thus it is a statement of **materialism**. Contrasts with **type physicalism**.

topic-neutral descriptions Descriptions of things that make no reference to their intrinsic nature. For example, if we can describe mental states solely in terms of their relations with stimuli or behavior, then we can leave it open whether they are physical states of the brain or states of an immaterial mind.

transparent, the In Aristotle's theory of vision, the substance in air and water that makes possible the transmission of color to the soul.

Turing Machine An abstract **digital computer** with unlimited storage capacities and no time constraints described by Alan Turing. Turing Machines are useful as simple and effective ways of describing the computing power of digital computers. Their operations are absolutely simple, and yet they are capable of mimicking the behavior of any digital computer, no matter how powerful. See also **Universal Turing Machine**.

Turing Machine functionalism A version of functionalism according to which mental state types are internal functional states described as states of a **Turing Machine**.

Turing Test A test proposed by Alan Turing as a criterion for deciding whether a machine possesses intelligence. Roughly, it requires the machine to answer questions in a way that would fool an interrogator into thinking the answers are written by a person.

type physicalism The position that every **mental type** is a **physical type**. This position is stronger than **token physicalism** for it asserts that whenever two **mental tokens** belong to the same mental type, then they must also belong to the same physical type. **Identity theory of mind** is a variety of type physicalism.

universals A characteristic or property that can be possessed by more than one object. For example, many objects can be red; what they have in common is the universal, redness.

Universal Turing Machine (UTM) A programmable **Turing Machine** that is constructed in such a way that, by writing the appropriate program onto its tape, it will imitate the behavior of any other Turing Machine, and hence also any other **digital computer**.

verifiability theory of meaning A theory about the meanings of sentences adopted by the **logical positivists**. The theory says that the meaning of any sentence is given by a description of the observable circumstances under which it would be true or false, or of the evidence that would demonstrate that it is true or false. If there are no such circumstances or evidence, then the sentence is held to be meaningless.

visible, the In Aristotle's theory of vision, that which is the object of the faculty of sight, i.e., that which is seen directly by the eye. The visible, according to Aristotle, is color.

ACKNOWLEDGMENTS

Akins, Kathleen A. "A Bat without Qualities?," Chapter 13 of *Consciousness: Psychological and Philosophical Essays*, edited by Martin Davies and Glyn W. Humphreys. Blackwell, 1993. Used with permission of John Wiley & Sons via Copyright Clearance Center, Inc. "The Role of the Flight Membranes in Insect Capture by Bats," in *Animal Behaviour* by Frederic A. Webster and Donald R. Griffin. Elsevier, July–October 1962. Reprinted with permission from Elsevier.

Aristotle. Selections from "On the Soul," and "Sense and Sensibilia," from *The Complete Works of Aristotle*, edited by Jonathan Barnes. Princeton, NJ: Princeton University Press, 1984. Reprinted with the permission of Princeton University Press via Copyright Clearance Center, Inc.

Armstrong, David M. "The Nature of Mind," from *The Mind-Brain Identity Theory*, edited by C.V. Borst. London: Palgrave, 1970. Republished with permission of Red Globe Press via Copyright Clearance Center, Inc.

Arnauld, Antoine. "Objections to Descartes' Meditations," from *The Philosophical Writings of Descartes*, Vol. 2, translated by John Cottingham, Robert Stoothoff, and Dugald Murdoch. Copyright © Cambridge University Press, 1984. Reproduced with permission of the Licensor through PLSclear.

Bayne, Tim. "The Sense of Agency," Chapter 18 of *The Senses: Classic and Contemporary Philosophical Perspectives*, edited by Fiona Macpherson. Copyright © 2011 by Oxford University Press, Inc. Reproduced with permission of the Licensor through PLSclear.

Berkeley, George. Selections from *A Treatise Concerning the Principles of Human Knowledge*, 1710.

Block, Ned. Selections from "Troubles with Functionalism," from "Perception and Cognition: Issues in the Foundations of Psychology," in *Minnesota Studies in the Philosophy of Science*, Vol. IX, edited by C.W. Savage. Minneapolis: University of Minnesota Press, 1978, pp. 261–325. (Abridged version as it appeared in *Philosophy of Mind: Classical Problems/Contemporary Issues*, edited by Brian Beakley and Peter Ludlow, MIT Press. Reprinted with the permission of the University of Minnesota Press.) Excerpts from "On a Confusion about a Function of Consciousness," in *Behavioral and Brain Sciences* 18.2 (June 1995): 227–47. Reproduced with permission.

Boden, Margaret A. "Escaping from the Chinese Room," first published in this form in *The Philosophy of Artificial Intelligence*, edited by Margaret A. Boden. Oxford: Oxford University Press, 1990. A modified version of Margaret A. Boden, *Computer Models of Mind*. Copyright © Cambridge University Press, 1988. Reproduced with permission.

Chalmers, David J. Excerpts from "Facing Up to the Problem of Consciousness," in *Journal of Consciousness Studies* 2.3 (1995): 200–19. Reprinted with the permission of David Chalmers. Excerpts from *The Conscious Mind: In Search of a Fundamental Theory*. Oxford University Press, 1997. Copyright © 1996 by David J. Chalmers. Reproduced with permission of the Licensor through PLSclear.

Chomsky, Noam. Excerpts from "A Review of B.F. Skinner's Verbal Behavior," in *Readings in the Philosophy of Psychology* 1, edited by Ned Block. Cambridge, MA: Harvard University Press, 1980. First published in *Language* 35.1 (1959): 26–58. Reprinted with the permission of ROAM Agency, New York.

Cohen, Michael A., and Daniel C. Dennett. "Consciousness Cannot Be Separated from Function," from *Trends in Cognitive Sciences* 15.8 (August 2011): 358–63. Copyright © 2011 Elsevier Ltd. Reprinted with permission from Elsevier.

Davidson, Donald. "Actions, Reasons, and Causes," from *The Journal of Philosophy* 60.23 (November 1963): 685–700. Reprinted with the permission of Dr. Marcia Cavell.

Dennett, Daniel C. "Quining Qualia," Chapter III of *Consciousness in Contemporary Science*, edited by A. Marcel and E. Bisiach. Oxford: Oxford University Press, 1992. Copyright © Daniel C. Dennett, 1988, 1992. Reproduced with permission of the Licensor through PLSclear.

Descartes, René. Selections from *The Philosophical Writings of Descartes*, Vol. 1, translated by John Cottingham, Robert Stoothoff, and Dugald Murdoch. Copyright © 1985 Cambridge University Press. Reproduced with permission of the Licensor through PLSclear. Excerpts from *Meditations on First Philosophy*, edited by Andrew Bailey and translated by Ian Johnston. Copyright © Broadview Press, 2013. Excerpts from *Discourse on Method*, edited by Andrew Bailey and translated by Ian Johnston. Copyright © Broadview Press, 2020 (forthcoming). "Reply to Antoine Arnauld," from *The Philosophical Writings of Descartes*, Vol. 2, translated by John Cottingham, Robert Stoothoff, and Dugald Murdoch. Copyright © Cambridge University Press, 1984. Reproduced with permission of the Licensor through PLSclear.

Descartes, René, and Elisabeth, Princess of Bohemia. Excerpt from *The Correspondence between Princess Elisabeth of Bohemia and René Descartes*, translated & edited by Lisa Shapiro. University of Chicago Press, 2007. Republished with the permission of The University of Chicago Press via Copyright Clearance Center, Inc.

From the Publisher

A name never says it all, but the word "Broadview" expresses a good
deal of the philosophy behind our company. We are open to a
broad range of academic approaches and political viewpoints. We pay
attention to the broad impact book publishing and book printing has in
the wider world; for some years now we have used 100% recycled
paper for most titles. Our publishing program is internationally oriented
and broad-ranging. Our individual titles often appeal to a broad
readership too; many are of interest as much to general readers as to
academics and students.

Founded in 1985, Broadview remains a fully independent
company owned by its shareholders—not an imprint or subsidiary
of a larger multinational.

For the most accurate information on our books (including information
on pricing, editions, and formats) please visit our website at
www.broadviewpress.com. Our print books and ebooks are also
available for sale on our site.

broadview press
www.broadviewpress.com